THE

ISRAELITE BIBLE

WITH APOCRYPHA

OLD AND NEW COVENANT SCRIPTURE

TRANSLATED OUT OF THE ORIGINAL TONGUES: AND WITH
THE FORMER TRANSLATIONS DILIGENTLY COMPARED
AND REVISED. BY HIS MAJESTY'S SPECIAL COMMAND

APPOINTED TO BE READ TO THE CHILDREN OF ISRAEL
AND THE STRANGERS ATTACHED TO THEM.

AUTHORIZED ISRAELITE BIBLE
RESTORED 1611 KJV EDITION
JUDAH MOBILE INTERNATIONAL
PUBLISHED IN CAPTIVITY

Book 2

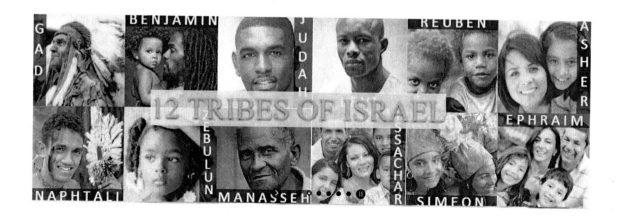

26 But the judgment shall sit, and they shall take away his dominion, to consume and to destroy *it* unto the end.

27 And the kingdom and dominion, and the greatness of the kingdom under the whole heaven, shall be given to the people of the saints of the most High, whose kingdom *is* an everlasting kingdom, and all dominions shall serve and obey him.

28 Hitherto *is* the end of the matter. As for me Daniel, my cogitations much troubled me, and my countenance changed in me: but I kept the matter in my heart.

CHAPTER 8

IN the third year of the reign of king Belshazzar a vision appeared unto me, *even unto* me Daniel, after that which appeared unto me at the first.

2 And I saw in a vision; and it came to pass, when I saw, that I *was* at Shushan *in* the palace, which *is* in the province of Elam; and I saw in a vision, and I was by the river of Ulai.

3 Then I lifted up mine eyes, and saw, and, behold, there stood before the river a ram which had *two* horns: and the *two* horns *were* high; but one *was* higher than the other, and the higher came up last.

4 I saw the ram pushing westward, and northward, and southward; so that no beasts might stand before him, neither *was there any* that could deliver out of his hand; but he did according to his will, and became great.

5 And as I was considering, behold, an he goat came from the west on the face of the whole earth, and touched not the ground: and the goat *had* a notable horn between his eyes.

6 And he came to the ram that had *two* horns, which I had seen standing before the river, and ran unto him in the fury of his power.

7 And I saw him come close unto the ram, and he was moved with choler against him, and smote the ram, and brake his two horns: and there was no power in the ram to stand before him, but he cast him down to the ground, and stamped upon him: and there was none that could deliver the ram out of his hand.

8 Therefore the he goat waxed very great: and when he was strong, the great horn was broken; and for it came up four notable ones toward the four winds of heaven.

9 And out of one of them came forth a little horn, which waxed exceeding great, toward the south, and toward the east, and toward the pleasant *land.*

10 And it waxed great, *even* to the host of heaven; and it cast down *some* of the host and of the stars to the ground, and stamped upon them.

11 Yea, he magnified *himself* even to the prince of the host, and by him the daily *sacrifice* was taken away, and the place of his sanctuary was cast down.

12 And an host was given *him* against the daily *sacrifice* by reason of transgression, and it cast down the truth to the ground; and it practised, and prospered.

13 ¶ Then I heard one saint speaking, and another saint said unto that certain *saint* which spake, How long *shall be* the vision *concerning* the daily *sacrifice,* and the transgression of desolation, to give both the sanctuary and the host to be trodden under foot?

14 And he said unto me, Unto two thousand and three hundred days; then shall the sanctuary be cleansed.

15 ¶ And it came to pass, when I, *even* I Daniel, had seen the vision, and sought for the meaning, then, behold, there stood before me as the appearance of a man.

16 And I heard a man's voice between *the banks of* Ulai, which called, and said, Gabriel, make this *man* to understand the vision.

17 So he came near where I stood: and when he came, I was afraid, and fell upon my face: but he said unto me, Understand, O son of man: for at the time of the end *shall be* the vision.

18 Now as he was speaking with me, I was in a deep sleep on my face toward the ground: but he touched me, and set me upright.

19 And he said, Behold, I will make thee know what shall be in the last end of the indignation: for at the time appointed the end *shall be.*

20 The ram which thou sawest having *two* horns *are* the kings of Media and Persia.

21 And the rough goat *is* the king of Grecia: and the great horn that *is* between his eyes *is* the first king.

22 Now that being broken, whereas four stood up for it, four kingdoms shall stand up out of the nation, but not in his power.

23 And in the latter time of their kingdom, when the transgressors are come to the full, a king of fierce countenance, and understanding dark sentences, shall stand up.

24 And his power shall be mighty, but not by his own power: and he shall destroy wonderfully, and shall prosper, and practise, and shall destroy the mighty and the holy people.

25 And through his policy also he shall cause craft to prosper in his hand; and he shall magnify *himself* in his heart, and by peace shall destroy many: he shall also stand up against the Prince of princes; but he shall be broken without hand.

26 And the vision of the evening and the morning which was told *is* true: wherefore shut thou up the vision; for it *shall be* for many days.

27 And I Daniel fainted, and was sick *certain* days; afterward I rose up, and did the king's business; and I was astonished at the vision, but none understood *it.*

CHAPTER 9

IN the first year of Darius the son of Ahasuerus, of the seed of the Medes, which was made king over the realm of the Chaldeans;

2 In the first year of his reign I Daniel understood by books the number of the years, whereof the word of the Lᴏʀᴅ came to Jeremiah the prophet, that he would accomplish seventy years in the desolations of Jerusalem.

3 ¶ And I set my face unto the Lord אֱלֹהִים, to seek by prayer and supplications, with fasting, and sackcloth, and ashes:

4 And I prayed unto the Lᴏʀᴅ my אֱלֹהִים, and made my confession, and said, O Lord, the great and dreadful אֱלֹהִים, keeping the covenant and mercy to them that love him, and to them that keep his commandments;

5 We have sinned, and have committed iniquity, and have done wickedly, and have rebelled, even by departing from thy precepts and from thy judgments:

6 Neither have we hearkened unto thy servants the prophets, which spake in thy name to our kings, our princes, and our fathers, and to all the people of the land.

7 O Lord, righteousness *belongeth* unto thee, but unto us confusion of faces, as at this day; to the men of Judah, and to the inhabitants of Jerusalem, and unto all Israel, *that are* near, and *that are* far off, through all the countries whither thou hast driven them, because of their trespass that they have trespassed against thee.

8 O Lord, to us *belongeth* confusion of face, to our kings, to our princes, and to our fathers, because we have sinned against thee.

9 To the Lord our אֱלֹהִים *belong* mercies and forgivenesses, though we have rebelled against him;

10 Neither have we obeyed the voice of the Lord our אֱ, to walk in his laws, which he set before us by his servants the prophets.

11 Yea, all Israel have transgressed thy law, even by departing, that they might not obey thy voice; therefore the curse is poured upon us, and the oath that *is* written in the law of Moses the servant of אֱלֹהִים, because we have sinned against him.

12 And he hath confirmed his words, which he spake against us, and against our judges that judged us, by bringing upon us a great evil: for under the whole heaven hath not been done as hath been done upon Jerusalem.

13 As *it is* written in the law of Moses, all this evil is come upon us: yet made we not our prayer before the Lord our אֱלֹהִים, that we might turn from our iniquities, and understand thy truth.

14 Therefore hath the Lord watched upon the evil, and brought it upon us: for the Lord our אֱלֹהִים *is* righteous in all his works which he doeth: for we obeyed not his voice.

15 And now, O Lord our אֱלֹהִים, that hast brought thy people forth out of the land of Egypt with a mighty hand, and hast gotten thee renown, as at this day; we have sinned, we have done wickedly.

16 ¶ O Lord, according to all thy righteousness, I beseech thee, let thine anger and thy fury be turned away from thy city Jerusalem, thy holy mountain: because for our sins, and for the iniquities of our fathers, Jerusalem and thy people *are become* a reproach to all *that are* about us.

17 Now therefore, O our אֱלֹהִים, hear the prayer of thy servant, and his supplications, and cause thy face to shine upon thy sanctuary that is desolate, for the Lord's sake.

18 O my אֱלֹהִים, incline thine ear, and hear; open thine eyes, and behold our desolations, and the city which is called by thy name: for we do not present our supplications before thee for our righteousnesses, but for thy great mercies.

19 O Lord, hear; O Lord, forgive; O Lord, hearken and do; defer not, for thine own sake, O my אֱלֹהִים: for thy city and thy people are called by thy name.

20 ¶ And whiles I *was* speaking, and praying, and confessing my sin and the sin of my people Israel, and presenting my supplication before the Lord my אֱלֹהִים for the holy mountain of my אֱלֹהִים;

21 Yea, whiles I *was* speaking in prayer, even the man Gabriel, whom I had seen in the vision at the beginning, being caused to fly swiftly, touched me about the time of the evening oblation.

22 And he informed *me*, and talked with me, and said, O Daniel, I am now come forth to give thee skill and understanding.

23 At the beginning of thy supplications the commandment came forth, and I am come to shew *thee;* for thou *art* greatly beloved: therefore understand the matter, and consider the vision.

24 Seventy weeks are determined upon thy people and upon thy holy city, to finish the transgression, and to make an end of sins, and to make reconciliation for iniquity, and to bring in everlasting righteousness, and to seal up the vision and prophecy, and to anoint the most Holy.

25 Know therefore and understand, *that* from the going forth of the commandment to restore and to build Jerusalem unto the Messiah the Prince *shall be* seven weeks, and threescore and two weeks: the street shall be built again, and the wall, even in troublous times.

26 And after threescore and two weeks shall Messiah be cut off, but not for himself: and the people of the prince that shall come shall destroy the city and the sanctuary; and the end thereof *shall be* with a flood, and unto the end of the war desolations are determined.

27 And he shall confirm the covenant with many for one week: and in the midst of the week he shall cause the sacrifice and the oblation to cease, and for the overspreading of abominations he shall make *it* desolate, even until the consummation, and that determined shall be poured upon the desolate.

CHAPTER 10

IN the third year of Cyrus king of Persia a thing was revealed unto Daniel, whose name was called Belteshazzar; and the thing *was* true, but the time appointed *was* long: and he understood the thing, and had understanding of the vision.

2 In those days I Daniel was mourning three full weeks.

3 I ate no pleasant bread, neither came flesh nor wine in my mouth, neither did I anoint myself at all, till three whole weeks were fulfilled.

4 And in the four and twentieth day of the first month, as I was by the side of the great river, which *is* Hiddekel;

5 Then I lifted up mine eyes, and looked, and behold a certain man clothed in linen, whose loins *were* girded with fine gold of Uphaz:

6 His body also *was* like the beryl, and his face as the appearance of lightning, and his eyes as lamps of fire, and his arms and his feet like in colour to polished brass, and the voice of his words like the voice of a multitude.

7 And I Daniel alone saw the vision: for the men that were with me saw not the vision; but a great quaking fell upon them, so that they fled to hide themselves.

8 Therefore I was left alone, and saw this great vision, and there remained no strength in me: for my comeliness was turned in me into corruption, and I retained no strength.

9 Yet heard I the voice of his words: and when I heard the voice of his words, then was I in a deep sleep on my face, and my face toward the ground.

10 ¶ And, behold, an hand touched me, which set me upon my knees and *upon* the palms of my hands.

11 And he said unto me, O Daniel, a man greatly beloved, understand the words that I speak unto thee, and stand upright: for unto thee am I now sent. And when he had spoken this word unto me, I stood trembling.

12 Then said he unto me, Fear not, Daniel: for from the first day that thou didst set thine heart to understand, and to chasten thyself before thy אֱ, thy words were heard, and I am come for thy words.

13 But the prince of the kingdom of Persia withstood me one and twenty days: but, lo, Michael, one of the chief princes, came to help me; and I remained there with the kings of Persia.

14 Now I am come to make thee understand what shall befall thy people in the latter days: for yet the vision *is* for *many* days.

15 And when he had spoken such words unto me, I set my face toward the ground, and I became dumb.

16 And, behold, *one* like the similitude of the sons of men touched my lips: then I opened my mouth, and spake, and said unto him that stood before me, O my lord, by the vision my sorrows are turned upon me, and I have retained no strength.

17 For how can the servant of this my lord talk with this my lord? for as for me, straightway there remained no strength in me, neither is there breath left in me.

18 Then there came again and touched me *one* like the appearance of a man, and he strengthened me,

19 And said, O man greatly beloved, fear not: peace *be* unto thee, be strong, yea, be strong. And when he had spoken unto me, I was strengthened, and said, Let my lord speak; for thou hast strengthened me.

20 Then said he, Knowest thou wherefore I come unto thee? and now will I return to fight with the prince of Persia: and when I am gone forth, lo, the prince of Grecia shall come.

21 But I will shew thee that which is noted in the scripture of truth: and *there is* none that holdeth with me in these things, but Michael your prince.

CHAPTER 11

ALSO I in the first year of Darius the Mede, *even* I, stood to confirm and to strengthen him.

2 And now will I shew thee the truth. Behold, there shall stand up yet three kings in Persia; and the fourth shall be far richer than *they* all: and by his strength through his riches he shall stir up all against the realm of Grecia.

3 And a mighty king shall stand up, that shall rule with great dominion, and do according to his will.

4 And when he shall stand up, his kingdom shall be broken, and shall be divided toward the four winds of heaven; and not to his posterity, nor according to his dominion which he ruled: for his kingdom shall be plucked up, even for others beside those.

5 ¶ And the king of the south shall be strong, and *one* of his princes; and he shall be strong above him, and have dominion; his dominion *shall be* a great dominion.

6 And in the end of years they shall join themselves together; for the king's daughter of the south shall come to the king of the north to make an agreement: but she shall not retain the power of the arm; neither shall he stand, nor his arm: but she shall be given up, and they that brought her, and he that begat her, and he that strengthened her in *these* times.

7 But out of a branch of her roots shall *one* stand up in his estate, which shall come with an army, and shall enter into the fortress of the king of the north, and shall deal against them, and shall prevail:

8 And shall also carry captives into Egypt their gods, with their princes, *and* with their precious vessels of silver and of gold; and he shall continue *more* years than the king of the north.

9 So the king of the south shall come into *his* kingdom, and shall return into his own land.

10 But his sons shall be stirred up, and shall assemble a multitude of great forces: and *one* shall certainly come, and overflow, and pass through: then shall he return, and be stirred up, *even* to his fortress.

11 And the king of the south shall be moved with choler, and shall come forth and fight with him, *even* with the king of the north: and he shall set forth a great multitude; but the multitude shall be given into his hand.

12 *And* when he hath taken away the multitude, his heart shall be lifted up; and he shall cast down *many* ten thousands: but he shall not be strengthened *by it.*

13 For the king of the north shall return, and shall set forth a multitude greater than the former, and shall certainly come after certain years with a great army and with much riches.

14 And in those times there shall many stand up against the king of the south: also the robbers of thy people shall exalt themselves to establish the vision; but they shall fall.

15 So the king of the north shall come, and cast up a mount, and take the most fenced cities: and the arms of the south shall not withstand, neither his chosen people, neither *shall there be any* strength to withstand.

16 But he that cometh against him shall do according to his own will, and none shall stand before him: and he shall stand in the glorious land, which by his hand shall be consumed.

17 He shall also set his face to enter with the strength of his whole kingdom, and upright ones with him; thus shall he do: and he shall give him the daughter of women, corrupting her: but she shall not stand *on his side,* neither be for him.

18 After this shall he turn his face unto the isles, and shall take many: but a prince for his own behalf shall cause the reproach offered by him to cease; without his own reproach he shall cause *it* to turn upon him.

19 Then he shall turn his face toward the fort of his own land: but he shall stumble and fall, and not be found.

20 Then shall stand up in his estate a raiser of taxes *in* the glory of the kingdom: but within few days he shall be destroyed, neither in anger, nor in battle.

21 And in his estate shall stand up a vile person, to whom they shall not give the honour of the kingdom: but he shall come in peaceably, and obtain the kingdom by flatteries.

22 And with the arms of a flood shall they be overflown from before him, and shall be broken; yea, also the prince of the covenant.

23 And after the league *made* with him he shall work deceitfully: for he shall come up, and shall become strong with a small people.

24 He shall enter peaceably even upon the fattest places of the province; and he shall do *that* which his fathers have not done, nor his fathers' fathers; he shall scatter among them the prey, and spoil, and riches: *yea,* and he shall forecast his devices against the strong holds, even for a time.

25 And he shall stir up his power and his courage against the king of the south with a great army; and the king of the south shall be stirred up to battle with a very great and mighty army; but he shall not stand: for they shall forecast devices against him.

26 Yea, they that feed of the portion of his meat shall destroy him, and his army shall overflow: and many shall fall down slain.

27 And both these kings' hearts *shall be* to do mischief, and they shall speak lies at one table; but it shall not prosper: for yet the end *shall be* at the time appointed.

28 Then shall he return into his land with great riches; and his heart *shall be* against the holy covenant; and he shall do *exploits,* and return to his own land.

29 At the time appointed he shall return, and come toward the south; but it shall not be as the former, or as the latter.

30 ¶ For the ships of Chittim shall come against him: therefore he shall be grieved, and return, and have indignation against the holy covenant: so shall he do; he shall even return, and have intelligence with them that forsake the holy covenant.

31 And arms shall stand on his part, and they shall pollute the sanctuary of strength, and shall take away the daily *sacrifice,* and they shall place the abomination that maketh desolate.

32 And such as do wickedly against the covenant shall he corrupt by flatteries: but the people that do know their אֱלֹהִים shall be strong, and do *exploits.*

33 And they that understand among the people shall instruct many: yet they shall fall by the sword, and by flame, by captivity, and by spoil, *many* days.

34 Now when they shall fall, they shall be holpen with a little help: but many shall cleave to them with flatteries.

35 And *some* of them of understanding shall fall, to try them, and to purge, and to make *them* white, *even* to the time of the end:

because *it is* yet for a time appointed.

36 And the king shall do according to his will; and he shall exalt himself, and magnify himself above every god, and shall speak marvellous things against the אֱלֹהִים of gods, and shall prosper till the indignation be accomplished: for that that is determined shall be done.

37 Neither shall he regard the אֱלֹהִים of his fathers, nor the desire of women, nor regard any god: for he shall magnify himself above all.

38 But in his estate shall he honour the אֱלֹהִים of forces: and a god whom his fathers knew not shall he honour with gold, and silver, and with precious stones, and pleasant things.

39 Thus shall he do in the most strong holds with a strange god, whom he shall acknowledge *and* increase with glory: and he shall cause them to rule over many, and shall divide the land for gain.

40 And at the time of the end shall the king of the south push at him: and the king of the north shall come against him like a whirlwind, with chariots, and with horsemen, and with many ships; and he shall enter into the countries, and shall overflow and pass over.

41 He shall enter also into the glorious land, and many *countries* shall be overthrown: but these shall escape out of his hand, *even* Edom, and Moab, and the chief of the children of Ammon.

42 He shall stretch forth his hand also upon the countries: and the land of Egypt shall not escape.

43 But he shall have power over the treasures of gold and of silver, and over all the precious things of Egypt: and the Libyans and the Ethiopians *shall be* at his steps.

44 But tidings out of the east and out of the north shall trouble him: therefore he shall go forth with great fury to destroy, and utterly to make away many.

45 And he shall plant the tabernacles of his palace between the seas in the glorious holy mountain; yet he shall come to his end, and none shall help him.

CHAPTER 12

AND at that time shall Michael stand up, the great prince which standeth for the children of thy people: and there shall be a time of trouble, such as never was since there was a nation *even* to that same time: and at that time thy people shall be delivered, every one that shall be found written in the book.

2 And many of them that sleep in the dust of the earth shall awake, some to everlasting life, and some to shame *and* everlasting contempt.

3 And they that be wise shall shine as the brightness of the firmament; and they that turn many to righteousness as the stars for ever and ever.

4 But thou, O Daniel, shut up the words, and seal the book, *even* to the time of the end: many shall run to and fro, and knowledge shall be increased.

5 ¶ Then I Daniel looked, and, behold, there stood other two, the one on this side of the bank of the river, and the other on that side of the bank of the river.

6 And *one* said to the man clothed in linen, which *was* upon the waters of the river, How long *shall it be to* the end of these wonders?

7 And I heard the man clothed in linen, which *was* upon the waters of the river, when he held up his right hand and his left hand unto heaven, and sware by him that liveth for ever that *it shall be* for a time, times, and an half; and when he shall have accomplished to scatter the power of the holy people, all these *things* shall be finished.

8 And I heard, but I understood not: then said I, O my Lord, what *shall be* the end of these *things?*

9 And he said, Go thy way, Daniel: for the words *are* closed up and sealed till the time of the end.

10 Many shall be purified, and made white, and tried; but the wicked shall do wickedly: and none of the wicked shall understand; but the wise shall understand.

11 And from the time *that* the daily *sacrifice* shall be taken away, and the abomination that maketh desolate set up, *there shall be* a thousand two hundred and ninety days.

12 Blessed *is* he that waiteth, and cometh to the thousand three hundred and five and thirty days.

13 But go thou thy way till the end *be*: for thou shalt rest, and stand in thy lot at the end of the days.

HOSEA.

CHAPTER 1

THE word of the LORD that came unto Hosea, the son of Beeri, in the days of Uzziah, Jotham, Ahaz, *and* Hezekiah, kings of Judah, and in the days of Jeroboam the son of Joash, king of Israel.

2 The beginning of the word of the LORD by Hosea. And the LORD said to Hosea, Go, take unto thee a wife of whoredoms and children of whoredoms: for the land hath committed great whoredom, *departing* from the LORD.

3 So he went and took Gomer the daughter of Diblaim; which conceived, and bare him a son.

4 And the LORD said unto him, Call his name Jezreel; for yet a little *while*, and I will avenge the blood of Jezreel upon the house of Jehu, and will cause to cease the kingdom of the house of Israel.

5 And it shall come to pass at that day, that I will break the bow of Israel in the valley of Jezreel.

6 ¶ And she conceived again, and bare a daughter. And אֱלֹהִים said unto him, Call her name Lo-ruhamah: for I will no more have mercy upon the house of Israel; but I will utterly take them away.

7 But I will have mercy upon the house of Judah, and will save them by the LORD their אֱלֹהִים, and will not save them by bow, nor by sword, nor by battle, by horses, nor by horsemen.

8 ¶ Now when she had weaned Lo-ruhamah, she conceived, and bare a son.

9 Then said אֱלֹהִים, Call his name Lo-ammi: for ye *are* not my people, and I will not be your אֱלֹהִים.

10 ¶ Yet the number of the children of Israel shall be as the sand of the sea, which cannot be measured nor numbered; and it shall come to pass, *that* in the place where it was said unto them, Ye *are* not my people, *there* it shall be said unto them, *Ye are* the sons of the living אֱלֹהִים.

11 Then shall the children of Judah and the children of Israel be gathered together, and appoint themselves one head, and they shall

come up out of the land: for great *shall be* the day of Jezreel.

CHAPTER 2

SAY ye unto your brethren, Ammi; and to your sisters, Ru-hamah.

2 Plead with your mother, plead: for she *is* not my wife, neither *am* I her husband: let her therefore put away her whoredoms out of her sight, and her adulteries from between her breasts;

3 Lest I strip her naked, and set her as in the day that she was born, and make her as a wilderness, and set her like a dry land, and slay her with thirst.

4 And I will not have mercy upon her children; for they *be* the children of whoredoms.

5 For their mother hath played the harlot: she that conceived them hath done shamefully: for she said, I will go after my lovers, that give *me* my bread and my water, my wool and my flax, mine oil and my drink.

6 ¶ Therefore, behold, I will hedge up thy way with thorns, and make a wall, that she shall not find her paths.

7 And she shall follow after her lovers, but she shall not overtake them; and she shall seek them, but shall not find *them*: then shall she say, I will go and return to my first husband; for then *was it* better with me than now.

8 For she did not know that I gave her corn, and wine, and oil, and multiplied her silver and gold, *which* they prepared for Baal.

9 Therefore will I return, and take away my corn in the time thereof, and my wine in the season thereof, and will recover my wool and my flax *given* to cover her nakedness.

10 And now will I discover her lewdness in the sight of her lovers, and none shall deliver her out of mine hand.

11 I will also cause all her mirth to cease, her feast days, her new moons, and her sabbaths, and all her solemn feasts.

12 And I will destroy her vines and her fig trees, whereof she hath said, These *are* my rewards that my lovers have given me: and I will make them a forest, and the beasts of the field shall eat them.

13 And I will visit upon her the days of Baalim, wherein she burned incense to them, and she decked herself with her earrings and her jewels, and she went after her lovers, and forgat me, saith the LORD.

14 ¶ Therefore, behold, I will allure her, and bring her into the wilderness, and speak comfortably unto her.

15 And I will give her her vineyards from thence, and the valley of Achor for a door of hope: and she shall sing there, as in the days of her youth, and as in the day when she came up out of the land of Egypt.

16 And it shall be at that day, saith the LORD, *that* thou shalt call me Ishi; and shalt call me no more Baali.

17 For I will take away the names of Baalim out of her mouth, and they shall no more be remembered by their name.

18 And in that day will I make a covenant for them with the beasts of the field, and with the fowls of heaven, and *with* the creeping things of the ground: and I will break the bow and the sword and the battle out of the earth, and will make them to lie down safely.

19 And I will betroth thee unto me for ever; yea, I will betroth thee unto me in righteousness, and in judgment, and in lovingkindness, and in mercies.

20 I will even betroth thee unto me in faithfulness: and thou shalt know the LORD.

21 And it shall come to pass in that day, I will hear, saith the LORD, I will hear the heavens, and they shall hear the earth;

22 And the earth shall hear the corn, and the wine, and the oil; and they shall hear Jezreel.

23 And I will sow her unto me in the earth; and I will have mercy upon her that had not obtained mercy; and I will say to *them which were* not my people, Thou *art* my people; and they shall say, *Thou art* my אֱלֹהִים.

CHAPTER 3

THEN said the LORD unto me, Go yet, love a woman beloved of *her* friend, yet an adulteress, according to the love of the LORD toward the children of Israel, who look to other gods, and love flagons of wine.

2 So I bought her to me for fifteen *pieces* of silver, and *for* an homer of barley, and an half homer of barley:

3 And I said unto her, Thou shalt abide for me many days; thou shalt not play the harlot, and thou shalt not be for *another* man: so *will* I also *be* for thee.

4 For the children of Israel shall abide many days without a king, and without a prince, and without a sacrifice, and without an image, and without an ephod, and *without* teraphim:

5 Afterward shall the children of Israel return, and seek the LORD their אֱלֹהִים, and David their king; and shall fear the LORD and his goodness in the latter days.

CHAPTER 4

HEAR the word of the LORD, ye children of Israel: for the LORD hath a controversy with the inhabitants of the land, because *there is* no truth, nor mercy, nor knowledge of אֱלֹהִים in the land.

2 By swearing, and lying, and killing, and stealing, and committing adultery, they break out, and blood toucheth blood.

3 Therefore shall the land mourn, and every one that dwelleth therein shall languish, with the beasts of the field, and with the fowls of heaven; yea, the fishes of the sea also shall be taken away.

4 Yet let no man strive, nor reprove another: for thy people *are* as they that strive with the priest.

5 Therefore shalt thou fall in the day, and the prophet also shall fall with thee in the night, and I will destroy thy mother.

6 ¶ My people are destroyed for lack of knowledge: because thou hast rejected knowledge, I will also reject thee, that thou shalt be no priest to me: seeing thou hast forgotten the law of thy אֱלֹהִים, I will also forget thy children.

7 As they were increased, so they sinned against me: *therefore* will I change their glory into shame.

8 They eat up the sin of my people, and they set their heart on their iniquity.

9 And there shall be, like people, like priest: and I will punish them for their ways, and reward them their doings.

10 For they shall eat, and not have enough: they shall commit whoredom, and shall not increase: because they have left off to take heed to the LORD.

11 Whoredom and wine and new wine take away the heart.

12 ¶ My people ask counsel at their stocks, and their staff declareth unto them: for the spirit of whoredoms hath caused *them* to err, and they have gone a whoring from under their אֱלֹהִים.

13 They sacrifice upon the tops of the mountains, and burn incense upon the hills, under oaks and poplars and elms, because the shadow thereof *is* good: therefore your daughters shall commit whoredom, and your spouses shall commit adultery.

14 I will not punish your daughters when they commit whoredom, nor your spouses when they commit adultery: for themselves are

separated with whores, and they sacrifice with harlots: therefore the people *that* doth not understand shall fall.

15 ¶ Though thou, Israel, play the harlot, *yet* let not Judah offend; and come not ye unto Gilgal, neither go ye up to Beth-aven, nor swear, The LORD liveth.

16 For Israel slideth back as a backsliding heifer: now the LORD will feed them as a lamb in a large place.

17 Ephraim *is* joined to idols: let him alone.

18 Their drink is sour: they have committed whoredom continually: her rulers *with* shame do love, Give ye.

19 The wind hath bound her up in her wings, and they shall be ashamed because of their sacrifices.

CHAPTER 5

HEAR ye this, O priests; and hearken, ye house of Israel; and give ye ear, O house of the king; for judgment *is* toward you, because ye have been a snare on Mizpah, and a net spread upon Tabor.

2 And the revolters are profound to make slaughter, though I *have been* a rebuker of them all.

3 I know Ephraim, and Israel is not hid from me: for now, O Ephraim, thou committest whoredom, *and* Israel is defiled.

4 They will not frame their doings to turn unto their אֱלֹהִים: for the spirit of whoredoms *is* in the midst of them, and they have not known the LORD.

5 And the pride of Israel doth testify to his face: therefore shall Israel and Ephraim fall in their iniquity; Judah also shall fall with them.

6 They shall go with their flocks and with their herds to seek the LORD; but they shall not find *him;* he hath withdrawn himself from them.

7 They have dealt treacherously against the LORD: for they have begotten strange children: now shall a month devour them with their portions.

8 Blow ye the cornet in Gibeah, *and* the trumpet in Ramah: cry aloud *at* Beth-aven, after thee, O Benjamin.

9 Ephraim shall be desolate in the day of rebuke: among the tribes of Israel have I made known that which shall surely be.

10 The princes of Judah were like them that remove the bound: *therefore* I will pour out my wrath upon them like water.

11 Ephraim *is* oppressed *and* broken in judgment, because he willingly walked after the commandment.

12 Therefore *will* I *be* unto Ephraim as a moth, and to the house of Judah as rottenness.

13 When Ephraim saw his sickness, and Judah *saw* his wound, then went Ephraim to the Assyrian, and sent to king Jareb: yet could he not heal you, nor cure you of your wound.

14 For I *will be* unto Ephraim as a lion, and as a young lion to the house of Judah: I, *even* I, will tear and go away; I will take away, and none shall rescue *him.*

15 ¶ I will go *and* return to my place, till they acknowledge their offence, and seek my face: in their affliction they will seek me early.

CHAPTER 6

COME, and let us return unto the LORD: for he hath torn, and he will heal us; he hath smitten, and he will bind us up.

2 After two days will he revive us: in the third day he will raise us up, and we shall live in his sight.

3 Then shall we know, *if* we follow on to know the LORD: his going forth is prepared as the morning; and he shall come unto us as the rain, as the latter *and* former rain unto the earth.

4 ¶ O Ephraim, what shall I do unto thee? O Judah, what shall I do unto thee? for your goodness *is* as a morning cloud, and as the early dew it goeth away.

5 Therefore have I hewed *them* by the prophets; I have slain them by the words of my mouth: and thy judgments *are as* the light *that* goeth forth.

6 For I desired mercy, and not sacrifice; and the knowledge of אֱלֹהִים more than burnt offerings.

7 But they like men have transgressed the covenant: there have they dealt treacherously against me.

8 Gilead *is* a city of them that work iniquity, *and is* polluted with blood.

9 And as troops of robbers wait for a man, *so* the company of priests murder in the way by consent: for they commit lewdness.

10 I have seen an horrible thing in the house of Israel: there *is* the whoredom of Ephraim, Israel is defiled.

11 Also, O Judah, he hath set an harvest for thee, when I returned the captivity of my people.

CHAPTER 7

WHEN I would have healed Israel, then the iniquity of Ephraim was discovered, and the wickedness of Samaria: for they commit falsehood; and the thief cometh in, *and* the troop of robbers spoileth without.

2 And they consider not in their hearts *that* I remember all their wickedness: now their own doings have beset them about; they are before my face.

3 They make the king glad with their wickedness, and the princes with their lies.

4 They *are* all adulterers, as an oven heated by the baker, *who* ceaseth from raising after he hath kneaded the dough, until it be leavened.

5 In the day of our king the princes have made *him* sick with bottles of wine; he stretched out his hand with scorners.

6 For they have made ready their heart like an oven, whiles they lie in wait: their baker sleepeth all the night; in the morning it burneth as a flaming fire.

7 They are all hot as an oven, and have devoured their judges; all their kings are fallen: *there is* none among them that calleth unto me.

8 Ephraim, he hath mixed himself among the people; Ephraim is a cake not turned.

9 Strangers have devoured his strength, and he knoweth *it* not: yea, gray hairs are here and there upon him, yet he knoweth not.

10 And the pride of Israel testifieth to his face: and they do not return to the LORD their אֱלֹהִים, nor seek him for all this.

11 ¶ Ephraim also is like a silly dove without heart: they call to Egypt, they go to Assyria.

12 When they shall go, I will spread my net upon them; I will bring them down as the fowls of the heaven; I will chastise them, as their congregation hath heard.

13 Woe unto them! for they have fled from me: destruction unto them! because they have transgressed against me: though I have redeemed them, yet they have spoken lies against me.

14 And they have not cried unto me with their heart, when they howled upon their beds: they assemble themselves for corn and wine, *and* they rebel against me.

15 Though I have bound *and* strengthened their arms, yet do they imagine mischief against me.

16 They return, *but* not to the most High: they are like a deceitful bow: their princes shall fall by the sword for the rage of their tongue: this *shall be* their derision in the land of Egypt.

CHAPTER 8

SET the trumpet to thy mouth. *He shall come* as an eagle against the house of the LORD, because they have transgressed my covenant, and trespassed against my law.

2 Israel shall cry unto me, My אֱלֹהִים, we know thee.

3 Israel hath cast off *the thing that is* good: the enemy shall pursue him.

4 They have set up kings, but not by me: they have made princes, and I knew *it* not: of their silver and their gold have they made them idols, that they may be cut off.

5 ¶ Thy calf, O Samaria, hath cast *thee* off; mine anger is kindled against them: how long *will it be* ere they attain to innocency?

6 For from Israel *was* it also: the workman made it; therefore it *is* not אֱלֹהִים: but the calf of Samaria shall be broken in pieces.

7 For they have sown the wind, and they shall reap the whirlwind: it hath no stalk: the bud shall yield no meal: if so be it yield, the strangers shall swallow it up.

8 Israel is swallowed up: now shall they be among the Gentiles as a vessel wherein *is* no pleasure.

9 For they are gone up to Assyria, a wild ass alone by himself: Ephraim hath hired lovers.

10 Yea, though they have hired among the nations, now will I gather them, and they shall sorrow a little for the burden of the king of princes.

11 Because Ephraim hath made many altars to sin, altars shall be unto him to sin.

12 I have written to him the great things of my law, *but* they were counted as a strange thing.

13 They sacrifice flesh *for* the sacrifices of mine offerings, and eat *it:* but the LORD accepteth them not; now will he remember their iniquity, and visit their sins: they shall return to Egypt.

14 For Israel hath forgotten his Maker, and buildeth temples; and Judah hath multiplied fenced cities: but I will send a fire upon his cities, and it shall devour the palaces thereof.

CHAPTER 9

REJOICE not, O Israel, for joy, as *other* people: for thou hast gone a whoring from thy אֱלֹהִים, thou hast loved a reward upon every cornfloor.

2 The floor and the winepress shall not feed them, and the new wine shall fail in her.

3 They shall not dwell in the LORD's land; but Ephraim shall return to Egypt, and they shall eat unclean *things* in Assyria.

4 They shall not offer wine *offerings* to the LORD, neither shall they be pleasing unto him: their sacrifices *shall be* unto them as the bread of mourners; all that eat thereof shall be polluted: for their bread for their soul shall not come into the house of the LORD.

5 What will ye do in the solemn day, and in the day of the feast of the LORD?

6 For, lo, they are gone because of destruction: Egypt shall gather them up, Memphis shall bury them: the pleasant *places* for their silver, nettles shall possess them: thorns *shall be* in their tabernacles.

7 The days of visitation are come, the days of recompence are come; Israel shall know *it:* the prophet *is* a fool, the spiritual man *is* mad, for the multitude of thine iniquity, and the great hatred.

8 The watchman of Ephraim *was* with my אֱלֹהִים: *but* the prophet *is* a snare of a fowler in all his ways, *and* hatred in the house of his אֱלֹהִים.

9 They have deeply corrupted *themselves,* as in the days of Gibeah: *therefore* he will remember their iniquity, he will visit their sins.

10 I found Israel like grapes in the wilderness; I saw your fathers as the firstripe in the fig tree at her first time: *but* they went to Baal-peor, and separated themselves unto *that* shame; and *their* abominations were according as they loved.

11 *As for* Ephraim, their glory shall fly away like a bird, from the birth, and from the womb, and from the conception.

12 Though they bring up their children, yet will I bereave them, *that there shall* not *be* a man *left:* yea, woe also to them when I depart from them!

13 Ephraim, as I saw Tyrus, *is* planted in a pleasant place: but Ephraim shall bring forth his children to the murderer.

14 Give them, O LORD: what wilt thou give? give them a miscarrying womb and dry breasts.

15 All their wickedness *is* in Gilgal: for there I hated them: for the wickedness of their doings I will drive them out of mine house, I will love them no more: all their princes *are* revolters.

16 Ephraim is smitten, their root is dried up, they shall bear no fruit: yea, though they bring forth, yet will I slay *even* the beloved *fruit* of their womb.

17 My אֱלֹהִים will cast them away, because they did not hearken unto him: and they shall be wanderers among the nations.

CHAPTER 10

ISRAEL *is* an empty vine, he bringeth forth fruit unto himself: according to the multitude of his fruit he hath increased the altars; according to the goodness of his land they have made goodly images.

2 Their heart is divided; now shall they be found faulty: he shall break down their altars, he shall spoil their images.

3 For now they shall say, We have no king, because we feared not the LORD; what then should a king do to us?

4 They have spoken words, swearing falsely in making a covenant: thus judgment springeth up as hemlock in the furrows of the field.

5 The inhabitants of Samaria shall fear because of the calves of Beth-aven: for the people thereof shall mourn over it, and the priests thereof *that* rejoiced on it, for the glory thereof, because it is departed from it.

6 It shall be also carried unto Assyria *for* a present to king Jareb: Ephraim shall receive shame, and Israel shall be ashamed of his own counsel.

7 *As for* Samaria, her king is cut off as the foam upon the water.

8 The high places also of Aven, the sin of Israel, shall be destroyed: the thorn and the thistle shall come up on their altars; and they shall say to the mountains, Cover us; and to the hills, Fall on us.

9 O Israel, thou hast sinned from the days of Gibeah: there they stood: the battle in Gibeah against the children of iniquity did not overtake them.

10 *It is* in my desire that I should chastise them; and the people shall be gathered against them, when they shall bind themselves in

their two furrows.

11 And Ephraim *is as* an heifer *that is* taught, *and* loveth to tread out *the corn:* but I passed over upon her fair neck: I will make Ephraim to ride; Judah shall plow, *and* Jacob shall break his clods.

12 Sow to yourselves in righteousness, reap in mercy; break up your fallow ground: for *it is* time to seek the LORD, till he come and rain righteousness upon you.

13 Ye have plowed wickedness, ye have reaped iniquity; ye have eaten the fruit of lies: because thou didst trust in thy way, in the multitude of thy mighty men.

14 Therefore shall a tumult arise among thy people, and all thy fortresses shall be spoiled, as Shalman spoiled Beth-arbel in the day of battle: the mother was dashed in pieces upon *her* children.

15 So shall Beth-el do unto you because of your great wickedness: in a morning shall the king of Israel utterly be cut off.

CHAPTER 11

WHEN Israel *was* a child, then I loved him, and called my son out of Egypt.

2 *As* they called them, so they went from them: they sacrificed unto Baalim, and burned incense to graven images.

3 I taught Ephraim also to go, taking them by their arms; but they knew not that I healed them.

4 I drew them with cords of a man, with bands of love: and I was to them as they that take off the yoke on their jaws, and I laid meat unto them.

5 ¶ He shall not return into the land of Egypt, but the Assyrian shall be his king, because they refused to return.

6 And the sword shall abide on his cities, and shall consume his branches, and devour *them,* because of their own counsels.

7 And my people are bent to backsliding from me: though they called them to the most High, none at all would exalt *him.*

8 How shall I give thee up, Ephraim? *how* shall I deliver thee, Israel? how shall I make thee as Admah? *how* shall I set thee as Zeboim? mine heart is turned within me, my repentings are kindled together.

9 I will not execute the fierceness of mine anger, I will not return to destroy Ephraim: for I *am* אֱלֹהִים, and not man; the Holy One in the midst of thee: and I will not enter into the city.

10 They shall walk after the LORD: he shall roar like a lion: when he shall roar, then the children shall tremble from the west.

11 They shall tremble as a bird out of Egypt, and as a dove out of the land of Assyria: and I will place them in their houses, saith the LORD.

12 Ephraim compasseth me about with lies, and the house of Israel with deceit: but Judah yet ruleth with אֱלֹהִים, and is faithful with the saints.

CHAPTER 12

EPHRAIM feedeth on wind, and followeth after the east wind: he daily increaseth lies and desolation; and they do make a covenant with the Assyrians, and oil is carried into Egypt.

2 The LORD hath also a controversy with Judah, and will punish Jacob according to his ways; according to his doings will he recompense him.

3 ¶ He took his brother by the heel in the womb, and by his strength he had power with אֱלֹהִים:

4 Yea, he had power over the angel, and prevailed: he wept, and made supplication unto him: he found him *in* Beth-el, and there he spake with us;

5 Even the LORD אֱלֹהִים of hosts; the LORD *is* his memorial.

6 Therefore turn thou to thy אֱלֹהִים: keep mercy and judgment, and wait on thy אֱלֹהִים continually.

7 ¶ *He is* a merchant, the balances of deceit *are* in his hand: he loveth to oppress.

8 And Ephraim said, Yet I am become rich, I have found me out substance: *in* all my labours they shall find none iniquity in me that *were* sin.

9 And I *that am* the LORD thy אֱלֹהִים from the land of Egypt will yet make thee to dwell in tabernacles, as in the days of the solemn feast.

10 I have also spoken by the prophets, and I have multiplied visions, and used similitudes, by the ministry of the prophets.

11 *Is there* iniquity *in* Gilead? surely they are vanity: they sacrifice bullocks in Gilgal; yea, their altars *are* as heaps in the furrows of the fields.

12 And Jacob fled into the country of Syria, and Israel served for a wife, and for a wife he kept *sheep.*

13 And by a prophet the LORD brought Israel out of Egypt, and by a prophet was he preserved.

14 Ephraim provoked *him* to anger most bitterly: therefore shall he leave his blood upon him, and his reproach shall his Lord return unto him.

CHAPTER 13

WHEN Ephraim spake trembling, he exalted himself in Israel; but when he offended in Baal, he died.

2 And now they sin more and more, and have made them molten images of their silver, *and* idols according to their own understanding, all of it the work of the craftsmen: they say of them, Let the men that sacrifice kiss the calves.

3 Therefore they shall be as the morning cloud, and as the early dew that passeth away, as the chaff *that* is driven with the whirlwind out of the floor, and as the smoke out of the chimney.

4 Yet I *am* the LORD thy אֱלֹהִים from the land of Egypt, and thou shalt know no god but me: for *there is* no saviour beside me.

5 ¶ I did know thee in the wilderness, in the land of great drought.

6 According to their pasture, so were they filled; they were filled, and their heart was exalted; therefore have they forgotten me.

7 Therefore I will be unto them as a lion: as a leopard by the way will I observe *them:*

8 I will meet them as a bear *that is* bereaved *of her whelps,* and will rend the caul of their heart, and there will I devour them like a lion: the wild beast shall tear them.

9 ¶ O Israel, thou hast destroyed thyself; but in me *is* thine help.

10 I will be thy king: where *is any other* that may save thee in all thy cities? and thy judges of whom thou saidst, Give me a king and princes?

11 I gave thee a king in mine anger, and took *him* away in my wrath.

12 The iniquity of Ephraim *is* bound up; his sin *is* hid.

13 The sorrows of a travailing woman shall come upon him: he *is* an unwise son; for he should not stay long in *the place of* the breaking forth of children.

14 I will ransom them from the power of the grave; I will redeem them from death: O death, I will be thy plagues; O grave, I will be thy destruction: repentance shall be hid from mine eyes.

15 ¶ Though he be fruitful among *his* brethren, an east wind shall come, the wind of the Lord shall come up from the wilderness, and his spring shall become dry, and his fountain shall be dried up: he shall spoil the treasure of all pleasant vessels.

16 Samaria shall become desolate; for she hath rebelled against her אֱלֹהִים: they shall fall by the sword: their infants shall be dashed in pieces, and their women with child shall be ripped up.

CHAPTER 14

O ISRAEL, return unto the Lord thy אֱלֹהִים; for thou hast fallen by thine iniquity.

2 Take with you words, and turn to the Lord: say unto him, Take away all iniquity, and receive *us* graciously: so will we render the calves of our lips.

3 Asshur shall not save us; we will not ride upon horses: neither will we say any more to the work of our hands, *Ye are* our gods: for in thee the fatherless findeth mercy.

4 ¶ I will heal their backsliding, I will love them freely: for mine anger is turned away from him.

5 I will be as the dew unto Israel: he shall grow as the lily, and cast forth his roots as Lebanon.

6 His branches shall spread, and his beauty shall be as the olive tree, and his smell as Lebanon.

7 They that dwell under his shadow shall return; they shall revive *as* the corn, and grow as the vine: the scent thereof *shall be* as the wine of Lebanon.

8 Ephraim *shall say*, What have I to do any more with idols? I have heard *him*, and observed him: I *am* like a green fir tree. From me is thy fruit found.

9 Who *is* wise, and he shall understand these *things?* prudent, and he shall know them? for the ways of the Lord *are* right, and the just shall walk in them: but the transgressors shall fall therein.

JOEL.

CHAPTER 1

THE word of the Lord that came to Joel the son of Pethuel.

2 Hear this, ye old men, and give ear, all ye inhabitants of the land. Hath this been in your days, or even in the days of your fathers?

3 Tell ye your children of it, and *let* your children *tell* their children, and their children another generation.

4 That which the palmerworm hath left hath the locust eaten; and that which the locust hath left hath the cankerworm eaten; and that which the cankerworm hath left hath the caterpiller eaten.

5 Awake, ye drunkards, and weep; and howl, all ye drinkers of wine, because of the new wine; for it is cut off from your mouth.

6 For a nation is come up upon my land, strong, and without number, whose teeth *are* the teeth of a lion, and he hath the cheek teeth of a great lion.

7 He hath laid my vine waste, and barked my fig tree: he hath made it clean bare, and cast *it* away; the branches thereof are made white.

8 ¶ Lament like a virgin girded with sackcloth for the husband of her youth.

9 The meat offering and the drink offering is cut off from the house of the Lord; the priests, the Lord's ministers, mourn.

10 The field is wasted, the land mourneth; for the corn is wasted: the new wine is dried up, the oil languisheth.

11 Be ye ashamed, O ye husbandmen; howl, O ye vinedressers, for the wheat and for the barley; because the harvest of the field is perished.

12 The vine is dried up, and the fig tree languisheth; the pomegranate tree, the palm tree also, and the apple tree, *even* all the trees of the field, are withered: because joy is withered away from the sons of men.

13 Gird yourselves, and lament, ye priests: howl, ye ministers of the altar: come, lie all night in sackcloth, ye ministers of my אֱלֹהִים: for the meat offering and the drink offering is withholden from the house of your אֱלֹהִים.

14 ¶ Sanctify ye a fast, call a solemn assembly, gather the elders *and* all the inhabitants of the land *into* the house of the Lord your אֱלֹהִים, and cry unto the Lord,

15 Alas for the day! for the day of the Lord *is* at hand, and as a destruction from the Almighty shall it come.

16 Is not the meat cut off before our eyes, *yea*, joy and gladness from the house of our אֱלֹהִים?

17 The seed is rotten under their clods, the garners are laid desolate, the barns are broken down; for the corn is withered.

18 How do the beasts groan! the herds of cattle are perplexed, because they have no pasture; yea, the flocks of sheep are made desolate.

19 O Lord, to thee will I cry: for the fire hath devoured the pastures of the wilderness, and the flame hath burned all the trees of the field.

20 The beasts of the field cry also unto thee: for the rivers of waters are dried up, and the fire hath devoured the pastures of the wilderness.

CHAPTER 2

BLOW ye the trumpet in Zion, and sound an alarm in my holy mountain: let all the inhabitants of the land tremble: for the day of the Lord cometh, for *it is* nigh at hand;

2 A day of darkness and of gloominess, a day of clouds and of thick darkness, as the morning spread upon the mountains: a great people and a strong; there hath not been ever the like, neither shall be any more after it, *even* to the years of many generations.

3 A fire devoureth before them; and behind them a flame burneth: the land *is* as the garden of Eden before them, and behind them a desolate wilderness; yea, and nothing shall escape them.

4 The appearance of them *is* as the appearance of horses; and as horsemen, so shall they run.

5 Like the noise of chariots on the tops of mountains shall they leap, like the noise of a flame of fire that devoureth the stubble, as a strong people set in battle array.

6 Before their face the people shall be much pained: all faces shall gather blackness.

7 They shall run like mighty men; they shall climb the wall like men of war; and they shall march every one on his ways, and they shall not break their ranks:

8 Neither shall one thrust another; they shall walk every one in his path: and *when* they fall upon the sword, they shall not be wounded.

9 They shall run to and fro in the city; they shall run upon the wall, they shall climb up upon the houses; they shall enter in at the windows like a thief.

10 The earth shall quake before them; the heavens shall tremble: the sun and the moon shall be dark, and the stars shall withdraw their shining:

11 And the LORD shall utter his voice before his army: for his camp *is* very great: for *he is* strong that executeth his word: for the day of the LORD *is* great and very terrible; and who can abide it?

12 ¶ Therefore also now, saith the LORD, turn ye *even* to me with all your heart, and with fasting, and with weeping, and with mourning:

13 And rend your heart, and not your garments, and turn unto the LORD your אֱלֹהִים: for he *is* gracious and merciful, slow to anger, and of great kindness, and repenteth him of the evil.

14 Who knoweth *if* he will return and repent, and leave a blessing behind him; *even* a meat offering and a drink offering unto the LORD your אֱלֹהִים?

15 ¶ Blow the trumpet in Zion, sanctify a fast, call a solemn assembly:

16 Gather the people, sanctify the congregation, assemble the elders, gather the children, and those that suck the breasts: let the bridegroom go forth of his chamber, and the bride out of her closet.

17 Let the priests, the ministers of the LORD, weep between the porch and the altar, and let them say, Spare thy people, O LORD, and give not thine heritage to reproach, that the heathen should rule over them: wherefore should they say among the people, Where *is* their אֱלֹהִים?

18 ¶ Then will the LORD be jealous for his land, and pity his people.

19 Yea, the LORD will answer and say unto his people, Behold, I will send you corn, and wine, and oil, and ye shall be satisfied therewith: and I will no more make you a reproach among the heathen:

20 But I will remove far off from you the northern *army*, and will drive him into a land barren and desolate, with his face toward the east sea, and his hinder part toward the utmost sea, and his stink shall come up, and his ill savour shall come up, because he hath done great things.

21 ¶ Fear not, O land; be glad and rejoice: for the LORD will do great things.

22 Be not afraid, ye beasts of the field: for the pastures of the wilderness do spring, for the tree beareth her fruit, the fig tree and the vine do yield their strength.

23 Be glad then, ye children of Zion, and rejoice in the LORD your אֱלֹהִים: for he hath given you the former rain moderately, and he will cause to come down for you the rain, the former rain, and the latter rain in the first *month*.

24 And the floors shall be full of wheat, and the fats shall overflow with wine and oil.

25 And I will restore to you the years that the locust hath eaten, the cankerworm, and the caterpiller, and the palmerworm, my great army which I sent among you.

26 And ye shall eat in plenty, and be satisfied, and praise the name of the LORD your אֱלֹהִים, that hath dealt wondrously with you: and my people shall never be ashamed.

27 And ye shall know that I *am* in the midst of Israel, and *that* I *am* the LORD your אֱלֹהִים, and none else: and my people shall never be ashamed.

28 ¶ And it shall come to pass afterward, *that* I will pour out my spirit upon all flesh; and your sons and your daughters shall prophesy, your old men shall dream dreams, your young men shall see visions:

29 And also upon the servants and upon the handmaids in those days will I pour out my spirit.

30 And I will shew wonders in the heavens and in the earth, blood, and fire, and pillars of smoke.

31 The sun shall be turned into darkness, and the moon into blood, before the great and the terrible day of the LORD come.

32 And it shall come to pass, *that* whosoever shall call on the name of the LORD shall be delivered: for in mount Zion and in Jerusalem shall be deliverance, as the LORD hath said, and in the remnant whom the LORD shall call.

CHAPTER 3

FOR, behold, in those days, and in that time, when I shall bring again the captivity of Judah and Jerusalem,

2 I will also gather all nations, and will bring them down into the valley of Jehoshaphat, and will plead with them there for my people and *for* my heritage Israel, whom they have scattered among the nations, and parted my land.

3 And they have cast lots for my people; and have given a boy for an harlot, and sold a girl for wine, that they might drink.

4 Yea, and what have ye to do with me, O Tyre, and Zidon, and all the coasts of Palestine? will ye render me a recompence? and if ye recompense me, swiftly *and* speedily will I return your recompence upon your own head;

5 Because ye have taken my silver and my gold, and have carried into your temples my goodly pleasant things:

6 The children also of Judah and the children of Jerusalem have ye sold unto the Grecians, that ye might remove them far from their border.

7 Behold, I will raise them out of the place whither ye have sold them, and will return your recompence upon your own head:

8 And I will sell your sons and your daughters into the hand of the children of Judah, and they shall sell them to the Sabeans, to a people far off: for the LORD hath spoken *it*.

9 ¶ Proclaim ye this among the Gentiles; Prepare war, wake up the mighty men, let all the men of war draw near; let them come up:

10 Beat your plowshares into swords, and your pruninghooks into spears: let the weak say, I *am* strong.

11 Assemble yourselves, and come, all ye heathen, and gather yourselves together round about: thither cause thy mighty ones to come down, O LORD.

12 Let the heathen be wakened, and come up to the valley of Jehoshaphat: for there will I sit to judge all the heathen round about.

13 Put ye in the sickle, for the harvest is ripe: come, get you down; for the press is full, the fats overflow; for their wickedness *is* great.

14 Multitudes, multitudes in the valley of decision: for the day of the LORD *is* near in the valley of decision.

15 The sun and the moon shall be darkened, and the stars shall withdraw their shining.

16 The Lord also shall roar out of Zion, and utter his voice from Jerusalem; and the heavens and the earth shall shake: but the Lord *will be* the hope of his people, and the strength of the children of Israel.

17 So shall ye know that I *am* the Lord your אֱלֹהִים dwelling in Zion, my holy mountain: then shall Jerusalem be holy, and there shall no strangers pass through her any more.

18 ¶ And it shall come to pass in that day, *that* the mountains shall drop down new wine, and the hills shall flow with milk, and all the rivers of Judah shall flow with waters, and a fountain shall come forth of the house of the Lord, and shall water the valley of Shittim.

19 Egypt shall be a desolation, and Edom shall be a desolate wilderness, for the violence *against* the children of Judah, because they have shed innocent blood in their land.

20 But Judah shall dwell for ever, and Jerusalem from generation to generation.

21 For I will cleanse their blood *that* I have not cleansed: for the Lord dwelleth in Zion.

AMOS.

CHAPTER 1

THE words of Amos, who was among the herdmen of Tekoa, which he saw concerning Israel in the days of Uzziah king of Judah, and in the days of Jeroboam the son of Joash king of Israel, two years before the earthquake.

2 And he said, The Lord will roar from Zion, and utter his voice from Jerusalem; and the habitations of the shepherds shall mourn, and the top of Carmel shall wither.

3 Thus saith the Lord; For three transgressions of Damascus, and for four, I will not turn away *the punishment* thereof; because they have threshed Gilead with threshing instruments of iron:

4 But I will send a fire into the house of Hazael, which shall devour the palaces of Ben-hadad.

5 I will break also the bar of Damascus, and cut off the inhabitant from the plain of Aven, and him that holdeth the sceptre from the house of Eden: and the people of Syria shall go into captivity unto Kir, saith the Lord.

6 ¶ Thus saith the Lord; For three transgressions of Gaza, and for four, I will not turn away *the punishment* thereof; because they carried away captive the whole captivity, to deliver *them* up to Edom:

7 But I will send a fire on the wall of Gaza, which shall devour the palaces thereof:

8 And I will cut off the inhabitant from Ashdod, and him that holdeth the sceptre from Ashkelon, and I will turn mine hand against Ekron: and the remnant of the Philistines shall perish, saith the Lord אֱלֹהִים.

9 ¶ Thus saith the Lord; For three transgressions of Tyrus, and for four, I will not turn away *the punishment* thereof; because they delivered up the whole captivity to Edom, and remembered not the brotherly covenant:

10 But I will send a fire on the wall of Tyrus, which shall devour the palaces thereof.

11 ¶ Thus saith the Lord; For three transgressions of Edom, and for four, I will not turn away *the punishment* thereof; because he did pursue his brother with the sword, and did cast off all pity, and his anger did tear perpetually, and he kept his wrath for ever:

12 But I will send a fire upon Teman, which shall devour the palaces of Bozrah.

13 ¶ Thus saith the Lord; For three transgressions of the children of Ammon, and for four, I will not turn away *the punishment* thereof; because they have ripped up the women with child of Gilead, that they might enlarge their border:

14 But I will kindle a fire in the wall of Rabbah, and it shall devour the palaces thereof, with shouting in the day of battle, with a tempest in the day of the whirlwind:

15 And their king shall go into captivity, he and his princes together, saith the Lord.

CHAPTER 2

THUS saith the Lord; For three transgressions of Moab, and for four, I will not turn away *the punishment* thereof; because he burned the bones of the king of Edom into lime:

2 But I will send a fire upon Moab, and it shall devour the palaces of Kerioth: and Moab shall die with tumult, with shouting, *and* with the sound of the trumpet:

3 And I will cut off the judge from the midst thereof, and will slay all the princes thereof with him, saith the Lord.

4 ¶ Thus saith the Lord; For three transgressions of Judah, and for four, I will not turn away *the punishment* thereof; because they have despised the law of the Lord, and have not kept his commandments, and their lies caused them to err, after the which their fathers have walked:

5 But I will send a fire upon Judah, and it shall devour the palaces of Jerusalem.

6 ¶ Thus saith the Lord; For three transgressions of Israel, and for four, I will not turn away *the punishment* thereof; because they sold the righteous for silver, and the poor for a pair of shoes;

7 That pant after the dust of the earth on the head of the poor, and turn aside the way of the meek: and a man and his father will go in unto the *same* maid, to profane my holy name:

8 And they lay *themselves* down upon clothes laid to pledge by every altar, and they drink the wine of the condemned *in* the house of their god.

9 ¶ Yet destroyed I the Amorite before them, whose height *was* like the height of the cedars, and he *was* strong as the oaks; yet I destroyed his fruit from above, and his roots from beneath.

10 Also I brought you up from the land of Egypt, and led you forty years through the wilderness, to possess the land of the Amorite.

11 And I raised up of your sons for prophets, and of your young men for Nazarites. *Is it* not even thus, O ye children of Israel? saith the Lord.

12 But ye gave the Nazarites wine to drink; and commanded the prophets, saying, Prophesy not.

13 Behold, I am pressed under you, as a cart is pressed *that is* full of sheaves.

14 Therefore the flight shall perish from the swift, and the strong shall not strengthen his force, neither shall the mighty deliver himself:

15 Neither shall he stand that handleth the bow; and *he that is* swift of foot shall not deliver *himself:* neither shall he that rideth the horse deliver himself.

16 And *he that is* courageous among the mighty shall flee away naked in that day, saith the Lord.

CHAPTER 3

HEAR this word that the LORD hath spoken against you, O children of Israel, against the whole family which I brought up from the land of Egypt, saying,

2 You only have I known of all the families of the earth: therefore I will punish you for all your iniquities.

3 Can two walk together, except they be agreed?

4 Will a lion roar in the forest, when he hath no prey? will a young lion cry out of his den, if he have taken nothing?

5 Can a bird fall in a snare upon the earth, where no gin *is* for him? shall *one* take up a snare from the earth, and have taken nothing at all?

6 Shall a trumpet be blown in the city, and the people not be afraid? shall there be evil in a city, and the LORD hath not done *it?*

7 Surely the Lord אֱלֹהִים will do nothing, but he revealeth his secret unto his servants the prophets.

8 The lion hath roared, who will not fear? the Lord אֱלֹהִים hath spoken, who can but prophesy?

9 ¶ Publish in the palaces at Ashdod, and in the palaces in the land of Egypt, and say, Assemble yourselves upon the mountains of Samaria, and behold the great tumults in the midst thereof, and the oppressed in the midst thereof.

10 For they know not to do right, saith the LORD, who store up violence and robbery in their palaces.

11 Therefore thus saith the Lord אֱלֹהִים; An adversary *there shall be* even round about the land; and he shall bring down thy strength from thee, and thy palaces shall be spoiled.

12 Thus saith the LORD; As the shepherd taketh out of the mouth of the lion two legs, or a piece of an ear; so shall the children of Israel be taken out that dwell in Samaria in the corner of a bed, and in Damascus *in* a couch.

13 Hear ye, and testify in the house of Jacob, saith the Lord אֱלֹהִים, the אֱלֹהִים of hosts,

14 That in the day that I shall visit the transgressions of Israel upon him I will also visit the altars of Beth-el: and the horns of the altar shall be cut off, and fall to the ground.

15 And I will smite the winter house with the summer house; and the houses of ivory shall perish, and the great houses shall have an end, saith the LORD.

CHAPTER 4

HEAR this word, ye kine of Bashan, that *are* in the mountain of Samaria, which oppress the poor, which crush the needy, which say to their masters, Bring, and let us drink.

2 The Lord אֱלֹהִים hath sworn by his holiness, that, lo, the days shall come upon you, that he will take you away with hooks, and your posterity with fishhooks.

3 And ye shall go out at the breaches, every *cow at that which is* before her; and ye shall cast *them* into the palace, saith the LORD.

4 ¶ Come to Beth-el, and transgress; at Gilgal multiply transgression; and bring your sacrifices every morning, *and* your tithes after three years:

5 And offer a sacrifice of thanksgiving with leaven, and proclaim *and* publish the free offerings: for this liketh you, O ye children of Israel, saith the Lord אֱלֹהִים.

6 ¶ And I also have given you cleanness of teeth in all your cities, and want of bread in all your places: yet have ye not returned unto me, saith the LORD.

7 And also I have withholden the rain from you, when *there were* yet three months to the harvest: and I caused it to rain upon one city, and caused it not to rain upon another city: one piece was rained upon, and the piece whereupon it rained not withered.

8 So two *or* three cities wandered unto one city, to drink water; but they were not satisfied: yet have ye not returned unto me, saith the LORD.

9 I have smitten you with blasting and mildew: when your gardens and your vineyards and your fig trees and your olive trees increased, the palmerworm devoured *them:* yet have ye not returned unto me, saith the LORD.

10 I have sent among you the pestilence after the manner of Egypt: your young men have I slain with the sword, and have taken away your horses; and I have made the stink of your camps to come up unto your nostrils: yet have ye not returned unto me, saith the LORD.

11 I have overthrown *some* of you, as אֱלֹהִים overthrew Sodom and Gomorrah, and ye were as a firebrand plucked out of the burning: yet have ye not returned unto me, saith the LORD.

12 Therefore thus will I do unto thee, O Israel: *and* because I will do this unto thee, prepare to meet thy אֱלֹהִים, O Israel.

13 For, lo, he that formeth the mountains, and createth the wind, and declareth unto man what *is* his thought, that maketh the morning darkness, and treadeth upon the high places of the earth, The LORD, The אֱלֹהִים of hosts, *is* his name.

CHAPTER 5

HEAR ye this word which I take up against you, *even* a lamentation, O house of Israel.

2 The virgin of Israel is fallen; she shall no more rise: she is forsaken upon her land; *there is* none to raise her up.

3 For thus saith the Lord אֱלֹהִים; The city that went out *by* a thousand shall leave an hundred, and that which went forth *by* an hundred shall leave ten, to the house of Israel.

4 ¶ For thus saith the LORD unto the house of Israel, Seek ye me, and ye shall live:

5 But seek not Beth-el, nor enter into Gilgal, and pass not to Beer-sheba: for Gilgal shall surely go into captivity, and Beth-el shall come to nought.

6 Seek the LORD, and ye shall live; lest he break out like fire in the house of Joseph, and devour *it,* and *there be* none to quench *it* in Beth-el.

7 Ye who turn judgment to wormwood, and leave off righteousness in the earth,

8 *Seek him* that maketh the seven stars and Orion, and turneth the shadow of death into the morning, and maketh the day dark with night: that calleth for the waters of the sea, and poureth them out upon the face of the earth: The LORD *is* his name:

9 That strengtheneth the spoiled against the strong, so that the spoiled shall come against the fortress.

10 They hate him that rebuketh in the gate, and they abhor him that speaketh uprightly.

11 Forasmuch therefore as your treading *is* upon the poor, and ye take from him burdens of wheat: ye have built houses of hewn stone, but ye shall not dwell in them; ye have planted pleasant vineyards, but ye shall not drink wine of them.

12 For I know your manifold transgressions and your mighty sins: they afflict the just, they take a bribe, and they turn aside the poor in the gate *from their right.*

13 Therefore the prudent shall keep silence in that time; for it *is* an evil time.

14 Seek good, and not evil, that ye may live: and so the Lᴏʀᴅ, the אֱלֹהִים of hosts, shall be with you, as ye have spoken.

15 Hate the evil, and love the good, and establish judgment in the gate: it may be that the Lᴏʀᴅ אֱלֹהִים of hosts will be gracious unto the remnant of Joseph.

16 Therefore the Lᴏʀᴅ, the אֱלֹהִים of hosts, the Lord, saith thus; Wailing *shall be* in all streets; and they shall say in all the highways, Alas! alas! and they shall call the husbandman to mourning, and such as are skilful of lamentation to wailing.

17 And in all vineyards *shall be* wailing: for I will pass through thee, saith the Lᴏʀᴅ.

18 Woe unto you that desire the day of the Lᴏʀᴅ! to what end *is* it for you? the day of the Lᴏʀᴅ *is* darkness, and not light.

19 As if a man did flee from a lion, and a bear met him; or went into the house, and leaned his hand on the wall, and a serpent bit him.

20 *Shall* not the day of the Lᴏʀᴅ *be* darkness, and not light? even very dark, and no brightness in it?

21 ¶ I hate, I despise your feast days, and I will not smell in your solemn assemblies.

22 Though ye offer me burnt offerings and your meat offerings, I will not accept *them:* neither will I regard the peace offerings of your fat beasts.

23 Take thou away from me the noise of thy songs; for I will not hear the melody of thy viols.

24 But let judgment run down as waters, and righteousness as a mighty stream.

25 Have ye offered unto me sacrifices and offerings in the wilderness forty years, O house of Israel?

26 But ye have borne the tabernacle of your Moloch and Chiun your images, the star of your god, which ye made to yourselves.

27 Therefore will I cause you to go into captivity beyond Damascus, saith the Lᴏʀᴅ, whose name *is* The אֱלֹהִים of hosts.

CHAPTER 6

WOE to them *that are* at ease in Zion, and trust in the mountain of Samaria, *which are* named chief of the nations, to whom the house of Israel came!

2 Pass ye unto Calneh, and see; and from thence go ye to Hamath the great: then go down to Gath of the Philistines: *be they* better than these kingdoms? or their border greater than your border?

3 Ye that put far away the evil day, and cause the seat of violence to come near;

4 That lie upon beds of ivory, and stretch themselves upon their couches, and eat the lambs out of the flock, and the calves out of the midst of the stall;

5 That chant to the sound of the viol, *and* invent to themselves instruments of musick, like David;

6 That drink wine in bowls, and anoint themselves with the chief ointments: but they are not grieved for the affliction of Joseph.

7 ¶ Therefore now shall they go captive with the first that go captive, and the banquet of them that stretched themselves shall be removed.

8 The Lord אֱלֹהִים hath sworn by himself, saith the Lᴏʀᴅ the אֱלֹהִים of hosts, I abhor the excellency of Jacob, and hate his palaces: therefore will I deliver up the city with all that is therein.

9 And it shall come to pass, if there remain ten men in one house, that they shall die.

10 And a man's uncle shall take him up, and he that burneth him, to bring out the bones out of the house, and shall say unto him that *is* by the sides of the house, *Is there* yet *any* with thee? and he shall say, No. Then shall he say, Hold thy tongue: for we may not make mention of the name of the Lᴏʀᴅ.

11 For, behold, the Lᴏʀᴅ commandeth, and he will smite the great house with breaches, and the little house with clefts.

12 ¶ Shall horses run upon the rock? will *one* plow *there* with oxen? for ye have turned judgment into gall, and the fruit of righteousness into hemlock:

13 Ye which rejoice in a thing of nought, which say, Have we not taken to us horns by our own strength?

14 But, behold, I will raise up against you a nation, O house of Israel, saith the Lᴏʀᴅ the אֱלֹהִים of hosts; and they shall afflict you from the entering in of Hemath unto the river of the wilderness.

CHAPTER 7

THUS hath the Lord אֱלֹהִים shewed unto me; and, behold, he formed grasshoppers in the beginning of the shooting up of the latter growth; and, lo, *it was* the latter growth after the king's mowings.

2 And it came to pass, *that* when they had made an end of eating the grass of the land, then I said, O Lord אֱלֹהִים, forgive, I beseech thee: by whom shall Jacob arise? for he *is* small.

3 The Lᴏʀᴅ repented for this: It shall not be, saith the Lᴏʀᴅ.

4 ¶ Thus hath the Lord אֱלֹהִים shewed unto me: and, behold, the Lord אֱלֹהִים called to contend by fire, and it devoured the great deep, and did eat up a part.

5 Then said I, O Lord אֱלֹהִים, cease, I beseech thee: by whom shall Jacob arise? for he *is* small.

6 The Lᴏʀᴅ repented for this: This also shall not be, saith the Lord אֱלֹהִים.

7 ¶ Thus he shewed me: and, behold, the Lord stood upon a wall *made* by a plumbline, with a plumbline in his hand.

8 And the Lᴏʀᴅ said unto me, Amos, what seest thou? And I said, A plumbline. Then said the Lord, Behold, I will set a plumbline in the midst of my people Israel: I will not again pass by them any more:

9 And the high places of Isaac shall be desolate, and the sanctuaries of Israel shall be laid waste; and I will rise against the house of Jeroboam with the sword.

10 ¶ Then Amaziah the priest of Beth-el sent to Jeroboam king of Israel, saying, Amos hath conspired against thee in the midst of the house of Israel: the land is not able to bear all his words.

11 For thus Amos saith, Jeroboam shall die by the sword, and Israel shall surely be led away captive out of their own land.

12 Also Amaziah said unto Amos, O thou seer, go, flee thee away into the land of Judah, and there eat bread, and prophesy there:

13 But prophesy not again any more at Beth-el: for it *is* the king's chapel, and it *is* the king's court.

14 ¶ Then answered Amos, and said to Amaziah, I *was* no prophet, neither *was* I a prophet's son; but I *was* an herdman, and a gatherer of sycomore fruit:

15 And the Lᴏʀᴅ took me as I followed the flock, and the Lᴏʀᴅ said unto me, Go, prophesy unto my people Israel.

16 ¶ Now therefore hear thou the word of the Lᴏʀᴅ: Thou sayest, Prophesy not against Israel, and drop not *thy word* against the house of Isaac.

17 Therefore thus saith the Lᴏʀᴅ; Thy wife shall be an harlot in the city, and thy sons and thy daughters shall fall by the sword, and thy land shall be divided by line; and thou shalt die in a polluted land: and Israel shall surely go into captivity forth of his land.

CHAPTER 8

THUS hath the Lord אֱלֹהִים shewed unto me: and behold a basket of summer fruit.

2 And he said, Amos, what seest thou? And I said, A basket of summer fruit. Then said the LORD unto me, The end is come upon my people of Israel; I will not again pass by them any more.

3 And the songs of the temple shall be howlings in that day, saith the Lord אֱלֹהִים: *there shall be* many dead bodies in every place; they shall cast *them* forth with silence.

4 ¶ Hear this, O ye that swallow up the needy, even to make the poor of the land to fail,

5 Saying, When will the new moon be gone, that we may sell corn? and the sabbath, that we may set forth wheat, making the ephah small, and the shekel great, and falsifying the balances by deceit?

6 That we may buy the poor for silver, and the needy for a pair of shoes; *yea,* and sell the refuse of the wheat?

7 The LORD hath sworn by the excellency of Jacob, Surely I will never forget any of their works.

8 Shall not the land tremble for this, and every one mourn that dwelleth therein? and it shall rise up wholly as a flood; and it shall be cast out and drowned, as *by* the flood of Egypt.

9 And it shall come to pass in that day, saith the Lord אֱלֹהִים, that I will cause the sun to go down at noon, and I will darken the earth in the clear day:

10 And I will turn your feasts into mourning, and all your songs into lamentation; and I will bring up sackcloth upon all loins, and baldness upon every head; and I will make it as the mourning of an only *son,* and the end thereof as a bitter day.

11 ¶ Behold, the days come, saith the Lord אֱלֹהִים, that I will send a famine in the land, not a famine of bread, nor a thirst for water, but of hearing the words of the LORD:

12 And they shall wander from sea to sea, and from the north even to the east, they shall run to and fro to seek the word of the LORD, and shall not find *it.*

13 In that day shall the fair virgins and young men faint for thirst.

14 They that swear by the sin of Samaria, and say, Thy god, O Dan, liveth; and, The manner of Beer-sheba liveth; even they shall fall, and never rise up again.

CHAPTER 9

I SAW the Lord standing upon the altar: and he said, Smite the lintel of the door, that the posts may shake: and cut them in the head, all of them; and I will slay the last of them with the sword: he that fleeth of them shall not flee away, and he that escapeth of them shall not be delivered.

2 Though they dig into hell, thence shall mine hand take them; though they climb up to heaven, thence will I bring them down:

3 And though they hide themselves in the top of Carmel, I will search and take them out thence; and though they be hid from my sight in the bottom of the sea, thence will I command the serpent, and he shall bite them:

4 And though they go into captivity before their enemies, thence will I command the sword, and it shall slay them: and I will set mine eyes upon them for evil, and not for good.

5 And the Lord אֱלֹהִים of hosts *is* he that toucheth the land, and it shall melt, and all that dwell therein shall mourn: and it shall rise up wholly like a flood; and shall be drowned, as *by* the flood of Egypt.

6 *It is* he that buildeth his stories in the heaven, and hath founded his troop in the earth; he that calleth for the waters of the sea, and poureth them out upon the face of the earth: The LORD *is* his name.

7 *Are* ye not as children of the Ethiopians unto me, O children of Israel? saith the LORD. Have not I brought up Israel out of the land of Egypt? and the Philistines from Caphtor, and the Syrians from Kir?

8 Behold, the eyes of the Lord אֱלֹהִים *are* upon the sinful kingdom, and I will destroy it from off the face of the earth; saving that I will not utterly destroy the house of Jacob, saith the LORD.

9 For, lo, I will command, and I will sift the house of Israel among all nations, like as *corn* is sifted in a sieve, yet shall not the least grain fall upon the earth.

10 All the sinners of my people shall die by the sword, which say, The evil shall not overtake nor prevent us.

11 ¶ In that day will I raise up the tabernacle of David that is fallen, and close up the breaches thereof; and I will raise up his ruins, and I will build it as in the days of old:

12 That they may possess the remnant of Edom, and of all the heathen, which are called by my name, saith the LORD that doeth this.

13 Behold, the days come, saith the LORD, that the plowman shall overtake the reaper, and the treader of grapes him that soweth seed; and the mountains shall drop sweet wine, and all the hills shall melt.

14 And I will bring again the captivity of my people of Israel, and they shall build the waste cities, and inhabit *them;* and they shall plant vineyards, and drink the wine thereof; they shall also make gardens, and eat the fruit of them.

15 And I will plant them upon their land, and they shall no more be pulled up out of their land which I have given them, saith the LORD thy אֱלֹהִים.

OBADIAH.

CHAPTER 1

THE vision of Obadiah. Thus saith the Lord אֱלֹהִים concerning Edom; We have heard a rumour from the LORD, and an ambassador is sent among the heathen, Arise ye, and let us rise up against her in battle.

2 Behold, I have made thee small among the heathen: thou art greatly despised.

3 ¶ The pride of thine heart hath deceived thee, thou that dwellest in the clefts of the rock, whose habitation *is* high; that saith in his heart, Who shall bring me down to the ground?

4 Though thou exalt *thyself* as the eagle, and though thou set thy nest among the stars, thence will I bring thee down, saith the LORD.

5 If thieves came to thee, if robbers by night, (how art thou cut off!) would they not have stolen till they had enough? if the grapegatherers came to thee, would they not leave *some* grapes?

6 How are *the things* of Esau searched out! how are his hidden things sought up!

7 All the men of thy confederacy have brought thee *even* to the border: the men that were at peace with thee have deceived thee, *and*

prevailed against thee; *they that eat* thy bread have laid a wound under thee: *there is* none understanding in him.

8 Shall I not in that day, saith the LORD, even destroy the wise *men* out of Edom, and understanding out of the mount of Esau?

9 And thy mighty *men*, O Teman, shall be dismayed, to the end that every one of the mount of Esau may be cut off by slaughter.

10 ¶ For *thy* violence against thy brother Jacob shame shall cover thee, and thou shalt be cut off for ever.

11 In the day that thou stoodest on the other side, in the day that the strangers carried away captive his forces, and foreigners entered into his gates, and cast lots upon Jerusalem, even thou *wast* as one of them.

12 But thou shouldest not have looked on the day of thy brother in the day that he became a stranger; neither shouldest thou have rejoiced over the children of Judah in the day of their destruction; neither shouldest thou have spoken proudly in the day of distress.

13 Thou shouldest not have entered into the gate of my people in the day of their calamity; yea, thou shouldest not have looked on their affliction in the day of their calamity, nor have laid *hands* on their substance in the day of their calamity;

14 Neither shouldest thou have stood in the crossway, to cut off those of his that did escape; neither shouldest thou have delivered up those of his that did remain in the day of distress.

15 For the day of the LORD *is* near upon all the heathen: as thou hast done, it shall be done unto thee: thy reward shall return upon thine own head.

16 For as ye have drunk upon my holy mountain, *so* shall all the heathen drink continually, yea, they shall drink, and they shall swallow down, and they shall be as though they had not been.

17 ¶ But upon mount Zion shall be deliverance, and there shall be holiness; and the house of Jacob shall possess their possessions.

18 And the house of Jacob shall be a fire, and the house of Joseph a flame, and the house of Esau for stubble, and they shall kindle in them, and devour them; and there shall not be *any* remaining of the house of Esau; for the LORD hath spoken *it*.

19 And *they of* the south shall possess the mount of Esau; and *they of* the plain the Philistines: and they shall possess the fields of Ephraim, and the fields of Samaria: and Benjamin *shall possess* Gilead.

20 And the captivity of this host of the children of Israel *shall possess* that of the Canaanites, *even* unto Zarephath; and the captivity of Jerusalem, which *is* in Sepharad, shall possess the cities of the south.

21 And saviours shall come up on mount Zion to judge the mount of Esau; and the kingdom shall be the LORD's.

JONAH.

CHAPTER 1

NOW the word of the LORD came unto Jonah the son of Amittai, saying,

2 Arise, go to Nineveh, that great city, and cry against it; for their wickedness is come up before me.

3 But Jonah rose up to flee unto Tarshish from the presence of the LORD, and went down to Joppa; and he found a ship going to Tarshish: so he paid the fare thereof, and went down into it, to go with them unto Tarshish from the presence of the LORD.

4 ¶ But the LORD sent out a great wind into the sea, and there was a mighty tempest in the sea, so that the ship was like to be broken.

5 Then the mariners were afraid, and cried every man unto his god, and cast forth the wares that *were* in the ship into the sea, to lighten *it* of them. But Jonah was gone down into the sides of the ship; and he lay, and was fast asleep.

6 So the shipmaster came to him, and said unto him, What meanest thou, O sleeper? arise, call upon thy אֱלֹהִים, if so be that אֱלֹהִים will think upon us, that we perish not.

7 And they said every one to his fellow, Come, and let us cast lots, that we may know for whose cause this evil *is* upon us. So they cast lots, and the lot fell upon Jonah.

8 Then said they unto him, Tell us, we pray thee, for whose cause this evil *is* upon us; What *is* thine occupation? and whence comest thou? what *is* thy country? and of what people *art* thou?

9 And he said unto them, I *am* an Hebrew; and I fear the LORD, the אֱלֹהִים of heaven, which hath made the sea and the dry *land*.

10 Then were the men exceedingly afraid, and said unto him, Why hast thou done this? For the men knew that he fled from the presence of the LORD, because he had told them.

11 ¶ Then said they unto him, What shall we do unto thee, that the sea may be calm unto us? for the sea wrought, and was tempestuous.

12 And he said unto them, Take me up, and cast me forth into the sea; so shall the sea be calm unto you: for I know that for my sake this great tempest *is* upon you.

13 Nevertheless the men rowed hard to bring *it* to the land; but they could not: for the sea wrought, and was tempestuous against them.

14 Wherefore they cried unto the LORD, and said, We beseech thee, O LORD, we beseech thee, let us not perish for this man's life, and lay not upon us innocent blood: for thou, O LORD, hast done as it pleased thee.

15 So they took up Jonah, and cast him forth into the sea: and the sea ceased from her raging.

16 Then the men feared the LORD exceedingly, and offered a sacrifice unto the LORD, and made vows.

17 ¶ Now the LORD had prepared a great fish to swallow up Jonah. And Jonah was in the belly of the fish three days and three nights.

CHAPTER 2

THEN Jonah prayed unto the LORD his אֱלֹהִים out of the fish's belly,

2 And said, I cried by reason of mine affliction unto the LORD, and he heard me; out of the belly of hell cried I, *and* thou heardest my voice.

3 For thou hadst cast me into the deep, in the midst of the seas; and the floods compassed me about: all thy billows and thy waves passed over me.

4 Then I said, I am cast out of thy sight; yet I will look again toward thy holy temple.

5 The waters compassed me about, *even* to the soul: the depth closed me round about, the weeds were wrapped about my head.

6 I went down to the bottoms of the mountains; the earth with her bars *was* about me for ever: yet hast thou brought up my life from corruption, O LORD my אֱלֹהִים.

7 When my soul fainted within me I remembered the LORD: and my prayer came in unto thee, into thine holy temple.

8 They that observe lying vanities forsake their own mercy.

9 But I will sacrifice unto thee with the voice of thanksgiving; I will pay *that* that I have vowed. Salvation *is* of the LORD.

10 ¶ And the LORD spake unto the fish, and it vomited out Jonah upon the dry *land*.

AND the word of the Lord came unto Jonah the second time, saying,

2 Arise, go unto Nineveh, that great city, and preach unto it the preaching that I bid thee.

3 So Jonah arose, and went unto Nineveh, according to the word of the Lord. Now Nineveh was an exceeding great city of three days' journey.

4 And Jonah began to enter into the city a day's journey, and he cried, and said, Yet forty days, and Nineveh shall be overthrown.

5 ¶ So the people of Nineveh believed אֱלֹהִים, and proclaimed a fast, and put on sackcloth, from the greatest of them even to the least of them.

6 For word came unto the king of Nineveh, and he arose from his throne, and he laid his robe from him, and covered *him* with sackcloth, and sat in ashes.

7 And he caused *it* to be proclaimed and published through Nineveh by the decree of the king and his nobles, saying, Let neither man nor beast, herd nor flock, taste any thing: let them not feed, nor drink water:

8 But let man and beast be covered with sackcloth, and cry mightily unto אֱלֹהִים: yea, let them turn every one from his evil way, and from the violence that *is* in their hands.

9 Who can tell *if* אֱלֹהִים will turn and repent, and turn away from his fierce anger, that we perish not?

10 ¶ And אֱלֹהִים saw their works, that they turned from their evil way; and אֱלֹהִים repented of the evil, that he had said that he would do unto them; and he did *it* not.

CHAPTER 4

BUT it displeased Jonah exceedingly, and he was very angry.

2 And he prayed unto the Lord, and said, I pray thee, O Lord, *was* not this my saying, when I was yet in my country? Therefore I fled before unto Tarshish: for I knew that thou *art* a gracious אֱלֹהִים, and merciful, slow to anger, and of great kindness, and repentest thee of the evil.

3 Therefore now, O Lord, take, I beseech thee, my life from me; for *it is* better for me to die than to live.

4 ¶ Then said the Lord, Doest thou well to be angry?

5 So Jonah went out of the city, and sat on the east side of the city, and there made him a booth, and sat under it in the shadow, till he might see what would become of the city.

6 And the Lord אֱלֹהִים prepared a gourd, and made *it* to come up over Jonah, that it might be a shadow over his head, to deliver him from his grief. So Jonah was exceeding glad of the gourd.

7 But אֱלֹהִים prepared a worm when the morning rose the next day, and it smote the gourd that it withered.

8 And it came to pass, when the sun did arise, that אֱלֹהִים prepared a vehement east wind; and the sun beat upon the head of Jonah, that he fainted, and wished in himself to die, and said, *It is* better for me to die than to live.

9 And אֱלֹהִים said to Jonah, Doest thou well to be angry for the gourd? And he said, I do well to be angry, *even* unto death.

10 Then said the Lord, Thou hast had pity on the gourd, for the which thou hast not laboured, neither madest it grow; which came up in a night, and perished in a night:

11 And should not I spare Nineveh, that great city, wherein are more than sixscore thousand persons that cannot discern between their right hand and their left hand; and *also* much cattle?

MICAH.

CHAPTER 1

THE word of the Lord that came to Micah the Morasthite in the days of Jotham, Ahaz, *and* Hezekiah, kings of Judah, which he saw concerning Samaria and Jerusalem.

2 Hear, all ye people; hearken, O earth, and all that therein is: and let the Lord אֱלֹהִים be witness against you, the Lord from his holy temple.

3 For, behold, the Lord cometh forth out of his place, and will come down, and tread upon the high places of the earth.

4 And the mountains shall be molten under him, and the valleys shall be cleft, as wax before the fire, *and* as the waters *that are* poured down a steep place.

5 For the transgression of Jacob *is* all this, and for the sins of the house of Israel. What *is* the transgression of Jacob? *is it* not Samaria? and what *are* the high places of Judah? *are they* not Jerusalem?

6 Therefore I will make Samaria as an heap of the field, *and* as plantings of a vineyard: and I will pour down the stones thereof into the valley, and I will discover the foundations thereof.

7 And all the graven images thereof shall be beaten to pieces, and all the hires thereof shall be burned with the fire, and all the idols thereof will I lay desolate: for she gathered *it* of the hire of an harlot, and they shall return to the hire of an harlot.

8 Therefore I will wail and howl, I will go stripped and naked: I will make a wailing like the dragons, and mourning as the owls.

9 For her wound *is* incurable; for it is come unto Judah; he is come unto the gate of my people, *even* to Jerusalem.

10 ¶ Declare ye *it* not at Gath, weep ye not at all: in the house of Aphrah roll thyself in the dust.

11 Pass ye away, thou inhabitant of Saphir, having thy shame naked: the inhabitant of Zaanan came not forth in the mourning of Beth-ezel; he shall receive of you his standing.

12 For the inhabitant of Maroth waited carefully for good: but evil came down from the Lord unto the gate of Jerusalem.

13 O thou inhabitant of Lachish, bind the chariot to the swift beast: she *is* the beginning of the sin to the daughter of Zion: for the transgressions of Israel were found in thee.

14 Therefore shalt thou give presents to Moresheth-gath: the houses of Achzib *shall be* a lie to the kings of Israel.

15 Yet will I bring an heir unto thee, O inhabitant of Mareshah: he shall come unto Adullam the glory of Israel.

16 Make thee bald, and poll thee for thy delicate children; enlarge thy baldness as the eagle; for they are gone into captivity from thee.

CHAPTER 2

WOE to them that devise iniquity, and work evil upon their beds! when the morning is light, they practise it, because it is in the power of their hand.

2 And they covet fields, and take *them* by violence; and houses, and take *them* away: so they oppress a man and his house, even a man and his heritage.

3 Therefore thus saith the LORD; Behold, against this family do I devise an evil, from which ye shall not remove your necks; neither shall ye go haughtily: for this time *is* evil.

4 ¶ In that day shall *one* take up a parable against you, and lament with a doleful lamentation, *and* say, We be utterly spoiled: he hath changed the portion of my people: how hath he removed *it* from me! turning away he hath divided our fields.

5 Therefore thou shalt have none that shall cast a cord by lot in the congregation of the LORD.

6 Prophesy ye not, *say they to them that* prophesy: they shall not prophesy to them, *that* they shall not take shame.

7 ¶ O *thou that art* named the house of Jacob, is the spirit of the LORD straitened? *are* these his doings? do not my words do good to him that walketh uprightly?

8 Even of late my people is risen up as an enemy: ye pull off the robe with the garment from them that pass by securely as men averse from war.

9 The women of my people have ye cast out from their pleasant houses; from their children have ye taken away my glory for ever.

10 Arise ye, and depart; for this *is* not *your* rest: because it is polluted, it shall destroy *you*, even with a sore destruction.

11 If a man walking in the spirit and falsehood do lie, *saying,* I will prophesy unto thee of wine and of strong drink; he shall even be the prophet of this people.

12 ¶ I will surely assemble, O Jacob, all of thee; I will surely gather the remnant of Israel; I will put them together as the sheep of Bozrah, as the flock in the midst of their fold: they shall make great noise by reason of *the multitude of* men.

13 The breaker is come up before them: they have broken up, and have passed through the gate, and are gone out by it: and their king shall pass before them, and the LORD on the head of them.

CHAPTER 3

AND I said, Hear, I pray you, O heads of Jacob, and ye princes of the house of Israel; *Is it* not for you to know judgment?

2 Who hate the good, and love the evil; who pluck off their skin from off them, and their flesh from off their bones;

3 Who also eat the flesh of my people, and flay their skin from off them; and they break their bones, and chop them in pieces, as for the pot, and as flesh within the caldron.

4 Then shall they cry unto the LORD, but he will not hear them: he will even hide his face from them at that time, as they have behaved themselves ill in their doings.

5 ¶ Thus saith the LORD concerning the prophets that make my people err, that bite with their teeth, and cry, Peace; and he that putteth not into their mouths, they even prepare war against him.

6 Therefore night *shall be* unto you, that ye shall not have a vision; and it shall be dark unto you, that ye shall not divine; and the sun shall go down over the prophets, and the day shall be dark over them.

7 Then shall the seers be ashamed, and the diviners confounded: yea, they shall all cover their lips; for *there is* no answer of אֱלֹהִים.

8 ¶ But truly I am full of power by the spirit of the LORD, and of judgment, and of might, to declare unto Jacob his transgression, and to Israel his sin.

9 Hear this, I pray you, ye heads of the house of Jacob, and princes of the house of Israel, that abhor judgment, and pervert all equity.

10 They build up Zion with blood, and Jerusalem with iniquity.

11 The heads thereof judge for reward, and the priests thereof teach for hire, and the prophets thereof divine for money: yet will they lean upon the LORD, and say, *Is* not the LORD among us? none evil can come upon us.

12 Therefore shall Zion for your sake be plowed *as* a field, and Jerusalem shall become heaps, and the mountain of the house as the high places of the forest.

CHAPTER 4

BUT in the last days it shall come to pass, *that* the mountain of the house of the LORD shall be established in the top of the mountains, and it shall be exalted above the hills; and people shall flow unto it.

2 And many nations shall come, and say, Come, and let us go up to the mountain of the LORD, and to the house of the אֱלֹהִים of Jacob; and he will teach us of his ways, and we will walk in his paths: for the law shall go forth of Zion, and the word of the LORD from Jerusalem.

3 ¶ And he shall judge among many people, and rebuke strong nations afar off; and they shall beat their swords into plowshares, and their spears into pruninghooks: nation shall not lift up a sword against nation, neither shall they learn war any more.

4 But they shall sit every man under his vine and under his fig tree; and none shall make *them* afraid: for the mouth of the LORD of hosts hath spoken *it*.

5 For all people will walk every one in the name of his god, and we will walk in the name of the LORD our אֱלֹהִים for ever and ever.

6 In that day, saith the LORD, will I assemble her that halteth, and I will gather her that is driven out, and her that I have afflicted;

7 And I will make her that halted a remnant, and her that was cast far off a strong nation: and the LORD shall reign over them in mount Zion from henceforth, even for ever.

8 ¶ And thou, O tower of the flock, the strong hold of the daughter of Zion, unto thee shall it come, even the first dominion; the kingdom shall come to the daughter of Jerusalem.

9 Now why dost thou cry out aloud? *is there* no king in thee? is thy counseller perished? for pangs have taken thee as a woman in travail.

10 Be in pain, and labour to bring forth, O daughter of Zion, like a woman in travail: for now shalt thou go forth out of the city, and thou shalt dwell in the field, and thou shalt go *even* to Babylon; there shalt thou be delivered; there the LORD shall redeem thee from the hand of thine enemies.

11 ¶ Now also many nations are gathered against thee, that say, Let her be defiled, and let our eye look upon Zion.

12 But they know not the thoughts of the LORD, neither understand they his counsel: for he shall gather them as the sheaves into the floor.

13 Arise and thresh, O daughter of Zion: for I will make thine horn iron, and I will make thy hoofs brass: and thou shalt beat in pieces many people: and I will consecrate their gain unto the LORD, and their substance unto the Lord of the whole earth.

CHAPTER 5

NOW gather thyself in troops, O daughter of troops: he hath laid siege against us: they shall smite the judge of Israel with a rod upon the cheek.

2 But thou, Beth-lehem Ephratah, *though* thou be little among the thousands of Judah, *yet* out of thee shall he come forth unto me *that is* to be ruler in Israel; whose goings forth *have been* from of old, from everlasting.

3 Therefore will he give them up, until the time *that* she which travaileth hath brought forth: then the remnant of his brethren shall return unto the children of Israel.

4 ¶ And he shall stand and feed in the strength of the Lord, in the majesty of the name of the Lord his אֱלֹהִים; and they shall abide: for now shall he be great unto the ends of the earth.

5 And this *man* shall be the peace, when the Assyrian shall come into our land: and when he shall tread in our palaces, then shall we raise against him seven shepherds, and eight principal men.

6 And they shall waste the land of Assyria with the sword, and the land of Nimrod in the entrances thereof: thus shall he deliver *us* from the Assyrian, when he cometh into our land, and when he treadeth within our borders.

7 And the remnant of Jacob shall be in the midst of many people as a dew from the Lord, as the showers upon the grass, that tarrieth not for man, nor waiteth for the sons of men.

8 ¶ And the remnant of Jacob shall be among the Gentiles in the midst of many people as a lion among the beasts of the forest, as a young lion among the flocks of sheep: who, if he go through, both treadeth down, and teareth in pieces, and none can deliver.

9 Thine hand shall be lifted up upon thine adversaries, and all thine enemies shall be cut off.

10 And it shall come to pass in that day, saith the Lord, that I will cut off thy horses out of the midst of thee, and I will destroy thy chariots:

11 And I will cut off the cities of thy land, and throw down all thy strong holds:

12 And I will cut off witchcrafts out of thine hand; and thou shalt have no *more* soothsayers:

13 Thy graven images also will I cut off, and thy standing images out of the midst of thee; and thou shalt no more worship the work of thine hands.

14 And I will pluck up thy groves out of the midst of thee: so will I destroy thy cities.

15 And I will execute vengeance in anger and fury upon the heathen, such as they have not heard.

CHAPTER 6

HEAR ye now what the Lord saith; Arise, contend thou before the mountains, and let the hills hear thy voice.

2 Hear ye, O mountains, the Lord's controversy, and ye strong foundations of the earth: for the Lord hath a controversy with his people, and he will plead with Israel.

3 O my people, what have I done unto thee? and wherein have I wearied thee? testify against me.

4 For I brought thee up out of the land of Egypt, and redeemed thee out of the house of servants; and I sent before thee Moses, Aaron, and Miriam.

5 O my people, remember now what Balak king of Moab consulted, and what Balaam the son of Beor answered him from Shittim unto Gilgal; that ye may know the righteousness of the Lord.

6 ¶ Wherewith shall I come before the Lord, *and* bow myself before the high אֱלֹהִים? shall I come before him with burnt offerings, with calves of a year old?

7 Will the Lord be pleased with thousands of rams, *or* with ten thousands of rivers of oil? shall I give my firstborn *for* my transgression, the fruit of my body *for* the sin of my soul?

8 He hath shewed thee, O man, what *is* good; and what doth the Lord require of thee, but to do justly, and to love mercy, and to walk humbly with thy אֱלֹהִים?

9 The Lord's voice crieth unto the city, and *the man of* wisdom shall see thy name: hear ye the rod, and who hath appointed it.

10 ¶ Are there yet the treasures of wickedness in the house of the wicked, and the scant measure *that is* abominable?

11 Shall I count *them* pure with the wicked balances, and with the bag of deceitful weights?

12 For the rich men thereof are full of violence, and the inhabitants thereof have spoken lies, and their tongue *is* deceitful in their mouth.

13 Therefore also will I make *thee* sick in smiting thee, in making *thee* desolate because of thy sins.

14 Thou shalt eat, but not be satisfied; and thy casting down *shall be* in the midst of thee; and thou shalt take hold, but shalt not deliver; and *that* which thou deliverest will I give up to the sword.

15 Thou shalt sow, but thou shalt not reap; thou shalt tread the olives, but thou shalt not anoint thee with oil; and sweet wine, but shalt not drink wine.

16 ¶ For the statutes of Omri are kept, and all the works of the house of Ahab, and ye walk in their counsels; that I should make thee a desolation, and the inhabitants thereof an hissing: therefore ye shall bear the reproach of my people.

CHAPTER 7

WOE is me! for I am as when they have gathered the summer fruits, as the grapegleanings of the vintage: *there is* no cluster to eat: my soul desired the firstripe fruit.

2 The good *man* is perished out of the earth: and *there is* none upright among men: they all lie in wait for blood; they hunt every man his brother with a net.

3 ¶ That they may do evil with both hands earnestly, the prince asketh, and the judge *asketh* for a reward; and the great *man*, he uttereth his mischievous desire: so they wrap it up.

4 The best of them *is* as a brier: the most upright *is sharper* than a thorn hedge: the day of thy watchmen *and* thy visitation cometh; now shall be their perplexity.

5 ¶ Trust ye not in a friend, put ye not confidence in a guide: keep the doors of thy mouth from her that lieth in thy bosom.

6 For the son dishonoureth the father, the daughter riseth up against her mother, the daughter in law against her mother in law; a man's enemies *are* the men of his own house.

7 Therefore I will look unto the Lord; I will wait for the אֱלֹהִים of my salvation: my אֱלֹהִים will hear me.

8 ¶ Rejoice not against me, O mine enemy: when I fall, I shall arise; when I sit in darkness, the Lord *shall be* a light unto me.

9 I will bear the indignation of the Lord, because I have sinned against him, until he plead my cause, and execute judgment for me: he

will bring me forth to the light, *and* I shall behold his righteousness.

10 Then *she that is* mine enemy shall see *it*, and shame shall cover her which said unto me, Where is the LORD thy אֱלֹהִים? mine eyes shall behold her: now shall she be trodden down as the mire of the streets.

11 *In* the day that thy walls are to be built, *in* that day shall the decree be far removed.

12 *In* that day *also* he shall come even to thee from Assyria, and *from* the fortified cities, and from the fortress even to the river, and from sea to sea, and *from* mountain to mountain.

13 Notwithstanding the land shall be desolate because of them that dwell therein, for the fruit of their doings.

14 ¶ Feed thy people with thy rod, the flock of thine heritage, which dwell solitarily *in* the wood, in the midst of Carmel: let them feed *in* Bashan and Gilead, as in the days of old.

15 According to the days of thy coming out of the land of Egypt will I shew unto him marvellous *things*.

16 ¶ The nations shall see and be confounded at all their might: they shall lay *their* hand upon *their* mouth, their ears shall be deaf.

17 They shall lick the dust like a serpent, they shall move out of their holes like worms of the earth: they shall be afraid of the LORD our אֱלֹהִים, and shall fear because of thee.

18 Who *is* a אֱלֹהִים like unto thee, that pardoneth iniquity, and passeth by the transgression of the remnant of his heritage? he retaineth not his anger for ever, because he delighteth *in* mercy.

19 He will turn again, he will have compassion upon us; he will subdue our iniquities; and thou wilt cast all their sins into the depths of the sea.

20 Thou wilt perform the truth to Jacob, *and* the mercy to Abraham, which thou hast sworn unto our fathers from the days of old.

NAHUM.

CHAPTER 1

THE burden of Nineveh. The book of the vision of Nahum the Elkoshite.

2 אֱלֹהִים *is* jealous, and the LORD revengeth; the LORD revengeth, and *is* furious; the LORD will take vengeance on his adversaries, and he reserveth *wrath* for his enemies.

3 The LORD *is* slow to anger, and great in power, and will not at all acquit *the wicked*: the LORD *hath* his way in the whirlwind and in the storm, and the clouds *are* the dust of his feet.

4 He rebuketh the sea, and maketh it dry, and drieth up all the rivers: Bashan languisheth, and Carmel, and the flower of Lebanon languisheth.

5 The mountains quake at him, and the hills melt, and the earth is burned at his presence, yea, the world, and all that dwell therein.

6 Who can stand before his indignation? and who can abide in the fierceness of his anger? his fury is poured out like fire, and the rocks are thrown down by him.

7 The LORD *is* good, a strong hold in the day of trouble; and he knoweth them that trust in him.

8 But with an overrunning flood he will make an utter end of the place thereof, and darkness shall pursue his enemies.

9 What do ye imagine against the LORD? he will make an utter end: affliction shall not rise up the second time.

10 For while *they be* folden together *as* thorns, and while they are drunken *as* drunkards, they shall be devoured as stubble fully dry.

11 There is *one* come out of thee, that imagineth evil against the LORD, a wicked counseller.

12 Thus saith the LORD; Though *they be* quiet, and likewise many, yet thus shall they be cut down, when he shall pass through. Though I have afflicted thee, I will afflict thee no more.

13 For now will I break his yoke from off thee, and will burst thy bonds in sunder.

14 And the LORD hath given a commandment concerning thee, *that* no more of thy name be sown: out of the house of thy gods will I cut off the graven image and the molten image: I will make thy grave; for thou art vile.

15 Behold upon the mountains the feet of him that bringeth good tidings, that publisheth peace! O Judah, keep thy solemn feasts, perform thy vows: for the wicked shall no more pass through thee; he is utterly cut off.

CHAPTER 2

HE that dasheth in pieces is come up before thy face: keep the munition, watch the way, make *thy* loins strong, fortify *thy* power mightily.

2 For the LORD hath turned away the excellency of Jacob, as the excellency of Israel: for the emptiers have emptied them out, and marred their vine branches.

3 The shield of his mighty men is made red, the valiant men *are* in scarlet: the chariots *shall be* with flaming torches in the day of his preparation, and the fir trees shall be terribly shaken.

4 The chariots shall rage in the streets, they shall justle one against another in the broad ways: they shall seem like torches, they shall run like the lightnings.

5 He shall recount his worthies: they shall stumble in their walk; they shall make haste to the wall thereof, and the defence shall be prepared.

6 The gates of the rivers shall be opened, and the palace shall be dissolved.

7 And Huzzab shall be led away captive, she shall be brought up, and her maids shall lead *her* as with the voice of doves, tabering upon their breasts.

8 But Nineveh *is* of old like a pool of water: yet they shall flee away. Stand, stand, *shall they cry*; but none shall look back.

9 Take ye the spoil of silver, take the spoil of gold: for *there is* none end of the store *and* glory out of all the pleasant furniture.

10 She is empty, and void, and waste: and the heart melteth, and the knees smite together, and much pain *is* in all loins, and the faces of them all gather blackness.

11 Where *is* the dwelling of the lions, and the feedingplace of the young lions, where the lion, *even* the old lion, walked, *and* the lion's whelp, and none made *them* afraid?

12 The lion did tear in pieces enough for his whelps, and strangled for his lionesses, and filled his holes with prey, and his dens with ravin.

13 Behold, I *am* against thee, saith the LORD of hosts, and I will burn her chariots in the smoke, and the sword shall devour thy young lions: and I will cut off thy prey from the earth, and the voice of thy messengers shall no more be heard.

WOE to the bloody city! it *is* all full of lies *and* robbery; the prey departeth not;

2 The noise of a whip, and the noise of the rattling of the wheels, and of the pransing horses, and of the jumping chariots.

3 The horseman lifteth up both the bright sword and the glittering spear: and *there is* a multitude of slain, and a great number of carcases; and *there is* none end of *their* corpses; they stumble upon their corpses:

4 Because of the multitude of the whoredoms of the wellfavoured harlot, the mistress of witchcrafts, that selleth nations through her whoredoms, and families through her witchcrafts.

5 Behold, I *am* against thee, saith the LORD of hosts; and I will discover thy skirts upon thy face, and I will shew the nations thy nakedness, and the kingdoms thy shame.

6 And I will cast abominable filth upon thee, and make thee vile, and will set thee as a gazingstock.

7 And it shall come to pass, *that* all they that look upon thee shall flee from thee, and say, Nineveh is laid waste: who will bemoan her? whence shall I seek comforters for thee?

8 Art thou better than populous No, that was situate among the rivers, *that had* the waters round about it, whose rampart *was* the sea, *and* her wall *was* from the sea?

9 Ethiopia and Egypt *were* her strength, and *it was* infinite; Put and Lubim were thy helpers.

10 Yet *was* she carried away, she went into captivity: her young children also were dashed in pieces at the top of all the streets: and they cast lots for her honourable men, and all her great men were bound in chains.

11 Thou also shalt be drunken: thou shalt be hid, thou also shalt seek strength because of the enemy.

12 All thy strong holds *shall be like* fig trees with the firstripe figs: if they be shaken, they shall even fall into the mouth of the eater.

13 Behold, thy people in the midst of thee *are* women: the gates of thy land shall be set wide open unto thine enemies: the fire shall devour thy bars.

14 Draw thee waters for the siege, fortify thy strong holds: go into clay, and tread the morter, make strong the brickkiln.

15 There shall the fire devour thee; the sword shall cut thee off, it shall eat thee up like the cankerworm: make thyself many as the cankerworm, make thyself many as the locusts.

16 Thou hast multiplied thy merchants above the stars of heaven: the cankerworm spoileth, and flieth away.

17 Thy crowned *are* as the locusts, and thy captains as the great grasshoppers, which camp in the hedges in the cold day, *but* when the sun ariseth they flee away, and their place is not known where they *are*.

18 Thy shepherds slumber, O king of Assyria: thy nobles shall dwell *in the dust:* thy people is scattered upon the mountains, and no man gathereth *them.*

19 *There is* no healing of thy bruise; thy wound is grievous: all that hear the bruit of thee shall clap the hands over thee: for upon whom hath not thy wickedness passed continually?

HABAKKUK.

CHAPTER 1

THE burden which Habakkuk the prophet did see.

2 O LORD, how long shall I cry, and thou wilt not hear! *even* cry out unto thee *of* violence, and thou wilt not save!

3 Why dost thou shew me iniquity, and cause *me* to behold grievance? for spoiling and violence *are* before me: and there are *that* raise up strife and contention.

4 Therefore the law is slacked, and judgment doth never go forth: for the wicked doth compass about the righteous; therefore wrong judgment proceedeth.

5 ¶ Behold ye among the heathen, and regard, and wonder marvellously: for *I* will work a work in your days, *which* ye will not believe, though it be told *you.*

6 For, lo, I raise up the Chaldeans, *that* bitter and hasty nation, which shall march through the breadth of the land, to possess the dwellingplaces *that are* not theirs.

7 They *are* terrible and dreadful: their judgment and their dignity shall proceed of themselves.

8 Their horses also are swifter than the leopards, and are more fierce than the evening wolves: and their horsemen shall spread themselves, and their horsemen shall come from far; they shall fly as the eagle *that* hasteth to eat.

9 They shall come all for violence: their faces shall sup up *as* the east wind, and they shall gather the captivity as the sand.

10 And they shall scoff at the kings, and the princes shall be a scorn unto them: they shall deride every strong hold; for they shall heap dust, and take it.

11 Then shall *his* mind change, and he shall pass over, and offend, *imputing* this his power unto his god.

12 ¶ *Art* thou not from everlasting, O LORD my אֱלֹהִים, mine Holy One? we shall not die. O LORD, thou hast ordained them for judgment; and, O mighty אֱלֹהִים, thou hast established them for correction.

13 *Thou art* of purer eyes than to behold evil, and canst not look on iniquity: wherefore lookest thou upon them that deal treacherously, *and* holdest thy tongue when the wicked devoureth *the man that is* more righteous than he?

14 And makest men as the fishes of the sea, as the creeping things, *that have* no ruler over them?

15 They take up all of them with the angle, they catch them in their net, and gather them in their drag: therefore they rejoice and are glad.

16 Therefore they sacrifice unto their net, and burn incense unto their drag; because by them their portion *is* fat, and their meat plenteous.

17 Shall they therefore empty their net, and not spare continually to slay the nations?

CHAPTER 2

I WILL stand upon my watch, and set me upon the tower, and will watch to see what he will say unto me, and what I shall answer when I am reproved.

2 And the LORD answered me, and said, Write the vision, and make *it* plain upon tables, that he may run that readeth it.

3 For the vision *is* yet for an appointed time, but at the end it shall speak, and not lie: though it tarry, wait for it; because it will surely

come, it will not tarry.

4 Behold, his soul *which* is lifted up is not upright in him: but the just shall live by his faith.

5 ¶ Yea also, because he transgresseth by wine, *he is* a proud man, neither keepeth at home, who enlargeth his desire as hell, and *is* as death, and cannot be satisfied, but gathereth unto him all nations, and heapeth unto him all people:

6 Shall not all these take up a parable against him, and a taunting proverb against him, and say, Woe to him that increaseth *that which is* not his! how long? and to him that ladeth himself with thick clay!

7 Shall they not rise up suddenly that shall bite thee, and awake that shall vex thee, and thou shalt be for booties unto them?

8 Because thou hast spoiled many nations, all the remnant of the people shall spoil thee; because of men's blood, and *for* the violence of the land, of the city, and of all that dwell therein.

9 ¶ Woe to him that coveteth an evil covetousness to his house, that he may set his nest on high, that he may be delivered from the power of evil!

10 Thou hast consulted shame to thy house by cutting off many people, and hast sinned *against* thy soul.

11 For the stone shall cry out of the wall, and the beam out of the timber shall answer it.

12 ¶ Woe to him that buildeth a town with blood, and stablisheth a city by iniquity!

13 Behold, *is it* not of the LORD of hosts that the people shall labour in the very fire, and the people shall weary themselves for very vanity?

14 For the earth shall be filled with the knowledge of the glory of the LORD, as the waters cover the sea.

15 ¶ Woe unto him that giveth his neighbour drink, that puttest thy bottle to *him*, and makest *him* drunken also, that thou mayest look on their nakedness!

16 Thou art filled with shame for glory: drink thou also, and let thy foreskin be uncovered: the cup of the LORD's right hand shall be turned unto thee, and shameful spewing *shall be* on thy glory.

17 For the violence of Lebanon shall cover thee, and the spoil of beasts, *which* made them afraid, because of men's blood, and for the violence of the land, of the city, and of all that dwell therein.

18 ¶ What profiteth the graven image that the maker thereof hath graven it; the molten image, and a teacher of lies, that the maker of his work trusteth therein, to make dumb idols?

19 Woe unto him that saith to the wood, Awake; to the dumb stone, Arise, it shall teach! Behold, it *is* laid over with gold and silver, and *there is* no breath at all in the midst of it.

20 But the LORD *is* in his holy temple: let all the earth keep silence before him.

CHAPTER 3

A PRAYER of Habakkuk the prophet upon Shigionoth.

2 O LORD, I have heard thy speech, *and* was afraid: O LORD, revive thy work in the midst of the years, in the midst of the years make known; in wrath remember mercy.

3 אֱלֹהִים came from Teman, and the Holy One from mount Paran. Selah. His glory covered the heavens, and the earth was full of his praise.

4 And *his* brightness was as the light; he had horns *coming* out of his hand: and there *was* the hiding of his power.

5 Before him went the pestilence, and burning coals went forth at his feet.

6 He stood, and measured the earth: he beheld, and drove asunder the nations; and the everlasting mountains were scattered, the perpetual hills did bow: his ways *are* everlasting.

7 I saw the tents of Cushan in affliction: *and* the curtains of the land of Midian did tremble.

8 Was the LORD displeased against the rivers? *was* thine anger against the rivers? *was* thy wrath against the sea, that thou didst ride upon thine horses *and* thy chariots of salvation?

9 Thy bow was made quite naked, *according* to the oaths of the tribes, *even thy* word. Selah. Thou didst cleave the earth with rivers.

10 The mountains saw thee, *and* they trembled: the overflowing of the water passed by: the deep uttered his voice, *and* lifted up his hands on high.

11 The sun *and* moon stood still in their habitation: at the light of thine arrows they went, *and* at the shining of thy glittering spear.

12 Thou didst march through the land in indignation, thou didst thresh the heathen in anger.

13 Thou wentest forth for the salvation of thy people, *even* for salvation with thine anointed; thou woundedst the head out of the house of the wicked, by discovering the foundation unto the neck. Selah.

14 Thou didst strike through with his staves the head of his villages: they came out as a whirlwind to scatter me: their rejoicing *was* as to devour the poor secretly.

15 Thou didst walk through the sea with thine horses, *through* the heap of great waters.

16 When I heard, my belly trembled; my lips quivered at the voice: rottenness entered into my bones, and I trembled in myself, that I might rest in the day of trouble: when he cometh up unto the people, he will invade them with his troops.

17 ¶ Although the fig tree shall not blossom, neither *shall* fruit *be* in the vines; the labour of the olive shall fail, and the fields shall yield no meat; the flock shall be cut off from the fold, and *there shall be* no herd in the stalls:

18 Yet I will rejoice in the LORD, I will joy in the אֱלֹהִים of my salvation.

19 The LORD אֱלֹהִים *is* my strength, and he will make my feet like hinds' *feet*, and he will make me to walk upon mine high places. To the chief singer on my stringed instruments.

ZEPHANIAH.

CHAPTER 1

THE word of the LORD which came unto Zephaniah the son of Cushi, the son of Gedaliah, the son of Amariah, the son of Hizkiah, in the days of Josiah the son of Amon, king of Judah.

2 I will utterly consume all *things* from off the land, saith the LORD.

3 I will consume man and beast; I will consume the fowls of the heaven, and the fishes of the sea, and the stumblingblocks with the wicked; and I will cut off man from off the land, saith the LORD.

4 I will also stretch out mine hand upon Judah, and upon all the inhabitants of Jerusalem; and I will cut off the remnant of Baal from

this place, *and* the name of the Chemarims with the priests;

5 And them that worship the host of heaven upon the housetops; and them that worship *and* that swear by the Lord, and that swear by Malcham;

6 And them that are turned back from the Lord; and *those* that have not sought the Lord, nor inquired for him.

7 Hold thy peace at the presence of the Lord אֱלֹהִים: for the day of the Lord *is* at hand: for the Lord hath prepared a sacrifice, he hath bid his guests.

8 And it shall come to pass in the day of the Lord's sacrifice, that I will punish the princes, and the king's children, and all such as are clothed with strange apparel.

9 In the same day also will I punish all those that leap on the threshold, which fill their masters' houses with violence and deceit.

10 And it shall come to pass in that day, saith the Lord, *that there shall be* the noise of a cry from the fish gate, and an howling from the second, and a great crashing from the hills.

11 Howl, ye inhabitants of Maktesh, for all the merchant people are cut down; all they that bear silver are cut off.

12 And it shall come to pass at that time, *that* I will search Jerusalem with candles, and punish the men that are settled on their lees: that say in their heart, The Lord will not do good, neither will he do evil.

13 Therefore their goods shall become a booty, and their houses a desolation: they shall also build houses, but not inhabit *them;* and they shall plant vineyards, but not drink the wine thereof.

14 The great day of the Lord *is* near, *it is* near, and hasteth greatly, *even* the voice of the day of the Lord: the mighty man shall cry there bitterly.

15 That day *is* a day of wrath, a day of trouble and distress, a day of wasteness and desolation, a day of darkness and gloominess, a day of clouds and thick darkness,

16 A day of the trumpet and alarm against the fenced cities, and against the high towers.

17 And I will bring distress upon men, that they shall walk like blind men, because they have sinned against the Lord: and their blood shall be poured out as dust, and their flesh as the dung.

18 Neither their silver nor their gold shall be able to deliver them in the day of the Lord's wrath; but the whole land shall be devoured by the fire of his jealousy: for he shall make even a speedy riddance of all them that dwell in the land.

CHAPTER 2

GATHER yourselves together, yea, gather together, O nation not desired;

2 Before the decree bring forth, *before* the day pass as the chaff, before the fierce anger of the Lord come upon you, before the day of the Lord's anger come upon you.

3 Seek ye the Lord, all ye meek of the earth, which have wrought his judgment; seek righteousness, seek meekness: it may be ye shall be hid in the day of the Lord's anger.

4 ¶ For Gaza shall be forsaken, and Ashkelon a desolation: they shall drive out Ashdod at the noon day, and Ekron shall be rooted up.

5 Woe unto the inhabitants of the sea coast, the nation of the Cherethites! the word of the Lord *is* against you; O Canaan, the land of the Philistines, I will even destroy thee, that there shall be no inhabitant.

6 And the sea coast shall be dwellings *and* cottages for shepherds, and folds for flocks.

7 And the coast shall be for the remnant of the house of Judah; they shall feed thereupon: in the houses of Ashkelon shall they lie down in the evening: for the Lord their אֱלֹהִים shall visit them, and turn away their captivity.

8 ¶ I have heard the reproach of Moab, and the revilings of the children of Ammon, whereby they have reproached my people, and magnified *themselves* against their border.

9 Therefore *as* I live, saith the Lord of hosts, the אֱלֹהִים of Israel, Surely Moab shall be as Sodom, and the children of Ammon as Gomorrah, *even* the breeding of nettles, and saltpits, and a perpetual desolation: the residue of my people shall spoil them, and the remnant of my people shall possess them.

10 This shall they have for their pride, because they have reproached and magnified *themselves* against the people of the Lord of hosts.

11 The Lord *will be* terrible unto them: for he will famish all the gods of the earth; and *men* shall worship him, every one from his place, *even* all the isles of the heathen.

12 ¶ Ye Ethiopians also, ye *shall be* slain by my sword.

13 And he will stretch out his hand against the north, and destroy Assyria; and will make Nineveh a desolation, *and* dry like a wilderness.

14 And flocks shall lie down in the midst of her, all the beasts of the nations: both the cormorant and the bittern shall lodge in the upper lintels of it; *their* voice shall sing in the windows; desolation *shall be* in the thresholds: for he shall uncover the cedar work.

15 This *is* the rejoicing city that dwelt carelessly, that said in her heart, I *am,* and *there is* none beside me: how is she become a desolation, a place for beasts to lie down in! every one that passeth by her shall hiss, *and* wag his hand.

CHAPTER 3

WOE to her that is filthy and polluted, to the oppressing city!

2 She obeyed not the voice; she received not correction; she trusted not in the Lord; she drew not near to her אֱלֹהֶ.

3 Her princes within her *are* roaring lions; her judges *are* evening wolves; they gnaw not the bones till the morrow.

4 Her prophets *are* light *and* treacherous persons: her priests have polluted the sanctuary, they have done violence to the law.

5 The just Lord *is* in the midst thereof; he will not do iniquity: every morning doth he bring his judgment to light, he faileth not; but the unjust knoweth no shame.

6 I have cut off the nations: their towers are desolate; I made their streets waste, that none passeth by: their cities are destroyed, so that there is no man, that there is none inhabitant.

7 I said, Surely thou wilt fear me, thou wilt receive instruction; so their dwelling should not be cut off, howsoever I punished them: but they rose early, *and* corrupted all their doings.

8 ¶ Therefore wait ye upon me, saith the Lord, until the day that I rise up to the prey: for my determination *is* to gather the nations, that I may assemble the kingdoms, to pour upon them mine indignation, *even* all my fierce anger: for all the earth shall be devoured with the fire of my jealousy.

9 For then will I turn to the people a pure language, that they may all call upon the name of the Lord, to serve him with one consent.

10 From beyond the rivers of Ethiopia my suppliants, *even* the daughter of my dispersed, shall bring mine offering.

11 In that day shalt thou not be ashamed for all thy doings, wherein thou hast transgressed against me: for then I will take away out of the midst of thee them that rejoice in thy pride, and thou shalt no more be haughty because of my holy mountain.

12 I will also leave in the midst of thee an afflicted and poor people, and they shall trust in the name of the LORD.

13 The remnant of Israel shall not do iniquity, nor speak lies; neither shall a deceitful tongue be found in their mouth: for they shall feed and lie down, and none shall make *them* afraid.

14 ¶ Sing, O daughter of Zion; shout, O Israel; be glad and rejoice with all the heart, O daughter of Jerusalem.

15 The LORD hath taken away thy judgments, he hath cast out thine enemy: the king of Israel, *even* the LORD, *is* in the midst of thee: thou shalt not see evil any more.

16 In that day it shall be said to Jerusalem, Fear thou not: *and to* Zion, Let not thine hands be slack.

17 The LORD thy אֱלֹהִים in the midst of thee *is* mighty; he will save, he will rejoice over thee with joy; he will rest in his love, he will joy over thee with singing.

18 I will gather *them that are* sorrowful for the solemn assembly, *who* are of thee, *to whom* the reproach of it *was* a burden.

19 Behold, at that time I will undo all that afflict thee: and I will save her that halteth, and gather her that was driven out; and I will get them praise and fame in every land where they have been put to shame.

20 At that time will I bring you *again*, even in the time that I gather you: for I will make you a name and a praise among all people of the earth, when I turn back your captivity before your eyes, saith the LORD.

HAGGAI.

CHAPTER 1

IN the second year of Darius the king, in the sixth month, in the first day of the month, came the word of the LORD by Haggai the prophet unto Zerubbabel the son of Shealtiel, governor of Judah, and to Joshua the son of Josedech, the high priest, saying,

2 Thus speaketh the LORD of hosts, saying, This people say, The time is not come, the time that the LORD's house should be built.

3 Then came the word of the LORD by Haggai the prophet, saying,

4 *Is it* time for you, O ye, to dwell in your cieled houses, and this house *lie* waste?

5 Now therefore thus saith the LORD of hosts; Consider your ways.

6 Ye have sown much, and bring in little; ye eat, but ye have not enough; ye drink, but ye are not filled with drink; ye clothe you, but there is none warm; and he that earneth wages earneth wages *to put it* into a bag with holes.

7 ¶ Thus saith the LORD of hosts; Consider your ways.

8 Go up to the mountain, and bring wood, and build the house; and I will take pleasure in it, and I will be glorified, saith the LORD.

9 Ye looked for much, and, lo, *it came* to little; and when ye brought *it* home, I did blow upon it. Why? saith the LORD of hosts. Because of mine house that *is* waste, and ye run every man unto his own house.

10 Therefore the heaven over you is stayed from dew, and the earth is stayed *from* her fruit.

11 And I called for a drought upon the land, and upon the mountains, and upon the corn, and upon the new wine, and upon the oil, and upon *that* which the ground bringeth forth, and upon men, and upon cattle, and upon all the labour of the hands.

12 ¶ Then Zerubbabel the son of Shealtiel, and Joshua the son of Josedech, the high priest, with all the remnant of the people, obeyed the voice of the LORD their אֱלֹהִים, and the words of Haggai the prophet, as the LORD their אֱלֹהִים had sent him, and the people did fear before the LORD.

13 Then spake Haggai the LORD's messenger in the LORD's message unto the people, saying, I *am* with you, saith the LORD.

14 And the LORD stirred up the spirit of Zerubbabel the son of Shealtiel, governor of Judah, and the spirit of Joshua the son of Josedech, the high priest, and the spirit of all the remnant of the people; and they came and did work in the house of the LORD of hosts, their אֱלֹהִים,

15 In the four and twentieth day of the sixth month, in the second year of Darius the king.

CHAPTER 2

IN the seventh *month*, in the one and twentieth *day* of the month, came the word of the LORD by the prophet Haggai, saying,

2 Speak now to Zerubbabel the son of Shealtiel, governor of Judah, and to Joshua the son of Josedech, the high priest, and to the residue of the people, saying,

3 Who *is* left among you that saw this house in her first glory? and how do ye see it now? *is it* not in your eyes in comparison of it as nothing?

4 Yet now be strong, O Zerubbabel, saith the LORD; and be strong, O Joshua, son of Josedech, the high priest; and be strong, all ye people of the land, saith the LORD, and work: for I *am* with you, saith the LORD of hosts:

5 *According to* the word that I covenanted with you when ye came out of Egypt, so my spirit remaineth among you: fear ye not.

6 For thus saith the LORD of hosts; Yet once, it *is* a little while, and I will shake the heavens, and the earth, and the sea, and the dry land;

7 And I will shake all nations, and the desire of all nations shall come: and I will fill this house with glory, saith the LORD of hosts.

8 The silver *is* mine, and the gold *is* mine, saith the LORD of hosts.

9 The glory of this latter house shall be greater than of the former, saith the LORD of hosts: and in this place will I give peace, saith the LORD of hosts.

10 ¶ In the four and twentieth *day* of the ninth *month*, in the second year of Darius, came the word of the LORD by Haggai the prophet, saying,

11 Thus saith the LORD of hosts; Ask now the priests *concerning* the law, saying,

12 If one bear holy flesh in the skirt of his garment, and with his skirt do touch bread, or pottage, or wine, or oil, or any meat, shall it be holy? And the priests answered and said, No.

13 Then said Haggai, If *one that is* unclean by a dead body touch any of these, shall it be unclean? And the priests answered and said, It shall be unclean.

14 Then answered Haggai, and said, So *is* this people, and so *is* this nation before me, saith the LORD; and so *is* every work of their hands; and that which they offer there *is* unclean.

15 And now, I pray you, consider from this day and upward, from before a stone was laid upon a stone in the temple of the LORD:

16 Since those *days* were, when *one* came to an heap of twenty *measures*, there were *but* ten: when *one* came to the pressfat for to draw out fifty *vessels* out of the press, there were *but* twenty.

17 I smote you with blasting and with mildew and with hail in all the labours of your hands; yet ye *turned* not to me, saith the LORD.

18 Consider now from this day and upward, from the four and twentieth day of the ninth *month, even* from the day that the foundation of the LORD's temple was laid, consider *it*.

19 Is the seed yet in the barn? yea, as yet the vine, and the fig tree, and the pomegranate, and the olive tree, hath not brought forth: from this day will I bless *you*.

20 ¶ And again the word of the LORD came unto Haggai in the four and twentieth *day* of the month, saying,

21 Speak to Zerubbabel, governor of Judah, saying, I will shake the heavens and the earth;

22 And I will overthrow the throne of kingdoms, and I will destroy the strength of the kingdoms of the heathen; and I will overthrow the chariots, and those that ride in them; and the horses and their riders shall come down, every one by the sword of his brother.

23 In that day, saith the LORD of hosts, will I take thee, O Zerubbabel, my servant, the son of Shealtiel, saith the LORD, and will make thee as a signet: for I have chosen thee, saith the LORD of hosts.

ZECHARIAH.

CHAPTER 1

IN the eighth month, in the second year of Darius, came the word of the LORD unto Zechariah, the son of Berechiah, the son of Iddo the prophet, saying,

2 The LORD hath been sore displeased with your fathers.

3 Therefore say thou unto them, Thus saith the LORD of hosts; Turn ye unto me, saith the LORD of hosts, and I will turn unto you, saith the LORD of hosts.

4 Be ye not as your fathers, unto whom the former prophets have cried, saying, Thus saith the LORD of hosts; Turn ye now from your evil ways, and *from* your evil doings: but they did not hear, nor hearken unto me, saith the LORD.

5 Your fathers, where *are* they? and the prophets, do they live for ever?

6 But my words and my statutes, which I commanded my servants the prophets, did they not take hold of your fathers? and they returned and said, Like as the LORD of hosts thought to do unto us, according to our ways, and according to our doings, so hath he dealt with us.

7 ¶ Upon the four and twentieth day of the eleventh month, which *is* the month Sebat, in the second year of Darius, came the word of the LORD unto Zechariah, the son of Berechiah, the son of Iddo the prophet, saying,

8 I saw by night, and behold a man riding upon a red horse, and he stood among the myrtle trees that *were* in the bottom; and behind him *were there* red horses, speckled, and white.

9 Then said I, O my lord, what *are* these? And the angel that talked with me said unto me, I will shew thee what these *be*.

10 And the man that stood among the myrtle trees answered and said, These *are they* whom the LORD hath sent to walk to and fro through the earth.

11 And they answered the angel of the LORD that stood among the myrtle trees, and said, We have walked to and fro through the earth, and, behold, all the earth sitteth still, and is at rest.

12 ¶ Then the angel of the LORD answered and said, O LORD of hosts, how long wilt thou not have mercy on Jerusalem and on the cities of Judah, against which thou hast had indignation these threescore and ten years?

13 And the LORD answered the angel that talked with me *with* good words *and* comfortable words.

14 So the angel that communed with me said unto me, Cry thou, saying, Thus saith the LORD of hosts; I am jealous for Jerusalem and for Zion with a great jealousy.

15 And I am very sore displeased with the heathen *that are* at ease: for I was but a little displeased, and they helped forward the affliction.

16 Therefore thus saith the LORD; I am returned to Jerusalem with mercies: my house shall be built in it, saith the LORD of hosts, and a line shall be stretched forth upon Jerusalem.

17 Cry yet, saying, Thus saith the LORD of hosts; My cities through prosperity shall yet be spread abroad; and the LORD shall yet comfort Zion, and shall yet choose Jerusalem.

18 ¶ Then lifted I up mine eyes, and saw, and behold four horns.

19 And I said unto the angel that talked with me, What *be* these? And he answered me, These *are* the horns which have scattered Judah, Israel, and Jerusalem.

20 And the LORD shewed me four carpenters.

21 Then said I, What come these to do? And he spake, saying, These *are* the horns which have scattered Judah, so that no man did lift up his head: but these are come to fray them, to cast out the horns of the Gentiles, which lifted up *their* horn over the land of Judah to scatter it.

CHAPTER 2

I LIFTED up mine eyes again, and looked, and behold a man with a measuring line in his hand.

2 Then said I, Whither goest thou? And he said unto me, To measure Jerusalem, to see what *is* the breadth thereof, and what *is* the length thereof.

3 And, behold, the angel that talked with me went forth, and another angel went out to meet him,

4 And said unto him, Run, speak to this young man, saying, Jerusalem shall be inhabited *as* towns without walls for the multitude of men and cattle therein:

5 For I, saith the LORD, will be unto her a wall of fire round about, and will be the glory in the midst of her.

6 ¶ Ho, ho, *come forth*, and flee from the land of the north, saith the LORD: for I have spread you abroad as the four winds of the heaven, saith the LORD.

7 Deliver thyself, O Zion, that dwellest *with* the daughter of Babylon.

8 For thus saith the LORD of hosts; After the glory hath he sent me unto the nations which spoiled you: for he that toucheth you

toucheth the apple of his eye.

9 For, behold, I will shake mine hand upon them, and they shall be a spoil to their servants: and ye shall know that the Lord of hosts hath sent me.

10 ¶ Sing and rejoice, O daughter of Zion: for, lo, I come, and I will dwell in the midst of thee, saith the Lord.

11 And many nations shall be joined to the Lord in that day, and shall be my people: and I will dwell in the midst of thee, and thou shalt know that the Lord of hosts hath sent me unto thee.

12 And the Lord shall inherit Judah his portion in the holy land, and shall choose Jerusalem again.

13 Be silent, O all flesh, before the Lord: for he is raised up out of his holy habitation.

CHAPTER 3

AND he shewed me Joshua the high priest standing before the angel of the Lord, and Satan standing at his right hand to resist him.

2 And the Lord said unto Satan, The Lord rebuke thee, O Satan; even the Lord that hath chosen Jerusalem rebuke thee: *is* not this a brand plucked out of the fire?

3 Now Joshua was clothed with filthy garments, and stood before the angel.

4 And he answered and spake unto those that stood before him, saying, Take away the filthy garments from him. And unto him he said, Behold, I have caused thine iniquity to pass from thee, and I will clothe thee with change of raiment.

5 And I said, Let them set a fair mitre upon his head. So they set a fair mitre upon his head, and clothed him with garments. And the angel of the Lord stood by.

6 And the angel of the Lord protested unto Joshua, saying,

7 Thus saith the Lord of hosts; If thou wilt walk in my ways, and if thou wilt keep my charge, then thou shalt also judge my house, and shalt also keep my courts, and I will give thee places to walk among these that stand by.

8 Hear now, O Joshua the high priest, thou, and thy fellows that sit before thee: for they *are* men wondered at: for, behold, I will bring forth my servant the BRANCH.

9 For behold the stone that I have laid before Joshua; upon one stone *shall be* seven eyes: behold, I will engrave the graving thereof, saith the Lord of hosts, and I will remove the iniquity of that land in one day.

10 In that day, saith the Lord of hosts, shall ye call every man his neighbour under the vine and under the fig tree.

CHAPTER 4

AND the angel that talked with me came again, and waked me, as a man that is wakened out of his sleep,

2 And said unto me, What seest thou? And I said, I have looked, and behold a candlestick all *of* gold, with a bowl upon the top of it, and his seven lamps thereon, and seven pipes to the seven lamps, which *are* upon the top thereof:

3 And two olive trees by it, one upon the right *side* of the bowl, and the other upon the left *side* thereof.

4 So I answered and spake to the angel that talked with me, saying, What *are* these, my lord?

5 Then the angel that talked with me answered and said unto me, Knowest thou not what these be? And I said, No, my lord.

6 Then he answered and spake unto me, saying, This *is* the word of the Lord unto Zerubbabel, saying, Not by might, nor by power, but by my spirit, saith the Lord of hosts.

7 Who *art* thou, O great mountain? before Zerubbabel *thou shalt become* a plain: and he shall bring forth the headstone *thereof with* shoutings, *crying*, Grace, grace unto it.

8 Moreover the word of the Lord came unto me, saying,

9 The hands of Zerubbabel have laid the foundation of this house; his hands shall also finish it; and thou shalt know that the Lord of hosts hath sent me unto you.

10 For who hath despised the day of small things? for they shall rejoice, and shall see the plummet in the hand of Zerubbabel *with* those seven; they *are* the eyes of the Lord, which run to and fro through the whole earth.

11 ¶ Then answered I, and said unto him, What *are* these two olive trees upon the right *side* of the candlestick and upon the left *side* thereof?

12 And I answered again, and said unto him, What *be these* two olive branches which through the two golden pipes empty the golden *oil* out of themselves?

13 And he answered me and said, Knowest thou not what these *be?* And I said, No, my lord.

14 Then said he, These *are* the two anointed ones, that stand by the Lord of the whole earth.

CHAPTER 5

THEN I turned, and lifted up mine eyes, and looked, and behold a flying roll.

2 And he said unto me, What seest thou? And I answered, I see a flying roll; the length thereof *is* twenty cubits, and the breadth thereof ten cubits.

3 Then said he unto me, This *is* the curse that goeth forth over the face of the whole earth: for every one that stealeth shall be cut off *as* on this side according to it; and every one that sweareth shall be cut off *as* on that side according to it.

4 I will bring it forth, saith the Lord of hosts, and it shall enter into the house of the thief, and into the house of him that sweareth falsely by my name: and it shall remain in the midst of his house, and shall consume it with the timber thereof and the stones thereof.

5 ¶ Then the angel that talked with me went forth, and said unto me, Lift up now thine eyes, and see what *is* this that goeth forth.

6 And I said, What *is* it? And he said, This *is* an ephah that goeth forth. He said moreover, This *is* their resemblance through all the earth.

7 And, behold, there was lifted up a talent of lead: and this *is* a woman that sitteth in the midst of the ephah.

8 And he said, This *is* wickedness. And he cast it into the midst of the ephah; and he cast the weight of lead upon the mouth thereof.

9 Then lifted I up mine eyes, and looked, and, behold, there came out two women, and the wind *was* in their wings; for they had wings like the wings of a stork: and they lifted up the ephah between the earth and the heaven.

10 Then said I to the angel that talked with me, Whither do these bear the ephah?

11 And he said unto me, To build it an house in the land of Shinar: and it shall be established, and set there upon her own base.

CHAPTER 6

AND I turned, and lifted up mine eyes, and looked, and, behold, there came four chariots out from between two mountains; and the mountains *were* mountains of brass.

2 In the first chariot *were* red horses; and in the second chariot black horses;

3 And in the third chariot white horses; and in the fourth chariot grisled and bay horses.

4 Then I answered and said unto the angel that talked with me, What *are* these, my lord?

5 And the angel answered and said unto me, These *are* the four spirits of the heavens, which go forth from standing before the Lord of all the earth.

6 The black horses which *are* therein go forth into the north country; and the white go forth after them; and the grisled go forth toward the south country.

7 And the bay went forth, and sought to go that they might walk to and fro through the earth: and he said, Get you hence, walk to and fro through the earth. So they walked to and fro through the earth.

8 Then cried he upon me, and spake unto me, saying, Behold, these that go toward the north country have quieted my spirit in the north country.

9 ¶ And the word of the Lord came unto me, saying,

10 Take of *them of* the captivity, *even* of Heldai, of Tobijah, and of Jedaiah, which are come from Babylon, and come thou the same day, and go into the house of Josiah the son of Zephaniah;

11 Then take silver and gold, and make crowns, and set *them* upon the head of Joshua the son of Josedech, the high priest;

12 And speak unto him, saying, Thus speaketh the Lord of hosts, saying, Behold the man whose name *is* The BRANCH; and he shall grow up out of his place, and he shall build the temple of the Lord:

13 Even he shall build the temple of the Lord; and he shall bear the glory, and shall sit and rule upon his throne; and he shall be a priest upon his throne: and the counsel of peace shall be between them both.

14 And the crowns shall be to Helem, and to Tobijah, and to Jedaiah, and to Hen the son of Zephaniah, for a memorial in the temple of the Lord.

15 And they *that are* far off shall come and build in the temple of the Lord, and ye shall know that the Lord of hosts hath sent me unto you. And *this* shall come to pass, if ye will diligently obey the voice of the Lord your אֱלֹהִים.

CHAPTER 7

AND it came to pass in the fourth year of king Darius, *that* the word of the Lord came unto Zechariah in the fourth *day* of the ninth month, *even* in Chisleu;

2 When they had sent unto the house of אֱלֹהִים Sherezer and Regem-melech, and their men, to pray before the Lord,

3 *And* to speak unto the priests which *were* in the house of the Lord of hosts, and to the prophets, saying, Should I weep in the fifth month, separating myself, as I have done these so many years?

4 ¶ Then came the word of the Lord of hosts unto me, saying,

5 Speak unto all the people of the land, and to the priests, saying, When ye fasted and mourned in the fifth and seventh *month*, even those seventy years, did ye at all fast unto me, *even* to me?

6 And when ye did eat, and when ye did drink, did not ye eat *for yourselves*, and drink *for yourselves?*

7 *Should ye* not *hear* the words which the Lord hath cried by the former prophets, when Jerusalem was inhabited and in prosperity, and the cities thereof round about her, when *men* inhabited the south and the plain?

8 ¶ And the word of the Lord came unto Zechariah, saying,

9 Thus speaketh the Lord of hosts, saying, Execute true judgment, and shew mercy and compassions every man to his brother:

10 And oppress not the widow, nor the fatherless, the stranger, nor the poor; and let none of you imagine evil against his brother in your heart.

11 But they refused to hearken, and pulled away the shoulder, and stopped their ears, that they should not hear.

12 Yea, they made their hearts *as* an adamant stone, lest they should hear the law, and the words which the Lord of hosts hath sent in his spirit by the former prophets: therefore came a great wrath from the Lord of hosts.

13 Therefore it is come to pass, *that* as he cried, and they would not hear; so they cried, and I would not hear, saith the Lord of hosts:

14 But I scattered them with a whirlwind among all the nations whom they knew not. Thus the land was desolate after them, that no man passed through nor returned: for they laid the pleasant land desolate.

CHAPTER 8

AGAIN the word of the Lord of hosts came *to me*, saying,

2 Thus saith the Lord of hosts; I was jealous for Zion with great jealousy, and I was jealous for her with great fury.

3 Thus saith the Lord; I am returned unto Zion, and will dwell in the midst of Jerusalem: and Jerusalem shall be called a city of truth; and the mountain of the Lord of hosts the holy mountain.

4 Thus saith the Lord of hosts; There shall yet old men and old women dwell in the streets of Jerusalem, and every man with his staff in his hand for very age.

5 And the streets of the city shall be full of boys and girls playing in the streets thereof.

6 Thus saith the Lord of hosts; If it be marvellous in the eyes of the remnant of this people in these days, should it also be marvellous in mine eyes? saith the Lord of hosts.

7 Thus saith the Lord of hosts; Behold, I will save my people from the east country, and from the west country;

8 And I will bring them, and they shall dwell in the midst of Jerusalem: and they shall be my people, and I will be their אֱלֹהִים, in truth and in righteousness.

9 ¶ Thus saith the Lord of hosts; Let your hands be strong, ye that hear in these days these words by the mouth of the prophets, which *were* in the day *that* the foundation of the house of the Lord of hosts was laid, that the temple might be built.

10 For before these days there was no hire for man, nor any hire for beast; neither *was there any* peace to him that went out or came in because of the affliction: for I set all men every one against his neighbour.

11 But now I *will* not *be* unto the residue of this people as in the former days, saith the Lord of hosts.

12 For the seed *shall be* prosperous; the vine shall give her fruit, and the ground shall give her increase, and the heavens shall give their dew; and I will cause the remnant of this people to possess all these *things*.

13 And it shall come to pass, *that* as ye were a curse among the heathen, O house of Judah, and house of Israel; so will I save you, and ye shall be a blessing: fear not, *but* let your hands be strong.

14 For thus saith the LORD of hosts; As I thought to punish you, when your fathers provoked me to wrath, saith the LORD of hosts, and I repented not:

15 So again have I thought in these days to do well unto Jerusalem and to the house of Judah: fear ye not.

16 ¶ These *are* the things that ye shall do; Speak ye every man the truth to his neighbour; execute the judgment of truth and peace in your gates:

17 And let none of you imagine evil in your hearts against his neighbour; and love no false oath: for all these *are things* that I hate, saith the LORD.

18 ¶ And the word of the LORD of hosts came unto me, saying,

19 Thus saith the LORD of hosts; The fast of the fourth *month*, and the fast of the fifth, and the fast of the seventh, and the fast of the tenth, shall be to the house of Judah joy and gladness, and cheerful feasts; therefore love the truth and peace.

20 Thus saith the LORD of hosts; *It shall* yet *come to pass*, that there shall come people, and the inhabitants of many cities:

21 And the inhabitants of one *city* shall go to another, saying, Let us go speedily to pray before the LORD, and to seek the LORD of hosts: I will go also.

22 Yea, many people and strong nations shall come to seek the LORD of hosts in Jerusalem, and to pray before the LORD.

23 Thus saith the LORD of hosts; In those days *it shall come to pass*, that ten men shall take hold out of all languages of the nations, even shall take hold of the skirt of him that is a Jew, saying, We will go with you: for we have heard *that* אֱלֹהִים *is* with you.

CHAPTER 9

THE burden of the word of the LORD in the land of Hadrach, and Damascus *shall be* the rest thereof: when the eyes of man, as of all the tribes of Israel, *shall be* toward the LORD.

2 And Hamath also shall border thereby; Tyrus, and Zidon, though it be very wise.

3 And Tyrus did build herself a strong hold, and heaped up silver as the dust, and fine gold as the mire of the streets.

4 Behold, the Lord will cast her out, and he will smite her power in the sea; and she shall be devoured with fire.

5 Ashkelon shall see *it*, and fear; Gaza also *shall see it*, and be very sorrowful, and Ekron; for her expectation shall be ashamed; and the king shall perish from Gaza, and Ashkelon shall not be inhabited.

6 And a bastard shall dwell in Ashdod, and I will cut off the pride of the Philistines.

7 And I will take away his blood out of his mouth, and his abominations from between his teeth: but he that remaineth, even he, *shall be* for our אֱלֹהִים, and he shall be as a governor in Judah, and Ekron as a Jebusite.

8 And I will encamp about mine house because of the army, because of him that passeth by, and because of him that returneth: and no oppressor shall pass through them any more: for now have I seen with mine eyes.

9 ¶ Rejoice greatly, O daughter of Zion; shout, O daughter of Jerusalem: behold, thy King cometh unto thee: he *is* just, and having salvation; lowly, and riding upon an ass, and upon a colt the foal of an ass.

10 And I will cut off the chariot from Ephraim, and the horse from Jerusalem, and the battle bow shall be cut off: and he shall speak peace unto the heathen: and his dominion *shall be* from sea *even* to sea, and from the river *even* to the ends of the earth.

11 As for thee also, by the blood of thy covenant I have sent forth thy prisoners out of the pit wherein *is* no water.

12 ¶ Turn you to the strong hold, ye prisoners of hope: even to day do I declare *that* I will render double unto thee;

13 When I have bent Judah for me, filled the bow with Ephraim, and raised up thy sons, O Zion, against thy sons, O Greece, and made thee as the sword of a mighty man.

14 And the LORD shall be seen over them, and his arrow shall go forth as the lightning: and the Lord אֱלֹהִים shall blow the trumpet, and shall go with whirlwinds of the south.

15 The LORD of hosts shall defend them; and they shall devour, and subdue with sling stones; and they shall drink, *and* make a noise as through wine; and they shall be filled like bowls, *and* as the corners of the altar.

16 And the LORD their אֱלֹהִים shall save them in that day as the flock of his people: for *they shall be as* the stones of a crown, lifted up as an ensign upon his land.

17 For how great *is* his goodness, and how great *is* his beauty! corn shall make the young men cheerful, and new wine the maids.

CHAPTER 10

ASK ye of the LORD rain in the time of the latter rain; *so* the LORD shall make bright clouds, and give them showers of rain, to every one grass in the field.

2 For the idols have spoken vanity, and the diviners have seen a lie, and have told false dreams; they comfort in vain: therefore they went their way as a flock, they were troubled, because *there was* no shepherd.

3 Mine anger was kindled against the shepherds, and I punished the goats: for the LORD of hosts hath visited his flock the house of Judah, and hath made them as his goodly horse in the battle.

4 Out of him came forth the corner, out of him the nail, out of him the battle bow, out of him every oppressor together.

5 ¶ And they shall be as mighty *men*, which tread down *their enemies* in the mire of the streets in the battle: and they shall fight, because the LORD *is* with them, and the riders on horses shall be confounded.

6 And I will strengthen the house of Judah, and I will save the house of Joseph, and I will bring them again to place them; for I have mercy upon them: and they shall be as though I had not cast them off: for I *am* the LORD their אֱלֹהִים, and will hear them.

7 And *they of* Ephraim shall be like a mighty *man*, and their heart shall rejoice as through wine: yea, their children shall see *it*, and be glad; their heart shall rejoice in the LORD.

8 I will hiss for them, and gather them; for I have redeemed them: and they shall increase as they have increased.

9 And I will sow them among the people: and they shall remember me in far countries; and they shall live with their children, and turn again.

10 I will bring them again also out of the land of Egypt, and gather them out of Assyria; and I will bring them into the land of Gilead and Lebanon; and *place* shall not be found for them.

11 And he shall pass through the sea with affliction, and shall smite the waves in the sea, and all the deeps of the river shall dry up: and the pride of Assyria shall be brought down, and the sceptre of Egypt shall depart away.

12 And I will strengthen them in the LORD; and they shall walk up and down in his name, saith the LORD.

CHAPTER 11

OPEN thy doors, O Lebanon, that the fire may devour thy cedars.

2 Howl, fir tree; for the cedar is fallen; because the mighty are spoiled: howl, O ye oaks of Bashan; for the forest of the vintage is come down.

3 ¶ *There is* a voice of the howling of the shepherds; for their glory is spoiled: a voice of the roaring of young lions; for the pride of Jordan is spoiled.

4 Thus saith the LORD my אֱלֹהִים: Feed the flock of the slaughter;

5 Whose possessors slay them, and hold themselves not guilty: and they that sell them say, Blessed *be* the LORD; for I am rich: and their own shepherds pity them not.

6 For I will no more pity the inhabitants of the land, saith the LORD: but, lo, I will deliver the men every one into his neighbour's hand, and into the hand of his king: and they shall smite the land, and out of their hand I will not deliver *them.*

7 And I will feed the flock of slaughter, *even* you, O poor of the flock. And I took unto me two staves; the one I called Beauty, and the other I called Bands; and I fed the flock.

8 Three shepherds also I cut off in one month; and my soul lothed them, and their soul also abhorred me.

9 Then said I, I will not feed you: that that dieth, let it die; and that that is to be cut off, let it be cut off; and let the rest eat every one the flesh of another.

10 ¶ And I took my staff, *even* Beauty, and cut it asunder, that I might break my covenant which I had made with all the people.

11 And it was broken in that day: and so the poor of the flock that waited upon me knew that it *was* the word of the LORD.

12 And I said unto them, If ye think good, give *me* my price; and if not, forbear. So they weighed for my price thirty *pieces* of silver.

13 And the LORD said unto me, Cast it unto the potter: a goodly price that I was prised at of them. And I took the thirty *pieces* of silver, and cast them to the potter in the house of the LORD.

14 Then I cut asunder mine other staff, *even* Bands, that I might break the brotherhood between Judah and Israel.

15 ¶ And the LORD said unto me, Take unto thee yet the instruments of a foolish shepherd.

16 For, lo, I will raise up a shepherd in the land, *which* shall not visit those that be cut off, neither shall seek the young one, nor heal that that is broken, nor feed that that standeth still: but he shall eat the flesh of the fat, and tear their claws in pieces.

17 Woe to the idol shepherd that leaveth the flock! the sword *shall be* upon his arm, and upon his right eye: his arm shall be clean dried up, and his right eye shall be utterly darkened.

CHAPTER 12

THE burden of the word of the LORD for Israel, saith the LORD, which stretcheth forth the heavens, and layeth the foundation of the earth, and formeth the spirit of man within him.

2 Behold, I will make Jerusalem a cup of trembling unto all the people round about, when they shall be in the siege both against Judah *and* against Jerusalem.

3 ¶ And in that day will I make Jerusalem a burdensome stone for all people: all that burden themselves with it shall be cut in pieces, though all the people of the earth be gathered together against it.

4 In that day, saith the LORD, I will smite every horse with astonishment, and his rider with madness: and I will open mine eyes upon the house of Judah, and will smite every horse of the people with blindness.

5 And the governors of Judah shall say in their heart, The inhabitants of Jerusalem *shall be* my strength in the LORD of hosts their אֱלֹהִים.

6 ¶ In that day will I make the governors of Judah like an hearth of fire among the wood, and like a torch of fire in a sheaf; and they shall devour all the people round about, on the right hand and on the left: and Jerusalem shall be inhabited again in her own place, *even* in Jerusalem.

7 The LORD also shall save the tents of Judah first, that the glory of the house of David and the glory of the inhabitants of Jerusalem do not magnify *themselves* against Judah.

8 In that day shall the LORD defend the inhabitants of Jerusalem; and he that is feeble among them at that day shall be as David; and the house of David *shall be* as אֱלֹהִים, as the angel of the LORD before them.

9 ¶ And it shall come to pass in that day, *that* I will seek to destroy all the nations that come against Jerusalem.

10 And I will pour upon the house of David, and upon the inhabitants of Jerusalem, the spirit of grace and of supplications: and they shall look upon me whom they have pierced, and they shall mourn for him, as one mourneth for *his* only *son*, and shall be in bitterness for him, as one that is in bitterness for *his* firstborn.

11 In that day shall there be a great mourning in Jerusalem, as the mourning of Hadadrimmon in the valley of Megiddon.

12 And the land shall mourn, every family apart; the family of the house of David apart, and their wives apart; the family of the house of Nathan apart, and their wives apart;

13 The family of the house of Levi apart, and their wives apart; the family of Shimei apart, and their wives apart;

14 All the families that remain, every family apart, and their wives apart.

CHAPTER 13

IN that day there shall be a fountain opened to the house of David and to the inhabitants of Jerusalem for sin and for uncleanness.

2 ¶ And it shall come to pass in that day, saith the LORD of hosts, *that* I will cut off the names of the idols out of the land, and they shall no more be remembered: and also I will cause the prophets and the unclean spirit to pass out of the land.

3 And it shall come to pass, *that* when any shall yet prophesy, then his father and his mother that begat him shall say unto him, Thou shalt not live; for thou speakest lies in the name of the LORD: and his father and his mother that begat him shall thrust him through when he prophesieth.

4 And it shall come to pass in that day, *that* the prophets shall be ashamed every one of his vision, when he hath prophesied; neither shall they wear a rough garment to deceive:

5 But he shall say, I *am* no prophet, I *am* an husbandman; for man taught me to keep cattle from my youth.

6 And *one* shall say unto him, What *are* these wounds in thine hands? Then he shall answer, *Those* with which I was wounded *in* the house of my friends.

7 ¶ Awake, O sword, against my shepherd, and against the man *that is* my fellow, saith the LORD of hosts: smite the shepherd, and the sheep shall be scattered: and I will turn mine hand upon the little ones.

8 And it shall come to pass, *that* in all the land, saith the LORD, two parts therein shall be cut off *and* die; but the third shall be left

therein.

9 And I will bring the third part through the fire, and will refine them as silver is refined, and will try them as gold is tried: they shall call on my name, and I will hear them: I will say, It *is* my people: and they shall say, The Lᴏʀᴅ *is* my אֱלֹהִים.

CHAPTER 14

BEHOLD, the day of the Lᴏʀᴅ cometh, and thy spoil shall be divided in the midst of thee.

2 For I will gather all nations against Jerusalem to battle; and the city shall be taken, and the houses rifled, and the women ravished; and half of the city shall go forth into captivity, and the residue of the people shall not be cut off from the city.

3 Then shall the Lᴏʀᴅ go forth, and fight against those nations, as when he fought in the day of battle.

4 ¶ And his feet shall stand in that day upon the mount of Olives, which *is* before Jerusalem on the east, and the mount of Olives shall cleave in the midst thereof toward the east and toward the west, *and there shall be* a very great valley; and half of the mountain shall remove toward the north, and half of it toward the south.

5 And ye shall flee *to* the valley of the mountains; for the valley of the mountains shall reach unto Azal: yea, ye shall flee, like as ye fled from before the earthquake in the days of Uzziah king of Judah: and the Lᴏʀᴅ my אֱלֹהַי shall come, *and* all the saints with thee.

6 And it shall come to pass in that day, *that* the light shall not be clear, *nor* dark:

7 But it shall be one day which shall be known to the Lᴏʀᴅ, not day, nor night: but it shall come to pass, *that* at evening time it shall be light.

8 And it shall be in that day, *that* living waters shall go out from Jerusalem; half of them toward the former sea, and half of them toward the hinder sea: in summer and in winter shall it be.

9 And the Lᴏʀᴅ shall be king over all the earth: in that day shall there be one Lᴏʀᴅ, and his name one.

10 All the land shall be turned as a plain from Geba to Rimmon south of Jerusalem: and it shall be lifted up, and inhabited in her place, from Benjamin's gate unto the place of the first gate, unto the corner gate, and *from* the tower of Hananeel unto the king's winepresses.

11 And *men* shall dwell in it, and there shall be no more utter destruction; but Jerusalem shall be safely inhabited.

12 ¶ And this shall be the plague wherewith the Lᴏʀᴅ will smite all the people that have fought against Jerusalem; Their flesh shall consume away while they stand upon their feet, and their eyes shall consume away in their holes, and their tongue shall consume away in their mouth.

13 And it shall come to pass in that day, *that* a great tumult from the Lᴏʀᴅ shall be among them; and they shall lay hold every one on the hand of his neighbour, and his hand shall rise up against the hand of his neighbour.

14 And Judah also shall fight at Jerusalem; and the wealth of all the heathen round about shall be gathered together, gold, and silver, and apparel, in great abundance.

15 And so shall be the plague of the horse, of the mule, of the camel, and of the ass, and of all the beasts that shall be in these tents, as this plague.

16 ¶ And it shall come to pass, *that* every one that is left of all the nations which came against Jerusalem shall even go up from year to year to worship the King, the Lᴏʀᴅ of hosts, and to keep the feast of tabernacles.

17 And it shall be, *that* whoso will not come up of *all* the families of the earth unto Jerusalem to worship the King, the Lᴏʀᴅ of hosts, even upon them shall be no rain.

18 And if the family of Egypt go not up, and come not, that *have* no *rain;* there shall be the plague, wherewith the Lᴏʀᴅ will smite the heathen that come not up to keep the feast of tabernacles.

19 This shall be the punishment of Egypt, and the punishment of all nations that come not up to keep the feast of tabernacles.

20 ¶ In that day shall there be upon the bells of the horses, HOLINESS UNTO THE LORD; and the pots in the Lᴏʀᴅ's house shall be like the bowls before the altar.

21 Yea, every pot in Jerusalem and in Judah shall be holiness unto the Lᴏʀᴅ of hosts: and all they that sacrifice shall come and take of them, and seethe therein: and in that day there shall be no more the Canaanite in the house of the Lᴏʀᴅ of hosts.

MALACHI.

CHAPTER 1

THE burden of the word of the Lᴏʀᴅ to Israel by Malachi.

2 I have loved you, saith the Lᴏʀᴅ. Yet ye say, Wherein hast thou loved us? *Was* not Esau Jacob's brother? saith the Lᴏʀᴅ: yet I loved Jacob,

3 And I hated Esau, and laid his mountains and his heritage waste for the dragons of the wilderness.

4 Whereas Edom saith, We are impoverished, but we will return and build the desolate places; thus saith the Lᴏʀᴅ of hosts, They shall build, but I will throw down; and they shall call them, The border of wickedness, and, The people against whom the Lᴏʀᴅ hath indignation for ever.

5 And your eyes shall see, and ye shall say, The Lᴏʀᴅ will be magnified from the border of Israel.

6 ¶ A son honoureth *his* father, and a servant his master: if then I *be* a father, where *is* mine honour? and if I *be* a master, where *is* my fear? saith the Lᴏʀᴅ of hosts unto you, O priests, that despise my name. And ye say, Wherein have we despised thy name?

7 Ye offer polluted bread upon mine altar; and ye say, Wherein have we polluted thee? In that ye say, The table of the Lᴏʀᴅ *is* contemptible.

8 And if ye offer the blind for sacrifice, *is it* not evil? and if ye offer the lame and sick, *is it* not evil? offer it now unto thy governor; will he be pleased with thee, or accept thy person? saith the Lᴏʀᴅ of hosts.

9 And now, I pray you, beseech אֵל that he will be gracious unto us: this hath been by your means: will he regard your persons? saith the Lᴏʀᴅ of hosts.

10 Who *is there* even among you that would shut the doors *for nought?* neither do ye kindle *fire* on mine altar for nought. I have no pleasure in you, saith the Lᴏʀᴅ of hosts, neither will I accept an offering at your hand.

11 For from the rising of the sun even unto the going down of the same my name *shall be* great among the Gentiles; and in every place incense *shall be* offered unto my name, and a pure offering: for my name *shall be* great among the heathen, saith the Lᴏʀᴅ of hosts.

12 ¶ But ye have profaned it, in that ye say, The table of the Lᴏʀᴅ *is* polluted; and the fruit thereof, *even* his meat, *is* contemptible.

13 Ye said also, Behold, what a weariness *is it!* and ye have snuffed at it, saith the Lord of hosts; and ye brought *that which was* torn, and the lame, and the sick; thus ye brought an offering: should I accept this of your hand? saith the Lord.

14 But cursed *be* the deceiver, which hath in his flock a male, and voweth, and sacrificeth unto the Lord a corrupt thing: for I *am* a great King, saith the Lord of hosts, and my name *is* dreadful among the heathen.

CHAPTER 2

AND now, O ye priests, this commandment *is* for you.

2 If ye will not hear, and if ye will not lay *it* to heart, to give glory unto my name, saith the Lord of hosts, I will even send a curse upon you, and I will curse your blessings: yea, I have cursed them already, because ye do not lay *it* to heart.

3 Behold, I will corrupt your seed, and spread dung upon your faces, *even* the dung of your solemn feasts; and *one* shall take you away with it.

4 And ye shall know that I have sent this commandment unto you, that my covenant might be with Levi, saith the Lord of hosts.

5 My covenant was with him of life and peace; and I gave them to him *for* the fear wherewith he feared me, and was afraid before my name.

6 The law of truth was in his mouth, and iniquity was not found in his lips: he walked with me in peace and equity, and did turn many away from iniquity.

7 For the priest's lips should keep knowledge, and they should seek the law at his mouth: for he *is* the messenger of the Lord of hosts.

8 But ye are departed out of the way; ye have caused many to stumble at the law; ye have corrupted the covenant of Levi, saith the Lord of hosts.

9 Therefore have I also made you contemptible and base before all the people, according as ye have not kept my ways, but have been partial in the law.

10 Have we not all one father? hath not one אֱלֹהִים created us? why do we deal treacherously every man against his brother, by profaning the covenant of our fathers?

11 ¶ Judah hath dealt treacherously, and an abomination is committed in Israel and in Jerusalem; for Judah hath profaned the holiness of the Lord which he loved, and hath married the daughter of a strange god.

12 The Lord will cut off the man that doeth this, the master and the scholar, out of the tabernacles of Jacob, and him that offereth an offering unto the Lord of hosts.

13 And this have ye done again, covering the altar of the Lord with tears, with weeping, and with crying out, insomuch that he regardeth not the offering any more, or receiveth *it* with good will at your hand.

14 ¶ Yet ye say, Wherefore? Because the Lord hath been witness between thee and the wife of thy youth, against whom thou hast dealt treacherously: yet *is* she thy companion, and the wife of thy covenant.

15 And did not he make one? Yet had he the residue of the spirit. And wherefore one? That he might seek a godly seed. Therefore take heed to your spirit, and let none deal treacherously against the wife of his youth.

16 For the Lord, the אֱלֹהִים of Israel, saith that he hateth putting away: for *one* covereth violence with his garment, saith the Lord of hosts: therefore take heed to your spirit, that ye deal not treacherously.

17 ¶ Ye have wearied the Lord with your words. Yet ye say, Wherein have we wearied *him?* When ye say, Every one that doeth evil *is* good in the sight of the Lord, and he delighteth in them; or, Where *is* the אֱלֹהִים of judgment?

CHAPTER 3

BEHOLD, I will send my messenger, and he shall prepare the way before me: and the Lord, whom ye seek, shall suddenly come to his temple, even the messenger of the covenant, whom ye delight in: behold, he shall come, saith the Lord of hosts.

2 But who may abide the day of his coming? and who shall stand when he appeareth? for he *is* like a refiner's fire, and like fullers' soap:

3 And he shall sit *as* a refiner and purifier of silver: and he shall purify the sons of Levi, and purge them as gold and silver, that they may offer unto the Lord an offering in righteousness.

4 Then shall the offering of Judah and Jerusalem be pleasant unto the Lord, as in the days of old, and as in former years.

5 And I will come near to you to judgment; and I will be a swift witness against the sorcerers, and against the adulterers, and against false swearers, and against those that oppress the hireling in *his* wages, the widow, and the fatherless, and that turn aside the stranger *from his right*, and fear not me, saith the Lord of hosts.

6 For I *am* the Lord, I change not; therefore ye sons of Jacob are not consumed.

7 ¶ Even from the days of your fathers ye are gone away from mine ordinances, and have not kept *them*. Return unto me, and I will return unto you, saith the Lord of hosts. But ye said, Wherein shall we return?

8 ¶ Will a man rob אֱלֹהִים? Yet ye have robbed me. But ye say, Wherein have we robbed thee? In tithes and offerings.

9 Ye *are* cursed with a curse: for ye have robbed me, *even* this whole nation.

10 Bring ye all the tithes into the storehouse, that there may be meat in mine house, and prove me now herewith, saith the Lord of hosts, if I will not open you the windows of heaven, and pour you out a blessing, that *there shall* not *be room* enough *to receive it.*

11 And I will rebuke the devourer for your sakes, and he shall not destroy the fruits of your ground; neither shall your vine cast her fruit before the time in the field, saith the Lord of hosts.

12 And all nations shall call you blessed: for ye shall be a delightsome land, saith the Lord of hosts.

13 ¶ Your words have been stout against me, saith the Lord. Yet ye say, What have we spoken *so much* against thee?

14 Ye have said, It *is* vain to serve אֱלֹהִים: and what profit *is it* that we have kept his ordinance, and that we have walked mournfully before the Lord of hosts?

15 And now we call the proud happy; yea, they that work wickedness are set up; yea, *they that* tempt אֱלֹהִים are even delivered.

16 ¶ Then they that feared the Lord spake often one to another: and the Lord hearkened, and heard *it*, and a book of remembrance was written before him for them that feared the Lord, and that thought upon his name.

17 And they shall be mine, saith the Lord of hosts, in that day when I make up my jewels; and I will spare them, as a man spareth his own son that serveth him.

18 Then shall ye return, and discern between the righteous and the wicked, between him that serveth אֱלֹהִים and him that serveth him not.

FOR, behold, the day cometh, that shall burn as an oven; and all the proud, yea, and all that do wickedly, shall be stubble: and the day that cometh shall burn them up, saith the LORD of hosts, that it shall leave them neither root nor branch.

2 ¶ But unto you that fear my name shall the Sun of righteousness arise with healing in his wings; and ye shall go forth, and grow up as calves of the stall.

3 And ye shall tread down the wicked; for they shall be ashes under the soles of your feet in the day that I shall do *this*, saith the LORD of hosts.

4 ¶ Remember ye the law of Moses my servant, which I commanded unto him in Horeb for all Israel, *with* the statutes and judgments.

5 ¶ Behold, I will send you Elijah the prophet before the coming of the great and dreadful day of the LORD:

6 And he shall turn the heart of the fathers to the children, and the heart of the children to their fathers, lest I come and smite the earth with a curse.

Es1|1|1|And Josias held the feast of the passover in Jerusalem unto his Lord, and offered the passover the fourteenth day of the first month;

Es1|1|2|Having set the priests according to their daily courses, being arrayed in long garments, in the temple of the Lord.

Es1|1|3|And he spake unto the Levites, the holy ministers of Israel, that they should hallow themselves unto the Lord, to set the holy ark of the Lord in the house that king Solomon the son of David had built:

Es1|1|4|And said, Ye shall no more bear the ark upon your shoulders: now therefore serve the Lord your אֱלֹהִים, and minister unto his people Israel, and prepare you after your families and kindreds,

Es1|1|5|According as David the king of Israel prescribed, and according to the magnificence of Solomon his son: and standing in the temple according to the several dignity of the families of you the Levites, who minister in the presence of your brethren the children of Israel,

Es1|1|6|Offer the passover in order, and make ready the sacrifices for your brethren, and keep the passover according to the commandment of the Lord, which was given unto Moses.

Es1|1|7|And unto the people that was found there Josias gave thirty thousand lambs and kids, and three thousand calves: these things were given of the king's allowance, according as he promised, to the people, to the priests, and to the Levites.

Es1|1|8|And Helkias, Zacharias, and Syelus, the governors of the temple, gave to the priests for the passover two thousand and six hundred sheep, and three hundred calves.

Es1|1|9|And Jeconias, and Samaias, and Nathanael his brother, and Assabias, and Ochiel, and Joram, captains over thousands, gave to the Levites for the passover five thousand sheep, and seven hundred calves.

Es1|1|10|And when these things were done, the priests and Levites, having the unleavened bread, stood in very comely order according to the kindreds,

Es1|1|11|And according to the several dignities of the fathers, before the people, to offer to the Lord, as it is written in the book of Moses: and thus did they in the morning.

Es1|1|12|And they roasted the passover with fire, as appertaineth: as for the sacrifices, they sod them in brass pots and pans with a good savour,

Es1|1|13|And set them before all the people: and afterward they prepared for themselves, and for the priests their brethren, the sons of Aaron.

Es1|1|14|For the priests offered the fat until night: and the Levites prepared for themselves, and the priests their brethren, the sons of Aaron.

Es1|1|15|The holy singers also, the sons of Asaph, were in their order, according to the appointment of David, to wit, Asaph, Zacharias, and Jeduthun, who was of the king's retinue.

Es1|1|16|Moreover the porters were at every gate; it was not lawful for any to go from his ordinary service: for their brethren the Levites prepared for them.

Es1|1|17|Thus were the things that belonged to the sacrifices of the Lord accomplished in that day, that they might hold the passover,

Es1|1|18|And offer sacrifices upon the altar of the Lord, according to the commandment of king Josias.

Es1|1|19|So the children of Israel which were present held the passover at that time, and the feast of sweet bread seven days.

Es1|1|20|And such a passover was not kept in Israel since the time of the prophet Samuel.

Es1|1|21|Yea, all the kings of Israel held not such a passover as Josias, and the priests, and the Levites, and the Jews, held with all Israel that were found dwelling at Jerusalem.

Es1|1|22|In the eighteenth year of the reign of Josias was this passover kept.

Es1|1|23|And the works or Josias were upright before his Lord with an heart full of godliness.

Es1|1|24|As for the things that came to pass in his time, they were written in former times, concerning those that sinned, and did wickedly against the Lord above all people and kingdoms, and how they grieved him exceedingly, so that the words of the Lord rose up against Israel.

Es1|1|25|Now after all these acts of Josias it came to pass, that Pharaoh the king of Egypt came to raise war at Carchamis upon Euphrates: and Josias went out against him.

Es1|1|26|But the king of Egypt sent to him, saying, What have I to do with thee, O king of Judea?

Es1|1|27|I am not sent out from the Lord אֱלֹהִים against thee; for my war is upon Euphrates: and now the Lord is with me, yea, the Lord is with me hasting me forward: depart from me, and be not against the Lord.

Es1|1|28|Howbeit Josias did not turn back his chariot from him, but undertook to fight with him, not regarding the words of the prophet Jeremy spoken by the mouth of the Lord:

Es1|1|29|But joined battle with him in the plain of Magiddo, and the princes came against king Josias.

Es1|1|30|Then said the king unto his servants, Carry me away out of the battle; for I am very weak. And immediately his servants took him away out of the battle.

Es1|1|31|Then gat he up upon his second chariot; and being brought back to Jerusalem died, and was buried in his father's sepulchre.

Es1|1|32|And in all Jewry they mourned for Josias, yea, Jeremy the prophet lamented for Josias, and the chief men with the women made lamentation for him unto this day: and this was given out for an ordinance to be done continually in all the nation of Israel.

Es1|1|33|These things are written in the book of the stories of the kings of Judah, and every one of the acts that Josias did, and his glory, and his understanding in the law of the Lord, and the things that he had done before, and the things now recited, are reported in the book of the kings of Israel and Judea.

Es1|1|34|And the people took Joachaz the son of Josias, and made him king instead of Josias his father, when he was twenty and three years old.

Es1|1|35|And he reigned in Judea and in Jerusalem three months: and then the king of Egypt deposed him from reigning in Jerusalem.

Es1|1|36|And he set a tax upon the land of an hundred talents of silver and one talent of gold.

Es1|1|37|The king of Egypt also made king Joacim his brother king of Judea and Jerusalem.

Es1|1|38|And he bound Joacim and the nobles: but Zaraces his brother he apprehended, and brought him out of Egypt.

Es1|1|39|Five and twenty years old was Joacim when he was made king in the land of Judea and Jerusalem; and he did evil before the Lord.

Es1|1|40|Wherefore against him Nabuchodonosor the king of Babylon came up, and bound him with a chain of brass, and carried him into Babylon.

Es1|1|41|Nabuchodonosor also took of the holy vessels of the Lord, and carried them away, and set them in his own temple at Babylon.

Es1|1|42|But those things that are recorded of him, and of his uncleaness and impiety, are written in the chronicles of the kings.

Es1|1|43|And Joacim his son reigned in his stead: he was made king being eighteen years old;

Es1|1|44|And reigned but three months and ten days in Jerusalem; and did evil before the Lord.

Es1|1|45|So after a year Nabuchodonosor sent and caused him to be brought into Babylon with the holy vessels of the Lord;

Es1|1|46|And made Zedechias king of Judea and Jerusalem, when he was one and twenty years old; and he reigned eleven years:

Es1|1|47|And he did evil also in the sight of the Lord, and cared not for the words that were spoken unto him by the prophet Jeremy from the mouth of the Lord.

Es1|1|48|And after that king Nabuchodonosor had made him to swear by the name of the Lord, he forswore himself, and rebelled; and hardening his neck, his heart, he transgressed the laws of the Lord אֱלֹהִים of Israel.

Es1|1|49|The governors also of the people and of the priests did many things against the laws, and passed all the pollutions of all nations, and defiled the temple of the Lord, which was sanctified in Jerusalem.

Es1|1|50|Nevertheless the אֱלֹהִים of their fathers sent by his messenger to call them back, because he spared them and his tabernacle also.

Es1|1|51|But they had his messengers in derision; and, look, when the Lord spake unto them, they made a sport of his prophets:

Es1|1|52|So far forth, that he, being wroth with his people for their great ungodliness, commanded the kings of the Chaldees to come up against them;

Es1|1|53|Who slew their young men with the sword, yea, even within the compass of their holy temple, and spared neither young man nor maid, old man nor child, among them; for he delivered all into their hands.

Es1|1|54|And they took all the holy vessels of the Lord, both great and small, with the vessels of the ark of אֱלֹהִים, and the king's treasures, and carried them away into Babylon.

Es1|1|55|As for the house of the Lord, they burnt it, and brake down the walls of Jerusalem, and set fire upon her towers:

Es1|1|56|And as for her glorious things, they never ceased till they had consumed and brought them all to nought: and the people that were not slain with the sword he carried unto Babylon:

Es1|1|57|Who became servants to him and his children, till the Persians reigned, to fulfil the word of the Lord spoken by the mouth of Jeremy:

Es1|1|58|Until the land had enjoyed her sabbaths, the whole time of her desolation shall she rest, until the full term of seventy years.

Es1|2|1|In the first year of Cyrus king of the Persians, that the word of the Lord might be accomplished, that he had promised by the mouth of Jeremy;

Es1|2|2|The Lord raised up the spirit of Cyrus the king of the Persians, and he made proclamation through all his kingdom, and also by writing,

Es1|2|3|Saying, Thus saith Cyrus king of the Persians; The Lord of Israel, the most high Lord, hath made me king of the whole world,

Es1|2|4|And commanded me to build him an house at Jerusalem in Jewry.

Es1|2|5|If therefore there be any of you that are of his people, let the Lord, even his Lord, be with him, and let him go up to Jerusalem that is in Judea, and build the house of the Lord of Israel: for he is the Lord that dwelleth in Jerusalem.

Es1|2|6|Whosoever then dwell in the places about, let them help him, those, I say, that are his neighbours, with gold, and with silver,

Es1|2|7|With gifts, with horses, and with cattle, and other things, which have been set forth by vow, for the temple of the Lord at Jerusalem.

Es1|2|8|Then the chief of the families of Judea and of the tribe of Benjamin stood up; the priests also, and the Levites, and all they whose mind the Lord had moved to go up, and to build an house for the Lord at Jerusalem,

Es1|2|9|And they that dwelt round about them, and helped them in all things with silver and gold, with horses and cattle, and with very many free gifts of a great number whose minds were stirred up thereto.

Es1|2|10|King Cyrus also brought forth the holy vessels, which Nabuchodonosor had carried away from Jerusalem, and had set up in his temple of idols.

Es1|2|11|Now when Cyrus king of the Persians had brought them forth, he delivered them to Mithridates his treasurer:

Es1|2|12|And by him they were delivered to Sanabassar the governor of Judea.

Es1|2|13|And this was the number of them; A thousand golden cups, and a thousand of silver, censers of silver twenty nine, vials of gold thirty, and of silver two thousand four hundred and ten, and a thousand other vessels.

Es1|2|14|So all the vessels of gold and of silver, which were carried away, were five thousand four hundred threescore and nine.

Es1|2|15|These were brought back by Sanabassar, together with them of the captivity, from Babylon to Jerusalem.

Es1|2|16|But in the time of Artexerxes king of the Persians Belemus, and Mithridates, and Tabellius, and Rathumus, and Beeltethmus, and Semellius the secretary, with others that were in commission with them, dwelling in Samaria and other places, wrote unto him against them that dwelt in Judea and Jerusalem these letters following;

Es1|2|17|To king Artexerxes our lord, Thy servants, Rathumus the storywriter, and Semellius the scribe, and the rest of their council, and the judges that are in Celosyria and Phenice.

Es1|2|18|Be it now known to the lord king, that the Jews that are up from you to us, being come into Jerusalem, that rebellious and wicked city, do build the marketplaces, and repair the walls of it and do lay the foundation of the temple.

Es1|2|19|Now if this city and the walls thereof be made up again, they will not only refuse to give tribute, but also rebel against kings.

Es1|2|20|And forasmuch as the things pertaining to the temple are now in hand, we think it meet not to neglect such a matter,

Es1|2|21|But to speak unto our lord the king, to the intent that, if it be thy pleasure it may be sought out in the books of thy fathers:

Es1|2|22|And thou shalt find in the chronicles what is written concerning these things, and shalt understand that that city was rebellious, troubling both kings and cities:

Es1|2|23|And that the Jews were rebellious, and raised always wars therein; for the which cause even this city was made desolate.

Es1|2|24|Wherefore now we do declare unto thee, O lord the king, that if this city be built again, and the walls thereof set up anew, thou shalt from henceforth have no passage into Celosyria and Phenice.

Es1|2|25|Then the king wrote back again to Rathumus the storywriter, to Beeltethmus, to Semellius the scribe, and to the rest that were in commission, and dwellers in Samaria and Syria and Phenice, after this manner;

Es1|2|26|I have read the epistle which ye have sent unto me: therefore I commanded to make diligent search, and it hath been found that that city was from the beginning practising against kings;

Es1|2|27|And the men therein were given to rebellion and war: and that mighty kings and fierce were in Jerusalem, who reigned and exacted tributes in Celosyria and Phenice.

Es1|2|28|Now therefore I have commanded to hinder those men from building the city, and heed to be taken that there be no more done in it;

Es1|2|29|And that those wicked workers proceed no further to the annoyance of kings,

Es1|2|30|Then king Artexerxes his letters being read, Rathumus, and Semellius the scribe, and the rest that were in commission with them, removing in haste toward Jerusalem with a troop of horsemen and a multitude of people in battle array, began to hinder the builders; and the building of the temple in Jerusalem ceased until the second year of the reign of Darius king of the Persians.

Es1|3|1|Now when Darius reigned, he made a great feast unto all his subjects, and unto all his household, and unto all the princes of Media and Persia,

Es1|3|2|And to all the governors and captains and lieutenants that were under him, from India unto Ethiopia, of an hundred twenty and seven provinces.

Es1|3|3|And when they had eaten and drunken, and being satisfied were gone home, then Darius the king went into his bedchamber, and slept, and soon after awaked.

Es1|3|4|Then three young men, that were of the guard that kept the king's body, spake one to another;

Es1|3|5|Let every one of us speak a sentence: he that shall overcome, and whose sentence shall seem wiser than the others, unto him shall the king Darius give great gifts, and great things in token of victory:

Es1|3|6|As, to be clothed in purple, to drink in gold, and to sleep upon gold, and a chariot with bridles of gold, and an headtire of fine linen, and a chain about his neck:

Es1|3|7|And he shall sit next to Darius because of his wisdom, and shall be called Darius his cousin.

Es1|3|8|And then every one wrote his sentence, sealed it, and laid it under king Darius his pillow;

Es1|3|9|And said that, when the king is risen, some will give him the writings; and of whose side the king and the three princes of Persia shall judge that his sentence is the wisest, to him shall the victory be given, as was appointed.

Es1|3|10|The first wrote, Wine is the strongest.

Es1|3|11|The second wrote, The king is strongest.

Es1|3|12|The third wrote, Women are strongest: but above all things Truth beareth away the victory.

Es1|3|13|Now when the king was risen up, they took their writings, and delivered them unto him, and so he read them:

Es1|3|14|And sending forth he called all the princes of Persia and Media, and the governors, and the captains, and the lieutenants, and the chief officers;

Es1|3|15|And sat him down in the royal seat of judgment; and the writings were read before them.

Es1|3|16|And he said, Call the young men, and they shall declare their own sentences. So they were called, and came in.

Es1|3|17|And he said unto them, Declare unto us your mind concerning the writings. Then began the first, who had spoken of the strength of wine;

Es1|3|18|And he said thus, O ye men, how exceeding strong is wine! it causeth all men to err that drink it:

Es1|3|19|It maketh the mind of the king and of the fatherless child to be all one; of the bondman and of the freeman, of the poor man and of the rich:

Es1|3|20|It turneth also every thought into jollity and mirth, so that a man remembereth neither sorrow nor debt:

Es1|3|21|And it maketh every heart rich, so that a man remembereth neither king nor governor; and it maketh to speak all things by talents:

Es1|3|22|And when they are in their cups, they forget their love both to friends and brethren, and a little after draw out swords:

Es1|3|23|But when they are from the wine, they remember not what they have done.

Es1|3|24|O ye men, is not wine the strongest, that enforceth to do thus? And when he had so spoken, he held his peace.

Es1|4|1|Then the second, that had spoken of the strength of the king, began to say,

Es1|4|2|O ye men, do not men excel in strength that bear rule over sea and land and all things in them?

Es1|4|3|But yet the king is more mighty: for he is lord of all these things, and hath dominion over them; and whatsoever he commandeth them they do.

Es1|4|4|If he bid them make war the one against the other, they do it: if he send them out against the enemies, they go, and break down mountains walls and towers.

Es1|4|5|They slay and are slain, and transgress not the king's commandment: if they get the victory, they bring all to the king, as well the spoil, as all things else.

Es1|4|6|Likewise for those that are no soldiers, and have not to do with wars, but use husbundry, when they have reaped again that which they had sown, they bring it to the king, and compel one another to pay tribute unto the king.

Es1|4|7|And yet he is but one man: if he command to kill, they kill; if he command to spare, they spare;

Es1|4|8|If he command to smite, they smite; if he command to make desolate, they make desolate; if he command to build, they build;

Es1|4|9|If he command to cut down, they cut down; if he command to plant, they plant.

Es1|4|10|So all his people and his armies obey him: furthermore he lieth down, he eateth and drinketh, and taketh his rest:

Es1|4|11|And these keep watch round about him, neither may any one depart, and do his own business, neither disobey they him in any thing.

Es1|4|12|O ye men, how should not the king be mightiest, when in such sort he is obeyed? And he held his tongue.

Es1|4|13|Then the third, who had spoken of women, and of the truth, (this was Zorobabel) began to speak.

Es1|4|14|O ye men, it is not the great king, nor the multitude of men, neither is it wine, that excelleth; who is it then that ruleth them, or hath the lordship over them? are they not women?

Es1|4|15|Women have borne the king and all the people that bear rule by sea and land.

Es1|4|16|Even of them came they: and they nourished them up that planted the vineyards, from whence the wine cometh.

Es1|4|17|These also make garments for men; these bring glory unto men; and without women cannot men be.

Es1|4|18|Yea, and if men have gathered together gold and silver, or any other goodly thing, do they not love a woman which is comely in favour and beauty?

Es1|4|19|And letting all those things go, do they not gape, and even with open mouth fix their eyes fast on her; and have not all men more desire unto her than unto silver or gold, or any goodly thing whatsoever?

Es1|4|20|A man leaveth his own father that brought him up, and his own country, and cleaveth unto his wife.

Es1|4|21|He sticketh not to spend his life with his wife. and remembereth neither father, nor mother, nor country.

Es1|4|22|By this also ye must know that women have dominion over you: do ye not labour and toil, and give and bring all to the woman?

Es1|4|23|Yea, a man taketh his sword, and goeth his way to rob and to steal, to sail upon the sea and upon rivers;

Es1|4|24|And looketh upon a lion, and goeth in the darkness; and when he hath stolen, spoiled, and robbed, he bringeth it to his love.

Es1|4|25|Wherefore a man loveth his wife better than father or mother.

Es1|4|26|Yea, many there be that have run out of their wits for women, and become servants for their sakes.

Es1|4|27|Many also have perished, have erred, and sinned, for women.

Es1|4|28|And now do ye not believe me? is not the king great in his power? do not all regions fear to touch him?

Es1|4|29|Yet did I see him and Apame the king's concubine, the daughter of the admirable Bartacus, sitting at the right hand of the king,

Es1|4|30|And taking the crown from the king's head, and setting it upon her own head; she also struck the king with her left hand.

Es1|4|31|And yet for all this the king gaped and gazed upon her with open mouth: if she laughed upon him, he laughed also: but if she took any displeasure at him, the king was fain to flatter, that she might be reconciled to him again.

Es1|4|32|O ye men, how can it be but women should be strong, seeing they do thus?

Es1|4|33|Then the king and the princes looked one upon another: so he began to speak of the truth.

Es1|4|34|O ye men, are not women strong? great is the earth, high is the heaven, swift is the sun in his course, for he compasseth the heavens round about, and fetcheth his course again to his own place in one day.

Es1|4|35|Is he not great that maketh these things? therefore great is the truth, and stronger than all things.

Es1|4|36|All the earth crieth upon the truth, and the heaven blesseth it: all works shake and tremble at it, and with it is no unrighteous thing.

Es1|4|37|Wine is wicked, the king is wicked, women are wicked, all the children of men are wicked, and such are all their wicked works; and there is no truth in them; in their unrighteousness also they shall perish.

Es1|4|38|As for the truth, it endureth, and is alwaYs strong; it liveth and conquereth for evermore.

Es1|4|39|With her there is no accepting of persons or rewards; but she doeth the things that are just, and refraineth from all unjust and wicked things; and all men do well like of her works.

Es1|4|40|Neither in her judgment is any unrighteousness; and she is the strength, kingdom, power, and majesty, of all ages. Blessed be the אֱלֹהִים of truth.

Es1|4|41|And with that he held his peace. And all the people then shouted, and said, Great is Truth, and mighty above all things.

Es1|4|42|Then said the king unto him, Ask what thou wilt more than is appointed in the writing, and we will give it thee, because thou art found wisest; and thou shalt sit next me, and shalt be called my cousin.

Es1|4|43|Then said he unto the king, Remember thy vow, which thou hast vowed to build Jerusalem, in the day when thou camest to thy kingdom,

Es1|4|44|And to send away all the vessels that were taken away out of Jerusalem, which Cyrus set apart, when he vowed to destroy Babylon, and to send them again thither.

Es1|4|45|Thou also hast vowed to build up the temple, which the Edomites burned when Judea was made desolate by the Chaldees.

Es1|4|46|And now, O lord the king, this is that which I require, and which I desire of thee, and this is the princely liberality proceeding from thyself: I desire therefore that thou make good the vow, the performance whereof with thine own mouth thou hast vowed to the King of heaven.

Es1|4|47|Then Darius the king stood up, and kissed him, and wrote letters for him unto all the treasurers and lieutenants and captains and governors, that they should safely convey on their way both him, and all those that go up with him to build Jerusalem.

Es1|4|48|He wrote letters also unto the lieutenants that were in Celosyria and Phenice, and unto them in Libanus, that they should bring cedar wood from Libanus unto Jerusalem, and that they should build the city with him.

Es1|4|49|Moreover he wrote for all the Jews that went out of his realm up into Jewry, concerning their freedom, that no officer, no ruler, no lieutenant, nor treasurer, should forcibly enter into their doors;

Es1|4|50|And that all the country which they hold should be free without tribute; and that the Edomites should give over the villages of the Jews which then they held:

Es1|4|51|Yea, that there should be yearly given twenty talents to the building of the temple, until the time that it were built;

Es1|4|52|And other ten talents yearly, to maintain the burnt offerings upon the altar every day, as they had a commandment to offer seventeen:

Es1|4|53|And that all they that went from Babylon to build the city should have free liberty, as well they as their posterity, and all the priests that went away.

Es1|4|54|He wrote also concerning. the charges, and the priests' vestments wherein they minister;

Es1|4|55|And likewise for the charges of the Levites, to be given them until the day that the house were finished, and Jerusalem builded up.

Es1|4|56|And he commanded to give to all that kept the city pensions and wages.

Es1|4|57|He sent away also all the vessels from Babylon, that Cyrus had set apart; and all that Cyrus had given in commandment, the same charged he also to be done, and sent unto Jerusalem.

Es1|4|58|Now when this young man was gone forth, he lifted up his face to heaven toward Jerusalem, and praised the King of heaven,

Es1|4|59|And said, From thee cometh victory, from thee cometh wisdom, and thine is the glory, and I am thy servant.

Es1|4|60|Blessed art thou, who hast given me wisdom: for to thee I give thanks, O Lord of our fathers.

Es1|4|61|And so he took the letters, and went out, and came unto Babylon, and told it all his brethren.

Es1|4|62|And they praised the אֱלֹהִים of their fathers, because he had given them freedom and liberty

Es1|4|63|To go up, and to build Jerusalem, and the temple which is called by his name: and they feasted with instruments of musick and gladness seven days.

Es1|5|1|After this were the principal men of the families chosen according to their tribes, to go up with their wives and sons and daughters, with their menservants and maidservants, and their cattle.

Es1|5|2|And Darius sent with them a thousand horsemen, till they had brought them back to Jerusalem safely, and with musical [instruments] tabrets and flutes.

Es1|5|3|And all their brethren played, and he made them go up together with them.

Es1|5|4|And these are the names of the men which went up, according to their families among their tribes, after their several heads.

Es1|5|5|The priests, the sons of Phinees the son of Aaron: Yashiyah the son of Josedec, the son of Saraias, and Joacim the son of Zorobabel, the son of Salathiel, of the house of David, out of the kindred of Phares, of the tribe of Judah;

Es1|5|6|Who spake wise sentences before Darius the king of Persia in the second year of his reign, in the month Nisan, which is the first month.

Es1|5|7|And these are they of Jewry that came up from the captivity, where they dwelt as strangers, whom Nabuchodonosor the king of Babylon had carried away unto Babylon.

Es1|5|8|And they returned unto Jerusalem, and to the other parts of Jewry, every man to his own city, who came with Zorobabel, with Yashiyah, Nehemias, and Zacharias, and Reesaias, Enenius, Mardocheus. Beelsarus, Aspharasus, Reelius, Roimus, and Baana, their guides.

Es1|5|9|The number of them of the nation, and their governors, sons of Phoros, two thousand an hundred seventy and two; the sons of Saphat, four hundred seventy and two:

Es1|5|10|The sons of Ares, seven hundred fifty and six:

Es1|5|11|The sons of Phaath Moab, two thousand eight hundred and twelve:

Es1|5|12|The sons of Elam, a thousand two hundred fifty and four: the sons of Zathul, nine hundred forty and five: the sons of Corbe, seven hundred and five: the sons of Bani, six hundred forty and eight:

Es1|5|13|The sons of Bebai, six hundred twenty and three: the sons of Sadas, three thousand two hundred twenty and two:

Es1|5|14|The sons of Adonikam, six hundred sixty and seven: the sons of Bagoi, two thousand sixty and six: the sons of Adin, four hundred fifty and four:

Es1|5|15|The sons of Aterezias, ninety and two: the sons of Ceilan and Azetas threescore and seven: the sons of Azuran, four hundred thirty and two:

Es1|5|16|The sons of Ananias, an hundred and one: the sons of Arom, thirty two: and the sons of Bassa, three hundred twenty and three: the sons of Azephurith, an hundred and two:

Es1|5|17|The sons of Meterus, three thousand and five: the sons of Bethlomon, an hundred twenty and three:

Es1|5|18|They of Netophah, fifty and five: they of Anathoth, an hundred fifty and eight: they of Bethsamos, forty and two:

Es1|5|19|They of Kiriathiarius, twenty and five: they of Caphira and Beroth, seven hundred forty and three: they of Pira, seven hundred:

Es1|5|20|They of Chadias and Ammidoi, four hundred twenty and two: they of Cirama and Gabdes, six hundred twenty and one:

Es1|5|21|They of Macalon, an hundred twenty and two: they of Betolius, fifty and two: the sons of Nephis, an hundred fifty and six:

Es1|5|22|The sons of Calamolalus and Onus, seven hundred twenty and five: the sons of Jerechus, two hundred forty and five:

Es1|5|23|The sons of Annas, three thousand three hundred and thirty.

Es1|5|24|The priests: the sons of Jeddu, the son of Yashiyah among the sons of Sanasib, nine hundred seventy and two: the sons of Meruth, a thousand fifty and two:

Es1|5|25|The sons of Phassaron, a thousand forty and seven: the sons of Carme, a thousand and seventeen.

Es1|5|26|The Levites: the sons of Jessue, and Cadmiel, and Banuas, and Sudias, seventy and four.

Es1|5|27|The holy singers: the sons of Asaph, an hundred twenty and eight.

Es1|5|28|The porters: the sons of Salum, the sons of Jatal, the sons of Talmon, the sons of Dacobi, the sons of Teta, the sons of Sami, in all an hundred thirty and nine.

Es1|5|29|The servants of the temple: the sons of Esau, the sons of Asipha, the sons of Tabaoth, the sons of Ceras, the sons of Sud, the sons of Phaleas, the sons of Labana, the sons of Graba,

Es1|5|30|The sons of Acua, the sons of Uta, the sons of Cetab, the sons of Agaba, the sons of Subai, the sons of Anan, the sons of Cathua, the sons of Geddur,

Es1|5|31|The sons of Airus, the sons of Daisan, the sons of Noeba, the sons of Chaseba, the sons of Gazera, the sons of Azia, the sons of Phinees, the sons of Azare, the sons of Bastai, the sons of Asana, the sons of Meani, the sons of Naphisi, the sons of Acub, the sons of Acipha, the sons of Assur, the sons of Pharacim, the sons of Basaloth,

Es1|5|32|The sons of Meeda, the sons of Coutha, the sons of Charea, the sons of Charcus, the sons of Aserer, the sons of Thomoi, the sons of Nasith, the sons of Atipha.

Es1|5|33|The sons of the servants of Solomon: the sons of Azaphion, the sons of Pharira, the sons of Jeeli, the sons of Lozon, the sons of Israel, the sons of Sapheth,

Es1|5|34|The sons of Hagia, the sons of Pharacareth, the sons of Sabi, the sons of Sarothie, the sons of Masias, the sons of Gar, the sons of Addus, the sons of Suba, the sons of Apherra, the sons of Barodis, the sons of Sabat, the sons of Allom.

Es1|5|35|All the ministers of the temple, and the sons of the servants of Solomon, were three hundred seventy and two.

Es1|5|36|These came up from Thermeleth and Thelersas, Charaathalar leading them, and Aalar;

Es1|5|37|Neither could they shew their families, nor their stock, how they were of Israel: the sons of Ladan, the son of Ban, the sons of Necodan, six hundred fifty and two.

Es1|5|38|And of the priests that usurped the office of the priesthood, and were not found: the sons of Obdia, the sons of Accoz, the sons of Addus, who married Augia one of the daughters of Barzelus, and was named after his name.

Es1|5|39|And when the description of the kindred of these men was sought in the register, and was not found, they were removed from executing the office of the priesthood:

Es1|5|40|For unto them said Nehemias and Atharias, that they should not be partakers of the holy things, till there arose up an high priest clothed with doctrine and truth.

Es1|5|41|So of Israel, from them of twelve years old and upward, they were all in number forty thousand, beside menservants and womenservants two thousand three hundred and sixty.

Es1|5|42|Their menservants and handmaids were seven thousand three hundred forty and seven: the singing men and singing women, two hundred forty and five:

Es1|5|43|Four hundred thirty and five camels, seven thousand thirty and six horses, two hundred forty and five mules, five thousand five hundred twenty and five beasts used to the yoke.

Es1|5|44|And certain of the chief of their families, when they came to the temple of אֱלֹהִים that is in Jerusalem, vowed to set up the house again in his own place according to their ability,

Es1|5|45|And to give into the holy treasury of the works a thousand pounds of gold, five thousand of silver, and an hundred priestly vestments.

Es1|5|46|And so dwelt the priests and the Levites and the people in Jerusalem, and in the country, the singers also and the porters; and all Israel in their villages.

Es1|5|47|But when the seventh month was at hand, and when the children of Israel were every man in his own place, they came all together with one consent into the open place of the first gate which is toward the east.

Es1|5|48|Then stood up Yashiyah the son of Josedec, and his brethren the priests and Zorobabel the son of Salathiel, and his brethren, and made ready the altar of the אֱלֹהִים of Israel,

Es1|5|49|To offer burnt sacrifices upon it, according as it is expressly commanded in the book of Moses the man of אֱלֹהִים.

Es1|5|50|And there were gathered unto them out of the other nations of the land, and they erected the altar upon his own place, because all the nations of the land were at enmity with them, and oppressed them; and they offered sacrifices according to the time, and burnt offerings to the Lord both morning and evening.

Es1|5|51|Also they held the feast of tabernacles, as it is commanded in the law, and offered sacrifices daily, as was meet:

Es1|5|52|And after that, the continual oblations, and the sacrifice of the sabbaths, and of the new moons, and of all holy feasts.

Es1|5|53|And all they that had made any vow to אֱלֹהִים began to offer sacrifices to אֱלֹהִים from the first day of the seventh month, although the temple of the Lord was not yet built.

Es1|5|54|And they gave unto the masons and carpenters money, meat, and drink, with cheerfulness.

Es1|5|55|Unto them of Zidon also and Tyre they gave carrs, that they should bring cedar trees from Libanus, which should be brought by floats to the haven of Joppa, according as it was commanded them by Cyrus king of the Persians.

Es1|5|56|And in the second year and second month after his coming to the temple of אֱלֹהִים at Jerusalem began Zorobabel the son of Salathiel, and Yashiyah the son of Josedec, and their brethren, and the priests, and the Levites, and all they that were come unto Jerusalem out of the captivity:

Es1|5|57|And they laid the foundation of the house of אֱלֹהִים in the first day of the second month, in the second year after they were come to Jewry and Jerusalem.

Es1|5|58|And they appointed the Levites from twenty years old over the works of the Lord. Then stood up Yashiyah, and his sons and brethren, and Cadmiel his brother, and the sons of Madiabun, with the sons of Joda the son of Eliadun, with their sons and brethren, all Levites, with one accord setters forward of the business, labouring to advance the works in the house of אֱלֹהִים. So the workmen built the temple of the Lord.

Es1|5|59|And the priests stood arrayed in their vestments with musical instruments and trumpets; and the Levites the sons of Asaph had cymbals,

Es1|5|60|Singing songs of thanksgiving, and praising the Lord, according as David the king of Israel had ordained.

Es1|5|61|And they sung with loud voices songs to the praise of the Lord, because his mercy and glory is for ever in all Israel.

Es1|5|62|And all the people sounded trumpets, and shouted with a loud voice, singing songs of thanksgiving unto the Lord for the rearing up of the house of the Lord.

Es1|5|63|Also of the priests and Levites, and of the chief of their families, the ancients who had seen the former house came to the building of this with weeping and great crying.

Es1|5|64|But many with trumpets and joy shouted with loud voice,

Es1|5|65|Insomuch that the trumpets might not be heard for the weeping of the people: yet the multitude sounded marvellously, so that it was heard afar off.

Es1|5|66|Wherefore when the enemies of the tribe of Judah and Benjamin heard it, they came to know what that noise of trumpets should mean.

Es1|5|67|And they perceived that they that were of the captivity did build the temple unto the Lord אֱלֹהִים of Israel.

Es1|5|68|So they went to Zorobabel and Yashiyah, and to the chief of the families, and said unto them, We will build together with you.

Es1|5|69|For we likewise, as ye, do obey your Lord, and do sacrifice unto him from the days of Azbazareth the king of the Assyrians, who brought us hither.

Es1|5|70|Then Zorobabel and Yashiyah and the chief of the families of Israel said unto them, It is not for us and you to build together an house unto the Lord our אֱלֹהִים.

Es1|5|71|We ourselves alone will build unto the Lord of Israel, according as Cyrus the king of the Persians hath commanded us.

Es1|5|72|But the heathen of the land lying heavy upon the inhabitants of Judea, and holding them strait, hindered their building;

Es1|5|73|And by their secret plots, and popular persuasions and commotions, they hindered the finishing of the building all the time that king Cyrus lived: so they were hindered from building for the space of two years, until the reign of Darius.

Es1|6|1|Now in the second year of the reign of Darius Aggeus and Zacharias the son of Addo, the prophets, prophesied unto the Jews in Jewry and Jerusalem in the name of the Lord אֱלֹהִים of Israel, which was upon them.

Es1|6|2|Then stood up Zorobabel the son of Salatiel, and Yashiyah the son of Josedec, and began to build the house of the Lord at Jerusalem, the prophets of the Lord being with them, and helping them.

Es1|6|3|At the same time came unto them Sisinnes the governor of Syria and Phenice, with Sathrabuzanes and his companions, and said unto them,

Es1|6|4|By whose appointment do ye build this house and this roof, and perform all the other things? and who are the workmen that perform these things?

Es1|6|5|Nevertheless the elders of the Jews obtained favour, because the Lord had visited the captivity:

Es1|6|6|And they were not hindered from building, until such time as signification was given unto Darius concerning them, and an answer received.

Es1|6|7|The copy of the letters which Sisinnes, governor of Syria and Phenice, and Sathrabuzanes, with their companions, rulers in Syria and Phenice, wrote and sent unto Darius; To king Darius, greeting:

Es1|6|8|Let all things be known unto our lord the king, that being come into the country of Judea, and entered into the city of Jerusalem we found in the city of Jerusalem the ancients of the Jews that were of the captivity

Es1|6|9|Building an house unto the Lord, great and new, of hewn and costly stones, and the timber already laid upon the walls.

Es1|6|10|And those works are done with great speed, and the work goeth on prosperously in their hands, and with all glory and diligence is it made.

Es1|6|11|Then asked we these elders, saying, By whose commandment build ye this house, and lay the foundations of these works?

Es1|6|12|Therefore to the intent that we might give knowledge unto thee by writing, we demanded of them who were the chief doers, and we required of them the names in writing of their principal men.

Es1|6|13|So they gave us this answer, We are the servants of the Lord which made heaven and earth.

Es1|6|14|And as for this house, it was builded many years ago by a king of Israel great and strong, and was finished.

Es1|6|15|But when our fathers provoked אֱלֹהִים unto wrath, and sinned against the Lord of Israel which is in heaven, he gave them over into the power of Nabuchodonosor king of Babylon, of the Chaldees;

Es1|6|16|Who pulled down the house, and burned it, and carried away the people captives unto Babylon.

Es1|6|17|But in the first year that king Cyrus reigned over the country of Babylon Cyrus the king wrote to build up this house.

Es1|6|18|And the holy vessels of gold and of silver, that Nabuchodonosor had carried away out of the house at Jerusalem, and had set them in his own temple those Cyrus the king brought forth again out of the temple at Babylon, and they were delivered to Zorobabel and to Sanabassarus the ruler,

Es1|6|19|With commandment that he should carry away the same vessels, and put them in the temple at Jerusalem; and that the temple of the Lord should be built in his place.

Es1|6|20|Then the same Sanabassarus, being come hither, laid the foundations of the house of the Lord at Jerusalem; and from that time to this being still a building, it is not yet fully ended.

Es1|6|21|Now therefore, if it seem good unto the king, let search be made among the records of king Cyrus:

Es1|6|22|And if it be found that the building of the house of the Lord at Jerusalem hath been done with the consent of king Cyrus, and if our lord the king be so minded, let him signify unto us thereof.

Es1|6|23|Then commanded king Darius to seek among the records at Babylon: and so at Ecbatane the palace, which is in the country of Media, there was found a roll wherein these things were recorded.

Es1|6|24|In the first year of the reign of Cyrus king Cyrus commanded that the house of the Lord at Jerusalem should be built again, where they do sacrifice with continual fire:

Es1|6|25|Whose height shall be sixty cubits and the breadth sixty cubits, with three rows of hewn stones, and one row of new wood of that country; and the expences thereof to be given out of the house of king Cyrus:

Es1|6|26|And that the holy vessels of the house of the Lord, both of gold and silver, that Nabuchodonosor took out of the house at Jerusalem, and brought to Babylon, should be restored to the house at Jerusalem, and be set in the place where they were before.

Es1|6|27|And also he commanded that Sisinnes the governor of Syria and Phenice, and Sathrabuzanes, and their companions, and those which were appointed rulers in Syria and Phenice, should be careful not to meddle with the place, but suffer Zorobabel, the servant of the Lord, and governor of Judea, and the elders of the Jews, to build the house of the Lord in that place.

Es1|6|28|I have commanded also to have it built up whole again; and that they look diligently to help those that be of the captivity of the Jews, till the house of the Lord be finished:

Es1|6|29|And out of the tribute of Celosyria and Phenice a portion carefully to be given these men for the sacrifices of the Lord, that is, to Zorobabel the governor, for bullocks, and rams, and lambs;

Es1|6|30|And also corn, salt, wine, and oil, and that continually every year without further question, according as the priests that be in Jerusalem shall signify to be daily spent:

Es1|6|31|That offerings may be made to the most high אֱלֹהִים for the king and for his children, and that they may pray for their lives.

Es1|6|32|And he commanded that whosoever should transgress, yea, or make light of any thing afore spoken or written, out of his own house should a tree be taken, and he thereon be hanged, and all his goods seized for the king.

Es1|6|33|The Lord therefore, whose name is there called upon, utterly destroy every king and nation, that stretcheth out his hand to hinder or endamage that house of the Lord in Jerusalem.

Es1|6|34|I Darius the king have ordained that according unto these things it be done with diligence.

Es1|7|1|Then Sisinnes the governor of Celosyria and Phenice, and Sathrabuzanes, with their companions following the commandments of king Darius,

Es1|7|2|Did very carefully oversee the holy works, assisting the ancients of the Jews and governors of the temple.

Es1|7|3|And so the holy works prospered, when Aggeus and Zacharias the prophets prophesied.

Es1|7|4|And they finished these things by the commandment of the Lord אֱלֹהִים of Israel, and with the consent of Cyrus, Darius, and Artexerxes, kings of Persia.

Es1|7|5|And thus was the holy house finished in the three and twentieth day of the month Adar, in the sixth year of Darius king of the Persians

Es1|7|6|And the children of Israel, the priests, and the Levites, and others that were of the captivity, that were added unto them, did according to the things written in the book of Moses.

Es1|7|7|And to the dedication of the temple of the Lord they offered an hundred bullocks two hundred rams, four hundred lambs;

Es1|7|8|And twelve goats for the sin of all Israel, according to the number of the chief of the tribes of Israel.

Es1|7|9|The priests also and the Levites stood arrayed in their vestments, according to their kindreds, in the service of the Lord אֱלֹהִים of Israel, according to the book of Moses: and the porters at every gate.

Es1|7|10|And the children of Israel that were of the captivity held the passover the fourteenth day of the first month, after that the priests and the Levites were sanctified.

Es1|7|11|They that were of the captivity were not all sanctified together: but the Levites were all sanctified together.

Es1|7|12|And so they offered the passover for all them of the captivity, and for their brethren the priests, and for themselves.

Es1|7|13|And the children of Israel that came out of the captivity did eat, even all they that had separated themselves from the abominations of the people of the land, and sought the Lord.

Es1|7|14|And they kept the feast of unleavened bread seven days, making merry before the Lord,

Es1|7|15|For that he had turned the counsel of the king of Assyria toward them, to strengthen their hands in the works of the Lord אֱלֹהִים of Israel.

Es1|8|1|And after these things, when Artexerxes the king of the Persians reigned came Esdras the son of Saraias, the son of Ezerias, the son of Helchiah, the son of Salum,

Es1|8|2|The son of Sadduc, the son of Achitob, the son of Amarias, the son of Ezias, the son of Meremoth, the son of Zaraias, the son of Savias, the son of Boccas, the son of Abisum, the son of Phinees, the son of Eleazar, the son of Aaron the chief priest.

Es1|8|3|This Esdras went up from Babylon, as a scribe, being very ready in the law of Moses, that was given by the אֱלֹהִים of Israel.

Es1|8|4|And the king did him honour: for he found grace in his sight in all his requests.

Es1|8|5|There went up with him also certain of the children of Israel, of the priest of the Levites, of the holy singers, porters, and ministers of the temple, unto Jerusalem,

Es1|8|6|In the seventh year of the reign of Artexerxes, in the fifth month, this was the king's seventh year; for they went from Babylon in the first day of the first month, and came to Jerusalem, according to the prosperous journey which the Lord gave them.

Es1|8|7|For Esdras had very great skill, so that he omitted nothing of the law and commandments of the Lord, but taught all Israel the ordinances and judgments.

Es1|8|8|Now the copy of the commission, which was written from Artexerxes the king, and came to Esdras the priest and reader of the law of the Lord, is this that followeth;

Es1|8|9|King Artexerxes unto Esdras the priest and reader of the law of the Lord sendeth greeting:

Es1|8|10|Having determined to deal graciously, I have given order, that such of the nation of the Jews, and of the priests and Levites being within our realm, as are willing and desirous should go with thee unto

Jerusalem.

Es1|8|11|As many therefore as have a mind thereunto, let them depart with thee, as it hath seemed good both to me and my seven friends the counsellors;

Es1|8|12|That they may look unto the affairs of Judea and Jerusalem, agreeably to that which is in the law of the Lord;

Es1|8|13|And carry the gifts unto the Lord of Israel to Jerusalem, which I and my friends have vowed, and all the gold and silver that in the country of Babylon can be found, to the Lord in Jerusalem,

Es1|8|14|With that also which is given of the people for the temple of the Lord their אֱלֹהִים at Jerusalem: and that silver and gold may be collected for bullocks, rams, and lambs, and things thereunto appertaining;

Es1|8|15|To the end that they may offer sacrifices unto the Lord upon the altar of the Lord their אֱלֹהִים, which is in Jerusalem.

Es1|8|16|And whatsoever thou and thy brethren will do with the silver and gold, that do, according to the will of thy אֱלֹהִים.

Es1|8|17|And the holy vessels of the Lord, which are given thee for the use of the temple of thy אֱלֹהִים, which is in Jerusalem, thou shalt set before thy אֱלֹהִים in Jerusalem.

Es1|8|18|And whatsoever thing else thou shalt remember for the use of the temple of thy אֱלֹהִים, thou shalt give it out of the king's treasury.

Es1|8|19|And I king Artexerxes have also commanded the keepers of the treasures in Syria and Phenice, that whatsoever Esdras the priest and the reader of the law of the most high אֱלֹהִים shall send for, they should give it him with speed,

Es1|8|20|To the sum of an hundred talents of silver, likewise also of wheat even to an hundred cors, and an hundred pieces of wine, and other things in abundance.

Es1|8|21|Let all things be performed after the law of אֱלֹהִים diligently unto the most high אֱלֹהִים, that wrath come not upon the kingdom of the king and his sons.

Es1|8|22|I command you also, that ye require no tax, nor any other imposition, of any of the priests, or Levites, or holy singers, or porters, or ministers of the temple, or of any that have doings in this temple, and that no man have authority to impose any thing upon them.

Es1|8|23|And thou, Esdras, according to the wisdom of אֱלֹהִים ordain judges and justices, that they may judge in all Syria and Phenice all those that know the law of thy אֱלֹהִים; and those that know it not thou shalt teach.

Es1|8|24|And whosoever shall transgress the law of thy אֱלֹהִים, and of the king, shall be punished diligently, whether it be by death, or other punishment, by penalty of money, or by imprisonment.

Es1|8|25|Then said Esdras the scribe, Blessed be the only Lord אֱלֹהִים of my fathers, who hath put these things into the heart of the king, to glorify his house that is in Jerusalem:

Es1|8|26|And hath honoured me in the sight of the king, and his counsellors, and all his friends and nobles.

Es1|8|27|Therefore was I encouraged by the help of the Lord my אֱלֹהִים, and gathered together men of Israel to go up with me.

Es1|8|28|And these are the chief according to their families and several dignities, that went up with me from Babylon in the reign of king Artexerxes:

Es1|8|29|Of the sons of Phinees, Gerson: of the sons of Ithamar, Gamael: of the sons of David, Lettus the son of Sechenias:

Es1|8|30|Of the sons of Pharez, Zacharias; and with him were counted an hundred and fifty men:

Es1|8|31|Of the sons of Pahath Moab, Eliaonias, the son of Zaraias, and with him two hundred men:

Es1|8|32|Of the sons of Zathoe, Sechenias the son of Jezelus, and with him three hundred men: of the sons of Adin, Obeth the son of Jonathan, and with him two hundred and fifty men:

Es1|8|33|Of the sons of Elam, Josias son of Gotholias, and with him seventy men:

Es1|8|34|Of the sons of Saphatias, Zaraias son of Michael, and with him threescore and ten men:

Es1|8|35|Of the sons of Joab, Abadias son of Jezelus, and with him two hundred and twelve men:

Es1|8|36|Of the sons of Banid, Assalimoth son of Josaphias, and with him an hundred and threescore men:

Es1|8|37|Of the sons of Babi, Zacharias son of Bebai, and with him twenty and eight men:

Es1|8|38|Of the sons of Astath, Johannes son of Acatan, and with him an hundred and ten men:

Es1|8|39|Of the sons of Adonikam the last, and these are the names of them, Eliphalet, Jewel, and Samaias, and with them seventy men:

Es1|8|40|Of the sons of Bago, Uthi the son of Istalcurus, and with him seventy men.

Es1|8|41|And these I gathered together to the river called Theras, where we pitched our tents three days: and then I surveyed them.

Es1|8|42|But when I had found there none of the priests and Levites,

Es1|8|43|Then sent I unto Eleazar, and Iduel, and Masman,

Es1|8|44|And Alnathan, and Mamaias, and Joribas, and Nathan, Eunatan, Zacharias, and Mosollamon, principal men and learned.

Es1|8|45|And I bade them that they should go unto Saddeus the captain, who was in the place of the treasury:

Es1|8|46|And commanded them that they should speak unto Daddeus, and to his brethren, and to the treasurers in that place, to send us such men as might execute the priests' office in the house of the Lord.

Es1|8|47|And by the mighty hand of our Lord they brought unto us skilful men of the sons of Moli the son of Levi, the son of Israel, Asebebia, and his sons, and his brethren, who were eighteen.

Es1|8|48|And Asebia, and Annus, and Osaias his brother, of the sons of Channuneus, and their sons, were twenty men.

Es1|8|49|And of the servants of the temple whom David had ordained, and the principal men for the service of the Levites to wit, the servants of the temple two hundred and twenty, the catalogue of whose names were shewed.

Es1|8|50|And there I vowed a fast unto the young men before our Lord, to desire of him a prosperous journey both for us and them that were with us, for our children, and for the cattle:

Es1|8|51|For I was ashamed to ask the king footmen, and horsemen, and conduct for safeguard against our adversaries.

Es1|8|52|For we had said unto the king, that the power of the Lord our אֱלֹהִים should be with them that seek him, to support them in all ways.

Es1|8|53|And again we besought our Lord as touching these things, and found him favourable unto us.

Es1|8|54|Then I separated twelve of the chief of the priests, Esebrias, and Assanias, and ten men of their brethren with them:

Es1|8|55|And I weighed them the gold, and the silver, and the holy vessels of the house of our Lord, which the king, and his council, and the princes, and all Israel, had given.

Es1|8|56|And when I had weighed it, I delivered unto them six hundred and fifty talents of silver, and silver vessels of an hundred talents, and an hundred talents of gold,

Es1|8|57|And twenty golden vessels, and twelve vessels of brass, even of fine brass, glittering like gold.

Es1|8|58|And I said unto them, Both ye are holy unto the Lord, and the vessels are holy, and the gold and the silver is a vow unto the Lord, the Lord of our fathers.

Es1|8|59|Watch ye, and keep them till ye deliver them to the chief of the priests and Levites, and to the principal men of the families of Israel, in Jerusalem, into the chambers of the house of our אֱלֹהִים.

Es1|8|60|So the priests and the Levites, who had received the silver and the gold and the vessels, brought them unto Jerusalem, into the temple of the Lord.

Es1|8|61|And from the river Theras we departed the twelfth day of the first month, and came to Jerusalem by the mighty hand of our Lord, which was with us: and from the beginning of our journey the Lord delivered us from every enemy, and so we came to Jerusalem.

Es1|8|62|And when we had been there three days, the gold and silver that was weighed was delivered in the house of our Lord on the fourth day unto Marmoth the priest the son of Iri.

Es1|8|63|And with him was Eleazar the son of Phinees, and with them were Josabad the son of Jesu and Moeth the son of Sabban, Levites: all was delivered them by number and weight.

Es1|8|64|And all the weight of them was written up the same hour.

Es1|8|65|Moreover they that were come out of the captivity offered sacrifice unto the Lord אֱלֹהִים of Israel, even twelve bullocks for all Israel, fourscore and sixteen rams,

Es1|8|66|Threescore and twelve lambs, goats for a peace offering, twelve; all of them a sacrifice to the Lord.

Es1|8|67|And they delivered the king's commandments unto the king's stewards' and to the governors of Celosyria and Phenice; and they honoured the people and the temple of אֱלֹהִים.

Es1|8|68|Now when these things were done, the rulers came unto me, and said,

Es1|8|69|The nation of Israel, the princes, the priests and Levites, have not put away from them the strange people of the land, nor the pollutions of the Gentiles to wit, of the Canaanites, Hittites, Pheresites, Jebusites, and the Moabites, Egyptians, and Edomites.

Es1|8|70|For both they and their sons have married with their daughters, and the holy seed is mixed with the strange people of the land; and from the beginning of this matter the rulers and the great men have been partakers of this iniquity.

Es1|8|71|And as soon as I had heard these things, I rent my clothes, and the holy garment, and pulled off the hair from off my head and beard, and sat me down sad and very heavy.

Es1|8|72|So all they that were then moved at the word of the Lord אֱלֹהִים of Israel assembled unto me, whilst I mourned for the iniquity: but I sat still full of heaviness until the evening sacrifice.

Es1|8|73|Then rising up from the fast with my clothes and the holy garment rent, and bowing my knees, and stretching forth my hands unto the Lord,

Es1|8|74|I said, O Lord, I am confounded and ashamed before thy face;

Es1|8|75|For our sins are multiplied above our heads, and our ignorances have reached up unto heaven.

Es1|8|76|For ever since the time of our fathers we have been and are in great sin, even unto this day.

Es1|8|77|And for our sins and our fathers' we with our brethren and our kings and our priests were given up unto the kings of the earth, to the sword, and to captivity, and for a prey with shame, unto this day.

Es1|8|78|And now in some measure hath mercy been shewed unto us from thee, O Lord, that there should be left us a root and a name in the place of thy sanctuary;

Es1|8|79|And to discover unto us a light in the house of the Lord our אֱלֹהִים, and to give us food in the time of our servitude.

Es1|8|80|Yea, when we were in bondage, we were not forsaken of our Lord; but he made us gracious before the kings of Persia, so that they gave us food;

Es1|8|81|Yea, and honoured the temple of our Lord, and raised up the desolate Sion, that they have given us a sure abiding in Jewry and Jerusalem.

Es1|8|82|And now, O Lord, what shall we say, having these things? for we have transgressed thy commandments, which thou gavest by the hand of thy servants the prophets, saying,

Es1|8|83|That the land, which ye enter into to possess as an heritage, is a land polluted with the pollutions of the strangers of the land, and they have filled it with their uncleanness.

Es1|8|84|Therefore now shall ye not join your daughters unto their sons, neither shall ye take their daughters unto your sons.

Es1|8|85|Moreover ye shall never seek to have peace with them, that ye may be strong, and eat the good things of the land, and that ye may leave the inheritance of the land unto your children for evermore.

Es1|8|86|And all that is befallen is done unto us for our wicked works and great sins; for thou, O Lord, didst make our sins light,

Es1|8|87|And didst give unto us such a root: but we have turned back again to transgress thy law, and to mingle ourselves with the uncleanness of the nations of the land.

Es1|8|88|Mightest not thou be angry with us to destroy us, till thou hadst left us neither root, seed, nor name?

Es1|8|89|O Lord of Israel, thou art true: for we are left a root this day.

Es1|8|90|Behold, now are we before thee in our iniquities, for we cannot stand any longer by reason of these things before thee.

Es1|8|91|And as Esdras in his prayer made his confession, weeping, and lying flat upon the ground before the temple, there gathered unto him from Jerusalem a very great multitude of men and women and children: for there was great weeping among the multitude.

Es1|8|92|Then Jechonias the son of Jeelus, one of the sons of Israel, called out, and said, O Esdras, we have sinned against the Lord אֱלֹהִים, we have married strange women of the nations of the land, and now is all Israel aloft.

Es1|8|93|Let us make an oath to the Lord, that we will put away all our wives, which we have taken of the heathen, with their children,

Es1|8|94|Like as thou hast decreed, and as many as do obey the law of the Lord.

Es1|8|95|Arise and put in execution: for to thee doth this matter appertain, and we will be with thee: do valiantly.

Es1|8|96|So Esdras arose, and took an oath of the chief of the priests and Levites of all Israel to do after these things; and so they sware.

Es1|9|1|Then Esdras rising from the court of the temple went to the chamber of Joanan the son of Eliasib,

Es1|9|2|And remained there, and did eat no meat nor drink water, mourning for the great iniquities of the multitude.

Es1|9|3|And there was a proclamation in all Jewry and Jerusalem to all them that were of the captivity, that they should be gathered together at Jerusalem:

Es1|9|4|And that whosoever met not there within two or three days according as the elders that bare rule appointed, their cattle should be seized to the use of the temple, and himself cast out from them that were of the captivity.

Es1|9|5|And in three days were all they of the tribe of Judah and Benjamin gathered together at Jerusalem the twentieth day of the ninth month.

Es1|9|6|And all the multitude sat trembling in the broad court of the temple because of the present foul weather.

Es1|9|7|So Esdras arose up, and said unto them, Ye have transgressed the law in marrying strange wives, thereby to increase the sins of Israel.

Es1|9|8|And now by confessing give glory unto the Lord אֱלֹהִים of our fathers,

Es1|9|9|And do his will, and separate yourselves from the heathen of the land, and from the strange women.

Es1|9|10|Then cried the whole multitude, and said with a loud voice, Like as thou hast spoken, so will we do.

Es1|9|11|But forasmuch as the people are many, and it is foul weather, so that we cannot stand without, and this is not a work of a day or two, seeing our sin in these things is spread far:

Es1|9|12|Therefore let the rulers of the multitude stay, and let all them of our habitations that have strange wives come at the time appointed,

Es1|9|13|And with them the rulers and judges of every place, till we turn away the wrath of the Lord from us for this matter.

Es1|9|14|Then Jonathan the son of Azael and Ezechias the son of Theocanus accordingly took this matter upon them: and Mosollam and Levis and Sabbatheus helped them.

Es1|9|15|And they that were of the captivity did according to all these things.

Es1|9|16|And Esdras the priest chose unto him the principal men of their families, all by name: and in the first day of the tenth month they sat together to examine the matter.

Es1|9|17|So their cause that held strange wives was brought to an end in the first day of the first month.

Es1|9|18|And of the priests that were come together, and had strange wives, there were found:

Es1|9|19|Of the sons of Yashiyah the son of Josedec, and his brethren; Matthelas and Eleazar, and Joribus and Joadanus.

Es1|9|20|And they gave their hands to put away their wives and to offer rams to make reconcilement for their errors.

Es1|9|21|And of the sons of Emmer; Ananias, and Zabdeus, and Eanes, and Sameius, and Hiereel, and Azarias.

Es1|9|22|And of the sons of Phaisur; Elionas, Massias Israel, and Nathanael, and Ocidelus and Talsas.

Es1|9|23|And of the Levites; Jozabad, and Semis, and Colius, who was called Calitas, and Patheus, and Judas, and Jonas.

Es1|9|24|Of the holy singers; Eleazurus, Bacchurus.

Es1|9|25|Of the porters; Sallumus, and Tolbanes.

Es1|9|26|Of them of Israel, of the sons of Phoros; Hiermas, and Eddias, and Melchias, and Maelus, and Eleazar, and Asibias, and Baanias.

Es1|9|27|Of the sons of Ela; Matthanias, Zacharias, and Hierielus, and Hieremoth, and Aedias.

Es1|9|28|And of the sons of Zamoth; Eliadas, Elisimus, Othonias, Jarimoth, and Sabatus, and Sardeus.

Es1|9|29|Of the sons of Babai; Johannes, and Ananias and Josabad, and Amatheis.

Es1|9|30|Of the sons of Mani; Olamus, Mamuchus, Jedeus, Jasubus, Jasael, and Hieremoth.

Es1|9|31|And of the sons of Addi; Naathus, and Moosias, Lacunus, and Naidus, and Mathanias, and Sesthel, Balnuus, and Manasseas.

Es1|9|32|And of the sons of Annas; Elionas and Aseas, and Melchias, and Sabbeus, and Simon Chosameus.

Es1|9|33|And of the sons of Asom; Altaneus, and Matthias, and Baanaia, Eliphalet, and Manasses, and Semei.

Es1|9|34|And of the sons of Maani; Jeremias, Momdis, Omaerus, Juel, Mabdai, and Pelias, and Anos, Carabasion, and Enasibus, and Mamnitanaimus, Eliasis, Bannus, Eliali, Samis, Selemias, Nathanias: and of the sons of Ozora; Sesis, Esril, Azaelus, Samatus, Zambis, Josephus.

Es1|9|35|And of the sons of Ethma; Mazitias, Zabadaias, Edes, Juel, Banaias.

Es1|9|36|All these had taken strange wives, and they put them away with their children.

Es1|9|37|And the priests and Levites, and they that were of Israel, dwelt in Jerusalem, and in the country, in the first day of the seventh month: so the children of Israel were in their habitations.

Es1|9|38|And the whole multitude came together with one accord into the broad place of the holy porch toward the east:

Es1|9|39|And they spake unto Esdras the priest and reader, that he would bring the law of Moses, that was given of the Lord אֱלֹהִים of Israel.

Es1|9|40|So Esdras the chief priest brought the law unto the whole multitude from man to woman, and to all the priests, to hear law in the first day of the seventh month.

Es1|9|41|And he read in the broad court before the holy porch from morning unto midday, before both men and women; and the multitude gave heed unto the law.

Es1|9|42|And Esdras the priest and reader of the law stood up upon a pulpit of wood, which was made for that purpose.

Es1|9|43|And there stood up by him Mattathias, Sammus, Ananias, Azarias, Urias, Ezecias, Balasamus, upon the right hand:

Es1|9|44|And upon his left hand stood Phaldaius, Misael, Melchias, Lothasubus, and Nabarias.

Es1|9|45|Then took Esdras the book of the law before the multitude: for he sat honourably in the first place in the sight of them all.

Es1|9|46|And when he opened the law, they stood all straight up. So Esdras blessed the Lord אֱלֹהִים most High, the אֱלֹהִים of hosts, Almighty.

Es1|9|47|And all the people answered, Amen; and lifting up their hands they fell to the ground, and worshipped the Lord.

Es1|9|48|Also Yashiyah, Anus, Sarabias, Adinus, Jacubus, Sabateas, Auteas, Maianeas, and Calitas, Asrias, and Joazabdus, and Ananias, Biatas, the Levites, taught the law of the Lord, making them withal to understand it.

Es1|9|49|Then spake Attharates unto Esdras the chief priest. and reader, and to the Levites that taught the multitude, even to all, saying,

Es1|9|50|This day is holy unto the Lord; (for they all wept when they heard the law:)

Es1|9|51|Go then, and eat the fat, and drink the sweet, and send part to them that have nothing;

Es1|9|52|For this day is holy unto the Lord: and be not sorrowful; for the Lord will bring you to honour.

Es1|9|53|So the Levites published all things to the people, saying, This day is holy to the Lord; be not sorrowful.

Es1|9|54|Then went they their way, every one to eat and drink, and make merry, and to give part to them that had nothing, and to make great cheer;

Es1|9|55|Because they understood the words wherein they were instructed, and for the which they had been assembled.

Es2|1|1|The second book of the prophet Esdras, the son of Saraias, the son of Azarias, the son of Helchias, the son of Sadamias, the sou of Sadoc, the son of Achitob,

Es2|1|2|The son of Achias, the son of Phinees, the son of Heli, the son of Amarias, the son of Aziei, the son of Marimoth, the son of And he spake unto the of Borith, the son of Abisei, the son of Phinees, the son of Eleazar,

Es2|1|3|The son of Aaron, of the tribe of Levi; which was captive in the land of the Medes, in the reign of Artexerxes king of the Persians.

Es2|1|4|And the word of the Lord came unto me, saying,

Es2|1|5|Go thy way, and shew my people their sinful deeds, and their children their wickedness which they have done against me; that they may tell their children's children:

Es2|1|6|Because the sins of their fathers are increased in them: for they have forgotten me, and have offered unto strange gods.

Es2|1|7|Am not I even he that brought them out of the land of Egypt, from the house of bondage? but they have provoked me unto wrath, and despised my counsels.

Es2|1|8|Pull thou off then the hair of thy head, and cast all evil upon them, for they have not been obedient unto my law, but it is a rebellious people.

Es2|1|9|How long shall I forbear them, into whom I have done so much good?

Es2|1|10|Many kings have I destroyed for their sakes; Pharaoh with his servants and all his power have I smitten down.

Es2|1|11|All the nations have I destroyed before them, and in the east I have scattered the people of two provinces, even of Tyrus and Sidon, and have slain all their enemies.

Es2|1|12|Speak thou therefore unto them, saying, Thus saith the Lord,

Es2|1|13|I led you through the sea and in the beginning gave you a large and safe passage; I gave you Moses for a leader, and Aaron for a priest.

Es2|1|14|I gave you light in a pillar of fire, and great wonders have I done among you; yet have ye forgotten me, saith the Lord.

Es2|1|15|Thus saith the Almighty Lord, The quails were as a token to you; I gave you tents for your safeguard: nevertheless ye murmured there,

Es2|1|16|And triumphed not in my name for the destruction of your enemies, but ever to this day do ye yet murmur.

Es2|1|17|Where are the benefits that I have done for you? when ye were hungry and thirsty in the wilderness, did ye not cry unto me,

Es2|1|18|Saying, Why hast thou brought us into this wilderness to kill us? it had been better for us to have served the Egyptians, than to die in this wilderness.

Es2|1|19|Then had I pity upon your mournings, and gave you manna to eat; so ye did eat angels' bread.

Es2|1|20|When ye were thirsty, did I not cleave the rock, and waters flowed out to your fill? for the heat I covered you with the leaves of the trees.

Es2|1|21|I divided among you a fruitful land, I cast out the Canaanites, the Pherezites, and the Philistines, before you: what shall I yet do more for you? saith the Lord.

Es2|1|22|Thus saith the Almighty Lord, When ye were in the wilderness, in the river of the Amorites, being athirst, and blaspheming my name,

Es2|1|23|I gave you not fire for your blasphemies, but cast a tree in the water, and made the river sweet.

Es2|1|24|What shall I do unto thee, O Jacob? thou, Juda, wouldest not obey me: I will turn me to other nations, and unto those will I give my name, that they may keep my statutes.

Es2|1|25|Seeing ye have forsaken me, I will forsake you also; when ye desire me to be gracious unto you, I shall have no mercy upon you.

Es2|1|26|Whensoever ye shall call upon me, I will not hear you: for ye have defiled your hands with blood, and your feet are swift to commit manslaughter.

Es2|1|27|Ye have not as it were forsaken me, but your own selves, saith the Lord.

Es2|1|28|Thus saith the Almighty Lord, Have I not prayed you as a father his sons, as a mother her daughters, and a nurse her young babes,

Es2|1|29|That ye would be my people, and I should be your אֱלֹהִים; that ye would be my children, and I should be your father?

Es2|1|30|I gathered you together, as a hen gathereth her chickens under her wings: but now, what shall I do unto you? I will cast you out from my face.

Es2|1|31|When ye offer unto me, I will turn my face from you: for your solemn feastdays, your new moons, and your circumcisions, have I forsaken.

Es2|1|32|I sent unto you my servants the prophets, whom ye have taken and slain, and torn their bodies in pieces, whose blood I will require of your hands, saith the Lord.

Es2|1|33|Thus saith the Almighty Lord, Your house is desolate, I will cast you out as the wind doth stubble.

Es2|1|34|And your children shall not be fruitful; for they have despised my commandment, and done the thing that is an evil before me.

Es2|1|35|Your houses will I give to a people that shall come; which not having heard of me yet shall believe me; to whom I have shewed no signs, yet they shall do that I have commanded them.

Es2|1|36|They have seen no prophets, yet they shall call their sins to remembrance, and acknowledge them.

Es2|1|37|I take to witness the grace of the people to come, whose little ones rejoice in gladness: and though they have not seen me with bodily eyes, yet in spirit they believe the thing that I say.

Es2|1|38|And now, brother, behold what glory; and see the people that come from the east:

Es2|1|39|Unto whom I will give for leaders, Abraham, Isaac, and Jacob, Oseas, Amos, and Micheas, Joel, Abdias, and Jonas,

Es2|1|40|Nahum, and Abacuc, Sophonias, Aggeus, Zachary, and Malachy, which is called also an angel of the Lord.

Es2|2|1|Thus saith the Lord, I brought this people out of bondage, and I gave them my commandments by menservants the prophets; whom they would not hear, but despised my counsels.

Es2|2|2|The mother that bare them saith unto them, Go your way, ye children; for I am a widow and forsaken.

Es2|2|3|I brought you up with gladness; but with sorrow and heaviness have I lost you: for ye have sinned before the Lord your אֱלֹהִים, and done that thing that is evil before him.

Es2|2|4|But what shall I now do unto you? I am a widow and forsaken: go your way, O my children, and ask mercy of the Lord.

Es2|2|5|As for me, O father, I call upon thee for a witness over the mother of these children, which would not keep my covenant,

Es2|2|6|That thou bring them to confusion, and their mother to a spoil, that there may be no offspring of them.

Es2|2|7|Let them be scattered abroad among the heathen, let their names be put out of the earth: for they have despised my covenant.

Es2|2|8|Woe be unto thee, Assur, thou that hidest the unrighteous in thee! O thou wicked people, remember what I did unto Sodom and Gomorrha;

Es2|2|9|Whose land lieth in clods of pitch and heaps of ashes: even so also will I do unto them that hear me not, saith the Almighty Lord.

Es2|2|10|Thus saith the Lord unto Esdras, Tell my people that I will give them the kingdom of Jerusalem, which I would have given unto Israel.

Es2|2|11|Their glory also will I take unto me, and give these the everlasting tabernacles, which I had prepared for them.

Es2|2|12|They shall have the tree of life for an ointment of sweet savour; they shall neither labour, nor be weary.

Es2|2|13|Go, and ye shall receive: pray for few days unto you, that they may be shortened: the kingdom is already prepared for you: watch.

Es2|2|14|Take heaven and earth to witness; for I have broken the evil in pieces, and created the good: for I live, saith the Lord.

Es2|2|15|Mother, embrace thy children, and bring them up with gladness, make their feet as fast as a pillar: for I have chosen thee, saith the Lord.

Es2|2|16|And those that be dead will I raise up again from their places, and bring them out of the graves: for I have known my name in Israel.

Es2|2|17|Fear not, thou mother of the children: for I have chosen thee, saith the Lord.

Es2|2|18|For thy help will I send my servants Esau and Jeremy, after whose counsel I have sanctified and prepared for thee twelve trees laden with divers fruits,

Es2|2|19|And as many fountains flowing with milk and honey, and seven mighty mountains, whereupon there grow roses and lilies, whereby I will fill thy children with joy.

Es2|2|20|Do right to the widow, judge for the fatherless, give to the poor, defend the orphan, clothe the naked,

Es2|2|21|Heal the broken and the weak, laugh not a lame man to scorn, defend the maimed, and let the blind man come into the sight of my clearness.

Es2|2|22|Keep the old and young within thy walls.

Es2|2|23|Wheresoever thou findest the dead, take them and bury them, and I will give thee the first place in my resurrection.

Es2|2|24|Abide still, O my people, and take thy rest, for thy quietness still come.

Es2|2|25|Nourish thy children, O thou good nurse; stablish their feet.

Es2|2|26|As for the servants whom I have given thee, there shall not one of them perish; for I will require them from among thy number.

Es2|2|27|Be not weary: for when the day of trouble and heaviness cometh, others shall weep and be sorrowful, but thou shalt be merry and have abundance.

Es2|2|28|The heathen shall envy thee, but they shall be able to do nothing against thee, saith the Lord.

Es2|2|29|My hands shall cover thee, so that thy children shall not see hell.

Es2|2|30|Be joyful, O thou mother, with thy children; for I will deliver thee, saith the Lord.

Es2|2|31|Remember thy children that sleep, for I shall bring them out of the sides of the earth, and shew mercy unto them: for I am merciful, saith the Lord Almighty.

Es2|2|32|Embrace thy children until I come and shew mercy unto them: for my wells run over, and my grace shall not fail.

Es2|2|33|I Esdras received a charge of the Lord upon the mount Oreb, that I should go unto Israel; but when I came unto them, they set me at nought, and despised the commandment of the Lord.

Es2|2|34|And therefore I say unto you, O ye heathen, that hear and understand, look for your Shepherd, he shall give you everlasting rest; for he is nigh at hand, that shall come in the end of the world.

Es2|2|35|Be ready to the reward of the kingdom, for the everlasting light shall shine upon you for evermore.

Es2|2|36|Flee the shadow of this world, receive the joyfulness of your glory: I testify my Saviour openly.

Es2|2|37|O receive the gift that is given you, and be glad, giving thanks unto him that hath led you to the heavenly kingdom.

Es2|2|38|Arise up and stand, behold the number of those that be sealed in the feast of the Lord;

Es2|2|39|Which are departed from the shadow of the world, and have received glorious garments of the Lord.

Es2|2|40|Take thy number, O Sion, and shut up those of thine that are clothed in white, which have fulfilled the law of the Lord.

Es2|2|41|The number of thy children, whom thou longedst for, is fulfilled: beseech the power of the Lord, that thy people, which have been called from the beginning, may be hallowed.

Es2|2|42|I Esdras saw upon the mount Sion a great people, whom I could not number, and they all praised the Lord with songs.

Es2|2|43|And in the midst of them there was a young man of a high stature, taller than all the rest, and upon every one of their heads he set crowns, and was more exalted; which I marvelled at greatly.

Es2|2|44|So I asked the angel, and said, Sir, what are these?

Es2|2|45|He answered and said unto me, These be they that have put off the mortal clothing, and put on the immortal, and have confessed the name of אֱלֹהִים: now are they crowned, and receive palms.

Es2|2|46|Then said I unto the angel, What young person is it that crowneth them, and giveth them palms in their hands?

Es2|2|47|So he answered and said unto me, It is the Son of אֱלֹהִים, whom they have confessed in the world. Then began I greatly to commend them that stood so stiffly for the name of the Lord.

Es2|2|48|Then the angel said unto me, Go thy way, and tell my people what manner of things, and how great wonders of the Lord thy אֱלֹהִים, thou hast seen.

Es2|3|1|In the thirtieth year after the ruin of the city I was in Babylon, and lay troubled upon my bed, and my thoughts came up over my heart:

Es2|3|2|For I saw the desolation of Sion, and the wealth of them that dwelt at Babylon.

Es2|3|3|And my spirit was sore moved, so that I began to speak words full of fear to the most High, and said,

Es2|3|4|O Lord, who bearest rule, thou spakest at the beginning, when thou didst plant the earth, and that thyself alone, and commandedst the people,

Es2|3|5|And gavest a body unto Adam without soul, which was the workmanship of thine hands, and didst breathe into him the breath of life, and he was made living before thee.

Es2|3|6|And thou leadest him into paradise, which thy right hand had planted, before ever the earth came forward.

Es2|3|7|And unto him thou gavest commandment to love thy way: which he transgressed, and immediately thou appointedst death in him and in his generations, of whom came nations, tribes, people, and kindreds, out of number.

Es2|3|8|And every people walked after their own will, and did wonderful things before thee, and despised thy commandments.

Es2|3|9|And again in process of time thou broughtest the flood upon those that dwelt in the world, and destroyedst them.

Es2|3|10|And it came to pass in every of them, that as death was to Adam, so was the flood to these.

Es2|3|11|Nevertheless one of them thou leftest, namely, Noah with his household, of whom came all righteous men.

Es2|3|12|And it happened, that when they that dwelt upon the earth began to multiply, and had gotten them many children, and were a great people, they began again to be more ungodly than the first.

Es2|3|13|Now when they lived so wickedly before thee, thou didst choose thee a man from among them, whose name was Abraham.

Es2|3|14|Him thou lovedst, and unto him only thou shewedst thy will:

Es2|3|15|And madest an everlasting covenant with him, promising him that thou wouldest never forsake his seed.

Es2|3|16|And unto him thou gavest Isaac, and unto Isaac also thou gavest Jacob and Esau. As for Jacob, thou didst choose him to thee, and put by Esau: and so Jacob became a great multitude.

Es2|3|17|And it came to pass, that when thou leadest his seed out of Egypt, thou broughtest them up to the mount Sinai.

Es2|3|18|And bowing the heavens, thou didst set fast the earth, movedst the whole world, and madest the depths to tremble, and troubledst the men of that age.

Es2|3|19|And thy glory went through four gates, of fire, and of earthquake, and of wind, and of cold; that thou mightest give the law unto the seed of Jacob, and diligence unto the generation of Israel.

Es2|3|20|And yet tookest thou not away from them a wicked heart, that thy law might bring forth fruit in them.

Es2|3|21|For the first Adam bearing a wicked heart transgressed, and was overcome; and so be all they that are born of him.

Es2|3|22|Thus infirmity was made permanent; and the law (also) in the heart of the people with the malignity of the root; so that the good departed away, and the evil abode still.

Es2|3|23|So the times passed away, and the years were brought to an end: then didst thou raise thee up a servant, called David:

Es2|3|24|Whom thou commandedst to build a city unto thy name, and to offer incense and oblations unto thee therein.

Es2|3|25|When this was done many years, then they that inhabited the city forsook thee,

Es2|3|26|And in all things did even as Adam and all his generations had done: for they also had a wicked heart:

Es2|3|27|And so thou gavest thy city over into the hands of thine enemies.

Es2|3|28|Are their deeds then any better that inhabit Babylon, that they should therefore have the dominion over Sion?

Es2|3|29|For when I came thither, and had seen impieties without number, then my soul saw many evildoers in this thirtieth year, so that my heart failed me.

Es2|3|30|For I have seen how thou sufferest them sinning, and hast spared wicked doers: and hast destroyed thy people, and hast preserved thine enemies, and hast not signified it.

Es2|3|31|I do not remember how this way may be left: Are they then of Babylon better than they of Sion?

Es2|3|32|Or is there any other people that knoweth thee beside Israel? or what generation hath so believed thy covenants as Jacob?

Es2|3|33|And yet their reward appeareth not, and their labour hath no fruit: for I have gone here and there through the heathen, and I see that they flow in wealth, and think not upon thy commandments.

Es2|3|34|Weigh thou therefore our wickedness now in the balance, and their's also that dwell the world; and so shall thy name no where be found but in Israel.

Es2|3|35|Or when was it that they which dwell upon the earth have not sinned in thy sight? or what people have so kept thy commandments?

Es2|3|36|Thou shalt find that Israel by name hath kept thy precepts; but not the heathen.

Es2|4|1|And the angel that was sent unto me, whose name was Uriel, gave me an answer,

Es2|4|2|And said, Thy heart hath gone to far in this world, and thinkest thou to comprehend the way of the most High?

Es2|4|3|Then said I, Yea, my lord. And he answered me, and said, I am sent to shew thee three ways, and to set forth three similitudes before thee:

Es2|4|4|Whereof if thou canst declare me one, I will shew thee also the way that thou desirest to see, and I shall shew thee from whence the wicked heart cometh.

Es2|4|5|And I said, Tell on, my lord. Then said he unto me, Go thy way, weigh me the weight of the fire, or measure me the blast of the wind, or call me again the day that is past.

Es2|4|6|Then answered I and said, What man is able to do that, that thou shouldest ask such things of me?

Es2|4|7|And he said unto me, If I should ask thee how great dwellings are in the midst of the sea, or how many springs are in the beginning of the deep, or how many springs are above the firmament, or which are the outgoings of paradise:

Es2|4|8|Peradventure thou wouldest say unto me, I never went down into the deep, nor as yet into hell, neither did I ever climb up into heaven.

Es2|4|9|Nevertheless now have I asked thee but only of the fire and wind, and of the day wherethrough thou hast passed, and of things from which thou canst not be separated, and yet canst thou give me no answer of them.

Es2|4|10|He said moreover unto me, Thine own things, and such as are grown up with thee, canst thou not know;

Es2|4|11|How should thy vessel then be able to comprehend the way of the Highest, and, the world being now outwardly corrupted to understand the corruption that is evident in my sight?

Es2|4|12|Then said I unto him, It were better that we were not at all, than that we should live still in wickedness, and to suffer, and not to know wherefore.

Es2|4|13|He answered me, and said, I went into a forest into a plain, and the trees took counsel,

Es2|4|14|And said, Come, let us go and make war against the sea that it may depart away before us, and that we may make us more woods.

Es2|4|15|The floods of the sea also in like manner took counsel, and said, Come, let us go up and subdue the woods of the plain, that there also we may make us another country.

Es2|4|16|The thought of the wood was in vain, for the fire came and consumed it.

Es2|4|17|The thought of the floods of the sea came likewise to nought, for the sand stood up and stopped them.

Es2|4|18|If thou wert judge now betwixt these two, whom wouldest thou begin to justify? or whom wouldest thou condemn?

Es2|4|19|I answered and said, Verily it is a foolish thought that they both have devised, for the ground is given unto the wood, and the sea also hath his place to bear his floods.

Es2|4|20|Then answered he me, and said, Thou hast given a right judgment, but why judgest thou not thyself also?

Es2|4|21|For like as the ground is given unto the wood, and the sea to his floods: even so they that dwell upon the earth may understand nothing but that which is upon the earth: and he that dwelleth above the heavens may only understand the things that are above the height of the heavens.

Es2|4|22|Then answered I and said, I beseech thee, O Lord, let me have understanding:

Es2|4|23|For it was not my mind to be curious of the high things, but of such as pass by us daily, namely, wherefore Israel is given up as a reproach to the heathen, and for what cause the people whom thou hast loved is given over unto ungodly nations, and why the law of our forefathers is brought to nought, and the written covenants come to none effect,

Es2|4|24|And we pass away out of the world as grasshoppers, and our life is astonishment and fear, and we are not worthy to obtain mercy.

Es2|4|25|What will he then do unto his name whereby we are called? of these things have I asked.

Es2|4|26|Then answered he me, and said, The more thou searchest, the more thou shalt marvel; for the world hasteth fast to pass away,

Es2|4|27|And cannot comprehend the things that are promised to the righteous in time to come: for this world is full of unrighteousness and infirmities.

Es2|4|28|But as concerning the things whereof thou askest me, I will tell thee; for the evil is sown, but the destruction thereof is not yet come.

Es2|4|29|If therefore that which is sown be not turned upside down, and if the place where the evil is sown pass not away, then cannot it come that is sown with good.

Es2|4|30|For the grain of evil seed hath been sown in the heart of Adam from the beginning, and how much ungodliness hath it brought up unto this time? and how much shall it yet bring forth until the time of threshing come?

Es2|4|31|Ponder now by thyself, how great fruit of wickedness the grain of evil seed hath brought forth.

Es2|4|32|And when the ears shall be cut down, which are without number, how great a floor shall they fill?

Es2|4|33|Then I answered and said, How, and when shall these things come to pass? wherefore are our years few and evil?

Es2|4|34|And he answered me, saying, Do not thou hasten above the most Highest: for thy haste is in vain to be above him, for thou hast much exceeded.

Es2|4|35|Did not the souls also of the righteous ask question of these things in their chambers, saying, How long shall I hope on this fashion? when cometh the fruit of the floor of our reward?

Es2|4|36|And unto these things Uriel the archangel gave them answer, and said, Even when the number of seeds is filled in you: for he hath weighed the world in the balance.

Es2|4|37|By measure hath he measured the times; and by number hath he numbered the times; and he doth not move nor stir them, until the said measure be fulfilled.

Es2|4|38|Then answered I and said, O Lord that bearest rule, even we all are full of impiety.

Es2|4|39|And for our sakes peradventure it is that the floors of the righteous are not filled, because of the sins of them that dwell upon the earth.

Es2|4|40|So he answered me, and said, Go thy way to a woman with child, and ask of her when she hath fulfilled her nine months, if her womb may keep the birth any longer within her.

Es2|4|41|Then said I, No, Lord, that can she not. And he said unto me, In the grave the chambers of souls are like the womb of a woman:

Es2|4|42|For like as a woman that travaileth maketh haste to escape the necessity of the travail: even so do these places haste to deliver those things that are committed unto them.

Es2|4|43|From the beginning, look, what thou desirest to see, it shall be shewed thee.

Es2|4|44|Then answered I and said, If I have found favour in thy sight, and if it be possible, and if I be meet therefore,

Es2|4|45|Shew me then whether there be more to come than is past, or more past than is to come.

Es2|4|46|What is past I know, but what is for to come I know not.

Es2|4|47|And he said unto me, Stand up upon the right side, and I shall expound the similitude unto thee.

Es2|4|48|So I stood, and saw, and, behold, an hot burning oven passed by before me: and it happened that when the flame was gone by I looked, and, behold, the smoke remained still.

Es2|4|49|After this there passed by before me a watery cloud, and sent down much rain with a storm; and when the stormy rain was past, the drops remained still.

Es2|4|50|Then said he unto me, Consider with thyself; as the rain is more than the drops, and as the fire is greater than the smoke; but the drops and the smoke remain behind: so the quantity which is past did more exceed.

Es2|4|51|Then I prayed, and said, May I live, thinkest thou, until that time? or what shall happen in those days?

Es2|4|52|He answered me, and said, As for the tokens whereof thou askest me, I may tell thee of them in part: but as touching thy life, I am not sent to shew thee; for I do not know it.

Es2|5|1|Nevertheless as coming the tokens, behold, the days shall come, that they which dwell upon earth shall be taken in a great number, and the way of truth shall be hidden, and the land shall be barren of faith.

Es2|5|2|But iniquity shall be increased above that which now thou seest, or that thou hast heard long ago.

Es2|5|3|And the land, that thou seest now to have root, shalt thou see wasted suddenly.

Es2|5|4|But if the most High grant thee to live, thou shalt see after the third trumpet that the sun shall suddenly shine again in the night, and the moon thrice in the day:

Es2|5|5|And blood shall drop out of wood, and the stone shall give his voice, and the people shall be troubled:

Es2|5|6|And even he shall rule, whom they look not for that dwell upon the earth, and the fowls shall take their flight away together:

Es2|5|7|And the Sodomitish sea shall cast out fish, and make a noise in the night, which many have not known: but they shall all hear the voice thereof.

Es2|5|8|There shall be a confusion also in many places, and the fire shall be oft sent out again, and the wild beasts shall change their places, and menstruous women shall bring forth monsters:

Es2|5|9|And salt waters shall be found in the sweet, and all friends shall destroy one another; then shall wit hide itself, and understanding withdraw itself into his secret chamber,

Es2|5|10|And shall be sought of many, and yet not be found: then shall unrighteousness and incontinency be multiplied upon earth.

Es2|5|11|One land also shall ask another, and say, Is righteousness that maketh a man righteous gone through thee? And it shall say, No.

Es2|5|12|At the same time shall men hope, but nothing obtain: they shall labour, but their ways shall not prosper.

Es2|5|13|To shew thee such tokens I have leave; and if thou wilt pray again, and weep as now, and fast even days, thou shalt hear yet greater things.

Es2|5|14|Then I awaked, and an extreme fearfulness went through all my body, and my mind was troubled, so that it fainted.

Es2|5|15|So the angel that was come to talk with me held me, comforted me, and set me up upon my feet.

Es2|5|16|And in the second night it came to pass, that Salathiel the captain of the people came unto me, saying, Where hast thou been? and why is thy countenance so heavy?

Es2|5|17|Knowest thou not that Israel is committed unto thee in the land of their captivity?

Es2|5|18|Up then, and eat bread, and forsake us not, as the shepherd that leaveth his flock in the hands of cruel wolves.

Es2|5|19|Then said I unto him, Go thy ways from me, and come not nigh me. And he heard what I said, and went from me.

Es2|5|20|And so I fasted seven days, mourning and weeping, like as Uriel the angel commanded me.

Es2|5|21|And after seven days so it was, that the thoughts of my heart were very grievous unto me again,

Es2|5|22|And my soul recovered the spirit of understanding, and I began to talk with the most High again,

Es2|5|23|And said, O Lord that bearest rule, of every wood of the earth, and of all the trees thereof, thou hast chosen thee one only vine:

Es2|5|24|And of all lands of the whole world thou hast chosen thee one pit: and of all the flowers thereof one lily:

Es2|5|25|And of all the depths of the sea thou hast filled thee one river: and of all builded cities thou hast hallowed Sion unto thyself:

Es2|5|26|And of all the fowls that are created thou hast named thee one dove: and of all the cattle that are made thou hast provided thee one sheep:

Es2|5|27|And among all the multitudes of people thou hast gotten thee one people: and unto this people, whom thou lovedst, thou gavest a law that is approved of all.

Es2|5|28|And now, O Lord, why hast thou given this one people over unto many? and upon the one root hast thou prepared others, and why hast thou scattered thy only one people among many?

Es2|5|29|And they which did gainsay thy promises, and believed not thy covenants, have trodden them down.

Es2|5|30|If thou didst so much hate thy people, yet shouldest thou punish them with thine own hands.

Es2|5|31|Now when I had spoken these words, the angel that came to me the night afore was sent unto me,

Es2|5|32|And said unto me, Hear me, and I will instruct thee; hearken to the thing that I say, and I shall tell thee more.

Es2|5|33|And I said, Speak on, my Lord. Then said he unto me, Thou art sore troubled in mind for Israel's sake: lovest thou that people better than he that made them?

Es2|5|34|And I said, No, Lord: but of very grief have I spoken: for my reins pain me every hour, while I labour to comprehend the way of the most High, and to seek out part of his judgment.

Es2|5|35|And he said unto me, Thou canst not. And I said, Wherefore, Lord? whereunto was I born then? or why was not my mother's womb then my grave, that I might not have seen the travail of Jacob, and the wearisome toil of the stock of Israel?

Es2|5|36|And he said unto me, Number me the things that are not yet come, gather me together the dross that are scattered abroad, make me the flowers green again that are withered,

Es2|5|37|Open me the places that are closed, and bring me forth the winds that in them are shut up, shew me the image of a voice: and then I will declare to thee the thing that thou labourest to know.

Es2|5|38|And I said, O Lord that bearest rule, who may know these things, but he that hath not his dwelling with men?

Es2|5|39|As for me, I am unwise: how may I then speak of these things whereof thou askest me?

Es2|5|40|Then said he unto me, Like as thou canst do none of these things that I have spoken of, even so canst thou not find out my judgment, or in the end the love that I have promised unto my people.

Es2|5|41|And I said, Behold, O Lord, yet art thou nigh unto them that be reserved till the end: and what shall they do that have been before me, or we that be now, or they that shall come after us?

Es2|5|42|And he said unto me, I will liken my judgment unto a ring: like as there is no slackness of the last, even so there is no swiftness of the first.

Es2|5|43|So I answered and said, Couldest thou not make those that have been made, and be now, and that are for to come, at once; that thou mightest shew thy judgment the sooner?

Es2|5|44|Then answered he me, and said, The creature may not haste above the maker; neither may the world hold them at once that shall be created therein.

Es2|5|45|And I said, As thou hast said unto thy servant, that thou, which givest life to all, hast given life at once to the creature that thou hast created, and the creature bare it: even so it might now also bear them that now be present at once.

Es2|5|46|And he said unto me, Ask the womb of a woman, and say unto her, If thou bringest forth children, why dost thou it not together, but one after another? pray her therefore to bring forth ten children at once.

Es2|5|47|And I said, She cannot: but must do it by distance of time.

Es2|5|48|Then said he unto me, Even so have I given the womb of the earth to those that be sown in it in their times.

Es2|5|49|For like as a young child may not bring forth the things that belong to the aged, even so have I disposed the world which I created.

Es2|5|50|And I asked, and said, Seeing thou hast now given me the way, I will proceed to speak before thee: for our mother, of whom thou hast told me that she is young, draweth now nigh unto age.

Es2|5|51|He answered me, and said, Ask a woman that beareth children, and she shall tell thee.

Es2|5|52|Say unto her, Wherefore are unto they whom thou hast now brought forth like those that were before, but less of stature?

Es2|5|53|And she shall answer thee, They that be born in the the strength of youth are of one fashion, and they that are born in the time of age, when the womb faileth, are otherwise.

Es2|5|54|Consider thou therefore also, how that ye are less of stature than those that were before you.

Es2|5|55|And so are they that come after you less than ye, as the creatures which now begin to be old, and have passed over the strength of youth.

Es2|5|56|Then said I, Lord, I beseech thee, if I have found favour in thy sight, shew thy servant by whom thou visitest thy creature.

Es2|6|1|And he said unto me, In the beginning, when the earth was made, before the borders of the world stood, or ever the winds blew,

Es2|6|2|Before it thundered and lightened, or ever the foundations of paradise were laid,

Es2|6|3|Before the fair flowers were seen, or ever the moveable powers were established, before the innumerable multitude of angels were gathered together,

Es2|6|4|Or ever the heights of the air were lifted up, before the measures of the firmament were named, or ever the chimneys in Sion were hot,

Es2|6|5|And ere the present years were sought out, and or ever the inventions of them that now sin were turned, before they were sealed that have gathered faith for a treasure:

Es2|6|6|Then did I consider these things, and they all were made through me alone, and through none other: by me also they shall be ended, and by none other.

Es2|6|7|Then answered I and said, What shall be the parting asunder of the times? or when shall be the end of the first, and the beginning of it that followeth?

Es2|6|8|And he said unto me, From Abraham unto Isaac, when Jacob and Esau were born of him, Jacob's hand held first the heel of Esau.

Es2|6|9|For Esau is the end of the world, and Jacob is the beginning of it that followeth.

Es2|6|10|The hand of man is betwixt the heel and the hand: other question, Esdras, ask thou not.

Es2|6|11|I answered then and said, O Lord that bearest rule, if I have found favour in thy sight,

Es2|6|12|I beseech thee, shew thy servant the end of thy tokens, whereof thou shewedst me part the last night.

Es2|6|13|So he answered and said unto me, Stand up upon thy feet, and hear a mighty sounding voice.

Es2|6|14|And it shall be as it were a great motion; but the place where thou standest shall not be moved.

Es2|6|15|And therefore when it speaketh be not afraid: for the word is of the end, and the foundation of the earth is understood.

Es2|6|16|And why? because the speech of these things trembleth and is moved: for it knoweth that the end of these things must be changed.

Es2|6|17|And it happened, that when I had heard it I stood up upon my feet, and hearkened, and, behold, there was a voice that spake, and the sound of it was like the sound of many waters.

Es2|6|18|And it said, Behold, the days come, that I will begin to draw nigh, and to visit them that dwell upon the earth,

Es2|6|19|And will begin to make inquisition of them, what they be that have hurt unjustly with their unrighteousness, and when the affliction of Sion shall be fulfilled;

Es2|6|20|And when the world, that shall begin to vanish away, shall be finished, then will I shew these tokens: the books shall be opened before the firmament, and they shall see all together:

Es2|6|21|And the children of a year old shall speak with their voices, the women with child shall bring forth untimely children of three or four months old, and they shall live, and be raised up.

Es2|6|22|And suddenly shall the sown places appear unsown, the full storehouses shall suddenly be found empty:

Es2|6|23|And tha trumpet shall give a sound, which when every man heareth, they shall be suddenly afraid.

Es2|6|24|At that time shall friends fight one against another like enemies, and the earth shall stand in fear with those that dwell therein, the springs of the fountains shall stand still, and in three hours they shall not run.

Es2|6|25|Whosoever remaineth from all these that I have told thee shall escape, and see my salvation, and the end of your world.

Es2|6|26|And the men that are received shall see it, who have not tasted death from their birth: and the heart of the inhabitants shall be changed, and turned into another meaning.

Es2|6|27|For evil shall be put out, and deceit shall be quenched.

Es2|6|28|As for faith, it shall flourish, corruption shall be overcome, and the truth, which hath been so long without fruit, shall be declared.

Es2|6|29|And when he talked with me, behold, I looked by little and little upon him before whom I stood.

Es2|6|30|And these words said he unto me; I am come to shew thee the time of the night to come.

Es2|6|31|If thou wilt pray yet more, and fast seven days again, I shall tell thee greater things by day than I have heard.

Es2|6|32|For thy voice is heard before the most High: for the Mighty hath seen thy righteous dealing, he hath seen also thy chastity, which thou hast had ever since thy youth.

Es2|6|33|And therefore hath he sent me to shew thee all these things, and to say unto thee, Be of good comfort and fear not

Es2|6|34|And hasten not with the times that are past, to think vain things, that thou mayest not hasten from the latter times.

Es2|6|35|And it came to pass after this, that I wept again, and fasted seven days in like manner, that I might fulfil the three weeks which he told me.

Es2|6|36|And in the eighth night was my heart vexed within me again, and I began to speak before the most High.

Es2|6|37|For my spirit was greatly set on fire, and my soul was in distress.

Es2|6|38|And I said, O Lord, thou spakest from the beginning of the creation, even the first day, and saidst thus; Let heaven and earth be made; and thy word was a perfect work.

Es2|6|39|And then was the spirit, and darkness and silence were on every side; the sound of man's voice was not yet formed.

Es2|6|40|Then commandedst thou a fair light to come forth of thy treasures, that thy work might appear.

Es2|6|41|Upon the second day thou madest the spirit of the firmament, and commandedst it to part asunder, and to make a division betwixt the waters, that the one part might go up, and the other remain beneath.

Es2|6|42|Upon the third day thou didst command that the waters should be gathered in the seventh part of the earth: six pats hast thou dried up, and kept them, to the intent that of these some being planted of אֱלֹהִים and tilled might serve thee.

Es2|6|43|For as soon as thy word went forth the work was made.

Es2|6|44|For immediately there was great and innumerable fruit, and many and divers pleasures for the taste, and flowers of unchangeable colour, and odours of wonderful smell: and this was done the third day.

Es2|6|45|Upon the fourth day thou commandedst that the sun should shine, and the moon give her light, and the stars should be in order:

Es2|6|46|And gavest them a charge to do service unto man, that was to be made.

Es2|6|47|Upon the fifth day thou saidst unto the seventh part, where the waters were gathered that it should bring forth living creatures, fowls and fishes: and so it came to pass.

Es2|6|48|For the dumb water and without life brought forth living things at the commandment of אֱלֹהִים, that all people might praise thy wondrous works.

Es2|6|49|Then didst thou ordain two living creatures, the one thou calledst Enoch, and the other Leviathan;

Es2|6|50|And didst separate the one from the other: for the seventh part, namely, where the water was gathered together, might not hold them both.

Es2|6|51|Unto Enoch thou gavest one part, which was dried up the third day, that he should dwell in the same part, wherein are a thousand hills:

Es2|6|52|But unto Leviathan thou gavest the seventh part, namely, the moist; and hast kept him to be devoured of whom thou wilt, and when.

Es2|6|53|Upon the sixth day thou gavest commandment unto the earth, that before thee it should bring forth beasts, cattle, and creeping things:

Es2|6|54|And after these, Adam also, whom thou madest lord of all thy creatures: of him come we all, and the people also whom thou hast chosen.

Es2|6|55|All this have I spoken before thee, O Lord, because thou madest the world for our sakes

Es2|6|56|As for the other people, which also come of Adam, thou hast said that they are nothing, but be like unto spittle: and hast likened the abundance of them unto a drop that falleth from a vessel.

Es2|6|57|And now, O Lord, behold, these heathen, which have ever been reputed as nothing, have begun to be lords over us, and to devour us.

Es2|6|58|But we thy people, whom thou hast called thy firstborn, thy only begotten, and thy fervent lover, are given into their hands.

Es2|6|59|If the world now be made for our sakes, why do we not possess an inheritance with the world? how long shall this endure?

Es2|7|1|And when I had made an end of speaking these words, there was sent unto me the angel which had been sent unto me the nights afore:

Es2|7|2|And he said unto me, Up, Esdras, and hear the words that I am come to tell thee.

Es2|7|3|And I said, Speak on, my אֱלֹהִים. Then said he unto me, The sea is set in a wide place, that it might be deep and great.

Es2|7|4|But put the case the entrance were narrow, and like a river:

Es2|7|5|Who then could go into the sea to look upon it, and to rule it? if he went not through the narrow, how could he come into the broad?

Es2|7|6|There is also another thing; A city is builded, and set upon a broad field, and is full of all good things:

Es2|7|7|The entrance thereof is narrow, and is set in a dangerous place to fall, like as if there were a fire on the right hand, and on the left a deep water:

Es2|7|8|And one only path between them both, even between the fire and the water, so small that there could but one man go there at once.

Es2|7|9|If this city now were given unto a man for an inheritance, if he never shall pass the danger set before it, how shall he receive this inheritance?

Es2|7|10|And I said, It is so, Lord. Then said he unto me, Even so also is Israel's portion.

Es2|7|11|Because for their sakes I made the world: and when Adam transgressed my statutes, then was decreed that now is done.

Es2|7|12|Then were the entrances of this world made narrow, full of sorrow and travail: they are but few and evil, full of perils,: and very painful.

Es2|7|13|For the entrances of the elder world were wide and sure, and brought immortal fruit.

Es2|7|14|If then they that live labour not to enter these strait and vain things, they can never receive those that are laid up for them.

Es2|7|15|Now therefore why disquietest thou thyself, seeing thou art but a corruptible man? and why art thou moved, whereas thou art but mortal?

Es2|7|16|Why hast thou not considered in thy mind this thing that is to come, rather than that which is present?

Es2|7|17|Then answered I and said, O Lord that bearest rule, thou hast ordained in thy law, that the righteous should inherit these things, but that the ungodly should perish.

Es2|7|18|Nevertheless the righteous shall suffer strait things, and hope for wide: for they that have done wickedly have suffered the strait things, and yet shall not see the wide.

Es2|7|19|And he said unto me, There is no judge above אֱלֹהִים, and none that hath understanding above the Highest.

Es2|7|20|For there be many that perish in this life, because they despise the law of אֱלֹהִים that is set before them.

Es2|7|21|For אֱלֹהִים hath given strait commandment to such as came, what they should do to live, even as they came, and what they should observe to avoid punishment.

Es2|7|22|Nevertheless they were not obedient unto him; but spake against him, and imagined vain things;

Es2|7|23|And deceived themselves by their wicked deeds; and said of the most High, that he is not; and knew not his ways:

Es2|7|24|But his law have they despised, and denied his covenants; in his statutes have they not been faithful, and have not performed his works.

Es2|7|25|And therefore, Esdras, for the empty are empty things, and for the full are the full things.

Es2|7|26|Behold, the time shall come, that these tokens which I have told thee shall come to pass, and the bride shall appear, and she coming forth shall be seen, that now is withdrawn from the earth.

Es2|7|27|And whosoever is delivered from the foresaid evils shall see my wonders.

Es2|7|28|For my son Yashiyah shall be revealed with those that be with him, and they that remain shall rejoice within four hundred years.

Es2|7|29|After these years shall my son Christ die, and all men that have life.

Es2|7|30|And the world shall be turned into the old silence seven days, like as in the former judgments: so that no man shall remain.

Es2|7|31|And after seven days the world, that yet awaketh not, shall be raised up, and that shall die that is corrupt

Es2|7|32|And the earth shall restore those that are asleep in her, and so shall the dust those that dwell in silence, and the secret places shall deliver those souls that were committed unto them.

Es2|7|33|And the most High shall appear upon the seat of judgment, and misery shall pass away, and the long suffering shall have an end:

Es2|7|34|But judgment only shall remain, truth shall stand, and faith shall wax strong:

Es2|7|35|And the work shall follow, and the reward shall be shewed, and the good deeds shall be of force, and wicked deeds shall bear no rule.

Es2|7|36|Then said I, Abraham prayed first for the Sodomites, and Moses for the fathers that sinned in the wilderness:

Es2|7|37|And Yashiyah after him for Israel in the time of Achan:

Es2|7|38|And Samuel and David for the destruction: and Solomon for them that should come to the sanctuary:

Es2|7|39|And Helias for those that received rain; and for the dead, that he might live:

Es2|7|40|And Ezechias for the people in the time of Sennacherib: and many for many.

Es2|7|41|Even so now, seeing corruption is grown up, and wickedness increased, and the righteous have prayed for the ungodly: wherefore shall it not be so now also?

Es2|7|42|He answered me, and said, This present life is not the end where much glory doth abide; therefore have they prayed for the weak.

Es2|7|43|But the day of doom shall be the end of this time, and the beginning of the immortality for to come, wherein corruption is past,

Es2|7|44|Intemperance is at an end, infidelity is cut off, righteousness is grown, and truth is sprung up.

Es2|7|45|Then shall no man be able to save him that is destroyed, nor to oppress him that hath gotten the victory.

Es2|7|46|I answered then and said, This is my first and last saying, that it had been better not to have given the earth unto Adam: or else, when it was given him, to have restrained him from sinning.

Es2|7|47|For what profit is it for men now in this present time to live in heaviness, and after death to look for punishment?

Es2|7|48|O thou Adam, what hast thou done? for though it was thou that sinned, thou art not fallen alone, but we all that come of thee.

Es2|7|49|For what profit is it unto us, if there be promised us an immortal time, whereas we have done the works that bring death?

Es2|7|50|And that there is promised us an everlasting hope, whereas ourselves being most wicked are made vain?

Es2|7|51|And that there are laid up for us dwellings of health and safety, whereas we have lived wickedly?

Es2|7|52|And that the glory of the most High is kept to defend them which have led a wary life, whereas we have walked in the most wicked ways of all?

Es2|7|53|And that there should be shewed a paradise, whose fruit endureth for ever, wherein is security and medicine, since we shall not enter into it?

Es2|7|54|(For we have walked in unpleasant places.)

Es2|7|55|And that the faces of them which have used abstinence shall shine above the stars, whereas our faces shall be blacker than darkness?

Es2|7|56|For while we lived and committed iniquity, we considered not that we should begin to suffer for it after death.

Es2|7|57|Then answered he me, and said, This is the condition of the battle, which man that is born upon the earth shall fight;

Es2|7|58|That, if he be overcome, he shall suffer as thou hast said: but if he get the victory, he shall receive the thing that I say.

Es2|7|59|For this is the life whereof Moses spake unto the people while he lived, saying, Choose thee life, that thou mayest live.

Es2|7|60|Nevertheless they believed not him, nor yet the prophets after him, no nor me which have spoken unto them,

Es2|7|61|That there should not be such heaviness in their destruction, as shall be joy over them that are persuaded to salvation.

Es2|7|62|I answered then, and said, I know, Lord, that the most High is called merciful, in that he hath mercy upon them which are not yet come into the world,

Es2|7|63|And upon those also that turn to his law;

Es2|7|64|And that he is patient, and long suffereth those that have sinned, as his creatures;

Es2|7|65|And that he is bountiful, for he is ready to give where it needeth;

Es2|7|66|And that he is of great mercy, for he multiplieth more and more mercies to them that are present, and that are past, and also to them which are to come.

Es2|7|67|For if he shall not multiply his mercies, the world would not continue with them that inherit therein.

Es2|7|68|And he pardoneth; for if he did not so of his goodness, that they which have committed iniquities might be eased of them, the ten thousandth part of men should not remain living.

Es2|7|69|And being judge, if he should not forgive them that are cured with his word, and put out the multitude of contentions,

Es2|7|70|There should be very few left peradventure in an innumerable multitude.

Es2|8|1|And he answered me, saying, The most High hath made this world for many, but the world to come for few.

Es2|8|2|I will tell thee a similitude, Esdras; As when thou askest the earth, it shall say unto thee, that it giveth much mould whereof earthen vessels are made, but little dust that gold cometh of: even so is the course of this present world.

Es2|8|3|There be many created, but few shall be saved.

Es2|8|4|So answered I and said, Swallow then down, O my soul, understanding, and devour wisdom.

Es2|8|5|For thou hast agreed to give ear, and art willing to prophesy: for thou hast no longer space than only to live.

Es2|8|6|O Lord, if thou suffer not thy servant, that we may pray before thee, and thou give us seed unto our heart, and culture to our understanding, that there may come fruit of it; how shall each man live that is corrupt, who beareth the place of a man?

Es2|8|7|For thou art alone, and we all one workmanship of thine hands, like as thou hast said.

Es2|8|8|For when the body is fashioned now in the mother's womb, and thou givest it members, thy creature is preserved in fire and water, and nine months doth thy workmanship endure thy creature which is created in her.

Es2|8|9|But that which keepeth and is kept shall both be preserved: and when the time cometh, the womb preserved delivereth up the things that grew in it.

Es2|8|10|For thou hast commanded out of the parts of the body, that is to say, out of the breasts, milk to be given, which is the fruit of the breasts,

Es2|8|11|That the thing which is fashioned may be nourished for a time, till thou disposest it to thy mercy.

Es2|8|12|Thou broughtest it up with thy righteousness, and nurturedst it in thy law, and reformedst it with thy judgment.

Es2|8|13|And thou shalt mortify it as thy creature, and quicken it as thy work.

Es2|8|14|If therefore thou shalt destroy him which with so great labour was fashioned, it is an easy thing to be ordained by thy commandment, that the thing which was made might be preserved.

Es2|8|15|Now therefore, Lord, I will speak; touching man in general, thou knowest best; but touching thy people, for whose sake I am sorry;

Es2|8|16|And for thine inheritance, for whose cause I mourn; and for Israel, for whom I am heavy; and for Jacob, for whose sake I am troubled;

Es2|8|17|Therefore will I begin to pray before thee for myself and for them: for I see the falls of us that dwell in the land.

Es2|8|18|But I have heard the swiftness of the judge which is to come.

Es2|8|19|Therefore hear my voice, and understand my words, and I shall speak before thee. This is the beginning of the words of Esdras, before he was taken up: and I said,

Es2|8|20|O Lord, thou that dwellest in everlastingness which beholdest from above things in the heaven and in the air;

Es2|8|21|Whose throne is inestimable; whose glory may not be comprehended; before whom the hosts of angels stand with trembling,

Es2|8|22|Whose service is conversant in wind and fire; whose word is true, and sayings constant; whose commandment is strong, and ordinance fearful;

Es2|8|23|Whose look drieth up the depths, and indignation maketh the mountains to melt away; which the truth witnesseth:

Es2|8|24|O hear the prayer of thy servant, and give ear to the petition of thy creature.

Es2|8|25|For while I live I will speak, and so long as I have understanding I will answer.

Es2|8|26|O look not upon the sins of thy people; but on them which serve thee in truth.

Es2|8|27|Regard not the wicked inventions of the heathen, but the desire of those that keep thy testimonies in afflictions.

Es2|8|28|Think not upon those that have walked feignedly before thee: but remember them, which according to thy will have known thy fear.

Es2|8|29|Let it not be thy will to destroy them which have lived like beasts; but to look upon them that have clearly taught thy law.

Es2|8|30|Take thou no indignation at them which are deemed worse than beasts; but love them that always put their trust in thy righteousness and glory.

Es2|8|31|For we and our fathers do languish of such diseases: but because of us sinners thou shalt be called merciful.

Es2|8|32|For if thou hast a desire to have mercy upon us, thou shalt be called merciful, to us namely, that have no works of righteousness.

Es2|8|33|For the just, which have many good works laid up with thee, shall out of their own deeds receive reward.

Es2|8|34|For what is man, that thou shouldest take displeasure at him? or what is a corruptible generation, that thou shouldest be so bitter toward it?

Es2|8|35|For in truth them is no man among them that be born, but he hath dealt wickedly; and among the faithful there is none which hath not done amiss.

Es2|8|36|For in this, O Lord, thy righteousness and thy goodness shall be declared, if thou be merciful unto them which have not the confidence of good works.

Es2|8|37|Then answered he me, and said, Some things hast thou spoken aright, and according unto thy words it shall be.

Es2|8|38|For indeed I will not think on the disposition of them which have sinned before death, before judgment, before destruction:

Es2|8|39|But I will rejoice over the disposition of the righteous, and I will remember also their pilgrimage, and the salvation, and the reward, that they shall have.

Es2|8|40|Like as I have spoken now, so shall it come to pass.

Es2|8|41|For as the husbandman soweth much seed upon the ground, and planteth many trees, and yet the thing that is sown good in his season cometh not up, neither doth all that is planted take root: even so is it of them that are sown in the world; they shall not all be saved.

Es2|8|42|I answered then and said, If I have found grace, let me speak.

Es2|8|43|Like as the husbandman's seed perisheth, if it come not up, and receive not thy rain in due season; or if there come too much rain, and corrupt it:

Es2|8|44|Even so perisheth man also, which is formed with thy hands, and is called thine own image, because thou art like unto him, for whose sake thou hast made all things, and likened him unto the husbandman's seed.

Es2|8|45|Be not wroth with us but spare thy people, and have mercy upon thine own inheritance: for thou art merciful unto thy creature.

Es2|8|46|Then answered he me, and said, Things present are for the present, and things to cometh for such as be to come.

Es2|8|47|For thou comest far short that thou shouldest be able to love my creature more than I: but I have ofttimes drawn nigh unto thee, and unto it, but never to the unrighteous.

Es2|8|48|In this also thou art marvellous before the most High:

Es2|8|49|In that thou hast humbled thyself, as it becometh thee, and hast not judged thyself worthy to be much glorified among the righteous.

Es2|8|50|For many great miseries shall be done to them that in the latter time shall dwell in the world, because they have walked in great pride.

Es2|8|51|But understand thou for thyself, and seek out the glory for such as be like thee.

Es2|8|52|For unto you is paradise opened, the tree of life is planted, the time to come is prepared, plenteousness is made ready, a city is builded, and rest is allowed, yea, perfect goodness and wisdom.

Es2|8|53|The root of evil is sealed up from you, weakness and the moth is hid from you, and corruption is fled into hell to be forgotten:

Es2|8|54|Sorrows are passed, and in the end is shewed the treasure of immortality.

Es2|8|55|And therefore ask thou no more questions concerning the multitude of them that perish.

Es2|8|56|For when they had taken liberty, they despised the most High, thought scorn of his law, and forsook his ways.

Es2|8|57|Moreover they have trodden down his righteous,

Es2|8|58|And said in their heart, that there is no אֱלֹהִים; yea, and that knowing they must die.

Es2|8|59|For as the things aforesaid shalt receive you, so thirst and pain are prepared for them: for it was not his will that men should come to nought:

Es2|8|60|But they which be created have defiled the name of him that made them, and were unthankful unto him which prepared life for them.

Es2|8|61|And therefore is my judgment now at hand.

Es2|8|62|These things have I not shewed unto all men, but unto thee, and a few like thee. Then answered I and said,

Es2|8|63|Behold, O Lord, now hast thou shewed me the multitude of the wonders, which thou wilt begin to do in the last times: but at what time, thou hast not shewed me.

Es2|9|1|He answered me then, and said, Measure thou the time diligently in itself: and when thou seest part of the signs past, which I have told thee before,

Es2|9|2|Then shalt thou understand, that it is the very same time, wherein the Highest will begin to visit the world which he made.

Es2|9|3|Therefore when there shall be seen earthquakes and uproars of the people in the world:

Es2|9|4|Then shalt thou well understand, that the most High spake of those things from the days that were before thee, even from the beginning.

Es2|9|5|For like as all that is made in the world hath a beginning and an end, and the end is manifest:

Es2|9|6|Even so the times also of the Highest have plain beginnings in wonder and powerful works, and endings in effects and signs.

Es2|9|7|And every one that shall be saved, and shall be able to escape by his works, and by faith, whereby ye have believed,

Es2|9|8|Shall be preserved from the said perils, and shall see my salvation in my land, and within my borders: for I have sanctified them for me from the beginning.

Es2|9|9|Then shall they be in pitiful case, which now have abused my ways: and they that have cast them away despitefully shall dwell in torments.

Es2|9|10|For such as in their life have received benefits, and have not known me;

Es2|9|11|And they that have loathed my law, while they had yet liberty, and, when as yet place of repentance was open unto them, understood not, but despised it;

Es2|9|12|The same must know it after death by pain.

Es2|9|13|And therefore be thou not curious how the ungodly shall be punished, and when: but enquire how the righteous shall be saved, whose the world is, and for whom the world is created.

Es2|9|14|Then answered I and said,

Es2|9|15|I have said before, and now do speak, and will speak it also hereafter, that there be many more of them which perish, than of them which shall be saved:

Es2|9|16|Like as a wave is greater than a drop.

Es2|9|17|And he answered me, saying, Like as the field is, so is also the seed; as the flowers be, such are the colours also; such as the workman is, such also is the work; and as the husbandman Is himself, so is his husbandry also: for it was the time of the world.

Es2|9|18|And now when I prepared the world, which was not yet made, even for them to dwell in that now live, no man spake against me.

Es2|9|19|For then every one obeyed: but now the manners of them which are created in this world that is made are corrupted by a perpetual seed, and by a law which is unsearchable rid themselves.

Es2|9|20|So I considered the world, and, behold, there was peril because of the devices that were come into it.

Es2|9|21|And I saw, and spared it greatly, and have kept me a grape of the cluster, and a plant of a great people.

Es2|9|22|Let the multitude perish then, which was born in vain; and let my grape be kept, and my plant; for with great labour have I made it perfect.

Es2|9|23|Nevertheless, if thou wilt cease yet seven days more, (but thou shalt not fast in them,

Es2|9|24|But go into a field of flowers, where no house is builded, and eat only the flowers of the field; taste no flesh, drink no wine, but eat flowers only;)

Es2|9|25|And pray unto the Highest continually, then will I come and talk with thee.

Es2|9|26|So I went my way into the field which is called Ardath, like as he commanded me; and there I sat among the flowers, and did eat of the herbs of the field, and the meat of the same satisfied me.

Es2|9|27|After seven days I sat upon the grass, and my heart was vexed within me, like as before:

Es2|9|28|And I opened my mouth, and began to talk before the most High, and said,

Es2|9|29|O Lord, thou that shewest thyself unto us, thou wast shewed unto our fathers in the wilderness, in a place where no man treadeth, in a barren place, when they came out of Egypt.

Es2|9|30|And thou spakest saying, Hear me, O Israel; and mark my words, thou seed of Jacob.

Es2|9|31|For, behold, I sow my law in you, and it shall bring fruit in you, and ye shall be honoured in it for ever.

Es2|9|32|But our fathers, which received the law, kept it not, and observed not thy ordinances: and though the fruit of thy law did not perish, neither could it, for it was thine;

Es2|9|33|Yet they that received it perished, because they kept not the thing that was sown in them.

Es2|9|34|And, lo, it is a custom, when the ground hath received seed, or the sea a ship, or any vessel meat or drink, that, that being perished wherein it was sown or cast into,

Es2|9|35|That thing also which was sown, or cast therein, or received, doth perish, and remaineth not with us: but with us it hath not happened so.

Es2|9|36|For we that have received the law perish by sin, and our heart also which received it

Es2|9|37|Notwithstanding the law perisheth not, but remaineth in his force.

Es2|9|38|And when I spake these things in my heart, I looked back with mine eyes, and upon the right side I saw a woman, and, behold, she mourned and wept with a loud voice, and was much grieved in heart, and her clothes were rent, and she had ashes upon her head.

Es2|9|39|Then let I my thoughts go that I was in, and turned me unto her,

Es2|9|40|And said unto her, Wherefore weepest thou? why art thou so grieved in thy mind?

Es2|9|41|And she said unto me, Sir, let me alone, that I may bewail myself, and add unto my sorrow, for I am sore vexed in my mind, and brought very low.

Es2|9|42|And I said unto her, What aileth thee? tell me.

Es2|9|43|She said unto me, I thy servant have been barren, and had no child, though I had an husband thirty years,

Es2|9|44|And those thirty years I did nothing else day and night, and every hour, but make my, prayer to the Highest.

Es2|9|45|After thirty years אֱלֹהִים heard me thine handmaid, looked upon my misery, considered my trouble, and gave me a son: and I was very glad of him, so was my husband also, and all my neighbours: and we gave great honour unto the Almighty.

Es2|9|46|And I nourished him with great travail.

Es2|9|47|So when he grew up, and came to the time that he should have a wife, I made a feast.

Es2|10|1|And it so came to pass, that when my son was entered into his wedding chamber, he fell down, and died.

Es2|10|2|Then we all overthrew the lights, and all my neighbours rose up to comfort me: so I took my rest unto the second day at night.

Es2|10|3|And it came to pass, when they had all left off to comfort me, to the end I might be quiet; then rose I up by night and fled, and came hither into this field, as thou seest.

Es2|10|4|And I do now purpose not to return into the city, but here to stay, and neither to eat nor drink, but continually to mourn and to fast until I die.

Es2|10|5|Then left I the meditations wherein I was, and spake to her in anger, saying,

Es2|10|6|Thou foolish woman above all other, seest thou not our mourning, and what happeneth unto us?

Es2|10|7|How that Sion our mother is full of all heaviness, and much humbled, mourning very sore?

Es2|10|8|And now, seeing we all mourn and are sad, for we are all in heaviness, art thou grieved for one son?

Es2|10|9|For ask the earth, and she shall tell thee, that it is she which ought to mourn for the fall of so many that grow upon her.

Es2|10|10|For out of her came all at the first, and out of her shall all others come, and, behold, they walk almost all into destruction, and a multitude of them is utterly rooted out.

Es2|10|11|Who then should make more mourning than she, that hath lost so great a multitude; and not thou, which art sorry but for one?

Es2|10|12|But if thou sayest unto me, My lamentation is not like the earth's, because I have lost the fruit of my womb, which I brought forth with pains, and bare with sorrows;

Es2|10|13|But the earth not so: for the multitude present in it according to the course of the earth is gone, as it came:

Es2|10|14|Then say I unto thee, Like as thou hast brought forth with labour; even so the earth also hath given her fruit, namely, man, ever since the beginning unto him that made her.

Es2|10|15|Now therefore keep thy sorrow to thyself, and bear with a good courage that which hath befallen thee.

Es2|10|16|For if thou shalt acknowledge the determination of אֱלֹהִים to be just, thou shalt both receive thy son in time, and shalt be commended among women.

Es2|10|17|Go thy way then into the city to thine husband.

Es2|10|18|And she said unto me, That will I not do: I will not go into the city, but here will I die.

Es2|10|19|So I proceeded to speak further unto her, and said,

Es2|10|20|Do not so, but be counselled. by me: for how many are the adversities of Sion? be comforted in regard of the sorrow of Jerusalem.

Es2|10|21|For thou seest that our sanctuary is laid waste, our altar broken down, our temple destroyed;

Es2|10|22|Our psaltery is laid on the ground, our song is put to silence, our rejoicing is at an end, the light of our candlestick is put out, the ark of our covenant is spoiled, our holy things are defiled, and the name that is called upon us is almost profaned: our children are put to shame, our priests are burnt, our Levites are gone into captivity, our virgins are defiled, and our wives ravished; our righteous men carried away, our little ones destroyed, our young men are brought in bondage, and our strong men are become weak;

Es2|10|23|And, which is the greatest of all, the seal of Sion hath now lost her honour; for she is delivered into the hands of them that hate us.

Es2|10|24|And therefore shake off thy great heaviness, and put away the multitude of sorrows, that the Mighty may be merciful unto thee again, and the Highest shall give thee rest and ease from thy labour.

Es2|10|25|And it came to pass while I was talking with her, behold, her face upon a sudden shined exceedingly, and her countenance glistered, so that I was afraid of her, and mused what it might be.

Es2|10|26|And, behold, suddenly she made a great cry very fearful: so that the earth shook at the noise of the woman.

Es2|10|27|And I looked, and, behold, the woman appeared unto me no more, but there was a city builded, and a large place shewed itself from the foundations: then was I afraid, and cried with a loud voice, and said,

Es2|10|28|Where is Uriel the angel, who came unto me at the first? for he hath caused me to fall into many trances, and mine end is turned into corruption, and my prayer to rebuke.

Es2|10|29|And as I was speaking these words behold, he came unto me, and looked upon me.

Es2|10|30|And, lo, I lay as one that had been dead, and mine understanding was taken from me: and he took me by the right hand, and comforted me, and set me upon my feet, and said unto me,

Es2|10|31|What aileth thee? and why art thou so disquieted? and why is thine understanding troubled, and the thoughts of thine heart?

Es2|10|32|And I said, Because thou hast forsaken me, and yet I did according to thy words, and I went into the field, and, lo, I have seen, and yet see, that I am not able to express.

Es2|10|33|And he said unto me, Stand up manfully, and I will advise thee.

Es2|10|34|Then said I, Speak on, my lord, in me; only forsake me not, lest I die frustrate of my hope.

Es2|10|35|For I have seen that I knew not, and hear that I do not know.

Es2|10|36|Or is my sense deceived, or my soul in a dream?

Es2|10|37|Now therefore I beseech thee that thou wilt shew thy servant of this vision.

Es2|10|38|He answered me then, and said, Hear me, and I shall inform thee, and tell thee wherefore thou art afraid: for the Highest will reveal many secret things unto thee.

Es2|10|39|He hath seen that thy way is right: for that thou sorrowest continually for thy people, and makest great lamentation for Sion.

Es2|10|40|This therefore is the meaning of the vision which thou lately sawest:

Es2|10|41|Thou sawest a woman mourning, and thou begannest to comfort her:

Es2|10|42|But now seest thou the likeness of the woman no more, but there appeared unto thee a city builded.

Es2|10|43|And whereas she told thee of the death of her son, this is the solution:

Es2|10|44|This woman, whom thou sawest is Sion: and whereas she said unto thee, even she whom thou seest as a city builded,

Es2|10|45|Whereas, I say, she said unto thee, that she hath been thirty years barren: those are the thirty years wherein there was no offering made in her.

Es2|10|46|But after thirty years Solomon builded the city and offered offerings: and then bare the barren a son.

Es2|10|47|And whereas she told thee that she nourished him with labour: that was the dwelling in Jerusalem.

Es2|10|48|But whereas she said unto thee, That my son coming into his marriage chamber happened to have a fail, and died: this was the destruction that came to Jerusalem.

Es2|10|49|And, behold, thou sawest her likeness, and because she mourned for her son, thou begannest to comfort her: and of these things which have chanced, these are to be opened unto thee.

Es2|10|50|For now the most High seeth that thou art grieved unfeignedly, and sufferest from thy whole heart for her, so hath he shewed thee the brightness of her glory, and the comeliness of her beauty:

Es2|10|51|And therefore I bade thee remain in the field where no house was builded:

Es2|10|52|For I knew that the Highest would shew this unto thee.

Es2|10|53|Therefore I commanded thee to go into the field, where no foundation of any building was.

Es2|10|54|For in the place wherein the Highest beginneth to shew his city, there can no man's building be able to stand.

Es2|10|55|And therefore fear not, let not thine heart be affrighted, but go thy way in, and see the beauty and greatness of the building, as much as thine eyes be able to see:

Es2|10|56|And then shalt thou hear as much as thine ears may comprehend.

Es2|10|57|For thou art blessed above many other, and art called with the Highest; and so are but few.

Es2|10|58|But to morrow at night thou shalt remain here;

Es2|10|59|And so shall the Highest shew thee visions of the high things, which the most High will do unto them that dwell upon the earth in the last days. So I slept that night and another, like as he commanded me.

Es2|11|1|Then saw I a dream, and, behold, there came up from the sea an eagle, which had twelve feathered wings, and three heads.

Es2|11|2|And I saw, and, behold, she spread her wings over all the earth, and all the winds of the air blew on her, and were gathered together.

Es2|11|3|And I beheld, and out of her feathers there grew other contrary feathers; and they became little feathers and small.

Es2|11|4|But her heads were at rest: the head in the midst was greater than the other, yet rested it with the residue.

Es2|11|5|Moreover I beheld, and, lo, the eagle flew with her feathers, and reigned upon earth, and over them that dwelt therein.

Es2|11|6|And I saw that all things under heaven were subject unto her, and no man spake against her, no, not one creature upon earth.

Es2|11|7|And I beheld, and, lo, the eagle rose upon her talons, and spake to her feathers, saying,

Es2|11|8|Watch not all at once: sleep every one in his own place, and watch by course:

Es2|11|9|But let the heads be preserved for the last.

Es2|11|10|And I beheld, and, lo, the voice went not out of her heads, but from the midst of her body.

Es2|11|11|And I numbered her contrary feathers, and, behold, there were eight of them.

Es2|11|12|And I looked, and, behold, on the right side there arose one feather, and reigned over all the earth;

Es2|11|13|And so it was, that when it reigned, the end of it came, and the place thereof appeared no more: so the next following stood up. and reigned, and had a great time;

Es2|11|14|And it happened, that when it reigned, the end of it came also, like as the first, so that it appeared no more.

Es2|11|15|Then came there a voice unto it, and said,

Es2|11|16|Hear thou that hast borne rule over the earth so long: this I say unto thee, before thou beginnest to appear no more,

Es2|11|17|There shall none after thee attain unto thy time, neither unto the half thereof.

Es2|11|18|Then arose the third, and reigned as the other before, and appeared no more also.

Es2|11|19|So went it with all the residue one after another, as that every one reigned, and then appeared no more.

Es2|11|20|Then I beheld, and, lo, in process of time the feathers that followed stood up upon the right side, that they might rule also; and some of them ruled, but within a while they appeared no more:

Es2|11|21|For some of them were set up, but ruled not.

Es2|11|22|After this I looked, and, behold, the twelve feathers appeared no more, nor the two little feathers:

Es2|11|23|And there was no more upon the eagle's body, but three heads that rested, and six little wings.

Es2|11|24|Then saw I also that two little feathers divided themselves from the six, and remained under the head that was upon the right side: for the four continued in their place.

Es2|11|25|And I beheld, and, lo, the feathers that were under the wing thought to set up themselves and to have the rule.

Es2|11|26|And I beheld, and, lo, there was one set up, but shortly it appeared no more.

Es2|11|27|And the second was sooner away than the first.

Es2|11|28|And I beheld, and, lo, the two that remained thought also in themselves to reign:

Es2|11|29|And when they so thought, behold, there awaked one of the heads that were at rest, namely, it that was in the midst; for that was greater than the two other heads.

Es2|11|30|And then I saw that the two other heads were joined with it.

Es2|11|31|And, behold, the head was turned with them that were with it, and did eat up the two feathers under the wing that would have reigned.

Es2|11|32|But this head put the whole earth in fear, and bare rule in it over all those that dwelt upon the earth with much oppression; and it had the governance of the world more than all the wings that had been.

Es2|11|33|And after this I beheld, and, lo, the head that was in the midst suddenly appeared no more, like as the wings.

Es2|11|34|But there remained the two heads, which also in like sort ruled upon the earth, and over those that dwelt therein.

Es2|11|35|And I beheld, and, lo, the head upon the right side devoured it that was upon the left side.

Es2|11|36|Then I head a voice, which said unto me, Look before thee, and consider the thing that thou seest.

Es2|11|37|And I beheld, and lo, as it were a roaring lion chased out of the wood: and I saw that he sent out a man's voice unto the eagle, and said,

Es2|11|38|Hear thou, I will talk with thee, and the Highest shall say unto thee,

Es2|11|39|Art not thou it that remainest of the four beasts, whom I made to reign in my world, that the end of their times might come through them?

Es2|11|40|And the fourth came, and overcame all the beasts that were past, and had power over the world with great fearfulness, and over the whole compass of the earth with much wicked oppression; and so long time dwelt he upon the earth with deceit.

Es2|11|41|For the earth hast thou not judged with truth.

Es2|11|42|For thou hast afflicted the meek, thou hast hurt the peaceable, thou hast loved liars, and destroyed the dwellings of them that brought forth fruit, and hast cast down the walls of such as did thee no harm.

Es2|11|43|Therefore is thy wrongful dealing come up unto the Highest, and thy pride unto the Mighty.

Es2|11|44|The Highest also hath looked upon the proud times, and, behold, they are ended, and his abominations are fulfilled.

Es2|11|45|And therefore appear no more, thou eagle, nor thy horrible wings, nor thy wicked feathers nor thy malicious heads, nor thy hurtful claws, nor all thy vain body:

Es2|11|46|That all the earth may be refreshed, and may return, being delivered from thy violence, and that she may hope for the judgment and mercy of him that made her.

Es2|12|1|And it came to pass, whiles the lion spake these words unto the eagle, I saw,

Es2|12|2|And, behold, the head that remained and the four wings appeared no more, and the two went unto it and set themselves up to reign, and their kingdom was small, and fill of uproar.

Es2|12|3|And I saw, and, behold, they appeared no more, and the whole body of the eagle was burnt so that the earth was in great fear: then awaked I out of the trouble and trance of my mind, and from great fear, and said unto my spirit,

Es2|12|4|Lo, this hast thou done unto me, in that thou searchest out the ways of the Highest.

Es2|12|5|Lo, yet am I weary in my mind, and very weak in my spirit; and little strength is there in me, for the great fear wherewith I was afflicted this night.

Es2|12|6|Therefore will I now beseech the Highest, that he will comfort me unto the end.

Es2|12|7|And I said, Lord that bearest rule, if I have found grace before thy sight, and if I am justified with thee before many others, and if my prayer indeed be come up before thy face;

Es2|12|8|Comfort me then, and shew me thy servant the interpretation and plain difference of this fearful vision, that thou mayest perfectly comfort my soul.

Es2|12|9|For thou hast judged me worthy to shew me the last times.

Es2|12|10|And he said unto me, This is the interpretation of the vision:

Es2|12|11|The eagle, whom thou sawest come up from the sea, is the kingdom which was seen in the vision of thy brother Daniel.

Es2|12|12|But it was not expounded unto him, therefore now I declare it unto thee.

Es2|12|13|Behold, the days will come, that there shall rise up a kingdom upon earth, and it shall be feared above all the kingdoms that were before it.

Es2|12|14|In the same shall twelve kings reign, one after another:

Es2|12|15|Whereof the second shall begin to reign, and shall have more time than any of the twelve.
Es2|12|16|And this do the twelve wings signify, which thou sawest.
Es2|12|17|As for the voice which thou heardest speak, and that thou sawest not to go out from the heads but from the midst of the body thereof, this is the interpretation:
Es2|12|18|That after the time of that kingdom there shall arise great strivings, and it shall stand in peril of failing: nevertheless it shall not then fall, but shall be restored again to his beginning.
Es2|12|19|And whereas thou sawest the eight small under feathers sticking to her wings, this is the interpretation:
Es2|12|20|That in him there shall arise eight kings, whose times shall be but small, and their years swift.
Es2|12|21|And two of them shall perish, the middle time approaching: four shall be kept until their end begin to approach: but two shall be kept unto the end.
Es2|12|22|And whereas thou sawest three heads resting, this is the interpretation:
Es2|12|23|In his last days shall the most High raise up three kingdoms, and renew many things therein, and they shall have the dominion of the earth,
Es2|12|24|And of those that dwell therein, with much oppression, above all those that were before them: therefore are they called the heads of the eagle.
Es2|12|25|For these are they that shall accomplish his wickedness, and that shall finish his last end.
Es2|12|26|And whereas thou sawest that the great head appeared no more, it signifieth that one of them shall die upon his bed, and yet with pain.
Es2|12|27|For the two that remain shall be slain with the sword.
Es2|12|28|For the sword of the one shall devour the other: but at the last shall he fall through the sword himself.
Es2|12|29|And whereas thou sawest two feathers under the wings passing over the head that is on the right side;
Es2|12|30|It signifieth that these are they, whom the Highest hath kept unto their end: this is the small kingdom and full of trouble, as thou sawest.
Es2|12|31|And the lion, whom thou sawest rising up out of the wood, and roaring, and speaking to the eagle, and rebuking her for her unrighteousness with all the words which thou hast heard;
Es2|12|32|This is the anointed, which the Highest hath kept for them and for their wickedness unto the end: he shall reprove them, and shall upbraid them with their cruelty.
Es2|12|33|For he shall set them before him alive in judgment, and shall rebuke them, and correct them.
Es2|12|34|For the rest of my people shall he deliver with mercy, those that have been pressed upon my borders, and he shall make them joyful until the coming of the day of judgment, whereof I have spoken unto thee from the the the beginning.
Es2|12|35|This is the dream that thou sawest, and these are the interpretations.
Es2|12|36|Thou only hast been meet to know this secret of the Highest.
Es2|12|37|Therefore write all these things that thou hast seen in a book, and hide them:
Es2|12|38|And teach them to the wise of the people, whose hearts thou knowest may comprehend and keep these secrets.
Es2|12|39|But wait thou here thyself yet seven days more, that it may be shewed thee, whatsoever it pleaseth the Highest to declare unto thee. And with that he went his way.
Es2|12|40|And it came to pass, when all the people saw that the seven days were past, and I not come again into the city, they gathered them all together, from the least unto the greatest, and came unto me, and said,
Es2|12|41|What have we offended thee? and what evil have we done against thee, that thou forsakest us, and sittest here in this place?
Es2|12|42|For of all the prophets thou only art left us, as a cluster of the vintage, and as a candle in a dark place, and as a haven or ship preserved from the tempest.
Es2|12|43|Are not the evils which are come to us sufficient?
Es2|12|44|If thou shalt forsake us, how much better had it been for us, if we also had been burned in the midst of Sion?
Es2|12|45|For we are not better than they that died there. And they wept with a loud voice. Then answered I them, and said,
Es2|12|46|Be of good comfort, O Israel; and be not heavy, thou house of Jacob:
Es2|12|47|For the Highest hath you in remembrance, and the Mighty hath not forgotten you in temptation.
Es2|12|48|As for me, I have not forsaken you, neither am I departed from you: but am come into this place, to pray for the desolation of Sion, and that I might seek mercy for the low estate of your sanctuary.

Es2|12|49|And now go your way home every man, and after these days will I come unto you.

Es2|12|50|So the people went their way into the city, like as I commanded them:

Es2|12|51|But I remained still in the field seven days, as the angel commanded me; and did eat only in those days of the flowers of the field, and had my meat of the herbs

Es2|13|1|And it came to pass after seven days, I dreamed a dream by night:

Es2|13|2|And, lo, there arose a wind from the sea, that it moved all the waves thereof.

Es2|13|3|And I beheld, and, lo, that man waxed strong with the thousands of heaven: and when he turned his countenance to look, all the things trembled that were seen under him.

Es2|13|4|And whensoever the voice went out of his mouth, all they burned that heard his voice, like as the earth faileth when it feeleth the fire.

Es2|13|5|And after this I beheld, and, lo, there was gathered together a multitude of men, out of number, from the four winds of the heaven, to subdue the man that came out of the sea

Es2|13|6|But I beheld, and, lo, he had graved himself a great mountain, and flew up upon it.

Es2|13|7|But I would have seen the region or place whereout the hill was graven, and I could not.

Es2|13|8|And after this I beheld, and, lo, all they which were gathered together to subdue him were sore afraid, and yet durst fight.

Es2|13|9|And, lo, as he saw the violence of the multitude that came, he neither lifted up his hand, nor held sword, nor any instrument of war:

Es2|13|10|But only I saw that he sent out of his mouth as it had been a blast of fire, and out of his lips a flaming breath, and out of his tongue he cast out sparks and tempests.

Es2|13|11|And they were all mixed together; the blast of fire, the flaming breath, and the great tempest; and fell with violence upon the multitude which was prepared to fight, and burned them up every one, so that upon a sudden of an innumerable multitude nothing was to be perceived, but only dust and smell of smoke: when I saw this I was afraid.

Es2|13|12|Afterward saw I the same man come down from the mountain, and call unto him another peaceable Multitude.

Es2|13|13|And there came much people unto him, whereof some were glad, some were sorry, and some of them were bound, and other some brought of them that were offered: then was I sick through great fear, and I awaked, and said,

Es2|13|14|Thou hast shewed thy servant these wonders from the beginning, and hast counted me worthy that thou shouldest receive my prayer:

Es2|13|15|Shew me now yet the interpretation of this dream.

Es2|13|16|For as I conceive in mine understanding, woe unto them that shall be left in those days and much more woe unto them that are not left behind!

Es2|13|17|For they that were not left were in heaviness.

Es2|13|18|Now understand I the things that are laid up in the latter days, which shall happen unto them, and to those that are left behind.

Es2|13|19|Therefore are they come into great perils and many necessities, like as these dreams declare.

Es2|13|20|Yet is it easier for him that is in danger to come into these things, than to pass away as a cloud out of the world, and not to see the things that happen in the last days. And he answered unto me, and said,

Es2|13|21|The interpretation of the vision shall I shew thee, and I will open unto thee the thing that thou hast required.

Es2|13|22|Whereas thou hast spoken of them that are left behind, this is the interpretation:

Es2|13|23|He that shall endure the peril in that time hath kept himself: they that be fallen into danger are such as have works, and faith toward the Almighty.

Es2|13|24|Know this therefore, that they which be left behind are more blessed than they that be dead.

Es2|13|25|This is the meaning of the vision: Whereas thou sawest a man coming up from the midst of the sea:

Es2|13|26|The same is he whom אֱלֹהִים the Highest hath kept a great season, which by his own self shall deliver his creature: and he shall order them that are left behind.

Es2|13|27|And whereas thou sawest, that out of his mouth there came as a blast of wind, and fire, and storm;

Es2|13|28|And that he held neither sword, nor any instrument of war, but that the rushing in of him destroyed the whole multitude that came to subdue him; this is the interpretation:

Es2|13|29|Behold, the days come, when the most High will begin to deliver them that are upon the earth.

Es2|13|30|And he shall come to the astonishment of them that dwell on the earth.

Es2|13|31|And one shall undertake to fight against another, one city against another, one place against another, one people against another, and one realm against another.

Es2|13|32|And the time shall be when these things shall come to pass, and the signs shall happen which I shewed thee before, and then shall my Son be declared, whom thou sawest as a man ascending.

Es2|13|33|And when all the people hear his voice, every man shall in their own land leave the battle they have one against another.

Es2|13|34|And an innumerable multitude shall be gathered together, as thou sawest them, willing to come, and to overcome him by fighting.

Es2|13|35|But he shall stand upon the top of the mount Sion.

Es2|13|36|And Sion shall come, and shall be shewed to all men, being prepared and builded, like as thou sawest the hill graven without hands.

Es2|13|37|And this my Son shall rebuke the wicked inventions of those nations, which for their wicked life are fallen into the tempest;

Es2|13|38|And shall lay before them their evil thoughts, and the torments wherewith they shall begin to be tormented, which are like unto a flame: and he shall destroy them without labour by the law which is like unto me.

Es2|13|39|And whereas thou sawest that he gathered another peaceable multitude unto him;

Es2|13|40|Those are the ten tribes, which were carried away prisoners out of their own land in the time of Osea the king, whom Salmanasar the king of Assyria led away captive, and he carried them over the waters, and so came they into another land.

Es2|13|41|But they took this counsel among themselves, that they would leave the multitude of the heathen, and go forth into a further country, where never mankind dwelt,

Es2|13|42|That they might there keep their statutes, which they never kept in their own land.

Es2|13|43|And they entered into Euphrates by the narrow places of the river.

Es2|13|44|For the most High then shewed signs for them, and held still the flood, till they were passed over.

Es2|13|45|For through that country there was a great way to go, namely, of a year and a half: and the same region is called Arsareth.

Es2|13|46|Then dwelt they there until the latter time; and now when they shall begin to come,

Es2|13|47|The Highest shall stay the springs of the stream again, that they may go through: therefore sawest thou the multitude with peace.

Es2|13|48|But those that be left behind of thy people are they that are found within my borders.

Es2|13|49|Now when he destroyeth the multitude of the nations that are gathered together, he shall defend his people that remain.

Es2|13|50|And then shall he shew them great wonders.

Es2|13|51|Then said I, O Lord that bearest rule, shew me this: Wherefore have I seen the man coming up from the midst of the sea?

Es2|13|52|And he said unto me, Like as thou canst neither seek out nor know the things that are in the deep of the sea: even so can no man upon earth see my Son, or those that be with him, but in the day time.

Es2|13|53|This is the interpretation of the dream which thou sawest, and whereby thou only art here lightened.

Es2|13|54|For thou hast forsaken thine own way, and applied thy diligence unto my law, and sought it.

Es2|13|55|Thy life hast thou ordered in wisdom, and hast called understanding thy mother.

Es2|13|56|And therefore have I shewed thee the treasures of the Highest: after other three days I will speak other things unto thee, and declare unto thee mighty and wondrous things.

Es2|13|57|Then went I forth into the field, giving praise and thanks greatly unto the most High because of his wonders which he did in time;

Es2|13|58|And because he governeth the same, and such things as fall in their seasons: and there I sat three days.

Es2|14|1|And it came to pass upon the third day, I sat under an oak, and, behold, there came a voice out of a bush over against me, and said, Esdras, Esdras.

Es2|14|2|And I said, Here am I, Lord And I stood up upon my feet.

Es2|14|3|Then said he unto me, In the bush I did manifestly reveal myself unto Moses, and talked with him, when my people served in Egypt:

Es2|14|4|And I sent him and led my people out of Egypt, and brought him up to the mount of where I held him by me a long season,

Es2|14|5|And told him many wondrous things, and shewed him the secrets of the times, and the end; and commanded him, saying,

Es2|14|6|These words shalt thou declare, and these shalt thou hide.

Es2|14|7|And now I say unto thee,

Es2|14|8|That thou lay up in thy heart the signs that I have shewed, and the dreams that thou hast seen, and the interpretations which thou hast heard:

Es2|14|9|For thou shalt be taken away from all, and from henceforth thou shalt remain with my Son, and with such as be like thee, until the times be ended.

Es2|14|10|For the world hath lost his youth, and the times begin to wax old.

Es2|14|11|For the world is divided into twelve parts, and the ten parts of it are gone already, and half of a tenth part:

Es2|14|12|And there remaineth that which is after the half of the tenth part.

Es2|14|13|Now therefore set thine house in order, and reprove thy people, comfort such of them as be in trouble, and now renounce corruption,

Es2|14|14|Let go from thee mortal thoughts, cast away the burdens of man, put off now the weak nature,

Es2|14|15|And set aside the thoughts that are most heavy unto thee, and haste thee to flee from these times.

Es2|14|16|For yet greater evils than those which thou hast seen happen shall be done hereafter.

Es2|14|17|For look how much the world shall be weaker through age, so much the more shall evils increase upon them that dwell therein.

Es2|14|18|For the time is fled far away, and leasing is hard at hand: for now hasteth the vision to come, which thou hast seen.

Es2|14|19|Then answered I before thee, and said,

Es2|14|20|Behold, Lord, I will go, as thou hast commanded me, and reprove the people which are present: but they that shall be born afterward, who shall admonish them? thus the world is set in darkness, and they that dwell therein are without light.

Es2|14|21|For thy law is burnt, therefore no man knoweth the things that are done of thee, or the work that shall begin.

Es2|14|22|But if I have found grace before thee, send the Holy Ghost into me, and I shall write all that hath been done in the world since the beginning, which were written in thy law, that men may find thy path, and that they which will live in the latter days may live.

Es2|14|23|And he answered me, saying, Go thy way, gather the people together, and say unto them, that they seek thee not for forty days.

Es2|14|24|But look thou prepare thee many box trees, and take with thee Sarea, Dabria, Selemia, Ecanus, and Asiel, these five which are ready to write swiftly;

Es2|14|25|And come hither, and I shall light a candle of understanding in thine heart, which shall not be put out, till the things be performed which thou shalt begin to write.

Es2|14|26|And when thou hast done, some things shalt thou publish, and some things shalt thou shew secretly to the wise: to morrow this hour shalt thou begin to write.

Es2|14|27|Then went I forth, as he commanded, and gathered all the people together, and said,

Es2|14|28|Hear these words, O Israel.

Es2|14|29|Our fathers at the beginning were strangers in Egypt, from whence they were delivered:

Es2|14|30|And received the law of life, which they kept not, which ye also have transgressed after them.

Es2|14|31|Then was the land, even the land of Sion, parted among you by lot: but your fathers, and ye yourselves, have done unrighteousness, and have not kept the ways which the Highest commanded you.

Es2|14|32|And forasmuch as he is a righteous judge, he took from you in time the thing that he had given you.

Es2|14|33|And now are ye here, and your brethren among you.

Es2|14|34|Therefore if so be that ye will subdue your own understanding, and reform your hearts, ye shall be kept alive and after death ye shall obtain mercy.

Es2|14|35|For after death shall the judgment come, when we shall live again: and then shall the names of the righteous be manifest, and the works of the ungodly shall be declared.

Es2|14|36|Let no man therefore come unto me now, nor seek after me these forty days.

Es2|14|37|So I took the five men, as he commanded me, and we went into the field, and remained there.

Es2|14|38|And the next day, behold, a voice called me, saying, Esdras, open thy mouth, and drink that I give thee to drink.

Es2|14|39|Then opened I my mouth, and, behold, he reached me a full cup, which was full as it were with water, but the colour of it was like fire.

Es2|14|40|And I took it, and drank: and when I had drunk of it, my heart uttered understanding, and wisdom grew in my breast, for my spirit strengthened my memory:

Es2|14|41|And my mouth was opened, and shut no more.

Es2|14|42|The Highest gave understanding unto the five men, and they wrote the wonderful visions of the night that were told, which they knew not: and they sat forty days, and they wrote in the day, and at night they ate bread.

Es2|14|43|As for me. I spake in the day, and I held not my tongue by night.

Es2|14|44|In forty days they wrote two hundred and four books.

Es2|14|45|And it came to pass, when the forty days were filled, that the Highest spake, saying, The first that thou hast written publish openly, that the worthy and unworthy may read it:

Es2|14|46|But keep the seventy last, that thou mayest deliver them only to such as be wise among the people:

Es2|14|47|For in them is the spring of understanding, the fountain of wisdom, and the stream of knowledge.

Es2|14|48|And I did so.

Es2|15|1|Behold, speak thou in the ears of my people the words of prophecy, which I will put in thy mouth, saith the Lord:

Es2|15|2|And cause them to be written in paper: for they are faithful and true.

Es2|15|3|Fear not the imaginations against thee, let not the incredulity of them trouble thee, that speak against thee.

Es2|15|4|For all the unfaithful shall die in their unfaithfulness.

Es2|15|5|Behold, saith the Lord, I will bring plagues upon the world; the sword, famine, death, and destruction.

Es2|15|6|For wickedness hath exceedingly polluted the whole earth, and their hurtful works are fulfilled.

Es2|15|7|Therefore saith the Lord,

Es2|15|8|I will hold my tongue no more as touching their wickedness, which they profanely commit, neither will I suffer them in those things, in which they wickedly exercise themselves: behold, the innocent and righteous blood crieth unto me, and the souls of the just complain continually.

Es2|15|9|And therefore, saith the Lord, I will surely avenge them, and receive unto me all the innocent blood from among them.

Es2|15|10|Behold, my people is led as a flock to the slaughter: I will not suffer them now to dwell in the land of Egypt:

Es2|15|11|But I will bring them with a mighty hand and a stretched out arm, and smite Egypt with plagues, as before, and will destroy all the land thereof.

Es2|15|12|Egypt shall mourn, and the foundation of it shall be smitten with the plague and punishment that אֱלֹהִים shall bring upon it.

Es2|15|13|They that till the ground shall mourn: for their seeds shall fail through the blasting and hail, and with a fearful constellation.

Es2|15|14|Woe to the world and them that dwell therein!

Es2|15|15|For the sword and their destruction draweth nigh, and one people shall stand up and fight against another, and swords in their hands.

Es2|15|16|For there shall be sedition among men, and invading one another; they shall not regard their kings nor princes, and the course of their actions shall stand in their power.

Es2|15|17|A man shall desire to go into a city, and shall not be able.

Es2|15|18|For because of their pride the cities shall be troubled, the houses shall be destroyed, and men shall be afraid.

Es2|15|19|A man shall have no pity upon his neighbour, but shall destroy their houses with the sword, and spoil their goods, because of the lack of bread, and for great tribulation.

Es2|15|20|Behold, saith אֱלֹהִים, I will call together all the kings of the earth to reverence me, which are from the rising of the sun, from the south, from the east, and Libanus; to turn themselves one against another, and repay the things that they have done to them.

Es2|15|21|Like as they do yet this day unto my chosen, so will I do also, and recompense in their bosom. Thus saith the Lord אֱלֹהִים;

Es2|15|22|My right hand shall not spare the sinners, and my sword shall not cease over them that shed innocent blood upon the earth.

Es2|15|23|The fire is gone forth from his wrath, and hath consumed the foundations of the earth, and the sinners, like the straw that is kindled.

Es2|15|24|Woe to them that sin, and keep not my commandments! saith the Lord.

Es2|15|25|I will not spare them: go your way, ye children, from the power, defile not my sanctuary.

Es2|15|26|For the Lord knoweth all them that sin against him, and therefore delivereth he them unto death and destruction.

Es2|15|27|For now are the plagues come upon the whole earth and ye shall remain in them: for אֱלֹהִים shall not deliver you, because ye have sinned against him.

Es2|15|28|Behold an horrible vision, and the appearance thereof from the east:

Es2|15|29|Where the nations of the dragons of Arabia shall come out with many chariots, and the multitude of them shall be carried as the wind upon earth, that all they which hear them may fear and tremble.

Es2|15|30|Also the Carmanians raging in wrath shall go forth as the wild boars of the wood, and with great power shall they come, and join battle with them, and shall waste a portion of the land of the Assyrians.

Es2|15|31|And then shall the dragons have the upper hand, remembering their nature; and if they shall turn themselves, conspiring together in great power to persecute them,

Es2|15|32|Then these shall be troubled bled, and keep silence through their power, and shall flee.

Es2|15|33|And from the land of the Assyrians shall the enemy besiege them, and consume some of them, and in their host shall be fear and dread, and strife among their kings.

Es2|15|34|Behold clouds from the east and from the north unto the south, and they are very horrible to look upon, full of wrath and storm.

Es2|15|35|They shall smite one upon another, and they shall smite down a great multitude of stars upon the earth, even their own star; and blood shall be from the sword unto the belly,

Es2|15|36|And dung of men unto the camel's hough.

Es2|15|37|And there shall be great fearfulness and trembling upon earth: and they that see the wrath shall be afraid, and trembling shall come upon them.

Es2|15|38|And then shall there come great storms from the south, and from the north, and another part from the west.

Es2|15|39|And strong winds shall arise from the east, and shall open it; and the cloud which he raised up in wrath, and the star stirred to cause fear toward the east and west wind, shall be destroyed.

Es2|15|40|The great and mighty clouds shall be puffed up full of wrath, and the star, that they may make all the earth afraid, and them that dwell therein; and they shall pour out over every high and eminent place an horrible star,

Es2|15|41|Fire, and hail, and flying swords, and many waters, that all fields may be full, and all rivers, with the abundance of great waters.

Es2|15|42|And they shall break down the cities and walls, mountains and hills, trees of the wood, and grass of the meadows, and their corn.

Es2|15|43|And they shall go stedfastly unto Babylon, and make her afraid.

Es2|15|44|They shall come to her, and besiege her, the star and all wrath shall they pour out upon her: then shall the dust and smoke go up unto the heaven, and all they that be about her shall bewail her.

Es2|15|45|And they that remain under her shall do service unto them that have put her in fear.

Es2|15|46|And thou, Asia, that art partaker of the hope of Babylon, and art the glory of her person:

Es2|15|47|Woe be unto thee, thou wretch, because thou hast made thyself like unto her; and hast decked thy daughters in whoredom, that they might please and glory in thy lovers, which have always desired to commit whoredom with thee.

Es2|15|48|Thou hast followed her that is hated in all her works and inventions: therefore saith אֱלֹהִים,

Es2|15|49|I will send plagues upon thee; widowhood, poverty, famine, sword, and pestilence, to waste thy houses with destruction and death.

Es2|15|50|And the glory of thy Power shall be dried up as a flower, the heat shall arise that is sent over thee.

Es2|15|51|Thou shalt be weakened as a poor woman with stripes, and as one chastised with wounds, so that the mighty and lovers shall not be able to receive thee.

Es2|15|52|Would I with jealousy have so proceeded against thee, saith the Lord,

Es2|15|53|If thou hadst not always slain my chosen, exalting the stroke of thine hands, and saying over their dead, when thou wast drunken,

Es2|15|54|Set forth the beauty of thy countenance?

Es2|15|55|The reward of thy whoredom shall be in thy bosom, therefore shalt thou receive recompence.

Es2|15|56|Like as thou hast done unto my chosen, saith the Lord, even so shall אֱלֹהִים do unto thee, and shall deliver thee into mischief

Es2|15|57|Thy children shall die of hunger, and thou shalt fall through the sword: thy cities shall be broken down, and all thine shall perish with the sword in the field.

Es2|15|58|They that be in the mountains shall die of hunger, and eat their own flesh, and drink their own blood, for very hunger of bread, and thirst of water.

Es2|15|59|Thou as unhappy shalt come through the sea, and receive plagues again.

Es2|15|60|And in the passage they shall rush on the idle city, and shall destroy some portion of thy land, and consume part of thy glory, and shall return to Babylon that was destroyed.

Es2|15|61|And thou shalt be cast down by them as stubble, and they shall be unto thee as fire;

Es2|15|62|And shall consume thee, and thy cities, thy land, and thy mountains; all thy woods and thy fruitful trees shall they burn up with fire.

Es2|15|63|Thy children shall they carry away captive, and, look, what thou hast, they shall spoil it, and mar the beauty of thy face.

Es2|16|1|Woe be unto thee, Babylon, and Asia! woe be unto thee, Egypt and Syria!

Es2|16|2|Gird up yourselves with cloths of sack and hair, bewail your children, and be sorry; for your destruction is at hand.

Es2|16|3|A sword is sent upon you, and who may turn it back?

Es2|16|4|A fire is sent among you, and who may quench it?

Es2|16|5|Plagues are sent unto you, and what is he that may drive them away?

Es2|16|6|May any man drive away an hungry lion in the wood? or may any one quench the fire in stubble, when it hath begun to burn?

Es2|16|7|May one turn again the arrow that is shot of a strong archer?

Es2|16|8|The mighty Lord sendeth the plagues and who is he that can drive them away?

Es2|16|9|A fire shall go forth from his wrath, and who is he that may quench it?

Es2|16|10|He shall cast lightnings, and who shall not fear? he shall thunder, and who shall not be afraid?

Es2|16|11|The Lord shall threaten, and who shall not be utterly beaten to powder at his presence?

Es2|16|12|The earth quaketh, and the foundations thereof; the sea ariseth up with waves from the deep, and the waves of it are troubled, and the fishes thereof also, before the Lord, and before the glory of his power:

Es2|16|13|For strong is his right hand that bendeth the bow, his arrows that he shooteth are sharp, and shall not miss, when they begin to be shot into the ends of the world.

Es2|16|14|Behold, the plagues are sent, and shall not return again, until they come upon the earth.

Es2|16|15|The fire is kindled, and shall not be put out, till it consume the foundation of the earth.

Es2|16|16|Like as an arrow which is shot of a mighty archer returneth not backward: even so the plagues that shall be sent upon earth shall not return again.

Es2|16|17|Woe is me! woe is me! who will deliver me in those days?

Es2|16|18|The beginning of sorrows and great mournings; the beginning of famine and great death; the beginning of wars, and the powers shall stand in fear; the beginning of evils! what shall I do when these evils shall come?

Es2|16|19|Behold, famine and plague, tribulation and anguish, are sent as scourges for amendment.

Es2|16|20|But for all these things they shall not turn from their wickedness, nor be always mindful of the scourges.

Es2|16|21|Behold, victuals shall be so good cheap upon earth, that they shall think themselves to be in good case, and even then shall evils grow upon earth, sword, famine, and great confusion.

Es2|16|22|For many of them that dwell upon earth shall perish of famine; and the other, that escape the hunger, shall the sword destroy.

Es2|16|23|And the dead shall be cast out as dung, and there shall be no man to comfort them: for the earth shall be wasted, and the cities shall be cast down.

Es2|16|24|There shall be no man left to till the earth, and to sow it

Es2|16|25|The trees shall give fruit, and who shall gather them?

Es2|16|26|The grapes shall ripen, and who shall tread them? for all places shall be desolate of men:

Es2|16|27|So that one man shall desire to see another, and to hear his voice.

Es2|16|28|For of a city there shall be ten left, and two of the field, which shall hide themselves in the thick groves, and in the clefts of the rocks.

Es2|16|29|As in an orchard of Olives upon every tree there are left three or four olives;

Es2|16|30|Or as when a vineyard is gathered, there are left some clusters of them that diligently seek through the vineyard:

Es2|16|31|Even so in those days there shall be three or four left by them that search their houses with the sword.

Es2|16|32|And the earth shall be laid waste, and the fields thereof shall wax old, and her ways and all her paths shall grow full of thorns, because no man shall travel therethrough.

Es2|16|33|The virgins shall mourn, having no bridegrooms; the women shall mourn, having no husbands; their daughters shall mourn, having no helpers.

Es2|16|34|In the wars shall their bridegrooms be destroyed, and their husbands shall perish of famine.

Es2|16|35|Hear now these things and understand them, ye servants of the Lord.

Es2|16|36|Behold, the word of the Lord, receive it: believe not the gods of whom the Lord spake.

Es2|16|37|Behold, the plagues draw nigh, and are not slack.

Es2|16|38|As when a woman with child in the ninth month bringeth forth her son, with two or three hours of her birth great pains compass her womb, which pains, when the child cometh forth, they slack not a moment:

Es2|16|39|Even so shall not the plagues be slack to come upon the earth, and the world shall mourn, and sorrows shall come upon it on every side.

Es2|16|40|O my people, hear my word: make you ready to thy battle, and in those evils be even as pilgrims upon the earth.

Es2|16|41|He that selleth, let him be as he that fleeth away: and he that buyeth, as one that will lose:

Es2|16|42|He that occupieth merchandise, as he that hath no profit by it: and he that buildeth, as he that shall not dwell therein:

Es2|16|43|He that soweth, as if he should not reap: so also he that planteth the vineyard, as he that shall not gather the grapes:

Es2|16|44|They that marry, as they that shall get no children; and they that marry not, as the widowers.

Es2|16|45|And therefore they that labour labour in vain:

Es2|16|46|For strangers shall reap their fruits, and spoil their goods, overthrow their houses, and take their children captives, for in captivity and famine shall they get children.

Es2|16|47|And they that occupy their merchandise with robbery, the more they deck their cities, their houses, their possessions, and their own persons:

Es2|16|48|The more will I be angry with them for their sin, saith the Lord.

Es2|16|49|Like as a whore envieth a right honest and virtuous woman:

Es2|16|50|So shall righteousness hate iniquity, when she decketh herself, and shall accuse her to her face, when he cometh that shall defend him that diligently searcheth out every sin upon earth.

Es2|16|51|And therefore be ye not like thereunto, nor to the works thereof.

Es2|16|52|For yet a little, and iniquity shall be taken away out of the earth, and righteousness shall reign among you.

Es2|16|53|Let not the sinner say that he hath not sinned: for אֱלֹהִים shall burn coals of fire upon his head, which saith before the Lord אֱלֹהִ and his glory, I have not sinned.

Es2|16|54|Behold, the Lord knoweth all the works of men, their imaginations, their thoughts, and their hearts:

Es2|16|55|Which spake but the word, Let the earth be made; and it was made: Let the heaven be made; and it was created.

Es2|16|56|In his word were the stars made, and he knoweth the number of them.

Es2|16|57|He searcheth the deep, and the treasures thereof; he hath measured the sea, and what it containeth.

Es2|16|58|He hath shut the sea in the midst of the waters, and with his word hath he hanged the earth upon the waters.

Es2|16|59|He spreadeth out the heavens like a vault; upon the waters hath he founded it.

Es2|16|60|In the desert hath he made springs of water, and pools upon the tops of the mountains, that the floods might pour down from the high rocks to water the earth.

Es2|16|61|He made man, and put his heart in the midst of the body, and gave him breath, life, and understanding.

Es2|16|62|Yea and the Spirit of Almighty אֱלֹהִים, which made all things, and searcheth out all hidden things in the secrets of the earth,

Es2|16|63|Surely he knoweth your inventions, and what ye think in your hearts, even them that sin, and would hide their sin.

Es2|16|64|Therefore hath the Lord exactly searched out all your works, and he will put you all to shame.

Es2|16|65|And when your sins are brought forth, ye shall be ashamed before men, and your own sins shall

be your accusers in that day.
Es2|16|66|What will ye do? or how will ye hide your sins before אֱלֹהִים and his angels?
Es2|16|67|Behold, אֱלֹהִים himself is the judge, fear him: leave off from your sins, and forget your iniquities, to meddle no more with them for ever: so shall אֱלֹהִים lead you forth, and deliver you from all trouble.
Es2|16|68|For, behold, the burning wrath of a great multitude is kindled over you, and they shall take away certain of you, and feed you, being idle, with things offered unto idols.
Es2|16|69|And they that consent unto them shall be had in derision and in reproach, and trodden under foot.
Es2|16|70|For there shall be in every place, and in the next cities, a great insurrection upon those that fear the Lord.
Es2|16|71|They shall be like mad men, sparing none, but still spoiling and destroying those that fear the Lord.
Es2|16|72|For they shall waste and take away their goods, and cast them out of their houses.
Es2|16|73|Then shall they be known, who are my chosen; and they shall be tried as the gold in the fire.
Es2|16|74|Hear, O ye my beloved, saith the Lord: behold, the days of trouble are at hand, but I will deliver you from the same.
Es2|16|75|Be ye not afraid neither doubt; for אֱלֹהִים is your guide,
Es2|16|76|And the guide of them who keep my commandments and precepts, saith the Lord אֱלֹהִים: let not your sins weigh you down, and let not your iniquities lift up themselves.
Es2|16|77|Woe be unto them that are bound with their sins, and covered with their iniquities like as a field is covered over with bushes, and the path thereof covered with thorns, that no man may travel through!
Es2|16|78|It is left undressed, and is cast into the fire to be consumed therewith.
Aes|10|4|Then Mardocheus said, אֱלֹהִים hath done these things.
Aes|10|5|For I remember a dream which I saw concerning these matters, and nothing thereof hath failed.
Aes|10|6|A little fountain became a river, and there was light, and the sun, and much water: this river is Esther, whom the king married, and made queen:
Aes|10|7|And the two dragons are I and Aman.
Aes|10|8|And the nations were those that were assembled to destroy the name of the Jews:
Aes|10|9|And my nation is this Israel, which cried to אֱלֹהִים, and were saved: for the Lord hath saved his people, and the Lord hath delivered us from all those evils, and אֱלֹהִים hath wrought signs and great wonders, which have not been done among the Gentiles.
Aes|10|10|Therefore hath he made two lots, one for the people of אֱלֹהִים, and another for all the Gentiles.
Aes|10|11|And these two lots came at the hour, and time, and day of judgment, before אֱלֹהִים among all nations.
Aes|10|12|So אֱלֹהִים remembered his people, and justified his inheritance.
Aes|10|13|Therefore those days shall be unto them in the month Adar, the fourteenth and fifteenth day of the same month, with an assembly, and joy, and with gladness before אֱלֹהִים, according to the generations for ever among his people.
Aes|11|1|In the fourth year of the reign of Ptolemeus and Cleopatra, Dositheus, who said he was a priest and Levite, and Ptolemeus his son, brought this epistle of Phurim, which they said was the same, and that Lysimachus the son of Ptolemeus, that was in Jerusalem, had interpreted it.
Aes|11|2|In the second year of the reign of Artexerxes the great, in the first day of the month Nisan, Mardocheus the son of Jairus, the son of Semei, the son of Cisai, of the tribe of Benjamin, had a dream;
Aes|11|3|Who was a Jew, and dwelt in the city of Susa, a great man, being a servitor in the king's court.
Aes|11|4|He was also one of the captives, which Nabuchodonosor the king of Babylon carried from Jerusalem with Jechonias king of Judea; and this was his dream:
Aes|11|5|Behold a noise of a tumult, with thunder, and earthquakes, and uproar in the land:
Aes|11|6|And, behold, two great dragons came forth ready to fight, and their cry was great.
Aes|11|7|And at their cry all nations were prepared to battle, that they might fight against the righteous people.
Aes|11|8|And lo a day of darkness and obscurity, tribulation and anguish, affliction and great uproar, upon earth.
Aes|11|9|And the whole righteous nation was troubled, fearing their own evils, and were ready to perish.
Aes|11|10|Then they cried unto אֱלֹהִים, and upon their cry, as it were from a little fountain, was made a great flood, even much water.
Aes|11|11|The light and the sun rose up, and the lowly were exalted, and devoured the glorious.
Aes|11|12|Now when Mardocheus, who had seen this dream, and what אֱלֹהִים had determined to do, was

awake, he bare this dream in mind, and until night by all means was desirous to know it.

Aes|12|1|And Mardocheus took his rest in the court with Gabatha and Tharra, the two eunuchs of the king, and keepers of the palace.

Aes|12|2|And he heard their devices, and searched out their purposes, and learned that they were about to lay hands upon Artexerxes the king; and so he certified the king of them.

Aes|12|3|Then the king examined the two eunuchs, and after that they had confessed it, they were strangled.

Aes|12|4|And the king made a record of these things, and Mardocheus also wrote thereof.

Aes|12|5|So the king commanded, Mardocheus to serve in the court, and for this he rewarded him.

Aes|12|6|Howbeit Aman the son of Amadathus the Agagite, who was in great honour with the king, sought to molest Mardocheus and his people because of the two eunuchs of the king.

Aes|13|1|The copy of the letters was this: The great king Artexerxes writeth these things to the princes and governours that are under him from India unto Ethiopia in an hundred and seven and twenty provinces.

Aes|13|2|After that I became lord over many nations and had dominion over the whole world, not lifted up with presumption of my authority, but carrying myself always with equity and mildness, I purposed to settle my subjects continually in a quiet life, and making my kingdom peaceable, and open for passage to the utmost coasts, to renew peace, which is desired of all men.

Aes|13|3|Now when I asked my counsellors how this might be brought to pass, Aman, that excelled in wisdom among us, and was approved for his constant good will and steadfast fidelity, and had the honour of the second place in the kingdom,

Aes|13|4|Declared unto us, that in all nations throughout the world there was scattered a certain malicious people, that had laws contrary to all nations, and continually despised the commandments of kings, so as the uniting of our kingdoms, honourably intended by us cannot go forward.

Aes|13|5|Seeing then we understand that this people alone is continually in opposition unto all men, differing in the strange manner of their laws, and evil affected to our state, working all the mischief they can that our kingdom may not be firmly established:

Aes|13|6|Therefore have we commanded, that all they that are signified in writing unto you by Aman, who is ordained over the affairs, and is next unto us, shall all, with their wives and children, be utterly destroyed by the sword of their enemies, without all mercy and pity, the fourteenth day of the twelfth month Adar of this present year:

Aes|13|7|That they, who of old and now also are malicious, may in one day with violence go into the grave, and so ever hereafter cause our affairs to be well settled, and without trouble.

Aes|13|8|Then Mardocheus thought upon all the works of the Lord, and made his prayer unto him,

Aes|13|9|Saying, O Lord, Lord, the King Almighty: for the whole world is in thy power, and if thou hast appointed to save Israel, there is no man that can gainsay thee:

Aes|13|10|For thou hast made heaven and earth, and all the wondrous things under the heaven.

Aes|13|11|Thou art Lord of all things, and and there is no man that can resist thee, which art the Lord.

Aes|13|12|Thou knowest all things, and thou knowest, Lord, that it was neither in contempt nor pride, nor for any desire of glory, that I did not bow down to proud Aman.

Aes|13|13|For I could have been content with good will for the salvation of Israel to kiss the soles of his feet.

Aes|13|14|But I did this, that I might not prefer the glory of man above the glory of אֱלֹהִים: neither will I worship any but thee, O אֱלֹהִים, neither will I do it in pride.

Aes|13|15|And now, O Lord אֱלֹהִים and King, spare thy people: for their eyes are upon us to bring us to nought; yea, they desire to destroy the inheritance, that hath been thine from the beginning.

Aes|13|16|Despise not the portion, which thou hast delivered out of Egypt for thine own self.

Aes|13|17|Hear my prayer, and be merciful unto thine inheritance: turn our sorrow into joy, that we may live, O Lord, and praise thy name: and destroy not the mouths of them that praise thee, O Lord.

Aes|13|18|All Israel in like manner cried most earnestly unto the Lord, because their death was before their eyes.

Aes|14|1|Queen Esther also, being in fear of death, resorted unto the Lord:

Aes|14|2|And laid away her glorious apparel, and put on the garments of anguish and mourning: and instead of precious ointments, she covered her head with ashes and dung, and she humbled her body greatly, and all the places of her joy she filled with her torn hair.

Aes|14|3|And she prayed unto the Lord אֱלֹהִים of Israel, saying, O my Lord, thou only art our King: help me, desolate woman, which have no helper but thee:

Aes|14|4|For my danger is in mine hand.

Aes|14|5|From my youth up I have heard in the tribe of my family that thou, O Lord, tookest Israel from among all people, and our fathers from all their predecessors, for a perpetual inheritance, and thou hast performed whatsoever thou didst promise them.

Aes|14|6|And now we have sinned before thee: therefore hast thou given us into the hands of our enemies,

Aes|14|7|Because we worshipped their gods: O Lord, thou art righteous.

Aes|14|8|Nevertheless it satisfieth them not, that we are in bitter captivity: but they have stricken hands with their idols,

Aes|14|9|That they will abolish the thing that thou with thy mouth hast ordained, and destroy thine inheritance, and stop the mouth of them that praise thee, and quench the glory of thy house, and of thine altar,

Aes|14|10|And open the mouths of the heathen to set forth the praises of the idols, and to magnify a fleshly king for ever.

Aes|14|11|O Lord, give not thy sceptre unto them that be nothing, and let them not laugh at our fall; but turn their device upon themselves, and make him an example, that hath begun this against us.

Aes|14|12|Remember, O Lord, make thyself known in time of our affliction, and give me boldness, O King of the nations, and Lord of all power.

Aes|14|13|Give me eloquent speech in my mouth before the lion: turn his heart to hate him that fighteth against us, that there may be an end of him, and of all that are likeminded to him:

Aes|14|14|But deliver us with thine hand, and help me that am desolate, and which have no other help but thee.

Aes|14|15|Thou knowest all things, O Lord; thou knowest that I hate the glory of the unrighteous, and abhor the bed of the uncircumcised, and of all the heathen.

Aes|14|16|Thou knowest my necessity: for I abhor the sign of my high estate, which is upon mine head in the days wherein I shew myself, and that I abhor it as a menstruous rag, and that I wear it not when I am private by myself.

Aes|14|17|And that thine handmaid hath not eaten at Aman's table, and that I have not greatly esteemed the king's feast, nor drunk the wine of the drink offerings.

Aes|14|18|Neither had thine handmaid any joy since the day that I was brought hither to this present, but in thee, O Lord אֱלֹהִים of Abraham.

Aes|14|19|O thou mighty אֱלֹהִים above all, hear the voice of the forlorn and deliver us out of the hands of the mischievous, and deliver me out of my fear.

Aes|15|1|And upon the third day, when she had ended her prayers, she laid away her mourning garments, and put on her glorious apparel.

Aes|15|2|And being gloriously adorned, after she had called upon אֱלֹהִים, who is the beholder and saviour of all things, she took two maids with her:

Aes|15|3|And upon the one she leaned, as carrying herself daintily;

Aes|15|4|And the other followed, bearing up her train.

Aes|15|5|And she was ruddy through the perfection of her beauty, and her countenance was cheerful and very amiable: but her heart was in anguish for fear.

Aes|15|6|Then having passed through all the doors, she stood before the king, who sat upon his royal throne, and was clothed with all his robes of majesty, all glittering with gold and precious stones; and he was very dreadful.

Aes|15|7|Then lifting up his countenance that shone with majesty, he looked very fiercely upon her: and the queen fell down, and was pale, and fainted, and bowed herself upon the head of the maid that went before her.

Aes|15|8|Then אֱלֹהִים changed the spirit of the king into mildness, who in a fear leaped from his throne, and took her in his arms, till she came to herself again, and comforted her with loving words and said unto her,

Aes|15|9|Esther, what is the matter? I am thy brother, be of good cheer:

Aes|15|10|Thou shalt not die, though our our commandment be general: come near.

Aes|15|11|And so be held up his golden sceptre, and laid it upon her neck,

Aes|15|12|And embraced her, and said, Speak unto me.

Aes|15|13|Then said she unto him, I saw thee, my lord, as an angel of אֱלֹהִים, and my heart was troubled for fear of thy majesty.

Aes|15|14|For wonderful art thou, lord, and thy countenance is full of grace.

Aes|15|15|And as she was speaking, she fell down for faintness.

Aes|15|16|Then the king was troubled, and ail his servants comforted her.

Aes|16|1|The great king Artexerxes unto the princes and governors of an hundred and seven and twenty provinces from India unto Ethiopia, and unto all our faithful subjects, greeting.

Aes|16|2|Many, the more often they are honoured with the great bounty of their gracious princes, the more proud they are waxen,

Aes|16|3|And endeavour to hurt not our subjects only, but not being able to bear abundance, do take in hand to practise also against those that do them good:

Aes|16|4|And take not only thankfulness away from among men, but also lifted up with the glorious words of lewd persons, that were never good, they think to escape the justice of אֱלֹהִים, that seeth all things and hateth evil.

Aes|16|5|Oftentimes also fair speech of those, that are put in trust to manage their friends' affairs, hath caused many that are in authority to be partakers of innocent blood, and hath enwrapped them in remediless calamities:

Aes|16|6|Beguiling with the falsehood and deceit of their lewd disposition the innocency and goodness of princes.

Aes|16|7|Now ye may see this, as we have declared, not so much by ancient histories, as ye may, if ye search what hath been wickedly done of late through the pestilent behaviour of them that are unworthily placed in authority.

Aes|16|8|And we must take care for the time to come, that our kingdom may be quiet and peaceable for all men,

Aes|16|9|Both by changing our purposes, and always judging things that are evident with more equal proceeding.

Aes|16|10|For Aman, a Macedonian, the son of Amadatha, being indeed a stranger from the Persian blood, and far distant from our goodness, and as a stranger received of us,

Aes|16|11|Had so far forth obtained the favour that we shew toward every nation, as that he was called our father, and was continually honoured of all the next person unto the king.

Aes|16|12|But he, not bearing his great dignity, went about to deprive us of our kingdom and life:

Aes|16|13|Having by manifold and cunning deceits sought of us the destruction, as well of Mardocheus, who saved our life, and continually procured our good, as also of blameless Esther, partaker of our kingdom, with their whole nation.

Aes|16|14|For by these means he thought, finding us destitute of friends to have translated the kingdom of the Persians to the Macedonians.

Aes|16|15|But we find that the Jews, whom this wicked wretch hath delivered to utter destruction, are no evildoers, but live by most just laws:

Aes|16|16|And that they be children of the most high and most mighty, living אֱלֹהִים, who hath ordered the kingdom both unto us and to our progenitors in the most excellent manner.

Aes|16|17|Wherefore ye shall do well not to put in execution the letters sent unto you by Aman the son of Amadatha.

Aes|16|18|For he that was the worker of these things, is hanged at the gates of Susa with all his family: אֱלֹהִים, who ruleth all things, speedily rendering vengeance to him according to his deserts.

Aes|16|19|Therefore ye shall publish the copy of this letter in all places, that the Jews may freely live after their own laws.

Aes|16|20|And ye shall aid them, that even the same day, being the thirteenth day of the twelfth month Adar, they may be avenged on them, who in the time of their affliction shall set upon them.

Aes|16|21|For Almighty אֱלֹהִים hath turned to joy unto them the day, wherein the chosen people should have perished.

Aes|16|22|Ye shall therefore among your solemn feasts keep it an high day with all feasting:

Aes|16|23|That both now and hereafter there may be safety to us and the well affected Persians; but to those which do conspire against us a memorial of destruction.

Aes|16|24|Therefore every city and country whatsoever, which shall not do according to these things, shall be destroyed without mercy with fire and sword, and shall be made not only unpassable for men, but also most hateful to wild beasts and fowls for ever.

Ma1|1|1|And it happened, after that Alexander son of Philip, the Macedonian, who came out of the land of Chettiim, had smitten Darius king of the Persians and Medes, that he reigned in his stead, the first over Greece,

Ma1|1|2|And made many wars, and won many strong holds, and slew the kings of the earth,

Ma1|1|3|And went through to the ends of the earth, and took spoils of many nations, insomuch that the earth was quiet before him; whereupon he was exalted and his heart was lifted up.

Ma1|1|4|And he gathered a mighty strong host and ruled over countries, and nations, and kings, who became tributaries unto him.

Ma1|1|5|And after these things he fell sick, and perceived that he should die.

Ma1|1|6|Wherefore he called his servants, such as were honourable, and had been brought up with him from his youth, and parted his kingdom among them, while he was yet alive.

Ma1|1|7|So Alexander reigned twelves years, and then died.

Ma1|1|8|And his servants bare rule every one in his place.

Ma1|1|9|And after his death they all put crowns upon themselves; so did their sons after them many years: and evils were multiplied in the earth.

Ma1|1|10|And there came out of them a wicked root Antiochus surnamed Epiphanes, son of Antiochus the king, who had been an hostage at Rome, and he reigned in the hundred and thirty and seventh year of the kingdom of the Greeks.

Ma1|1|11|In those days went there out of Israel wicked men, who persuaded many, saying, Let us go and make a covenant with the heathen that are round about us: for since we departed from them we have had much sorrow.

Ma1|1|12|So this device pleased them well.

Ma1|1|13|Then certain of the people were so forward herein, that they went to the king, who gave them licence to do after the ordinances of the heathen:

Ma1|1|14|Whereupon they built a place of exercise at Jerusalem according to the customs of the heathen:

Ma1|1|15|And made themselves uncircumcised, and forsook the holy covenant, and joined themselves to the heathen, and were sold to do mischief.

Ma1|1|16|Now when the kingdom was established before Antiochus, he thought to reign over Egypt that he might have the dominion of two realms.

Ma1|1|17|Wherefore he entered into Egypt with a great multitude, with chariots, and elephants, and horsemen, and a great navy,

Ma1|1|18|And made war against Ptolemee king of Egypt: but Ptolemee was afraid of him, and fled; and many were wounded to death.

Ma1|1|19|Thus they got the strong cities in the land of Egypt and he took the spoils thereof.

Ma1|1|20|And after that Antiochus had smitten Egypt, he returned again in the hundred forty and third year, and went up against Israel and Jerusalem with a great multitude,

Ma1|1|21|And entered proudly into the sanctuary, and took away the golden altar, and the candlestick of light, and all the vessels thereof,

Ma1|1|22|And the table of the shewbread, and the pouring vessels, and the vials. and the censers of gold, and the veil, and the crown, and the golden ornaments that were before the temple, all which he pulled off.

Ma1|1|23|He took also the silver and the gold, and the precious vessels: also he took the hidden treasures which he found.

Ma1|1|24|And when he had taken all away, he went into his own land, having made a great massacre, and spoken very proudly.

Ma1|1|25|Therefore there was a great mourning in Israel, in every place where they were;

Ma1|1|26|So that the princes and elders mourned, the virgins and young men were made feeble, and the beauty of women was changed.

Ma1|1|27|Every bridegroom took up lamentation, and she that sat in the marriage chamber was in heaviness,

Ma1|1|28|The land also was moved for the inhabitants thereof, and all the house of Jacob was covered with confusion.

Ma1|1|29|And after two years fully expired the king sent his chief collector of tribute unto the cities of Juda, who came unto Jerusalem with a great multitude,

Ma1|1|30|And spake peaceable words unto them, but all was deceit: for when they had given him credence, he fell suddenly upon the city, and smote it very sore, and destroyed much people of Israel.

Ma1|1|31|And when he had taken the spoils of the city, he set it on fire, and pulled down the houses and walls thereof on every side.

Ma1|1|32|But the women and children took they captive, and possessed the cattle.

Ma1|1|33|Then builded they the city of David with a great and strong wall, and with mighty towers, and made it a strong hold for them.

Ma1|1|34|And they put therein a sinful nation, wicked men, and fortified themselves therein.

Ma1|1|35|They stored it also with armour and victuals, and when they had gathered together the spoils of Jerusalem, they laid them up there, and so they became a sore snare:

Ma1|1|36|For it was a place to lie in wait against the sanctuary, and an evil adversary to Israel.

Ma1|1|37|Thus they shed innocent blood on every side of the sanctuary, and defiled it:

Ma1|1|38|Insomuch that the inhabitants of Jerusalem fled because of them: whereupon the city was made an habitation of strangers, and became strange to those that were born in her; and her own children left her.

Ma1|1|39|Her sanctuary was laid waste like a wilderness, her feasts were turned into mourning, her sabbaths into reproach her honour into contempt.

Ma1|1|40|As had been her glory, so was her dishonour increased, and her excellency was turned into mourning.

Ma1|1|41|Moreover king Antiochus wrote to his whole kingdom, that all should be one people,

Ma1|1|42|And every one should leave his laws: so all the heathen agreed according to the commandment of the king.

Ma1|1|43|Yea, many also of the Israelites consented to his religion, and sacrificed unto idols, and profaned the sabbath.

Ma1|1|44|For the king had sent letters by messengers unto Jerusalem and the cities of Juda that they should follow the strange laws of the land,

Ma1|1|45|And forbid burnt offerings, and sacrifice, and drink offerings, in the temple; and that they should profane the sabbaths and festival days:

Ma1|1|46|And pollute the sanctuary and holy people:

Ma1|1|47|Set up altars, and groves, and chapels of idols, and sacrifice swine's flesh, and unclean beasts:

Ma1|1|48|That they should also leave their children uncircumcised, and make their souls abominable with all manner of uncleanness and profanation:

Ma1|1|49|To the end they might forget the law, and change all the ordinances.

Ma1|1|50|And whosoever would not do according to the commandment of the king, he said, he should die.

Ma1|1|51|In the selfsame manner wrote he to his whole kingdom, and appointed overseers over all the people, commanding the cities of Juda to sacrifice, city by city.

Ma1|1|52|Then many of the people were gathered unto them, to wit every one that forsook the law; and so they committed evils in the land;

Ma1|1|53|And drove the Israelites into secret places, even wheresoever they could flee for succour.

Ma1|1|54|Now the fifteenth day of the month Casleu, in the hundred forty and fifth year, they set up the abomination of desolation upon the altar, and builded idol altars throughout the cities of Juda on every side;

Ma1|1|55|And burnt incense at the doors of their houses, and in the streets.

Ma1|1|56|And when they had rent in pieces the books of the law which they found, they burnt them with fire.

Ma1|1|57|And whosoever was found with any the book of the testament, or if any committed to the law, the king's commandment was, that they should put him to death.

Ma1|1|58|Thus did they by their authority unto the Israelites every month, to as many as were found in the cities.

Ma1|1|59|Now the five and twentieth day of the month they did sacrifice upon the idol altar, which was upon the altar of אֱלֹהִים.

Ma1|1|60|At which time according to the commandment they put to death certain women, that had caused their children to be circumcised.

Ma1|1|61|And they hanged the infants about their necks, and rifled their houses, and slew them that had circumcised them.

Ma1|1|62|Howbeit many in Israel were fully resolved and confirmed in themselves not to eat any unclean thing.

Ma1|1|63|Wherefore the rather to die, that they might not be defiled with meats, and that they might not profane the holy covenant: so then they died.

Ma1|1|64|And there was very great wrath upon Israel.

Ma1|2|1|In those days arose Mattathias the son of John, the son of Simeon, a priest of the sons of Joarib, from Jerusalem, and dwelt in Modin.

Ma1|2|2|And he had five sons, Joannan, called Caddis:

Ma1|2|3|Simon; called Thassi:

Ma1|2|4|Judas, who was called Maccabeus:

Ma1|2|5|Eleazar, called Avaran: and Jonathan, whose surname was Apphus.

Mal|2|6|And when he saw the blasphemies that were committed in Juda and Jerusalem,

Mal|2|7|He said, Woe is me! wherefore was I born to see this misery of my people, and of the holy city, and to dwell there, when it was delivered into the hand of the enemy, and the sanctuary into the hand of strangers?

Mal|2|8|Her temple is become as a man without glory.

Mal|2|9|Her glorious vessels are carried away into captivity, her infants are slain in the streets, her young men with the sword of the enemy.

Mal|2|10|What nation hath not had a part in her kingdom and gotten of her spoils?

Mal|2|11|All her ornaments are taken away; of a free woman she is become a bondslave.

Mal|2|12|And, behold, our sanctuary, even our beauty and our glory, is laid waste, and the Gentiles have profaned it.

Mal|2|13|To what end therefore shall we live any longer?

Mal|2|14|Then Mattathias and his sons rent their clothes, and put on sackcloth, and mourned very sore.

Mal|2|15|In the mean while the king's officers, such as compelled the people to revolt, came into the city Modin, to make them sacrifice.

Mal|2|16|And when many of Israel came unto them, Mattathias also and his sons came together.

Mal|2|17|Then answered the king's officers, and said to Mattathias on this wise, Thou art a ruler, and an honourable and great man in this city, and strengthened with sons and brethren:

Mal|2|18|Now therefore come thou first, and fulfil the king's commandment, like as all the heathen have done, yea, and the men of Juda also, and such as remain at Jerusalem: so shalt thou and thy house be in the number of the king's friends, and thou and thy children shall be honoured with silver and gold, and many rewards.

Mal|2|19|Then Mattathias answered and spake with a loud voice, Though all the nations that are under the king's dominion obey him, and fall away every one from the religion of their fathers, and give consent to his commandments:

Mal|2|20|Yet will I and my sons and my brethren walk in the covenant of our fathers.

Mal|2|21|אֱלֹהִים forbid that we should forsake the law and the ordinances.

Mal|2|22|We will not hearken to the king's words, to go from our religion, either on the right hand, or the left.

Mal|2|23|Now when he had left speaking these words, there came one of the Jews in the sight of all to sacrifice on the altar which was at Modin, according to the king's commandment.

Mal|2|24|Which thing when Mattathias saw, he was inflamed with zeal, and his reins trembled, neither could he forbear to shew his anger according to judgment: wherefore he ran, and slew him upon the altar.

Mal|2|25|Also the king's commissioner, who compelled men to sacrifice, he killed at that time, and the altar he pulled down.

Mal|2|26|Thus dealt he zealously for the law of אֱלֹהִים like as Phinees did unto Zambri the son of Salom.

Mal|2|27|And Mattathias cried throughout the city with a loud voice, saying, Whosoever is zealous of the law, and maintaineth the covenant, let him follow me.

Mal|2|28|So he and his sons fled into the mountains, and left all that ever they had in the city.

Mal|2|29|Then many that sought after justice and judgment went down into the wilderness, to dwell there:

Mal|2|30|Both they, and their children, and their wives; and their cattle; because afflictions increased sore upon them.

Mal|2|31|Now when it was told the king's servants, and the host that was at Jerusalem, in the city of David, that certain men, who had broken the king's commandment, were gone down into the secret places in the wilderness,

Mal|2|32|They pursued after them a great number, and having overtaken them, they camped against them, and made war against them on the sabbath day.

Mal|2|33|And they said unto them, Let that which ye have done hitherto suffice; come forth, and do according to the commandment of the king, and ye shall live.

Mal|2|34|But they said, We will not come forth, neither will we do the king's commandment, to profane the sabbath day.

Mal|2|35|So then they gave them the battle with all speed.

Mal|2|36|Howbeit they answered them not, neither cast they a stone at them, nor stopped the places where they lay hid;

Mal|2|37|But said, Let us die all in our innocency: heaven and earth will testify for us, that ye put us to death wrongfully.

Mal|2|38|So they rose up against them in battle on the sabbath, and they slew them, with their wives and children and their cattle, to the number of a thousand people.

Mal|2|39|Now when Mattathias and his friends understood hereof, they mourned for them right sore.

Mal|2|40|And one of them said to another, If we all do as our brethren have done, and fight not for our lives and laws against the heathen, they will now quickly root us out of the earth.

Mal|2|41|At that time therefore they decreed, saying, Whosoever shall come to make battle with us on the sabbath day, we will fight against him; neither will we die all, as our brethren that were murdered im the secret places.

Mal|2|42|Then came there unto him a company of Assideans who were mighty men of Israel, even all such as were voluntarily devoted unto the law.

Mal|2|43|Also all they that fled for persecution joined themselves unto them, and were a stay unto them.

Mal|2|44|So they joined their forces, and smote sinful men in their anger, and wicked men in their wrath: but the rest fled to the heathen for succour.

Mal|2|45|Then Mattathias and his friends went round about, and pulled down the altars:

Mal|2|46|And what children soever they found within the coast of Israel uncircumcised, those they circumcised valiantly.

Mal|2|47|They pursued also after the proud men, and the work prospered in their hand.

Mal|2|48|So they recovered the law out of the hand of the Gentiles, and out of the hand of kings, neither suffered they the sinner to triumph.

Mal|2|49|Now when the time drew near that Mattathias should die, he said unto his sons, Now hath pride and rebuke gotten strength, and the time of destruction, and the wrath of indignation:

Mal|2|50|Now therefore, my sons, be ye zealous for the law, and give your lives for the covenant of your fathers.

Mal|2|51|Call to remembrance what acts our fathers did in their time; so shall ye receive great honour and an everlasting name.

Mal|2|52|Was not Abraham found faithful in temptation, and it was imputed unto him for righteousness?

Mal|2|53|Joseph in the time of his distress kept the commandment and was made lord of Egypt.

Mal|2|54|Phinees our father in being zealous and fervent obtained the covenant of an everlasting priesthood.

Mal|2|55|Yashiyah for fulfilling the word was made a judge in Israel.

Mal|2|56|Caleb for bearing witness before the congregation received the heritage of the land.

Mal|2|57|David for being merciful possessed the throne of an everlasting kingdom.

Mal|2|58|Elias for being zealous and fervent for the law was taken up into heaven.

Mal|2|59|Ananias, Azarias, and Misael, by believing were saved out of the flame.

Mal|2|60|Daniel for his innocency was delivered from the mouth of lions.

Mal|2|61|And thus consider ye throughout all ages, that none that put their trust in him shall be overcome.

Mal|2|62|Fear not then the words of a sinful man: for his glory shall be dung and worms.

Mal|2|63|To day he shall be lifted up and to morrow he shall not be found, because he is returned into his dust, and his thought is come to nothing.

Mal|2|64|Wherefore, ye my sons, be valiant and shew yourselves men in the behalf of the law; for by it shall ye obtain glory.

Mal|2|65|And behold, I know that your brother Simon is a man of counsel, give ear unto him alway: he shall be a father unto you.

Mal|2|66|As for Judas Maccabeus, he hath been mighty and strong, even from his youth up: let him be your captain, and fight the battle of the people.

Mal|2|67|Take also unto you all those that observe the law, and avenge ye the wrong of your people.

Mal|2|68|Recompense fully the heathen, and take heed to the commandments of the law.

Mal|2|69|So he blessed them, and was gathered to his fathers.

Mal|2|70|And he died in the hundred forty and sixth year, and his sons buried him in the sepulchres of his fathers at Modin, and all Israel made great lamentation for him.

Mal|3|1|Then his son Judas, called Maccabeus, rose up in his stead.

Mal|3|2|And all his brethren helped him, and so did all they that held with his father, and they fought with cheerfulness the battle of Israel.

Mal|3|3|So he gat his people great honour, and put on a breastplate as a giant, and girt his warlike harness about him, and he made battles, protecting the host with his sword.

Mal|3|4|In his acts he was like a lion, and like a lion's whelp roaring for his prey.

Mal|3|5|For He pursued the wicked, and sought them out, and burnt up those that vexed his people.

Mal|3|6|Wherefore the wicked shrunk for fear of him, and all the workers of iniquity were troubled, because salvation prospered in his hand.

Mal|3|7|He grieved also many kings, and made Jacob glad with his acts, and his memorial is blessed for ever.

Mal|3|8|Moreover he went through the cities of Juda, destroying the ungodly out of them, and turning away wrath from Israel:

Mal|3|9|So that he was renowned unto the utmost part of the earth, and he received unto him such as were ready to perish.

Mal|3|10|Then Apollonius gathered the Gentiles together, and a great host out of Samaria, to fight against Israel.

Mal|3|11|Which thing when Judas perceived, he went forth to meet him, and so he smote him, and slew him: many also fell down slain, but the rest fled.

Mal|3|12|Wherefore Judas took their spoils, and Apollonius' sword also, and therewith he fought all his life long.

Mal|3|13|Now when Seron, a prince of the army of Syria, heard say that Judas had gathered unto him a multitude and company of the faithful to go out with him to war;

Mal|3|14|He said, I will get me a name and honour in the kingdom; for I will go fight with Judas and them that are with him, who despise the king's commandment.

Mal|3|15|So he made him ready to go up, and there went with him a mighty host of the ungodly to help him, and to be avenged of the children of Israel.

Mal|3|16|And when he came near to the going up of Bethhoron, Judas went forth to meet him with a small company:

Mal|3|17|Who, when they saw the host coming to meet them, said unto Judas, How shall we be able, being so few, to fight against so great a multitude and so strong, seeing we are ready to faint with fasting all this day?

Mal|3|18|Unto whom Judas answered, It is no hard matter for many to be shut up in the hands of a few; and with the אֱלֹהִים of heaven it is all one, to deliver with a great multitude, or a small company:

Mal|3|19|For the victory of battle standeth not in the multitude of an host; but strength cometh from heaven.

Mal|3|20|They come against us in much pride and iniquity to destroy us, and our wives and children, and to spoil us:

Mal|3|21|But we fight for our lives and our laws.

Mal|3|22|Wherefore the Lord himself will overthrow them before our face: and as for you, be ye not afraid of them.

Mal|3|23|Now as soon as he had left off speaking, he leapt suddenly upon them, and so Seron and his host was overthrown before him.

Mal|3|24|And they pursued them from the going down of Bethhoron unto the plain, where were slain about eight hundred men of them; and the residue fled into the land of the Philistines.

Mal|3|25|Then began the fear of Judas and his brethren, and an exceeding great dread, to fall upon the nations round about them:

Mal|3|26|Insomuch as his fame came unto the king, and all nations talked of the battles of Judas.

Mal|3|27|Now when king Antiochus heard these things, he was full of indignation: wherefore he sent and gathered together all the forces of his realm, even a very strong army.

Mal|3|28|He opened also his treasure, and gave his soldiers pay for a year, commanding them to be ready whensoever he should need them.

Mal|3|29|Nevertheless, when he saw that the money of his treasures failed and that the tributes in the country were small, because of the dissension and plague, which he had brought upon the land in taking away the laws which had been of old time;

Mal|3|30|He feared that he should not be able to bear the charges any longer, nor to have such gifts to give so liberally as he did before: for he had abounded above the kings that were before him.

Mal|3|31|Wherefore, being greatly perplexed in his mind, he determined to go into Persia, there to take the tributes of the countries, and to gather much money.

Mal|3|32|So he left Lysias, a nobleman, and one of the blood royal, to oversee the affairs of the king from the river Euphrates unto the borders of Egypt:

Mal|3|33|And to bring up his son Antiochus, until he came again.

Ma1|3|34|Moreover he delivered unto him the half of his forces, and the elephants, and gave him charge of all things that he would have done, as also concerning them that dwelt in Juda and Jerusalem:

Ma1|3|35|To wit, that he should send an army against them, to destroy and root out the strength of Israel, and the remnant of Jerusalem, and to take away their memorial from that place;

Ma1|3|36|And that he should place strangers in all their quarters, and divide their land by lot.

Ma1|3|37|So the king took the half of the forces that remained, and departed from Antioch, his royal city, the hundred forty and seventh year; and having passed the river Euphrates, he went through the high countries.

Ma1|3|38|Then Lysias chose Ptolemee the son of Dorymenes, Nicanor, and Gorgias, mighty men of the king's friends:

Ma1|3|39|And with them he sent forty thousand footmen, and seven thousand horsemen, to go into the land of Juda, and to destroy it, as the king commanded.

Ma1|3|40|So they went forth with all their power, and came and pitched by Emmaus in the plain country.

Ma1|3|41|And the merchants of the country, hearing the fame of them, took silver and gold very much, with servants, and came into the camp to buy the children of Israel for slaves: a power also of Syria and of the land of the Philistines joined themselves unto them.

Ma1|3|42|Now when Judas and his brethren saw that miseries were multiplied, and that the forces did encamp themselves in their borders: for they knew how the king had given commandment to destroy the people, and utterly abolish them;

Ma1|3|43|They said one to another, Let us restore the decayed fortune of our people, and let us fight for our people and the sanctuary.

Ma1|3|44|Then was the congregation gathered together, that they might be ready for battle, and that they might pray, and ask mercy and compassion.

Ma1|3|45|Now Jerusalem lay void as a wilderness, there was none of her children that went in or out: the sanctuary also was trodden down, and aliens kept the strong hold; the heathen had their habitation in that place; and joy was taken from Jacob, and the pipe with the harp ceased.

Ma1|3|46|Wherefore the Israelites assembled themselves together, and came to Maspha, over against Jerusalem; for in Maspha was the place where they prayed aforetime in Israel.

Ma1|3|47|Then they fasted that day, and put on sackcloth, and cast ashes upon their heads, and rent their clothes,

Ma1|3|48|And laid open the book of the law, wherein the heathen had sought to paint the likeness of their images.

Ma1|3|49|They brought also the priests' garments, and the firstfruits, and the tithes: and the Nazarites they stirred up, who had accomplished their days.

Ma1|3|50|Then cried they with a loud voice toward heaven, saying, What shall we do with these, and whither shall we carry them away?

Ma1|3|51|For thy sanctuary is trodden down and profaned, and thy priests are in heaviness, and brought low.

Ma1|3|52|And lo, the heathen are assembled together against us to destroy us: what things they imagine against us, thou knowest.

Ma1|3|53|How shall we be able to stand against them, except thou, O אֱלֹהִים, be our help?

Ma1|3|54|Then sounded they with trumpets, and cried with a loud voice.

Ma1|3|55|And after this Judas ordained captains over the people, even captains over thousands, and over hundreds, and over fifties, and over tens.

Ma1|3|56|But as for such as were building houses, or had betrothed wives, or were planting vineyards, or were fearful, those he commanded that they should return, every man to his own house, according to the law.

Ma1|3|57|So the camp removed, and pitched upon the south side of Emmaus.

Ma1|3|58|And Judas said, arm yourselves, and be valiant men, and see that ye be in readiness against the morning, that ye may fight with these nations, that are assembled together against us to destroy us and our sanctuary:

Ma1|3|59|For it is better for us to die in battle, than to behold the calamities of our people and our sanctuary.

Ma1|3|60|Nevertheless, as the will of אֱלֹהִים is in heaven, so let him do.

Ma1|4|1|Then took Gorgias five thousand footmen, and a thousand of the best horsemen, and removed out of the camp by night;

Ma1|4|2|To the end he might rush in upon the camp of the Jews, and smite them suddenly. And the men of the fortress were his guides.

Ma1|4|3|Now when Judas heard thereof he himself removed, and the valiant men with him, that he might smite the king's army which was at Emmaus,

Ma1|4|4|While as yet the forces were dispersed from the camp.

Ma1|4|5|In the mean season came Gorgias by night into the camp of Judas: and when he found no man there, he sought them in the mountains: for said he, These fellows flee from us

Ma1|4|6|But as soon as it was day, Judas shewed himself in the plain with three thousand men, who nevertheless had neither armour nor swords to their minds.

Ma1|4|7|And they saw the camp of the heathen, that it was strong and well harnessed, and compassed round about with horsemen; and these were expert of war.

Ma1|4|8|Then said Judas to the men that were with him, Fear ye not their multitude, neither be ye afraid of their assault.

Ma1|4|9|Remember how our fathers were delivered in the Red sea, when Pharaoh pursued them with an army.

Ma1|4|10|Now therefore let us cry unto heaven, if peradventure the Lord will have mercy upon us, and remember the covenant of our fathers, and destroy this host before our face this day:

Ma1|4|11|That so all the heathen may know that there is one who delivereth and saveth Israel.

Ma1|4|12|Then the strangers lifted up their eyes, and saw them coming over against them.

Ma1|4|13|Wherefore they went out of the camp to battle; but they that were with Judas sounded their trumpets.

Ma1|4|14|So they joined battle, and the heathen being discomfited fled into the plain.

Ma1|4|15|Howbeit all the hindmost of them were slain with the sword: for they pursued them unto Gazera, and unto the plains of Idumea, and Azotus, and Jamnia, so that there were slain of them upon a three thousand men.

Ma1|4|16|This done, Judas returned again with his host from pursuing them,

Ma1|4|17|And said to the people, Be not greedy of the spoil inasmuch as there is a battle before us,

Ma1|4|18|And Gorgias and his host are here by us in the mountain: but stand ye now against our enemies, and overcome them, and after this ye may boldly take the spoils.

Ma1|4|19|As Judas was yet speaking these words, there appeared a part of them looking out of the mountain:

Ma1|4|20|Who when they perceived that the Jews had put their host to flight and were burning the tents; for the smoke that was seen declared what was done:

Ma1|4|21|When therefore they perceived these things, they were sore afraid, and seeing also the host of Judas in the plain ready to fight,

Ma1|4|22|They fled every one into the land of strangers.

Ma1|4|23|Then Judas returned to spoil the tents, where they got much gold, and silver, and blue silk, and purple of the sea, and great riches.

Ma1|4|24|After this they went home, and sung a song of thanksgiving, and praised the Lord in heaven: because it is good, because his mercy endureth forever.

Ma1|4|25|Thus Israel had a great deliverance that day.

Ma1|4|26|Now all the strangers that had escaped came and told Lysias what had happened:

Ma1|4|27|Who, when he heard thereof, was confounded and discouraged, because neither such things as he would were done unto Israel, nor such things as the king commanded him were come to pass.

Ma1|4|28|The next year therefore following Lysias gathered together threescore thousand choice men of foot, and five thousand horsemen, that he might subdue them.

Ma1|4|29|So they came into Idumea, and pitched their tents at Bethsura, and Judas met them with ten thousand men.

Ma1|4|30|And when he saw that mighty army, he prayed and said, Blessed art thou, O Saviour of Israel, who didst quell the violence of the mighty man by the hand of thy servant David, and gavest the host of strangers into the hands of Jonathan the son of Saul, and his armourbearer;

Ma1|4|31|Shut up this army in the hand of thy people Israel, and let them be confounded in their power and horsemen:

Ma1|4|32|Make them to be of no courage, and cause the boldness of their strength to fall away, and let them quake at their destruction:

Ma1|4|33|Cast them down with the sword of them that love thee, and let all those that know thy name praise thee with thanksgiving.

Ma1|4|34|So they joined battle; and there were slain of the host of Lysias about five thousand men, even before them were they slain.

Ma1|4|35|Now when Lysias saw his army put to flight, and the manliness of Judas' soldiers, and how they were ready either to live or die valiantly, he went into Antiochia, and gathered together a company of strangers, and having made his army greater than it was, he purposed to come again into Judea.

Ma1|4|36|Then said Judas and his brethren, Behold, our enemies are discomfited: let us go up to cleanse and dedicate the sanctuary.

Ma1|4|37|Upon this all the host assembled themselves together, and went up into mount Sion.

Ma1|4|38|And when they saw the sanctuary desolate, and the altar profaned, and the gates burned up, and shrubs growing in the courts as in a forest, or in one of the mountains, yea, and the priests' chambers pulled down;

Ma1|4|39|They rent their clothes, and made great lamentation, and cast ashes upon their heads,

Ma1|4|40|And fell down flat to the ground upon their faces, and blew an alarm with the trumpets, and cried toward heaven.

Ma1|4|41|Then Judas appointed certain men to fight against those that were in the fortress, until he had cleansed the sanctuary.

Ma1|4|42|So he chose priests of blameless conversation, such as had pleasure in the law:

Ma1|4|43|Who cleansed the sanctuary, and bare out the defiled stones into an unclean place.

Ma1|4|44|And when as they consulted what to do with the altar of burnt offerings, which was profaned;

Ma1|4|45|They thought it best to pull it down, lest it should be a reproach to them, because the heathen had defiled it: wherefore they pulled it down,

Ma1|4|46|And laid up the stones in the mountain of the temple in a convenient place, until there should come a prophet to shew what should be done with them.

Ma1|4|47|Then they took whole stones according to the law, and built a new altar according to the former;

Ma1|4|48|And made up the sanctuary, and the things that were within the temple, and hallowed the courts.

Ma1|4|49|They made also new holy vessels, and into the temple they brought the candlestick, and the altar of burnt offerings, and of incense, and the table.

Ma1|4|50|And upon the altar they burned incense, and the lamps that were upon the candlestick they lighted, that they might give light in the temple.

Ma1|4|51|Furthermore they set the loaves upon the table, and spread out the veils, and finished all the works which they had begun to make.

Ma1|4|52|Now on the five and twentieth day of the ninth month, which is called the month Casleu, in the hundred forty and eighth year, they rose up betimes in the morning,

Ma1|4|53|And offered sacrifice according to the law upon the new altar of burnt offerings, which they had made.

Ma1|4|54|Look, at what time and what day the heathen had profaned it, even in that was it dedicated with songs, and citherns, and harps, and cymbals.

Ma1|4|55|Then all the people fell upon their faces, worshipping and praising the אֱלֹהִים of heaven, who had given them good success.

Ma1|4|56|And so they kept the dedication of the altar eight days and offered burnt offerings with gladness, and sacrificed the sacrifice of deliverance and praise.

Ma1|4|57|They decked also the forefront of the temple with crowns of gold, and with shields; and the gates and the chambers they renewed, and hanged doors upon them.

Ma1|4|58|Thus was there very great gladness among the people, for that the reproach of the heathen was put away.

Ma1|4|59|Moreover Judas and his brethren with the whole congregation of Israel ordained, that the days of the dedication of the altar should be kept in their season from year to year by the space of eight days, from the five and twentieth day of the month Casleu, with mirth and gladness.

Ma1|4|60|At that time also they builded up the mount Sion with high walls and strong towers round about, lest the Gentiles should come and tread it down as they had done before.

Ma1|4|61|And they set there a garrison to keep it, and fortified Bethsura to preserve it; that the people might have a defence against Idumea.

Ma1|5|1|Now when the nations round about heard that the altar was built and the sanctuary renewed as before, it displeased them very much.

Ma1|5|2|Wherefore they thought to destroy the generation of Jacob that was among them, and thereupon they began to slay and destroy the people.

Ma1|5|3|Then Judas fought against the children of Esau in Idumea at Arabattine, because they besieged Gael: and he gave them a great overthrow, and abated their courage, and took their spoils.

Ma1|5|4|Also he remembered the injury of the children of Bean, who had been a snare and an offence unto the people, in that they lay in wait for them in the ways.

Ma1|5|5|He shut them up therefore in the towers, and encamped against them, and destroyed them utterly, and burned the towers of that place with fire, and all that were therein.

Ma1|5|6|Afterward he passed over to the children of Ammon, where he found a mighty power, and much people, with Timotheus their captain.

Ma1|5|7|So he fought many battles with them, till at length they were discomfited before him; and he smote them.

Ma1|5|8|And when he had taken Jazar, with the towns belonging thereto, he returned into Judea.

Ma1|5|9|Then the heathen that were at Galaad assembled themselves together against the Israelites that were in their quarters, to destroy them; but they fled to the fortress of Dathema.

Ma1|5|10|And sent letters unto Judas and his brethren, The heathen that are round about us are assembled together against us to destroy us:

Ma1|5|11|And they are preparing to come and take the fortress whereunto we are fled, Timotheus being captain of their host.

Ma1|5|12|Come now therefore, and deliver us from their hands, for many of us are slain:

Ma1|5|13|Yea, all our brethren that were in the places of Tobie are put to death: their wives and their children also they have carried away captives, and borne away their stuff; and they have destroyed there about a thousand men.

Ma1|5|14|While these letters were yet reading, behold, there came other messengers from Galilee with their clothes rent, who reported on this wise,

Ma1|5|15|And said, They of Ptolemais, and of Tyrus, and Sidon, and all Galilee of the Gentiles, are assembled together against us to consume us.

Ma1|5|16|Now when Judas and the people heard these words, there assembled a great congregation together, to consult what they should do for their brethren, that were in trouble, and assaulted of them.

Ma1|5|17|Then said Judas unto Simon his brother, Choose thee out men, and go and deliver thy brethren that are in Galilee, for I and Jonathan my brother will go into the country of Galaad.

Ma1|5|18|So he left Joseph the son of Zacharias, and Azarias, captains of the people, with the remnant of the host in Judea to keep it.

Ma1|5|19|Unto whom he gave commandment, saying, Take ye the charge of this people, and see that ye make not war against the heathen until the time that we come again.

Ma1|5|20|Now unto Simon were given three thousand men to go into Galilee, and unto Judas eight thousand men for the country of Galaad.

Ma1|5|21|Then went Simon into Galilee, where he fought many battles with the heathen, so that the heathen were discomfited by him.

Ma1|5|22|And he pursued them unto the gate of Ptolemais; and there were slain of the heathen about three thousand men, whose spoils he took.

Ma1|5|23|And those that were in Galilee, and in Arbattis, with their wives and their children, and all that they had, took he away with him, and brought them into Judea with great joy.

Ma1|5|24|Judas Maccabeus also and his brother Jonathan went over Jordan, and travelled three days' journey in the wilderness,

Ma1|5|25|Where they met with the Nabathites, who came unto them in a peaceable manner, and told them every thing that had happened to their brethren in the land of Galaad:

Ma1|5|26|And how that many of them were shut up in Bosora, and Bosor, and Alema, Casphor, Maked, and Carnaim; all these cities are strong and great:

Ma1|5|27|And that they were shut up in the rest of the cities of the country of Galaad, and that against to morrow they had appointed to bring their host against the forts, and to take them, and to destroy them all in one day.

Ma1|5|28|Hereupon Judas and his host turned suddenly by the way of the wilderness unto Bosora; and when he had won the city, he slew all the males with the edge of the sword, and took all their spoils, and burned the city with fire,

Ma1|5|29|From whence he removed by night, and went till he came to the fortress.

Ma1|5|30|And betimes in the morning they looked up, and, behold, there was an innumerable people bearing ladders and other engines of war, to take the fortress: for they assaulted them.

Ma1|5|31|When Judas therefore saw that the battle was begun, and that the cry of the city went up to heaven, with trumpets, and a great sound,

Ma1|5|32|He said unto his host, Fight this day for your brethren.

Ma1|5|33|So he went forth behind them in three companies, who sounded their trumpets, and cried with prayer.

Ma1|5|34|Then the host of Timotheus, knowing that it was Maccabeus, fled from him: wherefore he smote them with a great slaughter; so that there were killed of them that day about eight thousand men.

Ma1|5|35|This done, Judas turned aside to Maspha; and after he had assaulted it he took and slew all the males therein, and received the spoils thereof and and burnt it with fire.

Ma1|5|36|From thence went he, and took Casphon, Maged, Bosor, and the other cities of the country of Galaad.

Ma1|5|37|After these things gathered Timotheus another host and encamped against Raphon beyond the brook.

Ma1|5|38|So Judas sent men to espy the host, who brought him word, saying, All the heathen that be round about us are assembled unto them, even a very great host.

Ma1|5|39|He hath also hired the Arabians to help them and they have pitched their tents beyond the brook, ready to come and fight against thee. Upon this Judas went to meet them.

Ma1|5|40|Then Timotheus said unto the captains of his host, When Judas and his host come near the brook, if he pass over first unto us, we shall not be able to withstand him; for he will mightily prevail against us:

Ma1|5|41|But if he be afraid, and camp beyond the river, we shall go over unto him, and prevail against him.

Ma1|5|42|Now when Judas came near the brook, he caused the scribes of the people to remain by the brook: unto whom he gave commandment, saying, Suffer no man to remain in the camp, but let all come to the battle.

Ma1|5|43|So he went first over unto them, and all the people after him: then all the heathen, being discomfited before him, cast away their weapons, and fled unto the temple that was at Carnaim.

Ma1|5|44|But they took the city, and burned the temple with all that were therein. Thus was Carnaim subdued, neither could they stand any longer before Judas.

Ma1|5|45|Then Judas gathered together all the Israelites that were in the country of Galaad, from the least unto the greatest, even their wives, and their children, and their stuff, a very great host, to the end they might come into the land of Judea.

Ma1|5|46|Now when they came unto Ephron, (this was a great city in the way as they should go, very well fortified) they could not turn from it, either on the right hand or the left, but must needs pass through the midst of it.

Ma1|5|47|Then they of the city shut them out, and stopped up the gates with stones.

Ma1|5|48|Whereupon Judas sent unto them in peaceable manner, saying, Let us pass through your land to go into our own country, and none shall do you any hurt; we will only pass through on foot: howbeit they would not open unto him.

Ma1|5|49|Wherefore Judas commanded a proclamation to be made throughout the host, that every man should pitch his tent in the place where he was.

Ma1|5|50|So the soldiers pitched, and assaulted the city all that day and all that night, till at the length the city was delivered into his hands:

Ma1|5|51|Who then slew all the males with the edge of the sword, and rased the city, and took the spoils thereof, and passed through the city over them that were slain.

Ma1|5|52|After this went they over Jordan into the great plain before Bethsan.

Ma1|5|53|And Judas gathered together those that came behind, and exhorted the people all the way through, till they came into the land of Judea.

Ma1|5|54|So they went up to mount Sion with joy and gladness, where they offered burnt offerings, because not one of them were slain until they had returned in peace.

Ma1|5|55|Now what time as Judas and Jonathan were in the land of Galaad, and Simon his brother in Galilee before Ptolemais,

Ma1|5|56|Joseph the son of Zacharias, and Azarias, captains of the garrisons, heard of the valiant acts and warlike deeds which they had done.

Ma1|5|57|Wherefore they said, Let us also get us a name, and go fight against the heathen that are round about us.

Ma1|5|58|So when they had given charge unto the garrison that was with them, they went toward Jamnia.

Ma1|5|59|Then came Gorgias and his men out of the city to fight against them.

Ma1|5|60|And so it was, that Joseph and Azaras were put to flight, and pursued unto the borders of Judea: and there were slain that day of the people of Israel about two thousand men.

Ma1|5|61|Thus was there a great overthrow among the children of Israel, because they were not obedient unto Judas and his brethren, but thought to do some valiant act.

Ma1|5|62|Moreover these men came not of the seed of those, by whose hand deliverance was given unto Israel.

Ma1|5|63|Howbeit the man Judas and his brethren were greatly renowned in the sight of all Israel, and of all the heathen, wheresoever their name was heard of;

Ma1|5|64|Insomuch as the the people assembled unto them with joyful acclamations.

Ma1|5|65|Afterward went Judas forth with his brethren, and fought against the children of Esau in the land toward the south, where he smote Hebron, and the towns thereof, and pulled down the fortress of it, and burned the towers thereof round about.

Ma1|5|66|From thence he removed to go into the land of the Philistines, and passed through Samaria.

Ma1|5|67|At that time certain priests, desirous to shew their valour, were slain in battle, for that they went out to fight unadvisedly.

Ma1|5|68|So Judas turned to Azotus in the land of the Philistines, and when he had pulled down their altars, and burned their carved images with fire, and spoiled their cities, he returned into the land of Judea.

Ma1|6|1|About that time king Antiochus travelling through the high countries heard say, that Elymais in the country of Persia was a city greatly renowned for riches, silver, and gold;

Ma1|6|2|And that there was in it a very rich temple, wherein were coverings of gold, and breastplates, and shields, which Alexander, son of Philip, the Macedonian king, who reigned first among the Grecians, had left there.

Ma1|6|3|Wherefore he came and sought to take the city, and to spoil it; but he was not able, because they of the city, having had warning thereof,

Ma1|6|4|Rose up against him in battle: so he fled, and departed thence with great heaviness, and returned to Babylon.

Ma1|6|5|Moreover there came one who brought him tidings into Persia, that the armies, which went against the land of Judea, were put to flight:

Ma1|6|6|And that Lysias, who went forth first with a great power was driven away of the Jews; and that they were made strong by the armour, and power, and store of spoils, which they had gotten of the armies, whom they had destroyed:

Ma1|6|7|Also that they had pulled down the abomination, which he had set up upon the altar in Jerusalem, and that they had compassed about the sanctuary with high walls, as before, and his city Bethsura.

Ma1|6|8|Now when the king heard these words, he was astonished and sore moved: whereupon he laid him down upon his bed, and fell sick for grief, because it had not befallen him as he looked for.

Ma1|6|9|And there he continued many days: for his grief was ever more and more, and he made account that he should die.

Ma1|6|10|Wherefore he called for all his friends, and said unto them, The sleep is gone from mine eyes, and my heart faileth for very care.

Ma1|6|11|And I thought with myself, Into what tribulation am I come, and how great a flood of misery is it, wherein now I am! for I was bountiful and beloved in my power.

Ma1|6|12|But now I remember the evils that I did at Jerusalem, and that I took all the vessels of gold and silver that were therein, and sent to destroy the inhabitants of Judea without a cause.

Ma1|6|13|I perceive therefore that for this cause these troubles are come upon me, and, behold, I perish through great grief in a strange land.

Ma1|6|14|Then called he for Philip, one of his friends, who he made ruler over all his realm,

Ma1|6|15|And gave him the crown, and his robe, and his signet, to the end he should bring up his son Antiochus, and nourish him up for the kingdom.

Ma1|6|16|So king Antiochus died there in the hundred forty and ninth year.

Ma1|6|17|Now when Lysias knew that the king was dead, he set up Antiochus his son, whom he had brought up being young, to reign in his stead, and his name he called Eupator.

Ma1|6|18|About this time they that were in the tower shut up the Israelites round about the sanctuary, and sought always their hurt, and the strengthening of the heathen.

Ma1|6|19|Wherefore Judas, purposing to destroy them, called all the people together to besiege them.

Ma1|6|20|So they came together, and besieged them in the hundred and fiftieth year, and he made mounts for shot against them, and other engines.

Ma1|6|21|Howbeit certain of them that were besieged got forth, unto whom some ungodly men of Israel joined themselves:

Ma1|6|22|And they went unto the king, and said, How long will it be ere thou execute judgment, and avenge our brethren?

Ma1|6|23|We have been willing to serve thy father, and to do as he would have us, and to obey his commandments;

Ma1|6|24|For which cause they of our nation besiege the tower, and are alienated from us: moreover as many of us as they could light on they slew, and spoiled our inheritance.

Ma1|6|25|Neither have they stretched out their hand against us only, but also against their borders.

Ma1|6|26|And, behold, this day are they besieging the tower at Jerusalem, to take it: the sanctuary also and Bethsura have they fortified.

Ma1|6|27|Wherefore if thou dost not prevent them quickly, they will do the greater things than these, neither shalt thou be able to rule them.

Ma1|6|28|Now when the king heard this, he was angry, and gathered together all his friends, and the captains of his army, and those that had charge of the horse.

Ma1|6|29|There came also unto him from other kingdoms, and from isles of the sea, bands of hired soldiers.

Ma1|6|30|So that the number of his army was an hundred thousand footmen, and twenty thousand horsemen, and two and thirty elephants exercised in battle.

Ma1|6|31|These went through Idumea, and pitched against Bethsura, which they assaulted many days, making engines of war; but they of Bethsura came out, and burned them with fire, and fought valiantly.

Ma1|6|32|Upon this Judas removed from the tower, and pitched in Bathzacharias, over against the king's camp.

Ma1|6|33|Then the king rising very early marched fiercely with his host toward Bathzacharias, where his armies made them ready to battle, and sounded the trumpets.

Ma1|6|34|And to the end they might provoke the elephants to fight, they shewed them the blood of grapes and mulberries.

Ma1|6|35|Moreover they divided the beasts among the armies, and for every elephant they appointed a thousand men, armed with coats of mail, and with helmets of brass on their heads; and beside this, for every beast were ordained five hundred horsemen of the best.

Ma1|6|36|These were ready at every occasion: wheresoever the beast was, and whithersoever the beast went, they went also, neither departed they from him.

Ma1|6|37|And upon the beasts were there strong towers of wood, which covered every one of them, and were girt fast unto them with devices: there were also upon every one two and thirty strong men, that fought upon them, beside the Indian that ruled him.

Ma1|6|38|As for the remnant of the horsemen, they set them on this side and that side at the two parts of the host giving them signs what to do, and being harnessed all over amidst the ranks.

Ma1|6|39|Now when the sun shone upon the shields of gold and brass, the mountains glistered therewith, and shined like lamps of fire.

Ma1|6|40|So part of the king's army being spread upon the high mountains, and part on the valleys below, they marched on safely and in order.

Ma1|6|41|Wherefore all that heard the noise of their multitude, and the marching of the company, and the rattling of the harness, were moved: for the army was very great and mighty.

Ma1|6|42|Then Judas and his host drew near, and entered into battle, and there were slain of the king's army six hundred men.

Ma1|6|43|Eleazar also, surnamed Savaran, perceiving that one of the beasts, armed with royal harness, was higher than all the rest, and supposing that the king was upon him,

Ma1|6|44|Put himself in jeopardy, to the end he might deliver his people, and get him a perpetual name:

Ma1|6|45|Wherefore he ran upon him courageously through the midst of the battle, slaying on the right hand and on the left, so that they were divided from him on both sides.

Ma1|6|46|Which done, he crept under the elephant, and thrust him under, and slew him: whereupon the elephant fell down upon him, and there he died.

Ma1|6|47|Howbeit the rest of the Jews seeing the strength of the king, and the violence of his forces, turned away from them.

Ma1|6|48|Then the king's army went up to Jerusalem to meet them, and the king pitched his tents against

Judea, and against mount Sion.

Mal|6|49|But with them that were in Bethsura he made peace: for they came out of the city, because they had no victuals there to endure the siege, it being a year of rest to the land.

Mal|6|50|So the king took Bethsura, and set a garrison there to keep it.

Mal|6|51|As for the sanctuary, he besieged it many days: and set there artillery with engines and instruments to cast fire and stones, and pieces to cast darts and slings.

Mal|6|52|Whereupon they also made engines against their engines, and held them battle a long season.

Mal|6|53|Yet at the last, their vessels being without victuals, (for that it was the seventh year, and they in Judea that were delivered from the Gentiles, had eaten up the residue of the store;)

Mal|6|54|There were but a few left in the sanctuary, because the famine did so prevail against them, that they were fain to disperse themselves, every man to his own place.

Mal|6|55|At that time Lysias heard say, that Philip, whom Antiochus the king, whiles he lived, had appointed to bring up his son Antiochus, that he might be king,

Mal|6|56|Was returned out of Persia and Media, and the king's host also that went with him, and that he sought to take unto him the ruling of the affairs.

Mal|6|57|Wherefore he went in all haste, and said to the king and the captains of the host and the company, We decay daily, and our victuals are but small, and the place we lay siege unto is strong, and the affairs of the kingdom lie upon us:

Mal|6|58|Now therefore let us be friends with these men, and make peace with them, and with all their nation;

Mal|6|59|And covenant with them, that they shall live after their laws, as they did before: for they are therefore displeased, and have done all these things, because we abolished their laws.

Mal|6|60|So the king and the princes were content: wherefore he sent unto them to make peace; and they accepted thereof.

Mal|6|61|Also the king and the princes made an oath unto them: whereupon they went out of the strong hold.

Mal|6|62|Then the king entered into mount Sion; but when he saw the strength of the place, he broke his oath that he had made, and gave commandment to pull down the wall round about.

Mal|6|63|Afterward departed he in all haste, and returned unto Antiochia, where he found Philip to be master of the city: so he fought against him, and took the city by force.

Mal|7|1|In the hundred and one and fiftieth year Demetrius the son of Seleucus departed from Rome, and came up with a few men unto a city of the sea coast, and reigned there.

Mal|7|2|And as he entered into the palace of his ancestors, so it was, that his forces had taken Antiochus and Lysias, to bring them unto him.

Mal|7|3|Wherefore, when he knew it, he said, Let me not see their faces.

Mal|7|4|So his host slew them. Now when Demetrius was set upon the throne of his kingdom,

Mal|7|5|There came unto him all the wicked and ungodly men of Israel, having Alcimus, who was desirous to be high priest, for their captain:

Mal|7|6|And they accused the people to the king, saying, Judas and his brethren have slain all thy friends, and driven us out of our own land.

Mal|7|7|Now therefore send some man whom thou trustest, and let him go and see what havock he hath made among us, and in the king's land, and let him punish them with all them that aid them.

Mal|7|8|Then the king chose Bacchides, a friend of the king, who ruled beyond the flood, and was a great man in the kingdom, and faithful to the king,

Mal|7|9|And him he sent with that wicked Alcimus, whom he made high priest, and commanded that he should take vengeance of the children of Israel.

Mal|7|10|So they departed, and came with a great power into the land of Judea, where they sent messengers to Judas and his brethren with peaceable words deceitfully.

Mal|7|11|But they gave no heed to their words; for they saw that they were come with a great power.

Mal|7|12|Then did there assemble unto Alcimus and Bacchides a company of scribes, to require justice.

Mal|7|13|Now the Assideans were the first among the children of Israel that sought peace of them:

Mal|7|14|For said they, One that is a priest of the seed of Aaron is come with this army, and he will do us no wrong.

Mal|7|15|So he spake unto them, peaceably, and sware unto them, saying, we will procure the harm neither of you nor your friends.

Mal|7|16|Whereupon they believed him: howbeit he took of them threescore men, and slew them in one day, according to the words which he wrote,

Ma1|7|17|The flesh of thy saints have they cast out, and their blood have they shed round about Jerusalem, and there was none to bury them.

Ma1|7|18|Wherefore the fear and dread of them fell upon all the people, who said, There is neither truth nor righteousness in them; for they have broken the covenant and oath that they made.

Ma1|7|19|After this, removed Bacchides from Jerusalem, and pitched his tents in Bezeth, where he sent and took many of the men that had forsaken him, and certain of the people also, and when he had slain them, he cast them into the great pit.

Ma1|7|20|Then committed he the country to Alcimus, and left with him a power to aid him: so Bacchides went to the king.

Ma1|7|21|But Alcimus contended for the high priesthood.

Ma1|7|22|And unto him resorted all such as troubled the people, who, after they had gotten the land of Juda into their power, did much hurt in Israel.

Ma1|7|23|Now when Judas saw all the mischief that Alcimus and his company had done among the Israelites, even above the heathen,

Ma1|7|24|He went out into all the coasts of Judea round about, and took vengeance of them that had revolted from him, so that they durst no more go forth into the country.

Ma1|7|25|On the other side, when Alcimus saw that Judas and his company had gotten the upper hand, and knew that he was not able to abide their force, he went again to the king, and said all the worst of them that he could.

Ma1|7|26|Then the king sent Nicanor, one of his honourable princes, a man that bare deadly hate unto Israel, with commandment to destroy the people.

Ma1|7|27|So Nicanor came to Jerusalem with a great force; and sent unto Judas and his brethren deceitfully with friendly words, saying,

Ma1|7|28|Let there be no battle between me and you; I will come with a few men, that I may see you in peace.

Ma1|7|29|He came therefore to Judas, and they saluted one another peaceably. Howbeit the enemies were prepared to take away Judas by violence.

Ma1|7|30|Which thing after it was known to Judas, to wit, that he came unto him with deceit, he was sore afraid of him, and would see his face no more.

Ma1|7|31|Nicanor also, when he saw that his counsel was discovered, went out to fight against Judas beside Capharsalama:

Ma1|7|32|Where there were slain of Nicanor's side about five thousand men, and the rest fled into the city of David.

Ma1|7|33|After this went Nicanor up to mount Sion, and there came out of the sanctuary certain of the priests and certain of the elders of the people, to salute him peaceably, and to shew him the burnt sacrifice that was offered for the king.

Ma1|7|34|But he mocked them, and laughed at them, and abused them shamefully, and spake proudly,

Ma1|7|35|And sware in his wrath, saying, Unless Judas and his host be now delivered into my hands, if ever I come again in safety, I will burn up this house: and with that he went out in a great rage.

Ma1|7|36|Then the priests entered in, and stood before the altar and the temple, weeping, and saying,

Ma1|7|37|Thou, O Lord, didst choose this house to be called by thy name, and to be a house of prayer and petition for thy people:

Ma1|7|38|Be avenged of this man and his host, and let them fall by the sword: remember their blasphemies, and suffer them not to continue any longer.

Ma1|7|39|So Nicanor went out of Jerusalem, and pitched his tents in Bethhoron, where an host out of Syria met him.

Ma1|7|40|But Judas pitched in Adasa with three thousand men, and there he prayed, saying,

Ma1|7|41|O Lord, when they that were sent from the king of the Assyrians blasphemed, thine angel went out, and smote an hundred fourscore and five thousand of them.

Ma1|7|42|Even so destroy thou this host before us this day, that the rest may know that he hath spoken blasphemously against thy sanctuary, and judge thou him according to his wickedness.

Ma1|7|43|So the thirteenth day of the month Adar the hosts joined battle: but Nicanor's host was discomfited, and he himself was first slain in the battle.

Ma1|7|44|Now when Nicanor's host saw that he was slain, they cast away their weapons, and fled.

Ma1|7|45|Then they pursued after them a day's journey, from Adasa unto Gazera, sounding an alarm after them with their trumpets.

Ma1|7|46|Whereupon they came forth out of all the towns of Judea round about, and closed them in; so that they, turning back upon them that pursued them, were all slain with the sword, and not one of them was left.

Ma1|7|47|Afterwards they took the spoils, and the prey, and smote off Nicanors head, and his right hand, which he stretched out so proudly, and brought them away, and hanged them up toward Jerusalem.

Ma1|7|48|For this cause the people rejoiced greatly, and they kept that day a day of great gladness.

Ma1|7|49|Moreover they ordained to keep yearly this day, being the thirteenth of Adar.

Ma1|7|50|Thus the land of Juda was in rest a little while.

Ma1|8|1|Now Judas had heard of the the Romans, that they were mighty and valiant men, and such as would lovingly accept all that joined themselves unto them, and make a league of amity with all that came unto them;

Ma1|8|2|And that they were men of great valour. It was told him also of their wars and noble acts which they had done among the Galatians, and how they had conquered them, and brought them under tribute;

Ma1|8|3|And what they had done in the country of Spain, for the winning of the mines of the silver and gold which is there;

Ma1|8|4|And that by their policy and patience they had conquered all the place, though it were very far from them; and the kings also that came against them from the uttermost part of the earth, till they had discomfited them, and given them a great overthrow, so that the rest did give them tribute every year:

Ma1|8|5|Beside this, how they had discomfited in battle Philip, and Perseus, king of the Citims, with others that lifted up themselves against them, and had overcome them:

Ma1|8|6|How also Antiochus the great king of Asia, that came against them in battle, having an hundred and twenty elephants, with horsemen, and chariots, and a very great army, was discomfited by them;

Ma1|8|7|And how they took him alive, and covenanted that he and such as reigned after him should pay a great tribute, and give hostages, and that which was agreed upon,

Ma1|8|8|And the country of India, and Media and Lydia and of the goodliest countries, which they took of him, and gave to king Eumenes:

Ma1|8|9|Moreover how the Grecians had determined to come and destroy them;

Ma1|8|10|And that they, having knowledge thereof sent against them a certain captain, and fighting with them slew many of them, and carried away captives their wives and their children, and spoiled them, and took possession of their lands, and pulled down their strong holds, and brought them to be their servants unto this day:

Ma1|8|11|It was told him besides, how they destroyed and brought under their dominion all other kingdoms and isles that at any time resisted them;

Ma1|8|12|But with their friends and such as relied upon them they kept amity: and that they had conquered kingdoms both far and nigh, insomuch as all that heard of their name were afraid of them:

Ma1|8|13|Also that, whom they would help to a kingdom, those reign; and whom again they would, they displace: finally, that they were greatly exalted:

Ma1|8|14|Yet for all this none of them wore a crown or was clothed in purple, to be magnified thereby:

Ma1|8|15|Moreover how they had made for themselves a senate house, wherein three hundred and twenty men sat in council daily, consulting alway for the people, to the end they might be well ordered:

Ma1|8|16|And that they committed their government to one man every year, who ruled over all their country, and that all were obedient to that one, and that there was neither envy nor emmulation among them.

Ma1|8|17|In consideration of these things, Judas chose Eupolemus the son of John, the son of Accos, and Jason the son of Eleazar, and sent them to Rome, to make a league of amity and confederacy with them,

Ma1|8|18|And to intreat them that they would take the yoke from them; for they saw that the kingdom of the Grecians did oppress Israel with servitude.

Ma1|8|19|They went therefore to Rome, which was a very great journey, and came into the senate, where they spake and said.

Ma1|8|20|Judas Maccabeus with his brethren, and the people of the Jews, have sent us unto you, to make a confederacy and peace with you, and that we might be registered your confederates and friends.

Ma1|8|21|So that matter pleased the Romans well.

Ma1|8|22|And this is the copy of the epistle which the senate wrote back again in tables of brass, and sent to Jerusalem, that there they might have by them a memorial of peace and confederacy:

Ma1|8|23|Good success be to the Romans, and to the people of the Jews, by sea and by land for ever: the sword also and enemy be far from them,

Ma1|8|24|If there come first any war upon the Romans or any of their confederates throughout all their dominion,

Ma1|8|25|The people of the Jews shall help them, as the time shall be appointed, with all their heart:

Ma1|8|26|Neither shall they give any thing unto them that make war upon them, or aid them with victuals, weapons, money, or ships, as it hath seemed good unto the Romans; but they shall keep their covenants without taking any thing therefore.

Ma1|8|27|In the same manner also, if war come first upon the nation of the Jews, the Romans shall help them with all their heart, according as the time shall be appointed them:

Ma1|8|28|Neither shall victuals be given to them that take part against them, or weapons, or money, or ships, as it hath seemed good to the Romans; but they shall keep their covenants, and that without deceit.

Ma1|8|29|According to these articles did the Romans make a covenant with the people of the Jews.

Ma1|8|30|Howbeit if hereafter the one party or the other shall think to meet to add or diminish any thing, they may do it at their pleasures, and whatsoever they shall add or take away shall be ratified.

Ma1|8|31|And as touching the evils that Demetrius doeth to the Jews, we have written unto him, saying, Wherefore thou made thy yoke heavy upon our friends and confederates the Jews?

Ma1|8|32|If therefore they complain any more against thee, we will do them justice, and fight with thee by sea and by land.

Ma1|9|1|Furthermore, when Demetrius heard the Nicanor and his host were slain in battle, he sent Bacchides and Alcimus into the land of Judea the second time, and with them the chief strength of his host:

Ma1|9|2|Who went forth by the way that leadeth to Galgala, and pitched their tents before Masaloth, which is in Arbela, and after they had won it, they slew much people.

Ma1|9|3|Also the first month of the hundred fifty and second year they encamped before Jerusalem:

Ma1|9|4|From whence they removed, and went to Berea, with twenty thousand footmen and two thousand horsemen.

Ma1|9|5|Now Judas had pitched his tents at Eleasa, and three thousand chosen men with him:

Ma1|9|6|Who seeing the multitude of the other army to he so great were sore afraid; whereupon many conveyed themselves out of the host, insomuch as abode of them no more but eight hundred men.

Ma1|9|7|When Judas therefore saw that his host slipt away, and that the battle pressed upon him, he was sore troubled in mind, and much distressed, for that he had no time to gather them together.

Ma1|9|8|Nevertheless unto them that remained he said, Let us arise and go up against our enemies, if peradventure we may be able to fight with them.

Ma1|9|9|But they dehorted him, saying, We shall never be able: let us now rather save our lives, and hereafter we will return with our brethren, and fight against them: for we are but few.

Ma1|9|10|Then Judas said, אֱלֹהִים forbid that I should do this thing, and flee away from them: if our time be come, let us die manfully for our brethren, and let us not stain our honour.

Ma1|9|11|With that the host of Bacchides removed out of their tents, and stood over against them, their horsemen being divided into two troops, and their slingers and archers going before the host and they that marched in the foreward were all mighty men.

Ma1|9|12|As for Bacchides, he was in the right wing: so the host drew near on the two parts, and sounded their trumpets.

Ma1|9|13|They also of Judas' side, even they sounded their trumpets also, so that the earth shook at the noise of the armies, and the battle continued from morning till night.

Ma1|9|14|Now when Judas perceived that Bacchides and the strength of his army were on the right side, he took with him all the hardy men,

Ma1|9|15|Who discomfited the right wing, and pursued them unto the mount Azotus.

Ma1|9|16|But when they of the left wing saw that they of the right wing were discomfited, they followed upon Judas and those that were with him hard at the heels from behind:

Ma1|9|17|Whereupon there was a sore battle, insomuch as many were slain on both parts.

Ma1|9|18|Judas also was killed, and the remnant fled.

Ma1|9|19|THen Jonathan and Simon took Judas their brother, and buried him in the sepulchre of his fathers in Modin.

Ma1|9|20|Moreover they bewailed him, and all Israel made great lamentation for him, and mourned many days, saying,

Ma1|9|21|How is the valiant man fallen, that delivered Israel!

Ma1|9|22|As for the other things concerning Judas and his wars, and the noble acts which he did, and his greatness, they are not written: for they were very many.

Ma1|9|23|Now after the death of Judas the wicked began to put forth their heads in all the coasts of Israel, and there arose up all such as wrought iniquity.

Ma1|9|24|In those days also was there a very great famine, by reason whereof the country revolted, and went with them.

Ma1|9|25|Then Bacchides chose the wicked men, and made them lords of the country.

Ma1|9|26|And they made enquiry and search for Judas' friends, and brought them unto Bacchides, who took vengeance of them, and used them despitefully.

Ma1|9|27|So was there a great affliction in Israel, the like whereof was not since the time that a prophet was not seen among them.

Ma1|9|28|For this cause all Judas' friends came together, and said unto Jonathan,

Ma1|9|29|Since thy brother Judas died, we have no man like him to go forth against our enemies, and Bacchides, and against them of our nation that are adversaries to us.

Ma1|9|30|Now therefore we have chosen thee this day to be our prince and captain in his stead, that thou mayest fight our battles.

Ma1|9|31|Upon this Jonathan took the governance upon him at that time, and rose up instead of his brother Judas.

Ma1|9|32|But when Bacchides gat knowledge thereof, he sought for to slay him

Ma1|9|33|Then Jonathan, and Simon his brother, and all that were with him, perceiving that, fled into the wilderness of Thecoe, and pitched their tents by the water of the pool Asphar.

Ma1|9|34|Which when Bacchides understood, he came near to Jordan with all his host upon the sabbath day.

Ma1|9|35|Now Jonathan had sent his brother John, a captain of the people, to pray his friends the Nabathites, that they might leave with them their carriage, which was much.

Ma1|9|36|But the children of Jambri came out of Medaba, and took John, and all that he had, and went their way with it.

Ma1|9|37|After this came word to Jonathan and Simon his brother, that the children of Jambri made a great marriage, and were bringing the bride from Nadabatha with a great train, as being the daughter of one of the great princes of Chanaan.

Ma1|9|38|Therefore they remembered John their brother, and went up, and hid themselves under the covert of the mountain:

Ma1|9|39|Where they lifted up their eyes, and looked, and, behold, there was much ado and great carriage: and the bridegroom came forth, and his friends and brethren, to meet them with drums, and instruments of musick, and many weapons.

Ma1|9|40|Then Jonathan and they that were with him rose up against them from the place where they lay in ambush, and made a slaughter of them in such sort, as many fell down dead, and the remnant fled into the mountain, and they took all their spoils.

Ma1|9|41|Thus was the marriage turned into mourning, and the noise of their melody into lamentation.

Ma1|9|42|So when they had avenged fully the blood of their brother, they turned again to the marsh of Jordan.

Ma1|9|43|Now when Bacchides heard hereof, he came on the sabbath day unto the banks of Jordan with a great power.

Ma1|9|44|Then Jonathan said to his company, Let us go up now and fight for our lives, for it standeth not with us to day, as in time past:

Ma1|9|45|For, behold, the battle is before us and behind us, and the water of Jordan on this side and that side, the marsh likewise and wood, neither is there place for us to turn aside.

Ma1|9|46|Wherefore cry ye now unto heaven, that ye may be delivered from the hand of your enemies.

Ma1|9|47|With that they joined battle, and Jonathan stretched forth his hand to smite Bacchides, but he turned back from him.

Ma1|9|48|Then Jonathan and they that were with him leapt into Jordan, and swam over unto the other bank: howbeit the other passed not over Jordan unto them.

Ma1|9|49|So there were slain of Bacchides' side that day about a thousand men.

Ma1|9|50|Afterward returned Bacchides to Jerusalem and repaired the strong cites in Judea; the fort in Jericho, and Emmaus, and Bethhoron, and Bethel, and Thamnatha, Pharathoni, and Taphon, these did he strengthen with high walls, with gates and with bars.

Ma1|9|51|And in them he set a garrison, that they might work malice upon Israel.

Ma1|9|52|He fortified also the city Bethsura, and Gazera, and the tower, and put forces in them, and provision of victuals.

Ma1|9|53|Besides, he took the chief men's sons in the country for hostages, and put them into the tower at Jerusalem to be kept.

Ma1|9|54|Moreover in the hundred fifty and third year, in the second month, Alcimus commanded that the wall of the inner court of the sanctuary should be pulled down; he pulled down also the works of the prophets

Ma1|9|55|And as he began to pull down, even at that time was Alcimus plagued, and his enterprizes hindered: for his mouth was stopped, and he was taken with a palsy, so that he could no more speak any thing, nor give order concerning his house.

Ma1|9|56|So Alcimus died at that time with great torment.

Ma1|9|57|Now when Bacchides saw that Alcimus was dead, he returned to the king: whereupon the land of Judea was in rest two years.

Ma1|9|58|Then all the ungodly men held a council, saying, Behold, Jonathan and his company are at ease, and dwell without care: now therefore we will bring Bacchides hither, who shall take them all in one night.

Ma1|9|59|So they went and consulted with him.

Ma1|9|60|Then removed he, and came with a great host, and sent letters privily to his adherents in Judea, that they should take Jonathan and those that were with him: howbeit they could not, because their counsel was known unto them.

Ma1|9|61|Wherefore they took of the men of the country, that were authors of that mischief, about fifty persons, and slew them.

Ma1|9|62|Afterward Jonathan, and Simon, and they that were with him, got them away to Bethbasi, which is in the wilderness, and they repaired the decays thereof, and made it strong.

Ma1|9|63|Which thing when Bacchides knew, he gathered together all his host, and sent word to them that were of Judea.

Ma1|9|64|Then went he and laid siege against Bethbasi; and they fought against it a long season and made engines of war.

Ma1|9|65|But Jonathan left his brother Simon in the city, and went forth himself into the country, and with a certain number went he forth.

Ma1|9|66|And he smote Odonarkes and his brethren, and the children of Phasiron in their tent.

Ma1|9|67|And when he began to smite them, and came up with his forces, Simon and his company went out of the city, and burned up the engines of war,

Ma1|9|68|And fought against Bacchides, who was discomfited by them, and they afflicted him sore: for his counsel and travail was in vain.

Ma1|9|69|Wherefore he was very wroth at the wicked men that gave him counsel to come into the country, inasmuch as he slew many of them, and purposed to return into his own country.

Ma1|9|70|Whereof when Jonathan had knowledge, he sent ambassadors unto him, to the end he should make peace with him, and deliver them the prisoners.

Ma1|9|71|Which thing he accepted, and did according to his demands, and sware unto him that he would never do him harm all the days of his life.

Ma1|9|72|When therefore he had restored unto him the prisoners that he had taken aforetime out of the land of Judea, he returned and went his way into his own land, neither came he any more into their borders.

Ma1|9|73|Thus the sword ceased from Israel: but Jonathan dwelt at Machmas, and began to govern the people; and he destroyed the ungodly men out of Israel.

Ma1|10|1|In the hundred and sixtieth year Alexander, the son of Antiochus surnamed Epiphanes, went up and took Ptolemais: for the people had received him, by means whereof he reigned there,

Ma1|10|2|Now when king Demetrius heard thereof, he gathered together an exceeding great host, and went forth against him to fight.

Ma1|10|3|Moreover Demetrius sent letters unto Jonathan with loving words, so as he magnified him.

Ma1|10|4|For said he, Let us first make peace with him, before he join with Alexander against us:

Ma1|10|5|Else he will remember all the evils that we have done against him, and against his brethren and his people.

Ma1|10|6|Wherefore he gave him authority to gather together an host, and to provide weapons, that he might aid him in battle: he commanded also that the hostages that were in the tower should be delivered him.

Ma1|10|7|Then came Jonathan to Jerusalem, and read the letters in the audience of all the people, and of them that were in the tower:

Ma1|10|8|Who were sore afraid, when they heard that the king had given him authority to gather together an host.

Ma1|10|9|Whereupon they of the tower delivered their hostages unto Jonathan, and he delivered them unto their parents.

Ma1|10|10|This done, Jonathan settled himself in Jerusalem, and began to build and repair the city.

Ma1|10|11|And he commanded the workmen to build the walls and the mount Sion and about with square stones for fortification; and they did so.

Ma1|10|12|Then the strangers, that were in the fortresses which Bacchides had built, fled away;

Ma1|10|13|Insomuch as every man left his place, and went into his own country.

Ma1|10|14|Only at Bethsura certain of those that had forsaken the law and the commandments remained still: for it was their place of refuge.

Ma1|10|15|Now when king Alexander had heard what promises Demetrius had sent unto Jonathan: when also it was told him of the battles and noble acts which he and his brethren had done, and of the pains that they had endured,

Ma1|10|16|He said, Shall we find such another man? now therefore we will make him our friend and confederate.

Ma1|10|17|Upon this he wrote a letter, and sent it unto him, according to these words, saying,

Ma1|10|18|King Alexander to his brother Jonathan sendeth greeting:

Ma1|10|19|We have heard of thee, that thou art a man of great power, and meet to be our friend.

Ma1|10|20|Wherefore now this day we ordain thee to be the high priest of thy nation, and to be called the king's friend; (and therewithal he sent him a purple robe and a crown of gold:) and require thee to take our part, and keep friendship with us.

Ma1|10|21|So in the seventh month of the hundred and sixtieth year, at the feast of the tabernacles, Jonathan put on the holy robe, and gathered together forces, and provided much armour.

Ma1|10|22|Whereof when Demetrius heard, he was very sorry, and said,

Ma1|10|23|What have we done, that Alexander hath prevented us in making amity with the Jews to strengthen himself?

Ma1|10|24|I also will write unto them words of encouragement, and promise them dignities and gifts, that I may have their aid.

Ma1|10|25|He sent unto them therefore to this effect: King Demetrius unto the people of the Jews sendeth greeting:

Ma1|10|26|Whereas ye have kept covenants with us, and continued in our friendship, not joining yourselves with our enemies, we have heard hereof, and are glad.

Ma1|10|27|Wherefore now continue ye still to be faithful unto us, and we will well recompense you for the things ye do in our behalf,

Ma1|10|28|And will grant you many immunities, and give you rewards.

Ma1|10|29|And now do I free you, and for your sake I release all the Jews, from tributes, and from the customs of salt, and from crown taxes,

Ma1|10|30|And from that which appertaineth unto me to receive for the third part or the seed, and the half of the fruit of the trees, I release it from this day forth, so that they shall not be taken of the land of Judea, nor of the three governments which are added thereunto out of the country of Samaria and Galilee, from this day forth for evermore.

Ma1|10|31|Let Jerusalem also be holy and free, with the borders thereof, both from tenths and tributes.

Ma1|10|32|And as for the tower which is at Jerusalem, I yield up authority over it, and give the high priest, that he may set in it such men as he shall choose to keep it.

Ma1|10|33|Moreover I freely set at liberty every one of the Jews, that were carried captives out of the land of Judea into any part of my kingdom, and I will that all my officers remit the tributes even of their cattle.

Ma1|10|34|Furthermore I will that all the feasts, and sabbaths, and new moons, and solemn days, and the three days before the feast, and the three days after the feast shall be all of immunity and freedom for all the Jews in my realm.

Ma1|10|35|Also no man shall have authority to meddle with or to molest any of them in any matter.

Ma1|10|36|I will further, that there be enrolled among the king's forces about thirty thousand men of the Jews, unto whom pay shall be given, as belongeth to all king's forces.

Ma1|10|37|And of them some shall be placed in the king's strong holds, of whom also some shall be set over the affairs of the kingdom, which are of trust: and I will that their overseers and governors be of themselves, and that they live after their own laws, even as the king hath commanded in the land of Judea.

Ma1|10|38|And concerning the three governments that are added to Judea from the country of Samaria, let them be joined with Judea, that they may be reckoned to be under one, nor bound to obey other authority than the high priest's.

Ma1|10|39|As for Ptolemais, and the land pertaining thereto, I give it as a free gift to the sanctuary at Jerusalem for the necessary expences of the sanctuary.

Ma1|10|40|Moreover I give every year fifteen thousand shekels of silver out of the king's accounts from the places appertaining.

Ma1|10|41|And all the overplus, which the officers payed not in as in former time, from henceforth shall be given toward the works of the temple.

Ma1|10|42|And beside this, the five thousand shekels of silver, which they took from the uses of the temple out of the accounts year by year, even those things shall be released, because they appertain to the priests that minister.

Ma1|10|43|And whosoever they be that flee unto the temple at Jerusalem, or be within the liberties hereof, being indebted unto the king, or for any other matter, let them be at liberty, and all that they have in my realm.

Ma1|10|44|For the building also and repairing of the works of the sanctuary expences shall be given of the king's accounts.

Ma1|10|45|Yea, and for the building of the walls of Jerusalem, and the fortifying thereof round about, expences shall be given out of the king's accounts, as also for the building of the walls in Judea.

Ma1|10|46|Now when Jonathan and the people heard these words, they gave no credit unto them, nor received them, because they remembered the great evil that he had done in Israel; for he had afflicted them very sore.

Ma1|10|47|But with Alexander they were well pleased, because he was the first that entreated of true peace with them, and they were confederate with him always.

Ma1|10|48|Then gathered king Alexander great forces, and camped over against Demetrius.

Ma1|10|49|And after the two kings had joined battle, Demetrius' host fled: but Alexander followed after him, and prevailed against them.

Ma1|10|50|And he continued the battle very sore until the sun went down: and that day was Demetrius slain.

Ma1|10|51|Afterward Alexander sent ambassadors to Ptolemee king of Egypt with a message to this effect:

Ma1|10|52|Forasmuch as I am come again to my realm, and am set in the throne of my progenitors, and have gotten the dominion, and overthrown Demetrius, and recovered our country;

Ma1|10|53|For after I had joined battle with him, both he and his host was discomfited by us, so that we sit in the throne of his kingdom:

Ma1|10|54|Now therefore let us make a league of amity together, and give me now thy daughter to wife: and I will be thy son in law, and will give both thee and her as according to thy dignity.

Ma1|10|55|Then Ptolemee the king gave answer, saying, Happy be the day wherein thou didst return into the land of thy fathers, and satest in the throne of their kingdom.

Ma1|10|56|And now will I do to thee, as thou hast written: meet me therefore at Ptolemais, that we may see one another; for I will marry my daughter to thee according to thy desire.

Ma1|10|57|So Ptolemee went out of Egypt with his daughter Cleopatra, and they came unto Ptolemais in the hundred threescore and second year:

Ma1|10|58|Where king Alexander meeting him, he gave unto him his daughter Cleopatra, and celebrated her marriage at Ptolemais with great glory, as the manner of kings is.

Ma1|10|59|Now king Alexander had written unto Jonathan, that he should come and meet him.

Ma1|10|60|Who thereupon went honourably to Ptolemais, where he met the two kings, and gave them and their friends silver and gold, and many presents, and found favour in their sight.

Ma1|10|61|At that time certain pestilent fellows of Israel, men of a wicked life, assembled themselves against him, to accuse him: but the king would not hear them.

Ma1|10|62|Yea more than that, the king commanded to take off his garments, and clothe him in purple: and they did so.

Ma1|10|63|And he made him sit by himself, and said into his princes, Go with him into the midst of the city, and make proclamation, that no man complain against him of any matter, and that no man trouble him for any manner of cause.

Ma1|10|64|Now when his accusers saw that he was honored according to the proclamation, and clothed in purple, they fled all away.

Ma1|10|65|So the king honoured him, and wrote him among his chief friends, and made him a duke, and partaker of his dominion.

Ma1|10|66|Afterward Jonathan returned to Jerusalem with peace and gladness.

Ma1|10|67|Furthermore in the; hundred threescore and fifth year came Demetrius son of Demetrius out of Crete into the land of his fathers:

Ma1|10|68|Whereof when king Alexander heard tell, he was right sorry, and returned into Antioch.

Ma1|10|69|Then Demetrius made Apollonius the governor of Celosyria his general, who gathered together a great host, and camped in Jamnia, and sent unto Jonathan the high priest, saying,

Ma1|10|70|Thou alone liftest up thyself against us, and I am laughed to scorn for thy sake, and reproached: and why dost thou vaunt thy power against us in the mountains?

Ma1|10|71|Now therefore, if thou trustest in thine own strength, come down to us into the plain field, and there let us try the matter together: for with me is the power of the cities.

Ma1|10|72|Ask and learn who I am, and the rest that take our part, and they shall tell thee that thy foot is not able to to flight in their own land.

Ma1|10|73|Wherefore now thou shalt not be able to abide the horsemen and so great a power in the plain, where is neither stone nor flint, nor place to flee unto.

Ma1|10|74|So when Jonathan heard these words of Apollonius, he was moved in his mind, and choosing ten thousand men he went out of Jerusalem, where Simon his brother met him for to help him.

Ma1|10|75|And he pitched his tents against Joppa: but; they of Joppa shut him out of the city, because Apollonius had a garrison there.

Ma1|10|76|Then Jonathan laid siege unto it: whereupon they of the city let him in for fear: and so Jonathan won Joppa.

Ma1|10|77|Whereof when Apollonius heard, he took three thousand horsemen, with a great host of footmen, and went to Azotus as one that journeyed, and therewithal drew him forth into the plain. because he had a great number of horsemen, in whom he put his trust.

Ma1|10|78|Then Jonathan followed after him to Azotus, where the armies joined battle.

Ma1|10|79|Now Apollonius had left a thousand horsemen in ambush.

Ma1|10|80|And Jonathan knew that there was an ambushment behind him; for they had compassed in his host, and cast darts at the people, from morning till evening.

Ma1|10|81|But the people stood still, as Jonathan had commanded them: and so the enemies' horses were tired.

Ma1|10|82|Then brought Simon forth his host, and set them against the footmen, (for the horsemen were spent) who were discomfited by him, and fled.

Ma1|10|83|The horsemen also, being scattered in the field, fled to Azotus, and went into Bethdagon, their idol's temple, for safety.

Ma1|10|84|But Jonathan set fire on Azotus, and the cities round about it, and took their spoils; and the temple of Dagon, with them that were fled into it, he burned with fire.

Ma1|10|85|Thus there were burned and slain with the sword well nigh eight thousand men.

Ma1|10|86|And from thence Jonathan removed his host, and camped against Ascalon, where the men of the city came forth, and met him with great pomp.

Ma1|10|87|After this returned Jonathan and his host unto Jerusalem, having any spoils.

Ma1|10|88|Now when king ALexander heard these things, he honoured Jonathan yet more.

Ma1|10|89|And sent him a buckle of gold, as the use is to be given to such as are of the king's blood: he gave him also Accaron with the borders thereof in possession.

Ma1|11|1|And the king of Egypt gathered together a great host, like the sand that lieth upon the sea shore, and many ships, and went about through deceit to get Alexander's kingdom, and join it to his own.

Ma1|11|2|Whereupon he took his journey into Spain in peaceable manner, so as they of the cities opened unto him, and met him: for king Alexander had commanded them so to do, because he was his brother in law.

Ma1|11|3|Now as Ptolemee entered into the cities, he set in every one of them a garrison of soldiers to keep it.

Ma1|11|4|And when he came near to Azotus, they shewed him the temple of Dagon that was burnt, and Azotus and the suburbs thereof that were destroyed, and the bodies that were cast abroad and them that he had burnt in the battle; for they had made heaps of them by the way where he should pass.

Ma1|11|5|Also they told the king whatsoever Jonathan had done, to the intent he might blame him: but the king held his peace.

Ma1|11|6|Then Jonathan met the king with great pomp at Joppa, where they saluted one another, and lodged.

Ma1|11|7|Afterward Jonathan, when he had gone with the king to the river called Eleutherus, returned again to Jerusalem.

Ma1|11|8|King Ptolemee therefore, having gotten the dominion of the cities by the sea unto Seleucia upon the sea coast, imagined wicked counsels against Alexander.

Ma1|11|9|Whereupon he sent ambasadors unto king Demetrius, saying, Come, let us make a league betwixt us, and I will give thee my daughter whom Alexander hath, and thou shalt reign in thy father's kingdom:

Ma1|11|10|For I repent that I gave my daughter unto him, for he sought to slay me.

Ma1|11|11|Thus did he slander him, because he was desirous of his kingdom.

Ma1|11|12|Wherefore he took his daughter from him, and gave her to Demetrius, and forsook Alexander, so that their hatred was openly known.

Ma1|11|13|Then Ptolemee entered into Antioch, where he set two crowns upon his head, the crown of Asia, and of Egypt.

Ma1|11|14|In the mean season was king Alexander in Cilicia, because those that dwelt in those parts had revolted from him.

Ma1|11|15|But when Alexander heard of this, he came to war against him: whereupon king Ptolemee brought forth his host, and met him with a mighty power, and put him to flight.

Ma1|11|16|So Alexander fled into Arabia there to be defended; but king Ptolemee was exalted:

Ma1|11|17|For Zabdiel the Arabian took off Alexander's head, and sent it unto Ptolemee.

Ma1|11|18|King Ptolemee also died the third day after, and they that were in the strong holds were slain one of another.

Ma1|11|19|By this means Demetrius reigned in the hundred threescore and seventh year.

Ma1|11|20|At the same time Jonathan gathered together them that were in Judea to take the tower that was in Jerusalem: and he made many engines of war against it.

Ma1|11|21|Then came ungodly persons, who hated their own people, went unto the king, and told him that Jonathan besieged the tower,

Ma1|11|22|Whereof when he heard, he was angry, and immediately removing, he came to Ptolemais, and wrote unto Jonathan, that he should not lay siege to the tower, but come and speak with him at Ptolemais in great haste.

Ma1|11|23|Nevertheless Jonathan, when he heard this, commanded to besiege it still: and he chose certain of the elders of Israel and the priests, and put himself in peril;

Ma1|11|24|And took silver and gold, and raiment, and divers presents besides, and went to Ptolemais unto the king, where he found favour in his sight.

Ma1|11|25|And though certain ungodly men of the people had made complaints against him,

Ma1|11|26|Yet the king entreated him as his predecessors had done before, and promoted him in the sight of all his friends,

Ma1|11|27|And confirmed him in the high priesthood, and in all the honours that he had before, and gave him preeminence among his chief friends.

Ma1|11|28|Then Jonathan desired the king, that he would make Judea free from tribute, as also the three governments, with the country of Samaria; and he promised him three hundred talents.

Ma1|11|29|So the king consented, and wrote letters unto Jonathan of all these things after this manner:

Ma1|11|30|King Demetrius unto his brother Jonathan, and unto the nation of the Jews, sendeth greeting:

Ma1|11|31|We send you here a copy of the letter which we did write unto our cousin Lasthenes concerning you, that ye might see it.

Ma1|11|32|King Demetrius unto his father Lasthenes sendeth greeting:

Ma1|11|33|We are determined to do good to the people of the Jews, who are our friends, and keep covenants with us, because of their good will toward us.

Ma1|11|34|Wherefore we have ratified unto them the borders of Judea, with the three governments of Apherema and Lydda and Ramathem, that are added unto Judea from the country of Samaria, and all things appertaining unto them, for all such as do sacrifice in Jerusalem, instead of the payments which the king received of them yearly aforetime out of the fruits of the earth and of trees.

Ma1|11|35|And as for other things that belong unto us, of the tithes and customs pertaining unto us, as also the saltpits, and the crown taxes, which are due unto us, we discharge them of them all for their relief.

Ma1|11|36|And nothing hereof shall be revoked from this time forth for ever.

Ma1|11|37|Now therefore see that thou make a copy of these things, and let it be delivered unto Jonathan, and set upon the holy mount in a conspicuous place.

Ma1|11|38|After this, when king Demetrius saw that the land was quiet before him, and that no resistance was made against him, he sent away all his forces, every one to his own place, except certain bands of strangers, whom he had gathered from the isles of the heathen: wherefore all the forces of his fathers hated him.

Ma1|11|39|Moreover there was one Tryphon, that had been of Alexander's part afore, who, seeing that all the host murmured against Demetrius, went to Simalcue the Arabian that brought up Antiochus the young son of Alexander,

Ma1|11|40|And lay sore upon him to deliver him this young Antiochus, that he might reign in his father's stead: he told him therefore all that Demetrius had done, and how his men of war were at enmity with him, and there he remained a long season.

Ma1|11|41|In the mean time Jonathan sent unto king Demetrius, that he would cast those of the tower out of Jerusalem, and those also in the fortresses: for they fought against Israel.

Ma1|11|42|So Demetrius sent unto Jonathan, saying, I will not only do this for thee and thy people, but I will greatly honour thee and thy nation, if opportunity serve.

Ma1|11|43|Now therefore thou shalt do well, if thou send me men to help me; for all my forces are gone from me.

Ma1|11|44|Upon this Jonathan sent him three thousand strong men unto Antioch: and when they came to the king, the king was very glad of their coming.

Ma1|11|45|Howbeit they that were of the city gathered themselves together into the midst of the city, to the number of an hundred and twenty thousand men, and would have slain the king.

Ma1|11|46|Wherefore the king fled into the court, but they of the city kept the passages of the city, and began to fight.

Ma1|11|47|Then the king called to the Jews for help, who came unto him all at once, and dispersing themselves through the city slew that day in the city to the number of an hundred thousand.

Ma1|11|48|Also they set fire on the city, and gat many spoils that day, and delivered the king.

Ma1|11|49|So when they of the city saw that the Jews had got the city as they would, their courage was abated: wherefore they made supplication to the king, and cried, saying,

Ma1|11|50|Grant us peace, and let the Jews cease from assaulting us and the city.

Ma1|11|51|With that they cast away their weapons, and made peace; and the Jews were honoured in the sight of the king, and in the sight of all that were in his realm; and they returned to Jerusalem, having great spoils.

Ma1|11|52|So king Demetrius sat on the throne of his kingdom, and the land was quiet before him.

Ma1|11|53|Nevertheless he dissembled in all that ever he spake, and estranged himself from Jonathan, neither rewarded he him according to the benefits which he had received of him, but troubled him very sore.

Ma1|11|54|After this returned Tryphon, and with him the young child Antiochus, who reigned, and was crowned.

Ma1|11|55|Then there gathered unto him all the men of war, whom Demetrius had put away, and they fought against Demetrius, who turned his back and fled.

Ma1|11|56|Moreover Tryphon took the elephants, and won Antioch.

Ma1|11|57|At that time young Antiochus wrote unto Jonathan, saying, I confirm thee in the high priesthood, and appoint thee ruler over the four governments, and to be one of the king's friends.

Ma1|11|58|Upon this he sent him golden vessels to be served in, and gave him leave to drink in gold, and to be clothed in purple, and to wear a golden buckle.

Ma1|11|59|His brother Simon also he made captain from the place called The ladder of Tyrus unto the borders of Egypt.

Ma1|11|60|Then Jonathan went forth, and passed through the cities beyond the water, and all the forces of Syria gathered themselves unto him for to help him: and when he came to Ascalon, they of the city met him honourably.

Ma1|11|61|From whence he went to Gaza, but they of Gaza shut him out; wherefore he laid siege unto it, and burned the suburbs thereof with fire, and spoiled them.

Ma1|11|62|Afterward, when they of Gaza made supplication unto Jonathan, he made peace with them, and took the sons of their chief men for hostages, and sent them to Jerusalem, and passed through the country unto Damascus.

Ma1|11|63|Now when Jonathan heard that Demetrius' princes were come to Cades, which is in Galilee, with a great power, purposing to remove him out of the country,

Ma1|11|64|He went to meet them, and left Simon his brother in the country.

Ma1|11|65|Then Simon encamped against Bethsura and fought against it a long season, and shut it up:

Ma1|11|66|But they desired to have peace with him, which he granted them, and then put them out from thence, and took the city, and set a garrison in it.

Ma1|11|67|As for Jonathan and his host, they pitched at the water of Gennesar, from whence betimes in the morning they gat them to the plain of Nasor.

Ma1|11|68|And, behold, the host of strangers met them in the plain, who, having laid men in ambush for him in the mountains, came themselves over against him.

Ma1|11|69|So when they that lay in ambush rose out of their places and joined battle, all that were of Jonathan's side fled:

Ma1|11|70|Insomuch as there was not one of them left, except Mattathias the son of Absalom, and Judas the son of Calphi, the captains of the host.

Ma1|11|71|Then Jonathan rent his clothes, and cast earth upon his head, and prayed.

Ma1|11|72|Afterwards turning again to battle, he put them to flight, and so they ran away.

Ma1|11|73|Now when his own men that were fled saw this, they turned again unto him, and with him pursued them to Cades, even unto their own tents, and there they camped.

Ma1|11|74|So there were slain of the heathen that day about three thousand men: but Jonathan returned to Jerusalem.

Ma1|12|1|Now when Jonathan saw that time served him, he chose certain men, and sent them to Rome, for to confirm and renew the friendship that they had with them.

Ma1|12|2|He sent letters also to the Lacedemonians, and to other places, for the same purpose.

Ma1|12|3|So they went unto Rome, and entered into the senate, and said, Jonathan the high priest, and the people of the Jews, sent us unto you, to the end ye should renew the friendship, which ye had with them, and league, as in former time.

Ma1|12|4|Upon this the Romans gave them letters unto the governors of every place that they should bring them into the land of Judea peaceably.

Ma1|12|5|And this is the copy of the letters which Jonathan wrote to the Lacedemonians:

Ma1|12|6|Jonathan the high priest, and the elders of the nation, and the priests, and the other of the Jews, unto the Lacedemonians their brethren send greeting:

Ma1|12|7|There were letters sent in times past unto Onias the high priest from Darius, who reigned then among you, to signify that ye are our brethren, as the copy here underwritten doth specify.

Ma1|12|8|At which time Onias entreated the ambassador that was sent honourably, and received the letters, wherein declaration was made of the league and friendship.

Ma1|12|9|Therefore we also, albeit we need none of these things, that we have the holy books of scripture in our hands to comfort us,

Ma1|12|10|Have nevertheless attempted to send unto you for the renewing of brotherhood and friendship, lest we should become strangers unto you altogether: for there is a long time passed since ye sent unto us.

Ma1|12|11|We therefore at all times without ceasing, both in our feasts, and other convenient days, do remember you in the sacrifices which we offer, and in our prayers, as reason is, and as it becometh us to think upon our brethren:

Ma1|12|12|And we are right glad of your honour.

Ma1|12|13|As for ourselves, we have had great troubles and wars on every side, forsomuch as the kings that are round about us have fought against us.

Ma1|12|14|Howbeit we would not be troublesome unto you, nor to others of our confederates and friends, in these wars:

Ma1|12|15|For we have help from heaven that succoureth us, so as we are delivered from our enemies, and our enemies are brought under foot.

Ma1|12|16|For this cause we chose Numenius the son of Antiochus, and Antipater he son of Jason, and sent them unto the Romans, to renew the amity that we had with them, and the former league.

Ma1|12|17|We commanded them also to go unto you, and to salute and to deliver you our letters concerning the renewing of our brotherhood.

Ma1|12|18|Wherefore now ye shall do well to give us an answer thereto.

Ma1|12|19|And this is the copy of the letters which Oniares sent.

Ma1|12|20|Areus king of the Lacedemonians to Onias the high priest, greeting:

Ma1|12|21|It is found in writing, that the Lacedemonians and Jews are brethren, and that they are of the stock of Abraham:

Ma1|12|22|Now therefore, since this is come to our knowledge, ye shall do well to write unto us of your prosperity.

Ma1|12|23|We do write back again to you, that your cattle and goods are our's, and our's are your's We do command therefore our ambassadors to make report unto you on this wise.

Ma1|12|24|Now when Jonathan heard that Demebius' princes were come to fight against him with a greater host than afore,

Ma1|12|25|He removed from Jerusalem, and met them in the land of Amathis: for he gave them no respite to enter his country.

Ma1|12|26|He sent spies also unto their tents, who came again, and told him that they were appointed to come upon them in the night season.

Ma1|12|27|Wherefore so soon as the sun was down, Jonathan commanded his men to watch, and to be in arms, that all the night long they might be ready to fight: also he sent forth centinels round about the host.

Ma1|12|28|But when the adversaries heard that Jonathan and his men were ready for battle, they feared, and trembled in their hearts, and they kindled fires in their camp.

Ma1|12|29|Howbeit Jonathan and his company knew it not till the morning: for they saw the lights burning.

Ma1|12|30|Then Jonathan pursued after them, but overtook them not: for they were gone over the river Eleutherus.

Ma1|12|31|Wherefore Jonathan turned to the Arabians, who were called Zabadeans, and smote them, and took their spoils.

Ma1|12|32|And removing thence, he came to Damascus, and so passed through all the country,

Ma1|12|33|Simon also went forth, and passed through the country unto Ascalon, and the holds there adjoining, from whence he turned aside to Joppa, and won it.

Ma1|12|34|For he had heard that they would deliver the hold unto them that took Demetrius' part; wherefore he set a garrison there to keep it.

Ma1|12|35|After this came Jonathan home again, and calling the elders of the people together, he consulted with them about building strong holds in Judea,

Ma1|12|36|And making the walls of Jerusalem higher, and raising a great mount between the tower and the city, for to separate it from the city, that so it might be alone, that men might neither sell nor buy in it.

Ma1|12|37|Upon this they came together to build up the city, forasmuch as part of the wall toward the brook on the east side was fallen down, and they repaired that which was called Caphenatha.

Ma1|12|38|Simon also set up Adida in Sephela, and made it strong with gates and bars.

Ma1|12|39|Now Tryphon went about to get the kingdom of Asia, and to kill Antiochus the king, that he might set the crown upon his own head.

Ma1|12|40|Howbeit he was afraid that Jonathan would not suffer him, and that he would fight against him; wherefore he sought a way how to take Jonathan, that he might kill him. So he removed, and came to Bethsan.

Ma1|12|41|Then Jonathan went out to meet him with forty thousand men chosen for the battle, and came to Bethsan.

Ma1|12|42|Now when Tryphon saw Jonathan came with so great a force, he durst not stretch his hand against him;

Ma1|12|43|But received him honourably, and commended him unto all his friends, and gave him gifts, and commanded his men of war to be as obedient unto him, as to himself.

Ma1|12|44|Unto Jonathan also he said, Why hast thou brought all this people to so great trouble, seeing there is no war betwixt us?

Ma1|12|45|Therefore send them now home again, and choose a few men to wait on thee, and come thou with me to Ptolemais, for I will give it thee, and the rest of the strong holds and forces, and all that have any charge: as for me, I will return and depart: for this is the cause of my coming.

Ma1|12|46|So Jonathan believing him did as he bade him, and sent away his host, who went into the land of Judea.

Ma1|12|47|And with himself he retained but three thousand men, of whom he sent two thousand into Galilee, and one thousand went with him.

Ma1|12|48|Now as soon as Jonathan entered into Ptolemais, they of Ptolemais shut the gates and took him, and all them that came with him they slew with the sword.

Ma1|12|49|Then sent Tryphon an host of footmen and horsemen into Galilee, and into the great plain, to destroy all Jonathan's company.

Ma1|12|50|But when they knew that Jonathan and they that were with him were taken and slain, they encouraged one another; and went close together, prepared to fight.

Ma1|12|51|They therefore that followed upon them, perceiving that they were ready to fight for their lives, turned back again.

Ma1|12|52|Whereupon they all came into the land of Judea peaceably, and there they bewailed Jonathan, and them that were with him, and they were sore afraid; wherefore all Israel made great lamentation.

Ma1|12|53|Then all the heathen that were round about then sought to destroy them: for said they, They have no captain, nor any to help them: now therefore let us make war upon them, and take away their memorial from among men.

Ma1|13|1|Now when Simon heard that Tryphon had gathered together a great host to invade the land of Judea, and destroy it,

Ma1|13|2|And saw that the people was in great trembling and fear, he went up to Jerusalem, and gathered the people together,

Ma1|13|3|And gave them exhortation, saying, Ye yourselves know what great things I, and my brethren, and my father's house, have done for the laws and the sanctuary, the battles also and troubles which we have seen.

Ma1|13|4|By reason whereof all my brethren are slain for Israel's sake, and I am left alone.

Ma1|13|5|Now therefore be it far from me, that I should spare mine own life in any time of trouble: for I am no better than my brethren.

Ma1|13|6|Doubtless I will avenge my nation, and the sanctuary, and our wives, and our children: for all the heathen are gathered to destroy us of very malice.

Ma1|13|7|Now as soon as the people heard these words, their spirit revived.

Ma1|13|8|And they answered with a loud voice, saying, Thou shalt be our leader instead of Judas and Jonathan thy brother.

Ma1|13|9|Fight thou our battles, and whatsoever, thou commandest us, that will we do.

Ma1|13|10|So then he gathered together all the men of war, and made haste to finish the walls of Jerusalem, and he fortified it round about.

Ma1|13|11|Also he sent Jonathan the son of Absolom, and with him a great power, to Joppa: who casting out them that were therein remained there in it.

Ma1|13|12|So Tryphon removed from Ptolemaus with a great power to invade the land of Judea, and Jonathan was with him in ward.

Ma1|13|13|But Simon pitched his tents at Adida, over against the plain.

Ma1|13|14|Now when Tryphon knew that Simon was risen up instead of his brother Jonathan, and meant to join battle with him, he sent messengers unto him, saying,

Ma1|13|15|Whereas we have Jonathan thy brother in hold, it is for money that he is owing unto the king's treasure, concerning the business that was committed unto him.

Ma1|13|16|Wherefore now send an hundred talents of silver, and two of his sons for hostages, that when he is at liberty he may not revolt from us, and we will let him go.

Ma1|13|17|Hereupon Simon, albeit he perceived that they spake deceitfully unto him yet sent he the money and the children, lest peradventure he should procure to himself great hatred of the people:

Ma1|13|18|Who might have said, Because I sent him not the money and the children, therefore is Jonathan dead.

Ma1|13|19|So he sent them the children and the hundred talents: howbeit Tryphon dissembled neither would he let Jonathan go.

Ma1|13|20|And after this came Tryphon to invade the land, and destroy it, going round about by the way that leadeth unto Adora: but Simon and his host marched against him in every place, wheresoever he went.

Ma1|13|21|Now they that were in the tower sent messengers unto Tryphon, to the end that he should hasten his coming unto them by the wilderness, and send them victuals.

Ma1|13|22|Wherefore Tryphon made ready all his horsemen to come that night: but there fell a very great snow, by reason whereof he came not. So he departed, and came into the country of Galaad.

Ma1|13|23|And when he came near to Bascama he slew Jonathan, who was buried there.

Ma1|13|24|Afterward Tryphon returned and went into his own land.

Ma1|13|25|Then sent Simon, and took the bones of Jonathan his brother, and buried them in Modin, the city of his fathers.

Ma1|13|26|And all Israel made great lamentation for him, and bewailed him many days.

Ma1|13|27|Simon also built a monument upon the sepulchre of his father and his brethren, and raised it aloft to the sight, with hewn stone behind and before.

Ma1|13|28|Moreover he set up seven pyramids, one against another, for his father, and his mother, and his four brethren.

Ma1|13|29|And in these he made cunning devices, about the which he set great pillars, and upon the pillars he made all their armour for a perpetual memory, and by the armour ships carved, that they might be seen of all that sail on the sea.

Ma1|13|30|This is the sepulchre which he made at Modin, and it standeth yet unto this day.

Ma1|13|31|Now Tryphon dealt deceitfully with the young king Antiochus, and slew him.

Ma1|13|32|And he reigned in his stead, and crowned himself king of Asia, and brought a great calamity upon the land.

Ma1|13|33|Then Simon built up the strong holds in Judea, and fenced them about with high towers, and great walls, and gates, and bars, and laid up victuals therein.

Ma1|13|34|Moreover Simon chose men, and sent to king Demetrius, to the end he should give the land an immunity, because all that Tryphon did was to spoil.

Ma1|13|35|Unto whom king Demetrius answered and wrote after this manner:

Ma1|13|36|King Demetrius unto Simon the high priest, and friend of kings, as also unto the elders and nation of the Jews, sendeth greeting:

Ma1|13|37|The golden crown, and the scarlet robe, which ye sent unto us, we have received: and we are ready to make a stedfast peace with you, yea, and to write unto our officers, to confirm the immunities which we have granted.

Ma1|13|38|And whatsoever covenants we have made with you shall stand; and the strong holds, which ye have builded, shall be your own.

Ma1|13|39|As for any oversight or fault committed unto this day, we forgive it, and the crown tax also, which ye owe us: and if there were any other tribute paid in Jerusalem, it shall no more be paid.

Ma1|13|40|And look who are meet among you to be in our court, let then be enrolled, and let there be peace betwixt us.

Ma1|13|41|Thus the yoke of the heathen was taken away from Israel in the hundred and seventieth year.

Ma1|13|42|Then the people of Israel began to write in their instruments and contracts, In the first year of Simon the high priest, the governor and leader of the Jews.

Ma1|13|43|In those days Simon camped against Gaza and besieged it round about; he made also an engine of war, and set it by the city, and battered a certain tower, and took it.

Ma1|13|44|And they that were in the engine leaped into the city; whereupon there was a great uproar in the city:

Ma1|13|45|Insomuch as the people of the city rent their clothes, and climbed upon the walls with their wives and children, and cried with a loud voice, beseeching Simon to grant them peace.

Ma1|13|46|And they said, Deal not with us according to our wickedness, but according to thy mercy.

Ma1|13|47|So Simon was appeased toward them, and fought no more against them, but put them out of the city, and cleansed the houses wherein the idols were, and so entered into it with songs and thanksgiving.

Ma1|13|48|Yea, he put all uncleanness out of it, and placed such men there as would keep the law, and made it stronger than it was before, and built therein a dwellingplace for himself.

Ma1|13|49|They also of the tower in Jerusalem were kept so strait, that they could neither come forth, nor go into the country, nor buy, nor sell: wherefore they were in great distress for want of victuals, and a great number of them perished through famine.

Ma1|13|50|Then cried they to Simon, beseeching him to be at one with them: which thing he granted them; and when he had put them out from thence, he cleansed the tower from pollutions:

Ma1|13|51|And entered into it the three and twentieth day of the second month in the hundred seventy and first year, with thanksgiving, and branches of palm trees, and with harps, and cymbals, and with viols, and hymns, and songs: because there was destroyed a great enemy out of Israel.

Ma1|13|52|He ordained also that that day should be kept every year with gladness. Moreover the hill of the temple that was by the tower he made stronger than it was, and there he dwelt himself with his company.

Ma1|13|53|And when Simon saw that John his son was a valiant man, he made him captain of all the hosts; and he dwelt in Gazera.

Ma1|14|1|Now in the hundred threescore and twelfth year king Demetrius gathered his forces together, and went into Media to get him help to fight against Tryphone.

Ma1|14|2|But when Arsaces, the king of Persia and Media, heard that Demetrius was entered within his borders, he sent one of his princes to take him alive:

Ma1|14|3|Who went and smote the host of Demetrius, and took him, and brought him to Arsaces, by whom he was put in ward.

Ma1|14|4|As for the land of Judea, that was quiet all the days of Simon; for he sought the good of his nation in such wise, as that evermore his authority and honour pleased them well.

Ma1|14|5|And as he was honourable in all his acts, so in this, that he took Joppa for an haven, and made an entrance to the isles of the sea,

Ma1|14|6|And enlarged the bounds of his nation, and recovered the country,

Ma1|14|7|And gathered together a great number of captives, and had the dominion of Gazera, and Bethsura, and the tower, out of the which he took all uncleaness, neither was there any that resisted him.

Ma1|14|8|Then did they till their ground in peace, and the earth gave her increase, and the trees of the field their fruit.

Ma1|14|9|The ancient men sat all in the streets, communing together of good things, and the young men put on glorious and warlike apparel.

Ma1|14|10|He provided victuals for the cities, and set in them all manner of munition, so that his honourable name was renowned unto the end of the world.

Ma1|14|11|He made peace in the land, and Israel rejoiced with great joy:

Ma1|14|12|For every man sat under his vine and his fig tree, and there was none to fray them:

Ma1|14|13|Neither was there any left in the land to fight against them: yea, the kings themselves were overthrown in those days.

Ma1|14|14|Moreover he strengthened all those of his people that were brought low: the law he searched out; and every contemner of the law and wicked person he took away.

Ma1|14|15|He beautified the sanctuary, and multiplied vessels of the temple.

Ma1|14|16|Now when it was heard at Rome, and as far as Sparta, that Jonathan was dead, they were very sorry.

Ma1|14|17|But as soon as they heard that his brother Simon was made high priest in his stead, and ruled the country, and the cities therein:

Ma1|14|18|They wrote unto him in tables of brass, to renew the friendship and league which they had made with Judas and Jonathan his brethren:

Ma1|14|19|Which writings were read before the congregation at Jerusalem.

Ma1|14|20|And this is the copy of the letters that the Lacedemonians sent; The rulers of the Lacedemonians, with the city, unto Simon the high priest, and the elders, and priests, and residue of the people of the Jews, our brethren, send greeting:

Ma1|14|21|The ambassadors that were sent unto our people certified us of your glory and honour: wherefore we were glad of their coming,

Ma1|14|22|And did register the things that they spake in the council of the people in this manner; Numenius son of Antiochus, and Antipater son of Jason, the Jews' ambassadors, came unto us to renew the friendship they had with us.

Ma1|14|23|And it pleased the people to entertain the men honourably, and to put the copy of their ambassage in publick records, to the end the people of the Lacedemonians might have a memorial thereof: furthermore we have written a copy thereof unto Simon the high priest.

Ma1|14|24|After this Simon sent Numenius to Rome with a great shield of gold of a thousand pound weight to confirm the league with them.

Ma1|14|25|Whereof when the people heard, they said, What thanks shall we give to Simon and his sons?

Ma1|14|26|For he and his brethren and the house of his father have established Israel, and chased away in fight their enemies from them, and confirmed their liberty.

Ma1|14|27|So then they wrote it in tables of brass, which they set upon pillars in mount Sion: and this is the copy of the writing; The eighteenth day of the month Elul, in the hundred threescore and twelfth year, being the third year of Simon the high priest,

Ma1|14|28|At Saramel in the great congregation of the priests, and people, and rulers of the nation, and elders of the country, were these things notified unto us.

Ma1|14|29|Forasmuch as oftentimes there have been wars in the country, wherein for the maintenance of their sanctuary, and the law, Simon the son of Mattathias, of the posterity of Jarib, together with his brethren, put themselves in jeopardy, and resisting the enemies of their nation did their nation great honour:

Ma1|14|30|(For after that Jonathan, having gathered his nation together, and been their high priest, was added to his people,

Ma1|14|31|Their enemies prepared to invade their country, that they might destroy it, and lay hands on the sanctuary:

Ma1|14|32|At which time Simon rose up, and fought for his nation, and spent much of his own substance, and armed the valiant men of his nation and gave them wages,

Ma1|14|33|And fortified the cities of Judea, together with Bethsura, that lieth upon the borders of Judea, where the armour of the enemies had been before; but he set a garrison of Jews there:

Ma1|14|34|Moreover he fortified Joppa, which lieth upon the sea, and Gazera, that bordereth upon Azotus, where the enemies had dwelt before: but he placed Jews there, and furnished them with all things convenient for the reparation thereof.)

Ma1|14|35|The people therefore sang the acts of Simon, and unto what glory he thought to bring his nation, made him their governor and chief priest, because he had done all these things, and for the justice and faith which he kept to his nation, and for that he sought by all means to exalt his people.

Ma1|14|36|For in his time things prospered in his hands, so that the heathen were taken out of their country, and they also that were in the city of David in Jerusalem, who had made themselves a tower, out of which they issued, and polluted all about the sanctuary, and did much hurt in the holy place:

Ma1|14|37|But he placed Jews therein. and fortified it for the safety of the country and the city, and raised up the walls of Jerusalem.

Ma1|14|38|King Demetrius also confirmed him in the high priesthood according to those things,

Ma1|14|39|And made him one of his friends, and honoured him with great honour.

Ma1|14|40|For he had heard say, that the Romans had called the Jews their friends and confederates and brethren; and that they had entertained the ambassadors of Simon honourably;

Ma1|14|41|Also that the Jews and priests were well pleased that Simon should be their governor and high priest for ever, until there should arise a faithful prophet;

Ma1|14|42|Moreover that he should be their captain, and should take charge of the sanctuary, to set them over their works, and over the country, and over the armour, and over the fortresses, that, I say, he should take charge of the sanctuary;

Ma1|14|43|Beside this, that he should be obeyed of every man, and that all the writings in the country should be made in his name, and that he should be clothed in purple, and wear gold:

Ma1|14|44|Also that it should be lawful for none of the people or priests to break any of these things, or to gainsay his words, or to gather an assembly in the country without him, or to be clothed in purple, or wear a buckle of gold;

Ma1|14|45|And whosoever should do otherwise, or break any of these things, he should be punished.

Ma1|14|46|Thus it liked all the people to deal with Simon, and to do as hath been said.

Ma1|14|47|Then Simon accepted hereof, and was well pleased to be high priest, and captain and governor of the Jews and priests, and to defend them all.

Ma1|14|48|So they commanded that this writing should be put in tables of brass, and that they should be set up within the compass of the sanctuary in a conspicuous place;

Ma1|14|49|Also that the copies thereof should be laid up in the treasury, to the end that Simon and his sons might have them.

Ma1|15|1|Moreover Antiochus son of Demetrius the king sent letters from the isles of the sea unto Simon the priest and prince of the Jews, and to all the people;

Ma1|15|2|The contents whereof were these: King Antiochus to Simon the high priest and prince of his nation, and to the people of the Jews, greeting:

Ma1|15|3|Forasmuch as certain pestilent men have usurped the kingdom of our fathers, and my purpose is to challenge it again, that I may restore it to the old estate, and to that end have gathered a multitude of foreign soldiers together, and prepared ships of war;

Ma1|15|4|My meaning also being to go through the country, that I may be avenged of them that have destroyed it, and made many cities in the kingdom desolate:

Ma1|15|5|Now therefore I confirm unto thee all the oblations which the kings before me granted thee, and whatsoever gifts besides they granted.

Ma1|15|6|I give thee leave also to coin money for thy country with thine own stamp.

Ma1|15|7|And as concerning Jerusalem and the sanctuary, let them be free; and all the armour that thou hast made, and fortresses that thou hast built, and keepest in thine hands, let them remain unto thee.

Ma1|15|8|And if anything be, or shall be, owing to the king, let it be forgiven thee from this time forth for evermore.

Ma1|15|9|Furthermore, when we have obtained our kingdom, we will honour thee, and thy nation, and thy temple, with great honour, so that your honour shall be known throughout the world.

Ma1|15|10|In the hundred threescore and fourteenth year went Antiochus into the land of his fathers: at which time all the forces came together unto him, so that few were left with Tryphon.

Ma1|15|11|Wherefore being pursued by king Antiochus, he fled unto Dora, which lieth by the sea side:

Ma1|15|12|For he saw that troubles came upon him all at once, and that his forces had forsaken him.

Ma1|15|13|Then camped Antiochus against Dora, having with him an hundred and twenty thousand men of war, and eight thousand horsemen.

Ma1|15|14|And when he had compassed the city round about, and joined ships close to the town on the sea side, he vexed the city by land and by sea, neither suffered he any to go out or in.

Ma1|15|15|In the mean season came Numenius and his company from Rome, having letters to the kings and countries; wherein were written these things:

Ma1|15|16|Lucius, consul of the Romans unto king Ptolemee, greeting:

Ma1|15|17|The Jews' ambassadors, our friends and confederates, came unto us to renew the old friendship and league, being sent from Simon the high priest, and from the people of the Jews:

Ma1|15|18|And they brought a shield of gold of a thousand pound.

Ma1|15|19|We thought it good therefore to write unto the kings and countries, that they should do them no harm, nor fight against them, their cities, or countries, nor yet aid their enemies against them.

Ma1|15|20|It seemed also good to us to receive the shield of them.

Ma1|15|21|If therefore there be any pestilent fellows, that have fled from their country unto you, deliver them unto Simon the high priest, that he may punish them according to their own law.

Ma1|15|22|The same things wrote he likewise unto Demetrius the king, and Attalus, to Ariarathes, and Arsaces,

Ma1|15|23|And to all the countries and to Sampsames, and the Lacedemonians, and to Delus, and Myndus, and Sicyon, and Caria, and Samos, and Pamphylia, and Lycia, and Halicarnassus, and Rhodus, and Aradus, and Cos, and Side, and Aradus, and Gortyna, and Cnidus, and Cyprus, and Cyrene.

Ma1|15|24|And the copy hereof they wrote to Simon the high priest.

Ma1|15|25|So Antiochus the king camped against Dora the second day, assaulting it continually, and making engines, by which means he shut up Tryphon, that he could neither go out nor in.

Ma1|15|26|At that time Simon sent him two thousand chosen men to aid him; silver also, and gold, and much armour.

Ma1|15|27|Nevertheless he would not receive them, but brake all the covenants which he had made with him afore, and became strange unto him.

Ma1|15|28|Furthermore he sent unto him Athenobius, one of his friends, to commune with him, and say, Ye withhold Joppa and Gazera; with the tower that is in Jerusalem, which are cities of my realm.

Ma1|15|29|The borders thereof ye have wasted, and done great hurt in the land, and got the dominion of many places within my kingdom.

Ma1|15|30|Now therefore deliver the cities which ye have taken, and the tributes of the places, whereof ye have gotten dominion without the borders of Judea:

Ma1|15|31|Or else give me for them five hundred talents of silver; and for the harm that ye have done, and the tributes of the cities, other five hundred talents: if not, we will come and fight against you

Ma1|15|32|So Athenobius the king's friend came to Jerusalem: and when he saw the glory of Simon, and the cupboard of gold and silver plate, and his great attendance, he was astonished, and told him the king's message.

Ma1|15|33|Then answered Simon, and said unto him, We have neither taken other men's land, nor holden that which appertaineth to others, but the inheritance of our fathers, which our enemies had wrongfully in possession a certain time.

Ma1|15|34|Wherefore we, having opportunity, hold the inheritance of our fathers.

Ma1|15|35|And whereas thou demandest Joppa and Gazera, albeit they did great harm unto the people in our country, yet will we give thee an hundred talents for them. Hereunto Athenobius answered him not a word;

Ma1|15|36|But returned in a rage to the king, and made report unto him of these speeches, and of the glory of Simon, and of all that he had seen: whereupon the king was exceeding wroth.

Ma1|15|37|In the mean time fled Tryphon by ship unto Orthosias.

Ma1|15|38|Then the king made Cendebeus captain of the sea coast, and gave him an host of footmen and horsemen,

Ma1|15|39|And commanded him to remove his host toward Judea; also he commanded him to build up

Cedron, and to fortify the gates, and to war against the people; but as for the king himself, he pursued Tryphon.

Ma1|15|40|So Cendebeus came to Jamnia and began to provoke the people and to invade Judea, and to take the people prisoners, and slay them.

Ma1|15|41|And when he had built up Cedrou, he set horsemen there, and an host of footmen, to the end that issuing out they might make outroads upon the ways of Judea, as the king had commanded him.

Ma1|16|1|Then came up John from Gazera, and told Simon his father what Cendebeus had done.

Ma1|16|2|Wherefore Simon called his two eldest sons, Judas and John, and said unto them, I, and my brethren, and my father's house, have ever from my youth unto this day fought against the enemies of Israel; and things have prospered so well in our hands, that we have delivered Israel oftentimes.

Ma1|16|3|But now I am old, and ye, by אֱלֹהִים's mercy, are of a sufficient age: be ye instead of me and my brother, and go and fight for our nation, and the help from heaven be with you.

Ma1|16|4|So he chose out of the country twenty thousand men of war with horsemen, who went out against Cendebeus, and rested that night at Modin.

Ma1|16|5|And when as they rose in the morning, and went into the plain, behold, a mighty great host both of footmen and horsemen came against them: howbeit there was a water brook betwixt them.

Ma1|16|6|So he and his people pitched over against them: and when he saw that the people were afraid to go over the water brook, he went first over himself, and then the men seeing him passed through after him.

Ma1|16|7|That done, he divided his men, and set the horsemen in the midst of the footmen: for the enemies' horsemen were very many.

Ma1|16|8|Then sounded they with the holy trumpets: whereupon Cendebeus and his host were put to flight, so that many of them were slain, and the remnant gat them to the strong hold.

Ma1|16|9|At that time was Judas John's brother wounded; but John still followed after them, until he came to Cedron, which Cendebeus had built.

Ma1|16|10|So they fled even unto the towers in the fields of Azotus; wherefore he burned it with fire: so that there were slain of them about two thousand men. Afterward he returned into the land of Judea in peace.

Ma1|16|11|Moreover in the plain of Jericho was Ptolemeus the son of Abubus made captain, and he had abundance of silver and gold:

Ma1|16|12|For he was the high priest's son in law.

Ma1|16|13|Wherefore his heart being lifted up, he thought to get the country to himself, and thereupon consulted deceitfully against Simon and his sons to destroy them.

Ma1|16|14|Now Simon was visiting the cities that were in the country, and taking care for the good ordering of them; at which time he came down himself to Jericho with his sons, Mattathias and Judas, in the hundred threescore and seventeenth year, in the eleventh month, called Sabat:

Ma1|16|15|Where the son of Abubus receiving them deceitfully into a little hold, called Docus, which he had built, made them a great banquet: howbeit he had hid men there.

Ma1|16|16|So when Simon and his sons had drunk largely, Ptolemee and his men rose up, and took their weapons, and came upon Simon into the banqueting place, and slew him, and his two sons, and certain of his servants.

Ma1|16|17|In which doing he committed a great treachery, and recompensed evil for good.

Ma1|16|18|Then Ptolemee wrote these things, and sent to the king, that he should send him an host to aid him, and he would deliver him the country and cities.

Ma1|16|19|He sent others also to Gazera to kill John: and unto the tribunes he sent letters to come unto him, that he might give them silver, and gold, and rewards.

Ma1|16|20|And others he sent to take Jerusalem, and the mountain of the temple.

Ma1|16|21|Now one had run afore to Gazera and told John that his father and brethren were slain, and, quoth he, Ptolemee hath sent to slay thee also.

Ma1|16|22|Hereof when he heard, he was sore astonished: so he laid hands on them that were come to destroy him, and slew them; for he knew that they sought to make him away.

Ma1|16|23|As concerning the rest of the acts of John, and his wars, and worthy deeds which he did, and the building of the walls which he made, and his doings,

Ma1|16|24|Behold, these are written in the chronicles of his priesthood, from the time he was made high priest after his father.

Ma2|1|1|The brethren, the Jews that be at Jerusalem and in the land of Judea, wish unto the brethren, the Jews that are throughout Egypt health and peace:

Ma2|1|2|אֱלֹהִים be gracious unto you, and remember his covenant that he made with Abraham, Isaac, and Jacob, his faithful servants;

Ma2|1|3|And give you all an heart to serve him, and to do his will, with a good courage and a willing mind;

Ma2|1|4|And open your hearts in his law and commandments, and send you peace,

Ma2|1|5|And hear your prayers, and be at one with you, and never forsake you in time of trouble.

Ma2|1|6|And now we be here praying for you.

Ma2|1|7|What time as Demetrius reigned, in the hundred threescore and ninth year, we the Jews wrote unto you in the extremity of trouble that came upon us in those years, from the time that Jason and his company revolted from the holy land and kingdom,

Ma2|1|8|And burned the porch, and shed innocent blood: then we prayed unto the Lord, and were heard; we offered also sacrifices and fine flour, and lighted the lamps, and set forth the loaves.

Ma2|1|9|And now see that ye keep the feast of tabernacles in the month Casleu.

Ma2|1|10|In the hundred fourscore and eighth year, the people that were at Jerusalem and in Judea, and the council, and Judas, sent greeting and health unto Aristobulus, king Ptolemeus' master, who was of the stock of the anointed priests, and to the Jews that were in Egypt:

Ma2|1|11|Insomuch as אֱלֹהִים hath delivered us from great perils, we thank him highly, as having been in battle against a king.

Ma2|1|12|For he cast them out that fought within the holy city.

Ma2|1|13|For when the leader was come into Persia, and the army with him that seemed invincible, they were slain in the temple of Nanea by the deceit of Nanea's priests.

Ma2|1|14|For Antiochus, as though he would marry her, came into the place, and his friends that were with him, to receive money in name of a dowry.

Ma2|1|15|Which when the priests of Nanea had set forth, and he was entered with a small company into the compass of the temple, they shut the temple as soon as Antiochus was come in:

Ma2|1|16|And opening a privy door of the roof, they threw stones like thunderbolts, and struck down the captain, hewed them in pieces, smote off their heads and cast them to those that were without.

Ma2|1|17|Blessed be our אֱלֹהִים in all things, who hath delivered up the ungodly.

Ma2|1|18|Therefore whereas we are now purposed to keep the purification of the temple upon the five and twentieth day of the month Casleu, we thought it necessary to certify you thereof, that ye also might keep it, as the feast of the tabernacles, and of the fire, which was given us when Neemias offered sacrifice, after that he had builded the temple and the altar.

Ma2|1|19|For when our fathers were led into Persia, the priests that were then devout took the fire of the altar privily, and hid it in an hollow place of a pit without water, where they kept it sure, so that the place was unknown to all men.

Ma2|1|20|Now after many years, when it pleased אֱלֹהִים, Neemias, being sent from the king of Persia, did send of the posterity of those priests that had hid it to the fire: but when they told us they found no fire, but thick water;

Ma2|1|21|Then commanded he them to draw it up, and to bring it; and when the sacrifices were laid on, Neemias commanded the priests to sprinkle the wood and the things laid thereupon with the water.

Ma2|1|22|When this was done, and the time came that the sun shone, which afore was hid in the cloud, there was a great fire kindled, so that every man marvelled.

Ma2|1|23|And the priests made a prayer whilst the sacrifice was consuming, I say, both the priests, and all the rest, Jonathan beginning, and the rest answering thereunto, as Neemias did.

Ma2|1|24|And the prayer was after this manner; O Lord, Lord אֱלֹהִים, Creator of all things, who art fearful and strong, and righteous, and merciful, and the only and gracious King,

Ma2|1|25|The only giver of all things, the only just, almighty, and everlasting, thou that deliverest Israel from all trouble, and didst choose the fathers, and sanctify them:

Ma2|1|26|Receive the sacrifice for thy whole people Israel, and preserve thine own portion, and sanctify it.

Ma2|1|27|Gather those together that are scattered from us, deliver them that serve among the heathen, look upon them that are despised and abhorred, and let the heathen know that thou art our אֱלֹהִים.

Ma2|1|28|Punish them that oppress us, and with pride do us wrong.

Ma2|1|29|Plant thy people again in thy holy place, as Moses hath spoken.

Ma2|1|30|And the priests sung psalms of thanksgiving.

Ma2|1|31|Now when the sacrifice was consumed, Neemias commanded the water that was left to be poured on the great stones.

Ma2|1|32|When this was done, there was kindled a flame: but it was consumed by the light that shined from the altar.

Ma2|1|33|So when this matter was known, it was told the king of Persia, that in the place, where the priests that were led away had hid the fire, there appeared water, and that Neemias had purified the sacrifices therewith.

Ma2|1|34|Then the king, inclosing the place, made it holy, after he had tried the matter.

Ma2|1|35|And the king took many gifts, and bestowed thereof on those whom he would gratify.

Ma2|1|36|And Neemias called this thing Naphthar, which is as much as to say, a cleansing: but many men call it Nephi.

Ma2|2|1|It is also found in the records, that Jeremy the prophet commanded them that were carried away to take of the fire, as it hath been signified:

Ma2|2|2|And how that the prophet, having given them the law, charged them not to forget the commandments of the Lord, and that they should not err in their minds, when they see images of silver and gold, with their ornaments.

Ma2|2|3|And with other such speeches exhorted he them, that the law should not depart from their hearts.

Ma2|2|4|It was also contained in the same writing, that the prophet, being warned of אֱלֹהִים, commanded the tabernacle and the ark to go with him, as he went forth into the mountain, where Moses climbed up, and saw the heritage of אֱלֹהִים.

Ma2|2|5|And when Jeremy came thither, he found an hollow cave, wherein he laid the tabernacle, and the ark, and the altar of incense, and so stopped the door.

Ma2|2|6|And some of those that followed him came to mark the way, but they could not find it.

Ma2|2|7|Which when Jeremy perceived, he blamed them, saying, As for that place, it shall be unknown until the time that אֱלֹהִים gather his people again together, and receive them unto mercy.

Ma2|2|8|Then shall the Lord shew them these things, and the glory of the Lord shall appear, and the cloud also, as it was shewed under Moses, and as when Solomon desired that the place might be honourably sanctified.

Ma2|2|9|It was also declared, that he being wise offered the sacrifice of dedication, and of the finishing of the temple.

Ma2|2|10|And as when Moses prayed unto the Lord, the fire came down from heaven, and consumed the sacrifices: even so prayed Solomon also, and the fire came down from heaven, and consumed the burnt offerings.

Ma2|2|11|And Moses said, Because the sin offering was not to be eaten, it was consumed.

Ma2|2|12|So Solomon kept those eight days.

Ma2|2|13|The same things also were reported in the writings and commentaries of Neemias; and how he founding a library gathered together the acts of the kings, and the prophets, and of David, and the epistles of the kings concerning the holy gifts.

Ma2|2|14|In like manner also Judas gathered together all those things that were lost by reason of the war we had, and they remain with us,

Ma2|2|15|Wherefore if ye have need thereof, send some to fetch them unto you.

Ma2|2|16|Whereas we then are about to celebrate the purification, we have written unto you, and ye shall do well, if ye keep the same days.

Ma2|2|17|We hope also, that the אֱלֹהִים, that delivered all his people, and gave them all an heritage, and the kingdom, and the priesthood, and the sanctuary,

Ma2|2|18|As he promised in the law, will shortly have mercy upon us, and gather us together out of every land under heaven into the holy place: for he hath delivered us out of great troubles, and hath purified the place.

Ma2|2|19|Now as concerning Judas Maccabeus, and his brethren, and the purification of the great temple, and the dedication of the altar,

Ma2|2|20|And the wars against Antiochus Epiphanes, and Eupator his son,

Ma2|2|21|And the manifest signs that came from heaven unto those that behaved themselves manfully to their honour for Judaism: so that, being but a few, they overcame the whole country, and chased barbarous multitudes,

Ma2|2|22|And recovered again the temple renowned all the world over, and freed the city, and upheld the laws which were going down, the Lord being gracious unto them with all favour:

Ma2|2|23|All these things, I say, being declared by Jason of Cyrene in five books, we will assay to abridge in one volume.

Ma2|2|24|For considering the infinite number, and the difficulty which they find that desire to look into the narrations of the story, for the variety of the matter,

Ma2|2|25|We have been careful, that they that will read may have delight, and that they that are desirous to commit to memory might have ease, and that all into whose hands it comes might have profit.

Ma2|2|26|Therefore to us, that have taken upon us this painful labour of abridging, it was not easy, but a matter of sweat and watching;

Ma2|2|27|Even as it is no ease unto him that prepareth a banquet, and seeketh the benefit of others: yet for the pleasuring of many we will undertake gladly this great pains;

Ma2|2|28|Leaving to the author the exact handling of every particular, and labouring to follow the rules of an abridgement.

Ma2|2|29|For as the master builder of a new house must care for the whole building; but he that undertaketh to set it out, and paint it, must seek out fit things for the adorning thereof: even so I think it is with us.

Ma2|2|30|To stand upon every point, and go over things at large, and to be curious in particulars, belongeth to the first author of the story:

Ma2|2|31|But to use brevity, and avoid much labouring of the work, is to be granted to him that will make an abridgment.

Ma2|2|32|Here then will we begin the story: only adding thus much to that which hath been said, that it is a foolish thing to make a long prologue, and to be short in the story itself.

Ma2|3|1|Now when the holy city was inhabited with all peace, and the laws were kept very well, because of the godliness of Onias the high priest, and his hatred of wickedness,

Ma2|3|2|It came to pass that even the kings themselves did honour the place, and magnify the temple with their best gifts;

Ma2|3|3|Insomuch that Seleucus of Asia of his own revenues bare all the costs belonging to the service of the sacrifices.

Ma2|3|4|But one Simon of the tribe of Benjamin, who was made governor of the temple, fell out with the high priest about disorder in the city.

Ma2|3|5|And when he could not overcome Onias, he gat him to Apollonius the son of Thraseas, who then was governor of Celosyria and Phenice,

Ma2|3|6|And told him that the treasury in Jerusalem was full of infinite sums of money, so that the multitude of their riches, which did not pertain to the account of the sacrifices, was innumerable, and that it was possible to bring all into the king's hand.

Ma2|3|7|Now when Apollonius came to the king, and had shewed him of the money whereof he was told, the king chose out Heliodorus his treasurer, and sent him with a commandment to bring him the foresaid money.

Ma2|3|8|So forthwith Heliodorus took his journey; under a colour of visiting the cities of Celosyria and Phenice, but indeed to fulfil the king's purpose.

Ma2|3|9|And when he was come to Jerusalem, and had been courteously received of the high priest of the city, he told him what intelligence was given of the money, and declared wherefore he came, and asked if these things were so indeed.

Ma2|3|10|Then the high priest told him that there was such money laid up for the relief of widows and fatherless children:

Ma2|3|11|And that some of it belonged to Hircanus son of Tobias, a man of great dignity, and not as that wicked Simon had misinformed: the sum whereof in all was four hundred talents of silver, and two hundred of gold:

Ma2|3|12|And that it was altogether impossible that such wrongs should be done unto them, that had committed it to the holiness of the place, and to the majesty and inviolable sanctity of the temple, honoured over all the world.

Ma2|3|13|But Heliodorus, because of the king's commandment given him, said, That in any wise it must be brought into the king's treasury.

Ma2|3|14|So at the day which he appointed he entered in to order this matter: wherefore there was no small agony throughout the whole city.

Ma2|3|15|But the priests, prostrating themselves before the altar in their priests' vestments, called unto heaven upon him that made a law concerning things given to he kept, that they should safely be preserved for such as had committed them to be kept.

Ma2|3|16|Then whoso had looked the high priest in the face, it would have wounded his heart: for his countenance and the changing of his colour declared the inward agony of his mind.

Ma2|3|17|For the man was so compassed with fear and horror of the body, that it was manifest to them that looked upon him, what sorrow he had now in his heart.

Ma2|3|18|Others ran flocking out of their houses to the general supplication, because the place was like to come into contempt.

Ma2|3|19|And the women, girt with sackcloth under their breasts, abounded in the streets, and the virgins that were kept in ran, some to the gates, and some to the walls, and others looked out of the windows.

Ma2|3|20|And all, holding their hands toward heaven, made supplication.

Ma2|3|21|Then it would have pitied a man to see the falling down of the multitude of all sorts, and the fear of the high priest being in such an agony.

Ma2|3|22|They then called upon the Almighty Lord to keep the things committed of trust safe and sure for those that had committed them.

Ma2|3|23|Nevertheless Heliodorus executed that which was decreed.

Ma2|3|24|Now as he was there present himself with his guard about the treasury, the Lord of spirits, and the Prince of all power, caused a great apparition, so that all that presumed to come in with him were astonished at the power of אֱלֹהִים, and fainted, and were sore afraid.

Ma2|3|25|For there appeared unto them an horse with a terrible rider upon him, and adorned with a very fair covering, and he ran fiercely, and smote at Heliodorus with his forefeet, and it seemed that he that sat upon the horse had complete harness of gold.

Ma2|3|26|Moreover two other young men appeared before him, notable in strength, excellent in beauty, and comely in apparel, who stood by him on either side; and scourged him continually, and gave him many sore stripes.

Ma2|3|27|And Heliodorus fell suddenly unto the ground, and was compassed with great darkness: but they that were with him took him up, and put him into a litter.

Ma2|3|28|Thus him, that lately came with a great train and with all his guard into the said treasury, they carried out, being unable to help himself with his weapons: and manifestly they acknowledged the power of אֱלֹהִים.

Ma2|3|29|For he by the hand of אֱלֹהִים was cast down, and lay speechless without all hope of life.

Ma2|3|30|But they praised the Lord, that had miraculously honoured his own place: for the temple; which a little afore was full of fear and trouble, when the Almighty Lord appeared, was filled with joy and gladness.

Ma2|3|31|Then straightways certain of Heliodorus' friends prayed Onias, that he would call upon the most High to grant him his life, who lay ready to give up the ghost.

Ma2|3|32|So the high priest, suspecting lest the king should misconceive that some treachery had been done to Heliodorus by the Jews, offered a sacrifice for the health of the man.

Ma2|3|33|Now as the high priest was making an atonement, the same young men in the same clothing appeared and stood beside Heliodorus, saying, Give Onias the high priest great thanks, insomuch as for his sake the Lord hath granted thee life:

Ma2|3|34|And seeing that thou hast been scourged from heaven, declare unto all men the mighty power of אֱלֹהִים. And when they had spoken these words, they appeared no more.

Ma2|3|35|So Heliodorus, after he had offered sacrifice unto the Lord, and made great vows unto him that had saved his life, and saluted Onias, returned with his host to the king.

Ma2|3|36|Then testified he to all men the works of the great אֱלֹהִים, which he had seen with his eyes.

Ma2|3|37|And when the king Heliodorus, who might be a fit man to be sent yet once again to Jerusalem, he said,

Ma2|3|38|If thou hast any enemy or traitor, send him thither, and thou shalt receive him well scourged, if he escape with his life: for in that place, no doubt; there is an especial power of אֱלֹהִים.

Ma2|3|39|For he that dwelleth in heaven hath his eye on that place, and defendeth it; and he beateth and destroyeth them that come to hurt it.

Ma2|3|40|And the things concerning Heliodorus, and the keeping of the treasury, fell out on this sort.

Ma2|4|1|This Simon now, of whom we spake afore, having been a betrayer of the money, and of his country, slandered Onias, as if he ha terrified Heliodorus, and been the worker of these evils.

Ma2|4|2|Thus was he bold to call him a traitor, that had deserved well of the city, and tendered his own nation, and was so zealous of the laws.

Ma2|4|3|But when their hatred went so far, that by one of Simon's faction murders were committed,

Ma2|4|4|Onias seeing the danger of this contention, and that Apollonius, as being the governor of Celosyria and Phenice, did rage, and increase Simon's malice,

Ma2|4|5|He went to the king, not to be an accuser of his countrymen, but seeking the good of all, both publick and private:

Ma2|4|6|For he saw that it was impossible that the state should continue quiet, and Simon leave his folly, unless the king did look thereunto.

Ma2|4|7|But after the death of Seleucus, when Antiochus, called Epiphanes, took the kingdom, Jason the brother of Onias laboured underhand to be high priest,

Ma2|4|8|Promising unto the king by intercession three hundred and threescore talents of silver, and of another revenue eighty talents:

Ma2|4|9|Beside this, he promised to assign an hundred and fifty more, if he might have licence to set him up a place for exercise, and for the training up of youth in the fashions of the heathen, and to write them of Jerusalem by the name of Antiochians.

Ma2|4|10|Which when the king had granted, and he had gotten into his hand the rule he forthwith brought his own nation to Greekish fashion.

Ma2|4|11|And the royal privileges granted of special favour to the Jews by the means of John the father of Eupolemus, who went ambassador to Rome for amity and aid, he took away; and putting down the governments which were according to the law, he brought up new customs against the law:

Ma2|4|12|For he built gladly a place of exercise under the tower itself, and brought the chief young men under his subjection, and made them wear a hat.

Ma2|4|13|Now such was the height of Greek fashions, and increase of heathenish manners, through the exceeding profaneness of Jason, that ungodly wretch, and no high priest;

Ma2|4|14|That the priests had no courage to serve any more at the altar, but despising the temple, and neglecting the sacrifices, hastened to be partakers of the unlawful allowance in the place of exercise, after the game of Discus called them forth;

Ma2|4|15|Not setting by the honours of their fathers, but liking the glory of the Grecians best of all.

Ma2|4|16|By reason whereof sore calamity came upon them: for they had them to be their enemies and avengers, whose custom they followed so earnestly, and unto whom they desired to be like in all things.

Ma2|4|17|For it is not a light thing to do wickedly against the laws of אֱלֹהִים: but the time following shall declare these things.

Ma2|4|18|Now when the game that was used every faith year was kept at Tyrus, the king being present,

Ma2|4|19|This ungracious Jason sent special messengers from Jerusalem, who were Antiochians, to carry three hundred drachms of silver to the sacrifice of Hercules, which even the bearers thereof thought fit not to bestow upon the sacrifice, because it was not convenient, but to be reserved for other charges.

Ma2|4|20|This money then, in regard of the sender, was appointed to Hercules' sacrifice; but because of the bearers thereof, it was employed to the making of gallies.

Ma2|4|21|Now when Apollonius the son of Menestheus was sent into Egypt for the coronation of king Ptolemeus Philometor, Antiochus, understanding him not to be well affected to his affairs, provided for his own safety: whereupon he came to Joppa, and from thence to Jerusalem:

Ma2|4|22|Where he was honourably received of Jason, and of the city, and was brought in with torch alight, and with great shoutings: and so afterward went with his host unto Phenice.

Ma2|4|23|Three years afterward Jason sent Menelaus, the aforesaid Simon's brother, to bear the money unto the king, and to put him in mind of certain necessary matters.

Ma2|4|24|But he being brought to the presence of the king, when he had magnified him for the glorious appearance of his power, got the priesthood to himself, offering more than Jason by three hundred talents of silver.

Ma2|4|25|So he came with the king's mandate, bringing nothing worthy the high priesthood, but having the fury of a cruel tyrant, and the rage of a savage beast.

Ma2|4|26|Then Jason, who had undermined his own brother, being undermined by another, was compelled to flee into the country of the Ammonites.

Ma2|4|27|So Menelaus got the principality: but as for the money that he had promised unto the king, he took no good order for it, albeit Sostratis the ruler of the castle required it:

Ma2|4|28|For unto him appertained the gathering of the customs. Wherefore they were both called before the king.

Ma2|4|29|Now Menelaus left his brother Lysimachus in his stead in the priesthood; and Sostratus left Crates, who was governor of the Cyprians.

Ma2|4|30|While those things were in doing, they of Tarsus and Mallos made insurrection, because they were given to the king's concubine, called Antiochus.

Ma2|4|31|Then came the king in all haste to appease matters, leaving Andronicus, a man in authority, for his deputy.

Ma2|4|32|Now Menelaus, supposing that he had gotten a convenient time, stole certain vessels of gold out of the temple, and gave some of them to Andronicus, and some he sold into Tyrus and the cities round about.

Ma2|4|33|Which when Onias knew of a surety, he reproved him, and withdrew himself into a sanctuary at Daphne, that lieth by Antiochia.

Ma2|4|34|Wherefore Menelaus, taking Andronicus apart, prayed, him to get Onias into his hands; who being persuaded thereunto, and coming to Onias in deceit, gave him his right hand with oaths; and though he were suspected by him, yet persuaded he him to come forth of the sanctuary: whom forthwith he shut up without regard of justice.

Ma2|4|35|For the which cause not only the Jews, but many also of other nations, took great indignation, and were much grieved for the unjust murder of the man.

Ma2|4|36|And when the king was come again from the places about Cilicia, the Jews that were in the city, and certain of the Greeks that abhorred the fact also, complained because Onias was slain without cause.

Ma2|4|37|Therefore Antiochus was heartily sorry, and moved to pity, and wept, because of the sober and modest behaviour of him that was dead.

Ma2|4|38|And being kindled with anger, forthwith he took away Andronicus his purple, and rent off his clothes, and leading him through the whole city unto that very place, where he had committed impiety against Onias, there slew he the cursed murderer. Thus the Lord rewarded him his punishment, as he had deserved.

Ma2|4|39|Now when many sacrileges had been committed in the city by Lysimachus with the consent of Menelaus, and the fruit thereof was spread abroad, the multitude gathered themselves together against Lysimachus, many vessels of gold being already carried away.

Ma2|4|40|Whereupon the common people rising, and being filled with rage, Lysimachus armed about three thousand men, and began first to offer violence; one Auranus being the leader, a man far gone in years, and no less in folly.

Ma2|4|41|They then seeing the attempt of Lysimachus, some of them caught stones, some clubs, others taking handfuls of dust, that was next at hand, cast them all together upon Lysimachus, and those that set upon them.

Ma2|4|42|Thus many of them they wounded, and some they struck to the ground, and all of them they forced to flee: but as for the churchrobber himself, him they killed beside the treasury.

Ma2|4|43|Of these matters therefore there was an accusation laid against Menelaus.

Ma2|4|44|Now when the king came to Tyrus, three men that were sent from the senate pleaded the cause before him:

Ma2|4|45|But Menelaus, being now convicted, promised Ptolemee the son of Dorymenes to give him much money, if he would pacify the king toward him.

Ma2|4|46|Whereupon Ptolemee taking the king aside into a certain gallery, as it were to take the air, brought him to be of another mind:

Ma2|4|47|Insomuch that he discharged Menelaus from the accusations, who notwithstanding was cause of all the mischief: and those poor men, who, if they had told their cause, yea, before the Scythians, should have been judged innocent, them he condemned to death.

Ma2|4|48|Thus they that followed the matter for the city, and for the people, and for the holy vessels, did soon suffer unjust punishment.

Ma2|4|49|Wherefore even they of Tyrus, moved with hatred of that wicked deed, caused them to be honourably buried.

Ma2|4|50|And so through the covetousness of them that were of power Menelaus remained still in authority, increasing in malice, and being a great traitor to the citizens.

Ma2|5|1|About the same time Antiochus prepared his second voyage into Egypt:

Ma2|5|2|And then it happened, that through all the city, for the space almost of forty days, there were seen horsemen running in the air, in cloth of gold, and armed with lances, like a band of soldiers,

Ma2|5|3|And troops of horsemen in array, encountering and running one against another, with shaking of shields, and multitude of pikes, and drawing of swords, and casting of darts, and glittering of golden ornaments, and harness of all sorts.

Ma2|5|4|Wherefore every man prayed that that apparition might turn to good.

Ma2|5|5|Now when there was gone forth a false rumour, as though Antiochus had been dead, Jason took at the least a thousand men, and suddenly made an assault upon the city; and they that were upon the walls being put back, and the city at length taken, Menelaus fled into the castle:

Ma2|5|6|But Jason slew his own citizens without mercy, not considering that to get the day of them of his own nation would be a most unhappy day for him; but thinking they had been his enemies, and not his countrymen, whom he conquered.

Ma2|5|7|Howbeit for all this he obtained not the principality, but at the last received shame for the reward of his treason, and fled again into the country of the Ammonites.

Ma2|5|8|In the end therefore he had an unhappy return, being accused before Aretas the king of the Arabians, fleeing from city to city, pursued of all men, hated as a forsaker of the laws, and being had in abomination as an open enemy of his country and countrymen, he was cast out into Egypt.

Ma2|5|9|Thus he that had driven many out of their country perished in a strange land, retiring to the Lacedemonians, and thinking there to find succour by reason of his kindred:

Ma2|5|10|And he that had cast out many unburied had none to mourn for him, nor any solemn funerals at all, nor sepulchre with his fathers.

Ma2|5|11|Now when this that was done came to the king's car, he thought that Judea had revolted: whereupon removing out of Egypt in a furious mind, he took the city by force of arms,

Ma2|5|12|And commanded his men of war not to spare such as they met, and to slay such as went up upon the houses.

Ma2|5|13|Thus there was killing of young and old, making away of men, women, and children, slaying of virgins and infants.

Ma2|5|14|And there were destroyed within the space of three whole days fourscore thousand, whereof forty thousand were slain in the conflict; and no fewer sold than slain.

Ma2|5|15|Yet was he not content with this, but presumed to go into the most holy temple of all the world; Menelaus, that traitor to the laws, and to his own country, being his guide:

Ma2|5|16|And taking the holy vessels with polluted hands, and with profane hands pulling down the things that were dedicated by other kings to the augmentation and glory and honour of the place, he gave them away.

Ma2|5|17|And so haughty was Antiochus in mind, that he considered not that the Lord was angry for a while for the sins of them that dwelt in the city, and therefore his eye was not upon the place.

Ma2|5|18|For had they not been formerly wrapped in many sins, this man, as soon as he had come, had forthwith been scourged, and put back from his presumption, as Heliodorus was, whom Seleucus the king sent to view the treasury.

Ma2|5|19|Nevertheless אֱלֹהִים did not choose the people for the place's sake, but the place far the people's sake.

Ma2|5|20|And therefore the place itself, that was partaker with them of the adversity that happened to the nation, did afterward communicate in the benefits sent from the Lord: and as it was forsaken in the wrath of the Almighty, so again, the great Lord being reconciled, it was set up with all glory.

Ma2|5|21|So when Antiochus had carried out of the temple a thousand and eight hundred talents, he departed in all haste unto Antiochia, weening in his pride to make the land navigable, and the sea passable by foot: such was the haughtiness of his mind.

Ma2|5|22|And he left governors to vex the nation: at Jerusalem, Philip, for his country a Phrygian, and for manners more barbarous than he that set him there;

Ma2|5|23|And at Garizim, Andronicus; and besides, Menelaus, who worse than all the rest bare an heavy hand over the citizens, having a malicious mind against his countrymen the Jews.

Ma2|5|24|He sent also that detestable ringleader Apollonius with an army of two and twenty thousand, commanding him to slay all those that were in their best age, and to sell the women and the younger sort:

Ma2|5|25|Who coming to Jerusalem, and pretending peace, did forbear till the holy day of the sabbath, when taking the Jews keeping holy day, he commanded his men to arm themselves.

Ma2|5|26|And so he slew all them that were gone to the celebrating of the sabbath, and running through the city with weapons slew great multitudes.

Ma2|5|27|But Judas Maccabeus with nine others, or thereabout, withdrew himself into the wilderness, and lived in the mountains after the manner of beasts, with his company, who fed on herbs continually, lest they should be partakers of the pollution.

Ma2|6|1|Not long after this the king sent an old man of Athens to compel the Jews to depart from the laws of their fathers, and not to live after the laws of אֱלֹהִים:

Ma2|6|2|And to pollute also the temple in Jerusalem, and to call it the temple of Jupiter Olympius; and that in Garizim, of Jupiter the Defender of strangers, as they did desire that dwelt in the place.

Ma2|6|3|The coming in of this mischief was sore and grievous to the people:

Ma2|6|4|For the temple was filled with riot and revelling by the Gentiles, who dallied with harlots, and had to do with women within the circuit of the holy places, and besides that brought in things that were not lawful.

Ma2|6|5|The altar also was filled with profane things, which the law forbiddeth.

Ma2|6|6|Neither was it lawful for a man to keep sabbath days or ancient fasts, or to profess himself at all to be a Jew.

Ma2|6|7|And in the day of the king's birth every month they were brought by bitter constraint to eat of the sacrifices; and when the fast of Bacchus was kept, the Jews were compelled to go in procession to Bacchus, carrying ivy.

Ma2|6|8|Moreover there went out a decree to the neighbour cities of the heathen, by the suggestion of Ptolemee, against the Jews, that they should observe the same fashions, and be partakers of their sacrifices:

Ma2|6|9|And whoso would not conform themselves to the manners of the Gentiles should be put to death. Then might a man have seen the present misery.

Ma2|6|10|For there were two women brought, who had circumcised their children; whom when they had openly led round about the city, the babes handing at their breasts, they cast them down headlong from the wall.

Ma2|6|11|And others, that had run together into caves near by, to keep the sabbath day secretly, being discovered by Philip, were all burnt together, because they made a conscience to help themselves for the honour of the most sacred day.

Ma2|6|12|Now I beseech those that read this book, that they be not discouraged for these calamities, but that they judge those punishments not to be for destruction, but for a chastening of our nation.

Ma2|6|13|For it is a token of his great goodness, when wicked doers are not suffered any long time, but forthwith punished.

Ma2|6|14|For not as with other nations, whom the Lord patiently forbeareth to punish, till they be come to the fulness of their sins, so dealeth he with us,

Ma2|6|15|Lest that, being come to the height of sin, afterwards he should take vengeance of us.

Ma2|6|16|And therefore he never withdraweth his mercy from us: and though he punish with adversity, yet doth he never forsake his people.

Ma2|6|17|But let this that we at spoken be for a warning unto us. And now will we come to the declaring of the matter in a few words.

Ma2|6|18|Eleazar, one of the principal scribes, an aged man, and of a well favoured countenance, was constrained to open his mouth, and to eat swine's flesh.

Ma2|6|19|But he, choosing rather to die gloriously, than to live stained with such an abomination, spit it forth, and came of his own accord to the torment,

Ma2|6|20|As it behoved them to come, that are resolute to stand out against such things, as are not lawful for love of life to be tasted.

Ma2|6|21|But they that had the charge of that wicked feast, for the old acquaintance they had with the man, taking him aside, besought him to bring flesh of his own provision, such as was lawful for him to use, and make as if he did eat of the flesh taken from the sacrifice commanded by the king;

Ma2|6|22|That in so doing he might be delivered from death, and for the old friendship with them find favour.

Ma2|6|23|But he began to consider discreetly, and as became his age, and the excellency of his ancient years, and the honour of his gray head, whereon was come, and his most honest education from a child, or rather the holy law made and given by אֱלֹהִים: therefore he answered accordingly, and willed them straightways to send him to the grave.

Ma2|6|24|For it becometh not our age, said he, in any wise to dissemble, whereby many young persons might think that Eleazar, being fourscore years old and ten, were now gone to a strange religion;

Ma2|6|25|And so they through mine hypocrisy, and desire to live a little time and a moment longer, should be deceived by me, and I get a stain to mine old age, and make it abominable.

Ma2|6|26|For though for the present time I should be delivered from the punishment of men: yet should I not escape the hand of the Almighty, neither alive, nor dead.

Ma2|6|27|Wherefore now, manfully changing this life, I will shew myself such an one as mine age requireth,

Ma2|6|28|And leave a notable example to such as be young to die willingly and courageously for the honourable and holy laws. And when he had said these words, immediately he went to the torment:

Ma2|6|29|They that led him changing the good will they bare him a little before into hatred, because the foresaid speeches proceeded, as they thought, from a desperate mind.

Ma2|6|30|But when he was ready to die with stripes, he groaned, and said, It is manifest unto the Lord, that hath the holy knowledge, that whereas I might have been delivered from death, I now endure sore pains in body by being beaten: but in soul am well content to suffer these things, because I fear him.

Ma2|6|31|And thus this man died, leaving his death for an example of a noble courage, and a memorial of virtue, not only unto young men, but unto all his nation.

Ma2|7|1|It came to pass also, that seven brethren with their mother were taken, and compelled by the king against the law to taste swine's flesh, and were tormented with scourges and whips.

Ma2|7|2|But one of them that spake first said thus, What wouldest thou ask or learn of us? we are ready to die, rather than to transgress the laws of our fathers.

Ma2|7|3|Then the king, being in a rage, commanded pans and caldrons to be made hot:

Ma2|7|4|Which forthwith being heated, he commanded to cut out the tongue of him that spake first, and to cut off the utmost parts of his body, the rest of his brethren and his mother looking on.

Ma2|7|5|Now when he was thus maimed in all his members, he commanded him being yet alive to be brought to the fire, and to be fried in the pan: and as the vapour of the pan was for a good space dispersed, they exhorted one another with the mother to die manfully, saying thus,

Ma2|7|6|The Lord אֱלֹהִים looketh upon us, and in truth hath comfort in us, as Moses in his song, which witnessed to their faces, declared, saying, And he shall be comforted in his servants.

Ma2|7|7|So when the first was dead after this number, they brought the second to make him a mocking stock: and when they had pulled off the skin of his head with the hair, they asked him, Wilt thou eat, before thou be punished throughout every member of thy body?

Ma2|7|8|But he answered in his own language, and said, No. Wherefore he also received the next torment in order, as the former did.

Ma2|7|9|And when he was at the last gasp, he said, Thou like a fury takest us out of this present life, but the King of the world shall raise us up, who have died for his laws, unto everlasting life.

Ma2|7|10|After him was the third made a mocking stock: and when he was required, he put out his tongue, and that right soon, holding forth his hands manfully.

Ma2|7|11|And said courageously, These I had from heaven; and for his laws I despise them; and from him I hope to receive them again.

Ma2|7|12|Insomuch that the king, and they that were with him, marvelled at the young man's courage, for that he nothing regarded the pains.

Ma2|7|13|Now when this man was dead also, they tormented and mangled the fourth in like manner.

Ma2|7|14|So when he was ready to die he said thus, It is good, being put to death by men, to look for hope from אֱלֹהִים to be raised up again by him: as for thee, thou shalt have no resurrection to life.

Ma2|7|15|Afterward they brought the fifth also, and mangled him.

Ma2|7|16|Then looked he unto the king, and said, Thou hast power over men, thou art corruptible, thou doest what thou wilt; yet think not that our nation is forsaken of אֱלֹהִים;

Ma2|7|17|But abide a while, and behold his great power, how he will torment thee and thy seed.

Ma2|7|18|After him also they brought the sixth, who being ready to die said, Be not deceived without cause: for we suffer these things for ourselves, having sinned against our אֱלֹהִים: therefore marvellous things are done unto us.

Ma2|7|19|But think not thou, that takest in hand to strive against אֱלֹהִים, that thou shalt escape unpunished.

Ma2|7|20|But the mother was marvellous above all, and worthy of honourable memory: for when she saw her seven sons slain within the space of one day, she bare it with a good courage, because of the hope that she had in the Lord.

Ma2|7|21|Yea, she exhorted every one of them in her own language, filled with courageous spirits; and stirring up her womanish thoughts with a manly stomach, she said unto them,

Ma2|7|22|I cannot tell how ye came into my womb: for I neither gave you breath nor life, neither was it I that formed the members of every one of you;

Ma2|7|23|But doubtless the Creator of the world, who formed the generation of man, and found out the beginning of all things, will also of his own mercy give you breath and life again, as ye now regard not your own selves for his laws' sake.

Ma2|7|24|Now Antiochus, thinking himself despised, and suspecting it to be a reproachful speech, whilst the youngest was yet alive, did not only exhort him by words, but also assured him with oaths, that he would make him both a rich and a happy man, if he would turn from the laws of his fathers; and that also he would take him for his friend, and trust him with affairs.

Ma2|7|25|But when the young man would in no case hearken unto him, the king called his mother, and exhorted her that she would counsel the young man to save his life.

Ma2|7|26|And when he had exhorted her with many words, she promised him that she would counsel her son.

Ma2|7|27|But she bowing herself toward him, laughing the cruel tyrant to scorn, spake in her country language on this manner; O my son, have pity upon me that bare thee nine months in my womb, and gave thee such three years, and nourished thee, and brought thee up unto this age, and endured the troubles of education.

Ma2|7|28|I beseech thee, my son, look upon the heaven and the earth, and all that is therein, and consider that אֱלֹהִים made them of things that were not; and so was mankind made likewise.

Ma2|7|29|Fear not this tormentor, but, being worthy of thy brethren, take thy death that I may receive thee again in mercy with thy brethren.

Ma2|7|30|Whiles she was yet speaking these words, the young man said, Whom wait ye for? I will not obey the king's commandment: but I will obey the commandment of the law that was given unto our fathers by Moses.

Ma2|7|31|And thou, that hast been the author of all mischief against the Hebrews, shalt not escape the hands of אֱלֹהִים.

Ma2|7|32|For we suffer because of our sins.

Ma2|7|33|And though the living Lord be angry with us a little while for our chastening and correction, yet shall he be at one again with his servants.

Ma2|7|34|But thou, O godless man, and of all other most wicked, be not lifted up without a cause, nor puffed up with uncertain hopes, lifting up thy hand against the servants of אֱלֹהִים:

Ma2|7|35|For thou hast not yet escaped the judgment of Almighty אֱלֹהִים, who seeth all things.

Ma2|7|36|For our brethren, who now have suffered a short pain, are dead under אֱלֹהִים's covenant of everlasting life: but thou, through the judgment of אֱלֹהִים, shalt receive just punishment for thy pride.

Ma2|7|37|But I, as my brethren, offer up my body and life for the laws of our fathers, beseeching אֱלֹהִים that he would speedily be merciful unto our nation; and that thou by torments and plagues mayest confess, that he alone is אֱלֹהִים;

Ma2|7|38|And that in me and my brethren the wrath of the Almighty, which is justly brought upon our nation, may cease.

Ma2|7|39|Than the king' being in a rage, handed him worse than all the rest, and took it grievously that he was mocked.

Ma2|7|40|So this man died undefiled, and put his whole trust in the Lord.

Ma2|7|41|Last of all after the sons the mother died.

Ma2|7|42|Let this be enough now to have spoken concerning the idolatrous feasts, and the extreme tortures.

Ma2|8|1|Then Judas Maccabeus, and they that were with him, went privily into the towns, and called their kinsfolks together, and took unto them all such as continued in the Jews' religion, and assembled about six thousand men.

Ma2|8|2|And they called upon the Lord, that he would look upon the people that was trodden down of all; and also pity the temple profaned of ungodly men;

Ma2|8|3|And that he would have compassion upon the city, sore defaced, and ready to be made even with the ground; and hear the blood that cried unto him,

Ma2|8|4|And remember the wicked slaughter of harmless infants, and the blasphemies committed against his name; and that he would shew his hatred against the wicked.

Ma2|8|5|Now when Maccabeus had his company about him, he could not be withstood by the heathen: for the wrath of the Lord was turned into mercy.

Ma2|8|6|Therefore he came at unawares, and burnt up towns and cities, and got into his hands the most commodious places, and overcame and put to flight no small number of his enemies.

Ma2|8|7|But specially took he advantage of the night for such privy attempts, insomuch that the fruit of his holiness was spread every where.

Ma2|8|8|So when Philip saw that this man increased by little and little, and that things prospered with him still more and more, he wrote unto Ptolemeus, the governor of Celosyria and Phenice, to yield more aid to the king's affairs.

Ma2|8|9|Then forthwith choosing Nicanor the son of Patroclus, one of his special friends, he sent him with no fewer than twenty thousand of all nations under him, to root out the whole generation of the Jews; and with him he joined also Gorgias a captain, who in matters of war had great experience.

Ma2|8|10|So Nicanor undertook to make so much money of the captive Jews, as should defray the tribute of two thousand talents, which the king was to pay to the Romans.

Ma2|8|11|Wherefore immediately he sent to the cities upon the sea coast, proclaiming a sale of the captive Jews, and promising that they should have fourscore and ten bodies for one talent, not expecting the vengeance that was to follow upon him from the Almighty אֱלֹהִים.

Ma2|8|12|Now when word was brought unto Judas of Nicanor's coming, and he had imparted unto those that were with him that the army was at hand,

Ma2|8|13|They that were fearful, and distrusted the justice of אֱלֹהִים, fled, and conveyed themselves away.

Ma2|8|14|Others sold all that they had left, and withal besought the Lord to deliver them, sold by the wicked Nicanor before they met together:

Ma2|8|15|And if not for their own sakes, yet for the covenants he had made with their fathers, and for his holy and glorious name's sake, by which they were called.

Ma2|8|16|So Maccabeus called his men together unto the number of six thousand, and exhorted them not to be stricken with terror of the enemy, nor to fear the great multitude of the heathen, who came wrongly against them; but to fight manfully,

Ma2|8|17|And to set before their eyes the injury that they had unjustly done to the holy place, and the cruel handling of the city, whereof they made a mockery, and also the taking away of the government of their forefathers:

Ma2|8|18|For they, said he, trust in their weapons and boldness; but our confidence is in the Almighty who at a beck can cast down both them that come against us, and also all the world.

Ma2|8|19|Moreover, he recounted unto them what helps their forefathers had found, and how they were delivered, when under Sennacherib an hundred fourscore and five thousand perished.

Ma2|8|20|And he told them of the battle that they had in Babylon with the Galatians, how they came but eight thousand in all to the business, with four thousand Macedonians, and that the Macedonians being perplexed, the eight thousand destroyed an hundred and twenty thousand because of the help that they had from heaven, and so received a great booty.

Ma2|8|21|Thus when he had made them bold with these words, and ready to die for the law and the country, he divided his army into four parts;

Ma2|8|22|And joined with himself his own brethren, leaders of each band, to wit Simon, and Joseph, and Jonathan, giving each one fifteen hundred men.

Ma2|8|23|Also he appointed Eleazar to read the holy book: and when he had given them this watchword, The help of אֱלֹהִים; himself leading the first band,

Ma2|8|24|And by the help of the Almighty they slew above nine thousand of their enemies, and wounded and maimed the most part of Nicanor's host, and so put all to flight;

Ma2|8|25|And took their money that came to buy them, and pursued them far: but lacking time they returned:

Ma2|8|26|For it was the day before the sabbath, and therefore they would no longer pursue them.

Ma2|8|27|So when they had gathered their armour together, and spoiled their enemies, they occupied themselves about the sabbath, yielding exceeding praise and thanks to the Lord, who had preserved them unto that day, which was the beginning of mercy distilling upon them.

Ma2|8|28|And after the sabbath, when they had given part of the spoils to the maimed, and the widows, and orphans, the residue they divided among themselves and their servants.

Ma2|8|29|When this was done, and they had made a common supplication, they besought the merciful Lord to be reconciled with his servants for ever.

Ma2|8|30|Moreover of those that were with Timotheus and Bacchides, who fought against them, they slew above twenty thousand, and very easily got high and strong holds, and divided among themselves many spoils more, and made the maimed, orphans, widows, yea, and the aged also, equal in spoils with themselves.

Ma2|8|31|And when they had gathered their armour together, they laid them up all carefully in convenient places, and the remnant of the spoils they brought to Jerusalem.

Ma2|8|32|They slew also Philarches, that wicked person, who was with Timotheus, and had annoyed the Jews many ways.

Ma2|8|33|Furthermore at such time as they kept the feast for the victory in their country they burnt Callisthenes, that had set fire upon the holy gates, who had fled into a little house; and so he received a reward meet for his wickedness.

Ma2|8|34|As for that most ungracious Nicanor, who had brought a thousand merchants to buy the Jews,

Ma2|8|35|He was through the help of the Lord brought down by them, of whom he made least account; and putting off his glorious apparel, and discharging his company, he came like a fugitive servant through the midland unto Antioch having very great dishonour, for that his host was destroyed.

Ma2|8|36|Thus he, that took upon him to make good to the Romans their tribute by means of captives in Jerusalem, told abroad, that the Jews had אֱלֹהִים to fight for them, and therefore they could not be hurt, because they followed the laws that he gave them.

Ma2|9|1|About that time came Antiochus with dishonour out of the country of Persia

Ma2|9|2|For he had entered the city called Persepolis, and went about to rob the temple, and to hold the city; whereupon the multitude running to defend themselves with their weapons put them to flight; and so it happened, that Antiochus being put to flight of the inhabitants returned with shame.

Ma2|9|3|Now when he came to Ecbatane, news was brought him what had happened unto Nicanor and Timotheus.

Ma2|9|4|Then swelling with anger. he thought to avenge upon the Jews the disgrace done unto him by those that made him flee. Therefore commanded he his chariotman to drive without ceasing, and to dispatch the journey, the judgment of GOd now following him. For he had spoken proudly in this sort, That he would come to Jerusalem and make it a common burying place of the Jews.

Ma2|9|5|But the Lord Almighty, the אֱלֹהִים of Isreal, smote him with an incurable and invisible plague: or as soon as he had spoken these words, a pain of the bowels that was remediless came upon him, and sore torments of the inner parts;

Ma2|9|6|And that most justly: for he had tormented other men's bowels with many and strange torments.

Ma2|9|7|Howbeit he nothing at all ceased from his bragging, but still was filled with pride, breathing out fire in his rage against the Jews, and commanding to haste the journey: but it came to pass that he fell down from his chariot, carried violently; so that having a sore fall, all the members of his body were much pained.

Ma2|9|8|And thus he that a little afore thought he might command the waves of the sea, (so proud was he beyond the condition of man) and weigh the high mountains in a balance, was now cast on the ground, and carried in an horselitter, shewing forth unto all the manifest power of אֱלֹהִים.

Ma2|9|9|So that the worms rose up out of the body of this wicked man, and whiles he lived in sorrow and pain, his flesh fell away, and the filthiness of his smell was noisome to all his army.

Ma2|9|10|And the man, that thought a little afore he could reach to the stars of heaven, no man could endure to carry for his intolerable stink.

Ma2|9|11|Here therefore, being plagued, he began to leave off his great pride, and to come to the knowledge of himself by the scourge of אֱלֹהִים, his pain increasing every moment.

Ma2|9|12|And when he himself could not abide his own smell, he said these words, It is meet to be subject unto אֱלֹהִים, and that a man that is mortal should not proudly think of himself if he were אֱלֹהִים.

Ma2|9|13|This wicked person vowed also unto the Lord, who now no more would have mercy upon him, saying thus,

Ma2|9|14|That the holy city (to the which he was going in haste to lay it even with the ground, and to make it a common buryingplace,) he would set at liberty:

Ma2|9|15|And as touching the Jews, whom he had judged not worthy so much as to be buried, but to be cast out with their children to be devoured of the fowls and wild beasts, he would make them all equals to the citizens of Athens:

Ma2|9|16|And the holy temple, which before he had spoiled, he would garnish with goodly gifts, and restore all the holy vessels with many more, and out of his own revenue defray the charges belonging to the sacrifices:

Ma2|9|17|Yea, and that also he would become a Jew himself, and go through all the world that was inhabited, and declare the power of אֱלֹהִים.

Ma2|9|18|But for all this his pains would not cease: for the just judgment of אֱלֹהִים was come upon him: therefore despairing of his health, he wrote unto the Jews the letter underwritten, containing the form of a supplication, after this manner:

Ma2|9|19|Antiochus, king and governor, to the good Jews his citizens wisheth much joy, health, and prosperity:

Ma2|9|20|If ye and your children fare well, and your affairs be to your contentment, I give very great thanks to אֱלֹהִים, having my hope in heaven.

Ma2|9|21|As for me, I was weak, or else I would have remembered kindly your honour and good will returning out of Persia, and being taken with a grievous disease, I thought it necessary to care for the common safety of all:

Ma2|9|22|Not distrusting mine health, but having great hope to escape this sickness.

Ma2|9|23|But considering that even my father, at what time he led an army into the high countries. appointed a successor,

Ma2|9|24|To the end that, if any thing fell out contrary to expectation, or if any tidings were brought that were grievous, they of the land, knowing to whom the state was left, might not be troubled:

Ma2|9|25|Again, considering how that the princes that are borderers and neighbours unto my kingdom wait for opportunities, and expect what shall be the event. I have appointed my son Antiochus king, whom I often committed and commended unto many of you, when I went up into the high provinces; to whom I have written as followeth:

Ma2|9|26|Therefore I pray and request you to remember the benefits that I have done unto you generally, and in special, and that every man will be still faithful to me and my son.

Ma2|9|27|For I am persuaded that he understanding my mind will favourably and graciously yield to your desires.

Ma2|9|28|Thus the murderer and blasphemer having suffered most grievously, as he entreated other men, so died he a miserable death in a strange country in the mountains.

Ma2|9|29|And Philip, that was brought up with him, carried away his body, who also fearing the son of Antiochus went into Egypt to Ptolemeus Philometor.

Ma2|10|1|Now Maccabeus and his company, the Lord guiding them, recovered the temple and the city:

Ma2|10|2|But the altars which the heathen had built in the open street, and also the chapels, they pulled down.

Ma2|10|3|And having cleansed the temple they made another altar, and striking stones they took fire out of them, and offered a sacrifice after two years, and set forth incense, and lights, and shewbread.

Ma2|10|4|When that was done, they fell flat down, and besought the Lord that they might come no more into such troubles; but if they sinned any more against him, that he himself would chasten them with mercy, and that they might not be delivered unto the blasphemous and barbarous nations.

Ma2|10|5|Now upon the same day that the strangers profaned the temple, on the very same day it was cleansed again, even the five and twentieth day of the same month, which is Casleu.

Ma2|10|6|And they kept the eight days with gladness, as in the feast of the tabernacles, remembering that not long afore they had held the feast of the tabernacles, when as they wandered in the mountains and dens like beasts.

Ma2|10|7|Therefore they bare branches, and fair boughs, and palms also, and sang psalms unto him that had given them good success in cleansing his place.

Ma2|10|8|They ordained also by a common statute and decree, That every year those days should be kept of the whole nation of the Jews.

Ma2|10|9|And this was the end of Antiochus, called Epiphanes.

Ma2|10|10|Now will we declare the acts of Antiochus Eupator, who was the son of this wicked man, gathering briefly the calamities of the wars.

Ma2|10|11|So when he was come to the crown, he set one Lysias over the affairs of his realm, and appointed him his chief governor of Celosyria and Phenice.

Ma2|10|12|For Ptolemeus, that was called Macron, choosing rather to do justice unto the Jews for the wrong that had been done unto them, endeavoured to continue peace with them.

Ma2|10|13|Whereupon being accused of the king's friends before Eupator, and called traitor at every word because he had left Cyprus, that Philometor had committed unto him, and departed to Antiochus Epiphanes, and seeing that he was in no honourable place, he was so discouraged, that he poisoned himself and died.

Ma2|10|14|But when Gorgias was governor of the holds, he hired soldiers, and nourished war continually with the Jews:

Ma2|10|15|And therewithall the Idumeans, having gotten into their hands the most commodious holds, kept the Jews occupied, and receiving those that were banished from Jerusalem, they went about to nourish war.

Ma2|10|16|Then they that were with Maccabeus made supplication, and besought אֱלֹהִים that he would be their helper; and so they ran with violence upon the strong holds of the Idumeans,

Ma2|10|17|And assaulting them strongly, they won the holds, and kept off all that fought upon the wall, and slew all that fell into their hands, and killed no fewer than twenty thousand.

Ma2|10|18|And because certain, who were no less than nine thousand, were fled together into two very strong castles, having all manner of things convenient to sustain the siege,

Ma2|10|19|Maccabeus left Simon and Joseph, and Zaccheus also, and them that were with him, who were enough to besiege them, and departed himself unto those places which more needed his help.

Ma2|10|20|Now they that were with Simon, being led with covetousness, were persuaded for money through certain of those that were in the castle, and took seventy thousand drachms, and let some of them escape.

Ma2|10|21|But when it was told Maccabeus what was done, he called the governors of the people together, and accused those men, that they had sold their brethren for money, and set their enemies free to fight against them.

Ma2|10|22|So he slew those that were found traitors, and immediately took the two castles.

Ma2|10|23|And having good success with his weapons in all things he took in hand, he slew in the two holds more than twenty thousand.

Ma2|10|24|Now Timotheus, whom the Jews had overcome before, when he had gathered a great multitude of foreign forces, and horses out of Asia not a few, came as though he would take Jewry by force of arms.

Ma2|10|25|But when he drew near, they that were with Maccabeus turned themselves to pray unto אֱלֹהִים, and sprinkled earth upon their heads, and girded their loins with sackcloth,

Ma2|10|26|And fell down at the foot of the altar, and besought him to be merciful to them, and to be an enemy to their enemies, and an adversary to their adversaries, as the law declareth.

Ma2|10|27|So after the prayer they took their weapons, and went on further from the city: and when they drew near to their enemies, they kept by themselves.

Ma2|10|28|Now the sun being newly risen, they joined both together; the one part having together with their virtue their refuge also unto the Lord for a pledge of their success and victory: the other side making their rage leader of their battle

Ma2|10|29|But when the battle waxed strong, there appeared unto the enemies from heaven five comely men upon horses, with bridles of gold, and two of them led the Jews,

Ma2|10|30|And took Maccabeus betwixt them, and covered him on every side weapons, and kept him safe, but shot arrows and lightnings against the enemies: so that being confounded with blindness, and full of trouble, they were killed.

Ma2|10|31|And there were slain of footmen twenty thousand and five hundred, and six hundred horsemen.

Ma2|10|32|As for Timotheus himself, he fled into a very strong hold, called Gawra, where Chereas was governor.

Ma2|10|33|But they that were with Maccabeus laid siege against the fortress courageously four days.

Ma2|10|34|And they that were within, trusting to the strength of the place, blasphemed exceedingly, and uttered wicked words.

Ma2|10|35|Nevertheless upon the fifth day early twenty young men of Maccabeus' company, inflamed with anger because of the blasphemies, assaulted the wall manly, and with a fierce courage killed all that they met withal.

Ma2|10|36|Others likewise ascending after them, whiles they were busied with them that were within, burnt the towers, and kindling fires burnt the blasphemers alive; and others broke open the gates, and, having received in the rest of the army, took the city,

Ma2|10|37|And killed Timotheus, that was hid in a certain pit, and Chereas his brother, with Apollophanes.

Ma2|10|38|When this was done, they praised the Lord with psalms and thanksgiving, who had done so great things for Israel, and given them the victory.

Ma2|11|1|Not long after the, Lysias the king's protector and cousin, who also managed the affairs, took sore displeasure for the things that were done.

Ma2|11|2|And when he had gathered about fourscore thousand with all the horsemen, he came against the Jews, thinking to make the city an habitation of the Gentiles,

Ma2|11|3|And to make a gain of the temple, as of the other chapels of the heathen, and to set the high priesthood to sale every year:

Ma2|11|4|Not at all considering the power of אֱלֹהִים but puffed up with his ten thousands of footmen, and his thousands of horsemen, and his fourscore elephants.

Ma2|11|5|So he came to Judea, and drew near to Bethsura, which was a strong town, but distant from Jerusalem about five furlongs, and he laid sore siege unto it.

Ma2|11|6|Now when they that were with Maccabeus heard that he besieged the holds, they and all the people with lamentation and tears besought the Lord that he would send a good angel to deliver Israel.

Ma2|11|7|Then Maccabeus himself first of all took weapons, exhorting the other that they would jeopard themselves together with him to help their brethren: so they went forth together with a willing mind.

Ma2|11|8|And as they were at Jerusalem, there appeared before them on horseback one in white clothing, shaking his armour of gold.

Ma2|11|9|Then they praised the merciful אֱלֹהִים all together, and took heart, insomuch that they were ready not only to fight with men, but with most cruel beasts, and to pierce through walls of iron.

Ma2|11|10|Thus they marched forward in their armour, having an helper from heaven: for the Lord was merciful unto them

Ma2|11|11|And giving a charge upon their enemies like lions, they slew eleven thousand footmen, and sixteen hundred horsemen, and put all the other to flight.

Ma2|11|12|Many of them also being wounded escaped naked; and Lysias himself fled away shamefully, and so escaped.

Ma2|11|13|Who, as he was a man of understanding, casting with himself what loss he had had, and considering that the Hebrews could not be overcome, because the Almighty אֱלֹהִים helped them, he sent unto them,

Ma2|11|14|And persuaded them to agree to all reasonable conditions, and promised that he would persuade the king that he must needs be a friend unto them.

Ma2|11|15|Then Maccabeus consented to all that Lysias desired, being careful of the common good; and whatsoever Maccabeus wrote unto Lysias concerning the Jews, the king granted it.

Ma2|11|16|For there were letters written unto the Jews from Lysias to this effect: Lysias unto the people of the Jews sendeth greeting:

Ma2|11|17|John and Absolom, who were sent from you, delivered me the petition subscribed, and made request for the performance of the contents thereof.

Ma2|11|18|Therefore what things soever were meet to be reported to the king, I have declared them, and he hath granted as much as might be.

Ma2|11|19|And if then ye will keep yourselves loyal to the state, hereafter also will I endeavour to be a means of your good.

Ma2|11|20|But of the particulars I have given order both to these and the other that came from me, to commune with you.

Ma2|11|21|Fare ye well. The hundred and eight and fortieth year, the four and twentieth day of the month Dioscorinthius.

Ma2|11|22|Now the king's letter contained these words: King Antiochus unto his brother Lysias sendeth greeting:

Ma2|11|23|Since our father is translated unto the gods, our will is, that they that are in our realm live quietly, that every one may attend upon his own affairs.

Ma2|11|24|We understand also that the Jews would not consent to our father, for to be brought unto the custom of the Gentiles, but had rather keep their own manner of living: for the which cause they require of us, that we should suffer them to live after their own laws.

Ma2|11|25|Wherefore our mind is, that this nation shall be in rest, and we have determined to restore them their temple, that they may live according to the customs of their forefathers.

Ma2|11|26|Thou shalt do well therefore to send unto them, and grant them peace, that when they are certified of our mind, they may be of good comfort, and ever go cheerfully about their own affairs.

Ma2|11|27|And the letter of the king unto the nation of the Jews was after this manner: King Antiochus sendeth greeting unto the council, and the rest of the Jews:

Ma2|11|28|If ye fare well, we have our desire; we are also in good health.

Ma2|11|29|Menelaus declared unto us, that your desire was to return home, and to follow your own business:

Ma2|11|30|Wherefore they that will depart shall have safe conduct till the thirtieth day of Xanthicus with security.

Ma2|11|31|And the Jews shall use their own kind of meats and laws, as before; and none of them any manner of ways shall be molested for things ignorantly done.

Ma2|11|32|I have sent also Menelaus, that he may comfort you.

Ma2|11|33|Fare ye well. In the hundred forty and eighth year, and the fifteenth day of the month Xanthicus.

Ma2|11|34|The Romans also sent unto them a letter containing these words: Quintus Memmius and Titus Manlius, ambassadors of the Romans, send greeting unto the people of the Jews.

Ma2|11|35|Whatsoever Lysias the king's cousin hath granted, therewith we also are well pleased.

Ma2|11|36|But touching such things as he judged to be referred to the king, after ye have advised thereof, send one forthwith, that we may declare as it is convenient for you: for we are now going to Antioch.

Ma2|11|37|Therefore send some with speed, that we may know what is your mind.

Ma2|11|38|Farewell. This hundred and eight and fortieth year, the fifteenth day of the month Xanthicus.

Ma2|12|1|When these covenants were made, Lysias went unto the king, and the Jews were about their husbandry.

Ma2|12|2|But of the governours of several places, Timotheus, and Apollonius the son of Genneus, also Hieronymus, and Demophon, and beside them Nicanor the governor of Cyprus, would not suffer them to be quiet and live in peace.

Ma2|12|3|The men of Joppa also did such an ungodly deed: they prayed the Jews that dwelt among them to go with their wives and children into the boats which they had prepared, as though they had meant them no hurt.

Ma2|12|4|Who accepted of it according to the common decree of the city, as being desirous to live in peace, and suspecting nothing: but when they were gone forth into the deep, they drowned no less than two hundred of them.

Ma2|12|5|When Judas heard of this cruelty done unto his countrymen, he commanded those that were with him to make them ready.

Ma2|12|6|And calling upon אֱלֹהִים the righteous Judge, he came against those murderers of his brethren, and burnt the haven by night, and set the boats on fire, and those that fled thither he slew.

Ma2|12|7|And when the town was shut up, he went backward, as if he would return to root out all them of the city of Joppa.

Ma2|12|8|But when he heard that the Jamnites were minded to do in like manner unto the Jews that dwelt among them,

Ma2|12|9|He came upon the Jamnites also by night, and set fire on the haven and the navy, so that the light of the fire was seen at Jerusalem two hundred and forty furlongs off.

Ma2|12|10|Now when they were gone from thence nine furlongs in their journey toward Timotheus, no fewer than five thousand men on foot and five hundred horsemen of the Arabians set upon him.

Ma2|12|11|Whereupon there was a very sore battle; but Judas' side by the help of אֱלֹהִים got the victory; so that the Nomades of Arabia, being overcome, besought Judas for peace, promising both to give him cattle, and to pleasure him otherwise.

Ma2|12|12|Then Judas, thinking indeed that they would be profitable in many things, granted them peace: whereupon they shook hands, and so they departed to their tents.

Ma2|12|13|He went also about to make a bridge to a certain strong city, which was fenced about with walls, and inhabited by people of divers countries; and the name of it was Caspis.

Ma2|12|14|But they that were within it put such trust in the strength of the walls and provision of victuals, that they behaved themselves rudely toward them that were with Judas, railing and blaspheming, and uttering such words as were not to be spoken.

Ma2|12|15|Wherefore Judas with his company, calling upon the great Lord of the world, who without rams or engines of war did cast down Jericho in the time of Joshua, gave a fierce assault against the walls,

Ma2|12|16|And took the city by the will of אֱלֹהִים, and made unspeakable slaughters, insomuch that a lake two furlongs broad near adjoining thereunto, being filled full, was seen running with blood.

Ma2|12|17|Then departed they from thence seven hundred and fifty furlongs, and came to Characa unto the Jews that are called Tubieni.

Ma2|12|18|But as for Timotheus, they found him not in the places: for before he had dispatched any thing, he departed from thence, having left a very strong garrison in a certain hold.

Ma2|12|19|Howbeit Dositheus and Sosipater, who were of Maccabeus' captains, went forth, and slew those that Timotheus had left in the fortress, above ten thousand men.

Ma2|12|20|And Maccabeus ranged his army by bands, and set them over the bands, and went against Timotheus, who had about him an hundred and twenty thousand men of foot, and two thousand and five hundred horsemen.

Ma2|12|21|Now when Timotheus had knowledge of Judas' coming, he sent the women and children and the other baggage unto a fortress called Carnion: for the town was hard to besiege, and uneasy to come unto, by reason of the straitness of all the places.

Ma2|12|22|But when Judas his first band came in sight, the enemies, being smitten with fear and terror through the appearing of him who seeth all things, fled amain, one running into this way, another that way, so as that they were often hurt of their own men, and wounded with the points of their own swords.

Ma2|12|23|Judas also was very earnest in pursuing them, killing those wicked wretches, of whom he slew about thirty thousand men.

Ma2|12|24|Moreover Timotheus himself fell into the hands of Dositheus and Sosipater, whom he besought with much craft to let him go with his life, because he had many of the Jews' parents, and the brethren of some of them, who, if they put him to death, should not be regarded.

Ma2|12|25|So when he had assured them with many words that he would restore them without hurt, according to the agreement, they let him go for the saving of their brethren.

Ma2|12|26|Then Maccabeus marched forth to Carnion, and to the temple of Atargatis, and there he slew five and twenty thousand persons.

Ma2|12|27|And after he had put to flight and destroyed them, Judas removed the host toward Ephron, a strong city, wherein Lysias abode, and a great multitude of divers nations, and the strong young men kept the walls, and defended them mightily: wherein also was great provision of engines and darts.

Ma2|12|28|But when Judas and his company had called upon Almighty אֱלֹהִים, who with his power breaketh the strength of his enemies, they won the city, and slew twenty and five thousand of them that were within,

Ma2|12|29|From thence they departed to Scythopolis, which lieth six hundred furlongs from Jerusalem,

Ma2|12|30|But when the Jews that dwelt there had testified that the Scythopolitans dealt lovingly with them, and entreated them kindly in the time of their adversity;

Ma2|12|31|They gave them thanks, desiring them to be friendly still unto them: and so they came to Jerusalem, the feast of the weeks approaching.

Ma2|12|32|And after the feast, called Pentecost, they went forth against Gorgias the governor of Idumea,

Ma2|12|33|Who came out with three thousand men of foot and four hundred horsemen.

Ma2|12|34|And it happened that in their fighting together a few of the Jews were slain.

Ma2|12|35|At which time Dositheus, one of Bacenor's company, who was on horseback, and a strong man, was still upon Gorgias, and taking hold of his coat drew him by force; and when he would have taken that cursed man alive, a horseman of Thracia coming upon him smote off his shoulder, so that Gorgias fled unto Marisa.

Ma2|12|36|Now when they that were with Gorgias had fought long, and were weary, Judas called upon the Lord, that he would shew himself to be their helper and leader of the battle.

Ma2|12|37|And with that he began in his own language, and sung psalms with a loud voice, and rushing unawares upon Gorgias' men, he put them to flight.

Ma2|12|38|So Judas gathered his host, and came into the city of Odollam, And when the seventh day came, they purified themselves, as the custom was, and kept the sabbath in the same place.

Ma2|12|39|And upon the day following, as the use had been, Judas and his company came to take up the bodies of them that were slain, and to bury them with their kinsmen in their fathers' graves.

Ma2|12|40|Now under the coats of every one that was slain they found things consecrated to the idols of the Jamnites, which is forbidden the Jews by the law. Then every man saw that this was the cause wherefore they were slain.

Ma2|12|41|All men therefore praising the Lord, the righteous Judge, who had opened the things that were hid,

Ma2|12|42|Betook themselves unto prayer, and besought him that the sin committed might wholly be put out of remembrance. Besides, that noble Judas exhorted the people to keep themselves from sin, forsomuch as they saw before their eyes the things that came to pass for the sins of those that were slain.

Ma2|12|43|And when he had made a gathering throughout the company to the sum of two thousand drachms of silver, he sent it to Jerusalem to offer a sin offering, doing therein very well and honestly, in that he was mindful of the resurrection:

Ma2|12|44|For if he had not hoped that they that were slain should have risen again, it had been superfluous and vain to pray for the dead.

Ma2|12|45|And also in that he perceived that there was great favour laid up for those that died godly, it was an holy and good thought. Whereupon he made a reconciliation for the dead, that they might be delivered from sin.

Ma2|13|1|In the hundred forty and ninth year it was told Judas, that Antiochus Eupator was coming with a great power into Judea,

Ma2|13|2|And with him Lysias his protector, and ruler of his affairs, having either of them a Grecian power of footmen, an hundred and ten thousand, and horsemen five thousand and three hundred, and elephants two and twenty, and three hundred chariots armed with hooks.

Ma2|13|3|Menelaus also joined himself with them, and with great dissimulation encouraged Antiochus, not for the safeguard of the country, but because he thought to have been made governor.

Ma2|13|4|But the King of kings moved Antiochus' mind against this wicked wretch, and Lysias informed the king that this man was the cause of all mischief, so that the king commanded to bring him unto Berea, and to put him to death, as the manner is in that place.

Ma2|13|5|Now there was in that place a tower of fifty cubits high, full of ashes, and it had a round instrument which on every side hanged down into the ashes.

Ma2|13|6|And whosoever was condemned of sacrilege, or had committed any other grievous crime, there did all men thrust him unto death.

Ma2|13|7|Such a death it happened that wicked man to die, not having so much as burial in the earth; and that most justly:

Ma2|13|8|For inasmuch as he had committed many sins about the altar, whose fire and ashes were holy, he received his death in ashes.

Ma2|13|9|Now the king came with a barbarous and haughty mind to do far worse to the Jews, than had been done in his father's time.

Ma2|13|10|Which things when Judas perceived, he commanded the multitude to call upon the Lord night and day, that if ever at any other time, he would now also help them, being at the point to be put from their law, from their country, and from the holy temple:

Ma2|13|11|And that he would not suffer the people, that had even now been but a little refreshed, to be in subjection to the blasphemous nations.

Ma2|13|12|So when they had all done this together, and besought the merciful Lord with weeping and fasting, and lying flat upon the ground three days long, Judas, having exhorted them, commanded they should be in a readiness.

Ma2|13|13|And Judas, being apart with the elders, determined, before the king's host should enter into Judea, and get the city, to go forth and try the matter in fight by the help of the Lord.

Ma2|13|14|So when he had committed all to the Creator of the world, and exhorted his soldiers to fight manfully, even unto death, for the laws, the temple, the city, the country, and the commonwealth, he camped by Modin:

Ma2|13|15|And having given the watchword to them that were about him, Victory is of אֱלֹהִים; with the most valiant and choice young men he went in into the king's tent by night, and slew in the camp about four thousand men, and the chiefest of the elephants, with all that were upon him.

Ma2|13|16|And at last they filled the camp with fear and tumult, and departed with good success.

Ma2|13|17|This was done in the break of the day, because the protection of the Lord did help him.

Ma2|13|18|Now when the king had taken a taste of the manliness of the Jews, he went about to take the holds by policy,

Ma2|13|19|And marched toward Bethsura, which was a strong hold of the Jews: but he was put to flight, failed, and lost of his men:

Ma2|13|20|For Judas had conveyed unto them that were in it such things as were necessary.

Ma2|13|21|But Rhodocus, who was in the Jews' host, disclosed the secrets to the enemies; therefore he was sought out, and when they had gotten him, they put him in prison.

Ma2|13|22|The king treated with them in Bethsum the second time, gave his hand, took their's, departed, fought with Judas, was overcome;

Ma2|13|23|Heard that Philip, who was left over the affairs in Antioch, was desperately bent, confounded, intreated the Jews, submitted himself, and sware to all equal conditions, agreed with them, and offered sacrifice, honoured the temple, and dealt kindly with the place,

Ma2|13|24|And accepted well of Maccabeus, made him principal governor from Ptolemais unto the Gerrhenians;

Ma2|13|25|Came to Ptolemais: the people there were grieved for the covenants; for they stormed, because they would make their covenants void:

Ma2|13|26|Lysias went up to the judgment seat, said as much as could be in defence of the cause, persuaded, pacified, made them well affected, returned to Antioch. Thus it went touching the king's coming and departing.

Ma2|14|1|After three years was Judas informed, that Demetrius the son of Seleucus, having entered by the haven of Tripolis with a great power and navy,

Ma2|14|2|Had taken the country, and killed Antiochus, and Lysias his protector.

Ma2|14|3|Now one Alcimus, who had been high priest, and had defiled himself wilfully in the times of their mingling with the Gentiles, seeing that by no means he could save himself, nor have any more access to the holy altar,

Ma2|14|4|Came to king Demetrius in the hundred and one and fiftieth year, presenting unto him a crown of gold, and a palm, and also of the boughs which were used solemnly in the temple: and so that day he held his peace.

Ma2|14|5|Howbeit having gotten opportunity to further his foolish enterprize, and being called into counsel by Demetrius, and asked how the Jews stood affected, and what they intended, he answered thereunto:

Ma2|14|6|Those of the Jews that he called Assideans, whose captain is Judas Maccabeus, nourish war and are seditious, and will not let the rest be in peace.

Ma2|14|7|Therefore I, being deprived of mine ancestors' honour, I mean the high priesthood, am now come hither:

Ma2|14|8|First, verily for the unfeigned care I have of things pertaining to the king; and secondly, even for that I intend the good of mine own countrymen: for all our nation is in no small misery through the unadvised dealing of them aforersaid.

Ma2|14|9|Wherefore, O king, seeing knowest all these things, be careful for the country, and our nation, which is pressed on every side, according to the clemency that thou readily shewest unto all.

Ma2|14|10|For as long as Judas liveth, it is not possible that the state should be quiet.

Ma2|14|11|This was no sooner spoken of him, but others of the king's friends, being maliciously set against Judas, did more incense Demetrius.

Ma2|14|12|And forthwith calling Nicanor, who had been master of the elephants, and making him governor over Judea, he sent him forth,

Ma2|14|13|Commanding him to slay Judas, and to scatter them that were with him, and to make Alcimus high priest of the great temple.

Ma2|14|14|Then the heathen, that had fled out of Judea from Judas, came to Nicanor by flocks, thinking the harm and calamities ot the Jews to be their welfare.

Ma2|14|15|Now when the Jews heard of Nicanor's coming, and that the heathen were up against them, they cast earth upon their heads, and made supplication to him that had established his people for ever, and who always helpeth his portion with manifestation of his presence.

Ma2|14|16|So at the commandment of the captain they removed straightways from thence, and came near unto them at the town of Dessau.

Ma2|14|17|Now Simon, Judas' brother, had joined battle with Nicanor, but was somewhat discomfited through the sudden silence of his enemies.

Ma2|14|18|Nevertheless Nicanor, hearing of the manliness of them that were with Judas, and the courageousness that they had to fight for their country, durst not try the matter by the sword.

Ma2|14|19|Wherefore he sent Posidonius, and Theodotus, and Mattathias, to make peace.

Ma2|14|20|So when they had taken long advisement thereupon, and the captain had made the multitude acquainted therewith, and it appeared that they were all of one mind, they consented to the covenants,

Ma2|14|21|And appointed a day to meet in together by themselves: and when the day came, and stools were set for either of them,

Ma2|14|22|Ludas placed armed men ready in convenient places, lest some treachery should be suddenly practised by the enemies: so they made a peaceable conference.

Ma2|14|23|Now Nicanor abode in Jerusalem, and did no hurt, but sent away the people that came flocking unto him.

Ma2|14|24|And he would not willingly have Judas out of his sight: for he love the man from his heart

Ma2|14|25|He prayed him also to take a wife, and to beget children: so he married, was quiet, and took part of this life.

Ma2|14|26|But Alcimus, perceiving the love that was betwixt them, and considering the covenants that were made, came to Demetrius, and told him that Nicanor was not well affected toward the state; for that he had ordained Judas, a traitor to his realm, to be the king's successor.

Ma2|14|27|Then the king being in a rage, and provoked with the accusations of the most wicked man, wrote to Nicanor, signifying that he was much displeased with the covenants, and commanding him that he should send Maccabeus prisoner in all haste unto Antioch.

Ma2|14|28|When this came to Nicanor's hearing, he was much confounded in himself, and took it grievously that he should make void the articles which were agreed upon, the man being in no fault.

Ma2|14|29|But because there was no dealing against the king, he watched his time to accomplish this thing by policy.

Ma2|14|30|Notwithstanding, when Maccabeus saw that Nicanor began to be churlish unto him, and that he entreated him more roughly than he was wont, perceiving that such sour behaviour came not of good, he gathered together not a few of his men, and withdrew himself from Nicanor.

Ma2|14|31|But the other, knowing that he was notably prevented by Judas' policy, came into the great and holy temple, and commanded the priests, that were offering their usual sacrifices, to deliver him the man.

Ma2|14|32|And when they sware that they could not tell where the man was whom he sought,

Ma2|14|33|He stretched out his right hand toward the temple, and made an oath in this manner: If ye will not deliver me Judas as a prisoner, I will lay this temple of אֱלֹהִים even with the ground, and I will break down the altar, and erect a notable temple unto Bacchus.

Ma2|14|34|After these words he departed. Then the priests lifted up their hands toward heaven, and besought him that was ever a defender of their nation, saying in this manner;

Ma2|14|35|Thou, O Lord of all things, who hast need of nothing, wast pleased that the temple of thine habitation should be among us:

Ma2|14|36|Therefore now, O holy Lord of all holiness, keep this house ever undefiled, which lately was cleansed, and stop every unrighteous mouth.

Ma2|14|37|Now was there accused unto Nicanor one Razis, one of the elders of Jerusalem, a lover of his countrymen, and a man of very good report, who for his kindness was called a father of the Jews.

Ma2|14|38|For in the former times, when they mingled not themselves with the Gentiles, he had been accused of Judaism, and did boldly jeopard his body and life with all vehemency for the religion of the Jews.

Ma2|14|39|So Nicanor, willing to declare the hate that he bare unto the Jews, sent above five hundred men of war to take him:

Ma2|14|40|For he thought by taking him to do the Jews much hurt.

Ma2|14|41|Now when the multitude would have taken the tower, and violently broken into the outer door, and bade that fire should be brought to burn it, he being ready to be taken on every side fell upon his sword;

Ma2|14|42|Choosing rather to die manfully, than to come into the hands of the wicked, to be abused otherwise than beseemed his noble birth:

Ma2|14|43|But missing his stroke through haste, the multitude also rushing within the doors, he ran boldly up to the wall, and cast himself down manfully among the thickest of them.

Ma2|14|44|But they quickly giving back, and a space being made, he fell down into the midst of the void place.

Ma2|14|45|Nevertheless, while there was yet breath within him, being inflamed with anger, he rose up; and though his blood gushed out like spouts of water, and his wounds were grievous, yet he ran through the midst of the throng; and standing upon a steep rock,

Ma2|14|46|When as his blood was now quite gone, he plucked out his bowels, and taking them in both his hands, he cast them upon the throng, and calling upon the Lord of life and spirit to restore him those again, he thus died.

Ma2|15|1|But Nicanor, hearing that Judas and his company were in the strong places about Samaria, resolved without any danger to set upon them on the sabbath day.

Ma2|15|2|Nevertheless the Jews that were compelled to go with him said, O destroy not so cruelly and barbarously, but give honour to that day, which he, that seeth all things, hath honoured with holiness above all other days.

Ma2|15|3|Then the most ungracious wretch demanded, if there were a Mighty one in heaven, that had commanded the sabbath day to be kept.

Ma2|15|4|And when they said, There is in heaven a living Lord, and mighty, who commanded the seventh day to be kept:

Ma2|15|5|Then said the other, And I also am mighty upon earth, and I command to take arms, and to do the king's business. Yet he obtained not to have his wicked will done.

Ma2|15|6|So Nicanor in exceeding pride and haughtiness determined to set up a publick monument of his victory over Judas and them that were with him.

Ma2|15|7|But Maccabeus had ever sure confidence that the Lord would help him:

Ma2|15|8|Wherefore he exhorted his people not to fear the coming of the heathen against them, but to remember the help which in former times they had received from heaven, and now to expect the victory and aid, which should come unto them from the Almighty.

Ma2|15|9|And so comforting them out of the law and the prophets, and withal putting them in mind of the battles that they won afore, he made them more cheerful.

Ma2|15|10|And when he had stirred up their minds, he gave them their charge, shewing them therewithall the falsehood of the heathen, and the breach of oaths.

Ma2|15|11|Thus he armed every one of them, not so much with defence of shields and spears, as with comfortable and good words: and beside that, he told them a dream worthy to be believed, as if it had been so indeed, which did not a little rejoice them.

Ma2|15|12|And this was his vision: That Onias, who had been high priest, a virtuous and a good man, reverend in conversation, gentle in condition, well spoken also, and exercised from a child in all points of virtue, holding up his hands prayed for the whole body of the Jews.

Ma2|15|13|This done, in like manner there appeared a man with gray hairs, and exceeding glorious, who was of a wonderful and excellent majesty.

Ma2|15|14|Then Onias answered, saying, This is a lover of the brethren, who prayeth much for the people, and for the holy city, to wit, Jeremias the prophet of אֱלֹהִים.

Ma2|15|15|Whereupon Jeremias holding forth his right hand gave to Judas a sword of gold, and in giving it spake thus,

Ma2|15|16|Take this holy sword, a gift from אֱלֹהִים, with the which thou shalt wound the adversaries.

Ma2|15|17|Thus being well comforted by the words of Judas, which were very good, and able to stir them up to valour, and to encourage the hearts of the young men, they determined not to pitch camp, but courageously to set upon them, and manfully to try the matter by conflict, because the city and the sanctuary and the temple were in danger.

Ma2|15|18|For the care that they took for their wives, and their children, their brethren, and folks, was in least account with them: but the greatest and principal fear was for the holy temple.

Ma2|15|19|Also they that were in the city took not the least care, being troubled for the conflict abroad.

Ma2|15|20|And now, when as all looked what should be the trial, and the enemies were already come near, and the army was set in array, and the beasts conveniently placed, and the horsemen set in wings,

Ma2|15|21|Maccabeus seeing the coming of the multitude, and the divers preparations of armour, and the fierceness of the beasts, stretched out his hands toward heaven, and called upon the Lord that worketh wonders, knowing that victory cometh not by arms, but even as it seemeth good to him, he giveth it to such as are worthy:

Ma2|15|22|Therefore in his prayer he said after this manner; O Lord, thou didst send thine angel in the time of Ezekias king of Judea, and didst slay in the host of Sennacherib an hundred fourscore and five thousand:

Ma2|15|23|Wherefore now also, O Lord of heaven, send a good angel before us for a fear and dread unto them;

Ma2|15|24|And through the might of thine arm let those be stricken with terror, that come against thy holy people to blaspheme. And he ended thus.

Ma2|15|25|Then Nicanor and they that were with him came forward with trumpets and songs.

Ma2|15|26|But Judas and his company encountered the enemies with invocation and prayer.

Ma2|15|27|So that fighting with their hands, and praying unto אֱלֹהִים with their hearts, they slew no less than thirty and five thousand men: for through the appearance of אֱלֹהִים they were greatly cheered.

Ma2|15|28|Now when the battle was done, returning again with joy, they knew that Nicanor lay dead in his harness.

Ma2|15|29|Then they made a great shout and a noise, praising the Almighty in their own language.

Ma2|15|30|And Judas, who was ever the chief defender of the citizens both in body and mind, and who continued his love toward his countrymen all his life, commanded to strike off Nicanor's head, and his hand with his shoulder, and bring them to Jerusalem.

Ma2|15|31|So when he was there, and called them of his nation together, and set the priests before the altar, he sent for them that were of the tower,

Ma2|15|32|And shewed them vile Nicanor's head, and the hand of that blasphemer, which with proud brags he had stretched out against the holy temple of the Almighty.

Ma2|15|33|And when he had cut out the tongue of that ungodly Nicanor, he commanded that they should give it by pieces unto the fowls, and hang up the reward of his madness before the temple.

Ma2|15|34|So every man praised toward the heaven the glorious Lord, saying, Blessed be he that hath kept his own place undefiled.

Ma2|15|35|He hanged also Nicanor's head upon the tower, an evident and manifest sign unto all of the help of the Lord.

Ma2|15|36|And they ordained all with a common decree in no case to let that day pass without solemnity, but to celebrate the thirtieth day of the twelfth month, which in the Syrian tongue is called Adar, the day before Mardocheus' day.

Ma2|15|37|Thus went it with Nicanor: and from that time forth the Hebrews had the city in their power. And here will I make an end.

Ma2|15|38|And if I have done well, and as is fitting the story, it is that which I desired: but if slenderly and meanly, it is that which I could attain unto.

Ma2|15|39|For as it is hurtful to drink wine or water alone; and as wine mingled with water is pleasant, and delighteth the taste: even so speech finely framed delighteth the ears of them that read the story. And here shall be an end.

Tob|1|1|The book of the words of Tobit, son of Tobiel, the son of Ananiel, the son of Aduel, the son of Gabael, of the seed of Asael, of the tribe of Nephthali;

Tob|1|2|Who in the time of Enemessar king of the Assyrians was led captive out of Thisbe, which is at the right hand of that city, which is called properly Nephthali in Galilee above Aser.

Tob|1|3|I Tobit have walked all the days of my life in the ways of truth and justice, and I did many almsdeeds to my brethren, and my nation, who came with me to Nineve, into the land of the Assyrians.

Tob|1|4|And when I was in mine own country, in the land of Israel being but young, all the tribe of Nephthali my father fell from the house of Jerusalem, which was chosen out of all the tribes of Israel, that all the tribes should sacrifice there, where the temple of the habitation of the most High was consecrated and built for all ages.

Tob|1|5|Now all the tribes which together revolted, and the house of my father Nephthali, sacrificed unto the heifer Baal.

Tob|1|6|But I alone went often to Jerusalem at the feasts, as it was ordained unto all the people of Israel by an everlasting decree, having the firstfruits and tenths of increase, with that which was first shorn; and them gave I at the altar to the priests the children of Aaron.

Tob|1|7|The first tenth part of all increase I gave to the sons of Aaron, who ministered at Jerusalem: another tenth part I sold away, and went, and spent it every year at Jerusalem:

Tob|1|8|And the third I gave unto them to whom it was meet, as Debora my father's mother had commanded me, because I was left an orphan by my father.

Tob|1|9|Furthermore, when I was come to the age of a man, I married Anna of mine own kindred, and of her I begat Tobias.

Tob|1|10|And when we were carried away captives to Nineve, all my brethren and those that were of my kindred did eat of the bread of the Gentiles.

Tob|1|11|But I kept myself from eating;

Tob|1|12|Because I remembered אֱלֹהִים with all my heart.

Tob|1|13|And the most High gave me grace and favour before Enemessar, so that I was his purveyor.

Tob|1|14|And I went into Media, and left in trust with Gabael, the brother of Gabrias, at Rages a city of Media ten talents of silver.

Tob|1|15|Now when Enemessar was dead, Sennacherib his son reigned in his stead; whose estate was troubled, that I could not go into Media.

Tob|1|16|And in the time of Enemessar I gave many alms to my brethren, and gave my bread to the hungry,

Tob|1|17|And my clothes to the naked: and if I saw any of my nation dead, or cast about the walls of Nineve, I buried him.

Tob|1|18|And if the king Sennacherib had slain any, when he was come, and fled from Judea, I buried them privily; for in his wrath he killed many; but the bodies were not found, when they were sought for of the king.

Tob|1|19|And when one of the Ninevites went and complained of me to the king, that I buried them, and hid myself; understanding that I was sought for to be put to death, I withdrew myself for fear.

Tob|1|20|Then all my goods were forcibly taken away, neither was there any thing left me, beside my wife Anna and my son Tobias.

Tob|1|21|And there passed not five and fifty days, before two of his sons killed him, and they fled into the mountains of Ararath; and Sarchedonus his son reigned in his stead; who appointed over his father's accounts, and over all his affairs, Achiacharus my brother Anael's son.

Tob|1|22|And Achiacharus intreating for me, I returned to Nineve. Now Achiacharus was cupbearer, and keeper of the signet, and steward, and overseer of the accounts: and Sarchedonus appointed him next unto him: and he was my brother's son.

Tob|2|1|Now when I was come home again, and my wife Anna was restored unto me, with my son Tobias, in the feast of Pentecost, which is the holy feast of the seven weeks, there was a good dinner prepared me, in the which I sat down to eat.

Tob|2|2|And when I saw abundance of meat, I said to my son, Go and bring what poor man soever thou shalt find out of our brethren, who is mindful of the Lord; and, lo, I tarry for thee.

Tob|2|3|But he came again, and said, Father, one of our nation is strangled, and is cast out in the marketplace.

Tob|2|4|Then before I had tasted of any meat, I started up, and took him up into a room until the going down of the sun.

Tob|2|5|Then I returned, and washed myself, and ate my meat in heaviness,

Tob|2|6|Remembering that prophecy of Amos, as he said, Your feasts shall be turned into mourning, and all your mirth into lamentation.

Tob|2|7|Therefore I wept: and after the going down of the sun I went and made a grave, and buried him.

Tob|2|8|But my neighbours mocked me, and said, This man is not yet afraid to be put to death for this matter: who fled away; and yet, lo, he burieth the dead again.

Tob|2|9|The same night also I returned from the burial, and slept by the wall of my courtyard, being polluted and my face was uncovered:

Tob|2|10|And I knew not that there were sparrows in the wall, and mine eyes being open, the sparrows muted warm dung into mine eyes, and a whiteness came in mine eyes: and I went to the physicians, but they helped me not: moreover Achiacharus did nourish me, until I went into Elymais.

Tob|2|11|And my wife Anna did take women's works to do.

Tob|2|12|And when she had sent them home to the owners, they paid her wages, and gave her also besides a kid.

Tob|2|13|And when it was in my house, and began to cry, I said unto her, From whence is this kid? is it not stolen? render it to the owners; for it is not lawful to eat any thing that is stolen.

Tob|2|14|But she replied upon me, It was given for a gift more than the wages. Howbeit I did not believe her, but bade her render it to the owners: and I was abashed at her. But she replied upon me, Where are thine alms and thy righteous deeds? behold, thou and all thy works are known.

Tob|3|1|Then I being grieved did weep, and in my sorrow prayed, saying,

Tob|3|2|O Lord, thou art just, and all thy works and all thy ways are mercy and truth, and thou judgest truly and justly for ever.

Tob|3|3|Remember me, and look on me, punish me not for my sins and ignorances, and the sins of mg fathers, who have sinned before thee:

Tob|3|4|For they obeyed not thy commandments: wherefore thou hast delivered us for a spoil, and unto captivity, and unto death, and for a proverb of reproach to all the nations among whom we are dispersed.

Tob|3|5|And now thy judgments are many and true: deal with me according to my sins and my fathers': because we have not kept thy commandments, neither have walked in truth before thee.

Tob|3|6|Now therefore deal with me as seemeth best unto thee, and command my spirit to be taken from me, that I may be dissolved, and become earth: for it is profitable for me to die rather than to live, because I have heard false reproaches, and have much sorrow: command therefore that I may now be delivered out of this distress, and go into the everlasting place: turn not thy face away from me.

Tob|3|7|It came to pass the same day, that in Ecbatane a city of Media Sara the daughter of Raguel was also reproached by her father's maids;

Tob|3|8|Because that she had been married to seven husbands, whom Asmodeus the evil spirit had killed, before they had lain with her. Dost thou not know, said they, that thou hast strangled thine husbands? thou hast had already seven husbands, neither wast thou named after any of them.

Tob|3|9|Wherefore dost thou beat us for them? if they be dead, go thy ways after them, let us never see of thee either son or daughter.

Tob|3|10|Whe she heard these things, she was very sorrowful, so that she thought to have strangled herself; and she said, I am the only daughter of my father, and if I do this, it shall be a reproach unto him, and I shall bring his old age with sorrow unto the grave.

Tob|3|11|Then she prayed toward the window, and said, Blessed art thou, O Lord my אֱלֹהִים, and thine holy and glorious name is blessed and honourable for ever: let all thy works praise thee for ever.

Tob|3|12|And now, O Lord, I set I mine eyes and my face toward thee,

Tob|3|13|And say, Take me out of the earth, that I may hear no more the reproach.

Tob|3|14|Thou knowest, Lord, that I am pure from all sin with man,

Tob|3|15|And that I never polluted my name, nor the name of my father, in the land of my captivity: I am the only daughter of my father, neither hath he any child to be his heir, neither any near kinsman, nor any son of his alive, to whom I may keep myself for a wife: my seven husbands are already dead; and why should I live? but if it please not thee that I should die, command some regard to be had of me, and pity taken of me, that I hear no more reproach.

Tob|3|16|So the prayers of them both were heard before the majesty of the great אֱלֹהִים.

Tob|3|17|And Raphael was sent to heal them both, that is, to scale away the whiteness of Tobit's eyes, and to give Sara the daughter of Raguel for a wife to Tobias the son of Tobit; and to bind Asmodeus the evil spirit; because she belonged to Tobias by right of inheritance. The selfsame time came Tobit home, and entered into his house, and Sara the daughter of Raguel came down from her upper chamber.

Tob|4|1|In that day Tobit remembered the money which he had committed to Gabael in Rages of Media,

Tob|4|2|And said with himself, I have wished for death; wherefore do I not call for my son Tobias that I may signify to him of the money before I die?

Tob|4|3|And when he had called him, he said, My son, when I am dead, bury me; and despise not thy mother, but honour her all the days of thy life, and do that which shall please her, and grieve her not.

Tob|4|4|Remember, my son, that she saw many dangers for thee, when thou wast in her womb: and when she is dead, bury her by me in one grave.

Tob|4|5|My son, be mindful of the Lord our אֱלֹהִים all thy days, and let not thy will be set to sin, or to transgress his commandments: do uprightly all thy life long, and follow not the ways of unrighteousness.

Tob|4|6|For if thou deal truly, thy doings shall prosperously succeed to thee, and to all them that live justly.

Tob|4|7|Give alms of thy substance; and when thou givest alms, let not thine eye be envious, neither turn thy face from any poor, and the face of אֱלֹהִים shall not be turned away from thee.

Tob|4|8|If thou hast abundance give alms accordingly: if thou have but a little, be not afraid to give according to that little:

Tob|4|9|For thou layest up a good treasure for thyself against the day of necessity.

Tob|4|10|Because that alms do deliver from death, and suffereth not to come into darkness.

Tob|4|11|For alms is a good gift unto all that give it in the sight of the most High.

Tob|4|12|Beware of all whoredom, my son, and chiefly take a wife of the seed of thy fathers, and take not a strange woman to wife, which is not of thy father's tribe: for we are the children of the prophets, Noe, Abraham, Isaac, and Jacob: remember, my son, that our fathers from the beginning, even that they all married wives of their own kindred, and were blessed in their children, and their seed shall inherit the land.

Tob|4|13|Now therefore, my son, love thy brethren, and despise not in thy heart thy brethren, the sons and daughters of thy people, in not taking a wife of them: for in pride is destruction and much trouble, and in lewdness is decay and great want: for lewdness is the mother of famine.

Tob|4|14|Let not the wages of any man, which hath wrought for thee, tarry with thee, but give him it out of hand: for if thou serve אֱלֹהִים, he will also repay thee: be circumspect my son, in all things thou doest, and be wise in all thy conversation.

Tob|4|15|Do that to no man which thou hatest: drink not wine to make thee drunken: neither let drunkenness go with thee in thy journey.

Tob|4|16|Give of thy bread to the hungry, and of thy garments to them that are naked; and according to thine abundance give alms: and let not thine eye be envious, when thou givest alms.

Tob|4|17|Pour out thy bread on the burial of the just, but give nothing to the wicked.

Tob|4|18|Ask counsel of all that are wise, and despise not any counsel that is profitable.

Tob|4|19|Bless the Lord thy אֱלֹהִים alway, and desire of him that thy ways may be directed, and that all thy paths and counsels may prosper: for every nation hath not counsel; but the Lord himself giveth all good things, and he humbleth whom he will, as he will; now therefore, my son, remember my commandments, neither let them be put out of thy mind.

Tob|4|20|And now I signify this to they that I committed ten talents to Gabael the son of Gabrias at Rages in Media.

Tob|4|21|And fear not, my son, that we are made poor: for thou hast much wealth, if thou fear אֱלֹהִים, and depart from all sin, and do that which is pleasing in his sight.

Tob|5|1|Tobias then answered and said, Father, I will do all things which thou hast commanded me:

Tob|5|2|But how can I receive the money, seeing I know him not?

Tob|5|3|Then he gave him the handwriting, and said unto him, Seek thee a man which may go with thee, whiles I yet live, and I will give him wages: and go and receive the money.

Tob|5|4|Therefore when he went to seek a man, he found Raphael that was an angel.

Tob|5|5|But he knew not; and he said unto him, Canst thou go with me to Rages? and knowest thou those places well?

Tob|5|6|To whom the angel said, I will go with thee, and I know the way well: for I have lodged with our brother Gabael.

Tob|5|7|Then Tobias said unto him, Tarry for me, till I tell my father.

Tob|5|8|Then he said unto him, Go and tarry not. So he went in and said to his father, Behold, I have found one which will go with me. Then he said, Call him unto me, that I may know of what tribe he is, and whether he be a trusty man to go with thee.

Tob|5|9|So he called him, and he came in, and they saluted one another.

Tob|5|10|Then Tobit said unto him, Brother, shew me of what tribe and family thou art.

Tob|5|11|To whom he said, Dost thou seek for a tribe or family, or an hired man to go with thy son? Then Tobit said unto him, I would know, brother, thy kindred and name.

Tob|5|12|Then he said, I am Azarias, the son of Ananias the great, and of thy brethren.

Tob|5|13|Then Tobit said, Thou art welcome, brother; be not now angry with me, because I have enquired to know thy tribe and thy family; for thou art my brother, of an honest and good stock: for I know Ananias and Jonathas, sons of that great Samaias, as we went together to Jerusalem to worship, and offered the firstborn, and the tenths of the fruits; and they were not seduced with the error of our brethren: my brother, thou art of a good stock.

Tob|5|14|But tell me, what wages shall I give thee? wilt thou a drachm a day, and things necessary, as to mine own son?

Tob|5|15|Yea, moreover, if ye return safe, I will add something to thy wages.

Tob|5|16|So they were well pleased. Then said he to Tobias, Prepare thyself for the journey, and אֱלֹהִים send you a good journey. And when his son had prepared all things far the journey, his father said, Go thou with this man, and אֱלֹהִים, which dwelleth in heaven, prosper your journey, and the angel of אֱלֹהִים keep you company. So they went forth both, and the young man's dog with them.

Tob|5|17|But Anna his mother wept, and said to Tobit, Why hast thou sent away our son? is he not the staff of our hand, in going in and out before us?

Tob|5|18|Be not greedy to add money to money: but let it be as refuse in respect of our child.

Tob|5|19|For that which the Lord hath given us to live with doth suffice us.

Tob|5|20|Then said Tobit to her, Take no care, my sister; he shall return in safety, and thine eyes shall see him.

Tob|5|21|For the good angel will keep him company, and his journey shall be prosperous, and he shall return safe.

Tob|5|22|Then she made an end of weeping.

Tob|6|1|And as they went on their journey, they came in the evening to the river Tigris, and they lodged there.

Tob|6|2|And when the young man went down to wash himself, a fish leaped out of the river, and would have devoured him.

Tob|6|3|Then the angel said unto him, Take the fish. And the young man laid hold of the fish, and drew it to land.

Tob|6|4|To whom the angel said, Open the fish, and take the heart and the liver and the gall, and put them up safely.

Tob|6|5|So the young man did as the angel commanded him; and when they had roasted the fish, they did eat it: then they both went on their way, till they drew near to Ecbatane.

Tob|6|6|Then the young man said to the angel, Brother Azarias, to what use is the heart and the liver and the gal of the fish?

Tob|6|7|And he said unto him, Touching the heart and the liver, if a devil or an evil spirit trouble any, we must make a smoke thereof before the man or the woman, and the party shall be no more vexed.

Tob|6|8|As for the gall, it is good to anoint a man that hath whiteness in his eyes, and he shall be healed.

Tob|6|9|And when they were come near to Rages,

Tob|6|10|The angel said to the young man, Brother, to day we shall lodge with Raguel, who is thy cousin; he also hath one only daughter, named Sara; I will speak for her, that she may be given thee for a wife.

Tob|6|11|For to thee doth the right of her appertain, seeing thou only art of her kindred.

Tob|6|12|And the maid is fair and wise: now therefore hear me, and I will speak to her father; and when we return from Rages we will celebrate the marriage: for I know that Raguel cannot marry her to another according to the law of Moses, but he shall be guilty of death, because the right of inheritance doth rather appertain to thee than to any other.

Tob|6|13|Then the young man answered the angel, I have heard, brother Azarias that this maid hath been given to seven men, who all died in the marriage chamber.

Tob|6|14|And now I am the only son of my father, and I am afraid, lest if I go in unto her, I die, as the other before: for a wicked spirit loveth her, which hurteth no body, but those which come unto her; wherefore I also fear lest I die, and bring my father's and my mother's life because of me to the grave with sorrow: for they have no other son to bury them.

Tob|6|15|Then the angel said unto him, Dost thou not remember the precepts which thy father gave thee, that thou shouldest marry a wife of thine own kindred? wherefore hear me, O my brother; for she shall be given thee to wife; and make thou no reckoning of the evil spirit; for this same night shall she be given thee in marriage.

Tob|6|16|And when thou shalt come into the marriage chamber, thou shalt take the ashes of perfume, and shalt lay upon them some of the heart and liver of the fish, and shalt make a smoke with it:

Tob|6|17|And the devil shall smell it, and flee away, and never come again any more: but when thou shalt come to her, rise up both of you, and pray to אֱלֹהִים which is merciful, who will have pity on you, and save you: fear not, for she is appointed unto thee from the beginning; and thou shalt preserve her, and she shall go with thee. Moreover I suppose that she shall bear thee children. Now when Tobias had heard these things, he loved her, and his heart was effectually joined to her.

Tob|7|1|And when they were come to Ecbatane, they came to the house of Raguel, and Sara met them: and after they had saluted one another, she brought them into the house.

Tob|7|2|Then said Raguel to Edna his wife, How like is this young man to Tobit my cousin!

Tob|7|3|And Raguel asked them, From whence are ye, brethren? To whom they said, We are of the sons of Nephthalim, which are captives in Nineve.

Tob|7|4|Then he said to them, Do ye know Tobit our kinsman? And they said, We know him. Then said he, Is he in good health?

Tob|7|5|And they said, He is both alive, and in good health: and Tobias said, He is my father.

Tob|7|6|Then Raguel leaped up, and kissed him, and wept,

Tob|7|7|And blessed him, and said unto him, Thou art the son of an honest and good man. But when he had heard that Tobit was blind, he was sorrowful, and wept.

Tob|7|8|And likewise Edna his wife and Sara his daughter wept. Moreover they entertained them cheerfully; and after that they had killed a ram of the flock, they set store of meat on the table. Then said Tobias to Raphael, Brother Azarias, speak of those things of which thou didst talk in the way, and let this business be dispatched.

Tob|7|9|So he communicated the matter with Raguel: and Raguel said to Tobias, Eat and drink, and make merry:

Tob|7|10|For it is meet that thou shouldest marry my daughter: nevertheless I will declare unto thee the truth.

Tob|7|11|I have given my daughter in marriage te seven men, who died that night they came in unto her: nevertheless for the present be merry. But Tobias said, I will eat nothing here, till we agree and swear one to another.

Tob|7|12|Raguel said, Then take her from henceforth according to the manner, for thou art her cousin, and she is thine, and the merciful אֱלֹהִים give you good success in all things.

Tob|7|13|Then he called his daughter Sara, and she came to her father, and he took her by the hand, and gave her to be wife to Tobias, saying, Behold, take her after the law of Moses, and lead her away to thy father. And he blessed them;

Tob|7|14|And called Edna his wife, and took paper, and did write an instrument of covenants, and sealed it.

Tob|7|15|Then they began to eat.

Tob|7|16|After Raguel called his wife Edna, and said unto her, Sister, prepare another chamber, and bring her in thither.

Tob|7|17|Which when she had done as he had bidden her, she brought her thither: and she wept, and she received the tears of her daughter, and said unto her,

Tob|7|18|Be of good comfort, my daughter; the Lord of heaven and earth give thee joy for this thy sorrow: be of good comfort, my daughter.

Tob|8|1|And when they had supped, they brought Tobias in unto her.

Tob|8|2|And as he went, he remembered the words of Raphael, and took the ashes of the perfumes, and put the heart and the liver of the fish thereupon, and made a smoke therewith.

Tob|8|3|The which smell when the evil spirit had smelled, he fled into the utmost parts of Egypt, and the angel bound him.

Tob|8|4|And after that they were both shut in together, Tobias rose out of the bed, and said, Sister, arise, and let us pray that אֱלֹהִים would have pity on us.

Tob|8|5|Then began Tobias to say, Blessed art thou, O אֱלֹהִים of our fathers, and blessed is thy holy and glorious name for ever; let the heavens bless thee, and all thy creatures.

Tob|8|6|Thou madest Adam, and gavest him Eve his wife for an helper and stay: of them came mankind: thou hast said, It is not good that man should be alone; let us make unto him an aid like unto himself.

Tob|8|7|And now, O Lord, I take not this my sister for lush but uprightly: therefore mercifully ordain that we may become aged together.

Tob|8|8|And she said with him, Amen.

Tob|8|9|So they slept both that night. And Raguel arose, and went and made a grave,

Tob|8|10|Saying, I fear lest he also be dead.

Tob|8|11|But when Raguel was come into his house,

Tob|8|12|He said unto his wife Edna. Send one of the maids, and let her see whether he be alive: if he be not, that we may bury him, and no man know it.

Tob|8|13|So the maid opened the door, and went in, and found them both asleep,

Tob|8|14|And came forth, and told them that he was alive.

Tob|8|15|Then Raguel praised אֱלֹהִים, and said, O אֱלֹהִים, thou art worthy to be praised with all pure and holy praise; therefore let thy saints praise thee with all thy creatures; and let all thine angels and thine elect praise thee for ever.

Tob|8|16|Thou art to be praised, for thou hast made me joyful; and that is not come to me which I suspected; but thou hast dealt with us according to thy great mercy.

Tob|8|17|Thou art to be praised because thou hast had mercy of two that were the only begotten children of their fathers: grant them mercy, O Lord, and finish their life in health with joy and mercy.

Tob|8|18|Then Raguel bade his servants to fill the grave.

Tob|8|19|And he kept the wedding feast fourteen days.

Tob|8|20|For before the days of the marriage were finished, Raguel had said unto him by an oath, that he should not depart till the fourteen days of the marriage were expired;

Tob|8|21|And then he should take the half of his goods, and go in safety to his father; and should have the rest when I and my wife be dead.

Tob|9|1|Then Tobias called Raphael, and said unto him,

Tob|9|2|Brother Azarias, take with thee a servant, and two camels, and go to Rages of Media to Gabael, and bring me the money, and bring him to the wedding.

Tob|9|3|For Raguel hath sworn that I shall not depart.

Tob|9|4|But my father counteth the days; and if I tarry long, he will be very sorry.

Tob|9|5|So Raphael went out, and lodged with Gabael, and gave him the handwriting: who brought forth bags which were sealed up, and gave them to him.

Tob|9|6|And early in the morning they went forth both together, and came to the wedding: and Tobias blessed his wife.

Tob|10|1|Now Tobit his father counted every day: and when the days of the journey were expired, and they came not,

Tob|10|2|Then Tobit said, Are they detained? or is Gabael dead, and there is no man to give him the money?

Tob|10|3|Therefore he was very sorry.

Tob|10|4|Then his wife said unto him, My son is dead, seeing he stayeth long; and she began to wail him, and said,

Tob|10|5|Now I care for nothing, my son, since I have let thee go, the light of mine eyes.

Tob|10|6|To whom Tobit said, Hold thy peace, take no care, for he is safe.

Tob|10|7|But she said, Hold thy peace, and deceive me not; my son is dead. And she went out every day into the way which they went, and did eat no meat on the daytime, and ceased not whole nights to bewail her son Tobias, until the fourteen days of the wedding were expired, which Raguel had sworn that he should spend there. Then Tobias said to Raguel, Let me go, for my father and my mother look no more to see me.

Tob|10|8|But his father in law said unto him, Tarry with me, and I will send to thy father, and they shall declare unto him how things go with thee.

Tob|10|9|But Tobias said, No; but let me go to my father.

Tob|10|10|Then Raguel arose, and gave him Sara his wife, and half his goods, servants, and cattle, and money:

Tob|10|11|And he blessed them, and sent them away, saying, The אֱלֹהִים of heaven give you a prosperous journey, my children.

Tob|10|12|And he said to his daughter, Honour thy father and thy mother in law, which are now thy parents, that I may hear good report of thee. And he kissed her. Edna also said to Tobias, The Lord of heaven restore thee, my dear brother, and grant that I may see thy children of my daughter Sara before I die, that I may rejoice before the Lord: behold, I commit my daughter unto thee of special trust; where are do not entreat her evil.

Tob|11|1|After these things Tobias went his way, praising אֱלֹהִים that he had given him a prosperous journey, and blessed Raguel and Edna his wife, and went on his way till they drew near unto Nineve.

Tob|11|2|Then Raphael said to Tobias, Thou knowest, brother, how thou didst leave thy father:

Tob|11|3|Let us haste before thy wife, and prepare the house.

Tob|11|4|And take in thine hand the gall of the fish. So they went their way, and the dog went after them.

Tob|11|5|Now Anna sat looking about toward the way for her son.

Tob|11|6|And when she espied him coming, she said to his father, Behold, thy son cometh, and the man that went with him.

Tob|11|7|Then said Raphael, I know, Tobias, that thy father will open his eyes.

Tob|11|8|Therefore anoint thou his eyes with the gall, and being pricked therewith, he shall rub, and the whiteness shall fall away, and he shall see thee.

Tob|11|9|Then Anna ran forth, and fell upon the neck of her son, and said unto him, Seeing I have seen thee, my son, from henceforth I am content to die. And they wept both.

Tob|11|10|Tobit also went forth toward the door, and stumbled: but his son ran unto him,

Tob|11|11|And took hold of his father: and he strake of the gall on his fathers' eyes, saying, Be of good hope, my father.

Tob|11|12|And when his eyes began to smart, he rubbed them;

Tob|11|13|And the whiteness pilled away from the corners of his eyes: and when he saw his son, he fell upon his neck.

Tob|11|14|And he wept, and said, Blessed art thou, O אֱלֹהִים, and blessed is thy name for ever; and blessed are all thine holy angels:

Tob|11|15|For thou hast scourged, and hast taken pity on me: for, behold, I see my son Tobias. And his son went in rejoicing, and told his father the great things that had happened to him in Media.

Tob|11|16|Then Tobit went out to meet his daughter in law at the gate of Nineve, rejoicing and praising אֱלֹהִים: and they which saw him go marvelled, because he had received his sight.

Tob|11|17|But Tobias gave thanks before them, because אֱלֹהִים had mercy on him. And when he came near to Sara his daughter in law, he blessed her, saying, Thou art welcome, daughter: אֱלֹהִים be blessed, which hath brought thee unto us, and blessed be thy father and thy mother. And there was joy among all his brethren which were at Nineve.

Tob|11|18|And Achiacharus, and Nasbas his brother's son, came:

Tob|11|19|And Tobias' wedding was kept seven days with great joy.

Tob|12|1|Then Tobit called his son Tobias, and said unto him, My son, see that the man have his wages, which went with thee, and thou must give him more.

Tob|12|2|And Tobias said unto him, O father, it is no harm to me to give him half of those things which I have brought:

Tob|12|3|For he hath brought me again to thee in safety, and made whole my wife, and brought me the money, and likewise healed thee.

Tob|12|4|Then the old man said, It is due unto him.

Tob|12|5|So he called the angel, and he said unto him, Take half of all that ye have brought and go away in safety.

Tob|12|6|Then he took them both apart, and said unto them, Bless אֱלֹהִים, praise him, and magnify him, and praise him for the things which he hath done unto you in the sight of all that live. It is good to praise אֱלֹהִים, and exalt his name, and honourably to shew forth the works of אֱלֹהִים; therefore be not slack to praise him.

Tob|12|7|It is good to keep close the secret of a king, but it is honourable to reveal the works of אֱלֹהִים. Do that which is good, and no evil shall touch you.

Tob|12|8|Prayer is good with fasting and alms and righteousness. A little with righteousness is better than much with unrighteousness. It is better to give alms than to lay up gold:

Tob|12|9|For alms doth deliver from death, and shall purge away all sin. Those that exercise alms and righteousness shall be filled with life:

Tob|12|10|But they that sin are enemies to their own life.

Tob|12|11|Surely I will keep close nothing from you. For I said, It was good to keep close the secret of a king, but that it was honourable to reveal the works of אֱלֹהִים.

Tob|12|12|Now therefore, when thou didst pray, and Sara thy daughter in law, I did bring the remembrance of your prayers before the Holy One: and when thou didst bury the dead, I was with thee likewise.

Tob|12|13|And when thou didst not delay to rise up, and leave thy dinner, to go and cover the dead, thy good deed was not hid from me: but I was with thee.

Tob|12|14|And now אֱלֹהִים hath sent me to heal thee and Sara thy daughter in law.

Tob|12|15|I am Raphael, one of the seven holy angels, which present the prayers of the saints, and which go in and out before the glory of the Holy One.

Tob|12|16|Then they were both troubled, and fell upon their faces: for they feared.

Tob|12|17|But he said unto them, Fear not, for it shall go well with you; praise אֱלֹהִים therefore.

Tob|12|18|For not of any favour of mine, but by the will of our אֱלֹהִים I came; wherefore praise him for ever.

Tob|12|19|All these days I did appear unto you; but I did neither eat nor drink, but ye did see a vision.

Tob|12|20|Now therefore give אֱלֹהִים thanks: for I go up to him that sent me; but write all things which are done in a book.

Tob|12|21|And when they arose, they saw him no more.

Tob|12|22|Then they confessed the great and wonderful works of אֱלֹהִים, and how the angel of the Lord had appeared unto them.

Tob|13|1|Then Tobit wrote a prayer of rejoicing, and said, Blessed be אֱלֹהִים that liveth for ever, and blessed be his kingdom.

Tob|13|2|For he doth scourge, and hath mercy: he leadeth down to hell, and bringeth up again: neither is there any that can avoid his hand.

Tob|13|3|Confess him before the Gentiles, ye children of Israel: for he hath scattered us among them.

Tob|13|4|There declare his greatness, and extol him before all the living: for he is our Lord, and he is the אֱלֹהִים our Father for ever.

Tob|13|5|And he will scourge us for our iniquities, and will have mercy again, and will gather us out of all nations, among whom he hath scattered us.

Tob|13|6|If ye turn to him with your whole heart, and with your whole mind, and deal uprightly before him, then will he turn unto you, and will not hide his face from you. Therefore see what he will do with you, and confess him with your whole mouth, and praise the Lord of might, and extol the everlasting King. In the land of my captivity do I praise him, and declare his might and majesty to a sinful nation. O ye sinners, turn and do justice before him: who can tell if he will accept you, and have mercy on you?

Tob|13|7|I will extol my אֱלֹהִים, and my soul shall praise the King of heaven, and shall rejoice in his greatness.

Tob|13|8|Let all men speak, and let all praise him for his righteousness.

Tob|13|9|O Jerusalem, the holy city, he will scourge thee for thy children's works, and will have mercy again on the sons of the righteous.

Tob|13|10|Give praise to the Lord, for he is good: and praise the everlasting King, that his tabernacle may be builded in thee again with joy, and let him make joyful there in thee those that are captives, and love in thee for ever those that are miserable.

Tob|13|11|Many nations shall come from far to the name of the Lord אֱלֹהִים with gifts in their hands, even gifts to the King of heaven; all generations shall praise thee with great joy.

Tob|13|12|Cursed are all they which hate thee, and blessed shall all be which love thee for ever.

Tob|13|13|Rejoice and be glad for the children of the just: for they shall be gathered together, and shall bless the Lord of the just.

Tob|13|14|O blessed are they which love thee, for they shall rejoice in thy peace: blessed are they which have been sorrowful for all thy scourges; for they shall rejoice for thee, when they have seen all thy glory, and shall be glad for ever.

Tob|13|15|Let my soul bless אֱלֹהִים the great King.

Tob|13|16|For Jerusalem shall be built up with sapphires and emeralds, and precious stone: thy walls and towers and battlements with pure gold.

Tob|13|17|And the streets of Jerusalem shall be paved with beryl and carbuncle and stones of Ophir.

Tob|13|18|And all her streets shall say, Alleluia; and they shall praise him, saying, Blessed be אֱלֹהִים, which hath extolled it for ever.

Tob|14|1|So Tobit made an end of praising אֱלֹהִים.

Tob|14|2|And he was eight and fifty years old when he lost his sight, which was restored to him after eight years: and he gave alms, and he increased in the fear of the Lord אֱלֹהִים, and praised him.

Tob|14|3|And when he was very aged he called his son, and the sons of his son, and said to him, My son, take thy children; for, behold, I am aged, and am ready to depart out of this life.

Tob|14|4|Go into Media my son, for I surely believe those things which Jonas the prophet spake of Nineve, that it shall be overthrown; and that for a time peace shall rather be in Media; and that our brethren shall lie scattered in the earth from that good land: and Jerusalem shall be desolate, and the house of אֱלֹהִים in it shall be burned, and shall be desolate for a time;

Tob|14|5|And that again אֱלֹהִים will have mercy on them, and bring them again into the land, where they shall build a temple, but not like to the first, until the time of that age be fulfilled; and afterward they shall return from all places of their captivity, and build up Jerusalem gloriously, and the house of אֱלֹהִים shall be built in it for ever with a glorious building, as the prophets have spoken thereof.

Tob|14|6|And all nations shall turn, and fear the Lord אֱלֹהִים truly, and shall bury their idols.

Tob|14|7|So shall all nations praise the Lord, and his people shall confess אֱלֹהִים, and the Lord shall exalt his people; and all those which love the Lord אֱלֹהִים in truth and justice shall rejoice, shewing mercy to our brethren.

Tob|14|8|And now, my son, depart out of Nineve, because that those things which the prophet Jonas spake shall surely come to pass.

Tob|14|9|But keep thou the law and the commandments, and shew thyself merciful and just, that it may go well with thee.

Tob|14|10|And bury me decently, and thy mother with me; but tarry no longer at Nineve. Remember, my son, how Aman handled Achiacharus that brought him up, how out of light he brought him into darkness, and how he rewarded him again: yet Achiacharus was saved, but the other had his reward: for he went down into darkness. Manasses gave alms, and escaped the snares of death which they had set for him: but Aman fell into the snare, and perished.

Tob|14|11|Wherefore now, my son, consider what alms doeth, and how righteousness doth deliver. When he had said these things, he gave up the ghost in the bed, being an hundred and eight and fifty years old; and he buried him honourably.

Tob|14|12|And when Anna his mother was dead, he buried her with his father. But Tobias departed with his wife and children to Ecbatane to Raguel his father in law,

Tob|14|13|Where he became old with honour, and he buried his father and mother in law honourably, and he inherited their substance, and his father Tobit's.

Tob|14|14|And he died at Ecbatane in Media, being an hundred and seven and twenty years old.

Tob|14|15|But before he died he heard of the destruction of Nineve, which was taken by Nabuchodonosor and Assuerus: and before his death he rejoiced over Nineve.

Jdt|1|1|In the twelfth year of the reign of Nabuchodonosor, who reigned in Nineve, the great city; in the days of Arphaxad, which reigned over the Medes in Ecbatane,

Jdt|1|2|And built in Ecbatane walls round about of stones hewn three cubits broad and six cubits long, and made the height of the wall seventy cubits, and the breadth thereof fifty cubits:

Jdt|1|3|And set the towers thereof upon the gates of it an hundred cubits high, and the breadth thereof in the foundation threescore cubits:

Jdt|1|4|And he made the gates thereof, even gates that were raised to the height of seventy cubits, and the breadth of them was forty cubits, for the going forth of his mighty armies, and for the setting in array of his footmen:

Jdt|1|5|Even in those days king Nabuchodonosor made war with king Arphaxad in the great plain, which is the plain in the borders of Ragau.

Jdt|1|6|And there came unto him all they that dwelt in the hill country, and all that dwelt by Euphrates, and Tigris and Hydaspes, and the plain of Arioch the king of the Elymeans, and very many nations of the sons of Chelod, assembled themselves to the battle.

Jdt|1|7|Then Nabuchodonosor king of the Assyrians sent unto all that dwelt in Persia, and to all that dwelt westward, and to those that dwelt in Cilicia, and Damascus, and Libanus, and Antilibanus, and to all that dwelt upon the sea coast,

Jdt|1|8|And to those among the nations that were of Carmel, and Galaad, and the higher Galilee, and the great plain of Esdrelom,

Jdt|1|9|And to all that were in Samaria and the cities thereof, and beyond Jordan unto Jerusalem, and Betane, and Chelus, and Kades, and the river of Egypt, and Taphnes, and Ramesse, and all the land of Gesem,

Jdt|1|10|Until ye come beyond Tanis and Memphis, and to all the inhabitants of Egypt, until ye come to the borders of Ethiopia.

Jdt|1|11|But all the inhabitants of the land made light of the commandment of Nabuchodonosor king of the Assyrians, neither went they with him to the battle; for they were not afraid of him: yea, he was before them as one man, and they sent away his ambassadors from them without effect, and with disgrace.

Jdt|1|12|Therefore Nabuchodonosor was very angry with all this country, and sware by his throne and kingdom, that he would surely be avenged upon all those coasts of Cilicia, and Damascus, and Syria, and that he would slay with the sword all the inhabitants of the land of Moab, and the children of Ammon, and all Judea, and all that were in Egypt, till ye come to the borders of the two seas.

Jdt|1|13|Then he marched in battle array with his power against king Arphaxad in the seventeenth year, and he prevailed in his battle: for he overthrew all the power of Arphaxad, and all his horsemen, and all his chariots,

Jdt|1|14|And became lord of his cities, and came unto Ecbatane, and took the towers, and spoiled the streets thereof, and turned the beauty thereof into shame.

Jdt|1|15|He took also Arphaxad in the mountains of Ragau, and smote him through with his darts, and destroyed him utterly that day.

Jdt|1|16|So he returned afterward to Nineve, both he and all his company of sundry nations being a very great multitude of men of war, and there he took his ease, and banqueted, both he and his army, an hundred and twenty days.

Jdt|2|1|And in the eighteenth year, the two and twentieth day of the first month, there was talk in the house of Nabuchodonosor king of the Assyrians that he should, as he said, avenge himself on all the earth.

Jdt|2|2|So he called unto him all his officers, and all his nobles, and communicated with them his secret counsel, and concluded the afflicting of the whole earth out of his own mouth.

Jdt|2|3|Then they decreed to destroy all flesh, that did not obey the commandment of his mouth.

Jdt|2|4|And when he had ended his counsel, Nabuchodonosor king of the Assyrians called Holofernes the chief captain of his army, which was next unto him, and said unto him.

Jdt|2|5|Thus saith the great king, the lord of the whole earth, Behold, thou shalt go forth from my presence, and take with thee men that trust in their own strength, of footmen an hundred and twenty thousand; and the number of horses with their riders twelve thousand.

Jdt|2|6|And thou shalt go against all the west country, because they disobeyed my commandment.

Jdt|2|7|And thou shalt declare unto that they prepare for me earth and water: for I will go forth in my wrath against them and will cover the whole face of the earth with the feet of mine army, and I will give them for a spoil unto them:

Jdt|2|8|So that their slain shall fill their valleys and brooks and the river shall be filled with their dead, till it overflow:

Jdt|2|9|And I will lead them captives to the utmost parts of all the earth.

Jdt|2|10|Thou therefore shalt go forth. and take beforehand for me all their coasts: and if they will yield themselves unto thee, thou shalt reserve them for me till the day of their punishment.

Jdt|2|11|But concerning them that rebel, let not thine eye spare them; but put them to the slaughter, and spoil them wheresoever thou goest.

Jdt|2|12|For as I live, and by the power of my kingdom, whatsoever I have spoken, that will I do by mine hand.

Jdt|2|13|And take thou heed that thou transgress none of the commandments of thy lord, but accomplish them fully, as I have commanded thee, and defer not to do them.

Jdt|2|14|Then Holofernes went forth from the presence of his lord, and called ail the governors and captains, and the officers of the army of Assur;

Jdt|2|15|And he mustered the chosen men for the battle, as his lord had commanded him, unto an hundred and twenty thousand, and twelve thousand archers on horseback;

Jdt|2|16|And he ranged them, as a great army is ordered for the war.

Jdt|2|17|And he took camels and asses for their carriages, a very great number; and sheep and oxen and goats without number for their provision:

Jdt|2|18|And plenty of victual for every man of the army, and very much gold and silver out of the king's house.

Jdt|2|19|Then he went forth and all his power to go before king Nabuchodonosor in the voyage, and to cover all the face of the earth westward with their chariots, and horsemen, and their chosen footmen.

Jdt|2|20|A great number also sundry countries came with them like locusts, and like the sand of the earth: for the multitude was without number.

Jdt|2|21|And they went forth of Nineve three days' journey toward the plain of Bectileth, and pitched from Bectileth near the mountain which is at the left hand of the upper Cilicia.

Jdt|2|22|Then he took all his army, his footmen, and horsemen and chariots, and went from thence into the hill country;

Jdt|2|23|And destroyed Phud and Lud, and spoiled all the children of Rasses, and the children of Israel, which were toward the wilderness at the south of the land of the Chellians.

Jdt|2|24|Then he went over Euphrates, and went through Mesopotamia, and destroyed all the high cities that were upon the river Arbonai, till ye come to the sea.

Jdt|2|25|And he took the borders of Cilicia, and killed all that resisted him, and came to the borders of Japheth, which were toward the south, over against Arabia.

Jdt|2|26|He compassed also all the children of Madian, and burned up their tabernacles, and spoiled their sheepcotes.

Jdt|2|27|Then he went down into the plain of Damascus in the time of wheat harvest, and burnt up all their fields, and destroyed their flocks and herds, also he spoiled their cities, and utterly wasted their countries, and smote all their young men with the edge of the sword.

Jdt|2|28|Therefore the fear and dread of him fell upon all the inhabitants of the sea coasts, which were in Sidon and Tyrus, and them that dwelt in Sur and Ocina, and all that dwelt in Jemnaan; and they that dwelt in Azotus and Ascalon feared him greatly.

Jdt|3|1|So they sent ambassadors unto him to treat of peace, saying,

Jdt|3|2|Behold, we the servants of Nabuchodonosor the great king lie before thee; use us as shall be good in thy sight.

Jdt|3|3|Behold, our houses, and all our places, and all our fields of wheat, and flocks, and herds, and all the lodges of our tents lie before thy face; use them as it pleaseth thee.

Jdt|3|4|Behold, even our cities and the inhabitants thereof are thy servants; come and deal with them as seemeth good unto thee.

Jdt|3|5|So the men came to Holofernes, and declared unto him after this manner.

Jdt|3|6|Then came he down toward the sea coast, both he and his army, and set garrisons in the high cities, and took out of them chosen men for aid.

Jdt|3|7|So they and all the country round about received them with garlands, with dances, and with timbrels.

Jdt|3|8|Yet he did cast down their frontiers, and cut down their groves: for he had decreed to destroy all the gods of the land, that all nations should worship Nabuchodonosor only, and that all tongues and tribes should call upon him as god.

Jdt|3|9|Also he came over against Esdraelon near unto Judea, over against the great strait of Judea.

Jdt|3|10|And he pitched between Geba and Scythopolis, and there he tarried a whole month, that he might gather together all the carriages of his army.

Jdt|4|1|Now the children of Israel, that dwelt in Judea, heard all that Holofernes the chief captain of Nabuchodonosor king of the Assyrians had done to the nations, and after what manner he had spoiled all their temples, and brought them to nought.

Jdt|4|2|Therefore they were exceedingly afraid of him, and were troubled for Jerusalem, and for the temple of the Lord their אֱלֹהִים:

Jdt|4|3|For they were newly returned from the captivity, and all the people of Judea were lately gathered together: and the vessels, and the altar, and the house, were sanctified after the profanation.

Jdt|4|4|Therefore they sent into all the coasts of Samaria, and the villages and to Bethoron, and Belmen, and Jericho, and to Choba, and Esora, and to the valley of Salem:

Jdt|4|5|And possessed themselves beforehand of all the tops of the high mountains, and fortified the villages that were in them, and laid up victuals for the provision of war: for their fields were of late reaped.

Jdt|4|6|Also Joacim the high priest, which was in those days in Jerusalem, wrote to them that dwelt in Bethulia, and Betomestham, which is over against Esdraelon toward the open country, near to Dothaim,

Jdt|4|7|Charging them to keep the passages of the hill country: for by them there was an entrance into Judea, and it was easy to stop them that would come up, because the passage was straight, for two men at the most.

Jdt|4|8|And the children of Israel did as Joacim the high priest had commanded them, with the ancients of all the people of Israel, which dwelt at Jerusalem.

Jdt|4|9|Then every man of Israel cried to אֱלֹהִים with great fervency, and with great vehemency did they humble their souls:

Jdt|4|10|Both they, and their wives and their children, and their cattle, and every stranger and hireling, and their servants bought with money, put sackcloth upon their loins.

Jdt|4|11|Thus every man and women, and the little children, and the inhabitants of Jerusalem, fell before the temple, and cast ashes upon their heads, and spread out their sackcloth before the face of the Lord: also they put sackcloth about the altar,

Jdt|4|12|And cried to the אֱלֹהִים of Israel all with one consent earnestly, that he would not give their children for a prey, and their wives for a spoil, and the cities of their inheritance to destruction, and the sanctuary to profanation and reproach, and for the nations to rejoice at.

Jdt|4|13|So אֱלֹהִים heard their prayers, and looked upon their afflictions: for the people fasted many days in all Judea and Jerusalem before the sanctuary of the Lord Almighty.

Jdt|4|14|And Joacim the high priest, and all the priests that stood before the Lord, and they which ministered unto the Lord, had their loins girt with sackcloth, and offered the daily burnt offerings, with the vows and free gifts of the people,

Jdt|4|15|And had ashes on their mitres, and cried unto the Lord with all their power, that he would look upon all the house of Israel graciously.

Jdt|5|1|Then was it declared to Holofernes, the chief captain of the army of Assur, that the children of Israel had prepared for war, and had shut up the passages of the hill country, and had fortified all the tops of the high hills and had laid impediments in the champaign countries:

Jdt|5|2|Wherewith he was very angry, and called all the princes of Moab, and the captains of Ammon, and all the governors of the sea coast,

Jdt|5|3|And he said unto them, Tell me now, ye sons of Chanaan, who this people is, that dwelleth in the hill country, and what are the cities that they inhabit, and what is the multitude of their army, and wherein is their power and strength, and what king is set over them, or captain of their army;

Jdt|5|4|And why have they determined not to come and meet me, more than all the inhabitants of the west.

Jdt|5|5|Then said Achior, the captain of all the sons of Ammon, Let my lord now hear a word from the mouth of thy servant, and I will declare unto thee the truth concerning this people, which dwelleth near thee, and inhabiteth the hill countries: and there shall no lie come out of the mouth of thy servant.

Jdt|5|6|This people are descended of the Chaldeans:

Jdt|5|7|And they sojourned heretofore in Mesopotamia, because they would not follow the gods of their fathers, which were in the land of Chaldea.

Jdt|5|8|For they left the way of their ancestors, and worshipped the אֱלֹהִים of heaven, the אֱלֹהִים whom they knew: so they cast them out from the face of their gods, and they fled into Mesopotamia, and sojourned there many days.

Jdt|5|9|Then their אֱלֹהִים commanded them to depart from the place where they sojourned, and to go into the land of Chanaan: where they dwelt, and were increased with gold and silver, and with very much cattle.

Jdt|5|10|But when a famine covered all the land of Chanaan, they went down into Egypt, and sojourned there, while they were nourished, and became there a great multitude, so that one could not number their nation.

Jdt|5|11|Therefore the king of Egypt rose up against them, and dealt subtilly with them, and brought them low with labouring in brick, and made them slaves.

Jdt|5|12|Then they cried unto their אֱלֹהִים, and he smote all the land of Egypt with incurable plagues: so the Egyptians cast them out of their sight.

Jdt|5|13|And אֱלֹהִים dried the Red sea before them,

Jdt|5|14|And brought them to mount Sina, and Cades-Barne, and cast forth all that dwelt in the wilderness.

Jdt|5|15|So they dwelt in the land of the Amorites, and they destroyed by their strength all them of Esebon, and passing over Jordan they possessed all the hill country.

Jdt|5|16|And they cast forth before them the Chanaanite, the Pherezite, the Jebusite, and the Sychemite, and all the Gergesites, and they dwelt in that country many days.

Jdt|5|17|And whilst they sinned not before their אֱלֹהִים, they prospered, because the אֱלֹהִים that hateth iniquity was with them.

Jdt|5|18|But when they departed from the way which he appointed them, they were destroyed in many battles very sore, and were led captives into a land that was not their's, and the temple of their אֱלֹהִים was cast to the ground, and their cities were taken by the enemies.

Jdt|5|19|But now are they returned to their אֱלֹהִים, and are come up from the places where they were scattered, and have possessed Jerusalem, where their sanctuary is, and are seated in the hill country; for it was desolate.

Jdt|5|20|Now therefore, my lord and governor, if there be any error against this people, and they sin against their אֱלֹהִים, let us consider that this shall be their ruin, and let us go up, and we shall overcome them.

Jdt|5|21|But if there be no iniquity in their nation, let my lord now pass by, lest their Lord defend them, and their אֱלֹהִים be for them, and we become a reproach before all the world.

Jdt|5|22|And when Achior had finished these sayings, all the people standing round about the tent murmured, and the chief men of Holofernes, and all that dwelt by the sea side, and in Moab, spake that he should kill him.

Jdt|5|23|For, say they, we will not be afraid of the face of the children of Israel: for, lo, it is a people that have no strength nor power for a strong battle

Jdt|5|24|Now therefore, lord Holofernes, we will go up, and they shall be a prey to be devoured of all thine army.

Jdt|6|1|And when the tumult of men that were about the council was ceased, Holofernes the chief captain of the army of Assur said unto Achior and all the Moabites before all the company of other nations,

Jdt|6|2|And who art thou, Achior, and the hirelings of Ephraim, that thou hast prophesied against us as to day, and hast said, that we should not make war with the people of Israel, because their אֱלֹהִים will defend them? and who is אֱלֹהִים but Nabuchodonosor?

Jdt|6|3|He will send his power, and will destroy them from the face of the earth, and their אֱלֹהִים shall not deliver them: but we his servants will destroy them as one man; for they are not able to sustain the power of our horses.

Jdt|6|4|For with them we will tread them under foot, and their mountains shall be drunken with their blood, and their fields shall be filled with their dead bodies, and their footsteps shall not be able to stand before us, for they shall utterly perish, saith king Nabuchodonosor, lord of all the earth: for he said, None of my words shall be in vain.

Jdt|6|5|And thou, Achior, an hireling of Ammon, which hast spoken these words in the day of thine iniquity, shalt see my face no more from this day, until I take vengeance of this nation that came out of Egypt.

Jdt|6|6|And then shall the sword of mine army, and the multitude of them that serve me, pass through thy sides, and thou shalt fall among their slain, when I return.

Jdt|6|7|Now therefore my servants shall bring thee back into the hill country, and shall set thee in one of the cities of the passages:

Jdt|6|8|And thou shalt not perish, till thou be destroyed with them.

Jdt|6|9|And if thou persuade thyself in thy mind that they shall be taken, let not thy countenance fall: I have spoken it, and none of my words shall be in vain.

Jdt|6|10|Then Holofernes commanded his servants, that waited in his tent, to take Achior, and bring him to Bethulia, and deliver him into the hands of the children of Israel.

Jdt|6|11|So his servants took him, and brought him out of the camp into the plain, and they went from the midst of the plain into the hill country, and came unto the fountains that were under Bethulia.

Jdt|6|12|And when the men of the city saw them, they took up their weapons, and went out of the city to the top of the hill: and every man that used a sling kept them from coming up by casting of stones against them.

Jdt|6|13|Nevertheless having gotten privily under the hill, they bound Achior, and cast him down, and left him at the foot of the hill, and returned to their lord.

Jdt|6|14|But the Israelites descended from their city, and came unto him, and loosed him, and brought him to Bethulia, and presented him to the governors of the city:

Jdt|6|15|Which were in those days Ozias the son of Micha, of the tribe of Simeon, and Chabris the son of Gothoniel, and Charmis the son of Melchiel.

Jdt|6|16|And they called together all the ancients of the city, and all their youth ran together, and their women, to the assembly, and they set Achior in the midst of all their people. Then Ozias asked him of that which was done.

Jdt|6|17|And he answered and declared unto them the words of the council of Holofernes, and all the words that he had spoken in the midst of the princes of Assur, and whatsoever Holofernes had spoken proudly against the house of Israel.

Jdt|6|18|Then the people fell down and worshipped אֱלֹהִים, and cried unto אֱלֹהִים. saying,

Jdt|6|19|O Lord אֱלֹהִים of heaven, behold their pride, and pity the low estate of our nation, and look upon the face of those that are sanctified unto thee this day.

Jdt|6|20|Then they comforted Achior, and praised him greatly.

Jdt|6|21|And Ozias took him out of the assembly unto his house, and made a feast to the elders; and they called on the אֱלֹהִים of Israel all that night for help.

Jdt|7|1|The next day Holofernes commanded all his army, and all his people which were come to take his part, that they should remove their camp against Bethulia, to take aforehand the ascents of the hill country, and to make war against the children of Israel.

Jdt|7|2|Then their strong men removed their camps in that day, and the army of the men of war was an hundred and seventy thousand footmen, and twelve thousand horsemen, beside the baggage, and other men that were afoot among them, a very great multitude.

Jdt|7|3|And they camped in the valley near unto Bethulia, by the fountain, and they spread themselves in breadth over Dothaim even to Belmaim, and in length from Bethulia unto Cynamon, which is over against Esdraelon.

Jdt|7|4|Now the children of Israel, when they saw the multitude of them, were greatly troubled, and said every one to his neighbour, Now will these men lick up the face of the earth; for neither the high mountains, nor the valleys, nor the hills, are able to bear their weight.

Jdt|7|5|Then every man took up his weapons of war, and when they had kindled fires upon their towers, they remained and watched all that night.

Jdt|7|6|But in the second day Holofernes brought forth all his horsemen in the sight of the children of Israel which were in Bethulia,

Jdt|7|7|And viewed the passages up to the city, and came to the fountains of their waters, and took them, and set garrisons of men of war over them, and he himself removed toward his people.

Jdt|7|8|Then came unto him all the chief of the children of Esau, and all the governors of the people of Moab, and the captains of the sea coast, and said,

Jdt|7|9|Let our lord now hear a word, that there be not an overthrow in thine army.

Jdt|7|10|For this people of the children of Israel do not trust in their spears, but in the height of the mountains wherein they dwell, because it is not easy to come up to the tops of their mountains.

Jdt|7|11|Now therefore, my lord, fight not against them in battle array, and there shall not so much as one man of thy people perish.

Jdt|7|12|Remain in thy camp, and keep all the men of thine army, and let thy servants get into their hands the fountain of water, which issueth forth of the foot of the mountain:

Jdt|7|13|For all the inhabitants of Bethulia have their water thence; so shall thirst kill them, and they shall give up their city, and we and our people shall go up to the tops of the mountains that are near, and will camp upon them, to watch that none go out of the city.

Jdt|7|14|So they and their wives and their children shall be consumed with fire, and before the sword come against them, they shall be overthrown in the streets where they dwell.

Jdt|7|15|Thus shalt thou render them an evil reward; because they rebelled, and met not thy person peaceably.

Jdt|7|16|And these words pleased Holofernes and all his servants, and he appointed to do as they had spoken.

Jdt|7|17|So the camp of the children of Ammon departed, and with them five thousand of the Assyrians, and they pitched in the valley, and took the waters, and the fountains of the waters of the children of Israel.

Jdt|7|18|Then the children of Esau went up with the children of Ammon, and camped in the hill country over against Dothaim: and they sent some of them toward the south, and toward the east over against Ekrebel, which is near unto Chusi, that is upon the brook Mochmur; and the rest of the army of the Assyrians camped in the plain, and covered the face of the whole land; and their tents and carriages were pitched to a very great multitude.

Jdt|7|19|Then the children of Israel cried unto the Lord their אֱלֹהִים, because their heart failed, for all their enemies had compassed them round about, and there was no way to escape out from among them.

Jdt|7|20|Thus all the company of Assur remained about them, both their footmen, chariots, and horsemen, four and thirty days, so that all their vessels of water failed all the inhabitants of Bethulia.

Jdt|7|21|And the cisterns were emptied, and they had not water to drink their fill for one day; for they gave them drink by measure.

Jdt|7|22|Therefore their young children were out of heart, and their women and young men fainted for thirst, and fell down in the streets of the city, and by the passages of the gates, and there was no longer any strength in them.

Jdt|7|23|Then all the people assembled to Ozias, and to the chief of the city, both young men, and women, and children, and cried with a loud voice, and said before all the elders,

Jdt|7|24|אֱלֹהִים be judge between us and you: for ye have done us great injury, in that ye have not required peace of the children of Assur.

Jdt|7|25|For now we have no helper: but אֱלֹהִים hath sold us into their hands, that we should be thrown down before them with thirst and great destruction.

Jdt|7|26|Now therefore call them unto you, and deliver the whole city for a spoil to the people of Holofernes, and to all his army.

Jdt|7|27|For it is better for us to be made a spoil unto them, than to die for thirst: for we will be his servants, that our souls may live, and not see the death of our infants before our eyes, nor our wives nor our children to die.

Jdt|7|28|We take to witness against you the heaven and the earth, and our אֱלֹהִים and Lord of our fathers, which punisheth us according to our sins and the sins of our fathers, that he do not according as we have said this day.

Jdt|7|29|Then there was great weeping with one consent in the midst of the assembly; and they cried unto the Lord אֱלֹהִים with a loud voice.

Jdt|7|30|Then said Ozias to them, Brethren, be of good courage, let us yet endure five days, in the which space the Lord our אֱלֹהִים may turn his mercy toward us; for he will not forsake us utterly.

Jdt|7|31|And if these days pass, and there come no help unto us, I will do according to your word.

Jdt|7|32|And he dispersed the people, every one to their own charge; and they went unto the walls and towers of their city, and sent the women and children into their houses: and they were very low brought in the city.

Jdt|8|1|Now at that time Judith heard thereof, which was the daughter of Merari, the son of Ox, the son of Joseph, the son of Ozel, the son of Elcia, the son of Ananias, the son of Gedeon, the son of Raphaim, the son of Acitho, the son of Eliu, the son of Eliab, the son of Nathanael, the son of Samael, the son of Salasadal, the son of Israel.

Jdt|8|2|And Manasses was her husband, of her tribe and kindred, who died in the barley harvest.

Jdt|8|3|For as he stood overseeing them that bound sheaves in the field, the heat came upon his head, and he fell on his bed, and died in the city of Bethulia: and they buried him with his fathers in the field between Dothaim and Balamo.

Jdt|8|4|So Judith was a widow in her house three years and four months.

Jdt|8|5|And she made her a tent upon the top of her house, and put on sackcloth upon her loins and ware her widow's apparel.

Jdt|8|6|And she fasted all the days of her widowhood, save the eves of the sabbaths, and the sabbaths, and the eves of the new moons, and the new moons and the feasts and solemn days of the house of Israel.

Jdt|8|7|She was also of a goodly countenance, and very beautiful to behold: and her husband Manasses had left her gold, and silver, and menservants and maidservants, and cattle, and lands; and she remained upon them.

Jdt|8|8|And there was none that gave her an ill word; ar she feared אֱלֹהִים greatly.

Jdt|8|9|Now when she heard the evil words of the people against the governor, that they fainted for lack of water; for Judith had heard all the words that Ozias had spoken unto them, and that he had sworn to deliver the city unto the Assyrians after five days;

Jdt|8|10|Then she sent her waitingwoman, that had the government of all things that she had, to call Ozias and Chabris and Charmis, the ancients of the city.

Jdt|8|11|And they came unto her, and she said unto them, Hear me now, O ye governors of the inhabitants of Bethulia: for your words that ye have spoken before the people this day are not right, touching this oath which ye made and pronounced between אֱלֹהִים and you, and have promised to deliver the city to our enemies, unless within these days the Lord turn to help you.

Jdt|8|12|And now who are ye that have tempted אֱלֹהִים this day, and stand instead of אֱלֹהִים among the children of men?

Jdt|8|13|And now try the Lord Almighty, but ye shall never know any thing.

Jdt|8|14|For ye cannot find the depth of the heart of man, neither can ye perceive the things that he thinketh: then how can ye search out אֱלֹהִים, that hath made all these things, and know his mind, or comprehend his purpose? Nay, my brethren, provoke not the Lord our אֱלֹהִים to anger.

Jdt|8|15|For if he will not help us within these five days, he hath power to defend us when he will, even every day, or to destroy us before our enemies.

Jdt|8|16|Do not bind the counsels of the Lord our אֱלֹהִים: for אֱלֹהִים is not as man, that he may be threatened; neither is he as the son of man, that he should be wavering.

Jdt|8|17|Therefore let us wait for salvation of him, and call upon him to help us, and he will hear our voice, if it please him.

Jdt|8|18|For there arose none in our age, neither is there any now in these days neither tribe, nor family, nor people, nor city among us, which worship gods made with hands, as hath been aforetime.

Jdt|8|19|For the which cause our fathers were given to the sword, and for a spoil, and had a great fall before our enemies.

Jdt|8|20|But we know none other god, therefore we trust that he will not dispise us, nor any of our nation.

Jdt|8|21|For if we be taken so, all Judea shall lie waste, and our sanctuary shall be spoiled; and he will require the profanation thereof at our mouth.

Jdt|8|22|And the slaughter of our brethren, and the captivity of the country, and the desolation of our inheritance, will he turn upon our heads among the Gentiles, wheresoever we shall be in bondage; and we shall be an offence and a reproach to all them that possess us.

Jdt|8|23|For our servitude shall not be directed to favour: but the Lord our אֱלֹהִים shall turn it to dishonour.

Jdt|8|24|Now therefore, O brethren, let us shew an example to our brethren, because their hearts depend upon us, and the sanctuary, and the house, and the altar, rest upon us.

Jdt|8|25|Moreover let us give thanks to the Lord our אֱלֹהִים, which trieth us, even as he did our fathers.

Jdt|8|26|Remember what things he did to Abraham, and how he tried Isaac, and what happened to Jacob in Mesopotamia of Syria, when he kept the sheep of Laban his mother's brother.

Jdt|8|27|For he hath not tried us in the fire, as he did them, for the examination of their hearts, neither hath he taken vengeance on us: but the Lord doth scourge them that come near unto him, to admonish them.

Jdt|8|28|Then said Ozias to her, All that thou hast spoken hast thou spoken with a good heart, and there is none that may gainsay thy words.

Jdt|8|29|For this is not the first day wherein thy wisdom is manifested; but from the beginning of thy days all the people have known thy understanding, because the disposition of thine heart is good.

Jdt|8|30|But the people were very thirsty, and compelled us to do unto them as we have spoken, and to bring an oath upon ourselves, which we will not break.

Jdt|8|31|Therefore now pray thou for us, because thou art a godly woman, and the Lord will send us rain to fill our cisterns, and we shall faint no more.

Jdt|8|32|Then said Judith unto them, Hear me, and I will do a thing, which shall go throughout all generations to the children of our nation.

Jdt|8|33|Ye shall stand this night in the gate, and I will go forth with my waitingwoman: and within the days that ye have promised to deliver the city to our enemies the Lord will visit Israel by mine hand.

Jdt|8|34|But enquire not ye of mine act: for I will not declare it unto you, till the things be finished that I do.

Jdt|8|35|Then said Ozias and the princes unto her, Go in peace, and the Lord אֱלֹהִים be before thee, to take vengeance on our enemies.

Jdt|8|36|So they returned from the tent, and went to their wards.

Jdt|9|1|Judith fell upon her face, and put ashes upon her head, and uncovered the sackcloth wherewith she was clothed; and about the time that the incense of that evening was offered in Jerusalem in the house of the Lord Judith cried with a loud voice, and said,

Jdt|9|2|O Lord אֱלֹהִים of my father Simeon, to whom thou gavest a sword to take vengeance of the strangers, who loosened the girdle of a maid to defile her, and discovered the thigh to her shame, and polluted her virginity to her reproach; for thou saidst, It shall not be so; and yet they did so:

Jdt|9|3|Wherefore thou gavest their rulers to be slain, so that they dyed their bed in blood, being deceived, and smotest the servants with their lords, and the lords upon their thrones;

Jdt|9|4|And hast given their wives for a prey, and their daughters to be captives, and all their spoils to be divided among thy dear children; which were moved with thy zeal, and abhorred the pollution of their blood, and called upon thee for aid: O אֱלֹהִים, O my אֱלֹהִים, hear me also a widow.

Jdt|9|5|For thou hast wrought not only those things, but also the things which fell out before, and which ensued after; thou hast thought upon the things which are now, and which are to come.

Jdt|9|6|Yea, what things thou didst determine were ready at hand, and said, Lo, we are here: for all thy ways are prepared, and thy judgments are in thy foreknowledge.

Jdt|9|7|For, behold, the Assyrians are multiplied in their power; they are exalted with horse and man; they glory in the strength of their footmen; they trust in shield, and spear, and bow, and sling; and know not that thou art the Lord that breakest the battles: the Lord is thy name.

Jdt|9|8|Throw down their strength in thy power, and bring down their force in thy wrath: for they have purposed to defile thy sanctuary, and to pollute the tabernacle where thy glorious name resteth and to cast down with sword the horn of thy altar.

Jdt|9|9|Behold their pride, and send thy wrath upon their heads: give into mine hand, which am a widow, the power that I have conceived.

Jdt|9|10|Smite by the deceit of my lips the servant with the prince, and the prince with the servant: break down their stateliness by the hand of a woman.

Jdt|9|11|For thy power standeth not in multitude nor thy might in strong men: for thou art a אֱלֹהִים of the afflicted, an helper of the oppressed, an upholder of the weak, a protector of the forlorn, a saviour of them that are without hope.

Jdt|9|12|I pray thee, I pray thee, O אֱלֹהִים of my father, and אֱלֹהִים of the inheritance of Israel, Lord of the heavens and earth, Creator of the waters, king of every creature, hear thou my prayer:

Jdt|9|13|And make my speech and deceit to be their wound and stripe, who have purposed cruel things against thy covenant, and thy hallowed house, and against the top of Sion, and against the house of the possession of thy children.

Jdt|9|14|And make every nation and tribe to acknowledge that thou art the אֱלֹהִים of all power and might, and that there is none other that protecteth the people of Israel but thou.

Jdt|10|1|Now after that she had ceased to cry unto the אֱלֹהִים of Israel, and bad made an end of all these words,

Jdt|10|2|She rose where she had fallen down, and called her maid, and went down into the house in the which she abode in the sabbath days, and in her feast days,

Jdt|10|3|And pulled off the sackcloth which she had on, and put off the garments of her widowhood, and washed her body all over with water, and anointed herself with precious ointment, and braided the hair of her head, and put on a tire upon it, and put on her garments of gladness, wherewith she was clad during the life of Manasses her husband.

Jdt|10|4|And she took sandals upon her feet, and put about her her bracelets, and her chains, and her rings, and her earrings, and all her ornaments, and decked herself bravely, to allure the eyes of all men that should see her.

Jdt|10|5|Then she gave her maid a bottle of wine, and a cruse of oil, and filled a bag with parched corn, and lumps of figs, and with fine bread; so she folded all these things together, and laid them upon her.

Jdt|10|6|Thus they went forth to the gate of the city of Bethulia, and found standing there Ozias and the ancients of the city, Chabris and Charmis.

Jdt|10|7|And when they saw her, that her countenance was altered, and her apparel was changed, they wondered at her beauty very greatly, and said unto her.

Jdt|10|8|The אֱלֹהִים, the אֱלֹהִים of our fathers give thee favour, and accomplish thine enterprizes to the glory of the children of Israel, and to the exaltation of Jerusalem. Then they worshipped אֱלֹהִים.

Jdt|10|9|And she said unto them, Command the gates of the city to be opened unto me, that I may go forth to accomplish the things whereof ye have spoken with me. So they commanded the young men to open unto her, as she had spoken.

Jdt|10|10|And when they had done so, Judith went out, she, and her maid with her; and the men of the city looked after her, until she was gone down the mountain, and till she had passed the valley, and could see her no more.

Jdt|10|11|Thus they went straight forth in the valley: and the first watch of the Assyrians met her,

Jdt|10|12|And took her, and asked her, Of what people art thou? and whence comest thou? and whither goest thou? And she said, I am a woman of the Hebrews, and am fled from them: for they shall be given you to be consumed:

Jdt|10|13|And I am coming before Holofernes the chief captain of your army, to declare words of truth; and I will shew him a way, whereby he shall go, and win all the hill country, without losing the body or life of any one of his men.

Jdt|10|14|Now when the men heard her words, and beheld her countenance, they wondered greatly at her beauty, and said unto her,

Jdt|10|15|Thou hast saved thy life, in that thou hast hasted to come down to the presence of our lord: now therefore come to his tent, and some of us shall conduct thee, until they have delivered thee to his hands.

Jdt|10|16|And when thou standest before him, be not afraid in thine heart, but shew unto him according to thy word; and he will entreat thee well.

Jdt|10|17|Then they chose out of them an hundred men to accompany her and her maid; and they brought her to the tent of Holofernes.

Jdt|10|18|Then was there a concourse throughout all the camp: for her coming was noised among the tents, and they came about her, as she stood without the tent of Holofernes, till they told him of her.

Jdt|10|19|And they wondered at her beauty, and admired the children of Israel because of her, and every one said to his neighbour, Who would despise this people, that have among them such women? surely it is not good that one man of them be left who being let go might deceive the whole earth.

Jdt|10|20|And they that lay near Holofernes went out, and all his servants and they brought her into the tent.

Jdt|10|21|Now Holofernes rested upon his bed under a canopy, which was woven with purple, and gold, and emeralds, and precious stones.

Jdt|10|22|So they shewed him of her; and he came out before his tent with silver lamps going before him.

Jdt|10|23|And when Judith was come before him and his servants they all marvelled at the beauty of her countenance; and she fell down upon her face, and did reverence unto him: and his servants took her up.

Jdt|11|1|Then said Holofernes unto her, Woman, be of good comfort, fear not in thine heart: for I never hurt any that was willing to serve Nabuchodonosor, the king of all the earth.

Jdt|11|2|Now therefore, if thy people that dwelleth in the mountains had not set light by me, I would not have lifted up my spear against them: but they have done these things to themselves.

Jdt|11|3|But now tell me wherefore thou art fled from them, and art come unto us: for thou art come for safeguard; be of good comfort, thou shalt live this night, and hereafter:

Jdt|11|4|For none shall hurt thee, but entreat thee well, as they do the servants of king Nabuchodonosor my lord.

Jdt|11|5|Then Judith said unto him, Receive the words of thy servant, and suffer thine handmaid to speak in thy presence, and I will declare no lie to my lord this night.

Jdt|11|6|And if thou wilt follow the words of thine handmaid, אֱלֹהִים will bring the thing perfectly to pass by thee; and my lord shall not fail of his purposes.

Jdt|11|7|As Nabuchodonosor king of all the earth liveth, and as his power liveth, who hath sent thee for the upholding of every living thing: for not only men shall serve him by thee, but also the beasts of the field, and the cattle, and the fowls of the air, shall live by thy power under Nabuchodonosor and all his house.

Jdt|11|8|For we have heard of thy wisdom and thy policies, and it is reported in all the earth, that thou only art excellent in all the kingdom, and mighty in knowledge, and wonderful in feats of war.

Jdt|11|9|Now as concerning the matter, which Achior did speak in thy council, we have heard his words; for the men of Bethulia saved him, and he declared unto them all that he had spoken unto thee.

Jdt|11|10|Therefore, O lord and governor, respect not his word; but lay it up in thine heart, for it is true: for our nation shall not be punished, neither can sword prevail against them, except they sin against their אֱלֹהִים.

Jdt|11|11|And now, that my lord be not defeated and frustrate of his purpose, even death is now fallen upon them, and their sin hath overtaken them, wherewith they will provoke their אֱלֹהִים to anger whensoever they shall do that which is not fit to be done:

Jdt|11|12|For their victuals fail them, and all their water is scant, and they have determined to lay hands upon their cattle, and purposed to consume all those things, that אֱלֹהִים hath forbidden them to eat by his laws:

Jdt|11|13|And are resolved to spend the firstfruits of the the tenths of wine and oil, which they had sanctified, and reserved for the priests that serve in Jerusalem before the face of our אֱלֹהִים; the which things it is not lawful for any of the people so much as to touch with their hands.

Jdt|11|14|For they have sent some to Jerusalem, because they also that dwell there have done the like, to bring them a licence from the senate.

Jdt|11|15|Now when they shall bring them word, they will forthwith do it, and they shall be given to thee to be destroyed the same day.

Jdt|11|16|Wherefore I thine handmaid, knowing all this, am fled from their presence; and אֱלֹהִים hath sent me to work things with thee, whereat all the earth shall be astonished, and whosoever shall hear it.

Jdt|11|17|For thy servant is religious, and serveth the אֱלֹהִים of heaven day and night: now therefore, my lord, I will remain with thee, and thy servant will go out by night into the valley, and I will pray unto אֱלֹהִים, and he will tell me when they have committed their sins:

Jdt|11|18|And I will come and shew it unto thee: then thou shalt go forth with all thine army, and there shall be none of them that shall resist thee.

Jdt|11|19|And I will lead thee through the midst of Judea, until thou come before Jerusalem; and I will set thy throne in the midst thereof; and thou shalt drive them as sheep that have no shepherd, and a dog shall not so much as open his mouth at thee: for these things were told me according to my foreknowledge, and they were declared unto me, and I am sent to tell thee.

Jdt|11|20|Then her words pleased Holofernes and all his servants; and they marvelled at her wisdom, and said,

Jdt|11|21|There is not such a woman from one end of the earth to the other, both for beauty of face, and wisdom of words.

Jdt|11|22|Likewise Holofernes said unto her, אֱלֹהִים hath done well to send thee before the people, that strength might be in our hands and destruction upon them that lightly regard my lord.

Jdt|11|23|And now thou art both beautiful in thy countenance, and witty in thy words: surely if thou do as thou hast spoken thy אֱלֹהִים shall be my אֱלֹהִים, and thou shalt dwell in the house of king Nabuchodonosor, and shalt be renowned through the whole earth.

Jdt|12|1|Then he commanded to bring her in where his plate was set; and bade that they should prepare for her of his own meats, and that she should drink of his own wine.

Jdt|12|2|And Judith said, I will not eat thereof, lest there be an offence: but provision shall be made for me of the things that I have brought.

Jdt|12|3|Then Holofernes said unto her, If thy provision should fail, how should we give thee the like? for there be none with us of thy nation.

Jdt|12|4|Then said Judith unto him As thy soul liveth, my lord, thine handmaid shall not spend those things that I have, before the Lord work by mine hand the things that he hath determined.

Jdt|12|5|Then the servants of Holofernes brought her into the tent, and she slept till midnight, and she arose when it was toward the morning watch,

Jdt|12|6|And sent to Holofernes, saying, Let my lord now command that thine handmaid may go forth unto prayer.

Jdt|12|7|Then Holofernes commanded his guard that they should not stay her: thus she abode in the camp three days, and went out in the night into the valley of Bethulia, and washed herself in a fountain of water by the camp.

Jdt|12|8|And when she came out, she besought the Lord אֱלֹהִים of Israel to direct her way to the raising up of the children of her people.

Jdt|12|9|So she came in clean, and remained in the tent, until she did eat her meat at evening.

Jdt|12|10|And in the fourth day Holofernes made a feast to his own servants only, and called none of the officers to the banquet.

Jdt|12|11|Then said he to Bagoas the eunuch, who had charge over all that he had, Go now, and persuade this Hebrew woman which is with thee, that she come unto us, and eat and drink with us.

Jdt|12|12|For, lo, it will be a shame for our person, if we shall let such a woman go, not having had her company; for if we draw her not unto us, she will laugh us to scorn.

Jdt|12|13|Then went Bagoas from the presence of Holofernes, and came to her, and he said, Let not this fair damsel fear to come to my lord, and to be honoured in his presence, and drink wine, and be merry with us and be made this day as one of the daughters of the Assyrians, which serve in the house of Nabuchodonosor.

Jdt|12|14|Then said Judith unto him, Who am I now, that I should gainsay my lord? surely whatsoever pleaseth him I will do speedily, and it shall be my joy unto the day of my death.

Jdt|12|15|So she arose, and decked herself with her apparel and all her woman's attire, and her maid went and laid soft skins on the ground for her over against Holofernes, which she had received of Bagoas far her daily use, that she might sit and eat upon them.

Jdt|12|16|Now when Judith came in and sat down, Holofernes his heart was ravished with her, and his mind was moved, and he desired greatly her company; for he waited a time to deceive her, from the day that he had seen her.

Jdt|12|17|Then said Holofernes unto her, Drink now, and be merry with us.

Jdt|12|18|So Judith said, I will drink now, my lord, because my life is magnified in me this day more than all the days since I was born.

Jdt|12|19|Then she took and ate and drank before him what her maid had prepared.

Jdt|12|20|And Holofernes took great delight in her, and drank more wine than he had drunk at any time in one day since he was born.

Jdt|13|1|Now when the evening was come, his servants made haste to depart, and Bagoas shut his tent without, and dismissed the waiters from the presence of his lord; and they went to their beds: for they were all weary, because the feast had been long.

Jdt|13|2|And Judith was left along in the tent, and Holofernes lying along upon his bed: for he was filled with wine.

Jdt|13|3|Now Judith had commanded her maid to stand without her bedchamber, and to wait for her. coming forth, as she did daily: for she said she would go forth to her prayers, and she spake to Bagoas according to the same purpose.

Jdt|13|4|So all went forth and none was left in the bedchamber, neither little nor great. Then Judith, standing by his bed, said in her heart, O Lord אֱלֹהִים of all power, look at this present upon the works of mine hands for the exaltation of Jerusalem.

Jdt|13|5|For now is the time to help thine inheritance, and to execute thine enterprizes to the destruction of the enemies which are risen against us.

Jdt|13|6|Then she came to the pillar of the bed, which was at Holofernes' head, and took down his fauchion from thence,

Jdt|13|7|And approached to his bed, and took hold of the hair of his head, and said, Strengthen me, O Lord אֱלֹהִים of Israel, this day.

Jdt|13|8|And she smote twice upon his neck with all her might, and she took away his head from him.

Jdt|13|9|And tumbled his body down from the bed, and pulled down the canopy from the pillars; and anon after she went forth, and gave Holofernes his head to her maid;

Jdt|13|10|And she put it in her bag of meat: so they twain went together according to their custom unto prayer: and when they passed the camp, they compassed the valley, and went up the mountain of Bethulia, and came to the gates thereof.

Jdt|13|11|Then said Judith afar off, to the watchmen at the gate, Open, open now the gate: אֱלֹהִים, even our אֱלֹהִים, is with us, to shew his power yet in Jerusalem, and his forces against the enemy, as he hath even done this day.

Jdt|13|12|Now when the men of her city heard her voice, they made haste to go down to the gate of their city, and they called the elders of the city.

Jdt|13|13|And then they ran all together, both small and great, for it was strange unto them that she was come: so they opened the gate, and received them, and made a fire for a light, and stood round about them.

Jdt|13|14|Then she said to them with a loud voice, Praise, praise אֱלֹהִים, praise אֱלֹהִים, I say, for he hath not taken away his mercy from the house of Israel, but hath destroyed our enemies by mine hands this night.

Jdt|13|15|So she took the head out of the bag, and shewed it, and said unto them, behold the head of Holofernes, the chief captain of the army of Assur, and behold the canopy, wherein he did lie in his drunkenness; and the Lord hath smitten him by the hand of a woman.

Jdt|13|16|As the Lord liveth, who hath kept me in my way that I went, my countenance hath deceived him to his destruction, and yet hath he not committed sin with me, to defile and shame me.

Jdt|13|17|Then all the people were wonderfully astonished, and bowed themselves and worshipped אֱלֹהִים, and said with one accord, Blessed be thou, O our אֱלֹהִים, which hast this day brought to nought the enemies of thy people.

Jdt|13|18|Then said Ozias unto her, O daughter, blessed art thou of the most high אֱלֹהִים above all the women upon the earth; and blessed be the Lord אֱלֹהִים, which hath created the heavens and the earth, which hath directed thee to the cutting off of the head of the chief of our enemies.

Jdt|13|19|For this thy confidence shall not depart from the heart of men, which remember the power of אֱלֹהִים for ever.

Jdt|13|20|And אֱלֹהִים turn these things to thee for a perpetual praise, to visit thee in good things because thou hast not spared thy life for the affliction of our nation, but hast revenged our ruin, walking a straight way before our אֱלֹהִים. And all the people said; So be it, so be it.

Jdt|14|1|Then said Judith unto them, Hear me now, my brethren, and take this head, and hang it upon the highest place of your walls.

Jdt|14|2|And so soon as the morning shall appear, and the sun shall come forth upon the earth, take ye every one his weapons, and go forth every valiant man out of the city, and set ye a captain over them, as though ye would go down into the field toward the watch of the Assyrians; but go not down.

Jdt|14|3|Then they shall take their armour, and shall go into their camp, and raise up the captains of the army of Assur, and shall run to the tent of Holofernes, but shall not find him: then fear shall fall upon them, and they shall flee before your face.

Jdt|14|4|So ye, and all that inhabit the coast of Israel, shall pursue them, and overthrow them as they go.

Jdt|14|5|But before ye do these things, call me Achior the Ammonite, that he may see and know him that despised the house of Israel, and that sent him to us as it were to his death.

Jdt|14|6|Then they called Achior out of the house of Ozias; and when he was come, and saw the head of Holofernes in a man's hand in the assembly of the people, he fell down on his face, and his spirit failed.

Jdt|14|7|But when they had recovered him, he fell at Judith's feet, and reverenced her, and said, Blessed art thou in all the tabernacles of Juda, and in all nations, which hearing thy name shall be astonished.

Jdt|14|8|Now therefore tell me all the things that thou hast done in these days. Then Judith declared unto him in the midst of the people all that she had done, from the day that she went forth until that hour she spake unto them.

Jdt|14|9|And when she had left off speaking, the people shouted with a loud voice, and made a joyful noise in their city.

Jdt|14|10|And when Achior had seen all that the אֱלֹהִים of Israel had done, he believed in אֱלֹהִים greatly, and circumcised the flesh of his foreskin, and was joined unto the house of Israel unto this day.

Jdt|14|11|And as soon as the morning arose, they hanged the head of Holofernes upon the wall, and every man took his weapons, and they went forth by bands unto the straits of the mountain.

Jdt|14|12|But when the Assyrians saw them, they sent to their leaders, which came to their captains and tribunes, and to every one of their rulers.

Jdt|14|13|So they came to Holofernes' tent, and said to him that had the charge of all his things, Waken now our lord: for the slaves have been bold to come down against us to battle, that they may be utterly destroyed.

Jdt|14|14|Then went in Bagoas, and knocked at the door of the tent; for he thought that he had slept with Judith.

Jdt|14|15|But because none answered, he opened it, and went into the bedchamber, and found him cast upon the floor dead, and his head was taken from him.

Jdt|14|16|Therefore he cried with a loud voice, with weeping, and sighing, and a mighty cry, and rent his garments.

Jdt|14|17|After he went into the tent where Judith lodged: and when he found her not, he leaped out to the people, and cried,

Jdt|14|18|These slaves have dealt treacherously; one woman of the Hebrews hath brought shame upon the house of king Nabuchodonosor: for, behold, Holofernes lieth upon the ground without a head.

Jdt|14|19|When the captains of the Assyrians' army heard these words, they rent their coats and their minds were wonderfully troubled, and there was a cry and a very great noise throughout the camp.

Jdt|15|1|And when they that were in the tents heard, they were astonished at the thing that was done.

Jdt|15|2|And fear and trembling fell upon them, so that there was no man that durst abide in the sight of his neighbour, but rushing out all together, they fled into every way of the plain, and of the hill country.

Jdt|15|3|They also that had camped in the mountains round about Bethulia fled away. Then the children of Israel, every one that was a warrior among them, rushed out upon them.

Jdt|15|4|Then sent Ozias to Betomasthem, and to Bebai, and Chobai, and Cola and to all the coasts of Israel, such as should tell the things that were done, and that all should rush forth upon their enemies to destroy them.

Jdt|15|5|Now when the children of Israel heard it, they all fell upon them with one consent, and slew them unto Chobai: likewise also they that came from Jerusalem, and from all the hill country, (for men had told them what things were done in the camp of their enemies) and they that were in Galaad, and in Galilee, chased them with a great slaughter, until they were past Damascus and the borders thereof.

Jdt|15|6|And the residue that dwelt at Bethulia, fell upon the camp of Assur, and spoiled them, and were greatly enriched.

Jdt|15|7|And the children of Israel that returned from the slaughter had that which remained; and the villages and the cities, that were in the mountains and in the plain, gat many spoils: for the multitude was very great.

Jdt|15|8|Then Joacim the high priest, and the ancients of the children of Israel that dwelt in Jerusalem, came to behold the good things that אֱלֹהִים had shewed to Israel, and to see Judith, and to salute her.

Jdt|15|9|And when they came unto her, they blessed her with one accord, and said unto her, Thou art the exaltation of Jerusalem, thou art the great glory of Israel, thou art the great rejoicing of our nation:

Jdt|15|10|Thou hast done all these things by thine hand: thou hast done much good to Israel, and אֱלֹהִים is pleased therewith: blessed be thou of the Almighty Lord for evermore. And all the people said, So be it.

Jdt|15|11|And the people spoiled the camp the space of thirty days: and they gave unto Judith Holofernes his tent, and all his plate, and beds, and vessels, and all his stuff: and she took it and laid it on her mule; and made ready her carts, and laid them thereon.

Jdt|15|12|Then all the women of Israel ran together to see her, and blessed her, and made a dance among them for her: and she took branches in her hand, and gave also to the women that were with her.

Jdt|15|13|And they put a garland of olive upon her and her maid that was with her, and she went before all the people in the dance, leading all the women: and all the men of Israel followed in their armour with garlands, and with songs in their mouths.

Jdt|16|1|Then Judith began to sing this thanksgiving in all Israel, and all the people sang after her this song of praise.

Jdt|16|2|And Judith said, Begin unto my אֱלֹהִים with timbrels, sing unto my Lord with cymbals: tune unto him a new psalm: exalt him, and call upon his name.

Jdt|16|3|For אֱלֹהִים breaketh the battles: for among the camps in the midst of the people he hath delivered me out of the hands of them that persecuted me.

Jdt|16|4|Assur came out of the mountains from the north, he came with ten thousands of his army, the multitude whereof stopped the torrents, and their horsemen have covered the hills.

Jdt|16|5|He bragged that he would burn up my borders, and kill my young men with the sword, and dash the sucking children against the ground, and make mine infants as a prey, and my virgins as a spoil.

Jdt|16|6|But the Almighty Lord hath disappointed them by the hand of a woman.

Jdt|16|7|For the mighty one did not fall by the young men, neither did the sons of the Titans smite him, nor high giants set upon him: but Judith the daughter of Merari weakened him with the beauty of her countenance.

Jdt|16|8|For she put off the garment of her widowhood for the exaltation of those that were oppressed in Israel, and anointed her face with ointment, and bound her hair in a tire, and took a linen garment to deceive him.

Jdt|16|9|Her sandals ravished his eyes, her beauty took his mind prisoner, and the fauchion passed through his neck.

Jdt|16|10|The Persians quaked at her boldness, and the Medes were daunted at her hardiness.

Jdt|16|11|Then my afflicted shouted for joy, and my weak ones cried aloud; but they were astonished: these lifted up their voices, but they were overthrown.

Jdt|16|12|The sons of the damsels have pierced them through, and wounded them as fugatives' children: they perished by the battle of the Lord.

Jdt|16|13|I will sing unto the Lord a new song: O Lord, thou art great and glorious, wonderful in strength, and invincible.

Jdt|16|14|Let all creatures serve thee: for thou spakest, and they were made, thou didst send forth thy spirit, and it created them, and there is none that can resist thy voice.

Jdt|16|15|For the mountains shall be moved from their foundations with the waters, the rocks shall melt as wax at thy presence: yet thou art merciful to them that fear thee.

Jdt|16|16|For all sacrifice is too little for a sweet savour unto thee, and all the fat is not sufficient for thy burnt offering: but he that feareth the Lord is great at all times.

Jdt|16|17|Woe to the nations that rise up against my kindred! the Lord Almighty will take vengeance of them in the day of judgment, in putting fire and worms in their flesh; and they shall feel them, and weep for ever.

Jdt|16|18|Now as soon as they entered into Jerusalem, they worshipped the Lord; and as soon as the people were purified, they offered their burnt offerings, and their free offerings, and their gifts.

Jdt|16|19|Judith also dedicated all the stuff of Holofernes, which the people had given her, and gave the canopy, which she had taken out of his bedchamber, for a gift unto the Lord.

Jdt|16|20|So the people continued feasting in Jerusalem before the sanctuary for the space of three months and Judith remained with them.

Jdt|16|21|After this time every one returned to his own inheritance, and Judith went to Bethulia, and remained in her own possession, and was in her time honourable in all the country.

Jdt|16|22|And many desired her, but none knew her all the days of her life, after that Manasses her husband was dead, and was gathered to his people.

Jdt|16|23|But she increased more and more in honour, and waxed old in her husband's house, being an hundred and five years old, and made her maid free; so she died in Bethulia: and they buried her in the cave of her husband Manasses.

Jdt|16|24|And the house of Israel lamented her seven days: and before she died, she did distribute her goods to all them that were nearest of kindred to Manasses her husband, and to them that were the nearest of her kindred.

Jdt|16|25|And there was none that made the children of Israel any more afraid in the days of Judith, nor a long time after her death.

Wis|1|1|Love righteousness, ye that be judges of the earth: think of the Lord with a good (heart,) and in simplicity of heart seek him.

Wis|1|2|For he will be found of them that tempt him not; and sheweth himself unto such as do not distrust him.

Wis|1|3|For froward thoughts separate from אֱלֹהִים: and his power, when it is tried, reproveth the unwise.

Wis|1|4|For into a malicious soul wisdom shall not enter; nor dwell in the body that is subject unto sin.

Wis|1|5|For the holy spirit of discipline will flee deceit, and remove from thoughts that are without understanding, and will not abide when unrighteousness cometh in.

Wis|1|6|For wisdom is a loving spirit; and will not acquit a blasphemer of his words: for אֱלֹהִים is witness of his reins, and a true beholder of his heart, and a hearer of his tongue.

Wis|1|7|For the Spirit of the Lord filleth the world: and that which containeth all things hath knowledge of the voice.

Wis|1|8|Therefore he that speaketh unrighteous things cannot be hid: neither shall vengeance, when it punisheth, pass by him.

Wis|1|9|For inquisition shall be made into the counsels of the ungodly: and the sound of his words shall come unto the Lord for the manifestation of his wicked deeds.

Wis|1|10|For the ear of jealousy heareth all things: and the noise of murmurings is not hid.

Wis|1|11|Therefore beware of murmuring, which is unprofitable; and refrain your tongue from backbiting: for there is no word so secret, that shall go for nought: and the mouth that belieth slayeth the soul.

Wis|1|12|Seek not death in the error of your life: and pull not upon yourselves destruction with the works of your hands.

Wis|1|13|For אֱלֹהִים made not death: neither hath he pleasure in the destruction of the living.

Wis|1|14|For he created all things, that they might have their being: and the generations of the world were healthful; and there is no poison of destruction in them, nor the kingdom of death upon the earth:

Wis|1|15|(For righteousness is immortal:)

Wis|1|16|But ungodly men with their works and words called it to them: for when they thought to have it their friend, they consumed to nought, and made a covenant with it, because they are worthy to take part with it.

Wis|2|1|For the ungodly said, reasoning with themselves, but not aright, Our life is short and tedious, and in the death of a man there is no remedy: neither was there any man known to have returned from the grave.

Wis|2|2|For we are born at all adventure: and we shall be hereafter as though we had never been: for the breath in our nostrils is as smoke, and a little spark in the moving of our heart:

Wis|2|3|Which being extinguished, our body shall be turned into ashes, and our spirit shall vanish as the soft air,

Wis|2|4|And our name shall be forgotten in time, and no man shall have our works in remembrance, and our life shall pass away as the trace of a cloud, and shall be dispersed as a mist, that is driven away with the beams of the sun, and overcome with the heat thereof.

Wis|2|5|For our time is a very shadow that passeth away; and after our end there is no returning: for it is fast sealed, so that no man cometh again.

Wis|2|6|Come on therefore, let us enjoy the good things that are present: and let us speedily use the creatures like as in youth.

Wis|2|7|Let us fill ourselves with costly wine and ointments: and let no flower of the spring pass by us:

Wis|2|8|Let us crown ourselves with rosebuds, before they be withered:

Wis|2|9|Let none of us go without his part of our voluptuousness: let us leave tokens of our joyfulness in every place: for this is our portion, and our lot is this.

Wis|2|10|Let us oppress the poor righteous man, let us not spare the widow, nor reverence the ancient gray hairs of the aged.

Wis|2|11|Let our strength be the law of justice: for that which is feeble is found to be nothing worth.

Wis|2|12|Therefore let us lie in wait for the righteous; because he is not for our turn, and he is clean contrary to our doings: he upbraideth us with our offending the law, and objecteth to our infamy the transgressings of our education.

Wis|2|13|He professeth to have the knowledge of אֱלֹהִים: and he calleth himself the child of the Lord.

Wis|2|14|He was made to reprove our thoughts.

Wis|2|15|He is grievous unto us even to behold: for his life is not like other men's, his ways are of another fashion.

Wis|2|16|We are esteemed of him as counterfeits: he abstaineth from our ways as from filthiness: he pronounceth the end of the just to be blessed, and maketh his boast that אֱלֹהִים is his father.

Wis|2|17|Let us see if his words be true: and let us prove what shall happen in the end of him.

Wis|2|18|For if the just man be the son of אֱלֹהִים, he will help him, and deliver him from the hand of his enemies.

Wis|2|19|Let us examine him with despitefulness and torture, that we may know his meekness, and prove his patience.

Wis|2|20|Let us condemn him with a shameful death: for by his own saying he shall be respected.

Wis|2|21|Such things they did imagine, and were deceived: for their own wickedness hath blinded them.

Wis|2|22|As for the mysteries of אֱלֹהִים, they kn ew them not: neither hoped they for the wages of righteousness, nor discerned a reward for blameless souls.

Wis|2|23|For אֱלֹהִים created man to be immortal, and made him to be an image of his own eternity.

Wis|2|24|Nevertheless through envy of the devil came death into the world: and they that do hold of his side do find it.

Wis|3|1|But the souls of the righteous are in the hand of אֱלֹהִים, and there shall no torment touch them.

Wis|3|2|In the sight of the unwise they seemed to die: and their departure is taken for misery,

Wis|3|3|And their going from us to be utter destruction: but they are in peace.

Wis|3|4|For though they be punished in the sight of men, yet is their hope full of immortality.

Wis|3|5|And having been a little chastised, they shall be greatly rewarded: for אֱלֹהִים proved them, and found them worthy for himself.

Wis|3|6|As gold in the furnace hath he tried them, and received them as a burnt offering.

Wis|3|7|And in the time of their visitation they shall shine, and run to and fro like sparks among the stubble.

Wis|3|8|They shall judge the nations, and have dominion over the people, and their Lord shall reign for ever.

Wis|3|9|They that put their trust in him shall understand the truth: and such as be faithful in love shall abide with him: for grace and mercy is to his saints, and he hath care for his elect.

Wis|3|10|But the ungodly shall be punished according to their own imaginations, which have neglected the righteous, and forsaken the Lord.

Wis|3|11|For whoso despiseth wisdom and nurture, he is miserable, and their hope is vain, their labours unfruitful, and their works unprofitable:

Wis|3|12|Their wives are foolish, and their children wicked:

Wis|3|13|Their offspring is cursed. Wherefore blessed is the barren that is undefiled, which hath not known the sinful bed: she shall have fruit in the visitation of souls.

Wis|3|14|And blessed is the eunuch, which with his hands hath wrought no iniquity, nor imagined wicked things against אֱלֹהִים: for unto him shall be given the special gift of faith, and an inheritance in the temple of the Lord more acceptable to his mind.

Wis|3|15|For glorious is the fruit of good labours: and the root of wisdom shall never fall away.

Wis|3|16|As for the children of adulterers, they shall not come to their perfection, and the seed of an unrighteous bed shall be rooted out.

Wis|3|17|For though they live long, yet shall they be nothing regarded: and their last age shall be without honour.

Wis|3|18|Or, if they die quickly, they have no hope, neither comfort in the day of trial.

Wis|3|19|For horrible is the end of the unrighteous generation.

Wis|4|1|Better it is to have no children, and to have virtue: for the memorial thereof is immortal: because it is known with אֱלֹהִים, and with men.

Wis|4|2|When it is present, men take example at it; and when it is gone, they desire it: it weareth a crown, and triumpheth for ever, having gotten the victory, striving for undefiled rewards.

Wis|4|3|But the multiplying brood of the ungodly shall not thrive, nor take deep rooting from bastard slips, nor lay any fast foundation.

Wis|4|4|For though they flourish in branches for a time; yet standing not last, they shall be shaken with the wind, and through the force of winds they shall be rooted out.

Wis|4|5|The imperfect branches shall be broken off, their fruit unprofitable, not ripe to eat, yea, meet for nothing.

Wis|4|6|For children begotten of unlawful beds are witnesses of wickedness against their parents in their trial.

Wis|4|7|But though the righteous be prevented with death, yet shall he be in rest.

Wis|4|8|For honourable age is not that which standeth in length of time, nor that is measured by number of years.

Wis|4|9|But wisdom is the gray hair unto men, and an unspotted life is old age.

Wis|4|10|He pleased אֱלֹהִים, and was beloved of him: so that living among sinners he was translated.

Wis|4|11|Yea speedily was he taken away, lest that wickedness should alter his understanding, or deceit beguile his soul.

Wis|4|12|For the bewitching of naughtiness doth obscure things that are honest; and the wandering of concupiscence doth undermine the simple mind.

Wis|4|13|He, being made perfect in a short time, fulfilled a long time:

Wis|4|14|For his soul pleased the Lord: therefore hasted he to take him away from among the wicked.

Wis|4|15|This the people saw, and understood it not, neither laid they up this in their minds, That his grace and mercy is with his saints, and that he hath respect unto his chosen.

Wis|4|16|Thus the righteous that is dead shall condemn the ungodly which are living; and youth that is soon perfected the many years and old age of the unrighteous.

Wis|4|17|For they shall see the end of the wise, and shall not understand what אֱלֹהִים in his counsel hath decreed of him, and to what end the Lord hath set him in safety.

Wis|4|18|They shall see him, and despise him; but אֱלֹהִים shall laugh them to scorn: and they shall hereafter be a vile carcase, and a reproach among the dead for evermore.

Wis|4|19|For he shall rend them, and cast them down headlong, that they shall be speechless; and he shall shake them from the foundation; and they shall be utterly laid waste, and be in sorrow; and their memorial shall perish.

Wis|4|20|And when they cast up the accounts of their sins, they shall come with fear: and their own iniquities shall convince them to their face.

Wis|5|1|Then shall the righteous man stand in great boldness before the face of such as have afflicted him, and made no account of his labours.

Wis|5|2|When they see it, they shall be troubled with terrible fear, and shall be amazed at the strangeness of his salvation, so far beyond all that they looked for.

Wis|5|3|And they repenting and groaning for anguish of spirit shall say within themselves, This was he, whom we had sometimes in derision, and a proverb of reproach:

Wis|5|4|We fools accounted his life madness, and his end to be without honour:

Wis|5|5|How is he numbered among the children of אֱלֹהִים, and his lot is among the saints!

Wis|5|6|Therefore have we erred from the way of truth, and the light of righteousness hath not shined unto us, and the sun of righteousness rose not upon us.

Wis|5|7|We wearied ourselves in the way of wickedness and destruction: yea, we have gone through deserts, where there lay no way: but as for the way of the Lord, we have not known it.

Wis|5|8|What hath pride profited us? or what good hath riches with our vaunting brought us?

Wis|5|9|All those things are passed away like a shadow, and as a post that hasted by;

Wis|5|10|And as a ship that passeth over the waves of the water, which when it is gone by, the trace thereof cannot be found, neither the pathway of the keel in the waves;

Wis|5|11|Or as when a bird hath flown through the air, there is no token of her way to be found, but the light air being beaten with the stroke of her wings and parted with the violent noise and motion of them, is passed through, and therein afterwards no sign where she went is to be found;

Wis|5|12|Or like as when an arrow is shot at a mark, it parteth the air, which immediately cometh together again, so that a man cannot know where it went through:

Wis|5|13|Even so we in like manner, as soon as we were born, began to draw to our end, and had no sign of virtue to shew; but were consumed in our own wickedness.

Wis|5|14|For the hope of the Godly is like dust that is blown away with the wind; like a thin froth that is driven away with the storm; like as the smoke which is dispersed here and there with a tempest, and passeth away as the remembrance of a guest that tarrieth but a day.

Wis|5|15|But the righteous live for evermore; their reward also is with the Lord, and the care of them is with the most High.

Wis|5|16|Therefore shall they receive a glorious kingdom, and a beautiful crown from the Lord's hand: for with his right hand shall he cover them, and with his arm shall he protect them.

Wis|5|17|He shall take to him his jealousy for complete armour, and make the creature his weapon for the revenge of his enemies.

Wis|5|18|He shall put on righteousness as a breastplate, and true judgment instead of an helmet.

Wis|5|19|He shall take holiness for an invincible shield.

Wis|5|20|His severe wrath shall he sharpen for a sword, and the world shall fight with him against the unwise.

Wis|5|21|Then shall the right aiming thunderbolts go abroad; and from the clouds, as from a well drawn bow, shall they fly to the mark.

Wis|5|22|And hailstones full of wrath shall be cast as out of a stone bow, and the water of the sea shall rage against them, and the floods shall cruelly drown them.

Wis|5|23|Yea, a mighty wind shall stand up against them, and like a storm shall blow them away: thus iniquity shall lay waste the whole earth, and ill dealing shall overthrow the thrones of the mighty.

Wis|6|1|Hear therefore, O ye kings, and understand; learn, ye that be judges of the ends of the earth.

Wis|6|2|Give ear, ye that rule the people, and glory in the multitude of nations.

Wis|6|3|For power is given you of the Lord, and sovereignty from the Highest, who shall try your works, and search out your counsels.

Wis|6|4|Because, being ministers of his kingdom, ye have not judged aright, nor kept the law, nor walked after the counsel of אֱלֹהִים;

Wis|6|5|Horribly and speedily shall he come upon you: for a sharp judgment shall be to them that be in high places.

Wis|6|6|For mercy will soon pardon the meanest: but mighty men shall be mightily tormented.

Wis|6|7|For he which is Lord over all shall fear no man's person, neither shall he stand in awe of any man's greatness: for he hath made the small and great, and careth for all alike.

Wis|6|8|But a sore trial shall come upon the mighty.

Wis|6|9|Unto you therefore, O kings, do I speak, that ye may learn wisdom, and not fall away.

Wis|6|10|For they that keep holiness holily shall be judged holy: and they that have learned such things shall find what to answer.

Wis|6|11|Wherefore set your affection upon my words; desire them, and ye shall be instructed.

Wis|6|12|Wisdom is glorious, and never fadeth away: yea, she is easily seen of them that love her, and found of such as seek her.

Wis|6|13|She preventeth them that desire her, in making herself first known unto them.

Wis|6|14|Whoso seeketh her early shall have no great travail: for he shall find her sitting at his doors.

Wis|6|15|To think therefore upon her is perfection of wisdom: and whoso watcheth for her shall quickly be without care.

Wis|6|16|For she goeth about seeking such as are worthy of her, sheweth herself favourably unto them in the ways, and meeteth them in every thought.

Wis|6|17|For the very true beginning of her is the desire of discipline; and the care of discipline is love;

Wis|6|18|And love is the keeping of her laws; and the giving heed unto her laws is the assurance of incorruption;

Wis|6|19|And incorruption maketh us near unto אֱלֹהִים:

Wis|6|20|Therefore the desire of wisdom bringeth to a kingdom.

Wis|6|21|If your delight be then in thrones and sceptres, O ye kings of the people, honour wisdom, that ye may reign for evermore.

Wis|6|22|As for wisdom, what she is, and how she came up, I will tell you, and will not hide mysteries from you: but will seek her out from the beginning of her nativity, and bring the knowledge of her into light, and will not pass over the truth.

Wis|6|23|Neither will I go with consuming envy; for such a man shall have no fellowship with wisdom.

Wis|6|24|But the multitude of the wise is the welfare of the world: and a wise king is the upholding of the people.

Wis|6|25|Receive therefore instruction through my words, and it shall do you good.

Wis|7|1|I myself also am a mortal man, like to all, and the offspring of him that was first made of the earth,

Wis|7|2|And in my mother's womb was fashioned to be flesh in the time of ten months, being compacted in blood, of the seed of man, and the pleasure that came with sleep.

Wis|7|3|And when I was born, I drew in the common air, and fell upon the earth, which is of like nature, and the first voice which I uttered was crying, as all others do.

Wis|7|4|I was nursed in swaddling clothes, and that with cares.

Wis|7|5|For there is no king that had any other beginning of birth.

Wis|7|6|For all men have one entrance into life, and the like going out.

Wis|7|7|Wherefore I prayed, and understanding was given me: I called upon אֱלֹהִים, and the spirit of wisdom came to me.

Wis|7|8|I preferred her before sceptres and thrones, and esteemed riches nothing in comparison of her.

Wis|7|9|Neither compared I unto her any precious stone, because all gold in respect of her is as a little sand,

and silver shall be counted as clay before her.

Wis|7|10|I loved her above health and beauty, and chose to have her instead of light: for the light that cometh from her never goeth out.

Wis|7|11|All good things together came to me with her, and innumerable riches in her hands.

Wis|7|12|And I rejoiced in them all, because wisdom goeth before them: and I knew not that she was the mother of them.

Wis|7|13|I learned diligently, and do communicate her liberally: I do not hide her riches.

Wis|7|14|For she is a treasure unto men that never faileth: which they that use become the friends of אֱלֹהִים, being commended for the gifts that come from learning.

Wis|7|15|אֱלֹהִים hath granted me to speak as I would, and to conceive as is meet for the things that are given me: because it is he that leadeth unto wisdom, and directeth the wise.

Wis|7|16|For in his hand are both we and our words; all wisdom also, and knowledge of workmanship.

Wis|7|17|For he hath given me certain knowledge of the things that are, namely, to know how the world was made, and the operation of the elements:

Wis|7|18|The beginning, ending, and midst of the times: the alterations of the turning of the sun, and the change of seasons:

Wis|7|19|The circuits of years, and the positions of stars:

Wis|7|20|The natures of living creatures, and the furies of wild beasts: the violence of winds, and the reasonings of men: the diversities of plants and the virtues of roots:

Wis|7|21|And all such things as are either secret or manifest, them I know.

Wis|7|22|For wisdom, which is the worker of all things, taught me: for in her is an understanding spirit holy, one only, manifold, subtil, lively, clear, undefiled, plain, not subject to hurt, loving the thing that is good quick, which cannot be letted, ready to do good,

Wis|7|23|Kind to man, steadfast, sure, free from care, having all power, overseeing all things, and going through all understanding, pure, and most subtil, spirits.

Wis|7|24|For wisdom is more moving than any motion: she passeth and goeth through all things by reason of her pureness.

Wis|7|25|For she is the breath of the power of אֱלֹהִים, and a pure influence flowing from the glory of the Almighty: therefore can no defiled thing fall into her.

Wis|7|26|For she is the brightness of the everlasting light, the unspotted mirror of the power of אֱלֹהִים, and the image of his goodness.

Wis|7|27|And being but one, she can do all things: and remaining in herself, she maketh all things new: and in all ages entering into holy souls, she maketh them friends of אֱלֹהִים, and prophets.

Wis|7|28|For אֱלֹהִים loveth none but him that dwelleth with wisdom.

Wis|7|29|For she is more beautiful than the sun, and above all the order of stars: being compared with the light, she is found before it.

Wis|7|30|For after this cometh night: but vice shall not prevail against wisdom.

Wis|8|1|Wisdom reacheth from one end to another mightily: and sweetly doth she order all things.

Wis|8|2|I loved her, and sought her out from my youth, I desired to make her my spouse, and I was a lover of her beauty.

Wis|8|3|In that she is conversant with אֱלֹהִים, she magnifieth her nobility: yea, the Lord of all things himself loved her.

Wis|8|4|For she is privy to the mysteries of the knowledge of אֱלֹהִים, and a lover of his works.

Wis|8|5|If riches be a possession to be desired in this life; what is richer than wisdom, that worketh all things?

Wis|8|6|And if prudence work; who of all that are is a more cunning workman than she?

Wis|8|7|And if a man love righteousness her labours are virtues: for she teacheth temperance and prudence, justice and fortitude: which are such things, as en can have nothing more profitable in their life.

Wis|8|8|If a man desire much experience, she knoweth things of old, and conjectureth aright what is to come: she knoweth the subtilties of speeches, and can expound dark sentences: she foreseeth signs and wonders, and the events of seasons and times.

Wis|8|9|Therefore I purposed to take her to me to live with me, knowing that she would be a counsellor of good things, and a comfort in cares and grief.

Wis|8|10|For her sake I shall have estimation among the multitude, and honour with the elders, though I be young.

Wis|8|11|I shall be found of a quick conceit in judgment, and shall be admired in the sight of great men.

Wis|8|12|When I hold my tongue, they shall bide my leisure, and when I speak, they shall give good ear unto me: if I talk much, they shall lay their hands upon their mouth.

Wis|8|13|Moreover by the means of her I shall obtain immortality, and leave behind me an everlasting memorial to them that come after me.

Wis|8|14|I shall set the people in order, and the nations shall be subject unto me.

Wis|8|15|Horrible tyrants shall be afraid, when they do but hear of me; I shall be found good among the multitude, and valiant in war.

Wis|8|16|After I am come into mine house, I will repose myself with her: for her conversation hath no bitterness; and to live with her hath no sorrow, but mirth and joy.

Wis|8|17|Now when I considered these things in myself, and pondered them in my heart, how that to be allied unto wisdom is immortality;

Wis|8|18|And great pleasure it is to have her friendship; and in the works of her hands are infinite riches; and in the exercise of conference with her, prudence; and in talking with her, a good report; I went about seeking how to take her to me.

Wis|8|19|For I was a witty child, and had a good spirit.

Wis|8|20|Yea rather, being good, I came into a body undefiled.

Wis|8|21|Nevertheless, when I perceived that I could not otherwise obtain her, except אֱלֹהִים gave her me; and that was a point of wisdom also to know whose gift she was; I prayed unto the Lord, and besought him, and with my whole heart I said,

Wis|9|1|O אֱלֹהִים of my fathers, and Lord of mercy, who hast made all things with thy word,

Wis|9|2|And ordained man through thy wisdom, that he should have dominion over the creatures which thou hast made,

Wis|9|3|And order the world according to equity and righteousness, and execute judgment with an upright heart:

Wis|9|4|Give me wisdom, that sitteth by thy throne; and reject me not from among thy children:

Wis|9|5|For I thy servant and son of thine handmaid am a feeble person, and of a short time, and too young for the understanding of judgment and laws.

Wis|9|6|For though a man be never so perfect among the children of men, yet if thy wisdom be not with him, he shall be nothing regarded.

Wis|9|7|Thou hast chosen me to be a king of thy people, and a judge of thy sons and daughters:

Wis|9|8|Thou hast commanded me to build a temple upon thy holy mount, and an altar in the city wherein thou dwellest, a resemblance of the holy tabernacle, which thou hast prepared from the beginning.

Wis|9|9|And wisdom was with thee: which knoweth thy works, and was present when thou madest the world, and knew what was acceptable in thy sight, and right in thy commandments.

Wis|9|10|O send her out of thy holy heavens, and from the throne of thy glory, that being present she may labour with me, that I may know what is pleasing unto thee.

Wis|9|11|For she knoweth and understandeth all things, and she shall lead me soberly in my doings, and preserve me in her power.

Wis|9|12|So shall my works be acceptable, and then shall I judge thy people righteously, and be worthy to sit in my father's seat.

Wis|9|13|For what man is he that can know the counsel of אֱלֹהִים? or who can think what the will of the Lord is?

Wis|9|14|For the thoughts of mortal men are miserable, and our devices are but uncertain.

Wis|9|15|For the corruptible body presseth down the soul, and the earthy tabernacle weigheth down the mind that museth upon many things.

Wis|9|16|And hardly do we guess aright at things that are upon earth, and with labour do we find the things that are before us: but the things that are in heaven who hath searched out?

Wis|9|17|And thy counsel who hath known, except thou give wisdom, and send thy Holy Spirit from above?

Wis|9|18|For so the ways of them which lived on the earth were reformed, and men were taught the things that are pleasing unto thee, and were saved through wisdom.

Wis|10|1|She preserved the first formed father of the world, that was created alone, and brought him out of his fall,

Wis|10|2|And gave him power to rule all things.

Wis|10|3|But when the unrighteous went away from her in his anger, he perished also in the fury wherewith he murdered his brother.

Wis|10|4|For whose cause the earth being drowned with the flood, wisdom again preserved it, and directed the course of the righteous in a piece of wood of small value.

Wis|10|5|Moreover, the nations in their wicked conspiracy being confounded, she found out the righteous, and preserved him blameless unto אֱלֹהִים, and kept him strong against his tender compassion toward his son.

Wis|10|6|When the ungodly perished, she delivered the righteous man, who fled from the fire which fell down upon the five cities.

Wis|10|7|Of whose wickedness even to this day the waste land that smoketh is a testimony, and plants bearing fruit that never come to ripeness: and a standing pillar of salt is a monument of an unbelieving soul.

Wis|10|8|For regarding not wisdom, they gat not only this hurt, that they knew not the things which were good; but also left behind them to the world a memorial of their foolishness: so that in the things wherein they offended they could not so much as be hid.

Wis|10|9|Rut wisdom delivered from pain those that attended upon her.

Wis|10|10|When the righteous fled from his brother's wrath she guided him in right paths, shewed him the kingdom of אֱלֹ, and gave him knowledge of holy things, made him rich in his travels, and multiplied the fruit of his labours.

Wis|10|11|In the covetousness of such as oppressed him she stood by him, and made him rich.

Wis|10|12|She defended him from his enemies, and kept him safe from those that lay in wait, and in a sore conflict she gave him the victory; that he might know that goodness is stronger than all.

Wis|10|13|When the righteous was sold, she forsook him not, but delivered him from sin: she went down with him into the pit,

Wis|10|14|And left him not in bonds, till she brought him the sceptre of the kingdom, and power against those that oppressed him: as for them that had accused him, she shewed them to be liars, and gave him perpetual glory.

Wis|10|15|She delivered the righteous people and blameless seed from the nation that oppressed them.

Wis|10|16|She entered into the soul of the servant of the Lord, and withstood dreadful kings in wonders and signs;

Wis|10|17|Rendered to the righteous a reward of their labours, guided them in a marvellous way, and was unto them for a cover by day, and a light of stars in the night season;

Wis|10|18|Brought them through the Red sea, and led them through much water:

Wis|10|19|But she drowned their enemies, and cast them up out of the bottom of the deep.

Wis|10|20|Therefore the righteous spoiled the ungodly, and praised thy holy name, O Lord, and magnified with one accord thine hand, that fought for them.

Wis|10|21|For wisdom opened the mouth of the dumb, and made the tongues of them that cannot speak eloquent.

Wis|11|1|She prospered their works in the hand of the holy prophet.

Wis|11|2|They went through the wilderness that was not inhabited, and pitched tents in places where there lay no way.

Wis|11|3|They stood against their enemies, and were avenged of their adversaries.

Wis|11|4|When they were thirsty, they called upon thee, and water was given them out of the flinty rock, and their thirst was quenched out of the hard stone.

Wis|11|5|For by what things their enemies were punished, by the same they in their need were benefited.

Wis|11|6|For instead of of a perpetual running river troubled with foul blood,

Wis|11|7|For a manifest reproof of that commandment, whereby the infants were slain, thou gavest unto them abundance of water by a means which they hoped not for:

Wis|11|8|Declaring by that thirst then how thou hadst punished their adversaries.

Wis|11|9|For when they were tried albeit but in mercy chastised, they knew how the ungodly were judged in wrath and tormented, thirsting in another manner than the just.

Wis|11|10|For these thou didst admonish and try, as a father: but the other, as a severe king, thou didst condemn and punish.

Wis|11|11|Whether they were absent or present, they were vexed alike.

Wis|11|12|For a double grief came upon them, and a groaning for the remembrance of things past.

Wis|11|13|For when they heard by their own punishments the other to be benefited, they had some feeling of the Lord.

Wis|11|14|For whom they respected with scorn, when he was long before thrown out at the casting forth of the infants, him in the end, when they saw what came to pass, they admired.

Wis|11|15|But for the foolish devices of their wickedness, wherewith being deceived they worshipped serpents void of reason, and vile beasts, thou didst send a multitude of unreasonable beasts upon them for vengeance;

Wis|11|16|That they might know, that wherewithal a man sinneth, by the same also shall he be punished.

Wis|11|17|For thy Almighty hand, that made the world of matter without form, wanted not means to send among them a multitude of bears or fierce lions,

Wis|11|18|Or unknown wild beasts, full of rage, newly created, breathing out either a fiery vapour, or filthy scents of scattered smoke, or shooting horrible sparkles out of their eyes:

Wis|11|19|Whereof not only the harm might dispatch them at once, but also the terrible sight utterly destroy them.

Wis|11|20|Yea, and without these might they have fallen down with one blast, being persecuted of vengeance, and scattered abroad through the breath of thy power: but thou hast ordered all things in measure and number and weight.

Wis|11|21|For thou canst shew thy great strength at all times when thou wilt; and who may withstand the power of thine arm?

Wis|11|22|For the whole world before thee is as a little grain of the balance, yea, as a drop of the morning dew that falleth down upon the earth.

Wis|11|23|But thou hast mercy upon all; for thou canst do all things, and winkest at the sins of men, because they should amend.

Wis|11|24|For thou lovest all the things that are, and abhorrest nothing which thou hast made: for never wouldest thou have made any thing, if thou hadst hated it.

Wis|11|25|And how could any thing have endured, if it had not been thy will? or been preserved, if not called by thee?

Wis|11|26|But thou sparest all: for they are thine, O Lord, thou lover of souls.

Wis|12|1|For thine incorruptible Spirit is in all things.

Wis|12|2|Therefore chastenest thou them by little and little that offend, and warnest them by putting them in remembrance wherein they have offended, that leaving their wickedness they may believe on thee, O Lord.

Wis|12|3|For it was thy will to destroy by the hands of our fathers both those old inhabitants of thy holy land,

Wis|12|4|Whom thou hatedst for doing most odious works of witchcrafts, and wicked sacrifices;

Wis|12|5|And also those merciless murderers of children, and devourers of man's flesh, and the feasts of blood,

Wis|12|6|With their priests out of the midst of their idolatrous crew, and the parents, that killed with their own hands souls destitute of help:

Wis|12|7|That the land, which thou esteemedst above all other, might receive a worthy colony of אֱלֹהִים's children.

Wis|12|8|Nevertheless even those thou sparedst as men, and didst send wasps, forerunners of thine host, to destroy them by little and little.

Wis|12|9|Not that thou wast unable to bring the ungodly under the hand of the righteous in battle, or to destroy them at once with cruel beasts, or with one rough word:

Wis|12|10|But executing thy judgments upon them by little and little, thou gavest them place of repentance, not being ignorant that they were a naughty generation, and that their malice was bred in them, and that their cogitation would never be changed.

Wis|12|11|For it was a cursed seed from the beginning; neither didst thou for fear of any man give them pardon for those things wherein they sinned.

Wis|12|12|For who shall say, What hast thou done? or who shall withstand thy judgment? or who shall accuse thee for the nations that perish, whom thou made? or who shall come to stand against thee, to be revenged for the unrighteous men?

Wis|12|13|For neither is there any אֱלֹהִים but thou that careth for all, to whom thou mightest shew that thy judgment is not unright.

Wis|12|14|Neither shall king or tyrant be able to set his face against thee for any whom thou hast punished.

Wis|12|15|Forsomuch then as thou art righteous thyself, thou orderest all things righteously: thinking it not agreeable with thy power to condemn him that hath not deserved to be punished.

Wis|12|16|For thy power is the beginning of righteousness, and because thou art the Lord of all, it maketh thee to be gracious unto all.

Wis|12|17|For when men will not believe that thou art of a full power, thou shewest thy strength, and among them that know it thou makest their boldness manifest.

Wis|12|18|But thou, mastering thy power, judgest with equity, and orderest us with great favour: for thou mayest use power when thou wilt.

Wis|12|19|But by such works hast thou taught thy people that the just man should be merciful, and hast made thy children to be of a good hope that thou givest repentance for sins.

Wis|12|20|For if thou didst punish the enemies of thy children, and the condemned to death, with such deliberation, giving them time and place, whereby they might be delivered from their malice:

Wis|12|21|With how great circumspection didst thou judge thine own sons, unto whose fathers thou hast sworn, and made covenants of good promises?

Wis|12|22|Therefore, whereas thou dost chasten us, thou scourgest our enemies a thousand times more, to the intent that, when we judge, we should carefully think of thy goodness, and when we ourselves are judged, we should look for mercy.

Wis|12|23|Wherefore, whereas men have lived dissolutely and unrighteously, thou hast tormented them with their own abominations.

Wis|12|24|For they went astray very far in the ways of error, and held them for gods, which even among the beasts of their enemies were despised, being deceived, as children of no understanding.

Wis|12|25|Therefore unto them, as to children without the use of reason, thou didst send a judgment to mock them.

Wis|12|26|But they that would not be reformed by that correction, wherein he dallied with them, shall feel a judgment worthy of אֱלֹהִים.

Wis|12|27|For, look, for what things they grudged, when they were punished, that is, for them whom they thought to be gods; [now] being punished in them, when they saw it, they acknowledged him to be the true אֱלֹהִים, whom before they denied to know: and therefore came extreme damnation upon them.

Wis|13|1|Surely vain are all men by nature, who are ignorant of אֱלֹהִים, and could not out of the good things that are seen know him that is: neither by considering the works did they acknowledge the workmaster;

Wis|13|2|But deemed either fire, or wind, or the swift air, or the circle of the stars, or the violent water, or the lights of heaven, to be the gods which govern the world.

Wis|13|3|With whose beauty if they being delighted took them to be gods; let them know how much better the Lord of them is: for the first author of beauty hath created them.

Wis|13|4|But if they were astonished at their power and virtue, let them understand by them, how much mightier he is that made them.

Wis|13|5|For by the greatness and beauty of the creatures proportionably the maker of them is seen.

Wis|13|6|But yet for this they are the less to be blamed: for they peradventure err, seeking אֱלֹהִים, and desirous to find him.

Wis|13|7|For being conversant in his works they search him diligently, and believe their sight: because the things are beautiful that are seen.

Wis|13|8|Howbeit neither are they to be pardoned.

Wis|13|9|For if they were able to know so much, that they could aim at the world; how did they not sooner find out the Lord thereof?

Wis|13|10|But miserable are they, and in dead things is their hope, who call them gods, which are the works of men's hands, gold and silver, to shew art in, and resemblances of beasts, or a stone good for nothing, the work of an ancient hand.

Wis|13|11|Now a carpenter that felleth timber, after he hath sawn down a tree meet for the purpose, and taken off all the bark skilfully round about, and hath wrought it handsomely, and made a vessel thereof fit for the service of man's life;

Wis|13|12|And after spending the refuse of his work to dress his meat, hath filled himself;

Wis|13|13|And taking the very refuse among those which served to no use, being a crooked piece of wood, and full of knots, hath carved it diligently, when he had nothing else to do, and formed it by the skill of his understanding, and fashioned it to the image of a man;

Wis|13|14|Or made it like some vile beast, laying it over with vermilion, and with paint colouring it red, and covering every spot therein;

Wis|13|15|And when he had made a convenient room for it, set it in a wall, and made it fast with iron:

Wis|13|16|For he provided for it that it might not fall, knowing that it was unable to help itself; for it is an image, and hath need of help:

Wis|13|17|Then maketh he prayer for his goods, for his wife and children, and is not ashamed to speak to that which hath no life.

Wis|13|18|For health he calleth upon that which is weak: for life prayeth to that which is dead; for aid humbly beseecheth that which hath least means to help: and for a good journey he asketh of that which cannot set a foot forward:

Wis|13|19|And for gaining and getting, and for good success of his hands, asketh ability to do of him, that is most unable to do any thing.

Wis|14|1|Again, one preparing himself to sail, and about to pass through the raging waves, calleth upon a piece of wood more rotten than the vessel that carrieth him.

Wis|14|2|For verily desire of gain devised that, and the workman built it by his skill.

Wis|14|3|But thy providence, O Father, governeth it: for thou hast made a way in the sea, and a safe path in the waves;

Wis|14|4|Shewing that thou canst save from all danger: yea, though a man went to sea without art.

Wis|14|5|Nevertheless thou wouldest not that the works of thy wisdom should be idle, and therefore do men commit their lives to a small piece of wood, and passing the rough sea in a weak vessel are saved.

Wis|14|6|For in the old time also, when the proud giants perished, the hope of the world governed by thy hand escaped in a weak vessel, and left to all ages a seed of generation.

Wis|14|7|For blessed is the wood whereby righteousness cometh.

Wis|14|8|But that which is made with hands is cursed, as well it, as he that made it: he, because he made it; and it, because, being corruptible, it was called god.

Wis|14|9|For the ungodly and his ungodliness are both alike hateful unto אֱלֹהִים.

Wis|14|10|For that which is made shall be punished together with him that made it.

Wis|14|11|Therefore even upon the idols of the Gentiles shall there be a visitation: because in the creature of אֱלֹהִים they are become an abomination, and stumblingblocks to the souls of men, and a snare to the feet of the unwise.

Wis|14|12|For the devising of idols was the beginning of spiritual fornication, and the invention of them the corruption of life.

Wis|14|13|For neither were they from the beginning, neither shall they be for ever.

Wis|14|14|For by the vain glory of men they entered into the world, and therefore shall they come shortly to an end.

Wis|14|15|For a father afflicted with untimely mourning, when he hath made an image of his child soon taken away, now honoured him as a god, which was then a dead man, and delivered to those that were under him ceremonies and sacrifices.

Wis|14|16|Thus in process of time an ungodly custom grown strong was kept as a law, and graven images were worshipped by the commandments of kings.

Wis|14|17|Whom men could not honour in presence, because they dwelt far off, they took the counterfeit of his visage from far, and made an express image of a king whom they honoured, to the end that by this their forwardness they might flatter him that was absent, as if he were present.

Wis|14|18|Also the singular diligence of the artificer did help to set forward the ignorant to more superstition.

Wis|14|19|For he, peradventure willing to please one in authority, forced all his skill to make the resemblance of the best fashion.

Wis|14|20|And so the multitude, allured by the grace of the work, took him now for a god, which a little before was but honoured.

Wis|14|21|And this was an occasion to deceive the world: for men, serving either calamity or tyranny, did ascribe unto stones and stocks the incommunicable name.

Wis|14|22|Moreover this was not enough for them, that they erred in the knowledge of אֱלֹהִים; but whereas they lived in the great war of ignorance, those so great plagues called they peace.

Wis|14|23|For whilst they slew their children in sacrifices, or used secret ceremonies, or made revellings of strange rites;

Wis|14|24|They kept neither lives nor marriages any longer undefiled: but either one slew another traiterously, or grieved him by adultery.

Wis|14|25|So that there reigned in all men without exception blood, manslaughter, theft, and dissimulation, corruption, unfaithfulness, tumults, perjury,

Wis|14|26|Disquieting of good men, forgetfulness of good turns, defiling of souls, changing of kind, disorder in marriages, adultery, and shameless uncleanness.

Wis|14|27|For the worshipping of idols not to be named is the beginning, the cause, and the end, of all evil.

Wis|14|28|For either they are mad when they be merry, or prophesy lies, or live unjustly, or else lightly forswear themselves.

Wis|14|29|For insomuch as their trust is in idols, which have no life; though they swear falsely, yet they look not to be hurt.

Wis|14|30|Howbeit for both causes shall they be justly punished: both because they thought not well of אֱלֹהִים, giving heed unto idols, and also unjustly swore in deceit, despising holiness.

Wis|14|31|For it is not the power of them by whom they swear: but it is the just vengeance of sinners, that punisheth always the offence of the ungodly.

Wis|15|1|But thou, O אֱלֹהִים, art gracious and true, longsuffering, and in mercy ordering all things,

Wis|15|2|For if we sin, we are thine, knowing thy power: but we will not sin, knowing that we are counted thine.

Wis|15|3|For to know thee is perfect righteousness: yea, to know thy power is the root of immortality.

Wis|15|4|For neither did the mischievous invention of men deceive us, nor an image spotted with divers colours, the painter's fruitless labour;

Wis|15|5|The sight whereof enticeth fools to lust after it, and so they desire the form of a dead image, that hath no breath.

Wis|15|6|Both they that make them, they that desire them, and they that worship them, are lovers of evil things, and are worthy to have such things to trust upon.

Wis|15|7|For the potter, tempering soft earth, fashioneth every vessel with much labour for our service: yea, of the same clay he maketh both the vessels that serve for clean uses, and likewise also all such as serve to the contrary: but what is the use of either sort, the potter himself is the judge.

Wis|15|8|And employing his labours lewdly, he maketh a vain god of the same clay, even he which a little before was made of earth himself, and within a little while after returneth to the same, out when his life which was lent him shall be demanded.

Wis|15|9|Notwithstanding his care is, not that he shall have much labour, nor that his life is short: but striveth to excel goldsmiths and silversmiths, and endeavoureth to do like the workers in brass, and counteth it his glory to make counterfeit things.

Wis|15|10|His heart is ashes, his hope is more vile than earth, and his life of less value than clay:

Wis|15|11|Forasmuch as he knew not his Maker, and him that inspired into him an active soul, and breathed in a living spirit.

Wis|15|12|But they counted our life a pastime, and our time here a market for gain: for, say they, we must be getting every way, though it be by evil means.

Wis|15|13|For this man, that of earthly matter maketh brittle vessels and graven images, knoweth himself to offend above all others.

Wis|15|14|And all the enemies of thy people, that hold them in subjection, are most foolish, and are more miserable than very babes.

Wis|15|15|For they counted all the idols of the heathen to be gods: which neither have the use of eyes to see, nor noses to draw breath, nor ears to hear, nor fingers of hands to handle; and as for their feet, they are slow to go.

Wis|15|16|For man made them, and he that borrowed his own spirit fashioned them: but no man can make a god like unto himself.

Wis|15|17|For being mortal, he worketh a dead thing with wicked hands: for he himself is better than the things which he worshippeth: whereas he lived once, but they never.

Wis|15|18|Yea, they worshipped those beasts also that are most hateful: for being compared together, some are worse than others.

Wis|15|19|Neither are they beautiful, so much as to be desired in respect of beasts: but they went without the praise of אֱלֹהִים and his blessing.

Wis|16|1|Therefore by the like were they punished worthily, and by the multitude of beasts tormented.

Wis|16|2|Instead of which punishment, dealing graciously with thine own people, thou preparedst for them meat of a strange taste, even quails to stir up their appetite:

Wis|16|3|To the end that they, desiring food, might for the ugly sight of the beasts sent among them lothe even that, which they must needs desire; but these, suffering penury for a short space, might be made partakers of a strange taste.

Wis|16|4|For it was requisite, that upon them exercising tyranny should come penury, which they could not avoid: but to these it should only be shewed how their enemies were tormented.

Wis|16|5|For when the horrible fierceness of beasts came upon these, and they perished with the stings of crooked serpents, thy wrath endured not for ever:

Wis|16|6|But they were troubled for a small season, that they might be admonished, having a sign of salvation, to put them in remembrance of the commandment of thy law.

Wis|16|7|For he that turned himself toward it was not saved by the thing that he saw, but by thee, that art the Saviour of all.

Wis|16|8|And in this thou madest thine enemies confess, that it is thou who deliverest from all evil:

Wis|16|9|For them the bitings of grasshoppers and flies killed, neither was there found any remedy for their life: for they were worthy to be punished by such.

Wis|16|10|But thy sons not the very teeth of venomous dragons overcame: for thy mercy was ever by them, and healed them.

Wis|16|11|For they were pricked, that they should remember thy words; and were quickly saved, that not falling into deep forgetfulness, they might be continually mindful of thy goodness.

Wis|16|12|For it was neither herb, nor mollifying plaister, that restored them to health: but thy word, O Lord, which healeth all things.

Wis|16|13|For thou hast power of life and death: thou leadest to the gates of hell, and bringest up again.

Wis|16|14|A man indeed killeth through his malice: and the spirit, when it is gone forth, returneth not; neither the soul received up cometh again.

Wis|16|15|But it is not possible to escape thine hand.

Wis|16|16|For the ungodly, that denied to know thee, were scourged by the strength of thine arm: with strange rains, hails, and showers, were they persecuted, that they could not avoid, and through fire were they consumed.

Wis|16|17|For, which is most to be wondered at, the fire had more force in the water, that quencheth all things: for the world fighteth for the righteous.

Wis|16|18|For sometime the flame was mitigated, that it might not burn up the beasts that were sent against the ungodly; but themselves might see and perceive that they were persecuted with the judgment of אֱלֹהִים.

Wis|16|19|And at another time it burneth even in the midst of water above the power of fire, that it might destroy the fruits of an unjust land.

Wis|16|20|Instead whereof thou feddest thine own people with angels' food, and didst send them from heaven bread prepared without their labour, able to content every man's delight, and agreeing to every taste.

Wis|16|21|For thy sustenance declared thy sweetness unto thy children, and serving to the appetite of the eater, tempered itself to every man's liking.

Wis|16|22|But snow and ice endured the fire, and melted not, that they might know that fire burning in the hail, and sparkling in the rain, did destroy the fruits of the enemies.

Wis|16|23|But this again did even forget his own strength, that the righteous might be nourished.

Wis|16|24|For the creature that serveth thee, who art the Maker increaseth his strength against the unrighteous for their punishment, and abateth his strength for the benefit of such as put their trust in thee.

Wis|16|25|Therefore even then was it altered into all fashions, and was obedient to thy grace, that nourisheth all things, according to the desire of them that had need:

Wis|16|26|That thy children, O Lord, whom thou lovest, might know, that it is not the growing of fruits that nourisheth man: but that it is thy word, which preserveth them that put their trust in thee.

Wis|16|27|For that which was not destroyed of the fire, being warmed with a little sunbeam, soon melted away:

Wis|16|28|That it might be known, that we must prevent the sun to give thee thanks, and at the dayspring pray unto thee.

Wis|16|29|For the hope of the unthankful shall melt away as the winter's hoar frost, and shall run away as unprofitable water.

Wis|17|1|For great are thy judgments, and cannot be expressed: therefore unnurtured souls have erred.

Wis|17|2|For when unrighteous men thought to oppress the holy nation; they being shut up in their houses, the prisoners of darkness, and fettered with the bonds of a long night, lay [there] exiled from the eternal providence.

Wis|17|3|For while they supposed to lie hid in their secret sins, they were scattered under a dark veil of forgetfulness, being horribly astonished, and troubled with [strange] apparitions.

Wis|17|4|For neither might the corner that held them keep them from fear: but noises [as of waters] falling down sounded about them, and sad visions appeared unto them with heavy countenances.

Wis|17|5|No power of the fire might give them light: neither could the bright flames of the stars endure to lighten that horrible night.

Wis|17|6|Only there appeared unto them a fire kindled of itself, very dreadful: for being much terrified, they thought the things which they saw to be worse than the sight they saw not.

Wis|17|7|As for the illusions of art magick, they were put down, and their vaunting in wisdom was reproved with disgrace.

Wis|17|8|For they, that promised to drive away terrors and troubles from a sick soul, were sick themselves of fear, worthy to be laughed at.

Wis|17|9|For though no terrible thing did fear them; yet being scared with beasts that passed by, and hissing of serpents,

Wis|17|10|They died for fear, denying that they saw the air, which could of no side be avoided.

Wis|17|11|For wickedness, condemned by her own witness, is very timorous, and being pressed with conscience, always forecasteth grievous things.

Wis|17|12|For fear is nothing else but a betraying of the succours which reason offereth.

Wis|17|13|And the expectation from within, being less, counteth the ignorance more than the cause which bringeth the torment.

Wis|17|14|But they sleeping the same sleep that night, which was indeed intolerable, and which came upon them out of the bottoms of inevitable hell,

Wis|17|15|Were partly vexed with monstrous apparitions, and partly fainted, their heart failing them: for a sudden fear, and not looked for, came upon them.

Wis|17|16|So then whosoever there fell down was straitly kept, shut up in a prison without iron bars,

Wis|17|17|For whether he were husbandman, or shepherd, or a labourer in the field, he was overtaken, and endured that necessity, which could not be avoided: for they were all bound with one chain of darkness.

Wis|17|18|Whether it were a whistling wind, or a melodious noise of birds among the spreading branches, or a pleasing fall of water running violently,

Wis|17|19|Or a terrible sound of stones cast down, or a running that could not be seen of skipping beasts, or a roaring voice of most savage wild beasts, or a rebounding echo from the hollow mountains; these things made them to swoon for fear.

Wis|17|20|For the whole world shined with clear light, and none were hindered in their labour:

Wis|17|21|Over them only was spread an heavy night, an image of that darkness which should afterward receive them: but yet were they unto themselves more grievous than the darkness.

Wis|18|1|Nevertheless thy saints had a very great light, whose voice they hearing, and not seeing their shape, because they also had not suffered the same things, they counted them happy.

Wis|18|2|But for that they did not hurt them now, of whom they had been wronged before, they thanked them, and besought them pardon for that they had been enemies.

Wis|18|3|Instead whereof thou gavest them a burning pillar of fire, both to be a guide of the unknown journey, and an harmless sun to entertain them honourably.

Wis|18|4|For they were worthy to be deprived of light and imprisoned in darkness, who had kept thy sons shut up, by whom the uncorrupt light of the law was to be given unto the world.

Wis|18|5|And when they had determined to slay the babes of the saints, one child being cast forth, and saved, to reprove them, thou tookest away the multitude of their children, and destroyedst them altogether in a mighty water.

Wis|18|6|Of that night were our fathers certified afore, that assuredly knowing unto what oaths they had given credence, they might afterwards be of good cheer.

Wis|18|7|So of thy people was accepted both the salvation of the righteous, and destruction of the enemies.

Wis|18|8|For wherewith thou didst punish our adversaries, by the same thou didst glorify us, whom thou hadst called.

Wis|18|9|For the righteous children of good men did sacrifice secretly, and with one consent made a holy law, that the saints should be like partakers of the same good and evil, the fathers now singing out the songs of praise.

Wis|18|10|But on the other side there sounded an ill according cry of the enemies, and a lamentable noise was carried abroad for children that were bewailed.

Wis|18|11|The master and the servant were punished after one manner; and like as the king, so suffered the common person.

Wis|18|12|So they all together had innumerable dead with one kind of death; neither were the living sufficient to bury them: for in one moment the noblest offspring of them was destroyed.

Wis|18|13|For whereas they would not believe any thing by reason of the enchantments; upon the destruction of the firstborn, they acknowledged this people to be the sons of אֱלֹהִים.

Wis|18|14|For while all things were in quiet silence, and that night was in the midst of her swift course,

Wis|18|15|Thine Almighty word leaped down from heaven out of thy royal throne, as a fierce man of war into the midst of a land of destruction,

Wis|18|16|And brought thine unfeigned commandment as a sharp sword, and standing up filled all things with death; and it touched the heaven, but it stood upon the earth.

Wis|18|17|Then suddenly visions of horrible dreams troubled them sore, and terrors came upon them unlooked for.

Wis|18|18|And one thrown here, and another there, half dead, shewed the cause of his death.

Wis|18|19|For the dreams that troubled them did foreshew this, lest they should perish, and not know why they were afflicted.

Wis|18|20|Yea, the tasting of death touched the righteous also, and there was a destruction of the multitude in the wilderness: but the wrath endured not long.

Wis|18|21|For then the blameless man made haste, and stood forth to defend them; and bringing the shield of his proper ministry, even prayer, and the propitiation of incense, set himself against the wrath, and so brought the calamity to an end, declaring that he was thy servant.

Wis|18|22|So he overcame the destroyer, not with strength of body, nor force of arms, but with a word subdued him that punished, alleging the oaths and covenants made with the fathers.

Wis|18|23|For when the dead were now fallen down by heaps one upon another, standing between, he stayed the wrath, and parted the way to the living.

Wis|18|24|For in the long garment was the whole world, and in the four rows of the stones was the glory of the fathers graven, and thy Majesty upon the daidem of his head.

Wis|18|25|Unto these the destroyer gave place, and was afraid of them: for it was enough that they only tasted of the wrath.

Wis|19|1|As for the ungodly, wrath came upon them without mercy unto the end: for he knew before what they would do;

Wis|19|2|How that having given them leave to depart, and sent them hastily away, they would repent and pursue them.

Wis|19|3|For whilst they were yet mourning and making lamentation at the graves of the dead, they added another foolish device, and pursued them as fugitives, whom they had intreated to be gone.

Wis|19|4|For the destiny, whereof they were worthy, drew them unto this end, and made them forget the things that had already happened, that they might fulfil the punishment which was wanting to their torments:

Wis|19|5|And that thy people might pass a wonderful way: but they might find a strange death.

Wis|19|6|For the whole creature in his proper kind was fashioned again anew, serving the peculiar commandments that were given unto them, that thy children might be kept without hurt:

Wis|19|7|As namely, a cloud shadowing the camp; and where water stood before, dry land appeared; and out of the Red sea a way without impediment; and out of the violent stream a green field:

Wis|19|8|Wherethrough all the people went that were defended with thy hand, seeing thy marvellous strange wonders.

Wis|19|9|For they went at large like horses, and leaped like lambs, praising thee, O Lord, who hadst delivered them.

Wis|19|10|For they were yet mindful of the things that were done while they sojourned in the strange land, how the ground brought forth flies instead of cattle, and how the river cast up a multitude of frogs instead of fishes.

Wis|19|11|But afterwards they saw a new generation of fowls, when, being led with their appetite, they asked delicate meats.

Wis|19|12|For quails came up unto them from the sea for their contentment.

Wis|19|13|And punishments came upon the sinners not without former signs by the force of thunders: for they suffered justly according to their own wickedness, insomuch as they used a more hard and hateful behaviour toward strangers.

Wis|19|14|For the Sodomites did not receive those, whom they knew not when they came: but these brought friends into bondage, that had well deserved of them.

Wis|19|15|And not only so, but peradventure some respect shall be had of those, because they used strangers not friendly:

Wis|19|16|But these very grievously afflicted them, whom they had received with feastings, and were already made partakers of the same laws with them.

Wis|19|17|Therefore even with blindness were these stricken, as those were at the doors of the righteous man: when, being compassed about with horrible great darkness, every one sought the passage of his own doors.

Wis|19|18|For the elements were changed in themselves by a kind of harmony, like as in a psaltery notes change the name of the tune, and yet are always sounds; which may well be perceived by the sight of the things that have been done.

Wis|19|19|For earthly things were turned into watery, and the things, that before swam in the water, now went upon the ground.

Wis|19|20|The fire had power in the water, forgetting his own virtue: and the water forgat his own quenching nature.

Wis|19|21|On the other side, the flames wasted not the flesh of the corruptible living things, though they walked therein; neither melted they the icy kind of heavenly meat that was of nature apt to melt.

Wis|19|22|For in all things, O Lord, thou didst magnify thy people, and glorify them, neither didst thou lightly regard them: but didst assist them in every time and place.

Sir|1|1|[The Prologue of the Wisdom of Yashiyah the Son of Sirach.] Whereas many and great things have been delivered unto us by the law and the prophets, and by others that have followed their steps, for the which things Israel ought to be commended for learning and wisdom; and whereof not only the readers must needs become skilful themselves, but also they that desire to learn be able to profit them which are without, both by speaking and writing: my grandfather Yashiyah, when he had much given himself to the reading of the law, and the prophets, and other books of our fathers, and had gotten therein good judgment, was drawn on also himself to write something pertaining to learning and wisdom; to the intent that those which are desirous to learn, and are addicted to these things, might profit much more in living according to the law. Wherefore let me intreat you to read it with favour and attention, and to pardon us, wherein we may seem to come short of some words, which we have laboured to interpret. For the same things uttered in Hebrew, and translated into another tongue, have not the same force in them: and not only these things, but the law itself, and the prophets, and the rest of the books, have no small difference, when they are spoken in their own language. For in the eight and thirtieth year coming into Egypt, when Euergetes was king, and continuing there some time, I found a book of no small learning: therefore I thought it most necessary for me to bestow some diligence and travail to interpret it; using great watchfulness and skill in that space to bring the book to an end, and set it forth for them also, which in a strange country are willing to learn, being prepared before in manners to live after the law. All wisdom cometh from the Lord, and is with him for ever.

Sir|1|2|Who can number the sand of the sea, and the drops of rain, and the days of eternity?

Sir|1|3|Who can find out the height of heaven, and the breadth of the earth, and the deep, and wisdom?

Sir|1|4|Wisdom hath been created before all things, and the understanding of prudence from everlasting.

Sir|1|5|The word of אֱלֹהִים most high is the fountain of wisdom; and her ways are everlasting commandments.

Sir|1|6|To whom hath the root of wisdom been revealed? or who hath known her wise counsels?

Sir|1|7|[Unto whom hath the knowledge of wisdom been made manifest? and who hath understood her great experience?]

Sir|1|8|There is one wise and greatly to be feared, the Lord sitting upon his throne.

Sir|1|9|He created her, and saw her, and numbered her, and poured her out upon all his works.

Sir|1|10|She is with all flesh according to his gift, and he hath given her to them that love him.

Sir|1|11|The fear of the Lord is honour, and glory, and gladness, and a crown of rejoicing.

Sir|1|12|The fear of the Lord maketh a merry heart, and giveth joy, and gladness, and a long life.

Sir|1|13|Whoso feareth the Lord, it shall go well with him at the last, and he shall find favour in the day of his death.

Sir|1|14|To fear the Lord is the beginning of wisdom: and it was created with the faithful in the womb.

Sir|1|15|She hath built an everlasting foundation with men, and she shall continue with their seed.

Sir|1|16|To fear the Lord is fulness of wisdom, and filleth men with her fruits.

Sir|1|17|She filleth all their house with things desirable, and the garners with her increase.

Sir|1|18|The fear of the Lord is a crown of wisdom, making peace and perfect health to flourish; both which are the gifts of אֱלֹהִים: and it enlargeth their rejoicing that love him.

Sir|1|19|Wisdom raineth down skill and knowledge of understanding standing, and exalteth them to honour that hold her fast.

Sir|1|20|The root of wisdom is to fear the Lord, and the branches thereof are long life.

Sir|1|21|The fear of the Lord driveth away sins: and where it is present, it turneth away wrath.

Sir|1|22|A furious man cannot be justified; for the sway of his fury shall be his destruction.

Sir|1|23|A patient man will tear for a time, and afterward joy shall spring up unto him.

Sir|1|24|He will hide his words for a time, and the lips of many shall declare his wisdom.

Sir|1|25|The parables of knowledge are in the treasures of wisdom: but godliness is an abomination to a sinner.

Sir|1|26|If thou desire wisdom, keep the commandments, and the Lord shall give her unto thee.

Sir|1|27|For the fear of the Lord is wisdom and instruction: and faith and meekness are his delight.

Sir|1|28|Distrust not the fear of the Lord when thou art poor: and come not unto him with a double heart.

Sir|1|29|Be not an hypocrite in the sight of men, and take good heed what thou speakest.

Sir|1|30|Exalt not thyself, lest thou fall, and bring dishonour upon thy soul, and so אֱלֹהִים discover thy secrets, and cast thee down in the midst of the congregation, because thou camest not in truth to the fear of the Lord, but thy heart is full of deceit.

Sir|2|1|My son, if thou come to serve the Lord, prepare thy soul for temptation.

Sir|2|2|Set thy heart aright, and constantly endure, and make not haste in time of trouble.

Sir|2|3|Cleave unto him, and depart not away, that thou mayest be increased at thy last end.

Sir|2|4|Whatsoever is brought upon thee take cheerfully, and be patient when thou art changed to a low estate.

Sir|2|5|For gold is tried in the fire, and acceptable men in the furnace of adversity.

Sir|2|6|Believe in him, and he will help thee; order thy way aright, and trust in him.

Sir|2|7|Ye that fear the Lord, wait for his mercy; and go not aside, lest ye fall.

Sir|2|8|Ye that fear the Lord, believe him; and your reward shall not fail.

Sir|2|9|Ye that fear the Lord, hope for good, and for everlasting joy and mercy.

Sir|2|10|Look at the generations of old, and see; did ever any trust in the Lord, and was confounded? or did any abide in his fear, and was forsaken? or whom did he ever despise, that called upon him?

Sir|2|11|For the Lord is full of compassion and mercy, longsuffering, and very pitiful, and forgiveth sins, and saveth in time of affliction.

Sir|2|12|Woe be to fearful hearts, and faint hands, and the sinner that goeth two ways!

Sir|2|13|Woe unto him that is fainthearted! for he believeth not; therefore shall he not be defended.

Sir|2|14|Woe unto you that have lost patience! and what will ye do when the Lord shall visit you?

Sir|2|15|They that fear the Lord will not disobey his Word; and they that love him will keep his ways.

Sir|2|16|They that fear the Lord will seek that which is well, pleasing unto him; and they that love him shall be filled with the law.

Sir|2|17|They that fear the Lord will prepare their hearts, and humble their souls in his sight,

Sir|2|18|Saying, We will fall into the hands of the Lord, and not into the hands of men: for as his majesty is, so is his mercy.

Sir|3|1|Hear me your father, O children, and do thereafter, that ye may be safe.

Sir|3|2|For the Lord hath given the father honour over the children, and hath confirmed the authority of the mother over the sons.

Sir|3|3|Whoso honoureth his father maketh an atonement for his sins:

Sir|3|4|And he that honoureth his mother is as one that layeth up treasure.

Sir|3|5|Whoso honoureth his father shall have joy of his own children; and when he maketh his prayer, he shall be heard.

Sir|3|6|He that honoureth his father shall have a long life; and he that is obedient unto the Lord shall be a comfort to his mother.

Sir|3|7|He that feareth the Lord will honour his father, and will do service unto his parents, as to his masters.

Sir|3|8|Honour thy father and mother both in word and deed, that a blessing may come upon thee from them.

Sir|3|9|For the blessing of the father establisheth the houses of children; but the curse of the mother rooteth out foundations.

Sir|3|10|Glory not in the dishonour of thy father; for thy father's dishonour is no glory unto thee.

Sir|3|11|For the glory of a man is from the honour of his father; and a mother in dishonour is a reproach to the children.

Sir|3|12|My son, help thy father in his age, and grieve him not as long as he liveth.

Sir|3|13|And if his understanding fail, have patience with him; and despise him not when thou art in thy full strength.

Sir|3|14|For the relieving of thy father shall not be forgotten: and instead of sins it shall be added to build thee up.

Sir|3|15|In the day of thine affliction it shall be remembered; thy sins also shall melt away, as the ice in the fair warm weather.

Sir|3|16|He that forsaketh his father is as a blasphemer; and he that angereth his mother is cursed: of אֱלֹהִים.

Sir|3|17|My son, go on with thy business in meekness; so shalt thou be beloved of him that is approved.

Sir|3|18|The greater thou art, the more humble thyself, and thou shalt find favour before the Lord.

Sir|3|19|Many are in high place, and of renown: but mysteries are revealed unto the meek.

Sir|3|20|For the power of the Lord is great, and he is honoured of the lowly.

Sir|3|21|Seek not out things that are too hard for thee, neither search the things that are above thy strength.

Sir|3|22|But what is commanded thee, think thereupon with reverence, for it is not needful for thee to see with thine eyes the things that are in secret.

Sir|3|23|Be not curious in unnecessary matters: for more things are shewed unto thee than men understand.

Sir|3|24|For many are deceived by their own vain opinion; and an evil suspicion hath overthrown their judgment.

Sir|3|25|Without eyes thou shalt want light: profess not the knowledge therefore that thou hast not.

Sir|3|26|A stubborn heart shall fare evil at the last; and he that loveth danger shall perish therein.

Sir|3|27|An obstinate heart shall be laden with sorrows; and the wicked man shall heap sin upon sin.

Sir|3|28|In the punishment of the proud there is no remedy; for the plant of wickedness hath taken root in him.

Sir|3|29|The heart of the prudent will understand a parable; and an attentive ear is the desire of a wise man.

Sir|3|30|Water will quench a flaming fire; and alms maketh an atonement for sins.

Sir|3|31|And he that requiteth good turns is mindful of that which may come hereafter; and when he falleth, he shall find a stay.

Sir|4|1|My son, defraud not the poor of his living, and make not the needy eyes to wait long.

Sir|4|2|Make not an hungry soul sorrowful; neither provoke a man in his distress.

Sir|4|3|Add not more trouble to an heart that is vexed; and defer not to give to him that is in need.

Sir|4|4|Reject not the supplication of the afflicted; neither turn away thy face from a poor man.

Sir|4|5|Turn not away thine eye from the needy, and give him none occasion to curse thee:

Sir|4|6|For if he curse thee in the bitterness of his soul, his prayer shall be heard of him that made him.

Sir|4|7|Get thyself the love of the congregation, and bow thy head to a great man.

Sir|4|8|Let it not grieve thee to bow down thine ear to the poor, and give him a friendly answer with meekness.

Sir|4|9|Deliver him that suffereth wrong from the hand of the oppressor; and be not fainthearted when thou sittest in judgment.

Sir|4|10|Be as a father unto the fatherless, and instead of an husband unto their mother: so shalt thou be as the son of the most High, and he shall love thee more than thy mother doth.

Sir|4|11|Wisdom exalteth her children, and layeth hold of them that seek her.

Sir|4|12|He that loveth her loveth life; and they that seek to her early shall be filled with joy.

Sir|4|13|He that holdeth her fast shall inherit glory; and wheresoever she entereth, the Lord will bless.

Sir|4|14|They that serve her shall minister to the Holy One: and them that love her the Lord doth love.

Sir|4|15|Whoso giveth ear unto her shall judge the nations: and he that attendeth unto her shall dwell securely.

Sir|4|16|If a man commit himself unto her, he shall inherit her; and his generation shall hold her in possession.

Sir|4|17|For at the first she will walk with him by crooked ways, and bring fear and dread upon him, and torment him with her discipline, until she may trust his soul, and try him by her laws.

Sir|4|18|Then will she return the straight way unto him, and comfort him, and shew him her secrets.

Sir|4|19|But if he go wrong, she will forsake him, and give him over to his own ruin.

Sir|4|20|Observe the opportunity, and beware of evil; and be not ashamed when it concerneth thy soul.

Sir|4|21|For there is a shame that bringeth sin; and there is a shame which is glory and grace.

Sir|4|22|Accept no person against thy soul, and let not the reverence of any man cause thee to fall.

Sir|4|23|And refrain not to speak, when there is occasion to do good, and hide not thy wisdom in her beauty.

Sir|4|24|For by speech wisdom shall be known: and learning by the word of the tongue.

Sir|4|25|In no wise speak against the truth; but be abashed of the error of thine ignorance.

Sir|4|26|Be not ashamed to confess thy sins; and force not the course of the river.

Sir|4|27|Make not thyself an underling to a foolish man; neither accept the person of the mighty.

Sir|4|28|Strive for the truth unto death, and the Lord shall fight for thee.

Sir|4|29|Be not hasty in thy tongue, and in thy deeds slack and remiss.

Sir|4|30|Be not as a lion in thy house, nor frantick among thy servants.

Sir|4|31|Let not thine hand be stretched out to receive, and shut when thou shouldest repay.

Sir|5|1|Set thy heart upon thy goods; and say not, I have enough for my life.

Sir|5|2|Follow not thine own mind and thy strength, to walk in the ways of thy heart:

Sir|5|3|And say not, Who shall controul me for my works? for the Lord will surely revenge thy pride.

Sir|5|4|Say not, I have sinned, and what harm hath happened unto me? for the Lord is longsuffering, he will in no wise let thee go.

Sir|5|5|Concerning propitiation, be not without fear to add sin unto sin:

Sir|5|6|And say not His mercy is great; he will be pacified for the multitude of my sins: for mercy and wrath come from him, and his indignation resteth upon sinners.

Sir|5|7|Make no tarrying to turn to the Lord, and put not off from day to day: for suddenly shall the wrath of the Lord come forth, and in thy security thou shalt be destroyed, and perish in the day of vengeance.

Sir|5|8|Set not thine heart upon goods unjustly gotten, for they shall not profit thee in the day of calamity.

Sir|5|9|Winnow not with every wind, and go not into every way: for so doth the sinner that hath a double tongue.

Sir|5|10|Be stedfast in thy understanding; and let thy word be the same.

Sir|5|11|Be swift to hear; and let thy life be sincere; and with patience give answer.

Sir|5|12|If thou hast understanding, answer thy neighbour; if not, lay thy hand upon thy mouth.

Sir|5|13|Honour and shame is in talk: and the tongue of man is his fall.

Sir|5|14|Be not called a whisperer, and lie not in wait with thy tongue: for a foul shame is upon the thief, and an evil condemnation upon the double tongue.

Sir|5|15|Be not ignorant of any thing in a great matter or a small.

Sir|6|1|Instead of a friend become not an enemy; for [thereby] thou shalt inherit an ill name, shame, and reproach: even so shall a sinner that hath a double tongue.

Sir|6|2|Extol not thyself in the counsel of thine own heart; that thy soul be not torn in pieces as a bull [straying alone.]

Sir|6|3|Thou shalt eat up thy leaves, and lose thy fruit, and leave thyself as a dry tree.

Sir|6|4|A wicked soul shall destroy him that hath it, and shall make him to be laughed to scorn of his enemies.

Sir|6|5|Sweet language will multiply friends: and a fairspeaking tongue will increase kind greetings.

Sir|6|6|Be in peace with many: nevertheless have but one counsellor of a thousand.

Sir|6|7|If thou wouldest get a friend, prove him first and be not hasty to credit him.

Sir|6|8|For some man is a friend for his own occasion, and will not abide in the day of thy trouble.

Sir|6|9|And there is a friend, who being turned to enmity, and strife will discover thy reproach.

Sir|6|10|Again, some friend is a companion at the table, and will not continue in the day of thy affliction.

Sir|6|11|But in thy prosperity he will be as thyself, and will be bold over thy servants.

Sir|6|12|If thou be brought low, he will be against thee, and will hide himself from thy face.

Sir|6|13|Separate thyself from thine enemies, and take heed of thy friends.

Sir|6|14|A faithfull friend is a strong defence: and he that hath found such an one hath found a treasure.

Sir|6|15|Nothing doth countervail a faithful friend, and his excellency is invaluable.

Sir|6|16|A faithful friend is the medicine of life; and they that fear the Lord shall find him.

Sir|6|17|Whoso feareth the Lord shall direct his friendship aright: for as he is, so shall his neighbour be also.

Sir|6|18|My son, gather instruction from thy youth up: so shalt thou find wisdom till thine old age.

Sir|6|19|Come unto her as one that ploweth and soweth, and wait for her good fruits: for thou shalt not toil much in labouring about her, but thou shalt eat of her fruits right soon.

Sir|6|20|She is very unpleasant to the unlearned: he that is without understanding will not remain with her.

Sir|6|21|She will lie upon him as a mighty stone of trial; and he will cast her from him ere it be long.

Sir|6|22|For wisdom is according to her name, and she is not manifest unto many.

Sir|6|23|Give ear, my son, receive my advice, and refuse not my counsel,

Sir|6|24|And put thy feet into her fetters, and thy neck into her chain.

Sir|6|25|Bow down thy shoulder, and bear her, and be not grieved with her bonds.

Sir|6|26|Come unto her with thy whole heart, and keep her ways with all thy power.

Sir|6|27|Search, and seek, and she shall be made known unto thee: and when thou hast got hold of her, let her not go.
Sir|6|28|For at the last thou shalt find her rest, and that shall be turned to thy joy.
Sir|6|29|Then shall her fetters be a strong defence for thee, and her chains a robe of glory.
Sir|6|30|For there is a golden ornament upon her, and her bands are purple lace.
Sir|6|31|Thou shalt put her on as a robe of honour, and shalt put her about thee as a crown of joy.
Sir|6|32|My son, if thou wilt, thou shalt be taught: and if thou wilt apply thy mind, thou shalt be prudent.
Sir|6|33|If thou love to hear, thou shalt receive understanding: and if thou bow thine ear, thou shalt be wise,
Sir|6|34|Stand in the multitude of the elders; and cleave unto him that is wise.
Sir|6|35|Be willing to hear every godly discourse; and let not the parables of understanding escape thee.
Sir|6|36|And if thou seest a man of understanding, get thee betimes unto him, and let thy foot wear the steps of his door.
Sir|6|37|Let thy mind be upon the ordinances of the Lord and meditate continually in his commandments: he shall establish thine heart, and give thee wisdom at thine owns desire.
Sir|7|1|Do no evil, so shall no harm come unto thee.
Sir|7|2|Depart from the unjust, and iniquity shall turn away from thee.
Sir|7|3|My son, sow not upon the furrows of unrighteousness, and thou shalt not reap them sevenfold.
Sir|7|4|Seek not of the Lord preeminence, neither of the king the seat of honour.
Sir|7|5|justify not thyself before the Lord; and boast not of thy wisdom before the king.
Sir|7|6|Seek not to be judge, being not able to take away iniquity; lest at any time thou fear the person of the mighty, an stumblingblock in the way of thy uprightness.
Sir|7|7|Offend not against the multitude of a city, and then thou shalt not cast thyself down among the people.
Sir|7|8|Bind not one sin upon another; for in one thou shalt not be unpunished.
Sir|7|9|Say not, אֱלֹהִים will look upon the multitude of my oblations, and when I offer to the most high אֱלֹהִים, he will accept it.
Sir|7|10|Be not fainthearted when thou makest thy prayer, and neglect not to give alms.
Sir|7|11|Laugh no man to scorn in the bitterness of his soul: for there is one which humbleth and exalteth.
Sir|7|12|Devise not a lie against thy brother; neither do the like to thy friend.
Sir|7|13|Use not to make any manner of lie: for the custom thereof is not good.
Sir|7|14|Use not many words in a multitude of elders, and make not much babbling when thou prayest.
Sir|7|15|Hate not laborious work, neither husbandry, which the most High hath ordained.
Sir|7|16|Number not thyself among the multitude of sinners, but remember that wrath will not tarry long.
Sir|7|17|Humble thyself greatly: for the vengeance of the ungodly is fire and worms.
Sir|7|18|Change not a friend for any good by no means; neither a faithful brother for the gold of Ophir.
Sir|7|19|Forego not a wise and good woman: for her grace is above gold.
Sir|7|20|Whereas thy servant worketh truly, entreat him not evil. nor the hireling that bestoweth himself wholly for thee.
Sir|7|21|Let thy soul love a good servant, and defraud him not of liberty.
Sir|7|22|Hast thou cattle? have an eye to them: and if they be for thy profit, keep them with thee.
Sir|7|23|Hast thou children? instruct them, and bow down their neck from their youth.
Sir|7|24|Hast thou daughters? have a care of their body, and shew not thyself cheerful toward them.
Sir|7|25|Marry thy daughter, and so shalt thou have performed a weighty matter: but give her to a man of understanding.
Sir|7|26|Hast thou a wife after thy mind? forsake her not: but give not thyself over to a light woman.
Sir|7|27|Honour thy father with thy whole heart, and forget not the sorrows of thy mother.
Sir|7|28|Remember that thou wast begotten of them; and how canst thou recompense them the things that they have done for thee?
Sir|7|29|Fear the Lord with all thy soul, and reverence his priests.
Sir|7|30|Love him that made thee with all thy strength, and forsake not his ministers.
Sir|7|31|Fear the Lord, and honor the priest; and give him his portion, as it is commanded thee; the firstfruits, and the trespass offering, and the gift of the shoulders, and the sacrifice of sanctification, and the firstfruits of the holy things.
Sir|7|32|And stretch thine hand unto the poor, that thy blessing may be perfected.
Sir|7|33|A gift hath grace in the sight of every man living; and for the dead detain it not.
Sir|7|34|Fail not to be with them that weep, and mourn with them that mourn.

Sir|7|35|Be not slow to visit the sick: for that shall make thee to be beloved.

Sir|7|36|Whatsoever thou takest in hand, remember the end, and thou shalt never do amiss.

Sir|8|1|Strive not with a mighty man' lest thou fall into his hands.

Sir|8|2|Be not at variance with a rich man, lest he overweigh thee: for gold hath destroyed many, and perverted the hearts of kings.

Sir|8|3|Strive not with a man that is full of tongue, and heap not wood upon his fire.

Sir|8|4|Jest not with a rude man, lest thy ancestors be disgraced.

Sir|8|5|Reproach not a man that turneth from sin, but remember that we are all worthy of punishment.

Sir|8|6|Dishonour not a man in his old age: for even some of us wax old.

Sir|8|7|Rejoice not over thy greatest enemy being dead, but remember that we die all.

Sir|8|8|Despise not the discourse of the wise, but acquaint thyself with their proverbs: for of them thou shalt learn instruction, and how to serve great men with ease.

Sir|8|9|Miss not the discourse of the elders: for they also learned of their fathers, and of them thou shalt learn understanding, and to give answer as need requireth.

Sir|8|10|Kindle not the coals of a sinner, lest thou be burnt with the flame of his fire.

Sir|8|11|Rise not up [in anger] at the presence of an injurious person, lest he lie in wait to entrap thee in thy words

Sir|8|12|Lend not unto him that is mightier than thyself; for if thou lendest him, count it but lost.

Sir|8|13|Be not surety above thy power: for if thou be surety, take care to pay it.

Sir|8|14|Go not to law with a judge; for they will judge for him according to his honour.

Sir|8|15|Travel not by the way with a bold fellow, lest he become grievous unto thee: for he will do according to his own will, and thou shalt perish with him through his folly.

Sir|8|16|Strive not with an angry man, and go not with him into a solitary place: for blood is as nothing in his sight, and where there is no help, he will overthrow thee.

Sir|8|17|Consult not with a fool; for he cannot keep counsel.

Sir|8|18|Do no secret thing before a stranger; for thou knowest not what he will bring forth.

Sir|8|19|Open not thine heart to every man, lest he requite thee with a shrewd turn.

Sir|9|1|Be not jealous over the wife of thy bosom, and teach her not an evil lesson against thyself.

Sir|9|2|Give not thy soul unto a woman to set her foot upon thy substance.

Sir|9|3|Meet not with an harlot, lest thou fall into her snares.

Sir|9|4|Use not much the company of a woman that is a singer, lest thou be taken with her attempts.

Sir|9|5|Gaze not on a maid, that thou fall not by those things that are precious in her.

Sir|9|6|Give not thy soul unto harlots, that thou lose not thine inheritance.

Sir|9|7|Look not round about thee in the streets of the city, neither wander thou in the solitary place thereof.

Sir|9|8|Turn away thine eye from a beautiful woman, and look not upon another's beauty; for many have been deceived by the beauty of a woman; for herewith love is kindled as a fire.

Sir|9|9|Sit not at all with another man's wife, nor sit down with her in thine arms, and spend not thy money with her at the wine; lest thine heart incline unto her, and so through thy desire thou fall into destruction.

Sir|9|10|Forsake not an old friend; for the new is not comparable to him: a new friend is as new wine; when it is old, thou shalt drink it with pleasure.

Sir|9|11|Envy not the glory of a sinner: for thou knowest not what shall be his end.

Sir|9|12|Delight not in the thing that the ungodly have pleasure in; but remember they shall not go unpunished unto their grave.

Sir|9|13|Keep thee far from the man that hath power to kill; so shalt thou not doubt the fear of death: and if thou come unto him, make no fault, lest he take away thy life presently: remember that thou goest in the midst of snares, and that thou walkest upon the battlements of the city.

Sir|9|14|As near as thou canst, guess at thy neighbour, and consult with the wise.

Sir|9|15|Let thy talk be with the wise, and all thy communication in the law of the most High.

Sir|9|16|And let just men eat and drink with thee; and let thy glorying be in the fear of the Lord.

Sir|9|17|For the hand of the artificer the work shall be commended: and the wise ruler of the people for his speech.

Sir|9|18|A man of an ill tongue is dangerous in his city; and he that is rash in his talk shall be hated.

Sir|10|1|A wise judge will instruct his people; and the government of a prudent man is well ordered.

Sir|10|2|As the judge of the people is himself, so are his officers; and what manner of man the ruler of the city is, such are all they that dwell therein.

Sir|10|3|An unwise king destroyeth his people; but through the prudence of them which are in authority the city shall be inhabited.

Sir|10|4|The power of the earth is in the hand of the Lord, and in due time he will set over it one that is profitable.

Sir|10|5|In the hand of אֱלֹהִים is the prosperity of man: and upon the person of the scribe shall he lay his honour.

Sir|10|6|Bear not hatred to thy neighbour for every wrong; and do nothing at all by injurious practices.

Sir|10|7|Pride is hateful before אֱלֹהִים and man: and by both doth one commit iniquity.

Sir|10|8|Because of unrighteous dealings, injuries, and riches got by deceit, the kingdom is translated from one people to another.

Sir|10|9|Why is earth and ashes proud? There is not a more wicked thing than a covetous man: for such an one setteth his own soul to sale; because while he liveth he casteth away his bowels.

Sir|10|10|The physician cutteth off a long disease; and he that is to day a king to morrow shall die.

Sir|10|11|For when a man is dead, he shall inherit creeping things, beasts, and worms.

Sir|10|12|The beginning of pride is when one departeth from אֱלֹהִים, and his heart is turned away from his Maker.

Sir|10|13|For pride is the beginning of sin, and he that hath it shall pour out abomination: and therefore the Lord brought upon them strange calamities, and overthrew them utterly.

Sir|10|14|The Lord hath cast down the thrones of proud princes, and set up the meek in their stead.

Sir|10|15|The Lord hath plucked up the roots of the proud nations, and planted the lowly in their place.

Sir|10|16|The Lord overthrew countries of the heathen, and destroyed them to the foundations of the earth.

Sir|10|17|He took some of them away, and destroyed them, and hath made their memorial to cease from the earth.

Sir|10|18|Pride was not made for men, nor furious anger for them that are born of a woman.

Sir|10|19|They that fear the Lord are a sure seed, and they that love him an honourable plant: they that regard not the law are a dishonourable seed; they that transgress the commandments are a deceivable seed.

Sir|10|20|Among brethren he that is chief is honorable; so are they that fear the Lord in his eyes.

Sir|10|21|The fear of the Lord goeth before the obtaining of authority: but roughness and pride is the losing thereof.

Sir|10|22|Whether he be rich, noble, or poor, their glory is the fear of the Lord.

Sir|10|23|It is not meet to despise the poor man that hath understanding; neither is it convenient to magnify a sinful man.

Sir|10|24|Great men, and judges, and potentates, shall be honoured; yet is there none of them greater than he that feareth the Lord.

Sir|10|25|Unto the servant that is wise shall they that are free do service: and he that hath knowledge will not grudge when he is reformed.

Sir|10|26|Be not overwise in doing thy business; and boast not thyself in the time of thy distress.

Sir|10|27|Better is he that laboureth, and aboundeth in all things, than he that boasteth himself, and wanteth bread.

Sir|10|28|My son, glorify thy soul in meekness, and give it honour according to the dignity thereof.

Sir|10|29|Who will justify him that sinneth against his own soul? and who will honour him that dishonoureth his own life?

Sir|10|30|The poor man is honoured for his skill, and the rich man is honoured for his riches.

Sir|10|31|He that is honoured in poverty, how much more in riches? and he that is dishonourable in riches, how much more in poverty?

Sir|11|1|Wisdom lifteth up the head of him that is of low degree, and maketh him to sit among great men.

Sir|11|2|Commend not a man for his beauty; neither abhor a man for his outward appearance.

Sir|11|3|The bee is little among such as fly; but her fruit is the chief of sweet things.

Sir|11|4|Boast not of thy clothing and raiment, and exalt not thyself in the day of honour: for the works of the Lord are wonderful, and his works among men are hidden.

Sir|11|5|Many kings have sat down upon the ground; and one that was never thought of hath worn the crown.

Sir|11|6|Many mighty men have been greatly disgraced; and the honourable delivered into other men's hands.

Sir|11|7|Blame not before thou hast examined the truth: understand first, and then rebuke.

Sir|11|8|Answer not before thou hast heard the cause: neither interrupt men in the midst of their talk.

Sir|11|9|Strive not in a matter that concerneth thee not; and sit not in judgment with sinners.

Sir|11|10|My son, meddle not with many matters: for if thou meddle much, thou shalt not be innocent; and if thou follow after, thou shalt not obtain, neither shalt thou escape by fleeing.

Sir|11|11|There is one that laboureth, and taketh pains, and maketh haste, and is so much the more behind.

Sir|11|12|Again, there is another that is slow, and hath need of help, wanting ability, and full of poverty; yet the eye of the Lord looked upon him for good, and set him up from his low estate,

Sir|11|13|And lifted up his head from misery; so that many that saw from him is peace over all the

Sir|11|14|Prosperity and adversity, life and death, poverty and riches, come of the Lord.

Sir|11|15|Wisdom, knowledge, and understanding of the law, are of the Lord: love, and the way of good works, are from him.

Sir|11|16|Error and darkness had their beginning together with sinners: and evil shall wax old with them that glory therein.

Sir|11|17|The gift of the Lord remaineth with the ungodly, and his favour bringeth prosperity for ever.

Sir|11|18|There is that waxeth rich by his wariness and pinching, and this his the portion of his reward:

Sir|11|19|Whereas he saith, I have found rest, and now will eat continually of my goods; and yet he knoweth not what time shall come upon him, and that he must leave those things to others, and die.

Sir|11|20|Be stedfast in thy covenant, and be conversant therein, and wax old in thy work.

Sir|11|21|Marvel not at the works of sinners; but trust in the Lord, and abide in thy labour: for it is an easy thing in the sight of the Lord on the sudden to make a poor man rich.

Sir|11|22|The blessing of the Lord is in the reward of the godly, and suddenly he maketh his blessing flourish.

Sir|11|23|Say not, What profit is there of my service? and what good things shall I have hereafter?

Sir|11|24|Again, say not, I have enough, and possess many things, and what evil shall I have hereafter?

Sir|11|25|In the day of prosperity there is a forgetfulness of affliction: and in the day of affliction there is no more remembrance of prosperity.

Sir|11|26|For it is an easy thing unto the Lord in the day of death to reward a man according to his ways.

Sir|11|27|The affliction of an hour maketh a man forget pleasure: and in his end his deeds shall be discovered.

Sir|11|28|Judge none blessed before his death: for a man shall be known in his children.

Sir|11|29|Bring not every man into thine house: for the deceitful man hath many trains.

Sir|11|30|Like as a partridge taken [and kept] in a cage, so is the heart of the proud; and like as a spy, watcheth he for thy fall:

Sir|11|31|For he lieth in wait, and turneth good into evil, and in things worthy praise will lay blame upon thee.

Sir|11|32|Of a spark of fire a heap of coals is kindled: and a sinful man layeth wait for blood.

Sir|11|33|Take heed of a mischievous man, for he worketh wickedness; lest he bring upon thee a perpetual blot.

Sir|11|34|Receive a stranger into thine house, and he will disturb thee, and turn thee out of thine own.

Sir|12|1|When thou wilt do good know to whom thou doest it; so shalt thou be thanked for thy benefits.

Sir|12|2|Do good to the godly man, and thou shalt find a recompence; and if not from him, yet from the most High.

Sir|12|3|There can no good come to him that is always occupied in evil, nor to him that giveth no alms.

Sir|12|4|Give to the godly man, and help not a sinner.

Sir|12|5|Do well unto him that is lowly, but give not to the ungodly: hold back thy bread, and give it not unto him, lest he overmaster thee thereby: for [else] thou shalt receive twice as much evil for all the good thou shalt have done unto him.

Sir|12|6|For the most High hateth sinners, and will repay vengeance unto the ungodly, and keepeth them against the mighty day of their punishment.

Sir|12|7|Give unto the good, and help not the sinner.

Sir|12|8|A friend cannot be known in prosperity: and an enemy cannot be hidden in adversity.

Sir|12|9|In the prosperity of a man enemies will be grieved: but in his adversity even a friend will depart.

Sir|12|10|Never trust thine enemy: for like as iron rusteth, so is his wickedness.

Sir|12|11|Though he humble himself, and go crouching, yet take good heed and beware of him, and thou shalt be unto him as if thou hadst wiped a lookingglass, and thou shalt know that his rust hath not been altogether wiped away.

Sir|12|12|Set him not by thee, lest, when he hath overthrown thee, he stand up in thy place; neither let him sit at thy right hand, lest he seek to take thy seat, and thou at the last remember my words, and be pricked therewith.

Sir|12|13|Who will pity a charmer that is bitten with a serpent, or any such as come nigh wild beasts?

Sir|12|14|So one that goeth to a sinner, and is defiled with him in his sins, who will pity?

Sir|12|15|For a while he will abide with thee, but if thou begin to fall, he will not tarry.

Sir|12|16|An enemy speaketh sweetly with his lips, but in his heart he imagineth how to throw thee into a pit: he will weep with his eyes, but if he find opportunity, he will not be satisfied with blood.

Sir|12|17|If adversity come upon thee, thou shalt find him there first; and though he pretend to help thee, yet shall he undermine thee.

Sir|12|18|He will shake his head, and clap his hands, and whisper much, and change his countenance.

Sir|13|1|He that toucheth pitch shall be defiled therewith; and he that hath fellowship with a proud man shall be like unto him.

Sir|13|2|Burden not thyself above thy power while thou livest; and have no fellowship with one that is mightier and richer than thyself: for how agree the kettle and the earthen pot together? for if the one be smitten against the other, it shall be broken.

Sir|13|3|The rich man hath done wrong, and yet he threateneth withal: the poor is wronged, and he must intreat also.

Sir|13|4|If thou be for his profit, he will use thee: but if thou have nothing, he will forsake thee.

Sir|13|5|If thou have any thing, he will live with thee: yea, he will make thee bare, and will not be sorry for it.

Sir|13|6|If he have need of thee, he will deceive thee, and smile upon thee, and put thee in hope; he will speak thee fair, and say, What wantest thou?

Sir|13|7|And he will shame thee by his meats, until he have drawn thee dry twice or thrice, and at the last he will laugh thee to scorn afterward, when he seeth thee, he will forsake thee, and shake his head at thee.

Sir|13|8|Beware that thou be not deceived and brought down in thy jollity.

Sir|13|9|If thou be invited of a mighty man, withdraw thyself, and so much the more will he invite thee.

Sir|13|10|Press thou not upon him, lest thou be put back; stand not far off, lest thou be forgotten.

Sir|13|11|Affect not to be made equal unto him in talk, and believe not his many words: for with much communication will he tempt thee, and smiling upon thee will get out thy secrets:

Sir|13|12|But cruelly he will lay up thy words, and will not spare to do thee hurt, and to put thee in prison.

Sir|13|13|Observe, and take good heed, for thou walkest in peril of thy overthrowing: when thou hearest these things, awake in thy sleep.

Sir|13|14|Love the Lord all thy life, and call upon him for thy salvation.

Sir|13|15|Every beast loveth his like, and every man loveth his neighbor.

Sir|13|16|All flesh consorteth according to kind, and a man will cleave to his like.

Sir|13|17|What fellowship hath the wolf with the lamb? so the sinner with the godly.

Sir|13|18|What agreement is there between the hyena and a dog? and what peace between the rich and the poor?

Sir|13|19|As the wild ass is the lion's prey in the wilderness: so the rich eat up the poor.

Sir|13|20|As the proud hate humility: so doth the rich abhor the poor.

Sir|13|21|A rich man beginning to fall is held up of his friends: but a poor man being down is thrust away by his friends.

Sir|13|22|When a rich man is fallen, he hath many helpers: he speaketh things not to be spoken, and yet men justify him: the poor man slipped, and yet they rebuked him too; he spake wisely, and could have no place.

Sir|13|23|When a rich man speaketh, every man holdeth his tongue, and, look, what he saith, they extol it to the clouds: but if the poor man speak, they say, What fellow is this? and if he stumble, they will help to overthrow him.

Sir|13|24|Riches are good unto him that hath no sin, and poverty is evil in the mouth of the ungodly.

Sir|13|25|The heart of a man changeth his countenance, whether it be for good or evil: and a merry heart maketh a cheerful countenance.

Sir|13|26|A cheerful countenance is a token of a heart that is in prosperity; and the finding out of parables is a wearisome labour of the mind.

Sir|14|1|Blessed is the man that hath not slipped with his mouth, and is not pricked with the multitude of sins.

Sir|14|2|Blessed is he whose conscience hath not condemned him, and who is not fallen from his hope in the Lord.

Sir|14|3|Riches are not comely for a niggard: and what should an envious man do with money?

Sir|14|4|He that gathereth by defrauding his own soul gathereth for others, that shall spend his goods riotously.

Sir|14|5|He that is evil to himself, to whom will he be good? he shall not take pleasure in his goods.

Sir|14|6|There is none worse than he that envieth himself; and this is a recompence of his wickedness.

Sir|14|7|And if he doeth good, he doeth it unwillingly; and at the last he will declare his wickedness.

Sir|14|8|The envious man hath a wicked eye; he turneth away his face, and despiseth men.

Sir|14|9|A covetous man's eye is not satisfied with his portion; and the iniquity of the wicked drieth up his soul.

Sir|14|10|A wicked eye envieth [his] bread, and he is a niggard at his table.

Sir|14|11|My son, according to thy ability do good to thyself, and give the Lord his due offering.

Sir|14|12|Remember that death will not be long in coming, and that the covenant of the grave is not shewed unto thee.

Sir|14|13|Do good unto thy friend before thou die, and according to thy ability stretch out thy hand and give to him.

Sir|14|14|Defraud not thyself of the good day, and let not the part of a good desire overpass thee.

Sir|14|15|Shalt thou not leave thy travails unto another? and thy labours to be divided by lot?

Sir|14|16|Give, and take, and sanctify thy soul; for there is no seeking of dainties in the grave.

Sir|14|17|All flesh waxeth old as a garment: for the covenant from the beginning is, Thou shalt die the death.

Sir|14|18|As of the green leaves on a thick tree, some fall, and some grow; so is the generation of flesh and blood, one cometh to an end, and another is born.

Sir|14|19|Every work rotteth and consumeth away, and the worker thereof shall go withal.

Sir|14|20|Blessed is the man that doth meditate good things in wisdom, and that reasoneth of holy things by his understanding. ing.

Sir|14|21|He that considereth her ways in his heart shall also have understanding in her secrets.

Sir|14|22|Go after her as one that traceth, and lie in wait in her ways.

Sir|14|23|He that prieth in at her windows shall also hearken at her doors.

Sir|14|24|He that doth lodge near her house shall also fasten a pin in her walls.

Sir|14|25|He shall pitch his tent nigh unto her, and shall lodge in a lodging where good things are.

Sir|14|26|He shall set his children under her shelter, and shall lodge under her branches.

Sir|14|27|By her he shall be covered from heat, and in her glory shall he dwell.

Sir|15|1|He that feareth the Lord will do good, and he that hath the knowledge of the law shall obtain her.

Sir|15|2|And as a mother shall she meet him, and receive him as a wife married of a virgin.

Sir|15|3|With the bread of understanding shall she feed him, and give him the water of wisdom to drink.

Sir|15|4|He shall be stayed upon her, and shall not be moved; and shall rely upon her, and shall not be confounded.

Sir|15|5|She shall exalt him above his neighbours, and in the midst of the congregation shall she open his mouth.

Sir|15|6|He shall find joy and a crown of gladness, and she shall cause him to inherit an everlasting name.

Sir|15|7|But foolish men shall not attain unto her, and sinners shall not see her.

Sir|15|8|For she is far from pride, and men that are liars cannot remember her.

Sir|15|9|Praise is not seemly in the mouth of a sinner, for it was not sent him of the Lord.

Sir|15|10|For praise shall be uttered in wisdom, and the Lord will prosper it.

Sir|15|11|Say not thou, It is through the Lord that I fell away: for thou oughtest not to do the things that he hateth.

Sir|15|12|Say not thou, He hath caused me to err: for he hath no need of the sinful man.

Sir|15|13|The Lord hateth all abomination; and they that fear אֱלֹהִים love it not.

Sir|15|14|He himself made man from the beginning, and left him in the hand of his counsel;

Sir|15|15|If thou wilt, to keep the commandments, and to perform acceptable faithfulness.

Sir|15|16|He hath set fire and water before thee: stretch forth thy hand unto whether thou wilt.

Sir|15|17|Before man is life and death; and whether him liketh shall be given him.

Sir|15|18|For the wisdom of the Lord is great, and he is mighty in power, and beholdeth all things:

Sir|15|19|And his eyes are upon them that fear him, and he knoweth every work of man.

Sir|15|20|He hath commanded no man to do wickedly, neither hath he given any man licence to sin.

Sir|16|1|Desire not a multitude of unprofitable children, neither delight in ungodly sons.

Sir|16|2|Though they multiply, rejoice not in them, except the fear of the Lord be with them.

Sir|16|3|Trust not thou in their life, neither respect their multitude: for one that is just is better than a thousand; and better it is to die without children, than to have them that are ungodly.

Sir|16|4|For by one that hath understanding shall the city be replenished: but the kindred of the wicked shall speedily become desolate.

Sir|16|5|Many such things have I seen with mine eyes, and mine ear hath heard greater things than these.

Sir|16|6|In the congregation of the ungodly shall a fire be kindled; and in a rebellious nation wrath is set on fire.

Sir|16|7|He was not pacified toward the old giants, who fell away in the strength of their foolishness.

Sir|16|8|Neither spared he the place where Lot sojourned, but abhorred them for their pride.

Sir|16|9|He pitied not the people of perdition, who were taken away in their sins:

Sir|16|10|Nor the six hundred thousand footmen, who were gathered together in the hardness of their hearts.

Sir|16|11|And if there be one stiffnecked among the people, it is marvel if he escape unpunished: for mercy and wrath are with him; he is mighty to forgive, and to pour out displeasure.

Sir|16|12|As his mercy is great, so is his correction also: he judgeth a man according to his works

Sir|16|13|The sinner shall not escape with his spoils: and the patience of the godly shall not be frustrate.

Sir|16|14|Make way for every work of mercy: for every man shall find according to his works.

Sir|16|15|The Lord hardened Pharaoh, that he should not know him, that his powerful works might be known to the world.

Sir|16|16|His mercy is manifest to every creature; and he hath separated his light from the darkness with an adamant.

Sir|16|17|Say not thou, I will hide myself from the Lord: shall any remember me from above? I shall not be remembered among so many people: for what is my soul among such an infinite number of creatures?

Sir|16|18|Behold, the heaven, and the heaven of heavens, the deep, and the earth, and all that therein is, shall be moved when he shall visit.

Sir|16|19|The mountains also and foundations of the earth be shaken with trembling, when the Lord looketh upon them.

Sir|16|20|No heart can think upon these things worthily: and who is able to conceive his ways?

Sir|16|21|It is a tempest which no man can see: for the most part of his works are hid.

Sir|16|22|Who can declare the works of his justice? or who can endure them? for his covenant is afar off, and the trial of all things is in the end.

Sir|16|23|He that wanteth understanding will think upon vain things: and a foolish man erring imagineth follies.

Sir|16|24|by son, hearken unto me, and learn knowledge, and mark my words with thy heart.

Sir|16|25|I will shew forth doctrine in weight, and declare his knowledge exactly.

Sir|16|26|The works of the Lord are done in judgment from the beginning: and from the time he made them he disposed the parts thereof.

Sir|16|27|He garnished his works for ever, and in his hand are the chief of them unto all generations: they neither labour, nor are weary, nor cease from their works.

Sir|16|28|None of them hindereth another, and they shall never disobey his word.

Sir|16|29|After this the Lord looked upon the earth, and filled it with his blessings.

Sir|16|30|With all manner of living things hath he covered the face thereof; and they shall return into it again.

Sir|17|1|The Lord created man of the earth, and turned him into it again.

Sir|17|2|He gave them few days, and a short time, and power also over the things therein.

Sir|17|3|He endued them with strength by themselves, and made them according to his image,

Sir|17|4|And put the fear of man upon all flesh, and gave him dominion over beasts and fowls.

Sir|17|5|They received the use of the five operations of the Lord, and in the sixth place he imparted them understanding, and in the seventh speech, an interpreter of the cogitations thereof.]

Sir|17|6|Counsel, and a tongue, and eyes, ears, and a heart, gave he them to understand.

Sir|17|7|Withal he filled them with the knowledge of understanding, and shewed them good and evil.

Sir|17|8|He set his eye upon their hearts, that he might shew them the greatness of his works.

Sir|17|9|He gave them to glory in his marvellous acts for ever, that they might declare his works with understanding.

Sir|17|10|And the elect shall praise his holy name.

Sir|17|11|Beside this he gave them knowledge, and the law of life for an heritage.

Sir|17|12|He made an everlasting covenant with them, and shewed them his judgments.

Sir|17|13|Their eyes saw the majesty of his glory, and their ears heard his glorious voice.

Sir|17|14|And he said unto them, Beware of all unrighteousness; and he gave every man commandment concerning his neighbour.

Sir|17|15|Their ways are ever before him, and shall not be hid from his eyes.

Sir|17|16|Every man from his youth is given to evil; neither could they make to themselves fleshy hearts for stony.

Sir|17|17|For in the division of the nations of the whole earth he set a ruler over every people; but Israel is the Lord's portion:

Sir|17|18|Whom, being his firstborn, he nourisheth with discipline, and giving him the light of his love doth not forsake him.

Sir|17|19|Therefore all their works are as the sun before him, and his eyes are continually upon their ways.

Sir|17|20|None of their unrighteous deeds are hid from him, but all their sins are before the Lord

Sir|17|21|But the Lord being gracious and knowing his workmanship, neither left nor forsook them, but spared them.

Sir|17|22|The alms of a man is as a signet with him, and he will keep the good deeds of man as the apple of the eye, and give repentance to his sons and daughters.

Sir|17|23|Afterwards he will rise up and reward them, and render their recompence upon their heads.

Sir|17|24|But unto them that repent, he granted them return, and comforted those that failed in patience.

Sir|17|25|Return unto the Lord, and forsake thy sins, make thy prayer before his face, and offend less.

Sir|17|26|Turn again to the most High, and turn away from iniquity: for he will lead thee out of darkness into the light of health, and hate thou abomination vehemently.

Sir|17|27|Who shall praise the most High in the grave, instead of them which live and give thanks?

Sir|17|28|Thanksgiving perisheth from the dead, as from one that is not: the living and sound in heart shall praise the Lord.

Sir|17|29|How great is the lovingkindness of the Lord our אֱלֹהִים, and his compassion unto such as turn unto him in holiness!

Sir|17|30|For all things cannot be in men, because the son of man is not immortal.

Sir|17|31|What is brighter than the sun? yet the light thereof faileth; and flesh and blood will imagine evil.

Sir|17|32|He vieweth the power of the height of heaven; and all men are but earth and ashes.

Sir|18|1|He that liveth for ever Hath created all things in general.

Sir|18|2|The Lord only is righteous, and there is none other but he,

Sir|18|3|Who governeth the world with the palm of his hand, and all things obey his will: for he is the King of all, by his power dividing holy things among them from profane.

Sir|18|4|To whom hath he given power to declare his works? and who shall find out his noble acts?

Sir|18|5|Who shall number the strength of his majesty? and who shall also tell out his mercies?

Sir|18|6|As for the wondrous works of the Lord, there may nothing be taken from them, neither may any thing be put unto them, neither can the ground of them be found out.

Sir|18|7|When a man hath done, then he beginneth; and when he leaveth off, then he shall be doubtful.

Sir|18|8|What is man, and whereto serveth he? what is his good, and what is his evil?

Sir|18|9|The number of a man's days at the most are an hundred years.

Sir|18|10|As a drop of water unto the sea, and a gravelstone in comparison of the sand; so are a thousand years to the days of eternity.

Sir|18|11|Therefore is אֱלֹהִים patient with them, and poureth forth his mercy upon them.

Sir|18|12|He saw and perceived their end to be evil; therefore he multiplied his compassion.

Sir|18|13|The mercy of man is toward his neighbour; but the mercy of the Lord is upon all flesh: he reproveth, and nurtureth, and teacheth and bringeth again, as a shepherd his flock.

Sir|18|14|He hath mercy on them that receive discipline, and that diligently seek after his judgments.

Sir|18|15|My son, blemish not thy good deeds, neither use uncomfortable words when thou givest any thing.

Sir|18|16|Shall not the dew asswage the heat? so is a word better than a gift.

Sir|18|17|Lo, is not a word better than a gift? but both are with a gracious man.

Sir|18|18|A fool will upbraid churlishly, and a gift of the envious consumeth the eyes.

Sir|18|19|Learn before thou speak, and use physick or ever thou be sick.

Sir|18|20|Before judgment examine thyself, and in the day of visitation thou shalt find mercy.

Sir|18|21|Humble thyself before thou be sick, and in the time of sins shew repentance.

Sir|18|22|Let nothing hinder thee to pay thy vow in due time, and defer not until death to be justified.

Sir|18|23|Before thou prayest, prepare thyself; and be not as one that tempteth the Lord.

Sir|18|24|Think upon the wrath that shall be at the end, and the time of vengeance, when he shall turn away his face.

Sir|18|25|When thou hast enough, remember the time of hunger: and when thou art rich, think upon poverty and need.

Sir|18|26|From the morning until the evening the time is changed, and all things are soon done before the Lord.

Sir|18|27|A wise man will fear in every thing, and in the day of sinning he will beware of offence: but a fool will not observe time.

Sir|18|28|Every man of understanding knoweth wisdom, and will give praise unto him that found her.

Sir|18|29|They that were of understanding in sayings became also wise themselves, and poured forth exquisite parables.

Sir|18|30|Go not after thy lusts, but refrain thyself from thine appetites.

Sir|18|31|If thou givest thy soul the desires that please her, she will make thee a laughingstock to thine enemies that malign thee.

Sir|18|32|Take not pleasure in much good cheer, neither be tied to the expence thereof.

Sir|18|33|Be not made a beggar by banqueting upon borrowing, when thou hast nothing in thy purse: for thou shalt lie in wait for thine own life, and be talked on.

Sir|19|1|A labouring man that A is given to drunkenness shall not be rich: and he that contemneth small things shall fall by little and little.

Sir|19|2|Wine and women will make men of understanding to fall away: and he that cleaveth to harlots will become impudent.

Sir|19|3|Moths and worms shall have him to heritage, and a bold man shall be taken away.

Sir|19|4|He that is hasty to give credit is lightminded; and he that sinneth shall offend against his own soul.

Sir|19|5|Whoso taketh pleasure in wickedness shall be condemned: but he that resisteth pleasures crowneth his life.

Sir|19|6|He that can rule his tongue shall live without strife; and he that hateth babbling shall have less evil.

Sir|19|7|Rehearse not unto another that which is told unto thee, and thou shalt fare never the worse.

Sir|19|8|Whether it be to friend or foe, talk not of other men's lives; and if thou canst without offence, reveal them not.

Sir|19|9|For he heard and observed thee, and when time cometh he will hate thee.

Sir|19|10|If thou hast heard a word, let it die with thee; and be bold, it will not burst thee.

Sir|19|11|A fool travaileth with a word, as a woman in labour of a child.

Sir|19|12|As an arrow that sticketh in a man's thigh, so is a word within a fool's belly.

Sir|19|13|Admonish a friend, it may be he hath not done it: and if he have done it, that he do it no more.

Sir|19|14|Admonish thy friend, it may be he hath not said it: and if he have, that he speak it not again.

Sir|19|15|Admonish a friend: for many times it is a slander, and believe not every tale.

Sir|19|16|There is one that slippeth in his speech, but not from his heart; and who is he that hath not offended with his tongue?

Sir|19|17|Admonish thy neighbour before thou threaten him; and not being angry, give place to the law of the most High.

Sir|19|18|The fear of the Lord is the first step to be accepted [of him,] and wisdom obtaineth his love.

Sir|19|19|The knowledge of the commandments of the Lord is the doctrine of life: and they that do things that please him shall receive the fruit of the tree of immortality.

Sir|19|20|The fear of the Lord is all wisdom; and in all wisdom is the performance of the law, and the knowledge of his omnipotency.

Sir|19|21|If a servant say to his master, I will not do as it pleaseth thee; though afterward he do it, he angereth him that nourisheth him.

Sir|19|22|The knowledge of wickedness is not wisdom, neither at any time the counsel of sinners prudence.

Sir|19|23|There is a wickedness, and the same an abomination; and there is a fool wanting in wisdom.

Sir|19|24|He that hath small understanding, and feareth אֱלֹהִים, is better than one that hath much wisdom, and transgresseth the law of the most High.

Sir|19|25|There is an exquisite subtilty, and the same is unjust; and there is one that turneth aside to make judgment appear; and there is a wise man that justifieth in judgment.

Sir|19|26|There is a wicked man that hangeth down his head sadly; but inwardly he is full of deceit,

Sir|19|27|Casting down his countenance, and making as if he heard not: where he is not known, he will do thee a mischief before thou be aware.

Sir|19|28|And if for want of power he be hindered from sinning, yet when he findeth opportunity he will do evil.

Sir|19|29|A man may be known by his look, and one that hath understanding by his countenance, when thou meetest him.

Sir|19|30|A man's attire, and excessive laughter, and gait, shew what he is.

Sir|20|1|There is a reproof that is not comely: again, some man holdeth his tongue, and he is wise.

Sir|20|2|It is much better to reprove, than to be angry secretly: and he that confesseth his fault shall be preserved from hurt.

Sir|20|3|How good is it, when thou art reproved, to shew repentance! for so shalt thou escape wilful sin.

Sir|20|4|As is the lust of an eunuch to deflower a virgin; so is he that executeth judgment with violence.

Sir|20|5|There is one that keepeth silence, and is found wise: and another by much babbling becometh hateful.

Sir|20|6|Some man holdeth his tongue, because he hath not to answer: and some keepeth silence, knowing his time.

Sir|20|7|A wise man will hold his tongue till he see opportunity: but a babbler and a fool will regard no time.

Sir|20|8|He that useth many words shall be abhorred; and he that taketh to himself authority therein shall be hated.

Sir|20|9|There is a sinner that hath good success in evil things; and there is a gain that turneth to loss.

Sir|20|10|There is a gift that shall not profit thee; and there is a gift whose recompence is double.

Sir|20|11|There is an abasement because of glory; and there is that lifteth up his head from a low estate.

Sir|20|12|There is that buyeth much for a little, and repayeth it sevenfold.

Sir|20|13|A wise man by his words maketh him beloved: but the graces of fools shall be poured out.

Sir|20|14|The gift of a fool shall do thee no good when thou hast it; neither yet of the envious for his necessity: for he looketh to receive many things for one.

Sir|20|15|He giveth little, and upbraideth much; he openeth his mouth like a crier; to day he lendeth, and to morrow will he ask it again: such an one is to be hated of אֱלֹהִים and man.

Sir|20|16|The fool saith, I have no friends, I have no thank for all my good deeds, and they that eat my bread speak evil of me.

Sir|20|17|How oft, and of how many shall he be laughed to scorn! for he knoweth not aright what it is to have; and it is all one unto him as if he had it not.

Sir|20|18|To slip upon a pavement is better than to slip with the tongue: so the fall of the wicked shall come speedily.

Sir|20|19|An unseasonable tale will always be in the mouth of the unwise.

Sir|20|20|A wise sentence shall be rejected when it cometh out of a fool's mouth; for he will not speak it in due season.

Sir|20|21|There is that is hindered from sinning through want: and when he taketh rest, he shall not be troubled.

Sir|20|22|There is that destroyeth his own soul through bashfulness, and by accepting of persons overthroweth himself.

Sir|20|23|There is that for bashfulness promiseth to his friend, and maketh him his enemy for nothing.

Sir|20|24|A lie is a foul blot in a man, yet it is continually in the mouth of the untaught.

Sir|20|25|A thief is better than a man that is accustomed to lie: but they both shall have destruction to heritage.

Sir|20|26|The disposition of a liar is dishonourable, and his shame is ever with him.

Sir|20|27|A wise man shall promote himself to honour with his words: and he that hath understanding will please great men.

Sir|20|28|He that tilleth his land shall increase his heap: and he that pleaseth great men shall get pardon for iniquity.

Sir|20|29|Presents and gifts blind the eyes of the wise, and stop up his mouth that he cannot reprove.

Sir|20|30|Wisdom that is hid, and treasure that is hoarded up, what profit is in them both?

Sir|20|31|Better is he that hideth his folly than a man that hideth his wisdom.

Sir|20|32|Necessary patience in seeking ing the Lord is better than he that leadeth his life without a guide.

Sir|21|1|My son, hast thou sinned? do so no more, but ask pardon for thy former sins.

Sir|21|2|Flee from sin as from the face of a serpent: for if thou comest too near it, it will bite thee: the teeth thereof are as the teeth of a lion, slaying the souls of men.

Sir|21|3|All iniquity is as a two edged sword, the wounds whereof cannot be healed.

Sir|21|4|To terrify and do wrong will waste riches: thus the house of proud men shall be made desolate.

Sir|21|5|A prayer out of a poor man's mouth reacheth to the ears of אֱלֹהִים, and his judgment cometh speedily.

Sir|21|6|He that hateth to be reproved is in the way of sinners: but he that feareth the Lord will repent from his heart.

Sir|21|7|An eloquent man is known far and near; but a man of understanding knoweth when he slippeth.

Sir|21|8|He that buildeth his house with other men's money is like one that gathereth himself stones for the tomb of his burial.

Sir|21|9|The congregation of the wicked is like tow wrapped together: and the end of them is a flame of fire to destroy them.

Sir|21|10|The way of sinners is made plain with stones, but at the end thereof is the pit of hell.

Sir|21|11|He that keepeth the law of the Lord getteth the understanding thereof: and the perfection of the fear of the Lord is wisdom.

Sir|21|12|He that is not wise will not be taught: but there is a wisdom which multiplieth bitterness.

Sir|21|13|The knowledge of a wise man shall abound like a flood: and his counsel is like a pure fountain of life.

Sir|21|14|The inner parts of a fool are like a broken vessel, and he will hold no knowledge as long as he liveth.

Sir|21|15|If a skilful man hear a wise word, he will commend it, and add unto it: but as soon as one of no understanding heareth it, it displeaseth him, and he casteth it behind his back.

Sir|21|16|The talking of a fool is like a burden in the way: but grace shall be found in the lips of the wise.

Sir|21|17|They enquire at the mouth of the wise man in the congregation, and they shall ponder his words in their heart.

Sir|21|18|As is a house that is destroyed, so is wisdom to a fool: and the knowledge of the unwise is as talk without sense.

Sir|21|19|Doctrine unto fools is as fetters on the feet, and like manacles on the right hand.

Sir|21|20|A fool lifteth up his voice with laughter; but a wise man doth scarce smile a little.

Sir|21|21|Learning is unto a wise man as an ornament of gold, and like a bracelet upon his right arm.

Sir|21|22|A foolish man's foot is soon in his [neighbour's] house: but a man of experience is ashamed of him.

Sir|21|23|A fool will peep in at the door into the house: but he that is well nurtured will stand without.

Sir|21|24|It is the rudeness of a man to hearken at the door: but a wise man will be grieved with the disgrace.

Sir|21|25|The lips of talkers will be telling such things as pertain not unto them: but the words of such as have understanding are weighed in the balance.

Sir|21|26|The heart of fools is in their mouth: but the mouth of the wise is in their heart.

Sir|21|27|When the ungodly curseth Satan, he curseth his own soul.

Sir|21|28|A whisperer defileth his own soul, and is hated wheresoever he dwelleth.

Sir|22|1|A slothful man is compared to a filthy stone, and every one will hiss him out to his disgrace.

Sir|22|2|A slothful man is compared to the filth of a dunghill: every man that takes it up will shake his hand.

Sir|22|3|An evilnurtured man is the dishonour of his father that begat him: and a [foolish] daughter is born to his loss.

Sir|22|4|A wise daughter shall bring an inheritance to her husband: but she that liveth dishonestly is her father's heaviness.

Sir|22|5|She that is bold dishonoureth both her father and her husband, but they both shall despise her.

Sir|22|6|A tale out of season [is as] musick in mourning: but stripes and correction of wisdom are never out of time.

Sir|22|7|Whoso teacheth a fool is as one that glueth a potsherd together, and as he that waketh one from a sound sleep.

Sir|22|8|He that telleth a tale to a fool speaketh to one in a slumber: when he hath told his tale, he will say, What is the matter?

Sir|22|9|If children live honestly, and have wherewithal, they shall cover the baseness of their parents.

Sir|22|10|But children, being haughty, through disdain and want of nurture do stain the nobility of their kindred.

Sir|22|11|Weep for the dead, for he hath lost the light: and weep for the fool, for he wanteth understanding: make little weeping for the dead, for he is at rest: but the life of the fool is worse than death.

Sir|22|12|Seven days do men mourn for him that is dead; but for a fool and an ungodly man all the days of his life.

Sir|22|13|Talk not much with a fool, and go not to him that hath no understanding: beware of him, lest thou have trouble, and thou shalt never be defiled with his fooleries: depart from him, and thou shalt find rest, and never be disquieted with madness.

Sir|22|14|What is heavier than lead? and what is the name thereof, but a fool?

Sir|22|15|Sand, and salt, and a mass of iron, is easier to bear, than a man without understanding.

Sir|22|16|As timber girt and bound together in a building cannot be loosed with shaking: so the heart that is stablished by advised counsel shall fear at no time.

Sir|22|17|A heart settled upon a thought of understanding is as a fair plaistering on the wall of a gallery.

Sir|22|18|Pales set on an high place will never stand against the wind: so a fearful heart in the imagination of a fool cannot stand against any fear.

Sir|22|19|He that pricketh the eye will make tears to fall: and he that pricketh the heart maketh it to shew her knowledge.

Sir|22|20|Whoso casteth a stone at the birds frayeth them away: and he that upbraideth his friend breaketh friendship.

Sir|22|21|Though thou drewest a sword at thy friend, yet despair not: for there may be a returning [to favour.]

Sir|22|22|If thou hast opened thy mouth against thy friend, fear not; for there may be a reconciliation: except for upbraiding, or pride, or disclosing of secrets, or a treacherous wound: for for these things every friend will depart.

Sir|22|23|Be faithful to thy neighbour in his poverty, that thou mayest rejoice in his prosperity: abide stedfast unto him in the time of his trouble, that thou mayest be heir with him in his heritage: for a mean estate is not always to be contemned: nor the rich that is foolish to be had in admiration.

Sir|22|24|As the vapour and smoke of a furnace goeth before the fire; so reviling before blood.

Sir|22|25|I will not be ashamed to defend a friend; neither will I hide myself from him.

Sir|22|26|And if any evil happen unto me by him, every one that heareth it will beware of him.

Sir|22|27|Who shall set a watch before my mouth, and a seal of wisdom upon my lips, that I fall not suddenly by them, and that my tongue destroy me not?

Sir|23|1|O Lord, Father and Governor of all my whole life, leave me not to their counsels, and let me not fall by them.

Sir|23|2|Who will set scourges over my thoughts, and the discipline of wisdom over mine heart? that they spare me not for mine ignorances, and it pass not by my sins:

Sir|23|3|Lest mine ignorances increase, and my sins abound to my destruction, and I fall before mine adversaries, and mine enemy rejoice over me, whose hope is far from thy mercy.

Sir|23|4|O Lord, Father and אֱלֹהִים of my life, give me not a proud look, but turn away from thy servants always a haughty mind.

Sir|23|5|Turn away from me vain hopes and concupiscence, and thou shalt hold him up that is desirous always to serve thee.

Sir|23|6|Let not the greediness of the belly nor lust of the flesh take hold of me; and give not over me thy servant into an impudent mind.

Sir|23|7|Hear, O ye children, the discipline of the mouth: he that keepeth it shall never be taken in his lips.

Sir|23|8|The sinner shall be left in his foolishness: both the evil speaker and the proud shall fall thereby.

Sir|23|9|Accustom not thy mouth to swearing; neither use thyself to the naming of the Holy One.

Sir|23|10|For as a servant that is continually beaten shall not be without a blue mark: so he that sweareth and nameth אֱלֹהִים continually shall not be faultless.

Sir|23|11|A man that useth much swearing shall be filled with iniquity, and the plague shall never depart from his house: if he shall offend, his sin shall be upon him: and if he acknowledge not his sin, he maketh a double offence: and if he swear in vain, he shall not be innocent, but his house shall be full of calamities.

Sir|23|12|There is a word that is clothed about with death: אֱלֹהִים grant that it be not found in the heritage of Jacob; for all such things shall be far from the godly, and they shall not wallow in their sins.

Sir|23|13|Use not thy mouth to intemperate swearing, for therein is the word of sin.

Sir|23|14|Remember thy father and thy mother, when thou sittest among great men. Be not forgetful before them, and so thou by thy custom become a fool, and wish that thou hadst not been born, and curse they day of thy nativity.

Sir|23|15|The man that is accustomed to opprobrious words will never be reformed all the days of his life.

Sir|23|16|Two sorts of men multiply sin, and the third will bring wrath: a hot mind is as a burning fire, it will never be quenched till it be consumed: a fornicator in the body of his flesh will never cease till he hath kindled a fire.

Sir|23|17|All bread is sweet to a whoremonger, he will not leave off till he die.

Sir|23|18|A man that breaketh wedlock, saying thus in his heart, Who seeth me? I am compassed about with darkness, the walls cover me, and no body seeth me; what need I to fear? the most High will not remember my sins:

Sir|23|19|Such a man only feareth the eyes of men, and knoweth not that the eyes of the Lord are ten thousand times brighter than the sun, beholding all the ways of men, and considering the most secret parts.

Sir|23|20|He knew all things ere ever they were created; so also after they were perfected he looked upon them all.

Sir|23|21|This man shall be punished in the streets of the city, and where he suspecteth not he shall be taken.

Sir|23|22|Thus shall it go also with the wife that leaveth her husband, and bringeth in an heir by another.

Sir|23|23|For first, she hath disobeyed the law of the most High; and secondly, she hath trespassed against her own husband; and thirdly, she hath played the whore in adultery, and brought children by another man.

Sir|23|24|She shall be brought out into the congregation, and inquisition shall be made of her children.

Sir|23|25|Her children shall not take root, and her branches shall bring forth no fruit.

Sir|23|26|She shall leave her memory to be cursed, and her reproach shall not be blotted out.

Sir|23|27|And they that remain shall know that there is nothing better than the fear of the Lord, and that there is nothing sweeter than to take heed unto the commandments of the Lord.

Sir|23|28|It is great glory to follow the Lord, and to be received of him is long life.

Sir|24|1|Wisdom shall praise herself, and shall glory in the midst of her people.

Sir|24|2|In the congregation of the most High shall she open her mouth, and triumph before his power.

Sir|24|3|I came out of the mouth of the most High, and covered the earth as a cloud.

Sir|24|4|I dwelt in high places, and my throne is in a cloudy pillar.

Sir|24|5|I alone compassed the circuit of heaven, and walked in the bottom of the deep.

Sir|24|6|In the waves of the sea and in all the earth, and in every people and nation, I got a possession.

Sir|24|7|With all these I sought rest: and in whose inheritance shall I abide?

Sir|24|8|So the Creator of all things gave me a commandment, and he that made me caused my tabernacle to rest, and said, Let thy dwelling be in Jacob, and thine inheritance in Israel.

Sir|24|9|He created me from the beginning before the world, and I shall never fail.

Sir|24|10|In the holy tabernacle I served before him; and so was I established in Sion.

Sir|24|11|Likewise in the beloved city he gave me rest, and in Jerusalem was my power.

Sir|24|12|And I took root in an honourable people, even in the portion of the Lord's inheritance.

Sir|24|13|I was exalted like a cedar in Libanus, and as a cypress tree upon the mountains of Hermon.

Sir|24|14|I was exalted like a palm tree in En-gaddi, and as a rose plant in Jericho, as a fair olive tree in a pleasant field, and grew up as a plane tree by the water.

Sir|24|15|I gave a sweet smell like cinnamon and aspalathus, and I yielded a pleasant odour like the best myrrh, as galbanum, and onyx, and sweet storax, and as the fume of frankincense in the tabernacle.

Sir|24|16|As the turpentine tree I stretched out my branches, and my branches are the branches of honour and grace.

Sir|24|17|As the vine brought I forth pleasant savour, and my flowers are the fruit of honour and riches.

Sir|24|18|I am the mother of fair love, and fear, and knowledge, and holy hope: I therefore, being eternal, am given to all my children which are named of him.

Sir|24|19|Come unto me, all ye that be desirous of me, and fill yourselves with my fruits.

Sir|24|20|For my memorial is sweeter than honey, and mine inheritance than the honeycomb.

Sir|24|21|They that eat me shall yet be hungry, and they that drink me shall yet be thirsty.

Sir|24|22|He that obeyeth me shall never be confounded, and they that work by me shall not do amiss.

Sir|24|23|All these things are the book of the covenant of the most high אֱלֹהִים, even the law which Moses commanded for an heritage unto the congregations of Jacob.

Sir|24|24|Faint not to be strong in the Lord; that he may confirm you, cleave unto him: for the Lord Almighty is אֱלֹהִים alone, and beside him there is no other Saviour.

Sir|24|25|He filleth all things with his wisdom, as Phison and as Tigris in the time of the new fruits.

Sir|24|26|He maketh the understanding to abound like Euphrates, and as Jordan in the time of the harvest.

Sir|24|27|He maketh the doctrine of knowledge appear as the light, and as Geon in the time of vintage.

Sir|24|28|The first man knew her not perfectly: no more shall the last find her out.

Sir|24|29|For her thoughts are more than the sea, and her counsels profounder than the great deep.

Sir|24|30|I also came out as a brook from a river, and as a conduit into a garden.

Sir|24|31|I said, I will water my best garden, and will water abundantly my garden bed: and, lo, my brook became a river, and my river became a sea.

Sir|24|32|I will yet make doctrine to shine as the morning, and will send forth her light afar off.

Sir|24|33|I will yet pour out doctrine as prophecy, and leave it to all ages for ever.

Sir|24|34|Behold that I have not laboured for myself only, but for all them that seek wisdom.

Sir|25|1|In three things I was beautified, and stood up beautiful both before אֱלֹהִים and men: the unity of brethren, the love of neighbours, a man and a wife that agree together.

Sir|25|2|Three sorts of men my soul hateth, and I am greatly offended at their life: a poor man that is proud, a rich man that is a liar, and an old adulterer that doateth.

Sir|25|3|If thou hast gathered nothing in thy youth, how canst thou find any thing in thine age?

Sir|25|4|O how comely a thing is judgment for gray hairs, and for ancient men to know counsel!

Sir|25|5|O how comely is the wisdom of old men, and understanding and counsel to men of honour.

Sir|25|6|Much experience is the crown of old men, and the fear of אֱלֹהִים is their glory.

Sir|25|7|There be nine things which I have judged in mine heart to be happy, and the tenth I will utter with my tongue: A man that hath joy of his children; and he that liveth to see the fall of his enemy:

Sir|25|8|Well is him that dwelleth with a wife of understanding, and that hath not slipped with his tongue, and that hath not served a man more unworthy than himself:

Sir|25|9|Well is him that hath found prudence, and he that speaketh in the ears of them that will hear:

Sir|25|10|O how great is he that findeth wisdom! yet is there none above him that feareth the Lord.

Sir|25|11|But the love of the Lord passeth all things for illumination: he that holdeth it, whereto shall he be likened?

Sir|25|12|The fear of the Lord is the beginning of his love: and faith is the beginning of cleaving unto him.

Sir|25|13|[Give me] any plague, but the plague of the heart: and any wickedness, but the wickedness of a woman:

Sir|25|14|And any affliction, but the affliction from them that hate me: and any revenge, but the revenge of enemies.

Sir|25|15|There is no head above the head of a serpent; and there is no wrath above the wrath of an enemy.

Sir|25|16|I had rather dwell with a lion and a dragon, than to keep house with a wicked woman.

Sir|25|17|The wickedness of a woman changeth her face, and darkeneth her countenance like sackcloth.

Sir|25|18|Her husband shall sit among his neighbours; and when he heareth it shall sigh bitterly.

Sir|25|19|All wickedness is but little to the wickedness of a woman: let the portion of a sinner fall upon her.

Sir|25|20|As the climbing up a sandy way is to the feet of the aged, so is a wife full of words to a quiet man.

Sir|25|21|Stumble not at the beauty of a woman, and desire her not for pleasure.

Sir|25|22|A woman, if she maintain her husband, is full of anger, impudence, and much reproach.

Sir|25|23|A wicked woman abateth the courage, maketh an heavy countenance and a wounded heart: a woman that will not comfort her husband in distress maketh weak hands and feeble knees.

Sir|25|24|Of the woman came the beginning of sin, and through her we all die.

Sir|25|25|Give the water no passage; neither a wicked woman liberty to gad abroad.

Sir|25|26|If she go not as thou wouldest have her, cut her off from thy flesh, and give her a bill of divorce, and let her go.

Sir|26|1|Blessed is the man that hath a virtuous wife, for the number of his days shall be double.

Sir|26|2|A virtuous woman rejoiceth her husband, and he shall fulfil the years of his life in peace.

Sir|26|3|A good wife is a good portion, which shall be given in the portion of them that fear the Lord.

Sir|26|4|Whether a man be rich or poor, if he have a good heart toward the Lord, he shall at all times rejoice with a cheerful countenance.

Sir|26|5|There be three things that mine heart feareth; and for the fourth I was sore afraid: the slander of a city, the gathering together of an unruly multitude, and a false accusation: all these are worse than death.

Sir|26|6|But a grief of heart and sorrow is a woman that is jealous over another woman, and a scourge of the tongue which communicateth with all.

Sir|26|7|An evil wife is a yoke shaken to and fro: he that hath hold of her is as though he held a scorpion.

Sir|26|8|A drunken woman and a gadder abroad causeth great anger, and she will not cover her own shame.

Sir|26|9|The whoredom of a woman may be known in her haughty looks and eyelids.

Sir|26|10|If thy daughter be shameless, keep her in straitly, lest she abuse herself through overmuch liberty.

Sir|26|11|Watch over an impudent eye: and marvel not if she trespass against thee.

Sir|26|12|She will open her mouth, as a thirsty traveller when he hath found a fountain, and drink of every water near her: by every hedge will she sit down, and open her quiver against every arrow.

Sir|26|13|The grace of a wife delighteth her husband, and her discretion will fatten his bones.

Sir|26|14|A silent and loving woman is a gift of the Lord; and there is nothing so much worth as a mind well instructed.

Sir|26|15|A shamefaced and faithful woman is a double grace, and her continent mind cannot be valued.

Sir|26|16|As the sun when it ariseth in the high heaven; so is the beauty of a good wife in the ordering of her house.

Sir|26|17|As the clear light is upon the holy candlestick; so is the beauty of the face in ripe age.

Sir|26|18|As the golden pillars are upon the sockets of silver; so are the fair feet with a constant heart.

Sir|26|19|My son, keep the flower of thine age sound; and give not thy strength to strangers.

Sir|26|20|When thou hast gotten a fruitful possession through all the field, sow it with thine own seed, trusting in the goodness of thy stock.

Sir|26|21|So thy race which thou leavest shall be magnified, having the confidence of their good descent.

Sir|26|22|An harlot shall be accounted as spittle; but a married woman is a tower against death to her husband.

Sir|26|23|A wicked woman is given as a portion to a wicked man: but a godly woman is given to him that feareth the Lord.

Sir|26|24|A dishonest woman contemneth shame: but an honest woman will reverence her husband.

Sir|26|25|A shameless woman shall be counted as a dog; but she that is shamefaced will fear the Lord.

Sir|26|26|A woman that honoureth her husband shall be judged wise of all; but she that dishonoureth him in her pride shall be counted ungodly of all.

Sir|26|27|A loud crying woman and a scold shall be sought out to drive away the enemies.

Sir|26|28|There be two things that grieve my heart; and the third maketh me angry: a man of war that suffereth poverty; and men of understanding that are not set by; and one that returneth from righteousness to sin; the Lord prepareth such an one for the sword.

Sir|26|29|A merchant shall hardly keep himself from doing wrong; and an huckster shall not be freed from sin.

Sir|27|1|Many have sinned for a small matter; and he that seeketh for abundance will turn his eyes away.

Sir|27|2|As a nail sticketh fast between the joinings of the stones; so doth sin stick close between buying and selling.

Sir|27|3|Unless a man hold himself diligently in the fear of the Lord, his house shall soon be overthrown.

Sir|27|4|As when one sifteth with a sieve, the refuse remaineth; so the filth of man in his talk.

Sir|27|5|The furnace proveth the potter's vessels; so the trial of man is in his reasoning.

Sir|27|6|The fruit declareth if the tree have been dressed; so is the utterance of a conceit in the heart of man.

Sir|27|7|Praise no man before thou hearest him speak; for this is the trial of men.

Sir|27|8|If thou followest righteousness, thou shalt obtain her, and put her on, as a glorious long robe.

Sir|27|9|The birds will resort unto their like; so will truth return unto them that practise in her.

Sir|27|10|As the lion lieth in wait for the prey; so sin for them that work iniquity.

Sir|27|11|The discourse of a godly man is always with wisdom; but a fool changeth as the moon.

Sir|27|12|If thou be among the indiscreet, observe the time; but be continually among men of understanding.

Sir|27|13|The discourse of fools is irksome, and their sport is the wantonness of sin.

Sir|27|14|The talk of him that sweareth much maketh the hair stand upright; and their brawls make one stop his ears.

Sir|27|15|The strife of the proud is bloodshedding, and their revilings are grievous to the ear.

Sir|27|16|Whoso discovereth secrets loseth his credit; and shall never find friend to his mind.

Sir|27|17|Love thy friend, and be faithful unto him: but if thou betrayest his secrets, follow no more after him.

Sir|27|18|For as a man hath destroyed his enemy; so hast thou lost the love of thy neighbor.

Sir|27|19|As one that letteth a bird go out of his hand, so hast thou let thy neighbour go, and shalt not get him again

Sir|27|20|Follow after him no more, for he is too far off; he is as a roe escaped out of the snare.

Sir|27|21|As for a wound, it may be bound up; and after reviling there may be reconcilement: but he that betrayeth secrets is without hope.

Sir|27|22|He that winketh with the eyes worketh evil: and he that knoweth him will depart from him.

Sir|27|23|When thou art present, he will speak sweetly, and will admire thy words: but at the last he will writhe his mouth, and slander thy sayings.

Sir|27|24|I have hated many things, but nothing like him; for the Lord will hate him.

Sir|27|25|Whoso casteth a stone on high casteth it on his own head; and a deceitful stroke shall make wounds.

Sir|27|26|Whoso diggeth a pit shall fall therein: and he that setteth a trap shall be taken therein.

Sir|27|27|He that worketh mischief, it shall fall upon him, and he shall not know whence it cometh.

Sir|27|28|Mockery and reproach are from the proud; but vengeance, as a lion, shall lie in wait for them.

Sir|27|29|They that rejoice at the fall of the righteous shall be taken in the snare; and anguish shall consume them before they die.

Sir|27|30|Malice and wrath, even these are abominations; and the sinful man shall have them both.

Sir|28|1|He that revengeth shall find vengeance from the Lord, and he will surely keep his sins [in remembrance.]

Sir|28|2|Forgive thy neighbour the hurt that he hath done unto thee, so shall thy sins also be forgiven when thou prayest.

Sir|28|3|One man beareth hatred against another, and doth he seek pardon from the Lord?

Sir|28|4|He sheweth no mercy to a man, which is like himself: and doth he ask forgiveness of his own sins?

Sir|28|5|If he that is but flesh nourish hatred, who will intreat for pardon of his sins?

Sir|28|6|Remember thy end, and let enmity cease; [remember] corruption and death, and abide in the commandments.

Sir|28|7|Remember the commandments, and bear no malice to thy neighbour: [remember] the covenant of the Highest, and wink at ignorance.

Sir|28|8|Abstain from strife, and thou shalt diminish thy sins: for a furious man will kindle strife,

Sir|28|9|A sinful man disquieteth friends, and maketh debate among them that be at peace.

Sir|28|10|As the matter of the fire is, so it burneth: and as a man's strength is, so is his wrath; and according to his riches his anger riseth; and the stronger they are which contend, the more they will be inflamed.

Sir|28|11|An hasty contention kindleth a fire: and an hasty fighting sheddeth blood.

Sir|28|12|If thou blow the spark, it shall burn: if thou spit upon it, it shall be quenched: and both these come out of thy mouth.

Sir|28|13|Curse the whisperer and doubletongued: for such have destroyed many that were at peace.

Sir|28|14|A backbiting tongue hath disquieted many, and driven them from nation to nation: strong cities hath it pulled down, and overthrown the houses of great men.

Sir|28|15|A backbiting tongue hath cast out virtuous women, and deprived them of their labours.

Sir|28|16|Whoso hearkeneth unto it shall never find rest, and never dwell quietly.

Sir|28|17|The stroke of the whip maketh marks in the flesh: but the stroke of the tongue breaketh the bones.

Sir|28|18|Many have fallen by the edge of the sword: but not so many as have fallen by the tongue.

Sir|28|19|Well is he that is defended through the venom thereof; who hath not drawn the yoke thereof, nor hath been bound in her bands.

Sir|28|20|For the yoke thereof is a yoke of iron, and the bands thereof are bands of brass.

Sir|28|21|The death thereof is an evil death, the grave were better than it.

Sir|28|22|It shall not have rule over them that fear אֱלֹהִים, neither shall they be burned with the flame thereof.

Sir|28|23|Such as forsake the Lord shall fall into it; and it shall burn in them, and not be quenched; it shall be sent upon them as a lion, and devour them as a leopard.

Sir|28|24|Look that thou hedge thy possession about with thorns, and bind up thy silver and gold,

Sir|28|25|And weigh thy words in a balance, and make a door and bar for thy mouth.

Sir|28|26|Beware thou slide not by it, lest thou fall before him that lieth in wait.

Sir|29|1|He that is merciful will lend unto his neighbour; and he that strengtheneth his hand keepeth the commandments.

Sir|29|2|Lend to thy neighbour in time of his need, and pay thou thy neighbour again in due season.

Sir|29|3|Keep thy word, and deal faithfully with him, and thou shalt always find the thing that is necessary for thee.

Sir|29|4|Many, when a thing was lent them, reckoned it to be found, and put them to trouble that helped them.

Sir|29|5|Till he hath received, he will kiss a man's hand; and for his neighbour's money he will speak submissly: but when he should repay, he will prolong the time, and return words of grief, and complain of the time.

Sir|29|6|If he prevail, he shall hardly receive the half, and he will count as if he had found it: if not, he hath deprived him of his money, and he hath gotten him an enemy without cause: he payeth him with cursings and railings; and for honour he will pay him disgrace.

Sir|29|7|Many therefore have refused to lend for other men's ill dealing, fearing to be defrauded.

Sir|29|8|Yet have thou patience with a man in poor estate, and delay not to shew him mercy.

Sir|29|9|Help the poor for the commandment's sake, and turn him not away because of his poverty.

Sir|29|10|Lose thy money for thy brother and thy friend, and let it not rust under a stone to be lost.

Sir|29|11|Lay up thy treasure according to the commandments of the most High, and it shall bring thee more profit than gold.

Sir|29|12|Shut up alms in thy storehouses: and it shall deliver thee from all affliction.

Sir|29|13|It shall fight for thee against thine enemies better than a mighty shield and strong spear.

Sir|29|14|An honest man is surety for his neighbour: but he that is impudent will forsake him.

Sir|29|15|Forget not the friendship of thy surety, for he hath given his life for thee.

Sir|29|16|A sinner will overthrow the good estate of his surety:

Sir|29|17|And he that is of an unthankful mind will leave him [in danger] that delivered him.

Sir|29|18|Suretiship hath undone many of good estate, and shaken them as a wave of the sea: mighty men hath it driven from their houses, so that they wandered among strange nations.

Sir|29|19|A wicked man transgressing the commandments of the Lord shall fall into suretiship: and he that undertaketh and followeth other men's business for gain shall fall into suits.

Sir|29|20|Help thy neighbour according to thy power, and beware that thou thyself fall not into the same.

Sir|29|21|The chief thing for life is water, and bread, and clothing, and an house to cover shame.

Sir|29|22|Better is the life of a poor man in a mean cottage, than delicate fare in another man's house.

Sir|29|23|Be it little or much, hold thee contented, that thou hear not the reproach of thy house.

Sir|29|24|For it is a miserable life to go from house to house: for where thou art a stranger, thou darest not open thy mouth.

Sir|29|25|Thou shalt entertain, and feast, and have no thanks: moreover thou shalt hear bitter words:

Sir|29|26|Come, thou stranger, and furnish a table, and feed me of that thou hast ready.

Sir|29|27|Give place, thou stranger, to an honourable man; my brother cometh to be lodged, and I have need of mine house.

Sir|29|28|These things are grievous to a man of understanding; the upbraiding of houseroom, and reproaching of the lender.

Sir|30|1|He that loveth his son causeth him oft to feel the rod, that he may have joy of him in the end.

Sir|30|2|He that chastiseth his son shall have joy in him, and shall rejoice of him among his acquaintance.

Sir|30|3|He that teacheth his son grieveth the enemy: and before his friends he shall rejoice of him.

Sir|30|4|Though his father die, yet he is as though he were not dead: for he hath left one behind him that is like himself.

Sir|30|5|While he lived, he saw and rejoiced in him: and when he died, he was not sorrowful.

Sir|30|6|He left behind him an avenger against his enemies, and one that shall requite kindness to his friends.

Sir|30|7|He that maketh too much of his son shall bind up his wounds; and his bowels will be troubled at every cry.

Sir|30|8|An horse not broken becometh headstrong: and a child left to himself will be wilful.

Sir|30|9|Cocker thy child, and he shall make thee afraid: play with him, and he will bring thee to heaviness.

Sir|30|10|Laugh not with him, lest thou have sorrow with him, and lest thou gnash thy teeth in the end.

Sir|30|11|Give him no liberty in his youth, and wink not at his follies.

Sir|30|12|Bow down his neck while he is young, and beat him on the sides while he is a child, lest he wax stubborn, and be disobedient unto thee, and so bring sorrow to thine heart.

Sir|30|13|Chastise thy son, and hold him to labour, lest his lewd behaviour be an offence unto thee.

Sir|30|14|Better is the poor, being sound and strong of constitution, than a rich man that is afflicted in his body.

Sir|30|15|Health and good estate of body are above all gold, and a strong body above infinite wealth.

Sir|30|16|There is no riches above a sound body, and no joy above the joy of the heart.

Sir|30|17|Death is better than a bitter life or continual sickness.

Sir|30|18|Delicates poured upon a mouth shut up are as messes of meat set upon a grave.

Sir|30|19|What good doeth the offering unto an idol? for neither can it eat nor smell: so is he that is persecuted of the Lord.

Sir|30|20|He seeth with his eyes and groaneth, as an eunuch that embraceth a virgin and sigheth.

Sir|30|21|Give not over thy mind to heaviness, and afflict not thyself in thine own counsel.

Sir|30|22|The gladness of the heart is the life of man, and the joyfulness of a man prolongeth his days.

Sir|30|23|Love thine own soul, and comfort thy heart, remove sorrow far from thee: for sorrow hath killed many, and there is no profit therein.

Sir|30|24|Envy and wrath shorten the life, and carefulness bringeth age before the time.

Sir|30|25|A cheerful and good heart will have a care of his meat and diet.

Sir|31|1|Watching for riches consumeth the flesh, and the care thereof driveth away sleep.

Sir|31|2|Watching care will not let a man slumber, as a sore disease breaketh sleep,

Sir|31|3|The rich hath great labour in gathering riches together; and when he resteth, he is filled with his delicates.

Sir|31|4|The poor laboureth in his poor estate; and when he leaveth off, he is still needy.

Sir|31|5|He that loveth gold shall not be justified, and he that followeth corruption shall have enough thereof.

Sir|31|6|Gold hath been the ruin of many, and their destruction was present.

Sir|31|7|It is a stumblingblock unto them that sacrifice unto it, and every fool shall be taken therewith.

Sir|31|8|Blessed is the rich that is found without blemish, and hath not gone after gold.

Sir|31|9|Who is he? and we will call him blessed: for wonderful things hath he done among his people.

Sir|31|10|Who hath been tried thereby, and found perfect? then let him glory. Who might offend, and hath not offended? or done evil, and hath not done it?

Sir|31|11|His goods shall be established, and the congregation shall declare his alms.

Sir|31|12|If thou sit at a bountiful table, be not greedy upon it, and say not, There is much meat on it.

Sir|31|13|Remember that a wicked eye is an evil thing: and what is created more wicked than an eye? therefore it weepeth upon every occasion.

Sir|31|14|Stretch not thine hand whithersoever it looketh, and thrust it not with him into the dish.

Sir|31|15|Judge not thy neighbour by thyself: and be discreet in every point.

Sir|31|16|Eat as it becometh a man, those things which are set before thee; and devour note, lest thou be hated.

Sir|31|17|Leave off first for manners' sake; and be not unsatiable, lest thou offend.

Sir|31|18|When thou sittest among many, reach not thine hand out first of all.

Sir|31|19|A very little is sufficient for a man well nurtured, and he fetcheth not his wind short upon his bed.

Sir|31|20|Sound sleep cometh of moderate eating: he riseth early, and his wits are with him: but the pain of watching, and choler, and pangs of the belly, are with an unsatiable man.

Sir|31|21|And if thou hast been forced to eat, arise, go forth, vomit, and thou shalt have rest.

Sir|31|22|My son, hear me, and despise me not, and at the last thou shalt find as I told thee: in all thy works be quick, so shall there no sickness come unto thee.

Sir|31|23|Whoso is liberal of his meat, men shall speak well of him; and the report of his good housekeeping will be believed.

Sir|31|24|But against him that is a niggard of his meat the whole city shall murmur; and the testimonies of his niggardness shall not be doubted of.

Sir|31|25|Shew not thy valiantness in wine; for wine hath destroyed many.

Sir|31|26|The furnace proveth the edge by dipping: so doth wine the hearts of the proud by drunkeness.

Sir|31|27|Wine is as good as life to a man, if it be drunk moderately: what life is then to a man that is without wine? for it was made to make men glad.

Sir|31|28|Wine measurably drunk and in season bringeth gladness of the heart, and cheerfulness of the mind:

Sir|31|29|But wine drunken with excess maketh bitterness of the mind, with brawling and quarrelling.

Sir|31|30|Drunkenness increaseth the rage of a fool till he offend: it diminisheth strength, and maketh wounds.

Sir|31|31|Rebuke not thy neighbour at the wine, and despise him not in his mirth: give him no despiteful words, and press not upon him with urging him [to drink.]

Sir|32|1|If thou be made the master [of a feast,] lift not thyself up, but be among them as one of the rest;

take diligent care for them, and so sit down.

Sir|32|2|And when thou hast done all thy office, take thy place, that thou mayest be merry with them, and receive a crown for thy well ordering of the feast.

Sir|32|3|Speak, thou that art the elder, for it becometh thee, but with sound judgment; and hinder not musick.

Sir|32|4|Pour not out words where there is a musician, and shew not forth wisdom out of time.

Sir|32|5|A concert of musick in a banquet of wine is as a signet of carbuncle set in gold.

Sir|32|6|As a signet of an emerald set in a work of gold, so is the melody of musick with pleasant wine.

Sir|32|7|Speak, young man, if there be need of thee: and yet scarcely when thou art twice asked.

Sir|32|8|Let thy speech be short, comprehending much in few words; be as one that knoweth and yet holdeth his tongue.

Sir|32|9|If thou be among great men, make not thyself equal with them; and when ancient men are in place, use not many words.

Sir|32|10|Before the thunder goeth lightning; and before a shamefaced man shall go favour.

Sir|32|11|Rise up betimes, and be not the last; but get thee home without delay.

Sir|32|12|There take thy pastime, and do what thou wilt: but sin not by proud speech.

Sir|32|13|And for these things bless him that made thee, and hath replenished thee with his good things.

Sir|32|14|Whoso feareth the Lord will receive his discipline; and they that seek him early shall find favour.

Sir|32|15|He that seeketh the law shall be filled therewith: but the hypocrite will be offended thereat.

Sir|32|16|They that fear the Lord shall find judgment, and shall kindle justice as a light.

Sir|32|17|A sinful man will not be reproved, but findeth an excuse according to his will.

Sir|32|18|A man of counsel will be considerate; but a strange and proud man is not daunted with fear, even when of himself he hath done without counsel.

Sir|32|19|Do nothing without advice; and when thou hast once done, repent not.

Sir|32|20|Go not in a way wherein thou mayest fall, and stumble not among the stones.

Sir|32|21|Be not confident in a plain way.

Sir|32|22|And beware of thine own children.

Sir|32|23|In every good work trust thy own soul; for this is the keeping of the commandments.

Sir|32|24|He that believeth in the Lord taketh heed to the commandment; and he that trusteth in him shall fare never the worse.

Sir|33|1|There shall no evil happen unto him that feareth the Lord; but in temptation even again he will deliver him.

Sir|33|2|A wise man hateth not the law; but he that is an hypocrite therein is as a ship in a storm.

Sir|33|3|A man of understanding trusteth in the law; and the law is faithful unto him, as an oracle.

Sir|33|4|Prepare what to say, and so thou shalt be heard: and bind up instruction, and then make answer.

Sir|33|5|The heart of the foolish is like a cartwheel; and his thoughts are like a rolling axletree.

Sir|33|6|A stallion horse is as a mocking friend, he neigheth under every one that sitteth upon him.

Sir|33|7|Why doth one day excel another, when as all the light of every day in the year is of the sun?

Sir|33|8|By the knowledge of the Lord they were distinguished: and he altered seasons and feasts.

Sir|33|9|Some of them hath he made high days, and hallowed them, and some of them hath he made ordinary days.

Sir|33|10|And all men are from the ground, and Adam was created of earth:

Sir|33|11|In much knowledge the Lord hath divided them, and made their ways diverse.

Sir|33|12|Some of them hath he blessed and exalted and some of them he sanctified, and set near himself: but some of them hath he cursed and brought low, and turned out of their places.

Sir|33|13|As the clay is in the potter's hand, to fashion it at his pleasure: so man is in the hand of him that made him, to render to them as liketh him best.

Sir|33|14|Good is set against evil, and life against death: so is the godly against the sinner, and the sinner against the godly.

Sir|33|15|So look upon all the works of the most High; and there are two and two, one against another.

Sir|33|16|I awaked up last of all, as one that gathereth after the grapegatherers: by the blessing of the Lord I profited, and trod my winepress like a gatherer of grapes.

Sir|33|17|Consider that I laboured not for myself only, but for all them that seek learning.

Sir|33|18|Hear me, O ye great men of the people, and hearken with your ears, ye rulers of the congregation.

Sir|33|19|Give not thy son and wife, thy brother and friend, power over thee while thou livest, and give not thy goods to another: lest it repent thee, and thou intreat for the same again.

Sir|33|20|As long as thou livest and hast breath in thee, give not thyself over to any.

Sir|33|21|For better it is that thy children should seek to thee, than that thou shouldest stand to their courtesy.

Sir|33|22|In all thy works keep to thyself the preeminence; leave not a stain in thine honour.

Sir|33|23|At the time when thou shalt end thy days, and finish thy life, distribute thine inheritance.

Sir|33|24|Fodder, a wand, and burdens, are for the ass; and bread, correction, and work, for a servant. .

Sir|33|25|If thou set thy servant to labour, thou shalt find rest: but if thou let him go idle, he shall seek liberty.

Sir|33|26|A yoke and a collar do bow the neck: so are tortures and torments for an evil servant.

Sir|33|27|Send him to labour, that he be not idle; for idleness teacheth much evil.

Sir|33|28|Set him to work, as is fit for him: if he be not obedient, put on more heavy fetters.

Sir|33|29|But be not excessive toward any; and without discretion do nothing.

Sir|33|30|If thou have a servant, let him be unto thee as thyself, because thou hast bought him with a price.

Sir|33|31|If thou have a servant, entreat him as a brother: for thou hast need of him, as of thine own soul: if thou entreat him evil, and he run from thee, which way wilt thou go to seek him?

Sir|34|1|The hopes of a man void of understanding are vain and false: and dreams lift up fools.

Sir|34|2|Whoso regardeth dreams is like him that catcheth at a shadow, and followeth after the wind.

Sir|34|3|The vision of dreams is the resemblance of one thing to another, even as the likeness of a face to a face.

Sir|34|4|Of an unclean thing what can be cleansed? and from that thing which is false what truth can come?

Sir|34|5|Divinations, and soothsayings, and dreams, are vain: and the heart fancieth, as a woman's heart in travail.

Sir|34|6|If they be not sent from the most High in thy visitation, set not thy heart upon them.

Sir|34|7|For dreams have deceived many, and they have failed that put their trust in them.

Sir|34|8|The law shall be found perfect without lies: and wisdom is perfection to a faithful mouth.

Sir|34|9|A man that hath travelled knoweth many things; and he that hath much experience will declare wisdom.

Sir|34|10|He that hath no experience knoweth little: but he that hath travelled is full of prudence.

Sir|34|11|When I travelled, I saw many things; and I understand more than I can express.

Sir|34|12|I was ofttimes in danger of death: yet I was delivered because of these things.

Sir|34|13|The spirit of those that fear the Lord shall live; for their hope is in him that saveth them.

Sir|34|14|Whoso feareth the Lord shall not fear nor be afraid; for he is his hope.

Sir|34|15|Blessed is the soul of him that feareth the Lord: to whom doth he look? and who is his strength?

Sir|34|16|For the eyes of the Lord are upon them that love him, he is their mighty protection and strong stay, a defence from heat, and a cover from the sun at noon, a preservation from stumbling, and an help from falling.

Sir|34|17|He raiseth up the soul, and lighteneth the eyes: he giveth health, life, and blessing.

Sir|34|18|He that sacrificeth of a thing wrongfully gotten, his offering is ridiculous; and the gifts of unjust men are not accepted.

Sir|34|19|The most High is not pleased with the offerings of the wicked; neither is he pacified for sin by the multitude of sacrifices.

Sir|34|20|Whoso bringeth an offering of the goods of the poor doeth as one that killeth the son before his father's eyes.

Sir|34|21|The bread of the needy is their life: he that defraudeth him thereof is a man of blood.

Sir|34|22|He that taketh away his neighbour's living slayeth him; and he that defraudeth the labourer of his hire is a bloodshedder.

Sir|34|23|When one buildeth, and another pulleth down, what profit have they then but labour?

Sir|34|24|When one prayeth, and another curseth, whose voice will the Lord hear?

Sir|34|25|He that washeth himself after the touching of a dead body, if he touch it again, what availeth his washing?

Sir|34|26|So is it with a man that fasteth for his sins, and goeth again, and doeth the same: who will hear his prayer? or what doth his humbling profit him?

Sir|35|1|He that keepeth the law bringeth offerings enough: he that taketh heed to the commandment offereth a peace offering.

Sir|35|2|He that requiteth a goodturn offereth fine flour; and he that giveth alms sacrificeth praise.

Sir|35|3|To depart from wickedness is a thing pleasing to the Lord; and to forsake unrighteousness is a propitiation.

Sir|35|4|Thou shalt not appear empty before the Lord.

Sir|35|5|For all these things [are to be done] because of the commandment.

Sir|35|6|The offering of the righteous maketh the altar fat, and the sweet savour thereof is before the most High.

Sir|35|7|The sacrifice of a just man is acceptable. and the memorial thereof shall never be forgotten.

Sir|35|8|Give the Lord his honour with a good eye, and diminish not the firstfruits of thine hands.

Sir|35|9|In all thy gifts shew a cheerful countenance, and dedicate thy tithes with gladness.

Sir|35|10|Give unto the most High according as he hath enriched thee; and as thou hast gotten, give with a cheerful eye.

Sir|35|11|For the Lord recompenseth, and will give thee seven times as much.

Sir|35|12|Do not think to corrupt with gifts; for such he will not receive: and trust not to unrighteous sacrifices; for the Lord is judge, and with him is no respect of persons.

Sir|35|13|He will not accept any person against a poor man, but will hear the prayer of the oppressed.

Sir|35|14|He will not despise the supplication of the fatherless; nor the widow, when she poureth out her complaint.

Sir|35|15|Do not the tears run down the widow's cheeks? and is not her cry against him that causeth them to fall?

Sir|35|16|He that serveth the Lord shall be accepted with favour, and his prayer shall reach unto the clouds.

Sir|35|17|The prayer of the humble pierceth the clouds: and till it come nigh, he will not be comforted; and will not depart, till the most High shall behold to judge righteously, and execute judgment.

Sir|35|18|For the Lord will not be slack, neither will the Mighty be patient toward them, till he have smitten in sunder the loins of the unmerciful, and repayed vengeance to the heathen; till he have taken away the multitude of the proud, and broken the sceptre of the unrighteous;

Sir|35|19|Till he have rendered to every man according to his deeds, and to the works of men according to their devices; till he have judged the cause of his people, and made them to rejoice in his mercy.

Sir|35|20|Mercy is seasonable in the time of affliction, as clouds of rain in the time of drought.

Sir|36|1|Have mercy upon us, O Lord אֱלֹהִים of all, and behold us:

Sir|36|2|And send thy fear upon all the nations that seek not after thee.

Sir|36|3|Lift up thy hand against the strange nations, and let them see thy power.

Sir|36|4|As thou wast sanctified in us before them: so be thou magnified among them before us.

Sir|36|5|And let them know thee, as we have known thee, that there is no אֱלֹהִים but only thou, O אֱלֹהִים.

Sir|36|6|Shew new signs, and make other strange wonders: glorify thy hand and thy right arm, that they may set forth thy wondrous works.

Sir|36|7|Raise up indignation, and pour out wrath: take away the adversary, and destroy the enemy.

Sir|36|8|Sake the time short, remember the covenant, and let them declare thy wonderful works.

Sir|36|9|Let him that escapeth be consumed by the rage of the fire; and let them perish that oppress the people.

Sir|36|10|Smite in sunder the heads of the rulers of the heathen, that say, There is none other but we.

Sir|36|11|Gather all the tribes of Jacob together, and inherit thou them, as from the beginning.

Sir|36|12|O Lord, have mercy upon the people that is called by thy name, and upon Israel, whom thou hast named thy firstborn.

Sir|36|13|O be merciful unto Jerusalem, thy holy city, the place of thy rest.

Sir|36|14|Fill Sion with thine unspeakable oracles, and thy people with thy glory:

Sir|36|15|Give testimony unto those that thou hast possessed from the beginning, and raise up prophets that have been in thy name.

Sir|36|16|Reward them that wait for thee, and let thy prophets be found faithful.

Sir|36|17|O Lord, hear the prayer of thy servants, according to the blessing of Aaron over thy people, that all they which dwell upon the earth may know that thou art the Lord, the eternal אֱלֹהִים.

Sir|36|18|The belly devoureth all meats, yet is one meat better than another.

Sir|36|19|As the palate tasteth divers kinds of venison: so doth an heart of understanding false speeches.

Sir|36|20|A froward heart causeth heaviness: but a man of experience will recompense him.

Sir|36|21|A woman will receive every man, yet is one daughter better than another.

Sir|36|22|The beauty of a woman cheereth the countenance, and a man loveth nothing better.

Sir|36|23|If there be kindness, meekness, and comfort, in her tongue, then is not her husband like other men.

Sir|36|24|He that getteth a wife beginneth a possession, a help like unto himself, and a pillar of rest.

Sir|36|25|Where no hedge is, there the possession is spoiled: and he that hath no wife will wander up and down mourning.

Sir|36|26|Who will trust a thief well appointed, that skippeth from city to city? so [who will believe] a man that hath no house, and lodgeth wheresoever the night taketh him?

Sir|37|1|Every friend saith, I am his friend also: but there is a friend, which is only a friend in name.

Sir|37|2|Is it not a grief unto death, when a companion and friend is turned to an enemy?

Sir|37|3|O wicked imagination, whence camest thou in to cover the earth with deceit?

Sir|37|4|There is a companion, which rejoiceth in the prosperity of a friend, but in the time of trouble will be against him.

Sir|37|5|There is a companion, which helpeth his friend for the belly, and taketh up the buckler against the enemy.

Sir|37|6|Forget not thy friend in thy mind, and be not unmindful of him in thy riches.

Sir|37|7|Every counsellor extolleth counsel; but there is some that counselleth for himself.

Sir|37|8|Beware of a counsellor, and know before what need he hath; for he will counsel for himself; lest he cast the lot upon thee,

Sir|37|9|And say unto thee, Thy way is good: and afterward he stand on the other side, to see what shall befall thee.

Sir|37|10|Consult not with one that suspecteth thee: and hide thy counsel from such as envy thee.

Sir|37|11|Neither consult with a woman touching her of whom she is jealous; neither with a coward in matters of war; nor with a merchant concerning exchange; nor with a buyer of selling; nor with an envious man of thankfulness; nor with an unmerciful man touching kindness; nor with the slothful for any work; nor with an hireling for a year of finishing work; nor with an idle servant of much business: hearken not unto these in any matter of counsel.

Sir|37|12|But be continually with a godly man, whom thou knowest to keep the commandments of the Lord, whose, mind is according to thy mind, and will sorrow with thee, if thou shalt miscarry.

Sir|37|13|And let the counsel of thine own heart stand: for there is no man more faithful unto thee than it.

Sir|37|14|For a man's mind is sometime wont to tell him more than seven watchmen, that sit above in an high tower.

Sir|37|15|And above all this pray to the most High, that he will direct thy way in truth.

Sir|37|16|Let reason go before every enterprize, and counsel before every action.

Sir|37|17|The countenance is a sign of changing of the heart.

Sir|37|18|Four manner of things appear: good and evil, life and death: but the tongue ruleth over them continually.

Sir|37|19|There is one that is wise and teacheth many, and yet is unprofitable to himself.

Sir|37|20|There is one that sheweth wisdom in words, and is hated: he shall be destitute of all food.

Sir|37|21|For grace is not given, him from the Lord, because he is deprived of all wisdom.

Sir|37|22|Another is wise to himself; and the fruits of understanding are commendable in his mouth.

Sir|37|23|A wise man instructeth his people; and the fruits of his understanding fail not.

Sir|37|24|A wise man shall be filled with blessing; and all they that see him shall count him happy.

Sir|37|25|The days of the life of man may be numbered: but the days of Israel are innumerable.

Sir|37|26|A wise man shall inherit glory among his people, and his name shall be perpetual.

Sir|37|27|My son, prove thy soul in thy life, and see what is evil for it, and give not that unto it.

Sir|37|28|For all things are not profitable for all men, neither hath every soul pleasure in every thing.

Sir|37|29|Be not unsatiable in any dainty thing, nor too greedy upon meats:

Sir|37|30|For excess of meats bringeth sickness, and surfeiting will turn into choler.

Sir|37|31|By surfeiting have many perished; but he that taketh heed prolongeth his life.

Sir|38|1|Honour a physician with the honour due unto him for the uses which ye may have of him: for the Lord hath created him.

Sir|38|2|For of the most High cometh healing, and he shall receive honour of the king.

Sir|38|3|The skill of the physician shall lift up his head: and in the sight of great men he shall be in admiration.

Sir|38|4|The Lord hath created medicines out of the earth; and he that is wise will not abhor them.

Sir|38|5|Was not the water made sweet with wood, that the virtue thereof might be known?

Sir|38|6|And he hath given men skill, that he might be honoured in his marvellous works.

Sir|38|7|With such doth he heal [men,] and taketh away their pains.

Sir|38|8|Of such doth the apothecary make a confection; and of his works there is no end; and from him is peace over all the earth,

Sir|38|9|My son, in thy sickness be not negligent: but pray unto the Lord, and he will make thee whole.

Sir|38|10|Leave off from sin, and order thine hands aright, and cleanse thy heart from all wickedness.

Sir|38|11|Give a sweet savour, and a memorial of fine flour; and make a fat offering, as not being.

Sir|38|12|Then give place to the physician, for the Lord hath created him: let him not go from thee, for thou hast need of him.

Sir|38|13|There is a time when in their hands there is good success.

Sir|38|14|For they shall also pray unto the Lord, that he would prosper that, which they give for ease and remedy to prolong life.

Sir|38|15|He that sinneth before his Maker, let him fall into the hand of the physician.

Sir|38|16|My son, let tears fall down over the dead, and begin to lament, as if thou hadst suffered great harm thyself; and then cover his body according to the custom, and neglect not his burial.

Sir|38|17|Weep bitterly, and make great moan, and use lamentation, as he is worthy, and that a day or two, lest thou be evil spoken of: and then comfort thyself for thy heaviness.

Sir|38|18|For of heaviness cometh death, and the heaviness of the heart breaketh strength.

Sir|38|19|In affliction also sorrow remaineth: and the life of the poor is the curse of the heart.

Sir|38|20|Take no heaviness to heart: drive it away, and member the last end.

Sir|38|21|Forget it not, for there is no turning again: thou shalt not do him good, but hurt thyself.

Sir|38|22|Remember my judgment: for thine also shall be so; yesterday for me, and to day for thee.

Sir|38|23|When the dead is at rest, let his remembrance rest; and be comforted for him, when his Spirit is departed from him.

Sir|38|24|The wisdom of a learned man cometh by opportunity of leisure: and he that hath little business shall become wise.

Sir|38|25|How can he get wisdom that holdeth the plough, and that glorieth in the goad, that driveth oxen, and is occupied in their labours, and whose talk is of bullocks?

Sir|38|26|He giveth his mind to make furrows; and is diligent to give the kine fodder.

Sir|38|27|So every carpenter and workmaster, that laboureth night and day: and they that cut and grave seals, and are diligent to make great variety, and give themselves to counterfeit imagery, and watch to finish a work:

Sir|38|28|The smith also sitting by the anvil, and considering the iron work, the vapour of the fire wasteth his flesh, and he fighteth with the heat of the furnace: the noise of the hammer and the anvil is ever in his ears, and his eyes look still upon the pattern of the thing that he maketh; he setteth his mind to finish his work, and watcheth to polish it perfectly:

Sir|38|29|So doth the potter sitting at his work, and turning the wheel about with his feet, who is alway carefully set at his work, and maketh all his work by number;

Sir|38|30|He fashioneth the clay with his arm, and boweth down his strength before his feet; he applieth himself to lead it over; and he is diligent to make clean the furnace:

Sir|38|31|All these trust to their hands: and every one is wise in his work.

Sir|38|32|Without these cannot a city be inhabited: and they shall not dwell where they will, nor go up and down:

Sir|38|33|They shall not be sought for in publick counsel, nor sit high in the congregation: they shall not sit on the judges' seat, nor understand the sentence of judgment: they cannot declare justice and judgment; and they shall not be found where parables are spoken.

Sir|38|34|But they will maintain the state of the world, and [all] their desire is in the work of their craft.

Sir|39|1|But he that giveth his mind to the law of the most High, and is occupied in the meditation thereof, will seek out the wisdom of all the ancient, and be occupied in prophecies.

Sir|39|2|He will keep the sayings of the renowned men: and where subtil parables are, he will be there also.

Sir|39|3|He will seek out the secrets of grave sentences, and be conversant in dark parables.

Sir|39|4|He shall serve among great men, and appear before princes: he will travel through strange countries; for he hath tried the good and the evil among men.

Sir|39|5|He will give his heart to resort early to the Lord that made him, and will pray before the most High, and will open his mouth in prayer, and make supplication for his sins.

Sir|39|6|When the great Lord will, he shall be filled with the spirit of understanding: he shall pour out wise sentences, and give thanks unto the Lord in his prayer.

Sir|39|7|He shall direct his counsel and knowledge, and in his secrets shall he meditate.

Sir|39|8|He shall shew forth that which he hath learned, and shall glory in the law of the covenant of the Lord.

Sir|39|9|Many shall commend his understanding; and so long as the world endureth, it shall not be blotted out; his memorial shall not depart away, and his name shall live from generation to generation.

Sir|39|10|Nations shall shew forth his wisdom, and the congregation shall declare his praise.

Sir|39|11|If he die, he shall leave a greater name than a thousand: and if he live, he shall increase it.

Sir|39|12|Yet have I more to say, which I have thought upon; for I am filled as the moon at the full.

Sir|39|13|Hearken unto me, ye holy children, and bud forth as a rose growing by the brook of the field:

Sir|39|14|And give ye a sweet savour as frankincense, and flourish as a lily, send forth a smell, and sing a song of praise, bless the Lord in all his works.

Sir|39|15|Magnify his name, and shew forth his praise with the songs of your lips, and with harps, and in praising him ye shall say after this manner:

Sir|39|16|All the works of the Lord are exceeding good, and whatsoever he commandeth shall be accomplished in due season.

Sir|39|17|And none may say, What is this? wherefore is that? for at time convenient they shall all be sought out: at his commandment the waters stood as an heap, and at the words of his mouth the receptacles of waters.

Sir|39|18|At his commandment is done whatsoever pleaseth him; and none can hinder, when he will save.

Sir|39|19|The works of all flesh are before him, and nothing can be hid from his eyes.

Sir|39|20|He seeth from everlasting to everlasting; and there is nothing wonderful before him.

Sir|39|21|A man need not to say, What is this? wherefore is that? for he hath made all things for their uses.

Sir|39|22|His blessing covered the dry land as a river, and watered it as a flood.

Sir|39|23|As he hath turned the waters into saltness: so shall the heathen inherit his wrath.

Sir|39|24|As his ways are plain unto the holy; so are they stumblingblocks unto the wicked.

Sir|39|25|For the good are good things created from the beginning: so evil things for sinners.

Sir|39|26|The principal things for the whole use of man's life are water, fire, iron, and salt, flour of wheat, honey, milk, and the blood of the grape, and oil, and clothing.

Sir|39|27|All these things are for good to the godly: so to the sinners they are turned into evil.

Sir|39|28|There be spirits that are created for vengeance, which in their fury lay on sore strokes; in the time of destruction they pour out their force, and appease the wrath of him that made them.

Sir|39|29|Fire, and hail, and famine, and death, all these were created for vengeance;

Sir|39|30|Teeth of wild beasts, and scorpions, serpents, and the sword punishing the wicked to destruction.

Sir|39|31|They shall rejoice in his commandment, and they shall be ready upon earth, when need is; and when their time is come, they shall not transgress his word.

Sir|39|32|Therefore from the beginning I was resolved, and thought upon these things, and have left them in writing.

Sir|39|33|All the works of the Lord are good: and he will give every needful thing in due season.

Sir|39|34|So that a man cannot say, This is worse than that: for in time they shall all be well approved.

Sir|39|35|And therefore praise ye the Lord with the whole heart and mouth, and bless the name of the Lord.

Sir|40|1|Great travail is created for every man, and an heavy yoke is upon the sons of Adam, from the day that they go out of their mother's womb, till the day that they return to the mother of all things.

Sir|40|2|Their imagination of things to come, and the day of death, [trouble] their thoughts, and [cause] fear of heart;

Sir|40|3|From him that sitteth on a throne of glory, unto him that is humbled in earth and ashes;

Sir|40|4|From him that weareth purple and a crown, unto him that is clothed with a linen frock.

Sir|40|5|Wrath, and envy, trouble, and unquietness, fear of death, and anger, and strife, and in the time of rest upon his bed his night sleep, do change his knowledge.

Sir|40|6|A little or nothing is his rest, and afterward he is in his sleep, as in a day of keeping watch, troubled in the vision of his heart, as if he were escaped out of a battle.

Sir|40|7|When all is safe, he awaketh, and marvelleth that the fear was nothing.

Sir|40|8|[Such things happen] unto all flesh, both man and beast, and that is sevenfold more upon sinners.

Sir|40|9|Death, and bloodshed, strife, and sword, calamities, famine, tribulation, and the scourge;

Sir|40|10|These things are created for the wicked, and for their sakes came the flood.

Sir|40|11|All things that are of the earth shall turn to the earth again: and that which is of the waters doth return into the sea.

Sir|40|12|All bribery and injustice shall be blotted out: but true dealing shall endure for ever.

Sir|40|13|The goods of the unjust shall be dried up like a river, and shall vanish with noise, like a great thunder in rain.
Sir|40|14|While he openeth his hand he shall rejoice: so shall transgressors come to nought.
Sir|40|15|The children of the ungodly shall not bring forth many branches: but are as unclean roots upon a hard rock.
Sir|40|16|The weed growing upon every water and bank of a river shall be pulled up before all grass.
Sir|40|17|Bountifulness is as a most fruitful garden, and mercifulness endureth for ever.
Sir|40|18|To labour, and to be content with that a man hath, is a sweet life: but he that findeth a treasure is above them both.
Sir|40|19|Children and the building of a city continue a man's name: but a blameless wife is counted above them both.
Sir|40|20|Wine and musick rejoice the heart: but the love of wisdom is above them both.
Sir|40|21|The pipe and the psaltery make sweet melody: but a pleasant tongue is above them both.
Sir|40|22|Thine eye desireth favour and beauty: but more than both corn while it is green.
Sir|40|23|A friend and companion never meet amiss: but above both is a wife with her husband.
Sir|40|24|Brethren and help are against time of trouble: but alms shall deliver more than them both.
Sir|40|25|Gold and silver make the foot stand sure: but counsel is esteemed above them both.
Sir|40|26|Riches and strength lift up the heart: but the fear of the Lord is above them both: there is no want in the fear of the Lord, and it needeth not to seek help.
Sir|40|27|The fear of the Lord is a fruitful garden, and covereth him above all glory.
Sir|40|28|My son, lead not a beggar's life; for better it is to die than to beg.
Sir|40|29|The life of him that dependeth on another man's table is not to be counted for a life; for he polluteth himself with other men's meat: but a wise man well nurtured will beware thereof.
Sir|40|30|Begging is sweet in the mouth of the shameless: but in his belly there shall burn a fire.
Sir|41|1|O death, how bitter is the remembrance of thee to a man that liveth at rest in his possessions, unto the man that hath nothing to vex him, and that hath prosperity in all things: yea, unto him that is yet able to receive meat!
Sir|41|2|O death, acceptable is thy sentence unto the needy, and unto him whose strength faileth, that is now in the last age, and is vexed with all things, and to him that despaireth, and hath lost patience!
Sir|41|3|Fear not the sentence of death, remember them that have been before thee, and that come after; for this is the sentence of the Lord over all flesh.
Sir|41|4|And why art thou against the pleasure of the most High? there is no inquisition in the grave, whether thou have lived ten, or an hundred, or a thousand years.
Sir|41|5|The children of sinners are abominable children, and they that are conversant in the dwelling of the ungodly.
Sir|41|6|The inheritance of sinners' children shall perish, and their posterity shall have a perpetual reproach.
Sir|41|7|The children will complain of an ungodly father, because they shall be reproached for his sake.
Sir|41|8|Woe be unto you, ungodly men, which have forsaken the law of the most high אֱלֹהִים! for if ye increase, it shall be to your destruction:
Sir|41|9|And if ye be born, ye shall be born to a curse: and if ye die, a curse shall be your portion.
Sir|41|10|All that are of the earth shall turn to earth again: so the ungodly shall go from a curse to destruction.
Sir|41|11|The mourning of men is about their bodies: but an ill name of sinners shall be blotted out.
Sir|41|12|Have regard to thy name; for that shall continue with thee above a thousand great treasures of gold.
Sir|41|13|A good life hath but few days: but a good name endureth for ever.
Sir|41|14|My children, keep discipline in peace: for wisdom that is hid, and a treasure that is not seen, what profit is in them both?
Sir|41|15|A man that hideth his foolishness is better than a man that hideth his wisdom.
Sir|41|16|Therefore be shamefaced according to my word: for it is not good to retain all shamefacedness; neither is it altogether approved in every thing.
Sir|41|17|Be ashamed of whoredom before father and mother: and of a lie before a prince and a mighty man;
Sir|41|18|Of an offence before a judge and ruler; of iniquity before a congregation and people; of unjust dealing before thy partner and friend;
Sir|41|19|And of theft in regard of the place where thou sojournest, and in regard of the truth of אֱלֹהִים and

his covenant; and to lean with thine elbow upon the meat; and of scorning to give and take;

Sir|41|20|And of silence before them that salute thee; and to look upon an harlot;

Sir|41|21|And to turn away thy face from thy kinsman; or to take away a portion or a gift; or to gaze upon another man's wife.

Sir|41|22|Or to be overbusy with his maid, and come not near her bed; or of upbraiding speeches before friends; and after thou hast given, upbraid not;

Sir|41|23|Or of iterating and speaking again that which thou hast heard; and of revealing of secrets.

Sir|41|24|So shalt thou be truly shamefaced and find favour before all men.

Sir|42|1|Of these things be not thou ashamed, and accept no person to sin thereby:

Sir|42|2|Of the law of the most High, and his covenant; and of judgment to justify the ungodly;

Sir|42|3|Of reckoning with thy partners and travellers; or of the gift of the heritage of friends;

Sir|42|4|Of exactness of balance and weights; or of getting much or little;

Sir|42|5|And of merchants' indifferent selling; of much correction of children; and to make the side of an evil servant to bleed.

Sir|42|6|Sure keeping is good, where an evil wife is; and shut up, where many hands are.

Sir|42|7|Deliver all things in number and weight; and put all in writing that thou givest out, or receivest in.

Sir|42|8|Be not ashamed to inform the unwise and foolish, and the extreme aged that contendeth with those that are young: thus shalt thou be truly learned, and approved of all men living.

Sir|42|9|The father waketh for the daughter, when no man knoweth; and the care for her taketh away sleep: when she is young, lest she pass away the flower of her age; and being married, lest she should be hated:

Sir|42|10|In her virginity, lest she should be defiled and gotten with child in her father's house; and having an husband, lest she should misbehave herself; and when she is married, lest she should be barren.

Sir|42|11|Keep a sure watch over a shameless daughter, lest she make thee a laughingstock to thine enemies, and a byword in the city, and a reproach among the people, and make thee ashamed before the multitude.

Sir|42|12|Behold not every body's beauty, and sit not in the midst of women.

Sir|42|13|For from garments cometh a moth, and from women wickedness.

Sir|42|14|Better is the churlishness of a man than a courteous woman, a woman, I say, which bringeth shame and reproach.

Sir|42|15|I will now remember the works of the Lord, and declare the things that I have seen: In the words of the Lord are his works.

Sir|42|16|The sun that giveth light looketh upon all things, and the work thereof is full of the glory of the Lord.

Sir|42|17|The Lord hath not given power to the saints to declare all his marvellous works, which the Almighty Lord firmly settled, that whatsoever is might be established for his glory.

Sir|42|18|He seeketh out the deep, and the heart, and considereth their crafty devices: for the Lord knoweth all that may be known, and he beholdeth the signs of the world.

Sir|42|19|He declareth the things that are past, and for to come, and revealeth the steps of hidden things.

Sir|42|20|No thought escapeth him, neither any word is hidden from him.

Sir|42|21|He hath garnished the excellent works of his wisdom, and he is from everlasting to everlasting: unto him may nothing be added, neither can he be diminished, and he hath no need of any counsellor.

Sir|42|22|Oh how desirable are all his works! and that a man may see even to a spark.

Sir|42|23|All these things live and remain for ever for all uses, and they are all obedient.

Sir|42|24|All things are double one against another: and he hath made nothing imperfect.

Sir|42|25|One thing establisheth the good or another: and who shall be filled with beholding his glory?

Sir|43|1|The pride of the height, the clear firmament, the beauty of heaven, with his glorious shew;

Sir|43|2|The sun when it appeareth, declaring at his rising a marvellous instrument, the work of the most High:

Sir|43|3|At noon it parcheth the country, and who can abide the burning heat thereof?

Sir|43|4|A man blowing a furnace is in works of heat, but the sun burneth the mountains three times more; breathing out fiery vapours, and sending forth bright beams, it dimmeth the eyes.

Sir|43|5|Great is the Lord that made it; and at his commandment runneth hastily.

Sir|43|6|He made the moon also to serve in her season for a declaration of times, and a sign of the world.

Sir|43|7|From the moon is the sign of feasts, a light that decreaseth in her perfection.

Sir|43|8|The month is called after her name, increasing wonderfully in her changing, being an instrument of the armies above, shining in the firmament of heaven;

Sir|43|9|The beauty of heaven, the glory of the stars, an ornament giving light in the highest places of the Lord.

Sir|43|10|At the commandment of the Holy One they will stand in their order, and never faint in their watches.

Sir|43|11|Look upon the rainbow, and praise him that made it; very beautiful it is in the brightness thereof.

Sir|43|12|It compasseth the heaven about with a glorious circle, and the hands of the most High have bended it.

Sir|43|13|By his commandment he maketh the snow to fall aplace, and sendeth swiftly the lightnings of his judgment.

Sir|43|14|Through this the treasures are opened: and clouds fly forth as fowls.

Sir|43|15|By his great power he maketh the clouds firm, and the hailstones are broken small.

Sir|43|16|At his sight the mountains are shaken, and at his will the south wind bloweth.

Sir|43|17|The noise of the thunder maketh the earth to tremble: so doth the northern storm and the whirlwind: as birds flying he scattereth the snow, and the falling down thereof is as the lighting of grasshoppers:

Sir|43|18|The eye marvelleth at the beauty of the whiteness thereof, and the heart is astonished at the raining of it.

Sir|43|19|The hoarfrost also as salt he poureth on the earth, and being congealed, it lieth on the top of sharp stakes.

Sir|43|20|When the cold north wind bloweth, and the water is congealed into ice, it abideth upon every gathering together of water, and clotheth the water as with a breastplate.

Sir|43|21|It devoureth the mountains, and burneth the wilderness, and consumeth the grass as fire.

Sir|43|22|A present remedy of all is a mist coming speedily, a dew coming after heat refresheth.

Sir|43|23|By his counsel he appeaseth the deep, and planteth islands therein.

Sir|43|24|They that sail on the sea tell of the danger thereof; and when we hear it with our ears, we marvel thereat.

Sir|43|25|For therein be strange and wondrous works, variety of all kinds of beasts and whales created.

Sir|43|26|By him the end of them hath prosperous success, and by his word all things consist.

Sir|43|27|We may speak much, and yet come short: wherefore in sum, he is all.

Sir|43|28|How shall we be able to magnify him? for he is great above all his works.

Sir|43|29|The Lord is terrible and very great, and marvellous is his power.

Sir|43|30|When ye glorify the Lord, exalt him as much as ye can; for even yet will he far exceed: and when ye exalt him, put forth all your strength, and be not weary; for ye can never go far enough.

Sir|43|31|Who hath seen him, that he might tell us? and who can magnify him as he is?

Sir|43|32|There are yet hid greater things than these be, for we have seen but a few of his works.

Sir|43|33|For the Lord hath made all things; and to the godly hath he given wisdom.

Sir|44|1|Let us now praise famous men, and our fathers that begat us.

Sir|44|2|The Lord hath wrought great glory by them through his great power from the beginning.

Sir|44|3|Such as did bear rule in their kingdoms, men renowned for their power, giving counsel by their understanding, and declaring prophecies:

Sir|44|4|Leaders of the people by their counsels, and by their knowledge of learning meet for the people, wise and eloquent are their instructions:

Sir|44|5|Such as found out musical tunes, and recited verses in writing:

Sir|44|6|Rich men furnished with ability, living peaceably in their habitations:

Sir|44|7|All these were honoured in their generations, and were the glory of their times.

Sir|44|8|There be of them, that have left a name behind them, that their praises might be reported.

Sir|44|9|And some there be, which have no memorial; who are perished, as though they had never been; and are become as though they had never been born; and their children after them.

Sir|44|10|But these were merciful men, whose righteousness hath not been forgotten.

Sir|44|11|With their seed shall continually remain a good inheritance, and their children are within the covenant.

Sir|44|12|Their seed standeth fast, and their children for their sakes.

Sir|44|13|Their seed shall remain for ever, and their glory shall not be blotted out.

Sir|44|14|Their bodies are buried in peace; but their name liveth for evermore.

Sir|44|15|The people will tell of their wisdom, and the congregation will shew forth their praise.

Sir|44|16|Enoch pleased the Lord, and was translated, being an example of repentance to all generations.

Sir|44|17|Noah was found perfect and righteous; in the time of wrath he was taken in exchange [for the world;] therefore was he left as a remnant unto the earth, when the flood came.

Sir|44|18|An everlasting covenant was made with him, that all flesh should perish no more by the flood.

Sir|44|19|Abraham was a great father of many people: in glory was there none like unto him;

Sir|44|20|Who kept the law of the most High, and was in covenant with him: he established the covenant in his flesh; and when he was proved, he was found faithful.

Sir|44|21|Therefore he assured him by an oath, that he would bless the nations in his seed, and that he would multiply him as the dust of the earth, and exalt his seed as the stars, and cause them to inherit from sea to sea, and from the river unto the utmost part of the land.

Sir|44|22|With Isaac did he establish likewise [for Abraham his father's sake] the blessing of all men, and the covenant, And made it rest upon the head of Jacob. He acknowledged him in his blessing, and gave him an heritage, and divided his portions; among the twelve tribes did he part them.

Sir|45|1|And he brought out of him a merciful man, which found favour in the sight of all flesh, even Moses, beloved of אֱלֹהִים and men, whose memorial is blessed.

Sir|45|2|He made him like to the glorious saints, and magnified him, so that his enemies stood in fear of him.

Sir|45|3|By his words he caused the wonders to cease, and he made him glorious in the sight of kings, and gave him a commandment for his people, and shewed him part of his glory.

Sir|45|4|He sanctified him in his faithfuless and meekness, and chose him out of all men.

Sir|45|5|He made him to hear his voice, and brought him into the dark cloud, and gave him commandments before his face, even the law of life and knowledge, that he might teach Jacob his covenants, and Israel his judgments.

Sir|45|6|He exalted Aaron, an holy man like unto him, even his brother, of the tribe of Levi.

Sir|45|7|An everlasting covenant he made with him and gave him the priesthood among the people; he beautified him with comely ornaments, and clothed him with a robe of glory.

Sir|45|8|He put upon him perfect glory; and strengthened him with rich garments, with breeches, with a long robe, and the ephod.

Sir|45|9|And he compassed him with pomegranates, and with many golden bells round about, that as he went there might be a sound, and a noise made that might be heard in the temple, for a memorial to the children of his people;

Sir|45|10|With an holy garment, with gold, and blue silk, and purple, the work of the embroidere, with a breastplate of judgment, and with Urim and Thummim;

Sir|45|11|With twisted scarlet, the work of the cunning workman, with precious stones graven like seals, and set in gold, the work of the jeweller, with a writing engraved for a memorial, after the number of the tribes of Israel.

Sir|45|12|He set a crown of gold upon the mitre, wherein was engraved Holiness, an ornament of honour, a costly work, the desires of the eyes, goodly and beautiful.

Sir|45|13|Before him there were none such, neither did ever any stranger put them on, but only his children and his children's children perpetually.

Sir|45|14|Their sacrifices shall be wholly consumed every day twice continually.

Sir|45|15|Moses consecrated him, and anointed him with holy oil: this was appointed unto him by an everlasting covenant, and to his seed, so long as the heavens should remain, that they should minister unto him, and execute the office of the priesthood, and bless the people in his name.

Sir|45|16|He chose him out of all men living to offer sacrifices to the Lord, incense, and a sweet savour, for a memorial, to make reconciliation for his people.

Sir|45|17|He gave unto him his commandments, and authority in the statutes of judgments, that he should teach Jacob the testimonies, and inform Israel in his laws.

Sir|45|18|Strangers conspired together against him, and maligned him in the wilderness, even the men that were of Dathan's and Abiron's side, and the congregation of Core, with fury and wrath.

Sir|45|19|This the Lord saw, and it displeased him, and in his wrathful indignation were they consumed: he did wonders upon them, to consume them with the fiery flame.

Sir|45|20|But he made Aaron more honourable, and gave him an heritage, and divided unto him the firstfruits of the increase; especially he prepared bread in abundance:

Sir|45|21|For they eat of the sacrifices of the Lord, which he gave unto him and his seed.

Sir|45|22|Howbeit in the land of the people he had no inheritance, neither had he any portion among the people: for the Lord himself is his portion and inheritance.

Sir|45|23|The third in glory is Phinees the son of Eleazar, because he had zeal in the fear of the Lord, and stood up with good courage of heart: when the people were turned back, and made reconciliation for Israel.
Sir|45|24|Therefore was there a covenant of peace made with him, that he should be the chief of the sanctuary and of his people, and that he and his posterity should have the dignity of the priesthood for ever:
Sir|45|25|According to the covenant made with David son of Jesse, of the tribe of Juda, that the inheritance of the king should be to his posterity alone: so the inheritance of Aaron should also be unto his seed.
Sir|45|26|אֱלֹהִים give you wisdom in your heart to judge his people in righteousness, that their good things be not abolished, and that their glory may endure for ever.
Sir|46|1|Yashiyah the son a Nave was valiant in the wars, and was the successor of Moses in prophecies, who according to his name was made great for the saving of the elect of אֱלֹהִים, and taking vengeance of the enemies that rose up against them, that he might set Israel in their inheritance.
Sir|46|2|How great glory gat he, when he did lift up his hands, and stretched out his sword against the cities!
Sir|46|3|Who before him so stood to it? for the Lord himself brought his enemies unto him.
Sir|46|4|Did not the sun go back by his means? and was not one day as long as two?
Sir|46|5|He called upon the most high Lord, when the enemies pressed upon him on every side; and the great Lord heard him.
Sir|46|6|And with hailstones of mighty power he made the battle to fall violently upon the nations, and in the descent [of Beth-horon] he destroyed them that resisted, that the nations might know all their strength, because he fought in the sight of the Lord, and he followed the Mighty One.
Sir|46|7|In the time of Moses also he did a work of mercy, he and Caleb the son of Jephunne, in that they withstood the congregation, and withheld the people from sin, and appeased the wicked murmuring.
Sir|46|8|And of six hundred thousand people on foot, they two were preserved to bring them in to the heritage, even unto the land that floweth with milk and honey.
Sir|46|9|The Lord gave strength also unto Caleb, which remained with him unto his old age: so that he entered upon the high places of the land, and his seed obtained it for an heritage:
Sir|46|10|That all the children of Israel might see that it is good to follow the Lord.
Sir|46|11|And concerning the judges, every one by name, whose heart went not a whoring, nor departed from the Lord, let their memory be blessed.
Sir|46|12|Let their bones flourish out of their place, and let the name of them that were honoured be continued upon their children.
Sir|46|13|Samuel, the prophet of the Lord, beloved of his Lord, established a kingdom, and anointed princes over his people.
Sir|46|14|By the law of the Lord he judged the congregation, and the Lord had respect unto Jacob.
Sir|46|15|By his faithfulness he was found a true prophet, and by his word he was known to be faithful in vision.
Sir|46|16|He called upon the mighty Lord, when his enemies pressed upon him on every side, when he offered the sucking lamb.
Sir|46|17|And the Lord thundered from heaven, and with a great noise made his voice to be heard.
Sir|46|18|And he destroyed the rulers of the Tyrians, and all the princes cf the Philistines.
Sir|46|19|And before his long sleep he made protestations in the sight of the Lord and his anointed, I have not taken any man's goods, so much as a shoe: and no man did accuse him.
Sir|46|20|And after his death he prophesied, and shewed the king his end, and lifted up his voice from the earth in prophecy, to blot out the wickedness of the people.
Sir|47|1|And after him rose up Nathan to prophesy in the time of David.
Sir|47|2|As is the fat taken away from the peace offering, so was David chosen out of the children of Israel.
Sir|47|3|He played with lions as with kids, and with bears as with lambs.
Sir|47|4|Slew he not a giant, when he was yet but young? and did he not take away reproach from the people, when he lifted up his hand with the stone in the sling, and beat down the boasting of Goliath?
Sir|47|5|For he called upon the most high Lord; and he gave him strength in his right hand to slay that mighty warrior, and set up the horn of his people.
Sir|47|6|So the people honoured him with ten thousands, and praised him in the blessings of the Lord, in that he gave him a crown of glory.
Sir|47|7|For he destroyed the enemies on every side, and brought to nought the Philistines his adversaries, and brake their horn in sunder unto this day.
Sir|47|8|In all his works he praised the Holy One most high with words of glory; with his whole heart he

sung songs, and loved him that made him.

Sir|47|9|He set singers also before the altar, that by their voices they might make sweet melody, and daily sing praises in their songs.

Sir|47|10|He beautified their feasts, and set in order the solemn times until the end, that they might praise his holy name, and that the temple might sound from morning.

Sir|47|11|The Lord took away his sins, and exalted his horn for ever: he gave him a covenant of kings, and a throne of glory in Israel.

Sir|47|12|After him rose up a wise son, and for his sake he dwelt at large.

Sir|47|13|Solomon reigned in a peaceable time, and was honoured; for אֱלֹהִים made all quiet round about him, that he might build an house in his name, and prepare his sanctuary for ever.

Sir|47|14|How wise wast thou in thy youth and, as a flood, filled with understanding!

Sir|47|15|Thy soul covered the whole earth, and thou filledst it with dark parables.

Sir|47|16|Thy name went far unto the islands; and for thy peace thou wast beloved.

Sir|47|17|The countries marvelled at thee for thy songs, and proverbs, and parables, and interpretations.

Sir|47|18|By the name of the Lord אֱלֹהִים, which is called the Lord אֱלֹהִים of Israel, thou didst gather gold as tin and didst multiply silver as lead.

Sir|47|19|Thou didst bow thy loins unto women, and by thy body thou wast brought into subjection.

Sir|47|20|Thou didst stain thy honour, and pollute thy seed: so that thou broughtest wrath upon thy children, and wast grieved for thy folly.

Sir|47|21|So the kingdom was divided, and out of Ephraim ruled a rebellious kingdom.

Sir|47|22|But the Lord will never leave off his mercy, neither shall any of his works perish, neither will he abolish the posterity of his elect, and the seed of him that loveth him he will not take away: wherefore he gave a remnant unto Jacob, and out of him a root unto David.

Sir|47|23|Thus rested Solomon with his fathers, and of his seed he left behind him Roboam, even the foolishness of the people, and one that had no understanding, who turned away the people through his counsel. There was also Jeroboam the son of Nebat, who caused Israel to sin, and shewed Ephraim the way of sin:

Sir|47|24|And their sins were multiplied exceedingly, that they were driven out of the land.

Sir|47|25|For they sought out all wickedness, till the vengeance came upon them.

Sir|48|1|Then stood up Elias the prophet as fire, and his word burned like a lamp.

Sir|48|2|He brought a sore famine upon them, and by his zeal he diminished their number.

Sir|48|3|By the word of the Lord he shut up the heaven, and also three times brought down fire.

Sir|48|4|O Elias, how wast thou honoured in thy wondrous deeds! and who may glory like unto thee!

Sir|48|5|Who didst raise up a dead man from death, and his soul from the place of the dead, by the word of the most High:

Sir|48|6|Who broughtest kings to destruction, and honorable men from their bed:

Sir|48|7|Who heardest the rebuke of the Lord in Sinai, and in Horeb the judgment of vengeance:

Sir|48|8|Who annointedst kings to take revenge, and prophets to succeed after him:

Sir|48|9|Who was taken up in a whirlwind of fire, and in a chariot of fiery horses:

Sir|48|10|Who wast ordained for reproofs in their times, to pacify the wrath of the Lord's judgment, before it brake forth into fury, and to turn the heart of the father unto the son, and to restore the tribes of Jacob.

Sir|48|11|Blessed are they that saw thee, and slept in love; for we shall surely live.

Sir|48|12|Elias it was, who was covered with a whirlwind: and Eliseus was filled with his spirit: whilst he lived, he was not moved with the presence of any prince, neither could any bring him into subjection.

Sir|48|13|No word could overcome him; and after his death his body prophesied.

Sir|48|14|He did wonders in his life, and at his death were his works marvellous.

Sir|48|15|For all this the people repented not, neither departed they from their sins, till they were spoiled and carried out of their land, and were scattered through all the earth: yet there remained a small people, and a ruler in the house of David:

Sir|48|16|Of whom some did that which was pleasing to אֱלֹהִים, and some multiplied sins.

Sir|48|17|Ezekias fortified his city, and brought in water into the midst thereof: he digged the hard rock with iron, and made wells for waters.

Sir|48|18|In his time Sennacherib came up, and sent Rabsaces, and lifted up his hand against Sion, and boasted proudly.

Sir|48|19|Then trembled their hearts and hands, and they were in pain, as women in travail.

Sir|48|20|But they called upon the Lord which is merciful, and stretched out their hands toward him: and immediately the Holy One heard them out of heaven, and delivered them by the ministry of Esay.

Sir|48|21|He smote the host of the Assyrians, and his angel destroyed them.

Sir|48|22|For Ezekias had done the thing that pleased the Lord, and was strong in the ways of David his father, as Esay the prophet, who was great and faithful in his vision, had commanded him.

Sir|48|23|In his time the sun went backward, and he lengthened the king's life.

Sir|48|24|He saw by an excellent spirit what should come to pass at the last, and he comforted them that mourned in Sion.

Sir|48|25|He shewed what should come to pass for ever, and secret things or ever they came.

Sir|49|1|The remembrance of Josias is like the composition of the perfume that is made by the art of the apothecary: it is sweet as honey in all mouths, and as musick at a banquet of wine.

Sir|49|2|He behaved himself uprightly in the conversion of the people, and took away the abominations of iniquity.

Sir|49|3|He directed his heart unto the Lord, and in the time of the ungodly he established the worship of אֱלֹהִים.

Sir|49|4|All, except David and Ezekias and Josias, were defective: for they forsook the law of the most High, even the kings of Juda failed.

Sir|49|5|Therefore he gave their power unto others, and their glory to a strange nation.

Sir|49|6|They burnt the chosen city of the sanctuary, and made the streets desolate, according to the prophecy of Jeremias.

Sir|49|7|For they entreated him evil, who nevertheless was a prophet, sanctified in his mother's womb, that he might root out, and afflict, and destroy; and that he might build up also, and plant.

Sir|49|8|It was Ezekiel who saw the glorious vision, which was shewed him upon the chariot of the cherubims.

Sir|49|9|For he made mention of the enemies under the figure of the rain, and directed them that went right.

Sir|49|10|And of the twelve prophets let the memorial be blessed, and let their bones flourish again out of their place: for they comforted Jacob, and delivered them by assured hope.

Sir|49|11|How shall we magnify Zorobabel? even he was as a signet on the right hand:

Sir|49|12|So was Yashiyah the son of Josedec: who in their time built the house, and set up an holy temple to the Lord, which was prepared for everlasting glory.

Sir|49|13|And among the elect was Neemias, whose renown is great, who raised up for us the walls that were fallen, and set up the gates and the bars, and raised up our ruins again.

Sir|49|14|But upon the earth was no man created like Enoch; for he was taken from the earth.

Sir|49|15|Neither was there a young man born like Joseph, a governor of his brethren, a stay of the people, whose bones were regarded of the Lord.

Sir|49|16|Sem and Seth were in great honour among men, and so was Adam above every living thing in creation.

Sir|50|1|Simon the high priest, the son of Onias, who in his life repaired the house again, and in his days fortified the temple:

Sir|50|2|And by him was built from the foundation the double height, the high fortress of the wall about the temple:

Sir|50|3|In his days the cistern to receive water, being in compass as the sea, was covered with plates of brass:

Sir|50|4|He took care of the temple that it should not fall, and fortified the city against besieging:

Sir|50|5|How was he honoured in the midst of the people in his coming out of the sanctuary!

Sir|50|6|He was as the morning star in the midst of a cloud, and as the moon at the full:

Sir|50|7|As the sun shining upon the temple of the most High, and as the rainbow giving light in the bright clouds:

Sir|50|8|And as the flower of roses in the spring of the year, as lilies by the rivers of waters, and as the branches of the frankincense tree in the time of summer:

Sir|50|9|As fire and incense in the censer, and as a vessel of beaten gold set with all manner of precious stones:

Sir|50|10|And as a fair olive tree budding forth fruit, and as a cypress tree which groweth up to the clouds.

Sir|50|11|When he put on the robe of honour, and was clothed with the perfection of glory, when he went up to the holy altar, he made the garment of holiness honourable.

Sir|50|12|When he took the portions out of the priests' hands, he himself stood by the hearth of the altar, compassed about, as a young cedar in Libanus; and as palm trees compassed they him round about.

Sir|50|13|So were all the sons of Aaron in their glory, and the oblations of the Lord in their hands, before all the congregation of Israel.

Sir|50|14|And finishing the service at the altar, that he might adorn the offering of the most high Almighty,

Sir|50|15|He stretched out his hand to the cup, and poured of the blood of the grape, he poured out at the foot of the altar a sweetsmelling savour unto the most high King of all.

Sir|50|16|Then shouted the sons of Aaron, and sounded the silver trumpets, and made a great noise to be heard, for a remembrance before the most High.

Sir|50|17|Then all the people together hasted, and fell down to the earth upon their faces to worship their Lord אֱלֹהִים Almighty, the most High.

Sir|50|18|The singers also sang praises with their voices, with great variety of sounds was there made sweet melody.

Sir|50|19|And the people besought the Lord, the most High, by prayer before him that is merciful, till the solemnity of the Lord was ended, and they had finished his service.

Sir|50|20|Then he went down, and lifted up his hands over the whole congregation of the children of Israel, to give the blessing of the Lord with his lips, and to rejoice in his name.

Sir|50|21|And they bowed themselves down to worship the second time, that they might receive a blessing from the most High.

Sir|50|22|Now therefore bless ye the אֱלֹהִים of all, which only doeth wondrous things every where, which exalteth our days from the womb, and dealeth with us according to his mercy.

Sir|50|23|He grant us joyfulness of heart, and that peace may be in our days in Israel for ever:

Sir|50|24|That he would confirm his mercy with us, and deliver us at his time!

Sir|50|25|There be two manner of nations which my heart abhorreth, and the third is no nation:

Sir|50|26|They that sit upon the mountain of Samaria, and they that dwell among the Philistines, and that foolish people that dwell in Sichem.

Sir|50|27|Yashiyah the son of Sirach of Jerusalem hath written in this book the instruction of understanding and knowledge, who out of his heart poured forth wisdom.

Sir|50|28|Blessed is he that shall be exercised in these things; and he that layeth them up in his heart shall become wise.

Sir|50|29|For if he do them, he shall be strong to all things: for the light of the Lord leadeth him, who giveth wisdom to the godly. Blessed be the name of the Lord for ever. Amen, Amen.

Sir|51|1|[A Prayer of Yashiyah the son of Sirach.] I will thank thee, O Lord and King, and praise thee, O אֱלֹהִים my Saviour: I do give praise unto thy name:

Sir|51|2|For thou art my defender and helper, and has preserved my body from destruction, and from the snare of the slanderous tongue, and from the lips that forge lies, and has been mine helper against mine adversaries:

Sir|51|3|And hast delivered me, according to the multitude of they mercies and greatness of thy name, from the teeth of them that were ready to devour me, and out of the hands of such as sought after my life, and from the manifold afflictions which I had;

Sir|51|4|From the choking of fire on every side, and from the midst of the fire which I kindled not;

Sir|51|5|From the depth of the belly of hell, from an unclean tongue, and from lying words.

Sir|51|6|By an accusation to the king from an unrighteous tongue my soul drew near even unto death, my life was near to the hell beneath.

Sir|51|7|They compassed me on every side, and there was no man to help me: I looked for the succour of men, but there was none.

Sir|51|8|Then thought I upon thy mercy, O Lord, and upon thy acts of old, how thou deliverest such as wait for thee, and savest them out of the hands of the enemies.

Sir|51|9|Then lifted I up my supplications from the earth, and prayed for deliverance from death.

Sir|51|10|I called upon the Lord, the Father of my Lord, that he would not leave me in the days of my trouble, and in the time of the proud, when there was no help.

Sir|51|11|I will praise thy name continually, and will sing praises with thanksgiving; and so my prayer was heard:

Sir|51|12|For thou savedst me from destruction, and deliveredst me from the evil time: therefore will I give thanks, and praise thee, and bless they name, O Lord.

Sir|51|13|When I was yet young, or ever I went abroad, I desired wisdom openly in my prayer.

Sir|51|14|I prayed for her before the temple, and will seek her out even to the end.

Sir|51|15|Even from the flower till the grape was ripe hath my heart delighted in her: my foot went the right way, from my youth up sought I after her.

Sir|51|16|I bowed down mine ear a little, and received her, and gat much learning.

Sir|51|17|I profited therein, therefore will I ascribe glory unto him that giveth me wisdom.

Sir|51|18|For I purposed to do after her, and earnestly I followed that which is good; so shall I not be confounded.

Sir|51|19|My soul hath wrestled with her, and in my doings I was exact: I stretched forth my hands to the heaven above, and bewailed my ignorances of her.

Sir|51|20|I directed my soul unto her, and I found her in pureness: I have had my heart joined with her from the beginning, therefore shall I not be foresaken.

Sir|51|21|My heart was troubled in seeking her: therefore have I gotten a good possession.

Sir|51|22|The Lord hath given me a tongue for my reward, and I will praise him therewith.

Sir|51|23|Draw near unto me, ye unlearned, and dwell in the house of learning.

Sir|51|24|Wherefore are ye slow, and what say ye to these things, seeing your souls are very thirsty?

Sir|51|25|I opened my mouth, and said, Buy her for yourselves without money.

Sir|51|26|Put your neck under the yoke, and let your soul receive instruction: she is hard at hand to find.

Sir|51|27|Behold with your eyes, how that I have but little labour, and have gotten unto me much rest.

Sir|51|28|Get learning with a great sum of money, and get much gold by her.

Sir|51|29|Let your soul rejoice in his mercy, and be not ashamed of his praise.

Sir|51|30|Work your work betimes, and in his time he will give you your reward.

Bar|1|1|And these are the words of the book, which Baruch the son of Nerias, the son of Maasias, the son of Sedecias, the son of Asadias, the son of Chelcias, wrote in Babylon,

Bar|1|2|In the fifth year, and in the seventh day of the month, what time as the Chaldeans took Jerusalem, and burnt it with fire.

Bar|1|3|And Baruch did read the words of this book in the hearing of Jechonias the son of Joachim king of Juda, and in the ears of all the people that came to hear the book,

Bar|1|4|And in the hearing of the nobles, and of the king's sons, and in the hearing of the elders, and of all the people, from the lowest unto the highest, even of all them that dwelt at Babylon by the river Sud.

Bar|1|5|Whereupon they wept, fasted, and prayed before the Lord.

Bar|1|6|They made also a collection of money according to every man's power:

Bar|1|7|And they sent it to Jerusalem unto Joachim the high priest, the son of Chelcias, son of Salom, and to the priests, and to all the people which were found with him at Jerusalem,

Bar|1|8|At the same time when he received the vessels of the house of the Lord, that were carried out of the temple, to return them into the land of Juda, the tenth day of the month Sivan, namely, silver vessels, which Sedecias the son of Josias king of Jada had made,

Bar|1|9|After that Nabuchodonosor king of Babylon had carried away Jechonias, and the princes, and the captives, and the mighty men, and the people of the land, from Jerusalem, and brought them unto Babylon.

Bar|1|10|And they said, Behold, we have sent you money to buy you burnt offerings, and sin offerings, and incense, and prepare ye manna, and offer upon the altar of the Lord our אֱלֹהִים;

Bar|1|11|And pray for the life of Nabuchodonosor king of Babylon, and for the life of Balthasar his son, that their days may be upon earth as the days of heaven:

Bar|1|12|And the Lord will give us strength, and lighten our eyes, and we shall live under the shadow of Nabuchodonosor king of Babylon, and under the shadow of Balthasar his son, and we shall serve them many days, and find favour in their sight.

Bar|1|13|Pray for us also unto the Lord our אֱלֹהִים, for we have sinned against the Lord our אֱלֹהִים; and unto this day the fury of the Lord and his wrath is not turned from us.

Bar|1|14|And ye shall read this book which we have sent unto you, to make confession in the house of the Lord, upon the feasts and solemn days.

Bar|1|15|And ye shall say, To the Lord our אֱלֹהִים belongeth righteousness, but unto us the confusion of faces, as it is come to pass this day, unto them of Juda, and to the inhabitants of Jerusalem,

Bar|1|16|And to our kings, and to our princes, and to our priests, and to our prophets, and to our fathers:

Bar|1|17|For we have sinned before the Lord,

Bar|1|18|And disobeyed him, and have not hearkened unto the voice of the Lord our אֱלֹהִים, to walk in the commandments that he gave us openly:

Bar|1|19|Since the day that the Lord brought our forefathers out of the land of Egypt, unto this present day, we have been disobedient unto the Lord our אֱלֹהִים, and we have been negligent in not hearing his voice.

Bar|1|20|Wherefore the evils cleaved unto us, and the curse, which the Lord appointed by Moses his servant at the time that he brought our fathers out of the land of Egypt, to give us a land that floweth with milk and honey, like as it is to see this day.

Bar|1|21|Nevertheless we have not hearkened unto the voice of the Lord our אֱלֹהִים, according unto all the words of the prophets, whom he sent unto us:

Bar|1|22|But every man followed the imagination of his own wicked heart, to serve strange gods, and to do evil in the sight of the Lord our אֱלֹהִים.

Bar|2|1|Therefore the Lord hath made good his word, which he pronounced against us, and against our judges that judged Israel, and against our kings, and against our princes, and against the men of Israel and Juda,

Bar|2|2|To bring upon us great plagues, such as never happened under the whole heaven, as it came to pass in Jerusalem, according to the things that were written in the law of Moses;

Bar|2|3|That a man should eat the flesh of his own son, and the flesh of his own daughter.

Bar|2|4|Moreover he hath delivered them to be in subjection to all the kingdoms that are round about us, to be as a reproach and desolation among all the people round about, where the Lord hath scattered them.

Bar|2|5|Thus we were cast down, and not exalted, because we have sinned against the Lord our אֱלֹהִים, and have not been obedient unto his voice.

Bar|2|6|To the Lord our אֱלֹהִים appertaineth righteousness: but unto us and to our fathers open shame, as appeareth this day.

Bar|2|7|For all these plagues are come upon us, which the Lord hath pronounced against us

Bar|2|8|Yet have we not prayed before the Lord, that we might turn every one from the imaginations of his wicked heart.

Bar|2|9|Wherefore the Lord watched over us for evil, and the Lord hath brought it upon us: for the Lord is righteous in all his works which he hath commanded us.

Bar|2|10|Yet we have not hearkened unto his voice, to walk in the commandments of the Lord, that he hath set before us.

Bar|2|11|And now, O Lord אֱלֹהִים of Israel, that hast brought thy people out of the land of Egypt with a mighty hand, and high arm, and with signs, and with wonders, and with great power, and hast gotten thyself a name, as appeareth this day:

Bar|2|12|O Lord our אֱלֹהִים, we have sinned, we have done ungodly, we have dealt unrighteously in all thine ordinances.

Bar|2|13|Let thy wrath turn from us: for we are but a few left among the heathen, where thou hast scattered us.

Bar|2|14|Hear our prayers, O Lord, and our petitions, and deliver us for thine own sake, and give us favour in the sight of them which have led us away:

Bar|2|15|That all the earth may know that thou art the Lord our אֱלֹהִים, because Israel and his posterity is called by thy name.

Bar|2|16|O Lord, look down from thine holy house, and consider us: bow down thine ear, O Lord, to hear us.

Bar|2|17|Open thine eyes, and behold; for the dead that are in the graves, whose souls are taken from their bodies, will give unto the Lord neither praise nor righteousness:

Bar|2|18|But the soul that is greatly vexed, which goeth stooping and feeble, and the eyes that fail, and the hungry soul, will give thee praise and righteousness, O Lord.

Bar|2|19|Therefore we do not make our humble supplication before thee, O Lord our אֱלֹהִים, for the righteousness of our fathers, and of our kings.

Bar|2|20|For thou hast sent out thy wrath and indignation upon us, as thou hast spoken by thy servants the prophets, saying,

Bar|2|21|Thus saith the Lord, Bow down your shoulders to serve the king of Babylon: so shall ye remain in the land that I gave unto your fathers.

Bar|2|22|But if ye will not hear the voice of the Lord, to serve the king of Babylon,

Bar|2|23|I will cause to cease out of the cites of Judah, and from without Jerusalem, the voice of mirth, and the voice of joy, the voice of the bridegroom, and the voice of the bride: and the whole land shall be desolate of inhabitants.

Bar|2|24|But we would not hearken unto thy voice, to serve the king of Babylon: therefore hast thou made good the words that thou spakest by thy servants the prophets, namely, that the bones of our kings, and the bones of our fathers, should be taken out of their place.

Bar|2|25|And, lo, they are cast out to the heat of the day, and to the frost of the night, and they died in great miseries by famine, by sword, and by pestilence.

Bar|2|26|And the house which is called by thy name hast thou laid waste, as it is to be seen this day, for the wickedness of the house of Israel and the house of Juda.

Bar|2|27|O Lord our אֱלֹהִים, thou hast dealt with us after all thy goodness, and according to all that great mercy of thine,

Bar|2|28|As thou spakest by thy servant Moses in the day when thou didst command him to write the law before the children of Israel, saying,

Bar|2|29|If ye will not hear my voice, surely this very great multitude shall be turned into a small number among the nations, where I will scatter them.

Bar|2|30|For I knew that they would not hear me, because it is a stiffnecked people: but in the land of their captivities they shall remember themselves.

Bar|2|31|And shall know that I am the Lord their אֱלֹהִים: for I will give them an heart, and ears to hear:

Bar|2|32|And they shall praise me in the land of their captivity, and think upon my name,

Bar|2|33|And return from their stiff neck, and from their wicked deeds: for they shall remember the way of their fathers, which sinned before the Lord.

Bar|2|34|And I will bring them again into the land which I promised with an oath unto their fathers, Abraham, Isaac, and Jacob, and they shall be lords of it: and I will increase them, and they shall not be diminished.

Bar|2|35|And I will make an everlasting covenant with them to be their אֱלֹהִים, and they shall be my people: and I will no more drive my people of Israel out of the land that I have given them.

Bar|3|1|O Lord Almighty, אֱלֹהִים of Israel, the soul in anguish the troubled spirit, crieth unto thee.

Bar|3|2|Hear, O Lord, and have mercy; ar thou art merciful: and have pity upon us, because we have sinned before thee.

Bar|3|3|For thou endurest for ever, and we perish utterly.

Bar|3|4|O Lord Almighty, thou אֱלֹהִים of Israel, hear now the prayers of the dead Israelites, and of their children, which have sinned before thee, and not hearkened unto the voice of thee their אֱלֹהִים: for the which cause these plagues cleave unto us.

Bar|3|5|Remember not the iniquities of our forefathers: but think upon thy power and thy name now at this time.

Bar|3|6|For thou art the Lord our אֱלֹהִים, and thee, O Lord, will we praise.

Bar|3|7|And for this cause thou hast put thy fear in our hearts, to the intent that we should call upon thy name, and praise thee in our captivity: for we have called to mind all the iniquity of our forefathers, that sinned before thee.

Bar|3|8|Behold, we are yet this day in our captivity, where thou hast scattered us, for a reproach and a curse, and to be subject to payments, according to all the iniquities of our fathers, which departed from the Lord our אֱלֹהִים.

Bar|3|9|Hear, Israel, the commandments of life: give ear to understand wisdom.

Bar|3|10|How happeneth it Israel, that thou art in thine enemies' land, that thou art waxen old in a strange country, that thou art defiled with the dead,

Bar|3|11|That thou art counted with them that go down into the grave?

Bar|3|12|Thou hast forsaken the fountain of wisdom.

Bar|3|13|For if thou hadst walked in the way of אֱלֹהִים, thou shouldest have dwelled in peace for ever.

Bar|3|14|Learn where is wisdom, where is strength, where is understanding; that thou mayest know also where is length of days, and life, where is the light of the eyes, and peace.

Bar|3|15|Who hath found out her place? or who hath come into her treasures ?

Bar|3|16|Where are the princes of the heathen become, and such as ruled the beasts upon the earth;

Bar|3|17|They that had their pastime with the fowls of the air, and they that hoarded up silver and gold, wherein men trust, and made no end of their getting?

Bar|3|18|For they that wrought in silver, and were so careful, and whose works are unsearchable,

Bar|3|19|They are vanished and gone down to the grave, and others are come up in their steads.

Bar|3|20|Young men have seen light, and dwelt upon the earth: but the way of knowledge have they not known,

Bar|3|21|Nor understood the paths thereof, nor laid hold of it: their children were far off from that way.

Bar|3|22|It hath not been heard of in Chanaan, neither hath it been seen in Theman.

Bar|3|23|The Agarenes that seek wisdom upon earth, the merchants of Meran and of Theman, the authors of fables, and searchers out of understanding; none of these have known the way of wisdom, or remember her paths.

Bar|3|24|O Israel, how great is the house of אֱלֹהִים! and how large is the place of his possession!

Bar|3|25|Great, and hath none end; high, and unmeasurable.

Bar|3|26|There were the giants famous from the beginning, that were of so great stature, and so expert in war.

Bar|3|27|Those did not the Lord choose, neither gave he the way of knowledge unto them:

Bar|3|28|But they were destroyed, because they had no wisdom, and perished through their own foolishness.

Bar|3|29|Who hath gone up into heaven, and taken her, and brought her down from the clouds?

Bar|3|30|Who hath gone over the sea, and found her, and will bring her for pure gold?

Bar|3|31|No man knoweth her way, nor thinketh of her path.

Bar|3|32|But he that knoweth all things knoweth her, and hath found her out with his understanding: he that prepared the earth for evermore hath filled it with fourfooted beasts:

Bar|3|33|He that sendeth forth light, and it goeth, calleth it again, and it obeyeth him with fear.

Bar|3|34|The stars shined in their watches, and rejoiced: when he calleth them, they say, Here we be; and so with cheerfulness they shewed light unto him that made them.

Bar|3|35|This is our אֱלֹהִים, and there shall none other be accounted of in comparison of him

Bar|3|36|He hath found out all the way of knowledge, and hath given it unto Jacob his servant, and to Israel his beloved.

Bar|3|37|Afterward did he shew himself upon earth, and conversed with men.

Bar|4|1|This is the book of the commandments of אֱלֹהִים, and the law that endureth for ever: all they that keep it shall come to life; but such as leave it shall die.

Bar|4|2|Turn thee, O Jacob, and take hold of it: walk in the presence of the light thereof, that thou mayest be illuminated.

Bar|4|3|Give not thine honour to another, nor the things that are profitable unto thee to a strange nation.

Bar|4|4|O Israel, happy are we: for things that are pleasing to אֱלֹהִים are made known unto us.

Bar|4|5|Be of good cheer, my people, the memorial of Israel.

Bar|4|6|Ye were sold to the nations, not for [your] destruction: but because ye moved אֱלֹהִים to wrath, ye were delivered unto the enemies.

Bar|4|7|For ye provoked him that made you by sacrificing unto devils, and not to אֱלֹהִים.

Bar|4|8|Ye have forgotten the everlasting אֱלֹהִים, that brought you up; and ye have grieved Jerusalem, that nursed you.

Bar|4|9|For when she saw the wrath of אֱלֹהִים coming upon you, she said, Hearken, O ye that dwell about Sion: אֱלֹהִים hath brought upon me great mourning;

Bar|4|10|For I saw the captivity of my sons and daughters, which the Everlasting brought upon them.

Bar|4|11|With joy did I nourish them; but sent them away with weeping and mourning.

Bar|4|12|Let no man rejoice over me, a widow, and forsaken of many, who for the sins of my children am left desolate; because they departed from the law of אֱלֹהִים.

Bar|4|13|They knew not his statutes, nor walked in the ways of his commandments, nor trod in the paths of discipline in his righteousness.

Bar|4|14|Let them that dwell about Sion come, and remember ye the captivity of my sons and daughters, which the Everlasting hath brought upon them.

Bar|4|15|For he hath brought a nation upon them from far, a shameless nation, and of a strange language, who neither reverenced old man, nor pitied child.

Bar|4|16|These have carried away the dear beloved children of the widow, and left her that was alone desolate without daughters.

Bar|4|17|But what can I help you?

Bar|4|18|For he that brought these plagues upon you will deliver you from the hands of your enemies.

Bar|4|19|Go your way, O my children, go your way: for I am left desolate.

Bar|4|20|I have put off the clothing of peace, and put upon me the sackcloth of my prayer: I will cry unto the Everlasting in my days.

Bar|4|21|Be of good cheer, O my children, cry unto the Lord, and he will deliver you from the power and hand of the enemies.

Bar|4|22|For my hope is in the Everlasting, that he will save you; and joy is come unto me from the Holy One, because of the mercy which shall soon come unto you from the Everlasting our Saviour.

Bar|4|23|For I sent you out with mourning and weeping: but אֱלֹהִים will give you to me again with joy and gladness for ever.

Bar|4|24|Like as now the neighbours of Sion have seen your captivity: so shall they see shortly your salvation from our אֱלֹהִים which shall come upon you with great glory, and brightness of the Everlasting.

Bar|4|25|My children, suffer patiently the wrath that is come upon you from אֱלֹהִים: for thine enemy hath persecuted thee; but shortly thou shalt see his destruction, and shalt tread upon his neck.

Bar|4|26|My delicate ones have gone rough ways, and were taken away as a flock caught of the enemies.

Bar|4|27|Be of good comfort, O my children, and cry unto אֱלֹהִים: for ye shall be remembered of him that brought these things upon you.

Bar|4|28|For as it was your mind to go astray from אֱלֹהִים: so, being returned, seek him ten times more.

Bar|4|29|For he that hath brought these plagues upon you shall bring you everlasting joy with your salvation.

Bar|4|30|Take a good heart, O Jerusalem: for he that gave thee that name will comfort thee.

Bar|4|31|Miserable are they that afflicted thee, and rejoiced at thy fall.

Bar|4|32|Miserable are the cities which thy children served: miserable is she that received thy sons.

Bar|4|33|For as she rejoiced at thy ruin, and was glad of thy fall: so shall she be grieved for her own desolation.

Bar|4|34|For I will take away the rejoicing of her great multitude, and her pride shall be turned into mourning.

Bar|4|35|For fire shall come upon her from the Everlasting, long to endure; and she shall be inhabited of devils for a great time.

Bar|4|36|O Jerusalem, look about thee toward the east, and behold the joy that cometh unto thee from אֱלֹהִים.

Bar|4|37|Lo, thy sons come, whom thou sentest away, they come gathered together from the east to the west by the word of the Holy One, rejoicing in the glory of אֱלֹהִים.

Bar|5|1|Put off, O Jerusalem, the garment of mourning and affliction, and put on the comeliness of the glory that cometh from אֱלֹהִים for ever.

Bar|5|2|Cast about thee a double garment of the righteousness which cometh from אֱלֹהִים; and set a diadem on thine head of the glory of the Everlasting.

Bar|5|3|For אֱלֹהִים will shew thy brightness unto every country under heaven.

Bar|5|4|For thy name shall be called of אֱלֹהִים for ever The peace of righteousness, and The glory of אֱלֹהִים's worship.

Bar|5|5|Arise, O Jerusalem, and stand on high, and look about toward the east, and behold thy children gathered from the west unto the east by the word of the Holy One, rejoicing in the remembrance of אֱלֹהִים.

Bar|5|6|For they departed from thee on foot, and were led away of their enemies: but אֱלֹהִים bringeth them unto thee exalted with glory, as children of the kingdom.

Bar|5|7|For אֱלֹהִים hath appointed that every high hill, and banks of long continuance, should be cast down, and valleys filled up, to make even the ground, that Israel may go safely in the glory of אֱלֹהִים,

Bar|5|8|Moreover even the woods and every sweetsmelling tree shall overshadow Israel by the commandment of אֱלֹהִים.

Bar|5|9|For אֱלֹהִים shall lead Israel with joy in the light of his glory with the mercy and righteousness that cometh from him.

Epj|6|1|A copy of an epistle, which Jeremy sent unto them which were to be led captives into Babylon by the king of the Babylonians, to certify them, as it was commanded him of אֱלֹהִים.

Epj|6|2|Because of the sins which ye have committed before אֱלֹהִים, ye shall be led away captives into Babylon by Nabuchodonosor king of the Babylonians.

Epj|6|3|So when ye be come unto Babylon, ye shall remain there many years, and for a long season, namely, seven generations: and after that I will bring you away peaceably from thence.

Epj|6|4|Now shall ye see in Babylon gods of silver, and of gold, and of wood, borne upon shoulders, which cause the nations to fear.

Epj|6|5|Beware therefore that ye in no wise be like to strangers, neither be ye and of them, when ye see the multitude before them and behind them, worshipping them.

Epj|6|6|But say ye in your hearts, O Lord, we must worship thee.

Epj|6|7|For mine angel is with you, and I myself caring for your souls.

Epj|6|8|As for their tongue, it is polished by the workman, and they themselves are gilded and laid over with silver; yet are they but false, and cannot speak.

Epj|6|9|And taking gold, as it were for a virgin that loveth to go gay, they make crowns for the heads of their gods.

Epj|6|10|Sometimes also the priests convey from their gods gold and silver, and bestow it upon themselves.

Epj|6|11|Yea, they will give thereof to the common harlots, and deck them as men with garments, [being] gods of silver, and gods of gold, and wood.

Epj|6|12|Yet cannot these gods save themselves from rust and moth, though they be covered with purple raiment.

Epj|6|13|They wipe their faces because of the dust of the temple, when there is much upon them.

Epj|6|14|And he that cannot put to death one that offendeth him holdeth a sceptre, as though he were a judge of the country.

Epj|6|15|He hath also in his right hand a dagger and an ax: but cannot deliver himself from war and thieves.

Epj|6|16|Whereby they are known not to be gods: therefore fear them not.

Epj|6|17|For like as a vessel that a man useth is nothing worth when it is broken; even so it is with their gods: when they be set up in the temple, their eyes be full of dust through the feet of them that come in.

Epj|6|18|And as the doors are made sure on every side upon him that offendeth the king, as being committed to suffer death: even so the priests make fast their temples with doors, with locks, and bars, lest their gods be spoiled with robbers.

Epj|6|19|They light them candles, yea, more than for themselves, whereof they cannot see one.

Epj|6|20|They are as one of the beams of the temple, yet they say their hearts are gnawed upon by things creeping out of the earth; and when they eat them and their clothes, they feel it not.

Epj|6|21|Their faces are blacked through the smoke that cometh out of the temple.

Epj|6|22|Upon their bodies and heads sit bats, swallows, and birds, and the cats also.

Epj|6|23|By this ye may know that they are no gods: therefore fear them not.

Epj|6|24|Notwithstanding the gold that is about them to make them beautiful, except they wipe off the rust, they will not shine: for neither when they were molten did they feel it.

Epj|6|25|The things wherein there is no breath are bought for a most high price.

Epj|6|26|They are borne upon shoulders, having no feet whereby they declare unto men that they be nothing worth.

Epj|6|27|They also that serve them are ashamed: for if they fall to the ground at any time, they cannot rise up again of themselves: neither, if one set them upright, can they move of themselves: neither, if they be bowed down, can they make themselves straight: but they set gifts before them as unto dead men.

Epj|6|28|As for the things that are sacrificed unto them, their priests sell and abuse; in like manner their wives lay up part thereof in salt; but unto the poor and impotent they give nothing of it.

Epj|6|29|Menstruous women and women in childbed eat their sacrifices: by these things ye may know that they are no gods: fear them not.

Epj|6|30|For how can they be called gods? because women set meat before the gods of silver, gold, and wood.

Epj|6|31|And the priests sit in their temples, having their clothes rent, and their heads and beards shaven, and nothing upon their heads.

Epj|6|32|They roar and cry before their gods, as men do at the feast when one is dead.

Epj|6|33|The priests also take off their garments, and clothe their wives and children.

Epj|6|34|Whether it be evil that one doeth unto them, or good, they are not able to recompense it: they can neither set up a king, nor put him down.

Epj|6|35|In like manner, they can neither give riches nor money: though a man make a vow unto them, and keep it not, they will not require it.

Epj|6|36|They can save no man from death, neither deliver the weak from the mighty.

Epj|6|37|They cannot restore a blind man to his sight, nor help any man in his distress.

Epj|6|38|They can shew no mercy to the widow, nor do good to the fatherless.

Epj|6|39|Their gods of wood, and which are overlaid with gold and silver, are like the stones that be hewn out of the mountain: they that worship them shall be confounded.

Epj|6|40|How should a man then think and say that they are gods, when even the Chaldeans themselves dishonour them?

Epj|6|41|Who if they shall see one dumb that cannot speak, they bring him, and intreat Bel that he may speak, as though he were able to understand.

Epj|6|42|Yet they cannot understand this themselves, and leave them: for they have no knowledge.

Epj|6|43|The women also with cords about them, sitting in the ways, burn bran for perfume: but if any of them, drawn by some that passeth by, lie with him, she reproacheth her fellow, that she was not thought as worthy as herself, nor her cord broken.

Epj|6|44|Whatsoever is done among them is false: how may it then be thought or said that they are gods?

Epj|6|45|They are made of carpenters and goldsmiths: they can be nothing else than the workmen will have them to be.

Epj|6|46|And they themselves that made them can never continue long; how should then the things that are made of them be gods?

Epj|6|47|For they left lies and reproaches to them that come after.

Epj|6|48|For when there cometh any war or plague upon them, the priests consult with themselves, where they may be hidden with them.

Epj|6|49|How then cannot men perceive that they be no gods, which can neither save themselves from war, nor from plague?

Epj|6|50|For seeing they be but of wood, and overlaid with silver and gold, it shall be known hereafter that they are false:

Epj|6|51|And it shall manifestly appear to all nations and kings that they are no gods, but the works of men's hands, and that there is no work of אֱלֹהִים in them.

Epj|6|52|Who then may not know that they are no gods?

Epj|6|53|For neither can they set up a king in the land, nor give rain unto men.

Epj|6|54|Neither can they judge their own cause, nor redress a wrong, being unable: for they are as crows between heaven and earth.

Epj|6|55|Whereupon when fire falleth upon the house of gods of wood, or laid over with gold or silver, their priests will flee away, and escape; but they themselves shall be burned asunder like beams.

Epj|6|56|Moreover they cannot withstand any king or enemies: how can it then be thought or said that they be gods?

Epj|6|57|Neither are those gods of wood, and laid over with silver or gold, able to escape either from thieves or robbers.

Epj|6|58|Whose gold, and silver, and garments wherewith they are clothed, they that are strong take, and go away withal: neither are they able to help themselves.

Epj|6|59|Therefore it is better to be a king that sheweth his power, or else a profitable vessel in an house, which the owner shall have use of, than such false gods; or to be a door in an house, to keep such things therein, than such false gods. or a pillar of wood in a a palace, than such false gods.

Epj|6|60|For sun, moon, and stars, being bright and sent to do their offices, are obedient.

Epj|6|61|In like manner the lightning when it breaketh forth is easy to be seen; and after the same manner the wind bloweth in every country.

Epj|6|62|And when אֱלֹהִים commandeth the clouds to go over the whole world, they do as they are bidden.

Epj|6|63|And the fire sent from above to consume hills and woods doeth as it is commanded: but these are like unto them neither in shew nor power.

Epj|6|64|Wherefore it is neither to be supposed nor said that they are gods, seeing, they are able neither to judge causes, nor to do good unto men.

Epj|6|65|Knowing therefore that they are no gods, fear them not,

Epj|6|66|For they can neither curse nor bless kings:

Epj|6|67|Neither can they shew signs in the heavens among the heathen, nor shine as the sun, nor give light as the moon.

Epj|6|68|The beasts are better than they: for they can get under a cover and help themselves.

Epj|6|69|It is then by no means manifest unto us that they are gods: therefore fear them not.

Epj|6|70|For as a scarecrow in a garden of cucumbers keepeth nothing: so are their gods of wood, and laid over with silver and gold.

Epj|6|71|And likewise their gods of wood, and laid over with silver and gold, are like to a white thorn in an orchard, that every bird sitteth upon; as also to a dead body, that is east into the dark.

Epj|6|72|And ye shall know them to be no gods by the bright purple that rotteth upon then1: and they themselves afterward shall be eaten, and shall be a reproach in the country.

Epj|6|73|Better therefore is the just man that hath none idols: for he shall be far from reproach.

Sus|1|1|There dwelt a man in Babylon, called Joacim:

Sus|1|2|And he took a wife, whose name was Susanna, the daughter of Chelcias, a very fair woman, and one that feared the Lord.

Sus|1|3|Her parents also were righteous, and taught their daughter according to the law of Moses.

Sus|1|4|Now Joacim was a great rich man, and had a fair garden joining unto his house: and to him resorted the Jews; because he was more honourable than all others.

Sus|1|5|The same year were appointed two of the ancients of the people to be judges, such as the Lord spake of, that wickedness came from Babylon from ancient judges, who seemed to govern the people.

Sus|1|6|These kept much at Joacim's house: and all that had any suits in law came unto them.

Sus|1|7|Now when the people departed away at noon, Susanna went into her husband's garden to walk.

Sus|1|8|And the two elders saw her going in every day, and walking; so that their lust was inflamed toward her.

Sus|1|9|And they perverted their own mind, and turned away their eyes, that they might not look unto heaven, nor remember just judgments.

Sus|1|10|And albeit they both were wounded with her love, yet durst not one shew another his grief.

Sus|1|11|For they were ashamed to declare their lust, that they desired to have to do with her.

Sus|1|12|Yet they watched diligently from day to day to see her.

Sus|1|13|And the one said to the other, Let us now go home: for it is dinner time.

Sus|1|14|So when they were gone out, they parted the one from the other, and turning back again they came to the same place; and after that they had asked one another the cause, they acknowledged their lust: then appointed they a time both together, when they might find her alone.

Sus|1|15|And it fell out, as they watched a fit time, she went in as before with two maids only, and she was desirous to wash herself in the garden: for it was hot.

Sus|1|16|And there was no body there save the two elders, that had hid themselves, and watched her.

Sus|1|17|Then she said to her maids, Bring me oil and washing balls, and shut the garden doors, that I may wash me.

Sus|1|18|And they did as she bade them, and shut the garden doors, and went out themselves at privy doors to fetch the things that she had commanded them: but they saw not the elders, because they were hid.

Sus|1|19|Now when the maids were gone forth, the two elders rose up, and ran unto her, saying,

Sus|1|20|Behold, the garden doors are shut, that no man can see us, and we are in love with thee; therefore consent unto us, and lie with us.

Sus|1|21|If thou wilt not, we will bear witness against thee, that a young man was with thee: and therefore thou didst send away thy maids from thee.

Sus|1|22|Then Susanna sighed, and said, I am straitened on every side: for if I do this thing, it is death unto me: and if I do it not I cannot escape your hands.

Sus|1|23|It is better for me to fall into your hands, and not do it, than to sin in the sight of the Lord.

Sus|1|24|With that Susanna cried with a loud voice: and the two elders cried out against her.

Sus|1|25|Then ran the one, and opened the garden door.

Sus|1|26|So when the servants of the house heard the cry in the garden, they rushed in at the privy door, to see what was done unto her.

Sus|1|27|But when the elders had declared their matter, the servants were greatly ashamed: for there was never such a report made of Susanna.

Sus|1|28|And it came to pass the next day, when the people were assembled to her husband Joacim, the two elders came also full of mischievous imagination against Susanna to put her to death;

Sus|1|29|And said before the people, Send for Susanna, the daughter of Chelcias, Joacim's wife. And so they sent.

Sus|1|30|So she came with her father and mother, her children, and all her kindred.

Sus|1|31|Now Susanna was a very delicate woman, and beauteous to behold.

Sus|1|32|And these wicked men commanded to uncover her face, (for she was covered) that they might be filled with her beauty.

Sus|1|33|Therefore her friends and all that saw her wept.

Sus|1|34|Then the two elders stood up in the midst of the people, and laid their hands upon her head.

Sus|1|35|And she weeping looked up toward heaven: for her heart trusted in the Lord.

Sus|1|36|And the elders said, As we walked in the garden alone, this woman came in with two maids, and shut the garden doors, and sent the maids away.

Sus|1|37|Then a young man, who there was hid, came unto her, and lay with her.

Sus|1|38|Then we that stood in a corner of the garden, seeing this wickedness, ran unto them.

Sus|1|39|And when we saw them together, the man we could not hold: for he was stronger than we, and opened the door, and leaped out.

Sus|1|40|But having taken this woman, we asked who the young man was, but she would not tell us: these things do we testify.

Sus|1|41|Then the assembly believed them as those that were the elders and judges of the people: so they condemned her to death.

Sus|1|42|Then Susanna cried out with a loud voice, and said, O everlasting אֱלֹהִים, that knowest the secrets, and knowest all things before they be:

Sus|1|43|Thou knowest that they have borne false witness against me, and, behold, I must die; whereas I never did such things as these men have maliciously invented against me.

Sus|1|44|And the Lord heard her voice.

Sus|1|45|Therefore when she was led to be put to death, the Lord raised up the holy spirit of a young youth whose name was Daniel:

Sus|1|46|Who cried with a loud voice, I am clear from the blood of this woman.

Sus|1|47|Then all the people turned them toward him, and said, What mean these words that thou hast spoken?

Sus|1|48|So he standing in the midst of them said, Are ye such fools, ye sons of Israel, that without examination or knowledge of the truth ye have condemned a daughter of Israel?

Sus|1|49|Return again to the place of judgment: for they have borne false witness against her.

Sus|1|50|Wherefore all the people turned again in haste, and the elders said unto him, Come, sit down among us, and shew it us, seeing אֱלֹהִים hath given thee the honour of an elder.

Sus|1|51|Then said Daniel unto them, Put these two aside one far from another, and I will examine them.

Sus|1|52|So when they were put asunder one from another, he called one of them, and said unto him, O thou that art waxen old in wickedness, now thy sins which thou hast committed aforetime are come to light.

Sus|1|53|For thou hast pronounced false judgment and hast condemned the innocent and hast let the guilty go free; albeit the Lord saith, The innocent and righteous shalt thou not slay.

Sus|1|54|Now then, if thou hast seen her, tell me, Under what tree sawest thou them companying together? Who answered, Under a mastick tree.

Sus|1|55|And Daniel said, Very well; thou hast lied against thine own head; for even now the angel of אֱלֹהִים hath received the sentence of אֱלֹהִים to cut thee in two.

Sus|1|56|So he put him aside, and commanded to bring the other, and said unto him, O thou seed of Chanaan, and not of Juda, beauty hath deceived thee, and lust hath perverted thine heart.

Sus|1|57|Thus have ye dealt with the daughters of Israel, and they for fear companied with you: but the daughter of Juda would not abide your wickedness.

Sus|1|58|Now therefore tell me, Under what tree didst thou take them companying together? Who answered, Under an holm tree.

Sus|1|59|Then said Daniel unto him, Well; thou hast also lied against thine own head: for the angel of אֱלֹהִים waiteth with the sword to cut thee in two, that he may destroy you.

Sus|1|60|With that all the assembly cried out with a loud voice, and praised אֱלֹהִים, who saveth them that trust in him.

Sus|1|61|And they arose against the two elders, for Daniel had convicted them of false witness by their own mouth:

Sus|1|62|And according to the law of Moses they did unto them in such sort as they maliciously intended to do to their neighbour: and they put them to death. Thus the innocent blood was saved the same day.

Sus|1|63|Therefore Chelcias and his wife praised אֱלֹהִים for their daughter Susanna, with Joacim her husband, and all the kindred, because there was no dishonesty found in her.

Sus|1|64|From that day forth was Daniel had in great reputation in the sight of the people.

Aza|1|1|And they walked in the midst of the fire, praising אֱלֹהִים, and blessing the Lord.

Aza|1|2|Then Azarias stood up, and prayed on this manner; and opening his mouth in the midst of the fire said,

Aza|1|3|Blessed art thou, O Lord אֱלֹהִים of our fathers: thy name is worthy to be praised and glorified for evermore:

Aza|1|4|For thou art righteous in all the things that thou hast done to us: yea, true are all thy works, thy ways are right, and all thy judgments truth.

Aza|1|5|In all the things that thou hast brought upon us, and upon the holy city of our fathers, even Jerusalem, thou hast executed true judgment: for according to truth and judgment didst thou bring all these things upon us because of our sins.

Aza|1|6|For we have sinned and committed iniquity, departing from thee.

Aza|1|7|In all things have we trespassed, and not obeyed thy commandments, nor kept them, neither done as thou hast commanded us, that it might go well with us.

Aza|1|8|Wherefore all that thou hast brought upon us, and every thing that thou hast done to us, thou hast done in true judgment.

Aza|1|9|And thou didst deliver us into the hands of lawless enemies, most hateful forsakers of אֱלֹהִים, and to an unjust king, and the most wicked in all the world.

Aza|1|10|And now we cannot open our mouths, we are become a shame and reproach to thy servants; and to them that worship thee.

Aza|1|11|Yet deliver us not up wholly, for thy name's sake, neither disannul thou thy covenant:

Aza|1|12|And cause not thy mercy to depart from us, for thy beloved Abraham's sake, for thy servant Issac's sake, and for thy holy Israel's sake;

Aza|1|13|To whom thou hast spoken and promised, that thou wouldest multiply their seed as the stars of heaven, and as the sand that lieth upon the seashore.

Aza|1|14|For we, O Lord, are become less than any nation, and be kept under this day in all the world because of our sins.

Aza|1|15|Neither is there at this time prince, or prophet, or leader, or burnt offering, or sacrifice, or oblation, or incense, or place to sacrifice before thee, and to find mercy.

Aza|1|16|Nevertheless in a contrite heart and an humble spirit let us be accepted.

Aza|1|17|Like as in the burnt offerings of rams and bullocks, and like as in ten thousands of fat lambs: so let our sacrifice be in thy sight this day, and grant that we may wholly go after thee: for they shall not be confounded that put their trust in thee.

Aza|1|18|And now we follow thee with all our heart, we fear thee, and seek thy face.

Aza|1|19|Put us not to shame: but deal with us after thy lovingkindness, and according to the multitude of thy mercies.

Aza|1|20|Deliver us also according to thy marvellous works, and give glory to thy name, O Lord: and let all them that do thy servants hurt be ashamed;

Aza|1|21|And let them be confounded in all their power and might, and let their strength be broken;

Aza|1|22|And let them know that thou art אֱלֹהִים, the only אֱלֹהִים, and glorious over the whole world.

Aza|1|23|And the king's servants, that put them in, ceased not to make the oven hot with rosin, pitch, tow, and small wood;

Aza|1|24|So that the flame streamed forth above the furnace forty and nine cubits.

Aza|1|25|And it passed through, and burned those Chaldeans it found about the furnace.

Aza|1|26|But the angel of the Lord came down into the oven together with Azarias and his fellows, and smote the flame of the fire out of the oven;

Aza|1|27|And made the midst of the furnace as it had been a moist whistling wind, so that the fire touched them not at all, neither hurt nor troubled them.

Aza|1|28|Then the three, as out of one mouth, praised, glorified, and blessed, אֱלֹהִים in the furnace, saying,

Aza|1|29|Blessed art thou, O Lord אֱלֹהִים of our fathers: and to be praised and exalted above all for ever.

Aza|1|30|And blessed is thy glorious and holy name: and to be praised and exalted above all for ever.

Aza|1|31|Blessed art thou in the temple of thine holy glory: and to be praised and glorified above all for ever.

Aza|1|32|Blessed art thou that beholdest the depths, and sittest upon the cherubims: and to be praised and exalted above all for ever.

Aza|1|33|Blessed art thou on the glorious throne of thy kingdom: and to be praised and glorified above all for ever.

Aza|1|34|Blessed art thou in the firmament of heaven: and above ail to be praised and glorified for ever.

Aza|1|35|O all ye works of the Lord, bless ye the Lord : praise and exalt him above all for ever,

Aza|1|36|O ye heavens, bless ye the Lord : praise and exalt him above all for ever.

Aza|1|37|O ye angels of the Lord, bless ye the Lord: praise and exalt him above all for ever.

Aza|1|38|O all ye waters that be above the heaven, bless ye the Lord: praise and exalt him above all for ever.

Aza|1|39|O all ye powers of the Lord, bless ye the Lord: praise and exalt him above all for ever.

Aza|1|40|O ye sun and moon, bless ye the Lord: praise and exalt him above all for ever.

Aza|1|41|O ye stars of heaven, bless ye the Lord: praise and exalt him above all for ever.

Aza|1|42|O every shower and dew, bless ye the Lord: praise and exalt him above all for ever.

Aza|1|43|O all ye winds, bless ye the Lord: praise and exalt him above all for ever,

Aza|1|44|O ye fire and heat, bless ye the Lord: praise and exalt him above all for ever.

Aza|1|45|O ye winter and summer, bless ye the Lord: praise and exalt him above all for ever.

Aza|1|46|0 ye dews and storms of snow, bless ye the Lord: praise and exalt him above all for ever.

Aza|1|47|O ye nights and days, bless ye the Lord: bless and exalt him above all for ever.

Aza|1|48|O ye light and darkness, bless ye the Lord: praise and exalt him above all for ever.

Aza|1|49|O ye ice and cold, bless ye the Lord: praise and exalt him above all for ever.

Aza|1|50|O ye frost and snow, bless ye the Lord: praise and exalt him above all for ever.

Aza|1|51|O ye lightnings and clouds, bless ye the Lord: praise and exalt him above all for ever.

Aza|1|52|O let the earth bless the Lord: praise and exalt him above all for ever.

Aza|1|53|O ye mountains and little hills, bless ye the Lord: praise and exalt him above all for ever.

Aza|1|54|O all ye things that grow in the earth, bless ye the Lord: praise and exalt him above all for ever.

Aza|1|55|O ye mountains, bless ye the Lord: Praise and exalt him above all for ever.

Aza|1|56|O ye seas and rivers, bless ye the Lord: praise and exalt him above all for ever.

Aza|1|57|O ye whales, and all that move in the waters, bless ye the Lord: praise and exalt him above all for ever.

Aza|1|58|O all ye fowls of the air, bless ye the Lord: praise and exalt him above all for ever.

Aza|1|59|O all ye beasts and cattle, bless ye the Lord: praise and exalt him above all for ever.

Aza|1|60|O ye children of men, bless ye the Lord: praise and exalt him above all for ever.

Aza|1|61|O Israel, bless ye the Lord: praise and exalt him above all for ever.

Aza|1|62|O ye priests of the Lord, bless ye the Lord: praise and exalt him above all for ever.

Aza|1|63|O ye servants of the Lord, bless ye the Lord: praise and exalt him above all for ever.

Aza|1|64|O ye spirits and souls of the righteous, bless ye the Lord: praise and exalt him above all for ever.

Aza|1|65|O ye holy and humble men of heart, bless ye the Lord: praise and exalt him above all for ever.

Aza|1|66|O Ananias, Azarias, and Misael, bless ye the Lord: praise and exalt him above all for ever: far he hath delivered us from hell, and saved us from the hand of death, and delivered us out of the midst of the furnace and burning flame: even out of the midst of the fire hath he delivered us.

Aza|1|67|O give thanks unto the Lord, because he is gracious: for his mercy endureth for ever.

Aza|1|68|O all ye that worship the Lord, bless the אֱלֹהִים of gods, praise him, and give him thanks: for his mercy endureth for ever.

Man|1|1|O Lord, Almighty אֱלֹהִים of our fathers, Abraham, Isaac, and Jacob, and of their righteous seed; who hast made heaven and earth, with all the ornament thereof; who hast bound the sea by the word of thy commandment; who hast shut up the deep, and sealed it by thy terrible and glorious name; whom all men fear, and tremble before thy power; for the majesty of thy glory cannot be borne, and thine angry threatening toward sinners is importable: but thy merciful promise is unmeasurable and unsearchable; for thou art the most high Lord, of great compassion, longsuffering, very merciful, and repentest of the evils of men. Thou, O Lord, according to thy great goodness hast promised repentance and forgiveness to them that have sinned against thee: and of thine infinite mercies hast appointed repentance unto sinners, that they may be saved. Thou therefore, O Lord, that art the אֱלֹהִים of the just, hast not appointed repentance to the just, as to Abraham, and Isaac, and Jacob, which have not sinned against thee; but thou hast appointed repentance unto me that am a sinner: for I have sinned above the number of the sands of the sea. My transgressions, O Lord, are multiplied: my transgressions are multiplied, and I am not worthy to behold and see the height of heaven for the multitude of mine iniquities. I am bowed down with many iron bands, that I cannot life up mine head, neither have any release: for I have provoked thy wrath, and done evil before thee: I did not thy will, neither kept I thy commandments: I have set up abominations, and have multiplied offences. Now therefore I bow the knee of mine heart, beseeching thee of grace. I have sinned, O Lord, I have sinned, and I acknowledge mine iniquities: wherefore, I humbly beseech thee, forgive me, O Lord, forgive me, and destroy me not with mine iniquites. Be not angry with me for ever, by reserving evil for me; neither condemn me to the lower parts of the earth. For thou art the אֱלֹהִים, even the אֱלֹהִים of them that repent; and in me thou wilt shew all thy goodness: for thou wilt save me, that am unworthy, according to thy great mercy. Therefore I will praise thee for ever all the days of my life: for all the powers of the heavens do praise thee, and thine is the glory for ever and ever. Amen.

Bel|1|1|And king Astyages was gathered to his fathers, and Cyrus of Persia received his kingdom.

Bel|1|2|And Daniel conversed with the king, and was honoured above all his friends.

Bel|1|3|Now the Babylons had an idol, called Bel, and there were spent upon him every day twelve great measures of fine flour, and forty sheep, and six vessels of wine.

Bel|1|4|And the king worshipped it and went daily to adore it: but Daniel worshipped his own אֱלֹהִים. And the king said unto him, Why dost not thou worship Bel?

Bel|1|5|Who answered and said, Because I may not worship idols made with hands, but the living אֱלֹהִים, who hath created the heaven and the earth, and hath sovereignty over all flesh.

Bel|1|6|Then said the king unto him, Thinkest thou not that Bel is a living אֱלֹהִים? seest thou not how much he eateth and drinketh every day?

Bel|1|7|Then Daniel smiled, and said, O king, be not deceived: for this is but clay within, and brass without, and did never eat or drink any thing.

Bel|1|8|So the king was wroth, and called for his priests, and said unto them, If ye tell me not who this is that devoureth these expences, ye shall die.

Bel|1|9|But if ye can certify me that Bel devoureth them, then Daniel shall die: for he hath spoken blasphemy against Bel. And Daniel said unto the king, Let it be according to thy word.

Bel|1|10|Now the priests of Bel were threescore and ten, beside their wives and children. And the king went with Daniel into the temple of Bel.

Bel|1|11|So Bel's priests said, Lo, we go out: but thou, O king, set on the meat, and make ready the wine, and shut the door fast and seal it with thine own signet;

Bel|1|12|And to morrow when thou comest in, if thou findest not that hath eaten up all, we will suffer death, or else Daniel, that speaketh falsely against us.

Bel|1|13|And they little regarded it: for under the table they had made a privy entrance, whereby they entered in continually, and consumed those things.

Bel|1|14|So when they were gone forth, the king set meats before Bel. Now Daniel had commanded his servants to bring ashes, and those they strewed throughout all the temple in the presence of the king alone: then went they out, and shut the door, and sealed it with the king's signet, and so departed.

Bel|1|15|Now in the night came the priests with their wives and children, as they were wont to do, and did eat and drinck up all.

Bel|1|16|In the morning betime the king arose, and Daniel with him.

Bel|1|17|And the king said, Daniel, are the seals whole? And he said, Yea, O king, they be whole.

Bel|1|18|And as soon as he had opened the dour, the king looked upon the table, and cried with a loud voice, Great art thou, O Bel, and with thee is no deceit at all.

Bel|1|19|Then laughed Daniel, and held the king that he should not go in, and said, Behold now the pavement, and mark well whose footsteps are these.

Bel|1|20|And the king said, I see the footsteps of men, women, and children. And then the king was angry,

Bel|1|21|And took the priests with their wives and children, who shewed him the privy doors, where they came in, and consumed such things as were upon the table.

Bel|1|22|Therefore the king slew them, and delivered Bel into Daniel's power, who destroyed him and his temple.

Bel|1|23|And in that same place there was a great dragon, which they of Babylon worshipped.

Bel|1|24|And the king said unto Daniel, Wilt thou also say that this is of brass? lo, he liveth, he eateth and drinketh; thou canst not say that he is no living god: therefore worship him.

Bel|1|25|Then said Daniel unto the king, I will worship the Lord my אֱלֹהִים: for he is the living אֱלֹהִים.

Bel|1|26|But give me leave, O king, and I shall slay this dragon without sword or staff. The king said, I give thee leave.

Bel|1|27|Then Daniel took pitch, and fat, and hair, and did seethe them together, and made lumps thereof: this he put in the dragon's mouth, and so the dragon burst in sunder : and Daniel said, Lo, these are the gods ye worship.

Bel|1|28|When they of Babylon heard that, they took great indignation, and conspired against the king, saying, The king is become a Jew, and he hath destroyed Bel, he hath slain the dragon, and put the priests to death.

Bel|1|29|So they came to the king, and said, Deliver us Daniel, or else we will destroy thee and thine house.

Bel|1|30|Now when the king saw that they pressed him sore, being constrained, he delivered Daniel unto them:

Bel|1|31|Who cast him into the lions' den: where he was six days.

Bel|1|32|And in the den there were seven lions, and they had given them every day two carcases, and two sheep: which then were not given to them, to the intent they might devour Daniel.

Bel|1|33|Now there was in Jewry a prophet, called Habbacuc, who had made pottage, and had broken bread in a bowl, and was going into the field, for to bring it to the reapers.

Bel|1|34|But the angel of the Lord said unto Habbacuc, Go, carry the dinner that thou hast into Babylon unto Daniel, who is in the lions' den.

Bel|1|35|And Habbacuc said, Lord, I never saw Babylon; neither do I know where the den is.

Bel|1|36|Then the angel of the Lord took him by the crown, and bare him by the hair of his head, and through the vehemency of his spirit set him in Babylon over the den.

Bel|1|37|And Habbacuc cried, saying, O Daniel, Daniel, take the dinner which אֱלֹהִים hath sent thee.

Bel|1|38|And Daniel said, Thou hast remembered me, O אֱלֹהִים: neither hast thou forsaken them that seek thee and love thee.

Bel|1|39|So Daniel arose, and did eat: and the angel of the Lord set Habbacuc in his own place again immediately.

Bel|1|40|Upon the seventh day the king went to bewail Daniel: and when he came to the den, he looked in, and behold, Daniel was sitting.

Bel|1|41|Then cried the king with a loud voice, saying, Great art Lord אֱלֹהִים of Daniel, and there is none other beside thee.

Bel|1|42|And he drew him out, and cast those that were the cause of his destruction into the den: and they were devoured in a moment before his face.

Lao|1|1|Paul, an apostle not of men nor by man, but by Yashiyah Christ, unto the brethren that are at Laodicea.

Lao|1|2|Grace be unto you and peace from אֱלֹהִים the Father and the Lord Yashiyah Christ.

Lao|1|3|I give thanks unto Christ in all my prayers, that ye continue in him and persevere in his works, looking for the promise at the day of judgement.

Lao|1|4|Neither do the vain talkings of some overset you, which creep in, that they may turn you away from the truth of the Gospel which is preached by me.

Lao|1|5|And now shall אֱלֹהִים cause that they that are of me shall continue ministering unto the increase of the truth of the Gospel and accomplishing goodness, and the work of salvation, even eternal life.

Lao|1|6|And now are my bonds seen of all men, which I suffer in Christ, wherein I rejoice and am glad.

Lao|1|7|And unto me this is for everlasting salvation, which also is brought about by your prayers, and the ministry of the Holy Ghost, whether by life or by death.

Lao|1|8|For verily to me life is in Christ, and to die is joy.

Lao|1|9|And unto him (or And also) shall he work his mercy in you that ye may have the same love, and be of one mind.

Lao|1|10|Therefore, dearly beloved, as ye have heard in my presence so hold fast and work in the fear of אֱלֹהִים, and it shall be unto you for life eternal.

Lao|1|11|For it is אֱלֹהִים that worketh in you.

Lao|1|12|And do ye without afterthought whatsoever ye do.

Lao|1|13|And for the rest, dearly beloved, rejoice in Christ, and beware of them that are filthy in lucre.

Lao|1|14|Let all your petitions be made openly before אֱלֹהִים, and be ye steadfast in the mind of Christ.

Lao|1|15|And what things are sound and true and sober and just and to be loved, do ye.

Lao|1|16|And what ye have heard and received, keep fast in your heart.

Lao|1|17|And peace shall be unto you.

Lao|1|18|The saints salute you.

Lao|1|19|The grace of the Lord Yashiyah be with your spirit.

Lao|1|20|& cause this epistle to be read unto them of Colossae, & the epistle of the Colossians to be read unto you.

THE END OF THE PROPHETS.

THE

NEW TESTAMENT

OF

OUR LORD AND SAVIOUR

YASHIYAH THE MESSIAH

TRANSLATED OUT OF THE ORIGINAL GREEK: AND WITH

THE GOSPEL ACCORDING TO
ST. MATTHEW.

CHAPTER 1

THE book of the generation of Yashiyah Christ, the son of David, the son of Abraham.

2 Abraham begat Isaac; and Isaac begat Jacob; and Jacob begat Judas and his brethren;

3 And Judas begat Phares and Zara of Thamar; and Phares begat Esrom; and Esrom begat Aram;

4 And Aram begat Aminadab; and Aminadab begat Naasson; and Naasson begat Salmon;

5 And Salmon begat Booz of Rachab; and Booz begat Obed of Ruth; and Obed begat Jesse;

6 And Jesse begat David the king; and David the king begat Solomon of her *that had been the wife* of Urias;

7 And Solomon begat Roboam; and Roboam begat Abia; and Abia begat Asa;

8 And Asa begat Josaphat; and Josaphat begat Joram; and Joram begat Ozias;

9 And Ozias begat Joatham; and Joatham begat Achaz; and Achaz begat Ezekias;

10 And Ezekias begat Manasses; and Manasses begat Amon; and Amon begat Josias;

11 And Josias begat Jechonias and his brethren, about the time they were carried away to Babylon:

12 And after they were brought to Babylon, Jechonias begat Salathiel; and Salathiel begat Zorobabel;

13 And Zorobabel begat Abiud; and Abiud begat Eliakim; and Eliakim begat Azor;

14 And Azor begat Sadoc; and Sadoc begat Achim; and Achim begat Eliud;

15 And Eliud begat Eleazar; and Eleazar begat Matthan; and Matthan begat Jacob;

16 And Jacob begat Joseph the husband of Mary, of whom was born Yashiyah, who is called Christ.

17 So all the generations from Abraham to David *are* fourteen generations; and from David until the carrying away into Babylon *are* fourteen generations; and from the carrying away into Babylon unto Christ *are* fourteen generations.

18 ¶ Now the birth of Yashiyah Christ was on this wise: When as his mother Mary was espoused to Joseph, before they came together, she was found with child of the Holy Ghost.

19 Then Joseph her husband, being a just *man*, and not willing to make her a publick example, was minded to put her away privily.

20 But while he thought on these things, behold, the angel of the Lord appeared unto him in a dream, saying, Joseph, thou son of David, fear not to take unto thee Mary thy wife: for that which is conceived in her is of the Holy Ghost.

21 And she shall bring forth a son, and thou shalt call his name JESUS: for he shall save his people from their sins.

22 Now all this was done, that it might be fulfilled which was spoken of the Lord by the prophet, saying,

23 Behold, a virgin shall be with child, and shall bring forth a son, and they shall call his name Emmanuel, which being interpreted is, אֱלֹהִים with us.

24 Then Joseph being raised from sleep did as the angel of the Lord had bidden him, and took unto him his wife:

25 And knew her not till she had brought forth her firstborn son: and he called his name JESUS.

CHAPTER 2

NOW when Yashiyah was born in Bethlehem of Judæa in the days of Herod the king, behold, there came wise men from the east to Jerusalem,

2 Saying, Where is he that is born King of the Jews? for we have seen his star in the east, and are come to worship him.

3 When Herod the king had heard *these things*, he was troubled, and all Jerusalem with him.

4 And when he had gathered all the chief priests and scribes of the people together, he demanded of them where Christ should be born.

5 And they said unto him, In Bethlehem of Judæa: for thus it is written by the prophet,

6 And thou Bethlehem, *in* the land of Juda, art not the least among the princes of Juda: for out of thee shall come a Governor, that shall rule my people Israel.

7 Then Herod, when he had privily called the wise men, inquired of them diligently what time the star appeared.

8 And he sent them to Bethlehem, and said, Go and search diligently for the young child; and when ye have found *him*, bring me word again, that I may come and worship him also.

9 When they had heard the king, they departed; and, lo, the star, which they saw in the east, went before them, till it came and stood over where the young child was.

10 When they saw the star, they rejoiced with exceeding great joy.

11 ¶ And when they were come into the house, they saw the young child with Mary his mother, and fell down, and worshipped him: and when they had opened their treasures, they presented unto him gifts; gold, and frankincense, and myrrh.

12 And being warned of אֱלֹהִים in a dream that they should not return to Herod, they departed into their own country another way.

13 And when they were departed, behold, the angel of the Lord appeareth to Joseph in a dream, saying, Arise, and take the young child and his mother, and flee into Egypt, and be thou there until I bring thee word: for Herod will seek the young child to destroy him.

14 When he arose, he took the young child and his mother by night, and departed into Egypt:

15 And was there until the death of Herod: that it might be fulfilled which was spoken of the Lord by the prophet, saying, Out of Egypt have I called my son.

16 ¶ Then Herod, when he saw that he was mocked of the wise men, was exceeding wroth, and sent forth, and slew all the children that were in Bethlehem, and in all the coasts thereof, from two years old and under, according to the time which he had diligently inquired of the wise men.

17 Then was fulfilled that which was spoken by Jeremy the prophet, saying,

18 In Rama was there a voice heard, lamentation, and weeping, and great mourning, Rachel weeping *for* her children, and would not be comforted, because they are not.

19 ¶ But when Herod was dead, behold, an angel of the Lord appeareth in a dream to Joseph in Egypt,

20 Saying, Arise, and take the young child and his mother, and go into the land of Israel: for they are dead which sought the young child's life.

21 And he arose, and took the young child and his mother, and came into the land of Israel.

22 But when he heard that Archelaus did reign in Judæa in the room of his father Herod, he was afraid to go thither: notwithstanding, being warned of אֱלֹהִים in a dream, he turned aside into the parts of Galilee:

23 And he came and dwelt in a city called Nazareth: that it might be fulfilled which was spoken by the prophets, He shall be called a Nazarene.

CHAPTER 3

IN those days came John the Baptist, preaching in the wilderness of Judæa,

2 And saying, Repent ye: for the kingdom of heaven is at hand.

3 For this is he that was spoken of by the prophet Esaias, saying, The voice of one crying in the wilderness, Prepare ye the way of the Lord, make his paths straight.

4 And the same John had his raiment of camel's hair, and a leathern girdle about his loins; and his meat was locusts and wild honey.

5 Then went out to him Jerusalem, and all Judæa, and all the region round about Jordan,

6 And were baptized of him in Jordan, confessing their sins.

7 ¶ But when he saw many of the Pharisees and Sadducees come to his baptism, he said unto them, O generation of vipers, who hath warned you to flee from the wrath to come?

8 Bring forth therefore fruits meet for repentance:

9 And think not to say within yourselves, We have Abraham to *our* father: for I say unto you, that אֱלֹהִים is able of these stones to raise up children unto Abraham.

10 And now also the axe is laid unto the root of the trees: therefore every tree which bringeth not forth good fruit is hewn down, and cast into the fire.

11 I indeed baptize you with water unto repentance: but he that cometh after me is mightier than I, whose shoes I am not worthy to bear: he shall baptize you with the Holy Ghost, and *with* fire:

12 Whose fan *is* in his hand, and he will throughly purge his floor, and gather his wheat into the garner; but he will burn up the chaff with unquenchable fire.

13 ¶ Then cometh Yashiyah from Galilee to Jordan unto John, to be baptized of him.

14 But John forbad him, saying, I have need to be baptized of thee, and comest thou to me?

15 And Yashiyah answering said unto him, Suffer *it to be so* now: for thus it becometh us to fulfil all righteousness. Then he suffered him.

16 And Yashiyah, when he was baptized, went up straightway out of the water: and, lo, the heavens were opened unto him, and he saw the Spirit of אֱלֹהִים descending like a dove, and lighting upon him:

17 And lo a voice from heaven, saying, This is my beloved Son, in whom I am well pleased.

CHAPTER 4

THEN was Yashiyah led up of the Spirit into the wilderness to be tempted of the devil.

2 And when he had fasted forty days and forty nights, he was afterward an hungred.

3 And when the tempter came to him, he said, If thou be the Son of אֱלֹהִים, command that these stones be made bread.

4 But he answered and said, It is written, Man shall not live by bread alone, but by every word that proceedeth out of the mouth of אֱלֹהִים.

5 Then the devil taketh him up into the holy city, and setteth him on a pinnacle of the temple,

6 And saith unto him, If thou be the Son of אֱלֹהִים, cast thyself down: for it is written, He shall give his angels charge concerning thee: and in *their* hands they shall bear thee up, lest at any time thou dash thy foot against a stone.

7 Yashiyah said unto him, It is written again, Thou shalt not tempt the Lord thy אֱלֹהִים.

8 Again, the devil taketh him up into an exceeding high mountain, and sheweth him all the kingdoms of the world, and the glory of them;

9 And saith unto him, All these things will I give thee, if thou wilt fall down and worship me.

10 Then saith Yashiyah unto him, Get thee hence, Satan: for it is written, Thou shalt worship the Lord thy אֱלֹהִים, and him only shalt thou serve.

11 Then the devil leaveth him, and, behold, angels came and ministered unto him.

12 ¶ Now when Yashiyah had heard that John was cast into prison, he departed into Galilee;

13 And leaving Nazareth, he came and dwelt in Capernaum, which is upon the sea coast, in the borders of Zabulon and Nephthalim:

14 That it might be fulfilled which was spoken by Esaias the prophet, saying,

15 The land of Zabulon, and the land of Nephthalim, *by* the way of the sea, beyond Jordan, Galilee of the Gentiles;

16 The people which sat in darkness saw great light; and to them which sat in the region and shadow of death light is sprung up.

17 ¶ From that time Yashiyah began to preach, and to say, Repent: for the kingdom of heaven is at hand.

18 ¶ And Yashiyah, walking by the sea of Galilee, saw two brethren, Simon called Peter, and Andrew his brother, casting a net into the sea: for they were fishers.

19 And he saith unto them, Follow me, and I will make you fishers of men.

20 And they straightway left *their* nets, and followed him.

21 And going on from thence, he saw other two brethren, James *the son* of Zebedee, and John his brother, in a ship with Zebedee their father, mending their nets; and he called them.

22 And they immediately left the ship and their father, and followed him.

23 ¶ And Yashiyah went about all Galilee, teaching in their synagogues, and preaching the gospel of the kingdom, and healing all manner of sickness and all manner of disease among the people.

24 And his fame went throughout all Syria: and they brought unto him all sick people that were taken with divers diseases and torments, and those which were possessed with devils, and those which were lunatick, and those that had the palsy; and he healed them.

25 And there followed him great multitudes of people from Galilee, and *from* Decapolis, and *from* Jerusalem, and *from* Judæa, and *from* beyond Jordan.

CHAPTER 5

AND seeing the multitudes, he went up into a mountain: and when he was set, his disciples came unto him:

2 And he opened his mouth, and taught them, saying,

3 Blessed *are* the poor in spirit: for theirs is the kingdom of heaven.

4 Blessed *are* they that mourn: for they shall be comforted.

5 Blessed *are* the meek: for they shall inherit the earth.

6 Blessed *are* they which do hunger and thirst after righteousness: for they shall be filled.

7 Blessed *are* the merciful: for they shall obtain mercy.

8 Blessed *are* the pure in heart: for they shall see אֱלֹהִים.

9 Blessed *are* the peacemakers: for they shall be called the children of אֱלֹהִים.

10 Blessed *are* they which are persecuted for righteousness' sake: for theirs is the kingdom of heaven.

11 Blessed are ye, when *men* shall revile you, and persecute *you*, and shall say all manner of evil against you falsely, for my sake.

12 Rejoice, and be exceeding glad: for great *is* your reward in heaven: for so persecuted they the prophets which were before you.

13 ¶ Ye are the salt of the earth: but if the salt have lost his savour, wherewith shall it be salted? it is thenceforth good for nothing, but to be cast out, and to be trodden under foot of men.

14 Ye are the light of the world. A city that is set on an hill cannot be hid.

15 Neither do men light a candle, and put it under a bushel, but on a candlestick; and it giveth light unto all that are in the house.

16 Let your light so shine before men, that they may see your good works, and glorify your Father which is in heaven.

17 ¶ Think not that I am come to destroy the law, or the prophets: I am not come to destroy, but to fulfil.

18 For verily I say unto you, Till heaven and earth pass, one jot or one tittle shall in no wise pass from the law, till all be fulfilled.

19 Whosoever therefore shall break one of these least commandments, and shall teach men so, he shall be called the least in the kingdom of heaven: but whosoever shall do and teach *them*, the same shall be called great in the kingdom of heaven.

20 For I say unto you, That except your righteousness shall exceed *the righteousness* of the scribes and Pharisees, ye shall in no case enter into the kingdom of heaven.

21 ¶ Ye have heard that it was said by them of old time, Thou shalt not kill; and whosoever shall kill shall be in danger of the judgment:

22 But I say unto you, That whosoever is angry with his brother without a cause shall be in danger of the judgment: and whosoever shall say to his brother, Raca, shall be in danger of the council: but whosoever shall say, Thou fool, shall be in danger of hell fire.

23 Therefore if thou bring thy gift to the altar, and there rememberest that thy brother hath ought against thee;

24 Leave there thy gift before the altar, and go thy way; first be reconciled to thy brother, and then come and offer thy gift.

25 Agree with thine adversary quickly, whiles thou art in the way with him; lest at any time the adversary deliver thee to the judge, and the judge deliver thee to the officer, and thou be cast into prison.

26 Verily I say unto thee, Thou shalt by no means come out thence, till thou hast paid the uttermost farthing.

27 ¶ Ye have heard that it was said by them of old time, Thou shalt not commit adultery:

28 But I say unto you, That whosoever looketh on a woman to lust after her hath committed adultery with her already in his heart.

29 And if thy right eye offend thee, pluck it out, and cast *it* from thee: for it is profitable for thee that one of thy members should perish, and not *that* thy whole body should be cast into hell.

30 And if thy right hand offend thee, cut it off, and cast *it* from thee: for it is profitable for thee that one of thy members should perish, and not *that* thy whole body should be cast into hell.

31 It hath been said, Whosoever shall put away his wife, let him give her a writing of divorcement:

32 But I say unto you, That whosoever shall put away his wife, saving for the cause of fornication, causeth her to commit adultery: and whosoever shall marry her that is divorced committeth adultery.

33 ¶ Again, ye have heard that it hath been said by them of old time, Thou shalt not forswear thyself, but shalt perform unto the Lord thine oaths:

34 But I say unto you, Swear not at all; neither by heaven; for it is אֱלֹהִים's throne:

35 Nor by the earth; for it is his footstool: neither by Jerusalem; for it is the city of the great King.

36 Neither shalt thou swear by thy head, because thou canst not make one hair white or black.

37 But let your communication be, Yea, yea; Nay, nay: for whatsoever is more than these cometh of evil.

38 ¶ Ye have heard that it hath been said, An eye for an eye, and a tooth for a tooth:

39 But I say unto you, That ye resist not evil: but whosoever shall smite thee on thy right cheek, turn to him the other also.

40 And if any man will sue thee at the law, and take away thy coat, let him have *thy* cloke also.

41 And whosoever shall compel thee to go a mile, go with him twain.

42 Give to him that asketh thee, and from him that would borrow of thee turn not thou away.

43 ¶ Ye have heard that it hath been said, Thou shalt love thy neighbour, and hate thine enemy.

44 But I say unto you, Love your enemies, bless them that curse you, do good to them that hate you, and pray for them which despitefully use you, and persecute you;

45 That ye may be the children of your Father which is in heaven: for he maketh his sun to rise on the evil and on the good, and sendeth rain on the just and on the unjust.

46 For if ye love them which love you, what reward have ye? do not even the publicans the same?

47 And if ye salute your brethren only, what do ye more *than others?* do not even the publicans so?

48 Be ye therefore perfect, even as your Father which is in heaven is perfect.

CHAPTER 6

TAKE heed that ye do not your alms before men, to be seen of them: otherwise ye have no reward of your Father which is in heaven.

2 Therefore when thou doest *thine* alms, do not sound a trumpet before thee, as the hypocrites do in the synagogues and in the streets, that they may have glory of men. Verily I say unto you, They have their reward.

3 But when thou doest alms, let not thy left hand know what thy right hand doeth:

4 That thine alms may be in secret: and thy Father which seeth in secret himself shall reward thee openly.

5 ¶ And when thou prayest, thou shalt not be as the hypocrites *are:* for they love to pray standing in the synagogues and in the corners of the streets, that they may be seen of men. Verily I say unto you, They have their reward.

6 But thou, when thou prayest, enter into thy closet, and when thou hast shut thy door, pray to thy Father which is in secret; and thy Father which seeth in secret shall reward thee openly.

7 But when ye pray, use not vain repetitions, as the heathen *do:* for they think that they shall be heard for their much speaking.

8 Be not ye therefore like unto them: for your Father knoweth what things ye have need of, before ye ask him.

9 After this manner therefore pray ye: Our Father which art in heaven, Hallowed be thy name.

10 Thy kingdom come. Thy will be done in earth, as *it is* in heaven.

11 Give us this day our daily bread.

12 And forgive us our debts, as we forgive our debtors.

13 And lead us not into temptation, but deliver us from evil: For thine is the kingdom, and the power, and the glory, for ever. Amen.

14 For if ye forgive men their trespasses, your heavenly Father will also forgive you:

15 But if ye forgive not men their trespasses, neither will your Father forgive your trespasses.

16 ¶ Moreover when ye fast, be not, as the hypocrites, of a sad countenance: for they disfigure their faces, that they may appear unto men to fast. Verily I say unto you, They have their reward.

17 But thou, when thou fastest, anoint thine head, and wash thy face;

18 That thou appear not unto men to fast, but unto thy Father which is in secret: and thy Father, which seeth in secret, shall reward thee openly.

19 ¶ Lay not up for yourselves treasures upon earth, where moth and rust doth corrupt, and where thieves break through and steal:

20 But lay up for yourselves treasures in heaven, where neither moth nor rust doth corrupt, and where thieves do not break through nor steal:

21 For where your treasure is, there will your heart be also.

22 The light of the body is the eye: if therefore thine eye be single, thy whole body shall be full of light.

23 But if thine eye be evil, thy whole body shall be full of darkness. If therefore the light that is in thee be darkness, how great *is* that darkness!

24 ¶ No man can serve two masters: for either he will hate the one, and love the other; or else he will hold to the one, and despise the other. Ye cannot serve אֱלֹהִים and mammon.

25 Therefore I say unto you, Take no thought for your life, what ye shall eat, or what ye shall drink; nor yet for your body, what ye shall put on. Is not the life more than meat, and the body than raiment?

26 Behold the fowls of the air: for they sow not, neither do they reap, nor gather into barns; yet your heavenly Father feedeth them. Are ye not much better than they?

27 Which of you by taking thought can add one cubit unto his stature?

28 And why take ye thought for raiment? Consider the lilies of the field, how they grow; they toil not, neither do they spin:

29 And yet I say unto you, That even Solomon in all his glory was not arrayed like one of these.

30 Wherefore, if אֱלֹהִים so clothe the grass of the field, which to day is, and to morrow is cast into the oven, *shall he* not much more *clothe* you, O ye of little faith?

31 Therefore take no thought, saying, What shall we eat? or, What shall we drink? or, Wherewithal shall we be clothed?

32 (For after all these things do the Gentiles seek:) for your heavenly Father knoweth that ye have need of all these things.

33 But seek ye first the kingdom of אֱלֹהִים, and his righteousness; and all these things shall be added unto you.

34 Take therefore no thought for the morrow: for the morrow shall take thought for the things of itself. Sufficient unto the day *is* the evil thereof.

CHAPTER 7

JUDGE not, that ye be not judged.

2 For with what judgment ye judge, ye shall be judged: and with what measure ye mete, it shall be measured to you again.

3 And why beholdest thou the mote that is in thy brother's eye, but considerest not the beam that is in thine own eye?

4 Or how wilt thou say to thy brother, Let me pull out the mote out of thine eye; and, behold, a beam *is* in thine own eye?

5 Thou hypocrite, first cast out the beam out of thine own eye; and then shalt thou see clearly to cast out the mote out of thy brother's eye.

6 ¶ Give not that which is holy unto the dogs, neither cast ye your pearls before swine, lest they trample them under their feet, and turn again and rend you.

7 ¶ Ask, and it shall be given you; seek, and ye shall find; knock, and it shall be opened unto you:

8 For every one that asketh receiveth; and he that seeketh findeth; and to him that knocketh it shall be opened.

9 Or what man is there of you, whom if his son ask bread, will he give him a stone?

10 Or if he ask a fish, will he give him a serpent?

11 If ye then, being evil, know how to give good gifts unto your children, how much more shall your Father which is in heaven give good things to them that ask him?

12 Therefore all things whatsoever ye would that men should do to you, do ye even so to them: for this is the law and the prophets.

13 ¶ Enter ye in at the strait gate: for wide *is* the gate, and broad *is* the way, that leadeth to destruction, and many there be which go in thereat:

14 Because strait *is* the gate, and narrow *is* the way, which leadeth unto life, and few there be that find it.

15 ¶ Beware of false prophets, which come to you in sheep's clothing, but inwardly they are ravening wolves.

16 Ye shall know them by their fruits. Do men gather grapes of thorns, or figs of thistles?

17 Even so every good tree bringeth forth good fruit; but a corrupt tree bringeth forth evil fruit.

18 A good tree cannot bring forth evil fruit, neither *can* a corrupt tree bring forth good fruit.

19 Every tree that bringeth not forth good fruit is hewn down, and cast into the fire.

20 Wherefore by their fruits ye shall know them.

21 ¶ Not every one that saith unto me, Lord, Lord, shall enter into the kingdom of heaven; but he that doeth the will of my Father which is in heaven.

22 Many will say to me in that day, Lord, Lord, have we not prophesied in thy name? and in thy name have cast out devils? and in thy name done many wonderful works?

23 And then will I profess unto them, I never knew you: depart from me, ye that work iniquity.

24 ¶ Therefore whosoever heareth these sayings of mine, and doeth them, I will liken him unto a wise man, which built his house upon a rock:

25 And the rain descended, and the floods came, and the winds blew, and beat upon that house; and it fell not: for it was founded upon a rock.

26 And every one that heareth these sayings of mine, and doeth them not, shall be likened unto a foolish man, which built his house upon the sand:

27 And the rain descended, and the floods came, and the winds blew, and beat upon that house; and it fell: and great was the fall of it.

28 And it came to pass, when Yashiyah had ended these sayings, the people were astonished at his doctrine:

29 For he taught them as *one* having authority, and not as the scribes.

CHAPTER 8

WHEN he was come down from the mountain, great multitudes followed him.

2 And, behold, there came a leper and worshipped him, saying, Lord, if thou wilt, thou canst make me clean.

3 And Yashiyah put forth *his* hand, and touched him, saying, I will; be thou clean. And immediately his leprosy was cleansed.

4 And Yashiyah saith unto him, See thou tell no man; but go thy way, shew thyself to the priest, and offer the gift that Moses commanded, for a testimony unto them.

5 ¶ And when Yashiyah was entered into Capernaum, there came unto him a centurion, beseeching him,

6 And saying, Lord, my servant lieth at home sick of the palsy, grievously tormented.

7 And Yashiyah saith unto him, I will come and heal him.

8 The centurion answered and said, Lord, I am not worthy that thou shouldest come under my roof: but speak the word only, and my servant shall be healed.

9 For I am a man under authority, having soldiers under me: and I say to this *man*, Go, and he goeth; and to another, Come, and he cometh; and to my servant, Do this, and he doeth *it*.

10 When Yashiyah heard *it*, he marvelled, and said to them that followed, Verily I say unto you, I have not found so great faith, no, not in Israel.

11 And I say unto you, That many shall come from the east and west, and shall sit down with Abraham, and Isaac, and Jacob, in the kingdom of heaven.

12 But the children of the kingdom shall be cast out into outer darkness: there shall be weeping and gnashing of teeth.

13 And Yashiyah said unto the centurion, Go thy way; and as thou hast believed, *so* be it done unto thee. And his servant was healed in the selfsame hour.

14 ¶ And when Yashiyah was come into Peter's house, he saw his wife's mother laid, and sick of a fever.

15 And he touched her hand, and the fever left her: and she arose, and ministered unto them.

16 ¶ When the even was come, they brought unto him many that were possessed with devils: and he cast out the spirits with *his* word, and healed all that were sick:

17 That it might be fulfilled which was spoken by Esaias the prophet, saying, Himself took our infirmities, and bare *our* sicknesses.

18 ¶ Now when Yashiyah saw great multitudes about him, he gave commandment to depart unto the other side.

19 And a certain scribe came, and said unto him, Master, I will follow thee whithersoever thou goest.

20 And Yashiyah saith unto him, The foxes have holes, and the birds of the air *have* nests; but the Son of man hath not where to lay *his* head.

21 And another of his disciples said unto him, Lord, suffer me first to go and bury my father.

22 But Yashiyah said unto him, Follow me; and let the dead bury their dead.

23 ¶ And when he was entered into a ship, his disciples followed him.

24 And, behold, there arose a great tempest in the sea, insomuch that the ship was covered with the waves: but he was asleep.

25 And his disciples came to *him*, and awoke him, saying, Lord, save us: we perish.

26 And he saith unto them, Why are ye fearful, O ye of little faith? Then he arose, and rebuked the winds and the sea; and there was a great calm.

27 But the men marvelled, saying, What manner of man is this, that even the winds and the sea obey him!

28 ¶ And when he was come to the other side into the country of the Gergesenes, there met him two possessed with devils, coming out of the tombs, exceeding fierce, so that no man might pass by that way.

29 And, behold, they cried out, saying, What have we to do with thee, Yashiyah, thou Son of אֱלֹהִים? art thou come hither to torment us before the time?

30 And there was a good way off from them an herd of many swine feeding.

31 So the devils besought him, saying, If thou cast us out, suffer us to go away into the herd of swine.

32 And he said unto them, Go. And when they were come out, they went into the herd of swine: and, behold, the whole herd of swine ran violently down a steep place into the sea, and perished in the waters.

33 And they that kept them fled, and went their ways into the city, and told every thing, and what was befallen to the possessed of the devils.

34 And, behold, the whole city came out to meet Yashiyah: and when they saw him, they besought *him* that he would depart out of their coasts.

CHAPTER 9

AND he entered into a ship, and passed over, and came into his own city.

2 And, behold, they brought to him a man sick of the palsy, lying on a bed: and Yashiyah seeing their faith said unto the sick of the palsy; Son, be of good cheer; thy sins be forgiven thee.

3 And, behold, certain of the scribes said within themselves, This *man* blasphemeth.

4 And Yashiyah knowing their thoughts said, Wherefore think ye evil in your hearts?

5 For whether is easier, to say, *Thy* sins be forgiven thee; or to say, Arise, and walk?

6 But that ye may know that the Son of man hath power on earth to forgive sins, (then saith he to the sick of the palsy,) Arise, take up thy bed, and go unto thine house.

7 And he arose, and departed to his house.

8 But when the multitudes saw *it*, they marvelled, and glorified אֱלֹהִים, which had given such power unto men.

9 ¶ And as Yashiyah passed forth from thence, he saw a man, named Matthew, sitting at the receipt of custom: and he saith unto him, Follow me. And he arose, and followed him.

10 ¶ And it came to pass, as Yashiyah sat at meat in the house, behold, many publicans and sinners came and sat down with him and his disciples.

11 And when the Pharisees saw *it*, they said unto his disciples, Why eateth your Master with publicans and sinners?

12 But when Yashiyah heard *that*, he said unto them, They that be whole need not a physician, but they that are sick.

13 But go ye and learn what *that* meaneth, I will have mercy, and not sacrifice: for I am not come to call the righteous, but sinners to repentance.

14 ¶ Then came to him the disciples of John, saying, Why do we and the Pharisees fast oft, but thy disciples fast not?

15 And Yashiyah said unto them, Can the children of the bridechamber mourn, as long as the bridegroom is with them? but the days will come, when the bridegroom shall be taken from them, and then shall they fast.

16 No man putteth a piece of new cloth unto an old garment, for that which is put in to fill it up taketh from the garment, and the rent is made worse.

17 Neither do men put new wine into old bottles: else the bottles break, and the wine runneth out, and the bottles perish: but they put new wine into new bottles, and both are preserved.

18 ¶ While he spake these things unto them, behold, there came a certain ruler, and worshipped him, saying, My daughter is even now dead: but come and lay thy hand upon her, and she shall live.

19 And Yashiyah arose, and followed him, and *so did* his disciples.

20 ¶ And, behold, a woman, which was diseased with an issue of blood twelve years, came behind *him*, and touched the hem of his garment:

21 For she said within herself, If I may but touch his garment, I shall be whole.

22 But Yashiyah turned him about, and when he saw her, he said, Daughter, be of good comfort; thy faith hath made thee whole. And the woman was made whole from that hour.

23 And when Yashiyah came into the ruler's house, and saw the minstrels and the people making a noise,

24 He said unto them, Give place: for the maid is not dead, but sleepeth. And they laughed him to scorn.

25 But when the people were put forth, he went in, and took her by the hand, and the maid arose.

26 And the fame hereof went abroad into all that land.

27 ¶ And when Yashiyah departed thence, two blind men followed him, crying, and saying, *Thou* Son of David, have mercy on us.

28 And when he was come into the house, the blind men came to him: and Yashiyah saith unto them, Believe ye that I am able to do this? They said unto him, Yea, Lord.

29 Then touched he their eyes, saying, According to your faith be it unto you.

30 And their eyes were opened; and Yashiyah straitly charged them, saying, See *that* no man know *it*.

31 But they, when they were departed, spread abroad his fame in all that country.

32 ¶ As they went out, behold, they brought to him a dumb man possessed with a devil.

33 And when the devil was cast out, the dumb spake: and the multitudes marvelled, saying, It was never so seen in Israel.

34 But the Pharisees said, He casteth out devils through the prince of the devils.

35 And Yashiyah went about all the cities and villages, teaching in their synagogues, and preaching the gospel of the kingdom, and healing every sickness and every disease among the people.

36 ¶ But when he saw the multitudes, he was moved with compassion on them, because they fainted, and were scattered abroad, as sheep having no shepherd.

37 Then saith he unto his disciples, The harvest truly *is* plenteous, but the labourers *are* few;

38 Pray ye therefore the Lord of the harvest, that he will send forth labourers into his harvest.

CHAPTER 10

AND when he had called unto *him* his twelve disciples, he gave them power *against* unclean spirits, to cast them out, and to heal all manner of sickness and all manner of disease.

2 Now the names of the twelve apostles are these; The first, Simon, who is called Peter, and Andrew his brother; James *the son* of Zebedee, and John his brother;

3 Philip, and Bartholomew; Thomas, and Matthew the publican; James *the son* of Alphæus, and Lebbæus, whose surname was Thaddæus;

4 Simon the Canaanite, and Judas Iscariot, who also betrayed him.

5 These twelve Yashiyah sent forth, and commanded them, saying, Go not into the way of the Gentiles, and into *any* city of the Samaritans enter ye not:

6 But go rather to the lost sheep of the house of Israel.

7 And as ye go, preach, saying, The kingdom of heaven is at hand.

8 Heal the sick, cleanse the lepers, raise the dead, cast out devils: freely ye have received, freely give.

9 Provide neither gold, nor silver, nor brass in your purses,

10 Nor scrip for *your* journey, neither two coats, neither shoes, nor yet staves: for the workman is worthy of his meat.

11 And into whatsoever city or town ye shall enter, inquire who in it is worthy; and there abide till ye go thence.

12 And when ye come into an house, salute it.

13 And if the house be worthy, let your peace come upon it: but if it be not worthy, let your peace return to you.

14 And whosoever shall not receive you, nor hear your words, when ye depart out of that house or city, shake off the dust of your feet.

15 Verily I say unto you, It shall be more tolerable for the land of Sodom and Gomorrha in the day of judgment, than for that city.

16 ¶ Behold, I send you forth as sheep in the midst of wolves: be ye therefore wise as serpents, and harmless as doves.

17 But beware of men: for they will deliver you up to the councils, and they will scourge you in their synagogues;

18 And ye shall be brought before governors and kings for my sake, for a testimony against them and the Gentiles.

19 But when they deliver you up, take no thought how or what ye shall speak: for it shall be given you in that same hour what ye shall speak.

20 For it is not ye that speak, but the Spirit of your Father which speaketh in you.

21 And the brother shall deliver up the brother to death, and the father the child: and the children shall rise up against *their* parents, and cause them to be put to death.

22 And ye shall be hated of all *men* for my name's sake: but he that endureth to the end shall be saved.

23 But when they persecute you in this city, flee ye into another: for verily I say unto you, Ye shall not have gone over the cities of Israel, till the Son of man be come.

24 The disciple is not above *his* master, nor the servant above his lord.

25 It is enough for the disciple that he be as his master, and the servant as his lord. If they have called the master of the house Beelzebub, how much more *shall they call* them of his household?

26 Fear them not therefore: for there is nothing covered, that shall not be revealed; and hid, that shall not be known.

27 What I tell you in darkness, *that* speak ye in light: and what ye hear in the ear, *that* preach ye upon the housetops.

28 And fear not them which kill the body, but are not able to kill the soul: but rather fear him which is able to destroy both soul and body in hell.

29 Are not two sparrows sold for a farthing? and one of them shall not fall on the ground without your Father.

30 But the very hairs of your head are all numbered.

31 Fear ye not therefore, ye are of more value than many sparrows.

32 Whosoever therefore shall confess me before men, him will I confess also before my Father which is in heaven.

33 But whosoever shall deny me before men, him will I also deny before my Father which is in heaven.

34 Think not that I am come to send peace on earth: I came not to send peace, but a sword.

35 For I am come to set a man at variance against his father, and the daughter against her mother, and the daughter in law against her mother in law.

36 And a man's foes *shall be* they of his own household.

37 He that loveth father or mother more than me is not worthy of me: and he that loveth son or daughter more than me is not worthy of me.

38 And he that taketh not his cross, and followeth after me, is not worthy of me.

39 He that findeth his life shall lose it: and he that loseth his life for my sake shall find it.

40 ¶ He that receiveth you receiveth me, and he that receiveth me receiveth him that sent me.

41 He that receiveth a prophet in the name of a prophet shall receive a prophet's reward; and he that receiveth a righteous man in the name of a righteous man shall receive a righteous man's reward.

42 And whosoever shall give to drink unto one of these little ones a cup of cold *water* only in the name of a disciple, verily I say unto you, he shall in no wise lose his reward.

CHAPTER 11

AND it came to pass, when Yashiyah had made an end of commanding his twelve disciples, he departed thence to teach and to preach in their cities.

2 Now when John had heard in the prison the works of Christ, he sent two of his disciples,

3 And said unto him, Art thou he that should come, or do we look for another?

4 Yashiyah answered and said unto them, Go and shew John again those things which ye do hear and see:

5 The blind receive their sight, and the lame walk, the lepers are cleansed, and the deaf hear, the dead are raised up, and the poor have the gospel preached to them.

6 And blessed is *he*, whosoever shall not be offended in me.

7 ¶ And as they departed, Yashiyah began to say unto the multitudes concerning John, What went ye out into the wilderness to see? A reed shaken with the wind?

8 But what went ye out for to see? A man clothed in soft raiment? behold, they that wear soft *clothing* are in kings' houses.

9 But what went ye out for to see? A prophet? yea, I say unto you, and more than a prophet.

10 For this is *he*, of whom it is written, Behold, I send my messenger before thy face, which shall prepare thy way before thee.

11 Verily I say unto you, Among them that are born of women there hath not risen a greater than John the Baptist: notwithstanding he that is least in the kingdom of heaven is greater than he.

12 And from the days of John the Baptist until now the kingdom of heaven suffereth violence, and the violent take it by force.

13 For all the prophets and the law prophesied until John.

14 And if ye will receive *it*, this is Elias, which was for to come.

15 He that hath ears to hear, let him hear.

16 ¶ But whereunto shall I liken this generation? It is like unto children sitting in the markets, and calling unto their fellows,

17 And saying, We have piped unto you, and ye have not danced; we have mourned unto you, and ye have not lamented.

18 For John came neither eating nor drinking, and they say, He hath a devil.

19 The Son of man came eating and drinking, and they say, Behold a man gluttonous, and a winebibber, a friend of publicans and sinners. But wisdom is justified of her children.

20 ¶ Then began he to upbraid the cities wherein most of his mighty works were done, because they repented not:

21 Woe unto thee, Chorazin! woe unto thee, Bethsaida! for if the mighty works, which were done in you, had been done in Tyre and Sidon, they would have repented long ago in sackcloth and ashes.

22 But I say unto you, It shall be more tolerable for Tyre and Sidon at the day of judgment, than for you.

23 And thou, Capernaum, which art exalted unto heaven, shalt be brought down to hell: for if the mighty works, which have been done in thee, had been done in Sodom, it would have remained until this day.

24 But I say unto you, That it shall be more tolerable for the land of Sodom in the day of judgment, than for thee.

25 ¶ At that time Yashiyah answered and said, I thank thee, O Father, Lord of heaven and earth, because thou hast hid these things from the wise and prudent, and hast revealed them unto babes.

26 Even so, Father: for so it seemed good in thy sight.

27 All things are delivered unto me of my Father: and no man knoweth the Son, but the Father; neither knoweth any man the Father, save the Son, and *he* to whomsoever the Son will reveal *him*.

28 ¶ Come unto me, all *ye* that labour and are heavy laden, and I will give you rest.

29 Take my yoke upon you, and learn of me; for I am meek and lowly in heart: and ye shall find rest unto your souls.

30 For my yoke *is* easy, and my burden is light.

CHAPTER 12

AT that time Yashiyah went on the sabbath day through the corn; and his disciples were an hungred, and began to pluck the ears of corn, and to eat.

2 But when the Pharisees saw *it*, they said unto him, Behold, thy disciples do that which is not lawful to do upon the sabbath day.

3 But he said unto them, Have ye not read what David did, when he was an hungred, and they that were with him;

4 How he entered into the house of אֱלֹהִים, and did eat the shewbread, which was not lawful for him to eat, neither for them which were with him, but only for the priests?

5 Or have ye not read in the law, how that on the sabbath days the priests in the temple profane the sabbath, and are blameless?

6 But I say unto you, That in this place is *one* greater than the temple.

7 But if ye had known what *this* meaneth, I will have mercy, and not sacrifice, ye would not have condemned the guiltless.

8 For the Son of man is Lord even of the sabbath day.

9 And when he was departed thence, he went into their synagogue:

10 ¶ And, behold, there was a man which had *his* hand withered. And they asked him, saying, Is it lawful to heal on the sabbath days? that they might accuse him.

11 And he said unto them, What man shall there be among you, that shall have one sheep, and if it fall into a pit on the sabbath day, will he not lay hold on it, and lift *it* out?

12 How much then is a man better than a sheep? Wherefore it is lawful to do well on the sabbath days.

13 Then saith he to the man, Stretch forth thine hand. And he stretched *it* forth; and it was restored whole, like as the other.

14 ¶ Then the Pharisees went out, and held a council against him, how they might destroy him.

15 But when Yashiyah knew *it*, he withdrew himself from thence: and great multitudes followed him, and he healed them all;

16 And charged them that they should not make him known:

17 That it might be fulfilled which was spoken by Esaias the prophet, saying,

18 Behold my servant, whom I have chosen; my beloved, in whom my soul is well pleased: I will put my spirit upon him, and he shall shew judgment to the Gentiles.

19 He shall not strive, nor cry; neither shall any man hear his voice in the streets.

20 A bruised reed shall he not break, and smoking flax shall he not quench, till he send forth judgment unto victory.

21 And in his name shall the Gentiles trust.

22 ¶ Then was brought unto him one possessed with a devil, blind, and dumb: and he healed him, insomuch that the blind and dumb both spake and saw.

23 And all the people were amazed, and said, Is not this the son of David?

24 But when the Pharisees heard *it*, they said, This *fellow* doth not cast out devils, but by Beelzebub the prince of the devils.

25 And Yashiyah knew their thoughts, and said unto them, Every kingdom divided against itself is brought to desolation; and every city or house divided against itself shall not stand:

26 And if Satan cast out Satan, he is divided against himself; how shall then his kingdom stand?

27 And if I by Beelzebub cast out devils, by whom do your children cast *them* out? therefore they shall be your judges.

28 But if I cast out devils by the Spirit of אֱלֹהִים, then the kingdom of אֱלֹהִים is come unto you.

29 Or else how can one enter into a strong man's house, and spoil his goods, except he first bind the strong man? and then he will spoil his house.

30 He that is not with me is against me; and he that gathereth not with me scattereth abroad.

31 ¶ Wherefore I say unto you, All manner of sin and blasphemy shall be forgiven unto men: but the blasphemy *against* the *Holy* Ghost shall not be forgiven unto men.

32 And whosoever speaketh a word against the Son of man, it shall be forgiven him: but whosoever speaketh against the Holy Ghost, it shall not be forgiven him, neither in this world, neither in the *world* to come.

33 Either make the tree good, and his fruit good; or else make the tree corrupt, and his fruit corrupt: for the tree is known by *his* fruit.

34 O generation of vipers, how can ye, being evil, speak good things? for out of the abundance of the heart the mouth speaketh.

35 A good man out of the good treasure of the heart bringeth forth good things: and an evil man out of the evil treasure bringeth forth evil things.

36 But I say unto you, That every idle word that men shall speak, they shall give account thereof in the day of judgment.

37 For by thy words thou shalt be justified, and by thy words thou shalt be condemned.

38 ¶ Then certain of the scribes and of the Pharisees answered, saying, Master, we would see a sign from thee.

39 But he answered and said unto them, An evil and adulterous generation seeketh after a sign; and there shall no sign be given to it, but the sign of the prophet Jonas:

40 For as Jonas was three days and three nights in the whale's belly; so shall the Son of man be three days and three nights in the heart of the earth.

41 The men of Nineveh shall rise in judgment with this generation, and shall condemn it: because they repented at the preaching of Jonas; and, behold, a greater than Jonas *is* here.

42 The queen of the south shall rise up in the judgment with this generation, and shall condemn it: for she came from the uttermost parts of the earth to hear the wisdom of Solomon; and, behold, a greater than Solomon *is* here.

43 When the unclean spirit is gone out of a man, he walketh through dry places, seeking rest, and findeth none.

44 Then he saith, I will return into my house from whence I came out; and when he is come, he findeth *it* empty, swept, and garnished.

45 Then goeth he, and taketh with himself seven other spirits more wicked than himself, and they enter in and dwell there: and the last *state* of that man is worse than the first. Even so shall it be also unto this wicked generation.

46 ¶ While he yet talked to the people, behold, *his* mother and his brethren stood without, desiring to speak with him.

47 Then one said unto him, Behold, thy mother and thy brethren stand without, desiring to speak with thee.

48 But he answered and said unto him that told him, Who is my mother? and who are my brethren?

49 And he stretched forth his hand toward his disciples, and said, Behold my mother and my brethren!

50 For whosoever shall do the will of my Father which is in heaven, the same is my brother, and sister, and mother.

CHAPTER 13

THE same day went Yashiyah out of the house, and sat by the sea side.

2 And great multitudes were gathered together unto him, so that he went into a ship, and sat; and the whole multitude stood on the shore.

3 And he spake many things unto them in parables, saying, Behold, a sower went forth to sow;

4 And when he sowed, some *seeds* fell by the way side, and the fowls came and devoured them up:

5 Some fell upon stony places, where they had not much earth: and forthwith they sprung up, because they had no deepness of earth:

6 And when the sun was up, they were scorched; and because they had no root, they withered away.

7 And some fell among thorns; and the thorns sprung up, and choked them:

8 But other fell into good ground, and brought forth fruit, some an hundredfold, some sixtyfold, some thirtyfold.

9 Who hath ears to hear, let him hear.

10 And the disciples came, and said unto him, Why speakest thou unto them in parables?

11 He answered and said unto them, Because it is given unto you to know the mysteries of the kingdom of heaven, but to them it is not given.

12 For whosoever hath, to him shall be given, and he shall have more abundance: but whosoever hath not, from him shall be taken away even that he hath.

13 Therefore speak I to them in parables: because they seeing see not; and hearing they hear not, neither do they understand.

14 And in them is fulfilled the prophecy of Esaias, which saith, By hearing ye shall hear, and shall not understand; and seeing ye shall see, and shall not perceive:

15 For this people's heart is waxed gross, and *their* ears are dull of hearing, and their eyes they have closed; lest at any time they should see with *their* eyes, and hear with *their* ears, and should understand with *their* heart, and should be converted, and I should heal them.

16 But blessed *are* your eyes, for they see: and your ears, for they hear.

17 For verily I say unto you, That many prophets and righteous *men* have desired to see *those things* which ye see, and have not seen *them*; and to hear *those things* which ye hear, and have not heard *them*.

18 ¶ Hear ye therefore the parable of the sower.

19 When any one heareth the word of the kingdom, and understandeth *it* not, then cometh the wicked *one*, and catcheth away that which was sown in his heart. This is he which received seed by the way side.

20 But he that received the seed into stony places, the same is he that heareth the word, and anon with joy receiveth it;

21 Yet hath he not root in himself, but dureth for a while: for when tribulation or persecution ariseth because of the word, by and by he is offended.

22 He also that received seed among the thorns is he that heareth the word; and the care of this world, and the deceitfulness of riches, choke the word, and he becometh unfruitful.

23 But he that received seed into the good ground is he that heareth the word, and understandeth *it*; which also beareth fruit, and bringeth forth, some an hundredfold, some sixty, some thirty.

24 ¶ Another parable put he forth unto them, saying, The kingdom of heaven is likened unto a man which sowed good seed in his field:

25 But while men slept, his enemy came and sowed tares among the wheat, and went his way.

26 But when the blade was sprung up, and brought forth fruit, then appeared the tares also.

27 So the servants of the householder came and said unto him, Sir, didst not thou sow good seed in thy field? from whence then hath it tares?

28 He said unto them, An enemy hath done this. The servants said unto him, Wilt thou then that we go and gather them up?

29 But he said, Nay; lest while ye gather up the tares, ye root up also the wheat with them.

30 Let both grow together until the harvest: and in the time of harvest I will say to the reapers, Gather ye together first the tares, and bind them in bundles to burn them: but gather the wheat into my barn.

31 ¶ Another parable put he forth unto them, saying, The kingdom of heaven is like to a grain of mustard seed, which a man took, and sowed in his field:

32 Which indeed is the least of all seeds: but when it is grown, it is the greatest among herbs, and becometh a tree, so that the birds of the air come and lodge in the branches thereof.

33 ¶ Another parable spake he unto them; The kingdom of heaven is like unto leaven, which a woman took, and hid in three measures of meal, till the whole was leavened.

34 All these things spake Yashiyah unto the multitude in parables; and without a parable spake he not unto them:

35 That it might be fulfilled which was spoken by the prophet, saying, I will open my mouth in parables; I will utter things which have been kept secret from the foundation of the world.

36 Then Yashiyah sent the multitude away, and went into the house: and his disciples came unto him, saying, Declare unto us the parable of the tares of the field.

37 He answered and said unto them, He that soweth the good seed is the Son of man;

38 The field is the world; the good seed are the children of the kingdom; but the tares are the children of the wicked *one:*

39 The enemy that sowed them is the devil; the harvest is the end of the world; and the reapers are the angels.

40 As therefore the tares are gathered and burned in the fire; so shall it be in the end of this world.

41 The Son of man shall send forth his angels, and they shall gather out of his kingdom all things that offend, and them which do iniquity;

42 And shall cast them into a furnace of fire: there shall be wailing and gnashing of teeth.

43 Then shall the righteous shine forth as the sun in the kingdom of their Father. Who hath ears to hear, let him hear.

44 ¶ Again, the kingdom of heaven is like unto treasure hid in a field; the which when a man hath found, he hideth, and for joy thereof goeth and selleth all that he hath, and buyeth that field.

45 ¶ Again, the kingdom of heaven is like unto a merchant man, seeking goodly pearls:

46 Who, when he had found one pearl of great price, went and sold all that he had, and bought it.

47 ¶ Again, the kingdom of heaven is like unto a net, that was cast into the sea, and gathered of every kind:

48 Which, when it was full, they drew to shore, and sat down, and gathered the good into vessels, but cast the bad away.

49 So shall it be at the end of the world: the angels shall come forth, and sever the wicked from among the just,

50 And shall cast them into the furnace of fire: there shall be wailing and gnashing of teeth.

51 Yashiyah saith unto them, Have ye understood all these things? They say unto him, Yea, Lord.

52 Then said he unto them, Therefore every scribe *which is* instructed unto the kingdom of heaven is like unto a man *that is* an householder, which bringeth forth out of his treasure *things* new and old.

53 ¶ And it came to pass, *that* when Yashiyah had finished these parables, he departed thence.

54 And when he was come into his own country, he taught them in their synagogue, insomuch that they were astonished, and said, Whence hath this *man* this wisdom, and *these* mighty works?

55 Is not this the carpenter's son? is not his mother called Mary? and his brethren, James, and Joses, and Simon, and Judas?

56 And his sisters, are they not all with us? Whence then hath this *man* all these things?

57 And they were offended in him. But Yashiyah said unto them, A prophet is not without honour, save in his own country, and in his own house.

58 And he did not many mighty works there because of their unbelief.

CHAPTER 14

AT that time Herod the tetrarch heard of the fame of Yashiyah,

2 And said unto his servants, This is John the Baptist; he is risen from the dead; and therefore mighty works do shew forth themselves in him.

3 ¶ For Herod had laid hold on John, and bound him, and put *him* in prison for Herodias' sake, his brother Philip's wife.

4 For John said unto him, It is not lawful for thee to have her.

5 And when he would have put him to death, he feared the multitude, because they counted him as a prophet.

6 But when Herod's birthday was kept, the daughter of Herodias danced before them, and pleased Herod.

7 Whereupon he promised with an oath to give her whatsoever she would ask.

8 And she, being before instructed of her mother, said, Give me here John Baptist's head in a charger.

9 And the king was sorry: nevertheless for the oath's sake, and them which sat with him at meat, he commanded *it* to be given *her.*

10 And he sent, and beheaded John in the prison.

11 And his head was brought in a charger, and given to the damsel: and she brought *it* to her mother.

12 And his disciples came, and took up the body, and buried it, and went and told Yashiyah.

13 ¶ When Yashiyah heard *of it,* he departed thence by ship into a desert place apart: and when the people had heard *thereof,* they followed him on foot out of the cities.

14 And Yashiyah went forth, and saw a great multitude, and was moved with compassion toward them, and he healed their sick.

15 ¶ And when it was evening, his disciples came to him, saying, This is a desert place, and the time is now past; send the multitude away, that they may go into the villages, and buy themselves victuals.

16 But Yashiyah said unto them, They need not depart; give ye them to eat.

17 And they say unto him, We have here but five loaves, and two fishes.

18 He said, Bring them hither to me.

19 And he commanded the multitude to sit down on the grass, and took the five loaves, and the two fishes, and looking up to heaven,

he blessed, and brake, and gave the loaves to *his* disciples, and the disciples to the multitude.

20 And they did all eat, and were filled: and they took up of the fragments that remained twelve baskets full.

21 And they that had eaten were about five thousand men, beside women and children.

22 ¶ And straightway Yashiyah constrained his disciples to get into a ship, and to go before him unto the other side, while he sent the multitudes away.

23 And when he had sent the multitudes away, he went up into a mountain apart to pray: and when the evening was come, he was there alone.

24 But the ship was now in the midst of the sea, tossed with waves: for the wind was contrary.

25 And in the fourth watch of the night Yashiyah went unto them, walking on the sea.

26 And when the disciples saw him walking on the sea, they were troubled, saying, It is a spirit; and they cried out for fear.

27 But straightway Yashiyah spake unto them, saying, Be of good cheer; it is I; be not afraid.

28 And Peter answered him and said, Lord, if it be thou, bid me come unto thee on the water.

29 And he said, Come. And when Peter was come down out of the ship, he walked on the water, to go to Yashiyah.

30 But when he saw the wind boisterous, he was afraid; and beginning to sink, he cried, saying, Lord, save me.

31 And immediately Yashiyah stretched forth *his* hand, and caught him, and said unto him, O thou of little faith, wherefore didst thou doubt?

32 And when they were come into the ship, the wind ceased.

33 Then they that were in the ship came and worshipped him, saying, Of a truth thou art the Son of אֱלֹהִים.

34 ¶ And when they were gone over, they came into the land of Gennesaret.

35 And when the men of that place had knowledge of him, they sent out into all that country round about, and brought unto him all that were diseased;

36 And besought him that they might only touch the hem of his garment: and as many as touched were made perfectly whole.

CHAPTER 15

THEN came to Yashiyah scribes and Pharisees, which were of Jerusalem, saying,

2 Why do thy disciples transgress the tradition of the elders? for they wash not their hands when they eat bread.

3 But he answered and said unto them, Why do ye also transgress the commandment of אֱלֹהִים by your tradition?

4 For אֱלֹהִים commanded, saying, Honour thy father and mother: and, He that curseth father or mother, let him die the death.

5 But ye say, Whosoever shall say to *his* father or *his* mother, *It is* a gift, by whatsoever thou mightest be profited by me;

6 And honour not his father or his mother, *he shall be free*. Thus have ye made the commandment of אֱלֹהִים of none effect by your tradition.

7 *Ye* hypocrites, well did Esaias prophesy of you, saying,

8 This people draweth nigh unto me with their mouth, and honoureth me with *their* lips; but their heart is far from me.

9 But in vain they do worship me, teaching *for* doctrines the commandments of men.

10 ¶ And he called the multitude, and said unto them, Hear, and understand:

11 Not that which goeth into the mouth defileth a man; but that which cometh out of the mouth, this defileth a man.

12 Then came his disciples, and said unto him, Knowest thou that the Pharisees were offended, after they heard this saying?

13 But he answered and said, Every plant, which my heavenly Father hath not planted, shall be rooted up.

14 Let them alone: they be blind leaders of the blind. And if the blind lead the blind, both shall fall into the ditch.

15 Then answered Peter and said unto him, Declare unto us this parable.

16 And Yashiyah said, Are ye also yet without understanding?

17 Do not ye yet understand, that whatsoever entereth in at the mouth goeth into the belly, and is cast out into the draught?

18 But those things which proceed out of the mouth come forth from the heart; and they defile the man.

19 For out of the heart proceed evil thoughts, murders, adulteries, fornications, thefts, false witness, blasphemies:

20 These are *the things* which defile a man: but to eat with unwashen hands defileth not a man.

21 ¶ Then Yashiyah went thence, and departed into the coasts of Tyre and Sidon.

22 And, behold, a woman of Canaan came out of the same coasts, and cried unto him, saying, Have mercy on me, O Lord, *thou* Son of David; my daughter is grievously vexed with a devil.

23 But he answered her not a word. And his disciples came and besought him, saying, Send her away; for she crieth after us.

24 But he answered and said, I am not sent but unto the lost sheep of the house of Israel.

25 Then came she and worshipped him, saying, Lord, help me.

26 But he answered and said, It is not meet to take the children's bread, and to cast *it* to dogs.

27 And she said, Truth, Lord: yet the dogs eat of the crumbs which fall from their masters' table.

28 Then Yashiyah answered and said unto her, O woman, great *is* thy faith: be it unto thee even as thou wilt. And her daughter was made whole from that very hour.

29 And Yashiyah departed from thence, and came nigh unto the sea of Galilee; and went up into a mountain, and sat down there.

30 And great multitudes came unto him, having with them *those that were* lame, blind, dumb, maimed, and many others, and cast them down at Yashiyah' feet; and he healed them:

31 Insomuch that the multitude wondered, when they saw the dumb to speak, the maimed to be whole, the lame to walk, and the blind to see: and they glorified the אֱלֹהִים of Israel.

32 ¶ Then Yashiyah called his disciples *unto him*, and said, I have compassion on the multitude, because they continue with me now three days, and have nothing to eat: and I will not send them away fasting, lest they faint in the way.

33 And his disciples say unto him, Whence should we have so much bread in the wilderness, as to fill so great a multitude?

34 And Yashiyah saith unto them, How many loaves have ye? And they said, Seven, and a few little fishes.

35 And he commanded the multitude to sit down on the ground.

36 And he took the seven loaves and the fishes, and gave thanks, and brake *them*, and gave to his disciples, and the disciples to the multitude.

37 And they did all eat, and were filled: and they took up of the broken *meat* that was left seven baskets full.

38 And they that did eat were four thousand men, beside women and children.

39 And he sent away the multitude, and took ship, and came into the coasts of Magdala.

CHAPTER 16

THE Pharisees also with the Sadducees came, and tempting desired him that he would shew them a sign from heaven.

2 He answered and said unto them, When it is evening, ye say, *It will be* fair weather: for the sky is red.

3 And in the morning, *It will be* foul weather to day: for the sky is red and lowring. O *ye* hypocrites, ye can discern the face of the sky; but can ye not *discern* the signs of the times?

4 A wicked and adulterous generation seeketh after a sign; and there shall no sign be given unto it, but the sign of the prophet Jonas. And he left them, and departed.

5 And when his disciples were come to the other side, they had forgotten to take bread.

6 ¶ Then Yashiyah said unto them, Take heed and beware of the leaven of the Pharisees and of the Sadducees.

7 And they reasoned among themselves, saying, *It is* because we have taken no bread.

8 *Which* when Yashiyah perceived, he said unto them, O ye of little faith, why reason ye among yourselves, because ye have brought no bread?

9 Do ye not yet understand, neither remember the five loaves of the five thousand, and how many baskets ye took up?

10 Neither the seven loaves of the four thousand, and how many baskets ye took up?

11 How is it that ye do not understand that I spake *it* not to you concerning bread, that ye should beware of the leaven of the Pharisees and of the Sadducees?

12 Then understood they how that he bade *them* not beware of the leaven of bread, but of the doctrine of the Pharisees and of the Sadducees.

13 ¶ When Yashiyah came into the coasts of Cæsarea Philippi, he asked his disciples, saying, Whom do men say that I the Son of man am?

14 And they said, Some *say that thou art* John the Baptist: some, Elias; and others, Jeremias, or one of the prophets.

15 He saith unto them, But whom say ye that I am?

16 And Simon Peter answered and said, Thou art the Christ, the Son of the living אֱלֹהִים.

17 And Yashiyah answered and said unto him, Blessed art thou, Simon Bar-jona: for flesh and blood hath not revealed *it* unto thee, but my Father which is in heaven.

18 And I say also unto thee, That thou art Peter, and upon this rock I will build my church; and the gates of hell shall not prevail against it.

19 And I will give unto thee the keys of the kingdom of heaven: and whatsoever thou shalt bind on earth shall be bound in heaven: and whatsoever thou shalt loose on earth shall be loosed in heaven.

20 Then charged he his disciples that they should tell no man that he was Yashiyah the Christ.

21 ¶ From that time forth began Yashiyah to shew unto his disciples, how that he must go unto Jerusalem, and suffer many things of the elders and chief priests and scribes, and be killed, and be raised again the third day.

22 Then Peter took him, and began to rebuke him, saying, Be it far from thee, Lord: this shall not be unto thee.

23 But he turned, and said unto Peter, Get thee behind me, Satan: thou art an offence unto me: for thou savourest not the things that be of אֱלֹהִים, but those that be of men.

24 ¶ Then said Yashiyah unto his disciples, If any *man* will come after me, let him deny himself, and take up his cross, and follow me.

25 For whosoever will save his life shall lose it: and whosoever will lose his life for my sake shall find it.

26 For what is a man profited, if he shall gain the whole world, and lose his own soul? or what shall a man give in exchange for his soul?

27 For the Son of man shall come in the glory of his Father with his angels; and then he shall reward every man according to his works.

28 Verily I say unto you, There be some standing here, which shall not taste of death, till they see the Son of man coming in his kingdom.

CHAPTER 17

AND after six days Yashiyah taketh Peter, James, and John his brother, and bringeth them up into an high mountain apart,

2 And was transfigured before them: and his face did shine as the sun, and his raiment was white as the light.

3 And, behold, there appeared unto them Moses and Elias talking with him.

4 Then answered Peter, and said unto Yashiyah, Lord, it is good for us to be here: if thou wilt, let us make here three tabernacles; one for thee, and one for Moses, and one for Elias.

5 While he yet spake, behold, a bright cloud overshadowed them: and behold a voice out of the cloud, which said, This is my beloved Son, in whom I am well pleased; hear ye him.

6 And when the disciples heard *it*, they fell on their face, and were sore afraid.

7 And Yashiyah came and touched them, and said, Arise, and be not afraid.

8 And when they had lifted up their eyes, they saw no man, save Yashiyah only.

9 And as they came down from the mountain, Yashiyah charged them, saying, Tell the vision to no man, until the Son of man be risen again from the dead.

10 And his disciples asked him, saying, Why then say the scribes that Elias must first come?

11 And Yashiyah answered and said unto them, Elias truly shall first come, and restore all things.

12 But I say unto you, That Elias is come already, and they knew him not, but have done unto him whatsoever they listed. Likewise shall also the Son of man suffer of them.

13 Then the disciples understood that he spake unto them of John the Baptist.

14 ¶ And when they were come to the multitude, there came to him a *certain* man, kneeling down to him, and saying,

15 Lord, have mercy on my son: for he is lunatick, and sore vexed: for ofttimes he falleth into the fire, and oft into the water.

16 And I brought him to thy disciples, and they could not cure him.

17 Then Yashiyah answered and said, O faithless and perverse generation, how long shall I be with you? how long shall I suffer you? bring him hither to me.

18 And Yashiyah rebuked the devil; and he departed out of him: and the child was cured from that very hour.

19 Then came the disciples to Yashiyah apart, and said, Why could not we cast him out?

20 And Yashiyah said unto them, Because of your unbelief: for verily I say unto you, If ye have faith as a grain of mustard seed, ye shall say unto this mountain, Remove hence to yonder place; and it shall remove; and nothing shall be impossible unto you.

21 Howbeit this kind goeth not out but by prayer and fasting.

22 ¶ And while they abode in Galilee, Yashiyah said unto them, The Son of man shall be betrayed into the hands of men:

23 And they shall kill him, and the third day he shall be raised again. And they were exceeding sorry.

24 ¶ And when they were come to Capernaum, they that received tribute *money* came to Peter, and said, Doth not your master pay tribute?

25 He saith, Yes. And when he was come into the house, Yashiyah prevented him, saying, What thinkest thou, Simon? of whom do the kings of the earth take custom or tribute? of their own children, or of strangers?

26 Peter saith unto him, Of strangers. Yashiyah saith unto him, Then are the children free.

27 Notwithstanding, lest we should offend them, go thou to the sea, and cast an hook, and take up the fish that first cometh up; and when thou hast opened his mouth, thou shalt find a piece of money: that take, and give unto them for me and thee.

CHAPTER 18

AT the same time came the disciples unto Yashiyah, saying, Who is the greatest in the kingdom of heaven?

2 And Yashiyah called a little child unto him, and set him in the midst of them,

3 And said, Verily I say unto you, Except ye be converted, and become as little children, ye shall not enter into the kingdom of heaven.

4 Whosoever therefore shall humble himself as this little child, the same is greatest in the kingdom of heaven.

5 And whoso shall receive one such little child in my name receiveth me.

6 But whoso shall offend one of these little ones which believe in me, it were better for him that a millstone were hanged about his neck, and *that* he were drowned in the depth of the sea.

7 ¶ Woe unto the world because of offences! for it must needs be that offences come; but woe to that man by whom the offence cometh!

8 Wherefore if thy hand or thy foot offend thee, cut them off, and cast *them* from thee: it is better for thee to enter into life halt or maimed, rather than having two hands or two feet to be cast into everlasting fire.

9 And if thine eye offend thee, pluck it out, and cast *it* from thee: it is better for thee to enter into life with one eye, rather than having two eyes to be cast into hell fire.

10 Take heed that ye despise not one of these little ones; for I say unto you, That in heaven their angels do always behold the face of my Father which is in heaven.

11 For the Son of man is come to save that which was lost.

12 How think ye? if a man have an hundred sheep, and one of them be gone astray, doth he not leave the ninety and nine, and goeth into the mountains, and seeketh that which is gone astray?

13 And if so be that he find it, verily I say unto you, he rejoiceth more of that *sheep*, than of the ninety and nine which went not astray.

14 Even so it is not the will of your Father which is in heaven, that one of these little ones should perish.

15 ¶ Moreover if thy brother shall trespass against thee, go and tell him his fault between thee and him alone: if he shall hear thee, thou hast gained thy brother.

16 But if he will not hear *thee, then* take with thee one or two more, that in the mouth of two or three witnesses every word may be established.

17 And if he shall neglect to hear them, tell *it* unto the church: but if he neglect to hear the church, let him be unto thee as an heathen man and a publican.

18 Verily I say unto you, Whatsoever ye shall bind on earth shall be bound in heaven: and whatsoever ye shall loose on earth shall be loosed in heaven.

19 Again I say unto you, That if two of you shall agree on earth as touching any thing that they shall ask, it shall be done for them of my Father which is in heaven.

20 For where two or three are gathered together in my name, there am I in the midst of them.

21 ¶ Then came Peter to him, and said, Lord, how oft shall my brother sin against me, and I forgive him? till seven times?

22 Yashiyah saith unto him, I say not unto thee, Until seven times: but, Until seventy times seven.

23 ¶ Therefore is the kingdom of heaven likened unto a certain king, which would take account of his servants.

24 And when he had begun to reckon, one was brought unto him, which owed him ten thousand talents.

25 But forasmuch as he had not to pay, his lord commanded him to be sold, and his wife, and children, and all that he had, and payment to be made.

26 The servant therefore fell down, and worshipped him, saying, Lord, have patience with me, and I will pay thee all.

27 Then the lord of that servant was moved with compassion, and loosed him, and forgave him the debt.

28 But the same servant went out, and found one of his fellowservants, which owed him an hundred pence: and he laid hands on him, and took *him* by the throat, saying, Pay me that thou owest.

29 And his fellowservant fell down at his feet, and besought him, saying, Have patience with me, and I will pay thee all.

30 And he would not: but went and cast him into prison, till he should pay the debt.

31 So when his fellowservants saw what was done, they were very sorry, and came and told unto their lord all that was done.

32 Then his lord, after that he had called him, said unto him, O thou wicked servant, I forgave thee all that debt, because thou desiredst me:

33 Shouldest not thou also have had compassion on thy fellowservant, even as I had pity on thee?

34 And his lord was wroth, and delivered him to the tormentors, till he should pay all that was due unto him.

35 So likewise shall my heavenly Father do also unto you, if ye from your hearts forgive not every one his brother their trespasses.

CHAPTER 19

AND it came to pass, *that* when Yashiyah had finished these sayings, he departed from Galilee, and came into the coasts of Judæa beyond Jordan;

2 And great multitudes followed him; and he healed them there.

3 ¶ The Pharisees also came unto him, tempting him, and saying unto him, Is it lawful for a man to put away his wife for every cause?

4 And he answered and said unto them, Have ye not read, that he which made *them* at the beginning made them male and female,

5 And said, For this cause shall a man leave father and mother, and shall cleave to his wife: and they twain shall be one flesh?

6 Wherefore they are no more twain, but one flesh. What therefore אֱלֹהִים hath joined together, let not man put asunder.

7 They say unto him, Why did Moses then command to give a writing of divorcement, and to put her away?

8 He saith unto them, Moses because of the hardness of your hearts suffered you to put away your wives: but from the beginning it was not so.

9 And I say unto you, Whosoever shall put away his wife, except *it be* for fornication, and shall marry another, committeth adultery: and whoso marrieth her which is put away doth commit adultery.

10 ¶ His disciples say unto him, If the case of the man be so with *his* wife, it is not good to marry.

11 But he said unto them, All *men* cannot receive this saying, save *they* to whom it is given.

12 For there are some eunuchs, which were so born from *their* mother's womb: and there are some eunuchs, which were made eunuchs of men: and there be eunuchs, which have made themselves eunuchs for the kingdom of heaven's sake. He that is able to receive *it*, let him receive *it*.

13 ¶ Then were there brought unto him little children, that he should put *his* hands on them, and pray: and the disciples rebuked them.

14 But Yashiyah said, Suffer little children, and forbid them not, to come unto me: for of such is the kingdom of heaven.

15 And he laid *his* hands on them, and departed thence.

16 ¶ And, behold, one came and said unto him, Good Master, what good thing shall I do, that I may have eternal life?

17 And he said unto him, Why callest thou me good? *there is* none good but one, *that is*, אֱלֹהִים: but if thou wilt enter into life, keep the commandments.

18 He saith unto him, Which? Yashiyah said, Thou shalt do no murder, Thou shalt not commit adultery, Thou shalt not steal, Thou shalt not bear false witness,

19 Honour thy father and *thy* mother: and, Thou shalt love thy neighbour as thyself.

20 The young man saith unto him, All these things have I kept from my youth up: what lack I yet?

21 Yashiyah said unto him, If thou wilt be perfect, go *and* sell that thou hast, and give to the poor, and thou shalt have treasure in heaven: and come *and* follow me.

22 But when the young man heard that saying, he went away sorrowful: for he had great possessions.

23 ¶ Then said Yashiyah unto his disciples, Verily I say unto you, That a rich man shall hardly enter into the kingdom of heaven.

24 And again I say unto you, It is easier for a camel to go through the eye of a needle, than for a rich man to enter into the kingdom of אֱלֹהִים.

25 When his disciples heard *it*, they were exceedingly amazed, saying, Who then can be saved?

26 But Yashiyah beheld *them*, and said unto them, With men this is impossible; but with אֱלֹהִים all things are possible.

27 ¶ Then answered Peter and said unto him, Behold, we have forsaken all, and followed thee; what shall we have therefore?

28 And Yashiyah said unto them, Verily I say unto you, That ye which have followed me, in the regeneration when the Son of man shall sit in the throne of his glory, ye also shall sit upon twelve thrones, judging the twelve tribes of Israel.

29 And every one that hath forsaken houses, or brethren, or sisters, or father, or mother, or wife, or children, or lands, for my name's sake, shall receive an hundredfold, and shall inherit everlasting life.

30 But many *that are* first shall be last; and the last *shall be* first.

CHAPTER 20

FOR the kingdom of heaven is like unto a man *that is* an householder, which went out early in the morning to hire labourers into his vineyard.

2 And when he had agreed with the labourers for a penny a day, he sent them into his vineyard.

3 And he went out about the third hour, and saw others standing idle in the marketplace,

4 And said unto them; Go ye also into the vineyard, and whatsoever is right I will give you. And they went their way.

5 Again he went out about the sixth and ninth hour, and did likewise.

6 And about the eleventh hour he went out, and found others standing idle, and saith unto them, Why stand ye here all the day idle?

7 They say unto him, Because no man hath hired us. He saith unto them, Go ye also into the vineyard; and whatsoever is right, *that* shall ye receive.

8 So when even was come, the lord of the vineyard saith unto his steward, Call the labourers, and give them *their* hire, beginning from the last unto the first.

9 And when they came that *were hired* about the eleventh hour, they received every man a penny.

10 But when the first came, they supposed that they should have received more; and they likewise received every man a penny.

11 And when they had received *it*, they murmured against the goodman of the house,

12 Saying, These last have wrought *but* one hour, and thou hast made them equal unto us, which have borne the burden and heat of the day.

13 But he answered one of them, and said, Friend, I do thee no wrong: didst not thou agree with me for a penny?

14 Take *that* thine *is*, and go thy way: I will give unto this last, even as unto thee.

15 Is it not lawful for me to do what I will with mine own? Is thine eye evil, because I am good?

16 So the last shall be first, and the first last: for many be called, but few chosen.

17 ¶ And Yashiyah going up to Jerusalem took the twelve disciples apart in the way, and said unto them,

18 Behold, we go up to Jerusalem; and the Son of man shall be betrayed unto the chief priests and unto the scribes, and they shall condemn him to death,

19 And shall deliver him to the Gentiles to mock, and to scourge, and to crucify *him*: and the third day he shall rise again.

20 ¶ Then came to him the mother of Zebedee's children with her sons, worshipping *him*, and desiring a certain thing of him.

21 And he said unto her, What wilt thou? She saith unto him, Grant that these my two sons may sit, the one on thy right hand, and the other on the left, in thy kingdom.

22 But Yashiyah answered and said, Ye know not what ye ask. Are ye able to drink of the cup that I shall drink of, and to be baptized with the baptism that I am baptized with? They say unto him, We are able.

23 And he saith unto them, Ye shall drink indeed of my cup, and be baptized with the baptism that I am baptized with: but to sit on my right hand, and on my left, is not mine to give, but *it shall be given to them* for whom it is prepared of my Father.

24 And when the ten heard *it*, they were moved with indignation against the two brethren.

25 But Yashiyah called them *unto him*, and said, Ye know that the princes of the Gentiles exercise dominion over them, and they that are great exercise authority upon them.

26 But it shall not be so among you: but whosoever will be great among you, let him be your minister;

27 And whosoever will be chief among you, let him be your servant:

28 Even as the Son of man came not to be ministered unto, but to minister, and to give his life a ransom for many.

29 And as they departed from Jericho, a great multitude followed him.

30 ¶ And, behold, two blind men sitting by the way side, when they heard that Yashiyah passed by, cried out, saying, Have mercy on us, O Lord, *thou* Son of David.

31 And the multitude rebuked them, because they should hold their peace: but they cried the more, saying, Have mercy on us, O Lord, *thou* Son of David.

32 And Yashiyah stood still, and called them, and said, What will ye that I shall do unto you?

33 They say unto him, Lord, that our eyes may be opened.

34 So Yashiyah had compassion *on them*, and touched their eyes: and immediately their eyes received sight, and they followed him.

CHAPTER 21

AND when they drew nigh unto Jerusalem, and were come to Bethphage, unto the mount of Olives, then sent Yashiyah two disciples,

2 Saying unto them, Go into the village over against you, and straightway ye shall find an ass tied, and a colt with her: loose *them*, and bring *them* unto me.

3 And if any *man* say ought unto you, ye shall say, The Lord hath need of them; and straightway he will send them.

4 All this was done, that it might be fulfilled which was spoken by the prophet, saying,

5 Tell ye the daughter of Sion, Behold, thy King cometh unto thee, meek, and sitting upon an ass, and a colt the foal of an ass.

6 And the disciples went, and did as Yashiyah commanded them,

7 And brought the ass, and the colt, and put on them their clothes, and they set *him* thereon.

8 And a very great multitude spread their garments in the way; others cut down branches from the trees, and strawed *them* in the way.

9 And the multitudes that went before, and that followed, cried, saying, Hosanna to the Son of David: Blessed *is* he that cometh in the name of the Lord; Hosanna in the highest.

10 And when he was come into Jerusalem, all the city was moved, saying, Who is this?

11 And the multitude said, This is Yashiyah the prophet of Nazareth of Galilee.

12 ¶ And Yashiyah went into the temple of אֱלֹהִים, and cast out all them that sold and bought in the temple, and overthrew the tables of the moneychangers, and the seats of them that sold doves,

13 And said unto them, It is written, My house shall be called the house of prayer; but ye have made it a den of thieves.

14 And the blind and the lame came to him in the temple; and he healed them.

15 And when the chief priests and scribes saw the wonderful things that he did, and the children crying in the temple, and saying, Hosanna to the Son of David; they were sore displeased,

16 And said unto him, Hearest thou what these say? And Yashiyah saith unto them, Yea; have ye never read, Out of the mouth of babes and sucklings thou hast perfected praise?

17 ¶ And he left them, and went out of the city into Bethany; and he lodged there.

18 Now in the morning as he returned into the city, he hungered.

19 And when he saw a fig tree in the way, he came to it, and found nothing thereon, but leaves only, and said unto it, Let no fruit grow on thee henceforward for ever. And presently the fig tree withered away.

20 And when the disciples saw *it*, they marvelled, saying, How soon is the fig tree withered away!

21 Yashiyah answered and said unto them, Verily I say unto you, If ye have faith, and doubt not, ye shall not only do this *which is done* to the fig tree, but also if ye shall say unto this mountain, Be thou removed, and be thou cast into the sea; it shall be done.

22 And all things, whatsoever ye shall ask in prayer, believing, ye shall receive.

23 ¶ And when he was come into the temple, the chief priests and the elders of the people came unto him as he was teaching, and said, By what authority doest thou these things? and who gave thee this authority?

24 And Yashiyah answered and said unto them, I also will ask you one thing, which if ye tell me, I in like wise will tell you by what authority I do these things.

25 The baptism of John, whence was it? from heaven, or of men? And they reasoned with themselves, saying, If we shall say, From heaven; he will say unto us, Why did ye not then believe him?

26 But if we shall say, Of men; we fear the people; for all hold John as a prophet.

27 And they answered Yashiyah, and said, We cannot tell. And he said unto them, Neither tell I you by what authority I do these things.

28 ¶ But what think ye? A *certain* man had two sons; and he came to the first, and said, Son, go work to day in my vineyard.

29 He answered and said, I will not: but afterward he repented, and went.

30 And he came to the second, and said likewise. And he answered and said, I *go*, sir: and went not.

31 Whether of them twain did the will of *his* father? They say unto him, The first. Yashiyah saith unto them, Verily I say unto you, That the publicans and the harlots go into the kingdom of אֱלֹהִים before you.

32 For John came unto you in the way of righteousness, and ye believed him not: but the publicans and the harlots believed him: and ye, when ye had seen *it*, repented not afterward, that ye might believe him.

33 ¶ Hear another parable: There was a certain householder, which planted a vineyard, and hedged it round about, and digged a winepress in it, and built a tower, and let it out to husbandmen, and went into a far country:

34 And when the time of the fruit drew near, he sent his servants to the husbandmen, that they might receive the fruits of it.

35 And the husbandmen took his servants, and beat one, and killed another, and stoned another.

36 Again, he sent other servants more than the first: and they did unto them likewise.

37 But last of all he sent unto them his son, saying, They will reverence my son.

38 But when the husbandmen saw the son, they said among themselves, This is the heir; come, let us kill him, and let us seize on his inheritance.

39 And they caught him, and cast *him* out of the vineyard, and slew *him*.

40 When the lord therefore of the vineyard cometh, what will he do unto those husbandmen?

41 They say unto him, He will miserably destroy those wicked men, and will let out *his* vineyard unto other husbandmen, which shall render him the fruits in their seasons.

42 Yashiyah saith unto them, Did ye never read in the scriptures, The stone which the builders rejected, the same is become the head of the corner: this is the Lord's doing, and it is marvellous in our eyes?

43 Therefore say I unto you, The kingdom of אֱלֹהִים shall be taken from you, and given to a nation bringing forth the fruits thereof.

44 And whosoever shall fall on this stone shall be broken: but on whomsoever it shall fall, it will grind him to powder.

45 And when the chief priests and Pharisees had heard his parables, they perceived that he spake of them.

46 But when they sought to lay hands on him, they feared the multitude, because they took him for a prophet.

CHAPTER 22

AND Yashiyah answered and spake unto them again by parables, and said,

2 The kingdom of heaven is like unto a certain king, which made a marriage for his son,

3 And sent forth his servants to call them that were bidden to the wedding: and they would not come.

4 Again, he sent forth other servants, saying, Tell them which are bidden, Behold, I have prepared my dinner: my oxen and *my* fatlings *are* killed, and all things *are* ready: come unto the marriage.

5 But they made light of *it*, and went their ways, one to his farm, another to his merchandise:

6 And the remnant took his servants, and entreated *them* spitefully, and slew *them*.

7 But when the king heard *thereof*, he was wroth: and he sent forth his armies, and destroyed those murderers, and burned up their city.

8 Then saith he to his servants, The wedding is ready, but they which were bidden were not worthy.

9 Go ye therefore into the highways, and as many as ye shall find, bid to the marriage.

10 So those servants went out into the highways, and gathered together all as many as they found, both bad and good: and the wedding was furnished with guests.

11 ¶ And when the king came in to see the guests, he saw there a man which had not on a wedding garment:

12 And he saith unto him, Friend, how camest thou in hither not having a wedding garment? And he was speechless.

13 Then said the king to the servants, Bind him hand and foot, and take him away, and cast *him* into outer darkness; there shall be weeping and gnashing of teeth.

14 For many are called, but few *are* chosen.

15 ¶ Then went the Pharisees, and took counsel how they might entangle him in *his* talk.

16 And they sent out unto him their disciples with the Herodians, saying, Master, we know that thou art true, and teachest the way of אֱלֹהִים in truth, neither carest thou for any *man:* for thou regardest not the person of men.

17 Tell us therefore, What thinkest thou? Is it lawful to give tribute unto Cæsar, or not?

18 But Yashiyah perceived their wickedness, and said, Why tempt ye me, *ye* hypocrites?

19 Shew me the tribute money. And they brought unto him a penny.

20 And he saith unto them, Whose *is* this image and superscription?

21 They say unto him, Cæsar's. Then saith he unto them, Render therefore unto Cæsar the things which are Cæsar's; and unto אֱלֹהִים the things that are אֱלֹהִים's.

22 When they had heard *these words*, they marvelled, and left him, and went their way.

23 ¶ The same day came to him the Sadducees, which say that there is no resurrection, and asked him,

24 Saying, Master, Moses said, If a man die, having no children, his brother shall marry his wife, and raise up seed unto his brother.

25 Now there were with us seven brethren: and the first, when he had married a wife, deceased, and, having no issue, left his wife unto his brother:

26 Likewise the second also, and the third, unto the seventh.

27 And last of all the woman died also.

28 Therefore in the resurrection whose wife shall she be of the seven? for they all had her.

29 Yashiyah answered and said unto them, Ye do err, not knowing the scriptures, nor the power of אֱלֹהִים.

30 For in the resurrection they neither marry, nor are given in marriage, but are as the angels of אֱלֹהִים in heaven.

31 But as touching the resurrection of the dead, have ye not read that which was spoken unto you by אֱלֹהִים, saying,

32 I am the אֱלֹהִים of Abraham, and the אֱלֹהִים of Isaac, and the אֱלֹהִים of Jacob? אֱלֹהִים is not the אֱלֹהִים of the dead, but of the living.

33 And when the multitude heard *this*, they were astonished at his doctrine.

34 ¶ But when the Pharisees had heard that he had put the Sadducees to silence, they were gathered together.

35 Then one of them, *which was* a lawyer, asked *him a question*, tempting him, and saying,

36 Master, which *is* the great commandment in the law?

37 Yashiyah said unto him, Thou shalt love the Lord thy אֱלֹהִים with all thy heart, and with all thy soul, and with all thy mind.

38 This is the first and great commandment.

39 And the second *is* like unto it, Thou shalt love thy neighbour as thyself.

40 On these two commandments hang all the law and the prophets.

41 ¶ While the Pharisees were gathered together, Yashiyah asked them,

42 Saying, What think ye of Christ? whose son is he? They say unto him, *The Son* of David.

43 He saith unto them, How then doth David in spirit call him Lord, saying,

44 The LORD said unto my Lord, Sit thou on my right hand, till I make thine enemies thy footstool?

45 If David then call him Lord, how is he his son?

46 And no man was able to answer him a word, neither durst any *man* from that day forth ask him any more *questions*.

CHAPTER 23

THEN spake Yashiyah to the multitude, and to his disciples,

2 Saying, The scribes and the Pharisees sit in Moses' seat:

3 All therefore whatsoever they bid you observe, *that* observe and do; but do not ye after their works: for they say, and do not.

4 For they bind heavy burdens and grievous to be borne, and lay *them* on men's shoulders; but they *themselves* will not move them

with one of their fingers.

5 But all their works they do for to be seen of men: they make broad their phylacteries, and enlarge the borders of their garments,

6 And love the uppermost rooms at feasts, and the chief seats in the synagogues,

7 And greetings in the markets, and to be called of men, Rabbi, Rabbi.

8 But be not ye called Rabbi: for one is your Master, *even* Christ; and all ye are brethren.

9 And call no *man* your father upon the earth: for one is your Father, which is in heaven.

10 Neither be ye called masters: for one is your Master, *even* Christ.

11 But he that is greatest among you shall be your servant.

12 And whosoever shall exalt himself shall be abased; and he that shall humble himself shall be exalted.

13 ¶ But woe unto you, scribes and Pharisees, hypocrites! for ye shut up the kingdom of heaven against men: for ye neither go in *yourselves*, neither suffer ye them that are entering to go in.

14 Woe unto you, scribes and Pharisees, hypocrites! for ye devour widows' houses, and for a pretence make long prayer: therefore ye shall receive the greater damnation.

15 Woe unto you, scribes and Pharisees, hypocrites! for ye compass sea and land to make one proselyte, and when he is made, ye make him twofold more the child of hell than yourselves.

16 Woe unto you, *ye* blind guides, which say, Whosoever shall swear by the temple, it is nothing; but whosoever shall swear by the gold of the temple, he is a debtor!

17 *Ye* fools and blind: for whether is greater, the gold, or the temple that sanctifieth the gold?

18 And, Whosoever shall swear by the altar, it is nothing; but whosoever sweareth by the gift that is upon it, he is guilty.

19 *Ye* fools and blind: for whether *is* greater, the gift, or the altar that sanctifieth the gift?

20 Whoso therefore shall swear by the altar, sweareth by it, and by all things thereon.

21 And whoso shall swear by the temple, sweareth by it, and by him that dwelleth therein.

22 And he that shall swear by heaven, sweareth by the throne of אֱלֹהִים, and by him that sitteth thereon.

23 Woe unto you, scribes and Pharisees, hypocrites! for ye pay tithe of mint and anise and cummin, and have omitted the weightier *matters* of the law, judgment, mercy, and faith: these ought ye to have done, and not to leave the other undone.

24 *Ye* blind guides, which strain at a gnat, and swallow a camel.

25 Woe unto you, scribes and Pharisees, hypocrites! for ye make clean the outside of the cup and of the platter, but within they are full of extortion and excess.

26 *Thou* blind Pharisee, cleanse first that *which is* within the cup and platter, that the outside of them may be clean also.

27 Woe unto you, scribes and Pharisees, hypocrites! for ye are like unto whited sepulchres, which indeed appear beautiful outward, but are within full of dead *men's* bones, and of all uncleanness.

28 Even so ye also outwardly appear righteous unto men, but within ye are full of hypocrisy and iniquity.

29 Woe unto you, scribes and Pharisees, hypocrites! because ye build the tombs of the prophets, and garnish the sepulchres of the righteous,

30 And say, If we had been in the days of our fathers, we would not have been partakers with them in the blood of the prophets.

31 Wherefore ye be witnesses unto yourselves, that ye are the children of them which killed the prophets.

32 Fill ye up then the measure of your fathers.

33 *Ye* serpents, *ye* generation of vipers, how can ye escape the damnation of hell?

34 ¶ Wherefore, behold, I send unto you prophets, and wise men, and scribes: and *some* of them ye shall kill and crucify; and *some* of them shall ye scourge in your synagogues, and persecute *them* from city to city:

35 That upon you may come all the righteous blood shed upon the earth, from the blood of righteous Abel unto the blood of Zacharias son of Barachias, whom ye slew between the temple and the altar.

36 Verily I say unto you, All these things shall come upon this generation.

37 O Jerusalem, Jerusalem, *thou* that killest the prophets, and stonest them which are sent unto thee, how often would I have gathered thy children together, even as a hen gathereth her chickens under *her* wings, and ye would not!

38 Behold, your house is left unto you desolate.

39 For I say unto you, Ye shall not see me henceforth, till ye shall say, Blessed *is* he that cometh in the name of the Lord.

CHAPTER 24

AND Yashiyah went out, and departed from the temple: and his disciples came to *him* for to shew him the buildings of the temple.

2 And Yashiyah said unto them, See ye not all these things? verily I say unto you, There shall not be left here one stone upon another, that shall not be thrown down.

3 ¶ And as he sat upon the mount of Olives, the disciples came unto him privately, saying, Tell us, when shall these things be? and what *shall be* the sign of thy coming, and of the end of the world?

4 And Yashiyah answered and said unto them, Take heed that no man deceive you.

5 For many shall come in my name, saying, I am Christ; and shall deceive many.

6 And ye shall hear of wars and rumours of wars: see that ye be not troubled: for all *these things* must come to pass, but the end is not yet.

7 For nation shall rise against nation, and kingdom against kingdom: and there shall be famines, and pestilences, and earthquakes, in divers places.

8 All these *are* the beginning of sorrows.

9 Then shall they deliver you up to be afflicted, and shall kill you: and ye shall be hated of all nations for my name's sake.

10 And then shall many be offended, and shall betray one another, and shall hate one another.

11 And many false prophets shall rise, and shall deceive many.

12 And because iniquity shall abound, the love of many shall wax cold.

13 But he that shall endure unto the end, the same shall be saved.

14 And this gospel of the kingdom shall be preached in all the world for a witness unto all nations; and then shall the end come.

15 When ye therefore shall see the abomination of desolation, spoken of by Daniel the prophet, stand in the holy place, (whoso readeth, let him understand:)

16 Then let them which be in Judæa flee into the mountains:

17 Let him which is on the housetop not come down to take any thing out of his house:

18 Neither let him which is in the field return back to take his clothes.

19 And woe unto them that are with child, and to them that give suck in those days!

20 But pray ye that your flight be not in the winter, neither on the sabbath day:

21 For then shall be great tribulation, such as was not since the beginning of the world to this time, no, nor ever shall be.

22 And except those days should be shortened, there should no flesh be saved: but for the elect's sake those days shall be shortened.

23 Then if any man shall say unto you, Lo, here *is* Christ, or there; believe *it* not.

24 For there shall arise false Christs, and false prophets, and shall shew great signs and wonders; insomuch that, if *it were* possible, they shall deceive the very elect.

25 Behold, I have told you before.

26 Wherefore if they shall say unto you, Behold, he is in the desert; go not forth: behold, *he is* in the secret chambers; believe *it* not.

27 For as the lightning cometh out of the east, and shineth even unto the west; so shall also the coming of the Son of man be.

28 For wheresoever the carcase is, there will the eagles be gathered together.

29 ¶ Immediately after the tribulation of those days shall the sun be darkened, and the moon shall not give her light, and the stars shall fall from heaven, and the powers of the heavens shall be shaken:

30 And then shall appear the sign of the Son of man in heaven: and then shall all the tribes of the earth mourn, and they shall see the Son of man coming in the clouds of heaven with power and great glory.

31 And he shall send his angels with a great sound of a trumpet, and they shall gather together his elect from the four winds, from one end of heaven to the other.

32 Now learn a parable of the fig tree; When his branch is yet tender, and putteth forth leaves, ye know that summer *is* nigh:

33 So likewise ye, when ye shall see all these things, know that it is near, *even* at the doors.

34 Verily I say unto you, This generation shall not pass, till all these things be fulfilled.

35 Heaven and earth shall pass away, but my words shall not pass away.

36 ¶ But of that day and hour knoweth no *man*, no, not the angels of heaven, but my Father only.

37 But as the days of Noe *were*, so shall also the coming of the Son of man be.

38 For as in the days that were before the flood they were eating and drinking, marrying and giving in marriage, until the day that Noe entered into the ark,

39 And knew not until the flood came, and took them all away; so shall also the coming of the Son of man be.

40 Then shall two be in the field; the one shall be taken, and the other left.

41 Two *women shall be* grinding at the mill; the one shall be taken, and the other left.

42 ¶ Watch therefore: for ye know not what hour your Lord doth come.

43 But know this, that if the goodman of the house had known in what watch the thief would come, he would have watched, and would not have suffered his house to be broken up.

44 Therefore be ye also ready: for in such an hour as ye think not the Son of man cometh.

45 Who then is a faithful and wise servant, whom his lord hath made ruler over his household, to give them meat in due season?

46 Blessed *is* that servant, whom his lord when he cometh shall find so doing.

47 Verily I say unto you, That he shall make him ruler over all his goods.

48 But and if that evil servant shall say in his heart, My lord delayeth his coming;

49 And shall begin to smite *his* fellowservants, and to eat and drink with the drunken;

50 The lord of that servant shall come in a day when he looketh not for *him*, and in an hour that he is not aware of,

51 And shall cut him asunder, and appoint *him* his portion with the hypocrites: there shall be weeping and gnashing of teeth.

CHAPTER 25

THEN shall the kingdom of heaven be likened unto ten virgins, which took their lamps, and went forth to meet the bridegroom.

2 And five of them were wise, and five *were* foolish.

3 They that *were* foolish took their lamps, and took no oil with them:

4 But the wise took oil in their vessels with their lamps.

5 While the bridegroom tarried, they all slumbered and slept.

6 And at midnight there was a cry made, Behold, the bridegroom cometh; go ye out to meet him.

7 Then all those virgins arose, and trimmed their lamps.

8 And the foolish said unto the wise, Give us of your oil; for our lamps are gone out.

9 But the wise answered, saying, *Not so;* lest there be not enough for us and you: but go ye rather to them that sell, and buy for yourselves.

10 And while they went to buy, the bridegroom came; and they that were ready went in with him to the marriage: and the door was shut.

11 Afterward came also the other virgins, saying, Lord, Lord, open to us.

12 But he answered and said, Verily I say unto you, I know you not.

13 Watch therefore, for ye know neither the day nor the hour wherein the Son of man cometh.

14 ¶ For *the kingdom of heaven is* as a man travelling into a far country, *who* called his own servants, and delivered unto them his goods.

15 And unto one he gave five talents, to another two, and to another one; to every man according to his several ability; and straightway took his journey.

16 Then he that had received the five talents went and traded with the same, and made *them* other five talents.

17 And likewise he that *had received* two, he also gained other two.

18 But he that had received one went and digged in the earth, and hid his lord's money.

19 After a long time the lord of those servants cometh, and reckoneth with them.

20 And so he that had received five talents came and brought other five talents, saying, Lord, thou deliveredst unto me five talents: behold, I have gained beside them five talents more.

21 His lord said unto him, Well done, *thou* good and faithful servant: thou hast been faithful over a few things, I will make thee ruler over many things: enter thou into the joy of thy lord.

22 He also that had received two talents came and said, Lord, thou deliveredst unto me two talents: behold, I have gained two other talents beside them.

23 His lord said unto him, Well done, good and faithful servant; thou hast been faithful over a few things, I will make thee ruler over many things: enter thou into the joy of thy lord.

24 Then he which had received the one talent came and said, Lord, I knew thee that thou art an hard man, reaping where thou hast not sown, and gathering where thou hast not strawed:

25 And I was afraid, and went and hid thy talent in the earth: lo, *there* thou hast *that is* thine.

26 His lord answered and said unto him, *Thou* wicked and slothful servant, thou knewest that I reap where I sowed not, and gather where I have not strawed:

27 Thou oughtest therefore to have put my money to the exchangers, and *then* at my coming I should have received mine own with usury.

28 Take therefore the talent from him, and give *it* unto him which hath ten talents.

29 For unto every one that hath shall be given, and he shall have abundance: but from him that hath not shall be taken away even that which he hath.

30 And cast ye the unprofitable servant into outer darkness: there shall be weeping and gnashing of teeth.

31 ¶ When the Son of man shall come in his glory, and all the holy angels with him, then shall he sit upon the throne of his glory:

32 And before him shall be gathered all nations: and he shall separate them one from another, as a shepherd divideth *his* sheep from the goats:

33 And he shall set the sheep on his right hand, but the goats on the left.

34 Then shall the King say unto them on his right hand, Come, ye blessed of my Father, inherit the kingdom prepared for you from the foundation of the world:

35 For I was an hungred, and ye gave me meat: I was thirsty, and ye gave me drink: I was a stranger, and ye took me in:

36 Naked, and ye clothed me: I was sick, and ye visited me: I was in prison, and ye came unto me.

37 Then shall the righteous answer him, saying, Lord, when saw we thee an hungred, and fed *thee?* or thirsty, and gave *thee* drink?

38 When saw we thee a stranger, and took *thee* in? or naked, and clothed *thee?*

39 Or when saw we thee sick, or in prison, and came unto thee?

40 And the King shall answer and say unto them, Verily I say unto you, Inasmuch as ye have done *it* unto one of the least of these my brethren, ye have done *it* unto me.

41 Then shall he say also unto them on the left hand, Depart from me, ye cursed, into everlasting fire, prepared for the devil and his angels:

42 For I was an hungred, and ye gave me no meat: I was thirsty, and ye gave me no drink:

43 I was a stranger, and ye took me not in: naked, and ye clothed me not: sick, and in prison, and ye visited me not.

44 Then shall they also answer him, saying, Lord, when saw we thee an hungred, or athirst, or a stranger, or naked, or sick, or in prison, and did not minister unto thee?

45 Then shall he answer them, saying, Verily I say unto you, Inasmuch as ye did *it* not to one of the least of these, ye did *it* not to me.

46 And these shall go away into everlasting punishment: but the righteous into life eternal.

CHAPTER 26

AND it came to pass, when Yashiyah had finished all these sayings, he said unto his disciples,

2 Ye know that after two days is *the feast of* the passover, and the Son of man is betrayed to be crucified.

3 Then assembled together the chief priests, and the scribes, and the elders of the people, unto the palace of the high priest, who was called Caiaphas,

4 And consulted that they might take Yashiyah by subtilty, and kill *him.*

5 But they said, Not on the feast *day*, lest there be an uproar among the people.

6 ¶ Now when Yashiyah was in Bethany, in the house of Simon the leper,

7 There came unto him a woman having an alabaster box of very precious ointment, and poured it on his head, as he sat *at meat.*

8 But when his disciples saw *it*, they had indignation, saying, To what purpose *is* this waste?

9 For this ointment might have been sold for much, and given to the poor.

10 When Yashiyah understood *it*, he said unto them, Why trouble ye the woman? for she hath wrought a good work upon me.

11 For ye have the poor always with you; but me ye have not always.

12 For in that she hath poured this ointment on my body, she did *it* for my burial.

13 Verily I say unto you, Wheresoever this gospel shall be preached in the whole world, *there* shall also this, that this woman hath done, be told for a memorial of her.

14 ¶ Then one of the twelve, called Judas Iscariot, went unto the chief priests,

15 And said *unto them*, What will ye give me, and I will deliver him unto you? And they covenanted with him for thirty pieces of silver.

16 And from that time he sought opportunity to betray him.

17 ¶ Now the first *day* of the *feast of* unleavened bread the disciples came to Yashiyah, saying unto him, Where wilt thou that we prepare for thee to eat the passover?

18 And he said, Go into the city to such a man, and say unto him, The Master saith, My time is at hand; I will keep the passover at thy house with my disciples.

19 And the disciples did as Yashiyah had appointed them; and they made ready the passover.

20 Now when the even was come, he sat down with the twelve.

21 And as they did eat, he said, Verily I say unto you, that one of you shall betray me.

22 And they were exceeding sorrowful, and began every one of them to say unto him, Lord, is it I?

23 And he answered and said, He that dippeth *his* hand with me in the dish, the same shall betray me.

24 The Son of man goeth as it is written of him: but woe unto that man by whom the Son of man is betrayed! it had been good for that man if he had not been born.

25 Then Judas, which betrayed him, answered and said, Master, is it I? He said unto him, Thou hast said.

26 ¶ And as they were eating, Yashiyah took bread, and blessed *it*, and brake *it*, and gave *it* to the disciples, and said, Take, eat; this is

my body.

27 And he took the cup, and gave thanks, and gave *it* to them, saying, Drink ye all of it;

28 For this is my blood of the new testament, which is shed for many for the remission of sins.

29 But I say unto you, I will not drink henceforth of this fruit of the vine, until that day when I drink it new with you in my Father's kingdom.

30 And when they had sung an hymn, they went out into the mount of Olives.

31 Then saith Yashiyah unto them, All ye shall be offended because of me this night: for it is written, I will smite the shepherd, and the sheep of the flock shall be scattered abroad.

32 But after I am risen again, I will go before you into Galilee.

33 Peter answered and said unto him, Though all *men* shall be offended because of thee, *yet* will I never be offended.

34 Yashiyah said unto him, Verily I say unto thee, That this night, before the cock crow, thou shalt deny me thrice.

35 Peter said unto him, Though I should die with thee, yet will I not deny thee. Likewise also said all the disciples.

36 ¶ Then cometh Yashiyah with them unto a place called Gethsemane, and saith unto the disciples, Sit ye here, while I go and pray yonder.

37 And he took with him Peter and the two sons of Zebedee, and began to be sorrowful and very heavy.

38 Then saith he unto them, My soul is exceeding sorrowful, even unto death: tarry ye here, and watch with me.

39 And he went a little further, and fell on his face, and prayed, saying, O my Father, if it be possible, let this cup pass from me: nevertheless not as I will, but as thou *wilt*.

40 And he cometh unto the disciples, and findeth them asleep, and saith unto Peter, What, could ye not watch with me one hour?

41 Watch and pray, that ye enter not into temptation: the spirit indeed *is* willing, but the flesh *is* weak.

42 He went away again the second time, and prayed, saying, O my Father, if this cup may not pass away from me, except I drink it, thy will be done.

43 And he came and found them asleep again: for their eyes were heavy.

44 And he left them, and went away again, and prayed the third time, saying the same words.

45 Then cometh he to his disciples, and saith unto them, Sleep on now, and take *your* rest: behold, the hour is at hand, and the Son of man is betrayed into the hands of sinners.

46 Rise, let us be going: behold, he is at hand that doth betray me.

47 ¶ And while he yet spake, lo, Judas, one of the twelve, came, and with him a great multitude with swords and staves, from the chief priests and elders of the people.

48 Now he that betrayed him gave them a sign, saying, Whomsoever I shall kiss, that same is he: hold him fast.

49 And forthwith he came to Yashiyah, and said, Hail, master; and kissed him.

50 And Yashiyah said unto him, Friend, wherefore art thou come? Then came they, and laid hands on Yashiyah, and took him.

51 And, behold, one of them which were with Yashiyah stretched out *his* hand, and drew his sword, and struck a servant of the high priest's, and smote off his ear.

52 Then said Yashiyah unto him, Put up again thy sword into his place: for all they that take the sword shall perish with the sword.

53 Thinkest thou that I cannot now pray to my Father, and he shall presently give me more than twelve legions of angels?

54 But how then shall the scriptures be fulfilled, that thus it must be?

55 In that same hour said Yashiyah to the multitudes, Are ye come out as against a thief with swords and staves for to take me? I sat daily with you teaching in the temple, and ye laid no hold on me.

56 But all this was done, that the scriptures of the prophets might be fulfilled. Then all the disciples forsook him, and fled.

57 ¶ And they that had laid hold on Yashiyah led *him* away to Caiaphas the high priest, where the scribes and the elders were assembled.

58 But Peter followed him afar off unto the high priest's palace, and went in, and sat with the servants, to see the end.

59 Now the chief priests, and elders, and all the council, sought false witness against Yashiyah, to put him to death;

60 But found none: yea, though many false witnesses came, *yet* found they none. At the last came two false witnesses,

61 And said, This *fellow* said, I am able to destroy the temple of אֱלֹהִים, and to build it in three days.

62 And the high priest arose, and said unto him, Answerest thou nothing? what *is it which* these witness against thee?

63 But Yashiyah held his peace. And the high priest answered and said unto him, I adjure thee by the living אֱלֹהִים, that thou tell us whether thou be the Christ, the Son of אֱלֹהִים.

64 Yashiyah saith unto him, Thou hast said: nevertheless I say unto you, Hereafter shall ye see the Son of man sitting on the right hand of power, and coming in the clouds of heaven.

65 Then the high priest rent his clothes, saying, He hath spoken blasphemy; what further need have we of witnesses? behold, now ye have heard his blasphemy.

66 What think ye? They answered and said, He is guilty of death.

67 Then did they spit in his face, and buffeted him; and others smote *him* with the palms of their hands,

68 Saying, Prophesy unto us, thou Christ, Who is he that smote thee?

69 ¶ Now Peter sat without in the palace: and a damsel came unto him, saying, Thou also wast with Yashiyah of Galilee.

70 But he denied before *them* all, saying, I know not what thou sayest.

71 And when he was gone out into the porch, another *maid* saw him, and said unto them that were there, This *fellow* was also with Yashiyah of Nazareth.

72 And again he denied with an oath, I do not know the man.

73 And after a while came unto *him* they that stood by, and said to Peter, Surely thou also art *one* of them; for thy speech bewrayeth thee.

74 Then began he to curse and to swear, *saying*, I know not the man. And immediately the cock crew.

75 And Peter remembered the word of Yashiyah, which said unto him, Before the cock crow, thou shalt deny me thrice. And he went out, and wept bitterly.

CHAPTER 27

WHEN the morning was come, all the chief priests and elders of the people took counsel against Yashiyah to put him to death:

2 And when they had bound him, they led *him* away, and delivered him to Pontius Pilate the governor.

3 ¶ Then Judas, which had betrayed him, when he saw that he was condemned, repented himself, and brought again the thirty pieces of silver to the chief priests and elders,

4 Saying, I have sinned in that I have betrayed the innocent blood. And they said, What *is that* to us? see thou *to that.*

5 And he cast down the pieces of silver in the temple, and departed, and went and hanged himself.

6 And the chief priests took the silver pieces, and said, It is not lawful for to put them into the treasury, because it is the price of blood.

7 And they took counsel, and bought with them the potter's field, to bury strangers in.

8 Wherefore that field was called, The field of blood, unto this day.

9 Then was fulfilled that which was spoken by Jeremy the prophet, saying, And they took the thirty pieces of silver, the price of him that was valued, whom they of the children of Israel did value;

10 And gave them for the potter's field, as the Lord appointed me.

11 And Yashiyah stood before the governor: and the governor asked him, saying, Art thou the King of the Jews? And Yashiyah said unto him, Thou sayest.

12 And when he was accused of the chief priests and elders, he answered nothing.

13 Then said Pilate unto him, Hearest thou not how many things they witness against thee?

14 And he answered him to never a word; insomuch that the governor marvelled greatly.

15 Now at *that* feast the governor was wont to release unto the people a prisoner, whom they would.

16 And they had then a notable prisoner, called Barabbas.

17 Therefore when they were gathered together, Pilate said unto them, Whom will ye that I release unto you? Barabbas, or Yashiyah which is called Christ?

18 For he knew that for envy they had delivered him.

19 ¶ When he was set down on the judgment seat, his wife sent unto him, saying, Have thou nothing to do with that just man: for I have suffered many things this day in a dream because of him.

20 But the chief priests and elders persuaded the multitude that they should ask Barabbas, and destroy Yashiyah.

21 The governor answered and said unto them, Whether of the twain will ye that I release unto you? They said, Barabbas.

22 Pilate saith unto them, What shall I do then with Yashiyah which is called Christ? *They* all say unto him, Let him be crucified.

23 And the governor said, Why, what evil hath he done? But they cried out the more, saying, Let him be crucified.

24 ¶ When Pilate saw that he could prevail nothing, but *that* rather a tumult was made, he took water, and washed *his* hands before the multitude, saying, I am innocent of the blood of this just person: see ye *to it.*

25 Then answered all the people, and said, His blood *be* on us, and on our children.

26 ¶ Then released he Barabbas unto them: and when he had scourged Yashiyah, he delivered *him* to be crucified.

27 Then the soldiers of the governor took Yashiyah into the common hall, and gathered unto him the whole band *of soldiers.*

28 And they stripped him, and put on him a scarlet robe.

29 ¶ And when they had platted a crown of thorns, they put *it* upon his head, and a reed in his right hand: and they bowed the knee before him, and mocked him, saying, Hail, King of the Jews!

30 And they spit upon him, and took the reed, and smote him on the head.

31 And after that they had mocked him, they took the robe off from him, and put his own raiment on him, and led him away to crucify *him.*

32 And as they came out, they found a man of Cyrene, Simon by name: him they compelled to bear his cross.

33 And when they were come unto a place called Golgotha, that is to say, a place of a skull,

34 ¶ They gave him vinegar to drink mingled with gall: and when he had tasted *thereof,* he would not drink.

35 And they crucified him, and parted his garments, casting lots: that it might be fulfilled which was spoken by the prophet, They parted my garments among them, and upon my vesture did they cast lots.

36 And sitting down they watched him there;

37 And set up over his head his accusation written, THIS IS JESUS THE KING OF THE JEWS.

38 Then were there two thieves crucified with him, one on the right hand, and another on the left.

39 ¶ And they that passed by reviled him, wagging their heads,

40 And saying, Thou that destroyest the temple, and buildest *it* in three days, save thyself. If thou be the Son of אֱלֹהִים, come down from the cross.

41 Likewise also the chief priests mocking *him,* with the scribes and elders, said,

42 He saved others; himself he cannot save. If he be the King of Israel, let him now come down from the cross, and we will believe him.

43 He trusted in אֱלֹהִים; let him deliver him now, if he will have him: for he said, I am the Son of אֱלֹהִים.

44 The thieves also, which were crucified with him, cast the same in his teeth.

45 Now from the sixth hour there was darkness over all the land unto the ninth hour.

46 And about the ninth hour Yashiyah cried with a loud voice, saying, Eli, Eli, lama sabachthani? that is to say, My אֱלֹהִים, my אֱ, why hast thou forsaken me?

47 Some of them that stood there, when they heard *that,* said, This *man* calleth for Elias.

48 And straightway one of them ran, and took a spunge, and filled *it* with vinegar, and put *it* on a reed, and gave him to drink.

49 The rest said, Let be, let us see whether Elias will come to save him.

50 ¶ Yashiyah, when he had cried again with a loud voice, yielded up the ghost.

51 And, behold, the veil of the temple was rent in twain from the top to the bottom; and the earth did quake, and the rocks rent;

52 And the graves were opened; and many bodies of the saints which slept arose,

53 And came out of the graves after his resurrection, and went into the holy city, and appeared unto many.

54 Now when the centurion, and they that were with him, watching Yashiyah, saw the earthquake, and those things that were done, they feared greatly, saying, Truly this was the Son of אֱלֹהִים.

55 And many women were there beholding afar off, which followed Yashiyah from Galilee, ministering unto him:

56 Among which was Mary Magdalene, and Mary the mother of James and Joses, and the mother of Zebedee's children.

57 When the even was come, there came a rich man of Arimathæa, named Joseph, who also himself was Yashiyah' disciple:

58 He went to Pilate, and begged the body of Yashiyah. Then Pilate commanded the body to be delivered.

59 And when Joseph had taken the body, he wrapped it in a clean linen cloth,

60 And laid it in his own new tomb, which he had hewn out in the rock: and he rolled a great stone to the door of the sepulchre, and departed.

61 And there was Mary Magdalene, and the other Mary, sitting over against the sepulchre.

62 ¶ Now the next day, that followed the day of the preparation, the chief priests and Pharisees came together unto Pilate,

63 Saying, Sir, we remember that that deceiver said, while he was yet alive, After three days I will rise again.

64 Command therefore that the sepulchre be made sure until the third day, lest his disciples come by night, and steal him away, and say unto the people, He is risen from the dead: so the last error shall be worse than the first.

65 Pilate said unto them, Ye have a watch: go your way, make *it* as sure as ye can.

66 So they went, and made the sepulchre sure, sealing the stone, and setting a watch.

CHAPTER 28

IN the end of the sabbath, as it began to dawn toward the first *day* of the week, came Mary Magdalene and the other Mary to see the sepulchre.

2 And, behold, there was a great earthquake: for the angel of the Lord descended from heaven, and came and rolled back the stone from the door, and sat upon it.

3 His countenance was like lightning, and his raiment white as snow:

4 And for fear of him the keepers did shake, and became as dead *men*.

5 And the angel answered and said unto the women, Fear not ye: for I know that ye seek Yashiyah, which was crucified.

6 He is not here: for he is risen, as he said. Come, see the place where the Lord lay.

7 And go quickly, and tell his disciples that he is risen from the dead; and, behold, he goeth before you into Galilee; there shall ye see him: lo, I have told you.

8 And they departed quickly from the sepulchre with fear and great joy; and did run to bring his disciples word.

9 ¶ And as they went to tell his disciples, behold, Yashiyah met them, saying, All hail. And they came and held him by the feet, and worshipped him.

10 Then said Yashiyah unto them, Be not afraid: go tell my brethren that they go into Galilee, and there shall they see me.

11 ¶ Now when they were going, behold, some of the watch came into the city, and shewed unto the chief priests all the things that were done.

12 And when they were assembled with the elders, and had taken counsel, they gave large money unto the soldiers,

13 Saying, Say ye, His disciples came by night, and stole him *away* while we slept.

14 And if this come to the governor's ears, we will persuade him, and secure you.

15 So they took the money, and did as they were taught: and this saying is commonly reported among the Jews until this day.

16 ¶ Then the eleven disciples went away into Galilee, into a mountain where Yashiyah had appointed them.

17 And when they saw him, they worshipped him: but some doubted.

18 And Yashiyah came and spake unto them, saying, All power is given unto me in heaven and in earth.

19 ¶ Go ye therefore, and teach all nations, baptizing them in the name of the Father, and of the Son, and of the Holy Ghost:

20 Teaching them to observe all things whatsoever I have commanded you: and, lo, I am with you alway, *even* unto the end of the world. Amen.

THE GOSPEL ACCORDING TO

ST. MARK.

CHAPTER 1

THE beginning of the gospel of Yashiyah Christ, the Son of אֱלֹהִים;

2 As it is written in the prophets, Behold, I send my messenger before thy face, which shall prepare thy way before thee.

3 The voice of one crying in the wilderness, Prepare ye the way of the Lord, make his paths straight.

4 John did baptize in the wilderness, and preach the baptism of repentance for the remission of sins.

5 And there went out unto him all the land of Judæa, and they of Jerusalem, and were all baptized of him in the river of Jordan, confessing their sins.

6 And John was clothed with camel's hair, and with a girdle of a skin about his loins; and he did eat locusts and wild honey;

7 And preached, saying, There cometh one mightier than I after me, the latchet of whose shoes I am not worthy to stoop down and unloose.

8 I indeed have baptized you with water: but he shall baptize you with the Holy Ghost.

9 And it came to pass in those days, that Yashiyah came from Nazareth of Galilee, and was baptized of John in Jordan.

10 And straightway coming up out of the water, he saw the heavens opened, and the Spirit like a dove descending upon him:

11 And there came a voice from heaven, *saying*, Thou art my beloved Son, in whom I am well pleased.

12 And immediately the Spirit driveth him into the wilderness.

13 And he was there in the wilderness forty days, tempted of Satan; and was with the wild beasts; and the angels ministered unto him.

14 Now after that John was put in prison, Yashiyah came into Galilee, preaching the gospel of the kingdom of אֱלֹהִים,

15 And saying, The time is fulfilled, and the kingdom of אֱלֹהִים is at hand: repent ye, and believe the gospel.

16 Now as he walked by the sea of Galilee, he saw Simon and Andrew his brother casting a net into the sea: for they were fishers.

17 And Yashiyah said unto them, Come ye after me, and I will make you to become fishers of men.

18 And straightway they forsook their nets, and followed him.

19 And when he had gone a little further thence, he saw James the *son* of Zebedee, and John his brother, who also were in the ship mending their nets.

20 And straightway he called them: and they left their father Zebedee in the ship with the hired servants, and went after him.

21 And they went into Capernaum; and straightway on the sabbath day he entered into the synagogue, and taught.

22 And they were astonished at his doctrine: for he taught them as one that had authority, and not as the scribes.

23 And there was in their synagogue a man with an unclean spirit; and he cried out,

24 Saying, Let *us* alone; what have we to do with thee, thou Yashiyah of Nazareth? art thou come to destroy us? I know thee who thou

art, the Holy One of אֱלֹהִים.

25 And Yashiyah rebuked him, saying, Hold thy peace, and come out of him.

26 And when the unclean spirit had torn him, and cried with a loud voice, he came out of him.

27 And they were all amazed, insomuch that they questioned among themselves, saying, What thing is this? what new doctrine *is* this? for with authority commandeth he even the unclean spirits, and they do obey him.

28 And immediately his fame spread abroad throughout all the region round about Galilee.

29 And forthwith, when they were come out of the synagogue, they entered into the house of Simon and Andrew, with James and John.

30 But Simon's wife's mother lay sick of a fever, and anon they tell him of her.

31 And he came and took her by the hand, and lifted her up; and immediately the fever left her, and she ministered unto them.

32 And at even, when the sun did set, they brought unto him all that were diseased, and them that were possessed with devils.

33 And all the city was gathered together at the door.

34 And he healed many that were sick of divers diseases, and cast out many devils; and suffered not the devils to speak, because they knew him.

35 And in the morning, rising up a great while before day, he went out, and departed into a solitary place, and there prayed.

36 And Simon and they that were with him followed after him.

37 And when they had found him, they said unto him, All *men* seek for thee.

38 And he said unto them, Let us go into the next towns, that I may preach there also: for therefore came I forth.

39 And he preached in their synagogues throughout all Galilee, and cast out devils.

40 And there came a leper to him, beseeching him, and kneeling down to him, and saying unto him, If thou wilt, thou canst make me clean.

41 And Yashiyah, moved with compassion, put forth *his* hand, and touched him, and saith unto him, I will; be thou clean.

42 And as soon as he had spoken, immediately the leprosy departed from him, and he was cleansed.

43 And he straitly charged him, and forthwith sent him away;

44 And saith unto him, See thou say nothing to any man: but go thy way, shew thyself to the priest, and offer for thy cleansing those things which Moses commanded, for a testimony unto them.

45 But he went out, and began to publish *it* much, and to blaze abroad the matter, insomuch that Yashiyah could no more openly enter into the city, but was without in desert places: and they came to him from every quarter.

CHAPTER 2

AND again he entered into Capernaum, after *some* days; and it was noised that he was in the house.

2 And straightway many were gathered together, insomuch that there was no room to receive *them*, no, not so much as about the door: and he preached the word unto them.

3 And they come unto him, bringing one sick of the palsy, which was borne of four.

4 And when they could not come nigh unto him for the press, they uncovered the roof where he was: and when they had broken *it* up, they let down the bed wherein the sick of the palsy lay.

5 When Yashiyah saw their faith, he said unto the sick of the palsy, Son, thy sins be forgiven thee.

6 But there were certain of the scribes sitting there, and reasoning in their hearts,

7 Why doth this *man* thus speak blasphemies? who can forgive sins but אֱלֹהִים only?

8 And immediately when Yashiyah perceived in his spirit that they so reasoned within themselves, he said unto them, Why reason ye these things in your hearts?

9 Whether is it easier to say to the sick of the palsy, *Thy* sins be forgiven thee; or to say, Arise, and take up thy bed, and walk?

10 But that ye may know that the Son of man hath power on earth to forgive sins, (he saith to the sick of the palsy,)

11 I say unto thee, Arise, and take up thy bed, and go thy way into thine house.

12 And immediately he arose, took up the bed, and went forth before them all; insomuch that they were all amazed, and glorified אֱלֹהִים, saying, We never saw it on this fashion.

13 And he went forth again by the sea side; and all the multitude resorted unto him, and he taught them.

14 And as he passed by, he saw Levi the *son* of Alphæus sitting at the receipt of custom, and said unto him, Follow me. And he arose and followed him.

15 And it came to pass, that, as Yashiyah sat at meat in his house, many publicans and sinners sat also together with Yashiyah and his disciples: for there were many, and they followed him.

16 And when the scribes and Pharisees saw him eat with publicans and sinners, they said unto his disciples, How is it that he eateth and drinketh with publicans and sinners?

17 When Yashiyah heard *it*, he saith unto them, They that are whole have no need of the physician, but they that are sick: I came not to call the righteous, but sinners to repentance.

18 And the disciples of John and of the Pharisees used to fast: and they come and say unto him, Why do the disciples of John and of the Pharisees fast, but thy disciples fast not? ◄

19 And Yashiyah said unto them, Can the children of the bridechamber fast, while the bridegroom is with them? as long as they have the bridegroom with them, they cannot fast.

20 But the days will come, when the bridegroom shall be taken away from them, and then shall they fast in those days.

21 No man also seweth a piece of new cloth on an old garment: else the new piece that filled it up taketh away from the old, and the rent is made worse.

22 And no man putteth new wine into old bottles: else the new wine doth burst the bottles, and the wine is spilled, and the bottles will be marred: but new wine must be put into new bottles.

23 And it came to pass, that he went through the corn fields on the sabbath day; and his disciples began, as they went, to pluck the ears of corn.

24 And the Pharisees said unto him, Behold, why do they on the sabbath day that which is not lawful?

25 And he said unto them, Have ye never read what David did, when he had need, and was an hungred, he, and they that were with him?

26 How he went into the house of אֱלֹהִים in the days of Abiathar the high priest, and did eat the shewbread, which is not lawful to eat

but for the priests, and gave also to them which were with him?

27 And he said unto them, The sabbath was made for man, and not man for the sabbath:

28 Therefore the Son of man is Lord also of the sabbath.

CHAPTER 3

AND he entered again into the synagogue; and there was a man there which had a withered hand.

2 And they watched him, whether he would heal him on the sabbath day; that they might accuse him.

3 And he saith unto the man which had the withered hand, Stand forth.

4 And he saith unto them, Is it lawful to do good on the sabbath days, or to do evil? to save life, or to kill? But they held their peace.

5 And when he had looked round about on them with anger, being grieved for the hardness of their hearts, he saith unto the man, Stretch forth thine hand. And he stretched *it* out: and his hand was restored whole as the other.

6 And the Pharisees went forth, and straightway took counsel with the Herodians against him, how they might destroy him.

7 But Yashiyah withdrew himself with his disciples to the sea: and a great multitude from Galilee followed him, and from Judæa,

8 And from Jerusalem, and from Idumæa, and *from* beyond Jordan; and they about Tyre and Sidon, a great multitude, when they had heard what great things he did, came unto him.

9 And he spake to his disciples, that a small ship should wait on him because of the multitude, lest they should throng him.

10 For he had healed many; insomuch that they pressed upon him for to touch him, as many as had plagues.

11 And unclean spirits, when they saw him, fell down before him, and cried, saying, Thou art the Son of אֱלֹהִים.

12 And he straitly charged them that they should not make him known.

13 And he goeth up into a mountain, and calleth *unto him* whom he would: and they came unto him.

14 And he ordained twelve, that they should be with him, and that he might send them forth to preach,

15 And to have power to heal sicknesses, and to cast out devils:

16 And Simon he surnamed Peter;

17 And James the *son* of Zebedee, and John the brother of James; and he surnamed them Boanerges, which is, The sons of thunder:

18 And Andrew, and Philip, and Bartholomew, and Matthew, and Thomas, and James the *son* of Alphæus, and Thaddæus, and Simon the Canaanite,

19 And Judas Iscariot, which also betrayed him: and they went into an house.

20 And the multitude cometh together again, so that they could not so much as eat bread.

21 And when his friends heard *of it*, they went out to lay hold on him: for they said, He is beside himself.

22 ¶ And the scribes which came down from Jerusalem said, He hath Beelzebub, and by the prince of the devils casteth he out devils.

23 And he called them *unto him*, and said unto them in parables, How can Satan cast out Satan?

24 And if a kingdom be divided against itself, that kingdom cannot stand.

25 And if a house be divided against itself, that house cannot stand.

26 And if Satan rise up against himself, and be divided, he cannot stand, but hath an end.

27 No man can enter into a strong man's house, and spoil his goods, except he will first bind the strong man; and then he will spoil his house.

28 Verily I say unto you, All sins shall be forgiven unto the sons of men, and blasphemies wherewith soever they shall blaspheme:

29 But he that shall blaspheme against the Holy Ghost hath never forgiveness, but is in danger of eternal damnation:

30 Because they said, He hath an unclean spirit.

31 ¶ There came then his brethren and his mother, and, standing without, sent unto him, calling him.

32 And the multitude sat about him, and they said unto him, Behold, thy mother and thy brethren without seek for thee.

33 And he answered them, saying, Who is my mother, or my brethren?

34 And he looked round about on them which sat about him, and said, Behold my mother and my brethren!

35 For whosoever shall do the will of אֱלֹהִים, the same is my brother, and my sister, and mother.

CHAPTER 4

AND he began again to teach by the sea side: and there was gathered unto him a great multitude, so that he entered into a ship, and sat in the sea; and the whole multitude was by the sea on the land.

2 And he taught them many things by parables, and said unto them in his doctrine,

3 Hearken; Behold, there went out a sower to sow:

4 And it came to pass, as he sowed, some fell by the way side, and the fowls of the air came and devoured it up.

5 And some fell on stony ground, where it had not much earth; and immediately it sprang up, because it had no depth of earth:

6 But when the sun was up, it was scorched; and because it had no root, it withered away.

7 And some fell among thorns, and the thorns grew up, and choked it, and it yielded no fruit.

8 And other fell on good ground, and did yield fruit that sprang up and increased; and brought forth, some thirty, and some sixty, and some an hundred.

9 And he said unto them, He that hath ears to hear, let him hear.

10 And when he was alone, they that were about him with the twelve asked of him the parable.

11 And he said unto them, Unto you it is given to know the mystery of the kingdom of אֱלֹהִים: but unto them that are without, all *these* things are done in parables:

12 That seeing they may see, and not perceive; and hearing they may hear, and not understand; lest at any time they should be converted, and *their* sins should be forgiven them.

13 And he said unto them, Know ye not this parable? and how then will ye know all parables?

14 ¶ The sower soweth the word.

15 And these are they by the way side, where the word is sown; but when they have heard, Satan cometh immediately, and taketh away the word that was sown in their hearts.

16 And these are they likewise which are sown on stony ground; who, when they have heard the word, immediately receive it with gladness;

17 And have no root in themselves, and so endure but for a time: afterward, when affliction or persecution ariseth for the word's sake, immediately they are offended.

18 And these are they which are sown among thorns; such as hear the word,

19 And the cares of this world, and the deceitfulness of riches, and the lusts of other things entering in, choke the word, and it becometh unfruitful.

20 And these are they which are sown on good ground; such as hear the word, and receive *it*, and bring forth fruit, some thirtyfold, some sixty, and some an hundred.

21 ¶ And he said unto them, Is a candle brought to be put under a bushel, or under a bed? and not to be set on a candlestick?

22 For there is nothing hid, which shall not be manifested; neither was any thing kept secret, but that it should come abroad.

23 If any man have ears to hear, let him hear.

24 And he said unto them, Take heed what ye hear: with what measure ye mete, it shall be measured to you: and unto you that hear shall more be given.

25 For he that hath, to him shall be given: and he that hath not, from him shall be taken even that which he hath.

26 ¶ And he said, So is the kingdom of אֱלֹהִים, as if a man should cast seed into the ground;

27 And should sleep, and rise night and day, and the seed should spring and grow up, he knoweth not how.

28 For the earth bringeth forth fruit of herself; first the blade, then the ear, after that the full corn in the ear.

29 But when the fruit is brought forth, immediately he putteth in the sickle, because the harvest is come.

30 ¶ And he said, Whereunto shall we liken the kingdom of אֱלֹהִים? or with what comparison shall we compare it?

31 *It is* like a grain of mustard seed, which, when it is sown in the earth, is less than all the seeds that be in the earth:

32 But when it is sown, it groweth up, and becometh greater than all herbs, and shooteth out great branches; so that the fowls of the air may lodge under the shadow of it.

33 And with many such parables spake he the word unto them, as they were able to hear *it*.

34 But without a parable spake he not unto them: and when they were alone, he expounded all things to his disciples.

35 And the same day, when the even was come, he saith unto them, Let us pass over unto the other side.

36 And when they had sent away the multitude, they took him even as he was in the ship. And there were also with him other little ships.

37 And there arose a great storm of wind, and the waves beat into the ship, so that it was now full.

38 And he was in the hinder part of the ship, asleep on a pillow: and they awake him, and say unto him, Master, carest thou not that we perish?

39 And he arose, and rebuked the wind, and said unto the sea, Peace, be still. And the wind ceased, and there was a great calm.

40 And he said unto them, Why are ye so fearful? how is it that ye have no faith?

41 And they feared exceedingly, and said one to another, What manner of man is this, that even the wind and the sea obey him?

CHAPTER 5

AND they came over unto the other side of the sea, into the country of the Gadarenes.

2 And when he was come out of the ship, immediately there met him out of the tombs a man with an unclean spirit,

3 Who had *his* dwelling among the tombs; and no man could bind him, no, not with chains:

4 Because that he had been often bound with fetters and chains, and the chains had been plucked asunder by him, and the fetters broken in pieces: neither could any *man* tame him.

5 And always, night and day, he was in the mountains, and in the tombs, crying, and cutting himself with stones.

6 But when he saw Yashiyah afar off, he ran and worshipped him,

7 And cried with a loud voice, and said, What have I to do with thee, Yashiyah, *thou* Son of the most high אֱלֹהִים? I adjure thee by אֱלֹהִים, that thou torment me not.

8 For he said unto him, Come out of the man, *thou* unclean spirit.

9 And he asked him, What *is* thy name? And he answered, saying, My name *is* Legion: for we are many.

10 And he besought him much that he would not send them away out of the country.

11 Now there was there nigh unto the mountains a great herd of swine feeding.

12 And all the devils besought him, saying, Send us into the swine, that we may enter into them.

13 And forthwith Yashiyah gave them leave. And the unclean spirits went out, and entered into the swine: and the herd ran violently down a steep place into the sea, (they were about two thousand;) and were choked in the sea.

14 And they that fed the swine fled, and told *it* in the city, and in the country. And they went out to see what it was that was done.

15 And they come to Yashiyah, and see him that was possessed with the devil, and had the legion, sitting, and clothed, and in his right mind: and they were afraid.

16 And they that saw *it* told them how it befell to him that was possessed with the devil, and *also* concerning the swine.

17 And they began to pray him to depart out of their coasts.

18 And when he was come into the ship, he that had been possessed with the devil prayed him that he might be with him.

19 Howbeit Yashiyah suffered him not, but saith unto him, Go home to thy friends, and tell them how great things the Lord hath done for thee, and hath had compassion on thee.

20 And he departed, and began to publish in Decapolis how great things Yashiyah had done for him: and all *men* did marvel.

21 And when Yashiyah was passed over again by ship unto the other side, much people gathered unto him: and he was nigh unto the sea.

22 And, behold, there cometh one of the rulers of the synagogue, Jairus by name; and when he saw him, he fell at his feet,

23 And besought him greatly, saying, My little daughter lieth at the point of death: *I pray thee*, come and lay thy hands on her, that she may be healed; and she shall live.

24 And *Yashiyah* went with him; and much people followed him, and thronged him.

25 And a certain woman, which had an issue of blood twelve years,

26 And had suffered many things of many physicians, and had spent all that she had, and was nothing bettered, but rather grew worse,

27 When she had heard of Yashiyah, came in the press behind, and touched his garment.

28 For she said, If I may touch but his clothes, I shall be whole.

29 And straightway the fountain of her blood was dried up; and she felt in *her* body that she was healed of that plague.

30 And Yashiyah, immediately knowing in himself that virtue had gone out of him, turned him about in the press, and said, Who touched my clothes?

31 And his disciples said unto him, Thou seest the multitude thronging thee, and sayest thou, Who touched me?

32 And he looked round about to see her that had done this thing.

33 But the woman fearing and trembling, knowing what was done in her, came and fell down before him, and told him all the truth.

34 And he said unto her, Daughter, thy faith hath made thee whole; go in peace, and be whole of thy plague.

35 While he yet spake, there came from the ruler of the synagogue's *house certain* which said, Thy daughter is dead: why troublest thou the Master any further?

36 As soon as Yashiyah heard the word that was spoken, he saith unto the ruler of the synagogue, Be not afraid, only believe.

37 And he suffered no man to follow him, save Peter, and James, and John the brother of James.

38 And he cometh to the house of the ruler of the synagogue, and seeth the tumult, and them that wept and wailed greatly.

39 And when he was come in, he saith unto them, Why make ye this ado, and weep? the damsel is not dead, but sleepeth.

40 And they laughed him to scorn. But when he had put them all out, he taketh the father and the mother of the damsel, and them that were with him, and entereth in where the damsel was lying.

41 And he took the damsel by the hand, and said unto her, Talitha cumi; which is, being interpreted, Damsel, I say unto thee, arise.

42 And straightway the damsel arose, and walked; for she was *of the age* of twelve years. And they were astonished with a great astonishment.

43 And he charged them straitly that no man should know it; and commanded that something should be given her to eat.

CHAPTER 6

AND he went out from thence, and came into his own country; and his disciples follow him.

2 And when the sabbath day was come, he began to teach in the synagogue: and many hearing *him* were astonished, saying, From whence hath this *man* these things? and what wisdom *is* this which is given unto him, that even such mighty works are wrought by his hands?

3 Is not this the carpenter, the son of Mary, the brother of James, and Joses, and of Juda, and Simon? and are not his sisters here with us? And they were offended at him.

4 But Yashiyah said unto them, A prophet is not without honour, but in his own country, and among his own kin, and in his own house.

5 And he could there do no mighty work, save that he laid his hands upon a few sick folk, and healed *them*.

6 And he marvelled because of their unbelief. And he went round about the villages, teaching.

7 ¶ And he called *unto him* the twelve, and began to send them forth by two and two; and gave them power over unclean spirits;

8 And commanded them that they should take nothing for *their* journey, save a staff only; no scrip, no bread, no money in *their* purse:

9 But *be* shod with sandals; and not put on two coats.

10 And he said unto them, In what place soever ye enter into an house, there abide till ye depart from that place.

11 And whosoever shall not receive you, nor hear you, when ye depart thence, shake off the dust under your feet for a testimony against them. Verily I say unto you, It shall be more tolerable for Sodom and Gomorrha in the day of judgment, than for that city.

12 And they went out, and preached that men should repent.

13 And they cast out many devils, and anointed with oil many that were sick, and healed *them*.

14 And king Herod heard *of him*: (for his name was spread abroad:) and he said, That John the Baptist was risen from the dead, and therefore mighty works do shew forth themselves in him.

15 Others said, That it is Elias. And others said, That it is a prophet, or as one of the prophets.

16 But when Herod heard *thereof*, he said, It is John, whom I beheaded: he is risen from the dead.

17 For Herod himself had sent forth and laid hold upon John, and bound him in prison for Herodias' sake, his brother Philip's wife: for he had married her.

18 For John had said unto Herod, It is not lawful for thee to have thy brother's wife.

19 Therefore Herodias had a quarrel against him, and would have killed him; but she could not:

20 For Herod feared John, knowing that he was a just man and an holy, and observed him; and when he heard him, he did many things, and heard him gladly.

21 And when a convenient day was come, that Herod on his birthday made a supper to his lords, high captains, and chief *estates* of Galilee;

22 And when the daughter of the said Herodias came in, and danced, and pleased Herod and them that sat with him, the king said unto the damsel, Ask of me whatsoever thou wilt, and I will give *it* thee.

23 And he sware unto her, Whatsoever thou shalt ask of me, I will give *it* thee, unto the half of my kingdom.

24 And she went forth, and said unto her mother, What shall I ask? And she said, The head of John the Baptist.

25 And she came in straightway with haste unto the king, and asked, saying, I will that thou give me by and by in a charger the head of John the Baptist.

26 And the king was exceeding sorry; *yet* for his oath's sake, and for their sakes which sat with him, he would not reject her.

27 And immediately the king sent an executioner, and commanded his head to be brought: and he went and beheaded him in the prison,

28 And brought his head in a charger, and gave it to the damsel: and the damsel gave it to her mother.

29 And when his disciples heard *of it*, they came and took up his corpse, and laid it in a tomb.

30 And the apostles gathered themselves together unto Yashiyah, and told him all things, both what they had done, and what they had taught.

31 And he said unto them, Come ye yourselves apart into a desert place, and rest a while: for there were many coming and going, and they had no leisure so much as to eat.

32 And they departed into a desert place by ship privately.

33 And the people saw them departing, and many knew him, and ran afoot thither out of all cities, and outwent them, and came together unto him.

34 And Yashiyah, when he came out, saw much people, and was moved with compassion toward them, because they were as sheep not having a shepherd: and he began to teach them many things.

35 And when the day was now far spent, his disciples came unto him, and said, This is a desert place, and now the time *is* far passed:

36 Send them away, that they may go into the country round about, and into the villages, and buy themselves bread: for they have

nothing to eat.

37 He answered and said unto them, Give ye them to eat. And they say unto him, Shall we go and buy two hundred pennyworth of bread, and give them to eat?

38 He saith unto them, How many loaves have ye? go and see. And when they knew, they say, Five, and two fishes.

39 And he commanded them to make all sit down by companies upon the green grass.

40 And they sat down in ranks, by hundreds, and by fifties.

41 And when he had taken the five loaves and the two fishes, he looked up to heaven, and blessed, and brake the loaves, and gave *them* to his disciples to set before them; and the two fishes divided he among them all.

42 And they did all eat, and were filled.

43 And they took up twelve baskets full of the fragments, and of the fishes.

44 And they that did eat of the loaves were about five thousand men.

45 And straightway he constrained his disciples to get into the ship, and to go to the other side before unto Bethsaida, while he sent away the people.

46 And when he had sent them away, he departed into a mountain to pray.

47 And when even was come, the ship was in the midst of the sea, and he alone on the land.

48 And he saw them toiling in rowing; for the wind was contrary unto them: and about the fourth watch of the night he cometh unto them, walking upon the sea, and would have passed by them.

49 But when they saw him walking upon the sea, they supposed it had been a spirit, and cried out:

50 For they all saw him, and were troubled. And immediately he talked with them, and saith unto them, Be of good cheer: it is I; be not afraid.

51 And he went up unto them into the ship; and the wind ceased: and they were sore amazed in themselves beyond measure, and wondered.

52 For they considered not *the miracle* of the loaves: for their heart was hardened.

53 And when they had passed over, they came into the land of Gennesaret, and drew to the shore.

54 And when they were come out of the ship, straightway they knew him,

55 And ran through that whole region round about, and began to carry about in beds those that were sick, where they heard he was.

56 And whithersoever he entered, into villages, or cities, or country, they laid the sick in the streets, and besought him that they might touch if it were but the border of his garment: and as many as touched him were made whole.

CHAPTER 7

THEN came together unto him the Pharisees, and certain of the scribes, which came from Jerusalem.

2 And when they saw some of his disciples eat bread with defiled, that is to say, with unwashen, hands, they found fault.

3 For the Pharisees, and all the Jews, except they wash *their* hands oft, eat not, holding the tradition of the elders.

4 And *when they come* from the market, except they wash, they eat not. And many other things there be, which they have received to hold, *as* the washing of cups, and pots, brasen vessels, and of tables.

5 Then the Pharisees and scribes asked him, Why walk not thy disciples according to the tradition of the elders, but eat bread with unwashen hands?

6 He answered and said unto them, Well hath Esaias prophesied of you hypocrites, as it is written, This people honoureth me with *their* lips, but their heart is far from me.

7 Howbeit in vain do they worship me, teaching *for* doctrines the commandments of men.

8 For laying aside the commandment of אֱלֹהִים, ye hold the tradition of men, *as* the washing of pots and cups: and many other such like things ye do.

9 And he said unto them, Full well ye reject the commandment of אֱלֹהִים, that ye may keep your own tradition.

10 For Moses said, Honour thy father and thy mother; and, Whoso curseth father or mother, let him die the death:

11 But ye say, If a man shall say to his father or mother, *It is* Corban, that is to say, a gift, by whatsoever thou mightest be profited by me; *he shall be free*.

12 And ye suffer him no more to do ought for his father or his mother;

13 Making the word of אֱלֹהִים of none effect through your tradition, which ye have delivered: and many such like things do ye.

14 ¶ And when he had called all the people *unto him*, he said unto them, Hearken unto me every one *of you*, and understand:

15 There is nothing from without a man, that entering into him can defile him: but the things which come out of him, those are they that defile the man.

16 If any man have ears to hear, let him hear.

17 And when he was entered into the house from the people, his disciples asked him concerning the parable.

18 And he saith unto them, Are ye so without understanding also? Do ye not perceive, that whatsoever thing from without entereth into the man, *it* cannot defile him;

19 Because it entereth not into his heart, but into the belly, and goeth out into the draught, purging all meats?

20 And he said, That which cometh out of the man, that defileth the man.

21 For from within, out of the heart of men, proceed evil thoughts, adulteries, fornications, murders,

22 Thefts, covetousness, wickedness, deceit, lasciviousness, an evil eye, blasphemy, pride, foolishness:

23 All these evil things come from within, and defile the man.

24 ¶ And from thence he arose, and went into the borders of Tyre and Sidon, and entered into an house, and would have no man know *it:* but he could not be hid.

25 For a *certain* woman, whose young daughter had an unclean spirit, heard of him, and came and fell at his feet:

26 The woman was a Greek, a Syrophenician by nation; and she besought him that he would cast forth the devil out of her daughter.

27 But Yashiyah said unto her, Let the children first be filled: for it is not meet to take the children's bread, and to cast *it* unto the dogs.

28 And she answered and said unto him, Yes, Lord: yet the dogs under the table eat of the children's crumbs.

29 And he said unto her, For this saying go thy way; the devil is gone out of thy daughter.

30 And when she was come to her house, she found the devil gone out, and her daughter laid upon the bed.

31 ¶ And again, departing from the coasts of Tyre and Sidon, he came unto the sea of Galilee, through the midst of the coasts of

Decapolis.

32 And they bring unto him one that was deaf, and had an impediment in his speech; and they beseech him to put his hand upon him.

33 And he took him aside from the multitude, and put his fingers into his ears, and he spit, and touched his tongue;

34 And looking up to heaven, he sighed, and saith unto him, Ephphatha, that is, Be opened.

35 And straightway his ears were opened, and the string of his tongue was loosed, and he spake plain.

36 And he charged them that they should tell no man: but the more he charged them, so much the more a great deal they published *it*;

37 And were beyond measure astonished, saying, He hath done all things well: he maketh both the deaf to hear, and the dumb to speak.

CHAPTER 8

IN those days the multitude being very great, and having nothing to eat, Yashiyah called his disciples *unto him*, and saith unto them,

2 I have compassion on the multitude, because they have now been with me three days, and have nothing to eat:

3 And if I send them away fasting to their own houses, they will faint by the way: for divers of them came from far.

4 And his disciples answered him, From whence can a man satisfy these *men* with bread here in the wilderness?

5 And he asked them, How many loaves have ye? And they said, Seven.

6 And he commanded the people to sit down on the ground: and he took the seven loaves, and gave thanks, and brake, and gave to his disciples to set before *them;* and they did set *them* before the people.

7 And they had a few small fishes: and he blessed, and commanded to set them also before *them*.

8 So they did eat, and were filled: and they took up of the broken *meat* that was left seven baskets.

9 And they that had eaten were about four thousand: and he sent them away.

10 ¶ And straightway he entered into a ship with his disciples, and came into the parts of Dalmanutha.

11 And the Pharisees came forth, and began to question with him, seeking of him a sign from heaven, tempting him.

12 And he sighed deeply in his spirit, and saith, Why doth this generation seek after a sign? verily I say unto you, There shall no sign be given unto this generation.

13 And he left them, and entering into the ship again departed to the other side.

14 ¶ Now *the disciples* had forgotten to take bread, neither had they in the ship with them more than one loaf.

15 And he charged them, saying, Take heed, beware of the leaven of the Pharisees, and *of* the leaven of Herod.

16 And they reasoned among themselves, saying, *It is* because we have no bread.

17 And when Yashiyah knew *it*, he saith unto them, Why reason ye, because ye have no bread? perceive ye not yet, neither understand? have ye your heart yet hardened?

18 Having eyes, see ye not? and having ears, hear ye not? and do ye not remember?

19 When I brake the five loaves among five thousand, how many baskets full of fragments took ye up? They say unto him, Twelve.

20 And when the seven among four thousand, how many baskets full of fragments took ye up? And they said, Seven.

21 And he said unto them, How is it that ye do not understand?

22 ¶ And he cometh to Bethsaida; and they bring a blind man unto him, and besought him to touch him.

23 And he took the blind man by the hand, and led him out of the town; and when he had spit on his eyes, and put his hands upon him, he asked him if he saw ought.

24 And he looked up, and said, I see men as trees, walking.

25 After that he put *his* hands again upon his eyes, and made him look up: and he was restored, and saw every man clearly.

26 And he sent him away to his house, saying, Neither go into the town, nor tell *it* to any in the town.

27 ¶ And Yashiyah went out, and his disciples, into the towns of Cæsarea Philippi: and by the way he asked his disciples, saying unto them, Whom do men say that I am?

28 And they answered, John the Baptist: but some *say*, Elias; and others, One of the prophets.

29 And he saith unto them, But whom say ye that I am? And Peter answereth and saith unto him, Thou art the Christ.

30 And he charged them that they should tell no man of him.

31 And he began to teach them, that the Son of man must suffer many things, and be rejected of the elders, and *of* the chief priests, and scribes, and be killed, and after three days rise again.

32 And he spake that saying openly. And Peter took him, and began to rebuke him.

33 But when he had turned about and looked on his disciples, he rebuked Peter, saying, Get thee behind me, Satan: for thou savourest not the things that be of אֱלֹהִים, but the things that be of men.

34 ¶ And when he had called the people *unto him* with his disciples also, he said unto them, Whosoever will come after me, let him deny himself, and take up his cross, and follow me.

35 For whosoever will save his life shall lose it; but whosoever shall lose his life for my sake and the gospel's, the same shall save it.

36 For what shall it profit a man, if he shall gain the whole world, and lose his own soul?

37 Or what shall a man give in exchange for his soul?

38 Whosoever therefore shall be ashamed of me and of my words in this adulterous and sinful generation; of him also shall the Son of man be ashamed, when he cometh in the glory of his Father with the holy angels.

CHAPTER 9

AND he said unto them, Verily I say unto you, That there be some of them that stand here, which shall not taste of death, till they have seen the kingdom of אֱלֹהִים come with power.

2 ¶ And after six days Yashiyah taketh *with him* Peter, and James, and John, and leadeth them up into an high mountain apart by themselves: and he was transfigured before them.

3 And his raiment became shining, exceeding white as snow; so as no fuller on earth can white them.

4 And there appeared unto them Elias with Moses: and they were talking with Yashiyah.

5 And Peter answered and said to Yashiyah, Master, it is good for us to be here: and let us make three tabernacles; one for thee, and one for Moses, and one for Elias.

6 For he wist not what to say; for they were sore afraid.

7 And there was a cloud that overshadowed them: and a voice came out of the cloud, saying, This is my beloved Son: hear him.

8 And suddenly, when they had looked round about, they saw no man any more, save Yashiyah only with themselves.

9 And as they came down from the mountain, he charged them that they should tell no man what things they had seen, till the Son of man were risen from the dead.

10 And they kept that saying with themselves, questioning one with another what the rising from the dead should mean.

11 ¶ And they asked him, saying, Why say the scribes that Elias must first come?

12 And he answered and told them, Elias verily cometh first, and restoreth all things; and how it is written of the Son of man, that he must suffer many things, and be set at nought.

13 But I say unto you, That Elias is indeed come, and they have done unto him whatsoever they listed, as it is written of him.

14 ¶ And when he came to *his* disciples, he saw a great multitude about them, and the scribes questioning with them.

15 And straightway all the people, when they beheld him, were greatly amazed, and running to *him* saluted him.

16 And he asked the scribes, What question ye with them?

17 And one of the multitude answered and said, Master, I have brought unto thee my son, which hath a dumb spirit;

18 And wheresoever he taketh him, he teareth him: and he foameth, and gnasheth with his teeth, and pineth away: and I spake to thy disciples that they should cast him out; and they could not.

19 He answereth him, and saith, O faithless generation, how long shall I be with you? how long shall I suffer you? bring him unto me.

20 And they brought him unto him: and when he saw him, straightway the spirit tare him; and he fell on the ground, and wallowed foaming.

21 And he asked his father, How long is it ago since this came unto him? And he said, Of a child.

22 And ofttimes it hath cast him into the fire, and into the waters, to destroy him: but if thou canst do any thing, have compassion on us, and help us.

23 Yashiyah said unto him, If thou canst believe, all things *are* possible to him that believeth.

24 And straightway the father of the child cried out, and said with tears, Lord, I believe; help thou mine unbelief.

25 When Yashiyah saw that the people came running together, he rebuked the foul spirit, saying unto him, *Thou* dumb and deaf spirit, I charge thee, come out of him, and enter no more into him.

26 And *the spirit* cried, and rent him sore, and came out of him: and he was as one dead; insomuch that many said, He is dead.

27 But Yashiyah took him by the hand, and lifted him up; and he arose.

28 And when he was come into the house, his disciples asked him privately, Why could not we cast him out?

29 And he said unto them, This kind can come forth by nothing, but by prayer and fasting.

30 ¶ And they departed thence, and passed through Galilee; and he would not that any man should know *it*.

31 For he taught his disciples, and said unto them, The Son of man is delivered into the hands of men, and they shall kill him; and after that he is killed, he shall rise the third day.

32 But they understood not that saying, and were afraid to ask him.

33 ¶ And he came to Capernaum: and being in the house he asked them, What was it that ye disputed among yourselves by the way?

34 But they held their peace: for by the way they had disputed among themselves, who *should be* the greatest.

35 And he sat down, and called the twelve, and saith unto them, If any man desire to be first, *the same* shall be last of all, and servant of all.

36 And he took a child, and set him in the midst of them: and when he had taken him in his arms, he said unto them,

37 Whosoever shall receive one of such children in my name, receiveth me: and whosoever shall receive me, receiveth not me, but him that sent me.

38 ¶ And John answered him, saying, Master, we saw one casting out devils in thy name, and he followeth not us: and we forbad him, because he followeth not us.

39 But Yashiyah said, Forbid him not: for there is no man which shall do a miracle in my name, that can lightly speak evil of me.

40 For he that is not against us is on our part.

41 For whosoever shall give you a cup of water to drink in my name, because ye belong to Christ, verily I say unto you, he shall not lose his reward.

42 And whosoever shall offend one of *these* little ones that believe in me, it is better for him that a millstone were hanged about his neck, and he were cast into the sea.

43 And if thy hand offend thee, cut it off: it is better for thee to enter into life maimed, than having two hands to go into hell, into the fire that never shall be quenched:

44 Where their worm dieth not, and the fire is not quenched.

45 And if thy foot offend thee, cut it off: it is better for thee to enter halt into life, than having two feet to be cast into hell, into the fire that never shall be quenched:

46 Where their worm dieth not, and the fire is not quenched.

47 And if thine eye offend thee, pluck it out: it is better for thee to enter into the kingdom of אֱלֹהִים with one eye, than having two eyes to be cast into hell fire:

48 Where their worm dieth not, and the fire is not quenched.

49 For every one shall be salted with fire, and every sacrifice shall be salted with salt.

50 Salt *is* good: but if the salt have lost his saltness, wherewith will ye season it? Have salt in yourselves, and have peace one with another.

CHAPTER 10

AND he arose from thence, and cometh into the coasts of Judæa by the farther side of Jordan: and the people resort unto him again; and, as he was wont, he taught them again.

2 ¶ And the Pharisees came to him, and asked him, Is it lawful for a man to put away *his* wife? tempting him.

3 And he answered and said unto them, What did Moses command you?

4 And they said, Moses suffered to write a bill of divorcement, and to put *her* away.

5 And Yashiyah answered and said unto them, For the hardness of your heart he wrote you this precept.

6 But from the beginning of the creation אֱלֹהִים made them male and female.

7 For this cause shall a man leave his father and mother, and cleave to his wife;

8 And they twain shall be one flesh: so then they are no more twain, but one flesh.

9 What therefore אֱלֹהִים hath joined together, let not man put asunder.

10 And in the house his disciples asked him again of the same *matter*.

11 And he saith unto them, Whosoever shall put away his wife, and marry another, committeth adultery against her.

12 And if a woman shall put away her husband, and be married to another, she committeth adultery.

13 ¶ And they brought young children to him, that he should touch them: and *his* disciples rebuked those that brought *them*.

14 But when Yashiyah saw *it*, he was much displeased, and said unto them, Suffer the little children to come unto me, and forbid them not: for of such is the kingdom of אֱלֹהִים.

15 Verily I say unto you, Whosoever shall not receive the kingdom of אֱלֹהִים as a little child, he shall not enter therein.

16 And he took them up in his arms, put *his* hands upon them, and blessed them.

17 ¶ And when he was gone forth into the way, there came one running, and kneeled to him, and asked him, Good Master, what shall I do that I may inherit eternal life?

18 And Yashiyah said unto him, Why callest thou me good? *there is* none good but one, *that is*, אֱלֹהִים.

19 Thou knowest the commandments, Do not commit adultery, Do not kill, Do not steal, Do not bear false witness, Defraud not, Honour thy father and mother.

20 And he answered and said unto him, Master, all these have I observed from my youth.

21 Then Yashiyah beholding him loved him, and said unto him, One thing thou lackest: go thy way, sell whatsoever thou hast, and give to the poor, and thou shalt have treasure in heaven: and come, take up the cross, and follow me.

22 And he was sad at that saying, and went away grieved: for he had great possessions.

23 ¶ And Yashiyah looked round about, and saith unto his disciples, How hardly shall they that have riches enter into the kingdom of אֱלֹהִים!

24 And the disciples were astonished at his words. But Yashiyah answereth again, and saith unto them, Children, how hard is it for them that trust in riches to enter into the kingdom of אֱלֹהִים!

25 It is easier for a camel to go through the eye of a needle, than for a rich man to enter into the kingdom of אֱלֹהִים.

26 And they were astonished out of measure, saying among themselves, Who then can be saved?

27 And Yashiyah looking upon them saith, With men *it is* impossible, but not with אֱלֹהִים: for with אֱלֹהִים all things are possible.

28 ¶ Then Peter began to say unto him, Lo, we have left all, and have followed thee.

29 And Yashiyah answered and said, Verily I say unto you, There is no man that hath left house, or brethren, or sisters, or father, or mother, or wife, or children, or lands, for my sake, and the gospel's,

30 But he shall receive an hundredfold now in this time, houses, and brethren, and sisters, and mothers, and children, and lands, with persecutions; and in the world to come eternal life.

31 But many *that are* first shall be last; and the last first.

32 ¶ And they were in the way going up to Jerusalem; and Yashiyah went before them: and they were amazed; and as they followed, they were afraid. And he took again the twelve, and began to tell them what things should happen unto him,

33 *Saying*, Behold, we go up to Jerusalem; and the Son of man shall be delivered unto the chief priests, and unto the scribes; and they shall condemn him to death, and shall deliver him to the Gentiles:

34 And they shall mock him, and shall scourge him, and shall spit upon him, and shall kill him: and the third day he shall rise again.

35 ¶ And James and John, the sons of Zebedee, come unto him, saying, Master, we would that thou shouldest do for us whatsoever we shall desire.

36 And he said unto them, What would ye that I should do for you?

37 They said unto him, Grant unto us that we may sit, one on thy right hand, and the other on thy left hand, in thy glory.

38 But Yashiyah said unto them, Ye know not what ye ask: can ye drink of the cup that I drink of? and be baptized with the baptism that I am baptized with?

39 And they said unto him, We can. And Yashiyah said unto them, Ye shall indeed drink of the cup that I drink of; and with the baptism that I am baptized withal shall ye be baptized:

40 But to sit on my right hand and on my left hand is not mine to give; but *it shall be given to them* for whom it is prepared.

41 And when the ten heard *it*, they began to be much displeased with James and John.

42 But Yashiyah called them *to him*, and saith unto them, Ye know that they which are accounted to rule over the Gentiles exercise lordship over them; and their great ones exercise authority upon them.

43 But so shall it not be among you: but whosoever will be great among you, shall be your minister:

44 And whosoever of you will be the chiefest, shall be servant of all.

45 For even the Son of man came not to be ministered unto, but to minister, and to give his life a ransom for many.

46 ¶ And they came to Jericho: and as he went out of Jericho with his disciples and a great number of people, blind Bartimæus, the son of Timæus, sat by the highway side begging.

47 And when he heard that it was Yashiyah of Nazareth, he began to cry out, and say, Yashiyah, *thou* Son of David, have mercy on me.

48 And many charged him that he should hold his peace: but he cried the more a great deal, *Thou* Son of David, have mercy on me.

49 And Yashiyah stood still, and commanded him to be called. And they call the blind man, saying unto him, Be of good comfort, rise; he calleth thee.

50 And he, casting away his garment, rose, and came to Yashiyah.

51 And Yashiyah answered and said unto him, What wilt thou that I should do unto thee? The blind man said unto him, Lord, that I might receive my sight.

52 And Yashiyah said unto him, Go thy way; thy faith hath made thee whole. And immediately he received his sight, and followed Yashiyah in the way.

CHAPTER 11

AND when they came nigh to Jerusalem, unto Bethphage and Bethany, at the mount of Olives, he sendeth forth two of his disciples,

2 And saith unto them, Go your way into the village over against you: and as soon as ye be entered into it, ye shall find a colt tied, whereon never man sat; loose him, and bring *him*.

3 And if any man say unto you, Why do ye this? say ye that the Lord hath need of him; and straightway he will send him hither.

4 And they went their way, and found the colt tied by the door without in a place where two ways met; and they loose him.

5 And certain of them that stood there said unto them, What do ye, loosing the colt?

6 And they said unto them even as Yashiyah had commanded: and they let them go.

7 And they brought the colt to Yashiyah, and cast their garments on him; and he sat upon him.

8 And many spread their garments in the way: and others cut down branches off the trees, and strawed *them* in the way.

9 And they that went before, and they that followed, cried, saying, Hosanna; Blessed *is* he that cometh in the name of the Lord:

10 Blessed *be* the kingdom of our father David, that cometh in the name of the Lord: Hosanna in the highest.

11 And Yashiyah entered into Jerusalem, and into the temple: and when he had looked round about upon all things, and now the eventide was come, he went out unto Bethany with the twelve.

12 ¶ And on the morrow, when they were come from Bethany, he was hungry:

13 And seeing a fig tree afar off having leaves, he came, if haply he might find any thing thereon: and when he came to it, he found nothing but leaves; for the time of figs was not *yet.*

14 And Yashiyah answered and said unto it, No man eat fruit of thee hereafter for ever. And his disciples heard *it.*

15 ¶ And they come to Jerusalem: and Yashiyah went into the temple, and began to cast out them that sold and bought in the temple, and overthrew the tables of the moneychangers, and the seats of them that sold doves;

16 And would not suffer that any man should carry *any* vessel through the temple.

17 And he taught, saying unto them, Is it not written, My house shall be called of all nations the house of prayer? but ye have made it a den of thieves.

18 And the scribes and chief priests heard *it,* and sought how they might destroy him: for they feared him, because all the people was astonished at his doctrine.

19 And when even was come, he went out of the city.

20 ¶ And in the morning, as they passed by, they saw the fig tree dried up from the roots.

21 And Peter calling to remembrance saith unto him, Master, behold, the fig tree which thou cursedst is withered away.

22 And Yashiyah answering saith unto them, Have faith in אֱלֹהִים.

23 For verily I say unto you, That whosoever shall say unto this mountain, Be thou removed, and be thou cast into the sea; and shall not doubt in his heart, but shall believe that those things which he saith shall come to pass; he shall have whatsoever he saith.

24 Therefore I say unto you, What things soever ye desire, when ye pray, believe that ye receive *them,* and ye shall have *them.*

25 And when ye stand praying, forgive, if ye have ought against any: that your Father also which is in heaven may forgive you your trespasses.

26 But if ye do not forgive, neither will your Father which is in heaven forgive your trespasses.

27 ¶ And they come again to Jerusalem: and as he was walking in the temple, there come to him the chief priests, and the scribes, and the elders,

28 And say unto him, By what authority doest thou these things? and who gave thee this authority to do these things?

29 And Yashiyah answered and said unto them, I will also ask of you one question, and answer me, and I will tell you by what authority I do these things.

30 The baptism of John, was *it* from heaven, or of men? answer me.

31 And they reasoned with themselves, saying, If we shall say, From heaven; he will say, Why then did ye not believe him?

32 But if we shall say, Of men; they feared the people: for all *men* counted John, that he was a prophet indeed.

33 And they answered and said unto Yashiyah, We cannot tell. And Yashiyah answering saith unto them, Neither do I tell you by what authority I do these things.

CHAPTER 12

AND he began to speak unto them by parables. A *certain* man planted a vineyard, and set an hedge about *it,* and digged *a place for* the winefat, and built a tower, and let it out to husbandmen, and went into a far country.

2 And at the season he sent to the husbandmen a servant, that he might receive from the husbandmen of the fruit of the vineyard.

3 And they caught *him,* and beat him, and sent *him* away empty.

4 And again he sent unto them another servant; and at him they cast stones, and wounded *him* in the head, and sent *him* away shamefully handled.

5 And again he sent another; and him they killed, and many others; beating some, and killing some.

6 Having yet therefore one son, his wellbeloved, he sent him also last unto them, saying, They will reverence my son.

7 But those husbandmen said among themselves, This is the heir; come, let us kill him, and the inheritance shall be ours.

8 And they took him, and killed *him,* and cast *him* out of the vineyard.

9 What shall therefore the lord of the vineyard do? he will come and destroy the husbandmen, and will give the vineyard unto others.

10 And have ye not read this scripture; The stone which the builders rejected is become the head of the corner:

11 This was the Lord's doing, and it is marvellous in our eyes?

12 And they sought to lay hold on him, but feared the people: for they knew that he had spoken the parable against them: and they left him, and went their way.

13 ¶ And they send unto him certain of the Pharisees and of the Herodians, to catch him in *his* words.

14 And when they were come, they say unto him, Master, we know that thou art true, and carest for no man: for thou regardest not the person of men, but teachest the way of אֱלֹהִים in truth: Is it lawful to give tribute to Cæsar, or not?

15 Shall we give, or shall we not give? But he, knowing their hypocrisy, said unto them, Why tempt ye me? bring me a penny, that I may see *it.*

16 And they brought *it.* And he saith unto them, Whose *is* this image and superscription? And they said unto him, Cæsar's.

17 And Yashiyah answering said unto them, Render to Cæsar the things that are Cæsar's, and to אֱלֹהִים the things that are אֱלֹהִים's. And they marvelled at him.

18 ¶ Then come unto him the Sadducees, which say there is no resurrection; and they asked him, saying,

19 Master, Moses wrote unto us, If a man's brother die, and leave *his* wife *behind him,* and leave no children, that his brother should take his wife, and raise up seed unto his brother.

20 Now there were seven brethren: and the first took a wife, and dying left no seed.

21 And the second took her, and died, neither left he any seed: and the third likewise.

22 And the seven had her, and left no seed: last of all the woman died also.

23 In the resurrection therefore, when they shall rise, whose wife shall she be of them? for the seven had her to wife.

24 And Yashiyah answering said unto them, Do ye not therefore err, because ye know not the scriptures, neither the power of אֱלֹהִים?

25 For when they shall rise from the dead, they neither marry, nor are given in marriage; but are as the angels which are in heaven.

26 And as touching the dead, that they rise: have ye not read in the book of Moses, how in the bush אֱלֹהִים spake unto him, saying, I *am* the אֱלֹהִים of Abraham, and the אֱלֹהִים of Isaac, and the אֱלֹהִים of Jacob?

27 He is not the אֱלֹהִים of the dead, but the אֱלֹהִים of the living: ye therefore do greatly err.

28 ¶ And one of the scribes came, and having heard them reasoning together, and perceiving that he had answered them well, asked him, Which is the first commandment of all?

29 And Yashiyah answered him, The first of all the commandments *is*, Hear, O Israel; The Lord our אֱלֹהִים is one Lord:

30 And thou shalt love the Lord thy אֱלֹהִים with all thy heart, and with all thy soul, and with all thy mind, and with all thy strength: this *is* the first commandment.

31 And the second *is* like, *namely* this, Thou shalt love thy neighbour as thyself. There is none other commandment greater than these.

32 And the scribe said unto him, Well, Master, thou hast said the truth: for there is one אֱלֹהִים; and there is none other but he:

33 And to love him with all the heart, and with all the understanding, and with all the soul, and with all the strength, and to love *his* neighbour as himself, is more than all whole burnt offerings and sacrifices.

34 And when Yashiyah saw that he answered discreetly, he said unto him, Thou art not far from the kingdom of אֱלֹהִים. And no man after that durst ask him *any question*.

35 ¶ And Yashiyah answered and said, while he taught in the temple, How say the scribes that Christ is the Son of David?

36 For David himself said by the Holy Ghost, The LORD said to my Lord, Sit thou on my right hand, till I make thine enemies thy footstool.

37 David therefore himself calleth him Lord; and whence is he *then* his son? And the common people heard him gladly.

38 ¶ And he said unto them in his doctrine, Beware of the scribes, which love to go in long clothing, and *love* salutations in the marketplaces,

39 And the chief seats in the synagogues, and the uppermost rooms at feasts:

40 Which devour widows' houses, and for a pretence make long prayers: these shall receive greater damnation.

41 ¶ And Yashiyah sat over against the treasury, and beheld how the people cast money into the treasury: and many that were rich cast in much.

42 And there came a certain poor widow, and she threw in two mites, which make a farthing.

43 And he called *unto him* his disciples, and saith unto them, Verily I say unto you, That this poor widow hath cast more in, than all they which have cast into the treasury:

44 For all *they* did cast in of their abundance; but she of her want did cast in all that she had, *even* all her living.

CHAPTER 13

AND as he went out of the temple, one of his disciples saith unto him, Master, see what manner of stones and what buildings *are* here!

2 And Yashiyah answering said unto him, Seest thou these great buildings? there shall not be left one stone upon another, that shall not be thrown down.

3 And as he sat upon the mount of Olives over against the temple, Peter and James and John and Andrew asked him privately,

4 Tell us, when shall these things be? and what *shall be* the sign when all these things shall be fulfilled?

5 And Yashiyah answering them began to say, Take heed lest any *man* deceive you:

6 For many shall come in my name, saying, I am *Christ;* and shall deceive many.

7 And when ye shall hear of wars and rumours of wars, be ye not troubled: for *such things* must needs be; but the end *shall* not *be* yet.

8 For nation shall rise against nation, and kingdom against kingdom: and there shall be earthquakes in divers places, and there shall be famines and troubles: these *are* the beginnings of sorrows.

9 ¶ But take heed to yourselves: for they shall deliver you up to councils; and in the synagogues ye shall be beaten: and ye shall be brought before rulers and kings for my sake, for a testimony against them.

10 And the gospel must first be published among all nations.

11 But when they shall lead *you*, and deliver you up, take no thought beforehand what ye shall speak, neither do ye premeditate: but whatsoever shall be given you in that hour, that speak ye: for it is not ye that speak, but the Holy Ghost.

12 Now the brother shall betray the brother to death, and the father the son; and children shall rise up against *their* parents, and shall cause them to be put to death.

13 And ye shall be hated of all *men* for my name's sake: but he that shall endure unto the end, the same shall be saved.

14 ¶ But when ye shall see the abomination of desolation, spoken of by Daniel the prophet, standing where it ought not, (let him that readeth understand,) then let them that be in Judæa flee to the mountains:

15 And let him that is on the housetop not go down into the house, neither enter *therein*, to take any thing out of his house:

16 And let him that is in the field not turn back again for to take up his garment.

17 But woe to them that are with child, and to them that give suck in those days!

18 And pray ye that your flight be not in the winter.

19 For *in* those days shall be affliction, such as was not from the beginning of the creation which אֱלֹהִים created unto this time, neither shall be.

20 And except that the Lord had shortened those days, no flesh should be saved: but for the elect's sake, whom he hath chosen, he hath shortened the days.

21 And then if any man shall say to you, Lo, here *is* Christ; or, lo, *he is* there; believe *him* not:

22 For false Christs and false prophets shall rise, and shall shew signs and wonders, to seduce, if *it were* possible, even the elect.

23 But take ye heed: behold, I have foretold you all things.

24 ¶ But in those days, after that tribulation, the sun shall be darkened, and the moon shall not give her light,

25 And the stars of heaven shall fall, and the powers that are in heaven shall be shaken.

26 And then shall they see the Son of man coming in the clouds with great power and glory.

27 And then shall he send his angels, and shall gather together his elect from the four winds, from the uttermost part of the earth to the uttermost part of heaven.

28 Now learn a parable of the fig tree; When her branch is yet tender, and putteth forth leaves, ye know that summer is near:

29 So ye in like manner, when ye shall see these things come to pass, know that it is nigh, *even* at the doors.

30 Verily I say unto you, that this generation shall not pass, till all these things be done.

31 Heaven and earth shall pass away: but my words shall not pass away.

32 ¶ But of that day and *that* hour knoweth no man, no, not the angels which are in heaven, neither the Son, but the Father.

33 Take ye heed, watch and pray: for ye know not when the time is.

34 *For the Son of man is* as a man taking a far journey, who left his house, and gave authority to his servants, and to every man his work, and commanded the porter to watch.

35 Watch ye therefore: for ye know not when the master of the house cometh, at even, or at midnight, or at the cockcrowing, or in the morning:

36 Lest coming suddenly he find you sleeping.

37 And what I say unto you I say unto all, Watch.

CHAPTER 14

AFTER two days was *the feast of* the passover, and of unleavened bread: and the chief priests and the scribes sought how they might take him by craft, and put *him* to death.

2 But they said, Not on the feast *day*, lest there be an uproar of the people.

3 ¶ And being in Bethany in the house of Simon the leper, as he sat at meat, there came a woman having an alabaster box of ointment of spikenard very precious; and she brake the box, and poured *it* on his head.

4 And there were some that had indignation within themselves, and said, Why was this waste of the ointment made?

5 For it might have been sold for more than three hundred pence, and have been given to the poor. And they murmured against her.

6 And Yashiyah said, Let her alone; why trouble ye her? she hath wrought a good work on me.

7 For ye have the poor with you always, and whensoever ye will ye may do them good: but me ye have not always.

8 She hath done what she could: she is come aforehand to anoint my body to the burying.

9 Verily I say unto you, Wheresoever this gospel shall be preached throughout the whole world, *this* also that she hath done shall be spoken of for a memorial of her.

10 ¶ And Judas Iscariot, one of the twelve, went unto the chief priests, to betray him unto them.

11 And when they heard *it*, they were glad, and promised to give him money. And he sought how he might conveniently betray him.

12 ¶ And the first day of unleavened bread, when they killed the passover, his disciples said unto him, Where wilt thou that we go and prepare that thou mayest eat the passover?

13 And he sendeth forth two of his disciples, and saith unto them, Go ye into the city, and there shall meet you a man bearing a pitcher of water: follow him.

14 And wheresoever he shall go in, say ye to the goodman of the house, The Master saith, Where is the guestchamber, where I shall eat the passover with my disciples?

15 And he will shew you a large upper room furnished *and* prepared: there make ready for us.

16 And his disciples went forth, and came into the city, and found as he had said unto them: and they made ready the passover.

17 And in the evening he cometh with the twelve.

18 And as they sat and did eat, Yashiyah said, Verily I say unto you, One of you which eateth with me shall betray me.

19 And they began to be sorrowful, and to say unto him one by one, *Is* it I? and another *said, Is* it I?

20 And he answered and said unto them, *It is* one of the twelve, that dippeth with me in the dish.

21 The Son of man indeed goeth, as it is written of him: but woe to that man by whom the Son of man is betrayed! good were it for that man if he had never been born.

22 ¶ And as they did eat, Yashiyah took bread, and blessed, and brake *it*, and gave to them, and said, Take, eat: this is my body.

23 And he took the cup, and when he had given thanks, he gave *it* to them: and they all drank of it.

24 And he said unto them, This is my blood of the new testament, which is shed for many.

25 Verily I say unto you, I will drink no more of the fruit of the vine, until that day that I drink it new in the kingdom of אֱלֹהִים.

26 ¶ And when they had sung an hymn, they went out into the mount of Olives.

27 And Yashiyah saith unto them, All ye shall be offended because of me this night: for it is written, I will smite the shepherd, and the sheep shall be scattered.

28 But after that I am risen, I will go before you into Galilee.

29 But Peter said unto him, Although all shall be offended, yet *will* not I.

30 And Yashiyah saith unto him, Verily I say unto thee, That this day, *even* in this night, before the cock crow twice, thou shalt deny me thrice.

31 But he spake the more vehemently, If I should die with thee, I will not deny thee in any wise. Likewise also said they all.

32 And they came to a place which was named Gethsemane: and he saith to his disciples, Sit ye here, while I shall pray.

33 And he taketh with him Peter and James and John, and began to be sore amazed, and to be very heavy;

34 And saith unto them, My soul is exceeding sorrowful unto death: tarry ye here, and watch.

35 And he went forward a little, and fell on the ground, and prayed that, if it were possible, the hour might pass from him.

36 And he said, Abba, Father, all things *are* possible unto thee; take away this cup from me: nevertheless not what I will, but what thou wilt.

37 And he cometh, and findeth them sleeping, and saith unto Peter, Simon, sleepest thou? couldest not thou watch one hour?

38 Watch ye and pray, lest ye enter into temptation. The spirit truly *is* ready, but the flesh *is* weak.

39 And again he went away, and prayed, and spake the same words.

40 And when he returned, he found them asleep again, (for their eyes were heavy,) neither wist they what to answer him.

41 And he cometh the third time, and saith unto them, Sleep on now, and take *your* rest: it is enough, the hour is come; behold, the Son of man is betrayed into the hands of sinners.

42 Rise up, let us go; lo, he that betrayeth me is at hand.

43 ¶ And immediately, while he yet spake, cometh Judas, one of the twelve, and with him a great multitude with swords and staves, from the chief priests and the scribes and the elders.

44 And he that betrayed him had given them a token, saying, Whomsoever I shall kiss, that same is he; take him, and lead *him* away safely.

45 And as soon as he was come, he goeth straightway to him, and saith, Master, master; and kissed him.

46 ¶ And they laid their hands on him, and took him.

47 And one of them that stood by drew a sword, and smote a servant of the high priest, and cut off his ear.

48 And Yashiyah answered and said unto them, Are ye come out, as against a thief, with swords and *with* staves to take me?

49 I was daily with you in the temple teaching, and ye took me not: but the scriptures must be fulfilled.

50 And they all forsook him, and fled.

51 And there followed him a certain young man, having a linen cloth cast about *his* naked *body*: and the young men laid hold on him:

52 And he left the linen cloth, and fled from them naked.

53 ¶ And they led Yashiyah away to the high priest: and with him were assembled all the chief priests and the elders and the scribes.

54 And Peter followed him afar off, even into the palace of the high priest: and he sat with the servants, and warmed himself at the fire.

55 And the chief priests and all the council sought for witness against Yashiyah to put him to death; and found none.

56 For many bare false witness against him, but their witness agreed not together.

57 And there arose certain, and bare false witness against him, saying,

58 We heard him say, I will destroy this temple that is made with hands, and within three days I will build another made without hands.

59 But neither so did their witness agree together.

60 And the high priest stood up in the midst, and asked Yashiyah, saying, Answerest thou nothing? what *is it which* these witness against thee?

61 But he held his peace, and answered nothing. Again the high priest asked him, and said unto him, Art thou the Christ, the Son of the Blessed?

62 And Yashiyah said, I am: and ye shall see the Son of man sitting on the right hand of power, and coming in the clouds of heaven.

63 Then the high priest rent his clothes, and saith, What need we any further witnesses?

64 Ye have heard the blasphemy: what think ye? And they all condemned him to be guilty of death.

65 And some began to spit on him, and to cover his face, and to buffet him, and to say unto him, Prophesy: and the servants did strike him with the palms of their hands.

66 ¶ And as Peter was beneath in the palace, there cometh one of the maids of the high priest:

67 And when she saw Peter warming himself, she looked upon him, and said, And thou also wast with Yashiyah of Nazareth.

68 But he denied, saying, I know not, neither understand I what thou sayest. And he went out into the porch; and the cock crew.

69 And a maid saw him again, and began to say to them that stood by, This is *one* of them.

70 And he denied it again. And a little after, they that stood by said again to Peter, Surely thou art *one* of them: for thou art a Galilæan, and thy speech agreeth *thereto*.

71 But he began to curse and to swear, *saying*, I know not this man of whom ye speak.

72 And the second time the cock crew. And Peter called to mind the word that Yashiyah said unto him, Before the cock crow twice, thou shalt deny me thrice. And when he thought thereon, he wept.

CHAPTER 15

AND straightway in the morning the chief priests held a consultation with the elders and scribes and the whole council, and bound Yashiyah, and carried *him* away, and delivered *him* to Pilate.

2 And Pilate asked him, Art thou the King of the Jews? And he answering said unto him, Thou sayest *it*.

3 And the chief priests accused him of many things: but he answered nothing.

4 And Pilate asked him again, saying, Answerest thou nothing? behold how many things they witness against thee.

5 But Yashiyah yet answered nothing; so that Pilate marvelled.

6 Now at *that* feast he released unto them one prisoner, whomsoever they desired.

7 And there was *one* named Barabbas, *which lay* bound with them that had made insurrection with him, who had committed murder in the insurrection.

8 And the multitude crying aloud began to desire *him to do* as he had ever done unto them.

9 But Pilate answered them, saying, Will ye that I release unto you the King of the Jews?

10 For he knew that the chief priests had delivered him for envy.

11 But the chief priests moved the people, that he should rather release Barabbas unto them.

12 And Pilate answered and said again unto them, What will ye then that I shall do *unto him* whom ye call the King of the Jews?

13 And they cried out again, Crucify him.

14 Then Pilate said unto them, Why, what evil hath he done? And they cried out the more exceedingly, Crucify him.

15 ¶ And *so* Pilate, willing to content the people, released Barabbas unto them, and delivered Yashiyah, when he had scourged *him*, to be crucified.

16 And the soldiers led him away into the hall, called Prætorium; and they call together the whole band.

17 And they clothed him with purple, and platted a crown of thorns, and put it about his *head*,

18 And began to salute him, Hail, King of the Jews!

19 And they smote him on the head with a reed, and did spit upon him, and bowing *their* knees worshipped him.

20 And when they had mocked him, they took off the purple from him, and put his own clothes on him, and led him out to crucify him.

21 And they compel one Simon a Cyrenian, who passed by, coming out of the country, the father of Alexander and Rufus, to bear his cross.

22 And they bring him unto the place Golgotha, which is, being interpreted, The place of a skull.

23 And they gave him to drink wine mingled with myrrh: but he received *it* not.

24 And when they had crucified him, they parted his garments, casting lots upon them, what every man should take.

25 And it was the third hour, and they crucified him.

26 And the superscription of his accusation was written over, THE KING OF THE JEWS.

27 And with him they crucify two thieves; the one on his right hand, and the other on his left.

28 And the scripture was fulfilled, which saith, And he was numbered with the transgressors.

29 And they that passed by railed on him, wagging their heads, and saying, Ah, thou that destroyest the temple, and buildest *it* in three days,

30 Save thyself, and come down from the cross.

31 Likewise also the chief priests mocking said among themselves with the scribes, He saved others; himself he cannot save.

32 Let Christ the King of Israel descend now from the cross, that we may see and believe. And they that were crucified with him reviled him.

33 And when the sixth hour was come, there was darkness over the whole land until the ninth hour.

34 And at the ninth hour Yashiyah cried with a loud voice, saying, Eloi, Eloi, lama sabachthani? which is, being interpreted, My אֱלֹהִים, my אֱלֹהִים, why hast thou forsaken me?

35 And some of them that stood by, when they heard *it*, said, Behold, he calleth Elias.

36 And one ran and filled a spunge full of vinegar, and put *it* on a reed, and gave him to drink, saying, Let alone; let us see whether Elias will come to take him down.

37 And Yashiyah cried with a loud voice, and gave up the ghost.

38 And the veil of the temple was rent in twain from the top to the bottom.

39 ¶ And when the centurion, which stood over against him, saw that he so cried out, and gave up the ghost, he said, Truly this man was the Son of אֱלֹהִים.

40 There were also women looking on afar off: among whom was Mary Magdalene, and Mary the mother of James the less and of Joses, and Salome;

41 (Who also, when he was in Galilee, followed him, and ministered unto him;) and many other women which came up with him unto Jerusalem.

42 ¶ And now when the even was come, because it was the preparation, that is, the day before the sabbath,

43 Joseph of Arimathæa, an honourable counseller, which also waited for the kingdom of אֱלֹהִים, came, and went in boldly unto Pilate, and craved the body of Yashiyah.

44 And Pilate marvelled if he were already dead: and calling *unto him* the centurion, he asked him whether he had been any while dead.

45 And when he knew *it* of the centurion, he gave the body to Joseph.

46 And he bought fine linen, and took him down, and wrapped him in the linen, and laid him in a sepulchre which was hewn out of a rock, and rolled a stone unto the door of the sepulchre.

47 And Mary Magdalene and Mary *the mother* of Joses beheld where he was laid.

CHAPTER 16

AND when the sabbath was past, Mary Magdalene, and Mary the *mother* of James, and Salome, had bought sweet spices, that they might come and anoint him.

2 And very early in the morning the first *day* of the week, they came unto the sepulchre at the rising of the sun.

3 And they said among themselves, Who shall roll us away the stone from the door of the sepulchre?

4 And when they looked, they saw that the stone was rolled away: for it was very great.

5 And entering into the sepulchre, they saw a young man sitting on the right side, clothed in a long white garment; and they were affrighted.

6 And he saith unto them, Be not affrighted: Ye seek Yashiyah of Nazareth, which was crucified: he is risen; he is not here: behold the place where they laid him.

7 But go your way, tell his disciples and Peter that he goeth before you into Galilee: there shall ye see him, as he said unto you.

8 And they went out quickly, and fled from the sepulchre; for they trembled and were amazed: neither said they any thing to any *man;* for they were afraid.

9 ¶ Now when *Yashiyah* was risen early the first *day* of the week, he appeared first to Mary Magdalene, out of whom he had cast seven devils.

10 *And* she went and told them that had been with him, as they mourned and wept.

11 And they, when they had heard that he was alive, and had been seen of her, believed not.

12 ¶ After that he appeared in another form unto two of them, as they walked, and went into the country.

13 And they went and told *it* unto the residue: neither believed they them.

14 ¶ Afterward he appeared unto the eleven as they sat at meat, and upbraided them with their unbelief and hardness of heart, because they believed not them which had seen him after he was risen.

15 And he said unto them, Go ye into all the world, and preach the gospel to every creature.

16 He that believeth and is baptized shall be saved; but he that believeth not shall be damned.

17 And these signs shall follow them that believe; In my name shall they cast out devils; they shall speak with new tongues;

18 They shall take up serpents; and if they drink any deadly thing, it shall not hurt them; they shall lay hands on the sick, and they shall recover.

19 ¶ So then after the Lord had spoken unto them, he was received up into heaven, and sat on the right hand of אֱלֹהִים.

20 And they went forth, and preached every where, the Lord working with *them*, and confirming the word with signs following. Amen.

THE GOSPEL ACCORDING TO
ST. LUKE.

CHAPTER 1

FORASMUCH as many have taken in hand to set forth in order a declaration of those things which are most surely believed among us,

2 Even as they delivered them unto us, which from the beginning were eyewitnesses, and ministers of the word;

3 It seemed good to me also, having had perfect understanding of all things from the very first, to write unto thee in order, most excellent Theophilus,

4 That thou mightest know the certainty of those things, wherein thou hast been instructed.

5 ¶ THERE was in the days of Herod, the king of Judæa, a certain priest named Zacharias, of the course of Abia: and his wife *was* of the daughters of Aaron, and her name *was* Elisabeth.

6 And they were both righteous before אֱלֹהִים, walking in all the commandments and ordinances of the Lord blameless.

7 And they had no child, because that Elisabeth was barren, and they both were *now* well stricken in years.

8 And it came to pass, that while he executed the priest's office before אֱלֹהִים in the order of his course,

9 According to the custom of the priest's office, his lot was to burn incense when he went into the temple of the Lord.

10 And the whole multitude of the people were praying without at the time of incense.

11 And there appeared unto him an angel of the Lord standing on the right side of the altar of incense.

12 And when Zacharias saw *him*, he was troubled, and fear fell upon him.

13 But the angel said unto him, Fear not, Zacharias: for thy prayer is heard; and thy wife Elisabeth shall bear thee a son, and thou shalt call his name John.

14 And thou shalt have joy and gladness; and many shall rejoice at his birth.

15 For he shall be great in the sight of the Lord, and shall drink neither wine nor strong drink; and he shall be filled with the Holy Ghost, even from his mother's womb.

16 And many of the children of Israel shall he turn to the Lord their אֱלֹהִים.

17 And he shall go before him in the spirit and power of Elias, to turn the hearts of the fathers to the children, and the disobedient to the wisdom of the just; to make ready a people prepared for the Lord.

18 And Zacharias said unto the angel, Whereby shall I know this? for I am an old man, and my wife well stricken in years.

19 And the angel answering said unto him, I am Gabriel, that stand in the presence of אֱלֹהִים; and am sent to speak unto thee, and to shew thee these glad tidings.

20 And, behold, thou shalt be dumb, and not able to speak, until the day that these things shall be performed, because thou believest not my words, which shall be fulfilled in their season.

21 And the people waited for Zacharias, and marvelled that he tarried so long in the temple.

22 And when he came out, he could not speak unto them: and they perceived that he had seen a vision in the temple: for he beckoned unto them, and remained speechless.

23 And it came to pass, that, as soon as the days of his ministration were accomplished, he departed to his own house.

24 And after those days his wife Elisabeth conceived, and hid herself five months, saying,

25 Thus hath the Lord dealt with me in the days wherein he looked on *me*, to take away my reproach among men.

26 And in the sixth month the angel Gabriel was sent from אֱלֹהִים unto a city of Galilee, named Nazareth,

27 To a virgin espoused to a man whose name was Joseph, of the house of David; and the virgin's name *was* Mary.

28 And the angel came in unto her, and said, Hail, *thou that art* highly favoured, the Lord *is* with thee: blessed *art* thou among women.

29 And when she saw *him*, she was troubled at his saying, and cast in her mind what manner of salutation this should be.

30 And the angel said unto her, Fear not, Mary: for thou hast found favour with אֱלֹהִים.

31 And, behold, thou shalt conceive in thy womb, and bring forth a son, and shalt call his name JESUS.

32 He shall be great, and shall be called the Son of the Highest: and the Lord אֱלֹהִים shall give unto him the throne of his father David:

33 And he shall reign over the house of Jacob for ever; and of his kingdom there shall be no end.

34 Then said Mary unto the angel, How shall this be, seeing I know not a man?

35 And the angel answered and said unto her, The Holy Ghost shall come upon thee, and the power of the Highest shall overshadow thee: therefore also that holy thing which shall be born of thee shall be called the Son of אֱלֹהִים.

36 And, behold, thy cousin Elisabeth, she hath also conceived a son in her old age: and this is the sixth month with her, who was called barren.

37 For with אֱלֹהִים nothing shall be impossible.

38 And Mary said, Behold the handmaid of the Lord; be it unto me according to thy word. And the angel departed from her.

39 And Mary arose in those days, and went into the hill country with haste, into a city of Juda;

40 And entered into the house of Zacharias, and saluted Elisabeth.

41 And it came to pass, that, when Elisabeth heard the salutation of Mary, the babe leaped in her womb; and Elisabeth was filled with the Holy Ghost:

42 And she spake out with a loud voice, and said, Blessed *art* thou among women, and blessed *is* the fruit of thy womb.

43 And whence *is* this to me, that the mother of my Lord should come to me?

44 For, lo, as soon as the voice of thy salutation sounded in mine ears, the babe leaped in my womb for joy.

45 And blessed *is* she that believed: for there shall be a performance of those things which were told her from the Lord.

46 And Mary said, My soul doth magnify the Lord,

47 And my spirit hath rejoiced in אֱלֹהִים my Saviour.

48 For he hath regarded the low estate of his handmaiden: for, behold, from henceforth all generations shall call me blessed.

49 For he that is mighty hath done to me great things; and holy *is* his name.

50 And his mercy *is* on them that fear him from generation to generation.

51 He hath shewed strength with his arm; he hath scattered the proud in the imagination of their hearts.

52 He hath put down the mighty from *their* seats, and exalted them of low degree.

53 He hath filled the hungry with good things; and the rich he hath sent empty away.

54 He hath holpen his servant Israel, in remembrance of *his* mercy;

55 As he spake to our fathers, to Abraham, and to his seed for ever.

56 And Mary abode with her about three months, and returned to her own house.

57 Now Elisabeth's full time came that she should be delivered; and she brought forth a son.

58 And her neighbours and her cousins heard how the Lord had shewed great mercy upon her; and they rejoiced with her.

59 And it came to pass, that on the eighth day they came to circumcise the child; and they called him Zacharias, after the name of his father.

60 And his mother answered and said, Not *so;* but he shall be called John.

61 And they said unto her, There is none of thy kindred that is called by this name.

62 And they made signs to his father, how he would have him called.

63 And he asked for a writing table, and wrote, saying, His name is John. And they marvelled all.

64 And his mouth was opened immediately, and his tongue *loosed*, and he spake, and praised אֱלֹהִים.

65 And fear came on all that dwelt round about them: and all these sayings were noised abroad throughout all the hill country of Judæa.

66 And all they that heard *them* laid *them* up in their hearts, saying, What manner of child shall this be! And the hand of the Lord was with him.

67 And his father Zacharias was filled with the Holy Ghost, and prophesied, saying,

68 Blessed *be* the Lord אֱלֹהִים of Israel; for he hath visited and redeemed his people,

69 And hath raised up an horn of salvation for us in the house of his servant David;

70 As he spake by the mouth of his holy prophets, which have been since the world began:

71 That we should be saved from our enemies, and from the hand of all that hate us;

72 To perform the mercy *promised* to our fathers, and to remember his holy covenant;

73 The oath which he sware to our father Abraham,

74 That he would grant unto us, that we being delivered out of the hand of our enemies might serve him without fear,

75 In holiness and righteousness before him, all the days of our life.

76 And thou, child, shalt be called the prophet of the Highest: for thou shalt go before the face of the Lord to prepare his ways;

77 To give knowledge of salvation unto his people by the remission of their sins,

78 Through the tender mercy of our אֱלֹהִים; whereby the dayspring from on high hath visited us,

79 To give light to them that sit in darkness and *in* the shadow of death, to guide our feet into the way of peace.

80 And the child grew, and waxed strong in spirit, and was in the deserts till the day of his shewing unto Israel.

CHAPTER 2

AND it came to pass in those days, that there went out a decree from Cæsar Augustus, that all the world should be taxed.

2 (*And* this taxing was first made when Cyrenius was governor of Syria.)

3 And all went to be taxed, every one into his own city.

4 And Joseph also went up from Galilee, out of the city of Nazareth, into Judæa, unto the city of David, which is called Bethlehem; (because he was of the house and lineage of David:)

5 To be taxed with Mary his espoused wife, being great with child.

6 And so it was, that, while they were there, the days were accomplished that she should be delivered.

7 And she brought forth her firstborn son, and wrapped him in swaddling clothes, and laid him in a manger; because there was no room for them in the inn.

8 And there were in the same country shepherds abiding in the field, keeping watch over their flock by night.

9 And, lo, the angel of the Lord came upon them, and the glory of the Lord shone round about them: and they were sore afraid.

10 And the angel said unto them, Fear not: for, behold, I bring you good tidings of great joy, which shall be to all people.

11 For unto you is born this day in the city of David a Saviour, which is Christ the Lord.

12 And this *shall be* a sign unto you; Ye shall find the babe wrapped in swaddling clothes, lying in a manger.

13 And suddenly there was with the angel a multitude of the heavenly host praising אֱלֹהִים, and saying,

14 Glory to אֱלֹהִים in the highest, and on earth peace, good will toward men.

15 And it came to pass, as the angels were gone away from them into heaven, the shepherds said one to another, Let us now go even unto Bethlehem, and see this thing which is come to pass, which the Lord hath made known unto us.

16 And they came with haste, and found Mary, and Joseph, and the babe lying in a manger.

17 And when they had seen *it*, they made known abroad the saying which was told them concerning this child.

18 And all they that heard *it* wondered at those things which were told them by the shepherds.

19 But Mary kept all these things, and pondered *them* in her heart.

20 And the shepherds returned, glorifying and praising אֱלֹהִים for all the things that they had heard and seen, as it was told unto them.

21 And when eight days were accomplished for the circumcising of the child, his name was called JESUS, which was so named of the angel before he was conceived in the womb.

22 And when the days of her purification according to the law of Moses were accomplished, they brought him to Jerusalem, to present *him* to the Lord;

23 (As it is written in the law of the Lord, Every male that openeth the womb shall be called holy to the Lord;)

24 And to offer a sacrifice according to that which is said in the law of the Lord, A pair of turtledoves, or two young pigeons.

25 And, behold, there was a man in Jerusalem, whose name *was* Simeon; and the same man *was* just and devout, waiting for the consolation of Israel: and the Holy Ghost was upon him.

26 And it was revealed unto him by the Holy Ghost, that he should not see death, before he had seen the Lord's Christ.

27 And he came by the Spirit into the temple: and when the parents brought in the child Yashiyah, to do for him after the custom of the law,

28 Then took he him up in his arms, and blessed אֱלֹהִים, and said,

29 Lord, now lettest thou thy servant depart in peace, according to thy word:

30 For mine eyes have seen thy salvation,

31 Which thou hast prepared before the face of all people;

32 A light to lighten the Gentiles, and the glory of thy people Israel.

33 And Joseph and his mother marvelled at those things which were spoken of him.

34 And Simeon blessed them, and said unto Mary his mother, Behold, this *child* is set for the fall and rising again of many in Israel; and for a sign which shall be spoken against;

35 (Yea, a sword shall pierce through thy own soul also,) that the thoughts of many hearts may be revealed.

36 And there was one Anna, a prophetess, the daughter of Phanuel, of the tribe of Aser: she was of a great age, and had lived with an husband seven years from her virginity;

37 And she *was* a widow of about fourscore and four years, which departed not from the temple, but served אֱלֹהִים with fastings and prayers night and day.

38 And she coming in that instant gave thanks likewise unto the Lord, and spake of him to all them that looked for redemption in Jerusalem.

39 And when they had performed all things according to the law of the Lord, they returned into Galilee, to their own city Nazareth.

40 And the child grew, and waxed strong in spirit, filled with wisdom: and the grace of אֱלֹהִים was upon him.

41 Now his parents went to Jerusalem every year at the feast of the passover.

42 And when he was twelve years old, they went up to Jerusalem after the custom of the feast.

43 And when they had fulfilled the days, as they returned, the child Yashiyah tarried behind in Jerusalem; and Joseph and his mother knew not *of it*.

44 But they, supposing him to have been in the company, went a day's journey; and they sought him among *their* kinsfolk and acquaintance.

45 And when they found him not, they turned back again to Jerusalem, seeking him.

46 And it came to pass, that after three days they found him in the temple, sitting in the midst of the doctors, both hearing them, and asking them questions.

47 And all that heard him were astonished at his understanding and answers.

48 And when they saw him, they were amazed: and his mother said unto him, Son, why hast thou thus dealt with us? behold, thy father and I have sought thee sorrowing.

49 And he said unto them, How is it that ye sought me? wist ye not that I must be about my Father's business?

50 And they understood not the saying which he spake unto them.

51 And he went down with them, and came to Nazareth, and was subject unto them: but his mother kept all these sayings in her heart.

52 And Yashiyah increased in wisdom and stature, and in favour with אֱלֹהִים and man.

CHAPTER 3

NOW in the fifteenth year of the reign of Tiberius Cæsar, Pontius Pilate being governor of Judæa, and Herod being tetrarch of Galilee, and his brother Philip tetrarch of Ituræa and of the region of Trachonitis, and Lysanias the tetrarch of Abilene,

2 Annas and Caiaphas being the high priests, the word of אֱלֹהִים came unto John the son of Zacharias in the wilderness.

3 And he came into all the country about Jordan, preaching the baptism of repentance for the remission of sins;

4 As it is written in the book of the words of Esaias the prophet, saying, The voice of one crying in the wilderness, Prepare ye the way of the Lord, make his paths straight.

5 Every valley shall be filled, and every mountain and hill shall be brought low; and the crooked shall be made straight, and the rough ways *shall be* made smooth;

6 And all flesh shall see the salvation of אֱלֹהִים.

7 Then said he to the multitude that came forth to be baptized of him, O generation of vipers, who hath warned you to flee from the wrath to come?

8 Bring forth therefore fruits worthy of repentance, and begin not to say within yourselves, We have Abraham to *our* father: for I say unto you, That אֱלֹהִים is able of these stones to raise up children unto Abraham.

9 And now also the axe is laid unto the root of the trees: every tree therefore which bringeth not forth good fruit is hewn down, and cast into the fire.

10 And the people asked him, saying, What shall we do then?

11 He answereth and saith unto them, He that hath two coats, let him impart to him that hath none; and he that hath meat, let him do likewise.

12 Then came also publicans to be baptized, and said unto him, Master, what shall we do?

13 And he said unto them, Exact no more than that which is appointed you.

14 And the soldiers likewise demanded of him, saying, And what shall we do? And he said unto them, Do violence to no man, neither accuse *any* falsely; and be content with your wages.

15 And as the people were in expectation, and all men mused in their hearts of John, whether he were the Christ, or not;

16 John answered, saying unto *them* all, I indeed baptize you with water; but one mightier than I cometh, the latchet of whose shoes I am not worthy to unloose: he shall baptize you with the Holy Ghost and with fire:

17 Whose fan *is* in his hand, and he will throughly purge his floor, and will gather the wheat into his garner; but the chaff he will burn with fire unquenchable.

18 And many other things in his exhortation preached he unto the people.

19 But Herod the tetrarch, being reproved by him for Herodias his brother Philip's wife, and for all the evils which Herod had done,

20 Added yet this above all, that he shut up John in prison.

21 Now when all the people were baptized, it came to pass, that Yashiyah also being baptized, and praying, the heaven was opened,

22 And the Holy Ghost descended in a bodily shape like a dove upon him, and a voice came from heaven, which said, Thou art my beloved Son; in thee I am well pleased.

23 And Yashiyah himself began to be about thirty years of age, being (as was supposed) the son of Joseph, which was *the son* of Heli,

24 Which was *the son* of Matthat, which was *the son* of Levi, which was *the son* of Melchi, which was *the son* of Janna, which was *the son* of Joseph,

25 Which was *the son* of Mattathias, which was *the son* of Amos, which was *the son* of Naum, which was *the son* of Esli, which was *the son* of Nagge,

26 Which was *the son* of Maath, which was *the son* of Mattathias, which was *the son* of Semei, which was *the son* of Joseph, which was *the son* of Juda,

27 Which was *the son* of Joanna, which was *the son* of Rhesa, which was *the son* of Zorobabel, which was *the son* of Salathiel, which was *the son* of Neri,

28 Which was *the son* of Melchi, which was *the son* of Addi, which was *the son* of Cosam, which was *the son* of Elmodam, which was *the son* of Er,

29 Which was *the son* of Jose, which was *the son* of Eliezer, which was *the son* of Jorim, which was *the son* of Matthat, which was *the son* of Levi,

30 Which was *the son* of Simeon, which was *the son* of Juda, which was *the son* of Joseph, which was *the son* of Jonan, which was *the son* of Eliakim,

31 Which was *the son* of Melea, which was *the son* of Menan, which was *the son* of Mattatha, which was *the son* of Nathan, which was *the son* of David,

32 Which was *the son* of Jesse, which was *the son* of Obed, which was *the son* of Booz, which was *the son* of Salmon, which was *the son* of Naasson,

33 Which was *the son* of Aminadab, which was *the son* of Aram, which was *the son* of Esrom, which was *the son* of Phares, which was *the son* of Juda,

34 Which was *the son* of Jacob, which was *the son* of Isaac, which was *the son* of Abraham, which was *the son* of Thara, which was *the son* of Nachor,

35 Which was *the son* of Saruch, which was *the son* of Ragau, which was *the son* of Phalec, which was *the son* of Heber, which was *the son* of Sala,

36 Which was *the son* of Cainan, which was *the son* of Arphaxad, which was *the son* of Sem, which was *the son* of Noe, which was *the son* of Lamech,

37 Which was *the son* of Mathusala, which was *the son* of Enoch, which was *the son* of Jared, which was *the son* of Maleleel, which was *the son* of Cainan,

38 Which was *the son* of Enos, which was *the son* of Seth, which was *the son* of Adam, which was *the son* of אֱלֹהִים.

CHAPTER 4

AND Yashiyah being full of the Holy Ghost returned from Jordan, and was led by the Spirit into the wilderness,

2 Being forty days tempted of the devil. And in those days he did eat nothing: and when they were ended, he afterward hungered.

3 And the devil said unto him, If thou be the Son of אֱלֹהִים, command this stone that it be made bread.

4 And Yashiyah answered him, saying, It is written, That man shall not live by bread alone, but by every word of אֱלֹהִים.

5 And the devil, taking him up into an high mountain, shewed unto him all the kingdoms of the world in a moment of time.

6 And the devil said unto him, All this power will I give thee, and the glory of them: for that is delivered unto me; and to whomsoever I will I give it.

7 If thou therefore wilt worship me, all shall be thine.

8 And Yashiyah answered and said unto him, Get thee behind me, Satan: for it is written, Thou shalt worship the Lord thy אֱלֹהִים, and him only shalt thou serve.

9 And he brought him to Jerusalem, and set him on a pinnacle of the temple, and said unto him, If thou be the Son of אֱלֹהִים, cast thyself down from hence:

10 For it is written, He shall give his angels charge over thee, to keep thee:

11 And in *their* hands they shall bear thee up, lest at any time thou dash thy foot against a stone.

12 And Yashiyah answering said unto him, It is said, Thou shalt not tempt the Lord thy אֱלֹהִים.

13 And when the devil had ended all the temptation, he departed from him for a season.

14 ¶ And Yashiyah returned in the power of the Spirit into Galilee: and there went out a fame of him through all the region round about.

15 And he taught in their synagogues, being glorified of all.

16 ¶ And he came to Nazareth, where he had been brought up: and, as his custom was, he went into the synagogue on the sabbath day, and stood up for to read.

17 And there was delivered unto him the book of the prophet Esaias. And when he had opened the book, he found the place where it was written,

18 The Spirit of the Lord *is* upon me, because he hath anointed me to preach the gospel to the poor; he hath sent me to heal the brokenhearted, to preach deliverance to the captives, and recovering of sight to the blind, to set at liberty them that are bruised,

19 To preach the acceptable year of the Lord.

20 And he closed the book, and he gave *it* again to the minister, and sat down. And the eyes of all them that were in the synagogue were fastened on him.

21 And he began to say unto them, This day is this scripture fulfilled in your ears.

22 And all bare him witness, and wondered at the gracious words which proceeded out of his mouth. And they said, Is not this Joseph's son?

23 And he said unto them, Ye will surely say unto me this proverb, Physician, heal thyself: whatsoever we have heard done in Capernaum, do also here in thy country.

24 And he said, Verily I say unto you, No prophet is accepted in his own country.

25 But I tell you of a truth, many widows were in Israel in the days of Elias, when the heaven was shut up three years and six months, when great famine was throughout all the land;

26 But unto none of them was Elias sent, save unto Sarepta, *a city* of Sidon, unto a woman *that was* a widow.

27 And many lepers were in Israel in the time of Eliseus the prophet; and none of them was cleansed, saving Naaman the Syrian.

28 And all they in the synagogue, when they heard these things, were filled with wrath,

29 And rose up, and thrust him out of the city, and led him unto the brow of the hill whereon their city was built, that they might cast him down headlong.

30 But he passing through the midst of them went his way,

31 And came down to Capernaum, a city of Galilee, and taught them on the sabbath days.

32 And they were astonished at his doctrine: for his word was with power.

33 ¶ And in the synagogue there was a man, which had a spirit of an unclean devil, and cried out with a loud voice,

34 Saying, Let *us* alone; what have we to do with thee, *thou* Yashiyah of Nazareth? art thou come to destroy us? I know thee who thou art; the Holy One of אֱלֹהִים.

35 And Yashiyah rebuked him, saying, Hold thy peace, and come out of him. And when the devil had thrown him in the midst, he came out of him, and hurt him not.

36 And they were all amazed, and spake among themselves, saying, What a word *is* this! for with authority and power he commandeth the unclean spirits, and they come out.

37 And the fame of him went out into every place of the country round about.

38 ¶ And he arose out of the synagogue, and entered into Simon's house. And Simon's wife's mother was taken with a great fever;

and they besought him for her.

39 And he stood over her, and rebuked the fever; and it left her: and immediately she arose and ministered unto them.

40 ¶ Now when the sun was setting, all they that had any sick with divers diseases brought them unto him; and he laid his hands on every one of them, and healed them.

41 And devils also came out of many, crying out, and saying, Thou art Christ the Son of אֱלֹהִים. And he rebuking *them* suffered them not to speak: for they knew that he was Christ.

42 And when it was day, he departed and went into a desert place: and the people sought him, and came unto him, and stayed him, that he should not depart from them.

43 And he said unto them, I must preach the kingdom of אֱלֹהִים to other cities also: for therefore am I sent.

44 And he preached in the synagogues of Galilee.

CHAPTER 5

AND it came to pass, that, as the people pressed upon him to hear the word of אֱלֹהִים, he stood by the lake of Gennesaret,

2 And saw two ships standing by the lake: but the fishermen were gone out of them, and were washing *their* nets.

3 And he entered into one of the ships, which was Simon's, and prayed him that he would thrust out a little from the land. And he sat down, and taught the people out of the ship.

4 Now when he had left speaking, he said unto Simon, Launch out into the deep, and let down your nets for a draught.

5 And Simon answering said unto him, Master, we have toiled all the night, and have taken nothing: nevertheless at thy word I will let down the net.

6 And when they had this done, they inclosed a great multitude of fishes: and their net brake.

7 And they beckoned unto *their* partners, which were in the other ship, that they should come and help them. And they came, and filled both the ships, so that they began to sink.

8 When Simon Peter saw *it*, he fell down at Yashiyah' knees, saying, Depart from me; for I am a sinful man, O Lord.

9 For he was astonished, and all that were with him, at the draught of the fishes which they had taken:

10 And so *was* also James, and John, the sons of Zebedee, which were partners with Simon. And Yashiyah said unto Simon, Fear not; from henceforth thou shalt catch men.

11 And when they had brought their ships to land, they forsook all, and followed him.

12 ¶ And it came to pass, when he was in a certain city, behold a man full of leprosy: who seeing Yashiyah fell on *his* face, and besought him, saying, Lord, if thou wilt, thou canst make me clean.

13 And he put forth *his* hand, and touched him, saying, I will: be thou clean. And immediately the leprosy departed from him.

14 And he charged him to tell no man: but go, and shew thyself to the priest, and offer for thy cleansing, according as Moses commanded, for a testimony unto them.

15 But so much the more went there a fame abroad of him: and great multitudes came together to hear, and to be healed by him of their infirmities.

16 ¶ And he withdrew himself into the wilderness, and prayed.

17 And it came to pass on a certain day, as he was teaching, that there were Pharisees and doctors of the law sitting by, which were come out of every town of Galilee, and Judæa, and Jerusalem: and the power of the Lord was *present* to heal them.

18 ¶ And, behold, men brought in a bed a man which was taken with a palsy: and they sought *means* to bring him in, and to lay *him* before him.

19 And when they could not find by what *way* they might bring him in because of the multitude, they went upon the housetop, and let him down through the tiling with *his* couch into the midst before Yashiyah.

20 And when he saw their faith, he said unto him, Man, thy sins are forgiven thee.

21 And the scribes and the Pharisees began to reason, saying, Who is this which speaketh blasphemies? Who can forgive sins, but אֱלֹהִים alone?

22 But when Yashiyah perceived their thoughts, he answering said unto them, What reason ye in your hearts?

23 Whether is easier, to say, Thy sins be forgiven thee; or to say, Rise up and walk?

24 But that ye may know that the Son of man hath power upon earth to forgive sins, (he said unto the sick of the palsy,) I say unto thee, Arise, and take up thy couch, and go into thine house.

25 And immediately he rose up before them, and took up that whereon he lay, and departed to his own house, glorifying אֱלֹהִים.

26 And they were all amazed, and they glorified אֱלֹהִים, and were filled with fear, saying, We have seen strange things to day.

27 ¶ And after these things he went forth, and saw a publican, named Levi, sitting at the receipt of custom: and he said unto him, Follow me.

28 And he left all, rose up, and followed him.

29 And Levi made him a great feast in his own house: and there was a great company of publicans and of others that sat down with them.

30 But their scribes and Pharisees murmured against his disciples, saying, Why do ye eat and drink with publicans and sinners?

31 And Yashiyah answering said unto them, They that are whole need not a physician; but they that are sick.

32 I came not to call the righteous, but sinners to repentance.

33 ¶ And they said unto him, Why do the disciples of John fast often, and make prayers, and likewise *the disciples* of the Pharisees; but thine eat and drink?

34 And he said unto them, Can ye make the children of the bridechamber fast, while the bridegroom is with them?

35 But the days will come, when the bridegroom shall be taken away from them, and then shall they fast in those days.

36 ¶ And he spake also a parable unto them; No man putteth a piece of a new garment upon an old; if otherwise, then both the new maketh a rent, and the piece that was *taken* out of the new agreeth not with the old.

37 And no man putteth new wine into old bottles; else the new wine will burst the bottles, and be spilled, and the bottles shall perish.

38 But new wine must be put into new bottles; and both are preserved.

39 No man also having drunk old *wine* straightway desireth new: for he saith, The old is better.

CHAPTER 6

AND it came to pass on the second sabbath after the first, that he went through the corn fields; and his disciples plucked the ears of corn, and did eat, rubbing *them* in *their* hands.

2 And certain of the Pharisees said unto them, Why do ye that which is not lawful to do on the sabbath days?

3 And Yashiyah answering them said, Have ye not read so much as this, what David did, when himself was an hungred, and they which were with him;

4 How he went into the house of אֱלֹהִים, and did take and eat the shewbread, and gave also to them that were with him; which it is not lawful to eat but for the priests alone?

5 And he said unto them, That the Son of man is Lord also of the sabbath.

6 And it came to pass also on another sabbath, that he entered into the synagogue and taught: and there was a man whose right hand was withered.

7 And the scribes and Pharisees watched him, whether he would heal on the sabbath day; that they might find an accusation against him.

8 But he knew their thoughts, and said to the man which had the withered hand, Rise up, and stand forth in the midst. And he arose and stood forth.

9 Then said Yashiyah unto them, I will ask you one thing; Is it lawful on the sabbath days to do good, or to do evil? to save life, or to destroy *it?*

10 And looking round about upon them all, he said unto the man, Stretch forth thy hand. And he did so: and his hand was restored whole as the other.

11 And they were filled with madness; and communed one with another what they might do to Yashiyah.

12 And it came to pass in those days, that he went out into a mountain to pray, and continued all night in prayer to אֱלֹהִים.

13 ¶ And when it was day, he called *unto him* his disciples: and of them he chose twelve, whom also he named apostles;

14 Simon, (whom he also named Peter,) and Andrew his brother, James and John, Philip and Bartholomew,

15 Matthew and Thomas, James the *son* of Alphæus, and Simon called Zelotes,

16 And Judas *the brother* of James, and Judas Iscariot, which also was the traitor.

17 ¶ And he came down with them, and stood in the plain, and the company of his disciples, and a great multitude of people out of all Judæa and Jerusalem, and from the sea coast of Tyre and Sidon, which came to hear him, and to be healed of their diseases;

18 And they that were vexed with unclean spirits: and they were healed.

19 And the whole multitude sought to touch him: for there went virtue out of him, and healed *them* all.

20 ¶ And he lifted up his eyes on his disciples, and said, Blessed *be ye* poor: for yours is the kingdom of אֱלֹהִים.

21 Blessed *are ye* that hunger now: for ye shall be filled. Blessed *are ye* that weep now: for ye shall laugh.

22 Blessed are ye, when men shall hate you, and when they shall separate you *from their company,* and shall reproach *you,* and cast out your name as evil, for the Son of man's sake.

23 Rejoice ye in that day, and leap for joy: for, behold, your reward *is* great in heaven: for in the like manner did their fathers unto the prophets.

24 But woe unto you that are rich! for ye have received your consolation.

25 Woe unto you that are full! for ye shall hunger. Woe unto you that laugh now! for ye shall mourn and weep.

26 Woe unto you, when all men shall speak well of you! for so did their fathers to the false prophets.

27 ¶ But I say unto you which hear, Love your enemies, do good to them which hate you,

28 Bless them that curse you, and pray for them which despitefully use you.

29 And unto him that smiteth thee on the *one* cheek offer also the other; and him that taketh away thy cloke forbid not *to take thy* coat also.

30 Give to every man that asketh of thee; and of him that taketh away thy goods ask *them* not again.

31 And as ye would that men should do to you, do ye also to them likewise.

32 For if ye love them which love you, what thank have ye? for sinners also love those that love them.

33 And if ye do good to them which do good to you, what thank have ye? for sinners also do even the same.

34 And if ye lend *to them* of whom ye hope to receive, what thank have ye? for sinners also lend to sinners, to receive as much again.

35 But love ye your enemies, and do good, and lend, hoping for nothing again; and your reward shall be great, and ye shall be the children of the Highest: for he is kind unto the unthankful and *to* the evil.

36 Be ye therefore merciful, as your Father also is merciful.

37 Judge not, and ye shall not be judged: condemn not, and ye shall not be condemned: forgive, and ye shall be forgiven:

38 Give, and it shall be given unto you; good measure, pressed down, and shaken together, and running over, shall men give into your bosom. For with the same measure that ye mete withal it shall be measured to you again.

39 And he spake a parable unto them, Can the blind lead the blind? shall they not both fall into the ditch?

40 The disciple is not above his master: but every one that is perfect shall be as his master.

41 And why beholdest thou the mote that is in thy brother's eye, but perceivest not the beam that is in thine own eye?

42 Either how canst thou say to thy brother, Brother, let me pull out the mote that is in thine eye, when thou thyself beholdest not the beam that is in thine own eye? Thou hypocrite, cast out first the beam out of thine own eye, and then shalt thou see clearly to pull out the mote that is in thy brother's eye.

43 For a good tree bringeth not forth corrupt fruit; neither doth a corrupt tree bring forth good fruit.

44 For every tree is known by his own fruit. For of thorns men do not gather figs, nor of a bramble bush gather they grapes.

45 A good man out of the good treasure of his heart bringeth forth that which is good; and an evil man out of the evil treasure of his heart bringeth forth that which is evil: for of the abundance of the heart his mouth speaketh.

46 ¶ And why call ye me, Lord, Lord, and do not the things which I say?

47 Whosoever cometh to me, and heareth my sayings, and doeth them, I will shew you to whom he is like:

48 He is like a man which built an house, and digged deep, and laid the foundation on a rock: and when the flood arose, the stream beat vehemently upon that house, and could not shake it: for it was founded upon a rock.

49 But he that heareth, and doeth not, is like a man that without a foundation built an house upon the earth; against which the stream did beat vehemently, and immediately it fell; and the ruin of that house was great.

CHAPTER 7

NOW when he had ended all his sayings in the audience of the people, he entered into Capernaum.

2 And a certain centurion's servant, who was dear unto him, was sick, and ready to die.

3 And when he heard of Yashiyah, he sent unto him the elders of the Jews, beseeching him that he would come and heal his servant.

4 And when they came to Yashiyah, they besought him instantly, saying, That he was worthy for whom he should do this:

5 For he loveth our nation, and he hath built us a synagogue.

6 Then Yashiyah went with them. And when he was now not far from the house, the centurion sent friends to him, saying unto him, Lord, trouble not thyself: for I am not worthy that thou shouldest enter under my roof:

7 Wherefore neither thought I myself worthy to come unto thee: but say in a word, and my servant shall be healed.

8 For I also am a man set under authority, having under me soldiers, and I say unto one, Go, and he goeth; and to another, Come, and he cometh; and to my servant, Do this, and he doeth *it*.

9 When Yashiyah heard these things, he marvelled at him, and turned him about, and said unto the people that followed him, I say unto you, I have not found so great faith, no, not in Israel.

10 And they that were sent, returning to the house, found the servant whole that had been sick.

11 ¶ And it came to pass the day after, that he went into a city called Nain; and many of his disciples went with him, and much people.

12 Now when he came nigh to the gate of the city, behold, there was a dead man carried out, the only son of his mother, and she was a widow: and much people of the city was with her.

13 And when the Lord saw her, he had compassion on her, and said unto her, Weep not.

14 And he came and touched the bier: and they that bare *him* stood still. And he said, Young man, I say unto thee, Arise.

15 And he that was dead sat up, and began to speak. And he delivered him to his mother.

16 And there came a fear on all: and they glorified אֱלֹהִים, saying, That a great prophet is risen up among us; and, That אֱלֹהִים hath visited his people.

17 And this rumour of him went forth throughout all Judæa, and throughout all the region round about.

18 And the disciples of John shewed him of all these things.

19 ¶ And John calling *unto him* two of his disciples sent *them* to Yashiyah, saying, Art thou he that should come? or look we for another?

20 When the men were come unto him, they said, John Baptist hath sent us unto thee, saying, Art thou he that should come? or look we for another?

21 And in that same hour he cured many of *their* infirmities and plagues, and of evil spirits; and unto many *that were* blind he gave sight.

22 Then Yashiyah answering said unto them, Go your way, and tell John what things ye have seen and heard; how that the blind see, the lame walk, the lepers are cleansed, the deaf hear, the dead are raised, to the poor the gospel is preached.

23 And blessed is *he*, whosoever shall not be offended in me.

24 ¶ And when the messengers of John were departed, he began to speak unto the people concerning John, What went ye out into the wilderness for to see? A reed shaken with the wind?

25 But what went ye out for to see? A man clothed in soft raiment? Behold, they which are gorgeously apparelled, and live delicately, are in kings' courts.

26 But what went ye out for to see? A prophet? Yea, I say unto you, and much more than a prophet.

27 This is *he*, of whom it is written, Behold, I send my messenger before thy face, which shall prepare thy way before thee.

28 For I say unto you, Among those that are born of women there is not a greater prophet than John the Baptist: but he that is least in the kingdom of אֱלֹהִים is greater than he.

29 And all the people that heard *him*, and the publicans, justified אֱלֹהִים, being baptized with the baptism of John.

30 But the Pharisees and lawyers rejected the counsel of אֱלֹהִים against themselves, being not baptized of him.

31 ¶ And the Lord said, Whereunto then shall I liken the men of this generation? and to what are they like?

32 They are like unto children sitting in the marketplace, and calling one to another, and saying, We have piped unto you, and ye have not danced; we have mourned to you, and ye have not wept.

33 For John the Baptist came neither eating bread nor drinking wine; and ye say, He hath a devil.

34 The Son of man is come eating and drinking; and ye say, Behold a gluttonous man, and a winebibber, a friend of publicans and sinners!

35 But wisdom is justified of all her children.

36 ¶ And one of the Pharisees desired him that he would eat with him. And he went into the Pharisee's house, and sat down to meat.

37 And, behold, a woman in the city, which was a sinner, when she knew that *Yashiyah* sat at meat in the Pharisee's house, brought an alabaster box of ointment,

38 And stood at his feet behind *him* weeping, and began to wash his feet with tears, and did wipe *them* with the hairs of her head, and kissed his feet, and anointed *them* with the ointment.

39 Now when the Pharisee which had bidden him saw *it*, he spake within himself, saying, This man, if he were a prophet, would have known who and what manner of woman *this is* that toucheth him: for she is a sinner.

40 And Yashiyah answering said unto him, Simon, I have somewhat to say unto thee. And he saith, Master, say on.

41 There was a certain creditor which had two debtors: the one owed five hundred pence, and the other fifty.

42 And when they had nothing to pay, he frankly forgave them both. Tell me therefore, which of them will love him most?

43 Simon answered and said, I suppose that *he*, to whom he forgave most. And he said unto him, Thou hast rightly judged.

44 And he turned to the woman, and said unto Simon, Seest thou this woman? I entered into thine house, thou gavest me no water for my feet: but she hath washed my feet with tears, and wiped *them* with the hairs of her head.

45 Thou gavest me no kiss: but this woman since the time I came in hath not ceased to kiss my feet.

46 My head with oil thou didst not anoint: but this woman hath anointed my feet with ointment.

47 Wherefore I say unto thee, Her sins, which are many, are forgiven; for she loved much: but to whom little is forgiven, *the same* loveth little.

48 And he said unto her, Thy sins are forgiven.

49 And they that sat at meat with him began to say within themselves, Who is this that forgiveth sins also?

50 And he said to the woman, Thy faith hath saved thee; go in peace.

CHAPTER 8

AND it came to pass afterward, that he went throughout every city and village, preaching and shewing the glad tidings of the kingdom of אֱלֹהִים: and the twelve *were* with him,

2 And certain women, which had been healed of evil spirits and infirmities, Mary called Magdalene, out of whom went seven devils,

3 And Joanna the wife of Chuza Herod's steward, and Susanna, and many others, which ministered unto him of their substance.

4 ¶ And when much people were gathered together, and were come to him out of every city, he spake by a parable:

5 A sower went out to sow his seed: and as he sowed, some fell by the way side; and it was trodden down, and the fowls of the air devoured it.

6 And some fell upon a rock; and as soon as it was sprung up, it withered away, because it lacked moisture.

7 And some fell among thorns; and the thorns sprang up with it, and choked it.

8 And other fell on good ground, and sprang up, and bare fruit an hundredfold. And when he had said these things, he cried, He that hath ears to hear, let him hear.

9 And his disciples asked him, saying, What might this parable be?

10 And he said, Unto you it is given to know the mysteries of the kingdom of אֱלֹהִים: but to others in parables; that seeing they might not see, and hearing they might not understand.

11 Now the parable is this: The seed is the word of אֱלֹהִים.

12 Those by the way side are they that hear; then cometh the devil, and taketh away the word out of their hearts, lest they should believe and be saved.

13 They on the rock *are they*, which, when they hear, receive the word with joy; and these have no root, which for a while believe, and in time of temptation fall away.

14 And that which fell among thorns are they, which, when they have heard, go forth, and are choked with cares and riches and pleasures of *this* life, and bring no fruit to perfection.

15 But that on the good ground are they, which in an honest and good heart, having heard the word, keep *it*, and bring forth fruit with patience.

16 ¶ No man, when he hath lighted a candle, covereth it with a vessel, or putteth *it* under a bed; but setteth *it* on a candlestick, that they which enter in may see the light.

17 For nothing is secret, that shall not be made manifest; neither *any thing* hid, that shall not be known and come abroad.

18 Take heed therefore how ye hear: for whosoever hath, to him shall be given; and whosoever hath not, from him shall be taken even that which he seemeth to have.

19 ¶ Then came to him *his* mother and his brethren, and could not come at him for the press.

20 And it was told him *by certain* which said, Thy mother and thy brethren stand without, desiring to see thee.

21 And he answered and said unto them, My mother and my brethren are these which hear the word of אֱלֹהִים, and do it.

22 ¶ Now it came to pass on a certain day, that he went into a ship with his disciples: and he said unto them, Let us go over unto the other side of the lake. And they launched forth.

23 But as they sailed he fell asleep: and there came down a storm of wind on the lake; and they were filled *with water*, and were in jeopardy.

24 And they came to him, and awoke him, saying, Master, master, we perish. Then he arose, and rebuked the wind and the raging of the water: and they ceased, and there was a calm.

25 And he said unto them, Where is your faith? And they being afraid wondered, saying one to another, What manner of man is this! for he commandeth even the winds and water, and they obey him.

26 ¶ And they arrived at the country of the Gadarenes, which is over against Galilee.

27 And when he went forth to land, there met him out of the city a certain man, which had devils long time, and ware no clothes, neither abode in *any* house, but in the tombs.

28 When he saw Yashiyah, he cried out, and fell down before him, and with a loud voice said, What have I to do with thee, Yashiyah, *thou* Son of אֱלֹהִים most high? I beseech thee, torment me not.

29 (For he had commanded the unclean spirit to come out of the man. For oftentimes it had caught him: and he was kept bound with chains and in fetters; and he brake the bands, and was driven of the devil into the wilderness.)

30 And Yashiyah asked him, saying, What is thy name? And he said, Legion: because many devils were entered into him.

31 And they besought him that he would not command them to go out into the deep.

32 And there was there an herd of many swine feeding on the mountain: and they besought him that he would suffer them to enter into them. And he suffered them.

33 Then went the devils out of the man, and entered into the swine: and the herd ran violently down a steep place into the lake, and were choked.

34 When they that fed *them* saw what was done, they fled, and went and told *it* in the city and in the country.

35 Then they went out to see what was done; and came to Yashiyah, and found the man, out of whom the devils were departed, sitting at the feet of Yashiyah, clothed, and in his right mind: and they were afraid.

36 They also which saw *it* told them by what means he that was possessed of the devils was healed.

37 ¶ Then the whole multitude of the country of the Gadarenes round about besought him to depart from them; for they were taken with great fear: and he went up into the ship, and returned back again.

38 Now the man out of whom the devils were departed besought him that he might be with him: but Yashiyah sent him away, saying,

39 Return to thine own house, and shew how great things אֱלֹהִים hath done unto thee. And he went his way, and published throughout the whole city how great things Yashiyah had done unto him.

40 And it came to pass, that, when Yashiyah was returned, the people *gladly* received him: for they were all waiting for him.

41 ¶ And, behold, there came a man named Jairus, and he was a ruler of the synagogue: and he fell down at Yashiyah' feet, and besought him that he would come into his house:

42 For he had one only daughter, about twelve years of age, and she lay a dying. But as he went the people thronged him.

43 ¶ And a woman having an issue of blood twelve years, which had spent all her living upon physicians, neither could be healed of any,

44 Came behind *him*, and touched the border of his garment: and immediately her issue of blood stanched.

45 And Yashiyah said, Who touched me? When all denied, Peter and they that were with him said, Master, the multitude throng thee and press *thee*, and sayest thou, Who touched me?

46 And Yashiyah said, Somebody hath touched me: for I perceive that virtue is gone out of me.

47 And when the woman saw that she was not hid, she came trembling, and falling down before him, she declared unto him before all the people for what cause she had touched him, and how she was healed immediately.

48 And he said unto her, Daughter, be of good comfort: thy faith hath made thee whole; go in peace.

49 ¶ While he yet spake, there cometh one from the ruler of the synagogue's *house*, saying to him, Thy daughter is dead; trouble not the Master.

50 But when Yashiyah heard *it*, he answered him, saying, Fear not: believe only, and she shall be made whole.

51 And when he came into the house, he suffered no man to go in, save Peter, and James, and John, and the father and the mother of the maiden.

52 And all wept, and bewailed her: but he said, Weep not; she is not dead, but sleepeth.

53 And they laughed him to scorn, knowing that she was dead.

54 And he put them all out, and took her by the hand, and called, saying, Maid, arise.

55 And her spirit came again, and she arose straightway: and he commanded to give her meat.

56 And her parents were astonished: but he charged them that they should tell no man what was done.

CHAPTER 9

THEN he called his twelve disciples together, and gave them power and authority over all devils, and to cure diseases.

2 And he sent them to preach the kingdom of אֱלֹהִים, and to heal the sick.

3 And he said unto them, Take nothing for *your* journey, neither staves, nor scrip, neither bread, neither money; neither have two coats apiece.

4 And whatsoever house ye enter into, there abide, and thence depart.

5 And whosoever will not receive you, when ye go out of that city, shake off the very dust from your feet for a testimony against them.

6 And they departed, and went through the towns, preaching the gospel, and healing every where.

7 ¶ Now Herod the tetrarch heard of all that was done by him: and he was perplexed, because that it was said of some, that John was risen from the dead;

8 And of some, that Elias had appeared; and of others, that one of the old prophets was risen again.

9 And Herod said, John have I beheaded: but who is this, of whom I hear such things? And he desired to see him.

10 ¶ And the apostles, when they were returned, told him all that they had done. And he took them, and went aside privately into a desert place belonging to the city called Bethsaida.

11 And the people, when they knew *it*, followed him: and he received them, and spake unto them of the kingdom of אֱלֹהִים, and healed them that had need of healing.

12 And when the day began to wear away, then came the twelve, and said unto him, Send the multitude away, that they may go into the towns and country round about, and lodge, and get victuals: for we are here in a desert place.

13 But he said unto them, Give ye them to eat. And they said, We have no more but five loaves and two fishes; except we should go and buy meat for all this people.

14 For they were about five thousand men. And he said to his disciples, Make them sit down by fifties in a company.

15 And they did so, and made them all sit down.

16 Then he took the five loaves and the two fishes, and looking up to heaven, he blessed them, and brake, and gave to the disciples to set before the multitude.

17 And they did eat, and were all filled: and there was taken up of fragments that remained to them twelve baskets.

18 ¶ And it came to pass, as he was alone praying, his disciples were with him: and he asked them, saying, Whom say the people that I am?

19 They answering said, John the Baptist; but some *say*, Elias; and others *say*, that one of the old prophets is risen again.

20 He said unto them, But whom say ye that I am? Peter answering said, The Christ of אֱלֹהִים.

21 And he straitly charged them, and commanded *them* to tell no man that thing;

22 Saying, The Son of man must suffer many things, and be rejected of the elders and chief priests and scribes, and be slain, and be raised the third day.

23 ¶ And he said to *them* all, If any *man* will come after me, let him deny himself, and take up his cross daily, and follow me.

24 For whosoever will save his life shall lose it: but whosoever will lose his life for my sake, the same shall save it.

25 For what is a man advantaged, if he gain the whole world, and lose himself, or be cast away?

26 For whosoever shall be ashamed of me and of my words, of him shall the Son of man be ashamed, when he shall come in his own glory, and *in his* Father's, and of the holy angels.

27 But I tell you of a truth, there be some standing here, which shall not taste of death, till they see the kingdom of אֱלֹהִים.

28 ¶ And it came to pass about an eight days after these sayings, he took Peter and John and James, and went up into a mountain to pray.

29 And as he prayed, the fashion of his countenance was altered, and his raiment *was* white *and* glistering.

30 And, behold, there talked with him two men, which were Moses and Elias:

31 Who appeared in glory, and spake of his decease which he should accomplish at Jerusalem.

32 But Peter and they that were with him were heavy with sleep: and when they were awake, they saw his glory, and the two men that stood with him.

33 And it came to pass, as they departed from him, Peter said unto Yashiyah, Master, it is good for us to be here: and let us make three tabernacles; one for thee, and one for Moses, and one for Elias: not knowing what he said.

34 While he thus spake, there came a cloud, and overshadowed them: and they feared as they entered into the cloud.

35 And there came a voice out of the cloud, saying, This is my beloved Son: hear him.

36 And when the voice was past, Yashiyah was found alone. And they kept *it* close, and told no man in those days any of those things which they had seen.

37 ¶ And it came to pass, that on the next day, when they were come down from the hill, much people met him.

38 And, behold, a man of the company cried out, saying, Master, I beseech thee, look upon my son: for he is mine only child.

39 And, lo, a spirit taketh him, and he suddenly crieth out; and it teareth him that he foameth again, and bruising him hardly departeth

from him.

40 And I besought thy disciples to cast him out; and they could not.

41 And Yashiyah answering said, O faithless and perverse generation, how long shall I be with you, and suffer you? Bring thy son hither.

42 And as he was yet a coming, the devil threw him down, and tare *him*. And Yashiyah rebuked the unclean spirit, and healed the child, and delivered him again to his father.

43 ¶ And they were all amazed at the mighty power of אֱלֹהִים. But while they wondered every one at all things which Yashiyah did, he said unto his disciples,

44 Let these sayings sink down into your ears: for the Son of man shall be delivered into the hands of men.

45 But they understood not this saying, and it was hid from them, that they perceived it not: and they feared to ask him of that saying.

46 ¶ Then there arose a reasoning among them, which of them should be greatest.

47 And Yashiyah, perceiving the thought of their heart, took a child, and set him by him,

48 And said unto them, Whosoever shall receive this child in my name receiveth me: and whosoever shall receive me receiveth him that sent me: for he that is least among you all, the same shall be great.

49 ¶ And John answered and said, Master, we saw one casting out devils in thy name; and we forbad him, because he followeth not with us.

50 And Yashiyah said unto him, Forbid *him* not: for he that is not against us is for us.

51 ¶ And it came to pass, when the time was come that he should be received up, he stedfastly set his face to go to Jerusalem,

52 And sent messengers before his face: and they went, and entered into a village of the Samaritans, to make ready for him.

53 And they did not receive him, because his face was as though he would go to Jerusalem.

54 And when his disciples James and John saw *this*, they said, Lord, wilt thou that we command fire to come down from heaven, and consume them, even as Elias did?

55 But he turned, and rebuked them, and said, Ye know not what manner of spirit ye are of.

56 For the Son of man is not come to destroy men's lives, but to save *them*. And they went to another village.

57 ¶ And it came to pass, that, as they went in the way, a certain *man* said unto him, Lord, I will follow thee whithersoever thou goest.

58 And Yashiyah said unto him, Foxes have holes, and birds of the air *have* nests; but the Son of man hath not where to lay *his* head.

59 And he said unto another, Follow me. But he said, Lord, suffer me first to go and bury my father.

60 Yashiyah said unto him, Let the dead bury their dead: but go thou and preach the kingdom of אֱלֹהִים.

61 And another also said, Lord, I will follow thee; but let me first go bid them farewell, which are at home at my house.

62 And Yashiyah said unto him, No man, having put his hand to the plough, and looking back, is fit for the kingdom of אֱלֹהִים.

CHAPTER 10

AFTER these things the Lord appointed other seventy also, and sent them two and two before his face into every city and place, whither he himself would come.

2 Therefore said he unto them, The harvest truly *is* great, but the labourers *are* few: pray ye therefore the Lord of the harvest, that he would send forth labourers into his harvest.

3 Go your ways: behold, I send you forth as lambs among wolves.

4 Carry neither purse, nor scrip, nor shoes: and salute no man by the way.

5 And into whatsoever house ye enter, first say, Peace *be* to this house.

6 And if the son of peace be there, your peace shall rest upon it: if not, it shall turn to you again.

7 And in the same house remain, eating and drinking such things as they give: for the labourer is worthy of his hire. Go not from house to house.

8 And into whatsoever city ye enter, and they receive you, eat such things as are set before you:

9 And heal the sick that are therein, and say unto them, The kingdom of אֱלֹהִים is come nigh unto you.

10 But into whatsoever city ye enter, and they receive you not, go your ways out into the streets of the same, and say,

11 Even the very dust of your city, which cleaveth on us, we do wipe off against you: notwithstanding be ye sure of this, that the kingdom of אֱלֹהִים is come nigh unto you.

12 But I say unto you, that it shall be more tolerable in that day for Sodom, than for that city.

13 Woe unto thee, Chorazin! woe unto thee, Bethsaida! for if the mighty works had been done in Tyre and Sidon, which have been done in you, they had a great while ago repented, sitting in sackcloth and ashes.

14 But it shall be more tolerable for Tyre and Sidon at the judgment, than for you.

15 And thou, Capernaum, which art exalted to heaven, shalt be thrust down to hell.

16 He that heareth you heareth me; and he that despiseth you despiseth me; and he that despiseth me despiseth him that sent me.

17 ¶ And the seventy returned again with joy, saying, Lord, even the devils are subject unto us through thy name.

18 And he said unto them, I beheld Satan as lightning fall from heaven.

19 Behold, I give unto you power to tread on serpents and scorpions, and over all the power of the enemy: and nothing shall by any means hurt you.

20 Notwithstanding in this rejoice not, that the spirits are subject unto you; but rather rejoice, because your names are written in heaven.

21 ¶ In that hour Yashiyah rejoiced in spirit, and said, I thank thee, O Father, Lord of heaven and earth, that thou hast hid these things from the wise and prudent, and hast revealed them unto babes: even so, Father; for so it seemed good in thy sight.

22 All things are delivered to me of my Father: and no man knoweth who the Son is, but the Father; and who the Father is, but the Son, and *he* to whom the Son will reveal *him*.

23 ¶ And he turned him unto *his* disciples, and said privately, Blessed *are* the eyes which see the things that ye see:

24 For I tell you, that many prophets and kings have desired to see those things which ye see, and have not seen *them*: and to hear those things which ye hear, and have not heard *them*.

25 ¶ And, behold, a certain lawyer stood up, and tempted him, saying, Master, what shall I do to inherit eternal life?

26 He said unto him, What is written in the law? how readest thou?

27 And he answering said, Thou shalt love the Lord thy אֱלֹהִים with all thy heart, and with all thy soul, and with all thy strength, and with all thy mind; and thy neighbour as thyself.

28 And he said unto him, Thou hast answered right: this do, and thou shalt live.

29 But he, willing to justify himself, said unto Yashiyah, And who is my neighbour?

30 And Yashiyah answering said, A certain *man* went down from Jerusalem to Jericho, and fell among thieves, which stripped him of his raiment, and wounded *him*, and departed, leaving *him* half dead.

31 And by chance there came down a certain priest that way: and when he saw him, he passed by on the other side.

32 And likewise a Levite, when he was at the place, came and looked *on him*, and passed by on the other side.

33 But a certain Samaritan, as he journeyed, came where he was: and when he saw him, he had compassion *on him*,

34 And went to *him*, and bound up his wounds, pouring in oil and wine, and set him on his own beast, and brought him to an inn, and took care of him.

35 And on the morrow when he departed, he took out two pence, and gave *them* to the host, and said unto him, Take care of him; and whatsoever thou spendest more, when I come again, I will repay thee.

36 Which now of these three, thinkest thou, was neighbour unto him that fell among the thieves?

37 And he said, He that shewed mercy on him. Then said Yashiyah unto him, Go, and do thou likewise.

38 ¶ Now it came to pass, as they went, that he entered into a certain village: and a certain woman named Martha received him into her house.

39 And she had a sister called Mary, which also sat at Yashiyah' feet, and heard his word.

40 But Martha was cumbered about much serving, and came to him, and said, Lord, dost thou not care that my sister hath left me to serve alone? bid her therefore that she help me.

41 And Yashiyah answered and said unto her, Martha, Martha, thou art careful and troubled about many things:

42 But one thing is needful: and Mary hath chosen that good part, which shall not be taken away from her.

CHAPTER 11

AND it came to pass, that, as he was praying in a certain place, when he ceased, one of his disciples said unto him, Lord, teach us to pray, as John also taught his disciples.

2 And he said unto them, When ye pray, say, Our Father which art in heaven, Hallowed be thy name. Thy kingdom come. Thy will be done, as in heaven, so in earth.

3 Give us day by day our daily bread.

4 And forgive us our sins; for we also forgive every one that is indebted to us. And lead us not into temptation; but deliver us from evil.

5 And he said unto them, Which of you shall have a friend, and shall go unto him at midnight, and say unto him, Friend, lend me three loaves;

6 For a friend of mine in his journey is come to me, and I have nothing to set before him?

7 And he from within shall answer and say, Trouble me not: the door is now shut, and my children are with me in bed; I cannot rise and give thee.

8 I say unto you, Though he will not rise and give him, because he is his friend, yet because of his importunity he will rise and give him as many as he needeth.

9 And I say unto you, Ask, and it shall be given you; seek, and ye shall find; knock, and it shall be opened unto you.

10 For every one that asketh receiveth; and he that seeketh findeth; and to him that knocketh it shall be opened.

11 If a son shall ask bread of any of you that is a father, will he give him a stone? or if *he ask* a fish, will he for a fish give him a serpent?

12 Or if he shall ask an egg, will he offer him a scorpion?

13 If ye then, being evil, know how to give good gifts unto your children: how much more shall *your* heavenly Father give the Holy Spirit to them that ask him?

14 ¶ And he was casting out a devil, and it was dumb. And it came to pass, when the devil was gone out, the dumb spake; and the people wondered.

15 But some of them said, He casteth out devils through Beelzebub the chief of the devils.

16 And others, tempting *him*, sought of him a sign from heaven.

17 But he, knowing their thoughts, said unto them, Every kingdom divided against itself is brought to desolation; and a house *divided* against a house falleth.

18 If Satan also be divided against himself, how shall his kingdom stand? because ye say that I cast out devils through Beelzebub.

19 And if I by Beelzebub cast out devils, by whom do your sons cast *them* out? therefore shall they be your judges.

20 But if I with the finger of אֱלֹהִים cast out devils, no doubt the kingdom of אֱלֹהִים is come upon you.

21 When a strong man armed keepeth his palace, his goods are in peace:

22 But when a stronger than he shall come upon him, and overcome him, he taketh from him all his armour wherein he trusted, and divideth his spoils.

23 He that is not with me is against me: and he that gathereth not with me scattereth.

24 When the unclean spirit is gone out of a man, he walketh through dry places, seeking rest; and finding none, he saith, I will return unto my house whence I came out.

25 And when he cometh, he findeth *it* swept and garnished.

26 Then goeth he, and taketh *to him* seven other spirits more wicked than himself; and they enter in, and dwell there: and the last *state* of that man is worse than the first.

27 ¶ And it came to pass, as he spake these things, a certain woman of the company lifted up her voice, and said unto him, Blessed *is* the womb that bare thee, and the paps which thou hast sucked.

28 But he said, Yea rather, blessed *are* they that hear the word of אֵל, and keep it.

29 ¶ And when the people were gathered thick together, he began to say, This is an evil generation: they seek a sign; and there shall no sign be given it, but the sign of Jonas the prophet.

30 For as Jonas was a sign unto the Ninevites, so shall also the Son of man be to this generation.

31 The queen of the south shall rise up in the judgment with the men of this generation, and condemn them: for she came from the utmost parts of the earth to hear the wisdom of Solomon; and, behold, a greater than Solomon *is* here.

32 The men of Nineve shall rise up in the judgment with this generation, and shall condemn it: for they repented at the preaching of

Jonas; and, behold, a greater than Jonas *is* here.

33 No man, when he hath lighted a candle, putteth *it* in a secret place, neither under a bushel, but on a candlestick, that they which come in may see the light.

34 The light of the body is the eye: therefore when thine eye is single, thy whole body also is full of light; but when *thine eye* is evil, thy body also *is* full of darkness.

35 Take heed therefore that the light which is in thee be not darkness.

36 If thy whole body therefore *be* full of light, having no part dark, the whole shall be full of light, as when the bright shining of a candle doth give thee light.

37 ¶ And as he spake, a certain Pharisee besought him to dine with him: and he went in, and sat down to meat.

38 And when the Pharisee saw *it*, he marvelled that he had not first washed before dinner.

39 And the Lord said unto him, Now do ye Pharisees make clean the outside of the cup and the platter; but your inward part is full of ravening and wickedness.

40 *Ye* fools, did not he that made that which is without make that which is within also?

41 But rather give alms of such things as ye have; and, behold, all things are clean unto you.

42 But woe unto you, Pharisees! for ye tithe mint and rue and all manner of herbs, and pass over judgment and the love of אֱלֹהִים: these ought ye to have done, and not to leave the other undone.

43 Woe unto you, Pharisees! for ye love the uppermost seats in the synagogues, and greetings in the markets.

44 Woe unto you, scribes and Pharisees, hypocrites! for ye are as graves which appear not, and the men that walk over *them* are not aware *of them*.

45 ¶ Then answered one of the lawyers, and said unto him, Master, thus saying thou reproachest us also.

46 And he said, Woe unto you also, *ye* lawyers! for ye lade men with burdens grievous to be borne, and ye yourselves touch not the burdens with one of your fingers.

47 Woe unto you! for ye build the sepulchres of the prophets, and your fathers killed them.

48 Truly ye bear witness that ye allow the deeds of your fathers: for they indeed killed them, and ye build their sepulchres.

49 Therefore also said the wisdom of אֱלֹהִים, I will send them prophets and apostles, and *some* of them they shall slay and persecute:

50 That the blood of all the prophets, which was shed from the foundation of the world, may be required of this generation;

51 From the blood of Abel unto the blood of Zacharias, which perished between the altar and the temple: verily I say unto you, It shall be required of this generation.

52 Woe unto you, lawyers! for ye have taken away the key of knowledge: ye entered not in yourselves, and them that were entering in ye hindered.

53 And as he said these things unto them, the scribes and the Pharisees began to urge *him* vehemently, and to provoke him to speak of many things:

54 Laying wait for him, and seeking to catch something out of his mouth, that they might accuse him.

CHAPTER 12

IN the mean time, when there were gathered together an innumerable multitude of people, insomuch that they trode one upon another, he began to say unto his disciples first of all, Beware ye of the leaven of the Pharisees, which is hypocrisy.

2 For there is nothing covered, that shall not be revealed; neither hid, that shall not be known.

3 Therefore whatsoever ye have spoken in darkness shall be heard in the light; and that which ye have spoken in the ear in closets shall be proclaimed upon the housetops.

4 And I say unto you my friends, Be not afraid of them that kill the body, and after that have no more that they can do.

5 But I will forewarn you whom ye shall fear: Fear him, which after he hath killed hath power to cast into hell; yea, I say unto you, Fear him.

6 Are not five sparrows sold for two farthings, and not one of them is forgotten before אֱלֹהִים?

7 But even the very hairs of your head are all numbered. Fear not therefore: ye are of more value than many sparrows.

8 Also I say unto you, Whosoever shall confess me before men, him shall the Son of man also confess before the angels of אֱלֹהִים:

9 But he that denieth me before men shall be denied before the angels of אֱ.

10 And whosoever shall speak a word against the Son of man, it shall be forgiven him: but unto him that blasphemeth against the Holy Ghost it shall not be forgiven.

11 And when they bring you unto the synagogues, and *unto* magistrates, and powers, take ye no thought how or what thing ye shall answer, or what ye shall say:

12 For the Holy Ghost shall teach you in the same hour what ye ought to say.

13 ¶ And one of the company said unto him, Master, speak to my brother, that he divide the inheritance with me.

14 And he said unto him, Man, who made me a judge or a divider over you?

15 And he said unto them, Take heed, and beware of covetousness: for a man's life consisteth not in the abundance of the things which he possesseth.

16 And he spake a parable unto them, saying, The ground of a certain rich man brought forth plentifully:

17 And he thought within himself, saying, What shall I do, because I have no room where to bestow my fruits?

18 And he said, This will I do: I will pull down my barns, and build greater; and there will I bestow all my fruits and my goods.

19 And I will say to my soul, Soul, thou hast much goods laid up for many years; take thine ease, eat, drink, *and* be merry.

20 But אֱלֹהִים said unto him, *Thou* fool, this night thy soul shall be required of thee: then whose shall those things be, which thou hast provided?

21 So *is* he that layeth up treasure for himself, and is not rich toward אֱלֹהִים.

22 ¶ And he said unto his disciples, Therefore I say unto you, Take no thought for your life, what ye shall eat; neither for the body, what ye shall put on.

23 The life is more than meat, and the body *is more* than raiment.

24 Consider the ravens: for they neither sow nor reap; which neither have storehouse nor barn; and אֱלֹהִים feedeth them: how much more are ye better than the fowls?

25 And which of you with taking thought can add to his stature one cubit?

26 If ye then be not able to do that thing which is least, why take ye thought for the rest?

27 Consider the lilies how they grow: they toil not, they spin not; and yet I say unto you, that Solomon in all his glory was not arrayed like one of these.

28 If then אֱלֹהִים so clothe the grass, which is to day in the field, and to morrow is cast into the oven; how much more *will he clothe* you, O ye of little faith?

29 And seek not ye what ye shall eat, or what ye shall drink, neither be ye of doubtful mind.

30 For all these things do the nations of the world seek after: and your Father knoweth that ye have need of these things.

31 ¶ But rather seek ye the kingdom of אֱלֹהִים; and all these things shall be added unto you.

32 Fear not, little flock; for it is your Father's good pleasure to give you the kingdom.

33 Sell that ye have, and give alms; provide yourselves bags which wax not old, a treasure in the heavens that faileth not, where no thief approacheth, neither moth corrupteth.

34 For where your treasure is, there will your heart be also.

35 Let your loins be girded about, and *your* lights burning;

36 And ye yourselves like unto men that wait for their lord, when he will return from the wedding; that when he cometh and knocketh, they may open unto him immediately.

37 Blessed *are* those servants, whom the lord when he cometh shall find watching: verily I say unto you, that he shall gird himself, and make them to sit down to meat, and will come forth and serve them.

38 And if he shall come in the second watch, or come in the third watch, and find *them* so, blessed are those servants.

39 And this know, that if the goodman of the house had known what hour the thief would come, he would have watched, and not have suffered his house to be broken through.

40 Be ye therefore ready also: for the Son of man cometh at an hour when ye think not.

41 ¶ Then Peter said unto him, Lord, speakest thou this parable unto us, or even to all?

42 And the Lord said, Who then is that faithful and wise steward, whom *his* lord shall make ruler over his household, to give *them their* portion of meat in due season?

43 Blessed *is* that servant, whom his lord when he cometh shall find so doing.

44 Of a truth I say unto you, that he will make him ruler over all that he hath.

45 But and if that servant say in his heart, My lord delayeth his coming; and shall begin to beat the menservants and maidens, and to eat and drink, and to be drunken;

46 The lord of that servant will come in a day when he looketh not for *him*, and at an hour when he is not aware, and will cut him in sunder, and will appoint him his portion with the unbelievers.

47 And that servant, which knew his lord's will, and prepared not *himself*, neither did according to his will, shall be beaten with many *stripes*.

48 But he that knew not, and did commit things worthy of stripes, shall be beaten with few *stripes*. For unto whomsoever much is given, of him shall be much required: and to whom men have committed much, of him they will ask the more.

49 ¶ I am come to send fire on the earth; and what will I, if it be already kindled?

50 But I have a baptism to be baptized with; and how am I straitened till it be accomplished!

51 Suppose ye that I am come to give peace on earth? I tell you, Nay; but rather division:

52 For from henceforth there shall be five in one house divided, three against two, and two against three.

53 The father shall be divided against the son, and the son against the father; the mother against the daughter, and the daughter against the mother; the mother in law against her daughter in law, and the daughter in law against her mother in law.

54 ¶ And he said also to the people, When ye see a cloud rise out of the west, straightway ye say, There cometh a shower; and so it is.

55 And when *ye see* the south wind blow, ye say, There will be heat; and it cometh to pass.

56 *Ye* hypocrites, ye can discern the face of the sky and of the earth; but how is it that ye do not discern this time?

57 Yea, and why even of yourselves judge ye not what is right?

58 ¶ When thou goest with thine adversary to the magistrate, *as thou art* in the way, give diligence that thou mayest be delivered from him; lest he hale thee to the judge, and the judge deliver thee to the officer, and the officer cast thee into prison.

59 I tell thee, thou shalt not depart thence, till thou hast paid the very last mite.

CHAPTER 13

THERE were present at that season some that told him of the Galilæans, whose blood Pilate had mingled with their sacrifices.

2 And Yashiyah answering said unto them, Suppose ye that these Galilæans were sinners above all the Galilæans, because they suffered such things?

3 I tell you, Nay: but, except ye repent, ye shall all likewise perish.

4 Or those eighteen, upon whom the tower in Siloam fell, and slew them, think ye that they were sinners above all men that dwelt in Jerusalem?

5 I tell you, Nay: but, except ye repent, ye shall all likewise perish.

6 ¶ He spake also this parable; A certain *man* had a fig tree planted in his vineyard; and he came and sought fruit thereon, and found none.

7 Then said he unto the dresser of his vineyard, Behold, these three years I come seeking fruit on this fig tree, and find none: cut it down; why cumbereth it the ground?

8 And he answering said unto him, Lord, let it alone this year also, till I shall dig about it, and dung *it:*

9 And if it bear fruit, *well:* and if not, *then* after that thou shalt cut it down.

10 And he was teaching in one of the synagogues on the sabbath.

11 ¶ And, behold, there was a woman which had a spirit of infirmity eighteen years, and was bowed together, and could in no wise lift up *herself.*

12 And when Yashiyah saw her, he called *her to him,* and said unto her, Woman, thou art loosed from thine infirmity.

13 And he laid *his* hands on her: and immediately she was made straight, and glorified אֱלֹהִים.

14 And the ruler of the synagogue answered with indignation, because that Yashiyah had healed on the sabbath day, and said unto the people, There are six days in which men ought to work: in them therefore come and be healed, and not on the sabbath day.

15 The Lord then answered him, and said, *Thou* hypocrite, doth not each one of you on the sabbath loose his ox or *his* ass from the stall, and lead *him* away to watering?

16 And ought not this woman, being a daughter of Abraham, whom Satan hath bound, lo, these eighteen years, be loosed from this bond on the sabbath day?

17 And when he had said these things, all his adversaries were ashamed: and all the people rejoiced for all the glorious things that were done by him.

18 ¶ Then said he, Unto what is the kingdom of אֱלֹהִים like? and whereunto shall I resemble it?

19 It is like a grain of mustard seed, which a man took, and cast into his garden; and it grew, and waxed a great tree; and the fowls of the air lodged in the branches of it.

20 And again he said, Whereunto shall I liken the kingdom of אֱלֹהִים?

21 It is like leaven, which a woman took and hid in three measures of meal, till the whole was leavened.

22 And he went through the cities and villages, teaching, and journeying toward Jerusalem.

23 Then said one unto him, Lord, are there few that be saved? And he said unto them,

24 ¶ Strive to enter in at the strait gate: for many, I say unto you, will seek to enter in, and shall not be able.

25 When once the master of the house is risen up, and hath shut to the door, and ye begin to stand without, and to knock at the door, saying, Lord, Lord, open unto us; and he shall answer and say unto you, I know you not whence ye are:

26 Then shall ye begin to say, We have eaten and drunk in thy presence, and thou hast taught in our streets.

27 But he shall say, I tell you, I know you not whence ye are; depart from me, all *ye* workers of iniquity.

28 There shall be weeping and gnashing of teeth, when ye shall see Abraham, and Isaac, and Jacob, and all the prophets, in the kingdom of אֱלֹהִים, and you *yourselves* thrust out.

29 And they shall come from the east, and *from* the west, and from the north, and *from* the south, and shall sit down in the kingdom of אֱלֹהִים.

30 And, behold, there are last which shall be first, and there are first which shall be last.

31 ¶ The same day there came certain of the Pharisees, saying unto him, Get thee out, and depart hence: for Herod will kill thee.

32 And he said unto them, Go ye, and tell that fox, Behold, I cast out devils, and I do cures to day and to morrow, and the third *day* I shall be perfected.

33 Nevertheless I must walk to day, and to morrow, and the *day* following: for it cannot be that a prophet perish out of Jerusalem.

34 O Jerusalem, Jerusalem, which killest the prophets, and stonest them that are sent unto thee; how often would I have gathered thy children together, as a hen *doth gather* her brood under *her* wings, and ye would not!

35 Behold, your house is left unto you desolate: and verily I say unto you, Ye shall not see me, until *the time* come when ye shall say, Blessed *is* he that cometh in the name of the Lord.

CHAPTER 14

AND it came to pass, as he went into the house of one of the chief Pharisees to eat bread on the sabbath day, that they watched him.

2 And, behold, there was a certain man before him which had the dropsy.

3 And Yashiyah answering spake unto the lawyers and Pharisees, saying, Is it lawful to heal on the sabbath day?

4 And they held their peace. And he took *him*, and healed him, and let him go;

5 And answered them, saying, Which of you shall have an ass or an ox fallen into a pit, and will not straightway pull him out on the sabbath day?

6 And they could not answer him again to these things.

7 ¶ And he put forth a parable to those which were bidden, when he marked how they chose out the chief rooms; saying unto them,

8 When thou art bidden of any *man* to a wedding, sit not down in the highest room; lest a more honourable man than thou be bidden of him;

9 And he that bade thee and him come and say to thee, Give this man place; and thou begin with shame to take the lowest room.

10 But when thou art bidden, go and sit down in the lowest room; that when he that bade thee cometh, he may say unto thee, Friend, go up higher: then shalt thou have worship in the presence of them that sit at meat with thee.

11 For whosoever exalteth himself shall be abased; and he that humbleth himself shall be exalted.

12 ¶ Then said he also to him that bade him, When thou makest a dinner or a supper, call not thy friends, nor thy brethren, neither thy kinsmen, nor *thy* rich neighbours; lest they also bid thee again, and a recompence be made thee.

13 But when thou makest a feast, call the poor, the maimed, the lame, the blind:

14 And thou shalt be blessed; for they cannot recompense thee: for thou shalt be recompensed at the resurrection of the just.

15 ¶ And when one of them that sat at meat with him heard these things, he said unto him, Blessed *is* he that shall eat bread in the kingdom of אֱלֹהִים.

16 Then said he unto him, A certain man made a great supper, and bade many:

17 And sent his servant at supper time to say to them that were bidden, Come; for all things are now ready.

18 And they all with one *consent* began to make excuse. The first said unto him, I have bought a piece of ground, and I must needs go and see it: I pray thee have me excused.

19 And another said, I have bought five yoke of oxen, and I go to prove them: I pray thee have me excused.

20 And another said, I have married a wife, and therefore I cannot come.

21 So that servant came, and shewed his lord these things. Then the master of the house being angry said to his servant, Go out quickly into the streets and lanes of the city, and bring in hither the poor, and the maimed, and the halt, and the blind.

22 And the servant said, Lord, it is done as thou hast commanded, and yet there is room.

23 And the lord said unto the servant, Go out into the highways and hedges, and compel *them* to come in, that my house may be filled.

24 For I say unto you, That none of those men which were bidden shall taste of my supper.

25 ¶ And there went great multitudes with him: and he turned, and said unto them,

26 If any *man* come to me, and hate not his father, and mother, and wife, and children, and brethren, and sisters, yea, and his own life also, he cannot be my disciple.

27 And whosoever doth not bear his cross, and come after me, cannot be my disciple.

28 For which of you, intending to build a tower, sitteth not down first, and counteth the cost, whether he have *sufficient* to finish *it*?

29 Lest haply, after he hath laid the foundation, and is not able to finish *it*, all that behold *it* begin to mock him,

30 Saying, This man began to build, and was not able to finish.

31 Or what king, going to make war against another king, sitteth not down first, and consulteth whether he be able with ten thousand

to meet him that cometh against him with twenty thousand?

32 Or else, while the other is yet a great way off, he sendeth an ambassage, and desireth conditions of peace.

33 So likewise, whosoever he be of you that forsaketh not all that he hath, he cannot be my disciple.

34 ¶ Salt *is* good: but if the salt have lost his savour, wherewith shall it be seasoned?

35 It is neither fit for the land, nor yet for the dunghill; *but* men cast it out. He that hath ears to hear, let him hear.

CHAPTER 15

THEN drew near unto him all the publicans and sinners for to hear him.

2 And the Pharisees and scribes murmured, saying, This man receiveth sinners, and eateth with them.

3 ¶ And he spake this parable unto them, saying,

4 What man of you, having an hundred sheep, if he lose one of them, doth not leave the ninety and nine in the wilderness, and go after that which is lost, until he find it?

5 And when he hath found *it*, he layeth *it* on his shoulders, rejoicing.

6 And when he cometh home, he calleth together *his* friends and neighbours, saying unto them, Rejoice with me; for I have found my sheep which was lost.

7 I say unto you, that likewise joy shall be in heaven over one sinner that repenteth, more than over ninety and nine just persons, which need no repentance.

8 ¶ Either what woman having ten pieces of silver, if she lose one piece, doth not light a candle, and sweep the house, and seek diligently till she find *it*?

9 And when she hath found *it*, she calleth *her* friends and *her* neighbours together, saying, Rejoice with me; for I have found the piece which I had lost.

10 Likewise, I say unto you, there is joy in the presence of the angels of אֱלֹהִים over one sinner that repenteth.

11 ¶ And he said, A certain man had two sons:

12 And the younger of them said to *his* father, Father, give me the portion of goods that falleth *to me*. And he divided unto them *his* living.

13 And not many days after the younger son gathered all together, and took his journey into a far country, and there wasted his substance with riotous living.

14 And when he had spent all, there arose a mighty famine in that land; and he began to be in want.

15 And he went and joined himself to a citizen of that country; and he sent him into his fields to feed swine.

16 And he would fain have filled his belly with the husks that the swine did eat: and no man gave unto him.

17 And when he came to himself, he said, How many hired servants of my father's have bread enough and to spare, and I perish with hunger!

18 I will arise and go to my father, and will say unto him, Father, I have sinned against heaven, and before thee,

19 And am no more worthy to be called thy son: make me as one of thy hired servants.

20 And he arose, and came to his father. But when he was yet a great way off, his father saw him, and had compassion, and ran, and fell on his neck, and kissed him.

21 And the son said unto him, Father, I have sinned against heaven, and in thy sight, and am no more worthy to be called thy son.

22 But the father said to his servants, Bring forth the best robe, and put *it* on him; and put a ring on his hand, and shoes on *his* feet:

23 And bring hither the fatted calf, and kill *it;* and let us eat, and be merry:

24 For this my son was dead, and is alive again; he was lost, and is found. And they began to be merry.

25 Now his elder son was in the field: and as he came and drew nigh to the house, he heard musick and dancing.

26 And he called one of the servants, and asked what these things meant.

27 And he said unto him, Thy brother is come; and thy father hath killed the fatted calf, because he hath received him safe and sound.

28 And he was angry, and would not go in: therefore came his father out, and intreated him.

29 And he answering said to *his* father, Lo, these many years do I serve thee, neither transgressed I at any time thy commandment: and yet thou never gavest me a kid, that I might make merry with my friends:

30 But as soon as this thy son was come, which hath devoured thy living with harlots, thou hast killed for him the fatted calf.

31 And he said unto him, Son, thou art ever with me, and all that I have is thine.

32 It was meet that we should make merry, and be glad: for this thy brother was dead, and is alive again; and was lost, and is found.

CHAPTER 16

AND he said also unto his disciples, There was a certain rich man, which had a steward; and the same was accused unto him that he had wasted his goods.

2 And he called him, and said unto him, How is it that I hear this of thee? give an account of thy stewardship; for thou mayest be no longer steward.

3 Then the steward said within himself, What shall I do? for my lord taketh away from me the stewardship: I cannot dig; to beg I am ashamed.

4 I am resolved what to do, that, when I am put out of the stewardship, they may receive me into their houses.

5 So he called every one of his lord's debtors *unto him*, and said unto the first, How much owest thou unto my lord?

6 And he said, An hundred measures of oil. And he said unto him, Take thy bill, and sit down quickly, and write fifty.

7 Then said he to another, And how much owest thou? And he said, An hundred measures of wheat. And he said unto him, Take thy bill, and write fourscore.

8 And the lord commended the unjust steward, because he had done wisely: for the children of this world are in their generation wiser than the children of light.

9 And I say unto you, Make to yourselves friends of the mammon of unrighteousness; that, when ye fail, they may receive you into everlasting habitations.

10 He that is faithful in that which is least is faithful also in much: and he that is unjust in the least is unjust also in much.

11 If therefore ye have not been faithful in the unrighteous mammon, who will commit to your trust the true *riches?*

12 And if ye have not been faithful in that which is another man's, who shall give you that which is your own?

13 ¶ No servant can serve two masters: for either he will hate the one, and love the other; or else he will hold to the one, and despise

the other. Ye cannot serve אֱלֹהִים and mammon.

14 And the Pharisees also, who were covetous, heard all these things: and they derided him.

15 And he said unto them, Ye are they which justify yourselves before men; but אֱלֹהִים knoweth your hearts: for that which is highly esteemed among men is abomination in the sight of אֱלֹהִים.

16 The law and the prophets *were* until John: since that time the kingdom of אֱלֹהִים is preached, and every man presseth into it.

17 And it is easier for heaven and earth to pass, than one tittle of the law to fail.

18 Whosoever putteth away his wife, and marrieth another, committeth adultery: and whosoever marrieth her that is put away from *her* husband committeth adultery.

19 ¶ There was a certain rich man, which was clothed in purple and fine linen, and fared sumptuously every day:

20 And there was a certain beggar named Lazarus, which was laid at his gate, full of sores,

21 And desiring to be fed with the crumbs which fell from the rich man's table: moreover the dogs came and licked his sores.

22 And it came to pass, that the beggar died, and was carried by the angels into Abraham's bosom: the rich man also died, and was buried;

23 And in hell he lift up his eyes, being in torments, and seeth Abraham afar off, and Lazarus in his bosom.

24 And he cried and said, Father Abraham, have mercy on me, and send Lazarus, that he may dip the tip of his finger in water, and cool my tongue; for I am tormented in this flame.

25 But Abraham said, Son, remember that thou in thy lifetime receivedst thy good things, and likewise Lazarus evil things: but now he is comforted, and thou art tormented.

26 And beside all this, between us and you there is a great gulf fixed: so that they which would pass from hence to you cannot; neither can they pass to us, that *would come* from thence.

27 Then he said, I pray thee therefore, father, that thou wouldest send him to my father's house:

28 For I have five brethren; that he may testify unto them, lest they also come into this place of torment.

29 Abraham saith unto him, They have Moses and the prophets; let them hear them.

30 And he said, Nay, father Abraham: but if one went unto them from the dead, they will repent.

31 And he said unto him, If they hear not Moses and the prophets, neither will they be persuaded, though one rose from the dead.

CHAPTER 17

THEN said he unto the disciples, It is impossible but that offences will come: but woe *unto him*, through whom they come!

2 It were better for him that a millstone were hanged about his neck, and he cast into the sea, than that he should offend one of these little ones.

3 ¶ Take heed to yourselves: If thy brother trespass against thee, rebuke him; and if he repent, forgive him.

4 And if he trespass against thee seven times in a day, and seven times in a day turn again to thee, saying, I repent; thou shalt forgive him.

5 And the apostles said unto the Lord, Increase our faith.

6 And the Lord said, If ye had faith as a grain of mustard seed, ye might say unto this sycamine tree, Be thou plucked up by the root, and be thou planted in the sea; and it should obey you.

7 But which of you, having a servant plowing or feeding cattle, will say unto him by and by, when he is come from the field, Go and sit down to meat?

8 And will not rather say unto him, Make ready wherewith I may sup, and gird thyself, and serve me, till I have eaten and drunken; and afterward thou shalt eat and drink?

9 Doth he thank that servant because he did the things that were commanded him? I trow not.

10 So likewise ye, when ye shall have done all those things which are commanded you, say, We are unprofitable servants: we have done that which was our duty to do.

11 ¶ And it came to pass, as he went to Jerusalem, that he passed through the midst of Samaria and Galilee.

12 And as he entered into a certain village, there met him ten men that were lepers, which stood afar off:

13 And they lifted up *their* voices, and said, Yashiyah, Master, have mercy on us.

14 And when he saw *them*, he said unto them, Go shew yourselves unto the priests. And it came to pass, that, as they went, they were cleansed.

15 And one of them, when he saw that he was healed, turned back, and with a loud voice glorified אֱלֹהִים,

16 And fell down on *his* face at his feet, giving him thanks: and he was a Samaritan.

17 And Yashiyah answering said, Were there not ten cleansed? but where *are* the nine?

18 There are not found that returned to give glory to אֱ, save this stranger.

19 And he said unto him, Arise, go thy way: thy faith hath made thee whole.

20 ¶ And when he was demanded of the Pharisees, when the kingdom of אֱלֹהִים should come, he answered them and said, The kingdom of אֱלֹהִים cometh not with observation:

21 Neither shall they say, Lo here! or, lo there! for, behold, the kingdom of אֱלֹהִים is within you.

22 And he said unto the disciples, The days will come, when ye shall desire to see one of the days of the Son of man, and ye shall not see *it*.

23 And they shall say to you, See here; or, see there: go not after *them*, nor follow *them*.

24 For as the lightning, that lighteneth out of the one *part* under heaven, shineth unto the other *part* under heaven; so shall also the Son of man be in his day.

25 But first must he suffer many things, and be rejected of this generation.

26 And as it was in the days of Noe, so shall it be also in the days of the Son of man.

27 They did eat, they drank, they married wives, they were given in marriage, until the day that Noe entered into the ark, and the flood came, and destroyed them all.

28 Likewise also as it was in the days of Lot; they did eat, they drank, they bought, they sold, they planted, they builded;

29 But the same day that Lot went out of Sodom it rained fire and brimstone from heaven, and destroyed *them* all.

30 Even thus shall it be in the day when the Son of man is revealed.

31 In that day, he which shall be upon the housetop, and his stuff in the house, let him not come down to take it away: and he that is in the field, let him likewise not return back.

32 Remember Lot's wife.

33 Whosoever shall seek to save his life shall lose it; and whosoever shall lose his life shall preserve it.

34 I tell you, in that night there shall be two *men* in one bed; the one shall be taken, and the other shall be left.

35 Two *women* shall be grinding together; the one shall be taken, and the other left.

36 Two *men* shall be in the field; the one shall be taken, and the other left.

37 And they answered and said unto him, Where, Lord? And he said unto them, Wheresoever the body *is*, thither will the eagles be gathered together.

CHAPTER 18

AND he spake a parable unto them *to this end*, that men ought always to pray, and not to faint;

2 Saying, There was in a city a judge, which feared not אֱלֹהִים, neither regarded man:

3 And there was a widow in that city; and she came unto him, saying, Avenge me of mine adversary.

4 And he would not for a while: but afterward he said within himself, Though I fear not אֱלֹהִים, nor regard man;

5 Yet because this widow troubleth me, I will avenge her, lest by her continual coming she weary me.

6 And the Lord said, Hear what the unjust judge saith.

7 And shall not אֱלֹהִים avenge his own elect, which cry day and night unto him, though he bear long with them?

8 I tell you that he will avenge them speedily. Nevertheless when the Son of man cometh, shall he find faith on the earth?

9 And he spake this parable unto certain which trusted in themselves that they were righteous, and despised others:

10 Two men went up into the temple to pray; the one a Pharisee, and the other a publican.

11 The Pharisee stood and prayed thus with himself, אֱלֹהִים, I thank thee, that I am not as other men *are*, extortioners, unjust, adulterers, or even as this publican.

12 I fast twice in the week, I give tithes of all that I possess.

13 And the publican, standing afar off, would not lift up so much as *his* eyes unto heaven, but smote upon his breast, saying, אֱלֹהִים be merciful to me a sinner.

14 I tell you, this man went down to his house justified *rather* than the other: for every one that exalteth himself shall be abased; and he that humbleth himself shall be exalted.

15 And they brought unto him also infants, that he would touch them: but when *his* disciples saw *it*, they rebuked them.

16 But Yashiyah called them *unto him*, and said, Suffer little children to come unto me, and forbid them not: for of such is the kingdom of אֱלֹהִים.

17 Verily I say unto you, Whosoever shall not receive the kingdom of אֱלֹהִים as a little child shall in no wise enter therein.

18 And a certain ruler asked him, saying, Good Master, what shall I do to inherit eternal life?

19 And Yashiyah said unto him, Why callest thou me good? none *is* good, save one, *that is*, אֱלֹהִים.

20 Thou knowest the commandments, Do not commit adultery, Do not kill, Do not steal, Do not bear false witness, Honour thy father and thy mother.

21 And he said, All these have I kept from my youth up.

22 Now when Yashiyah heard these things, he said unto him, Yet lackest thou one thing: sell all that thou hast, and distribute unto the poor, and thou shalt have treasure in heaven: and come, follow me.

23 And when he heard this, he was very sorrowful: for he was very rich.

24 And when Yashiyah saw that he was very sorrowful, he said, How hardly shall they that have riches enter into the kingdom of אֱלֹהִים!

25 For it is easier for a camel to go through a needle's eye, than for a rich man to enter into the kingdom of אֱלֹהִים.

26 And they that heard *it* said, Who then can be saved?

27 And he said, The things which are impossible with men are possible with אֱלֹהִים.

28 Then Peter said, Lo, we have left all, and followed thee.

29 And he said unto them, Verily I say unto you, There is no man that hath left house, or parents, or brethren, or wife, or children, for the kingdom of אֱלֹהִים's sake,

30 Who shall not receive manifold more in this present time, and in the world to come life everlasting.

31 ¶ Then he took *unto him* the twelve, and said unto them, Behold, we go up to Jerusalem, and all things that are written by the prophets concerning the Son of man shall be accomplished.

32 For he shall be delivered unto the Gentiles, and shall be mocked, and spitefully entreated, and spitted on:

33 And they shall scourge *him*, and put him to death: and the third day he shall rise again.

34 And they understood none of these things: and this saying was hid from them, neither knew they the things which were spoken.

35 ¶ And it came to pass, that as he was come nigh unto Jericho, a certain blind man sat by the way side begging:

36 And hearing the multitude pass by, he asked what it meant.

37 And they told him, that Yashiyah of Nazareth passeth by.

38 And he cried, saying, Yashiyah, *thou* Son of David, have mercy on me.

39 And they which went before rebuked him, that he should hold his peace: but he cried so much the more, *Thou* Son of David, have mercy on me.

40 And Yashiyah stood, and commanded him to be brought unto him: and when he was come near, he asked him,

41 Saying, What wilt thou that I shall do unto thee? And he said, Lord, that I may receive my sight.

42 And Yashiyah said unto him, Receive thy sight: thy faith hath saved thee.

43 And immediately he received his sight, and followed him, glorifying אֱלֹהִים: and all the people, when they saw *it*, gave praise unto אֱלֹהִים.

CHAPTER 19

AND *Yashiyah* entered and passed through Jericho.

2 And, behold, *there was* a man named Zacchæus, which was the chief among the publicans, and he was rich.

3 And he sought to see Yashiyah who he was; and could not for the press, because he was little of stature.

4 And he ran before, and climbed up into a sycomore tree to see him: for he was to pass that *way*.

5 And when Yashiyah came to the place, he looked up, and saw him, and said unto him, Zacchæus, make haste, and come down; for

to day I must abide at thy house.

6 And he made haste, and came down, and received him joyfully.

7 And when they saw *it*, they all murmured, saying, That he was gone to be guest with a man that is a sinner.

8 And Zacchæus stood, and said unto the Lord; Behold, Lord, the half of my goods I give to the poor; and if I have taken any thing from any man by false accusation, I restore *him* fourfold.

9 And Yashiyah said unto him, This day is salvation come to this house, forsomuch as he also is a son of Abraham.

10 For the Son of man is come to seek and to save that which was lost.

11 And as they heard these things, he added and spake a parable, because he was nigh to Jerusalem, and because they thought that the kingdom of אֱלֹהִים should immediately appear.

12 He said therefore, A certain nobleman went into a far country to receive for himself a kingdom, and to return.

13 And he called his ten servants, and delivered them ten pounds, and said unto them, Occupy till I come.

14 But his citizens hated him, and sent a message after him, saying, We will not have this *man* to reign over us.

15 And it came to pass, that when he was returned, having received the kingdom, then he commanded these servants to be called unto him, to whom he had given the money, that he might know how much every man had gained by trading.

16 Then came the first, saying, Lord, thy pound hath gained ten pounds.

17 And he said unto him, Well, thou good servant: because thou hast been faithful in a very little, have thou authority over ten cities.

18 And the second came, saying, Lord, thy pound hath gained five pounds.

19 And he said likewise to him, Be thou also over five cities.

20 And another came, saying, Lord, behold, *here is* thy pound, which I have kept laid up in a napkin:

21 For I feared thee, because thou art an austere man: thou takest up that thou layedst not down, and reapest that thou didst not sow.

22 And he saith unto him, Out of thine own mouth will I judge thee, *thou* wicked servant. Thou knewest that I was an austere man, taking up that I laid not down, and reaping that I did not sow:

23 Wherefore then gavest not thou my money into the bank, that at my coming I might have required mine own with usury?

24 And he said unto them that stood by, Take from him the pound, and give *it* to him that hath ten pounds.

25 (And they said unto him, Lord, he hath ten pounds.)

26 For I say unto you, That unto every one which hath shall be given; and from him that hath not, even that he hath shall be taken away from him.

27 But those mine enemies, which would not that I should reign over them, bring hither, and slay *them* before me.

28 ¶ And when he had thus spoken, he went before, ascending up to Jerusalem.

29 And it came to pass, when he was come nigh to Bethphage and Bethany, at the mount called *the mount* of Olives, he sent two of his disciples,

30 Saying, Go ye into the village over against *you*; in the which at your entering ye shall find a colt tied, whereon yet never man sat: loose him, and bring *him hither*.

31 And if any man ask you, Why do ye loose *him?* thus shall ye say unto him, Because the Lord hath need of him.

32 And they that were sent went their way, and found even as he had said unto them.

33 And as they were loosing the colt, the owners thereof said unto them, Why loose ye the colt?

34 And they said, The Lord hath need of him.

35 And they brought him to Yashiyah: and they cast their garments upon the colt, and they set Yashiyah thereon.

36 And as he went, they spread their clothes in the way.

37 And when he was come nigh, even now at the descent of the mount of Olives, the whole multitude of the disciples began to rejoice and praise אֱלֹהִים with a loud voice for all the mighty works that they had seen;

38 Saying, Blessed *be* the King that cometh in the name of the Lord: peace in heaven, and glory in the highest.

39 And some of the Pharisees from among the multitude said unto him, Master, rebuke thy disciples.

40 And he answered and said unto them, I tell you that, if these should hold their peace, the stones would immediately cry out.

41 ¶ And when he was come near, he beheld the city, and wept over it,

42 Saying, If thou hadst known, even thou, at least in this thy day, the things *which belong* unto thy peace! but now they are hid from thine eyes.

43 For the days shall come upon thee, that thine enemies shall cast a trench about thee, and compass thee round, and keep thee in on every side,

44 And shall lay thee even with the ground, and thy children within thee; and they shall not leave in thee one stone upon another; because thou knewest not the time of thy visitation.

45 And he went into the temple, and began to cast out them that sold therein, and them that bought;

46 Saying unto them, It is written, My house is the house of prayer: but ye have made it a den of thieves.

47 And he taught daily in the temple. But the chief priests and the scribes and the chief of the people sought to destroy him,

48 And could not find what they might do: for all the people were very attentive to hear him.

CHAPTER 20

AND it came to pass, *that* on one of those days, as he taught the people in the temple, and preached the gospel, the chief priests and the scribes came upon *him* with the elders,

2 And spake unto him, saying, Tell us, by what authority doest thou these things? or who is he that gave thee this authority?

3 And he answered and said unto them, I will also ask you one thing; and answer me:

4 The baptism of John, was it from heaven, or of men?

5 And they reasoned with themselves, saying, If we shall say, From heaven; he will say, Why then believed ye him not?

6 But and if we say, Of men; all the people will stone us: for they be persuaded that John was a prophet.

7 And they answered, that they could not tell whence *it was.*

8 And Yashiyah said unto them, Neither tell I you by what authority I do these things.

9 Then began he to speak to the people this parable; A certain man planted a vineyard, and let it forth to husbandmen, and went into a far country for a long time.

10 And at the season he sent a servant to the husbandmen, that they should give him of the fruit of the vineyard: but the husbandmen beat him, and sent *him* away empty.

11 And again he sent another servant: and they beat him also, and entreated *him* shamefully, and sent *him* away empty.

12 And again he sent a third: and they wounded him also, and cast *him* out.

13 Then said the lord of the vineyard, What shall I do? I will send my beloved son: it may be they will reverence *him* when they see him.

14 But when the husbandmen saw him, they reasoned among themselves, saying, This is the heir: come, let us kill him, that the inheritance may be ours.

15 So they cast him out of the vineyard, and killed *him*. What therefore shall the lord of the vineyard do unto them?

16 He shall come and destroy these husbandmen, and shall give the vineyard to others. And when they heard *it*, they said, אֱלֹהִים forbid.

17 And he beheld them, and said, What is this then that is written, The stone which the builders rejected, the same is become the head of the corner?

18 Whosoever shall fall upon that stone shall be broken; but on whomsoever it shall fall, it will grind him to powder.

19 ¶ And the chief priests and the scribes the same hour sought to lay hands on him; and they feared the people: for they perceived that he had spoken this parable against them.

20 And they watched *him*, and sent forth spies, which should feign themselves just men, that they might take hold of his words, that so they might deliver him unto the power and authority of the governor.

21 And they asked him, saying, Master, we know that thou sayest and teachest rightly, neither acceptest thou the person *of any*, but teachest the way of אֱלֹהִים truly:

22 Is it lawful for us to give tribute unto Cæsar, or no?

23 But he perceived their craftiness, and said unto them, Why tempt ye me?

24 Shew me a penny. Whose image and superscription hath it? They answered and said, Cæsar's.

25 And he said unto them, Render therefore unto Cæsar the things which be Cæsar's, and unto אֱלֹהִים the things which be אֱלֹהִים's.

26 And they could not take hold of his words before the people: and they marvelled at his answer, and held their peace.

27 ¶ Then came to *him* certain of the Sadducees, which deny that there is any resurrection; and they asked him,

28 Saying, Master, Moses wrote unto us, If any man's brother die, having a wife, and he die without children, that his brother should take his wife, and raise up seed unto his brother.

29 There were therefore seven brethren: and the first took a wife, and died without children.

30 And the second took her to wife, and he died childless.

31 And the third took her; and in like manner the seven also: and they left no children, and died.

32 Last of all the woman died also.

33 Therefore in the resurrection whose wife of them is she? for seven had her to wife.

34 And Yashiyah answering said unto them, The children of this world marry, and are given in marriage:

35 But they which shall be accounted worthy to obtain that world, and the resurrection from the dead, neither marry, nor are given in marriage:

36 Neither can they die any more: for they are equal unto the angels; and are the children of אֱלֹהִים, being the children of the resurrection.

37 Now that the dead are raised, even Moses shewed at the bush, when he calleth the Lord the אֱלֹהִים of Abraham, and the אֱלֹהִים of Isaac, and the אֱלֹהִים of Jacob.

38 For he is not a אֱלֹהִים of the dead, but of the living: for all live unto him.

39 ¶ Then certain of the scribes answering said, Master, thou hast well said.

40 And after that they durst not ask him any *question at all*.

41 And he said unto them, How say they that Christ is David's son?

42 And David himself saith in the book of Psalms, The Lᴏʀᴅ said unto my Lord, Sit thou on my right hand,

43 Till I make thine enemies thy footstool.

44 David therefore calleth him Lord, how is he then his son?

45 ¶ Then in the audience of all the people he said unto his disciples,

46 Beware of the scribes, which desire to walk in long robes, and love greetings in the markets, and the highest seats in the synagogues, and the chief rooms at feasts;

47 Which devour widows' houses, and for a shew make long prayers: the same shall receive greater damnation.

CHAPTER 21

AND he looked up, and saw the rich men casting their gifts into the treasury.

2 And he saw also a certain poor widow casting in thither two mites.

3 And he said, Of a truth I say unto you, that this poor widow hath cast in more than they all:

4 For all these have of their abundance cast in unto the offerings of אֱלֹהִים: but she of her penury hath cast in all the living that she had.

5 ¶ And as some spake of the temple, how it was adorned with goodly stones and gifts, he said,

6 *As for* these things which ye behold, the days will come, in the which there shall not be left one stone upon another, that shall not be thrown down.

7 And they asked him, saying, Master, but when shall these things be? and what sign *will there be* when these things shall come to pass?

8 And he said, Take heed that ye be not deceived: for many shall come in my name, saying, I am *Christ*; and the time draweth near: go ye not therefore after them.

9 But when ye shall hear of wars and commotions, be not terrified: for these things must first come to pass; but the end *is* not by and by.

10 Then said he unto them, Nation shall rise against nation, and kingdom against kingdom:

11 And great earthquakes shall be in divers places, and famines, and pestilences; and fearful sights and great signs shall there be from heaven.

12 But before all these, they shall lay their hands on you, and persecute *you*, delivering *you* up to the synagogues, and into prisons, being brought before kings and rulers for my name's sake.

13 And it shall turn to you for a testimony.

14 Settle *it* therefore in your hearts, not to meditate before what ye shall answer:

15 For I will give you a mouth and wisdom, which all your adversaries shall not be able to gainsay nor resist.

16 And ye shall be betrayed both by parents, and brethren, and kinsfolks, and friends; and *some* of you shall they cause to be put to death.

17 And ye shall be hated of all *men* for my name's sake.

18 But there shall not an hair of your head perish.

19 In your patience possess ye your souls.

20 And when ye shall see Jerusalem compassed with armies, then know that the desolation thereof is nigh.

21 Then let them which are in Judæa flee to the mountains; and let them which are in the midst of it depart out; and let not them that are in the countries enter thereinto.

22 For these be the days of vengeance, that all things which are written may be fulfilled.

23 But woe unto them that are with child, and to them that give suck, in those days! for there shall be great distress in the land, and wrath upon this people.

24 And they shall fall by the edge of the sword, and shall be led away captive into all nations: and Jerusalem shall be trodden down of the Gentiles, until the times of the Gentiles be fulfilled.

25 ¶ And there shall be signs in the sun, and in the moon, and in the stars; and upon the earth distress of nations, with perplexity; the sea and the waves roaring;

26 Men's hearts failing them for fear, and for looking after those things which are coming on the earth: for the powers of heaven shall be shaken.

27 And then shall they see the Son of man coming in a cloud with power and great glory.

28 And when these things begin to come to pass, then look up, and lift up your heads; for your redemption draweth nigh.

29 And he spake to them a parable; Behold the fig tree, and all the trees;

30 When they now shoot forth, ye see and know of your own selves that summer is now nigh at hand.

31 So likewise ye, when ye see these things come to pass, know ye that the kingdom of אֱלֹהִים is nigh at hand.

32 Verily I say unto you, This generation shall not pass away, till all be fulfilled.

33 Heaven and earth shall pass away: but my words shall not pass away.

34 ¶ And take heed to yourselves, lest at any time your hearts be overcharged with surfeiting, and drunkenness, and cares of this life, and *so* that day come upon you unawares.

35 For as a snare shall it come on all them that dwell on the face of the whole earth.

36 Watch ye therefore, and pray always, that ye may be accounted worthy to escape all these things that shall come to pass, and to stand before the Son of man.

37 And in the day time he was teaching in the temple; and at night he went out, and abode in the mount that is called *the mount* of Olives.

38 And all the people came early in the morning to him in the temple, for to hear him.

CHAPTER 22

NOW the feast of unleavened bread drew nigh, which is called the Passover.

2 And the chief priests and scribes sought how they might kill him; for they feared the people.

3 ¶ Then entered Satan into Judas surnamed Iscariot, being of the number of the twelve.

4 And he went his way, and communed with the chief priests and captains, how he might betray him unto them.

5 And they were glad, and covenanted to give him money.

6 And he promised, and sought opportunity to betray him unto them in the absence of the multitude.

7 ¶ Then came the day of unleavened bread, when the passover must be killed.

8 And he sent Peter and John, saying, Go and prepare us the passover, that we may eat.

9 And they said unto him, Where wilt thou that we prepare?

10 And he said unto them, Behold, when ye are entered into the city, there shall a man meet you, bearing a pitcher of water; follow him into the house where he entereth in.

11 And ye shall say unto the goodman of the house, The Master saith unto thee, Where is the guestchamber, where I shall eat the passover with my disciples?

12 And he shall shew you a large upper room furnished: there make ready.

13 And they went, and found as he had said unto them: and they made ready the passover.

14 And when the hour was come, he sat down, and the twelve apostles with him.

15 And he said unto them, With desire I have desired to eat this passover with you before I suffer:

16 For I say unto you, I will not any more eat thereof, until it be fulfilled in the kingdom of אֱלֹהִים.

17 And he took the cup, and gave thanks, and said, Take this, and divide *it* among yourselves:

18 For I say unto you, I will not drink of the fruit of the vine, until the kingdom of אֱלֹהִים shall come.

19 ¶ And he took bread, and gave thanks, and brake *it*, and gave unto them, saying, This is my body which is given for you: this do in remembrance of me.

20 Likewise also the cup after supper, saying, This cup *is* the new testament in my blood, which is shed for you.

21 ¶ But, behold, the hand of him that betrayeth me *is* with me on the table.

22 And truly the Son of man goeth, as it was determined: but woe unto that man by whom he is betrayed!

23 And they began to inquire among themselves, which of them it was that should do this thing.

24 ¶ And there was also a strife among them, which of them should be accounted the greatest.

25 And he said unto them, The kings of the Gentiles exercise lordship over them; and they that exercise authority upon them are called benefactors.

26 But ye *shall* not *be* so: but he that is greatest among you, let him be as the younger; and he that is chief, as he that doth serve.

27 For whether *is* greater, he that sitteth at meat, or he that serveth? *is* not he that sitteth at meat? but I am among you as he that serveth.

28 Ye are they which have continued with me in my temptations.

29 And I appoint unto you a kingdom, as my Father hath appointed unto me;

30 That ye may eat and drink at my table in my kingdom, and sit on thrones judging the twelve tribes of Israel.

31 ¶ And the Lord said, Simon, Simon, behold, Satan hath desired *to have* you, that he may sift *you* as wheat:

32 But I have prayed for thee, that thy faith fail not: and when thou art converted, strengthen thy brethren.

33 And he said unto him, Lord, I am ready to go with thee, both into prison, and to death.

34 And he said, I tell thee, Peter, the cock shall not crow this day, before that thou shalt thrice deny that thou knowest me.

35 And he said unto them, When I sent you without purse, and scrip, and shoes, lacked ye any thing? And they said, Nothing.

36 Then said he unto them, But now, he that hath a purse, let him take *it*, and likewise *his* scrip: and he that hath no sword, let him sell his garment, and buy one.

37 For I say unto you, that this that is written must yet be accomplished in me, And he was reckoned among the transgressors: for the things concerning me have an end.

38 And they said, Lord, behold, here *are* two swords. And he said unto them, It is enough.

39 ¶ And he came out, and went, as he was wont, to the mount of Olives; and his disciples also followed him.

40 And when he was at the place, he said unto them, Pray that ye enter not into temptation.

41 And he was withdrawn from them about a stone's cast, and kneeled down, and prayed,

42 Saying, Father, if thou be willing, remove this cup from me: nevertheless not my will, but thine, be done.

43 And there appeared an angel unto him from heaven, strengthening him.

44 And being in an agony he prayed more earnestly: and his sweat was as it were great drops of blood falling down to the ground.

45 And when he rose up from prayer, and was come to his disciples, he found them sleeping for sorrow,

46 And said unto them, Why sleep ye? rise and pray, lest ye enter into temptation.

47 ¶ And while he yet spake, behold a multitude, and he that was called Judas, one of the twelve, went before them, and drew near unto Yashiyah to kiss him.

48 But Yashiyah said unto him, Judas, betrayest thou the Son of man with a kiss?

49 When they which were about him saw what would follow, they said unto him, Lord, shall we smite with the sword?

50 ¶ And one of them smote the servant of the high priest, and cut off his right ear.

51 And Yashiyah answered and said, Suffer ye thus far. And he touched his ear, and healed him.

52 Then Yashiyah said unto the chief priests, and captains of the temple, and the elders, which were come to him, Be ye come out, as against a thief, with swords and staves?

53 When I was daily with you in the temple, ye stretched forth no hands against me: but this is your hour, and the power of darkness.

54 ¶ Then took they him, and led *him*, and brought him into the high priest's house. And Peter followed afar off.

55 And when they had kindled a fire in the midst of the hall, and were set down together, Peter sat down among them.

56 But a certain maid beheld him as he sat by the fire, and earnestly looked upon him, and said, This man was also with him.

57 And he denied him, saying, Woman, I know him not.

58 And after a little while another saw him, and said, Thou art also of them. And Peter said, Man, I am not.

59 And about the space of one hour after another confidently affirmed, saying, Of a truth this *fellow* also was with him: for he is a Galilæan.

60 And Peter said, Man, I know not what thou sayest. And immediately, while he yet spake, the cock crew.

61 And the Lord turned, and looked upon Peter. And Peter remembered the word of the Lord, how he had said unto him, Before the cock crow, thou shalt deny me thrice.

62 And Peter went out, and wept bitterly.

63 ¶ And the men that held Yashiyah mocked him, and smote *him*.

64 And when they had blindfolded him, they struck him on the face, and asked him, saying, Prophesy, who is it that smote thee?

65 And many other things blasphemously spake they against him.

66 ¶ And as soon as it was day, the elders of the people and the chief priests and the scribes came together, and led him into their council, saying,

67 Art thou the Christ? tell us. And he said unto them, If I tell you, ye will not believe:

68 And if I also ask *you*, ye will not answer me, nor let *me* go.

69 Hereafter shall the Son of man sit on the right hand of the power of אֱלֹהִים.

70 Then said they all, Art thou then the Son of אֱלֹהִים? And he said unto them, Ye say that I am.

71 And they said, What need we any further witness? for we ourselves have heard of his own mouth.

CHAPTER 23

AND the whole multitude of them arose, and led him unto Pilate.

2 And they began to accuse him, saying, We found this *fellow* perverting the nation, and forbidding to give tribute to Cæsar, saying that he himself is Christ a King.

3 And Pilate asked him, saying, Art thou the King of the Jews? And he answered him and said, Thou sayest *it*.

4 Then said Pilate to the chief priests and *to* the people, I find no fault in this man.

5 And they were the more fierce, saying, He stirreth up the people, teaching throughout all Jewry, beginning from Galilee to this place.

6 When Pilate heard of Galilee, he asked whether the man were a Galilæan.

7 And as soon as he knew that he belonged unto Herod's jurisdiction, he sent him to Herod, who himself also was at Jerusalem at that time.

8 ¶ And when Herod saw Yashiyah, he was exceeding glad: for he was desirous to see him of a long *season*, because he had heard many things of him; and he hoped to have seen some miracle done by him.

9 Then he questioned with him in many words; but he answered him nothing.

10 And the chief priests and scribes stood and vehemently accused him.

11 And Herod with his men of war set him at nought, and mocked *him*, and arrayed him in a gorgeous robe, and sent him again to Pilate.

12 ¶ And the same day Pilate and Herod were made friends together: for before they were at enmity between themselves.

13 ¶ And Pilate, when he had called together the chief priests and the rulers and the people,

14 Said unto them, Ye have brought this man unto me, as one that perverteth the people: and, behold, I, having examined *him* before

you, have found no fault in this man touching those things whereof ye accuse him:

15 No, nor yet Herod: for I sent you to him; and, lo, nothing worthy of death is done unto him.

16 I will therefore chastise him, and release *him*.

17 (For of necessity he must release one unto them at the feast.)

18 And they cried out all at once, saying, Away with this *man*, and release unto us Barabbas:

19 (Who for a certain sedition made in the city, and for murder, was cast into prison.)

20 Pilate therefore, willing to release Yashiyah, spake again to them.

21 But they cried, saying, Crucify *him*, crucify him.

22 And he said unto them the third time, Why, what evil hath he done? I have found no cause of death in him: I will therefore chastise him, and let *him* go.

23 And they were instant with loud voices, requiring that he might be crucified. And the voices of them and of the chief priests prevailed.

24 And Pilate gave sentence that it should be as they required.

25 And he released unto them him that for sedition and murder was cast into prison, whom they had desired; but he delivered Yashiyah to their will.

26 And as they led him away, they laid hold upon one Simon, a Cyrenian, coming out of the country, and on him they laid the cross, that he might bear *it* after Yashiyah.

27 ¶ And there followed him a great company of people, and of women, which also bewailed and lamented him.

28 But Yashiyah turning unto them said, Daughters of Jerusalem, weep not for me, but weep for yourselves, and for your children.

29 For, behold, the days are coming, in the which they shall say, Blessed *are* the barren, and the wombs that never bare, and the paps which never gave suck.

30 Then shall they begin to say to the mountains, Fall on us; and to the hills, Cover us.

31 For if they do these things in a green tree, what shall be done in the dry?

32 And there were also two other, malefactors, led with him to be put to death.

33 And when they were come to the place, which is called Calvary, there they crucified him, and the malefactors, one on the right hand, and the other on the left.

34 ¶ Then said Yashiyah, Father, forgive them; for they know not what they do. And they parted his raiment, and cast lots.

35 And the people stood beholding. And the rulers also with them derided *him*, saying, He saved others; let him save himself, if he be Christ, the chosen of אֱלֹהִים.

36 And the soldiers also mocked him, coming to him, and offering him vinegar,

37 And saying, If thou be the king of the Jews, save thyself.

38 And a superscription also was written over him in letters of Greek, and Latin, and Hebrew, THIS IS THE KING OF THE JEWS.

39 ¶ And one of the malefactors which were hanged railed on him, saying, If thou be Christ, save thyself and us.

40 But the other answering rebuked him, saying, Dost not thou fear אֱלֹהִים, seeing thou art in the same condemnation?

41 And we indeed justly; for we receive the due reward of our deeds: but this man hath done nothing amiss.

42 And he said unto Yashiyah, Lord, remember me when thou comest into thy kingdom.

43 And Yashiyah said unto him, Verily I say unto thee, To day shalt thou be with me in paradise.

44 And it was about the sixth hour, and there was a darkness over all the earth until the ninth hour.

45 And the sun was darkened, and the veil of the temple was rent in the midst.

46 ¶ And when Yashiyah had cried with a loud voice, he said, Father, into thy hands I commend my spirit: and having said thus, he gave up the ghost.

47 Now when the centurion saw what was done, he glorified אֱלֹהִים, saying, Certainly this was a righteous man.

48 And all the people that came together to that sight, beholding the things which were done, smote their breasts, and returned.

49 And all his acquaintance, and the women that followed him from Galilee, stood afar off, beholding these things.

50 ¶ And, behold, *there was* a man named Joseph, a counseller; *and he was* a good man, and a just:

51 (The same had not consented to the counsel and deed of them;) he was of Arimathæa, a city of the Jews: who also himself waited for the kingdom of אֱלֹהִים.

52 This *man* went unto Pilate, and begged the body of Yashiyah.

53 And he took it down, and wrapped it in linen, and laid it in a sepulchre that was hewn in stone, wherein never man before was laid.

54 And that day was the preparation, and the sabbath drew on.

55 And the women also, which came with him from Galilee, followed after, and beheld the sepulchre, and how his body was laid.

56 And they returned, and prepared spices and ointments; and rested the sabbath day according to the commandment.

CHAPTER 24

NOW upon the first *day* of the week, very early in the morning, they came unto the sepulchre, bringing the spices which they had prepared, and certain *others* with them.

2 And they found the stone rolled away from the sepulchre.

3 And they entered in, and found not the body of the Lord Yashiyah.

4 And it came to pass, as they were much perplexed thereabout, behold, two men stood by them in shining garments:

5 And as they were afraid, and bowed down *their* faces to the earth, they said unto them, Why seek ye the living among the dead?

6 He is not here, but is risen: remember how he spake unto you when he was yet in Galilee,

7 Saying, The Son of man must be delivered into the hands of sinful men, and be crucified, and the third day rise again.

8 And they remembered his words,

9 And returned from the sepulchre, and told all these things unto the eleven, and to all the rest.

10 It was Mary Magdalene, and Joanna, and Mary *the mother* of James, and other *women that were* with them, which told these things unto the apostles.

11 And their words seemed to them as idle tales, and they believed them not.

12 Then arose Peter, and ran unto the sepulchre; and stooping down, he beheld the linen clothes laid by themselves, and departed, wondering in himself at that which was come to pass.

13 ¶ And, behold, two of them went that same day to a village called Emmaus, which was from Jerusalem *about* threescore furlongs.

14 And they talked together of all these things which had happened.

15 And it came to pass, that, while they communed *together* and reasoned, Yashiyah himself drew near, and went with them.

16 But their eyes were holden that they should not know him.

17 And he said unto them, What manner of communications *are* these that ye have one to another, as ye walk, and are sad?

18 And the one of them, whose name was Cleopas, answering said unto him, Art thou only a stranger in Jerusalem, and hast not known the things which are come to pass there in these days?

19 And he said unto them, What things? And they said unto him, Concerning Yashiyah of Nazareth, which was a prophet mighty in deed and word before אֱלֹהִים and all the people:

20 And how the chief priests and our rulers delivered him to be condemned to death, and have crucified him.

21 But we trusted that it had been he which should have redeemed Israel: and beside all this, to day is the third day since these things were done.

22 Yea, and certain women also of our company made us astonished, which were early at the sepulchre;

23 And when they found not his body, they came, saying, that they had also seen a vision of angels, which said that he was alive.

24 And certain of them which were with us went to the sepulchre, and found *it* even so as the women had said: but him they saw not.

25 Then he said unto them, O fools, and slow of heart to believe all that the prophets have spoken:

26 Ought not Christ to have suffered these things, and to enter into his glory?

27 And beginning at Moses and all the prophets, he expounded unto them in all the scriptures the things concerning himself.

28 And they drew nigh unto the village, whither they went: and he made as though he would have gone further.

29 But they constrained him, saying, Abide with us: for it is toward evening, and the day is far spent. And he went in to tarry with them.

30 And it came to pass, as he sat at meat with them, he took bread, and blessed *it*, and brake, and gave to them.

31 And their eyes were opened, and they knew him; and he vanished out of their sight.

32 And they said one to another, Did not our heart burn within us, while he talked with us by the way, and while he opened to us the scriptures?

33 And they rose up the same hour, and returned to Jerusalem, and found the eleven gathered together, and them that were with them,

34 Saying, The Lord is risen indeed, and hath appeared to Simon.

35 And they told what things *were done* in the way, and how he was known of them in breaking of bread.

36 ¶ And as they thus spake, Yashiyah himself stood in the midst of them, and saith unto them, Peace *be* unto you.

37 But they were terrified and affrighted, and supposed that they had seen a spirit.

38 And he said unto them, Why are ye troubled? and why do thoughts arise in your hearts?

39 Behold my hands and my feet, that it is I myself: handle me, and see; for a spirit hath not flesh and bones, as ye see me have.

40 And when he had thus spoken, he shewed them *his* hands and *his* feet.

41 And while they yet believed not for joy, and wondered, he said unto them, Have ye here any meat?

42 And they gave him a piece of a broiled fish, and of an honeycomb.

43 And he took *it*, and did eat before them.

44 And he said unto them, These *are* the words which I spake unto you, while I was yet with you, that all things must be fulfilled, which were written in the law of Moses, and *in* the prophets, and *in* the psalms, concerning me.

45 Then opened he their understanding, that they might understand the scriptures,

46 And said unto them, Thus it is written, and thus it behoved Christ to suffer, and to rise from the dead the third day:

47 And that repentance and remission of sins should be preached in his name among all nations, beginning at Jerusalem.

48 And ye are witnesses of these things.

49 ¶ And, behold, I send the promise of my Father upon you: but tarry ye in the city of Jerusalem, until ye be endued with power from on high.

50 ¶ And he led them out as far as to Bethany, and he lifted up his hands, and blessed them.

51 And it came to pass, while he blessed them, he was parted from them, and carried up into heaven.

52 And they worshipped him, and returned to Jerusalem with great joy:

53 And were continually in the temple, praising and blessing אֱלֹהִים. Amen.

THE GOSPEL ACCORDING TO
ST. JOHN.

CHAPTER 1

IN the beginning was the Word, and the Word was with אֱלֹהִים, and the Word was אֱלֹהִים.

2 The same was in the beginning with אֱלֹהִים.

3 All things were made by him; and without him was not any thing made that was made.

4 In him was life; and the life was the light of men.

5 And the light shineth in darkness; and the darkness comprehended it not.

6 ¶ There was a man sent from אֱלֹהִים, whose name *was* John.

7 The same came for a witness, to bear witness of the Light, that all *men* through him might believe.

8 He was not that Light, but *was sent* to bear witness of that Light.

9 *That* was the true Light, which lighteth every man that cometh into the world.

10 He was in the world, and the world was made by him, and the world knew him not.

11 He came unto his own, and his own received him not.

12 But as many as received him, to them gave he power to become the sons of אֱלֹהִים, *even* to them that believe on his name:

13 Which were born, not of blood, nor of the will of the flesh, nor of the will of man, but of אֱלֹהִים.

14 And the Word was made flesh, and dwelt among us, (and we beheld his glory, the glory as of the only begotten of the Father,) full of grace and truth.

15 ¶ John bare witness of him, and cried, saying, This was he of whom I spake, He that cometh after me is preferred before me: for he was before me.

16 And of his fulness have all we received, and grace for grace.

17 For the law was given by Moses, *but* grace and truth came by Yashiyah Christ.

18 No man hath seen אֱלֹהִים at any time; the only begotten Son, which is in the bosom of the Father, he hath declared *him*.

19 ¶ And this is the record of John, when the Jews sent priests and Levites from Jerusalem to ask him, Who art thou?

20 And he confessed, and denied not; but confessed, I am not the Christ.

21 And they asked him, What then? Art thou Elias? And he saith, I am not. Art thou that prophet? And he answered, No.

22 Then said they unto him, Who art thou? that we may give an answer to them that sent us. What sayest thou of thyself?

23 He said, I *am* the voice of one crying in the wilderness, Make straight the way of the Lord, as said the prophet Esaias.

24 And they which were sent were of the Pharisees.

25 And they asked him, and said unto him, Why baptizest thou then, if thou be not that Christ, nor Elias, neither that prophet?

26 John answered them, saying, I baptize with water: but there standeth one among you, whom ye know not;

27 He it is, who coming after me is preferred before me, whose shoe's latchet I am not worthy to unloose.

28 These things were done in Bethabara beyond Jordan, where John was baptizing.

29 ¶ The next day John seeth Yashiyah coming unto him, and saith, Behold the Lamb of אֱלֹהִים, which taketh away the sin of the world.

30 This is he of whom I said, After me cometh a man which is preferred before me: for he was before me.

31 And I knew him not: but that he should be made manifest to Israel, therefore am I come baptizing with water.

32 And John bare record, saying, I saw the Spirit descending from heaven like a dove, and it abode upon him.

33 And I knew him not: but he that sent me to baptize with water, the same said unto me, Upon whom thou shalt see the Spirit descending, and remaining on him, the same is he which baptizeth with the Holy Ghost.

34 And I saw, and bare record that this is the Son of אֱלֹהִים.

35 ¶ Again the next day after John stood, and two of his disciples;

36 And looking upon Yashiyah as he walked, he saith, Behold the Lamb of אֱלֹהִים!

37 And the two disciples heard him speak, and they followed Yashiyah.

38 Then Yashiyah turned, and saw them following, and saith unto them, What seek ye? They said unto him, Rabbi, (which is to say, being interpreted, Master,) where dwellest thou?

39 He saith unto them, Come and see. They came and saw where he dwelt, and abode with him that day: for it was about the tenth hour.

40 One of the two which heard John *speak*, and followed him, was Andrew, Simon Peter's brother.

41 He first findeth his own brother Simon, and saith unto him, We have found the Messias, which is, being interpreted, the Christ.

42 And he brought him to Yashiyah. And when Yashiyah beheld him, he said, Thou art Simon the son of Jona: thou shalt be called Cephas, which is by interpretation, A stone.

43 ¶ The day following Yashiyah would go forth into Galilee, and findeth Philip, and saith unto him, Follow me.

44 Now Philip was of Bethsaida, the city of Andrew and Peter.

45 Philip findeth Nathanael, and saith unto him, We have found him, of whom Moses in the law, and the prophets, did write, Yashiyah of Nazareth, the son of Joseph.

46 And Nathanael said unto him, Can there any good thing come out of Nazareth? Philip saith unto him, Come and see.

47 Yashiyah saw Nathanael coming to him, and saith of him, Behold an Israelite indeed, in whom is no guile!

48 Nathanael saith unto him, Whence knowest thou me? Yashiyah answered and said unto him, Before that Philip called thee, when thou wast under the fig tree, I saw thee.

49 Nathanael answered and saith unto him, Rabbi, thou art the Son of אֱלֹהִים; thou art the King of Israel.

50 Yashiyah answered and said unto him, Because I said unto thee, I saw thee under the fig tree, believest thou? thou shalt see greater things than these.

51 And he saith unto him, Verily, verily, I say unto you, Hereafter ye shall see heaven open, and the angels of אֱלֹהִים ascending and descending upon the Son of man.

CHAPTER 2

AND the third day there was a marriage in Cana of Galilee; and the mother of Yashiyah was there:

2 And both Yashiyah was called, and his disciples, to the marriage.

3 And when they wanted wine, the mother of Yashiyah saith unto him, They have no wine.

4 Yashiyah saith unto her, Woman, what have I to do with thee? mine hour is not yet come.

5 His mother saith unto the servants, Whatsoever he saith unto you, do *it*.

6 And there were set there six waterpots of stone, after the manner of the purifying of the Jews, containing two or three firkins apiece.

7 Yashiyah saith unto them, Fill the waterpots with water. And they filled them up to the brim.

8 And he saith unto them, Draw out now, and bear unto the governor of the feast. And they bare *it*.

9 When the ruler of the feast had tasted the water that was made wine, and knew not whence it was: (but the servants which drew the water knew;) the governor of the feast called the bridegroom,

10 And saith unto him, Every man at the beginning doth set forth good wine; and when men have well drunk, then that which is worse: *but* thou hast kept the good wine until now.

11 This beginning of miracles did Yashiyah in Cana of Galilee, and manifested forth his glory; and his disciples believed on him.

12 ¶ After this he went down to Capernaum, he, and his mother, and his brethren, and his disciples: and they continued there not many days.

13 ¶ And the Jews' passover was at hand, and Yashiyah went up to Jerusalem,

14 And found in the temple those that sold oxen and sheep and doves, and the changers of money sitting:

15 And when he had made a scourge of small cords, he drove them all out of the temple, and the sheep, and the oxen; and poured out the changers' money, and overthrew the tables;

16 And said unto them that sold doves, Take these things hence; make not my Father's house an house of merchandise.

17 And his disciples remembered that it was written, The zeal of thine house hath eaten me up.

18 ¶ Then answered the Jews and said unto him, What sign shewest thou unto us, seeing that thou doest these things?

19 Yashiyah answered and said unto them, Destroy this temple, and in three days I will raise it up.

20 Then said the Jews, Forty and six years was this temple in building, and wilt thou rear it up in three days?

21 But he spake of the temple of his body.

22 When therefore he was risen from the dead, his disciples remembered that he had said this unto them; and they believed the scripture, and the word which Yashiyah had said.

23 ¶ Now when he was in Jerusalem at the passover, in the feast *day*, many believed in his name, when they saw the miracles which he did.

24 But Yashiyah did not commit himself unto them, because he knew all *men*,

25 And needed not that any should testify of man: for he knew what was in man.

CHAPTER 3

THERE was a man of the Pharisees, named Nicodemus, a ruler of the Jews:

2 The same came to Yashiyah by night, and said unto him, Rabbi, we know that thou art a teacher come from אֱלֹהִים: for no man can do these miracles that thou doest, except אֱלֹהִים be with him.

3 Yashiyah answered and said unto him, Verily, verily, I say unto thee, Except a man be born again, he cannot see the kingdom of אֱלֹהִים.

4 Nicodemus saith unto him, How can a man be born when he is old? can he enter the second time into his mother's womb, and be born?

5 Yashiyah answered, Verily, verily, I say unto thee, Except a man be born of water and *of* the Spirit, he cannot enter into the kingdom of אֱלֹהִים.

6 That which is born of the flesh is flesh; and that which is born of the Spirit is spirit.

7 Marvel not that I said unto thee, Ye must be born again.

8 The wind bloweth where it listeth, and thou hearest the sound thereof, but canst not tell whence it cometh, and whither it goeth: so is every one that is born of the Spirit.

9 Nicodemus answered and said unto him, How can these things be?

10 Yashiyah answered and said unto him, Art thou a master of Israel, and knowest not these things?

11 Verily, verily, I say unto thee, We speak that we do know, and testify that we have seen; and ye receive not our witness.

12 If I have told you earthly things, and ye believe not, how shall ye believe, if I tell you *of* heavenly things?

13 And no man hath ascended up to heaven, but he that came down from heaven, *even* the Son of man which is in heaven.

14 ¶ And as Moses lifted up the serpent in the wilderness, even so must the Son of man be lifted up:

15 That whosoever believeth in him should not perish, but have eternal life.

16 ¶ For אֱלֹהִים so loved the world, that he gave his only begotten Son, that whosoever believeth in him should not perish, but have everlasting life.

17 For אֱלֹהִים sent not his Son into the world to condemn the world; but that the world through him might be saved.

18 ¶ He that believeth on him is not condemned: but he that believeth not is condemned already, because he hath not believed in the name of the only begotten Son of אֱלֹהִים.

19 And this is the condemnation, that light is come into the world, and men loved darkness rather than light, because their deeds were evil.

20 For every one that doeth evil hateth the light, neither cometh to the light, lest his deeds should be reproved.

21 But he that doeth truth cometh to the light, that his deeds may be made manifest, that they are wrought in אֱלֹהִים.

22 ¶ After these things came Yashiyah and his disciples into the land of Judæa; and there he tarried with them, and baptized.

23 ¶ And John also was baptizing in Ænon near to Salim, because there was much water there: and they came, and were baptized.

24 For John was not yet cast into prison.

25 ¶ Then there arose a question between *some* of John's disciples and the Jews about purifying.

26 And they came unto John, and said unto him, Rabbi, he that was with thee beyond Jordan, to whom thou barest witness, behold, the same baptizeth, and all *men* come to him.

27 John answered and said, A man can receive nothing, except it be given him from heaven.

28 Ye yourselves bear me witness, that I said, I am not the Christ, but that I am sent before him.

29 He that hath the bride is the bridegroom: but the friend of the bridegroom, which standeth and heareth him, rejoiceth greatly because of the bridegroom's voice: this my joy therefore is fulfilled.

30 He must increase, but I *must* decrease.

31 He that cometh from above is above all: he that is of the earth is earthly, and speaketh of the earth: he that cometh from heaven is above all.

32 And what he hath seen and heard, that he testifieth; and no man receiveth his testimony.

33 He that hath received his testimony hath set to his seal that אֱלֹהִים is true.

34 For he whom אֱלֹהִים hath sent speaketh the words of אֱלֹהִים: for אֱלֹהִים giveth not the Spirit by measure *unto him*.

35 The Father loveth the Son, and hath given all things into his hand.

36 He that believeth on the Son hath everlasting life: and he that believeth not the Son shall not see life; but the wrath of אֱלֹהִים abideth on him.

CHAPTER 4

WHEN therefore the Lord knew how the Pharisees had heard that Yashiyah made and baptized more disciples than John,

2 (Though Yashiyah himself baptized not, but his disciples,)

3 He left Judæa, and departed again into Galilee.

4 And he must needs go through Samaria.

5 Then cometh he to a city of Samaria, which is called Sychar, near to the parcel of ground that Jacob gave to his son Joseph.

6 Now Jacob's well was there. Yashiyah therefore, being wearied with *his* journey, sat thus on the well: *and* it was about the sixth hour.

7 There cometh a woman of Samaria to draw water: Yashiyah saith unto her, Give me to drink.

8 (For his disciples were gone away unto the city to buy meat.)

9 Then saith the woman of Samaria unto him, How is it that thou, being a Jew, askest drink of me, which am a woman of Samaria? for

the Jews have no dealings with the Samaritans.

10 Yashiyah answered and said unto her, If thou knewest the gift of אֱלֹהִים, and who it is that saith to thee, Give me to drink; thou wouldest have asked of him, and he would have given thee living water.

11 The woman saith unto him, Sir, thou hast nothing to draw with, and the well is deep: from whence then hast thou that living water?

12 Art thou greater than our father Jacob, which gave us the well, and drank thereof himself, and his children, and his cattle?

13 Yashiyah answered and said unto her, Whosoever drinketh of this water shall thirst again:

14 But whosoever drinketh of the water that I shall give him shall never thirst; but the water that I shall give him shall be in him a well of water springing up into everlasting life.

15 The woman saith unto him, Sir, give me this water, that I thirst not, neither come hither to draw.

16 Yashiyah saith unto her, Go, call thy husband, and come hither.

17 The woman answered and said, I have no husband. Yashiyah said unto her, Thou hast well said, I have no husband:

18 For thou hast had five husbands; and he whom thou now hast is not thy husband: in that saidst thou truly.

19 The woman saith unto him, Sir, I perceive that thou art a prophet.

20 Our fathers worshipped in this mountain; and ye say, that in Jerusalem is the place where men ought to worship.

21 Yashiyah saith unto her, Woman, believe me, the hour cometh, when ye shall neither in this mountain, nor yet at Jerusalem, worship the Father.

22 Ye worship ye know not what: we know what we worship: for salvation is of the Jews.

23 But the hour cometh, and now is, when the true worshippers shall worship the Father in spirit and in truth: for the Father seeketh such to worship him.

24 אֱלֹהִים is a Spirit: and they that worship him must worship *him* in spirit and in truth.

25 The woman saith unto him, I know that Messias cometh, which is called Christ: when he is come, he will tell us all things.

26 Yashiyah saith unto her, I that speak unto thee am *he*.

27 ¶ And upon this came his disciples, and marvelled that he talked with the woman: yet no man said, What seekest thou? or, Why talkest thou with her?

28 The woman then left her waterpot, and went her way into the city, and saith to the men,

29 Come, see a man, which told me all things that ever I did: is not this the Christ?

30 Then they went out of the city, and came unto him.

31 ¶ In the mean while his disciples prayed him, saying, Master, eat.

32 But he said unto them, I have meat to eat that ye know not of.

33 Therefore said the disciples one to another, Hath any man brought him *ought* to eat?

34 Yashiyah saith unto them, My meat is to do the will of him that sent me, and to finish his work.

35 Say not ye, There are yet four months, and *then* cometh harvest? behold, I say unto you, Lift up your eyes, and look on the fields; for they are white already to harvest.

36 And he that reapeth receiveth wages, and gathereth fruit unto life eternal: that both he that soweth and he that reapeth may rejoice together.

37 And herein is that saying true, One soweth, and another reapeth.

38 I sent you to reap that whereon ye bestowed no labour: other men laboured, and ye are entered into their labours.

39 ¶ And many of the Samaritans of that city believed on him for the saying of the woman, which testified, He told me all that ever I did.

40 So when the Samaritans were come unto him, they besought him that he would tarry with them: and he abode there two days.

41 And many more believed because of his own word;

42 And said unto the woman, Now we believe, not because of thy saying: for we have heard *him* ourselves, and know that this is indeed the Christ, the Saviour of the world.

43 ¶ Now after two days he departed thence, and went into Galilee.

44 For Yashiyah himself testified, that a prophet hath no honour in his own country.

45 Then when he was come into Galilee, the Galilæans received him, having seen all the things that he did at Jerusalem at the feast: for they also went unto the feast.

46 So Yashiyah came again into Cana of Galilee, where he made the water wine. And there was a certain nobleman, whose son was sick at Capernaum.

47 When he heard that Yashiyah was come out of Judæa into Galilee, he went unto him, and besought him that he would come down, and heal his son: for he was at the point of death.

48 Then said Yashiyah unto him, Except ye see signs and wonders, ye will not believe.

49 The nobleman saith unto him, Sir, come down ere my child die.

50 Yashiyah saith unto him, Go thy way; thy son liveth. And the man believed the word that Yashiyah had spoken unto him, and he went his way.

51 And as he was now going down, his servants met him, and told *him*, saying, Thy son liveth.

52 Then inquired he of them the hour when he began to amend. And they said unto him, Yesterday at the seventh hour the fever left him.

53 So the father knew that *it was* at the same hour, in the which Yashiyah said unto him, Thy son liveth: and himself believed, and his whole house.

54 This *is* again the second miracle *that* Yashiyah did, when he was come out of Judæa into Galilee.

CHAPTER 5

AFTER this there was a feast of the Jews; and Yashiyah went up to Jerusalem.

2 Now there is at Jerusalem by the sheep *market* a pool, which is called in the Hebrew tongue Bethesda, having five porches.

3 In these lay a great multitude of impotent folk, of blind, halt, withered, waiting for the moving of the water.

4 For an angel went down at a certain season into the pool, and troubled the water: whosoever then first after the troubling of the water stepped in was made whole of whatsoever disease he had.

5 And a certain man was there, which had an infirmity thirty and eight years.

6 When Yashiyah saw him lie, and knew that he had been now a long time *in that case*, he saith unto him, Wilt thou be made whole?

7 The impotent man answered him, Sir, I have no man, when the water is troubled, to put me into the pool: but while I am coming, another steppeth down before me.

8 Yashiyah saith unto him, Rise, take up thy bed, and walk.

9 And immediately the man was made whole, and took up his bed, and walked: and on the same day was the sabbath.

10 ¶ The Jews therefore said unto him that was cured, It is the sabbath day: it is not lawful for thee to carry *thy* bed.

11 He answered them, He that made me whole, the same said unto me, Take up thy bed, and walk.

12 Then asked they him, What man is that which said unto thee, Take up thy bed, and walk?

13 And he that was healed wist not who it was: for Yashiyah had conveyed himself away, a multitude being in *that* place.

14 Afterward Yashiyah findeth him in the temple, and said unto him, Behold, thou art made whole: sin no more, lest a worse thing come unto thee.

15 The man departed, and told the Jews that it was Yashiyah, which had made him whole.

16 And therefore did the Jews persecute Yashiyah, and sought to slay him, because he had done these things on the sabbath day.

17 ¶ But Yashiyah answered them, My Father worketh hitherto, and I work.

18 Therefore the Jews sought the more to kill him, because he not only had broken the sabbath, but said also that אֱלֹהִים was his Father, making himself equal with אֱלֹהִים.

19 Then answered Yashiyah and said unto them, Verily, verily, I say unto you, The Son can do nothing of himself, but what he seeth the Father do: for what things soever he doeth, these also doeth the Son likewise.

20 For the Father loveth the Son, and sheweth him all things that himself doeth: and he will shew him greater works than these, that ye may marvel.

21 For as the Father raiseth up the dead, and quickeneth *them;* even so the Son quickeneth whom he will.

22 For the Father judgeth no man, but hath committed all judgment unto the Son:

23 That all *men* should honour the Son, even as they honour the Father. He that honoureth not the Son honoureth not the Father which hath sent him.

24 Verily, verily, I say unto you, He that heareth my word, and believeth on him that sent me, hath everlasting life, and shall not come into condemnation; but is passed from death unto life.

25 Verily, verily, I say unto you, The hour is coming, and now is, when the dead shall hear the voice of the Son of אֱלֹהִים: and they that hear shall live.

26 For as the Father hath life in himself; so hath he given to the Son to have life in himself;

27 And hath given him authority to execute judgment also, because he is the Son of man.

28 Marvel not at this: for the hour is coming, in the which all that are in the graves shall hear his voice,

29 And shall come forth; they that have done good, unto the resurrection of life; and they that have done evil, unto the resurrection of damnation.

30 I can of mine own self do nothing: as I hear, I judge: and my judgment is just; because I seek not mine own will, but the will of the Father which hath sent me.

31 If I bear witness of myself, my witness is not true.

32 ¶ There is another that beareth witness of me; and I know that the witness which he witnesseth of me is true.

33 Ye sent unto John, and he bare witness unto the truth.

34 But I receive not testimony from man: but these things I say, that ye might be saved.

35 He was a burning and a shining light: and ye were willing for a season to rejoice in his light.

36 ¶ But I have greater witness than *that* of John: for the works which the Father hath given me to finish, the same works that I do, bear witness of me, that the Father hath sent me.

37 And the Father himself, which hath sent me, hath borne witness of me. Ye have neither heard his voice at any time, nor seen his shape.

38 And ye have not his word abiding in you: for whom he hath sent, him ye believe not.

39 ¶ Search the scriptures; for in them ye think ye have eternal life: and they are they which testify of me.

40 And ye will not come to me, that ye might have life.

41 I receive not honour from men.

42 But I know you, that ye have not the love of אֱלֹהִים in you.

43 I am come in my Father's name, and ye receive me not: if another shall come in his own name, him ye will receive.

44 How can ye believe, which receive honour one of another, and seek not the honour that *cometh* from אֱלֹהִים only?

45 Do not think that I will accuse you to the Father: there is *one* that accuseth you, *even* Moses, in whom ye trust.

46 For had ye believed Moses, ye would have believed me: for he wrote of me.

47 But if ye believe not his writings, how shall ye believe my words?

CHAPTER 6

AFTER these things Yashiyah went over the sea of Galilee, which is *the sea* of Tiberias.

2 And a great multitude followed him, because they saw his miracles which he did on them that were diseased.

3 And Yashiyah went up into a mountain, and there he sat with his disciples.

4 And the passover, a feast of the Jews, was nigh.

5 ¶ When Yashiyah then lifted up *his* eyes, and saw a great company come unto him, he saith unto Philip, Whence shall we buy bread, that these may eat?

6 And this he said to prove him: for he himself knew what he would do.

7 Philip answered him, Two hundred pennyworth of bread is not sufficient for them, that every one of them may take a little.

8 One of his disciples, Andrew, Simon Peter's brother, saith unto him,

9 There is a lad here, which hath five barley loaves, and two small fishes: but what are they among so many?

10 And Yashiyah said, Make the men sit down. Now there was much grass in the place. So the men sat down, in number about five thousand.

11 And Yashiyah took the loaves; and when he had given thanks, he distributed to the disciples, and the disciples to them that were set down; and likewise of the fishes as much as they would.

12 When they were filled, he said unto his disciples, Gather up the fragments that remain, that nothing be lost.

13 Therefore they gathered *them* together, and filled twelve baskets with the fragments of the five barley loaves, which remained over and above unto them that had eaten.

14 Then those men, when they had seen the miracle that Yashiyah did, said, This is of a truth that prophet that should come into the world.

15 ¶ When Yashiyah therefore perceived that they would come and take him by force, to make him a king, he departed again into a mountain himself alone.

16 And when even was *now* come, his disciples went down unto the sea,

17 And entered into a ship, and went over the sea toward Capernaum. And it was now dark, and Yashiyah was not come to them.

18 And the sea arose by reason of a great wind that blew.

19 So when they had rowed about five and twenty or thirty furlongs, they see Yashiyah walking on the sea, and drawing nigh unto the ship: and they were afraid.

20 But he saith unto them, It is I; be not afraid.

21 Then they willingly received him into the ship: and immediately the ship was at the land whither they went.

22 ¶ The day following, when the people which stood on the other side of the sea saw that there was none other boat there, save that one whereinto his disciples were entered, and that Yashiyah went not with his disciples into the boat, but *that* his disciples were gone away alone;

23 (Howbeit there came other boats from Tiberias nigh unto the place where they did eat bread, after that the Lord had given thanks:)

24 When the people therefore saw that Yashiyah was not there, neither his disciples, they also took shipping, and came to Capernaum, seeking for Yashiyah.

25 And when they had found him on the other side of the sea, they said unto him, Rabbi, when camest thou hither?

26 Yashiyah answered them and said, Verily, verily, I say unto you, Ye seek me, not because ye saw the miracles, but because ye did eat of the loaves, and were filled.

27 Labour not for the meat which perisheth, but for that meat which endureth unto everlasting life, which the Son of man shall give unto you: for him hath אֱלֹהִים the Father sealed.

28 Then said they unto him, What shall we do, that we might work the works of אֱלֹהִים?

29 Yashiyah answered and said unto them, This is the work of אֱלֹהִים, that ye believe on him whom he hath sent.

30 They said therefore unto him, What sign shewest thou then, that we may see, and believe thee? what dost thou work?

31 Our fathers did eat manna in the desert; as it is written, He gave them bread from heaven to eat.

32 Then Yashiyah said unto them, Verily, verily, I say unto you, Moses gave you not that bread from heaven; but my Father giveth you the true bread from heaven.

33 For the bread of אֱלֹהִים is he which cometh down from heaven, and giveth life unto the world.

34 Then said they unto him, Lord, evermore give us this bread.

35 And Yashiyah said unto them, I am the bread of life: he that cometh to me shall never hunger; and he that believeth on me shall never thirst.

36 But I said unto you, That ye also have seen me, and believe not.

37 All that the Father giveth me shall come to me; and him that cometh to me I will in no wise cast out.

38 For I came down from heaven, not to do mine own will, but the will of him that sent me.

39 And this is the Father's will which hath sent me, that of all which he hath given me I should lose nothing, but should raise it up again at the last day.

40 And this is the will of him that sent me, that every one which seeth the Son, and believeth on him, may have everlasting life: and I will raise him up at the last day.

41 The Jews then murmured at him, because he said, I am the bread which came down from heaven.

42 And they said, Is not this Yashiyah, the son of Joseph, whose father and mother we know? how is it then that he saith, I came down from heaven?

43 Yashiyah therefore answered and said unto them, Murmur not among yourselves.

44 No man can come to me, except the Father which hath sent me draw him: and I will raise him up at the last day.

45 It is written in the prophets, And they shall be all taught of אֱלֹהִים. Every man therefore that hath heard, and hath learned of the Father, cometh unto me.

46 Not that any man hath seen the Father, save he which is of אֱלֹהִים, he hath seen the Father.

47 Verily, verily, I say unto you, He that believeth on me hath everlasting life.

48 I am that bread of life.

49 Your fathers did eat manna in the wilderness, and are dead.

50 This is the bread which cometh down from heaven, that a man may eat thereof, and not die.

51 I am the living bread which came down from heaven: if any man eat of this bread, he shall live for ever: and the bread that I will give is my flesh, which I will give for the life of the world.

52 The Jews therefore strove among themselves, saying, How can this man give us *his* flesh to eat?

53 Then Yashiyah said unto them, Verily, verily, I say unto you, Except ye eat the flesh of the Son of man, and drink his blood, ye have no life in you.

54 Whoso eateth my flesh, and drinketh my blood, hath eternal life; and I will raise him up at the last day.

55 For my flesh is meat indeed, and my blood is drink indeed.

56 He that eateth my flesh, and drinketh my blood, dwelleth in me, and I in him.

57 As the living Father hath sent me, and I live by the Father: so he that eateth me, even he shall live by me.

58 This is that bread which came down from heaven: not as your fathers did eat manna, and are dead: he that eateth of this bread shall live for ever.

59 These things said he in the synagogue, as he taught in Capernaum.

60 Many therefore of his disciples, when they had heard *this*, said, This is an hard saying; who can hear it?

61 When Yashiyah knew in himself that his disciples murmured at it, he said unto them, Doth this offend you?

62 *What* and if ye shall see the Son of man ascend up where he was before?

63 It is the spirit that quickeneth; the flesh profiteth nothing: the words that I speak unto you, *they* are spirit, and *they* are life.

64 But there are some of you that believe not. For Yashiyah knew from the beginning who they were that believed not, and who

should betray him.

65 And he said, Therefore said I unto you, that no man can come unto me, except it were given unto him of my Father.

66 ¶ From that *time* many of his disciples went back, and walked no more with him.

67 Then said Yashiyah unto the twelve, Will ye also go away?

68 Then Simon Peter answered him, Lord, to whom shall we go? thou hast the words of eternal life.

69 And we believe and are sure that thou art that Christ, the Son of the living אֱלֹהִים.

70 Yashiyah answered them, Have not I chosen you twelve, and one of you is a devil?

71 He spake of Judas Iscariot *the son* of Simon: for he it was that should betray him, being one of the twelve.

CHAPTER 7

AFTER these things Yashiyah walked in Galilee: for he would not walk in Jewry, because the Jews sought to kill him.

2 Now the Jews' feast of tabernacles was at hand.

3 His brethren therefore said unto him, Depart hence, and go into Judæa, that thy disciples also may see the works that thou doest.

4 For *there is* no man *that* doeth any thing in secret, and he himself seeketh to be known openly. If thou do these things, shew thyself to the world.

5 For neither did his brethren believe in him.

6 Then Yashiyah said unto them, My time is not yet come: but your time is alway ready.

7 The world cannot hate you; but me it hateth, because I testify of it, that the works thereof are evil.

8 Go ye up unto this feast: I go not up yet unto this feast; for my time is not yet full come.

9 When he had said these words unto them, he abode *still* in Galilee.

10 ¶ But when his brethren were gone up, then went he also up unto the feast, not openly, but as it were in secret.

11 Then the Jews sought him at the feast, and said, Where is he?

12 And there was much murmuring among the people concerning him: for some said, He is a good man: others said, Nay; but he deceiveth the people.

13 Howbeit no man spake openly of him for fear of the Jews.

14 ¶ Now about the midst of the feast Yashiyah went up into the temple, and taught.

15 And the Jews marvelled, saying, How knoweth this man letters, having never learned?

16 Yashiyah answered them, and said, My doctrine is not mine, but his that sent me.

17 If any man will do his will, he shall know of the doctrine, whether it be of אֱלֹהִים, or *whether* I speak of myself.

18 He that speaketh of himself seeketh his own glory: but he that seeketh his glory that sent him, the same is true, and no unrighteousness is in him.

19 Did not Moses give you the law, and *yet* none of you keepeth the law? Why go ye about to kill me?

20 The people answered and said, Thou hast a devil: who goeth about to kill thee?

21 Yashiyah answered and said unto them, I have done one work, and ye all marvel.

22 Moses therefore gave unto you circumcision; (not because it is of Moses, but of the fathers;) and ye on the sabbath day circumcise a man.

23 If a man on the sabbath day receive circumcision, that the law of Moses should not be broken; are ye angry at me, because I have made a man every whit whole on the sabbath day?

24 Judge not according to the appearance, but judge righteous judgment.

25 Then said some of them of Jerusalem, Is not this he, whom they seek to kill?

26 But, lo, he speaketh boldly, and they say nothing unto him. Do the rulers know indeed that this is the very Christ?

27 Howbeit we know this man whence he is: but when Christ cometh, no man knoweth whence he is.

28 Then cried Yashiyah in the temple as he taught, saying, Ye both know me, and ye know whence I am: and I am not come of myself, but he that sent me is true, whom ye know not.

29 But I know him: for I am from him, and he hath sent me.

30 Then they sought to take him: but no man laid hands on him, because his hour was not yet come.

31 And many of the people believed on him, and said, When Christ cometh, will he do more miracles than these which this *man* hath done?

32 ¶ The Pharisees heard that the people murmured such things concerning him; and the Pharisees and the chief priests sent officers to take him.

33 Then said Yashiyah unto them, Yet a little while am I with you, and *then* I go unto him that sent me.

34 Ye shall seek me, and shall not find *me:* and where I am, *thither* ye cannot come.

35 Then said the Jews among themselves, Whither will he go, that we shall not find him? will he go unto the dispersed among the Gentiles, and teach the Gentiles?

36 What *manner of* saying is this that he said, Ye shall seek me, and shall not find *me:* and where I am, *thither* ye cannot come?

37 In the last day, that great *day* of the feast, Yashiyah stood and cried, saying, If any man thirst, let him come unto me, and drink.

38 He that believeth on me, as the scripture hath said, out of his belly shall flow rivers of living water.

39 (But this spake he of the Spirit, which they that believe on him should receive: for the Holy Ghost was not yet *given;* because that Yashiyah was not yet glorified.)

40 ¶ Many of the people therefore, when they heard this saying, said, Of a truth this is the Prophet.

41 Others said, This is the Christ. But some said, Shall Christ come out of Galilee?

42 Hath not the scripture said, That Christ cometh of the seed of David, and out of the town of Bethlehem, where David was?

43 So there was a division among the people because of him.

44 And some of them would have taken him; but no man laid hands on him.

45 ¶ Then came the officers to the chief priests and Pharisees; and they said unto them, Why have ye not brought him?

46 The officers answered, Never man spake like this man.

47 Then answered them the Pharisees, Are ye also deceived?

48 Have any of the rulers or of the Pharisees believed on him?

49 But this people who knoweth not the law are cursed.

50 Nicodemus saith unto them, (he that came to Yashiyah by night, being one of them,)

51 Doth our law judge *any* man, before it hear him, and know what he doeth?

52 They answered and said unto him, Art thou also of Galilee? Search, and look: for out of Galilee ariseth no prophet.

53 And every man went unto his own house.

CHAPTER 8

JESUS went unto the mount of Olives.

2 And early in the morning he came again into the temple, and all the people came unto him; and he sat down, and taught them.

3 And the scribes and Pharisees brought unto him a woman taken in adultery; and when they had set her in the midst,

4 They say unto him, Master, this woman was taken in adultery, in the very act.

5 Now Moses in the law commanded us, that such should be stoned: but what sayest thou?

6 This they said, tempting him, that they might have to accuse him. But Yashiyah stooped down, and with *his* finger wrote on the ground, *as though he heard them not.*

7 So when they continued asking him, he lifted up himself, and said unto them, He that is without sin among you, let him first cast a stone at her.

8 And again he stooped down, and wrote on the ground.

9 And they which heard *it*, being convicted by *their own* conscience, went out one by one, beginning at the eldest, *even* unto the last: and Yashiyah was left alone, and the woman standing in the midst.

10 When Yashiyah had lifted up himself, and saw none but the woman, he said unto her, Woman, where are those thine accusers? hath no man condemned thee?

11 She said, No man, Lord. And Yashiyah said unto her, Neither do I condemn thee: go, and sin no more.

12 ¶ Then spake Yashiyah again unto them, saying, I am the light of the world: he that followeth me shall not walk in darkness, but shall have the light of life.

13 The Pharisees therefore said unto him, Thou bearest record of thyself; thy record is not true.

14 Yashiyah answered and said unto them, Though I bear record of myself, *yet* my record is true: for I know whence I came, and whither I go; but ye cannot tell whence I come, and whither I go.

15 Ye judge after the flesh; I judge no man.

16 And yet if I judge, my judgment is true: for I am not alone, but I and the Father that sent me.

17 It is also written in your law, that the testimony of two men is true.

18 I am one that bear witness of myself, and the Father that sent me beareth witness of me.

19 Then said they unto him, Where is thy Father? Yashiyah answered, Ye neither know me, nor my Father: if ye had known me, ye should have known my Father also.

20 These words spake Yashiyah in the treasury, as he taught in the temple: and no man laid hands on him; for his hour was not yet come.

21 Then said Yashiyah again unto them, I go my way, and ye shall seek me, and shall die in your sins: whither I go, ye cannot come.

22 Then said the Jews, Will he kill himself? because he saith, Whither I go, ye cannot come.

23 And he said unto them, Ye are from beneath; I am from above: ye are of this world; I am not of this world.

24 I said therefore unto you, that ye shall die in your sins: for if ye believe not that I am *he*, ye shall die in your sins.

25 Then said they unto him, Who art thou? And Yashiyah saith unto them, Even *the same* that I said unto you from the beginning.

26 I have many things to say and to judge of you: but he that sent me is true; and I speak to the world those things which I have heard of him.

27 They understood not that he spake to them of the Father.

28 Then said Yashiyah unto them, When ye have lifted up the Son of man, then shall ye know that I am *he*, and *that* I do nothing of myself; but as my Father hath taught me, I speak these things.

29 And he that sent me is with me: the Father hath not left me alone; for I do always those things that please him.

30 As he spake these words, many believed on him.

31 Then said Yashiyah to those Jews which believed on him, If ye continue in my word, *then* are ye my disciples indeed;

32 And ye shall know the truth, and the truth shall make you free.

33 ¶ They answered him, We be Abraham's seed, and were never in bondage to any man: how sayest thou, Ye shall be made free?

34 Yashiyah answered them, Verily, verily, I say unto you, Whosoever committeth sin is the servant of sin.

35 And the servant abideth not in the house for ever: *but* the Son abideth ever.

36 If the Son therefore shall make you free, ye shall be free indeed.

37 I know that ye are Abraham's seed; but ye seek to kill me, because my word hath no place in you.

38 I speak that which I have seen with my Father: and ye do that which ye have seen with your father.

39 They answered and said unto him, Abraham is our father. Yashiyah saith unto them, If ye were Abraham's children, ye would do the works of Abraham.

40 But now ye seek to kill me, a man that hath told you the truth, which I have heard of אֱלֹהִים: this did not Abraham.

41 Ye do the deeds of your father. Then said they to him, We be not born of fornication; we have one Father, *even* אֱלֹהִים.

42 Yashiyah said unto them, If אֱלֹהִים were your Father, ye would love me: for I proceeded forth and came from אֱלֹהִים; neither came I of myself, but he sent me.

43 Why do ye not understand my speech? *even* because ye cannot hear my word.

44 Ye are of *your* father the devil, and the lusts of your father ye will do. He was a murderer from the beginning, and abode not in the truth, because there is no truth in him. When he speaketh a lie, he speaketh of his own: for he is a liar, and the father of it.

45 And because I tell *you* the truth, ye believe me not.

46 Which of you convinceth me of sin? And if I say the truth, why do ye not believe me?

47 He that is of אֱלֹהִים heareth אֱלֹהִים's words: ye therefore hear *them* not, because ye are not of אֱלֹהִים.

48 Then answered the Jews, and said unto him, Say we not well that thou art a Samaritan, and hast a devil?

49 Yashiyah answered, I have not a devil; but I honour my Father, and ye do dishonour me.

50 And I seek not mine own glory: there is one that seeketh and judgeth.

51 Verily, verily, I say unto you, If a man keep my saying, he shall never see death.

52 Then said the Jews unto him, Now we know that thou hast a devil. Abraham is dead, and the prophets; and thou sayest, If a man

keep my saying, he shall never taste of death.

53 Art thou greater than our father Abraham, which is dead? and the prophets are dead: whom makest thou thyself?

54 Yashiyah answered, If I honour myself, my honour is nothing: it is my Father that honoureth me; of whom ye say, that he is your אֱלֹהִים:

55 Yet ye have not known him; but I know him: and if I should say, I know him not, I shall be a liar like unto you: but I know him, and keep his saying.

56 Your father Abraham rejoiced to see my day: and he saw *it*, and was glad.

57 Then said the Jews unto him, Thou art not yet fifty years old, and hast thou seen Abraham?

58 Yashiyah said unto them, Verily, verily, I say unto you, Before Abraham was, I am.

59 Then took they up stones to cast at him: but Yashiyah hid himself, and went out of the temple, going through the midst of them, and so passed by.

CHAPTER 9

AND as *Yashiyah* passed by, he saw a man which was blind from *his* birth.

2 And his disciples asked him, saying, Master, who did sin, this man, or his parents, that he was born blind?

3 Yashiyah answered, Neither hath this man sinned, nor his parents: but that the works of אֱלֹהִים should be made manifest in him.

4 I must work the works of him that sent me, while it is day: the night cometh, when no man can work.

5 As long as I am in the world, I am the light of the world.

6 When he had thus spoken, he spat on the ground, and made clay of the spittle, and he anointed the eyes of the blind man with the clay,

7 And said unto him, Go, wash in the pool of Siloam, (which is by interpretation, Sent.) He went his way therefore, and washed, and came seeing.

8 ¶ The neighbours therefore, and they which before had seen him that he was blind, said, Is not this he that sat and begged?

9 Some said, This is he: others *said*, He is like him: *but* he said, I am *he*.

10 Therefore said they unto him, How were thine eyes opened?

11 He answered and said, A man that is called Yashiyah made clay, and anointed mine eyes, and said unto me, Go to the pool of Siloam, and wash: and I went and washed, and I received sight.

12 Then said they unto him, Where is he? He said, I know not.

13 ¶ They brought to the Pharisees him that aforetime was blind.

14 And it was the sabbath day when Yashiyah made the clay, and opened his eyes.

15 Then again the Pharisees also asked him how he had received his sight. He said unto them, He put clay upon mine eyes, and I washed, and do see.

16 Therefore said some of the Pharisees, This man is not of אֱלֹהִים, because he keepeth not the sabbath day. Others said, How can a man that is a sinner do such miracles? And there was a division among them.

17 They say unto the blind man again, What sayest thou of him, that he hath opened thine eyes? He said, He is a prophet.

18 But the Jews did not believe concerning him, that he had been blind, and received his sight, until they called the parents of him that had received his sight.

19 And they asked them, saying, Is this your son, who ye say was born blind? how then doth he now see?

20 His parents answered them and said, We know that this is our son, and that he was born blind:

21 But by what means he now seeth, we know not; or who hath opened his eyes, we know not: he is of age; ask him: he shall speak for himself.

22 These *words* spake his parents, because they feared the Jews: for the Jews had agreed already, that if any man did confess that he was Christ, he should be put out of the synagogue.

23 Therefore said his parents, He is of age; ask him.

24 Then again called they the man that was blind, and said unto him, Give אֱלֹהִים the praise: we know that this man is a sinner.

25 He answered and said, Whether he be a sinner *or no*, I know not: one thing I know, that, whereas I was blind, now I see.

26 Then said they to him again, What did he to thee? how opened he thine eyes?

27 He answered them, I have told you already, and ye did not hear: wherefore would ye hear *it* again? will ye also be his disciples?

28 Then they reviled him, and said, Thou art his disciple; but we are Moses' disciples.

29 We know that אֱלֹהִים spake unto Moses: *as for* this *fellow*, we know not from whence he is.

30 The man answered and said unto them, Why herein is a marvellous thing, that ye know not from whence he is, and *yet* he hath opened mine eyes.

31 Now we know that אֱלֹהִים heareth not sinners: but if any man be a worshipper of אֱלֹהִים, and doeth his will, him he heareth.

32 Since the world began was it not heard that any man opened the eyes of one that was born blind.

33 If this man were not of אֱלֹהִים, he could do nothing.

34 They answered and said unto him, Thou wast altogether born in sins, and dost thou teach us? And they cast him out.

35 Yashiyah heard that they had cast him out; and when he had found him, he said unto him, Dost thou believe on the Son of אֱלֹהִים?

36 He answered and said, Who is he, Lord, that I might believe on him?

37 And Yashiyah said unto him, Thou hast both seen him, and it is he that talketh with thee.

38 And he said, Lord, I believe. And he worshipped him.

39 ¶ And Yashiyah said, For judgment I am come into this world, that they which see not might see; and that they which see might be made blind.

40 And *some* of the Pharisees which were with him heard these words, and said unto him, Are we blind also?

41 Yashiyah said unto them, If ye were blind, ye should have no sin: but now ye say, We see; therefore your sin remaineth.

CHAPTER 10

VERILY, verily, I say unto you, He that entereth not by the door into the sheepfold, but climbeth up some other way, the same is a thief and a robber.

2 But he that entereth in by the door is the shepherd of the sheep.

3 To him the porter openeth; and the sheep hear his voice: and he calleth his own sheep by name, and leadeth them out.

4 And when he putteth forth his own sheep, he goeth before them, and the sheep follow him: for they know his voice.

5 And a stranger will they not follow, but will flee from him: for they know not the voice of strangers.

6 This parable spake Yashiyah unto them: but they understood not what things they were which he spake unto them.

7 Then said Yashiyah unto them again, Verily, verily, I say unto you, I am the door of the sheep.

8 All that ever came before me are thieves and robbers: but the sheep did not hear them.

9 I am the door: by me if any man enter in, he shall be saved, and shall go in and out, and find pasture.

10 The thief cometh not, but for to steal, and to kill, and to destroy: I am come that they might have life, and that they might have *it* more abundantly.

11 I am the good shepherd: the good shepherd giveth his life for the sheep.

12 But he that is an hireling, and not the shepherd, whose own the sheep are not, seeth the wolf coming, and leaveth the sheep, and fleeth: and the wolf catcheth them, and scattereth the sheep.

13 The hireling fleeth, because he is an hireling, and careth not for the sheep.

14 I am the good shepherd, and know my *sheep*, and am known of mine.

15 As the Father knoweth me, even so know I the Father: and I lay down my life for the sheep.

16 And other sheep I have, which are not of this fold: them also I must bring, and they shall hear my voice; and there shall be one fold, *and* one shepherd.

17 Therefore doth my Father love me, because I lay down my life, that I might take it again.

18 No man taketh it from me, but I lay it down of myself. I have power to lay it down, and I have power to take it again. This commandment have I received of my Father.

19 ¶ There was a division therefore again among the Jews for these sayings.

20 And many of them said, He hath a devil, and is mad; why hear ye him?

21 Others said, These are not the words of him that hath a devil. Can a devil open the eyes of the blind?

22 ¶ And it was at Jerusalem the feast of the dedication, and it was winter.

23 And Yashiyah walked in the temple in Solomon's porch.

24 Then came the Jews round about him, and said unto him, How long dost thou make us to doubt? If thou be the Christ, tell us plainly.

25 Yashiyah answered them, I told you, and ye believed not: the works that I do in my Father's name, they bear witness of me.

26 But ye believe not, because ye are not of my sheep, as I said unto you.

27 My sheep hear my voice, and I know them, and they follow me:

28 And I give unto them eternal life; and they shall never perish, neither shall any *man* pluck them out of my hand.

29 My Father, which gave *them* me, is greater than all; and no *man* is able to pluck *them* out of my Father's hand.

30 I and *my* Father are one.

31 Then the Jews took up stones again to stone him.

32 Yashiyah answered them, Many good works have I shewed you from my Father; for which of those works do ye stone me?

33 The Jews answered him, saying, For a good work we stone thee not; but for blasphemy; and because that thou, being a man, makest thyself אֱלֹהִים.

34 Yashiyah answered them, Is it not written in your law, I said, Ye are gods?

35 If he called them gods, unto whom the word of אֱלֹהִים came, and the scripture cannot be broken;

36 Say ye of him, whom the Father hath sanctified, and sent into the world, Thou blasphemest; because I said, I am the Son of אֱלֹהִים?

37 If I do not the works of my Father, believe me not.

38 But if I do, though ye believe not me, believe the works: that ye may know, and believe, that the Father *is* in me, and I in him.

39 Therefore they sought again to take him: but he escaped out of their hand,

40 And went away again beyond Jordan into the place where John at first baptized; and there he abode.

41 And many resorted unto him, and said, John did no miracle: but all things that John spake of this man were true.

42 And many believed on him there.

CHAPTER 11

NOW a certain *man* was sick, *named* Lazarus, of Bethany, the town of Mary and her sister Martha.

2 (It was *that* Mary which anointed the Lord with ointment, and wiped his feet with her hair, whose brother Lazarus was sick.)

3 Therefore his sisters sent unto him, saying, Lord, behold, he whom thou lovest is sick.

4 When Yashiyah heard *that*, he said, This sickness is not unto death, but for the glory of אֱלֹהִים, that the Son of אֱלֹהִים might be glorified thereby.

5 Now Yashiyah loved Martha, and her sister, and Lazarus.

6 When he had heard therefore that he was sick, he abode two days still in the same place where he was.

7 Then after that saith he to *his* disciples, Let us go into Judæa again.

8 *His* disciples say unto him, Master, the Jews of late sought to stone thee; and goest thou thither again?

9 Yashiyah answered, Are there not twelve hours in the day? If any man walk in the day, he stumbleth not, because he seeth the light of this world.

10 But if a man walk in the night, he stumbleth, because there is no light in him.

11 These things said he: and after that he saith unto them, Our friend Lazarus sleepeth; but I go, that I may awake him out of sleep.

12 Then said his disciples, Lord, if he sleep, he shall do well.

13 Howbeit Yashiyah spake of his death: but they thought that he had spoken of taking of rest in sleep.

14 Then said Yashiyah unto them plainly, Lazarus is dead.

15 And I am glad for your sakes that I was not there, to the intent ye may believe; nevertheless let us go unto him.

16 Then said Thomas, which is called Didymus, unto his fellowdisciples, Let us also go, that we may die with him.

17 Then when Yashiyah came, he found that he had *lain* in the grave four days already.

18 Now Bethany was nigh unto Jerusalem, about fifteen furlongs off:

19 And many of the Jews came to Martha and Mary, to comfort them concerning their brother.

20 Then Martha, as soon as she heard that Yashiyah was coming, went and met him: but Mary sat *still* in the house.

21 Then said Martha unto Yashiyah, Lord, if thou hadst been here, my brother had not died.

22 But I know, that even now, whatsoever thou wilt ask of אֱלֹהִים, אֱלֹהִים will give *it* thee.

23 Yashiyah saith unto her, Thy brother shall rise again.

24 Martha saith unto him, I know that he shall rise again in the resurrection at the last day.

25 Yashiyah said unto her, I am the resurrection, and the life: he that believeth in me, though he were dead, yet shall he live:

26 And whosoever liveth and believeth in me shall never die. Believest thou this?

27 She saith unto him, Yea, Lord: I believe that thou art the Christ, the Son of אֱלֹהִים, which should come into the world.

28 And when she had so said, she went her way, and called Mary her sister secretly, saying, The Master is come, and calleth for thee.

29 As soon as she heard *that*, she arose quickly, and came unto him.

30 Now Yashiyah was not yet come into the town, but was in that place where Martha met him.

31 The Jews then which were with her in the house, and comforted her, when they saw Mary, that she rose up hastily and went out, followed her, saying, She goeth unto the grave to weep there.

32 Then when Mary was come where Yashiyah was, and saw him, she fell down at his feet, saying unto him, Lord, if thou hadst been here, my brother had not died.

33 When Yashiyah therefore saw her weeping, and the Jews also weeping which came with her, he groaned in the spirit, and was troubled,

34 And said, Where have ye laid him? They said unto him, Lord, come and see.

35 Yashiyah wept.

36 Then said the Jews, Behold how he loved him!

37 And some of them said, Could not this man, which opened the eyes of the blind, have caused that even this man should not have died?

38 Yashiyah therefore again groaning in himself cometh to the grave. It was a cave, and a stone lay upon it.

39 Yashiyah said, Take ye away the stone. Martha, the sister of him that was dead, saith unto him, Lord, by this time he stinketh: for he hath been *dead* four days.

40 Yashiyah saith unto her, Said I not unto thee, that, if thou wouldest believe, thou shouldest see the glory of אֱלֹהִים?

41 Then they took away the stone *from the place* where the dead was laid. And Yashiyah lifted up *his* eyes, and said, Father, I thank thee that thou hast heard me.

42 And I knew that thou hearest me always: but because of the people which stand by I said *it*, that they may believe that thou hast sent me.

43 And when he thus had spoken, he cried with a loud voice, Lazarus, come forth.

44 And he that was dead came forth, bound hand and foot with graveclothes: and his face was bound about with a napkin. Yashiyah saith unto them, Loose him, and let him go.

45 Then many of the Jews which came to Mary, and had seen the things which Yashiyah did, believed on him.

46 But some of them went their ways to the Pharisees, and told them what things Yashiyah had done.

47 ¶ Then gathered the chief priests and the Pharisees a council, and said, What do we? for this man doeth many miracles.

48 If we let him thus alone, all *men* will believe on him: and the Romans shall come and take away both our place and nation.

49 And one of them, *named* Caiaphas, being the high priest that same year, said unto them, Ye know nothing at all,

50 Nor consider that it is expedient for us, that one man should die for the people, and that the whole nation perish not.

51 And this spake he not of himself: but being high priest that year, he prophesied that Yashiyah should die for that nation;

52 And not for that nation only, but that also he should gather together in one the children of אֱלֹהִים that were scattered abroad.

53 Then from that day forth they took counsel together for to put him to death.

54 Yashiyah therefore walked no more openly among the Jews; but went thence unto a country near to the wilderness, into a city called Ephraim, and there continued with his disciples.

55 ¶ And the Jews' passover was nigh at hand: and many went out of the country up to Jerusalem before the passover, to purify themselves.

56 Then sought they for Yashiyah, and spake among themselves, as they stood in the temple, What think ye, that he will not come to the feast?

57 Now both the chief priests and the Pharisees had given a commandment, that, if any man knew where he were, he should shew *it*, that they might take him.

CHAPTER 12

THEN Yashiyah six days before the passover came to Bethany, where Lazarus was which had been dead, whom he raised from the dead.

2 There they made him a supper; and Martha served: but Lazarus was one of them that sat at the table with him.

3 Then took Mary a pound of ointment of spikenard, very costly, and anointed the feet of Yashiyah, and wiped his feet with her hair: and the house was filled with the odour of the ointment.

4 Then saith one of his disciples, Judas Iscariot, Simon's *son*, which should betray him,

5 Why was not this ointment sold for three hundred pence, and given to the poor?

6 This he said, not that he cared for the poor; but because he was a thief, and had the bag, and bare what was put therein.

7 Then said Yashiyah, Let her alone: against the day of my burying hath she kept this.

8 For the poor always ye have with you; but me ye have not always.

9 Much people of the Jews therefore knew that he was there: and they came not for Yashiyah' sake only, but that they might see Lazarus also, whom he had raised from the dead.

10 ¶ But the chief priests consulted that they might put Lazarus also to death;

11 Because that by reason of him many of the Jews went away, and believed on Yashiyah.

12 ¶ On the next day much people that were come to the feast, when they heard that Yashiyah was coming to Jerusalem,

13 Took branches of palm trees, and went forth to meet him, and cried, Hosanna: Blessed *is* the King of Israel that cometh in the name of the Lord.

14 And Yashiyah, when he had found a young ass, sat thereon; as it is written,

15 Fear not, daughter of Sion: behold, thy King cometh, sitting on an ass's colt.

16 These things understood not his disciples at the first: but when Yashiyah was glorified, then remembered they that these things

were written of him, and *that* they had done these things unto him.

17 The people therefore that was with him when he called Lazarus out of his grave, and raised him from the dead, bare record.

18 For this cause the people also met him, for that they heard that he had done this miracle.

19 The Pharisees therefore said among themselves, Perceive ye how ye prevail nothing? behold, the world is gone after him.

20 ¶ And there were certain Greeks among them that came up to worship at the feast:

21 The same came therefore to Philip, which was of Bethsaida of Galilee, and desired him, saying, Sir, we would see Yashiyah.

22 Philip cometh and telleth Andrew: and again Andrew and Philip tell Yashiyah.

23 ¶ And Yashiyah answered them, saying, The hour is come, that the Son of man should be glorified.

24 Verily, verily, I say unto you, Except a corn of wheat fall into the ground and die, it abideth alone: but if it die, it bringeth forth much fruit.

25 He that loveth his life shall lose it; and he that hateth his life in this world shall keep it unto life eternal.

26 If any man serve me, let him follow me; and where I am, there shall also my servant be: if any man serve me, him will *my* Father honour.

27 Now is my soul troubled; and what shall I say? Father, save me from this hour: but for this cause came I unto this hour.

28 Father, glorify thy name. Then came there a voice from heaven, *saying*, I have both glorified *it*, and will glorify *it* again.

29 The people therefore, that stood by, and heard *it*, said that it thundered: others said, An angel spake to him.

30 Yashiyah answered and said, This voice came not because of me, but for your sakes.

31 Now is the judgment of this world: now shall the prince of this world be cast out.

32 And I, if I be lifted up from the earth, will draw all *men* unto me.

33 This he said, signifying what death he should die.

34 The people answered him, We have heard out of the law that Christ abideth for ever: and how sayest thou, The Son of man must be lifted up? who is this Son of man?

35 Then Yashiyah said unto them, Yet a little while is the light with you. Walk while ye have the light, lest darkness come upon you: for he that walketh in darkness knoweth not whither he goeth.

36 While ye have light, believe in the light, that ye may be the children of light. These things spake Yashiyah, and departed, and did hide himself from them.

37 ¶ But though he had done so many miracles before them, yet they believed not on him:

38 That the saying of Esaias the prophet might be fulfilled, which he spake, Lord, who hath believed our report? and to whom hath the arm of the Lord been revealed?

39 Therefore they could not believe, because that Esaias said again,

40 He hath blinded their eyes, and hardened their heart; that they should not see with *their* eyes, nor understand with *their* heart, and be converted, and I should heal them.

41 These things said Esaias, when he saw his glory, and spake of him.

42 ¶ Nevertheless among the chief rulers also many believed on him; but because of the Pharisees they did not confess *him*, lest they should be put out of the synagogue:

43 For they loved the praise of men more than the praise of אֱלֹהִים.

44 ¶ Yashiyah cried and said, He that believeth on me, believeth not on me, but on him that sent me.

45 And he that seeth me seeth him that sent me.

46 I am come a light into the world, that whosoever believeth on me should not abide in darkness.

47 And if any man hear my words, and believe not, I judge him not: for I came not to judge the world, but to save the world.

48 He that rejecteth me, and receiveth not my words, hath one that judgeth him: the word that I have spoken, the same shall judge him in the last day.

49 For I have not spoken of myself; but the Father which sent me, he gave me a commandment, what I should say, and what I should speak.

50 And I know that his commandment is life everlasting: whatsoever I speak therefore, even as the Father said unto me, so I speak.

CHAPTER 13

NOW before the feast of the passover, when Yashiyah knew that his hour was come that he should depart out of this world unto the Father, having loved his own which were in the world, he loved them unto the end.

2 And supper being ended, the devil having now put into the heart of Judas Iscariot, Simon's *son*, to betray him;

3 Yashiyah knowing that the Father had given all things into his hands, and that he was come from אֱלֹהִים, and went to אֱלֹהִים;

4 He riseth from supper, and laid aside his garments; and took a towel, and girded himself.

5 After that he poureth water into a bason, and began to wash the disciples' feet, and to wipe *them* with the towel wherewith he was girded.

6 Then cometh he to Simon Peter: and Peter saith unto him, Lord, dost thou wash my feet?

7 Yashiyah answered and said unto him, What I do thou knowest not now; but thou shalt know hereafter.

8 Peter saith unto him, Thou shalt never wash my feet. Yashiyah answered him, If I wash thee not, thou hast no part with me.

9 Simon Peter saith unto him, Lord, not my feet only, but also *my* hands and *my* head.

10 Yashiyah saith to him, He that is washed needeth not save to wash *his* feet, but is clean every whit: and ye are clean, but not all.

11 For he knew who should betray him; therefore said he, Ye are not all clean.

12 So after he had washed their feet, and had taken his garments, and was set down again, he said unto them, Know ye what I have done to you?

13 Ye call me Master and Lord: and ye say well; for *so* I am.

14 If I then, *your* Lord and Master, have washed your feet; ye also ought to wash one another's feet.

15 For I have given you an example, that ye should do as I have done to you.

16 Verily, verily, I say unto you, The servant is not greater than his lord; neither he that is sent greater than he that sent him.

17 If ye know these things, happy are ye if ye do them.

18 ¶ I speak not of you all: I know whom I have chosen: but that the scripture may be fulfilled, He that eateth bread with me hath lifted up his heel against me.

19 Now I tell you before it come, that, when it is come to pass, ye may believe that I am *he*.

20 Verily, verily, I say unto you, He that receiveth whomsoever I send receiveth me; and he that receiveth me receiveth him that sent me.

21 When Yashiyah had thus said, he was troubled in spirit, and testified, and said, Verily, verily, I say unto you, that one of you shall betray me.

22 Then the disciples looked one on another, doubting of whom he spake.

23 Now there was leaning on Yashiyah' bosom one of his disciples, whom Yashiyah loved.

24 Simon Peter therefore beckoned to him, that he should ask who it should be of whom he spake.

25 He then lying on Yashiyah' breast saith unto him, Lord, who is it?

26 Yashiyah answered, He it is, to whom I shall give a sop, when I have dipped *it*. And when he had dipped the sop, he gave *it* to Judas Iscariot, *the son* of Simon.

27 And after the sop Satan entered into him. Then said Yashiyah unto him, That thou doest, do quickly.

28 Now no man at the table knew for what intent he spake this unto him.

29 For some *of them* thought, because Judas had the bag, that Yashiyah had said unto him, Buy *those things* that we have need of against the feast; or, that he should give something to the poor.

30 He then having received the sop went immediately out: and it was night.

31 ¶ Therefore, when he was gone out, Yashiyah said, Now is the Son of man glorified, and אֱלֹהִים is glorified in him.

32 If אֱלֹהִים be glorified in him, אֱלֹהִים shall also glorify him in himself, and shall straightway glorify him.

33 Little children, yet a little while I am with you. Ye shall seek me: and as I said unto the Jews, Whither I go, ye cannot come; so now I say to you.

34 A new commandment I give unto you, That ye love one another; as I have loved you, that ye also love one another.

35 By this shall all *men* know that ye are my disciples, if ye have love one to another.

36 ¶ Simon Peter said unto him, Lord, whither goest thou? Yashiyah answered him, Whither I go, thou canst not follow me now; but thou shalt follow me afterwards.

37 Peter said unto him, Lord, why cannot I follow thee now? I will lay down my life for thy sake.

38 Yashiyah answered him, Wilt thou lay down thy life for my sake? Verily, verily, I say unto thee, The cock shall not crow, till thou hast denied me thrice.

CHAPTER 14

LET not your heart be troubled: ye believe in אֱלֹהִים, believe also in me.

2 In my Father's house are many mansions: if *it were* not *so*, I would have told you. I go to prepare a place for you.

3 And if I go and prepare a place for you, I will come again, and receive you unto myself; that where I am, *there* ye may be also.

4 And whither I go ye know, and the way ye know.

5 Thomas saith unto him, Lord, we know not whither thou goest; and how can we know the way?

6 Yashiyah saith unto him, I am the way, the truth, and the life: no man cometh unto the Father, but by me.

7 If ye had known me, ye should have known my Father also: and from henceforth ye know him, and have seen him.

8 Philip saith unto him, Lord, shew us the Father, and it sufficeth us.

9 Yashiyah saith unto him, Have I been so long time with you, and yet hast thou not known me, Philip? he that hath seen me hath seen the Father; and how sayest thou *then*, Shew us the Father?

10 Believest thou not that I am in the Father, and the Father in me? the words that I speak unto you I speak not of myself: but the Father that dwelleth in me, he doeth the works.

11 Believe me that I *am* in the Father, and the Father in me: or else believe me for the very works' sake.

12 Verily, verily, I say unto you, He that believeth on me, the works that I do shall he do also; and greater *works* than these shall he do; because I go unto my Father.

13 And whatsoever ye shall ask in my name, that will I do, that the Father may be glorified in the Son.

14 If ye shall ask any thing in my name, I will do *it*.

15 ¶ If ye love me, keep my commandments.

16 And I will pray the Father, and he shall give you another Comforter, that he may abide with you for ever;

17 *Even* the Spirit of truth; whom the world cannot receive, because it seeth him not, neither knoweth him: but ye know him; for he dwelleth with you, and shall be in you.

18 I will not leave you comfortless: I will come to you.

19 Yet a little while, and the world seeth me no more; but ye see me: because I live, ye shall live also.

20 At that day ye shall know that I *am* in my Father, and ye in me, and I in you.

21 He that hath my commandments, and keepeth them, he it is that loveth me: and he that loveth me shall be loved of my Father, and I will love him, and will manifest myself to him.

22 Judas saith unto him, not Iscariot, Lord, how is it that thou wilt manifest thyself unto us, and not unto the world?

23 Yashiyah answered and said unto him, If a man love me, he will keep my words: and my Father will love him, and we will come unto him, and make our abode with him.

24 He that loveth me not keepeth not my sayings: and the word which ye hear is not mine, but the Father's which sent me.

25 These things have I spoken unto you, being *yet* present with you.

26 But the Comforter, *which is* the Holy Ghost, whom the Father will send in my name, he shall teach you all things, and bring all things to your remembrance, whatsoever I have said unto you.

27 Peace I leave with you, my peace I give unto you: not as the world giveth, give I unto you. Let not your heart be troubled, neither let it be afraid.

28 Ye have heard how I said unto you, I go away, and come *again* unto you. If ye loved me, ye would rejoice, because I said, I go unto the Father: for my Father is greater than I.

29 And now I have told you before it come to pass, that, when it is come to pass, ye might believe.

30 Hereafter I will not talk much with you: for the prince of this world cometh, and hath nothing in me.

31 But that the world may know that I love the Father; and as the Father gave me commandment, even so I do. Arise, let us go hence.

CHAPTER 15

I AM the true vine, and my Father is the husbandman.

2 Every branch in me that beareth not fruit he taketh away: and every *branch* that beareth fruit, he purgeth it, that it may bring forth more fruit.

3 Now ye are clean through the word which I have spoken unto you.

4 Abide in me, and I in you. As the branch cannot bear fruit of itself, except it abide in the vine; no more can ye, except ye abide in me.

5 I am the vine, ye *are* the branches: He that abideth in me, and I in him, the same bringeth forth much fruit: for without me ye can do nothing.

6 If a man abide not in me, he is cast forth as a branch, and is withered; and men gather them, and cast *them* into the fire, and they are burned.

7 If ye abide in me, and my words abide in you, ye shall ask what ye will, and it shall be done unto you.

8 Herein is my Father glorified, that ye bear much fruit; so shall ye be my disciples.

9 As the Father hath loved me, so have I loved you: continue ye in my love.

10 If ye keep my commandments, ye shall abide in my love; even as I have kept my Father's commandments, and abide in his love.

11 These things have I spoken unto you, that my joy might remain in you, and *that* your joy might be full.

12 This is my commandment, That ye love one another, as I have loved you.

13 Greater love hath no man than this, that a man lay down his life for his friends.

14 Ye are my friends, if ye do whatsoever I command you.

15 Henceforth I call you not servants; for the servant knoweth not what his lord doeth: but I have called you friends; for all things that I have heard of my Father I have made known unto you.

16 Ye have not chosen me, but I have chosen you, and ordained you, that ye should go and bring forth fruit, and *that* your fruit should remain: that whatsoever ye shall ask of the Father in my name, he may give it you.

17 These things I command you, that ye love one another.

18 If the world hate you, ye know that it hated me before *it hated* you.

19 If ye were of the world, the world would love his own: but because ye are not of the world, but I have chosen you out of the world, therefore the world hateth you.

20 Remember the word that I said unto you, The servant is not greater than his lord. If they have persecuted me, they will also persecute you; if they have kept my saying, they will keep yours also.

21 But all these things will they do unto you for my name's sake, because they know not him that sent me.

22 If I had not come and spoken unto them, they had not had sin: but now they have no cloke for their sin.

23 He that hateth me hateth my Father also.

24 If I had not done among them the works which none other man did, they had not had sin: but now have they both seen and hated both me and my Father.

25 But *this cometh to pass*, that the word might be fulfilled that is written in their law, They hated me without a cause.

26 But when the Comforter is come, whom I will send unto you from the Father, *even* the Spirit of truth, which proceedeth from the Father, he shall testify of me:

27 And ye also shall bear witness, because ye have been with me from the beginning.

CHAPTER 16

THESE things have I spoken unto you, that ye should not be offended.

2 They shall put you out of the synagogues: yea, the time cometh, that whosoever killeth you will think that he doeth אֱלֹהִים service.

3 And these things will they do unto you, because they have not known the Father, nor me.

4 But these things have I told you, that when the time shall come, ye may remember that I told you of them. And these things I said not unto you at the beginning, because I was with you.

5 But now I go my way to him that sent me; and none of you asketh me, Whither goest thou?

6 But because I have said these things unto you, sorrow hath filled your heart.

7 Nevertheless I tell you the truth; It is expedient for you that I go away: for if I go not away, the Comforter will not come unto you; but if I depart, I will send him unto you.

8 And when he is come, he will reprove the world of sin, and of righteousness, and of judgment:

9 Of sin, because they believe not on me;

10 Of righteousness, because I go to my Father, and ye see me no more;

11 Of judgment, because the prince of this world is judged.

12 I have yet many things to say unto you, but ye cannot bear them now.

13 Howbeit when he, the Spirit of truth, is come, he will guide you into all truth: for he shall not speak of himself; but whatsoever he shall hear, *that* shall he speak: and he will shew you things to come.

14 He shall glorify me: for he shall receive of mine, and shall shew *it* unto you.

15 All things that the Father hath are mine: therefore said I, that he shall take of mine, and shall shew *it* unto you.

16 A little while, and ye shall not see me: and again, a little while, and ye shall see me, because I go to the Father.

17 Then said *some* of his disciples among themselves, What is this that he saith unto us, A little while, and ye shall not see me: and again, a little while, and ye shall see me: and, Because I go to the Father?

18 They said therefore, What is this that he saith, A little while? we cannot tell what he saith.

19 Now Yashiyah knew that they were desirous to ask him, and said unto them, Do ye inquire among yourselves of that I said, A little while, and ye shall not see me: and again, a little while, and ye shall see me?

20 Verily, verily, I say unto you, That ye shall weep and lament, but the world shall rejoice: and ye shall be sorrowful, but your sorrow shall be turned into joy.

21 A woman when she is in travail hath sorrow, because her hour is come: but as soon as she is delivered of the child, she remembereth no more the anguish, for joy that a man is born into the world.

22 And ye now therefore have sorrow: but I will see you again, and your heart shall rejoice, and your joy no man taketh from you.

23 And in that day ye shall ask me nothing. Verily, verily, I say unto you, Whatsoever ye shall ask the Father in my name, he will give *it* you.

24 Hitherto have ye asked nothing in my name: ask, and ye shall receive, that your joy may be full.

25 These things have I spoken unto you in proverbs: but the time cometh, when I shall no more speak unto you in proverbs, but I shall shew you plainly of the Father.

26 At that day ye shall ask in my name: and I say not unto you, that I will pray the Father for you:

27 For the Father himself loveth you, because ye have loved me, and have believed that I came out from אֱלֹהִים.

28 I came forth from the Father, and am come into the world: again, I leave the world, and go to the Father.

29 His disciples said unto him, Lo, now speakest thou plainly, and speakest no proverb.

30 Now are we sure that thou knowest all things, and needest not that any man should ask thee: by this we believe that thou camest forth from אֱלֹהִים.

31 Yashiyah answered them, Do ye now believe?

32 Behold, the hour cometh, yea, is now come, that ye shall be scattered, every man to his own, and shall leave me alone: and yet I am not alone, because the Father is with me.

33 These things I have spoken unto you, that in me ye might have peace. In the world ye shall have tribulation: but be of good cheer; I have overcome the world.

CHAPTER 17

THESE words spake Yashiyah, and lifted up his eyes to heaven, and said, Father, the hour is come; glorify thy Son, that thy Son also may glorify thee:

2 As thou hast given him power over all flesh, that he should give eternal life to as many as thou hast given him.

3 And this is life eternal, that they might know thee the only true אֱלֹהִים, and Yashiyah Christ, whom thou hast sent.

4 I have glorified thee on the earth: I have finished the work which thou gavest me to do.

5 And now, O Father, glorify thou me with thine own self with the glory which I had with thee before the world was.

6 I have manifested thy name unto the men which thou gavest me out of the world: thine they were, and thou gavest them me; and they have kept thy word.

7 Now they have known that all things whatsoever thou hast given me are of thee.

8 For I have given unto them the words which thou gavest me; and they have received *them*, and have known surely that I came out from thee, and they have believed that thou didst send me.

9 I pray for them: I pray not for the world, but for them which thou hast given me; for they are thine.

10 And all mine are thine, and thine are mine; and I am glorified in them.

11 And now I am no more in the world, but these are in the world, and I come to thee. Holy Father, keep through thine own name those whom thou hast given me, that they may be one, as we *are*.

12 While I was with them in the world, I kept them in thy name: those that thou gavest me I have kept, and none of them is lost, but the son of perdition; that the scripture might be fulfilled.

13 And now come I to thee; and these things I speak in the world, that they might have my joy fulfilled in themselves.

14 I have given them thy word; and the world hath hated them, because they are not of the world, even as I am not of the world.

15 I pray not that thou shouldest take them out of the world, but that thou shouldest keep them from the evil.

16 They are not of the world, even as I am not of the world.

17 Sanctify them through thy truth: thy word is truth.

18 As thou hast sent me into the world, even so have I also sent them into the world.

19 And for their sakes I sanctify myself, that they also might be sanctified through the truth.

20 Neither pray I for these alone, but for them also which shall believe on me through their word;

21 That they all may be one; as thou, Father, *art* in me, and I in thee, that they also may be one in us: that the world may believe that thou hast sent me.

22 And the glory which thou gavest me I have given them; that they may be one, even as we are one:

23 I in them, and thou in me, that they may be made perfect in one; and that the world may know that thou hast sent me, and hast loved them, as thou hast loved me.

24 Father, I will that they also, whom thou hast given me, be with me where I am; that they may behold my glory, which thou hast given me: for thou lovedst me before the foundation of the world.

25 O righteous Father, the world hath not known thee: but I have known thee, and these have known that thou hast sent me.

26 And I have declared unto them thy name, and will declare *it:* that the love wherewith thou hast loved me may be in them, and I in them.

CHAPTER 18

WHEN Yashiyah had spoken these words, he went forth with his disciples over the brook Cedron, where was a garden, into the which he entered, and his disciples.

2 And Judas also, which betrayed him, knew the place: for Yashiyah ofttimes resorted thither with his disciples.

3 Judas then, having received a band *of men* and officers from the chief priests and Pharisees, cometh thither with lanterns and torches and weapons.

4 Yashiyah therefore, knowing all things that should come upon him, went forth, and said unto them, Whom seek ye?

5 They answered him, Yashiyah of Nazareth. Yashiyah saith unto them, I am *he*. And Judas also, which betrayed him, stood with them.

6 As soon then as he had said unto them, I am *he*, they went backward, and fell to the ground.

7 Then asked he them again, Whom seek ye? And they said, Yashiyah of Nazareth.

8 Yashiyah answered, I have told you that I am *he:* if therefore ye seek me, let these go their way:

9 That the saying might be fulfilled, which he spake, Of them which thou gavest me have I lost none.

10 Then Simon Peter having a sword drew it, and smote the high priest's servant, and cut off his right ear. The servant's name was Malchus.

11 Then said Yashiyah unto Peter, Put up thy sword into the sheath: the cup which my Father hath given me, shall I not drink it?

12 Then the band and the captain and officers of the Jews took Yashiyah, and bound him,

13 And led him away to Annas first; for he was father in law to Caiaphas, which was the high priest that same year.

14 Now Caiaphas was he, which gave counsel to the Jews, that it was expedient that one man should die for the people.

15 ¶ And Simon Peter followed Yashiyah, and *so did* another disciple: that disciple was known unto the high priest, and went in with Yashiyah into the palace of the high priest.

16 But Peter stood at the door without. Then went out that other disciple, which was known unto the high priest, and spake unto her that kept the door, and brought in Peter.

17 Then saith the damsel that kept the door unto Peter, Art not thou also *one* of this man's disciples? He saith, I am not.

18 And the servants and officers stood there, who had made a fire of coals; for it was cold: and they warmed themselves: and Peter stood with them, and warmed himself.

19 ¶ The high priest then asked Yashiyah of his disciples, and of his doctrine.

20 Yashiyah answered him, I spake openly to the world; I ever taught in the synagogue, and in the temple, whither the Jews always resort; and in secret have I said nothing.

21 Why askest thou me? ask them which heard me, what I have said unto them: behold, they know what I said.

22 And when he had thus spoken, one of the officers which stood by struck Yashiyah with the palm of his hand, saying, Answerest thou the high priest so?

23 Yashiyah answered him, If I have spoken evil, bear witness of the evil: but if well, why smitest thou me?

24 Now Annas had sent him bound unto Caiaphas the high priest.

25 And Simon Peter stood and warmed himself. They said therefore unto him, Art not thou also *one* of his disciples? He denied *it*, and said, I am not.

26 One of the servants of the high priest, being *his* kinsman whose ear Peter cut off, saith, Did not I see thee in the garden with him?

27 Peter then denied again: and immediately the cock crew.

28 ¶ Then led they Yashiyah from Caiaphas unto the hall of judgment: and it was early; and they themselves went not into the judgment hall, lest they should be defiled; but that they might eat the passover.

29 Pilate then went out unto them, and said, What accusation bring ye against this man?

30 They answered and said unto him, If he were not a malefactor, we would not have delivered him up unto thee.

31 Then said Pilate unto them, Take ye him, and judge him according to your law. The Jews therefore said unto him, It is not lawful for us to put any man to death:

32 That the saying of Yashiyah might be fulfilled, which he spake, signifying what death he should die.

33 Then Pilate entered into the judgment hall again, and called Yashiyah, and said unto him, Art thou the King of the Jews?

34 Yashiyah answered him, Sayest thou this thing of thyself, or did others tell it thee of me?

35 Pilate answered, Am I a Jew? Thine own nation and the chief priests have delivered thee unto me: what hast thou done?

36 Yashiyah answered, My kingdom is not of this world: if my kingdom were of this world, then would my servants fight, that I should not be delivered to the Jews: but now is my kingdom not from hence.

37 Pilate therefore said unto him, Art thou a king then? Yashiyah answered, Thou sayest that I am a king. To this end was I born, and for this cause came I into the world, that I should bear witness unto the truth. Every one that is of the truth heareth my voice.

38 Pilate saith unto him, What is truth? And when he had said this, he went out again unto the Jews, and saith unto them, I find in him no fault *at all*.

39 But ye have a custom, that I should release unto you one at the passover: will ye therefore that I release unto you the King of the Jews?

40 Then cried they all again, saying, Not this man, but Barabbas. Now Barabbas was a robber.

CHAPTER 19

THEN Pilate therefore took Yashiyah, and scourged *him*.

2 And the soldiers platted a crown of thorns, and put *it* on his head, and they put on him a purple robe,

3 And said, Hail, King of the Jews! and they smote him with their hands.

4 Pilate therefore went forth again, and saith unto them, Behold, I bring him forth to you, that ye may know that I find no fault in him.

5 Then came Yashiyah forth, wearing the crown of thorns, and the purple robe. And *Pilate* saith unto them, Behold the man!

6 When the chief priests therefore and officers saw him, they cried out, saying, Crucify *him*, crucify *him*. Pilate saith unto them, Take ye him, and crucify *him*: for I find no fault in him.

7 The Jews answered him, We have a law, and by our law he ought to die, because he made himself the Son of אֱלֹהִים.

8 ¶ When Pilate therefore heard that saying, he was the more afraid;

9 And went again into the judgment hall, and saith unto Yashiyah, Whence art thou? But Yashiyah gave him no answer.

10 Then saith Pilate unto him, Speakest thou not unto me? knowest thou not that I have power to crucify thee, and have power to release thee?

11 Yashiyah answered, Thou couldest have no power *at all* against me, except it were given thee from above: therefore he that delivered me unto thee hath the greater sin.

12 And from thenceforth Pilate sought to release him: but the Jews cried out, saying, If thou let this man go, thou art not Cæsar's friend: whosoever maketh himself a king speaketh against Cæsar.

13 ¶ When Pilate therefore heard that saying, he brought Yashiyah forth, and sat down in the judgment seat in a place that is called the Pavement, but in the Hebrew, Gabbatha.

14 And it was the preparation of the passover, and about the sixth hour: and he saith unto the Jews, Behold your King!

15 But they cried out, Away with *him*, away with *him*, crucify him. Pilate saith unto them, Shall I crucify your King? The chief priests answered, We have no king but Cæsar.

16 Then delivered he him therefore unto them to be crucified. And they took Yashiyah, and led *him* away.

17 And he bearing his cross went forth into a place called *the place* of a skull, which is called in the Hebrew Golgotha:

18 Where they crucified him, and two other with him, on either side one, and Yashiyah in the midst.

19 ¶ And Pilate wrote a title, and put *it* on the cross. And the writing was, JESUS OF NAZARETH THE KING OF THE JEWS.

20 This title then read many of the Jews: for the place where Yashiyah was crucified was nigh to the city: and it was written in Hebrew, *and* Greek, *and* Latin.

21 Then said the chief priests of the Jews to Pilate, Write not, The King of the Jews; but that he said, I am King of the Jews.

22 Pilate answered, What I have written I have written.

23 ¶ Then the soldiers, when they had crucified Yashiyah, took his garments, and made four parts, to every soldier a part; and also *his* coat: now the coat was without seam, woven from the top throughout.

24 They said therefore among themselves, Let us not rend it, but cast lots for it, whose it shall be: that the scripture might be fulfilled, which saith, They parted my raiment among them, and for my vesture they did cast lots. These things therefore the soldiers did.

25 ¶ Now there stood by the cross of Yashiyah his mother, and his mother's sister, Mary the *wife* of Cleophas, and Mary Magdalene.

26 When Yashiyah therefore saw his mother, and the disciple standing by, whom he loved, he saith unto his mother, Woman, behold thy son!

27 Then saith he to the disciple, Behold thy mother! And from that hour that disciple took her unto his own *home.*

28 ¶ After this, Yashiyah knowing that all things were now accomplished, that the scripture might be fulfilled, saith, I thirst.

29 Now there was set a vessel full of vinegar: and they filled a spunge with vinegar, and put *it* upon hyssop, and put *it* to his mouth.

30 When Yashiyah therefore had received the vinegar, he said, It is finished: and he bowed his head, and gave up the ghost.

31 The Jews therefore, because it was the preparation, that the bodies should not remain upon the cross on the sabbath day, (for that sabbath day was an high day,) besought Pilate that their legs might be broken, and *that* they might be taken away.

32 Then came the soldiers, and brake the legs of the first, and of the other which was crucified with him.

33 But when they came to Yashiyah, and saw that he was dead already, they brake not his legs:

34 But one of the soldiers with a spear pierced his side, and forthwith came there out blood and water.

35 And he that saw *it* bare record, and his record is true: and he knoweth that he saith true, that ye might believe.

36 For these things were done, that the scripture should be fulfilled, A bone of him shall not be broken.

37 And again another scripture saith, They shall look on him whom they pierced.

38 ¶ And after this Joseph of Arimathæa, being a disciple of Yashiyah, but secretly for fear of the Jews, besought Pilate that he might take away the body of Yashiyah: and Pilate gave *him* leave. He came therefore, and took the body of Yashiyah.

39 And there came also Nicodemus, which at the first came to Yashiyah by night, and brought a mixture of myrrh and aloes, about an hundred pound *weight.*

40 Then took they the body of Yashiyah, and wound it in linen clothes with the spices, as the manner of the Jews is to bury.

41 Now in the place where he was crucified there was a garden; and in the garden a new sepulchre, wherein was never man yet laid.

42 There laid they Yashiyah therefore because of the Jews' preparation *day:* for the sepulchre was nigh at hand.

CHAPTER 20

THE first *day* of the week cometh Mary Magdalene early, when it was yet dark, unto the sepulchre, and seeth the stone taken away from the sepulchre.

2 Then she runneth, and cometh to Simon Peter, and to the other disciple, whom Yashiyah loved, and saith unto them, They have taken away the Lord out of the sepulchre, and we know not where they have laid him.

3 Peter therefore went forth, and that other disciple, and came to the sepulchre.

4 So they ran both together: and the other disciple did outrun Peter, and came first to the sepulchre.

5 And he stooping down, *and looking in,* saw the linen clothes lying; yet went he not in.

6 Then cometh Simon Peter following him, and went into the sepulchre, and seeth the linen clothes lie,

7 And the napkin, that was about his head, not lying with the linen clothes, but wrapped together in a place by itself.

8 Then went in also that other disciple, which came first to the sepulchre, and he saw, and believed.

9 For as yet they knew not the scripture, that he must rise again from the dead.

10 Then the disciples went away again unto their own home.

11 ¶ But Mary stood without at the sepulchre weeping: and as she wept, she stooped down, *and looked* into the sepulchre,

12 And seeth two angels in white sitting, the one at the head, and the other at the feet, where the body of Yashiyah had lain.

13 And they say unto her, Woman, why weepest thou? She saith unto them, Because they have taken away my Lord, and I know not where they have laid him.

14 And when she had thus said, she turned herself back, and saw Yashiyah standing, and knew not that it was Yashiyah.

15 Yashiyah saith unto her, Woman, why weepest thou? whom seekest thou? She, supposing him to be the gardener, saith unto him, Sir, if thou have borne him hence, tell me where thou hast laid him, and I will take him away.

16 Yashiyah saith unto her, Mary. She turned herself, and saith unto him, Rabboni; which is to say, Master.

17 Yashiyah saith unto her, Touch me not; for I am not yet ascended to my Father: but go to my brethren, and say unto them, I ascend unto my Father, and your Father; and *to* my אֱלֹהִים, and your אֱלֹהִים.

18 Mary Magdalene came and told the disciples that she had seen the Lord, and *that* he had spoken these things unto her.

19 ¶ Then the same day at evening, being the first *day* of the week, when the doors were shut where the disciples were assembled for fear of the Jews, came Yashiyah and stood in the midst, and saith unto them, Peace *be* unto you.

20 And when he had so said, he shewed unto them *his* hands and his side. Then were the disciples glad, when they saw the Lord.

21 Then said Yashiyah to them again, Peace *be* unto you: as *my* Father hath sent me, even so send I you.

22 And when he had said this, he breathed on *them,* and saith unto them, Receive ye the Holy Ghost:

23 Whose soever sins ye remit, they are remitted unto them; *and* whose soever *sins* ye retain, they are retained.

24 ¶ But Thomas, one of the twelve, called Didymus, was not with them when Yashiyah came.

25 The other disciples therefore said unto him, We have seen the Lord. But he said unto them, Except I shall see in his hands the print of the nails, and put my finger into the print of the nails, and thrust my hand into his side, I will not believe.

26 ¶ And after eight days again his disciples were within, and Thomas with them: *then* came Yashiyah, the doors being shut, and stood in the midst, and said, Peace *be* unto you.

27 Then saith he to Thomas, Reach hither thy finger, and behold my hands; and reach hither thy hand, and thrust *it* into my side: and be not faithless, but believing.

28 And Thomas answered and said unto him, My Lord and my אֱלֹהִים.

29 Yashiyah saith unto him, Thomas, because thou hast seen me, thou hast believed: blessed *are* they that have not seen, and *yet* have believed.

30 ¶ And many other signs truly did Yashiyah in the presence of his disciples, which are not written in this book:

31 But these are written, that ye might believe that Yashiyah is the Christ, the Son of אֱלֹהִים; and that believing ye might have life through his name.

AFTER these things Yashiyah shewed himself again to the disciples at the sea of Tiberias; and on this wise shewed he *himself.*

2 There were together Simon Peter, and Thomas called Didymus, and Nathanael of Cana in Galilee, and the *sons* of Zebedee, and two other of his disciples.

3 Simon Peter saith unto them, I go a fishing. They say unto him, We also go with thee. They went forth, and entered into a ship immediately; and that night they caught nothing.

4 But when the morning was now come, Yashiyah stood on the shore: but the disciples knew not that it was Yashiyah.

5 Then Yashiyah saith unto them, Children, have ye any meat? They answered him, No.

6 And he said unto them, Cast the net on the right side of the ship, and ye shall find. They cast therefore, and now they were not able to draw it for the multitude of fishes.

7 Therefore that disciple whom Yashiyah loved saith unto Peter, It is the Lord. Now when Simon Peter heard that it was the Lord, he girt *his* fisher's coat *unto him,* (for he was naked,) and did cast himself into the sea.

8 And the other disciples came in a little ship; (for they were not far from land, but as it were two hundred cubits,) dragging the net with fishes.

9 As soon then as they were come to land, they saw a fire of coals there, and fish laid thereon, and bread.

10 Yashiyah saith unto them, Bring of the fish which ye have now caught.

11 Simon Peter went up, and drew the net to land full of great fishes, an hundred and fifty and three: and for all there were so many, yet was not the net broken.

12 Yashiyah saith unto them, Come *and* dine. And none of the disciples durst ask him, Who art thou? knowing that it was the Lord.

13 Yashiyah then cometh, and taketh bread, and giveth them, and fish likewise.

14 This is now the third time that Yashiyah shewed himself to his disciples, after that he was risen from the dead.

15 ¶ So when they had dined, Yashiyah saith to Simon Peter, Simon, *son* of Jonas, lovest thou me more than these? He saith unto him, Yea, Lord; thou knowest that I love thee. He saith unto him, Feed my lambs.

16 He saith to him again the second time, Simon, *son* of Jonas, lovest thou me? He saith unto him, Yea, Lord; thou knowest that I love thee. He saith unto him, Feed my sheep.

17 He saith unto him the third time, Simon, *son* of Jonas, lovest thou me? Peter was grieved because he said unto him the third time, Lovest thou me? And he said unto him, Lord, thou knowest all things; thou knowest that I love thee. Yashiyah saith unto him, Feed my sheep.

18 Verily, verily, I say unto thee, When thou wast young, thou girdedst thyself, and walkedst whither thou wouldest: but when thou shalt be old, thou shalt stretch forth thy hands, and another shall gird thee, and carry *thee* whither thou wouldest not.

19 This spake he, signifying by what death he should glorify אֱלֹהִים. And when he had spoken this, he saith unto him, Follow me.

20 Then Peter, turning about, seeth the disciple whom Yashiyah loved following; which also leaned on his breast at supper, and said, Lord, which is he that betrayeth thee?

21 Peter seeing him saith to Yashiyah, Lord, and what *shall* this man *do?*

22 Yashiyah saith unto him, If I will that he tarry till I come, what *is that* to thee? follow thou me.

23 Then went this saying abroad among the brethren, that that disciple should not die: yet Yashiyah said not unto him, He shall not die; but, If I will that he tarry till I come, what *is that* to thee?

24 This is the disciple which testifieth of these things, and wrote these things: and we know that his testimony is true.

25 And there are also many other things which Yashiyah did, the which, if they should be written every one, I suppose that even the world itself could not contain the books that should be written. Amen.

THE
ACTS OF THE APOSTLES.

CHAPTER 1

THE former treatise have I made, O Theophilus, of all that Yashiyah began both to do and teach,

2 Until the day in which he was taken up, after that he through the Holy Ghost had given commandments unto the apostles whom he had chosen:

3 To whom also he shewed himself alive after his passion by many infallible proofs, being seen of them forty days, and speaking of the things pertaining to the kingdom of אֱלֹהִים:

4 And, being assembled together with *them,* commanded them that they should not depart from Jerusalem, but wait for the promise of the Father, which, *saith he,* ye have heard of me.

5 For John truly baptized with water; but ye shall be baptized with the Holy Ghost not many days hence.

6 When they therefore were come together, they asked of him, saying, Lord, wilt thou at this time restore again the kingdom to Israel?

7 And he said unto them, It is not for you to know the times or the seasons, which the Father hath put in his own power.

8 But ye shall receive power, after that the Holy Ghost is come upon you: and ye shall be witnesses unto me both in Jerusalem, and in all Judæa, and in Samaria, and unto the uttermost part of the earth.

9 And when he had spoken these things, while they beheld, he was taken up; and a cloud received him out of their sight.

10 And while they looked stedfastly toward heaven as he went up, behold, two men stood by them in white apparel;

11 Which also said, Ye men of Galilee, why stand ye gazing up into heaven? this same Yashiyah, which is taken up from you into heaven, shall so come in like manner as ye have seen him go into heaven.

12 Then returned they unto Jerusalem from the mount called Olivet, which is from Jerusalem a sabbath day's journey.

13 And when they were come in, they went up into an upper room, where abode both Peter, and James, and John, and Andrew, Philip, and Thomas, Bartholomew, and Matthew, James *the son* of Alphæus, and Simon Zelotes, and Judas *the brother* of James.

14 These all continued with one accord in prayer and supplication, with the women, and Mary the mother of Yashiyah, and with his brethren.

15 ¶ And in those days Peter stood up in the midst of the disciples, and said, (the number of names together were about an hundred and twenty,)

16 Men *and* brethren, this scripture must needs have been fulfilled, which the Holy Ghost by the mouth of David spake before concerning Judas, which was guide to them that took Yashiyah.

17 For he was numbered with us, and had obtained part of this ministry.

18 Now this man purchased a field with the reward of iniquity; and falling headlong, he burst asunder in the midst, and all his bowels gushed out.

19 And it was known unto all the dwellers at Jerusalem; insomuch as that field is called in their proper tongue, Aceldama, that is to say, The field of blood.

20 For it is written in the book of Psalms, Let his habitation be desolate, and let no man dwell therein: and his bishoprick let another take.

21 Wherefore of these men which have companied with us all the time that the Lord Yashiyah went in and out among us,

22 Beginning from the baptism of John, unto that same day that he was taken up from us, must one be ordained to be a witness with us of his resurrection.

23 And they appointed two, Joseph called Barsabas, who was surnamed Justus, and Matthias.

24 And they prayed, and said, Thou, Lord, which knowest the hearts of all *men*, shew whether of these two thou hast chosen,

25 That he may take part of this ministry and apostleship, from which Judas by transgression fell, that he might go to his own place.

26 And they gave forth their lots; and the lot fell upon Matthias; and he was numbered with the eleven apostles.

CHAPTER 2

AND when the day of Pentecost was fully come, they were all with one accord in one place.

2 And suddenly there came a sound from heaven as of a rushing mighty wind, and it filled all the house where they were sitting.

3 And there appeared unto them cloven tongues like as of fire, and it sat upon each of them.

4 And they were all filled with the Holy Ghost, and began to speak with other tongues, as the Spirit gave them utterance.

5 And there were dwelling at Jerusalem Jews, devout men, out of every nation under heaven.

6 Now when this was noised abroad, the multitude came together, and were confounded, because that every man heard them speak in his own language.

7 And they were all amazed and marvelled, saying one to another, Behold, are not all these which speak Galilæans?

8 And how hear we every man in our own tongue, wherein we were born?

9 Parthians, and Medes, and Elamites, and the dwellers in Mesopotamia, and in Judæa, and Cappadocia, in Pontus, and Asia,

10 Phrygia, and Pamphylia, in Egypt, and in the parts of Libya about Cyrene, and strangers of Rome, Jews and proselytes,

11 Cretes and Arabians, we do hear them speak in our tongues the wonderful works of אֱלֹהִים.

12 And they were all amazed, and were in doubt, saying one to another, What meaneth this?

13 Others mocking said, These men are full of new wine.

14 ¶ But Peter, standing up with the eleven, lifted up his voice, and said unto them, Ye men of Judæa, and all *ye* that dwell at Jerusalem, be this known unto you, and hearken to my words:

15 For these are not drunken, as ye suppose, seeing it is *but* the third hour of the day.

16 But this is that which was spoken by the prophet Joel;

17 And it shall come to pass in the last days, saith אֱלֹהִים, I will pour out of my Spirit upon all flesh: and your sons and your daughters shall prophesy, and your young men shall see visions, and your old men shall dream dreams:

18 And on my servants and on my handmaidens I will pour out in those days of my Spirit; and they shall prophesy:

19 And I will shew wonders in heaven above, and signs in the earth beneath; blood, and fire, and vapour of smoke:

20 The sun shall be turned into darkness, and the moon into blood, before that great and notable day of the Lord come:

21 And it shall come to pass, *that* whosoever shall call on the name of the Lord shall be saved.

22 Ye men of Israel, hear these words; Yashiyah of Nazareth, a man approved of אֱלֹהִים among you by miracles and wonders and signs, which אֱלֹהִים did by him in the midst of you, as ye yourselves also know:

23 Him, being delivered by the determinate counsel and foreknowledge of אֱלֹהִים, ye have taken, and by wicked hands have crucified and slain:

24 Whom אֱלֹהִים hath raised up, having loosed the pains of death: because it was not possible that he should be holden of it.

25 For David speaketh concerning him, I foresaw the Lord always before my face, for he is on my right hand, that I should not be moved:

26 Therefore did my heart rejoice, and my tongue was glad; moreover also my flesh shall rest in hope:

27 Because thou wilt not leave my soul in hell, neither wilt thou suffer thine Holy One to see corruption.

28 Thou hast made known to me the ways of life; thou shalt make me full of joy with thy countenance.

29 Men *and* brethren, let me freely speak unto you of the patriarch David, that he is both dead and buried, and his sepulchre is with us unto this day.

30 Therefore being a prophet, and knowing that אֱלֹהִים had sworn with an oath to him, that of the fruit of his loins, according to the flesh, he would raise up Christ to sit on his throne;

31 He seeing this before spake of the resurrection of Christ, that his soul was not left in hell, neither his flesh did see corruption.

32 This Yashiyah hath אֱלֹהִים raised up, whereof we all are witnesses.

33 Therefore being by the right hand of אֱלֹהִים exalted, and having received of the Father the promise of the Holy Ghost, he hath shed forth this, which ye now see and hear.

34 For David is not ascended into the heavens: but he saith himself, The LORD said unto my Lord, Sit thou on my right hand,

35 Until I make thy foes thy footstool.

36 Therefore let all the house of Israel know assuredly, that אֱלֹהִים hath made that same Yashiyah, whom ye have crucified, both Lord and Christ.

37 ¶ Now when they heard *this*, they were pricked in their heart, and said unto Peter and to the rest of the apostles, Men *and* brethren, what shall we do?

38 Then Peter said unto them, Repent, and be baptized every one of you in the name of Yashiyah Christ for the remission of sins, and ye shall receive the gift of the Holy Ghost.

39 For the promise is unto you, and to your children, and to all that are afar off, *even* as many as the Lord our אֱלֹהִים shall call.

40 And with many other words did he testify and exhort, saying, Save yourselves from this untoward generation.

41 ¶ Then they that gladly received his word were baptized: and the same day there were added *unto them* about three thousand souls.

42 And they continued stedfastly in the apostles' doctrine and fellowship, and in breaking of bread, and in prayers.

43 And fear came upon every soul: and many wonders and signs were done by the apostles.

44 And all that believed were together, and had all things common;

45 And sold their possessions and goods, and parted them to all *men*, as every man had need.

46 And they, continuing daily with one accord in the temple, and breaking bread from house to house, did eat their meat with gladness and singleness of heart,

47 Praising אֱלֹהִים, and having favour with all the people. And the Lord added to the church daily such as should be saved.

CHAPTER 3

NOW Peter and John went up together into the temple at the hour of prayer, *being* the ninth *hour*.

2 And a certain man lame from his mother's womb was carried, whom they laid daily at the gate of the temple which is called Beautiful, to ask alms of them that entered into the temple;

3 Who seeing Peter and John about to go into the temple asked an alms.

4 And Peter, fastening his eyes upon him with John, said, Look on us.

5 And he gave heed unto them, expecting to receive something of them.

6 Then Peter said, Silver and gold have I none; but such as I have give I thee: In the name of Yashiyah Christ of Nazareth rise up and walk.

7 And he took him by the right hand, and lifted *him* up: and immediately his feet and ancle bones received strength.

8 And he leaping up stood, and walked, and entered with them into the temple, walking, and leaping, and praising אֱלֹהִים.

9 And all the people saw him walking and praising אֱלֹהִים:

10 And they knew that it was he which sat for alms at the Beautiful gate of the temple: and they were filled with wonder and amazement at that which had happened unto him.

11 And as the lame man which was healed held Peter and John, all the people ran together unto them in the porch that is called Solomon's, greatly wondering.

12 ¶ And when Peter saw *it*, he answered unto the people, Ye men of Israel, why marvel ye at this? or why look ye so earnestly on us, as though by our own power or holiness we had made this man to walk?

13 The אֱלֹהִים of Abraham, and of Isaac, and of Jacob, the אֱלֹהִים of our fathers, hath glorified his Son Yashiyah; whom ye delivered up, and denied him in the presence of Pilate, when he was determined to let *him* go.

14 But ye denied the Holy One and the Just, and desired a murderer to be granted unto you;

15 And killed the Prince of life, whom אֱלֹהִים hath raised from the dead; whereof we are witnesses.

16 And his name through faith in his name hath made this man strong, whom ye see and know: yea, the faith which is by him hath given him this perfect soundness in the presence of you all.

17 And now, brethren, I wot that through ignorance ye did *it*, as *did* also your rulers.

18 But those things, which אֱלֹהִים before had shewed by the mouth of all his prophets, that Christ should suffer, he hath so fulfilled.

19 ¶ Repent ye therefore, and be converted, that your sins may be blotted out, when the times of refreshing shall come from the presence of the Lord;

20 And he shall send Yashiyah Christ, which before was preached unto you:

21 Whom the heaven must receive until the times of restitution of all things, which אֱלֹהִים hath spoken by the mouth of all his holy prophets since the world began.

22 For Moses truly said unto the fathers, A prophet shall the Lord your אֱלֹהִים raise up unto you of your brethren, like unto me; him shall ye hear in all things whatsoever he shall say unto you.

23 And it shall come to pass, *that* every soul, which will not hear that prophet, shall be destroyed from among the people.

24 Yea, and all the prophets from Samuel and those that follow after, as many as have spoken, have likewise foretold of these days.

25 Ye are the children of the prophets, and of the covenant which אֱלֹהִים made with our fathers, saying unto Abraham, And in thy seed shall all the kindreds of the earth be blessed.

26 Unto you first אֱלֹהִים, having raised up his Son Yashiyah, sent him to bless you, in turning away every one of you from his iniquities.

CHAPTER 4

AND as they spake unto the people, the priests, and the captain of the temple, and the Sadducees, came upon them,

2 Being grieved that they taught the people, and preached through Yashiyah the resurrection from the dead.

3 And they laid hands on them, and put *them* in hold unto the next day: for it was now eventide.

4 Howbeit many of them which heard the word believed; and the number of the men was about five thousand.

5 ¶ And it came to pass on the morrow, that their rulers, and elders, and scribes,

6 And Annas the high priest, and Caiaphas, and John, and Alexander, and as many as were of the kindred of the high priest, were gathered together at Jerusalem.

7 And when they had set them in the midst, they asked, By what power, or by what name, have ye done this?

8 Then Peter, filled with the Holy Ghost, said unto them, Ye rulers of the people, and elders of Israel,

9 If we this day be examined of the good deed done to the impotent man, by what means he is made whole;

10 Be it known unto you all, and to all the people of Israel, that by the name of Yashiyah Christ of Nazareth, whom ye crucified, whom אֱלֹהִים raised from the dead, *even* by him doth this man stand here before you whole.

11 This is the stone which was set at nought of you builders, which is become the head of the corner.

12 Neither is there salvation in any other: for there is none other name under heaven given among men, whereby we must be saved.

13 ¶ Now when they saw the boldness of Peter and John, and perceived that they were unlearned and ignorant men, they marvelled; and they took knowledge of them, that they had been with Yashiyah.

14 And beholding the man which was healed standing with them, they could say nothing against it.

15 But when they had commanded them to go aside out of the council, they conferred among themselves,

16 Saying, What shall we do to these men? for that indeed a notable miracle hath been done by them *is* manifest to all them that dwell in Jerusalem; and we cannot deny *it*.

17 But that it spread no further among the people, let us straitly threaten them, that they speak henceforth to no man in this name.

18 And they called them, and commanded them not to speak at all nor teach in the name of Yashiyah.

19 But Peter and John answered and said unto them, Whether it be right in the sight of אֱלֹהִים to hearken unto you more than unto אֱלֹהִים, judge ye.

20 For we cannot but speak the things which we have seen and heard.

21 So when they had further threatened them, they let them go, finding nothing how they might punish them, because of the people: for all *men* glorified אֱלֹהִים for that which was done.

22 For the man was above forty years old, on whom this miracle of healing was shewed.

23 ¶ And being let go, they went to their own company, and reported all that the chief priests and elders had said unto them.

24 And when they heard that, they lifted up their voice to אֱלֹהִים with one accord, and said, Lord, thou *art* אֱלֹהִים, which hast made heaven, and earth, and the sea, and all that in them is:

25 Who by the mouth of thy servant David hast said, Why did the heathen rage, and the people imagine vain things?

26 The kings of the earth stood up, and the rulers were gathered together against the Lord, and against his Christ.

27 For of a truth against thy holy child Yashiyah, whom thou hast anointed, both Herod, and Pontius Pilate, with the Gentiles, and the people of Israel, were gathered together,

28 For to do whatsoever thy hand and thy counsel determined before to be done.

29 And now, Lord, behold their threatenings: and grant unto thy servants, that with all boldness they may speak thy word,

30 By stretching forth thine hand to heal; and that signs and wonders may be done by the name of thy holy child Yashiyah.

31 ¶ And when they had prayed, the place was shaken where they were assembled together; and they were all filled with the Holy Ghost, and they spake the word of אֱלֹהִים with boldness.

32 And the multitude of them that believed were of one heart and of one soul: neither said any *of them* that ought of the things which he possessed was his own; but they had all things common.

33 And with great power gave the apostles witness of the resurrection of the Lord Yashiyah: and great grace was upon them all.

34 Neither was there any among them that lacked: for as many as were possessors of lands or houses sold them, and brought the prices of the things that were sold,

35 And laid *them* down at the apostles' feet: and distribution was made unto every man according as he had need.

36 And Joses, who by the apostles was surnamed Barnabas, (which is, being interpreted, The son of consolation,) a Levite, *and* of the country of Cyprus,

37 Having land, sold *it*, and brought the money, and laid *it* at the apostles' feet.

CHAPTER 5

BUT a certain man named Ananias, with Sapphira his wife, sold a possession,

2 And kept back *part* of the price, his wife also being privy *to it*, and brought a certain part, and laid *it* at the apostles' feet.

3 But Peter said, Ananias, why hath Satan filled thine heart to lie to the Holy Ghost, and to keep back *part* of the price of the land?

4 Whiles it remained, was it not thine own? and after it was sold, was it not in thine own power? why hast thou conceived this thing in thine heart? thou hast not lied unto men, but unto אֱלֹהִים.

5 And Ananias hearing these words fell down, and gave up the ghost: and great fear came on all them that heard these things.

6 And the young men arose, wound him up, and carried *him* out, and buried *him*.

7 And it was about the space of three hours after, when his wife, not knowing what was done, came in.

8 And Peter answered unto her, Tell me whether ye sold the land for so much? And she said, Yea, for so much.

9 Then Peter said unto her, How is it that ye have agreed together to tempt the Spirit of the Lord? behold, the feet of them which have buried thy husband *are* at the door, and shall carry thee out.

10 Then fell she down straightway at his feet, and yielded up the ghost: and the young men came in, and found her dead, and, carrying *her* forth, buried *her* by her husband.

11 And great fear came upon all the church, and upon as many as heard these things.

12 ¶ And by the hands of the apostles were many signs and wonders wrought among the people; (and they were all with one accord in Solomon's porch.

13 And of the rest durst no man join himself to them: but the people magnified them.

14 And believers were the more added to the Lord, multitudes both of men and women.)

15 Insomuch that they brought forth the sick into the streets, and laid *them* on beds and couches, that at the least the shadow of Peter passing by might overshadow some of them.

16 There came also a multitude *out* of the cities round about unto Jerusalem, bringing sick folks, and them which were vexed with unclean spirits: and they were healed every one.

17 ¶ Then the high priest rose up, and all they that were with him, (which is the sect of the Sadducees,) and were filled with indignation,

18 And laid their hands on the apostles, and put them in the common prison.

19 But the angel of the Lord by night opened the prison doors, and brought them forth, and said,

20 Go, stand and speak in the temple to the people all the words of this life.

21 And when they heard *that*, they entered into the temple early in the morning, and taught. But the high priest came, and they that were with him, and called the council together, and all the senate of the children of Israel, and sent to the prison to have them brought.

22 But when the officers came, and found them not in the prison, they returned, and told,

23 Saying, The prison truly found we shut with all safety, and the keepers standing without before the doors: but when we had opened, we found no man within.

24 Now when the high priest and the captain of the temple and the chief priests heard these things, they doubted of them whereunto this would grow.

25 Then came one and told them, saying, Behold, the men whom ye put in prison are standing in the temple, and teaching the people.

26 Then went the captain with the officers, and brought them without violence: for they feared the people, lest they should have been stoned.

27 And when they had brought them, they set *them* before the council: and the high priest asked them,

28 Saying, Did not we straitly command you that ye should not teach in this name? and, behold, ye have filled Jerusalem with your

doctrine, and intend to bring this man's blood upon us.

29 ¶ Then Peter and the *other* apostles answered and said, We ought to obey אֱלֹהִים rather than men.

30 The אֱלֹהִים of our fathers raised up Yashiyah, whom ye slew and hanged on a tree.

31 Him hath אֱלֹהִים exalted with his right hand *to be* a Prince and a Saviour, for to give repentance to Israel, and forgiveness of sins.

32 And we are his witnesses of these things; and *so is* also the Holy Ghost, whom אֱלֹהִים hath given to them that obey him.

33 ¶ When they heard *that*, they were cut *to the heart*, and took counsel to slay them.

34 Then stood there up one in the council, a Pharisee, named Gamaliel, a doctor of the law, had in reputation among all the people, and commanded to put the apostles forth a little space;

35 And said unto them, Ye men of Israel, take heed to yourselves what ye intend to do as touching these men.

36 For before these days rose up Theudas, boasting himself to be somebody; to whom a number of men, about four hundred, joined themselves: who was slain; and all, as many as obeyed him, were scattered, and brought to nought.

37 After this man rose up Judas of Galilee in the days of the taxing, and drew away much people after him: he also perished; and all, *even* as many as obeyed him, were dispersed.

38 And now I say unto you, Refrain from these men, and let them alone: for if this counsel or this work be of men, it will come to nought:

39 But if it be of אֱלֹהִים, ye cannot overthrow it; lest haply ye be found even to fight against אֱלֹהִים.

40 And to him they agreed: and when they had called the apostles, and beaten *them*, they commanded that they should not speak in the name of Yashiyah, and let them go.

41 ¶ And they departed from the presence of the council, rejoicing that they were counted worthy to suffer shame for his name.

42 And daily in the temple, and in every house, they ceased not to teach and preach Yashiyah Christ.

CHAPTER 6

AND in those days, when the number of the disciples was multiplied, there arose a murmuring of the Grecians against the Hebrews, because their widows were neglected in the daily ministration.

2 Then the twelve called the multitude of the disciples *unto them*, and said, It is not reason that we should leave the word of אֱלֹהִים, and serve tables.

3 Wherefore, brethren, look ye out among you seven men of honest report, full of the Holy Ghost and wisdom, whom we may appoint over this business.

4 But we will give ourselves continually to prayer, and to the ministry of the word.

5 ¶ And the saying pleased the whole multitude: and they chose Stephen, a man full of faith and of the Holy Ghost, and Philip, and Prochorus, and Nicanor, and Timon, and Parmenas, and Nicolas a proselyte of Antioch:

6 Whom they set before the apostles: and when they had prayed, they laid *their* hands on them.

7 And the word of אֱלֹהִים increased; and the number of the disciples multiplied in Jerusalem greatly; and a great company of the priests were obedient to the faith.

8 And Stephen, full of faith and power, did great wonders and miracles among the people.

9 ¶ Then there arose certain of the synagogue, which is called *the synagogue* of the Libertines, and Cyrenians, and Alexandrians, and of them of Cilicia and of Asia, disputing with Stephen.

10 And they were not able to resist the wisdom and the spirit by which he spake.

11 Then they suborned men, which said, We have heard him speak blasphemous words against Moses, and *against* אֱלֹהִים.

12 And they stirred up the people, and the elders, and the scribes, and came upon *him*, and caught him, and brought *him* to the council,

13 And set up false witnesses, which said, This man ceaseth not to speak blasphemous words against this holy place, and the law:

14 For we have heard him say, that this Yashiyah of Nazareth shall destroy this place, and shall change the customs which Moses delivered us.

15 And all that sat in the council, looking stedfastly on him, saw his face as it had been the face of an angel.

CHAPTER 7

THEN said the high priest, Are these things so?

2 And he said, Men, brethren, and fathers, hearken; The אֱלֹהִים of glory appeared unto our father Abraham, when he was in Mesopotamia, before he dwelt in Charran,

3 And said unto him, Get thee out of thy country, and from thy kindred, and come into the land which I shall shew thee.

4 Then came he out of the land of the Chaldæans, and dwelt in Charran: and from thence, when his father was dead, he removed him into this land, wherein ye now dwell.

5 And he gave him none inheritance in it, no, not *so much as* to set his foot on: yet he promised that he would give it to him for a possession, and to his seed after him, when *as yet* he had no child.

6 And אֱלֹהִים spake on this wise, That his seed should sojourn in a strange land; and that they should bring them into bondage, and entreat *them* evil four hundred years.

7 And the nation to whom they shall be in bondage will I judge, said אֱלֹהִים: and after that shall they come forth, and serve me in this place.

8 And he gave him the covenant of circumcision: and so *Abraham* begat Isaac, and circumcised him the eighth day; and Isaac *begat* Jacob; and Jacob *begat* the twelve patriarchs.

9 And the patriarchs, moved with envy, sold Joseph into Egypt: but אֱלֹהִים was with him,

10 And delivered him out of all his afflictions, and gave him favour and wisdom in the sight of Pharaoh king of Egypt; and he made him governor over Egypt and all his house.

11 Now there came a dearth over all the land of Egypt and Chanaan, and great affliction: and our fathers found no sustenance.

12 But when Jacob heard that there was corn in Egypt, he sent out our fathers first.

13 And at the second *time* Joseph was made known to his brethren; and Joseph's kindred was made known unto Pharaoh.

14 Then sent Joseph, and called his father Jacob to *him*, and all his kindred, threescore and fifteen souls.

15 So Jacob went down into Egypt, and died, he, and our fathers,

16 And were carried over into Sychem, and laid in the sepulchre that Abraham bought for a sum of money of the sons of Emmor *the father* of Sychem.

17 But when the time of the promise drew nigh, which אֱלֹהִים had sworn to Abraham, the people grew and multiplied in Egypt,

18 Till another king arose, which knew not Joseph.

19 The same dealt subtilly with our kindred, and evil entreated our fathers, so that they cast out their young children, to the end they might not live.

20 In which time Moses was born, and was exceeding fair, and nourished up in his father's house three months:

21 And when he was cast out, Pharaoh's daughter took him up, and nourished him for her own son.

22 And Moses was learned in all the wisdom of the Egyptians, and was mighty in words and in deeds.

23 And when he was full forty years old, it came into his heart to visit his brethren the children of Israel.

24 And seeing one *of them* suffer wrong, he defended *him*, and avenged him that was oppressed, and smote the Egyptian:

25 For he supposed his brethren would have understood how that אֱלֹהִים by his hand would deliver them: but they understood not.

26 And the next day he shewed himself unto them as they strove, and would have set them at one again, saying, Sirs, ye are brethren; why do ye wrong one to another?

27 But he that did his neighbour wrong thrust him away, saying, Who made thee a ruler and a judge over us?

28 Wilt thou kill me, as thou diddest the Egyptian yesterday?

29 Then fled Moses at this saying, and was a stranger in the land of Madian, where he begat two sons.

30 And when forty years were expired, there appeared to him in the wilderness of mount Sina an angel of the Lord in a flame of fire in a bush.

31 When Moses saw *it*, he wondered at the sight: and as he drew near to behold *it*, the voice of the Lord came unto him,

32 *Saying*, I *am* the אֱלֹהִים of thy fathers, the אֱלֹהִים of Abraham, and the אֱלֹהִים of Isaac, and the אֱלֹהִים of Jacob. Then Moses trembled, and durst not behold.

33 Then said the Lord to him, Put off thy shoes from thy feet: for the place where thou standest is holy ground.

34 I have seen, I have seen the affliction of my people which is in Egypt, and I have heard their groaning, and am come down to deliver them. And now come, I will send thee into Egypt.

35 This Moses whom they refused, saying, Who made thee a ruler and a judge? the same did אֱלֹהִים send *to be* a ruler and a deliverer by the hand of the angel which appeared to him in the bush.

36 He brought them out, after that he had shewed wonders and signs in the land of Egypt, and in the Red sea, and in the wilderness forty years.

37 ¶ This is that Moses, which said unto the children of Israel, A prophet shall the Lord your אֱלֹהִים raise up unto you of your brethren, like unto me; him shall ye hear.

38 This is he, that was in the church in the wilderness with the angel which spake to him in the mount Sina, and *with* our fathers: who received the lively oracles to give unto us:

39 To whom our fathers would not obey, but thrust *him* from them, and in their hearts turned back again into Egypt,

40 Saying unto Aaron, Make us gods to go before us: for *as for* this Moses, which brought us out of the land of Egypt, we wot not what is become of him.

41 And they made a calf in those days, and offered sacrifice unto the idol, and rejoiced in the works of their own hands.

42 Then אֱלֹהִים turned, and gave them up to worship the host of heaven; as it is written in the book of the prophets, O ye house of Israel, have ye offered to me slain beasts and sacrifices *by the space of* forty years in the wilderness?

43 Yea, ye took up the tabernacle of Moloch, and the star of your god Remphan, figures which ye made to worship them: and I will carry you away beyond Babylon.

44 Our fathers had the tabernacle of witness in the wilderness, as he had appointed, speaking unto Moses, that he should make it according to the fashion that he had seen.

45 Which also our fathers that came after brought in with Yashiyah into the possession of the Gentiles, whom אֱלֹהִים drave out before the face of our fathers, unto the days of David;

46 Who found favour before אֱלֹהִים, and desired to find a tabernacle for the אֱלֹהִים of Jacob.

47 But Solomon built him an house.

48 Howbeit the most High dwelleth not in temples made with hands; as saith the prophet,

49 Heaven *is* my throne, and earth *is* my footstool: what house will ye build me? saith the Lord: or what *is* the place of my rest?

50 Hath not my hand made all these things?

51 ¶ Ye stiffnecked and uncircumcised in heart and ears, ye do always resist the Holy Ghost: as your fathers *did*, so *do* ye.

52 Which of the prophets have not your fathers persecuted? and they have slain them which shewed before of the coming of the Just One; of whom ye have been now the betrayers and murderers:

53 Who have received the law by the disposition of angels, and have not kept *it*.

54 ¶ When they heard these things, they were cut to the heart, and they gnashed on him with *their* teeth.

55 But he, being full of the Holy Ghost, looked up stedfastly into heaven, and saw the glory of אֱלֹהִים, and Yashiyah standing on the right hand of אֱלֹהִים,

56 And said, Behold, I see the heavens opened, and the Son of man standing on the right hand of אֱלֹהִים.

57 Then they cried out with a loud voice, and stopped their ears, and ran upon him with one accord,

58 And cast *him* out of the city, and stoned *him*: and the witnesses laid down their clothes at a young man's feet, whose name was Saul.

59 And they stoned Stephen, calling upon אֱלֹהִים, and saying, Lord Yashiyah, receive my spirit.

60 And he kneeled down, and cried with a loud voice, Lord, lay not this sin to their charge. And when he had said this, he fell asleep.

CHAPTER 8

AND Saul was consenting unto his death. And at that time there was a great persecution against the church which was at Jerusalem; and they were all scattered abroad throughout the regions of Judæa and Samaria, except the apostles.

2 And devout men carried Stephen *to his burial*, and made great lamentation over him.

3 As for Saul, he made havock of the church, entering into every house, and haling men and women committed *them* to prison.

4 Therefore they that were scattered abroad went every where preaching the word.

5 Then Philip went down to the city of Samaria, and preached Christ unto them.

6 And the people with one accord gave heed unto those things which Philip spake, hearing and seeing the miracles which he did.

7 For unclean spirits, crying with loud voice, came out of many that were possessed *with them*: and many taken with palsies, and that were lame, were healed.

8 And there was great joy in that city.

9 But there was a certain man, called Simon, which beforetime in the same city used sorcery, and bewitched the people of Samaria, giving out that himself was some great one:

10 To whom they all gave heed, from the least to the greatest, saying, This man is the great power of אֱלֹהִים.

11 And to him they had regard, because that of long time he had bewitched them with sorceries.

12 But when they believed Philip preaching the things concerning the kingdom of אֱלֹהִים, and the name of Yashiyah Christ, they were baptized, both men and women.

13 Then Simon himself believed also: and when he was baptized, he continued with Philip, and wondered, beholding the miracles and signs which were done.

14 Now when the apostles which were at Jerusalem heard that Samaria had received the word of אֱלֹהִים, they sent unto them Peter and John:

15 Who, when they were come down, prayed for them, that they might receive the Holy Ghost:

16 (For as yet he was fallen upon none of them: only they were baptized in the name of the Lord Yashiyah.)

17 Then laid they *their* hands on them, and they received the Holy Ghost.

18 And when Simon saw that through laying on of the apostles' hands the Holy Ghost was given, he offered them money,

19 Saying, Give me also this power, that on whomsoever I lay hands, he may receive the Holy Ghost.

20 But Peter said unto him, Thy money perish with thee, because thou hast thought that the gift of אֱלֹהִים may be purchased with money.

21 Thou hast neither part nor lot in this matter: for thy heart is not right in the sight of אֱלֹהִים.

22 Repent therefore of this thy wickedness, and pray אֱלֹהִים, if perhaps the thought of thine heart may be forgiven thee.

23 For I perceive that thou art in the gall of bitterness, and *in* the bond of iniquity.

24 Then answered Simon, and said, Pray ye to the Lord for me, that none of these things which ye have spoken come upon me.

25 And they, when they had testified and preached the word of the Lord, returned to Jerusalem, and preached the gospel in many villages of the Samaritans.

26 And the angel of the Lord spake unto Philip, saying, Arise, and go toward the south unto the way that goeth down from Jerusalem unto Gaza, which is desert.

27 And he arose and went: and, behold, a man of Ethiopia, an eunuch of great authority under Candace queen of the Ethiopians, who had the charge of all her treasure, and had come to Jerusalem for to worship,

28 Was returning, and sitting in his chariot read Esaias the prophet.

29 Then the Spirit said unto Philip, Go near, and join thyself to this chariot.

30 And Philip ran thither to *him*, and heard him read the prophet Esaias, and said, Understandest thou what thou readest?

31 And he said, How can I, except some man should guide me? And he desired Philip that he would come up and sit with him.

32 The place of the scripture which he read was this, He was led as a sheep to the slaughter; and like a lamb dumb before his shearer, so opened he not his mouth:

33 In his humiliation his judgment was taken away: and who shall declare his generation? for his life is taken from the earth.

34 And the eunuch answered Philip, and said, I pray thee, of whom speaketh the prophet this? of himself, or of some other man?

35 Then Philip opened his mouth, and began at the same scripture, and preached unto him Yashiyah.

36 And as they went on *their* way, they came unto a certain water: and the eunuch said, See, *here is* water; what doth hinder me to be baptized?

37 And Philip said, If thou believest with all thine heart, thou mayest. And he answered and said, I believe that Yashiyah Christ is the Son of אֱלֹהִים.

38 And he commanded the chariot to stand still: and they went down both into the water, both Philip and the eunuch; and he baptized him.

39 And when they were come up out of the water, the Spirit of the Lord caught away Philip, that the eunuch saw him no more: and he went on his way rejoicing.

40 But Philip was found at Azotus: and passing through he preached in all the cities, till he came to Cæsarea.

CHAPTER 9

AND Saul, yet breathing out threatenings and slaughter against the disciples of the Lord, went unto the high priest,

2 And desired of him letters to Damascus to the synagogues, that if he found any of this way, whether they were men or women, he might bring them bound unto Jerusalem.

3 And as he journeyed, he came near Damascus: and suddenly there shined round about him a light from heaven:

4 And he fell to the earth, and heard a voice saying unto him, Saul, Saul, why persecutest thou me?

5 And he said, Who art thou, Lord? And the Lord said, I am Yashiyah whom thou persecutest: *it is* hard for thee to kick against the pricks.

6 And he trembling and astonished said, Lord, what wilt thou have me to do? And the Lord *said* unto him, Arise, and go into the city, and it shall be told thee what thou must do.

7 And the men which journeyed with him stood speechless, hearing a voice, but seeing no man.

8 And Saul arose from the earth; and when his eyes were opened, he saw no man: but they led him by the hand, and brought *him* into Damascus.

9 And he was three days without sight, and neither did eat nor drink.

10 ¶ And there was a certain disciple at Damascus, named Ananias; and to him said the Lord in a vision, Ananias. And he said, Behold, I *am here*, Lord.

11 And the Lord *said* unto him, Arise, and go into the street which is called Straight, and inquire in the house of Judas for *one* called Saul, of Tarsus: for, behold, he prayeth,

12 And hath seen in a vision a man named Ananias coming in, and putting *his* hand on him, that he might receive his sight.

13 Then Ananias answered, Lord, I have heard by many of this man, how much evil he hath done to thy saints at Jerusalem:

14 And here he hath authority from the chief priests to bind all that call on thy name.

15 But the Lord said unto him, Go thy way: for he is a chosen vessel unto me, to bear my name before the Gentiles, and kings, and the children of Israel:

16 For I will shew him how great things he must suffer for my name's sake.

17 And Ananias went his way, and entered into the house; and putting his hands on him said, Brother Saul, the Lord, *even* Yashiyah, that appeared unto thee in the way as thou camest, hath sent me, that thou mightest receive thy sight, and be filled with the Holy Ghost.

18 And immediately there fell from his eyes as it had been scales: and he received sight forthwith, and arose, and was baptized.

19 And when he had received meat, he was strengthened. Then was Saul certain days with the disciples which were at Damascus.

20 And straightway he preached Christ in the synagogues, that he is the Son of אֱלֹהִים.

21 But all that heard *him* were amazed, and said; Is not this he that destroyed them which called on this name in Jerusalem, and came hither for that intent, that he might bring them bound unto the chief priests?

22 But Saul increased the more in strength, and confounded the Jews which dwelt at Damascus, proving that this is very Christ.

23 ¶ And after that many days were fulfilled, the Jews took counsel to kill him:

24 But their laying await was known of Saul. And they watched the gates day and night to kill him.

25 Then the disciples took him by night, and let *him* down by the wall in a basket.

26 And when Saul was come to Jerusalem, he assayed to join himself to the disciples: but they were all afraid of him, and believed not that he was a disciple.

27 But Barnabas took him, and brought *him* to the apostles, and declared unto them how he had seen the Lord in the way, and that he had spoken to him, and how he had preached boldly at Damascus in the name of Yashiyah.

28 And he was with them coming in and going out at Jerusalem.

29 And he spake boldly in the name of the Lord Yashiyah, and disputed against the Grecians: but they went about to slay him.

30 *Which* when the brethren knew, they brought him down to Cæsarea, and sent him forth to Tarsus.

31 Then had the churches rest throughout all Judæa and Galilee and Samaria, and were edified; and walking in the fear of the Lord, and in the comfort of the Holy Ghost, were multiplied.

32 ¶ And it came to pass, as Peter passed throughout all *quarters*, he came down also to the saints which dwelt at Lydda.

33 And there he found a certain man named Æneas, which had kept his bed eight years, and was sick of the palsy.

34 And Peter said unto him, Æneas, Yashiyah Christ maketh thee whole: arise, and make thy bed. And he arose immediately.

35 And all that dwelt at Lydda and Saron saw him, and turned to the Lord.

36 ¶ Now there was at Joppa a certain disciple named Tabitha, which by interpretation is called Dorcas: this woman was full of good works and almsdeeds which she did.

37 And it came to pass in those days, that she was sick, and died: whom when they had washed, they laid *her* in an upper chamber.

38 And forasmuch as Lydda was nigh to Joppa, and the disciples had heard that Peter was there, they sent unto him two men, desiring *him* that he would not delay to come to them.

39 Then Peter arose and went with them. When he was come, they brought him into the upper chamber: and all the widows stood by him weeping, and shewing the coats and garments which Dorcas made, while she was with them.

40 But Peter put them all forth, and kneeled down, and prayed; and turning *him* to the body said, Tabitha, arise. And she opened her eyes: and when she saw Peter, she sat up.

41 And he gave her *his* hand, and lifted her up, and when he had called the saints and widows, presented her alive.

42 And it was known throughout all Joppa; and many believed in the Lord.

43 And it came to pass, that he tarried many days in Joppa with one Simon a tanner.

CHAPTER 10

THERE was a certain man in Cæsarea called Cornelius, a centurion of the band called the Italian *band*,

2 *A* devout *man*, and one that feared אֱלֹהִים with all his house, which gave much alms to the people, and prayed to אֱלֹהִים alway.

3 He saw in a vision evidently about the ninth hour of the day an angel of אֱלֹהִים coming in to him, and saying unto him, Cornelius.

4 And when he looked on him, he was afraid, and said, What is it, Lord? And he said unto him, Thy prayers and thine alms are come up for a memorial before אֱלֹהִים.

5 And now send men to Joppa, and call for *one* Simon, whose surname is Peter:

6 He lodgeth with one Simon a tanner, whose house is by the sea side: he shall tell thee what thou oughtest to do.

7 And when the angel which spake unto Cornelius was departed, he called two of his household servants, and a devout soldier of them that waited on him continually;

8 And when he had declared all *these* things unto them, he sent them to Joppa.

9 ¶ On the morrow, as they went on their journey, and drew nigh unto the city, Peter went up upon the housetop to pray about the sixth hour:

10 And he became very hungry, and would have eaten: but while they made ready, he fell into a trance,

11 And saw heaven opened, and a certain vessel descending unto him, as it had been a great sheet knit at the four corners, and let down to the earth:

12 Wherein were all manner of fourfooted beasts of the earth, and wild beasts, and creeping things, and fowls of the air.

13 And there came a voice to him, Rise, Peter; kill, and eat.

14 But Peter said, Not so, Lord; for I have never eaten any thing that is common or unclean.

15 And the voice *spake* unto him again the second time, What אֱלֹהִים hath cleansed, *that* call not thou common.

16 This was done thrice: and the vessel was received up again into heaven.

17 Now while Peter doubted in himself what this vision which he had seen should mean, behold, the men which were sent from Cornelius had made inquiry for Simon's house, and stood before the gate,

18 And called, and asked whether Simon, which was surnamed Peter, were lodged there.

19 ¶ While Peter thought on the vision, the Spirit said unto him, Behold, three men seek thee.

20 Arise therefore, and get thee down, and go with them, doubting nothing: for I have sent them.

21 Then Peter went down to the men which were sent unto him from Cornelius; and said, Behold, I am he whom ye seek: what *is* the cause wherefore ye are come?

22 And they said, Cornelius the centurion, a just man, and one that feareth אֱלֹהִים, and of good report among all the nation of the Jews,

was warned from אֱלֹהִים by an holy angel to send for thee into his house, and to hear words of thee.

23 Then called he them in, and lodged *them*. And on the morrow Peter went away with them, and certain brethren from Joppa accompanied him.

24 And the morrow after they entered into Cæsarea. And Cornelius waited for them, and had called together his kinsmen and near friends.

25 And as Peter was coming in, Cornelius met him, and fell down at his feet, and worshipped *him*.

26 But Peter took him up, saying, Stand up; I myself also am a man.

27 And as he talked with him, he went in, and found many that were come together.

28 And he said unto them, Ye know how that it is an unlawful thing for a man that is a Jew to keep company, or come unto one of another nation; but אֱלֹהִים hath shewed me that I should not call any man common or unclean.

29 Therefore came I *unto you* without gainsaying, as soon as I was sent for: I ask therefore for what intent ye have sent for me?

30 And Cornelius said, Four days ago I was fasting until this hour; and at the ninth hour I prayed in my house, and, behold, a man stood before me in bright clothing,

31 And said, Cornelius, thy prayer is heard, and thine alms are had in remembrance in the sight of אֱלֹהִים.

32 Send therefore to Joppa, and call hither Simon, whose surname is Peter; he is lodged in the house of *one* Simon a tanner by the sea side: who, when he cometh, shall speak unto thee.

33 Immediately therefore I sent to thee; and thou hast well done that thou art come. Now therefore are we all here present before אֱלֹהִים, to hear all things that are commanded thee of אֱלֹהִים.

34 ¶ Then Peter opened *his* mouth, and said, Of a truth I perceive that אֱלֹהִים is no respecter of persons:

35 But in every nation he that feareth him, and worketh righteousness, is accepted with him.

36 The word which אֱלֹהִים sent unto the children of Israel, preaching peace by Yashiyah Christ: (he is Lord of all:)

37 That word, *I say*, ye know, which was published throughout all Judæa, and began from Galilee, after the baptism which John preached;

38 How אֱלֹהִים anointed Yashiyah of Nazareth with the Holy Ghost and with power: who went about doing good, and healing all that were oppressed of the devil; for אֱלֹהִים was with him.

39 And we are witnesses of all things which he did both in the land of the Jews, and in Jerusalem; whom they slew and hanged on a tree:

40 Him אֱלֹהִים raised up the third day, and shewed him openly;

41 Not to all the people, but unto witnesses chosen before of אֱלֹהִים, *even* to us, who did eat and drink with him after he rose from the dead.

42 And he commanded us to preach unto the people, and to testify that it is he which was ordained of אֱלֹהִים *to be* the Judge of quick and dead.

43 To him give all the prophets witness, that through his name whosoever believeth in him shall receive remission of sins.

44 ¶ While Peter yet spake these words, the Holy Ghost fell on all them which heard the word.

45 And they of the circumcision which believed were astonished, as many as came with Peter, because that on the Gentiles also was poured out the gift of the Holy Ghost.

46 For they heard them speak with tongues, and magnify אֱלֹהִים. Then answered Peter,

47 Can any man forbid water, that these should not be baptized, which have received the Holy Ghost as well as we?

48 And he commanded them to be baptized in the name of the Lord. Then prayed they him to tarry certain days.

CHAPTER 11

AND the apostles and brethren that were in Judæa heard that the Gentiles had also received the word of אֱלֹהִים.

2 And when Peter was come up to Jerusalem, they that were of the circumcision contended with him,

3 Saying, Thou wentest in to men uncircumcised, and didst eat with them.

4 But Peter rehearsed *the matter* from the beginning, and expounded *it* by order unto them, saying,

5 I was in the city of Joppa praying: and in a trance I saw a vision, A certain vessel descend, as it had been a great sheet, let down from heaven by four corners; and it came even to me:

6 Upon the which when I had fastened mine eyes, I considered, and saw fourfooted beasts of the earth, and wild beasts, and creeping things, and fowls of the air.

7 And I heard a voice saying unto me, Arise, Peter; slay and eat.

8 But I said, Not so, Lord: for nothing common or unclean hath at any time entered into my mouth.

9 But the voice answered me again from heaven, What אֱלֹהִים hath cleansed, *that* call not thou common.

10 And this was done three times: and all were drawn up again into heaven.

11 And, behold, immediately there were three men already come unto the house where I was, sent from Cæsarea unto me.

12 And the spirit bade me go with them, nothing doubting. Moreover these six brethren accompanied me, and we entered into the man's house:

13 And he shewed us how he had seen an angel in his house, which stood and said unto him, Send men to Joppa, and call for Simon, whose surname is Peter;

14 Who shall tell thee words, whereby thou and all thy house shall be saved.

15 And as I began to speak, the Holy Ghost fell on them, as on us at the beginning.

16 Then remembered I the word of the Lord, how that he said, John indeed baptized with water; but ye shall be baptized with the Holy Ghost.

17 Forasmuch then as אֱלֹהִים gave them the like gift as *he did* unto us, who believed on the Lord Yashiyah Christ; what was I, that I could withstand אֱלֹהִים?

18 When they heard these things, they held their peace, and glorified אֱלֹהִים, saying, Then hath אֱלֹהִים also to the Gentiles granted repentance unto life.

19 ¶ Now they which were scattered abroad upon the persecution that arose about Stephen travelled as far as Phenice, and Cyprus, and Antioch, preaching the word to none but unto the Jews only.

20 And some of them were men of Cyprus and Cyrene, which, when they were come to Antioch, spake unto the Grecians, preaching the Lord Yashiyah.

21 And the hand of the Lord was with them: and a great number believed, and turned unto the Lord.

22 ¶ Then tidings of these things came unto the ears of the church which was in Jerusalem: and they sent forth Barnabas, that he should go as far as Antioch.

23 Who, when he came, and had seen the grace of אֱלֹהִים, was glad, and exhorted them all, that with purpose of heart they would cleave unto the Lord.

24 For he was a good man, and full of the Holy Ghost and of faith: and much people was added unto the Lord.

25 Then departed Barnabas to Tarsus, for to seek Saul:

26 And when he had found him, he brought him unto Antioch. And it came to pass, that a whole year they assembled themselves with the church, and taught much people. And the disciples were called Christians first in Antioch.

27 ¶ And in these days came prophets from Jerusalem unto Antioch.

28 And there stood up one of them named Agabus, and signified by the spirit that there should be great dearth throughout all the world: which came to pass in the days of Claudius Cæsar.

29 Then the disciples, every man according to his ability, determined to send relief unto the brethren which dwelt in Judæa:

30 Which also they did, and sent it to the elders by the hands of Barnabas and Saul.

CHAPTER 12

NOW about that time Herod the king stretched forth *his* hands to vex certain of the church.

2 And he killed James the brother of John with the sword.

3 And because he saw it pleased the Jews, he proceeded further to take Peter also. (Then were the days of unleavened bread.)

4 And when he had apprehended him, he put *him* in prison, and delivered *him* to four quaternions of soldiers to keep him; intending after Easter to bring him forth to the people.

5 Peter therefore was kept in prison: but prayer was made without ceasing of the church unto אֱלֹהִים for him.

6 And when Herod would have brought him forth, the same night Peter was sleeping between two soldiers, bound with two chains: and the keepers before the door kept the prison.

7 And, behold, the angel of the Lord came upon *him*, and a light shined in the prison: and he smote Peter on the side, and raised him up, saying, Arise up quickly. And his chains fell off from *his* hands.

8 And the angel said unto him, Gird thyself, and bind on thy sandals. And so he did. And he saith unto him, Cast thy garment about thee, and follow me.

9 And he went out, and followed him; and wist not that it was true which was done by the angel; but thought he saw a vision.

10 When they were past the first and the second ward, they came unto the iron gate that leadeth unto the city; which opened to them of his own accord: and they went out, and passed on through one street; and forthwith the angel departed from him.

11 And when Peter was come to himself, he said, Now I know of a surety, that the Lord hath sent his angel, and hath delivered me out of the hand of Herod, and *from* all the expectation of the people of the Jews.

12 And when he had considered *the thing*, he came to the house of Mary the mother of John, whose surname was Mark; where many were gathered together praying.

13 And as Peter knocked at the door of the gate, a damsel came to hearken, named Rhoda.

14 And when she knew Peter's voice, she opened not the gate for gladness, but ran in, and told how Peter stood before the gate.

15 And they said unto her, Thou art mad. But she constantly affirmed that it was even so. Then said they, It is his angel.

16 But Peter continued knocking: and when they had opened *the door*, and saw him, they were astonished.

17 But he, beckoning unto them with the hand to hold their peace, declared unto them how the Lord had brought him out of the prison. And he said, Go shew these things unto James, and to the brethren. And he departed, and went into another place.

18 Now as soon as it was day, there was no small stir among the soldiers, what was become of Peter.

19 And when Herod had sought for him, and found him not, he examined the keepers, and commanded that *they* should be put to death. And he went down from Judæa to Cæsarea, and *there* abode.

20 ¶ And Herod was highly displeased with them of Tyre and Sidon: but they came with one accord to him, and, having made Blastus the king's chamberlain their friend, desired peace; because their country was nourished by the king's *country*.

21 And upon a set day Herod, arrayed in royal apparel, sat upon his throne, and made an oration unto them.

22 And the people gave a shout, *saying, It is* the voice of a god, and not of a man.

23 And immediately the angel of the Lord smote him, because he gave not אֱלֹהִים the glory: and he was eaten of worms, and gave up the ghost.

24 ¶ But the word of אֱלֹהִים grew and multiplied.

25 And Barnabas and Saul returned from Jerusalem, when they had fulfilled *their* ministry, and took with them John, whose surname was Mark.

CHAPTER 13

NOW there were in the church that was at Antioch certain prophets and teachers; as Barnabas, and Simeon that was called Niger, and Lucius of Cyrene, and Manaen, which had been brought up with Herod the tetrarch, and Saul.

2 As they ministered to the Lord, and fasted, the Holy Ghost said, Separate me Barnabas and Saul for the work whereunto I have called them.

3 And when they had fasted and prayed, and laid *their* hands on them, they sent *them* away.

4 ¶ So they, being sent forth by the Holy Ghost, departed unto Seleucia; and from thence they sailed to Cyprus.

5 And when they were at Salamis, they preached the word of אֱלֹהִים in the synagogues of the Jews: and they had also John to *their* minister.

6 And when they had gone through the isle unto Paphos, they found a certain sorcerer, a false prophet, a Jew, whose name *was* Bar-jesus:

7 Which was with the deputy of the country, Sergius Paulus, a prudent man; who called for Barnabas and Saul, and desired to hear the word of אֱלֹהִים.

8 But Elymas the sorcerer (for so is his name by interpretation) withstood them, seeking to turn away the deputy from the faith.

9 Then Saul, (who also *is called* Paul,) filled with the Holy Ghost, set his eyes on him,

10 And said, O full of all subtilty and all mischief, *thou* child of the devil, *thou* enemy of all righteousness, wilt thou not cease to

pervert the right ways of the Lord?

11 And now, behold, the hand of the Lord *is* upon thee, and thou shalt be blind, not seeing the sun for a season. And immediately there fell on him a mist and a darkness; and he went about seeking some to lead him by the hand.

12 Then the deputy, when he saw what was done, believed, being astonished at the doctrine of the Lord.

13 Now when Paul and his company loosed from Paphos, they came to Perga in Pamphylia: and John departing from them returned to Jerusalem.

14 ¶ But when they departed from Perga, they came to Antioch in Pisidia, and went into the synagogue on the sabbath day, and sat down.

15 And after the reading of the law and the prophets the rulers of the synagogue sent unto them, saying, *Ye* men *and* brethren, if ye have any word of exhortation for the people, say on.

16 Then Paul stood up, and beckoning with *his* hand said, Men of Israel, and ye that fear אֱלֹהִים, give audience.

17 The אֱלֹהִים of this people of Israel chose our fathers, and exalted the people when they dwelt as strangers in the land of Egypt, and with an high arm brought he them out of it.

18 And about the time of forty years suffered he their manners in the wilderness.

19 And when he had destroyed seven nations in the land of Chanaan, he divided their land to them by lot.

20 And after that he gave *unto them* judges about the space of four hundred and fifty years, until Samuel the prophet.

21 And afterward they desired a king: and אֱלֹהִים gave unto them Saul the son of Cis, a man of the tribe of Benjamin, by the space of forty years.

22 And when he had removed him, he raised up unto them David to be their king; to whom also he gave testimony, and said, I have found David the *son* of Jesse, a man after mine own heart, which shall fulfil all my will.

23 Of this man's seed hath אֱלֹהִים according to *his* promise raised unto Israel a Saviour, Yashiyah:

24 When John had first preached before his coming the baptism of repentance to all the people of Israel.

25 And as John fulfilled his course, he said, Whom think ye that I am? I am not *he*. But, behold, there cometh one after me, whose shoes of *his* feet I am not worthy to loose.

26 Men *and* brethren, children of the stock of Abraham, and whosoever among you feareth אֱלֹהִים, to you is the word of this salvation sent.

27 For they that dwell at Jerusalem, and their rulers, because they knew him not, nor yet the voices of the prophets which are read every sabbath day, they have fulfilled *them* in condemning *him*.

28 And though they found no cause of death *in him*, yet desired they Pilate that he should be slain.

29 And when they had fulfilled all that was written of him, they took *him* down from the tree, and laid *him* in a sepulchre.

30 But אֱלֹהִים raised him from the dead:

31 And he was seen many days of them which came up with him from Galilee to Jerusalem, who are his witnesses unto the people.

32 And we declare unto you glad tidings, how that the promise which was made unto the fathers,

33 אֱלֹהִים hath fulfilled the same unto us their children, in that he hath raised up Yashiyah again; as it is also written in the second psalm, Thou art my Son, this day have I begotten thee.

34 And as concerning that he raised him up from the dead, *now* no more to return to corruption, he said on this wise, I will give you the sure mercies of David.

35 Wherefore he saith also in another *psalm*, Thou shalt not suffer thine Holy One to see corruption.

36 For David, after he had served his own generation by the will of אֱלֹהִים, fell on sleep, and was laid unto his fathers, and saw corruption:

37 But he, whom אֱלֹהִים raised again, saw no corruption.

38 ¶ Be it known unto you therefore, men *and* brethren, that through this man is preached unto you the forgiveness of sins:

39 And by him all that believe are justified from all things, from which ye could not be justified by the law of Moses.

40 Beware therefore, lest that come upon you, which is spoken of in the prophets;

41 Behold, ye despisers, and wonder, and perish: for I work a work in your days, a work which ye shall in no wise believe, though a man declare it unto you.

42 And when the Jews were gone out of the synagogue, the Gentiles besought that these words might be preached to them the next sabbath.

43 Now when the congregation was broken up, many of the Jews and religious proselytes followed Paul and Barnabas: who, speaking to them, persuaded them to continue in the grace of אֱלֹהִים.

44 ¶ And the next sabbath day came almost the whole city together to hear the word of אֱלֹהִים.

45 But when the Jews saw the multitudes, they were filled with envy, and spake against those things which were spoken by Paul, contradicting and blaspheming.

46 Then Paul and Barnabas waxed bold, and said, It was necessary that the word of אֱלֹהִים should first have been spoken to you: but seeing ye put it from you, and judge yourselves unworthy of everlasting life, lo, we turn to the Gentiles.

47 For so hath the Lord commanded us, *saying*, I have set thee to be a light of the Gentiles, that thou shouldest be for salvation unto the ends of the earth.

48 And when the Gentiles heard this, they were glad, and glorified the word of the Lord: and as many as were ordained to eternal life believed.

49 And the word of the Lord was published throughout all the region.

50 But the Jews stirred up the devout and honourable women, and the chief men of the city, and raised persecution against Paul and Barnabas, and expelled them out of their coasts.

51 But they shook off the dust of their feet against them, and came unto Iconium.

52 And the disciples were filled with joy, and with the Holy Ghost.

CHAPTER 14

AND it came to pass in Iconium, that they went both together into the synagogue of the Jews, and so spake, that a great multitude both of the Jews and also of the Greeks believed.

2 But the unbelieving Jews stirred up the Gentiles, and made their minds evil affected against the brethren.

3 Long time therefore abode they speaking boldly in the Lord, which gave testimony unto the word of his grace, and granted signs and

wonders to be done by their hands.

4 But the multitude of the city was divided: and part held with the Jews, and part with the apostles.

5 And when there was an assault made both of the Gentiles, and also of the Jews with their rulers, to use *them* despitefully, and to stone them,

6 They were ware of *it*, and fled unto Lystra and Derbe, cities of Lycaonia, and unto the region that lieth round about:

7 And there they preached the gospel.

8 ¶ And there sat a certain man at Lystra, impotent in his feet, being a cripple from his mother's womb, who never had walked:

9 The same heard Paul speak: who stedfastly beholding him, and perceiving that he had faith to be healed,

10 Said with a loud voice, Stand upright on thy feet. And he leaped and walked.

11 And when the people saw what Paul had done, they lifted up their voices, saying in the speech of Lycaonia, The gods are come down to us in the likeness of men.

12 And they called Barnabas, Jupiter; and Paul, Mercurius, because he was the chief speaker.

13 Then the priest of Jupiter, which was before their city, brought oxen and garlands unto the gates, and would have done sacrifice with the people.

14 *Which* when the apostles, Barnabas and Paul, heard *of*, they rent their clothes, and ran in among the people, crying out,

15 And saying, Sirs, why do ye these things? We also are men of like passions with you, and preach unto you that ye should turn from these vanities unto the living אֱלֹהִים, which made heaven, and earth, and the sea, and all things that are therein:

16 Who in times past suffered all nations to walk in their own ways.

17 Nevertheless he left not himself without witness, in that he did good, and gave us rain from heaven, and fruitful seasons, filling our hearts with food and gladness.

18 And with these sayings scarce restrained they the people, that they had not done sacrifice unto them.

19 ¶ And there came thither *certain* Jews from Antioch and Iconium, who persuaded the people, and, having stoned Paul, drew *him* out of the city, supposing he had been dead.

20 Howbeit, as the disciples stood round about him, he rose up, and came into the city: and the next day he departed with Barnabas to Derbe.

21 And when they had preached the gospel to that city, and had taught many, they returned again to Lystra, and *to* Iconium, and Antioch,

22 Confirming the souls of the disciples, *and* exhorting them to continue in the faith, and that we must through much tribulation enter into the kingdom of אֱלֹהִים.

23 And when they had ordained them elders in every church, and had prayed with fasting, they commended them to the Lord, on whom they believed.

24 And after they had passed throughout Pisidia, they came to Pamphylia.

25 And when they had preached the word in Perga, they went down into Attalia:

26 And thence sailed to Antioch, from whence they had been recommended to the grace of אֱלֹהִים for the work which they fulfilled.

27 And when they were come, and had gathered the church together, they rehearsed all that אֱלֹהִים had done with them, and how he had opened the door of faith unto the Gentiles.

28 And there they abode long time with the disciples.

CHAPTER 15

AND certain men which came down from Judæa taught the brethren, *and said*, Except ye be circumcised after the manner of Moses, ye cannot be saved.

2 When therefore Paul and Barnabas had no small dissension and disputation with them, they determined that Paul and Barnabas, and certain other of them, should go up to Jerusalem unto the apostles and elders about this question.

3 And being brought on their way by the church, they passed through Phenice and Samaria, declaring the conversion of the Gentiles: and they caused great joy unto all the brethren.

4 And when they were come to Jerusalem, they were received of the church, and *of* the apostles and elders, and they declared all things that אֱלֹהִים had done with them.

5 But there rose up certain of the sect of the Pharisees which believed, saying, That it was needful to circumcise them, and to command *them* to keep the law of Moses.

6 ¶ And the apostles and elders came together for to consider of this matter.

7 And when there had been much disputing, Peter rose up, and said unto them, Men *and* brethren, ye know how that a good while ago אֱלֹהִים made choice among us, that the Gentiles by my mouth should hear the word of the gospel, and believe.

8 And אֱלֹהִים, which knoweth the hearts, bare them witness, giving them the Holy Ghost, even as *he did* unto us;

9 And put no difference between us and them, purifying their hearts by faith.

10 Now therefore why tempt ye אֱלֹהִים, to put a yoke upon the neck of the disciples, which neither our fathers nor we were able to bear?

11 But we believe that through the grace of the Lord Yashiyah Christ we shall be saved, even as they.

12 ¶ Then all the multitude kept silence, and gave audience to Barnabas and Paul, declaring what miracles and wonders אֱלֹהִים had wrought among the Gentiles by them.

13 ¶ And after they had held their peace, James answered, saying, Men *and* brethren, hearken unto me:

14 Simeon hath declared how אֱלֹהִים at the first did visit the Gentiles, to take out of them a people for his name.

15 And to this agree the words of the prophets; as it is written,

16 After this I will return, and will build again the tabernacle of David, which is fallen down; and I will build again the ruins thereof, and I will set it up:

17 That the residue of men might seek after the Lord, and all the Gentiles, upon whom my name is called, saith the Lord, who doeth all these things.

18 Known unto אֱלֹהִים are all his works from the beginning of the world.

19 Wherefore my sentence is, that we trouble not them, which from among the Gentiles are turned to אֱלֹהִים:

20 But that we write unto them, that they abstain from pollutions of idols, and *from* fornication, and *from* things strangled, and *from* blood.

21 For Moses of old time hath in every city them that preach him, being read in the synagogues every sabbath day.

22 Then pleased it the apostles and elders, with the whole church, to send chosen men of their own company to Antioch with Paul and Barnabas; *namely*, Judas surnamed Barsabas, and Silas, chief men among the brethren:

23 And they wrote *letters* by them after this manner; The apostles and elders and brethren *send* greeting unto the brethren which are of the Gentiles in Antioch and Syria and Cilicia:

24 Forasmuch as we have heard, that certain which went out from us have troubled you with words, subverting your souls, saying, *Ye must* be circumcised, and keep the law: to whom we gave no *such* commandment:

25 It seemed good unto us, being assembled with one accord, to send chosen men unto you with our beloved Barnabas and Paul,

26 Men that have hazarded their lives for the name of our Lord Yashiyah Christ.

27 We have sent therefore Judas and Silas, who shall also tell *you* the same things by mouth.

28 For it seemed good to the Holy Ghost, and to us, to lay upon you no greater burden than these necessary things;

29 That ye abstain from meats offered to idols, and from blood, and from things strangled, and from fornication: from which if ye keep yourselves, ye shall do well. Fare ye well.

30 So when they were dismissed, they came to Antioch: and when they had gathered the multitude together, they delivered the epistle:

31 *Which* when they had read, they rejoiced for the consolation.

32 And Judas and Silas, being prophets also themselves, exhorted the brethren with many words, and confirmed *them*.

33 And after they had tarried *there* a space, they were let go in peace from the brethren unto the apostles.

34 Notwithstanding it pleased Silas to abide there still.

35 Paul also and Barnabas continued in Antioch, teaching and preaching the word of the Lord, with many others also.

36 ¶ And some days after Paul said unto Barnabas, Let us go again and visit our brethren in every city where we have preached the word of the Lord, *and see* how they do.

37 And Barnabas determined to take with them John, whose surname was Mark.

38 But Paul thought not good to take him with them, who departed from them from Pamphylia, and went not with them to the work.

39 And the contention was so sharp between them, that they departed asunder one from the other: and so Barnabas took Mark, and sailed unto Cyprus;

40 And Paul chose Silas, and departed, being recommended by the brethren unto the grace of אֱלֹהִים.

41 And he went through Syria and Cilicia, confirming the churches.

CHAPTER 16

THEN came he to Derbe and Lystra: and, behold, a certain disciple was there, named Timotheus, the son of a certain woman, which was a Jewess, and believed; but his father *was* a Greek:

2 Which was well reported of by the brethren that were at Lystra and Iconium.

3 Him would Paul have to go forth with him; and took and circumcised him because of the Jews which were in those quarters: for they knew all that his father was a Greek.

4 And as they went through the cities, they delivered them the decrees for to keep, that were ordained of the apostles and elders which were at Jerusalem.

5 And so were the churches established in the faith, and increased in number daily.

6 Now when they had gone throughout Phrygia and the region of Galatia, and were forbidden of the Holy Ghost to preach the word in Asia,

7 After they were come to Mysia, they assayed to go into Bithynia: but the Spirit suffered them not.

8 And they passing by Mysia came down to Troas.

9 And a vision appeared to Paul in the night; There stood a man of Macedonia, and prayed him, saying, Come over into Macedonia, and help us.

10 And after he had seen the vision, immediately we endeavoured to go into Macedonia, assuredly gathering that the Lord had called us for to preach the gospel unto them.

11 Therefore loosing from Troas, we came with a straight course to Samothracia, and the next *day* to Neapolis;

12 And from thence to Philippi, which is the chief city of that part of Macedonia, *and* a colony: and we were in that city abiding certain days.

13 And on the sabbath we went out of the city by a river side, where prayer was wont to be made; and we sat down, and spake unto the women which resorted *thither*.

14 ¶ And a certain woman named Lydia, a seller of purple, of the city of Thyatira, which worshipped אֱלֹהִים, heard *us:* whose heart the Lord opened, that she attended unto the things which were spoken of Paul.

15 And when she was baptized, and her household, she besought *us*, saying, If ye have judged me to be faithful to the Lord, come into my house, and abide *there*. And she constrained us.

16 ¶ And it came to pass, as we went to prayer, a certain damsel possessed with a spirit of divination met us, which brought her masters much gain by soothsaying:

17 The same followed Paul and us, and cried, saying, These men are the servants of the most high אֱל, which shew unto us the way of salvation.

18 And this did she many days. But Paul, being grieved, turned and said to the spirit, I command thee in the name of Yashiyah Christ to come out of her. And he came out the same hour.

19 ¶ And when her masters saw that the hope of their gains was gone, they caught Paul and Silas, and drew *them* into the marketplace unto the rulers,

20 And brought them to the magistrates, saying, These men, being Jews, do exceedingly trouble our city,

21 And teach customs, which are not lawful for us to receive, neither to observe, being Romans.

22 And the multitude rose up together against them: and the magistrates rent off their clothes, and commanded to beat *them*.

23 And when they had laid many stripes upon them, they cast *them* into prison, charging the jailor to keep them safely:

24 Who, having received such a charge, thrust them into the inner prison, and made their feet fast in the stocks.

25 ¶ And at midnight Paul and Silas prayed, and sang praises unto אֱלֹהִים: and the prisoners heard them.

26 And suddenly there was a great earthquake, so that the foundations of the prison were shaken: and immediately all the doors were opened, and every one's bands were loosed.

27 And the keeper of the prison awaking out of his sleep, and seeing the prison doors open, he drew out his sword, and would have killed himself, supposing that the prisoners had been fled.

28 But Paul cried with a loud voice, saying, Do thyself no harm: for we are all here.

29 Then he called for a light, and sprang in, and came trembling, and fell down before Paul and Silas,

30 And brought them out, and said, Sirs, what must I do to be saved?

31 And they said, Believe on the Lord Yashiyah Christ, and thou shalt be saved, and thy house.

32 And they spake unto him the word of the Lord, and to all that were in his house.

33 And he took them the same hour of the night, and washed *their* stripes; and was baptized, he and all his, straightway.

34 And when he had brought them into his house, he set meat before them, and rejoiced, believing in אֱלֹהִים with all his house.

35 And when it was day, the magistrates sent the serjeants, saying, Let those men go.

36 And the keeper of the prison told this saying to Paul, The magistrates have sent to let you go: now therefore depart, and go in peace.

37 But Paul said unto them, They have beaten us openly uncondemned, being Romans, and have cast *us* into prison; and now do they thrust us out privily? nay verily; but let them come themselves and fetch us out.

38 And the serjeants told these words unto the magistrates: and they feared, when they heard that they were Romans.

39 And they came and besought them, and brought *them* out, and desired *them* to depart out of the city.

40 And they went out of the prison, and entered into *the house of* Lydia: and when they had seen the brethren, they comforted them, and departed.

CHAPTER 17

NOW when they had passed through Amphipolis and Apollonia, they came to Thessalonica, where was a synagogue of the Jews:

2 And Paul, as his manner was, went in unto them, and three sabbath days reasoned with them out of the scriptures,

3 Opening and alleging, that Christ must needs have suffered, and risen again from the dead; and that this Yashiyah, whom I preach unto you, is Christ.

4 And some of them believed, and consorted with Paul and Silas; and of the devout Greeks a great multitude, and of the chief women not a few.

5 ¶ But the Jews which believed not, moved with envy, took unto them certain lewd fellows of the baser sort, and gathered a company, and set all the city on an uproar, and assaulted the house of Jason, and sought to bring them out to the people.

6 And when they found them not, they drew Jason and certain brethren unto the rulers of the city, crying, These that have turned the world upside down are come hither also;

7 Whom Jason hath received: and these all do contrary to the decrees of Cæsar, saying that there is another king, *one* Yashiyah.

8 And they troubled the people and the rulers of the city, when they heard these things.

9 And when they had taken security of Jason, and of the other, they let them go.

10 ¶ And the brethren immediately sent away Paul and Silas by night unto Berea: who coming *thither* went into the synagogue of the Jews.

11 These were more noble than those in Thessalonica, in that they received the word with all readiness of mind, and searched the scriptures daily, whether those things were so.

12 Therefore many of them believed; also of honourable women which were Greeks, and of men, not a few.

13 But when the Jews of Thessalonica had knowledge that the word of אֱלֹהִים was preached of Paul at Berea, they came thither also, and stirred up the people.

14 And then immediately the brethren sent away Paul to go as it were to the sea: but Silas and Timotheus abode there still.

15 And they that conducted Paul brought him unto Athens: and receiving a commandment unto Silas and Timotheus for to come to him with all speed, they departed.

16 ¶ Now while Paul waited for them at Athens, his spirit was stirred in him, when he saw the city wholly given to idolatry.

17 Therefore disputed he in the synagogue with the Jews, and with the devout persons, and in the market daily with them that met with him.

18 Then certain philosophers of the Epicureans, and of the Stoicks, encountered him. And some said, What will this babbler say? other some, He seemeth to be a setter forth of strange gods: because he preached unto them Yashiyah, and the resurrection.

19 And they took him, and brought him unto Areopagus, saying, May we know what this new doctrine, whereof thou speakest, *is?*

20 For thou bringest certain strange things to our ears: we would know therefore what these things mean.

21 (For all the Athenians and strangers which were there spent their time in nothing else, but either to tell, or to hear some new thing.)

22 ¶ Then Paul stood in the midst of Mars' hill, and said, *Ye* men of Athens, I perceive that in all things ye are too superstitious.

23 For as I passed by, and beheld your devotions, I found an altar with this inscription, TO THE UNKNOWN GOD. Whom therefore ye ignorantly worship, him declare I unto you.

24 אֱלֹהִים that made the world and all things therein, seeing that he is Lord of heaven and earth, dwelleth not in temples made with hands;

25 Neither is worshipped with men's hands, as though he needed any thing, seeing he giveth to all life, and breath, and all things;

26 And hath made of one blood all nations of men for to dwell on all the face of the earth, and hath determined the times before appointed, and the bounds of their habitation;

27 That they should seek the Lord, if haply they might feel after him, and find him, though he be not far from every one of us:

28 For in him we live, and move, and have our being; as certain also of your own poets have said, For we are also his offspring.

29 Forasmuch then as we are the offspring of אֱלֹהִים, we ought not to think that the Godhead is like unto gold, or silver, or stone, graven by art and man's device.

30 And the times of this ignorance אֱלֹהִים winked at; but now commandeth all men every where to repent:

31 Because he hath appointed a day, in the which he will judge the world in righteousness by *that* man whom he hath ordained; *whereof* he hath given assurance unto all *men*, in that he hath raised him from the dead.

32 ¶ And when they heard of the resurrection of the dead, some mocked: and others said, We will hear thee again of this *matter.*

33 So Paul departed from among them.

34 Howbeit certain men clave unto him, and believed: among the which *was* Dionysius the Areopagite, and a woman named Damaris, and others with them.

CHAPTER 18

AFTER these things Paul departed from Athens, and came to Corinth;

2 And found a certain Jew named Aquila, born in Pontus, lately come from Italy, with his wife Priscilla; (because that Claudius had commanded all Jews to depart from Rome:) and came unto them.

3 And because he was of the same craft, he abode with them, and wrought: for by their occupation they were tentmakers.

4 And he reasoned in the synagogue every sabbath, and persuaded the Jews and the Greeks.

5 And when Silas and Timotheus were come from Macedonia, Paul was pressed in the spirit, and testified to the Jews *that* Yashiyah *was* Christ.

6 And when they opposed themselves, and blasphemed, he shook *his* raiment, and said unto them, Your blood *be* upon your own heads; I *am* clean: from henceforth I will go unto the Gentiles.

7 ¶ And he departed thence, and entered into a certain *man's* house, named Justus, *one* that worshipped אֱלֹהִים, whose house joined hard to the synagogue.

8 And Crispus, the chief ruler of the synagogue, believed on the Lord with all his house; and many of the Corinthians hearing believed, and were baptized.

9 Then spake the Lord to Paul in the night by a vision, Be not afraid, but speak, and hold not thy peace:

10 For I am with thee, and no man shall set on thee to hurt thee: for I have much people in this city.

11 And he continued *there* a year and six months, teaching the word of אֱלֹהִים among them.

12 ¶ And when Gallio was the deputy of Achaia, the Jews made insurrection with one accord against Paul, and brought him to the judgment seat,

13 Saying, This *fellow* persuadeth men to worship אֱלֹהִים contrary to the law.

14 And when Paul was now about to open *his* mouth, Gallio said unto the Jews, If it were a matter of wrong or wicked lewdness, O ye Jews, reason would that I should bear with you:

15 But if it be a question of words and names, and *of* your law, look ye *to it;* for I will be no judge of such *matters.*

16 And he drave them from the judgment seat.

17 Then all the Greeks took Sosthenes, the chief ruler of the synagogue, and beat *him* before the judgment seat. And Gallio cared for none of those things.

18 ¶ And Paul *after this* tarried *there* yet a good while, and then took his leave of the brethren, and sailed thence into Syria, and with him Priscilla and Aquila; having shorn *his* head in Cenchrea: for he had a vow.

19 And he came to Ephesus, and left them there: but he himself entered into the synagogue, and reasoned with the Jews.

20 When they desired *him* to tarry longer time with them, he consented not;

21 But bade them farewell, saying, I must by all means keep this feast that cometh in Jerusalem: but I will return again unto you, if אֱלֹהִים will. And he sailed from Ephesus.

22 And when he had landed at Cæsarea, and gone up, and saluted the church, he went down to Antioch.

23 And after he had spent some time *there,* he departed, and went over *all* the country of Galatia and Phrygia in order, strengthening all the disciples.

24 ¶ And a certain Jew named Apollos, born at Alexandria, an eloquent man, *and* mighty in the scriptures, came to Ephesus.

25 This man was instructed in the way of the Lord; and being fervent in the spirit, he spake and taught diligently the things of the Lord, knowing only the baptism of John.

26 And he began to speak boldly in the synagogue: whom when Aquila and Priscilla had heard, they took him unto *them,* and expounded unto him the way of אֱלֹהִים more perfectly.

27 And when he was disposed to pass into Achaia, the brethren wrote, exhorting the disciples to receive him: who, when he was come, helped them much which had believed through grace:

28 For he mightily convinced the Jews, *and that* publickly, shewing by the scriptures that Yashiyah was Christ.

CHAPTER 19

AND it came to pass, that, while Apollos was at Corinth, Paul having passed through the upper coasts came to Ephesus: and finding certain disciples,

2 He said unto them, Have ye received the Holy Ghost since ye believed? And they said unto him, We have not so much as heard whether there be any Holy Ghost.

3 And he said unto them, Unto what then were ye baptized? And they said, Unto John's baptism.

4 Then said Paul, John verily baptized with the baptism of repentance, saying unto the people, that they should believe on him which should come after him, that is, on Christ Yashiyah.

5 When they heard *this,* they were baptized in the name of the Lord Yashiyah.

6 And when Paul had laid *his* hands upon them, the Holy Ghost came on them; and they spake with tongues, and prophesied.

7 And all the men were about twelve.

8 And he went into the synagogue, and spake boldly for the space of three months, disputing and persuading the things concerning the kingdom of אֱלֹהִים.

9 But when divers were hardened, and believed not, but spake evil of that way before the multitude, he departed from them, and separated the disciples, disputing daily in the school of one Tyrannus.

10 And this continued by the space of two years; so that all they which dwelt in Asia heard the word of the Lord Yashiyah, both Jews and Greeks.

11 And אֱלֹהִים wrought special miracles by the hands of Paul:

12 So that from his body were brought unto the sick handkerchiefs or aprons, and the diseases departed from them, and the evil spirits went out of them.

13 ¶ Then certain of the vagabond Jews, exorcists, took upon them to call over them which had evil spirits the name of the Lord Yashiyah, saying, We adjure you by Yashiyah whom Paul preacheth.

14 And there were seven sons of *one* Sceva, a Jew, *and* chief of the priests, which did so.

15 And the evil spirit answered and said, Yashiyah I know, and Paul I know; but who are ye?

16 And the man in whom the evil spirit was leaped on them, and overcame them, and prevailed against them, so that they fled out of

that house naked and wounded.

17 And this was known to all the Jews and Greeks also dwelling at Ephesus; and fear fell on them all, and the name of the Lord Yashiyah was magnified.

18 And many that believed came, and confessed, and shewed their deeds.

19 Many of them also which used curious arts brought their books together, and burned them before all *men:* and they counted the price of them, and found *it* fifty thousand *pieces* of silver.

20 So mightily grew the word of אֱלֹהִים and prevailed.

21 ¶ After these things were ended, Paul purposed in the spirit, when he had passed through Macedonia and Achaia, to go to Jerusalem, saying, After I have been there, I must also see Rome.

22 So he sent into Macedonia two of them that ministered unto him, Timotheus and Erastus; but he himself stayed in Asia for a season.

23 And the same time there arose no small stir about that way.

24 For a certain *man* named Demetrius, a silversmith, which made silver shrines for Diana, brought no small gain unto the craftsmen;

25 Whom he called together with the workmen of like occupation, and said, Sirs, ye know that by this craft we have our wealth.

26 Moreover ye see and hear, that not alone at Ephesus, but almost throughout all Asia, this Paul hath persuaded and turned away much people, saying that they be no gods, which are made with hands:

27 So that not only this our craft is in danger to be set at nought; but also that the temple of the great goddess Diana should be despised, and her magnificence should be destroyed, whom all Asia and the world worshippeth.

28 And when they heard *these sayings*, they were full of wrath, and cried out, saying, Great *is* Diana of the Ephesians.

29 And the whole city was filled with confusion: and having caught Gaius and Aristarchus, men of Macedonia, Paul's companions in travel, they rushed with one accord into the theatre.

30 And when Paul would have entered in unto the people, the disciples suffered him not.

31 And certain of the chief of Asia, which were his friends, sent unto him, desiring *him* that he would not adventure himself into the theatre.

32 Some therefore cried one thing, and some another: for the assembly was confused; and the more part knew not wherefore they were come together.

33 And they drew Alexander out of the multitude, the Jews putting him forward. And Alexander beckoned with the hand, and would have made his defence unto the people.

34 But when they knew that he was a Jew, all with one voice about the space of two hours cried out, Great *is* Diana of the Ephesians.

35 And when the townclerk had appeased the people, he said, *Ye* men of Ephesus, what man is there that knoweth not how that the city of the Ephesians is a worshipper of the great goddess Diana, and of the *image* which fell down from Jupiter?

36 Seeing then that these things cannot be spoken against, ye ought to be quiet, and to do nothing rashly.

37 For ye have brought hither these men, which are neither robbers of churches, nor yet blasphemers of your goddess.

38 Wherefore if Demetrius, and the craftsmen which are with him, have a matter against any man, the law is open, and there are deputies: let them implead one another.

39 But if ye inquire any thing concerning other matters, it shall be determined in a lawful assembly.

40 For we are in danger to be called in question for this day's uproar, there being no cause whereby we may give an account of this concourse.

41 And when he had thus spoken, he dismissed the assembly.

CHAPTER 20

AND after the uproar was ceased, Paul called unto *him* the disciples, and embraced *them*, and departed for to go into Macedonia.

2 And when he had gone over those parts, and had given them much exhortation, he came into Greece,

3 And *there* abode three months. And when the Jews laid wait for him, as he was about to sail into Syria, he purposed to return through Macedonia.

4 And there accompanied him into Asia Sopater of Berea; and of the Thessalonians, Aristarchus and Secundus; and Gaius of Derbe, and Timotheus; and of Asia, Tychicus and Trophimus.

5 These going before tarried for us at Troas.

6 And we sailed away from Philippi after the days of unleavened bread, and came unto them to Troas in five days; where we abode seven days.

7 And upon the first *day* of the week, when the disciples came together to break bread, Paul preached unto them, ready to depart on the morrow; and continued his speech until midnight.

8 And there were many lights in the upper chamber, where they were gathered together.

9 And there sat in a window a certain young man named Eutychus, being fallen into a deep sleep: and as Paul was long preaching, he sunk down with sleep, and fell down from the third loft, and was taken up dead.

10 And Paul went down, and fell on him, and embracing *him* said, Trouble not yourselves; for his life is in him.

11 When he therefore was come up again, and had broken bread, and eaten, and talked a long while, even till break of day, so he departed.

12 And they brought the young man alive, and were not a little comforted.

13 ¶ And we went before to ship, and sailed unto Assos, there intending to take in Paul: for so had he appointed, minding himself to go afoot.

14 And when he met with us at Assos, we took him in, and came to Mitylene.

15 And we sailed thence, and came the next *day* over against Chios; and the next *day* we arrived at Samos, and tarried at Trogyllium; and the next *day* we came to Miletus.

16 For Paul had determined to sail by Ephesus, because he would not spend the time in Asia: for he hasted, if it were possible for him, to be at Jerusalem the day of Pentecost.

17 ¶ And from Miletus he sent to Ephesus, and called the elders of the church.

18 And when they were come to him, he said unto them, Ye know, from the first day that I came into Asia, after what manner I have been with you at all seasons,

19 Serving the Lord with all humility of mind, and with many tears, and temptations, which befell me by the lying in wait of the Jews:

20 *And* how I kept back nothing that was profitable *unto you*, but have shewed you, and have taught you publickly, and from house to house,

21 Testifying both to the Jews, and also to the Greeks, repentance toward אֱלֹהִים, and faith toward our Lord Yashiyah Christ.

22 And now, behold, I go bound in the spirit unto Jerusalem, not knowing the things that shall befall me there:

23 Save that the Holy Ghost witnesseth in every city, saying that bonds and afflictions abide me.

24 But none of these things move me, neither count I my life dear unto myself, so that I might finish my course with joy, and the ministry, which I have received of the Lord Yashiyah, to testify the gospel of the grace of אֱלֹהִים.

25 And now, behold, I know that ye all, among whom I have gone preaching the kingdom of אֱלֹהִים, shall see my face no more.

26 Wherefore I take you to record this day, that I *am* pure from the blood of all *men*.

27 For I have not shunned to declare unto you all the counsel of אֱלֹהִים.

28 ¶ Take heed therefore unto yourselves, and to all the flock, over the which the Holy Ghost hath made you overseers, to feed the church of אֱלֹהִים, which he hath purchased with his own blood.

29 For I know this, that after my departing shall grievous wolves enter in among you, not sparing the flock.

30 Also of your own selves shall men arise, speaking perverse things, to draw away disciples after them.

31 Therefore watch, and remember, that by the space of three years I ceased not to warn every one night and day with tears.

32 And now, brethren, I commend you to אֱלֹהִים, and to the word of his grace, which is able to build you up, and to give you an inheritance among all them which are sanctified.

33 I have coveted no man's silver, or gold, or apparel.

34 Yea, ye yourselves know, that these hands have ministered unto my necessities, and to them that were with me.

35 I have shewed you all things, how that so labouring ye ought to support the weak, and to remember the words of the Lord Yashiyah, how he said, It is more blessed to give than to receive.

36 ¶ And when he had thus spoken, he kneeled down, and prayed with them all.

37 And they all wept sore, and fell on Paul's neck, and kissed him,

38 Sorrowing most of all for the words which he spake, that they should see his face no more. And they accompanied him unto the ship.

CHAPTER 21

AND it came to pass, that after we were gotten from them, and had launched, we came with a straight course unto Coos, and the *day* following unto Rhodes, and from thence unto Patara:

2 And finding a ship sailing over unto Phenicia, we went aboard, and set forth.

3 Now when we had discovered Cyprus, we left it on the left hand, and sailed into Syria, and landed at Tyre: for there the ship was to unlade her burden.

4 And finding disciples, we tarried there seven days: who said to Paul through the Spirit, that he should not go up to Jerusalem.

5 And when we had accomplished those days, we departed and went our way; and they all brought us on our way, with wives and children, till *we were* out of the city: and we kneeled down on the shore, and prayed.

6 And when we had taken our leave one of another, we took ship; and they returned home again.

7 And when we had finished *our* course from Tyre, we came to Ptolemais, and saluted the brethren, and abode with them one day.

8 And the next *day* we that were of Paul's company departed, and came unto Cæsarea: and we entered into the house of Philip the evangelist, which was *one* of the seven; and abode with him.

9 And the same man had four daughters, virgins, which did prophesy.

10 And as we tarried *there* many days, there came down from Judæa a certain prophet, named Agabus.

11 And when he was come unto us, he took Paul's girdle, and bound his own hands and feet, and said, Thus saith the Holy Ghost, So shall the Jews at Jerusalem bind the man that oweth this girdle, and shall deliver *him* into the hands of the Gentiles.

12 And when we heard these things, both we, and they of that place, besought him not to go up to Jerusalem.

13 Then Paul answered, What mean ye to weep and to break mine heart? for I am ready not to be bound only, but also to die at Jerusalem for the name of the Lord Yashiyah.

14 And when he would not be persuaded, we ceased, saying, The will of the Lord be done.

15 And after those days we took up our carriages, and went up to Jerusalem.

16 There went with us also *certain* of the disciples of Cæsarea, and brought with them one Mnason of Cyprus, an old disciple, with whom we should lodge.

17 And when we were come to Jerusalem, the brethren received us gladly.

18 And the *day* following Paul went in with us unto James; and all the elders were present.

19 And when he had saluted them, he declared particularly what things אֱלֹהִים had wrought among the Gentiles by his ministry.

20 And when they heard *it*, they glorified the Lord, and said unto him, Thou seest, brother, how many thousands of Jews there are which believe; and they are all zealous of the law:

21 And they are informed of thee, that thou teachest all the Jews which are among the Gentiles to forsake Moses, saying that they ought not to circumcise *their* children, neither to walk after the customs.

22 What is it therefore? the multitude must needs come together: for they will hear that thou art come.

23 Do therefore this that we say to thee: We have four men which have a vow on them;

24 Them take, and purify thyself with them, and be at charges with them, that they may shave *their* heads: and all may know that those things, whereof they were informed concerning thee, are nothing; but *that* thou thyself also walkest orderly, and keepest the law.

25 As touching the Gentiles which believe, we have written *and* concluded that they observe no such thing, save only that they keep themselves from *things* offered to idols, and from blood, and from strangled, and from fornication.

26 Then Paul took the men, and the next day purifying himself with them entered into the temple, to signify the accomplishment of the days of purification, until that an offering should be offered for every one of them.

27 And when the seven days were almost ended, the Jews which were of Asia, when they saw him in the temple, stirred up all the people, and laid hands on him,

28 Crying out, Men of Israel, help: This is the man, that teacheth all *men* every where against the people, and the law, and this place: and further brought Greeks also into the temple, and hath polluted this holy place.

29 (For they had seen before with him in the city Trophimus an Ephesian, whom they supposed that Paul had brought into the temple.)

30 And all the city was moved, and the people ran together: and they took Paul, and drew him out of the temple: and forthwith the doors were shut.

31 And as they went about to kill him, tidings came unto the chief captain of the band, that all Jerusalem was in an uproar.

32 Who immediately took soldiers and centurions, and ran down unto them: and when they saw the chief captain and the soldiers, they left beating of Paul.

33 Then the chief captain came near, and took him, and commanded *him* to be bound with two chains; and demanded who he was, and what he had done.

34 And some cried one thing, some another, among the multitude: and when he could not know the certainty for the tumult, he commanded him to be carried into the castle.

35 And when he came upon the stairs, so it was, that he was borne of the soldiers for the violence of the people.

36 For the multitude of the people followed after, crying, Away with him.

37 And as Paul was to be led into the castle, he said unto the chief captain, May I speak unto thee? Who said, Canst thou speak Greek?

38 Art not thou that Egyptian, which before these days madest an uproar, and leddest out into the wilderness four thousand men that were murderers?

39 But Paul said, I am a man *which am* a Jew of Tarsus, *a city* in Cilicia, a citizen of no mean city: and, I beseech thee, suffer me to speak unto the people.

40 And when he had given him licence, Paul stood on the stairs, and beckoned with the hand unto the people. And when there was made a great silence, he spake unto *them* in the Hebrew tongue, saying,

CHAPTER 22

MEN, brethren, and fathers, hear ye my defence *which I make* now unto you.

2 (And when they heard that he spake in the Hebrew tongue to them, they kept the more silence: and he saith,)

3 I am verily a man *which am* a Jew, born in Tarsus, *a city* in Cilicia, yet brought up in this city at the feet of Gamaliel, *and* taught according to the perfect manner of the law of the fathers, and was zealous toward אֱלֹהִים, as ye all are this day.

4 And I persecuted this way unto the death, binding and delivering into prisons both men and women.

5 As also the high priest doth bear me witness, and all the estate of the elders: from whom also I received letters unto the brethren, and went to Damascus, to bring them which were there bound unto Jerusalem, for to be punished.

6 And it came to pass, that, as I made my journey, and was come nigh unto Damascus about noon, suddenly there shone from heaven a great light round about me.

7 And I fell unto the ground, and heard a voice saying unto me, Saul, Saul, why persecutest thou me?

8 And I answered, Who art thou, Lord? And he said unto me, I am Yashiyah of Nazareth, whom thou persecutest.

9 And they that were with me saw indeed the light, and were afraid; but they heard not the voice of him that spake to me.

10 And I said, What shall I do, Lord? And the Lord said unto me, Arise, and go into Damascus; and there it shall be told thee of all things which are appointed for thee to do.

11 And when I could not see for the glory of that light, being led by the hand of them that were with me, I came into Damascus.

12 And one Ananias, a devout man according to the law, having a good report of all the Jews which dwelt *there*,

13 Came unto me, and stood, and said unto me, Brother Saul, receive thy sight. And the same hour I looked up upon him.

14 And he said, The אֱלֹהִים of our fathers hath chosen thee, that thou shouldest know his will, and see that Just One, and shouldest hear the voice of his mouth.

15 For thou shalt be his witness unto all men of what thou hast seen and heard.

16 And now why tarriest thou? arise, and be baptized, and wash away thy sins, calling on the name of the Lord.

17 And it came to pass, that, when I was come again to Jerusalem, even while I prayed in the temple, I was in a trance;

18 And saw him saying unto me, Make haste, and get thee quickly out of Jerusalem: for they will not receive thy testimony concerning me.

19 And I said, Lord, they know that I imprisoned and beat in every synagogue them that believed on thee:

20 And when the blood of thy martyr Stephen was shed, I also was standing by, and consenting unto his death, and kept the raiment of them that slew him.

21 And he said unto me, Depart: for I will send thee far hence unto the Gentiles.

22 And they gave him audience unto this word, and *then* lifted up their voices, and said, Away with such a *fellow* from the earth: for it is not fit that he should live.

23 And as they cried out, and cast off *their* clothes, and threw dust into the air,

24 The chief captain commanded him to be brought into the castle, and bade that he should be examined by scourging; that he might know wherefore they cried so against him.

25 And as they bound him with thongs, Paul said unto the centurion that stood by, Is it lawful for you to scourge a man that is a Roman, and uncondemned?

26 When the centurion heard *that*, he went and told the chief captain, saying, Take heed what thou doest: for this man is a Roman.

27 Then the chief captain came, and said unto him, Tell me, art thou a Roman? He said, Yea.

28 And the chief captain answered, With a great sum obtained I this freedom. And Paul said, But I was *free* born.

29 Then straightway they departed from him which should have examined him: and the chief captain also was afraid, after he knew that he was a Roman, and because he had bound him.

30 On the morrow, because he would have known the certainty wherefore he was accused of the Jews, he loosed him from *his* bands, and commanded the chief priests and all their council to appear, and brought Paul down, and set him before them.

CHAPTER 23

AND Paul, earnestly beholding the council, said, Men *and* brethren, I have lived in all good conscience before אֱלֹהִים until this day.

2 And the high priest Ananias commanded them that stood by him to smite him on the mouth.

3 Then said Paul unto him, אֱלֹ shall smite thee, *thou* whited wall: for sittest thou to judge me after the law, and commandest me to be smitten contrary to the law?

4 And they that stood by said, Revilest thou אֱלֹהִים's high priest?

5 Then said Paul, I wist not, brethren, that he was the high priest: for it is written, Thou shalt not speak evil of the ruler of thy people.

6 But when Paul perceived that the one part were Sadducees, and the other Pharisees, he cried out in the council, Men *and* brethren, I am a Pharisee, the son of a Pharisee: of the hope and resurrection of the dead I am called in question.

7 And when he had so said, there arose a dissension between the Pharisees and the Sadducees: and the multitude was divided.

8 For the Sadducees say that there is no resurrection, neither angel, nor spirit: but the Pharisees confess both.

9 And there arose a great cry: and the scribes *that were* of the Pharisees' part arose, and strove, saying, We find no evil in this man: but if a spirit or an angel hath spoken to him, let us not fight against אֱלֹהִים.

10 And when there arose a great dissension, the chief captain, fearing lest Paul should have been pulled in pieces of them, commanded the soldiers to go down, and to take him by force from among them, and to bring *him* into the castle.

11 And the night following the Lord stood by him, and said, Be of good cheer, Paul: for as thou hast testified of me in Jerusalem, so must thou bear witness also at Rome.

12 And when it was day, certain of the Jews banded together, and bound themselves under a curse, saying that they would neither eat nor drink till they had killed Paul.

13 And they were more than forty which had made this conspiracy.

14 And they came to the chief priests and elders, and said, We have bound ourselves under a great curse, that we will eat nothing until we have slain Paul.

15 Now therefore ye with the council signify to the chief captain that he bring him down unto you to morrow, as though ye would inquire something more perfectly concerning him: and we, or ever he come near, are ready to kill him.

16 And when Paul's sister's son heard of their lying in wait, he went and entered into the castle, and told Paul.

17 Then Paul called one of the centurions unto *him*, and said, Bring this young man unto the chief captain: for he hath a certain thing to tell him.

18 So he took him, and brought *him* to the chief captain, and said, Paul the prisoner called me unto *him*, and prayed me to bring this young man unto thee, who hath something to say unto thee.

19 Then the chief captain took him by the hand, and went *with him* aside privately, and asked *him*, What is that thou hast to tell me?

20 And he said, The Jews have agreed to desire thee that thou wouldest bring down Paul to morrow into the council, as though they would inquire somewhat of him more perfectly.

21 But do not thou yield unto them: for there lie in wait for him of them more than forty men, which have bound themselves with an oath, that they will neither eat nor drink till they have killed him: and now are they ready, looking for a promise from thee.

22 So the chief captain *then* let the young man depart, and charged *him, See thou* tell no man that thou hast shewed these things to me.

23 And he called unto *him* two centurions, saying, Make ready two hundred soldiers to go to Cæsarea, and horsemen threescore and ten, and spearmen two hundred, at the third hour of the night;

24 And provide *them* beasts, that they may set Paul on, and bring *him* safe unto Felix the governor.

25 And he wrote a letter after this manner:

26 Claudius Lysias unto the most excellent governor Felix *sendeth* greeting.

27 This man was taken of the Jews, and should have been killed of them: then came I with an army, and rescued him, having understood that he was a Roman.

28 And when I would have known the cause wherefore they accused him, I brought him forth into their council:

29 Whom I perceived to be accused of questions of their law, but to have nothing laid to his charge worthy of death or of bonds.

30 And when it was told me how that the Jews laid wait for the man, I sent straightway to thee, and gave commandment to his accusers also to say before thee what *they had* against him. Farewell.

31 Then the soldiers, as it was commanded them, took Paul, and brought *him* by night to Antipatris.

32 On the morrow they left the horsemen to go with him, and returned to the castle:

33 Who, when they came to Cæsarea, and delivered the epistle to the governor, presented Paul also before him.

34 And when the governor had read *the letter*, he asked of what province he was. And when he understood that *he was* of Cilicia;

35 I will hear thee, said he, when thine accusers are also come. And he commanded him to be kept in Herod's judgment hall.

CHAPTER 24

AND after five days Ananias the high priest descended with the elders, and *with* a certain orator *named* Tertullus, who informed the governor against Paul.

2 And when he was called forth, Tertullus began to accuse *him*, saying, Seeing that by thee we enjoy great quietness, and that very worthy deeds are done unto this nation by thy providence,

3 We accept *it* always, and in all places, most noble Felix, with all thankfulness.

4 Notwithstanding, that I be not further tedious unto thee, I pray thee that thou wouldest hear us of thy clemency a few words.

5 For we have found this man *a* pestilent *fellow*, and a mover of sedition among all the Jews throughout the world, and a ringleader of the sect of the Nazarenes:

6 Who also hath gone about to profane the temple: whom we took, and would have judged according to our law.

7 But the chief captain Lysias came *upon us*, and with great violence took *him* away out of our hands,

8 Commanding his accusers to come unto thee: by examining of whom thyself mayest take knowledge of all these things, whereof we accuse him.

9 And the Jews also assented, saying that these things were so.

10 Then Paul, after that the governor had beckoned unto him to speak, answered, Forasmuch as I know that thou hast been of many years a judge unto this nation, I do the more cheerfully answer for myself:

11 Because that thou mayest understand, that there are yet but twelve days since I went up to Jerusalem for to worship.

12 And they neither found me in the temple disputing with any man, neither raising up the people, neither in the synagogues, nor in the city:

13 Neither can they prove the things whereof they now accuse me.

14 But this I confess unto thee, that after the way which they call heresy, so worship I the אֱלֹהִים of my fathers, believing all things which are written in the law and in the prophets:

15 And have hope toward אֱלֹהִים, which they themselves also allow, that there shall be a resurrection of the dead, both of the just and unjust.

16 And herein do I exercise myself, to have always a conscience void of offence toward אֱלֹהִים, and *toward* men.

17 Now after many years I came to bring alms to my nation, and offerings.

18 Whereupon certain Jews from Asia found me purified in the temple, neither with multitude, nor with tumult.

19 Who ought to have been here before thee, and object, if they had ought against me.

20 Or else let these same *here* say, if they have found any evil doing in me, while I stood before the council,

21 Except it be for this one voice, that I cried standing among them, Touching the resurrection of the dead I am called in question by you this day.

22 And when Felix heard these things, having more perfect knowledge of *that* way, he deferred them, and said, When Lysias the chief captain shall come down, I will know the uttermost of your matter.

23 And he commanded a centurion to keep Paul, and to let *him* have liberty, and that he should forbid none of his acquaintance to minister or come unto him.

24 And after certain days, when Felix came with his wife Drusilla, which was a Jewess, he sent for Paul, and heard him concerning the faith in Christ.

25 And as he reasoned of righteousness, temperance, and judgment to come, Felix trembled, and answered, Go thy way for this time; when I have a convenient season, I will call for thee.

26 He hoped also that money should have been given him of Paul, that he might loose him: wherefore he sent for him the oftener, and communed with him.

27 But after two years Porcius Festus came into Felix' room: and Felix, willing to shew the Jews a pleasure, left Paul bound.

CHAPTER 25

NOW when Festus was come into the province, after three days he ascended from Cæsarea to Jerusalem.

2 Then the high priest and the chief of the Jews informed him against Paul, and besought him,

3 And desired favour against him, that he would send for him to Jerusalem, laying wait in the way to kill him.

4 But Festus answered, that Paul should be kept at Cæsarea, and that he himself would depart shortly *thither*.

5 Let them therefore, said he, which among you are able, go down with *me*, and accuse this man, if there be any wickedness in him.

6 And when he had tarried among them more than ten days, he went down unto Cæsarea; and the next day sitting on the judgment seat commanded Paul to be brought.

7 And when he was come, the Jews which came down from Jerusalem stood round about, and laid many and grievous complaints against Paul, which they could not prove.

8 While he answered for himself, Neither against the law of the Jews, neither against the temple, nor yet against Cæsar, have I offended any thing at all.

9 But Festus, willing to do the Jews a pleasure, answered Paul, and said, Wilt thou go up to Jerusalem, and there be judged of these things before me?

10 Then said Paul, I stand at Cæsar's judgment seat, where I ought to be judged: to the Jews have I done no wrong, as thou very well knowest.

11 For if I be an offender, or have committed any thing worthy of death, I refuse not to die: but if there be none of these things whereof these accuse me, no man may deliver me unto them. I appeal unto Cæsar.

12 Then Festus, when he had conferred with the council, answered, Hast thou appealed unto Cæsar? unto Cæsar shalt thou go.

13 And after certain days king Agrippa and Bernice came unto Cæsarea to salute Festus.

14 And when they had been there many days, Festus declared Paul's cause unto the king, saying, There is a certain man left in bonds by Felix:

15 About whom, when I was at Jerusalem, the chief priests and the elders of the Jews informed *me*, desiring *to have* judgment against him.

16 To whom I answered, It is not the manner of the Romans to deliver any man to die, before that he which is accused have the accusers face to face, and have licence to answer for himself concerning the crime laid against him.

17 Therefore, when they were come hither, without any delay on the morrow I sat on the judgment seat, and commanded the man to be brought forth.

18 Against whom when the accusers stood up, they brought none accusation of such things as I supposed:

19 But had certain questions against him of their own superstition, and of one Yashiyah, which was dead, whom Paul affirmed to be alive.

20 And because I doubted of such manner of questions, I asked *him* whether he would go to Jerusalem, and there be judged of these matters.

21 But when Paul had appealed to be reserved unto the hearing of Augustus, I commanded him to be kept till I might send him to Cæsar.

22 Then Agrippa said unto Festus, I would also hear the man myself. To morrow, said he, thou shalt hear him.

23 And on the morrow, when Agrippa was come, and Bernice, with great pomp, and was entered into the place of hearing, with the chief captains, and principal men of the city, at Festus' commandment Paul was brought forth.

24 And Festus said, King Agrippa, and all men which are here present with us, ye see this man, about whom all the multitude of the Jews have dealt with me, both at Jerusalem, and *also* here, crying that he ought not to live any longer.

25 But when I found that he had committed nothing worthy of death, and that he himself hath appealed to Augustus, I have determined to send him.

26 Of whom I have no certain thing to write unto my lord. Wherefore I have brought him forth before you, and specially before thee, O king Agrippa, that, after examination had, I might have somewhat to write.

27 For it seemeth to me unreasonable to send a prisoner, and not withal to signify the crimes *laid* against him.

CHAPTER 26

THEN Agrippa said unto Paul, Thou art permitted to speak for thyself. Then Paul stretched forth the hand, and answered for himself:

2 I think myself happy, king Agrippa, because I shall answer for myself this day before thee touching all the things whereof I am accused of the Jews:

3 Especially *because I know* thee to be expert in all customs and questions which are among the Jews: wherefore I beseech thee to hear me patiently.

4 My manner of life from my youth, which was at the first among mine own nation at Jerusalem, know all the Jews;

5 Which knew me from the beginning, if they would testify, that after the most straitest sect of our religion I lived a Pharisee.

6 And now I stand and am judged for the hope of the promise made of אֱלֹהִים unto our fathers:

7 Unto which *promise* our twelve tribes, instantly serving אֱלֹהִים day and night, hope to come. For which hope's sake, king Agrippa, I am accused of the Jews.

8 Why should it be thought a thing incredible with you, that אֱלֹהִים should raise the dead?

9 I verily thought with myself, that I ought to do many things contrary to the name of Yashiyah of Nazareth.

10 Which thing I also did in Jerusalem: and many of the saints did I shut up in prison, having received authority from the chief priests; and when they were put to death, I gave my voice against *them.*

11 And I punished them oft in every synagogue, and compelled *them* to blaspheme; and being exceedingly mad against them, I persecuted *them* even unto strange cities.

12 Whereupon as I went to Damascus with authority and commission from the chief priests,

13 At midday, O king, I saw in the way a light from heaven, above the brightness of the sun, shining round about me and them which journeyed with me.

14 And when we were all fallen to the earth, I heard a voice speaking unto me, and saying in the Hebrew tongue, Saul, Saul, why persecutest thou me? *it is* hard for thee to kick against the pricks.

15 And I said, Who art thou, Lord? And he said, I am Yashiyah whom thou persecutest.

16 But rise, and stand upon thy feet: for I have appeared unto thee for this purpose, to make thee a minister and a witness both of these things which thou hast seen, and of those things in the which I will appear unto thee;

17 Delivering thee from the people, and *from* the Gentiles, unto whom now I send thee,

18 To open their eyes, *and* to turn *them* from darkness to light, and *from* the power of Satan unto אֱלֹהִים, that they may receive forgiveness of sins, and inheritance among them which are sanctified by faith that is in me.

19 Whereupon, O king Agrippa, I was not disobedient unto the heavenly vision:

20 But shewed first unto them of Damascus, and at Jerusalem, and throughout all the coasts of Judæa, and *then* to the Gentiles, that they should repent and turn to אֱלֹהִים, and do works meet for repentance.

21 For these causes the Jews caught me in the temple, and went about to kill *me.*

22 Having therefore obtained help of אֱלֹהִים, I continue unto this day, witnessing both to small and great, saying none other things than those which the prophets and Moses did say should come:

23 That Christ should suffer, *and* that he should be the first that should rise from the dead, and should shew light unto the people, and to the Gentiles.

24 And as he thus spake for himself, Festus said with a loud voice, Paul, thou art beside thyself; much learning doth make thee mad.

25 But he said, I am not mad, most noble Festus; but speak forth the words of truth and soberness.

26 For the king knoweth of these things, before whom also I speak freely: for I am persuaded that none of these things are hidden from him; for this thing was not done in a corner.

27 King Agrippa, believest thou the prophets? I know that thou believest.

28 Then Agrippa said unto Paul, Almost thou persuadest me to be a Christian.

29 And Paul said, I would to אֱלֹהִים, that not only thou, but also all that hear me this day, were both almost, and altogether such as I am, except these bonds.

30 And when he had thus spoken, the king rose up, and the governor, and Bernice, and they that sat with them:

31 And when they were gone aside, they talked between themselves, saying, This man doeth nothing worthy of death or of bonds.

32 Then said Agrippa unto Festus, This man might have been set at liberty, if he had not appealed unto Cæsar.

CHAPTER 27

AND when it was determined that we should sail into Italy, they delivered Paul and certain other prisoners unto *one* named Julius, a centurion of Augustus' band.

2 And entering into a ship of Adramyttium, we launched, meaning to sail by the coasts of Asia; *one* Aristarchus, a Macedonian of Thessalonica, being with us.

3 And the next *day* we touched at Sidon. And Julius courteously entreated Paul, and gave *him* liberty to go unto his friends to refresh himself.

4 And when we had launched from thence, we sailed under Cyprus, because the winds were contrary.

5 And when we had sailed over the sea of Cilicia and Pamphylia, we came to Myra, *a city* of Lycia.

6 And there the centurion found a ship of Alexandria sailing into Italy; and he put us therein.

7 And when we had sailed slowly many days, and scarce were come over against Cnidus, the wind not suffering us, we sailed under Crete, over against Salmone;

8 And, hardly passing it, came unto a place which is called The fair havens; nigh whereunto was the city *of* Lasea.

9 Now when much time was spent, and when sailing was now dangerous, because the fast was now already past, Paul admonished *them,*

10 And said unto them, Sirs, I perceive that this voyage will be with hurt and much damage, not only of the lading and ship, but also of our lives.

11 Nevertheless the centurion believed the master and the owner of the ship, more than those things which were spoken by Paul.

12 And because the haven was not commodious to winter in, the more part advised to depart thence also, if by any means they might attain to Phenice, *and there* to winter; which is an haven of Crete, and lieth toward the south west and north west.

13 And when the south wind blew softly, supposing that they had obtained *their* purpose, loosing *thence,* they sailed close by Crete.

14 But not long after there arose against it a tempestuous wind, called Euroclydon.

15 And when the ship was caught, and could not bear up into the wind, we let *her* drive.

16 And running under a certain island which is called Clauda, we had much work to come by the boat:

17 Which when they had taken up, they used helps, undergirding the ship; and, fearing lest they should fall into the quicksands, strake sail, and so were driven.

18 And we being exceedingly tossed with a tempest, the next *day* they lightened the ship;

19 And the third *day* we cast out with our own hands the tackling of the ship.

20 And when neither sun nor stars in many days appeared, and no small tempest lay on *us*, all hope that we should be saved was then taken away.

21 But after long abstinence Paul stood forth in the midst of them, and said, Sirs, ye should have hearkened unto me, and not have loosed from Crete, and to have gained this harm and loss.

22 And now I exhort you to be of good cheer: for there shall be no loss of *any man's* life among you, but of the ship.

23 For there stood by me this night the angel of אֱלֹהִים, whose I am, and whom I serve,

24 Saying, Fear not, Paul; thou must be brought before Cæsar: and, lo, אֱלֹהִים hath given thee all them that sail with thee.

25 Wherefore, sirs, be of good cheer: for I believe אֱלֹהִים, that it shall be even as it was told me.

26 Howbeit we must be cast upon a certain island.

27 But when the fourteenth night was come, as we were driven up and down in Adria, about midnight the shipmen deemed that they drew near to some country;

28 And sounded, and found *it* twenty fathoms: and when they had gone a little further, they sounded again, and found *it* fifteen fathoms.

29 Then fearing lest we should have fallen upon rocks, they cast four anchors out of the stern, and wished for the day.

30 And as the shipmen were about to flee out of the ship, when they had let down the boat into the sea, under colour as though they would have cast anchors out of the foreship,

31 Paul said to the centurion and to the soldiers, Except these abide in the ship, ye cannot be saved.

32 Then the soldiers cut off the ropes of the boat, and let her fall off.

33 And while the day was coming on, Paul besought *them* all to take meat, saying, This day is the fourteenth day that ye have tarried and continued fasting, having taken nothing.

34 Wherefore I pray you to take *some* meat: for this is for your health: for there shall not an hair fall from the head of any of you.

35 And when he had thus spoken, he took bread, and gave thanks to אֱלֹהִים in presence of them all: and when he had broken *it*, he began to eat.

36 Then were they all of good cheer, and they also took *some* meat.

37 And we were in all in the ship two hundred threescore and sixteen souls.

38 And when they had eaten enough, they lightened the ship, and cast out the wheat into the sea.

39 And when it was day, they knew not the land: but they discovered a certain creek with a shore, into the which they were minded, if it were possible, to thrust in the ship.

40 And when they had taken up the anchors, they committed *themselves* unto the sea, and loosed the rudder bands, and hoised up the mainsail to the wind, and made toward shore.

41 And falling into a place where two seas met, they ran the ship aground; and the forepart stuck fast, and remained unmoveable, but the hinder part was broken with the violence of the waves.

42 And the soldiers' counsel was to kill the prisoners, lest any of them should swim out, and escape.

43 But the centurion, willing to save Paul, kept them from *their* purpose; and commanded that they which could swim should cast *themselves* first *into the sea*, and get to land:

44 And the rest, some on boards, and some on *broken pieces* of the ship. And so it came to pass, that they escaped all safe to land.

CHAPTER 28

AND when they were escaped, then they knew that the island was called Melita.

2 And the barbarous people shewed us no little kindness: for they kindled a fire, and received us every one, because of the present rain, and because of the cold.

3 And when Paul had gathered a bundle of sticks, and laid *them* on the fire, there came a viper out of the heat, and fastened on his hand.

4 And when the barbarians saw the *venomous* beast hang on his hand, they said among themselves, No doubt this man is a murderer, whom, though he hath escaped the sea, yet vengeance suffereth not to live.

5 And he shook off the beast into the fire, and felt no harm.

6 Howbeit they looked when he should have swollen, or fallen down dead suddenly: but after they had looked a great while, and saw no harm come to him, they changed their minds, and said that he was a god.

7 In the same quarters were possessions of the chief man of the island, whose name was Publius; who received us, and lodged us three days courteously.

8 And it came to pass, that the father of Publius lay sick of a fever and of a bloody flux: to whom Paul entered in, and prayed, and laid his hands on him, and healed him.

9 So when this was done, others also, which had diseases in the island, came, and were healed:

10 Who also honoured us with many honours; and when we departed, they laded *us* with such things as were necessary.

11 And after three months we departed in a ship of Alexandria, which had wintered in the isle, whose sign was Castor and Pollux.

12 And landing at Syracuse, we tarried *there* three days.

13 And from thence we fetched a compass, and came to Rhegium: and after one day the south wind blew, and we came the next day to Puteoli:

14 Where we found brethren, and were desired to tarry with them seven days: and so we went toward Rome.

15 And from thence, when the brethren heard of us, they came to meet us as far as Appii forum, and The three taverns: whom when Paul saw, he thanked אֱלֹהִים, and took courage.

16 And when we came to Rome, the centurion delivered the prisoners to the captain of the guard: but Paul was suffered to dwell by himself with a soldier that kept him.

17 And it came to pass, that after three days Paul called the chief of the Jews together: and when they were come together, he said unto them, Men *and* brethren, though I have committed nothing against the people, or customs of our fathers, yet was I delivered prisoner from Jerusalem into the hands of the Romans.

18 Who, when they had examined me, would have let *me* go, because there was no cause of death in me.

19 But when the Jews spake against *it*, I was constrained to appeal unto Cæsar; not that I had ought to accuse my nation of.

20 For this cause therefore have I called for you, to see *you*, and to speak with *you*: because that for the hope of Israel I am bound with this chain.

21 And they said unto him, We neither received letters out of Judæa concerning thee, neither any of the brethren that came shewed or spake any harm of thee.

22 But we desire to hear of thee what thou thinkest: for as concerning this sect, we know that every where it is spoken against.

23 And when they had appointed him a day, there came many to him into *his* lodging; to whom he expounded and testified the kingdom of אֱלֹהִים, persuading them concerning Yashiyah, both out of the law of Moses, and *out of* the prophets, from morning till evening.

24 And some believed the things which were spoken, and some believed not.

25 And when they agreed not among themselves, they departed, after that Paul had spoken one word, Well spake the Holy Ghost by Esaias the prophet unto our fathers,

26 Saying, Go unto this people, and say, Hearing ye shall hear, and shall not understand; and seeing ye shall see, and not perceive:

27 For the heart of this people is waxed gross, and their ears are dull of hearing, and their eyes have they closed; lest they should see with *their* eyes, and hear with *their* ears, and understand with *their* heart, and should be converted, and I should heal them.

28 Be it known therefore unto you, that the salvation of אֱלֹהִים is sent unto the Gentiles, and *that* they will hear it.

29 And when he had said these words, the Jews departed, and had great reasoning among themselves.

30 And Paul dwelt two whole years in his own hired house, and received all that came in unto him,

31 Preaching the kingdom of אֱלֹהִים, and teaching those things which concern the Lord Yashiyah Christ, with all confidence, no man forbidding him.

THE EPISTLE OF PAUL THE APOSTLE
TO THE
ROMANS.

CHAPTER 1

PAUL, a servant of Yashiyah Christ, called *to be* an apostle, separated unto the gospel of אֱלֹהִים,

2 (Which he had promised afore by his prophets in the holy scriptures,)

3 Concerning his Son Yashiyah Christ our Lord, which was made of the seed of David according to the flesh;

4 And declared *to be* the Son of אֱלֹהִים with power, according to the spirit of holiness, by the resurrection from the dead:

5 By whom we have received grace and apostleship, for obedience to the faith among all nations, for his name:

6 Among whom are ye also the called of Yashiyah Christ:

7 To all that be in Rome, beloved of אֱלֹהִים, called *to be* saints: Grace to you and peace from אֱלֹהִים our Father, and the Lord Yashiyah Christ.

8 First, I thank my אֱלֹהִים through Yashiyah Christ for you all, that your faith is spoken of throughout the whole world.

9 For אֱלֹהִים is my witness, whom I serve with my spirit in the gospel of his Son, that without ceasing I make mention of you always in my prayers;

10 Making request, if by any means now at length I might have a prosperous journey by the will of אֱלֹהִים to come unto you.

11 For I long to see you, that I may impart unto you some spiritual gift, to the end ye may be established;

12 That is, that I may be comforted together with you by the mutual faith both of you and me.

13 Now I would not have you ignorant, brethren, that oftentimes I purposed to come unto you, (but was let hitherto,) that I might have some fruit among you also, even as among other Gentiles.

14 I am debtor both to the Greeks, and to the Barbarians; both to the wise, and to the unwise.

15 So, as much as in me is, I am ready to preach the gospel to you that are at Rome also.

16 For I am not ashamed of the gospel of Christ: for it is the power of אֱלֹהִים unto salvation to every one that believeth; to the Jew first, and also to the Greek.

17 For therein is the righteousness of אֱלֹהִים revealed from faith to faith: as it is written, The just shall live by faith.

18 For the wrath of אֱלֹהִים is revealed from heaven against all ungodliness and unrighteousness of men, who hold the truth in unrighteousness;

19 Because that which may be known of אֱלֹהִים is manifest in them; for אֱלֹהִים hath shewed *it* unto them.

20 For the invisible things of him from the creation of the world are clearly seen, being understood by the things that are made, *even* his eternal power and Godhead; so that they are without excuse:

21 Because that, when they knew אֱלֹהִים, they glorified *him* not as אֱלֹהִים, neither were thankful; but became vain in their imaginations, and their foolish heart was darkened.

22 Professing themselves to be wise, they became fools,

23 And changed the glory of the uncorruptible אֱלֹהִים into an image made like to corruptible man, and to birds, and fourfooted beasts, and creeping things.

24 Wherefore אֱלֹהִים also gave them up to uncleanness through the lusts of their own hearts, to dishonour their own bodies between themselves:

25 Who changed the truth of אֱלֹהִים into a lie, and worshipped and served the creature more than the Creator, who is blessed for ever. Amen.

26 For this cause אֱלֹהִים gave them up unto vile affections: for even their women did change the natural use into that which is against nature:

27 And likewise also the men, leaving the natural use of the woman, burned in their lust one toward another; men with men working that which is unseemly, and receiving in themselves that recompence of their error which was meet.

28 And even as they did not like to retain אֱלֹהִים in *their* knowledge, אֱלֹהִים gave them over to a reprobate mind, to do those things which are not convenient;

29 Being filled with all unrighteousness, fornication, wickedness, covetousness, maliciousness; full of envy, murder, debate, deceit, malignity; whisperers,

30 Backbiters, haters of אֱלֹהִים, despiteful, proud, boasters, inventors of evil things, disobedient to parents,

31 Without understanding, covenantbreakers, without natural affection, implacable, unmerciful:

32 Who knowing the judgment of אֱלֹהִים, that they which commit such things are worthy of death, not only do the same, but have

pleasure in them that do them.

CHAPTER 2

THEREFORE thou art inexcusable, O man, whosoever thou art that judgest: for wherein thou judgest another, thou condemnest thyself; for thou that judgest doest the same things.

2 But we are sure that the judgment of אֱלֹהִים is according to truth against them which commit such things.

3 And thinkest thou this, O man, that judgest them which do such things, and doest the same, that thou shalt escape the judgment of אֱלֹהִים?

4 Or despisest thou the riches of his goodness and forbearance and longsuffering; not knowing that the goodness of אֱלֹהִים leadeth thee to repentance?

5 But after thy hardness and impenitent heart treasurest up unto thyself wrath against the day of wrath and revelation of the righteous judgment of אֱלֹהִים;

6 Who will render to every man according to his deeds:

7 To them who by patient continuance in well doing seek for glory and honour and immortality, eternal life:

8 But unto them that are contentious, and do not obey the truth, but obey unrighteousness, indignation and wrath,

9 Tribulation and anguish, upon every soul of man that doeth evil, of the Jew first, and also of the Gentile;

10 But glory, honour, and peace, to every man that worketh good, to the Jew first, and also to the Gentile:

11 For there is no respect of persons with אֱלֹהִים.

12 For as many as have sinned without law shall also perish without law: and as many as have sinned in the law shall be judged by the law;

13 (For not the hearers of the law *are* just before אֱלֹהִים, but the doers of the law shall be justified.

14 For when the Gentiles, which have not the law, do by nature the things contained in the law, these, having not the law, are a law unto themselves:

15 Which shew the work of the law written in their hearts, their conscience also bearing witness, and *their* thoughts the mean while accusing or else excusing one another;)

16 In the day when אֱלֹהִים shall judge the secrets of men by Yashiyah Christ according to my gospel.

17 Behold, thou art called a Jew, and restest in the law, and makest thy boast of אֱלֹהִים,

18 And knowest *his* will, and approvest the things that are more excellent, being instructed out of the law;

19 And art confident that thou thyself art a guide of the blind, a light of them which are in darkness,

20 An instructor of the foolish, a teacher of babes, which hast the form of knowledge and of the truth in the law.

21 Thou therefore which teachest another, teachest thou not thyself? thou that preachest a man should not steal, dost thou steal?

22 Thou that sayest a man should not commit adultery, dost thou commit adultery? thou that abhorrest idols, dost thou commit sacrilege?

23 Thou that makest thy boast of the law, through breaking the law dishonourest thou אֱלֹהִים?

24 For the name of אֱלֹהִים is blasphemed among the Gentiles through you, as it is written.

25 For circumcision verily profiteth, if thou keep the law: but if thou be a breaker of the law, thy circumcision is made uncircumcision.

26 Therefore if the uncircumcision keep the righteousness of the law, shall not his uncircumcision be counted for circumcision?

27 And shall not uncircumcision which is by nature, if it fulfil the law, judge thee, who by the letter and circumcision dost transgress the law?

28 For he is not a Jew, which is one outwardly; neither *is that* circumcision, which is outward in the flesh:

29 But he *is* a Jew, which is one inwardly; and circumcision *is that* of the heart, in the spirit, *and* not in the letter; whose praise *is* not of men, but of אֱלֹהִים.

CHAPTER 3

WHAT advantage then hath the Jew? or what profit *is there* of circumcision?

2 Much every way: chiefly, because that unto them were committed the oracles of אֱלֹהִים.

3 For what if some did not believe? shall their unbelief make the faith of אֱלֹהִים without effect?

4 אֱלֹהִים forbid: yea, let אֱלֹהִים be true, but every man a liar; as it is written, That thou mightest be justified in thy sayings, and mightest overcome when thou art judged.

5 But if our unrighteousness commend the righteousness of אֱלֹהִים, what shall we say? *Is* אֱלֹהִים unrighteous who taketh vengeance? (I speak as a man)

6 אֱלֹהִים forbid: for then how shall אֱלֹהִים judge the world?

7 For if the truth of אֱלֹהִים hath more abounded through my lie unto his glory; why yet am I also judged as a sinner?

8 And not *rather*, (as we be slanderously reported, and as some affirm that we say,) Let us do evil, that good may come? whose damnation is just.

9 What then? are we better *than they?* No, in no wise: for we have before proved both Jews and Gentiles, that they are all under sin;

10 As it is written, There is none righteous, no, not one:

11 There is none that understandeth, there is none that seeketh after אֱלֹהִים.

12 They are all gone out of the way, they are together become unprofitable; there is none that doeth good, no, not one.

13 Their throat *is* an open sepulchre; with their tongues they have used deceit; the poison of asps *is* under their lips:

14 Whose mouth *is* full of cursing and bitterness:

15 Their feet *are* swift to shed blood:

16 Destruction and misery *are* in their ways:

17 And the way of peace have they not known:

18 There is no fear of אֱלֹהִים before their eyes.

19 Now we know that what things soever the law saith, it saith to them who are under the law: that every mouth may be stopped, and all the world may become guilty before אֱלֹהִים.

20 Therefore by the deeds of the law there shall no flesh be justified in his sight: for by the law *is* the knowledge of sin.

21 But now the righteousness of אֱלֹהִים without the law is manifested, being witnessed by the law and the prophets;

22 Even the righteousness of אֱלֹהִים *which is* by faith of Yashiyah Christ unto all and upon all them that believe: for there is no difference:

23 For all have sinned, and come short of the glory of אֱלֹהִים;

24 Being justified freely by his grace through the redemption that is in Christ Yashiyah:

25 Whom אֱלֹהִים hath set forth *to be* a propitiation through faith in his blood, to declare his righteousness for the remission of sins that are past, through the forbearance of אֱלֹהִים;

26 To declare, *I say*, at this time his righteousness: that he might be just, and the justifier of him which believeth in Yashiyah.

27 Where *is* boasting then? It is excluded. By what law? of works? Nay: but by the law of faith.

28 Therefore we conclude that a man is justified by faith without the deeds of the law.

29 *Is he* the אֱלֹהִים of the Jews only? *is he* not also of the Gentiles? Yes, of the Gentiles also:

30 Seeing *it is* one אֱלֹהִים, which shall justify the circumcision by faith, and uncircumcision through faith.

31 Do we then make void the law through faith? אֱלֹהִים forbid: yea, we establish the law.

CHAPTER 4

WHAT shall we say then that Abraham our father, as pertaining to the flesh, hath found?

2 For if Abraham were justified by works, he hath *whereof* to glory; but not before אֱלֹהִים.

3 For what saith the scripture? Abraham believed אֱלֹהִים, and it was counted unto him for righteousness.

4 Now to him that worketh is the reward not reckoned of grace, but of debt.

5 But to him that worketh not, but believeth on him that justifieth the ungodly, his faith is counted for righteousness.

6 Even as David also describeth the blessedness of the man, unto whom אֱלֹהִים imputeth righteousness without works,

7 *Saying*, Blessed *are* they whose iniquities are forgiven, and whose sins are covered.

8 Blessed *is* the man to whom the Lord will not impute sin.

9 *Cometh* this blessedness then upon the circumcision *only*, or upon the uncircumcision also? for we say that faith was reckoned to Abraham for righteousness.

10 How was it then reckoned? when he was in circumcision, or in uncircumcision? Not in circumcision, but in uncircumcision.

11 And he received the sign of circumcision, a seal of the righteousness of the faith which *he had yet* being uncircumcised: that he might be the father of all them that believe, though they be not circumcised; that righteousness might be imputed unto them also:

12 And the father of circumcision to them who are not of the circumcision only, but who also walk in the steps of that faith of our father Abraham, which *he had* being *yet* uncircumcised.

13 For the promise, that he should be the heir of the world, *was* not to Abraham, or to his seed, through the law, but through the righteousness of faith.

14 For if they which are of the law *be* heirs, faith is made void, and the promise made of none effect:

15 Because the law worketh wrath: for where no law is, *there is* no transgression.

16 Therefore *it is* of faith, that *it might be* by grace; to the end the promise might be sure to all the seed; not to that only which is of the law, but to that also which is of the faith of Abraham; who is the father of us all,

17 (As it is written, I have made thee a father of many nations,) before him whom he believed, *even* אֱלֹהִים, who quickeneth the dead, and calleth those things which be not as though they were.

18 Who against hope believed in hope, that he might become the father of many nations; according to that which was spoken, So shall thy seed be.

19 And being not weak in faith, he considered not his own body now dead, when he was about an hundred years old, neither yet the deadness of Sara's womb:

20 He staggered not at the promise of אֱלֹהִים through unbelief; but was strong in faith, giving glory to אֱלֹהִים;

21 And being fully persuaded that, what he had promised, he was able also to perform.

22 And therefore it was imputed to him for righteousness.

23 Now it was not written for his sake alone, that it was imputed to him;

24 But for us also, to whom it shall be imputed, if we believe on him that raised up Yashiyah our Lord from the dead;

25 Who was delivered for our offences, and was raised again for our justification.

CHAPTER 5

THEREFORE being justified by faith, we have peace with אֱלֹהִים through our Lord Yashiyah Christ:

2 By whom also we have access by faith into this grace wherein we stand, and rejoice in hope of the glory of אֱלֹהִים.

3 And not only *so*, but we glory in tribulations also: knowing that tribulation worketh patience;

4 And patience, experience; and experience, hope:

5 And hope maketh not ashamed; because the love of אֱלֹהִים is shed abroad in our hearts by the Holy Ghost which is given unto us.

6 For when we were yet without strength, in due time Christ died for the ungodly.

7 For scarcely for a righteous man will one die: yet peradventure for a good man some would even dare to die.

8 But אֱלֹהִים commendeth his love toward us, in that, while we were yet sinners, Christ died for us.

9 Much more then, being now justified by his blood, we shall be saved from wrath through him.

10 For if, when we were enemies, we were reconciled to אֱלֹהִים by the death of his Son, much more, being reconciled, we shall be saved by his life.

11 And not only *so*, but we also joy in אֱלֹהִים through our Lord Yashiyah Christ, by whom we have now received the atonement.

12 Wherefore, as by one man sin entered into the world, and death by sin; and so death passed upon all men, for that all have sinned:

13 (For until the law sin was in the world: but sin is not imputed when there is no law.

14 Nevertheless death reigned from Adam to Moses, even over them that had not sinned after the similitude of Adam's transgression, who is the figure of him that was to come.

15 But not as the offence, so also *is* the free gift. For if through the offence of one many be dead, much more the grace of אֱלֹהִים, and the gift by grace, *which is* by one man, Yashiyah Christ, hath abounded unto many.

16 And not as *it was* by one that sinned, *so is* the gift: for the judgment *was* by one to condemnation, but the free gift *is* of many offences unto justification.

17 For if by one man's offence death reigned by one; much more they which receive abundance of grace and of the gift of

righteousness shall reign in life by one, Yashiyah Christ.)

18 Therefore as by the offence of one *judgment came* upon all men to condemnation; even so by the righteousness of one *the free gift came* upon all men unto justification of life.

19 For as by one man's disobedience many were made sinners, so by the obedience of one shall many be made righteous.

20 Moreover the law entered, that the offence might abound. But where sin abounded, grace did much more abound:

21 That as sin hath reigned unto death, even so might grace reign through righteousness unto eternal life by Yashiyah Christ our Lord.

CHAPTER 6

WHAT shall we say then? Shall we continue in sin, that grace may abound?

2 אֱלֹהִים forbid. How shall we, that are dead to sin, live any longer therein?

3 Know ye not, that so many of us as were baptized into Yashiyah Christ were baptized into his death?

4 Therefore we are buried with him by baptism into death: that like as Christ was raised up from the dead by the glory of the Father, even so we also should walk in newness of life.

5 For if we have been planted together in the likeness of his death, we shall be also *in the likeness* of *his* resurrection:

6 Knowing this, that our old man is crucified with *him*, that the body of sin might be destroyed, that henceforth we should not serve sin.

7 For he that is dead is freed from sin.

8 Now if we be dead with Christ, we believe that we shall also live with him:

9 Knowing that Christ being raised from the dead dieth no more; death hath no more dominion over him.

10 For in that he died, he died unto sin once: but in that he liveth, he liveth unto אֱלֹהִים.

11 Likewise reckon ye also yourselves to be dead indeed unto sin, but alive unto אֱלֹ through Yashiyah Christ our Lord.

12 Let not sin therefore reign in your mortal body, that ye should obey it in the lusts thereof.

13 Neither yield ye your members *as* instruments of unrighteousness unto sin: but yield yourselves unto אֱלֹהִים, as those that are alive from the dead, and your members *as* instruments of righteousness unto אֱלֹהִים.

14 For sin shall not have dominion over you: for ye are not under the law, but under grace.

15 What then? shall we sin, because we are not under the law, but under grace? אֱלֹהִים forbid.

16 Know ye not, that to whom ye yield yourselves servants to obey, his servants ye are to whom ye obey; whether of sin unto death, or of obedience unto righteousness?

17 But אֱלֹהִים be thanked, that ye were the servants of sin, but ye have obeyed from the heart that form of doctrine which was delivered you.

18 Being then made free from sin, ye became the servants of righteousness.

19 I speak after the manner of men because of the infirmity of your flesh: for as ye have yielded your members servants to uncleanness and to iniquity unto iniquity; even so now yield your members servants to righteousness unto holiness.

20 For when ye were the servants of sin, ye were free from righteousness.

21 What fruit had ye then in those things whereof ye are now ashamed? for the end of those things *is* death.

22 But now being made free from sin, and become servants to אֱלֹהִים, ye have your fruit unto holiness, and the end everlasting life.

23 For the wages of sin *is* death; but the gift of אֱלֹהִים *is* eternal life through Yashiyah Christ our Lord.

CHAPTER 7

KNOW ye not, brethren, (for I speak to them that know the law,) how that the law hath dominion over a man as long as he liveth?

2 For the woman which hath an husband is bound by the law to *her* husband so long as he liveth; but if the husband be dead, she is loosed from the law of *her* husband.

3 So then if, while *her* husband liveth, she be married to another man, she shall be called an adulteress: but if her husband be dead, she is free from that law; so that she is no adulteress, though she be married to another man.

4 Wherefore, my brethren, ye also are become dead to the law by the body of Christ; that ye should be married to another, *even* to him who is raised from the dead, that we should bring forth fruit unto אֱלֹהִים.

5 For when we were in the flesh, the motions of sins, which were by the law, did work in our members to bring forth fruit unto death.

6 But now we are delivered from the law, that being dead wherein we were held; that we should serve in newness of spirit, and not *in* the oldness of the letter.

7 What shall we say then? *Is* the law sin? אֱלֹהִים forbid. Nay, I had not known sin, but by the law: for I had not known lust, except the law had said, Thou shalt not covet.

8 But sin, taking occasion by the commandment, wrought in me all manner of concupiscence. For without the law sin *was* dead.

9 For I was alive without the law once: but when the commandment came, sin revived, and I died.

10 And the commandment, which *was ordained* to life, I found *to be* unto death.

11 For sin, taking occasion by the commandment, deceived me, and by it slew *me*.

12 Wherefore the law *is* holy, and the commandment holy, and just, and good.

13 Was then that which is good made death unto me? אֱלֹהִים forbid. But sin, that it might appear sin, working death in me by that which is good; that sin by the commandment might become exceeding sinful.

14 For we know that the law is spiritual: but I am carnal, sold under sin.

15 For that which I do I allow not: for what I would, that do I not; but what I hate, that do I.

16 If then I do that which I would not, I consent unto the law that *it is* good.

17 Now then it is no more I that do it, but sin that dwelleth in me.

18 For I know that in me (that is, in my flesh,) dwelleth no good thing: for to will is present with me; but *how* to perform that which is good I find not.

19 For the good that I would I do not: but the evil which I would not, that I do.

20 Now if I do that I would not, it is no more I that do it, but sin that dwelleth in me.

21 I find then a law, that, when I would do good, evil is present with me.

22 For I delight in the law of אֱלֹהִים after the inward man:

23 But I see another law in my members, warring against the law of my mind, and bringing me into captivity to the law of sin which is in my members.

24 O wretched man that I am! who shall deliver me from the body of this death?

25 I thank אֱלֹהִים through Yashiyah Christ our Lord. So then with the mind I myself serve the law of אֱלֹהִים: but with the flesh the law of sin.

CHAPTER 8

THERE *is* therefore now no condemnation to them which are in Christ Yashiyah, who walk not after the flesh, but after the Spirit.

2 For the law of the Spirit of life in Christ Yashiyah hath made me free from the law of sin and death.

3 For what the law could not do, in that it was weak through the flesh, אֱלֹהִים sending his own Son in the likeness of sinful flesh, and for sin, condemned sin in the flesh:

4 That the righteousness of the law might be fulfilled in us, who walk not after the flesh, but after the Spirit.

5 For they that are after the flesh do mind the things of the flesh; but they that are after the Spirit the things of the Spirit.

6 For to be carnally minded *is* death; but to be spiritually minded *is* life and peace.

7 Because the carnal mind *is* enmity against אֱלֹהִים: for it is not subject to the law of אֱלֹהִים, neither indeed can be.

8 So then they that are in the flesh cannot please אֱלֹהִים.

9 But ye are not in the flesh, but in the Spirit, if so be that the Spirit of אֱלֹהִים dwell in you. Now if any man have not the Spirit of Christ, he is none of his.

10 And if Christ *be* in you, the body *is* dead because of sin; but the Spirit *is* life because of righteousness.

11 But if the Spirit of him that raised up Yashiyah from the dead dwell in you, he that raised up Christ from the dead shall also quicken your mortal bodies by his Spirit that dwelleth in you.

12 Therefore, brethren, we are debtors, not to the flesh, to live after the flesh.

13 For if ye live after the flesh, ye shall die: but if ye through the Spirit do mortify the deeds of the body, ye shall live.

14 For as many as are led by the Spirit of אֱלֹהִים, they are the sons of אֱלֹהִים.

15 For ye have not received the spirit of bondage again to fear; but ye have received the Spirit of adoption, whereby we cry, Abba, Father.

16 The Spirit itself beareth witness with our spirit, that we are the children of אֱלֹהִים:

17 And if children, then heirs; heirs of אֱלֹהִים, and joint-heirs with Christ; if so be that we suffer with *him*, that we may be also glorified together.

18 For I reckon that the sufferings of this present time *are* not worthy *to be compared* with the glory which shall be revealed in us.

19 For the earnest expectation of the creature waiteth for the manifestation of the sons of אֱלֹהִים.

20 For the creature was made subject to vanity, not willingly, but by reason of him who hath subjected *the same* in hope,

21 Because the creature itself also shall be delivered from the bondage of corruption into the glorious liberty of the children of אֱלֹהִים.

22 For we know that the whole creation groaneth and travaileth in pain together until now.

23 And not only *they*, but ourselves also, which have the firstfruits of the Spirit, even we ourselves groan within ourselves, waiting for the adoption, *to wit*, the redemption of our body.

24 For we are saved by hope: but hope that is seen is not hope: for what a man seeth, why doth he yet hope for?

25 But if we hope for that we see not, *then* do we with patience wait for *it*.

26 Likewise the Spirit also helpeth our infirmities: for we know not what we should pray for as we ought: but the Spirit itself maketh intercession for us with groanings which cannot be uttered.

27 And he that searcheth the hearts knoweth what *is* the mind of the Spirit, because he maketh intercession for the saints according to *the will of* אֱלֹהִים.

28 And we know that all things work together for good to them that love אֱלֹהִים, to them who are the called according to *his* purpose.

29 For whom he did foreknow, he also did predestinate *to be* conformed to the image of his Son, that he might be the firstborn among many brethren.

30 Moreover whom he did predestinate, them he also called: and whom he called, them he also justified: and whom he justified, them he also glorified.

31 What shall we then say to these things? If אֱלֹהִים *be* for us, who *can be* against us?

32 He that spared not his own Son, but delivered him up for us all, how shall he not with him also freely give us all things?

33 Who shall lay any thing to the charge of אֱלֹהִים's elect? *It is* אֱלֹהִים that justifieth.

34 Who *is* he that condemneth? *It is* Christ that died, yea rather, that is risen again, who is even at the right hand of אֱלֹהִים, who also maketh intercession for us.

35 Who shall separate us from the love of Christ? *shall* tribulation, or distress, or persecution, or famine, or nakedness, or peril, or sword?

36 As it is written, For thy sake we are killed all the day long; we are accounted as sheep for the slaughter.

37 Nay, in all these things we are more than conquerors through him that loved us.

38 For I am persuaded, that neither death, nor life, nor angels, nor principalities, nor powers, nor things present, nor things to come,

39 Nor height, nor depth, nor any other creature, shall be able to separate us from the love of אֱלֹהִים, which is in Christ Yashiyah our Lord.

CHAPTER 9

I SAY the truth in Christ, I lie not, my conscience also bearing me witness in the Holy Ghost,

2 That I have great heaviness and continual sorrow in my heart.

3 For I could wish that myself were accursed from Christ for my brethren, my kinsmen according to the flesh:

4 Who are Israelites; to whom *pertaineth* the adoption, and the glory, and the covenants, and the giving of the law, and the service *of* אֱלֹהִים, and the promises;

5 Whose *are* the fathers, and of whom as concerning the flesh Christ *came*, who is over all, אֱלֹהִים blessed for ever. Amen.

6 Not as though the word of אֱלֹהִים hath taken none effect. For they *are* not all Israel, which are of Israel:

7 Neither, because they are the seed of Abraham, *are they* all children: but, In Isaac shall thy seed be called.

8 That is, They which are the children of the flesh, these *are* not the children of אֱלֹהִים: but the children of the promise are counted for the seed.

9 For this *is* the word of promise, At this time will I come, and Sara shall have a son.

10 And not only *this;* but when Rebecca also had conceived by one, *even* by our father Isaac;

11 (For *the children* being not yet born, neither having done any good or evil, that the purpose of אֱלֹהִים according to election might stand, not of works, but of him that calleth;)

12 It was said unto her, The elder shall serve the younger.

13 As it is written, Jacob have I loved, but Esau have I hated.

14 What shall we say then? *Is there* unrighteousness with אֱלֹהִים? אֱלֹהִים forbid.

15 For he saith to Moses, I will have mercy on whom I will have mercy, and I will have compassion on whom I will have compassion.

16 So then *it is* not of him that willeth, nor of him that runneth, but of אֱלֹהִים that sheweth mercy.

17 For the scripture saith unto Pharaoh, Even for this same purpose have I raised thee up, that I might shew my power in thee, and that my name might be declared throughout all the earth.

18 Therefore hath he mercy on whom he will *have mercy,* and whom he will he hardeneth.

19 Thou wilt say then unto me, Why doth he yet find fault? For who hath resisted his will?

20 Nay but, O man, who art thou that repliest against אֱלֹהִים? Shall the thing formed say to him that formed *it,* Why hast thou made me thus?

21 Hath not the potter power over the clay, of the same lump to make one vessel unto honour, and another unto dishonour?

22 *What* if אֱלֹהִים, willing to shew *his* wrath, and to make his power known, endured with much longsuffering the vessels of wrath fitted to destruction:

23 And that he might make known the riches of his glory on the vessels of mercy, which he had afore prepared unto glory,

24 Even us, whom he hath called, not of the Jews only, but also of the Gentiles?

25 As he saith also in Osee, I will call them my people, which were not my people; and her beloved, which was not beloved.

26 And it shall come to pass, *that* in the place where it was said unto them, Ye *are* not my people; there shall they be called the children of the living אֱלֹהִים.

27 Esaias also crieth concerning Israel, Though the number of the children of Israel be as the sand of the sea, a remnant shall be saved:

28 For he will finish the work, and cut *it* short in righteousness: because a short work will the Lord make upon the earth.

29 And as Esaias said before, Except the Lord of Sabaoth had left us a seed, we had been as Sodoma, and been made like unto Gomorrha.

30 What shall we say then? That the Gentiles, which followed not after righteousness, have attained to righteousness, even the righteousness which is of faith.

31 But Israel, which followed after the law of righteousness, hath not attained to the law of righteousness.

32 Wherefore? Because *they sought it* not by faith, but as it were by the works of the law. For they stumbled at that stumblingstone;

33 As it is written, Behold, I lay in Sion a stumblingstone and rock of offence: and whosoever believeth on him shall not be ashamed.

CHAPTER 10

BRETHREN, my heart's desire and prayer to אֱלֹהִים for Israel is, that they might be saved.

2 For I bear them record that they have a zeal of אֱלֹהִים, but not according to knowledge.

3 For they being ignorant of אֱלֹהִים's righteousness, and going about to establish their own righteousness, have not submitted themselves unto the righteousness of אֱלֹהִים.

4 For Christ *is* the end of the law for righteousness to every one that believeth.

5 For Moses describeth the righteousness which is of the law, That the man which doeth those things shall live by them.

6 But the righteousness which is of faith speaketh on this wise, Say not in thine heart, Who shall ascend into heaven? (that is, to bring Christ down *from above:*)

7 Or, Who shall descend into the deep? (that is, to bring up Christ again from the dead.)

8 But what saith it? The word is nigh thee, *even* in thy mouth, and in thy heart: that is, the word of faith, which we preach;

9 That if thou shalt confess with thy mouth the Lord Yashiyah, and shalt believe in thine heart that אֱלֹהִים hath raised him from the dead, thou shalt be saved.

10 For with the heart man believeth unto righteousness; and with the mouth confession is made unto salvation.

11 For the scripture saith, Whosoever believeth on him shall not be ashamed.

12 For there is no difference between the Jew and the Greek: for the same Lord over all is rich unto all that call upon him.

13 For whosoever shall call upon the name of the Lord shall be saved.

14 How then shall they call on him in whom they have not believed? and how shall they believe in him of whom they have not heard? and how shall they hear without a preacher?

15 And how shall they preach, except they be sent? as it is written, How beautiful are the feet of them that preach the gospel of peace, and bring glad tidings of good things!

16 But they have not all obeyed the gospel. For Esaias saith, Lord, who hath believed our report?

17 So then faith *cometh* by hearing, and hearing by the word of אֱלֹהִים.

18 But I say, Have they not heard? Yes verily, their sound went into all the earth, and their words unto the ends of the world.

19 But I say, Did not Israel know? First Moses saith, I will provoke you to jealousy by *them that are* no people, *and* by a foolish nation I will anger you.

20 But Esaias is very bold, and saith, I was found of them that sought me not; I was made manifest unto them that asked not after me.

21 But to Israel he saith, All day long I have stretched forth my hands unto a disobedient and gainsaying people.

CHAPTER 11

I SAY then, Hath אֱלֹהִים cast away his people? אֱלֹהִים forbid. For I also am an Israelite, of the seed of Abraham, *of* the tribe of Benjamin.

2 אֱלֹהִים hath not cast away his people which he foreknew. Wot ye not what the scripture saith of Elias? how he maketh intercession to אֱלֹהִים against Israel, saying,

3 Lord, they have killed thy prophets, and digged down thine altars; and I am left alone, and they seek my life.

4 But what saith the answer of אֱלֹהִים unto him? I have reserved to myself seven thousand men, who have not bowed the knee to *the image of* Baal.

5 Even so then at this present time also there is a remnant according to the election of grace.

6 And if by grace, then *is it* no more of works: otherwise grace is no more grace. But if *it be* of works, then is it no more grace: otherwise work is no more work.

7 What then? Israel hath not obtained that which he seeketh for; but the election hath obtained it, and the rest were blinded

8 (According as it is written, אֱלֹהִים hath given them the spirit of slumber, eyes that they should not see, and ears that they should not hear;) unto this day.

9 And David saith, Let their table be made a snare, and a trap, and a stumblingblock, and a recompence unto them:

10 Let their eyes be darkened, that they may not see, and bow down their back alway.

11 I say then, Have they stumbled that they should fall? אֱלֹהִים forbid: but *rather* through their fall salvation *is come* unto the Gentiles, for to provoke them to jealousy.

12 Now if the fall of them *be* the riches of the world, and the diminishing of them the riches of the Gentiles; how much more their fulness?

13 For I speak to you Gentiles, inasmuch as I am the apostle of the Gentiles, I magnify mine office:

14 If by any means I may provoke to emulation *them which are* my flesh, and might save some of them.

15 For if the casting away of them *be* the reconciling of the world, what *shall* the receiving *of them be*, but life from the dead?

16 For if the firstfruit *be* holy, the lump *is* also *holy*: and if the root *be* holy, so *are* the branches.

17 And if some of the branches be broken off, and thou, being a wild olive tree, wert graffed in among them, and with them partakest of the root and fatness of the olive tree;

18 Boast not against the branches. But if thou boast, thou bearest not the root, but the root thee.

19 Thou wilt say then, The branches were broken off, that I might be graffed in.

20 Well; because of unbelief they were broken off, and thou standest by faith. Be not highminded, but fear:

21 For if אֱלֹהִים spared not the natural branches, *take heed* lest he also spare not thee.

22 Behold therefore the goodness and severity of אֱלֹהִים: on them which fell, severity; but toward thee, goodness, if thou continue in *his* goodness: otherwise thou also shalt be cut off.

23 And they also, if they abide not still in unbelief, shall be graffed in: for אֱלֹהִים is able to graff them in again.

24 For if thou wert cut out of the olive tree which is wild by nature, and wert graffed contrary to nature into a good olive tree: how much more shall these, which be the natural *branches*, be graffed into their own olive tree?

25 For I would not, brethren, that ye should be ignorant of this mystery, lest ye should be wise in your own conceits; that blindness in part is happened to Israel, until the fulness of the Gentiles be come in.

26 And so all Israel shall be saved: as it is written, There shall come out of Sion the Deliverer, and shall turn away ungodliness from Jacob:

27 For this *is* my covenant unto them, when I shall take away their sins.

28 As concerning the gospel, *they are* enemies for your sakes: but as touching the election, *they are* beloved for the fathers' sakes.

29 For the gifts and calling of אֱלֹהִים *are* without repentance.

30 For as ye in times past have not believed אֱלֹהִים, yet have now obtained mercy through their unbelief:

31 Even so have these also now not believed, that through your mercy they also may obtain mercy.

32 For אֱלֹהִים hath concluded them all in unbelief, that he might have mercy upon all.

33 O the depth of the riches both of the wisdom and knowledge of אֱלֹהִים! how unsearchable *are* his judgments, and his ways past finding out!

34 For who hath known the mind of the Lord? or who hath been his counseller?

35 Or who hath first given to him, and it shall be recompensed unto him again?

36 For of him, and through him, and to him, *are* all things: to whom *be* glory for ever. Amen.

CHAPTER 12

1 BESEECH you therefore, brethren, by the mercies of אֱלֹהִים, that ye present your bodies a living sacrifice, holy, acceptable unto אֱלֹהִים, *which is* your reasonable service.

2 And be not conformed to this world: but be ye transformed by the renewing of your mind, that ye may prove what *is* that good, and acceptable, and perfect, will of אֱלֹהִים.

3 For I say, through the grace given unto me, to every man that is among you, not to think *of himself* more highly than he ought to think; but to think soberly, according as אֱלֹהִים hath dealt to every man the measure of faith.

4 For as we have many members in one body, and all members have not the same office:

5 So we, *being* many, are one body in Christ, and every one members one of another.

6 Having then gifts differing according to the grace that is given to us, whether prophecy, *let us prophesy* according to the proportion of faith;

7 Or ministry, *let us wait* on *our* ministering: or he that teacheth, on teaching;

8 Or he that exhorteth, on exhortation: he that giveth, *let him do it* with simplicity; he that ruleth, with diligence; he that sheweth mercy, with cheerfulness.

9 *Let* love be without dissimulation. Abhor that which is evil; cleave to that which is good.

10 *Be* kindly affectioned one to another with brotherly love; in honour preferring one another;

11 Not slothful in business; fervent in spirit; serving the Lord;

12 Rejoicing in hope; patient in tribulation; continuing instant in prayer;

13 Distributing to the necessity of saints; given to hospitality.

14 Bless them which persecute you: bless, and curse not.

15 Rejoice with them that do rejoice, and weep with them that weep.

16 *Be* of the same mind one toward another. Mind not high things, but condescend to men of low estate. Be not wise in your own conceits.

17 Recompense to no man evil for evil. Provide things honest in the sight of all men.

18 If it be possible, as much as lieth in you, live peaceably with all men.

19 Dearly beloved, avenge not yourselves, but *rather* give place unto wrath: for it is written, Vengeance *is* mine; I will repay, saith the Lord.

20 Therefore if thine enemy hunger, feed him; if he thirst, give him drink: for in so doing thou shalt heap coals of fire on his head.

21 Be not overcome of evil, but overcome evil with good.

CHAPTER 13

LET every soul be subject unto the higher powers. For there is no power but of אֱלֹהִים: the powers that be are ordained of אֱלֹהִים.

2 Whosoever therefore resisteth the power, resisteth the ordinance of אֱלֹהִים: and they that resist shall receive to themselves damnation.

3 For rulers are not a terror to good works, but to the evil. Wilt thou then not be afraid of the power? do that which is good, and thou shalt have praise of the same:

4 For he is the minister of אֱלֹהִים to thee for good. But if thou do that which is evil, be afraid; for he beareth not the sword in vain: for he is the minister of אֱלֹהִים, a revenger to *execute* wrath upon him that doeth evil.

5 Wherefore *ye* must needs be subject, not only for wrath, but also for conscience sake.

6 For for this cause pay ye tribute also: for they are אֱלֹהִים's ministers, attending continually upon this very thing.

7 Render therefore to all their dues: tribute to whom tribute *is due;* custom to whom custom; fear to whom fear; honour to whom honour.

8 Owe no man any thing, but to love one another: for he that loveth another hath fulfilled the law.

9 For this, Thou shalt not commit adultery, Thou shalt not kill, Thou shalt not steal, Thou shalt not bear false witness, Thou shalt not covet; and if *there be* any other commandment, it is briefly comprehended in this saying, namely, Thou shalt love thy neighbour as thyself.

10 Love worketh no ill to his neighbour: therefore love *is* the fulfilling of the law.

11 And that, knowing the time, that now *it is* high time to awake out of sleep: for now *is* our salvation nearer than when we believed.

12 The night is far spent, the day is at hand: let us therefore cast off the works of darkness, and let us put on the armour of light.

13 Let us walk honestly, as in the day; not in rioting and drunkenness, not in chambering and wantonness, not in strife and envying.

14 But put ye on the Lord Yashiyah Christ, and make not provision for the flesh, to *fulfil* the lusts *thereof.*

CHAPTER 14

HIM that is weak in the faith receive ye, *but* not to doubtful disputations.

2 For one believeth that he may eat all things: another, who is weak, eateth herbs.

3 Let not him that eateth despise him that eateth not; and let not him which eateth not judge him that eateth: for אֱלֹהִים hath received him.

4 Who art thou that judgest another man's servant? to his own master he standeth or falleth. Yea, he shall be holden up: for אֱלֹהִים is able to make him stand.

5 One man esteemeth one day above another: another esteemeth every day *alike.* Let every man be fully persuaded in his own mind.

6 He that regardeth the day, regardeth *it* unto the Lord; and he that regardeth not the day, to the Lord he doth not regard *it.* He that eateth, eateth to the Lord, for he giveth אֱלֹהִים thanks; and he that eateth not, to the Lord he eateth not, and giveth אֱלֹהִים thanks.

7 For none of us liveth to himself, and no man dieth to himself.

8 For whether we live, we live unto the Lord; and whether we die, we die unto the Lord: whether we live therefore, or die, we are the Lord's.

9 For to this end Christ both died, and rose, and revived, that he might be Lord both of the dead and living.

10 But why dost thou judge thy brother? or why dost thou set at nought thy brother? for we shall all stand before the judgment seat of Christ.

11 For it is written, *As* I live, saith the Lord, every knee shall bow to me, and every tongue shall confess to אֱלֹהִים.

12 So then every one of us shall give account of himself to אֱלֹהִים.

13 Let us not therefore judge one another any more: but judge this rather, that no man put a stumblingblock or an occasion to fall in *his* brother's way.

14 I know, and am persuaded by the Lord Yashiyah, that *there is* nothing unclean of itself: but to him that esteemeth any thing to be unclean, to him *it is* unclean.

15 But if thy brother be grieved with *thy* meat, now walkest thou not charitably. Destroy not him with thy meat, for whom Christ died.

16 Let not then your good be evil spoken of:

17 For the kingdom of אֱלֹהִים is not meat and drink; but righteousness, and peace, and joy in the Holy Ghost.

18 For he that in these things serveth Christ *is* acceptable to אֱלֹהִים, and approved of men.

19 Let us therefore follow after the things which make for peace, and things wherewith one may edify another.

20 For meat destroy not the work of אֱלֹהִים. All things indeed *are* pure; but *it is* evil for that man who eateth with offence.

21 *It is* good neither to eat flesh, nor to drink wine, nor *any thing* whereby thy brother stumbleth, or is offended, or is made weak.

22 Hast thou faith? have *it* to thyself before אֱלֹהִים. Happy *is* he that condemneth not himself in that thing which he alloweth.

23 And he that doubteth is damned if he eat, because *he eateth* not of faith: for whatsoever *is* not of faith is sin.

CHAPTER 15

WE then that are strong ought to bear the infirmities of the weak, and not to please ourselves.

2 Let every one of us please *his* neighbour for *his* good to edification.

3 For even Christ pleased not himself; but, as it is written, The reproaches of them that reproached thee fell on me.

4 For whatsoever things were written aforetime were written for our learning, that we through patience and comfort of the scriptures might have hope.

5 Now the אֱלֹהִים of patience and consolation grant you to be likeminded one toward another according to Christ Yashiyah:

6 That ye may with one mind *and* one mouth glorify אֱלֹהִים, even the Father of our Lord Yashiyah Christ.

7 Wherefore receive ye one another, as Christ also received us to the glory of אֱלֹהִים.

8 Now I say that Yashiyah Christ was a minister of the circumcision for the truth of אֱלֹהִים, to confirm the promises *made* unto the fathers:

9 And that the Gentiles might glorify אֱלֹהִים for *his* mercy; as it is written, For this cause I will confess to thee among the Gentiles, and sing unto thy name.

10 And again he saith, Rejoice, ye Gentiles, with his people.

11 And again, Praise the Lord, all ye Gentiles; and laud him, all ye people.

12 And again, Esaias saith, There shall be a root of Jesse, and he that shall rise to reign over the Gentiles; in him shall the Gentiles trust.

13 Now the אֱלֹהִים of hope fill you with all joy and peace in believing, that ye may abound in hope, through the power of the Holy Ghost.

14 And I myself also am persuaded of you, my brethren, that ye also are full of goodness, filled with all knowledge, able also to admonish one another.

15 Nevertheless, brethren, I have written the more boldly unto you in some sort, as putting you in mind, because of the grace that is given to me of אֱלֹהִים,

16 That I should be the minister of Yashiyah Christ to the Gentiles, ministering the gospel of אֱלֹהִים, that the offering up of the Gentiles might be acceptable, being sanctified by the Holy Ghost.

17 I have therefore whereof I may glory through Yashiyah Christ in those things which pertain to אֱלֹהִים.

18 For I will not dare to speak of any of those things which Christ hath not wrought by me, to make the Gentiles obedient, by word and deed,

19 Through mighty signs and wonders, by the power of the Spirit of אֱלֹ; so that from Jerusalem, and round about unto Illyricum, I have fully preached the gospel of Christ.

20 Yea, so have I strived to preach the gospel, not where Christ was named, lest I should build upon another man's foundation:

21 But as it is written, To whom he was not spoken of, they shall see: and they that have not heard shall understand.

22 For which cause also I have been much hindered from coming to you.

23 But now having no more place in these parts, and having a great desire these many years to come unto you;

24 Whensoever I take my journey into Spain, I will come to you: for I trust to see you in my journey, and to be brought on my way thitherward by you, if first I be somewhat filled with your *company*.

25 But now I go unto Jerusalem to minister unto the saints.

26 For it hath pleased them of Macedonia and Achaia to make a certain contribution for the poor saints which are at Jerusalem.

27 It hath pleased them verily; and their debtors they are. For if the Gentiles have been made partakers of their spiritual things, their duty is also to minister unto them in carnal things.

28 When therefore I have performed this, and have sealed to them this fruit, I will come by you into Spain.

29 And I am sure that, when I come unto you, I shall come in the fulness of the blessing of the gospel of Christ.

30 Now I beseech you, brethren, for the Lord Yashiyah Christ's sake, and for the love of the Spirit, that ye strive together with me in *your* prayers to אֱלֹהִים for me;

31 That I may be delivered from them that do not believe in Judæa; and that my service which *I have* for Jerusalem may be accepted of the saints;

32 That I may come unto you with joy by the will of אֱלֹהִים, and may with you be refreshed.

33 Now the אֱלֹהִים of peace *be* with you all. Amen.

CHAPTER 16

1 COMMEND unto you Phebe our sister, which is a servant of the church which is at Cenchrea:

2 That ye receive her in the Lord, as becometh saints, and that ye assist her in whatsoever business she hath need of you: for she hath been a succourer of many, and of myself also.

3 Greet Priscilla and Aquila my helpers in Christ Yashiyah:

4 Who have for my life laid down their own necks: unto whom not only I give thanks, but also all the churches of the Gentiles.

5 Likewise *greet* the church that is in their house. Salute my wellbeloved Epænetus, who is the firstfruits of Achaia unto Christ.

6 Greet Mary, who bestowed much labour on us.

7 Salute Andronicus and Junia, my kinsmen, and my fellowprisoners, who are of note among the apostles, who also were in Christ before me.

8 Greet Amplias my beloved in the Lord.

9 Salute Urbane, our helper in Christ, and Stachys my beloved.

10 Salute Apelles approved in Christ. Salute them which are of Aristobulus' *household*.

11 Salute Herodion my kinsman. Greet them that be of the *household* of Narcissus, which are in the Lord.

12 Salute Tryphena and Tryphosa, who labour in the Lord. Salute the beloved Persis, which laboured much in the Lord.

13 Salute Rufus chosen in the Lord, and his mother and mine.

14 Salute Asyncritus, Phlegon, Hermas, Patrobas, Hermes, and the brethren which are with them.

15 Salute Philologus, and Julia, Nereus, and his sister, and Olympas, and all the saints which are with them.

16 Salute one another with an holy kiss. The churches of Christ salute you.

17 Now I beseech you, brethren, mark them which cause divisions and offences contrary to the doctrine which ye have learned; and avoid them.

18 For they that are such serve not our Lord Yashiyah Christ, but their own belly; and by good words and fair speeches deceive the hearts of the simple.

19 For your obedience is come abroad unto all *men*. I am glad therefore on your behalf: but yet I would have you wise unto that which is good, and simple concerning evil.

20 And the אֱלֹהִים of peace shall bruise Satan under your feet shortly. The grace of our Lord Yashiyah Christ *be* with you. Amen.

21 Timotheus my workfellow, and Lucius, and Jason, and Sosipater, my kinsmen, salute you.

22 I Tertius, who wrote *this* epistle, salute you in the Lord.

23 Gaius mine host, and of the whole church, saluteth you. Erastus the chamberlain of the city saluteth you, and Quartus a brother.

24 The grace of our Lord Yashiyah Christ *be* with you all. Amen.

25 Now to him that is of power to stablish you according to my gospel, and the preaching of Yashiyah Christ, according to the revelation of the mystery, which was kept secret since the world began,

26 But now is made manifest, and by the scriptures of the prophets, according to the commandment of the everlasting אֱלֹהִים, made known to all nations for the obedience of faith:

27 To אֱלֹהִים only wise, *be* glory through Yashiyah Christ for ever. Amen.

¶ Written to the Romans from Corinthus, *and sent* by Phebe servant of the church at Cenchrea.

THE
FIRST EPISTLE OF PAUL THE APOSTLE
TO THE
CORINTHIANS.

CHAPTER 1

PAUL, called *to be* an apostle of Yashiyah Christ through the will of אֱלֹהִים, and Sosthenes *our* brother,

2 Unto the church of אֱלֹהִים which is at Corinth, to them that are sanctified in Christ Yashiyah, called *to be* saints, with all that in every place call upon the name of Yashiyah Christ our Lord, both theirs and ours:

3 Grace *be* unto you, and peace, from אֱלֹהִים our Father, and *from* the Lord Yashiyah Christ.

4 I thank my אֱלֹהִים always on your behalf, for the grace of אֱלֹהִים which is given you by Yashiyah Christ;

5 That in every thing ye are enriched by him, in all utterance, and *in* all knowledge;

6 Even as the testimony of Christ was confirmed in you:

7 So that ye come behind in no gift; waiting for the coming of our Lord Yashiyah Christ:

8 Who shall also confirm you unto the end, *that ye may be* blameless in the day of our Lord Yashiyah Christ.

9 אֱלֹהִים *is* faithful, by whom ye were called unto the fellowship of his Son Yashiyah Christ our Lord.

10 Now I beseech you, brethren, by the name of our Lord Yashiyah Christ, that ye all speak the same thing, and *that* there be no divisions among you; but *that* ye be perfectly joined together in the same mind and in the same judgment.

11 For it hath been declared unto me of you, my brethren, by them *which are of the house* of Chloe, that there are contentions among you.

12 Now this I say, that every one of you saith, I am of Paul; and I of Apollos; and I of Cephas; and I of Christ.

13 Is Christ divided? was Paul crucified for you? or were ye baptized in the name of Paul?

14 I thank אֱלֹהִים that I baptized none of you, but Crispus and Gaius;

15 Lest any should say that I had baptized in mine own name.

16 And I baptized also the household of Stephanas: besides, I know not whether I baptized any other.

17 For Christ sent me not to baptize, but to preach the gospel: not with wisdom of words, lest the cross of Christ should be made of none effect.

18 For the preaching of the cross is to them that perish foolishness; but unto us which are saved it is the power of אֱלֹהִים.

19 For it is written, I will destroy the wisdom of the wise, and will bring to nothing the understanding of the prudent.

20 Where *is* the wise? where *is* the scribe? where *is* the disputer of this world? hath not אֱלֹהִים made foolish the wisdom of this world?

21 For after that in the wisdom of אֱלֹהִים the world by wisdom knew not אֱלֹהִים, it pleased אֱלֹהִים by the foolishness of preaching to save them that believe.

22 For the Jews require a sign, and the Greeks seek after wisdom:

23 But we preach Christ crucified, unto the Jews a stumblingblock, and unto the Greeks foolishness;

24 But unto them which are called, both Jews and Greeks, Christ the power of אֱלֹהִים, and the wisdom of אֱלֹהִים.

25 Because the foolishness of אֱלֹהִים is wiser than men; and the weakness of אֱלֹהִים is stronger than men.

26 For ye see your calling, brethren, how that not many wise men after the flesh, not many mighty, not many noble, *are called*:

27 But אֱלֹהִים hath chosen the foolish things of the world to confound the wise; and אֱלֹהִים hath chosen the weak things of the world to confound the things which are mighty;

28 And base things of the world, and things which are despised, hath אֱלֹהִים chosen, *yea*, and things which are not, to bring to nought things that are:

29 That no flesh should glory in his presence.

30 But of him are ye in Christ Yashiyah, who of אֱלֹהִים is made unto us wisdom, and righteousness, and sanctification, and redemption:

31 That, according as it is written, He that glorieth, let him glory in the Lord.

CHAPTER 2

AND I, brethren, when I came to you, came not with excellency of speech or of wisdom, declaring unto you the testimony of אֱלֹהִים.

2 For I determined not to know any thing among you, save Yashiyah Christ, and him crucified.

3 And I was with you in weakness, and in fear, and in much trembling.

4 And my speech and my preaching *was* not with enticing words of man's wisdom, but in demonstration of the Spirit and of power:

5 That your faith should not stand in the wisdom of men, but in the power of אֱלֹהִים.

6 Howbeit we speak wisdom among them that are perfect: yet not the wisdom of this world, nor of the princes of this world, that come to nought:

7 But we speak the wisdom of אֱלֹהִים in a mystery, *even* the hidden *wisdom*, which אֱלֹהִים ordained before the world unto our glory:

8 Which none of the princes of this world knew: for had they known *it*, they would not have crucified the Lord of glory.

9 But as it is written, Eye hath not seen, nor ear heard, neither have entered into the heart of man, the things which אֱלֹהִים hath prepared for them that love him.

10 But אֱלֹהִים hath revealed *them* unto us by his Spirit: for the Spirit searcheth all things, yea, the deep things of אֱלֹהִים.

11 For what man knoweth the things of a man, save the spirit of man which is in him? even so the things of אֱלֹהִים knoweth no man, but the Spirit of אֱלֹהִים.

12 Now we have received, not the spirit of the world, but the spirit which is of אֱלֹהִים; that we might know the things that are freely given to us of אֱלֹהִים.

13 Which things also we speak, not in the words which man's wisdom teacheth, but which the Holy Ghost teacheth; comparing spiritual things with spiritual.

14 But the natural man receiveth not the things of the Spirit of אֱלֹהִים: for they are foolishness unto him: neither can he know *them*, because they are spiritually discerned.

15 But he that is spiritual judgeth all things, yet he himself is judged of no man.

16 For who hath known the mind of the Lord, that he may instruct him? But we have the mind of Christ.

CHAPTER 3

AND I, brethren, could not speak unto you as unto spiritual, but as unto carnal, *even* as unto babes in Christ.

2 I have fed you with milk, and not with meat: for hitherto ye were not able *to bear it*, neither yet now are ye able.

3 For ye are yet carnal: for whereas *there is* among you envying, and strife, and divisions, are ye not carnal, and walk as men?

4 For while one saith, I am of Paul; and another, I *am* of Apollos; are ye not carnal?

5 Who then is Paul, and who *is* Apollos, but ministers by whom ye believed, even as the Lord gave to every man?

6 I have planted, Apollos watered; but אֱלֹהִים gave the increase.

7 So then neither is he that planteth any thing, neither he that watereth; but אֱלֹהִים that giveth the increase.

8 Now he that planteth and he that watereth are one: and every man shall receive his own reward according to his own labour.

9 For we are labourers together with אֱלֹהִים: ye are אֱלֹהִים's husbandry, *ye are* אֱלֹהִים's building.

10 According to the grace of אֱלֹהִים which is given unto me, as a wise masterbuilder, I have laid the foundation, and another buildeth thereon. But let every man take heed how he buildeth thereupon.

11 For other foundation can no man lay than that is laid, which is Yashiyah Christ.

12 Now if any man build upon this foundation gold, silver, precious stones, wood, hay, stubble;

13 Every man's work shall be made manifest: for the day shall declare it, because it shall be revealed by fire; and the fire shall try every man's work of what sort it is.

14 If any man's work abide which he hath built thereupon, he shall receive a reward.

15 If any man's work shall be burned, he shall suffer loss: but he himself shall be saved; yet so as by fire.

16 Know ye not that ye are the temple of אֱלֹהִים, and *that* the Spirit of אֱלֹהִים dwelleth in you?

17 If any man defile the temple of אֱלֹהִים, him shall אֱלֹהִים destroy; for the temple of אֱלֹהִים is holy, which *temple* ye are.

18 Let no man deceive himself. If any man among you seemeth to be wise in this world, let him become a fool, that he may be wise.

19 For the wisdom of this world is foolishness with אֱלֹהִים. For it is written, He taketh the wise in their own craftiness.

20 And again, The Lord knoweth the thoughts of the wise, that they are vain.

21 Therefore let no man glory in men. For all things are yours;

22 Whether Paul, or Apollos, or Cephas, or the world, or life, or death, or things present, or things to come; all are yours;

23 And ye are Christ's; and Christ *is* אֱלֹהִים's.

CHAPTER 4

LET a man so account of us, as of the ministers of Christ, and stewards of the mysteries of אֱלֹהִים.

2 Moreover it is required in stewards, that a man be found faithful.

3 But with me it is a very small thing that I should be judged of you, or of man's judgment: yea, I judge not mine own self.

4 For I know nothing by myself; yet am I not hereby justified: but he that judgeth me is the Lord.

5 Therefore judge nothing before the time, until the Lord come, who both will bring to light the hidden things of darkness, and will make manifest the counsels of the hearts: and then shall every man have praise of אֱלֹהִים.

6 And these things, brethren, I have in a figure transferred to myself and *to* Apollos for your sakes; that ye might learn in us not to think *of men* above that which is written, that no one of you be puffed up for one against another.

7 For who maketh thee to differ *from another?* and what hast thou that thou didst not receive? now if thou didst receive *it*, why dost thou glory, as if thou hadst not received *it?*

8 Now ye are full, now ye are rich, ye have reigned as kings without us: and I would to אֱלֹהִים ye did reign, that we also might reign with you.

9 For I think that אֱלֹהִים hath set forth us the apostles last, as it were appointed to death: for we are made a spectacle unto the world, and to angels, and to men.

10 We *are* fools for Christ's sake, but ye *are* wise in Christ; we *are* weak, but ye *are* strong; ye *are* honourable, but we *are* despised.

11 Even unto this present hour we both hunger, and thirst, and are naked, and are buffeted, and have no certain dwellingplace;

12 And labour, working with our own hands: being reviled, we bless; being persecuted, we suffer it:

13 Being defamed, we intreat: we are made as the filth of the world, *and are* the offscouring of all things unto this day.

14 I write not these things to shame you, but as my beloved sons I warn *you*.

15 For though ye have ten thousand instructors in Christ, yet *have ye* not many fathers: for in Christ Yashiyah I have begotten you through the gospel.

16 Wherefore I beseech you, be ye followers of me.

17 For this cause have I sent unto you Timotheus, who is my beloved son, and faithful in the Lord, who shall bring you into remembrance of my ways which be in Christ, as I teach every where in every church.

18 Now some are puffed up, as though I would not come to you.

19 But I will come to you shortly, if the Lord will, and will know, not the speech of them which are puffed up, but the power.

20 For the kingdom of אֱלֹהִים *is* not in word, but in power.

21 What will ye? shall I come unto you with a rod, or in love, and *in* the spirit of meekness?

CHAPTER 5

IT is reported commonly *that there is* fornication among you, and such fornication as is not so much as named among the Gentiles, that one should have his father's wife.

2 And ye are puffed up, and have not rather mourned, that he that hath done this deed might be taken away from among you.

3 For I verily, as absent in body, but present in spirit, have judged already, as though I were present, *concerning* him that hath so done this deed,

4 In the name of our Lord Yashiyah Christ, when ye are gathered together, and my spirit, with the power of our Lord Yashiyah Christ,

5 To deliver such an one unto Satan for the destruction of the flesh, that the spirit may be saved in the day of the Lord Yashiyah.

6 Your glorying *is* not good. Know ye not that a little leaven leaveneth the whole lump?

7 Purge out therefore the old leaven, that ye may be a new lump, as ye are unleavened. For even Christ our passover is sacrificed for us:

8 Therefore let us keep the feast, not with old leaven, neither with the leaven of malice and wickedness; but with the unleavened

bread of sincerity and truth.

9 I wrote unto you in an epistle not to company with fornicators:

10 Yet not altogether with the fornicators of this world, or with the covetous, or extortioners, or with idolaters; for then must ye needs go out of the world.

11 But now I have written unto you not to keep company, if any man that is called a brother be a fornicator, or covetous, or an idolater, or a railer, or a drunkard, or an extortioner; with such an one no not to eat.

12 For what have I to do to judge them also that are without? do not ye judge them that are within?

13 But them that are without אֱלֹהִים judgeth. Therefore put away from among yourselves that wicked person.

CHAPTER 6

DARE any of you, having a matter against another, go to law before the unjust, and not before the saints?

2 Do ye not know that the saints shall judge the world? and if the world shall be judged by you, are ye unworthy to judge the smallest matters?

3 Know ye not that we shall judge angels? how much more things that pertain to this life?

4 If then ye have judgments of things pertaining to this life, set them to judge who are least esteemed in the church.

5 I speak to your shame. Is it so, that there is not a wise man among you? no, not one that shall be able to judge between his brethren?

6 But brother goeth to law with brother, and that before the unbelievers.

7 Now therefore there is utterly a fault among you, because ye go to law one with another. Why do ye not rather take wrong? why do ye not rather *suffer yourselves to* be defrauded?

8 Nay, ye do wrong, and defraud, and that *your* brethren.

9 Know ye not that the unrighteous shall not inherit the kingdom of אֱלֹהִים? Be not deceived: neither fornicators, nor idolaters, nor adulterers, nor effeminate, nor abusers of themselves with mankind,

10 Nor thieves, nor covetous, nor drunkards, nor revilers, nor extortioners, shall inherit the kingdom of אֱלֹהִים.

11 And such were some of you: but ye are washed, but ye are sanctified, but ye are justified in the name of the Lord Yashiyah, and by the Spirit of our אֱלֹהִים.

12 All things are lawful unto me, but all things are not expedient: all things are lawful for me, but I will not be brought under the power of any.

13 Meats for the belly, and the belly for meats: but אֱלֹהִים shall destroy both it and them. Now the body *is* not for fornication, but for the Lord; and the Lord for the body.

14 And אֱלֹהִים hath both raised up the Lord, and will also raise up us by his own power.

15 Know ye not that your bodies are the members of Christ? shall I then take the members of Christ, and make *them* the members of an harlot? אֱלֹהִים forbid.

16 What? know ye not that he which is joined to an harlot is one body? for two, saith he, shall be one flesh.

17 But he that is joined unto the Lord is one spirit.

18 Flee fornication. Every sin that a man doeth is without the body; but he that committeth fornication sinneth against his own body.

19 What? know ye not that your body is the temple of the Holy Ghost *which is* in you, which ye have of אֱלֹהִים, and ye are not your own?

20 For ye are bought with a price: therefore glorify אֱלֹהִים in your body, and in your spirit, which are אֱלֹהִים's.

CHAPTER 7

NOW concerning the things whereof ye wrote unto me: *It is* good for a man not to touch a woman.

2 Nevertheless, *to avoid* fornication, let every man have his own wife, and let every woman have her own husband.

3 Let the husband render unto the wife due benevolence: and likewise also the wife unto the husband.

4 The wife hath not power of her own body, but the husband: and likewise also the husband hath not power of his own body, but the wife.

5 Defraud ye not one the other, except *it be* with consent for a time, that ye may give yourselves to fasting and prayer; and come together again, that Satan tempt you not for your incontinency.

6 But I speak this by permission, *and* not of commandment.

7 For I would that all men were even as I myself. But every man hath his proper gift of אֱלֹהִים, one after this manner, and another after that.

8 I say therefore to the unmarried and widows, It is good for them if they abide even as I.

9 But if they cannot contain, let them marry: for it is better to marry than to burn.

10 And unto the married I command, *yet* not I, but the Lord, Let not the wife depart from *her* husband:

11 But and if she depart, let her remain unmarried, or be reconciled to *her* husband: and let not the husband put away *his* wife.

12 But to the rest speak I, not the Lord: If any brother hath a wife that believeth not, and she be pleased to dwell with him, let him not put her away.

13 And the woman which hath an husband that believeth not, and if he be pleased to dwell with her, let her not leave him.

14 For the unbelieving husband is sanctified by the wife, and the unbelieving wife is sanctified by the husband: else were your children unclean; but now are they holy.

15 But if the unbelieving depart, let him depart. A brother or a sister is not under bondage in such *cases:* but אֱלֹהִים hath called us to peace.

16 For what knowest thou, O wife, whether thou shalt save *thy* husband? or how knowest thou, O man, whether thou shalt save *thy* wife?

17 But as אֱלֹהִים hath distributed to every man, as the Lord hath called every one, so let him walk. And so ordain I in all churches.

18 Is any man called being circumcised? let him not become uncircumcised. Is any called in uncircumcision? let him not be circumcised.

19 Circumcision is nothing, and uncircumcision is nothing, but the keeping of the commandments of אֱלֹהִים.

20 Let every man abide in the same calling wherein he was called.

21 Art thou called *being* a servant? care not for it: but if thou mayest be made free, use *it* rather.

22 For he that is called in the Lord, *being* a servant, is the Lord's freeman: likewise also he that is called, *being* free, is Christ's

servant.

23 Ye are bought with a price: be not ye the servants of men.

24 Brethren, let every man, wherein he is called, therein abide with אֱלֹהִים.

25 Now concerning virgins I have no commandment of the Lord: yet I give my judgment, as one that hath obtained mercy of the Lord to be faithful.

26 I suppose therefore that this is good for the present distress, *I say*, that *it is* good for a man so to be.

27 Art thou bound unto a wife? seek not to be loosed. Art thou loosed from a wife? seek not a wife.

28 But and if thou marry, thou hast not sinned; and if a virgin marry, she hath not sinned. Nevertheless such shall have trouble in the flesh: but I spare you.

29 But this I say, brethren, the time *is* short: it remaineth, that both they that have wives be as though they had none;

30 And they that weep, as though they wept not; and they that rejoice, as though they rejoiced not; and they that buy, as though they possessed not;

31 And they that use this world, as not abusing *it:* for the fashion of this world passeth away.

32 But I would have you without carefulness. He that is unmarried careth for the things that belong to the Lord, how he may please the Lord:

33 But he that is married careth for the things that are of the world, how he may please *his* wife.

34 There is difference *also* between a wife and a virgin. The unmarried woman careth for the things of the Lord, that she may be holy both in body and in spirit: but she that is married careth for the things of the world, how she may please *her* husband.

35 And this I speak for your own profit; not that I may cast a snare upon you, but for that which is comely, and that ye may attend upon the Lord without distraction.

36 But if any man think that he behaveth himself uncomely toward his virgin, if she pass the flower of *her* age, and need so require, let him do what he will, he sinneth not: let them marry.

37 Nevertheless he that standeth stedfast in his heart, having no necessity, but hath power over his own will, and hath so decreed in his heart that he will keep his virgin, doeth well.

38 So then he that giveth *her* in marriage doeth well; but he that giveth *her* not in marriage doeth better.

39 The wife is bound by the law as long as her husband liveth; but if her husband be dead, she is at liberty to be married to whom she will; only in the Lord.

40 But she is happier if she so abide, after my judgment: and I think also that I have the Spirit of אֱלֹהִים.

CHAPTER 8

NOW as touching things offered unto idols, we know that we all have knowledge. Knowledge puffeth up, but charity edifieth.

2 And if any man think that he knoweth any thing, he knoweth nothing yet as he ought to know.

3 But if any man love אֱלֹהִים, the same is known of him.

4 As concerning therefore the eating of those things that are offered in sacrifice unto idols, we know that an idol *is* nothing in the world, and that *there is* none other אֱלֹהִים but one.

5 For though there be that are called gods, whether in heaven or in earth, (as there be gods many, and lords many,)

6 But to us *there is but* one אֱלֹהִים, the Father, of whom *are* all things, and we in him; and one Lord Yashiyah Christ, by whom *are* all things, and we by him.

7 Howbeit *there is* not in every man that knowledge: for some with conscience of the idol unto this hour eat *it* as a thing offered unto an idol; and their conscience being weak is defiled.

8 But meat commendeth us not to אֱלֹהִים: for neither, if we eat, are we the better; neither, if we eat not, are we the worse.

9 But take heed lest by any means this liberty of yours become a stumblingblock to them that are weak.

10 For if any man see thee which hast knowledge sit at meat in the idol's temple, shall not the conscience of him which is weak be emboldened to eat those things which are offered to idols;

11 And through thy knowledge shall the weak brother perish, for whom Christ died?

12 But when ye sin so against the brethren, and wound their weak conscience, ye sin against Christ.

13 Wherefore, if meat make my brother to offend, I will eat no flesh while the world standeth, lest I make my brother to offend.

CHAPTER 9

AM I not an apostle? am I not free? have I not seen Yashiyah Christ our Lord? are not ye my work in the Lord?

2 If I be not an apostle unto others, yet doubtless I am to you: for the seal of mine apostleship are ye in the Lord.

3 Mine answer to them that do examine me is this,

4 Have we not power to eat and to drink?

5 Have we not power to lead about a sister, a wife, as well as other apostles, and *as* the brethren of the Lord, and Cephas?

6 Or I only and Barnabas, have not we power to forbear working?

7 Who goeth a warfare any time at his own charges? who planteth a vineyard, and eateth not of the fruit thereof? or who feedeth a flock, and eateth not of the milk of the flock?

8 Say I these things as a man? or saith not the law the same also?

9 For it is written in the law of Moses, Thou shalt not muzzle the mouth of the ox that treadeth out the corn. Doth אֱלֹהִים take care for oxen?

10 Or saith he *it* altogether for our sakes? For our sakes, no doubt, *this* is written: that he that ploweth should plow in hope; and that he that thresheth in hope should be partaker of his hope.

11 If we have sown unto you spiritual things, *is it* a great thing if we shall reap your carnal things?

12 If others be partakers of *this* power over you, *are* not we rather? Nevertheless we have not used this power; but suffer all things, lest we should hinder the gospel of Christ.

13 Do ye not know that they which minister about holy things live *of the things* of the temple? and they which wait at the altar are partakers with the altar?

14 Even so hath the Lord ordained that they which preach the gospel should live of the gospel.

15 But I have used none of these things: neither have I written these things, that it should be so done unto me: for *it were* better for me to die, than that any man should make my glorying void.

16 For though I preach the gospel, I have nothing to glory of: for necessity is laid upon me; yea, woe is unto me, if I preach not the gospel!

17 For if I do this thing willingly, I have a reward: but if against my will, a dispensation *of the gospel* is committed unto me.

18 What is my reward then? *Verily* that, when I preach the gospel, I may make the gospel of Christ without charge, that I abuse not my power in the gospel.

19 For though I be free from all *men*, yet have I made myself servant unto all, that I might gain the more.

20 And unto the Jews I became as a Jew, that I might gain the Jews; to them that are under the law, as under the law, that I might gain them that are under the law;

21 To them that are without law, as without law, (being not without law to אֱלֹהִים, but under the law to Christ,) that I might gain them that are without law.

22 To the weak became I as weak, that I might gain the weak: I am made all things to all *men*, that I might by all means save some.

23 And this I do for the gospel's sake, that I might be partaker thereof with *you*.

24 Know ye not that they which run in a race run all, but one receiveth the prize? So run, that ye may obtain.

25 And every man that striveth for the mastery is temperate in all things. Now they *do it* to obtain a corruptible crown; but we an incorruptible.

26 I therefore so run, not as uncertainly; so fight I, not as one that beateth the air:

27 But I keep under my body, and bring *it* into subjection: lest that by any means, when I have preached to others, I myself should be a castaway.

CHAPTER 10

MOREOVER, brethren, I would not that ye should be ignorant, how that all our fathers were under the cloud, and all passed through the sea;

2 And were all baptized unto Moses in the cloud and in the sea;

3 And did all eat the same spiritual meat;

4 And did all drink the same spiritual drink: for they drank of that spiritual Rock that followed them: and that Rock was Christ.

5 But with many of them אֱלֹהִים was not well pleased: for they were overthrown in the wilderness.

6 Now these things were our examples, to the intent we should not lust after evil things, as they also lusted.

7 Neither be ye idolaters, as *were* some of them; as it is written, The people sat down to eat and drink, and rose up to play.

8 Neither let us commit fornication, as some of them committed, and fell in one day three and twenty thousand.

9 Neither let us tempt Christ, as some of them also tempted, and were destroyed of serpents.

10 Neither murmur ye, as some of them also murmured, and were destroyed of the destroyer.

11 Now all these things happened unto them for ensamples: and they are written for our admonition, upon whom the ends of the world are come.

12 Wherefore let him that thinketh he standeth take heed lest he fall.

13 There hath no temptation taken you but such as is common to man: but אֱלֹהִים *is* faithful, who will not suffer you to be tempted above that ye are able; but will with the temptation also make a way to escape, that ye may be able to bear *it*.

14 Wherefore, my dearly beloved, flee from idolatry.

15 I speak as to wise men; judge ye what I say.

16 The cup of blessing which we bless, is it not the communion of the blood of Christ? The bread which we break, is it not the communion of the body of Christ?

17 For we *being* many are one bread, *and* one body: for we are all partakers of that one bread.

18 Behold Israel after the flesh: are not they which eat of the sacrifices partakers of the altar?

19 What say I then? that the idol is any thing, or that which is offered in sacrifice to idols is any thing?

20 But *I say*, that the things which the Gentiles sacrifice, they sacrifice to devils, and not to אֱלֹהִים: and I would not that ye should have fellowship with devils.

21 Ye cannot drink the cup of the Lord, and the cup of devils: ye cannot be partakers of the Lord's table, and of the table of devils.

22 Do we provoke the Lord to jealousy? are we stronger than he?

23 All things are lawful for me, but all things are not expedient: all things are lawful for me, but all things edify not.

24 Let no man seek his own, but every man another's *wealth*.

25 Whatsoever is sold in the shambles, *that* eat, asking no question for conscience sake:

26 For the earth *is* the Lord's, and the fulness thereof.

27 If any of them that believe not bid you *to a feast*, and ye be disposed to go; whatsoever is set before you, eat, asking no question for conscience sake.

28 But if any man say unto you, This is offered in sacrifice unto idols, eat not for his sake that shewed it, and for conscience sake: for the earth *is* the Lord's, and the fulness thereof:

29 Conscience, I say, not thine own, but of the other: for why is my liberty judged of another *man's* conscience?

30 For if I by grace be a partaker, why am I evil spoken of for that for which I give thanks?

31 Whether therefore ye eat, or drink, or whatsoever ye do, do all to the glory of אֱלֹהִים.

32 Give none offence, neither to the Jews, nor to the Gentiles, nor to the church of אֱלֹהִים:

33 Even as I please all *men* in all *things*, not seeking mine own profit, but the *profit* of many, that they may be saved.

CHAPTER 11

BE ye followers of me, even as I also *am* of Christ.

2 Now I praise you, brethren, that ye remember me in all things, and keep the ordinances, as I delivered *them* to you.

3 But I would have you know, that the head of every man is Christ; and the head of the woman *is* the man; and the head of Christ *is* אֱלֹהִים.

4 Every man praying or prophesying, having *his* head covered, dishonoureth his head.

5 But every woman that prayeth or prophesieth with *her* head uncovered dishonoureth her head: for that is even all one as if she were shaven.

6 For if the woman be not covered, let her also be shorn: but if it be a shame for a woman to be shorn or shaven, let her be covered.

7 For a man indeed ought not to cover *his* head, forasmuch as he is the image and glory of אֱלֹהִים: but the woman is the glory of the man.

8 For the man is not of the woman; but the woman of the man.

9 Neither was the man created for the woman; but the woman for the man.

10 For this cause ought the woman to have power on *her* head because of the angels.

11 Nevertheless neither is the man without the woman, neither the woman without the man, in the Lord.

12 For as the woman *is* of the man, even so *is* the man also by the woman; but all things of אֱלֹהִים.

13 Judge in yourselves: is it comely that a woman pray unto אֱלֹהִים uncovered?

14 Doth not even nature itself teach you, that, if a man have long hair, it is a shame unto him?

15 But if a woman have long hair, it is a glory to her: for *her* hair is given her for a covering.

16 But if any man seem to be contentious, we have no such custom, neither the churches of אֱלֹהִים.

17 Now in this that I declare *unto you* I praise *you* not, that ye come together not for the better, but for the worse.

18 For first of all, when ye come together in the church, I hear that there be divisions among you; and I partly believe it.

19 For there must be also heresies among you, that they which are approved may be made manifest among you.

20 When ye come together therefore into one place, *this* is not to eat the Lord's supper.

21 For in eating every one taketh before *other* his own supper: and one is hungry, and another is drunken.

22 What? have ye not houses to eat and to drink in? or despise ye the church of אֱלֹ, and shame them that have not? What shall I say to you? shall I praise you in this? I praise *you* not.

23 For I have received of the Lord that which also I delivered unto you, That the Lord Yashiyah the *same* night in which he was betrayed took bread:

24 And when he had given thanks, he brake *it*, and said, Take, eat: this is my body, which is broken for you: this do in remembrance of me.

25 After the same manner also *he took* the cup, when he had supped, saying, This cup is the new testament in my blood: this do ye, as oft as ye drink *it*, in remembrance of me.

26 For as often as ye eat this bread, and drink this cup, ye do shew the Lord's death till he come.

27 Wherefore whosoever shall eat this bread, and drink *this* cup of the Lord, unworthily, shall be guilty of the body and blood of the Lord.

28 But let a man examine himself, and so let him eat of *that* bread, and drink of *that* cup.

29 For he that eateth and drinketh unworthily, eateth and drinketh damnation to himself, not discerning the Lord's body.

30 For this cause many *are* weak and sickly among you, and many sleep.

31 For if we would judge ourselves, we should not be judged.

32 But when we are judged, we are chastened of the Lord, that we should not be condemned with the world.

33 Wherefore, my brethren, when ye come together to eat, tarry one for another.

34 And if any man hunger, let him eat at home; that ye come not together unto condemnation. And the rest will I set in order when I come.

CHAPTER 12

NOW concerning spiritual *gifts*, brethren, I would not have you ignorant.

2 Ye know that ye were Gentiles, carried away unto these dumb idols, even as ye were led.

3 Wherefore I give you to understand, that no man speaking by the Spirit of אֱלֹהִים calleth Yashiyah accursed: and *that* no man can say that Yashiyah is the Lord, but by the Holy Ghost.

4 Now there are diversities of gifts, but the same Spirit.

5 And there are differences of administrations, but the same Lord.

6 And there are diversities of operations, but it is the same אֱלֹ which worketh all in all.

7 But the manifestation of the Spirit is given to every man to profit withal.

8 For to one is given by the Spirit the word of wisdom; to another the word of knowledge by the same Spirit;

9 To another faith by the same Spirit; to another the gifts of healing by the same Spirit;

10 To another the working of miracles; to another prophecy; to another discerning of spirits; to another *divers* kinds of tongues; to another the interpretation of tongues:

11 But all these worketh that one and the selfsame Spirit, dividing to every man severally as he will.

12 For as the body is one, and hath many members, and all the members of that one body, being many, are one body: so also *is* Christ.

13 For by one Spirit are we all baptized into one body, whether *we be* Jews or Gentiles, whether *we be* bond or free; and have been all made to drink into one Spirit.

14 For the body is not one member, but many.

15 If the foot shall say, Because I am not the hand, I am not of the body; is it therefore not of the body?

16 And if the ear shall say, Because I am not the eye, I am not of the body; is it therefore not of the body?

17 If the whole body *were* an eye, where *were* the hearing? If the whole *were* hearing, where *were* the smelling?

18 But now hath אֱלֹ set the members every one of them in the body, as it hath pleased him.

19 And if they were all one member, where *were* the body?

20 But now *are they* many members, yet but one body.

21 And the eye cannot say unto the hand, I have no need of thee: nor again the head to the feet, I have no need of you.

22 Nay, much more those members of the body, which seem to be more feeble, are necessary:

23 And those *members* of the body, which we think to be less honourable, upon these we bestow more abundant honour; and our uncomely *parts* have more abundant comeliness.

24 For our comely *parts* have no need: but אֱלֹ hath tempered the body together, having given more abundant honour to that *part* which lacked:

25 That there should be no schism in the body; but *that* the members should have the same care one for another.

26 And whether one member suffer, all the members suffer with it; or one member be honoured, all the members rejoice with it.

27 Now ye are the body of Christ, and members in particular.

28 And אֱלֹהִים hath set some in the church, first apostles, secondarily prophets, thirdly teachers, after that miracles, then gifts of

healings, helps, governments, diversities of tongues.

29 *Are* all apostles? *are* all prophets? *are* all teachers? *are* all workers of miracles?

30 Have all the gifts of healing? do all speak with tongues? do all interpret?

31 But covet earnestly the best gifts: and yet shew I unto you a more excellent way.

CHAPTER 13

THOUGH I speak with the tongues of men and of angels, and have not charity, I am become *as* sounding brass, or a tinkling cymbal.

2 And though I have *the gift of* prophecy, and understand all mysteries, and all knowledge; and though I have all faith, so that I could remove mountains, and have not charity, I am nothing.

3 And though I bestow all my goods to feed *the poor*, and though I give my body to be burned, and have not charity, it profiteth me nothing.

4 Charity suffereth long, *and* is kind; charity envieth not; charity vaunteth not itself, is not puffed up,

5 Doth not behave itself unseemly, seeketh not her own, is not easily provoked, thinketh no evil;

6 Rejoiceth not in iniquity, but rejoiceth in the truth;

7 Beareth all things, believeth all things, hopeth all things, endureth all things.

8 Charity never faileth: but whether *there be* prophecies, they shall fail; whether *there be* tongues, they shall cease; whether *there be* knowledge, it shall vanish away.

9 For we know in part, and we prophesy in part.

10 But when that which is perfect is come, then that which is in part shall be done away.

11 When I was a child, I spake as a child, I understood as a child, I thought as a child: but when I became a man, I put away childish things.

12 For now we see through a glass, darkly; but then face to face: now I know in part; but then shall I know even as also I am known.

13 And now abideth faith, hope, charity, these three; but the greatest of these *is* charity.

CHAPTER 14

FOLLOW after charity, and desire spiritual *gifts*, but rather that ye may prophesy.

2 For he that speaketh in an *unknown* tongue speaketh not unto men, but unto אֱלֹהִים: for no man understandeth *him*; howbeit in the spirit he speaketh mysteries.

3 But he that prophesieth speaketh unto men *to* edification, and exhortation, and comfort.

4 He that speaketh in an *unknown* tongue edifieth himself; but he that prophesieth edifieth the church.

5 I would that ye all spake with tongues, but rather that ye prophesied: for greater *is* he that prophesieth than he that speaketh with tongues, except he interpret, that the church may receive edifying.

6 Now, brethren, if I come unto you speaking with tongues, what shall I profit you, except I shall speak to you either by revelation, or by knowledge, or by prophesying, or by doctrine?

7 And even things without life giving sound, whether pipe or harp, except they give a distinction in the sounds, how shall it be known what is piped or harped?

8 For if the trumpet give an uncertain sound, who shall prepare himself to the battle?

9 So likewise ye, except ye utter by the tongue words easy to be understood, how shall it be known what is spoken? for ye shall speak into the air.

10 There are, it may be, so many kinds of voices in the world, and none of them *is* without signification.

11 Therefore if I know not the meaning of the voice, I shall be unto him that speaketh a barbarian, and he that speaketh *shall be* a barbarian unto me.

12 Even so ye, forasmuch as ye are zealous of spiritual *gifts*, seek that ye may excel to the edifying of the church.

13 Wherefore let him that speaketh in an *unknown* tongue pray that he may interpret.

14 For if I pray in an *unknown* tongue, my spirit prayeth, but my understanding is unfruitful.

15 What is it then? I will pray with the spirit, and I will pray with the understanding also: I will sing with the spirit, and I will sing with the understanding also.

16 Else when thou shalt bless with the spirit, how shall he that occupieth the room of the unlearned say Amen at thy giving of thanks, seeing he understandeth not what thou sayest?

17 For thou verily givest thanks well, but the other is not edified.

18 I thank my אֱלֹהִים, I speak with tongues more than ye all:

19 Yet in the church I had rather speak five words with my understanding, that *by my voice* I might teach others also, than ten thousand words in an *unknown* tongue.

20 Brethren, be not children in understanding: howbeit in malice be ye children, but in understanding be men.

21 In the law it is written, With *men of* other tongues and other lips will I speak unto this people; and yet for all that will they not hear me, saith the Lord.

22 Wherefore tongues are for a sign, not to them that believe, but to them that believe not: but prophesying *serveth* not for them that believe not, but for them which believe.

23 If therefore the whole church be come together into one place, and all speak with tongues, and there come in *those that are* unlearned, or unbelievers, will they not say that ye are mad?

24 But if all prophesy, and there come in one that believeth not, or *one* unlearned, he is convinced of all, he is judged of all:

25 And thus are the secrets of his heart made manifest; and so falling down on *his* face he will worship אֱלֹהִים, and report that אֱלֹהִים is in you of a truth.

26 How is it then, brethren? when ye come together, every one of you hath a psalm, hath a doctrine, hath a tongue, hath a revelation, hath an interpretation. Let all things be done unto edifying.

27 If any man speak in an *unknown* tongue, *let it be* by two, or at the most *by* three, and *that* by course; and let one interpret.

28 But if there be no interpreter, let him keep silence in the church; and let him speak to himself, and to אֱלֹהִים.

29 Let the prophets speak two or three, and let the other judge.

30 If *any thing* be revealed to another that sitteth by, let the first hold his peace.

31 For ye may all prophesy one by one, that all may learn, and all may be comforted.

32 And the spirits of the prophets are subject to the prophets.

33 For אֱלֹהִים is not *the author* of confusion, but of peace, as in all churches of the saints.

34 Let your women keep silence in the churches: for it is not permitted unto them to speak; but *they are commanded* to be under obedience, as also saith the law.

35 And if they will learn any thing, let them ask their husbands at home: for it is a shame for women to speak in the church.

36 What? came the word of אֱלֹהִים out from you? or came it unto you only?

37 If any man think himself to be a prophet, or spiritual, let him acknowledge that the things that I write unto you are the commandments of the Lord.

38 But if any man be ignorant, let him be ignorant.

39 Wherefore, brethren, covet to prophesy, and forbid not to speak with tongues.

40 Let all things be done decently and in order.

CHAPTER 15

MOREOVER, brethren, I declare unto you the gospel which I preached unto you, which also ye have received, and wherein ye stand;

2 By which also ye are saved, if ye keep in memory what I preached unto you, unless ye have believed in vain.

3 For I delivered unto you first of all that which I also received, how that Christ died for our sins according to the scriptures;

4 And that he was buried, and that he rose again the third day according to the scriptures:

5 And that he was seen of Cephas, then of the twelve:

6 After that, he was seen of above five hundred brethren at once; of whom the greater part remain unto this present, but some are fallen asleep.

7 After that, he was seen of James; then of all the apostles.

8 And last of all he was seen of me also, as of one born out of due time.

9 For I am the least of the apostles, that am not meet to be called an apostle, because I persecuted the church of אֱלֹהִים.

10 But by the grace of אֱלֹהִים I am what I am: and his grace which *was bestowed* upon me was not in vain; but I laboured more abundantly than they all: yet not I, but the grace of אֱלֹהִים which was with me.

11 Therefore whether *it were* I or they, so we preach, and so ye believed.

12 Now if Christ be preached that he rose from the dead, how say some among you that there is no resurrection of the dead?

13 But if there be no resurrection of the dead, then is Christ not risen:

14 And if Christ be not risen, then *is* our preaching vain, and your faith *is* also vain.

15 Yea, and we are found false witnesses of אֱלֹהִים; because we have testified of אֱלֹהִים that he raised up Christ: whom he raised not up, if so be that the dead rise not.

16 For if the dead rise not, then is not Christ raised:

17 And if Christ be not raised, your faith *is* vain; ye are yet in your sins.

18 Then they also which are fallen asleep in Christ are perished.

19 If in this life only we have hope in Christ, we are of all men most miserable.

20 But now is Christ risen from the dead, *and* become the firstfruits of them that slept.

21 For since by man *came* death, by man *came* also the resurrection of the dead.

22 For as in Adam all die, even so in Christ shall all be made alive.

23 But every man in his own order: Christ the firstfruits; afterward they that are Christ's at his coming.

24 Then *cometh* the end, when he shall have delivered up the kingdom to אֱלֹהִים, even the Father; when he shall have put down all rule and all authority and power.

25 For he must reign, till he hath put all enemies under his feet.

26 The last enemy *that* shall be destroyed *is* death.

27 For he hath put all things under his feet. But when he saith, all things are put under *him, it is* manifest that he is excepted, which did put all things under him.

28 And when all things shall be subdued unto him, then shall the Son also himself be subject unto him that put all things under him, that אֱלֹהִים may be all in all.

29 Else what shall they do which are baptized for the dead, if the dead rise not at all? why are they then baptized for the dead?

30 And why stand we in jeopardy every hour?

31 I protest by your rejoicing which I have in Christ Yashiyah our Lord, I die daily.

32 If after the manner of men I have fought with beasts at Ephesus, what advantageth it me, if the dead rise not? let us eat and drink; for to morrow we die.

33 Be not deceived: evil communications corrupt good manners.

34 Awake to righteousness, and sin not; for some have not the knowledge of אֱלֹהִים: I speak *this* to your shame.

35 But some *man* will say, How are the dead raised up? and with what body do they come?

36 *Thou* fool, that which thou sowest is not quickened, except it die:

37 And that which thou sowest, thou sowest not that body that shall be, but bare grain, it may chance of wheat, or of some other grain:

38 But אֱלֹהִים giveth it a body as it hath pleased him, and to every seed his own body.

39 All flesh *is* not the same flesh: but *there is* one *kind of* flesh of men, another flesh of beasts, another of fishes, *and* another of birds.

40 *There are* also celestial bodies, and bodies terrestrial: but the glory of the celestial *is* one, and the *glory* of the terrestrial *is* another.

41 *There is* one glory of the sun, and another glory of the moon, and another glory of the stars: for *one* star differeth from *another* star in glory.

42 So also *is* the resurrection of the dead. It is sown in corruption; it is raised in incorruption:

43 It is sown in dishonour; it is raised in glory: it is sown in weakness; it is raised in power:

44 It is sown a natural body; it is raised a spiritual body. There is a natural body, and there is a spiritual body.

45 And so it is written, The first man Adam was made a living soul; the last Adam *was made* a quickening spirit.

46 Howbeit that *was* not first which is spiritual, but that which is natural; and afterward that which is spiritual.

47 The first man *is* of the earth, earthy: the second man *is* the Lord from heaven.

48 As *is* the earthy, such *are* they also that are earthy: and as *is* the heavenly, such *are* they also that are heavenly.

49 And as we have borne the image of the earthy, we shall also bear the image of the heavenly.

50 Now this I say, brethren, that flesh and blood cannot inherit the kingdom of אֱלֹהִים; neither doth corruption inherit incorruption.

51 Behold, I shew you a mystery; We shall not all sleep, but we shall all be changed,

52 In a moment, in the twinkling of an eye, at the last trump: for the trumpet shall sound, and the dead shall be raised incorruptible, and we shall be changed.

53 For this corruptible must put on incorruption, and this mortal *must* put on immortality.

54 So when this corruptible shall have put on incorruption, and this mortal shall have put on immortality, then shall be brought to pass the saying that is written, Death is swallowed up in victory.

55 O death, where *is* thy sting? O grave, where *is* thy victory?

56 The sting of death *is* sin; and the strength of sin *is* the law.

57 But thanks *be* to אֱלֹהִים, which giveth us the victory through our Lord Yashiyah Christ.

58 Therefore, my beloved brethren, be ye stedfast, unmoveable, always abounding in the work of the Lord, forasmuch as ye know that your labour is not in vain in the Lord.

CHAPTER 16

NOW concerning the collection for the saints, as I have given order to the churches of Galatia, even so do ye.

2 Upon the first *day* of the week let every one of you lay by him in store, as אֱלֹהִים hath prospered him, that there be no gatherings when I come.

3 And when I come, whomsoever ye shall approve by *your* letters, them will I send to bring your liberality unto Jerusalem.

4 And if it be meet that I go also, they shall go with me.

5 Now I will come unto you, when I shall pass through Macedonia: for I do pass through Macedonia.

6 And it may be that I will abide, yea, and winter with you, that ye may bring me on my journey whithersoever I go.

7 For I will not see you now by the way; but I trust to tarry a while with you, if the Lord permit.

8 But I will tarry at Ephesus until Pentecost.

9 For a great door and effectual is opened unto me, and *there are* many adversaries.

10 Now if Timotheus come, see that he may be with you without fear: for he worketh the work of the Lord, as I also *do*.

11 Let no man therefore despise him: but conduct him forth in peace, that he may come unto me: for I look for him with the brethren.

12 As touching *our* brother Apollos, I greatly desired him to come unto you with the brethren: but his will was not at all to come at this time; but he will come when he shall have convenient time.

13 Watch ye, stand fast in the faith, quit you like men, be strong.

14 Let all your things be done with charity.

15 I beseech you, brethren, (ye know the house of Stephanas, that it is the firstfruits of Achaia, and *that* they have addicted themselves to the ministry of the saints,)

16 That ye submit yourselves unto such, and to every one that helpeth with *us*, and laboureth.

17 I am glad of the coming of Stephanas and Fortunatus and Achaicus: for that which was lacking on your part they have supplied.

18 For they have refreshed my spirit and yours: therefore acknowledge ye them that are such.

19 The churches of Asia salute you. Aquila and Priscilla salute you much in the Lord, with the church that is in their house.

20 All the brethren greet you. Greet ye one another with an holy kiss.

21 The salutation of *me* Paul with mine own hand.

22 If any man love not the Lord Yashiyah Christ, let him be Anathema Maran-atha.

23 The grace of our Lord Yashiyah Christ *be* with you.

24 My love *be* with you all in Christ Yashiyah. Amen.

¶ The first *epistle* to the Corinthians was written from Philippi by Stephanas, and Fortunatus, and Achaicus, and Timotheus.

THE
SECOND EPISTLE OF PAUL THE APOSTLE
TO THE
CORINTHIANS.

CHAPTER 1

PAUL, an apostle of Yashiyah Christ by the will of אֱלֹהִים, and Timothy *our* brother, unto the church of אֱלֹהִים which is at Corinth, with all the saints which are in all Achaia:

2 Grace *be* to you and peace from אֱלֹהִים our Father, and *from* the Lord Yashiyah Christ.

3 Blessed *be* אֱלֹהִים, even the Father of our Lord Yashiyah Christ, the Father of mercies, and the אֱלֹהִים of all comfort;

4 Who comforteth us in all our tribulation, that we may be able to comfort them which are in any trouble, by the comfort wherewith we ourselves are comforted of אֱלֹהִים.

5 For as the sufferings of Christ abound in us, so our consolation also aboundeth by Christ.

6 And whether we be afflicted, *it is* for your consolation and salvation, which is effectual in the enduring of the same sufferings which we also suffer: or whether we be comforted, *it is* for your consolation and salvation.

7 And our hope of you *is* stedfast, knowing, that as ye are partakers of the sufferings, so *shall ye be* also of the consolation.

8 For we would not, brethren, have you ignorant of our trouble which came to us in Asia, that we were pressed out of measure, above strength, insomuch that we despaired even of life:

9 But we had the sentence of death in ourselves, that we should not trust in ourselves, but in אֱלֹהִים which raiseth the dead:

10 Who delivered us from so great a death, and doth deliver: in whom we trust that he will yet deliver *us*;

11 Ye also helping together by prayer for us, that for the gift *bestowed* upon us by the means of many persons thanks may be given by many on our behalf.

12 For our rejoicing is this, the testimony of our conscience, that in simplicity and godly sincerity, not with fleshly wisdom, but by the grace of אֱלֹהִים, we have had our conversation in the world, and more abundantly to you-ward.

13 For we write none other things unto you, than what ye read or acknowledge; and I trust ye shall acknowledge even to the end;

14 As also ye have acknowledged us in part, that we are your rejoicing, even as ye also *are* ours in the day of the Lord Yashiyah.

15 And in this confidence I was minded to come unto you before, that ye might have a second benefit;

16 And to pass by you into Macedonia, and to come again out of Macedonia unto you, and of you to be brought on my way toward Judæa.

17 When I therefore was thus minded, did I use lightness? or the things that I purpose, do I purpose according to the flesh, that with me there should be yea yea, and nay nay?

18 But *as* אֱלֹהִים *is* true, our word toward you was not yea and nay.

19 For the Son of אֱלֹהִים, Yashiyah Christ, who was preached among you by us, *even* by me and Silvanus and Timotheus, was not yea and nay, but in him was yea.

20 For all the promises of אֱלֹהִים in him *are* yea, and in him Amen, unto the glory of אֱלֹהִים by us.

21 Now he which stablisheth us with you in Christ, and hath anointed us, *is* אֱלֹהִים;

22 Who hath also sealed us, and given the earnest of the Spirit in our hearts.

23 Moreover I call אֱלֹהִים for a record upon my soul, that to spare you I came not as yet unto Corinth.

24 Not for that we have dominion over your faith, but are helpers of your joy: for by faith ye stand.

CHAPTER 2

BUT I determined this with myself, that I would not come again to you in heaviness.

2 For if I make you sorry, who is he then that maketh me glad, but the same which is made sorry by me?

3 And I wrote this same unto you, lest, when I came, I should have sorrow from them of whom I ought to rejoice; having confidence in you all, that my joy is *the joy* of you all.

4 For out of much affliction and anguish of heart I wrote unto you with many tears; not that ye should be grieved, but that ye might know the love which I have more abundantly unto you.

5 But if any have caused grief, he hath not grieved me, but in part: that I may not overcharge you all.

6 Sufficient to such a man *is* this punishment, which *was inflicted* of many.

7 So that contrariwise ye *ought* rather to forgive *him*, and comfort *him*, lest perhaps such a one should be swallowed up with overmuch sorrow.

8 Wherefore I beseech you that ye would confirm *your* love toward him.

9 For to this end also did I write, that I might know the proof of you, whether ye be obedient in all things.

10 To whom ye forgive any thing, I *forgive* also: for if I forgave any thing, to whom I forgave *it*, for your sakes *forgave I it* in the person of Christ;

11 Lest Satan should get an advantage of us: for we are not ignorant of his devices.

12 Furthermore, when I came to Troas to *preach* Christ's gospel, and a door was opened unto me of the Lord,

13 I had no rest in my spirit, because I found not Titus my brother: but taking my leave of them, I went from thence into Macedonia.

14 Now thanks *be* unto אֱלֹהִים, which always causeth us to triumph in Christ, and maketh manifest the savour of his knowledge by us in every place.

15 For we are unto אֱלֹהִים a sweet savour of Christ, in them that are saved, and in them that perish:

16 To the one *we are* the savour of death unto death; and to the other the savour of life unto life. And who *is* sufficient for these things?

17 For we are not as many, which corrupt the word of אֱלֹהִים: but as of sincerity, but as of אֱלֹהִים, in the sight of אֱלֹהִים speak we in Christ.

CHAPTER 3

DO we begin again to commend ourselves? or need we, as some *others*, epistles of commendation to you, or *letters* of commendation from you?

2 Ye are our epistle written in our hearts, known and read of all men:

3 *Forasmuch as ye are* manifestly declared to be the epistle of Christ ministered by us, written not with ink, but with the Spirit of the living אֱלֹהִים; not in tables of stone, but in fleshy tables of the heart.

4 And such trust have we through Christ to אֱלֹהִים-ward:

5 Not that we are sufficient of ourselves to think any thing as of ourselves; but our sufficiency *is* of אֱלֹהִים;

6 Who also hath made us able ministers of the new testament; not of the letter, but of the spirit: for the letter killeth, but the spirit giveth life.

7 But if the ministration of death, written *and* engraven in stones, was glorious, so that the children of Israel could not stedfastly behold the face of Moses for the glory of his countenance; which *glory* was to be done away:

8 How shall not the ministration of the spirit be rather glorious?

9 For if the ministration of condemnation *be* glory, much more doth the ministration of righteousness exceed in glory.

10 For even that which was made glorious had no glory in this respect, by reason of the glory that excelleth.

11 For if that which is done away *was* glorious, much more that which remaineth *is* glorious.

12 Seeing then that we have such hope, we use great plainness of speech:

13 And not as Moses, *which* put a vail over his face, that the children of Israel could not stedfastly look to the end of that which is abolished:

14 But their minds were blinded: for until this day remaineth the same vail untaken away in the reading of the old testament; which *vail* is done away in Christ.

15 But even unto this day, when Moses is read, the vail is upon their heart.

16 Nevertheless when it shall turn to the Lord, the vail shall be taken away.

17 Now the Lord is that Spirit: and where the Spirit of the Lord *is*, there *is* liberty.

18 But we all, with open face beholding as in a glass the glory of the Lord, are changed into the same image from glory to glory, *even* as by the Spirit of the Lord.

CHAPTER 4

THEREFORE seeing we have this ministry, as we have received mercy, we faint not;

2 But have renounced the hidden things of dishonesty, not walking in craftiness, nor handling the word of אֱלֹהִים deceitfully; but by manifestation of the truth commending ourselves to every man's conscience in the sight of אֱלֹהִים.

3 But if our gospel be hid, it is hid to them that are lost:

4 In whom the god of this world hath blinded the minds of them which believe not, lest the light of the glorious gospel of Christ, who is the image of אֱלֹהִים, should shine unto them.

5 For we preach not ourselves, but Christ Yashiyah the Lord; and ourselves your servants for Yashiyah' sake.

6 For אֱלֹהִים, who commanded the light to shine out of darkness, hath shined in our hearts, to *give* the light of the knowledge of the glory of אֱלֹהִים in the face of Yashiyah Christ.

7 But we have this treasure in earthen vessels, that the excellency of the power may be of אֱלֹהִים, and not of us.

8 *We are* troubled on every side, yet not distressed; *we are* perplexed, but not in despair;

9 Persecuted, but not forsaken; cast down, but not destroyed;

10 Always bearing about in the body the dying of the Lord Yashiyah, that the life also of Yashiyah might be made manifest in our body.

11 For we which live are alway delivered unto death for Yashiyah' sake, that the life also of Yashiyah might be made manifest in our mortal flesh.

12 So then death worketh in us, but life in you.

13 We having the same spirit of faith, according as it is written, I believed, and therefore have I spoken; we also believe, and therefore speak;

14 Knowing that he which raised up the Lord Yashiyah shall raise up us also by Yashiyah, and shall present *us* with you.

15 For all things *are* for your sakes, that the abundant grace might through the thanksgiving of many redound to the glory of אֱלֹהִים.

16 For which cause we faint not; but though our outward man perish, yet the inward *man* is renewed day by day.

17 For our light affliction, which is but for a moment, worketh for us a far more exceeding *and* eternal weight of glory;

18 While we look not at the things which are seen, but at the things which are not seen: for the things which are seen *are* temporal; but the things which are not seen *are* eternal.

CHAPTER 5

FOR we know that if our earthly house of *this* tabernacle were dissolved, we have a building of אֱלֹהִים, an house not made with hands, eternal in the heavens.

2 For in this we groan, earnestly desiring to be clothed upon with our house which is from heaven:

3 If so be that being clothed we shall not be found naked.

4 For we that are in *this* tabernacle do groan, being burdened: not for that we would be unclothed, but clothed upon, that mortality might be swallowed up of life.

5 Now he that hath wrought us for the selfsame thing *is* אֱלֹהִים, who also hath given unto us the earnest of the Spirit.

6 Therefore *we are* always confident, knowing that, whilst we are at home in the body, we are absent from the Lord:

7 (For we walk by faith, not by sight:)

8 We are confident, *I say*, and willing rather to be absent from the body, and to be present with the Lord.

9 Wherefore we labour, that, whether present or absent, we may be accepted of him.

10 For we must all appear before the judgment seat of Christ; that every one may receive the things *done* in *his* body, according to that he hath done, whether *it be* good or bad.

11 Knowing therefore the terror of the Lord, we persuade men; but we are made manifest unto אֱלֹהִים; and I trust also are made manifest in your consciences.

12 For we commend not ourselves again unto you, but give you occasion to glory on our behalf, that ye may have somewhat to *answer* them which glory in appearance, and not in heart.

13 For whether we be beside ourselves, *it is* to אֱלֹהִים: or whether we be sober, *it is* for your cause.

14 For the love of Christ constraineth us; because we thus judge, that if one died for all, then were all dead:

15 And *that* he died for all, that they which live should not henceforth live unto themselves, but unto him which died for them, and rose again.

16 Wherefore henceforth know we no man after the flesh: yea, though we have known Christ after the flesh, yet now henceforth know we *him* no more.

17 Therefore if any man *be* in Christ, *he is* a new creature: old things are passed away; behold, all things are become new.

18 And all things *are* of אֱלֹהִים, who hath reconciled us to himself by Yashiyah Christ, and hath given to us the ministry of reconciliation;

19 To wit, that אֱלֹהִים was in Christ, reconciling the world unto himself, not imputing their trespasses unto them; and hath committed unto us the word of reconciliation.

20 Now then we are ambassadors for Christ, as though אֱלֹהִים did beseech *you* by us: we pray *you* in Christ's stead, be ye reconciled to אֱלֹהִים.

21 For he hath made him *to be* sin for us, who knew no sin; that we might be made the righteousness of אֱלֹהִים in him.

CHAPTER 6

WE then, *as* workers together *with him*, beseech *you* also that ye receive not the grace of אֱלֹהִים in vain.

2 (For he saith, I have heard thee in a time accepted, and in the day of salvation have I succoured thee: behold, now *is* the accepted time; behold, now *is* the day of salvation.)

3 Giving no offence in any thing, that the ministry be not blamed:

4 But in all *things* approving ourselves as the ministers of אֱלֹהִים, in much patience, in afflictions, in necessities, in distresses,

5 In stripes, in imprisonments, in tumults, in labours, in watchings, in fastings;

6 By pureness, by knowledge, by longsuffering, by kindness, by the Holy Ghost, by love unfeigned,

7 By the word of truth, by the power of אֱלֹהִים, by the armour of righteousness on the right hand and on the left,

8 By honour and dishonour, by evil report and good report: as deceivers, and *yet* true;

9 As unknown, and *yet* well known; as dying, and, behold, we live; as chastened, and not killed;

10 As sorrowful, yet alway rejoicing; as poor, yet making many rich; as having nothing, and *yet* possessing all things.

11 O *ye* Corinthians, our mouth is open unto you, our heart is enlarged.

12 Ye are not straitened in us, but ye are straitened in your own bowels.

13 Now for a recompence in the same, (I speak as unto *my* children,) be ye also enlarged.

14 Be ye not unequally yoked together with unbelievers: for what fellowship hath righteousness with unrighteousness? and what communion hath light with darkness?

15 And what concord hath Christ with Belial? or what part hath he that believeth with an infidel?

16 And what agreement hath the temple of אֱלֹהִים with idols? for ye are the temple of the living אֱלֹהִים; as אֱלֹהִים hath said, I will dwell in them, and walk in *them:* and I will be their אֱלֹהִים, and they shall be my people.

17 Wherefore come out from among them, and be ye separate, saith the Lord, and touch not the unclean *thing:* and I will receive you,

18 And will be a Father unto you, and ye shall be my sons and daughters, saith the Lord Almighty.

CHAPTER 7

HAVING therefore these promises, dearly beloved, let us cleanse ourselves from all filthiness of the flesh and spirit, perfecting holiness in the fear of אֱלֹהִים.

2 Receive us; we have wronged no man, we have corrupted no man, we have defrauded no man.

3 I speak not *this* to condemn *you:* for I have said before, that ye are in our hearts to die and live with *you.*

4 Great *is* my boldness of speech toward you, great *is* my glorying of you: I am filled with comfort, I am exceeding joyful in all our tribulation.

5 For, when we were come into Macedonia, our flesh had no rest, but we were troubled on every side; without *were* fightings, within *were* fears.

6 Nevertheless אֱלֹהִים, that comforteth those that are cast down, comforted us by the coming of Titus;

7 And not by his coming only, but by the consolation wherewith he was comforted in you, when he told us your earnest desire, your mourning, your fervent mind toward me; so that I rejoiced the more.

8 For though I made you sorry with a letter, I do not repent, though I did repent: for I perceive that the same epistle hath made you sorry, though *it were* but for a season.

9 Now I rejoice, not that ye were made sorry, but that ye sorrowed to repentance: for ye were made sorry after a godly manner, that ye might receive damage by us in nothing.

10 For godly sorrow worketh repentance to salvation not to be repented of: but the sorrow of the world worketh death.

11 For behold this selfsame thing, that ye sorrowed after a godly sort, what carefulness it wrought in you, yea, *what* clearing of yourselves, yea, *what* indignation, yea, *what* fear, yea, *what* vehement desire, yea, *what* zeal, yea, *what* revenge! In all *things* ye have approved yourselves to be clear in this matter.

12 Wherefore, though I wrote unto you, *I did it* not for his cause that had done the wrong, nor for his cause that suffered wrong, but that our care for you in the sight of אֱלֹהִים might appear unto you.

13 Therefore we were comforted in your comfort: yea, and exceedingly the more joyed we for the joy of Titus, because his spirit was refreshed by you all.

14 For if I have boasted any thing to him of you, I am not ashamed; but as we spake all things to you in truth, even so our boasting, which *I made* before Titus, is found a truth.

15 And his inward affection is more abundant toward you, whilst he remembereth the obedience of you all, how with fear and trembling ye received him.

16 I rejoice therefore that I have confidence in you in all *things.*

CHAPTER 8

MOREOVER, brethren, we do you to wit of the grace of אֱלֹהִים bestowed on the churches of Macedonia;

2 How that in a great trial of affliction the abundance of their joy and their deep poverty abounded unto the riches of their liberality.

3 For to *their* power, I bear record, yea, and beyond *their* power *they were* willing of themselves;

4 Praying us with much intreaty that we would receive the gift, and *take upon us* the fellowship of the ministering to the saints.

5 And *this they did,* not as we hoped, but first gave their own selves to the Lord, and unto us by the will of אֱלֹהִים.

6 Insomuch that we desired Titus, that as he had begun, so he would also finish in you the same grace also.

7 Therefore, as ye abound in every *thing, in* faith, and utterance, and knowledge, and *in* all diligence, and *in* your love to us, *see* that ye abound in this grace also.

8 I speak not by commandment, but by occasion of the forwardness of others, and to prove the sincerity of your love.

9 For ye know the grace of our Lord Yashiyah Christ, that, though he was rich, yet for your sakes he became poor, that ye through his poverty might be rich.

10 And herein I give *my* advice: for this is expedient for you, who have begun before, not only to do, but also to be forward a year ago.

11 Now therefore perform the doing *of it;* that as *there was* a readiness to will, so *there may be* a performance also out of that which ye have.

12 For if there be first a willing mind, *it is* accepted according to that a man hath, *and* not according to that he hath not.

13 For *I mean* not that other men be eased, and ye burdened:

14 But by an equality, *that* now at this time your abundance *may be a supply* for their want, that their abundance also may be *a supply* for your want: that there may be equality:

15 As it is written, He that *had gathered* much had nothing over; and he that *had gathered* little had no lack.

16 But thanks *be* to אֱלֹהִים, which put the same earnest care into the heart of Titus for you.

17 For indeed he accepted the exhortation; but being more forward, of his own accord he went unto you.

18 And we have sent with him the brother, whose praise *is* in the gospel throughout all the churches;

19 And not *that* only, but who was also chosen of the churches to travel with us with this grace, which is administered by us to the glory of the same Lord, and *declaration of* your ready mind:

20 Avoiding this, that no man should blame us in this abundance which is administered by us:

21 Providing for honest things, not only in the sight of the Lord, but also in the sight of men.

22 And we have sent with them our brother, whom we have oftentimes proved diligent in many things, but now much more diligent, upon the great confidence which *I have* in you.

23 Whether *any do inquire* of Titus, *he is* my partner and fellowhelper concerning you: or our brethren *be inquired of, they are* the messengers of the churches, *and* the glory of Christ.

24 Wherefore shew ye to them, and before the churches, the proof of your love, and of our boasting on your behalf.

CHAPTER 9

FOR as touching the ministering to the saints, it is superfluous for me to write to you:

2 For I know the forwardness of your mind, for which I boast of you to them of Macedonia, that Achaia was ready a year ago; and your zeal hath provoked very many.

3 Yet have I sent the brethren, lest our boasting of you should be in vain in this behalf; that, as I said, ye may be ready:

4 Lest haply if they of Macedonia come with me, and find you unprepared, we (that we say not, ye) should be ashamed in this same confident boasting.

5 Therefore I thought it necessary to exhort the brethren, that they would go before unto you, and make up beforehand your bounty, whereof ye had notice before, that the same might be ready, as *a matter of* bounty, and not as *of* covetousness.

6 But this *I say*, He which soweth sparingly shall reap also sparingly; and he which soweth bountifully shall reap also bountifully.

7 Every man according as he purposeth in his heart, *so let him give:* not grudgingly, or of necessity: for אֱלֹהִים loveth a cheerful giver.

8 And אֱלֹהִים *is* able to make all grace abound toward you; that ye, always having all sufficiency in all *things*, may abound to every good work:

9 (As it is written, He hath dispersed abroad; he hath given to the poor: his righteousness remaineth for ever.

10 Now he that ministereth seed to the sower both minister bread for *your* food, and multiply your seed sown, and increase the fruits of your righteousness;)

11 Being enriched in every thing to all bountifulness, which causeth through us thanksgiving to אֱלֹהִים.

12 For the administration of this service not only supplieth the want of the saints, but is abundant also by many thanksgivings unto אֱלֹהִים;

13 Whiles by the experiment of this ministration they glorify אֱלֹהִים for your professed subjection unto the gospel of Christ, and for *your* liberal distribution unto them, and unto all *men;*

14 And by their prayer for you, which long after you for the exceeding grace of אֱלֹהִים in you.

15 Thanks *be* unto אֱלֹהִים for his unspeakable gift.

CHAPTER 10

NOW I Paul myself beseech you by the meekness and gentleness of Christ, who in presence *am* base among you, but being absent am bold toward you:

2 But I beseech *you*, that I may not be bold when I am present with that confidence, wherewith I think to be bold against some, which think of us as if we walked according to the flesh.

3 For though we walk in the flesh, we do not war after the flesh:

4 (For the weapons of our warfare *are* not carnal, but mighty through אֱלֹהִים to the pulling down of strong holds;)

5 Casting down imaginations, and every high thing that exalteth itself against the knowledge of אֱלֹהִים, and bringing into captivity every thought to the obedience of Christ;

6 And having in a readiness to revenge all disobedience, when your obedience is fulfilled.

7 Do ye look on things after the outward appearance? If any man trust to himself that he is Christ's, let him of himself think this again, that, as he *is* Christ's, even so *are* we Christ's.

8 For though I should boast somewhat more of our authority, which the Lord hath given us for edification, and not for your destruction, I should not be ashamed:

9 That I may not seem as if I would terrify you by letters.

10 For *his* letters, say they, *are* weighty and powerful; but *his* bodily presence *is* weak, and *his* speech contemptible.

11 Let such an one think this, that, such as we are in word by letters when we are absent, such *will we be* also in deed when we are present.

12 For we dare not make ourselves of the number, or compare ourselves with some that commend themselves: but they measuring themselves by themselves, and comparing themselves among themselves, are not wise.

13 But we will not boast of things without *our* measure, but according to the measure of the rule which אֱלֹהִים hath distributed to us, a measure to reach even unto you.

14 For we stretch not ourselves beyond *our measure*, as though we reached not unto you: for we are come as far as to you also in *preaching* the gospel of Christ:

15 Not boasting of things without *our* measure, *that is*, of other men's labours; but having hope, when your faith is increased, that we shall be enlarged by you according to our rule abundantly,

16 To preach the gospel in the *regions* beyond you, *and* not to boast in another man's line of things made ready to our hand.

17 But he that glorieth, let him glory in the Lord.

18 For not he that commendeth himself is approved, but whom the Lord commendeth.

CHAPTER 11

WOULD to אֱלֹהִים ye could bear with me a little in *my* folly: and indeed bear with me.

2 For I am jealous over you with godly jealousy: for I have espoused you to one husband, that I may present *you as* a chaste virgin to Christ.

3 But I fear, lest by any means, as the serpent beguiled Eve through his subtilty, so your minds should be corrupted from the simplicity that is in Christ.

4 For if he that cometh preacheth another Yashiyah, whom we have not preached, or *if* ye receive another spirit, which ye have not received, or another gospel, which ye have not accepted, ye might well bear with *him*.

5 For I suppose I was not a whit behind the very chiefest apostles.

6 But though *I be* rude in speech, yet not in knowledge; but we have been throughly made manifest among you in all things.

7 Have I committed an offence in abasing myself that ye might be exalted, because I have preached to you the gospel of אֱלֹהִים freely?

8 I robbed other churches, taking wages *of them*, to do you service.

9 And when I was present with you, and wanted, I was chargeable to no man: for that which was lacking to me the brethren which came from Macedonia supplied: and in all *things* I have kept myself from being burdensome unto you, and *so* will I keep *myself*.

10 As the truth of Christ is in me, no man shall stop me of this boasting in the regions of Achaia.

11 Wherefore? because I love you not? אֱלֹהִים knoweth.

12 But what I do, that I will do, that I may cut off occasion from them which desire occasion; that wherein they glory, they may be found even as we.

13 For such *are* false apostles, deceitful workers, transforming themselves into the apostles of Christ.

14 And no marvel; for Satan himself is transformed into an angel of light.

15 Therefore *it is* no great thing if his ministers also be transformed as the ministers of righteousness; whose end shall be according to their works.

16 I say again, Let no man think me a fool; if otherwise, yet as a fool receive me, that I may boast myself a little.

17 That which I speak, I speak *it* not after the Lord, but as it were foolishly, in this confidence of boasting.

18 Seeing that many glory after the flesh, I will glory also.

19 For ye suffer fools gladly, seeing ye *yourselves* are wise.

20 For ye suffer, if a man bring you into bondage, if a man devour *you*, if a man take *of you*, if a man exalt himself, if a man smite you on the face.

21 I speak as concerning reproach, as though we had been weak. Howbeit whereinsoever any is bold, (I speak foolishly,) I am bold also.

22 Are they Hebrews? so *am* I. Are they Israelites? so *am* I. Are they the seed of Abraham? so *am* I.

23 Are they ministers of Christ? (I speak as a fool) I *am* more; in labours more abundant, in stripes above measure, in prisons more frequent, in deaths oft.

24 Of the Jews five times received I forty *stripes* save one.

25 Thrice was I beaten with rods, once was I stoned, thrice I suffered shipwreck, a night and a day I have been in the deep;

26 *In* journeyings often, *in* perils of waters, *in* perils of robbers, *in* perils by *mine own* countrymen, *in* perils by the heathen, *in* perils in the city, *in* perils in the wilderness, *in* perils in the sea, *in* perils among false brethren;

27 In weariness and painfulness, in watchings often, in hunger and thirst, in fastings often, in cold and nakedness.

28 Beside those things that are without, that which cometh upon me daily, the care of all the churches.

29 Who is weak, and I am not weak? who is offended, and I burn not?

30 If I must needs glory, I will glory of the things which concern mine infirmities.

31 The אֱלֹהִים and Father of our Lord Yashiyah Christ, which is blessed for evermore, knoweth that I lie not.

32 In Damascus the governor under Aretas the king kept the city of the Damascenes with a garrison, desirous to apprehend me:

33 And through a window in a basket was I let down by the wall, and escaped his hands.

CHAPTER 12

IT is not expedient for me doubtless to glory. I will come to visions and revelations of the Lord.

2 I knew a man in Christ above fourteen years ago, (whether in the body, I cannot tell; or whether out of the body, I cannot tell: אֱלֹהִים knoweth;) such an one caught up to the third heaven.

3 And I knew such a man, (whether in the body, or out of the body, I cannot tell: אֱלֹהִים knoweth;)

4 How that he was caught up into paradise, and heard unspeakable words, which it is not lawful for a man to utter.

5 Of such an one will I glory: yet of myself I will not glory, but in mine infirmities.

6 For though I would desire to glory, I shall not be a fool; for I will say the truth: but *now* I forbear, lest any man should think of me above that which he seeth me *to be*, or *that* he heareth of me.

7 And lest I should be exalted above measure through the abundance of the revelations, there was given to me a thorn in the flesh, the messenger of Satan to buffet me, lest I should be exalted above measure.

8 For this thing I besought the Lord thrice, that it might depart from me.

9 And he said unto me, My grace is sufficient for thee: for my strength is made perfect in weakness. Most gladly therefore will I rather glory in my infirmities, that the power of Christ may rest upon me.

10 Therefore I take pleasure in infirmities, in reproaches, in necessities, in persecutions, in distresses for Christ's sake: for when I am weak, then am I strong.

11 I am become a fool in glorying; ye have compelled me: for I ought to have been commended of you: for in nothing am I behind the very chiefest apostles, though I be nothing.

12 Truly the signs of an apostle were wrought among you in all patience, in signs, and wonders, and mighty deeds.

13 For what is it wherein ye were inferior to other churches, except *it be* that I myself was not burdensome to you? forgive me this wrong.

14 Behold, the third time I am ready to come to you; and I will not be burdensome to you: for I seek not yours, but you: for the children ought not to lay up for the parents, but the parents for the children.

15 And I will very gladly spend and be spent for you; though the more abundantly I love you, the less I be loved.

16 But be it so, I did not burden you: nevertheless, being crafty, I caught you with guile.

17 Did I make a gain of you by any of them whom I sent unto you?

18 I desired Titus, and with *him* I sent a brother. Did Titus make a gain of you? walked we not in the same spirit? *walked we* not in the same steps?

19 Again, think ye that we excuse ourselves unto you? we speak before אֱלֹהִים in Christ: but *we do* all things, dearly beloved, for your edifying.

20 For I fear, lest, when I come, I shall not find you such as I would, and *that* I shall be found unto you such as ye would not: lest *there be* debates, envyings, wraths, strifes, backbitings, whisperings, swellings, tumults:

21 *And* lest, when I come again, my אֱלֹהִים will humble me among you, and *that* I shall bewail many which have sinned already, and have not repented of the uncleanness and fornication and lasciviousness which they have committed.

CHAPTER 13

THIS *is* the third *time* I am coming to you. In the mouth of two or three witnesses shall every word be established.

2 I told you before, and foretell you, as if I were present, the second time; and being absent now I write to them which heretofore have sinned, and to all other, that, if I come again, I will not spare:

3 Since ye seek a proof of Christ speaking in me, which to you-ward is not weak, but is mighty in you.

4 For though he was crucified through weakness, yet he liveth by the power of אֱלֹהִים. For we also are weak in him, but we shall live with him by the power of אֱלֹהִים toward you.

5 Examine yourselves, whether ye be in the faith; prove your own selves. Know ye not your own selves, how that Yashiyah Christ is in you, except ye be reprobates?

6 But I trust that ye shall know that we are not reprobates.

7 Now I pray to אֱלֹהִים that ye do no evil; not that we should appear approved, but that ye should do that which is honest, though we be as reprobates.

8 For we can do nothing against the truth, but for the truth.

9 For we are glad, when we are weak, and ye are strong: and this also we wish, *even* your perfection.

10 Therefore I write these things being absent, lest being present I should use sharpness, according to the power which the Lord hath given me to edification, and not to destruction.

11 Finally, brethren, farewell. Be perfect, be of good comfort, be of one mind, live in peace; and the אֱלֹהִים of love and peace shall be with you.

12 Greet one another with an holy kiss.

13 All the saints salute you.

14 The grace of the Lord Yashiyah Christ, and the love of אֱלֹהִים, and the communion of the Holy Ghost, *be* with you all. Amen.

¶ The second *epistle* to the Corinthians was written from Philippi, *a city* of Macedonia, by Titus and Lucas.

THE EPISTLE OF PAUL THE APOSTLE
TO THE
GALATIANS.

CHAPTER 1

PAUL, an apostle, (not of men, neither by man, but by Yashiyah Christ, and אֱלֹהִים the Father, who raised him from the dead;)

2 And all the brethren which are with me, unto the churches of Galatia:

3 Grace *be* to you and peace from אֱלֹהִים the Father, and *from* our Lord Yashiyah Christ,

4 Who gave himself for our sins, that he might deliver us from this present evil world, according to the will of אֱלֹהִים and our Father:

5 To whom *be* glory for ever and ever. Amen.

6 I marvel that ye are so soon removed from him that called you into the grace of Christ unto another gospel:

7 Which is not another; but there be some that trouble you, and would pervert the gospel of Christ.

8 But though we, or an angel from heaven, preach any other gospel unto you than that which we have preached unto you, let him be accursed.

9 As we said before, so say I now again, If any *man* preach any other gospel unto you than that ye have received, let him be accursed.

10 For do I now persuade men, or אֱלֹהִים? or do I seek to please men? for if I yet pleased men, I should not be the servant of Christ.

11 But I certify you, brethren, that the gospel which was preached of me is not after man.

12 For I neither received it of man, neither was I taught *it*, but by the revelation of Yashiyah Christ.

13 For ye have heard of my conversation in time past in the Jews' religion, how that beyond measure I persecuted the church of אֱלֹהִים, and wasted it:

14 And profited in the Jews' religion above many my equals in mine own nation, being more exceedingly zealous of the traditions of my fathers.

15 But when it pleased אֱלֹהִים, who separated me from my mother's womb, and called *me* by his grace,

16 To reveal his Son in me, that I might preach him among the heathen; immediately I conferred not with flesh and blood:

17 Neither went I up to Jerusalem to them which were apostles before me; but I went into Arabia, and returned again unto Damascus.

18 Then after three years I went up to Jerusalem to see Peter, and abode with him fifteen days.

19 But other of the apostles saw I none, save James the Lord's brother.

20 Now the things which I write unto you, behold, before אֱלֹהִים, I lie not.

21 Afterwards I came into the regions of Syria and Cilicia;

22 And was unknown by face unto the churches of Judæa which were in Christ:

23 But they had heard only, That he which persecuted us in times past now preacheth the faith which once he destroyed.

24 And they glorified אֱלֹהִים in me.

CHAPTER 2

THEN fourteen years after I went up again to Jerusalem with Barnabas, and took Titus with *me* also.

2 And I went up by revelation, and communicated unto them that gospel which I preach among the Gentiles, but privately to them which were of reputation, lest by any means I should run, or had run, in vain.

3 But neither Titus, who was with me, being a Greek, was compelled to be circumcised:

4 And that because of false brethren unawares brought in, who came in privily to spy out our liberty which we have in Christ Yashiyah, that they might bring us into bondage:

5 To whom we gave place by subjection, no, not for an hour; that the truth of the gospel might continue with you.

6 But of these who seemed to be somewhat, (whatsoever they were, it maketh no matter to me: אֱלֹהִים accepteth no man's person:) for they who seemed *to be somewhat* in conference added nothing to me:

7 But contrariwise, when they saw that the gospel of the uncircumcision was committed unto me, as *the gospel* of the circumcision *was* unto Peter;

8 (For he that wrought effectually in Peter to the apostleship of the circumcision, the same was mighty in me toward the Gentiles:)

9 And when James, Cephas, and John, who seemed to be pillars, perceived the grace that was given unto me, they gave to me and Barnabas the right hands of fellowship; that we *should go* unto the heathen, and they unto the circumcision.

10 Only *they would* that we should remember the poor; the same which I also was forward to do.

11 But when Peter was come to Antioch, I withstood him to the face, because he was to be blamed.

12 For before that certain came from James, he did eat with the Gentiles: but when they were come, he withdrew and separated himself, fearing them which were of the circumcision.

13 And the other Jews dissembled likewise with him; insomuch that Barnabas also was carried away with their dissimulation.

14 But when I saw that they walked not uprightly according to the truth of the gospel, I said unto Peter before *them* all, If thou, being a Jew, livest after the manner of Gentiles, and not as do the Jews, why compellest thou the Gentiles to live as do the Jews?

15 We *who are* Jews by nature, and not sinners of the Gentiles,

16 Knowing that a man is not justified by the works of the law, but by the faith of Yashiyah Christ, even we have believed in Yashiyah Christ, that we might be justified by the faith of Christ, and not by the works of the law: for by the works of the law shall no flesh be justified.

17 But if, while we seek to be justified by Christ, we ourselves also are found sinners, *is* therefore Christ the minister of sin? אֱלֹהִים forbid.

18 For if I build again the things which I destroyed, I make myself a transgressor.

19 For I through the law am dead to the law, that I might live unto אֱלֹהִים.

20 I am crucified with Christ: nevertheless I live; yet not I, but Christ liveth in me: and the life which I now live in the flesh I live by the faith of the Son of אֱלֹהִים, who loved me, and gave himself for me.

21 I do not frustrate the grace of אֱלֹהִים: for if righteousness *come* by the law, then Christ is dead in vain.

CHAPTER 3

O FOOLISH Galatians, who hath bewitched you, that ye should not obey the truth, before whose eyes Yashiyah Christ hath been evidently set forth, crucified among you?

2 This only would I learn of you, Received ye the Spirit by the works of the law, or by the hearing of faith?

3 Are ye so foolish? having begun in the Spirit, are ye now made perfect by the flesh?

4 Have ye suffered so many things in vain? if *it be* yet in vain.

5 He therefore that ministereth to you the Spirit, and worketh miracles among you, *doeth he it* by the works of the law, or by the hearing of faith?

6 Even as Abraham believed אֱלֹהִים, and it was accounted to him for righteousness.

7 Know ye therefore that they which are of faith, the same are the children of Abraham.

8 And the scripture, foreseeing that אֱלֹהִים would justify the heathen through faith, preached before the gospel unto Abraham, *saying*, In thee shall all nations be blessed.

9 So then they which be of faith are blessed with faithful Abraham.

10 For as many as are of the works of the law are under the curse: for it is written, Cursed *is* every one that continueth not in all things which are written in the book of the law to do them.

11 But that no man is justified by the law in the sight of אֱלֹהִים, *it is* evident: for, The just shall live by faith.

12 And the law is not of faith: but, The man that doeth them shall live in them.

13 Christ hath redeemed us from the curse of the law, being made a curse for us: for it is written, Cursed *is* every one that hangeth on a tree:

14 That the blessing of Abraham might come on the Gentiles through Yashiyah Christ; that we might receive the promise of the Spirit through faith.

15 Brethren, I speak after the manner of men; Though *it be* but a man's covenant, yet *if it be* confirmed, no man disannulleth, or addeth thereto.

16 Now to Abraham and his seed were the promises made. He saith not, And to seeds, as of many; but as of one, And to thy seed, which is Christ.

17 And this I say, *that* the covenant, that was confirmed before of אֱלֹהִים in Christ, the law, which was four hundred and thirty years after, cannot disannul, that it should make the promise of none effect.

18 For if the inheritance *be* of the law, *it is* no more of promise: but אֱלֹהִים gave *it* to Abraham by promise.

19 Wherefore then *serveth* the law? It was added because of transgressions, till the seed should come to whom the promise was made; *and it was* ordained by angels in the hand of a mediator.

20 Now a mediator is not *a mediator* of one, but אֱלֹהִים is one.

21 *Is* the law then against the promises of אֱלֹהִים? אֱלֹהִים forbid: for if there had been a law given which could have given life, verily righteousness should have been by the law.

22 But the scripture hath concluded all under sin, that the promise by faith of Yashiyah Christ might be given to them that believe.

23 But before faith came, we were kept under the law, shut up unto the faith which should afterwards be revealed.

24 Wherefore the law was our schoolmaster *to bring us* unto Christ, that we might be justified by faith.

25 But after that faith is come, we are no longer under a schoolmaster.

26 For ye are all the children of אֱלֹהִים by faith in Christ Yashiyah.

27 For as many of you as have been baptized into Christ have put on Christ.

28 There is neither Jew nor Greek, there is neither bond nor free, there is neither male nor female: for ye are all one in Christ Yashiyah.

29 And if ye *be* Christ's, then are ye Abraham's seed, and heirs according to the promise.

CHAPTER 4

NOW I say, *That* the heir, as long as he is a child, differeth nothing from a servant, though he be lord of all;

2 But is under tutors and governors until the time appointed of the father.

3 Even so we, when we were children, were in bondage under the elements of the world:

4 But when the fulness of the time was come, אֱלֹהִים sent forth his Son, made of a woman, made under the law,

5 To redeem them that were under the law, that we might receive the adoption of sons.

6 And because ye are sons, אֱלֹהִים hath sent forth the Spirit of his Son into your hearts, crying, Abba, Father.

7 Wherefore thou art no more a servant, but a son; and if a son, then an heir of אֱלֹהִים through Christ.

8 Howbeit then, when ye knew not אֱלֹהִים, ye did service unto them which by nature are no gods.

9 But now, after that ye have known אֱלֹהִים, or rather are known of אֱלֹהִים, how turn ye again to the weak and beggarly elements, whereunto ye desire again to be in bondage?

10 Ye observe days, and months, and times, and years.

11 I am afraid of you, lest I have bestowed upon you labour in vain.

12 Brethren, I beseech you, be as I *am*; for I *am* as ye *are*: ye have not injured me at all.

13 Ye know how through infirmity of the flesh I preached the gospel unto you at the first.

14 And my temptation which was in my flesh ye despised not, nor rejected; but received me as an angel of אֱלֹהִים, *even* as Christ Yashiyah.

15 Where is then the blessedness ye spake of? for I bear you record, that, if *it had been* possible, ye would have plucked out your own eyes, and have given them to me.

16 Am I therefore become your enemy, because I tell you the truth?

17 They zealously affect you, *but* not well; yea, they would exclude you, that ye might affect them.

18 But *it is* good to be zealously affected always in *a* good *thing*, and not only when I am present with you.

19 My little children, of whom I travail in birth again until Christ be formed in you,

20 I desire to be present with you now, and to change my voice; for I stand in doubt of you.

21 Tell me, ye that desire to be under the law, do ye not hear the law?

22 For it is written, that Abraham had two sons, the one by a bondmaid, the other by a freewoman.

23 But he *who was* of the bondwoman was born after the flesh; but he of the freewoman *was* by promise.

24 Which things are an allegory: for these are the two covenants; the one from the mount Sinai, which gendereth to bondage, which is Agar.

25 For this Agar is mount Sinai in Arabia, and answereth to Jerusalem which now is, and is in bondage with her children.

26 But Jerusalem which is above is free, which is the mother of us all.

27 For it is written, Rejoice, *thou* barren that bearest not; break forth and cry, thou that travailest not: for the desolate hath many more children than she which hath an husband.

28 Now we, brethren, as Isaac was, are the children of promise.

29 But as then he that was born after the flesh persecuted him *that was born* after the Spirit, even so *it is* now.

30 Nevertheless what saith the scripture? Cast out the bondwoman and her son: for the son of the bondwoman shall not be heir with the son of the freewoman.

31 So then, brethren, we are not children of the bondwoman, but of the free.

CHAPTER 5

STAND fast therefore in the liberty wherewith Christ hath made us free, and be not entangled again with the yoke of bondage.

2 Behold, I Paul say unto you, that if ye be circumcised, Christ shall profit you nothing.

3 For I testify again to every man that is circumcised, that he is a debtor to do the whole law.

4 Christ is become of no effect unto you, whosoever of you are justified by the law; ye are fallen from grace.

5 For we through the Spirit wait for the hope of righteousness by faith.

6 For in Yashiyah Christ neither circumcision availeth any thing, nor uncircumcision; but faith which worketh by love.

7 Ye did run well; who did hinder you that ye should not obey the truth?

8 This persuasion *cometh* not of him that calleth you.

9 A little leaven leaveneth the whole lump.

10 I have confidence in you through the Lord, that ye will be none otherwise minded: but he that troubleth you shall bear his judgment, whosoever he be.

11 And I, brethren, if I yet preach circumcision, why do I yet suffer persecution? then is the offence of the cross ceased.

12 I would they were even cut off which trouble you.

13 For, brethren, ye have been called unto liberty; only *use* not liberty for an occasion to the flesh, but by love serve one another.

14 For all the law is fulfilled in one word, *even* in this; Thou shalt love thy neighbour as thyself.

15 But if ye bite and devour one another, take heed that ye be not consumed one of another.

16 *This* I say then, Walk in the Spirit, and ye shall not fulfil the lust of the flesh.

17 For the flesh lusteth against the Spirit, and the Spirit against the flesh: and these are contrary the one to the other: so that ye cannot do the things that ye would.

18 But if ye be led of the Spirit, ye are not under the law.

19 Now the works of the flesh are manifest, which are *these*; Adultery, fornication, uncleanness, lasciviousness,

20 Idolatry, witchcraft, hatred, variance, emulations, wrath, strife, seditions, heresies,

21 Envyings, murders, drunkenness, revellings, and such like: of the which I tell you before, as I have also told *you* in time past, that they which do such things shall not inherit the kingdom of אֱלֹהִים.

22 But the fruit of the Spirit is love, joy, peace, longsuffering, gentleness, goodness, faith,

23 Meekness, temperance: against such there is no law.

24 And they that are Christ's have crucified the flesh with the affections and lusts.

25 If we live in the Spirit, let us also walk in the Spirit.

26 Let us not be desirous of vain glory, provoking one another, envying one another.

CHAPTER 6

BRETHREN, if a man be overtaken in a fault, ye which are spiritual, restore such an one in the spirit of meekness; considering thyself, lest thou also be tempted.

2 Bear ye one another's burdens, and so fulfil the law of Christ.

3 For if a man think himself to be something, when he is nothing, he deceiveth himself.

4 But let every man prove his own work, and then shall he have rejoicing in himself alone, and not in another.

5 For every man shall bear his own burden.

6 Let him that is taught in the word communicate unto him that teacheth in all good things.

7 Be not deceived; אֱלֹהִים is not mocked: for whatsoever a man soweth, that shall he also reap.

8 For he that soweth to his flesh shall of the flesh reap corruption; but he that soweth to the Spirit shall of the Spirit reap life everlasting.

9 And let us not be weary in well doing: for in due season we shall reap, if we faint not.

10 As we have therefore opportunity, let us do good unto all *men*, especially unto them who are of the household of faith.

11 Ye see how large a letter I have written unto you with mine own hand.

12 As many as desire to make a fair shew in the flesh, they constrain you to be circumcised; only lest they should suffer persecution for the cross of Christ.

13 For neither they themselves who are circumcised keep the law; but desire to have you circumcised, that they may glory in your flesh.

14 But אֱלֹהִים forbid that I should glory, save in the cross of our Lord Yashiyah Christ, by whom the world is crucified unto me, and I unto the world.

15 For in Christ Yashiyah neither circumcision availeth any thing, nor uncircumcision, but a new creature.

16 And as many as walk according to this rule, peace *be* on them, and mercy, and upon the Israel of אֱלֹהִים.

17 From henceforth let no man trouble me: for I bear in my body the marks of the Lord Yashiyah.

18 Brethren, the grace of our Lord Yashiyah Christ *be* with your spirit. Amen.

¶ Unto the Galatians written from Rome.

THE EPISTLE OF PAUL THE APOSTLE
TO THE
EPHESIANS.

CHAPTER 1

PAUL, an apostle of Yashiyah Christ by the will of אֱלֹהִים, to the saints which are at Ephesus, and to the faithful in Christ Yashiyah:

2 Grace *be* to you, and peace, from אֱלֹהִים our Father, and *from* the Lord Yashiyah Christ.

3 Blessed *be* the אֱלֹהִים and Father of our Lord Yashiyah Christ, who hath blessed us with all spiritual blessings in heavenly *places* in Christ:

4 According as he hath chosen us in him before the foundation of the world, that we should be holy and without blame before him in love:

5 Having predestinated us unto the adoption of children by Yashiyah Christ to himself, according to the good pleasure of his will,

6 To the praise of the glory of his grace, wherein he hath made us accepted in the beloved.

7 In whom we have redemption through his blood, the forgiveness of sins, according to the riches of his grace;

8 Wherein he hath abounded toward us in all wisdom and prudence;

9 Having made known unto us the mystery of his will, according to his good pleasure which he hath purposed in himself:

10 That in the dispensation of the fulness of times he might gather together in one all things in Christ, both which are in heaven, and which are on earth; *even* in him:

11 In whom also we have obtained an inheritance, being predestinated according to the purpose of him who worketh all things after the counsel of his own will:

12 That we should be to the praise of his glory, who first trusted in Christ.

13 In whom ye also *trusted*, after that ye heard the word of truth, the gospel of your salvation: in whom also after that ye believed, ye were sealed with that holy Spirit of promise,

14 Which is the earnest of our inheritance until the redemption of the purchased possession, unto the praise of his glory.

15 Wherefore I also, after I heard of your faith in the Lord Yashiyah, and love unto all the saints,

16 Cease not to give thanks for you, making mention of you in my prayers;

17 That the אֱלֹהִים of our Lord Yashiyah Christ, the Father of glory, may give unto you the spirit of wisdom and revelation in the knowledge of him:

18 The eyes of your understanding being enlightened; that ye may know what is the hope of his calling, and what the riches of the glory of his inheritance in the saints,

19 And what *is* the exceeding greatness of his power to us-ward who believe, according to the working of his mighty power,

20 Which he wrought in Christ, when he raised him from the dead, and set *him* at his own right hand in the heavenly *places*,

21 Far above all principality, and power, and might, and dominion, and every name that is named, not only in this world, but also in that which is to come:

22 And hath put all *things* under his feet, and gave him *to be* the head over all *things* to the church,

23 Which is his body, the fulness of him that filleth all in all.

CHAPTER 2

AND you *hath he quickened*, who were dead in trespasses and sins;

2 Wherein in time past ye walked according to the course of this world, according to the prince of the power of the air, the spirit that now worketh in the children of disobedience:

3 Among whom also we all had our conversation in times past in the lusts of our flesh, fulfilling the desires of the flesh and of the mind; and were by nature the children of wrath, even as others.

4 But אֱלֹהִים, who is rich in mercy, for his great love wherewith he loved us,

5 Even when we were dead in sins, hath quickened us together with Christ, (by grace ye are saved;)

6 And hath raised *us* up together, and made *us* sit together in heavenly *places* in Christ Yashiyah:

7 That in the ages to come he might shew the exceeding riches of his grace in *his* kindness toward us through Christ Yashiyah.

8 For by grace are ye saved through faith; and that not of yourselves: *it is* the gift of אֱלֹהִים:

9 Not of works, lest any man should boast.

10 For we are his workmanship, created in Christ Yashiyah unto good works, which אֱלֹהִים hath before ordained that we should walk in them.

11 Wherefore remember, that ye *being* in time past Gentiles in the flesh, who are called Uncircumcision by that which is called the Circumcision in the flesh made by hands;

12 That at that time ye were without Christ, being aliens from the commonwealth of Israel, and strangers from the covenants of promise, having no hope, and without אֱלֹהִים in the world:

13 But now in Christ Yashiyah ye who sometimes were far off are made nigh by the blood of Christ.

14 For he is our peace, who hath made both one, and hath broken down the middle wall of partition *between us;*

15 Having abolished in his flesh the enmity, *even* the law of commandments *contained* in ordinances; for to make in himself of twain one new man, *so* making peace;

16 And that he might reconcile both unto אֱלֹהִים in one body by the cross, having slain the enmity thereby:

17 And came and preached peace to you which were afar off, and to them that were nigh.

18 For through him we both have access by one Spirit unto the Father.

19 Now therefore ye are no more strangers and foreigners, but fellowcitizens with the saints, and of the household of אֱלֹהִים;

20 And are built upon the foundation of the apostles and prophets, Yashiyah Christ himself being the chief corner *stone;*

21 In whom all the building fitly framed together groweth unto an holy temple in the Lord:

22 In whom ye also are builded together for an habitation of אֱלֹהִים through the Spirit.

CHAPTER 3

FOR this cause I Paul, the prisoner of Yashiyah Christ for you Gentiles,

2 If ye have heard of the dispensation of the grace of אֱלֹהִים which is given me to you-ward:

3 How that by revelation he made known unto me the mystery; (as I wrote afore in few words,

4 Whereby, when ye read, ye may understand my knowledge in the mystery of Christ)

5 Which in other ages was not made known unto the sons of men, as it is now revealed unto his holy apostles and prophets by the Spirit;

6 That the Gentiles should be fellowheirs, and of the same body, and partakers of his promise in Christ by the gospel:

7 Whereof I was made a minister, according to the gift of the grace of אֱלֹהִים given unto me by the effectual working of his power.

8 Unto me, who am less than the least of all saints, is this grace given, that I should preach among the Gentiles the unsearchable riches of Christ;

9 And to make all *men* see what *is* the fellowship of the mystery, which from the beginning of the world hath been hid in אֱלֹהִים, who created all things by Yashiyah Christ:

10 To the intent that now unto the principalities and powers in heavenly *places* might be known by the church the manifold wisdom of אֱלֹהִים,

11 According to the eternal purpose which he purposed in Christ Yashiyah our Lord:

12 In whom we have boldness and access with confidence by the faith of him.

13 Wherefore I desire that ye faint not at my tribulations for you, which is your glory.

14 For this cause I bow my knees unto the Father of our Lord Yashiyah Christ,

15 Of whom the whole family in heaven and earth is named,

16 That he would grant you, according to the riches of his glory, to be strengthened with might by his Spirit in the inner man;

17 That Christ may dwell in your hearts by faith; that ye, being rooted and grounded in love,

18 May be able to comprehend with all saints what *is* the breadth, and length, and depth, and height;

19 And to know the love of Christ, which passeth knowledge, that ye might be filled with all the fulness of אֱלֹהִים.

20 Now unto him that is able to do exceeding abundantly above all that we ask or think, according to the power that worketh in us,

21 Unto him *be* glory in the church by Christ Yashiyah throughout all ages, world without end. Amen.

CHAPTER 4

I THEREFORE, the prisoner of the Lord, beseech you that ye walk worthy of the vocation wherewith ye are called,

2 With all lowliness and meekness, with longsuffering, forbearing one another in love;

3 Endeavouring to keep the unity of the Spirit in the bond of peace.

4 *There is* one body, and one Spirit, even as ye are called in one hope of your calling;

5 One Lord, one faith, one baptism,

6 One אֱלֹהִים and Father of all, who *is* above all, and through all, and in you all.

7 But unto every one of us is given grace according to the measure of the gift of Christ.

8 Wherefore he saith, When he ascended up on high, he led captivity captive, and gave gifts unto men.

9 (Now that he ascended, what is it but that he also descended first into the lower parts of the earth?

10 He that descended is the same also that ascended up far above all heavens, that he might fill all things.)

11 And he gave some, apostles; and some, prophets; and some, evangelists; and some, pastors and teachers;

12 For the perfecting of the saints, for the work of the ministry, for the edifying of the body of Christ:

13 Till we all come in the unity of the faith, and of the knowledge of the Son of אֱלֹהִים, unto a perfect man, unto the measure of the stature of the fulness of Christ:

14 That we *henceforth* be no more children, tossed to and fro, and carried about with every wind of doctrine, by the sleight of men, *and* cunning craftiness, whereby they lie in wait to deceive;

15 But speaking the truth in love, may grow up into him in all things, which is the head, *even* Christ:

16 From whom the whole body fitly joined together and compacted by that which every joint supplieth, according to the effectual working in the measure of every part, maketh increase of the body unto the edifying of itself in love.

17 This I say therefore, and testify in the Lord, that ye henceforth walk not as other Gentiles walk, in the vanity of their mind,

18 Having the understanding darkened, being alienated from the life of אֱלֹהִים through the ignorance that is in them, because of the blindness of their heart:

19 Who being past feeling have given themselves over unto lasciviousness, to work all uncleanness with greediness.

20 But ye have not so learned Christ;

21 If so be that ye have heard him, and have been taught by him, as the truth is in Yashiyah:

22 That ye put off concerning the former conversation the old man, which is corrupt according to the deceitful lusts;

23 And be renewed in the spirit of your mind;

24 And that ye put on the new man, which after אֱלֹהִים is created in righteousness and true holiness.

25 Wherefore putting away lying, speak every man truth with his neighbour: for we are members one of another.

26 Be ye angry, and sin not: let not the sun go down upon your wrath:

27 Neither give place to the devil.

28 Let him that stole steal no more: but rather let him labour, working with *his* hands the thing which is good, that he may have to give to him that needeth.

29 Let no corrupt communication proceed out of your mouth, but that which is good to the use of edifying, that it may minister grace unto the hearers.

30 And grieve not the holy Spirit of אֱלֹהִים, whereby ye are sealed unto the day of redemption.

31 Let all bitterness, and wrath, and anger, and clamour, and evil speaking, be put away from you, with all malice:

32 And be ye kind one to another, tenderhearted, forgiving one another, even as אֱלֹהִים for Christ's sake hath forgiven you.

CHAPTER 5

BE ye therefore followers of אֱלֹהִים, as dear children;

2 And walk in love, as Christ also hath loved us, and hath given himself for us an offering and a sacrifice to אֱלֹהִים for a sweetsmelling savour.

3 But fornication, and all uncleanness, or covetousness, let it not be once named among you, as becometh saints;

4 Neither filthiness, nor foolish talking, nor jesting, which are not convenient: but rather giving of thanks.

5 For this ye know, that no whoremonger, nor unclean person, nor covetous man, who is an idolater, hath any inheritance in the kingdom of Christ and of אֱלֹהִים.

6 Let no man deceive you with vain words: for because of these things cometh the wrath of אֱלֹהִים upon the children of disobedience.

7 Be not ye therefore partakers with them.

8 For ye were sometimes darkness, but now *are ye* light in the Lord: walk as children of light:

9 (For the fruit of the Spirit *is* in all goodness and righteousness and truth;)

10 Proving what is acceptable unto the Lord.

11 And have no fellowship with the unfruitful works of darkness, but rather reprove *them.*

12 For it is a shame even to speak of those things which are done of them in secret.

13 But all things that are reproved are made manifest by the light: for whatsoever doth make manifest is light.

14 Wherefore he saith, Awake thou that sleepest, and arise from the dead, and Christ shall give thee light.

15 See then that ye walk circumspectly, not as fools, but as wise,

16 Redeeming the time, because the days are evil.

17 Wherefore be ye not unwise, but understanding what the will of the Lord *is.*

18 And be not drunk with wine, wherein is excess; but be filled with the Spirit;

19 Speaking to yourselves in psalms and hymns and spiritual songs, singing and making melody in your heart to the Lord;

20 Giving thanks always for all things unto אֱלֹהִים and the Father in the name of our Lord Yashiyah Christ;

21 Submitting yourselves one to another in the fear of אֱלֹהִים.

22 Wives, submit yourselves unto your own husbands, as unto the Lord.

23 For the husband is the head of the wife, even as Christ is the head of the church: and he is the saviour of the body.

24 Therefore as the church is subject unto Christ, so *let* the wives *be* to their own husbands in every thing.

25 Husbands, love your wives, even as Christ also loved the church, and gave himself for it;

26 That he might sanctify and cleanse it with the washing of water by the word,

27 That he might present it to himself a glorious church, not having spot, or wrinkle, or any such thing; but that it should be holy and without blemish.

28 So ought men to love their wives as their own bodies. He that loveth his wife loveth himself.

29 For no man ever yet hated his own flesh; but nourisheth and cherisheth it, even as the Lord the church:

30 For we are members of his body, of his flesh, and of his bones.

31 For this cause shall a man leave his father and mother, and shall be joined unto his wife, and they two shall be one flesh.

32 This is a great mystery: but I speak concerning Christ and the church.

33 Nevertheless let every one of you in particular so love his wife even as himself; and the wife *see* that she reverence *her* husband.

CHAPTER 6

CHILDREN, obey your parents in the Lord: for this is right.

2 Honour thy father and mother; (which is the first commandment with promise;)

3 That it may be well with thee, and thou mayest live long on the earth.

4 And, ye fathers, provoke not your children to wrath: but bring them up in the nurture and admonition of the Lord.

5 Servants, be obedient to them that are *your* masters according to the flesh, with fear and trembling, in singleness of your heart, as unto Christ;

6 Not with eyeservice, as menpleasers; but as the servants of Christ, doing the will of אֱלֹהִים from the heart;

7 With good will doing service, as to the Lord, and not to men:

8 Knowing that whatsoever good thing any man doeth, the same shall he receive of the Lord, whether *he be* bond or free.

9 And, ye masters, do the same things unto them, forbearing threatening: knowing that your Master also is in heaven; neither is there respect of persons with him.

10 Finally, my brethren, be strong in the Lord, and in the power of his might.

11 Put on the whole armour of אֱלֹהִים, that ye may be able to stand against the wiles of the devil.

12 For we wrestle not against flesh and blood, but against principalities, against powers, against the rulers of the darkness of this world, against spiritual wickedness in high *places.*

13 Wherefore take unto you the whole armour of אֱלֹהִים, that ye may be able to withstand in the evil day, and having done all, to stand.

14 Stand therefore, having your loins girt about with truth, and having on the breastplate of righteousness;

15 And your feet shod with the preparation of the gospel of peace;

16 Above all, taking the shield of faith, wherewith ye shall be able to quench all the fiery darts of the wicked.

17 And take the helmet of salvation, and the sword of the Spirit, which is the word of אֱלֹהִים:

18 Praying always with all prayer and supplication in the Spirit, and watching thereunto with all perseverance and supplication for all saints;

19 And for me, that utterance may be given unto me, that I may open my mouth boldly, to make known the mystery of the gospel,

20 For which I am an ambassador in bonds: that therein I may speak boldly, as I ought to speak.

21 But that ye also may know my affairs, *and* how I do, Tychicus, a beloved brother and faithful minister in the Lord, shall make known to you all things:

22 Whom I have sent unto you for the same purpose, that ye might know our affairs, and *that* he might comfort your hearts.

23 Peace *be* to the brethren, and love with faith, from אֱלֹהִים the Father and the Lord Yashiyah Christ.

24 Grace *be* with all them that love our Lord Yashiyah Christ in sincerity. Amen.

¶ Written from Rome unto the Ephesians by Tychicus.

THE EPISTLE OF PAUL THE APOSTLE
TO THE
PHILIPPIANS.

CHAPTER 1

PAUL and Timotheus, the servants of Yashiyah Christ, to all the saints in Christ Yashiyah which are at Philippi, with the bishops and deacons:

2 Grace *be* unto you, and peace, from אֱלֹהִים our Father, and *from* the Lord Yashiyah Christ.

3 I thank my אֱלֹהִים upon every remembrance of you,

4 Always in every prayer of mine for you all making request with joy,

5 For your fellowship in the gospel from the first day until now;

6 Being confident of this very thing, that he which hath begun a good work in you will perform *it* until the day of Yashiyah Christ:

7 Even as it is meet for me to think this of you all, because I have you in my heart; inasmuch as both in my bonds, and in the defence and confirmation of the gospel, ye all are partakers of my grace.

8 For אֱלֹהִים is my record, how greatly I long after you all in the bowels of Yashiyah Christ.

9 And this I pray, that your love may abound yet more and more in knowledge and *in* all judgment;

10 That ye may approve things that are excellent; that ye may be sincere and without offence till the day of Christ;

11 Being filled with the fruits of righteousness, which are by Yashiyah Christ, unto the glory and praise of אֱלֹהִים.

12 But I would ye should understand, brethren, that the things *which happened* unto me have fallen out rather unto the furtherance of the gospel;

13 So that my bonds in Christ are manifest in all the palace, and in all other *places;*

14 And many of the brethren in the Lord, waxing confident by my bonds, are much more bold to speak the word without fear.

15 Some indeed preach Christ even of envy and strife; and some also of good will:

16 The one preach Christ of contention, not sincerely, supposing to add affliction to my bonds:

17 But the other of love, knowing that I am set for the defence of the gospel.

18 What then? notwithstanding, every way, whether in pretence, or in truth, Christ is preached; and I therein do rejoice, yea, and will rejoice.

19 For I know that this shall turn to my salvation through your prayer, and the supply of the Spirit of Yashiyah Christ,

20 According to my earnest expectation and *my* hope, that in nothing I shall be ashamed, but *that* with all boldness, as always, *so* now also Christ shall be magnified in my body, whether *it be* by life, or by death.

21 For to me to live *is* Christ, and to die *is* gain.

22 But if I live in the flesh, this *is* the fruit of my labour: yet what I shall choose I wot not.

23 For I am in a strait betwixt two, having a desire to depart, and to be with Christ; which is far better:

24 Nevertheless to abide in the flesh *is* more needful for you.

25 And having this confidence, I know that I shall abide and continue with you all for your furtherance and joy of faith;

26 That your rejoicing may be more abundant in Yashiyah Christ for me by my coming to you again.

27 Only let your conversation be as it becometh the gospel of Christ: that whether I come and see you, or else be absent, I may hear of your affairs, that ye stand fast in one spirit, with one mind striving together for the faith of the gospel;

28 And in nothing terrified by your adversaries: which is to them an evident token of perdition, but to you of salvation, and that of אֱלֹהִים.

29 For unto you it is given in the behalf of Christ, not only to believe on him, but also to suffer for his sake;

30 Having the same conflict which ye saw in me, and now hear *to be* in me.

CHAPTER 2

IF *there be* therefore any consolation in Christ, if any comfort of love, if any fellowship of the Spirit, if any bowels and mercies,

2 Fulfil ye my joy, that ye be likeminded, having the same love, *being* of one accord, of one mind.

3 *Let* nothing *be done* through strife or vainglory; but in lowliness of mind let each esteem other better than themselves.

4 Look not every man on his own things, but every man also on the things of others.

5 Let this mind be in you, which was also in Christ Yashiyah:

6 Who, being in the form of אֱלֹהִים, thought it not robbery to be equal with אֱלֹהִים:

7 But made himself of no reputation, and took upon him the form of a servant, and was made in the likeness of men:

8 And being found in fashion as a man, he humbled himself, and became obedient unto death, even the death of the cross.

9 Wherefore אֱלֹהִים also hath highly exalted him, and given him a name which is above every name:

10 That at the name of Yashiyah every knee should bow, of *things* in heaven, and *things* in earth, and *things* under the earth;

11 And *that* every tongue should confess that Yashiyah Christ *is* Lord, to the glory of אֱלֹהִים the Father.

12 Wherefore, my beloved, as ye have always obeyed, not as in my presence only, but now much more in my absence, work out your

own salvation with fear and trembling.

13 For it is אֱלֹהִים which worketh in you both to will and to do of *his* good pleasure.

14 Do all things without murmurings and disputings:

15 That ye may be blameless and harmless, the sons of אֱלֹהִים, without rebuke, in the midst of a crooked and perverse nation, among whom ye shine as lights in the world;

16 Holding forth the word of life; that I may rejoice in the day of Christ, that I have not run in vain, neither laboured in vain.

17 Yea, and if I be offered upon the sacrifice and service of your faith, I joy, and rejoice with you all.

18 For the same cause also do ye joy, and rejoice with me.

19 But I trust in the Lord Yashiyah to send Timotheus shortly unto you, that I also may be of good comfort, when I know your state.

20 For I have no man likeminded, who will naturally care for your state.

21 For all seek their own, not the things which are Yashiyah Christ's.

22 But ye know the proof of him, that, as a son with the father, he hath served with me in the gospel.

23 Him therefore I hope to send presently, so soon as I shall see how it will go with me.

24 But I trust in the Lord that I also myself shall come shortly.

25 Yet I supposed it necessary to send to you Epaphroditus, my brother, and companion in labour, and fellowsoldier, but your messenger, and he that ministered to my wants.

26 For he longed after you all, and was full of heaviness, because that ye had heard that he had been sick.

27 For indeed he was sick nigh unto death: but אֱלֹהִים had mercy on him; and not on him only, but on me also, lest I should have sorrow upon sorrow.

28 I sent him therefore the more carefully, that, when ye see him again, ye may rejoice, and that I may be the less sorrowful.

29 Receive him therefore in the Lord with all gladness; and hold such in reputation:

30 Because for the work of Christ he was nigh unto death, not regarding his life, to supply your lack of service toward me.

CHAPTER 3

FINALLY, my brethren, rejoice in the Lord. To write the same things to you, to me indeed *is* not grievous, but for you *it is* safe.

2 Beware of dogs, beware of evil workers, beware of the concision.

3 For we are the circumcision, which worship אֱלֹהִים in the spirit, and rejoice in Christ Yashiyah, and have no confidence in the flesh.

4 Though I might also have confidence in the flesh. If any other man thinketh that he hath whereof he might trust in the flesh, I more:

5 Circumcised the eighth day, of the stock of Israel, *of* the tribe of Benjamin, an Hebrew of the Hebrews; as touching the law, a Pharisee;

6 Concerning zeal, persecuting the church; touching the righteousness which is in the law, blameless.

7 But what things were gain to me, those I counted loss for Christ.

8 Yea doubtless, and I count all things *but* loss for the excellency of the knowledge of Christ Yashiyah my Lord: for whom I have suffered the loss of all things, and do count them *but* dung, that I may win Christ,

9 And be found in him, not having mine own righteousness, which is of the law, but that which is through the faith of Christ, the righteousness which is of אֱלֹהִים by faith:

10 That I may know him, and the power of his resurrection, and the fellowship of his sufferings, being made conformable unto his death;

11 If by any means I might attain unto the resurrection of the dead.

12 Not as though I had already attained, either were already perfect: but I follow after, if that I may apprehend that for which also I am apprehended of Christ Yashiyah.

13 Brethren, I count not myself to have apprehended: but *this* one thing *I do*, forgetting those things which are behind, and reaching forth unto those things which are before,

14 I press toward the mark for the prize of the high calling of אֱלֹהִים in Christ Yashiyah.

15 Let us therefore, as many as be perfect, be thus minded: and if in any thing ye be otherwise minded, אֱלֹהִים shall reveal even this unto you.

16 Nevertheless, whereto we have already attained, let us walk by the same rule, let us mind the same thing.

17 Brethren, be followers together of me, and mark them which walk so as ye have us for an ensample.

18 (For many walk, of whom I have told you often, and now tell you even weeping, *that they are* the enemies of the cross of Christ:

19 Whose end *is* destruction, whose אֱלֹהִים *is their* belly, and *whose* glory *is* in their shame, who mind earthly things.)

20 For our conversation is in heaven; from whence also we look for the Saviour, the Lord Yashiyah Christ:

21 Who shall change our vile body, that it may be fashioned like unto his glorious body, according to the working whereby he is able even to subdue all things unto himself.

CHAPTER 4

THEREFORE, my brethren dearly beloved and longed for, my joy and crown, so stand fast in the Lord, *my* dearly beloved.

2 I beseech Euodias, and beseech Syntyche, that they be of the same mind in the Lord.

3 And I intreat thee also, true yokefellow, help those women which laboured with me in the gospel, with Clement also, and *with* other my fellowlabourers, whose names *are* in the book of life.

4 Rejoice in the Lord alway: *and* again I say, Rejoice.

5 Let your moderation be known unto all men. The Lord *is* at hand.

6 Be careful for nothing; but in every thing by prayer and supplication with thanksgiving let your requests be made known unto אֱלֹהִים.

7 And the peace of אֱלֹהִים, which passeth all understanding, shall keep your hearts and minds through Christ Yashiyah.

8 Finally, brethren, whatsoever things are true, whatsoever things *are* honest, whatsoever things *are* just, whatsoever things *are* pure, whatsoever things *are* lovely, whatsoever things *are* of good report; if *there be* any virtue, and if *there be* any praise, think on these things.

9 Those things, which ye have both learned, and received, and heard, and seen in me, do: and the אֱלֹהִים of peace shall be with you.

10 But I rejoiced in the Lord greatly, that now at the last your care of me hath flourished again; wherein ye were also careful, but ye lacked opportunity.

11 Not that I speak in respect of want: for I have learned, in whatsoever state I am, *therewith* to be content.

12 I know both how to be abased, and I know how to abound: every where and in all things I am instructed both to be full and to be hungry, both to abound and to suffer need.

13 I can do all things through Christ which strengtheneth me.

14 Notwithstanding ye have well done, that ye did communicate with my affliction.

15 Now ye Philippians know also, that in the beginning of the gospel, when I departed from Macedonia, no church communicated with me as concerning giving and receiving, but ye only.

16 For even in Thessalonica ye sent once and again unto my necessity.

17 Not because I desire a gift: but I desire fruit that may abound to your account.

18 But I have all, and abound: I am full, having received of Epaphroditus the things *which were sent* from you, an odour of a sweet smell, a sacrifice acceptable, wellpleasing to אֱלֹהִים.

19 But my אֱלֹהִים shall supply all your need according to his riches in glory by Christ Yashiyah.

20 Now unto אֱלֹהִים and our Father *be* glory for ever and ever. Amen.

21 Salute every saint in Christ Yashiyah. The brethren which are with me greet you.

22 All the saints salute you, chiefly they that are of Cæsar's household.

23 The grace of our Lord Yashiyah Christ *be* with you all. Amen.

¶ It was written to the Philippians from Rome by Epaphroditus.

THE EPISTLE OF PAUL THE APOSTLE
TO THE
COLOSSIANS.

CHAPTER 1

PAUL, an apostle of Yashiyah Christ by the will of אֱלֹהִים, and Timotheus *our* brother,

2 To the saints and faithful brethren in Christ which are at Colosse: Grace *be* unto you, and peace, from אֱלֹהִים our Father and the Lord Yashiyah Christ.

3 We give thanks to אֱלֹהִים and the Father of our Lord Yashiyah Christ, praying always for you,

4 Since we heard of your faith in Christ Yashiyah, and of the love *which ye have* to all the saints,

5 For the hope which is laid up for you in heaven, whereof ye heard before in the word of the truth of the gospel;

6 Which is come unto you, as *it is* in all the world; and bringeth forth fruit, as *it doth* also in you, since the day ye heard *of it*, and knew the grace of אֱלֹהִים in truth:

7 As ye also learned of Epaphras our dear fellowservant, who is for you a faithful minister of Christ;

8 Who also declared unto us your love in the Spirit.

9 For this cause we also, since the day we heard *it*, do not cease to pray for you, and to desire that ye might be filled with the knowledge of his will in all wisdom and spiritual understanding;

10 That ye might walk worthy of the Lord unto all pleasing, being fruitful in every good work, and increasing in the knowledge of אֱלֹהִים;

11 Strengthened with all might, according to his glorious power, unto all patience and longsuffering with joyfulness;

12 Giving thanks unto the Father, which hath made us meet to be partakers of the inheritance of the saints in light:

13 Who hath delivered us from the power of darkness, and hath translated *us* into the kingdom of his dear Son:

14 In whom we have redemption through his blood, *even* the forgiveness of sins:

15 Who is the image of the invisible אֱלֹהִים, the firstborn of every creature:

16 For by him were all things created, that are in heaven, and that are in earth, visible and invisible, whether *they be* thrones, or dominions, or principalities, or powers: all things were created by him, and for him:

17 And he is before all things, and by him all things consist.

18 And he is the head of the body, the church: who is the beginning, the firstborn from the dead; that in all *things* he might have the preeminence.

19 For it pleased *the Father* that in him should all fulness dwell;

20 And, having made peace through the blood of his cross, by him to reconcile all things unto himself; by him, *I say*, whether *they be* things in earth, or things in heaven.

21 And you, that were sometime alienated and enemies in *your* mind by wicked works, yet now hath he reconciled

22 In the body of his flesh through death, to present you holy and unblameable and unreproveable in his sight:

23 If ye continue in the faith grounded and settled, and *be* not moved away from the hope of the gospel, which ye have heard, *and* which was preached to every creature which is under heaven; whereof I Paul am made a minister;

24 Who now rejoice in my sufferings for you, and fill up that which is behind of the afflictions of Christ in my flesh for his body's sake, which is the church:

25 Whereof I am made a minister, according to the dispensation of אֱלֹהִים which is given to me for you, to fulfil the word of אֱלֹהִים;

26 *Even* the mystery which hath been hid from ages and from generations, but now is made manifest to his saints:

27 To whom אֱלֹהִים would make known what *is* the riches of the glory of this mystery among the Gentiles; which is Christ in you, the hope of glory:

28 Whom we preach, warning every man, and teaching every man in all wisdom; that we may present every man perfect in Christ Yashiyah:

29 Whereunto I also labour, striving according to his working, which worketh in me mightily.

CHAPTER 2

FOR I would that ye knew what great conflict I have for you, and *for* them at Laodicea, and *for* as many as have not seen my face in the flesh;

2 That their hearts might be comforted, being knit together in love, and unto all riches of the full assurance of understanding, to the acknowledgement of the mystery of אֱלֹהִים, and of the Father, and of Christ;

3 In whom are hid all the treasures of wisdom and knowledge.

4 And this I say, lest any man should beguile you with enticing words.

5 For though I be absent in the flesh, yet am I with you in the spirit, joying and beholding your order, and the stedfastness of your faith in Christ.

6 As ye have therefore received Christ Yashiyah the Lord, *so* walk ye in him:

7 Rooted and built up in him, and stablished in the faith, as ye have been taught, abounding therein with thanksgiving.

8 Beware lest any man spoil you through philosophy and vain deceit, after the tradition of men, after the rudiments of the world, and not after Christ.

9 For in him dwelleth all the fulness of the Godhead bodily.

10 And ye are complete in him, which is the head of all principality and power:

11 In whom also ye are circumcised with the circumcision made without hands, in putting off the body of the sins of the flesh by the circumcision of Christ:

12 Buried with him in baptism, wherein also ye are risen with *him* through the faith of the operation of אֱלֹהִים, who hath raised him from the dead.

13 And you, being dead in your sins and the uncircumcision of your flesh, hath he quickened together with him, having forgiven you all trespasses;

14 Blotting out the handwriting of ordinances that was against us, which was contrary to us, and took it out of the way, nailing it to his cross;

15 *And* having spoiled principalities and powers, he made a shew of them openly, triumphing over them in it.

16 Let no man therefore judge you in meat, or in drink, or in respect of an holyday, or of the new moon, or of the sabbath *days:*

17 Which are a shadow of things to come; but the body *is* of Christ.

18 Let no man beguile you of your reward in a voluntary humility and worshipping of angels, intruding into those things which he hath not seen, vainly puffed up by his fleshly mind,

19 And not holding the Head, from which all the body by joints and bands having nourishment ministered, and knit together, increaseth with the increase of אֱלֹהִים.

20 Wherefore if ye be dead with Christ from the rudiments of the world, why, as though living in the world, are ye subject to ordinances,

21 (Touch not; taste not; handle not;

22 Which all are to perish with the using;) after the commandments and doctrines of men?

23 Which things have indeed a shew of wisdom in will worship, and humility, and neglecting of the body; not in any honour to the satisfying of the flesh.

CHAPTER 3

IF ye then be risen with Christ, seek those things which are above, where Christ sitteth on the right hand of אֱלֹהִים.

2 Set your affection on things above, not on things on the earth.

3 For ye are dead, and your life is hid with Christ in אֱלֹהִים.

4 When Christ, *who is* our life, shall appear, then shall ye also appear with him in glory.

5 Mortify therefore your members which are upon the earth; fornication, uncleanness, inordinate affection, evil concupiscence, and covetousness, which is idolatry:

6 For which things' sake the wrath of אֱלֹהִים cometh on the children of disobedience:

7 In the which ye also walked some time, when ye lived in them.

8 But now ye also put off all these; anger, wrath, malice, blasphemy, filthy communication out of your mouth.

9 Lie not one to another, seeing that ye have put off the old man with his deeds;

10 And have put on the new *man*, which is renewed in knowledge after the image of him that created him:

11 Where there is neither Greek nor Jew, circumcision nor uncircumcision, Barbarian, Scythian, bond *nor* free: but Christ *is* all, and in all.

12 Put on therefore, as the elect of אֱלֹהִים, holy and beloved, bowels of mercies, kindness, humbleness of mind, meekness, longsuffering;

13 Forbearing one another, and forgiving one another, if any man have a quarrel against any: even as Christ forgave you, so also *do* ye.

14 And above all these things *put on* charity, which is the bond of perfectness.

15 And let the peace of אֱלֹהִים rule in your hearts, to the which also ye are called in one body; and be ye thankful.

16 Let the word of Christ dwell in you richly in all wisdom; teaching and admonishing one another in psalms and hymns and spiritual songs, singing with grace in your hearts to the Lord.

17 And whatsoever ye do in word or deed, *do* all in the name of the Lord Yashiyah, giving thanks to אֱלֹהִים and the Father by him.

18 Wives, submit yourselves unto your own husbands, as it is fit in the Lord.

19 Husbands, love *your* wives, and be not bitter against them.

20 Children, obey *your* parents in all things: for this is well pleasing unto the Lord.

21 Fathers, provoke not your children *to anger*, lest they be discouraged.

22 Servants, obey in all things *your* masters according to the flesh; not with eyeservice, as menpleasers; but in singleness of heart, fearing אֱלֹהִים:

23 And whatsoever ye do, do *it* heartily, as to the Lord, and not unto men;

24 Knowing that of the Lord ye shall receive the reward of the inheritance: for ye serve the Lord Christ.

25 But he that doeth wrong shall receive for the wrong which he hath done: and there is no respect of persons.

CHAPTER 4

MASTERS, give unto *your* servants that which is just and equal; knowing that ye also have a Master in heaven.

2 Continue in prayer, and watch in the same with thanksgiving;

3 Withal praying also for us, that אֱלֹהִים would open unto us a door of utterance, to speak the mystery of Christ, for which I am also in bonds:

4 That I may make it manifest, as I ought to speak.

5 Walk in wisdom toward them that are without, redeeming the time.

6 Let your speech be alway with grace, seasoned with salt, that ye may know how ye ought to answer every man.

7 All my state shall Tychicus declare unto you, who is a beloved brother, and a faithful minister and fellowservant in the Lord:

8 Whom I have sent unto you for the same purpose, that he might know your estate, and comfort your hearts;

9 With Onesimus, a faithful and beloved brother, who is one of you. They shall make known unto you all things which are done here.

10 Aristarchus my fellowprisoner saluteth you, and Marcus, sister's son to Barnabas, (touching whom ye received commandments: if he come unto you, receive him;)

11 And Yashiyah, which is called Justus, who are of the circumcision. These only are my fellowworkers unto the kingdom of אֱלֹהִים, which have been a comfort unto me.

12 Epaphras, who is one of you, a servant of Christ, saluteth you, always labouring fervently for you in prayers, that ye may stand perfect and complete in all the will of אֱלֹהִים.

13 For I bear him record, that he hath a great zeal for you, and them that are in Laodicea, and them in Hierapolis.

14 Luke, the beloved physician, and Demas, greet you.

15 Salute the brethren which are in Laodicea, and Nymphas, and the church which is in his house.

16 And when this epistle is read among you, cause that it be read also in the church of the Laodiceans; and that ye likewise read the epistle from Laodicea.

17 And say to Archippus, Take heed to the ministry which thou hast received in the Lord, that thou fulfil it.

18 The salutation by the hand of me Paul. Remember my bonds. Grace be with you. Amen.

¶ Written from Rome to the Colossians by Tychicus and Onesimus

THE
FIRST EPISTLE OF PAUL THE APOSTLE
TO THE
THESSALONIANS.

CHAPTER 1

PAUL, and Silvanus, and Timotheus, unto the church of the Thessalonians which is in אֱלֹהִים the Father and in the Lord Yashiyah Christ: Grace be unto you, and peace, from אֱלֹהִים our Father, and the Lord Yashiyah Christ.

2 We give thanks to אֱלֹהִים always for you all, making mention of you in our prayers;

3 Remembering without ceasing your work of faith, and labour of love, and patience of hope in our Lord Yashiyah Christ, in the sight of אֱלֹהִים and our Father;

4 Knowing, brethren beloved, your election of אֱלֹהִים.

5 For our gospel came not unto you in word only, but also in power, and in the Holy Ghost, and in much assurance; as ye know what manner of men we were among you for your sake.

6 And ye became followers of us, and of the Lord, having received the word in much affliction, with joy of the Holy Ghost:

7 So that ye were ensamples to all that believe in Macedonia and Achaia.

8 For from you sounded out the word of the Lord not only in Macedonia and Achaia, but also in every place your faith to אֱלֹהִים-ward is spread abroad; so that we need not to speak any thing.

9 For they themselves shew of us what manner of entering in we had unto you, and how ye turned to אֱלֹהִים from idols to serve the living and true אֱלֹהִים;

10 And to wait for his Son from heaven, whom he raised from the dead, even Yashiyah, which delivered us from the wrath to come.

CHAPTER 2

FOR yourselves, brethren, know our entrance in unto you, that it was not in vain:

2 But even after that we had suffered before, and were shamefully entreated, as ye know, at Philippi, we were bold in our אֱלֹהִים to speak unto you the gospel of אֱלֹהִים with much contention.

3 For our exhortation was not of deceit, nor of uncleanness, nor in guile:

4 But as we were allowed of אֱלֹהִים to be put in trust with the gospel, even so we speak; not as pleasing men, but אֱלֹהִים, which trieth our hearts.

5 For neither at any time used we flattering words, as ye know, nor a cloke of covetousness; אֱלֹהִים is witness:

6 Nor of men sought we glory, neither of you, nor yet of others, when we might have been burdensome, as the apostles of Christ.

7 But we were gentle among you, even as a nurse cherisheth her children:

8 So being affectionately desirous of you, we were willing to have imparted unto you, not the gospel of אֱלֹהִים only, but also our own souls, because ye were dear unto us.

9 For ye remember, brethren, our labour and travail: for labouring night and day, because we would not be chargeable unto any of you, we preached unto you the gospel of אֱלֹהִים.

10 Ye are witnesses, and אֱלֹהִים also, how holily and justly and unblameably we behaved ourselves among you that believe:

11 As ye know how we exhorted and comforted and charged every one of you, as a father doth his children,

12 That ye would walk worthy of אֱלֹהִים, who hath called you unto his kingdom and glory.

13 For this cause also thank we אֱלֹהִים without ceasing, because, when ye received the word of אֱלֹהִים which ye heard of us, ye received it not as the word of men, but as it is in truth, the word of אֱלֹהִים, which effectually worketh also in you that believe.

14 For ye, brethren, became followers of the churches of אֱלֹהִים which in Judæa are in Christ Yashiyah: for ye also have suffered like things of your own countrymen, even as they have of the Jews:

15 Who both killed the Lord Yashiyah, and their own prophets, and have persecuted us; and they please not אֱלֹהִים, and are contrary to all men:

16 Forbidding us to speak to the Gentiles that they might be saved, to fill up their sins alway: for the wrath is come upon them to the uttermost.

17 But we, brethren, being taken from you for a short time in presence, not in heart, endeavoured the more abundantly to see your face with great desire.

18 Wherefore we would have come unto you, even I Paul, once and again; but Satan hindered us.

19 For what *is* our hope, or joy, or crown of rejoicing? *Are* not even ye in the presence of our Lord Yashiyah Christ at his coming?

20 For ye are our glory and joy.

CHAPTER 3

WHEREFORE when we could no longer forbear, we thought it good to be left at Athens alone;

2 And sent Timotheus, our brother, and minister of אֱלֹהִים, and our fellowlabourer in the gospel of Christ, to establish you, and to comfort you concerning your faith:

3 That no man should be moved by these afflictions: for yourselves know that we are appointed thereunto.

4 For verily, when we were with you, we told you before that we should suffer tribulation; even as it came to pass, and ye know.

5 For this cause, when I could no longer forbear, I sent to know your faith, lest by some means the tempter have tempted you, and our labour be in vain.

6 But now when Timotheus came from you unto us, and brought us good tidings of your faith and charity, and that ye have good remembrance of us always, desiring greatly to see us, as we also *to see* you:

7 Therefore, brethren, we were comforted over you in all our affliction and distress by your faith:

8 For now we live, if ye stand fast in the Lord.

9 For what thanks can we render to אֱלֹהִים again for you, for all the joy wherewith we joy for your sakes before our אֱלֹהִים;

10 Night and day praying exceedingly that we might see your face, and might perfect that which is lacking in your faith?

11 Now אֱלֹהִים himself and our Father, and our Lord Yashiyah Christ, direct our way unto you.

12 And the Lord make you to increase and abound in love one toward another, and toward all *men*, even as we *do* toward you:

13 To the end he may stablish your hearts unblameable in holiness before אֱלֹהִים, even our Father, at the coming of our Lord Yashiyah Christ with all his saints.

CHAPTER 4

FURTHERMORE then we beseech you, brethren, and exhort *you* by the Lord Yashiyah, that as ye have received of us how ye ought to walk and to please אֱלֹהִים, *so* ye would abound more and more.

2 For ye know what commandments we gave you by the Lord Yashiyah.

3 For this is the will of אֱלֹהִים, *even* your sanctification, that ye should abstain from fornication:

4 That every one of you should know how to possess his vessel in sanctification and honour;

5 Not in the lust of concupiscence, even as the Gentiles which know not אֱלֹהִים:

6 That no *man* go beyond and defraud his brother in *any* matter: because that the Lord *is* the avenger of all such, as we also have forewarned you and testified.

7 For אֱלֹהִים hath not called us unto uncleanness, but unto holiness.

8 He therefore that despiseth, despiseth not man, but אֱלֹהִים, who hath also given unto us his holy Spirit.

9 But as touching brotherly love ye need not that I write unto you: for ye yourselves are taught of אֱלֹהִים to love one another.

10 And indeed ye do it toward all the brethren which are in all Macedonia: but we beseech you, brethren, that ye increase more and more;

11 And that ye study to be quiet, and to do your own business, and to work with your own hands, as we commanded you;

12 That ye may walk honestly toward them that are without, and *that* ye may have lack of nothing.

13 But I would not have you to be ignorant, brethren, concerning them which are asleep, that ye sorrow not, even as others which have no hope.

14 For if we believe that Yashiyah died and rose again, even so them also which sleep in Yashiyah will אֱלֹהִים bring with him.

15 For this we say unto you by the word of the Lord, that we which are alive *and* remain unto the coming of the Lord shall not prevent them which are asleep.

16 For the Lord himself shall descend from heaven with a shout, with the voice of the archangel, and with the trump of אֱלֹהִים: and the dead in Christ shall rise first:

17 Then we which are alive *and* remain shall be caught up together with them in the clouds, to meet the Lord in the air: and so shall we ever be with the Lord.

18 Wherefore comfort one another with these words.

CHAPTER 5

BUT of the times and the seasons, brethren, ye have no need that I write unto you.

2 For yourselves know perfectly that the day of the Lord so cometh as a thief in the night.

3 For when they shall say, Peace and safety; then sudden destruction cometh upon them, as travail upon a woman with child; and they shall not escape.

4 But ye, brethren, are not in darkness, that that day should overtake you as a thief.

5 Ye are all the children of light, and the children of the day: we are not of the night, nor of darkness.

6 Therefore let us not sleep, as *do* others; but let us watch and be sober.

7 For they that sleep sleep in the night; and they that be drunken are drunken in the night.

8 But let us, who are of the day, be sober, putting on the breastplate of faith and love; and for an helmet, the hope of salvation.

9 For אֱלֹהִים hath not appointed us to wrath, but to obtain salvation by our Lord Yashiyah Christ,

10 Who died for us, that, whether we wake or sleep, we should live together with him.

11 Wherefore comfort yourselves together, and edify one another, even as also ye do.

12 And we beseech you, brethren, to know them which labour among you, and are over you in the Lord, and admonish you;

13 And to esteem them very highly in love for their work's sake. *And* be at peace among yourselves.

14 Now we exhort you, brethren, warn them that are unruly, comfort the feebleminded, support the weak, be patient toward all *men*.

15 See that none render evil for evil unto any *man;* but ever follow that which is good, both among yourselves, and to all *men*.

16 Rejoice evermore.

17 Pray without ceasing.

18 In every thing give thanks: for this is the will of אֱלֹהִים in Christ Yashiyah concerning you.

19 Quench not the Spirit.

20 Despise not prophesyings.

21 Prove all things; hold fast that which is good.

22 Abstain from all appearance of evil.

23 And the very אֱלֹהִים of peace sanctify you wholly; and *I pray* אֱלֹהִים your whole spirit and soul and body be preserved blameless unto the coming of our Lord Yashiyah Christ.

24 Faithful *is* he that calleth you, who also will do *it*.

25 Brethren, pray for us.

26 Greet all the brethren with an holy kiss.

27 I charge you by the Lord that this epistle be read unto all the holy brethren.

28 The grace of our Lord Yashiyah Christ *be* with you. Amen.

¶ The first *epistle* unto the Thessalonians was written from Athens.

THE
SECOND EPISTLE OF PAUL THE APOSTLE
TO THE
THESSALONIANS.

CHAPTER 1

PAUL, and Silvanus, and Timotheus, unto the church of the Thessalonians in אֱלֹהִים our Father and the Lord Yashiyah Christ:

2 Grace unto you, and peace, from אֱלֹהִים our Father and the Lord Yashiyah Christ.

3 We are bound to thank אֱלֹהִים always for you, brethren, as it is meet, because that your faith groweth exceedingly, and the charity of every one of you all toward each other aboundeth;

4 So that we ourselves glory in you in the churches of אֱלֹהִים for your patience and faith in all your persecutions and tribulations that ye endure:

5 *Which is* a manifest token of the righteous judgment of אֱלֹהִים, that ye may be counted worthy of the kingdom of אֱלֹהִים, for which ye also suffer:

6 Seeing *it is* a righteous thing with אֱלֹהִים to recompense tribulation to them that trouble you;

7 And to you who are troubled rest with us, when the Lord Yashiyah shall be revealed from heaven with his mighty angels,

8 In flaming fire taking vengeance on them that know not אֱלֹהִים, and that obey not the gospel of our Lord Yashiyah Christ:

9 Who shall be punished with everlasting destruction from the presence of the Lord, and from the glory of his power;

10 When he shall come to be glorified in his saints, and to be admired in all them that believe (because our testimony among you was believed) in that day.

11 Wherefore also we pray always for you, that our אֱלֹהִים would count you worthy of *this* calling, and fulfil all the good pleasure of *his* goodness, and the work of faith with power:

12 That the name of our Lord Yashiyah Christ may be glorified in you, and ye in him, according to the grace of our אֱלֹהִים and the Lord Yashiyah Christ.

CHAPTER 2

NOW we beseech you, brethren, by the coming of our Lord Yashiyah Christ, and *by* our gathering together unto him,

2 That ye be not soon shaken in mind, or be troubled, neither by spirit, nor by word, nor by letter as from us, as that the day of Christ is at hand.

3 Let no man deceive you by any means: for *that day shall not come*, except there come a falling away first, and that man of sin be revealed, the son of perdition;

4 Who opposeth and exalteth himself above all that is called אֱלֹהִים, or that is worshipped; so that he as אֱלֹהִים sitteth in the temple of אֱלֹהִים, shewing himself that he is אֱלֹהִים.

5 Remember ye not, that, when I was yet with you, I told you these things?

6 And now ye know what withholdeth that he might be revealed in his time.

7 For the mystery of iniquity doth already work: only he who now letteth *will let*, until he be taken out of the way.

8 And then shall that Wicked be revealed, whom the Lord shall consume with the spirit of his mouth, and shall destroy with the brightness of his coming:

9 *Even him*, whose coming is after the working of Satan with all power and signs and lying wonders,

10 And with all deceivableness of unrighteousness in them that perish; because they received not the love of the truth, that they might be saved.

11 And for this cause אֱלֹהִים shall send them strong delusion, that they should believe a lie:

12 That they all might be damned who believed not the truth, but had pleasure in unrighteousness.

13 But we are bound to give thanks alway to אֱלֹהִים for you, brethren beloved of the Lord, because אֱלֹהִים hath from the beginning chosen you to salvation through sanctification of the Spirit and belief of the truth:

14 Whereunto he called you by our gospel, to the obtaining of the glory of our Lord Yashiyah Christ.

15 Therefore, brethren, stand fast, and hold the traditions which ye have been taught, whether by word, or our epistle.

16 Now our Lord Yashiyah Christ himself, and אֱלֹהִים, even our Father, which hath loved us, and hath given *us* everlasting consolation and good hope through grace,

17 Comfort your hearts, and stablish you in every good word and work.

CHAPTER 3

FINALLY, brethren, pray for us, that the word of the Lord may have *free* course, and be glorified, even as *it is* with you:

2 And that we may be delivered from unreasonable and wicked men: for all *men* have not faith.

3 But the Lord is faithful, who shall stablish you, and keep *you* from evil.

4 And we have confidence in the Lord touching you, that ye both do and will do the things which we command you.

5 And the Lord direct your hearts into the love of אֱלֹהִים, and into the patient waiting for Christ.

6 Now we command you, brethren, in the name of our Lord Yashiyah Christ, that ye withdraw yourselves from every brother that walketh disorderly, and not after the tradition which he received of us.

7 For yourselves know how ye ought to follow us: for we behaved not ourselves disorderly among you;

8 Neither did we eat any man's bread for nought; but wrought with labour and travail night and day, that we might not be chargeable to any of you:

9 Not because we have not power, but to make ourselves an ensample unto you to follow us.

10 For even when we were with you, this we commanded you, that if any would not work, neither should he eat.

11 For we hear that there are some which walk among you disorderly, working not at all, but are busybodies.

12 Now them that are such we command and exhort by our Lord Yashiyah Christ, that with quietness they work, and eat their own bread.

13 But ye, brethren, be not weary in well doing.

14 And if any man obey not our word by this epistle, note that man, and have no company with him, that he may be ashamed.

15 Yet count *him* not as an enemy, but admonish *him* as a brother.

16 Now the Lord of peace himself give you peace always by all means. The Lord *be* with you all.

17 The salutation of Paul with mine own hand, which is the token in every epistle: so I write.

18 The grace of our Lord Yashiyah Christ *be* with you all. Amen.

¶ The second *epistle* to the Thessalonians was written from Athens.

THE FIRST
EPISTLE OF PAUL THE APOSTLE TO
TIMOTHY.

CHAPTER 1

PAUL, an apostle of Yashiyah Christ by the commandment of אֱלֹהִים our Saviour, and Lord Yashiyah Christ, *which is* our hope;

2 Unto Timothy, *my* own son in the faith: Grace, mercy, *and* peace, from אֱלֹהִים our Father and Yashiyah Christ our Lord.

3 As I besought thee to abide still at Ephesus, when I went into Macedonia, that thou mightest charge some that they teach no other doctrine,

4 Neither give heed to fables and endless genealogies, which minister questions, rather than godly edifying which is in faith: *so do.*

5 Now the end of the commandment is charity out of a pure heart, and *of* a good conscience, and *of* faith unfeigned:

6 From which some having swerved have turned aside unto vain jangling;

7 Desiring to be teachers of the law; understanding neither what they say, nor whereof they affirm.

8 But we know that the law *is* good, if a man use it lawfully;

9 Knowing this, that the law is not made for a righteous man, but for the lawless and disobedient, for the ungodly and for sinners, for unholy and profane, for murderers of fathers and murderers of mothers, for manslayers,

10 For whoremongers, for them that defile themselves with mankind, for menstealers, for liars, for perjured persons, and if there be any other thing that is contrary to sound doctrine;

11 According to the glorious gospel of the blessed אֱלֹהִים, which was committed to my trust.

12 And I thank Christ Yashiyah our Lord, who hath enabled me, for that he counted me faithful, putting me into the ministry;

13 Who was before a blasphemer, and a persecutor, and injurious: but I obtained mercy, because I did *it* ignorantly in unbelief.

14 And the grace of our Lord was exceeding abundant with faith and love which is in Christ Yashiyah.

15 This *is* a faithful saying, and worthy of all acceptation, that Christ Yashiyah came into the world to save sinners; of whom I am chief.

16 Howbeit for this cause I obtained mercy, that in me first Yashiyah Christ might shew forth all longsuffering, for a pattern to them which should hereafter believe on him to life everlasting.

17 Now unto the King eternal, immortal, invisible, the only wise אֱלֹהִים, *be* honour and glory for ever and ever. Amen.

18 This charge I commit unto thee, son Timothy, according to the prophecies which went before on thee, that thou by them mightest war a good warfare;

19 Holding faith, and a good conscience; which some having put away concerning faith have made shipwreck:

20 Of whom is Hymenæus and Alexander; whom I have delivered unto Satan, that they may learn not to blaspheme.

CHAPTER 2

I EXHORT therefore, that, first of all, supplications, prayers, intercessions, *and* giving of thanks, be made for all men;

2 For kings, and *for* all that are in authority; that we may lead a quiet and peaceable life in all godliness and honesty.

3 For this *is* good and acceptable in the sight of אֱלֹהִים our Saviour;

4 Who will have all men to be saved, and to come unto the knowledge of the truth.

5 For *there is* one אֱלֹהִים, and one mediator between אֱלֹהִים and men, the man Christ Yashiyah;

6 Who gave himself a ransom for all, to be testified in due time.

7 Whereunto I am ordained a preacher, and an apostle, (I speak the truth in Christ, *and* lie not;) a teacher of the Gentiles in faith and verity.

8 I will therefore that men pray every where, lifting up holy hands, without wrath and doubting.

9 In like manner also, that women adorn themselves in modest apparel, with shamefacedness and sobriety; not with broided hair, or gold, or pearls, or costly array;

10 But (which becometh women professing godliness) with good works.

11 Let the woman learn in silence with all subjection.

12 But I suffer not a woman to teach, nor to usurp authority over the man, but to be in silence.

13 For Adam was first formed, then Eve.

14 And Adam was not deceived, but the woman being deceived was in the transgression.

15 Notwithstanding she shall be saved in childbearing, if they continue in faith and charity and holiness with sobriety.

CHAPTER 3

THIS *is* a true saying, If a man desire the office of a bishop, he desireth a good work.

2 A bishop then must be blameless, the husband of one wife, vigilant, sober, of good behaviour, given to hospitality, apt to teach;

3 Not given to wine, no striker, not greedy of filthy lucre; but patient, not a brawler, not covetous;

4 One that ruleth well his own house, having his children in subjection with all gravity;

5 (For if a man know not how to rule his own house, how shall he take care of the church of אֱלֹהִים?)

6 Not a novice, lest being lifted up with pride he fall into the condemnation of the devil.

7 Moreover he must have a good report of them which are without; lest he fall into reproach and the snare of the devil.

8 Likewise *must* the deacons *be* grave, not doubletongued, not given to much wine, not greedy of filthy lucre;

9 Holding the mystery of the faith in a pure conscience.

10 And let these also first be proved; then let them use the office of a deacon, being *found* blameless.

11 Even so *must their* wives *be* grave, not slanderers, sober, faithful in all things.

12 Let the deacons be the husbands of one wife, ruling their children and their own houses well.

13 For they that have used the office of a deacon well purchase to themselves a good degree, and great boldness in the faith which is in Christ Yashiyah.

14 These things write I unto thee, hoping to come unto thee shortly:

15 But if I tarry long, that thou mayest know how thou oughtest to behave thyself in the house of אֱלֹהִים, which is the church of the living אֱלֹהִים, the pillar and ground of the truth.

16 And without controversy great is the mystery of godliness: אֱלֹהִים was manifest in the flesh, justified in the Spirit, seen of angels, preached unto the Gentiles, believed on in the world, received up into glory.

CHAPTER 4

NOW the Spirit speaketh expressly, that in the latter times some shall depart from the faith, giving heed to seducing spirits, and doctrines of devils;

2 Speaking lies in hypocrisy; having their conscience seared with a hot iron;

3 Forbidding to marry, *and commanding* to abstain from meats, which אֱלֹהִים hath created to be received with thanksgiving of them which believe and know the truth.

4 For every creature of אֱלֹהִים *is* good, and nothing to be refused, if it be received with thanksgiving:

5 For it is sanctified by the word of אֱלֹהִים and prayer.

6 If thou put the brethren in remembrance of these things, thou shalt be a good minister of Yashiyah Christ, nourished up in the words of faith and of good doctrine, whereunto thou hast attained.

7 But refuse profane and old wives' fables, and exercise thyself *rather* unto godliness.

8 For bodily exercise profiteth little: but godliness is profitable unto all things, having promise of the life that now is, and of that which is to come.

9 This *is* a faithful saying and worthy of all acceptation.

10 For therefore we both labour and suffer reproach, because we trust in the living אֱלֹהִים, who is the Saviour of all men, specially of those that believe.

11 These things command and teach.

12 Let no man despise thy youth; but be thou an example of the believers, in word, in conversation, in charity, in spirit, in faith, in purity.

13 Till I come, give attendance to reading, to exhortation, to doctrine.

14 Neglect not the gift that is in thee, which was given thee by prophecy, with the laying on of the hands of the presbytery.

15 Meditate upon these things; give thyself wholly to them; that thy profiting may appear to all.

16 Take heed unto thyself, and unto the doctrine; continue in them: for in doing this thou shalt both save thyself, and them that hear thee.

CHAPTER 5

REBUKE not an elder, but intreat *him* as a father; *and* the younger men as brethren;

2 The elder women as mothers; the younger as sisters, with all purity.

3 Honour widows that are widows indeed.

4 But if any widow have children or nephews, let them learn first to shew piety at home, and to requite their parents: for that is good and acceptable before אֱלֹהִים.

5 Now she that is a widow indeed, and desolate, trusteth in אֱלֹהִים, and continueth in supplications and prayers night and day.

6 But she that liveth in pleasure is dead while she liveth.

7 And these things give in charge, that they may be blameless.

8 But if any provide not for his own, and specially for those of his own house, he hath denied the faith, and is worse than an infidel.

9 Let not a widow be taken into the number under threescore years old, having been the wife of one man,

10 Well reported of for good works; if she have brought up children, if she have lodged strangers, if she have washed the saints' feet, if she have relieved the afflicted, if she have diligently followed every good work.

11 But the younger widows refuse: for when they have begun to wax wanton against Christ, they will marry;

12 Having damnation, because they have cast off their first faith.

13 And withal they learn *to be* idle, wandering about from house to house; and not only idle, but tattlers also and busybodies, speaking things which they ought not.

14 I will therefore that the younger women marry, bear children, guide the house, give none occasion to the adversary to speak reproachfully.

15 For some are already turned aside after Satan.

16 If any man or woman that believeth have widows, let them relieve them, and let not the church be charged; that it may relieve them that are widows indeed.

17 Let the elders that rule well be counted worthy of double honour, especially they who labour in the word and doctrine.

18 For the scripture saith, Thou shalt not muzzle the ox that treadeth out the corn. And, The labourer *is* worthy of his reward.

19 Against an elder receive not an accusation, but before two or three witnesses.

20 Them that sin rebuke before all, that others also may fear.

21 I charge *thee* before אֱלֹהִים, and the Lord Yashiyah Christ, and the elect angels, that thou observe these things without preferring one before another, doing nothing by partiality.

22 Lay hands suddenly on no man, neither be partaker of other men's sins: keep thyself pure.

23 Drink no longer water, but use a little wine for thy stomach's sake and thine often infirmities.

24 Some men's sins are open beforehand, going before to judgment; and some *men* they follow after.

25 Likewise also the good works *of some* are manifest beforehand; and they that are otherwise cannot be hid.

CHAPTER 6

LET as many servants as are under the yoke count their own masters worthy of all honour, that the name of אֱלֹהִים and *his* doctrine be not blasphemed.

2 And they that have believing masters, let them not despise *them*, because they are brethren; but rather do *them* service, because they are faithful and beloved, partakers of the benefit. These things teach and exhort.

3 If any man teach otherwise, and consent not to wholesome words, *even* the words of our Lord Yashiyah Christ, and to the doctrine which is according to godliness;

4 He is proud, knowing nothing, but doting about questions and strifes of words, whereof cometh envy, strife, railings, evil surmisings,

5 Perverse disputings of men of corrupt minds, and destitute of the truth, supposing that gain is godliness: from such withdraw thyself.

6 But godliness with contentment is great gain.

7 For we brought nothing into *this* world, *and it is* certain we can carry nothing out.

8 And having food and raiment let us be therewith content.

9 But they that will be rich fall into temptation and a snare, and *into* many foolish and hurtful lusts, which drown men in destruction and perdition.

10 For the love of money is the root of all evil: which while some coveted after, they have erred from the faith, and pierced themselves through with many sorrows.

11 But thou, O man of אֱלֹהִים, flee these things; and follow after righteousness, godliness, faith, love, patience, meekness.

12 Fight the good fight of faith, lay hold on eternal life, whereunto thou art also called, and hast professed a good profession before many witnesses.

13 I give thee charge in the sight of אֱלֹהִים, who quickeneth all things, and *before* Christ Yashiyah, who before Pontius Pilate witnessed a good confession;

14 That thou keep *this* commandment without spot, unrebukeable, until the appearing of our Lord Yashiyah Christ:

15 Which in his times he shall shew, *who is* the blessed and only Potentate, the King of kings, and Lord of lords;

16 Who only hath immortality, dwelling in the light which no man can approach unto; whom no man hath seen, nor can see: to whom *be* honour and power everlasting. Amen.

17 Charge them that are rich in this world, that they be not highminded, nor trust in uncertain riches, but in the living אֱלֹהִים, who giveth us richly all things to enjoy;

18 That they do good, that they be rich in good works, ready to distribute, willing to communicate;

19 Laying up in store for themselves a good foundation against the time to come, that they may lay hold on eternal life.

20 O Timothy, keep that which is committed to thy trust, avoiding profane *and* vain babblings, and oppositions of science falsely so called:

21 Which some professing have erred concerning the faith. Grace *be* with thee. Amen.

¶ The first to Timothy was written from Laodicea, which is the chiefest city of Phrygia Pacatiana.

THE SECOND
EPISTLE OF PAUL THE APOSTLE TO
TIMOTHY.

CHAPTER 1

PAUL, an apostle of Yashiyah Christ by the will of אֱלֹהִים, according to the promise of life which is in Christ Yashiyah,

2 To Timothy, *my* dearly beloved son: Grace, mercy, *and* peace, from אֱלֹהִים the Father and Christ Yashiyah our Lord.

3 I thank אֱלֹהִים, whom I serve from *my* forefathers with pure conscience, that without ceasing I have remembrance of thee in my prayers night and day;

4 Greatly desiring to see thee, being mindful of thy tears, that I may be filled with joy;

5 When I call to remembrance the unfeigned faith that is in thee, which dwelt first in thy grandmother Lois, and thy mother Eunice; and I am persuaded that in thee also.

6 Wherefore I put thee in remembrance that thou stir up the gift of אֱלֹהִים, which is in thee by the putting on of my hands.

7 For אֱלֹהִים hath not given us the spirit of fear; but of power, and of love, and of a sound mind.

8 Be not thou therefore ashamed of the testimony of our Lord, nor of me his prisoner: but be thou partaker of the afflictions of the gospel according to the power of אֱלֹהִים;

9 Who hath saved us, and called *us* with an holy calling, not according to our works, but according to his own purpose and grace, which was given us in Christ Yashiyah before the world began,

10 But is now made manifest by the appearing of our Saviour Yashiyah Christ, who hath abolished death, and hath brought life and immortality to light through the gospel:

11 Whereunto I am appointed a preacher, and an apostle, and a teacher of the Gentiles.

12 For the which cause I also suffer these things: nevertheless I am not ashamed: for I know whom I have believed, and am persuaded that he is able to keep that which I have committed unto him against that day.

13 Hold fast the form of sound words, which thou hast heard of me, in faith and love which is in Christ Yashiyah.

14 That good thing which was committed unto thee keep by the Holy Ghost which dwelleth in us.

15 This thou knowest, that all they which are in Asia be turned away from me; of whom are Phygellus and Hermogenes.

16 The Lord give mercy unto the house of Onesiphorus; for he oft refreshed me, and was not ashamed of my chain:

17 But, when he was in Rome, he sought me out very diligently, and found *me*.

18 The Lord grant unto him that he may find mercy of the Lord in that day: and in how many things he ministered unto me at Ephesus, thou knowest very well.

CHAPTER 2

THOU therefore, my son, be strong in the grace that is in Christ Yashiyah.

2 And the things that thou hast heard of me among many witnesses, the same commit thou to faithful men, who shall be able to teach others also.

3 Thou therefore endure hardness, as a good soldier of Yashiyah Christ.

4 No man that warreth entangleth himself with the affairs of *this* life; that he may please him who hath chosen him to be a soldier.

5 And if a man also strive for masteries, *yet* is he not crowned, except he strive lawfully.

6 The husbandman that laboureth must be first partaker of the fruits.

7 Consider what I say; and the Lord give thee understanding in all things.

8 Remember that Yashiyah Christ of the seed of David was raised from the dead according to my gospel:

9 Wherein I suffer trouble, as an evil doer, *even* unto bonds; but the word of אֱלֹהִים is not bound.

10 Therefore I endure all things for the elect's sakes, that they may also obtain the salvation which is in Christ Yashiyah with eternal glory.

11 *It is* a faithful saying: For if we be dead with *him*, we shall also live with *him*:

12 If we suffer, we shall also reign with *him*: if we deny *him*, he also will deny us:

13 If we believe not, *yet* he abideth faithful: he cannot deny himself.

14 Of these things put *them* in remembrance, charging *them* before the Lord that they strive not about words to no profit, *but* to the subverting of the hearers.

15 Study to shew thyself approved unto אֱלֹהִים, a workman that needeth not to be ashamed, rightly dividing the word of truth.

16 But shun profane *and* vain babblings: for they will increase unto more ungodliness.

17 And their word will eat as doth a canker: of whom is Hymenæus and Philetus;

18 Who concerning the truth have erred, saying that the resurrection is past already; and overthrow the faith of some.

19 Nevertheless the foundation of אֱלֹהִים standeth sure, having this seal, The Lord knoweth them that are his. And, Let every one that nameth the name of Christ depart from iniquity.

20 But in a great house there are not only vessels of gold and of silver, but also of wood and of earth; and some to honour, and some to dishonour.

21 If a man therefore purge himself from these, he shall be a vessel unto honour, sanctified, and meet for the master's use, *and* prepared unto every good work.

22 Flee also youthful lusts: but follow righteousness, faith, charity, peace, with them that call on the Lord out of a pure heart.

23 But foolish and unlearned questions avoid, knowing that they do gender strifes.

24 And the servant of the Lord must not strive; but be gentle unto all *men*, apt to teach, patient,

25 In meekness instructing those that oppose themselves; if אֱלֹהִים peradventure will give them repentance to the acknowledging of the truth;

26 And *that* they may recover themselves out of the snare of the devil, who are taken captive by him at his will.

CHAPTER 3

THIS know also, that in the last days perilous times shall come.

2 For men shall be lovers of their own selves, covetous, boasters, proud, blasphemers, disobedient to parents, unthankful, unholy,

3 Without natural affection, trucebreakers, false accusers, incontinent, fierce, despisers of those that are good,

4 Traitors, heady, highminded, lovers of pleasures more than lovers of אֱלֹהִים;

5 Having a form of godliness, but denying the power thereof: from such turn away.

6 For of this sort are they which creep into houses, and lead captive silly women laden with sins, led away with divers lusts,

7 Ever learning, and never able to come to the knowledge of the truth.

8 Now as Jannes and Jambres withstood Moses, so do these also resist the truth: men of corrupt minds, reprobate concerning the faith.

9 But they shall proceed no further: for their folly shall be manifest unto all *men*, as theirs also was.

10 But thou hast fully known my doctrine, manner of life, purpose, faith, longsuffering, charity, patience,

11 Persecutions, afflictions, which came unto me at Antioch, at Iconium, at Lystra; what persecutions I endured: but out of *them* all the Lord delivered me.

12 Yea, and all that will live godly in Christ Yashiyah shall suffer persecution.

13 But evil men and seducers shall wax worse and worse, deceiving, and being deceived.

14 But continue thou in the things which thou hast learned and hast been assured of, knowing of whom thou hast learned *them*;

15 And that from a child thou hast known the holy scriptures, which are able to make thee wise unto salvation through faith which is in Christ Yashiyah.

16 All scripture *is* given by inspiration of אֱלֹהִים, and *is* profitable for doctrine, for reproof, for correction, for instruction in righteousness:

17 That the man of אֱלֹהִים may be perfect, throughly furnished unto all good works.

CHAPTER 4

I CHARGE *thee* therefore before אֱלֹהִים, and the Lord Yashiyah Christ, who shall judge the quick and the dead at his appearing and his kingdom;

2 Preach the word; be instant in season, out of season; reprove, rebuke, exhort with all longsuffering and doctrine.

3 For the time will come when they will not endure sound doctrine; but after their own lusts shall they heap to themselves teachers, having itching ears;

4 And they shall turn away *their* ears from the truth, and shall be turned unto fables.

5 But watch thou in all things, endure afflictions, do the work of an evangelist, make full proof of thy ministry.

6 For I am now ready to be offered, and the time of my departure is at hand.

7 I have fought a good fight, I have finished *my* course, I have kept the faith:

8 Henceforth there is laid up for me a crown of righteousness, which the Lord, the righteous judge, shall give me at that day: and not to me only, but unto all them also that love his appearing.

9 Do thy diligence to come shortly unto me:

10 For Demas hath forsaken me, having loved this present world, and is departed unto Thessalonica; Crescens to Galatia, Titus unto Dalmatia.

11 Only Luke is with me. Take Mark, and bring him with thee: for he is profitable to me for the ministry.

12 And Tychicus have I sent to Ephesus.

13 The cloke that I left at Troas with Carpus, when thou comest, bring *with thee*, and the books, *but* especially the parchments.

14 Alexander the coppersmith did me much evil: the Lord reward him according to his works:

15 Of whom be thou ware also; for he hath greatly withstood our words.

16 At my first answer no man stood with me, but all *men* forsook me: *I pray* אֱלֹהִים that it may not be laid to their charge.

17 Notwithstanding the Lord stood with me, and strengthened me; that by me the preaching might be fully known, and *that* all the Gentiles might hear: and I was delivered out of the mouth of the lion.

18 And the Lord shall deliver me from every evil work, and will preserve *me* unto his heavenly kingdom: to whom *be* glory for ever and ever. Amen.

19 Salute Prisca and Aquila, and the household of Onesiphorus.

20 Erastus abode at Corinth: but Trophimus have I left at Miletum sick.

21 Do thy diligence to come before winter. Eubulus greeteth thee, and Pudens, and Linus, and Claudia, and all the brethren.

22 The Lord Yashiyah Christ *be* with thy spirit. Grace *be* with you. Amen.

¶ The second *epistle* unto Timotheus, ordained the first bishop of the church of the Ephesians, was written from Rome, when Paul was brought before Nero the second time.

THE EPISTLE OF PAUL TO
TITUS.

CHAPTER 1

PAUL, a servant of אֱלֹהִים, and an apostle of Yashiyah Christ, according to the faith of אֱלֹהִים's elect, and the acknowledging of the truth which is after godliness;

2 In hope of eternal life, which אֱלֹהִים, that cannot lie, promised before the world began;

3 But hath in due times manifested his word through preaching, which is committed unto me according to the commandment of אֱלֹהִים our Saviour;

4 To Titus, *mine* own son after the common faith: Grace, mercy, *and* peace, from אֱלֹהִים the Father and the Lord Yashiyah Christ our Saviour.

5 For this cause left I thee in Crete, that thou shouldest set in order the things that are wanting, and ordain elders in every city, as I had appointed thee:

6 If any be blameless, the husband of one wife, having faithful children not accused of riot or unruly.

7 For a bishop must be blameless, as the steward of אֱלֹהִים; not selfwilled, not soon angry, not given to wine, no striker, not given to filthy lucre;

8 But a lover of hospitality, a lover of good men, sober, just, holy, temperate;

9 Holding fast the faithful word as he hath been taught, that he may be able by sound doctrine both to exhort and to convince the gainsayers.

10 For there are many unruly and vain talkers and deceivers, specially they of the circumcision:

11 Whose mouths must be stopped, who subvert whole houses, teaching things which they ought not, for filthy lucre's sake.

12 One of themselves, *even* a prophet of their own, said, The Cretians *are* alway liars, evil beasts, slow bellies.

13 This witness is true. Wherefore rebuke them sharply, that they may be sound in the faith;

14 Not giving heed to Jewish fables, and commandments of men, that turn from the truth.

15 Unto the pure all things *are* pure: but unto them that are defiled and unbelieving *is* nothing pure; but even their mind and conscience is defiled.

16 They profess that they know אֱלֹהִים; but in works they deny *him*, being abominable, and disobedient, and unto every good work reprobate.

CHAPTER 2

BUT speak thou the things which become sound doctrine:

2 That the aged men be sober, grave, temperate, sound in faith, in charity, in patience.

3 The aged women likewise, that *they be* in behaviour as becometh holiness, not false accusers, not given to much wine, teachers of good things;

4 That they may teach the young women to be sober, to love their husbands, to love their children,

5 *To be* discreet, chaste, keepers at home, good, obedient to their own husbands, that the word of אֱלֹהִים be not blasphemed.

6 Young men likewise exhort to be sober minded.

7 In all things shewing thyself a pattern of good works: in doctrine *shewing* uncorruptness, gravity, sincerity,

8 Sound speech, that cannot be condemned; that he that is of the contrary part may be ashamed, having no evil thing to say of you.

9 *Exhort* servants to be obedient unto their own masters, *and* to please *them* well in all *things;* not answering again;

10 Not purloining, but shewing all good fidelity; that they may adorn the doctrine of אֱלֹהִים our Saviour in all things.

11 For the grace of אֱלֹהִים that bringeth salvation hath appeared to all men,

12 Teaching us that, denying ungodliness and worldly lusts, we should live soberly, righteously, and godly, in this present world;

13 Looking for that blessed hope, and the glorious appearing of the great אֱלֹהִים and our Saviour Yashiyah Christ;

14 Who gave himself for us, that he might redeem us from all iniquity, and purify unto himself a peculiar people, zealous of good works.

15 These things speak, and exhort, and rebuke with all authority. Let no man despise thee.

CHAPTER 3

PUT them in mind to be subject to principalities and powers, to obey magistrates, to be ready to every good work,

2 To speak evil of no man, to be no brawlers, *but* gentle, shewing all meekness unto all men.

3 For we ourselves also were sometimes foolish, disobedient, deceived, serving divers lusts and pleasures, living in malice and envy, hateful, *and* hating one another.

4 But after that the kindness and love of אֱלֹהִים our Saviour toward man appeared,

5 Not by works of righteousness which we have done, but according to his mercy he saved us, by the washing of regeneration, and renewing of the Holy Ghost;

6 Which he shed on us abundantly through Yashiyah Christ our Saviour;

7 That being justified by his grace, we should be made heirs according to the hope of eternal life.

8 *This is* a faithful saying, and these things I will that thou affirm constantly, that they which have believed in אֱלֹהִים might be careful to maintain good works. These things are good and profitable unto men.

9 But avoid foolish questions, and genealogies, and contentions, and strivings about the law; for they are unprofitable and vain.

10 A man that is an heretick after the first and second admonition reject;

11 Knowing that he that is such is subverted, and sinneth, being condemned of himself.

12 When I shall send Artemas unto thee, or Tychicus, be diligent to come unto me to Nicopolis: for I have determined there to winter.

13 Bring Zenas the lawyer and Apollos on their journey diligently, that nothing be wanting unto them.

14 And let ours also learn to maintain good works for necessary uses, that they be not unfruitful.

15 All that are with me salute thee. Greet them that love us in the faith. Grace *be* with you all. Amen.

¶ It was written to Titus, ordained the first bishop of the church of the Cretians, from Nicopolis of Macedonia.

THE EPISTLE OF PAUL TO

PHILEMON.

CHAPTER 1

PAUL, a prisoner of Yashiyah Christ, and Timothy *our* brother, unto Philemon our dearly beloved, and fellowlabourer,

2 And to *our* beloved Apphia, and Archippus our fellowsoldier, and to the church in thy house:

3 Grace to you, and peace, from אֱלֹהִים our Father and the Lord Yashiyah Christ.

4 I thank my אֱלֹהִים, making mention of thee always in my prayers,

5 Hearing of thy love and faith, which thou hast toward the Lord Yashiyah, and toward all saints;

6 That the communication of thy faith may become effectual by the acknowledging of every good thing which is in you in Christ Yashiyah.

7 For we have great joy and consolation in thy love, because the bowels of the saints are refreshed by thee, brother.

8 Wherefore, though I might be much bold in Christ to enjoin thee that which is convenient,

9 Yet for love's sake I rather beseech *thee*, being such an one as Paul the aged, and now also a prisoner of Yashiyah Christ.

10 I beseech thee for my son Onesimus, whom I have begotten in my bonds:

11 Which in time past was to thee unprofitable, but now profitable to thee and to me:

12 Whom I have sent again: thou therefore receive him, that is, mine own bowels:

13 Whom I would have retained with me, that in thy stead he might have ministered unto me in the bonds of the gospel:

14 But without thy mind would I do nothing; that thy benefit should not be as it were of necessity, but willingly.

15 For perhaps he therefore departed for a season, that thou shouldest receive him for ever;

16 Not now as a servant, but above a servant, a brother beloved, specially to me, but how much more unto thee, both in the flesh, and in the Lord?

17 If thou count me therefore a partner, receive him as myself.

18 If he hath wronged thee, or oweth *thee* ought, put that on mine account;

19 I Paul have written *it* with mine own hand, I will repay *it*: albeit I do not say to thee how thou owest unto me even thine own self besides.

20 Yea, brother, let me have joy of thee in the Lord: refresh my bowels in the Lord.

21 Having confidence in thy obedience I wrote unto thee, knowing that thou wilt also do more than I say.

22 But withal prepare me also a lodging: for I trust that through your prayers I shall be given unto you.

23 There salute thee Epaphras, my fellowprisoner in Christ Yashiyah;

24 Marcus, Aristarchus, Demas, Lucas, my fellowlabourers.

25 The grace of our Lord Yashiyah Christ *be* with your spirit. Amen.

¶ Written from Rome to Philemon, by Onesimus a servant.

THE EPISTLE OF PAUL THE APOSTLE
TO THE

HEBREWS.

CHAPTER 1

GOD, who at sundry times and in divers manners spake in time past unto the fathers by the prophets,

2 Hath in these last days spoken unto us by *his* Son, whom he hath appointed heir of all things, by whom also he made the worlds;

3 Who being the brightness of *his* glory, and the express image of his person, and upholding all things by the word of his power, when he had by himself purged our sins, sat down on the right hand of the Majesty on high;

4 Being made so much better than the angels, as he hath by inheritance obtained a more excellent name than they.

5 For unto which of the angels said he at any time, Thou art my Son, this day have I begotten thee? And again, I will be to him a Father, and he shall be to me a Son?

6 And again, when he bringeth in the firstbegotten into the world, he saith, And let all the angels of אֱלֹהִים worship him.

7 And of the angels he saith, Who maketh his angels spirits, and his ministers a flame of fire.

8 But unto the Son he saith, Thy throne, O אֱלֹהִים, is for ever and ever: a sceptre of righteousness is the sceptre of thy kingdom.

9 Thou hast loved righteousness, and hated iniquity; therefore אֱלֹהִים, even thy אֱלֹהִים, hath anointed thee with the oil of gladness above thy fellows.

10 And, Thou, Lord, in the beginning hast laid the foundation of the earth; and the heavens are the works of thine hands:

11 They shall perish; but thou remainest; and they all shall wax old as doth a garment;

12 And as a vesture shalt thou fold them up, and they shall be changed: but thou art the same, and thy years shall not fail.

13 But to which of the angels said he at any time, Sit on my right hand, until I make thine enemies thy footstool?

14 Are they not all ministering spirits, sent forth to minister for them who shall be heirs of salvation?

CHAPTER 2

THEREFORE we ought to give the more earnest heed to the things which we have heard, lest at any time we should let them slip.

2 For if the word spoken by angels was stedfast, and every transgression and disobedience received a just recompence of reward;

3 How shall we escape, if we neglect so great salvation; which at the first began to be spoken by the Lord, and was confirmed unto us by them that heard him;

4 אֱלֹהִים also bearing them witness, both with signs and wonders, and with divers miracles, and gifts of the Holy Ghost, according to his own will?

5 For unto the angels hath he not put in subjection the world to come, whereof we speak.

6 But one in a certain place testified, saying, What is man, that thou art mindful of him? or the son of man, that thou visitest him?

7 Thou madest him a little lower than the angels; thou crownedst him with glory and honour, and didst set him over the works of thy hands:

8 Thou hast put all things in subjection under his feet. For in that he put all in subjection under him, he left nothing that is not put under him. But now we see not yet all things put under him.

9 But we see Yashiyah, who was made a little lower than the angels for the suffering of death, crowned with glory and honour; that he by the grace of אֱלֹהִים should taste death for every man.

10 For it became him, for whom are all things, and by whom are all things, in bringing many sons unto glory, to make the captain of their salvation perfect through sufferings.

11 For both he that sanctifieth and they who are sanctified are all of one: for which cause he is not ashamed to call them brethren,

12 Saying, I will declare thy name unto my brethren, in the midst of the church will I sing praise unto thee.

13 And again, I will put my trust in him. And again, Behold I and the children which אֱלֹהִים hath given me.

14 Forasmuch then as the children are partakers of flesh and blood, he also himself likewise took part of the same; that through death he might destroy him that had the power of death, that is, the devil;

15 And deliver them who through fear of death were all their lifetime subject to bondage.

16 For verily he took not on him the nature of angels; but he took on him the seed of Abraham.

17 Wherefore in all things it behoved him to be made like unto his brethren, that he might be a merciful and faithful high priest in things pertaining to אֱלֹהִים, to make reconciliation for the sins of the people.

18 For in that he himself hath suffered being tempted, he is able to succour them that are tempted.

CHAPTER 3

WHEREFORE, holy brethren, partakers of the heavenly calling, consider the Apostle and High Priest of our profession, Christ Yashiyah;

2 Who was faithful to him that appointed him, as also Moses was faithful in all his house.

3 For this man was counted worthy of more glory than Moses, inasmuch as he who hath builded the house hath more honour than the house.

4 For every house is builded by some man; but he that built all things is אֱלֹהִים.

5 And Moses verily was faithful in all his house, as a servant, for a testimony of those things which were to be spoken after;

6 But Christ as a son over his own house; whose house are we, if we hold fast the confidence and the rejoicing of the hope firm unto the end.

7 Wherefore (as the Holy Ghost saith, To day if ye will hear his voice,

8 Harden not your hearts, as in the provocation, in the day of temptation in the wilderness:

9 When your fathers tempted me, proved me, and saw my works forty years.

10 Wherefore I was grieved with that generation, and said, They do alway err in their heart; and they have not known my ways.

11 So I sware in my wrath, They shall not enter into my rest.)

12 Take heed, brethren, lest there be in any of you an evil heart of unbelief, in departing from the living אֱלֹהִים.

13 But exhort one another daily, while it is called To day; lest any of you be hardened through the deceitfulness of sin.

14 For we are made partakers of Christ, if we hold the beginning of our confidence stedfast unto the end;

15 While it is said, To day if ye will hear his voice, harden not your hearts, as in the provocation.

16 For some, when they had heard, did provoke: howbeit not all that came out of Egypt by Moses.

17 But with whom was he grieved forty years? was it not with them that had sinned, whose carcases fell in the wilderness?

18 And to whom sware he that they should not enter into his rest, but to them that believed not?

19 So we see that they could not enter in because of unbelief.

CHAPTER 4

LET us therefore fear, lest, a promise being left us of entering into his rest, any of you should seem to come short of it.

2 For unto us was the gospel preached, as well as unto them: but the word preached did not profit them, not being mixed with faith in them that heard it.

3 For we which have believed do enter into rest, as he said, As I have sworn in my wrath, if they shall enter into my rest: although the works were finished from the foundation of the world.

4 For he spake in a certain place of the seventh *day* on this wise, And אֱלֹהִים did rest the seventh day from all his works.

5 And in this *place* again, If they shall enter into my rest.

6 Seeing therefore it remaineth that some must enter therein, and they to whom it was first preached entered not in because of unbelief:

7 Again, he limiteth a certain day, saying in David, To day, after so long a time; as it is said, To day if ye will hear his voice, harden not your hearts.

8 For if Yashiyah had given them rest, then would he not afterward have spoken of another day.

9 There remaineth therefore a rest to the people of אֱלֹהִים.

10 For he that is entered into his rest, he also hath ceased from his own works, as אֱלֹהִים *did* from his.

11 Let us labour therefore to enter into that rest, lest any man fall after the same example of unbelief.

12 For the word of אֱלֹהִים *is* quick, and powerful, and sharper than any twoedged sword, piercing even to the dividing asunder of soul and spirit, and of the joints and marrow, and *is* a discerner of the thoughts and intents of the heart.

13 Neither is there any creature that is not manifest in his sight: but all things *are* naked and opened unto the eyes of him with whom we have to do.

14 Seeing then that we have a great high priest, that is passed into the heavens, Yashiyah the Son of אֱלֹהִים, let us hold fast *our* profession.

15 For we have not an high priest which cannot be touched with the feeling of our infirmities; but was in all points tempted like as *we are*, *yet* without sin.

16 Let us therefore come boldly unto the throne of grace, that we may obtain mercy, and find grace to help in time of need.

CHAPTER 5

FOR every high priest taken from among men is ordained for men in things *pertaining* to אֱלֹהִים, that he may offer both gifts and sacrifices for sins:

2 Who can have compassion on the ignorant, and on them that are out of the way; for that he himself also is compassed with infirmity.

3 And by reason hereof he ought, as for the people, so also for himself, to offer for sins.

4 And no man taketh this honour unto himself, but he that is called of אֱלֹהִים, as *was* Aaron.

5 So also Christ glorified not himself to be made an high priest; but he that said unto him, Thou art my Son, to day have I begotten thee.

6 As he saith also in another *place*, Thou *art* a priest for ever after the order of Melchisedec.

7 Who in the days of his flesh, when he had offered up prayers and supplications with strong crying and tears unto him that was able to save him from death, and was heard in that he feared;

8 Though he were a Son, yet learned he obedience by the things which he suffered;

9 And being made perfect, he became the author of eternal salvation unto all them that obey him;

10 Called of אֱלֹהִים an high priest after the order of Melchisedec.

11 Of whom we have many things to say, and hard to be uttered, seeing ye are dull of hearing.

12 For when for the time ye ought to be teachers, ye have need that one teach you again which *be* the first principles of the oracles of אֱלֹהִים; and are become such as have need of milk, and not of strong meat.

13 For every one that useth milk *is* unskilful in the word of righteousness: for he is a babe.

14 But strong meat belongeth to them that are of full age, *even* those who by reason of use have their senses exercised to discern both good and evil.

CHAPTER 6

THEREFORE leaving the principles of the doctrine of Christ, let us go on unto perfection; not laying again the foundation of repentance from dead works, and of faith toward אֱלֹהִים,

2 Of the doctrine of baptisms, and of laying on of hands, and of resurrection of the dead, and of eternal judgment.

3 And this will we do, if אֱלֹהִים permit.

4 For *it is* impossible for those who were once enlightened, and have tasted of the heavenly gift, and were made partakers of the Holy Ghost,

5 And have tasted the good word of אֱלֹהִים, and the powers of the world to come,

6 If they shall fall away, to renew them again unto repentance; seeing they crucify to themselves the Son of אֱלֹהִים afresh, and put *him* to an open shame.

7 For the earth which drinketh in the rain that cometh oft upon it, and bringeth forth herbs meet for them by whom it is dressed, receiveth blessing from אֱלֹהִים:

8 But that which beareth thorns and briers *is* rejected, and *is* nigh unto cursing; whose end *is* to be burned.

9 But, beloved, we are persuaded better things of you, and things that accompany salvation, though we thus speak.

10 For אֱלֹהִים *is* not unrighteous to forget your work and labour of love, which ye have shewed toward his name, in that ye have ministered to the saints, and do minister.

11 And we desire that every one of you do shew the same diligence to the full assurance of hope unto the end:

12 That ye be not slothful, but followers of them who through faith and patience inherit the promises.

13 For when אֱלֹהִים made promise to Abraham, because he could swear by no greater, he sware by himself,

14 Saying, Surely blessing I will bless thee, and multiplying I will multiply thee.

15 And so, after he had patiently endured, he obtained the promise.

16 For men verily swear by the greater: and an oath for confirmation *is* to them an end of all strife.

17 Wherein אֱלֹהִים, willing more abundantly to shew unto the heirs of promise the immutability of his counsel, confirmed *it* by an oath:

18 That by two immutable things, in which *it was* impossible for אֱלֹהִים to lie, we might have a strong consolation, who have fled for refuge to lay hold upon the hope set before us:

19 Which *hope* we have as an anchor of the soul, both sure and stedfast, and which entereth into that within the veil;

20 Whither the forerunner is for us entered, *even* Yashiyah, made an high priest for ever after the order of Melchisedec.

CHAPTER 7

FOR this Melchisedec, king of Salem, priest of the most high אֱלֹהִים, who met Abraham returning from the slaughter of the kings, and blessed him:

2 To whom also Abraham gave a tenth part of all; first being by interpretation King of righteousness, and after that also King of Salem, which is, King of peace;

3 Without father, without mother, without descent, having neither beginning of days, nor end of life; but made like unto the Son of אֱלֹהִים; abideth a priest continually.

4 Now consider how great this man *was*, unto whom even the patriarch Abraham gave the tenth of the spoils.

5 And verily they that are of the sons of Levi, who receive the office of the priesthood, have a commandment to take tithes of the people according to the law, that is, of their brethren, though they come out of the loins of Abraham:

6 But he whose descent is not counted from them received tithes of Abraham, and blessed him that had the promises.

7 And without all contradiction the less is blessed of the better.

8 And here men that die receive tithes; but there he *receiveth them*, of whom it is witnessed that he liveth.

9 And as I may so say, Levi also, who receiveth tithes, payed tithes in Abraham.

10 For he was yet in the loins of his father, when Melchisedec met him.

11 If therefore perfection were by the Levitical priesthood, (for under it the people received the law,) what further need *was there* that another priest should rise after the order of Melchisedec, and not be called after the order of Aaron?

12 For the priesthood being changed, there is made of necessity a change also of the law.

13 For he of whom these things are spoken pertaineth to another tribe, of which no man gave attendance at the altar.

14 For *it is* evident that our Lord sprang out of Juda; of which tribe Moses spake nothing concerning priesthood.

15 And it is yet far more evident: for that after the similitude of Melchisedec there ariseth another priest,

16 Who is made, not after the law of a carnal commandment, but after the power of an endless life.

17 For he testifieth, Thou *art* a priest for ever after the order of Melchisedec.

18 For there is verily a disannulling of the commandment going before for the weakness and unprofitableness thereof.

19 For the law made nothing perfect, but the bringing in of a better hope *did*: by the which we draw nigh unto אֱלֹהִים.

20 And inasmuch as not without an oath *he was made priest*:

21 (For those priests were made without an oath; but this with an oath by him that said unto him, The Lord sware and will not repent, Thou *art* a priest for ever after the order of Melchisedec:)

22 By so much was Yashiyah made a surety of a better testament.

23 And they truly were many priests, because they were not suffered to continue by reason of death:

24 But this *man*, because he continueth ever, hath an unchangeable priesthood.

25 Wherefore he is able also to save them to the uttermost that come unto אֱלֹהִים by him, seeing he ever liveth to make intercession for them.

26 For such an high priest became us, *who is* holy, harmless, undefiled, separate from sinners, and made higher than the heavens;

27 Who needeth not daily, as those high priests, to offer up sacrifice, first for his own sins, and then for the people's: for this he did once, when he offered up himself.

28 For the law maketh men high priests which have infirmity; but the word of the oath, which was since the law, *maketh* the Son, who is consecrated for evermore.

CHAPTER 8

NOW of the things which we have spoken *this is* the sum: We have such an high priest, who is set on the right hand of the throne of the Majesty in the heavens;

2 A minister of the sanctuary, and of the true tabernacle, which the Lord pitched, and not man.

3 For every high priest is ordained to offer gifts and sacrifices: wherefore *it is* of necessity that this man have somewhat also to offer.

4 For if he were on earth, he should not be a priest, seeing that there are priests that offer gifts according to the law:

5 Who serve unto the example and shadow of heavenly things, as Moses was admonished of אֱלֹהִים when he was about to make the tabernacle: for, See, saith he, *that* thou make all things according to the pattern shewed to thee in the mount.

6 But now hath he obtained a more excellent ministry, by how much also he is the mediator of a better covenant, which was established upon better promises.

7 For if that first *covenant* had been faultless, then should no place have been sought for the second.

8 For finding fault with them, he saith, Behold, the days come, saith the Lord, when I will make a new covenant with the house of Israel and with the house of Judah:

9 Not according to the covenant that I made with their fathers in the day when I took them by the hand to lead them out of the land of Egypt; because they continued not in my covenant, and I regarded them not, saith the Lord.

10 For this *is* the covenant that I will make with the house of Israel after those days, saith the Lord; I will put my laws into their mind, and write them in their hearts: and I will be to them a אֱלֹהִים, and they shall be to me a people:

11 And they shall not teach every man his neighbour, and every man his brother, saying, Know the Lord: for all shall know me, from the least to the greatest.

12 For I will be merciful to their unrighteousness, and their sins and their iniquities will I remember no more.

13 In that he saith, A new *covenant*, he hath made the first old. Now that which decayeth and waxeth old *is* ready to vanish away.

CHAPTER 9

THEN verily the first *covenant* had also ordinances of divine service, and a worldly sanctuary.

2 For there was a tabernacle made; the first, wherein *was* the candlestick, and the table, and the shewbread; which is called the sanctuary.

3 And after the second veil, the tabernacle which is called the Holiest of all;

4 Which had the golden censer, and the ark of the covenant overlaid round about with gold, wherein *was* the golden pot that had manna, and Aaron's rod that budded, and the tables of the covenant;

5 And over it the cherubims of glory shadowing the mercyseat; of which we cannot now speak particularly.

6 Now when these things were thus ordained, the priests went always into the first tabernacle, accomplishing the service of אֱלֹהִים.

7 But into the second *went* the high priest alone once every year, not without blood, which he offered for himself, and *for* the errors of the people:

8 The Holy Ghost this signifying, that the way into the holiest of all was not yet made manifest, while as the first tabernacle was yet standing:

9 Which *was* a figure for the time then present, in which were offered both gifts and sacrifices, that could not make him that did the service perfect, as pertaining to the conscience;

10 *Which stood* only in meats and drinks, and divers washings, and carnal ordinances, imposed *on them* until the time of reformation.

11 But Christ being come an high priest of good things to come, by a greater and more perfect tabernacle, not made with hands, that is to say, not of this building;

12 Neither by the blood of goats and calves, but by his own blood he entered in once into the holy place, having obtained eternal redemption *for us*.

13 For if the blood of bulls and of goats, and the ashes of an heifer sprinkling the unclean, sanctifieth to the purifying of the flesh:

14 How much more shall the blood of Christ, who through the eternal Spirit offered himself without spot to אֱלֹהִים, purge your conscience from dead works to serve the living אֱלֹהִים?

15 And for this cause he is the mediator of the new testament, that by means of death, for the redemption of the transgressions *that were* under the first testament, they which are called might receive the promise of eternal inheritance.

16 For where a testament *is*, there must also of necessity be the death of the testator.

17 For a testament *is* of force after men are dead: otherwise it is of no strength at all while the testator liveth.

18 Whereupon neither the first *testament* was dedicated without blood.

19 For when Moses had spoken every precept to all the people according to the law, he took the blood of calves and of goats, with water, and scarlet wool, and hyssop, and sprinkled both the book, and all the people,

20 Saying, This *is* the blood of the testament which אֱלֹהִים hath enjoined unto you.

21 Moreover he sprinkled with blood both the tabernacle, and all the vessels of the ministry.

22 And almost all things are by the law purged with blood; and without shedding of blood is no remission.

23 *It was* therefore necessary that the patterns of things in the heavens should be purified with these; but the heavenly things themselves with better sacrifices than these.

24 For Christ is not entered into the holy places made with hands, *which are* the figures of the true; but into heaven itself, now to appear in the presence of אֱלֹהִים for us:

25 Nor yet that he should offer himself often, as the high priest entereth into the holy place every year with blood of others;

26 For then must he often have suffered since the foundation of the world: but now once in the end of the world hath he appeared to put away sin by the sacrifice of himself.

27 And as it is appointed unto men once to die, but after this the judgment:

28 So Christ was once offered to bear the sins of many; and unto them that look for him shall he appear the second time without sin unto salvation.

CHAPTER 10

FOR the law having a shadow of good things to come, *and* not the very image of the things, can never with those sacrifices which they offered year by year continually make the comers thereunto perfect.

2 For then would they not have ceased to be offered? because that the worshippers once purged should have had no more conscience of sins.

3 But in those *sacrifices there is* a remembrance again *made* of sins every year.

4 For *it is* not possible that the blood of bulls and of goats should take away sins.

5 Wherefore when he cometh into the world, he saith, Sacrifice and offering thou wouldest not, but a body hast thou prepared me:

6 In burnt offerings and *sacrifices* for sin thou hast had no pleasure.

7 Then said I, Lo, I come (in the volume of the book it is written of me,) to do thy will, O אֱלֹהִים.

8 Above when he said, Sacrifice and offering and burnt offerings and *offering* for sin thou wouldest not, neither hadst pleasure *therein;* which are offered by the law;

9 Then said he, Lo, I come to do thy will, O אֱלֹהִים. He taketh away the first, that he may establish the second.

10 By the which will we are sanctified through the offering of the body of Yashiyah Christ once *for all*.

11 And every priest standeth daily ministering and offering oftentimes the same sacrifices, which can never take away sins:

12 But this man, after he had offered one sacrifice for sins for ever, sat down on the right hand of אֱלֹהִים;

13 From henceforth expecting till his enemies be made his footstool.

14 For by one offering he hath perfected for ever them that are sanctified.

15 *Whereof* the Holy Ghost also is a witness to us: for after that he had said before,

16 This *is* the covenant that I will make with them after those days, saith the Lord, I will put my laws into their hearts, and in their minds will I write them;

17 And their sins and iniquities will I remember no more.

18 Now where remission of these *is*, there *is* no more offering for sin.

19 Having therefore, brethren, boldness to enter into the holiest by the blood of Yashiyah,

20 By a new and living way, which he hath consecrated for us, through the veil, that is to say, his flesh;

21 And *having* an high priest over the house of אֱלֹהִים;

22 Let us draw near with a true heart in full assurance of faith, having our hearts sprinkled from an evil conscience, and our bodies washed with pure water.

23 Let us hold fast the profession of *our* faith without wavering; (for he *is* faithful that promised;)

24 And let us consider one another to provoke unto love and to good works:

25 Not forsaking the assembling of ourselves together, as the manner of some *is;* but exhorting *one another:* and so much the more, as ye see the day approaching.

26 For if we sin wilfully after that we have received the knowledge of the truth, there remaineth no more sacrifice for sins,

27 But a certain fearful looking for of judgment and fiery indignation, which shall devour the adversaries.

28 He that despised Moses' law died without mercy under two or three witnesses:

29 Of how much sorer punishment, suppose ye, shall he be thought worthy, who hath trodden under foot the Son of אֱלֹהִים, and hath counted the blood of the covenant, wherewith he was sanctified, an unholy thing, and hath done despite unto the Spirit of grace?

30 For we know him that hath said, Vengeance *belongeth* unto me, I will recompense, saith the Lord. And again, The Lord shall judge his people.

31 *It is* a fearful thing to fall into the hands of the living אֱלֹהִים.

32 But call to remembrance the former days, in which, after ye were illuminated, ye endured a great fight of afflictions;

33 Partly, whilst ye were made a gazingstock both by reproaches and afflictions; and partly, whilst ye became companions of them that were so used.

34 For ye had compassion of me in my bonds, and took joyfully the spoiling of your goods, knowing in yourselves that ye have in heaven a better and an enduring substance.

35 Cast not away therefore your confidence, which hath great recompence of reward.

36 For ye have need of patience, that, after ye have done the will of אֱלֹהִים, ye might receive the promise.

37 For yet a little while, and he that shall come will come, and will not tarry.

38 Now the just shall live by faith: but if *any man* draw back, my soul shall have no pleasure in him.

39 But we are not of them who draw back unto perdition; but of them that believe to the saving of the soul.

CHAPTER 11

NOW faith is the substance of things hoped for, the evidence of things not seen.

2 For by it the elders obtained a good report.

3 Through faith we understand that the worlds were framed by the word of אֱלֹהִים, so that things which are seen were not made of things which do appear.

4 By faith Abel offered unto אֱלֹהִים a more excellent sacrifice than Cain, by which he obtained witness that he was righteous, אֱלֹהִים testifying of his gifts: and by it he being dead yet speaketh.

5 By faith Enoch was translated that he should not see death; and was not found, because אֱלֹהִים had translated him: for before his translation he had this testimony, that he pleased אֱלֹהִים.

6 But without faith *it is* impossible to please *him:* for he that cometh to אֱלֹהִים must believe that he is, and *that* he is a rewarder of them that diligently seek him.

7 By faith Noah, being warned of אֱלֹהִים of things not seen as yet, moved with fear, prepared an ark to the saving of his house; by the which he condemned the world, and became heir of the righteousness which is by faith.

8 By faith Abraham, when he was called to go out into a place which he should after receive for an inheritance, obeyed; and he went out, not knowing whither he went.

9 By faith he sojourned in the land of promise, as *in* a strange country, dwelling in tabernacles with Isaac and Jacob, the heirs with him of the same promise:

10 For he looked for a city which hath foundations, whose builder and maker *is* אֱלֹהִים.

11 Through faith also Sara herself received strength to conceive seed, and was delivered of a child when she was past age, because she judged him faithful who had promised.

12 Therefore sprang there even of one, and him as good as dead, *so many* as the stars of the sky in multitude, and as the sand which is by the sea shore innumerable.

13 These all died in faith, not having received the promises, but having seen them afar off, and were persuaded of *them,* and embraced *them,* and confessed that they were strangers and pilgrims on the earth.

14 For they that say such things declare plainly that they seek a country.

15 And truly, if they had been mindful of that *country* from whence they came out, they might have had opportunity to have returned.

16 But now they desire a better *country,* that is, an heavenly: wherefore אֱלֹהִים is not ashamed to be called their אֱלֹהִים: for he hath prepared for them a city.

17 By faith Abraham, when he was tried, offered up Isaac: and he that had received the promises offered up his only begotten *son,*

18 Of whom it was said, That in Isaac shall thy seed be called:

19 Accounting that אֱלֹהִים *was* able to raise *him* up, even from the dead; from whence also he received him in a figure.

20 By faith Isaac blessed Jacob and Esau concerning things to come.

21 By faith Jacob, when he was a dying, blessed both the sons of Joseph; and worshipped, *leaning* upon the top of his staff.

22 By faith Joseph, when he died, made mention of the departing of the children of Israel; and gave commandment concerning his bones.

23 By faith Moses, when he was born, was hid three months of his parents, because they saw *he was* a proper child; and they were not afraid of the king's commandment.

24 By faith Moses, when he was come to years, refused to be called the son of Pharaoh's daughter;

25 Choosing rather to suffer affliction with the people of אֱלֹהִים, than to enjoy the pleasures of sin for a season;

26 Esteeming the reproach of Christ greater riches than the treasures in Egypt: for he had respect unto the recompence of the reward.

27 By faith he forsook Egypt, not fearing the wrath of the king: for he endured, as seeing him who is invisible.

28 Through faith he kept the passover, and the sprinkling of blood, lest he that destroyed the firstborn should touch them.

29 By faith they passed through the Red sea as by dry *land:* which the Egyptians assaying to do were drowned.

30 By faith the walls of Jericho fell down, after they were compassed about seven days.

31 By faith the harlot Rahab perished not with them that believed not, when she had received the spies with peace.

32 And what shall I more say? for the time would fail me to tell of Gedeon, and *of* Barak, and *of* Samson, and *of* Jephthae; *of* David also, and Samuel, and *of* the prophets:

33 Who through faith subdued kingdoms, wrought righteousness, obtained promises, stopped the mouths of lions,

34 Quenched the violence of fire, escaped the edge of the sword, out of weakness were made strong, waxed valiant in fight, turned to flight the armies of the aliens.

35 Women received their dead raised to life again: and others were tortured, not accepting deliverance; that they might obtain a better resurrection:

36 And others had trial of *cruel* mockings and scourgings, yea, moreover of bonds and imprisonment:

37 They were stoned, they were sawn asunder, were tempted, were slain with the sword: they wandered about in sheepskins and goatskins; being destitute, afflicted, tormented;

38 (Of whom the world was not worthy:) they wandered in deserts, and *in* mountains, and *in* dens and caves of the earth.

39 And these all, having obtained a good report through faith, received not the promise:

40 אֱלֹהִים having provided some better thing for us, that they without us should not be made perfect.

CHAPTER 12

WHEREFORE seeing we also are compassed about with so great a cloud of witnesses, let us lay aside every weight, and the sin which doth so easily beset *us*, and let us run with patience the race that is set before us,

2 Looking unto Yashiyah the author and finisher of *our* faith; who for the joy that was set before him endured the cross, despising the shame, and is set down at the right hand of the throne of אֱלֹהִים.

3 For consider him that endured such contradiction of sinners against himself, lest ye be wearied and faint in your minds.

4 Ye have not yet resisted unto blood, striving against sin.

5 And ye have forgotten the exhortation which speaketh unto you as unto children, My son, despise not thou the chastening of the Lord, nor faint when thou art rebuked of him:

6 For whom the Lord loveth he chasteneth, and scourgeth every son whom he receiveth.

7 If ye endure chastening, אֱלֹהִים dealeth with you as with sons; for what son is he whom the father chasteneth not?

8 But if ye be without chastisement, whereof all are partakers, then are ye bastards, and not sons.

9 Furthermore we have had fathers of our flesh which corrected *us*, and we gave *them* reverence: shall we not much rather be in subjection unto the Father of spirits, and live?

10 For they verily for a few days chastened *us* after their own pleasure; but he for *our* profit, that *we* might be partakers of his holiness.

11 Now no chastening for the present seemeth to be joyous, but grievous: nevertheless afterward it yieldeth the peaceable fruit of righteousness unto them which are exercised thereby.

12 Wherefore lift up the hands which hang down, and the feeble knees;

13 And make straight paths for your feet, lest that which is lame be turned out of the way; but let it rather be healed.

14 Follow peace with all *men*, and holiness, without which no man shall see the Lord:

15 Looking diligently lest any man fail of the grace of אֱלֹהִים; lest any root of bitterness springing up trouble *you*, and thereby many be defiled;

16 Lest there *be* any fornicator, or profane person, as Esau, who for one morsel of meat sold his birthright.

17 For ye know how that afterward, when he would have inherited the blessing, he was rejected: for he found no place of repentance, though he sought it carefully with tears.

18 For ye are not come unto the mount that might be touched, and that burned with fire, nor unto blackness, and darkness, and tempest,

19 And the sound of a trumpet, and the voice of words; which *voice* they that heard intreated that the word should not be spoken to them any more:

20 (For they could not endure that which was commanded, And if so much as a beast touch the mountain, it shall be stoned, or thrust through with a dart:

21 And so terrible was the sight, *that* Moses said, I exceedingly fear and quake:)

22 But ye are come unto mount Sion, and unto the city of the living אֱלֹהִים, the heavenly Jerusalem, and to an innumerable company of angels,

23 To the general assembly and church of the firstborn, which are written in heaven, and to אֱלֹהִים the Judge of all, and to the spirits of just men made perfect,

24 And to Yashiyah the mediator of the new covenant, and to the blood of sprinkling, that speaketh better things than *that of* Abel.

25 See that ye refuse not him that speaketh. For if they escaped not who refused him that spake on earth, much more *shall not* we escape, if we turn away from him that *speaketh* from heaven:

26 Whose voice then shook the earth: but now he hath promised, saying, Yet once more I shake not the earth only, but also heaven.

27 And this *word*, Yet once more, signifieth the removing of those things that are shaken, as of things that are made, that those things which cannot be shaken may remain.

28 Wherefore we receiving a kingdom which cannot be moved, let us have grace, whereby we may serve אֱלֹהִים acceptably with reverence and godly fear:

29 For our אֱלֹהִים *is* a consuming fire.

CHAPTER 13

LET brotherly love continue.

2 Be not forgetful to entertain strangers: for thereby some have entertained angels unawares.

3 Remember them that are in bonds, as bound with them; *and* them which suffer adversity, as being yourselves also in the body.

4 Marriage *is* honourable in all, and the bed undefiled: but whoremongers and adulterers אֱלֹהִים will judge.

5 *Let your* conversation *be* without covetousness; *and be* content with such things as ye have: for he hath said, I will never leave thee, nor forsake thee.

6 So that we may boldly say, The Lord *is* my helper, and I will not fear what man shall do unto me.

7 Remember them which have the rule over you, who have spoken unto you the word of אֱלֹהִים: whose faith follow, considering the end of *their* conversation.

8 Yashiyah Christ the same yesterday, and to day, and for ever.

9 Be not carried about with divers and strange doctrines. For *it is* a good thing that the heart be established with grace; not with meats, which have not profited them that have been occupied therein.

10 We have an altar, whereof they have no right to eat which serve the tabernacle.

11 For the bodies of those beasts, whose blood is brought into the sanctuary by the high priest for sin, are burned without the camp.

12 Wherefore Yashiyah also, that he might sanctify the people with his own blood, suffered without the gate.

13 Let us go forth therefore unto him without the camp, bearing his reproach.

14 For here have we no continuing city, but we seek one to come.

15 By him therefore let us offer the sacrifice of praise to אֱלֹהִים continually, that is, the fruit of *our* lips giving thanks to his name.

16 But to do good and to communicate forget not: for with such sacrifices אֱלֹהִים is well pleased.

17 Obey them that have the rule over you, and submit yourselves: for they watch for your souls, as they that must give account, that they may do it with joy, and not with grief: for that *is* unprofitable for you.

18 Pray for us: for we trust we have a good conscience, in all things willing to live honestly.

19 But I beseech *you* the rather to do this, that I may be restored to you the sooner.

20 Now the אֱלֹהִים of peace, that brought again from the dead our Lord Yashiyah, that great shepherd of the sheep, through the blood of the everlasting covenant,

21 Make you perfect in every good work to do his will, working in you that which is wellpleasing in his sight, through Yashiyah Christ; to whom *be* glory for ever and ever. Amen.

22 And I beseech you, brethren, suffer the word of exhortation: for I have written a letter unto you in few words.

23 Know ye that *our* brother Timothy is set at liberty; with whom, if he come shortly, I will see you.

24 Salute all them that have the rule over you, and all the saints. They of Italy salute you.

25 Grace *be* with you all. Amen.

¶ Written to the Hebrews from Italy by Timothy.

THE GENERAL EPISTLE OF
JAMES.

CHAPTER 1

JAMES, a servant of אֱלֹהִים and of the Lord Yashiyah Christ, to the twelve tribes which are scattered abroad, greeting.

2 My brethren, count it all joy when ye fall into divers temptations;

3 Knowing *this*, that the trying of your faith worketh patience.

4 But let patience have *her* perfect work, that ye may be perfect and entire, wanting nothing.

5 If any of you lack wisdom, let him ask of אֱלֹהִים, that giveth to all *men* liberally, and upbraideth not; and it shall be given him.

6 But let him ask in faith, nothing wavering. For he that wavereth is like a wave of the sea driven with the wind and tossed.

7 For let not that man think that he shall receive any thing of the Lord.

8 A double minded man *is* unstable in all his ways.

9 Let the brother of low degree rejoice in that he is exalted:

10 But the rich, in that he is made low: because as the flower of the grass he shall pass away.

11 For the sun is no sooner risen with a burning heat, but it withereth the grass, and the flower thereof falleth, and the grace of the fashion of it perisheth: so also shall the rich man fade away in his ways.

12 Blessed *is* the man that endureth temptation: for when he is tried, he shall receive the crown of life, which the Lord hath promised to them that love him.

13 Let no man say when he is tempted, I am tempted of אֱלֹהִים: for אֱלֹהִים cannot be tempted with evil, neither tempteth he any man:

14 But every man is tempted, when he is drawn away of his own lust, and enticed.

15 Then when lust hath conceived, it bringeth forth sin: and sin, when it is finished, bringeth forth death.

16 Do not err, my beloved brethren.

17 Every good gift and every perfect gift is from above, and cometh down from the Father of lights, with whom is no variableness, neither shadow of turning.

18 Of his own will begat he us with the word of truth, that we should be a kind of firstfruits of his creatures.

19 Wherefore, my beloved brethren, let every man be swift to hear, slow to speak, slow to wrath:

20 For the wrath of man worketh not the righteousness of אֱלֹהִים.

21 Wherefore lay apart all filthiness and superfluity of naughtiness, and receive with meekness the engrafted word, which is able to save your souls.

22 But be ye doers of the word, and not hearers only, deceiving your own selves.

23 For if any be a hearer of the word, and not a doer, he is like unto a man beholding his natural face in a glass:

24 For he beholdeth himself, and goeth his way, and straightway forgetteth what manner of man he was.

25 But whoso looketh into the perfect law of liberty, and continueth *therein*, he being not a forgetful hearer, but a doer of the work, this man shall be blessed in his deed.

26 If any man among you seem to be religious, and bridleth not his tongue, but deceiveth his own heart, this man's religion *is* vain.

27 Pure religion and undefiled before אֱלֹהִים and the Father is this, To visit the fatherless and widows in their affliction, *and* to keep himself unspotted from the world.

CHAPTER 2

MY brethren, have not the faith of our Lord Yashiyah Christ, *the Lord* of glory, with respect of persons.

2 For if there come unto your assembly a man with a gold ring, in goodly apparel, and there come in also a poor man in vile raiment;

3 And ye have respect to him that weareth the gay clothing, and say unto him, Sit thou here in a good place; and say to the poor, Stand thou there, or sit here under my footstool:

4 Are ye not then partial in yourselves, and are become judges of evil thoughts?

5 Hearken, my beloved brethren, Hath not אֱלֹהִים chosen the poor of this world rich in faith, and heirs of the kingdom which he hath promised to them that love him?

6 But ye have despised the poor. Do not rich men oppress you, and draw you before the judgment seats?

7 Do not they blaspheme that worthy name by the which ye are called?

8 If ye fulfil the royal law according to the scripture, Thou shalt love thy neighbour as thyself, ye do well:

9 But if ye have respect to persons, ye commit sin, and are convinced of the law as transgressors.

10 For whosoever shall keep the whole law, and yet offend in one *point*, he is guilty of all.

11 For he that said, Do not commit adultery, said also, Do not kill. Now if thou commit no adultery, yet if thou kill, thou art become a

transgressor of the law.

12 So speak ye, and so do, as they that shall be judged by the law of liberty.

13 For he shall have judgment without mercy, that hath shewed no mercy; and mercy rejoiceth against judgment.

14 What *doth it* profit, my brethren, though a man say he hath faith, and have not works? can faith save him?

15 If a brother or sister be naked, and destitute of daily food,

16 And one of you say unto them, Depart in peace, be *ye* warmed and filled; notwithstanding ye give them not those things which are needful to the body; what *doth it* profit?

17 Even so faith, if it hath not works, is dead, being alone.

18 Yea, a man may say, Thou hast faith, and I have works: shew me thy faith without thy works, and I will shew thee my faith by my works.

19 Thou believest that there is one אֱלֹהִים; thou doest well: the devils also believe, and tremble.

20 But wilt thou know, O vain man, that faith without works is dead?

21 Was not Abraham our father justified by works, when he had offered Isaac his son upon the altar?

22 Seest thou how faith wrought with his works, and by works was faith made perfect?

23 And the scripture was fulfilled which saith, Abraham believed אֱלֹהִים, and it was imputed unto him for righteousness: and he was called the Friend of אֱלֹהִים.

24 Ye see then how that by works a man is justified, and not by faith only.

25 Likewise also was not Rahab the harlot justified by works, when she had received the messengers, and had sent *them* out another way?

26 For as the body without the spirit is dead, so faith without works is dead also.

CHAPTER 3

MY brethren, be not many masters, knowing that we shall receive the greater condemnation.

2 For in many things we offend all. If any man offend not in word, the same *is* a perfect man, *and* able also to bridle the whole body.

3 Behold, we put bits in the horses' mouths, that they may obey us; and we turn about their whole body.

4 Behold also the ships, which though *they be* so great, and *are* driven of fierce winds, yet are they turned about with a very small helm, whithersoever the governor listeth.

5 Even so the tongue is a little member, and boasteth great things. Behold, how great a matter a little fire kindleth!

6 And the tongue *is* a fire, a world of iniquity: so is the tongue among our members, that it defileth the whole body, and setteth on fire the course of nature; and it is set on fire of hell.

7 For every kind of beasts, and of birds, and of serpents, and of things in the sea, is tamed, and hath been tamed of mankind:

8 But the tongue can no man tame; *it is* an unruly evil, full of deadly poison.

9 Therewith bless we אֱלֹהִים, even the Father; and therewith curse we men, which are made after the similitude of אֱלֹהִים.

10 Out of the same mouth proceedeth blessing and cursing. My brethren, these things ought not so to be.

11 Doth a fountain send forth at the same place sweet *water* and bitter?

12 Can the fig tree, my brethren, bear olive berries? either a vine, figs? so *can* no fountain both yield salt water and fresh.

13 Who *is* a wise man and endued with knowledge among you? let him shew out of a good conversation his works with meekness of wisdom.

14 But if ye have bitter envying and strife in your hearts, glory not, and lie not against the truth.

15 This wisdom descendeth not from above, but *is* earthly, sensual, devilish.

16 For where envying and strife *is*, there *is* confusion and every evil work.

17 But the wisdom that is from above is first pure, then peaceable, gentle, *and* easy to be intreated, full of mercy and good fruits, without partiality, and without hypocrisy.

18 And the fruit of righteousness is sown in peace of them that make peace.

CHAPTER 4

FROM whence *come* wars and fightings among you? *come they* not hence, *even* of your lusts that war in your members?

2 Ye lust, and have not: ye kill, and desire to have, and cannot obtain: ye fight and war, yet ye have not, because ye ask not.

3 Ye ask, and receive not, because ye ask amiss, that ye may consume *it* upon your lusts.

4 Ye adulterers and adulteresses, know ye not that the friendship of the world is enmity with אֱלֹהִים? whosoever therefore will be a friend of the world is the enemy of אֱלֹהִים.

5 Do ye think that the scripture saith in vain, The spirit that dwelleth in us lusteth to envy?

6 But he giveth more grace. Wherefore he saith, אֱלֹהִים resisteth the proud, but giveth grace unto the humble.

7 Submit yourselves therefore to אֱלֹהִים. Resist the devil, and he will flee from you.

8 Draw nigh to אֱלֹהִים, and he will draw nigh to you. Cleanse *your* hands, *ye* sinners; and purify *your* hearts, *ye* double minded.

9 Be afflicted, and mourn, and weep: let your laughter be turned to mourning, and *your* joy to heaviness.

10 Humble yourselves in the sight of the Lord, and he shall lift you up.

11 Speak not evil one of another, brethren. He that speaketh evil of *his* brother, and judgeth his brother, speaketh evil of the law, and judgeth the law: but if thou judge the law, thou art not a doer of the law, but a judge.

12 There is one lawgiver, who is able to save and to destroy: who art thou that judgest another?

13 Go to now, ye that say, To day or to morrow we will go into such a city, and continue there a year, and buy and sell, and get gain:

14 Whereas ye know not what *shall be* on the morrow. For what *is* your life? It is even a vapour, that appeareth for a little time, and then vanisheth away.

15 For that ye *ought* to say, If the Lord will, we shall live, and do this, or that.

16 But now ye rejoice in your boastings: all such rejoicing is evil.

17 Therefore to him that knoweth to do good, and doeth *it* not, to him it is sin.

CHAPTER 5

GO to now, *ye* rich men, weep and howl for your miseries that shall come upon *you.*

2 Your riches are corrupted, and your garments are motheaten.

3 Your gold and silver is cankered; and the rust of them shall be a witness against you, and shall eat your flesh as it were fire. Ye have heaped treasure together for the last days.

4 Behold, the hire of the labourers who have reaped down your fields, which is of you kept back by fraud, crieth: and the cries of them which have reaped are entered into the ears of the Lord of sabaoth.

5 Ye have lived in pleasure on the earth, and been wanton; ye have nourished your hearts, as in a day of slaughter.

6 Ye have condemned *and* killed the just; *and* he doth not resist you.

7 Be patient therefore, brethren, unto the coming of the Lord. Behold, the husbandman waiteth for the precious fruit of the earth, and hath long patience for it, until he receive the early and latter rain.

8 Be ye also patient; stablish your hearts: for the coming of the Lord draweth nigh.

9 Grudge not one against another, brethren, lest ye be condemned: behold, the judge standeth before the door.

10 Take, my brethren, the prophets, who have spoken in the name of the Lord, for an example of suffering affliction, and of patience.

11 Behold, we count them happy which endure. Ye have heard of the patience of Job, and have seen the end of the Lord; that the Lord is very pitiful, and of tender mercy.

12 But above all things, my brethren, swear not, neither by heaven, neither by the earth, neither by any other oath: but let your yea be yea; and *your* nay, nay; lest ye fall into condemnation.

13 Is any among you afflicted? let him pray. Is any merry? let him sing psalms.

14 Is any sick among you? let him call for the elders of the church; and let them pray over him, anointing him with oil in the name of the Lord:

15 And the prayer of faith shall save the sick, and the Lord shall raise him up; and if he have committed sins, they shall be forgiven him.

16 Confess *your* faults one to another, and pray one for another, that ye may be healed. The effectual fervent prayer of a righteous man availeth much.

17 Elias was a man subject to like passions as we are, and he prayed earnestly that it might not rain: and it rained not on the earth by the space of three years and six months.

18 And he prayed again, and the heaven gave rain, and the earth brought forth her fruit.

19 Brethren, if any of you do err from the truth, and one convert him;

20 Let him know, that he which converteth the sinner from the error of his way shall save a soul from death, and shall hide a multitude of sins.

THE FIRST EPISTLE GENERAL OF
PETER.

CHAPTER 1

PETER, an apostle of Yashiyah Christ, to the strangers scattered throughout Pontus, Galatia, Cappadocia, Asia, and Bithynia,

2 Elect according to the foreknowledge of אֱלֹהִים the Father, through sanctification of the Spirit, unto obedience and sprinkling of the blood of Yashiyah Christ: Grace unto you, and peace, be multiplied.

3 Blessed *be* the אֱלֹהִים and Father of our Lord Yashiyah Christ, which according to his abundant mercy hath begotten us again unto a lively hope by the resurrection of Yashiyah Christ from the dead,

4 To an inheritance incorruptible, and undefiled, and that fadeth not away, reserved in heaven for you,

5 Who are kept by the power of אֱלֹהִים through faith unto salvation ready to be revealed in the last time.

6 Wherein ye greatly rejoice, though now for a season, if need be, ye are in heaviness through manifold temptations:

7 That the trial of your faith, being much more precious than of gold that perisheth, though it be tried with fire, might be found unto praise and honour and glory at the appearing of Yashiyah Christ:

8 Whom having not seen, ye love; in whom, though now ye see *him* not, yet believing, ye rejoice with joy unspeakable and full of glory:

9 Receiving the end of your faith, *even* the salvation of *your* souls.

10 Of which salvation the prophets have inquired and searched diligently, who prophesied of the grace *that should come* unto you:

11 Searching what, or what manner of time the Spirit of Christ which was in them did signify, when it testified beforehand the sufferings of Christ, and the glory that should follow.

12 Unto whom it was revealed, that not unto themselves, but unto us they did minister the things, which are now reported unto you by them that have preached the gospel unto you with the Holy Ghost sent down from heaven; which things the angels desire to look into.

13 Wherefore gird up the loins of your mind, be sober, and hope to the end for the grace that is to be brought unto you at the revelation of Yashiyah Christ;

14 As obedient children, not fashioning yourselves according to the former lusts in your ignorance:

15 But as he which hath called you is holy, so be ye holy in all manner of conversation;

16 Because it is written, Be ye holy; for I am holy.

17 And if ye call on the Father, who without respect of persons judgeth according to every man's work, pass the time of your sojourning *here* in fear:

18 Forasmuch as ye know that ye were not redeemed with corruptible things, *as* silver and gold, from your vain conversation *received* by tradition from your fathers;

19 But with the precious blood of Christ, as of a lamb without blemish and without spot:

20 Who verily was foreordained before the foundation of the world, but was manifest in these last times for you,

21 Who by him do believe in אֱלֹהִים, that raised him up from the dead, and gave him glory; that your faith and hope might be in אֱלֹהִים.

22 Seeing ye have purified your souls in obeying the truth through the Spirit unto unfeigned love of the brethren, *see that ye* love one another with a pure heart fervently:

23 Being born again, not of corruptible seed, but of incorruptible, by the word of אֱלֹהִים, which liveth and abideth for ever.

24 For all flesh *is* as grass, and all the glory of man as the flower of grass. The grass withereth, and the flower thereof falleth away:

25 But the word of the Lord endureth for ever. And this is the word which by the gospel is preached unto you.

WHEREFORE laying aside all malice, and all guile, and hypocrisies, and envies, and all evil speakings,

2 As newborn babes, desire the sincere milk of the word, that ye may grow thereby:

3 If so be ye have tasted that the Lord *is* gracious.

4 To whom coming, *as unto* a living stone, disallowed indeed of men, but chosen of אֱלֹהִים, *and* precious,

5 Ye also, as lively stones, are built up a spiritual house, an holy priesthood, to offer up spiritual sacrifices, acceptable to אֱלֹהִים by Yashiyah Christ.

6 Wherefore also it is contained in the scripture, Behold, I lay in Sion a chief corner stone, elect, precious: and he that believeth on him shall not be confounded.

7 Unto you therefore which believe *he is* precious: but unto them which be disobedient, the stone which the builders disallowed, the same is made the head of the corner,

8 And a stone of stumbling, and a rock of offence, *even to them* which stumble at the word, being disobedient: whereunto also they were appointed.

9 But ye *are* a chosen generation, a royal priesthood, an holy nation, a peculiar people; that ye should shew forth the praises of him who hath called you out of darkness into his marvellous light:

10 Which in time past *were* not a people, but *are* now the people of אֱלֹהִים: which had not obtained mercy, but now have obtained mercy.

11 Dearly beloved, I beseech *you* as strangers and pilgrims, abstain from fleshly lusts, which war against the soul;

12 Having your conversation honest among the Gentiles: that, whereas they speak against you as evildoers, they may by *your* good works, which they shall behold, glorify אֱלֹהִים in the day of visitation.

13 Submit yourselves to every ordinance of man for the Lord's sake: whether it be to the king, as supreme;

14 Or unto governors, as unto them that are sent by him for the punishment of evildoers, and for the praise of them that do well.

15 For so is the will of אֱלֹהִים, that with well doing ye may put to silence the ignorance of foolish men:

16 As free, and not using *your* liberty for a cloke of maliciousness, but as the servants of אֱלֹהִים.

17 Honour all *men.* Love the brotherhood. Fear אֱלֹהִים. Honour the king.

18 Servants, *be* subject to *your* masters with all fear; not only to the good and gentle, but also to the froward.

19 For this *is* thankworthy, if a man for conscience toward אֱלֹהִים endure grief, suffering wrongfully.

20 For what glory *is it,* if, when ye be buffeted for your faults, ye shall take it patiently? but if, when ye do well, and suffer *for it,* ye take it patiently, this *is* acceptable with אֱלֹהִים.

21 For even hereunto were ye called: because Christ also suffered for us, leaving us an example, that ye should follow his steps:

22 Who did no sin, neither was guile found in his mouth:

23 Who, when he was reviled, reviled not again; when he suffered, he threatened not; but committed *himself* to him that judgeth righteously:

24 Who his own self bare our sins in his own body on the tree, that we, being dead to sins, should live unto righteousness: by whose stripes ye were healed.

25 For ye were as sheep going astray; but are now returned unto the Shepherd and Bishop of your souls.

CHAPTER 3

LIKEWISE, ye wives, *be* in subjection to your own husbands; that, if any obey not the word, they also may without the word be won by the conversation of the wives;

2 While they behold your chaste conversation *coupled* with fear.

3 Whose adorning let it not be that outward *adorning* of plaiting the hair, and of wearing of gold, or of putting on of apparel;

4 But *let it be* the hidden man of the heart, in that which is not corruptible, *even the ornament* of a meek and quiet spirit, which is in the sight of אֱלֹהִים of great price.

5 For after this manner in the old time the holy women also, who trusted in אֱלֹהִים, adorned themselves, being in subjection unto their own husbands:

6 Even as Sara obeyed Abraham, calling him lord: whose daughters ye are, as long as ye do well, and are not afraid with any amazement.

7 Likewise, ye husbands, dwell with *them* according to knowledge, giving honour unto the wife, as unto the weaker vessel, and as being heirs together of the grace of life; that your prayers be not hindered.

8 Finally, *be ye* all of one mind, having compassion one of another, love as brethren, *be* pitiful, *be* courteous:

9 Not rendering evil for evil, or railing for railing: but contrariwise blessing; knowing that ye are thereunto called, that ye should inherit a blessing.

10 For he that will love life, and see good days, let him refrain his tongue from evil, and his lips that they speak no guile:

11 Let him eschew evil, and do good; let him seek peace, and ensue it.

12 For the eyes of the Lord *are* over the righteous, and his ears *are open* unto their prayers: but the face of the Lord *is* against them that do evil.

13 And who *is* he that will harm you, if ye be followers of that which is good?

14 But and if ye suffer for righteousness' sake, happy *are ye:* and be not afraid of their terror, neither be troubled;

15 But sanctify the Lord אֱלֹהִים in your hearts: and *be* ready always to *give* an answer to every man that asketh you a reason of the hope that is in you with meekness and fear:

16 Having a good conscience; that, whereas they speak evil of you, as of evildoers, they may be ashamed that falsely accuse your good conversation in Christ.

17 For *it is* better, if the will of אֱלֹהִים be so, that ye suffer for well doing, than for evil doing.

18 For Christ also hath once suffered for sins, the just for the unjust, that he might bring us to אֱלֹהִים, being put to death in the flesh, but quickened by the Spirit:

19 By which also he went and preached unto the spirits in prison;

20 Which sometime were disobedient, when once the longsuffering of אֱלֹהִים waited in the days of Noah, while the ark was a preparing, wherein few, that is, eight souls were saved by water.

21 The like figure whereunto *even* baptism doth also now save us (not the putting away of the filth of the flesh, but the answer of a

good conscience toward אֱלֹהִים.) by the resurrection of Yashiyah Christ:

22 Who is gone into heaven, and is on the right hand of אֱלֹהִים; angels and authorities and powers being made subject unto him.

CHAPTER 4

FORASMUCH then as Christ hath suffered for us in the flesh, arm yourselves likewise with the same mind: for he that hath suffered in the flesh hath ceased from sin;

2 That he no longer should live the rest of *his* time in the flesh to the lusts of men, but to the will of אֱלֹהִים.

3 For the time past of *our* life may suffice us to have wrought the will of the Gentiles, when we walked in lasciviousness, lusts, excess of wine, revellings, banquetings, and abominable idolatries:

4 Wherein they think it strange that ye run not with *them* to the same excess of riot, speaking evil of *you*:

5 Who shall give account to him that is ready to judge the quick and the dead.

6 For for this cause was the gospel preached also to them that are dead, that they might be judged according to men in the flesh, but live according to אֱלֹהִים in the spirit.

7 But the end of all things is at hand: be ye therefore sober, and watch unto prayer.

8 And above all things have fervent charity among yourselves: for charity shall cover the multitude of sins.

9 Use hospitality one to another without grudging.

10 As every man hath received the gift, *even so* minister the same one to another, as good stewards of the manifold grace of אֱלֹהִים.

11 If any man speak, *let him speak* as the oracles of אֱלֹהִים; if any man minister, *let him do it* as of the ability which אֱלֹהִים giveth: that אֱלֹהִים in all things may be glorified through Yashiyah Christ, to whom be praise and dominion for ever and ever. Amen.

12 Beloved, think it not strange concerning the fiery trial which is to try you, as though some strange thing happened unto you:

13 But rejoice, inasmuch as ye are partakers of Christ's sufferings; that, when his glory shall be revealed, ye may be glad also with exceeding joy.

14 If ye be reproached for the name of Christ, happy *are ye*; for the spirit of glory and of אֱלֹהִים resteth upon you: on their part he is evil spoken of, but on your part he is glorified.

15 But let none of you suffer as a murderer, or *as* a thief, or *as* an evildoer, or as a busybody in other men's matters.

16 Yet if *any man suffer* as a Christian, let him not be ashamed; but let him glorify אֱלֹהִים on this behalf.

17 For the time *is come* that judgment must begin at the house of אֱלֹהִים: and if *it* first *begin* at us, what shall the end *be* of them that obey not the gospel of אֱלֹהִים?

18 And if the righteous scarcely be saved, where shall the ungodly and the sinner appear?

19 Wherefore let them that suffer according to the will of אֱלֹהִים commit the keeping of their souls *to him* in well doing, as unto a faithful Creator.

CHAPTER 5

THE elders which are among you I exhort, who am also an elder, and a witness of the sufferings of Christ, and also a partaker of the glory that shall be revealed:

2 Feed the flock of אֱלֹהִים which is among you, taking the oversight *thereof*, not by constraint, but willingly; not for filthy lucre, but of a ready mind;

3 Neither as being lords over אֱלֹהִים*'s* heritage, but being ensamples to the flock.

4 And when the chief Shepherd shall appear, ye shall receive a crown of glory that fadeth not away.

5 Likewise, ye younger, submit yourselves unto the elder. Yea, all *of you* be subject one to another, and be clothed with humility: for אֱלֹהִים resisteth the proud, and giveth grace to the humble.

6 Humble yourselves therefore under the mighty hand of אֱלֹהִים, that he may exalt you in due time:

7 Casting all your care upon him; for he careth for you.

8 Be sober, be vigilant; because your adversary the devil, as a roaring lion, walketh about, seeking whom he may devour:

9 Whom resist stedfast in the faith, knowing that the same afflictions are accomplished in your brethren that are in the world.

10 But the אֱלֹהִים of all grace, who hath called us unto his eternal glory by Christ Yashiyah, after that ye have suffered a while, make you perfect, stablish, strengthen, settle *you*.

11 To him *be* glory and dominion for ever and ever. Amen.

12 By Silvanus, a faithful brother unto you, as I suppose, I have written briefly, exhorting, and testifying that this is the true grace of אֱלֹהִים wherein ye stand.

13 The *church that is* at Babylon, elected together with *you*, saluteth you; and *so doth* Marcus my son.

14 Greet ye one another with a kiss of charity. Peace *be* with you all that are in Christ Yashiyah. Amen.

THE SECOND EPISTLE GENERAL OF

PETER.

CHAPTER 1

SIMON Peter, a servant and an apostle of Yashiyah Christ, to them that have obtained like precious faith with us through the righteousness of אֱלֹהִים and our Saviour Yashiyah Christ:

2 Grace and peace be multiplied unto you through the knowledge of אֱלֹהִים, and of Yashiyah our Lord,

3 According as his divine power hath given unto us all things that *pertain* unto life and godliness, through the knowledge of him that hath called us to glory and virtue:

4 Whereby are given unto us exceeding great and precious promises: that by these ye might be partakers of the divine nature, having escaped the corruption that is in the world through lust.

5 And beside this, giving all diligence, add to your faith virtue; and to virtue knowledge;

6 And to knowledge temperance; and to temperance patience; and to patience godliness;

7 And to godliness brotherly kindness; and to brotherly kindness charity.

8 For if these things be in you, and abound, they make *you that ye shall* neither *be* barren nor unfruitful in the knowledge of our Lord Yashiyah Christ.

9 But he that lacketh these things is blind, and cannot see afar off, and hath forgotten that he was purged from his old sins.

10 Wherefore the rather, brethren, give diligence to make your calling and election sure: for if ye do these things, ye shall never fall:

11 For so an entrance shall be ministered unto you abundantly into the everlasting kingdom of our Lord and Saviour Yashiyah Christ.

12 Wherefore I will not be negligent to put you always in remembrance of these things, though ye know *them*, and be established in the present truth.

13 Yea, I think it meet, as long as I am in this tabernacle, to stir you up by putting *you* in remembrance;

14 Knowing that shortly I must put off *this* my tabernacle, even as our Lord Yashiyah Christ hath shewed me.

15 Moreover I will endeavour that ye may be able after my decease to have these things always in remembrance.

16 For we have not followed cunningly devised fables, when we made known unto you the power and coming of our Lord Yashiyah Christ, but were eyewitnesses of his majesty.

17 For he received from אֱלֹהִים the Father honour and glory, when there came such a voice to him from the excellent glory, This is my beloved Son, in whom I am well pleased.

18 And this voice which came from heaven we heard, when we were with him in the holy mount.

19 We have also a more sure word of prophecy; whereunto ye do well that ye take heed, as unto a light that shineth in a dark place, until the day dawn, and the day star arise in your hearts:

20 Knowing this first, that no prophecy of the scripture is of any private interpretation.

21 For the prophecy came not in old time by the will of man: but holy men of אֱלֹהִים spake *as they were* moved by the Holy Ghost.

CHAPTER 2

BUT there were false prophets also among the people, even as there shall be false teachers among you, who privily shall bring in damnable heresies, even denying the Lord that bought them, and bring upon themselves swift destruction.

2 And many shall follow their pernicious ways; by reason of whom the way of truth shall be evil spoken of.

3 And through covetousness shall they with feigned words make merchandise of you: whose judgment now of a long time lingereth not, and their damnation slumbereth not.

4 For if אֱלֹהִים spared not the angels that sinned, but cast *them* down to hell, and delivered *them* into chains of darkness, to be reserved unto judgment;

5 And spared not the old world, but saved Noah the eighth *person*, a preacher of righteousness, bringing in the flood upon the world of the ungodly;

6 And turning the cities of Sodom and Gomorrha into ashes condemned *them* with an overthrow, making *them* an ensample unto those that after should live ungodly;

7 And delivered just Lot, vexed with the filthy conversation of the wicked:

8 (For that righteous man dwelling among them, in seeing and hearing, vexed *his* righteous soul from day to day with *their* unlawful deeds;)

9 The Lord knoweth how to deliver the godly out of temptations, and to reserve the unjust unto the day of judgment to be punished:

10 But chiefly them that walk after the flesh in the lust of uncleanness, and despise government. Presumptuous *are they*, selfwilled, they are not afraid to speak evil of dignities.

11 Whereas angels, which are greater in power and might, bring not railing accusation against them before the Lord.

12 But these, as natural brute beasts, made to be taken and destroyed, speak evil of the things that they understand not; and shall utterly perish in their own corruption;

13 And shall receive the reward of unrighteousness, *as* they that count it pleasure to riot in the day time. Spots *they are* and blemishes, sporting themselves with their own deceivings while they feast with you;

14 Having eyes full of adultery, and that cannot cease from sin; beguiling unstable souls: an heart they have exercised with covetous practices; cursed children:

15 Which have forsaken the right way, and are gone astray, following the way of Balaam *the son* of Bosor, who loved the wages of unrighteousness;

16 But was rebuked for his iniquity: the dumb ass speaking with man's voice forbad the madness of the prophet.

17 These are wells without water, clouds that are carried with a tempest; to whom the mist of darkness is reserved for ever.

18 For when they speak great swelling *words* of vanity, they allure through the lusts of the flesh, *through much* wantonness, those that were clean escaped from them who live in error.

19 While they promise them liberty, they themselves are the servants of corruption: for of whom a man is overcome, of the same is he brought in bondage.

20 For if after they have escaped the pollutions of the world through the knowledge of the Lord and Saviour Yashiyah Christ, they are again entangled therein, and overcome, the latter end is worse with them than the beginning.

21 For it had been better for them not to have known the way of righteousness, than, after they have known *it*, to turn from the holy commandment delivered unto them.

22 But it is happened unto them according to the true proverb, The dog *is* turned to his own vomit again; and the sow that was washed to her wallowing in the mire.

CHAPTER 3

THIS second epistle, beloved, I now write unto you; in *both* which I stir up your pure minds by way of remembrance:

2 That ye may be mindful of the words which were spoken before by the holy prophets, and of the commandment of us the apostles of the Lord and Saviour:

3 Knowing this first, that there shall come in the last days scoffers, walking after their own lusts,

4 And saying, Where is the promise of his coming? for since the fathers fell asleep, all things continue as *they were* from the beginning of the creation.

5 For this they willingly are ignorant of, that by the word of אֱלֹהִים the heavens were of old, and the earth standing out of the water and in the water:

6 Whereby the world that then was, being overflowed with water, perished:

7 But the heavens and the earth, which are now, by the same word are kept in store, reserved unto fire against the day of judgment and perdition of ungodly men.

8 But, beloved, be not ignorant of this one thing, that one day *is* with the Lord as a thousand years, and a thousand years as one day.

9 The Lord is not slack concerning his promise, as some men count slackness; but is longsuffering to us-ward, not willing that any should perish, but that all should come to repentance.

10 But the day of the Lord will come as a thief in the night; in the which the heavens shall pass away with a great noise, and the elements shall melt with fervent heat, the earth also and the works that are therein shall be burned up.

11 *Seeing* then *that* all these things shall be dissolved, what manner *of persons* ought ye to be in *all* holy conversation and godliness,

12 Looking for and hasting unto the coming of the day of אֱלֹהִים, wherein the heavens being on fire shall be dissolved, and the elements shall melt with fervent heat?

13 Nevertheless we, according to his promise, look for new heavens and a new earth, wherein dwelleth righteousness.

14 Wherefore, beloved, seeing that ye look for such things, be diligent that ye may be found of him in peace, without spot, and blameless.

15 And account *that* the longsuffering of our Lord *is* salvation; even as our beloved brother Paul also according to the wisdom given unto him hath written unto you;

16 As also in all *his* epistles, speaking in them of these things; in which are some things hard to be understood, which they that are unlearned and unstable wrest, as *they do* also the other scriptures, unto their own destruction.

17 Ye therefore, beloved, seeing ye know *these things* before, beware lest ye also, being led away with the error of the wicked, fall from your own stedfastness.

18 But grow in grace, and *in* the knowledge of our Lord and Saviour Yashiyah Christ. To him *be* glory both now and for ever. Amen.

THE FIRST EPISTLE GENERAL OF
JOHN.

CHAPTER 1

THAT which was from the beginning, which we have heard, which we have seen with our eyes, which we have looked upon, and our hands have handled, of the Word of life;

2 (For the life was manifested, and we have seen *it*, and bear witness, and shew unto you that eternal life, which was with the Father, and was manifested unto us;)

3 That which we have seen and heard declare we unto you, that ye also may have fellowship with us: and truly our fellowship *is* with the Father, and with his Son Yashiyah Christ.

4 And these things write we unto you, that your joy may be full.

5 This then is the message which we have heard of him, and declare unto you, that אֱלֹהִים is light, and in him is no darkness at all.

6 If we say that we have fellowship with him, and walk in darkness, we lie, and do not the truth:

7 But if we walk in the light, as he is in the light, we have fellowship one with another, and the blood of Yashiyah Christ his Son cleanseth us from all sin.

8 If we say that we have no sin, we deceive ourselves, and the truth is not in us.

9 If we confess our sins, he is faithful and just to forgive us *our* sins, and to cleanse us from all unrighteousness.

10 If we say that we have not sinned, we make him a liar, and his word is not in us.

CHAPTER 2

MY little children, these things write I unto you, that ye sin not. And if any man sin, we have an advocate with the Father, Yashiyah Christ the righteous:

2 And he is the propitiation for our sins: and not for ours only, but also for *the sins of* the whole world.

3 And hereby we do know that we know him, if we keep his commandments.

4 He that saith, I know him, and keepeth not his commandments, is a liar, and the truth is not in him.

5 But whoso keepeth his word, in him verily is the love of אֱלֹהִים perfected: hereby know we that we are in him.

6 He that saith he abideth in him ought himself also so to walk, even as he walked.

7 Brethren, I write no new commandment unto you, but an old commandment which ye had from the beginning. The old commandment is the word which ye have heard from the beginning.

8 Again, a new commandment I write unto you, which thing is true in him and in you: because the darkness is past, and the true light now shineth.

9 He that saith he is in the light, and hateth his brother, is in darkness even until now.

10 He that loveth his brother abideth in the light, and there is none occasion of stumbling in him.

11 But he that hateth his brother is in darkness, and walketh in darkness, and knoweth not whither he goeth, because that darkness hath blinded his eyes.

12 I write unto you, little children, because your sins are forgiven you for his name's sake.

13 I write unto you, fathers, because ye have known him *that is* from the beginning. I write unto you, young men, because ye have overcome the wicked one. I write unto you, little children, because ye have known the Father.

14 I have written unto you, fathers, because ye have known him *that is* from the beginning. I have written unto you, young men, because ye are strong, and the word of אֱלֹהִים abideth in you, and ye have overcome the wicked one.

15 Love not the world, neither the things *that are* in the world. If any man love the world, the love of the Father is not in him.

16 For all that *is* in the world, the lust of the flesh, and the lust of the eyes, and the pride of life, is not of the Father, but is of the world.

17 And the world passeth away, and the lust thereof: but he that doeth the will of אֱלֹהִים abideth for ever.

18 Little children, it is the last time: and as ye have heard that antichrist shall come, even now are there many antichrists; whereby we know that it is the last time.

19 They went out from us, but they were not of us; for if they had been of us, they would *no doubt* have continued with us: but *they went out*, that they might be made manifest that they were not all of us.

20 But ye have an unction from the Holy One, and ye know all things.

21 I have not written unto you because ye know not the truth, but because ye know it, and that no lie is of the truth.

22 Who is a liar but he that denieth that Yashiyah is the Christ? He is antichrist, that denieth the Father and the Son.

23 Whosoever denieth the Son, the same hath not the Father: [*but*] *he that acknowledgeth the Son hath the Father also.*

24 Let that therefore abide in you, which ye have heard from the beginning. If that which ye have heard from the beginning shall remain in you, ye also shall continue in the Son, and in the Father.

25 And this is the promise that he hath promised us, *even* eternal life.

26 These *things* have I written unto you concerning them that seduce you.

27 But the anointing which ye have received of him abideth in you, and ye need not that any man teach you: but as the same anointing teacheth you of all things, and is truth, and is no lie, and even as it hath taught you, ye shall abide in him.

28 And now, little children, abide in him; that, when he shall appear, we may have confidence, and not be ashamed before him at his coming.

29 If ye know that he is righteous, ye know that every one that doeth righteousness is born of him.

CHAPTER 3

BEHOLD, what manner of love the Father hath bestowed upon us, that we should be called the sons of אֱלֹהִים: therefore the world knoweth us not, because it knew him not.

2 Beloved, now are we the sons of אֱלֹהִים, and it doth not yet appear what we shall be: but we know that, when he shall appear, we shall be like him; for we shall see him as he is.

3 And every man that hath this hope in him purifieth himself, even as he is pure.

4 Whosoever committeth sin transgresseth also the law: for sin is the transgression of the law.

5 And ye know that he was manifested to take away our sins; and in him is no sin.

6 Whosoever abideth in him sinneth not: whosoever sinneth hath not seen him, neither known him.

7 Little children, let no man deceive you: he that doeth righteousness is righteous, even as he is righteous.

8 He that committeth sin is of the devil; for the devil sinneth from the beginning. For this purpose the Son of אֱלֹהִים was manifested, that he might destroy the works of the devil.

9 Whosoever is born of אֱלֹהִים doth not commit sin; for his seed remaineth in him: and he cannot sin, because he is born of אֱלֹהִים.

10 In this the children of אֱלֹהִים are manifest, and the children of the devil: whosoever doeth not righteousness is not of אֱלֹהִים, neither he that loveth not his brother.

11 For this is the message that ye heard from the beginning, that we should love one another.

12 Not as Cain, *who* was of that wicked one, and slew his brother. And wherefore slew he him? Because his own works were evil, and his brother's righteous.

13 Marvel not, my brethren, if the world hate you.

14 We know that we have passed from death unto life, because we love the brethren. He that loveth not *his* brother abideth in death.

15 Whosoever hateth his brother is a murderer: and ye know that no murderer hath eternal life abiding in him.

16 Hereby perceive we the love *of* אֱל, because he laid down his life for us: and we ought to lay down *our* lives for the brethren.

17 But whoso hath this world's good, and seeth his brother have need, and shutteth up his bowels *of compassion* from him, how dwelleth the love of אֱלֹהִים in him?

18 My little children, let us not love in word, neither in tongue; but in deed and in truth.

19 And hereby we know that we are of the truth, and shall assure our hearts before him.

20 For if our heart condemn us, אֱלֹהִים is greater than our heart, and knoweth all things.

21 Beloved, if our heart condemn us not, *then* have we confidence toward אֱלֹהִים.

22 And whatsoever we ask, we receive of him, because we keep his commandments, and do those things that are pleasing in his sight.

23 And this is his commandment, That we should believe on the name of his Son Yashiyah Christ, and love one another, as he gave us commandment.

24 And he that keepeth his commandments dwelleth in him, and he in him. And hereby we know that he abideth in us, by the Spirit which he hath given us.

CHAPTER 4

BELOVED, believe not every spirit, but try the spirits whether they are of אֱלֹהִים: because many false prophets are gone out into the world.

2 Hereby know ye the Spirit of אֱלֹהִים: Every spirit that confesseth that Yashiyah Christ is come in the flesh is of אֱל:

3 And every spirit that confesseth not that Yashiyah Christ is come in the flesh is not of אֱלֹהִים: and this is that *spirit* of antichrist, whereof ye have heard that it should come; and even now already is it in the world.

4 Ye are of אֱלֹהִים, little children, and have overcome them: because greater is he that is in you, than he that is in the world.

5 They are of the world: therefore speak they of the world, and the world heareth them.

6 We are of אֱל: he that knoweth אֱלֹהִים heareth us; he that is not of אֱלֹהִים heareth not us. Hereby know we the spirit of truth, and the spirit of error.

7 Beloved, let us love one another: for love is of אֱל; and every one that loveth is born of אֱלֹהִים, and knoweth אֱלֹהִים.

8 He that loveth not knoweth not אֱלֹהִים; for אֱלֹהִים is love.

9 In this was manifested the love of אֱלֹהִים toward us, because that אֱלֹהִים sent his only begotten Son into the world, that we might live through him.

10 Herein is love, not that we loved אֱלֹהִים, but that he loved us, and sent his Son *to be* the propitiation for our sins.

11 Beloved, if אֱלֹהִים so loved us, we ought also to love one another.

12 No man hath seen אֱלֹהִים at any time. If we love one another, אֱלֹהִים dwelleth in us, and his love is perfected in us.

13 Hereby know we that we dwell in him, and he in us, because he hath given us of his Spirit.

14 And we have seen and do testify that the Father sent the Son *to be* the Saviour of the world.

15 Whosoever shall confess that Yashiyah is the Son of אֱלֹהִים, אֱלֹהִים dwelleth in him, and he in אֱלֹהִים.

16 And we have known and believed the love that אֱלֹהִים hath to us. אֱלֹהִים is love; and he that dwelleth in love dwelleth in אֱלֹהִים, and אֱלֹהִים in him.

17 Herein is our love made perfect, that we may have boldness in the day of judgment: because as he is, so are we in this world.

18 There is no fear in love; but perfect love casteth out fear: because fear hath torment. He that feareth is not made perfect in love.

19 We love him, because he first loved us.

20 If a man say, I love אֱלֹהִים, and hateth his brother, he is a liar: for he that loveth not his brother whom he hath seen, how can he love אֱלֹהִים whom he hath not seen?

21 And this commandment have we from him, That he who loveth אֱלֹהִים love his brother also.

CHAPTER 5

WHOSOEVER believeth that Yashiyah is the Christ is born of אֱלֹהִים: and every one that loveth him that begat loveth him also that is begotten of him.

2 By this we know that we love the children of אֱלֹהִים, when we love אֱלֹהִים, and keep his commandments.

3 For this is the love of אֱלֹהִים, that we keep his commandments: and his commandments are not grievous.

4 For whatsoever is born of אֱלֹהִים overcometh the world: and this is the victory that overcometh the world, *even* our faith.

5 Who is he that overcometh the world, but he that believeth that Yashiyah is the Son of אֱלֹהִים?

6 This is he that came by water and blood, *even* Yashiyah Christ; not by water only, but by water and blood. And it is the Spirit that beareth witness, because the Spirit is truth.

7 For there are three that bear record in heaven, the Father, the Word, and the Holy Ghost: and these three are one.

8 And there are three that bear witness in earth, the spirit, and the water, and the blood: and these three agree in one.

9 If we receive the witness of men, the witness of אֱלֹהִים is greater: for this is the witness of אֱלֹהִים which he hath testified of his Son.

10 He that believeth on the Son of אֱלֹהִים hath the witness in himself: he that believeth not אֱלֹהִים hath made him a liar; because he believeth not the record that אֱלֹהִים gave of his Son.

11 And this is the record, that אֱלֹהִים hath given to us eternal life, and this life is in his Son.

12 He that hath the Son hath life; *and* he that hath not the Son of אֱלֹהִים hath not life.

13 These things have I written unto you that believe on the name of the Son of אֱלֹהִים; that ye may know that ye have eternal life, and that ye may believe on the name of the Son of אֱלֹהִים.

14 And this is the confidence that we have in him, that, if we ask any thing according to his will, he heareth us:

15 And if we know that he hear us, whatsoever we ask, we know that we have the petitions that we desired of him.

16 If any man see his brother sin a sin *which is* not unto death, he shall ask, and he shall give him life for them that sin not unto death. There is a sin unto death: I do not say that he shall pray for it.

17 All unrighteousness is sin: and there is a sin not unto death.

18 We know that whosoever is born of אֱלֹהִים sinneth not; but he that is begotten of אֱלֹהִים keepeth himself, and that wicked one toucheth him not.

19 *And* we know that we are of אֱלֹהִים, and the whole world lieth in wickedness.

20 And we know that the Son of אֱלֹהִים is come, and hath given us an understanding, that we may know him that is true, and we are in him that is true, *even* in his Son Yashiyah Christ. This is the true אֱלֹהִים, and eternal life.

21 Little children, keep yourselves from idols. Amen.

THE SECOND EPISTLE OF

JOHN.

CHAPTER 1

THE elder unto the elect lady and her children, whom I love in the truth; and not I only, but also all they that have known the truth;

2 For the truth's sake, which dwelleth in us, and shall be with us for ever.

3 Grace be with you, mercy, *and* peace, from אֱלֹהִים the Father, and from the Lord Yashiyah Christ, the Son of the Father, in truth and love.

4 I rejoiced greatly that I found of thy children walking in truth, as we have received a commandment from the Father.

5 And now I beseech thee, lady, not as though I wrote a new commandment unto thee, but that which we had from the beginning, that we love one another.

6 And this is love, that we walk after his commandments. This is the commandment, That, as ye have heard from the beginning, ye should walk in it.

7 For many deceivers are entered into the world, who confess not that Yashiyah Christ is come in the flesh. This is a deceiver and an antichrist.

8 Look to yourselves, that we lose not those things which we have wrought, but that we receive a full reward.

9 Whosoever transgresseth, and abideth not in the doctrine of Christ, hath not אֱלֹהִים. He that abideth in the doctrine of Christ, he hath both the Father and the Son.

10 If there come any unto you, and bring not this doctrine, receive him not into *your* house, neither bid him אֱלֹהִים speed:

11 For he that biddeth him אֱלֹהִים speed is partaker of his evil deeds.

12 Having many things to write unto you, I would not *write* with paper and ink: but I trust to come unto you, and speak face to face, that our joy may be full.

13 The children of thy elect sister greet thee. Amen.

THE THIRD EPISTLE OF

JOHN.

CHAPTER 1

THE elder unto the wellbeloved Gaius, whom I love in the truth.

2 Beloved, I wish above all things that thou mayest prosper and be in health, even as thy soul prospereth.

3 For I rejoiced greatly, when the brethren came and testified of the truth that is in thee, even as thou walkest in the truth.

4 I have no greater joy than to hear that my children walk in truth.

5 Beloved, thou doest faithfully whatsoever thou doest to the brethren, and to strangers;

6 Which have borne witness of thy charity before the church: whom if thou bring forward on their journey after a godly sort, thou shalt do well:

7 Because that for his name's sake they went forth, taking nothing of the Gentiles.

8 We therefore ought to receive such, that we might be fellowhelpers to the truth.

9 I wrote unto the church: but Diotrephes, who loveth to have the preeminence among them, receiveth us not.

10 Wherefore, if I come, I will remember his deeds which he doeth, prating against us with malicious words: and not content therewith, neither doth he himself receive the brethren, and forbiddeth them that would, and casteth *them* out of the church.

11 Beloved, follow not that which is evil, but that which is good. He that doeth good is of אֱלֹהִים: but he that doeth evil hath not seen אֱלֹהִים.

12 Demetrius hath good report of all *men*, and of the truth itself: yea, and we *also* bear record; and ye know that our record is true.

13 I had many things to write, but I will not with ink and pen write unto thee:

14 But I trust I shall shortly see thee, and we shall speak face to face. Peace *be* to thee. *Our* friends salute thee. Greet the friends by name.

THE GENERAL EPISTLE OF
JUDE.

CHAPTER 1

JUDE, the servant of Yashiyah Christ, and brother of James, to them that are sanctified by אֱלֹהִים the Father, and preserved in Yashiyah Christ, *and* called:

2 Mercy unto you, and peace, and love, be multiplied.

3 Beloved, when I gave all diligence to write unto you of the common salvation, it was needful for me to write unto you, and exhort *you* that ye should earnestly contend for the faith which was once delivered unto the saints.

4 For there are certain men crept in unawares, who were before of old ordained to this condemnation, ungodly men, turning the grace of our אֱלֹהִים into lasciviousness, and denying the only Lord אֱלֹהִים, and our Lord Yashiyah Christ.

5 I will therefore put you in remembrance, though ye once knew this, how that the Lord, having saved the people out of the land of Egypt, afterward destroyed them that believed not.

6 And the angels which kept not their first estate, but left their own habitation, he hath reserved in everlasting chains under darkness unto the judgment of the great day.

7 Even as Sodom and Gomorrha, and the cities about them in like manner, giving themselves over to fornication, and going after strange flesh, are set forth for an example, suffering the vengeance of eternal fire.

8 Likewise also these *filthy* dreamers defile the flesh, despise dominion, and speak evil of dignities.

9 Yet Michael the archangel, when contending with the devil he disputed about the body of Moses, durst not bring against him a railing accusation, but said, The Lord rebuke thee.

10 But these speak evil of those things which they know not: but what they know naturally, as brute beasts, in those things they corrupt themselves.

11 Woe unto them! for they have gone in the way of Cain, and ran greedily after the error of Balaam for reward, and perished in the gainsaying of Core.

12 These are spots in your feasts of charity, when they feast with you, feeding themselves without fear: clouds *they are* without water, carried about of winds; trees whose fruit withereth, without fruit, twice dead, plucked up by the roots;

13 Raging waves of the sea, foaming out their own shame; wandering stars, to whom is reserved the blackness of darkness for ever.

14 And Enoch also, the seventh from Adam, prophesied of these, saying, Behold, the Lord cometh with ten thousands of his saints,

15 To execute judgment upon all, and to convince all that are ungodly among them of all their ungodly deeds which they have ungodly committed, and of all their hard *speeches* which ungodly sinners have spoken against him.

16 These are murmurers, complainers, walking after their own lusts; and their mouth speaketh great swelling *words*, having men's persons in admiration because of advantage.

17 But, beloved, remember ye the words which were spoken before of the apostles of our Lord Yashiyah Christ;

18 How that they told you there should be mockers in the last time, who should walk after their own ungodly lusts.

19 These be they who separate themselves, sensual, having not the Spirit.

20 But ye, beloved, building up yourselves on your most holy faith, praying in the Holy Ghost,

21 Keep yourselves in the love of אֱלֹהִים, looking for the mercy of our Lord Yashiyah Christ unto eternal life.

22 And of some have compassion, making a difference:

23 And others save with fear, pulling *them* out of the fire; hating even the garment spotted by the flesh.

24 Now unto him that is able to keep you from falling, and to present *you* faultless before the presence of his glory with exceeding joy,

25 To the only wise אֱלֹהִים our Saviour, *be* glory and majesty, dominion and power, both now and ever. Amen.

THE REVELATION
OF
ST. JOHN THE DIVINE.

CHAPTER 1

THE Revelation of Yashiyah Christ, which אֱלֹהִים gave unto him, to shew unto his servants things which must shortly come to pass; and he sent and signified *it* by his angel unto his servant John:

2 Who bare record of the word of אֱלֹהִים, and of the testimony of Yashiyah Christ, and of all things that he saw.

3 Blessed *is* he that readeth, and they that hear the words of this prophecy, and keep those things which are written therein: for the time *is* at hand.

4 JOHN to the seven churches which are in Asia: Grace *be* unto you, and peace, from him which is, and which was, and which is to come; and from the seven Spirits which are before his throne;

5 And from Yashiyah Christ, *who is* the faithful witness, *and* the first begotten of the dead, and the prince of the kings of the earth. Unto him that loved us, and washed us from our sins in his own blood,

6 And hath made us kings and priests unto אֱלֹהִים and his Father; to him *be* glory and dominion for ever and ever. Amen.

7 Behold, he cometh with clouds; and every eye shall see him, and they *also* which pierced him: and all kindreds of the earth shall wail because of him. Even so, Amen.

8 I am Alpha and Omega, the beginning and the ending, saith the Lord, which is, and which was, and which is to come, the Almighty.

9 I John, who also am your brother, and companion in tribulation, and in the kingdom and patience of Yashiyah Christ, was in the isle that is called Patmos, for the word of אֱלֹהִים, and for the testimony of Yashiyah Christ.

10 I was in the Spirit on the Lord's day, and heard behind me a great voice, as of a trumpet,

11 Saying, I am Alpha and Omega, the first and the last: and, What thou seest, write in a book, and send *it* unto the seven churches which are in Asia; unto Ephesus, and unto Smyrna, and unto Pergamos, and unto Thyatira, and unto Sardis, and unto Philadelphia, and unto Laodicea.

12 And I turned to see the voice that spake with me. And being turned, I saw seven golden candlesticks;

13 And in the midst of the seven candlesticks *one* like unto the Son of man, clothed with a garment down to the foot, and girt about the paps with a golden girdle.

14 His head and *his* hairs *were* white like wool, as white as snow; and his eyes *were* as a flame of fire;

15 And his feet like unto fine brass, as if they burned in a furnace; and his voice as the sound of many waters.

16 And he had in his right hand seven stars: and out of his mouth went a sharp twoedged sword: and his countenance *was* as the sun shineth in his strength.

17 And when I saw him, I fell at his feet as dead. And he laid his right hand upon me, saying unto me, Fear not; I am the first and the last:

18 *I am* he that liveth, and was dead; and, behold, I am alive for evermore, Amen; and have the keys of hell and of death.

19 Write the things which thou hast seen, and the things which are, and the things which shall be hereafter;

20 The mystery of the seven stars which thou sawest in my right hand, and the seven golden candlesticks. The seven stars are the angels of the seven churches: and the seven candlesticks which thou sawest are the seven churches.

CHAPTER 2

UNTO the angel of the church of Ephesus write; These things saith he that holdeth the seven stars in his right hand, who walketh in the midst of the seven golden candlesticks;

2 I know thy works, and thy labour, and thy patience, and how thou canst not bear them which are evil: and thou hast tried them which say they are apostles, and are not, and hast found them liars:

3 And hast borne, and hast patience, and for my name's sake hast laboured, and hast not fainted.

4 Nevertheless I have *somewhat* against thee, because thou hast left thy first love.

5 Remember therefore from whence thou art fallen, and repent, and do the first works; or else I will come unto thee quickly, and will remove thy candlestick out of his place, except thou repent.

6 But this thou hast, that thou hatest the deeds of the Nicolaitans, which I also hate.

7 He that hath an ear, let him hear what the Spirit saith unto the churches; To him that overcometh will I give to eat of the tree of life, which is in the midst of the paradise of אֱלֹהִים.

8 And unto the angel of the church in Smyrna write; These things saith the first and the last, which was dead, and is alive;

9 I know thy works, and tribulation, and poverty, (but thou art rich) and *I know* the blasphemy of them which say they are Jews, and are not, but *are* the synagogue of Satan.

10 Fear none of those things which thou shalt suffer: behold, the devil shall cast *some* of you into prison, that ye may be tried; and ye shall have tribulation ten days: be thou faithful unto death, and I will give thee a crown of life.

11 He that hath an ear, let him hear what the Spirit saith unto the churches; He that overcometh shall not be hurt of the second death.

12 And to the angel of the church in Pergamos write; These things saith he which hath the sharp sword with two edges;

13 I know thy works, and where thou dwellest, *even* where Satan's seat *is:* and thou holdest fast my name, and hast not denied my faith, even in those days wherein Antipas *was* my faithful martyr, who was slain among you, where Satan dwelleth.

14 But I have a few things against thee, because thou hast there them that hold the doctrine of Balaam, who taught Balac to cast a stumblingblock before the children of Israel, to eat things sacrificed unto idols, and to commit fornication.

15 So hast thou also them that hold the doctrine of the Nicolaitans, which thing I hate.

16 Repent; or else I will come unto thee quickly, and will fight against them with the sword of my mouth.

17 He that hath an ear, let him hear what the Spirit saith unto the churches; To him that overcometh will I give to eat of the hidden manna, and will give him a white stone, and in the stone a new name written, which no man knoweth saving he that receiveth *it*.

18 And unto the angel of the church in Thyatira write; These things saith the Son of אֱלֹהִים, who hath his eyes like unto a flame of fire, and his feet *are* like fine brass;

19 I know thy works, and charity, and service, and faith, and thy patience, and thy works; and the last *to be* more than the first.

20 Notwithstanding I have a few things against thee, because thou sufferest that woman Jezebel, which calleth herself a prophetess, to teach and to seduce my servants to commit fornication, and to eat things sacrificed unto idols.

21 And I gave her space to repent of her fornication; and she repented not.

22 Behold, I will cast her into a bed, and them that commit adultery with her into great tribulation, except they repent of their deeds.

23 And I will kill her children with death; and all the churches shall know that I am he which searcheth the reins and hearts: and I will give unto every one of you according to your works.

24 But unto you I say, and unto the rest in Thyatira, as many as have not this doctrine, and which have not known the depths of Satan, as they speak; I will put upon you none other burden.

25 But that which ye have *already* hold fast till I come.

26 And he that overcometh, and keepeth my works unto the end, to him will I give power over the nations:

27 And he shall rule them with a rod of iron; as the vessels of a potter shall they be broken to shivers: even as I received of my Father.

28 And I will give him the morning star.

29 He that hath an ear, let him hear what the Spirit saith unto the churches.

CHAPTER 3

AND unto the angel of the church in Sardis write; These things saith he that hath the seven Spirits of אֱלֹהִים, and the seven stars; I know thy works, that thou hast a name that thou livest, and art dead.

2 Be watchful, and strengthen the things which remain, that are ready to die: for I have not found thy works perfect before אֱלֹהִים.

3 Remember therefore how thou hast received and heard, and hold fast, and repent. If therefore thou shalt not watch, I will come on thee as a thief, and thou shalt not know what hour I will come upon thee.

4 Thou hast a few names even in Sardis which have not defiled their garments; and they shall walk with me in white: for they are worthy.

5 He that overcometh, the same shall be clothed in white raiment; and I will not blot out his name out of the book of life, but I will confess his name before my Father, and before his angels.

6 He that hath an ear, let him hear what the Spirit saith unto the churches.

7 And to the angel of the church in Philadelphia write; These things saith he that is holy, he that is true, he that hath the key of David, he that openeth, and no man shutteth; and shutteth, and no man openeth;

8 I know thy works: behold, I have set before thee an open door, and no man can shut it: for thou hast a little strength, and hast kept my word, and hast not denied my name.

9 Behold, I will make them of the synagogue of Satan, which say they are Jews, and are not, but do lie; behold, I will make them to come and worship before thy feet, and to know that I have loved thee.

10 Because thou hast kept the word of my patience, I also will keep thee from the hour of temptation, which shall come upon all the world, to try them that dwell upon the earth.

11 Behold, I come quickly: hold that fast which thou hast, that no man take thy crown.

12 Him that overcometh will I make a pillar in the temple of my אֱלֹהִים, and he shall go no more out: and I will write upon him the name of my אֱלֹהִים, and the name of the city of my אֱלֹהִים, *which is* new Jerusalem, which cometh down out of heaven from my אֱלֹהִים: and *I will write upon him* my new name.

13 He that hath an ear, let him hear what the Spirit saith unto the churches.

14 And unto the angel of the church of the Laodiceans write; These things saith the Amen, the faithful and true witness, the beginning of the creation of אֱלֹהִים;

15 I know thy works, that thou art neither cold nor hot: I would thou wert cold or hot.

16 So then because thou art lukewarm, and neither cold nor hot, I will spue thee out of my mouth.

17 Because thou sayest, I am rich, and increased with goods, and have need of nothing; and knowest not that thou art wretched, and miserable, and poor, and blind, and naked:

18 I counsel thee to buy of me gold tried in the fire, that thou mayest be rich; and white raiment, that thou mayest be clothed, and *that* the shame of thy nakedness do not appear; and anoint thine eyes with eyesalve, that thou mayest see.

19 As many as I love, I rebuke and chasten: be zealous therefore, and repent.

20 Behold, I stand at the door, and knock: if any man hear my voice, and open the door, I will come in to him, and will sup with him, and he with me.

21 To him that overcometh will I grant to sit with me in my throne, even as I also overcame, and am set down with my Father in his throne.

22 He that hath an ear, let him hear what the Spirit saith unto the churches.

CHAPTER 4

AFTER this I looked, and, behold, a door *was* opened in heaven: and the first voice which I heard *was* as it were of a trumpet talking with me; which said, Come up hither, and I will shew thee things which must be hereafter.

2 And immediately I was in the spirit: and, behold, a throne was set in heaven, and *one* sat on the throne.

3 And he that sat was to look upon like a jasper and a sardine stone: and *there was* a rainbow round about the throne, in sight like unto an emerald.

4 And round about the throne *were* four and twenty seats: and upon the seats I saw four and twenty elders sitting, clothed in white raiment; and they had on their heads crowns of gold.

5 And out of the throne proceeded lightnings and thunderings and voices: and *there were* seven lamps of fire burning before the throne, which are the seven Spirits of אֱלֹהִים.

6 And before the throne *there was* a sea of glass like unto crystal: and in the midst of the throne, and round about the throne, *were* four beasts full of eyes before and behind.

7 And the first beast *was* like a lion, and the second beast like a calf, and the third beast had a face as a man, and the fourth beast *was* like a flying eagle.

8 And the four beasts had each of them six wings about *him;* and *they were* full of eyes within: and they rest not day and night, saying, Holy, holy, holy, Lord אֱלֹהִים Almighty, which was, and is, and is to come.

9 And when those beasts give glory and honour and thanks to him that sat on the throne, who liveth for ever and ever,

10 The four and twenty elders fall down before him that sat on the throne, and worship him that liveth for ever and ever, and cast their crowns before the throne, saying,

11 Thou art worthy, O Lord, to receive glory and honour and power: for thou hast created all things, and for thy pleasure they are and were created.

CHAPTER 5

AND I saw in the right hand of him that sat on the throne a book written within and on the backside, sealed with seven seals.

2 And I saw a strong angel proclaiming with a loud voice, Who is worthy to open the book, and to loose the seals thereof?

3 And no man in heaven, nor in earth, neither under the earth, was able to open the book, neither to look thereon.

4 And I wept much, because no man was found worthy to open and to read the book, neither to look thereon.

5 And one of the elders saith unto me, Weep not: behold, the Lion of the tribe of Juda, the Root of David, hath prevailed to open the book, and to loose the seven seals thereof.

6 And I beheld, and, lo, in the midst of the throne and of the four beasts, and in the midst of the elders, stood a Lamb as it had been slain, having seven horns and seven eyes, which are the seven Spirits of אֱלֹהִים sent forth into all the earth.

7 And he came and took the book out of the right hand of him that sat upon the throne.

8 And when he had taken the book, the four beasts and four *and* twenty elders fell down before the Lamb, having every one of them harps, and golden vials full of odours, which are the prayers of saints.

9 And they sung a new song, saying, Thou art worthy to take the book, and to open the seals thereof: for thou wast slain, and hast redeemed us to אֱלֹהִים by thy blood out of every kindred, and tongue, and people, and nation;

10 And hast made us unto our אֱלֹהִים kings and priests: and we shall reign on the earth.

11 And I beheld, and I heard the voice of many angels round about the throne and the beasts and the elders: and the number of them was ten thousand times ten thousand, and thousands of thousands;

12 Saying with a loud voice, Worthy is the Lamb that was slain to receive power, and riches, and wisdom, and strength, and honour, and glory, and blessing.

13 And every creature which is in heaven, and on the earth, and under the earth, and such as are in the sea, and all that are in them, heard I saying, Blessing, and honour, and glory, and power, *be* unto him that sitteth upon the throne, and unto the Lamb for ever and ever.

14 And the four beasts said, Amen. And the four *and* twenty elders fell down and worshipped him that liveth for ever and ever.

CHAPTER 6

AND I saw when the Lamb opened one of the seals, and I heard, as it were the noise of thunder, one of the four beasts saying, Come and see.

2 And I saw, and behold a white horse: and he that sat on him had a bow; and a crown was given unto him: and he went forth conquering, and to conquer.

3 And when he had opened the second seal, I heard the second beast say, Come and see.

4 And there went out another horse *that was* red: and *power* was given to him that sat thereon to take peace from the earth, and that they should kill one another: and there was given unto him a great sword.

5 And when he had opened the third seal, I heard the third beast say, Come and see. And I beheld, and lo a black horse; and he that sat on him had a pair of balances in his hand.

6 And I heard a voice in the midst of the four beasts say, A measure of wheat for a penny, and three measures of barley for a penny; and *see* thou hurt not the oil and the wine.

7 And when he had opened the fourth seal, I heard the voice of the fourth beast say, Come and see.

8 And I looked, and behold a pale horse: and his name that sat on him was Death, and Hell followed with him. And power was given unto them over the fourth part of the earth, to kill with sword, and with hunger, and with death, and with the beasts of the earth.

9 And when he had opened the fifth seal, I saw under the altar the souls of them that were slain for the word of אֱלֹהִים, and for the testimony which they held:

10 And they cried with a loud voice, saying, How long, O Lord, holy and true, dost thou not judge and avenge our blood on them that dwell on the earth?

11 And white robes were given unto every one of them; and it was said unto them, that they should rest yet for a little season, until their fellowservants also and their brethren, that should be killed as they *were*, should be fulfilled.

12 And I beheld when he had opened the sixth seal, and, lo, there was a great earthquake; and the sun became black as sackcloth of hair, and the moon became as blood;

13 And the stars of heaven fell unto the earth, even as a fig tree casteth her untimely figs, when she is shaken of a mighty wind.

14 And the heaven departed as a scroll when it is rolled together; and every mountain and island were moved out of their places.

15 And the kings of the earth, and the great men, and the rich men, and the chief captains, and the mighty men, and every bondman, and every free man, hid themselves in the dens and in the rocks of the mountains;

16 And said to the mountains and rocks, Fall on us, and hide us from the face of him that sitteth on the throne, and from the wrath of the Lamb:

17 For the great day of his wrath is come; and who shall be able to stand?

CHAPTER 7

AND after these things I saw four angels standing on the four corners of the earth, holding the four winds of the earth, that the wind should not blow on the earth, nor on the sea, nor on any tree.

2 And I saw another angel ascending from the east, having the seal of the living אֱלֹהִים: and he cried with a loud voice to the four angels, to whom it was given to hurt the earth and the sea,

3 Saying, Hurt not the earth, neither the sea, nor the trees, till we have sealed the servants of our אֱלֹהִים in their foreheads.

4 And I heard the number of them which were sealed: *and there were* sealed an hundred *and* forty *and* four thousand of all the tribes of the children of Israel.

5 Of the tribe of Juda *were* sealed twelve thousand. Of the tribe of Reuben *were* sealed twelve thousand. Of the tribe of Gad *were* sealed twelve thousand.

6 Of the tribe of Aser *were* sealed twelve thousand. Of the tribe of Nepthalim *were* sealed twelve thousand. Of the tribe of Manasses *were* sealed twelve thousand.

7 Of the tribe of Simeon *were* sealed twelve thousand. Of the tribe of Levi *were* sealed twelve thousand. Of the tribe of Issachar *were* sealed twelve thousand.

8 Of the tribe of Zabulon *were* sealed twelve thousand. Of the tribe of Joseph *were* sealed twelve thousand. Of the tribe of Benjamin *were* sealed twelve thousand.

9 After this I beheld, and, lo, a great multitude, which no man could number, of all nations, and kindreds, and people, and tongues, stood before the throne, and before the Lamb, clothed with white robes, and palms in their hands;

10 And cried with a loud voice, saying, Salvation to our אֱלֹהִים which sitteth upon the throne, and unto the Lamb.

11 And all the angels stood round about the throne, and *about* the elders and the four beasts, and fell before the throne on their faces, and worshipped אֱלֹהִים,

12 Saying, Amen: Blessing, and glory, and wisdom, and thanksgiving, and honour, and power, and might, *be* unto our אֱלֹהִים for ever

and ever. Amen.

13 And one of the elders answered, saying unto me, What are these which are arrayed in white robes? and whence came they?

14 And I said unto him, Sir, thou knowest. And he said to me, These are they which came out of great tribulation, and have washed their robes, and made them white in the blood of the Lamb.

15 Therefore are they before the throne of אֱלֹהִים, and serve him day and night in his temple: and he that sitteth on the throne shall dwell among them.

16 They shall hunger no more, neither thirst any more; neither shall the sun light on them, nor any heat.

17 For the Lamb which is in the midst of the throne shall feed them, and shall lead them unto living fountains of waters: and אֱלֹהִים shall wipe away all tears from their eyes.

CHAPTER 8

AND when he had opened the seventh seal, there was silence in heaven about the space of half an hour.

2 And I saw the seven angels which stood before אֱלֹהִים; and to them were given seven trumpets.

3 And another angel came and stood at the altar, having a golden censer; and there was given unto him much incense, that he should offer *it* with the prayers of all saints upon the golden altar which was before the throne.

4 And the smoke of the incense, *which came* with the prayers of the saints, ascended up before אֱלֹהִים out of the angel's hand.

5 And the angel took the censer, and filled it with fire of the altar, and cast *it* into the earth: and there were voices, and thunderings, and lightnings, and an earthquake.

6 And the seven angels which had the seven trumpets prepared themselves to sound.

7 The first angel sounded, and there followed hail and fire mingled with blood, and they were cast upon the earth: and the third part of trees was burnt up, and all green grass was burnt up.

8 And the second angel sounded, and as it were a great mountain burning with fire was cast into the sea: and the third part of the sea became blood;

9 And the third part of the creatures which were in the sea, and had life, died; and the third part of the ships were destroyed.

10 And the third angel sounded, and there fell a great star from heaven, burning as it were a lamp, and it fell upon the third part of the rivers, and upon the fountains of waters;

11 And the name of the star is called Wormwood: and the third part of the waters became wormwood; and many men died of the waters, because they were made bitter.

12 And the fourth angel sounded, and the third part of the sun was smitten, and the third part of the moon, and the third part of the stars; so as the third part of them was darkened, and the day shone not for a third part of it, and the night likewise.

13 And I beheld, and heard an angel flying through the midst of heaven, saying with a loud voice, Woe, woe, woe, to the inhabiters of the earth by reason of the other voices of the trumpet of the three angels, which are yet to sound!

CHAPTER 9

AND the fifth angel sounded, and I saw a star fall from heaven unto the earth: and to him was given the key of the bottomless pit.

2 And he opened the bottomless pit; and there arose a smoke out of the pit, as the smoke of a great furnace; and the sun and the air were darkened by reason of the smoke of the pit.

3 And there came out of the smoke locusts upon the earth: and unto them was given power, as the scorpions of the earth have power.

4 And it was commanded them that they should not hurt the grass of the earth, neither any green thing, neither any tree; but only those men which have not the seal of אֱלֹהִים in their foreheads.

5 And to them it was given that they should not kill them, but that they should be tormented five months: and their torment *was* as the torment of a scorpion, when he striketh a man.

6 And in those days shall men seek death, and shall not find it; and shall desire to die, and death shall flee from them.

7 And the shapes of the locusts *were* like unto horses prepared unto battle; and on their heads *were* as it were crowns like gold, and their faces *were* as the faces of men.

8 And they had hair as the hair of women, and their teeth were as *the teeth* of lions.

9 And they had breastplates, as it were breastplates of iron; and the sound of their wings *was* as the sound of chariots of many horses running to battle.

10 And they had tails like unto scorpions, and there were stings in their tails: and their power *was* to hurt men five months.

11 And they had a king over them, *which is* the angel of the bottomless pit, whose name in the Hebrew tongue *is* Abaddon, but in the Greek tongue hath *his* name Apollyon.

12 One woe is past; *and*, behold, there come two woes more hereafter.

13 And the sixth angel sounded, and I heard a voice from the four horns of the golden altar which is before אֱלֹהִים,

14 Saying to the sixth angel which had the trumpet, Loose the four angels which are bound in the great river Euphrates.

15 And the four angels were loosed, which were prepared for an hour, and a day, and a month, and a year, for to slay the third part of men.

16 And the number of the army of the horsemen *were* two hundred thousand thousand: and I heard the number of them.

17 And thus I saw the horses in the vision, and them that sat on them, having breastplates of fire, and of jacinth, and brimstone: and the heads of the horses *were* as the heads of lions; and out of their mouths issued fire and smoke and brimstone.

18 By these three was the third part of men killed, by the fire, and by the smoke, and by the brimstone, which issued out of their mouths.

19 For their power is in their mouth, and in their tails: for their tails *were* like unto serpents, and had heads, and with them they do hurt.

20 And the rest of the men which were not killed by these plagues yet repented not of the works of their hands, that they should not worship devils, and idols of gold, and silver, and brass, and stone, and of wood: which neither can see, nor hear, nor walk:

21 Neither repented they of their murders, nor of their sorceries, nor of their fornication, nor of their thefts.

CHAPTER 10

AND I saw another mighty angel come down from heaven, clothed with a cloud: and a rainbow *was* upon his head, and his face *was* as it were the sun, and his feet as pillars of fire:

2 And he had in his hand a little book open: and he set his right foot upon the sea, and *his* left *foot* on the earth,

3 And cried with a loud voice, as *when* a lion roareth: and when he had cried, seven thunders uttered their voices.

4 And when the seven thunders had uttered their voices, I was about to write: and I heard a voice from heaven saying unto me, Seal up those things which the seven thunders uttered, and write them not.

5 And the angel which I saw stand upon the sea and upon the earth lifted up his hand to heaven,

6 And sware by him that liveth for ever and ever, who created heaven, and the things that therein are, and the earth, and the things that therein are, and the sea, and the things which are therein, that there should be time no longer:

7 But in the days of the voice of the seventh angel, when he shall begin to sound, the mystery of אֱלֹהִים should be finished, as he hath declared to his servants the prophets.

8 And the voice which I heard from heaven spake unto me again, and said, Go *and* take the little book which is open in the hand of the angel which standeth upon the sea and upon the earth.

9 And I went unto the angel, and said unto him, Give me the little book. And he said unto me, Take *it*, and eat it up; and it shall make thy belly bitter, but it shall be in thy mouth sweet as honey.

10 And I took the little book out of the angel's hand, and ate it up; and it was in my mouth sweet as honey: and as soon as I had eaten it, my belly was bitter.

11 And he said unto me, Thou must prophesy again before many peoples, and nations, and tongues, and kings.

CHAPTER 11

AND there was given me a reed like unto a rod: and the angel stood, saying, Rise, and measure the temple of אֱלֹהִים, and the altar, and them that worship therein.

2 But the court which is without the temple leave out, and measure it not; for it is given unto the Gentiles: and the holy city shall they tread under foot forty *and* two months.

3 And I will give *power* unto my two witnesses, and they shall prophesy a thousand two hundred *and* threescore days, clothed in sackcloth.

4 These are the two olive trees, and the two candlesticks standing before the אֱלֹהִים of the earth.

5 And if any man will hurt them, fire proceedeth out of their mouth, and devoureth their enemies: and if any man will hurt them, he must in this manner be killed.

6 These have power to shut heaven, that it rain not in the days of their prophecy: and have power over waters to turn them to blood, and to smite the earth with all plagues, as often as they will.

7 And when they shall have finished their testimony, the beast that ascendeth out of the bottomless pit shall make war against them, and shall overcome them, and kill them.

8 And their dead bodies *shall lie* in the street of the great city, which spiritually is called Sodom and Egypt, where also our Lord was crucified.

9 And they of the people and kindreds and tongues and nations shall see their dead bodies three days and an half, and shall not suffer their dead bodies to be put in graves.

10 And they that dwell upon the earth shall rejoice over them, and make merry, and shall send gifts one to another; because these two prophets tormented them that dwelt on the earth.

11 And after three days and an half the Spirit of life from אֱלֹהִים entered into them, and they stood upon their feet; and great fear fell upon them which saw them.

12 And they heard a great voice from heaven saying unto them, Come up hither. And they ascended up to heaven in a cloud; and their enemies beheld them.

13 And the same hour was there a great earthquake, and the tenth part of the city fell, and in the earthquake were slain of men seven thousand: and the remnant were affrighted, and gave glory to the אֱלֹהִים of heaven.

14 The second woe is past; *and*, behold, the third woe cometh quickly.

15 And the seventh angel sounded; and there were great voices in heaven, saying, The kingdoms of this world are become *the kingdoms* of our Lord, and of his Christ; and he shall reign for ever and ever.

16 And the four and twenty elders, which sat before אֱלֹהִים on their seats, fell upon their faces, and worshipped אֱלֹהִים,

17 Saying, We give thee thanks, O Lord אֱלֹהִים Almighty, which art, and wast, and art to come; because thou hast taken to thee thy great power, and hast reigned.

18 And the nations were angry, and thy wrath is come, and the time of the dead, that they should be judged, and that thou shouldest give reward unto thy servants the prophets, and to the saints, and them that fear thy name, small and great; and shouldest destroy them which destroy the earth.

19 And the temple of אֱלֹהִים was opened in heaven, and there was seen in his temple the ark of his testament: and there were lightnings, and voices, and thunderings, and an earthquake, and great hail.

CHAPTER 12

AND there appeared a great wonder in heaven; a woman clothed with the sun, and the moon under her feet, and upon her head a crown of twelve stars:

2 And she being with child cried, travailing in birth, and pained to be delivered.

3 And there appeared another wonder in heaven; and behold a great red dragon, having seven heads and ten horns, and seven crowns upon his heads.

4 And his tail drew the third part of the stars of heaven, and did cast them to the earth: and the dragon stood before the woman which was ready to be delivered, for to devour her child as soon as it was born.

5 And she brought forth a man child, who was to rule all nations with a rod of iron: and her child was caught up unto אֱלֹהִים, and *to* his throne.

6 And the woman fled into the wilderness, where she hath a place prepared of אֱלֹהִים, that they should feed her there a thousand two hundred *and* threescore days.

7 And there was war in heaven: Michael and his angels fought against the dragon; and the dragon fought and his angels,

8 And prevailed not; neither was their place found any more in heaven.

9 And the great dragon was cast out, that old serpent, called the Devil, and Satan, which deceiveth the whole world: he was cast out

into the earth, and his angels were cast out with him.

10 And I heard a loud voice saying in heaven, Now is come salvation, and strength, and the kingdom of our אֱלֹהִים, and the power of his Christ: for the accuser of our brethren is cast down, which accused them before our אֱלֹהִים day and night.

11 And they overcame him by the blood of the Lamb, and by the word of their testimony; and they loved not their lives unto the death.

12 Therefore rejoice, *ye* heavens, and ye that dwell in them. Woe to the inhabiters of the earth and of the sea! for the devil is come down unto you, having great wrath, because he knoweth that he hath but a short time.

13 And when the dragon saw that he was cast unto the earth, he persecuted the woman which brought forth the man *child*.

14 And to the woman were given two wings of a great eagle, that she might fly into the wilderness, into her place, where she is nourished for a time, and times, and half a time, from the face of the serpent.

15 And the serpent cast out of his mouth water as a flood after the woman, that he might cause her to be carried away of the flood.

16 And the earth helped the woman, and the earth opened her mouth, and swallowed up the flood which the dragon cast out of his mouth.

17 And the dragon was wroth with the woman, and went to make war with the remnant of her seed, which keep the commandments of אֱלֹהִים, and have the testimony of Yashiyah Christ.

CHAPTER 13

AND I stood upon the sand of the sea, and saw a beast rise up out of the sea, having seven heads and ten horns, and upon his horns ten crowns, and upon his heads the name of blasphemy.

2 And the beast which I saw was like unto a leopard, and his feet were as *the feet* of a bear, and his mouth as the mouth of a lion: and the dragon gave him his power, and his seat, and great authority.

3 And I saw one of his heads as it were wounded to death; and his deadly wound was healed: and all the world wondered after the beast.

4 And they worshipped the dragon which gave power unto the beast: and they worshipped the beast, saying, Who *is* like unto the beast? who is able to make war with him?

5 And there was given unto him a mouth speaking great things and blasphemies; and power was given unto him to continue forty *and* two months.

6 And he opened his mouth in blasphemy against אֱלֹהִים, to blaspheme his name, and his tabernacle, and them that dwell in heaven.

7 And it was given unto him to make war with the saints, and to overcome them: and power was given him over all kindreds, and tongues, and nations.

8 And all that dwell upon the earth shall worship him, whose names are not written in the book of life of the Lamb slain from the foundation of the world.

9 If any man have an ear, let him hear.

10 He that leadeth into captivity shall go into captivity: he that killeth with the sword must be killed with the sword. Here is the patience and the faith of the saints.

11 And I beheld another beast coming up out of the earth; and he had two horns like a lamb, and he spake as a dragon.

12 And he exerciseth all the power of the first beast before him, and causeth the earth and them which dwell therein to worship the first beast, whose deadly wound was healed.

13 And he doeth great wonders, so that he maketh fire come down from heaven on the earth in the sight of men,

14 And deceiveth them that dwell on the earth by *the means of* those miracles which he had power to do in the sight of the beast; saying to them that dwell on the earth, that they should make an image to the beast, which had the wound by a sword, and did live.

15 And he had power to give life unto the image of the beast, that the image of the beast should both speak, and cause that as many as would not worship the image of the beast should be killed.

16 And he causeth all, both small and great, rich and poor, free and bond, to receive a mark in their right hand, or in their foreheads:

17 And that no man might buy or sell, save he that had the mark, or the name of the beast, or the number of his name.

18 Here is wisdom. Let him that hath understanding count the number of the beast: for it is the number of a man; and his number *is* Six hundred threescore *and* six.

CHAPTER 14

AND I looked, and, lo, a Lamb stood on the mount Sion, and with him an hundred forty *and* four thousand, having his Father's name written in their foreheads.

2 And I heard a voice from heaven, as the voice of many waters, and as the voice of a great thunder: and I heard the voice of harpers harping with their harps:

3 And they sung as it were a new song before the throne, and before the four beasts, and the elders: and no man could learn that song but the hundred *and* forty *and* four thousand, which were redeemed from the earth.

4 These are they which were not defiled with women; for they are virgins. These are they which follow the Lamb whithersoever he goeth. These were redeemed from among men, *being* the firstfruits unto אֱלֹהִים and to the Lamb.

5 And in their mouth was found no guile: for they are without fault before the throne of אֱלֹהִים.

6 And I saw another angel fly in the midst of heaven, having the everlasting gospel to preach unto them that dwell on the earth, and to every nation, and kindred, and tongue, and people,

7 Saying with a loud voice, Fear אֱלֹהִים, and give glory to him; for the hour of his judgment is come: and worship him that made heaven, and earth, and the sea, and the fountains of waters.

8 And there followed another angel, saying, Babylon is fallen, is fallen, that great city, because she made all nations drink of the wine of the wrath of her fornication.

9 And the third angel followed them, saying with a loud voice, If any man worship the beast and his image, and receive *his* mark in his forehead, or in his hand,

10 The same shall drink of the wine of the wrath of אֱלֹהִים, which is poured out without mixture into the cup of his indignation; and he shall be tormented with fire and brimstone in the presence of the holy angels, and in the presence of the Lamb:

11 And the smoke of their torment ascendeth up for ever and ever: and they have no rest day nor night, who worship the beast and his image, and whosoever receiveth the mark of his name.

12 Here is the patience of the saints: here *are* they that keep the commandments of אֱלֹהִים, and the faith of Yashiyah.

13 And I heard a voice from heaven saying unto me, Write, Blessed *are* the dead which die in the Lord from henceforth: Yea, saith the Spirit, that they may rest from their labours; and their works do follow them.

14 And I looked, and behold a white cloud, and upon the cloud *one* sat like unto the Son of man, having on his head a golden crown, and in his hand a sharp sickle.

15 And another angel came out of the temple, crying with a loud voice to him that sat on the cloud, Thrust in thy sickle, and reap: for the time is come for thee to reap; for the harvest of the earth is ripe.

16 And he that sat on the cloud thrust in his sickle on the earth; and the earth was reaped.

17 And another angel came out of the temple which is in heaven, he also having a sharp sickle.

18 And another angel came out from the altar, which had power over fire; and cried with a loud cry to him that had the sharp sickle, saying, Thrust in thy sharp sickle, and gather the clusters of the vine of the earth; for her grapes are fully ripe.

19 And the angel thrust in his sickle into the earth, and gathered the vine of the earth, and cast *it* into the great winepress of the wrath of אֱלֹהִים.

20 And the winepress was trodden without the city, and blood came out of the winepress, even unto the horse bridles, by the space of a thousand *and* six hundred furlongs.

CHAPTER 15

AND I saw another sign in heaven, great and marvellous, seven angels having the seven last plagues; for in them is filled up the wrath of אֱלֹהִים.

2 And I saw as it were a sea of glass mingled with fire: and them that had gotten the victory over the beast, and over his image, and over his mark, *and* over the number of his name, stand on the sea of glass, having the harps of אֱלֹהִים.

3 And they sing the song of Moses the servant of אֱלֹהִים, and the song of the Lamb, saying, Great and marvellous *are* thy works, Lord אֱלֹהִים Almighty; just and true *are* thy ways, thou King of saints.

4 Who shall not fear thee, O Lord, and glorify thy name? for *thou* only *art* holy: for all nations shall come and worship before thee; for thy judgments are made manifest.

5 And after that I looked, and, behold, the temple of the tabernacle of the testimony in heaven was opened:

6 And the seven angels came out of the temple, having the seven plagues, clothed in pure and white linen, and having their breasts girded with golden girdles.

7 And one of the four beasts gave unto the seven angels seven golden vials full of the wrath of אֱלֹהִים, who liveth for ever and ever.

8 And the temple was filled with smoke from the glory of אֱלֹהִים, and from his power; and no man was able to enter into the temple, till the seven plagues of the seven angels were fulfilled.

CHAPTER 16

AND I heard a great voice out of the temple saying to the seven angels, Go your ways, and pour out the vials of the wrath of אֱלֹהִים upon the earth.

2 And the first went, and poured out his vial upon the earth; and there fell a noisome and grievous sore upon the men which had the mark of the beast, and *upon* them which worshipped his image.

3 And the second angel poured out his vial upon the sea; and it became as the blood of a dead *man:* and every living soul died in the sea.

4 And the third angel poured out his vial upon the rivers and fountains of waters; and they became blood.

5 And I heard the angel of the waters say, Thou art righteous, O Lord, which art, and wast, and shalt be, because thou hast judged thus.

6 For they have shed the blood of saints and prophets, and thou hast given them blood to drink; for they are worthy.

7 And I heard another out of the altar say, Even so, Lord אֱלֹהִים Almighty, true and righteous *are* thy judgments.

8 And the fourth angel poured out his vial upon the sun; and power was given unto him to scorch men with fire.

9 And men were scorched with great heat, and blasphemed the name of אֱלֹהִים, which hath power over these plagues: and they repented not to give him glory.

10 And the fifth angel poured out his vial upon the seat of the beast; and his kingdom was full of darkness; and they gnawed their tongues for pain,

11 And blasphemed the אֱלֹהִים of heaven because of their pains and their sores, and repented not of their deeds.

12 And the sixth angel poured out his vial upon the great river Euphrates; and the water thereof was dried up, that the way of the kings of the east might be prepared.

13 And I saw three unclean spirits like frogs *come* out of the mouth of the dragon, and out of the mouth of the beast, and out of the mouth of the false prophet.

14 For they are the spirits of devils, working miracles, *which* go forth unto the kings of the earth and of the whole world, to gather them to the battle of that great day of אֱלֹהִים Almighty.

15 Behold, I come as a thief. Blessed *is* he that watcheth, and keepeth his garments, lest he walk naked, and they see his shame.

16 And he gathered them together into a place called in the Hebrew tongue Armageddon.

17 And the seventh angel poured out his vial into the air; and there came a great voice out of the temple of heaven, from the throne, saying, It is done.

18 And there were voices, and thunders, and lightnings; and there was a great earthquake, such as was not since men were upon the earth, so mighty an earthquake, *and* so great.

19 And the great city was divided into three parts, and the cities of the nations fell: and great Babylon came in remembrance before אֱלֹהִים, to give unto her the cup of the wine of the fierceness of his wrath.

20 And every island fled away, and the mountains were not found.

21 And there fell upon men a great hail out of heaven, *every stone* about the weight of a talent: and men blasphemed אֱלֹהִים because of the plague of the hail; for the plague thereof was exceeding great.

CHAPTER 17

AND there came one of the seven angels which had the seven vials, and talked with me, saying unto me, Come hither; I will shew unto thee the judgment of the great whore that sitteth upon many waters:

2 With whom the kings of the earth have committed fornication, and the inhabitants of the earth have been made drunk with the wine

of her fornication.

3 So he carried me away in the spirit into the wilderness: and I saw a woman sit upon a scarlet coloured beast, full of names of blasphemy, having seven heads and ten horns.

4 And the woman was arrayed in purple and scarlet colour, and decked with gold and precious stones and pearls, having a golden cup in her hand full of abominations and filthiness of her fornication:

5 And upon her forehead *was* a name written, MYSTERY, BABYLON THE GREAT, THE MOTHER OF HARLOTS AND ABOMINATIONS OF THE EARTH.

6 And I saw the woman drunken with the blood of the saints, and with the blood of the martyrs of Yashiyah: and when I saw her, I wondered with great admiration.

7 And the angel said unto me, Wherefore didst thou marvel? I will tell thee the mystery of the woman, and of the beast that carrieth her, which hath the seven heads and ten horns.

8 The beast that thou sawest was, and is not; and shall ascend out of the bottomless pit, and go into perdition: and they that dwell on the earth shall wonder, whose names were not written in the book of life from the foundation of the world, when they behold the beast that was, and is not, and yet is.

9 And here *is* the mind which hath wisdom. The seven heads are seven mountains, on which the woman sitteth.

10 And there are seven kings: five are fallen, and one is, *and* the other is not yet come; and when he cometh, he must continue a short space.

11 And the beast that was, and is not, even he is the eighth, and is of the seven, and goeth into perdition.

12 And the ten horns which thou sawest are ten kings, which have received no kingdom as yet; but receive power as kings one hour with the beast.

13 These have one mind, and shall give their power and strength unto the beast.

14 These shall make war with the Lamb, and the Lamb shall overcome them: for he is Lord of lords, and King of kings: and they that are with him *are* called, and chosen, and faithful.

15 And he saith unto me, The waters which thou sawest, where the whore sitteth, are peoples, and multitudes, and nations, and tongues.

16 And the ten horns which thou sawest upon the beast, these shall hate the whore, and shall make her desolate and naked, and shall eat her flesh, and burn her with fire.

17 For אֱלֹהִים hath put in their hearts to fulfil his will, and to agree, and give their kingdom unto the beast, until the words of אֱלֹהִים shall be fulfilled.

18 And the woman which thou sawest is that great city, which reigneth over the kings of the earth.

CHAPTER 18

AND after these things I saw another angel come down from heaven, having great power; and the earth was lightened with his glory.

2 And he cried mightily with a strong voice, saying, Babylon the great is fallen, is fallen, and is become the habitation of devils, and the hold of every foul spirit, and a cage of every unclean and hateful bird.

3 For all nations have drunk of the wine of the wrath of her fornication, and the kings of the earth have committed fornication with her, and the merchants of the earth are waxed rich through the abundance of her delicacies.

4 And I heard another voice from heaven, saying, Come out of her, my people, that ye be not partakers of her sins, and that ye receive not of her plagues.

5 For her sins have reached unto heaven, and אֱלֹהִים hath remembered her iniquities.

6 Reward her even as she rewarded you, and double unto her double according to her works: in the cup which she hath filled fill to her double.

7 How much she hath glorified herself, and lived deliciously, so much torment and sorrow give her: for she saith in her heart, I sit a queen, and am no widow, and shall see no sorrow.

8 Therefore shall her plagues come in one day, death, and mourning, and famine; and she shall be utterly burned with fire: for strong *is* the Lord אֱלֹהִים who judgeth her.

9 And the kings of the earth, who have committed fornication and lived deliciously with her, shall bewail her, and lament for her, when they shall see the smoke of her burning,

10 Standing afar off for the fear of her torment, saying, Alas, alas, that great city Babylon, that mighty city! for in one hour is thy judgment come.

11 And the merchants of the earth shall weep and mourn over her; for no man buyeth their merchandise any more:

12 The merchandise of gold, and silver, and precious stones, and of pearls, and fine linen, and purple, and silk, and scarlet, and all thyine wood, and all manner vessels of ivory, and all manner vessels of most precious wood, and of brass, and iron, and marble,

13 And cinnamon, and odours, and ointments, and frankincense, and wine, and oil, and fine flour, and wheat, and beasts, and sheep, and horses, and chariots, and slaves, and souls of men.

14 And the fruits that thy soul lusted after are departed from thee, and all things which were dainty and goodly are departed from thee, and thou shalt find them no more at all.

15 The merchants of these things, which were made rich by her, shall stand afar off for the fear of her torment, weeping and wailing,

16 And saying, Alas, alas, that great city, that was clothed in fine linen, and purple, and scarlet, and decked with gold, and precious stones, and pearls!

17 For in one hour so great riches is come to nought. And every shipmaster, and all the company in ships, and sailors, and as many as trade by sea, stood afar off,

18 And cried when they saw the smoke of her burning, saying, What *city is* like unto this great city!

19 And they cast dust on their heads, and cried, weeping and wailing, saying, Alas, alas, that great city, wherein were made rich all that had ships in the sea by reason of her costliness! for in one hour is she made desolate.

20 Rejoice over her, *thou* heaven, and *ye* holy apostles and prophets; for אֱלֹהִים hath avenged you on her.

21 And a mighty angel took up a stone like a great millstone, and cast *it* into the sea, saying, Thus with violence shall that great city Babylon be thrown down, and shall be found no more at all.

22 And the voice of harpers, and musicians, and of pipers, and trumpeters, shall be heard no more at all in thee; and no craftsman, of whatsoever craft *he be*, shall be found any more in thee; and the sound of a millstone shall be heard no more at all in thee;

23 And the light of a candle shall shine no more at all in thee; and the voice of the bridegroom and of the bride shall be heard no more at all in thee: for thy merchants were the great men of the earth; for by thy sorceries were all nations deceived.

24 And in her was found the blood of prophets, and of saints, and of all that were slain upon the earth.

CHAPTER 19

AND after these things I heard a great voice of much people in heaven, saying, Alleluia; Salvation, and glory, and honour, and power, unto the Lord our אֱלֹהִים:

2 For true and righteous *are* his judgments: for he hath judged the great whore, which did corrupt the earth with her fornication, and hath avenged the blood of his servants at her hand.

3 And again they said, Alleluia. And her smoke rose up for ever and ever.

4 And the four and twenty elders and the four beasts fell down and worshipped אֱלֹהִים that sat on the throne, saying, Amen; Alleluia.

5 And a voice came out of the throne, saying, Praise our אֱלֹהִים, all ye his servants, and ye that fear him, both small and great.

6 And I heard as it were the voice of a great multitude, and as the voice of many waters, and as the voice of mighty thunderings, saying, Alleluia: for the Lord אֱלֹהִים omnipotent reigneth.

7 Let us be glad and rejoice, and give honour to him: for the marriage of the Lamb is come, and his wife hath made herself ready.

8 And to her was granted that she should be arrayed in fine linen, clean and white: for the fine linen is the righteousness of saints.

9 And he saith unto me, Write, Blessed *are* they which are called unto the marriage supper of the Lamb. And he saith unto me, These are the true sayings of אֱלֹהִים.

10 And I fell at his feet to worship him. And he said unto me, See *thou do it* not: I am thy fellowservant, and of thy brethren that have the testimony of Yashiyah: worship אֱלֹהִים: for the testimony of Yashiyah is the spirit of prophecy.

11 And I saw heaven opened, and behold a white horse; and he that sat upon him *was* called Faithful and True, and in righteousness he doth judge and make war.

12 His eyes *were* as a flame of fire, and on his head *were* many crowns; and he had a name written, that no man knew, but he himself.

13 And he *was* clothed with a vesture dipped in blood: and his name is called The Word of אֱלֹהִים.

14 And the armies *which were* in heaven followed him upon white horses, clothed in fine linen, white and clean.

15 And out of his mouth goeth a sharp sword, that with it he should smite the nations: and he shall rule them with a rod of iron: and he treadeth the winepress of the fierceness and wrath of Almighty אֱלֹהִים.

16 And he hath on *his* vesture and on his thigh a name written, KING OF KINGS, AND LORD OF LORDS.

17 And I saw an angel standing in the sun; and he cried with a loud voice, saying to all the fowls that fly in the midst of heaven, Come and gather yourselves together unto the supper of the great אֱלֹהִים;

18 That ye may eat the flesh of kings, and the flesh of captains, and the flesh of mighty men, and the flesh of horses, and of them that sit on them, and the flesh of all *men*, *both* free and bond, both small and great.

19 And I saw the beast, and the kings of the earth, and their armies, gathered together to make war against him that sat on the horse, and against his army.

20 And the beast was taken, and with him the false prophet that wrought miracles before him, with which he deceived them that had received the mark of the beast, and them that worshipped his image. These both were cast alive into a lake of fire burning with brimstone.

21 And the remnant were slain with the sword of him that sat upon the horse, which *sword* proceeded out of his mouth: and all the fowls were filled with their flesh.

CHAPTER 20

AND I saw an angel come down from heaven, having the key of the bottomless pit and a great chain in his hand.

2 And he laid hold on the dragon, that old serpent, which is the Devil, and Satan, and bound him a thousand years,

3 And cast him into the bottomless pit, and shut him up, and set a seal upon him, that he should deceive the nations no more, till the thousand years should be fulfilled: and after that he must be loosed a little season.

4 And I saw thrones, and they sat upon them, and judgment was given unto them: and *I saw* the souls of them that were beheaded for the witness of Yashiyah, and for the word of אֱלֹהִים, and which had not worshipped the beast, neither his image, neither had received *his* mark upon their foreheads, or in their hands; and they lived and reigned with Christ a thousand years.

5 But the rest of the dead lived not again until the thousand years were finished. This *is* the first resurrection.

6 Blessed and holy *is* he that hath part in the first resurrection: on such the second death hath no power, but they shall be priests of אֱלֹהִים and of Christ, and shall reign with him a thousand years.

7 And when the thousand years are expired, Satan shall be loosed out of his prison,

8 And shall go out to deceive the nations which are in the four quarters of the earth, Gog and Magog, to gather them together to battle: the number of whom *is* as the sand of the sea.

9 And they went up on the breadth of the earth, and compassed the camp of the saints about, and the beloved city: and fire came down from אֱלֹהִים out of heaven, and devoured them.

10 And the devil that deceived them was cast into the lake of fire and brimstone, where the beast and the false prophet *are*, and shall be tormented day and night for ever and ever.

11 And I saw a great white throne, and him that sat on it, from whose face the earth and the heaven fled away; and there was found no place for them.

12 And I saw the dead, small and great, stand before אֱלֹהִים; and the books were opened: and another book was opened, which is *the book* of life: and the dead were judged out of those things which were written in the books, according to their works.

13 And the sea gave up the dead which were in it; and death and hell delivered up the dead which were in them: and they were judged every man according to their works.

14 And death and hell were cast into the lake of fire. This is the second death.

15 And whosoever was not found written in the book of life was cast into the lake of fire.

CHAPTER 21

AND I saw a new heaven and a new earth: for the first heaven and the first earth were passed away; and there was no more sea.

2 And I John saw the holy city, new Jerusalem, coming down from אֱלֹהִים out of heaven, prepared as a bride adorned for her husband.

3 And I heard a great voice out of heaven saying, Behold, the tabernacle of אֱלֹהִים is with men, and he will dwell with them, and they shall be his people, and אֱלֹהִים himself shall be with them, *and be* their אֱלֹהִים.

4 And אֱלֹהִים shall wipe away all tears from their eyes; and there shall be no more death, neither sorrow, nor crying, neither shall there be any more pain: for the former things are passed away.

5 And he that sat upon the throne said, Behold, I make all things new. And he said unto me, Write: for these words are true and faithful.

6 And he said unto me, It is done. I am Alpha and Omega, the beginning and the end. I will give unto him that is athirst of the fountain of the water of life freely.

7 He that overcometh shall inherit all things; and I will be his אֱלֹהִים, and he shall be my son.

8 But the fearful, and unbelieving, and the abominable, and murderers, and whoremongers, and sorcerers, and idolaters, and all liars, shall have their part in the lake which burneth with fire and brimstone: which is the second death.

9 And there came unto me one of the seven angels which had the seven vials full of the seven last plagues, and talked with me, saying, Come hither, I will shew thee the bride, the Lamb's wife.

10 And he carried me away in the spirit to a great and high mountain, and shewed me that great city, the holy Jerusalem, descending out of heaven from אֱלֹהִים,

11 Having the glory of אֱלֹהִים: and her light *was* like unto a stone most precious, even like a jasper stone, clear as crystal;

12 And had a wall great and high, *and* had twelve gates, and at the gates twelve angels, and names written thereon, which are *the names* of the twelve tribes of the children of Israel:

13 On the east three gates; on the north three gates; on the south three gates; and on the west three gates.

14 And the wall of the city had twelve foundations, and in them the names of the twelve apostles of the Lamb.

15 And he that talked with me had a golden reed to measure the city, and the gates thereof, and the wall thereof.

16 And the city lieth foursquare, and the length is as large as the breadth: and he measured the city with the reed, twelve thousand furlongs. The length and the breadth and the height of it are equal.

17 And he measured the wall thereof, an hundred *and* forty *and* four cubits, *according to* the measure of a man, that is, of the angel.

18 And the building of the wall of it was *of* jasper: and the city *was* pure gold, like unto clear glass.

19 And the foundations of the wall of the city *were* garnished with all manner of precious stones. The first foundation *was* jasper; the second, sapphire; the third, a chalcedony; the fourth, an emerald;

20 The fifth, sardonyx; the sixth, sardius; the seventh, chrysolite; the eighth, beryl; the ninth, a topaz; the tenth, a chrysoprasus; the eleventh, a jacinth; the twelfth, an amethyst.

21 And the twelve gates *were* twelve pearls; every several gate was of one pearl: and the street of the city *was* pure gold, as it were transparent glass.

22 And I saw no temple therein: for the Lord אֱלֹהִים Almighty and the Lamb are the temple of it.

23 And the city had no need of the sun, neither of the moon, to shine in it: for the glory of אֱלֹהִים did lighten it, and the Lamb *is* the light thereof.

24 And the nations of them which are saved shall walk in the light of it: and the kings of the earth do bring their glory and honour into it.

25 And the gates of it shall not be shut at all by day: for there shall be no night there.

26 And they shall bring the glory and honour of the nations into it.

27 And there shall in no wise enter into it any thing that defileth, neither *whatsoever* worketh abomination, or *maketh* a lie: but they which are written in the Lamb's book of life.

CHAPTER 22

AND he shewed me a pure river of water of life, clear as crystal, proceeding out of the throne of אֱלֹהִים and of the Lamb.

2 In the midst of the street of it, and on either side of the river, *was there* the tree of life, which bare twelve *manner of* fruits, *and* yielded her fruit every month: and the leaves of the tree *were* for the healing of the nations.

3 And there shall be no more curse: but the throne of אֱלֹהִים and of the Lamb shall be in it; and his servants shall serve him:

4 And they shall see his face; and his name *shall be* in their foreheads.

5 And there shall be no night there; and they need no candle, neither light of the sun; for the Lord אֱלֹהִים giveth them light: and they shall reign for ever and ever.

6 And he said unto me, These sayings *are* faithful and true: and the Lord אֱלֹהִים of the holy prophets sent his angel to shew unto his servants the things which must shortly be done.

7 Behold, I come quickly: blessed *is* he that keepeth the sayings of the prophecy of this book.

8 And I John saw these things, and heard *them*. And when I had heard and seen, I fell down to worship before the feet of the angel which shewed me these things.

9 Then saith he unto me, See *thou do it* not: for I am thy fellowservant, and of thy brethren the prophets, and of them which keep the sayings of this book: worship אֱלֹהִים.

10 And he saith unto me, Seal not the sayings of the prophecy of this book: for the time is at hand.

11 He that is unjust, let him be unjust still: and he which is filthy, let him be filthy still: and he that is righteous, let him be righteous still: and he that is holy, let him be holy still.

12 And, behold, I come quickly; and my reward *is* with me, to give every man according as his work shall be.

13 I am Alpha and Omega, the beginning and the end, the first and the last.

14 Blessed *are* they that do his commandments, that they may have right to the tree of life, and may enter in through the gates into the city.

15 For without *are* dogs, and sorcerers, and whoremongers, and murderers, and idolaters, and whosoever loveth and maketh a lie.

16 I Yashiyah have sent mine angel to testify unto you these things in the churches. I am the root and the offspring of David, *and* the bright and morning star.

17 And the Spirit and the bride say, Come. And let him that heareth say, Come. And let him that is athirst come. And whosoever will, let him take the water of life freely.

18 For I testify unto every man that heareth the words of the prophecy of this book, If any man shall add unto these things, אֱלֹהִים shall add unto him the plagues that are written in this book:

19 And if any man shall take away from the words of the book of this prophecy, אלהים shall take away his part out of the book of life, and out of the holy city, and *from* the things which are written in this book.

20 He which testifieth these things saith, Surely I come quickly. Amen. Even so, come, Lord Yashiyah.

21 The grace of our Lord Yashiyah Christ *be* with you all. Amen.

THE END.

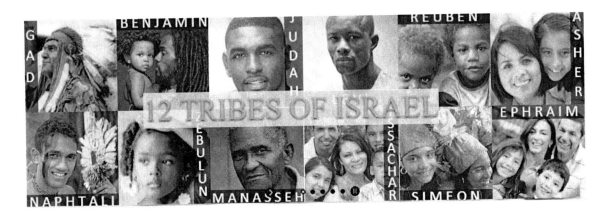

CPSIA information can be obtained
at www.ICGtesting.com
Printed in the USA
FFOW01n1306200217
32664FF

9 781530 913817